MW00366152

CONSUMER FINANCE

Aspen Casebook Series

CONSUMER FINANCE
Markets and Regulation

ADAM J. LEVITIN
Agnes N. Williams Research Professor and Professor of Law
Georgetown University Law Center

Published by Wolters Kluwer in New York.

Wolters Kluwer Legal & Regulatory U.S. serves customers worldwide with CCH, Aspen Publishers, and Kluwer Law International products. (www.WKLegaledu.com)

To contact Customer Service, e-mail customer.service@wolterskluwer.com, call 1-800-234-1660, fax 1-800-901-9075, or mail correspondence to:

Wolters Kluwer
Attn: Order Department
PO Box 990
Frederick, MD 21705

Printed in the United States of America.

1 2 3 4 5 6 7 8 9 0

ISBN 978-1-4548-6906-1

Library of Congress Cataloging-in-Publication Data

Names: Levitin, Adam Jeremiah, author.
Title: Consumer finance : markets and regulation / Adam J. Levitin, Agnes N. Williams Research Professor and Professor of Law, Georgetown University Law Center.
Description: New York : Wolters Kluwer, [2018] | Series: Aspen casebook series | Includes bibliographical references and index.
Identifiers: LCCN 2018026849 | ISBN 9781454869061
Subjects: LCSH: Consumer credit—Law and legislation—United States | Loans, Personal—Law and legislation—United States. | Mortgage loans—Law and legislation—United States. | Consumer protection—Law and legislation—United States. | Debtor and creditor—United States. | LCGFT: Casebooks (Law)
Classification: LCC KF1040 .L48 2018 | DDC 346.7307/3—dc23 LC record available at https://lccn.loc.gov/2018026849

About Wolters Kluwer Legal & Regulatory U.S.

Wolters Kluwer Legal & Regulatory U.S. delivers expert content and solutions in the areas of law, corporate compliance, health compliance, reimbursement, and legal education. Its practical solutions help customers successfully navigate the demands of a changing environment to drive their daily activities, enhance decision quality and inspire confident outcomes.

Serving customers worldwide, its legal and regulatory portfolio includes products under the Aspen Publishers, CCH Incorporated, Kluwer Law International, ftwilliam.com and MediRegs names. They are regarded as exceptional and trusted resources for general legal and practice-specific knowledge, compliance and risk management, dynamic workflow solutions, and expert commentary.

To my family

כי עוד נפשי דרור שואפת
לא מכרתיה לעגל פז
כי עוד אאמין באדם
גם ברוחו, רוח עז.

SUMMARY OF CONTENTS

CONTENTS

CHAPTER 3
Procedural Limits on Private Enforcement: Arbitration and Class Action Waivers 43

Section B
Regulation by Public Law 73

CHAPTER 4
State Regulation and UDAP 75

PREFACE

Until less than a decade ago, if one wanted to study consumer finance from a legal perspective, there was one clear place to go: bankruptcy court. From the 1980s until 2010, consumer bankruptcy scholarship was the primary lens for examining consumer finance. The pioneering empirical work of Teresa Sullivan, Elizabeth Warren, and Jay Westbrook on consumer bankruptcy was so powerful not because it was bankruptcy scholarship but because it was a lens into the realities facing American consumers. Bankruptcy cases generated the data for examining consumer finances at a time when other data sources were quite limited, and this data told the story of families struggling to hang on to life in the middle class.

Consumer finance markets completely changed during this period. First there was the rise of credit cards in the 1980s, then the invention of payday loans and increased use of debit cards in the 1990s, and then the explosive growth of subprime mortgage lending and the movement online of financial services in the 2000s. All the while the credit reporting system expanded.

Yet despite the sea changes in consumer finance, regulation was largely moribund. Yes, states had to come up with new regulatory regimes to deal with payday lending and the problems of identity theft raised by the increasingly electronic nature of commerce, but otherwise the regulatory regime remained relatively static after the 1970s other than a race to the bottom in usury regulation set off by the Supreme Court's 1978 *Marquette* decision.

All of that changed in 2010. The financial crisis of 2009 paved the way for the passage of the CARD Act in 2009, followed by the Dodd-Frank Wall Street Reform and Consumer Protection Act in 2010. The Dodd-Frank Act fundamentally changed the dynamics of consumer finance regulation by creating the Consumer Financial Protection Bureau (CFPB).

The CFPB's creation meant three critical things for consumer finance regulation from an academic's perspective. First, it meant that consumer finance regulation would be done on the federal level through a single agency rather than through a dozen different agencies (although the Departments of Defense, Education, and Housing and Urban Development still play roles in some parts of the market even today). That made it a lot easier to focus a course. Second, it meant that consumer finance was now going to be regulated on the front end through the regulatory process of rulemaking, supervision, and enforcement, rather than on the back end in the (primarily bankruptcy) courts. As a result, the action in consumer finance has shifted from the study of consumer bankruptcy to the study of the CFPB. And third, the CFPB meant that there would be a lot more and better quality data about the consumer finance industry available. It has not disappointed.

These three factors have made it possible for the creation of a new course that I hope will become a standard offering in the law school curriculum. I began teaching a consumer finance class in 2011 based on these ideas. I also saw the moment as analogous to that in 1934, following the creation of the Securities and Exchange Commission. Securities law was not yet a part of the law school curriculum, but by the 1940s it was a standard offering. Today there is a major and powerful federal agency that regulates consumer finance, which affects an enormous part of the U.S. economy. It only makes sense that it should receive coverage in the law school curriculum, but without a book that is hard to do. My hope is that this book will serve as the catalyst for making consumer finance a standard offering in the law school curriculum.

The course this book is designed to teach is a course on the regulation of retail financial services. There is, of course, a well-established financial institutions regulation course in the law school curriculum. But the banking law class is largely focused on prudential regulation—that is, safety-and-soundness regulation to ensure that banks do not fail—which involves only the banks and their regulators. To understand the retail banking market and its regulation, it is necessary to also understand another party—the consumers. Moreover, consumer finance involves a much broader range of financial institutions than are covered by a typical bank regulation class, which focuses on the regulation of depositories.

There is also a well-established "consumer law" class in the law school curriculum, but that course, too, differs materially from the one this book seeks to facilitate. Consumer law courses are focused on the experience of the consumer, particularly the *protection* of the consumer. Consumer law is also not particularly concerned with the substance of the transaction or about the risk incurred by other parties to the transaction. Moreover, consumer law covers an enormous range of topics from financial transactions to sales of goods and services, from mortgages to telemarketing and used car sales. This range of topics makes it impossible for a consumer law course to focus on the substance of the transactions. In contrast, I see the substance of the transactions—the particular product markets involved—as a major focus of consumer finance in part because some products are (imperfect) substitutes for others. Thus, consumer finance is neither bank regulation nor consumer law but a distinct field that combines some elements of those courses with a brand new regulatory agency and a focus on both the consumer *and* businesses involved in consumer financial transactions.

In my vision, the substance of a consumer finance course itself—and the design of the book—has two components: regulation and markets. The first component deals with the questions of who regulates consumer finance and how. Is regulation to be done by private law (contract and tort) or by public law? If by public law, should it be done on the state or federal level? If on the federal level, by which regulator? And if public law, what tools should be used? Disclosure requirements? Licensing requirements? Bright-line rules prohibiting or requiring particular practices or product terms? Standards prohibiting unfair, deceptive, or abusive acts and practices? Accordingly, this is the coverage of the first part of the book. This part of the book is on regulation, generally, but taught through a particular focus on consumer finance.

The second component deals with particular consumer financial products and their regulation. This is the markets part of the book. The chapters in this part of the book seek to acquaint students with various consumer financial products, make sure they understand how the products work and what they are used for, what their market structures look like, what risks the products pose for *both* consumers and businesses and the policy concerns these engender, and then what the regulatory regimes for these products look like and how well they address the policy concerns.

The initial challenge for a consumer finance book, in terms of both components, is scope of coverage. Consumer finance as a field (broadly) is functionally defined to include moving funds between parties in the present (payments), moving funds from the future to the present (credit), moving funds from the present to the future (savings and investment), contingent movements of funds to manage risk (insurance), and also advice and information services related to movements of funds (financial advisers and data intermediaries). *See* Peter Tufano, *Consumer Finance,* 1 Ann. Rev. Fin. Econ. 227 (2009).

Conceptually, one might wish for a consumer finance book that covers all these areas. Such a book, however, would be a truly unwieldy tome, unsuitable for teaching a law school course with a reasonable number of credits. While payments, credit, and certain ancillary services (plus a smidgen of savings and insurance) fall into the regulatory ambit of the CFPB, investments and insurance and associated ancillary services are in the bailiwick of other regulators, such as the SEC, CFTC, and state insurance regulators, that administer detailed and complex regulatory regimes. Moreover, these other regulatory regimes—securities, commodities, and insurance—are not consumer-specific regimes, but regimes that cover both consumers and businesses. In contrast, there is relatively little regulation of payments and credit other than for consumers; business credit is largely unregulated, and business payments are much more thinly regulated than consumer payments.

As a result, I have not attempted to cover insurance or investment products in this book. Those are topics best left for other books and other courses. Instead, I have focused on consumer payments and credit—conveniently the regulatory reach of the CFPB—and also regulation of consumer financial data. The development of consumer data markets has been key to creating a national consumer finance market and moving from retail credit to financial institution credit. Data is also an area that links payments and credit. Payments generate a tremendous amount of consumer data that can then be used for underwriting credit. Moreover, the theft of consumer payments data is often used for fraudulent credit purchases. The CFPB plays an important role in data privacy, although less so in data security—yet it is hard to fully understand either consumer payments markets or credit reporting markets without understanding the consumer financial data ecosystem and its regulation.

The book is organized in two parts with an introductory chapter. The introductory chapter provides an overview of consumers' finances and the consumer finance industry using a median-income family, the Smiths. The key point in that chapter is about why consumer finance is so important. Without payment systems, modern life is impossible, while because of the state of American consumers' economics, most of them are like the Smiths and cannot, without credit, finance any large purchases—a house, a car, education, or even a new furnace. The Smiths' reliance on credit, however, is a Catch-22, making their financial state ever more precarious. The Smiths' reliance on credit also points to the importance of financial data—data that is critical to creditors' ability to underwrite credit for the Smiths. Without that data, the Smiths' opportunities would be much more constrained.

After setting the scene about why payments, credit, and data matter, the book then turns to the first part, Chapters 2-13, which deals with who regulates and how. It is divided into three sections. Section *A* covers private law regulation, including limitations imposed by arbitration agreements. Section *B* covers public law regulation. It begins with state regulation of consumer financial services and then turns to federal regulation with a deep dive into the scope of the CFPB's regulatory authority for its different powers—rulemaking, supervision, and enforcement—as well as a close look at the CFPB's organic power of prohibiting unfair, deceptive, and abusive acts and practices. Section *C* rounds out Part I with an examination of disclosure mandates and behavioral economics as general tools in the regulatory toolkit.

The second part, Chapters 14-37, deals with specific product markets and their regulation. The second part is also divided into three sections. Section *A* covers payments. It starts with deposit accounts, which are the lynchpin of most modern payment systems, and then covers overdraft, the unbanked, prepaid cards, anti-money laundering regulations, paper- and electronic-based payment systems and emerging payment technologies (mobile wallets, cryptocurrencies), and the critical rules covering liability for unauthorized transactions and error resolution in payments.

Section *B* turns to credit products. It begins with some chapters on topics of general applicability to credit: basic terminology, usury, fair lending, and Truth in Lending regulation, before turning to specific products—auto loans, credit cards, mortgages, small-dollar loans, and student loans—and then addresses secondary markets and debt collection. Section *C* deals with the regulation of consumer data: credit reporting, financial privacy, and financial data security and identity theft.

The book's structure enables it to be used with course conceptions that differ from mine. Some might consider using it to teach a more discrete course on consumer credit (focusing on the third part with possible selections from the first part). Alternatively, some might consider using it to teach a course on consumer payments, combining the second and fourth parts. (To be clear, though, it would *not* be a traditional UCC Articles 3/4/4A payment systems course, not least because the UCC is relatively unimportant as a source of law for consumer payments.) The point is that it is possible to teach parts of the book without teaching all of it, as the chapters are generally standalone pieces.

The other real challenge for a consumer finance book is its depth of coverage. The sum total of consumer financial regulations is immense; one cannot possibly master all of the regulations that apply to payments, credits, and financial data. And yet the details of some of these regulations matter quite a bit for understanding how and why consumer finance works (or doesn't work). Students may feel somewhat deluged by the amount of information contained in this book—there are new agencies and products to learn, and on top of that some detailed statutes and regulations, and occasional cases on top of that. If students come away with the big picture—who regulates and what the products do and the policy issues involved—plus a knowledge of the key regulations, I will consider the book a success. It is not meant to be a treatise, but a sophisticated guide into the world of consumer finance.

The book has relatively few cases in it—indeed, I do not call it a "casebook," but a "textbook." Court rulings play only a secondary role in consumer finance regulation. As students will see, the economics of consumer finance makes litigation the exception, rather than the rule. Instead, the real action is in the statutes and regulations implementing those statutes, but those statutes and regulations are filled with terms that are open to interpretation. That means there are a lot of unanswered questions. Students need to get comfortable with that as a fact of life in consumer finance, and, indeed, to see it as a good thing for them professionally, for it means that they cannot be readily automated away. When there are judgment calls involved in legal compliance, lawyers have business.

Instead of cases, the book has a large amount of expository text, quite a few graphics, some regulatory materials, but also, in some instances, a type of material students are unlikely to have encountered elsewhere in their law books—complaints. A complaint is just one party's opinion, not law, but when a complaint is filed by a government agency, it gives a reasonably good impression of how that government agency interprets the law, and when the typical reality of enforcement actions is settlement, rather than trial, the government's interpretation of the law, rather than a court's, is what matters.

Each chapter of the book concludes with a problem set. The book is designed so that the problem sets can constitute all or the majority of class discussion. They are not the only way to teach the book—one can skip the problem sets entirely and teach the book as a lecture course or as a Socratic dialogue—but the problems are meant to reinforce what I think are the important pieces of the business issues and the regulatory regimes for various products. They are also meant to provide realistic issues that consumer finance lawyers must address and to underscore the interaction between legal regimes (and their uncertainty) and business concerns. Most chapters' problem sets also contain a question that sets the stage for a more open-ended discussion on consumer finance policy.

Finally, a word about what's not in the book: politics. Consumer finance regulation has become an intensely politicized and increasingly partisan area. This book does not attempt to cover the politics of consumer finance in any systematic way. It does contain an occasional observation about the political dynamics that led to particular regulations or the defeat of particular proposals, and I suppose it is unavoidable that my own political priors occasionally color the text, but I have striven to ensure that this is not a political book.

My concern that this not be a political book is reflected in its very conception as a consumer finance book rather than a "consumer law" book. The consumer finance focus is not just about the focus on financial products rather than, say, odometer fraud. Instead, it is because consumer finance is a field that necessarily involves consideration of both the consumer and the financier. Throughout the book, I have emphasized the concerns of financial services firms and of merchants in consumer transactions, as well as those of consumers. While this is not politics of a partisan sort, it is a different type of politics, one that does not see everything solely from the vantage point of the put-upon consumer, but also considers the concerns of other parties to the transaction. Part of the need for this approach is because students are as likely to find themselves representing financial institutions or merchants as consumers, but ultimately it is driven by a conviction that an informed approach to consumer finance regulation requires understanding the concerns of all parties to transactions. With any luck that is what students will come away with from this book.

Adam J. Levitin
Somerset, Maryland
July 2018

ACKNOWLEDGMENTS

I've learned the consumer finance field with a lot of help from a lot of different people. Elizabeth Warren bears the blame for getting me interested in this area in the first place when I was her student, and then for going and creating the CFPB. It's hard to think of a single individual who has had greater impact on the consumer finance field over the last quarter century, but her influence was also quite personal: a 3L paper I wrote for her about credit card merchant fees turned out to launch my career and ultimately this book, and Elizabeth has continually encouraged me in this endeavor.

Thomas Brown, Mallory Duncan, Liz Garner, Douglas Kantor, and Barrie Van Brackle have been patient with teaching me the payments world over the years; Chris Hoofnagle provided valuable suggestions about data privacy and security; and Larry Cordell, Laurie Goodman, and Susan Wachter have all helped me learn aspects of the mortgage world. A number of CFPB staffers whom I will not name given the politics of the area have answered questions throughout the years. I've also learned quite a bit from expert witness engagements, and I am particularly grateful to those attorneys who trusted in my expertise when I was an unproven young scholar.

Bob Lawless bravely taught a draft of the materials in the fall of 2017, and his comments were invaluable. Susan Block-Lieb, Matthew Bruckner, and Mark Fenster also used some of draft chapters in their courses and provided useful feedback. David Frey, Justin Horton, Devin Mauney, and Laura Mumm all provided valuable research assistance. Additionally, students at Georgetown and Harvard served as guinea pigs for draft versions of this book, and their feedback, and, in some cases, detailed line edits, helped improve the manuscript.

My editors at Wolters Kluwer and the Froebe Group have also worked hard to make this book a reality. In particular, Richard Mixter, Dena Kaufman, and Sarah Hains helped shepherd this book to fruition. Comments from several reviewers also saved me from (at least some) embarrassing mistakes. In a book this size, there are still bound to be some substantive mistakes from which no editor could save me, and those mistakes are all my own.

My deepest thanks go to my family. The time spent writing this book is time that I didn't spend with them. My love for them compounds daily and does not amortize. (But, if they will forgive the pun, it amor-izes.) This book is dedicated to them.

CHAPTER 1

INTRODUCTION TO CONSUMER FINANCE

I. CONSUMER FINANCIAL SERVICES

This book is about the regulation of consumer financial products and services. We all need financial products and services to live our daily lives. Imagine how the world would work without financial products and services. How would you get paid, and how would you pay for your expenses? You'd get paid in cash and need to find somewhere safe to hide that cash until you were ready to spend it. A mattress? A piggy bank? A strongbox? Those devices might fend off robbers, but you'd be losing time value every second your money was tucked away under your mattress, and payments would be very awkward. You'd have to go around everywhere with a wallet full of cash and pay in person. That might be fine for small, local transactions, such as groceries, but it would preclude transactions with non-local merchants. Internet commerce? Out of the question. And large transactions, even if local, would be difficult. You'd have to schlep thousands of dollars of cash to the bank every month for your mortgage payment. Your lender would, by definition, be local, which would limit competition and result in higher costs to you and regional disparities in credit availability and terms.

Speaking of mortgages, where would you get a loan absent specialized financial services firms? A rich uncle, perhaps, or the local miser, but without specialized lending institutions sources of credit would be severely constrained, making loans harder to get and more expensive.

Without credit, certain things in life would be much more difficult or impossible. You'd need to have cash to make all purchases, so you couldn't make a purchase if you didn't have enough in your wallet at that very moment. Not only would that mean that you'd have to make sure you had enough cash in your wallet every day when you left home, but you'd also simply be unable to make big ticket purchases unless you had managed to hoard up enough cash in advance. A car? A house? An education? All would be difficult to finance, and that would change what life was like.

Without cars, transportation options are more limited and would constrain employment options. Similarly, education affects earning potential. And without the ability to purchase a house, rental would be the only possibility. Humanity could certainly survive in such circumstances, but society would look very different. Financial services that provide payments and credit are essential for the operation of our modern way of life. A modern commercial economy cannot function without financial services.

Consumer financial services are about shifting of consumption ability—either between parties or between time periods. Payments allow for shifting of value between parties. Provision of a common medium of exchange for payments—such as dollars—is perhaps the most basic financial service, one that we often take for granted despite its relative novelty in the United States.[1] Cash payments, however, are but one of the ways consumers can transfer value. Checks, payment cards (debit and credit), money orders, wire transfers, automated clearing house (ACH) transactions, and online systems like PayPal all provide means of transferring value between parties in the present. While the modern dollar is a fiat currency, meaning it is not pegged to any extrinsic unit of value, such as gold, it nevertheless represents a unit of consumption, even if variable. That is to say, when I transfer a dollar to you, I am transferring to you the ability to consume whatever goods or services you can purchase for a dollar. Payment systems are the plumbing of modern commerce, and they depend on the use of financial institution intermediaries that stand between the payor and the payee.

Consumption ability can also be shifted temporally, either from the present to the future (savings and investments) or from the future to the present (borrowing). The ability to shift consumption from the present to the future enables consumers to save for periods of reduced income or increased expense. Absent the ability to save and invest, we would have to consume all of our income in the present. How would that affect someone with seasonal income, such as a farmer or an owner of a beachfront restaurant? And how would it affect our ability to retire or to have a nest egg to address unexpected expenses? Consumers use a range of financial products and services to shift their consumption from the present to the future. These include: bank products, such as savings accounts and certificates of deposit; mutual funds; annuities; pension plans; and government-mandated retirement savings in the form of Social Security.

Consumption can also be shifted from the future to the present through borrowing. Absent the ability to borrow, our present consumption would be limited to present income. That would preclude larger-ticket purchases, many of which—cars and education—are key to generating income.

Borrowing takes a variety of forms. Some borrowing is secured by collateral, for example mortgage loans, auto and auto title loans, pawn loans, and margin loans (with securities or derivatives as collateral). Other borrowing is unsecured, for example student loans, credit and charge cards, payday loans, and bank overdrafts. Some borrowing is formally cast as loans, while other forms of borrowing, such as rent-to-own or bank overdrafts, are not.

Likewise, value transfers between parties can be contingent on the occurrence of events. The ability to make contingent value transfers enables risk management.

1. The United States did not start to have a standard medium of exchange until the middle of the Civil War. Instead, various private bank notes and coins were used. The modern dollar bill did not fully take root until 1935 when Federal Reserve Notes became the sole circulating paper currency.

Consumers can contract for contingent value transfers to protect themselves from risk. There are some risks that are beyond our control and others that we cannot easily protect against. Even if we are careful, we might get sick or hurt or our property might get damaged. Either way, our ability to consume is reduced, as our income or assets are diminished. Others, however, might be better positioned to bear certain risks, and we can contract for them to transfer value to us in the future in the event that a risk is realized. Thus, consumers utilize a variety of types of insurance (health, life, property and casualty, disability), as well as financial products such as put options to protect against the decline of asset values. Government welfare programs also provide a type of contingent value transfer system.

From this we can see four basic consumer financial functions: payments, savings and investment, credit, and insurance. *See* Peter Tufano, *Consumer Finance*, 1 Ann. Rev. Fin. Econ. 227 (2009). To these four basic functions, we might add a fifth, ancillary function, namely advice services regarding the four basic functions.

Before we turn to a consideration of *why* we regulate consumer financial products and services, it's worth having some understanding of the people who use them and the firms that provide them. The following sections provide an overview of U.S. consumers and the consumer finance industry.

II. CONSUMERS: MEET THE MEDIAN-INCOME SMITHS

There is tremendous variation among U.S. consumers in terms of income, wealth, education, and financial sophistication. Regional, gender, and racial differences, among others, can also be significant among consumers. In other words, there is hardly a "typical" consumer.

Not surprisingly, U.S. consumers have varying needs in terms of financial products. While all consumers need to be able to make regular payments to domestic merchants, some consumers have unusual payment needs. Some consumers need to be able to transfer funds to loved ones who are in prison. Others need to be able to transfer funds to family overseas. Likewise, consumers' credit needs vary. Some need credit to finance an education, others for the purchase of a home or a vehicle or household appliances or jewelry. Others need credit to finance their small businesses. Some consumers need advice regarding what financial products to use; others don't need (or just don't want) such advice.

Understanding that there's no "typical" consumer, it is still helpful to have a picture of at least a "median" U.S. consumer. Our "median" consumer is the Smith family, a hypothetical median-income family featuring the most common names and household size in the United States. The Smiths live in Missouri (the geographic center of the U.S. population as of 2010) and are non-Hispanic whites, like almost 63% of the U.S. population.

The Smith household consists of two adults—Jim and Mary, both age 38—and two children, Patty, age 12, and John, age 10. Both Jim and Mary work. Jim works as a morgue attendant and Mary is an art teacher at the local elementary school.

In 2018, the Smiths' pre-tax household income was $59,039, exactly the U.S. household median. The Smiths, like all patriotic Americans, pay taxes. First, part of their paychecks is withheld for Old Age, Survivors, and Disability Insurance (OASDI or Social Security) taxes and Medicare taxes, 6.2% and 1.45% of their income respectively, totaling $4,516.

The Smiths also pay federal and state income taxes every year. Assuming that they file jointly and claim standard deductions of $24,000, their adjusted gross income, on which they are taxed, is $35,039. The federal government taxes the Smiths 10% on the first $19,050 of this income and 12% on the rest, for a total federal income tax liability of $3,824. Against this liability, the Smiths can offset $2,000 per child in child tax credits because their income is less than $400,000. Thus, their final federal income tax bill is zero, and they are actually eligible for a refund of $176. (They avoid the Alternative Minimum Tax.)

Let's assume a state and local income tax bill of another $2,188. In total, then, the Smiths pay $6,704 (11.4% of their income) in various income-based taxes, so the Smiths' post-tax income (known as "disposable personal income") is $52,335.

The Smiths own a median-priced home that they recently purchased for $240,000. They put 20% down and have a 30-year fixed-rate mortgage securing a purchase money loan of $192,000. Their mortgage interest rate is 4%, and their monthly payments are $917. They are also subject to property taxes at 1.5% for an annual property tax bill of $3,600. Total annual housing expenses, then, are $14,604 or 25% of the Smiths' annual income.

The Smiths own a single 2015 model Honda Civic for which the fuel runs $220/month and repairs and insurance average $180/month. They purchased the car with a $15,000 loan at 3% interest. Monthly payments are $270, and they still owe $3,182 on the loan. In total the car costs the Smiths $670/month.

The Smiths also have a variety of other regular expenses:

- utilities (electricity, gas, water, phone, cable, Internet, mobile) ($450/month)
- insurance (health, life) ($325/month)
- food and alcohol ($850/month)
- clothing ($250/month)
- miscellany (including household maintenance and recreation) ($400/month).

Thus, the Smith family's total non-tax, non-housing, non-vehicle expenses are $2,275/month. Obviously, these figures could vary significantly, but they are largely based on Census estimates. Notice that there are all kinds of potential expenses we have *not* accounted for, such as dry cleaning, summer camp for the kids, the expenses of maintaining Johnny Squeaky, the pet Dachshund, or birthday presents for the kids' friends. Using these estimates, however, the Smiths should be saving about $200/month or $2,400 annually.

This is a lot of numbers, so here's the big-picture breakdown. The Smiths are paying about 11% of their income in income-based taxes. They are spending 25% of their income on housing (including property taxes and insurance). 14% of their income goes to car-related expenses (transportation), and 45% of their income covers food, clothing, utility bills, etc. The Smiths' annual savings rate is 4% of their gross income, and 4.6% of their disposable personal income. Figure 1.1 summarizes graphically.

Figure 1.1 How the Smiths Spend Their Money

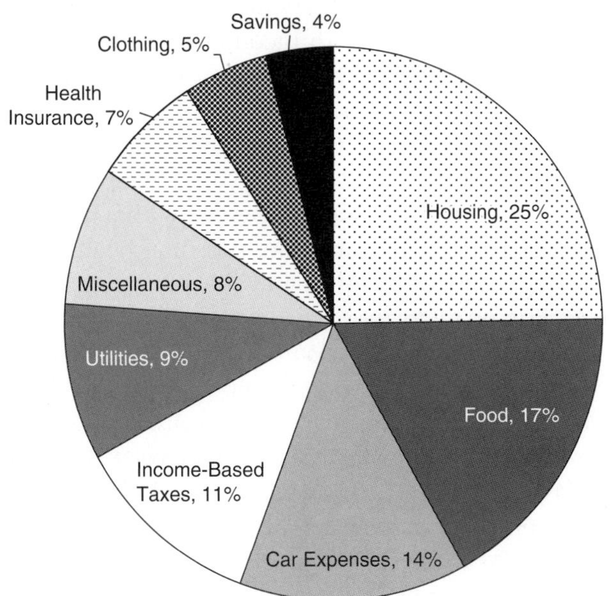

If the Smiths' savings rate seems low to you, it isn't. It's basically in line with the national average savings rate. Figure 1.2 shows the savings rate (that is, savings as a percentage of disposable personal income) over time. As you can see, it has fallen significantly since the mid-1970s. What's been going on with U.S. consumers? Why are they saving less?

Figure 1.2 U.S. Household Savings Rate[2]

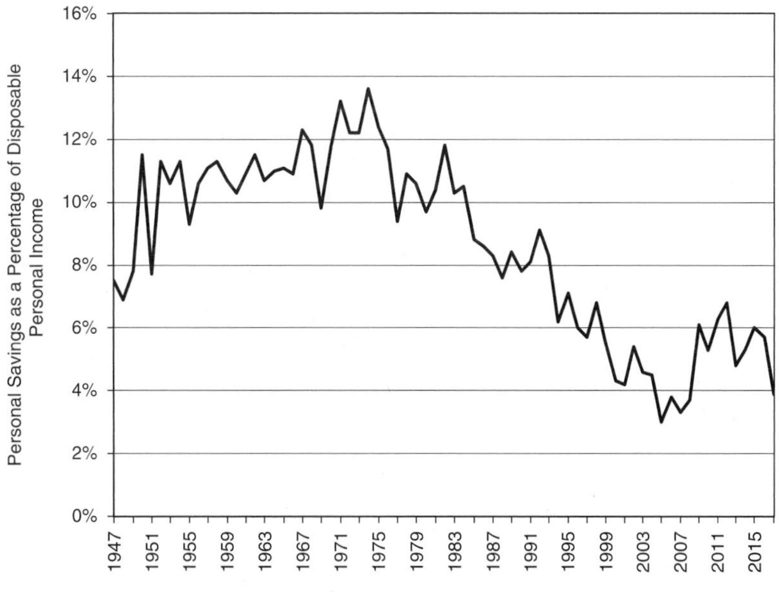

2. Federal Reserve Economic Data.

The answer is straightforward on some level. Until the late 1970s, as U.S. productivity rose, so too did incomes. (Workers were getting gains from increased productivity.) Living costs also kept pace with incomes until the mid-1970s. Since the mid-1970s, however, U.S. household incomes have stagnated, while costs of living have risen, particularly the costs of housing, education, and health care. Figure 1.3 illustrates part of this period, showing that from 1987 to 2017, real income rose 16%, but real housing prices increased 290%. During this same period (not depicted), tuition at private four-year colleges increased by 502% and tuition at public four-year colleges increased by 682%, and per capita personal health care expenditures rose over 362%.[3] With stagnant real incomes and sharply rising housing, education, and medical expenses, it is no surprise that the savings rate has plummeted. Why incomes have stagnated and costs have risen are issues beyond the scope of this book, but there are two implications of note for us.

The first implication of decreased personal savings is that households have less ability to absorb economic shocks. This means that economic volatility is more problematic for U.S. households than in the past because they have less ability to "self-insure" against such volatility through their own savings. *See* Jacob Hacker, *The Great Risk Shift* (2006). The result is more strain on the social safety net and more downward social mobility.

Historically, a key component of U.S. households' ability to self-insure against economic volatility was the ability to deploy an additional earner. U.S. households were historically one-income households: in 1960, only around a quarter of

Figure 1.3 U.S. Household Income, Home Price Index, and Savings Rate[4]

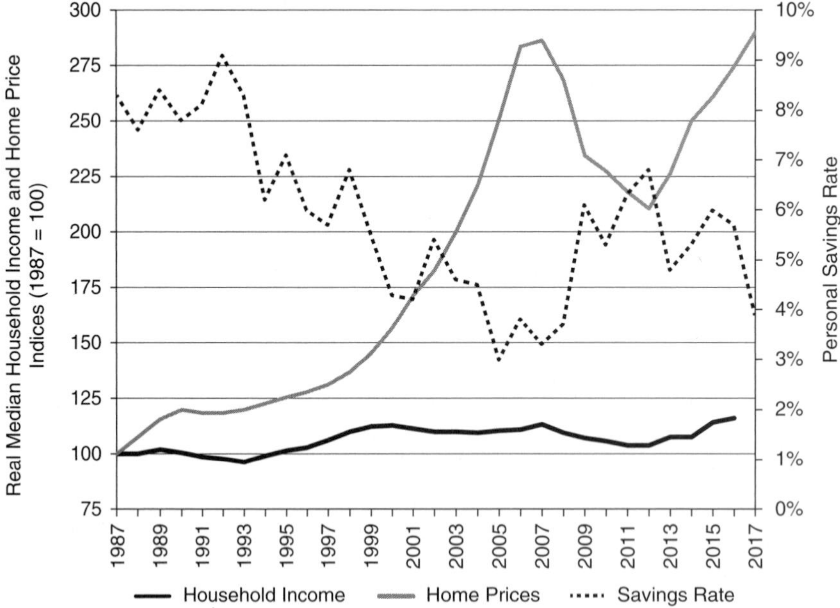

3. College Board data; Centers for Medicare and Medicaid, National Health Care Expenditure Data (1990 to 2017 comparison).

4. Federal Reserve Economic Data; Bureau of Labor Statistics.

households had two earners, and single-earner households almost always had a male earner. Thus, during an era when women were not generally in the workforce, women served as a safety net of sorts for households. If dad couldn't work for some reason, mom could always go out into the workforce. She wasn't likely to earn as much as dad, but she could still put bread on the table.

As women entered the workforce after the Second World War, the built-in safety net of a second potential earner has become tapped out. By 1990, around 60% of households were two-income households. Two-income households like the Smiths' are now the rule, not the exception, meaning that there is no longer a safety net of a second potential earner. *See* Elizabeth Warren & Amelia Warren-Tyagi, *The Two-Income Trap* (2003). And, increasingly, American households are single-parent households, which, by definition, lack the second-earner safety net. And for both single-parent households and two-income households, there is now the added expense of childcare for younger children.

The second implication of decreased personal savings is that consumer finance is increasingly called on to bridge the gap between income and expenses. In particular, as housing and education costs have risen, consumers have borrowed more and more to pay for housing and education. This has created the phenomenon that then professor, now Senator Elizabeth Warren termed the "Cement Life Raft": consumer financial services can be a lifesaver, but they can also sink a family. *Id.*

Recall, now, that our previous examination of the Smiths' finances shows that *assuming no unexpected expenses*, a median-income, average-expense household should be saving less than $2,500 annually. Pause and think about how that compares to your law school tuition or even the price of this book (which is beyond your humble author's control).

Let's assume that the Smiths plan to retire in 30 years, when they turn 68. How much should the Smiths have managed to save over 30 years at this rate? Let's assume they can get a 5% average return on their savings. That suggests that they should have just under $178,000 in present dollar value of savings *if* they manage to put away $2,400 every year at 5% compound interest. (In nominal dollars, they should have more because annual contributions will go up with inflation.) However we look at it, though, the Smiths will have saved around 3 years of income over 30 years—*assuming* that there are no unexpected expenses over that 30-year span.

They will, of course, have Social Security (one hopes) when they retire, but they won't have much else saved up in cash. Instead, their one major retirement asset is their home. Their mortgage should be paid off in 30 years, at which point their expenses will drop substantially. Moreover, if home prices remain stable, by paying off their mortgage they will basically double their retirement assets, and it's quite possible that their home will appreciate. The Smiths' home, then, is not simply their home. It is likely their largest single investment asset, and their equity in it is growing at a steady and guaranteed rate, unlike many investment options. Still, even with the home, the Smiths are on pace for about $400,000 in assets when they hit retirement, but many of their expenses will remain, and their income will be less.

If this is a bit depressing, it gets worse. We haven't assumed any unexpected expenses or unfortunate occurrences for the Smiths. Their financial situation is so precarious that they have little room for things to go wrong. The small things, like a bank fee, might not change the financial picture for the Smiths on their own, but in aggregate such things can. And then there are major life events—death, delivery (of a baby), disability, dismissal, and divorce (the five "Ds")—that can have enormous impacts on household economics.

Now remember, the Smiths are a *median*-income household. This means half of U.S. households earn *less* than the Smiths, while half earn more. The finances of many American households are precarious.

The Smiths' inability to save more than a modest amount (assuming that everything goes well) means that they have no choice but to borrow to finance their major, and unavoidable, expenses: housing, transportation, and eventually education for Patty and John. The only way the Smiths can afford large-ticket expenses is to use credit products to shift consumption from the future to the present. Hence the mortgage and car loan, and likely a student loan in the future. Indeed, if things are tight for the Smiths it might not only be large-ticket items that get financed; they sometimes carry a balance on a credit card. The Smiths aren't happy to admit it, but once Mary took out a payday loan to help cover their expenses when times were tight. It wasn't a happy experience, as the fees ate into their savings for quite a while, and she's avoided payday loans ever since.

The Smiths' reliance on credit products puts them in a Catch-22. Because the Smiths are indebted, they are in a much more precarious situation if they encounter any bumps in the road. While the Smiths can always tighten their belts and have hot dogs instead of steak, reducing their present consumption, they can't readily reduce their debt service payments. Those payments, like taxes, are fixed obligations that do not adjust to the Smiths' financial state. The Smiths have $14,244 in annual mortgage and car payments and another $10,284 in tax payments. That means that the Smiths have largely unadjustable obligations that constitute over 40% of their gross income. In other words, the Smiths rely on credit to give them financial flexibility, but that credit in turn reduces their financial flexibility.

While credit products are what both help and constrain the Smiths' finances, they are not the only financial products in the Smiths' lives. The Smiths use a variety of financial products: they have a deposit account at a bank, they make payments with cash, checks, debit cards, credit cards, and using automated clearing houses (even though they probably don't know what an ACH is). They also receive payments in cash, checks, and via ACH. The Smiths also have various insurance policies and a tax-advantaged retirement savings account. Use of this range of financial products is totally typical of American households. Let's turn now to look at the firms that provide these products and services.

III. U.S. CONSUMERS: AN AGGREGATE PICTURE

The Smiths are just one fictional median family. They don't give the aggregate picture of the U.S. consumer population. Perhaps the most notable thing about U.S. consumers is how indebted they are.

U.S. consumers owe, in aggregate, around $13 trillion as of the end of the third quarter of 2017. With roughly 125 million households in the country, this translates into an average debt burden of a bit over $100,000 per household—roughly two years of gross income for the median family. The overwhelming majority of this debt is related to home ownership.

Figure 1.4 shows the breakdown of consumer liabilities by category. Mortgages are 68% of total consumer debt, with home equity lines of credit making up another 4%. In other words, 72% of consumer debt is secured by consumers' homes. Auto loans make up 9% of total consumer debt, while credit card balances make up 6%. Because credit cards are revolving lines of credit that are constantly repaid and borrowed against, a snapshot of balances at any point in time understates their importance to consumer finance. Finally, student loans make up the other large category of consumer debt, accounting for 11% of total debt.

What these figures do not show, however, is the distribution of debts within the population. Not surprisingly, debt obligations are not distributed evenly. Roughly a third of households rent, so they do not have mortgage obligations. Likewise, some homeowners own their homes outright. Thus, only around 40% of households have mortgage debt obligations, meaning that almost three-quarters of consumer debt is concentrated in 40% of households.

Similarly, student loans are a large debt burden that is highly concentrated in a limited part of the population: out of a total population of 323 million, 44.2 million Americans have student loan debt. In contrast, there are 106 million auto loans outstanding and 450 million credit card accounts outstanding as of the end of 2017. While these figures are far from telling us the complete picture of consumer finances, they indicate that debt burdens are far from being spread evenly among the population.

Figure 1.4 Composition of Consumer Debt[5]

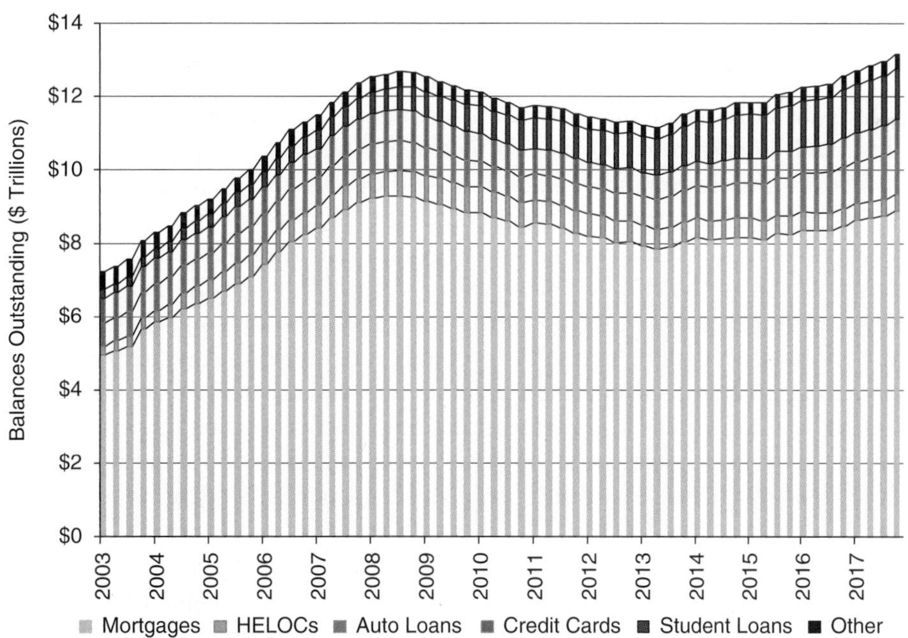

5. New York Fed Consumer Credit Panel/Equifax.

Debt figures, however, do not tell the whole story. American families also have significant assets to offset these liabilities: $10.6 trillion in bank deposits and money market funds plus another $13.4 trillion in home equity, as well as trillions of dollars in various personalty items (including vehicles) and investments. Note the importance of this breakdown—the bank deposits and money market funds are all liquid assets that can readily be used to pay obligations as they come due. In contrast, personalty and home equity value are harder for consumers to tap; doing so involves either selling the asset or, if the consumer wishes to keep the asset and tap only part of its value, borrowing against it.

Having shown you all these numbers, it's time to let you in on a dirty little secret about consumer finance statistics: our knowledge of consumers' finances is quite imperfect. The three main national data sources are the Federal Reserve Board's triennial Survey of Consumer Finances (SCF), the Federal Reserve Board's quarterly Financial Accounts of the United States (FAUS), and the NY Fed Consumer Credit Panel/Equifax (NYFCCP/E). All three sources have their limitations.

SCF is an excellent source built off of surveys of individual households. It contains a wealth of data on individual households and thus mean and median households for its sample, but it does not contain national aggregate data.

Conversely, the data in FAUS is aggregated from a number of sources, such as data submissions to regulators filed by financial institutions. It's not built directly on individual-level data, so it contains only national aggregate data. Unfortunately, consumers appear in FAUS as "Households and Non-Profits," which is the residual category for FAUS, meaning that any assets and liabilities not assigned to other entities are assigned to Households and Non-Profits. Further complicating things, the category of "Households and Non-Profits" is defined to include not just consumers and non-profit organizations, but also "domestic hedge funds, private equity funds, and personal trusts." This means that the aggregate national "consumer" data is actually substantially mixed with data from entities that are decidedly not "consumers." While certain categories of financial holdings, such as home mortgage liabilities, are clearly consumer liabilities, and others, such as municipal securities liabilities, clearly are not (these are liabilities of certain non-profits like hospitals), there are categories, such as ownership of equity in businesses, that could be either consumer assets or the assets of hedge funds and private equity funds.

The NYFCCP/E data is derived from a set of credit reports and then extrapolated to the national population. While it is probably the best source available, it is important to recognize that credit reporting data is a mix of account-level and individual-level data, and that there are always potential problems when extrapolating from a sample. More importantly, the NYFCCP/E only tells us about certain household debts. It does not tell us about other obligations, such as rent, or about household assets.

Taken together, this means that we need to take certain types of aggregate national consumer finance data with a grain of salt. The data is better for things like home mortgages, credit cards, and auto loans, and worse for things like securities holdings. What might be surprising here is the lack of precision of our knowledge about consumers' finances despite their central role in the economy. If regulators don't have good data, how can they produce good regulatory policy?

IV. THE CONSUMER FINANCE BUSINESS: BIG AND SMALL

While it is possible to imagine a median U.S. household, there really is no equivalent on the business side of consumer finance. Consumer finance involves a great variety of institutions, some managing enormous amounts of assets and operating on a national (or global) scale, and some much more modest and local. Some specialize in one particular product; others offer a range of products across financial functions. Even among firms offering the same general type of product, different firms may target different segments of the consumer market or have different business models. Some deal directly with consumers, while others provide support services or make secondary markets. Some are regulated federally, while others are regulated by states, and some are both at both levels.

Still, there are some common points that can be made about the consumer financial services business. Consumer financial services is a big business built on small transactions. As noted above, consumers had around $13.9 trillion in debt as of the end of 2017, and trillions in assets, including $14.4 trillion in home equity and $11.4 trillion in bank deposits and money market funds. Consumers don't just sit on these assets and liabilities. *See* Federal Reserve Statistical Release Z.1, Financial Accounts of the United States, table B.101, Balance Sheet of Households and Nonprofit Organizations. They also transact—a lot. There were some 185 billion consumer payment transactions made in 2016, accounting for over $9.9 trillion in payments. Nilson Report #1122 (Dec. 2017), at 10-11. Of these, 102.5 billion payments for $5.7 trillion dollars were made on credit and debit cards. *Id.*

Despite these large aggregate numbers, most consumer financial transactions are quite small. (*See* Figure 1.5.) For example, the most common type of consumer payment transaction is with a debit card; there were nearly 68 billion debit card transactions in 2016, but the average debit card payment was for $38. *Id.*

The small size of most consumer financial transactions affects the economics of the consumer finance industry in significant ways. The relatively small unit size means that the cost of prospecting for customers or overhead may account for a large part of the cost of the service. Small unit sizes also encourage automation and discourage financial service providers from spending significant resources on individual transactions or customers.

Small units also mean that consumers are unlikely to bring litigation over perceived wrongs, absent the ability to proceed as a class; the costs of litigation are simply too great to justify most individual consumers' claims. Businesses are keenly aware of this reality and frequently attempt to insulate themselves from liability by limiting consumers' ability to litigate as a class.

Lastly, small units mean that even when marginal costs for performing a single transaction might be small, there can be "lumpy" jumps in the cost of performing multiple additional transactions. Processing a single additional transaction might

Figure 1.5 Average Transaction Amount of U.S. Consumer Payments, 2016[6]

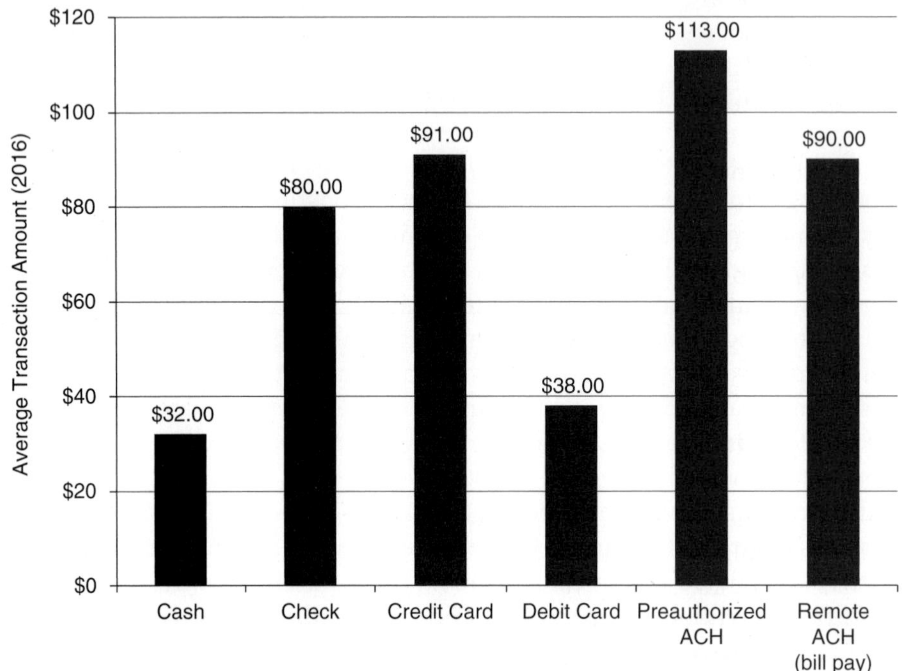

have virtually no marginal cost, but adding a million transactions might require investing in new infrastructure and employees. *See* John Y. Campbell *et al.*, *The Regulation of Consumer Financial Products: An Introductory Essay with Four Case Studies* (2010).

Enabling consumer transactions are a vast range of firms and individuals providing consumer financial services. Some are financial institutions that deal directly with consumers, such as depositaries (banks and thrifts), credit unions, insurance companies, finance companies, stockbrokers, and mutual fund advisors. Some of these are publicly traded companies that are among the largest firms in the world, while others are small, often family-owned, firms, such as many community banks.

While some consumer finance businesses interface directly with consumers, others offer critical support services to the direct providers of consumer financial services: payment processors, credit reporting agencies, and law firms. While the consumer finance market is primarily a business-to-consumer (b2c) market, there are numerous supporting business-to-business (b2b) roles, such as facilitating payments between financial institutions.

Yet other businesses in the consumer finance industry operate solely in b2b secondary markets. These firms are not providing support services, but are instead engaged in risk transfers with primary market firms. Examples of this are the government-sponsored enterprises Fannie Mae and Freddie Mac and government

6. *Id.*

agency Ginnie Mae, as well as insurers such as private mortgage insurance companies and the Federal Housing Administration. These secondary market firms often set the terms under which the primary (b2c) consumer market operates based on the transactions they are willing to fund or process, so they function as a type of indirect or "hydraulic" regulation on primary markets.

Some consumer finance providers are incorporated firms, while others may be unincorporated individuals, such as accountants, financial advisors, and lawyers. Yet others are actually government agencies, such as the Federal Housing Administration or Department of Veterans Affairs. Finally, other types of consumer finance businesses are perhaps less obvious: rent-to-own stores and retailers offering financing (including through deferred payment), tax preparers who facilitate tax refund anticipation loans, realtors who broker sales and sometimes arrange financing.

V. REGULATION OF CONSUMER FINANCE

Consumer finance is heavily regulated by federal, state, and sometimes local law. The particular regulations that apply can vary depending on the product involved, the provider of the product, and the identity of the consumer. Regulation of consumer finance can take a variety of forms, including: market self-regulation (including third-party bonding); common law tort and contract law; disclosure requirements; anti-fraud rules; conflict of interest requirements; licensing requirements; reporting requirements; mandatory default terms; mandatory terms; term and practice prohibitions (including anti-discrimination); price controls or rate regulation; and consumer education requirements.

First and most foundationally, consumer finance involves market relationships. This means that there will be some degree of market discipline regarding products and practices. Yet markets are not perfect. Sometimes markets fail, and sometimes the competitive pressures of markets create rather than solve problems in consumer finance. This means other forms of regulation are sometimes necessary.

Because consumer finance involves market relationships, it also almost always involves contractual relationships. This means that basic common law contract principles, such as rules regarding when parties are bound to a contract, contract interpretation, implied covenants of good faith and fair dealing, and defenses to contract enforcement such as duress, incapacity, fraud, mistake, misrepresentation, and unconscionability all apply. Similarly, common law torts, such as concealment, conversion, and fraud, also apply. Indeed, contract and tort law are the first level of consumer finance regulation.

Contract is a two-way street. While contract sets forth the rights of consumers against consumer finance providers, it also sets forth the limits of consumer finance providers' rights, such as when and how they may take action against a consumer to collect money owed or terminate a business relationship. While much of the material in this book focuses on statute and regulation, it is important not to overlook the enormous role of contract in consumer finance, as almost all consumer financial relationships are contractual. Contract is where we start in Chapter 2, and we will return to it at various intervals, including in the context of arbitration, in which contracts are used to limit consumers' rights, and mortgage lending, where there is substantial standardization of contracts such that it is possible to make a meaningful inquiry into the particular risk allocations in the mortgage contract.

State (and local) statutory law may also apply to consumer financial transactions. The Uniform Commercial Code governs some consumer financial transactions, while various non-uniform state statutes and regulations may also regulate specific products. States also license and regulate some providers of consumer financial services, including some banks, but also pawnshops, check cashers, payday lenders, auto title lenders, finance companies, and money transmitters. State laws tend to be in the nature of licensing requirements, broad anti-fraud type statutes (prohibiting "unfair and deceptive acts and practices"), and rate regulation via usury statutes. States also have their own anti-discrimination laws and some do have other product term or disclosure regulations.

Additionally, there is an extensive federal financial regulatory array that affects consumer financial transactions. Some of these regulations are statutes specifically applicable only to consumer financial transactions, such as the Consumer Credit Protection Act of 1968 or the Consumer Financial Protection Act of 2010 and the regulations adopted thereunder. These tend to be product-focused regulations, although they vary sometimes depending on the nature of the consumer. Frequently these federal regulations focus on disclosure, but sometimes they mandate or prohibit product terms or practices, and for debit cards they actually impose rate regulations. Additionally, there are broad federal anti-discrimination laws for housing and credit.

Importantly, federal and state regulation are not exclusive. While federal law sometimes preempts state law, there are many areas in which there is overlapping regulation and enforcement. The result is an often-confusing hodgepodge of regulatory authority. As you might imagine, this creates policy coordination issues both because of bureaucratic turf wars and because the politics of regulation on the federal level do not always track with those on the state level. Whether this lack of coordination is a virtue or vice is another matter. While it can send conflicting messages, it also makes it much less likely that there will be a full-court press for either more intense regulation or less intense regulation. In other words, overlapping authority might have the effect of smoothing the overall level of regulation, even if the nature and focus of that regulation differs substantially between state and federal regulation.

Other federal regulation of consumer finance is not actually specific to consumer finance, but is instead part of the complex federal regulatory systems for banks, securities firms, and government-sponsored entities. The applicability of these regulations depends on the identity of the financial services provider. In addition, federal bankruptcy or tax law plays a major role in shaping consumer financial markets; bankruptcy law is critical to shaping credit markets, while tax law affects consumers' investment and borrowing decisions. Further federal regulation affecting consumer finance comes through the government's own market activities as the provider of mortgage insurance and student loans. Additionally, federal anti-money laundering regulations have a significant impact on payment services.

In addition to this formal legal regulation there is also sometimes industry self-regulation. Payments made using the ACH system, such as direct deposits and online bill payments, are regulated by the National Automated Clearing House

Association (NACHA), a private organization. Likewise, realtors are subject to their own industry's standards of conduct.

Beyond the questions of private versus public regulation and state versus federal regulation, there is question of firm-based or product-based regulation. The variety of firms engaged in the consumer finance business presents significant challenge for regulation. On the one hand, firm-based regulation might make sense because the regulatory schemes that might be appropriate for one type of firm might not be appropriate for another. Yet on the other hand, having firm-based regulation invites regulatory arbitrage based on firm type, when from the consumer perspective the particular features of a counterparty may not matter. As it happens consumer finance regulation is of two minds on the issue, sometimes doing firm-based regulation and sometimes product-based.

Like any area of regulation, consumer finance faces the question of rules- or standards-based regulation. There are well-known trade-offs between rules and standards, and the difference may not always be as sharp as the dichotomy suggests. But in the consumer finance context, there may be different appeals of rules and standards to consumers and businesses. As it happens, modern consumer finance regulation has a belt-and-suspenders approach consisting of a battery of detailed rules backstopped by broad standards-based prohibitions.

The first half of this book is focused on these questions of regulatory design: private or public regulation, state or federal regulation, firm-based or product-based regulation, and rules-based or standards-based regulation. It also covers the surprisingly complex question of jurisdiction, which differs for enforcement, regulation, and "supervision"—the ability to engage in active auditing and monitoring of financial services firms' activities. This jurisdiction line has both state versus federal and inter-federal components, as we shall see.

There is a tremendous governmental apparatus that regulates consumer financial products and services. But why does the government do it? The answer would seem to tell us much about *how* the products should be regulated. The following essay excerpt summarizes many of the major arguments for the regulation of consumer financial products and services.

John Y. Campbell, Howell E. Jackson, Bridgette C. Madrian & Peter Tufano
The Regulation of Consumer Financial Products: An Introductory Essay with Four Case Studies (excerpts)

Working Paper (Nov. 17, 2010)

A. TRADITIONAL ECONOMIC JUSTIFICATIONS FOR CONSUMER FINANCIAL REGULATION

The first rationale for consumer financial regulation is to facilitate enforcement of financial contracts. Many consumer financial transactions span long time horizons or entail the transfer of wealth over considerable geographic distance. The temporal aspect of financial products gives firms the ability to engage in moral hazard in a way that may impede market efficiency. In markets such as those for retirement savings or life insurance, performance occurs over a long period of time, well after consumers and firms enter into a contractual commitment. Consumers are unlikely to be able to engage in continuous monitoring, and reputation may be insufficient to discipline firms that are tempted to expropriate their clients' wealth. In this case, mandatory capital requirements and other forms of on-going supervision may be needed to ensure the development of well-functioning markets. Such regulation is valuable not only for consumers, but also for firms, as it provides a commitment device that enables them to win business that would otherwise be unavailable.

A second rationale for consumer financial regulation is that of externalities: individual financial behavior may affect others in ways that are not reflected in market prices. Positive externalities from human capital accumulation and home ownership have been used to justify government subsidies to student loans and home mortgages. Conversely, foreclosures have social costs that are not taken into account by mortgage borrowers and lenders. More generally, correlated investment strategies may increase the systemic risk in financial markets and thus warrant supervisory intervention.

A third rationale for consumer financial regulation is to counter that market power that is facilitated by high consumer search costs. Price dispersion is a feature of many retail markets. It can be sustained by the existence of search costs that make some consumers willing to pay higher prices than they might find elsewhere. These search costs give retailers a degree of market power, allowing them to charge prices above marginal cost. One example in the financial arena is Standard and Poor's 500 index funds—providers charge a wide range of fees for an essentially identical product. Search costs can be addressed by providing information on market prices (for example, Medicare Part D prescription drug plan decision aids), by standardizing the provision of information (for example, requiring firms to quote interest rates as an annualized percentage rate, or by mandating uniform disclosure of fees and past returns in mutual fund prospectuses), or by directly regulating prices. More general responses to market power include limitations on the scale or scope of financial service firms or enhanced anti-trust requirements.

The role of information as a public good provides yet another rationale of consumer financial regulation. To make informed decisions, consumers often need information about financial products that they cannot efficiently generate themselves and for which joint production with other consumers is not easily coordinated. Often the financial provider will be the most efficient supplier of this information. Disclosure requirements—mandates that the firm produce and disseminate certain types of information—are an example of interventions that address this type of market failure. Anti-fraud rules backed by judicial enforcement mechanisms serve a similar purpose, although traditionally they were limited to intentional affirmative misrepresentations.

There are other information failures that also provide a basis for consumer financial regulation. Indeed, consumer finance provides the textbook cases of information problems: the underprovision of insurance and consumer credit as a result of adverse selection and moral hazard. The regulatory responses to this type of market failure include mandating the purchase of insurance (for example, auto insurance), the public provision of universal insurance programs such as social security to mitigate adverse selection, and the subsidization of private insurance purchases through the tax system.

In some cases, the government "solution" to ill-functioning private insurance markets may itself create moral hazard that might justify further intervention. For example, the social safety net might encourage individuals to assume excessive financial risks that will result in some suffering large financial losses that qualify them for public aid. Government can mitigate this moral hazard by restricting financial risk-taking, such as placing limits on employer stock holdings in retirement accounts.

Finally, the complexity of many consumer financial products generates both information asymmetries (firms know more about the products than consumers do) and transaction costs that make it difficult for even the most sophisticated individuals to comparison shop. This complexity may suppress the development of robust markets for certain consumer financial products. In these circumstances, constraints on the variation in product terms may actually improve social welfare, albeit at the cost of inhibiting consumer choice.

B. JUSTIFICATIONS BASED ON BEHAVIORAL AND COGNITIVE LIMITATIONS OF CONSUMERS

In addition to the traditional market failures described above, recent research in behavioral economics has highlighted the potential for inefficient market outcomes that result from consumers' cognitive limitations. . .

The first behavioral justification for consumer financial regulation is that consumers have preferences that are biased toward the present. These so-called present-biased preferences generate a type of externality in which the decisions of an individual today negatively affect the welfare of the same individual in the future in a way that is not internally consistent and that implies future regret. This type of negative externality is sometimes referred to as an "internality." Present-biased preferences have been used to explain behaviors as diverse as failing to save for retirement and taking up smoking. The proposed policy responses to such preferences are to constrain today's self from taking actions that would be too detrimental to the future self, and could include limiting early access to retirement saving or taxing consumption of cigarettes.

A second behavioral justification for consumer financial regulation is individual cognitive limitations. Recent research has documented a pervasive lack of basic financial literacy. . . .

If consumers cannot maximize their own welfare, there is no reason to believe that competitive markets will be efficient. A social planner can in principle achieve better outcomes, judged using the true welfare function of consumers, than a free market that responds to the biased decisions that financially illiterate consumers make. This is true both because financially illiterate consumers may pick inappropriate financial products, and because real resources may be wasted as firms seek to persuade consumers to purchase excessively expensive, and hence profitable, products. Such rent-seeking behavior creates deadweight loss. . . .

Another behavioral justification for consumer financial regulation is the role of trust in consumer financial markets. Consumers with cognitive limitations may use rules of thumb to guide their behavior. One such rule of thumb is to avoid the use of certain financial products altogether. This has been interpreted as a lack of trust in the financial system. Since lack of financial market participation can be a serious mistake, there is a case for regulation to improve consumer trust through restrictions on insider trading, suitability and fiduciary requirements, and other measures that convey a sense of strong supervisory oversight. There is evidence that mutual fund markets with stronger levels of investor protection are larger than those with lower levels of protection, perhaps working through this channel of trust.

A final behavioral justification for consumer financial regulation is individual lack of self-knowledge. Markets may work poorly if consumers do not correctly understand their own time-inconsistent preferences or cognitive limitations, in other words, if they lack self-knowledge. For example, consumers may choose a bank account with "free" checking, underestimating the extent to which they will pay penalty fees for overdrawing their accounts in the future. Such lack of self-knowledge leads to several problems. First, naïve consumers may purchase too many bank services because they underestimate the total cost to them. Second, banks compete away the excess profits they obtain through overdraft fees by keeping base charges low on checking accounts. This implies that naïve consumers cross-subsidize sophisticated consumers who do not overdraw their accounts. Products that allocate costs more equally across naïve and sophisticated consumers cannot be successfully brought to market as sophisticated consumers find it attractive to retain the cross-subsidies embedded in existing products. Nor is it profitable for firms to educate naïve consumers, because educated consumers become sophisticated and then demand fewer high-cost financial services. Finally, there are troubling distributional implications because naïve consumers are likely to have lower incomes than sophisticated consumers. . . .

C. DISTRIBUTIONAL CONSIDERATIONS AND CONSUMER FINANCIAL REGULATION

Even when unregulated markets are efficient, they may generate unacceptable distributional outcomes. While in principle this can be addressed by social welfare programs and progressive income taxation, distributional considerations also motivate some consumer financial regulation. As noted, consumers with high search costs are likely to pay higher prices in unregulated markets. In some contexts, search costs are higher for those with a high value of time and are likely to be positively correlated with income. . . . [F]or example, . . . middle-aged consumers pay higher prices than retired consumers because they spend less time shopping. In consumer financial markets, however, search costs may be correlated more with cognitive ability and financial experience than with the value of time. Individuals of limited cognitive ability or financial expertise may have higher search costs because they lack easy access to information or the capacity to process it, and thus may pay high prices for financial products even though they have low incomes. Distributional considerations thus strengthen the case for measures to reduce search costs or to limit the ability of firms to exercise market power over consumers with high search costs.

We might add another reason for consumer finance regulation to those given by Professor Campbell and his co-authors: managing the macroeconomic consequences of consumer finance. Consumer spending *is* the U.S. economy. Personal consumption expenditures are approximately 70% of gross domestic product. Consumer spending of all sorts is possible only because of payment systems, and consumer spending for large-ticket items is heavily facilitated through credit.

While the direct cost of consumer financial services accounts for only 8% of consumer spending, spending on financial services presents one of the ways for consumers to alter their spending, by shifting consumption from the future to the present or vice versa. To the extent that consumer financial decisions result in contraction (or growth) in consumer spending patterns, there can be profound macroeconomic consequences. Indeed, the mortgage market is one of the major channels through which Federal Reserve monetary policy translates into real economic effects. Lower borrowing costs, through lower interest rates, encourage home purchases, and with that economic activity in home building and furnishings. Higher borrowing costs, through higher interest rates, have the inverse effect.

Let's imagine, then, that our median-income family, the Smiths, feel that their expenses are too high for their current income and savings and therefore cut back on their consumption in an attempt to balance the household budget. When they do so, it affects other households. If the Smiths spend less on food, maybe cutting out eating at restaurants, those restaurants will have less revenue. That in turn might lead to the restaurants cutting back their employment or reducing wages. The restaurant employees who are now earning less will spend less themselves in an attempt to balance household budgets. And a downward cycle of economic contraction will emerge.

What the Smiths pay for consumer financial services is not necessarily lost from the economy. The financial institution—let's call it a bank—that gets the fees can use that money to fund new projects by making new loans. It could increase its own employment and compensation, make acquisitions, or otherwise reinvest in its own facilities. Or it could dividend the money to its shareholders.

But will the bank do this? What if it is concerned about the risks posed by potential borrowers and investments and wants to have cash on hand, just in case? To the extent that the money is hoarded by financial institutions and not reloaned, reinvested, or dividended, it is effectively being removed from the economy, resulting in economic contraction.

Let's say the Smith family's expenses are such that their savings rate becomes negative. Let's assume that they cannot increase their income. What does that mean in terms of their lifestyle? The Smiths might be living off of accumulated savings in addition to current income. That is, they might have money in the bank that they are using to pay for current expenses. That money will not be available for the future when the Smiths retire and their current income declines. What will happen then? The social safety net—Social Security and Medicare—will ensure a minimal level of living for the Smiths, but not much.

It's also possible that if the Smith family's expenses rise beyond current income and accumulated savings, the Smiths might be able to continue maintaining their current consumption levels—and thus keep up with their neighbors, the Joneses—by borrowing. But this is going to be a short-term strategy, as their debt service expenses will rise and eventually they will find themselves shut out of credit markets as too risky. What happens to the Smiths then?

One possibility is that they will slough off some of their debt through bankruptcy. But many, if not most, consumers in financial distress do not file for bankruptcy, not least because of the expense of doing so. What else might they do? They might muddle along. But consider what sort of incentives the Smiths would have if every additional dollar they made went to their creditors. Would there be any incentive for them to work harder and advance in the world? Not unless there was a light at the end of the tunnel. If consumers end up with too much debt, there can be a "debt overhang" problem that discourages productivity and innovation. At some point we might find the Smiths on the public dole.

Of course, the Smiths don't have to keep borrowing. They could instead reduce their consumption. Let's suppose that the Smiths decide to tighten their belts and cut out any "unnecessary" expenses. Which expenses are "unnecessary"? The daily latte? Piano lessons? Braces? The car? Their cellphones? The Internet? Johnny Squeaky? What does trimming expenses mean for the Smiths? We know it means that they aren't keeping up with their more successful median-income friends, the Joneses.

In economic jargon, the Smiths are reducing consumption. The Smiths are still surviving—they aren't starving—but as their consumption declines, their lives become rather different with ramifications for where the Smiths fit into society (or at least how they believe they fit and others perceive them), which has consequences for social and political stability.

VI. OVERVIEW OF THIS BOOK

As noted above, consumer finance writ large covers five transactional functions: payments, credit, savings and investment, insurance, and advice services. This book focuses on a subset of these five consumer financial functions and their regulation: savings, payments, and credit, along with associated advice services. This particular focus follows from the divisions of regulatory authority over different areas of consumer finance. Savings, payments, and credit are the core services offered by depository institutions (banks) and are under a separate regulatory regime than securities-based investment products and insurance. While many of the firms that offer payment, credit, and savings products and services are not banks, the regulatory framework for these products is closely tied to retail banking regulation. Moreover, since 2011, savings, payments, and credit have all been within the regulatory purview of a powerful new federal regulatory agency, the Consumer Financial Protection Bureau (CFPB); this book largely tracks the scope of the CFPB's regulatory authority.

The rest of this book is divided into two main parts. Part I is the "Regulation" part of the book. It covers the various modes and levels of regulation of consumer finance: common law and equity; state statutory schemes; and federal statutory schemes. Part I also covers general issues with disclosure regulation and consumer rationality. Part I is divided in to three sections. Section A begins with the most basic level of consumer finance regulation—common law tort and contract—through the lens of a case that is familiar to virtually every law student from first-year contracts—*Williams v. Walker-Thomas Furniture Co.* While you have probably read it as a contracts case on unconscionability, it is also a consumer finance case. The *Walker-Thomas* case is a microcosm of many of the issues involved in consumer finance and provides a useful touchstone for discussions later in the course.

Section A then looks at the economic and procedural obstacles to regulation through private enforcement. There are significant barriers to private enforcement of consumer finance contracts and rights. Not surprisingly, consumer finance regulation is often public regulation. Section B covers the general architecture of public regulation of consumer finance markets—who regulates what products and with what powers. Public regulation occurs at both the state and federal level. Section B begins with an examination of state money transmitter regulation as a window into state regulatory regimes before turning to the central player in consumer finance regulation, the Consumer Financial Protection Bureau. The bulk of Section B is devoted to an examination of the history and policy behind the CFPB and the scope of the CFPB's rulemaking, supervision, and enforcement authorities. Understanding exactly which entities and products are subject to which regulator's jurisdiction is a critical part of understanding how the consumer finance regulatory system operates. Section C then concludes Part I with a consideration of disclosure regulation, one of the most ubiquitous forms of regulation, and the insights and limitations of behavioral economics.

Part II is the "Markets" part of the book and is divided into three sections. Section A covers various savings and payment products, while Section B looks at consumer credit products, and Section C covers markets in consumer financial data—credit reporting, privacy, and data security—which are used for making credit decisions and for authorizing payments. The chapters in these sections provide an overview of different financial products, explaining how they operate, the players involved, the benefits produced, and the risks created, as well as the regulatory responses. Some of the chapters are specific to particular products, such as credit cards or mortgages, but other chapters deal with broader cross-product regulatory approaches, such as usury restrictions, data security, and fair lending laws. Throughout Part II, the book strives to present the issues involved in consumer finance from both the consumer and business sides.

Finally, a word about using the book. It might be different than what you're used to in other courses, as there aren't a lot of cases in the book. Instead, there's a fair amount of expository text, occasional graphics, and other assorted materials like complaints from litigation, rather than judicial opinions. Most notably, though, every chapter of the book concludes with a problem set. The problem sets are not incidental. They are integral to how the book is designed to be taught.

Sometimes the problems are designed to make you think broadly about policy issues or transactional problems; other times they are about close reading of statutes. Overall, though, they are designed to get you thinking about consumer finance as a lawyer. Most of the problems have a statutory citation following the problem. It's not there because it looks good. It's there because it points you to the answer. (Would that such citations abounded in real life!) To get the most out of this book you need to do the problems and to do the problems right you need to look up the statutory citations.

Problem Set 1

1. List all of the types of financial transactions you undertook in the last year. How many transactions of each type do you think you made? How many worked as planned? How many were problematic? How did you address the problematic transactions?

2. Why are the Smiths saving so little? Is it that they're profligate? Is it a high tax burden? Is it a deeper structural problem? What would need to happen to materially change the Smiths' financial situation? And how much *should* they be saving?

3. How do the following events affect the Smiths financially?

- **a.** The Smiths accidentally overdraw their bank account and get charged a $35 overdraft fee.
- **b.** The Smiths' bank starts to charge them a monthly $12.50 account fee.
- **c.** The Smiths' furnace needs to be replaced at a cost of $3,000. They can finance the purchase on a credit card at 18% annual interest.[7]
- **d.** Patty has a lateral lisp and speech therapy ($75/week for a year) is not covered by insurance.
- **e.** The Smiths' mortgage rate rises from 4% to 6%, so their monthly mortgage payments rise from $917 to $1,151.
- **f.** Jim and Mary get divorced and set up separate households.

4. Consider the Smiths' bad luck from the perspective of First Bank of Springfield, where the Smiths have their bank account, and which is also their mortgage lender. First Bank of Springfield has assets of $12 billion, annual net income of $110 million, and around 800,000 depositors (consumers and businesses).

- **a.** Which of the events in problem 3 is likely to materially affect the Smiths' ability to repay their mortgage loan?
- **b.** The Smiths have applied for a credit card from your bank. How large of a credit limit are you comfortable giving the Smiths?
- **c.** How much do the monthly account fee and overdraft fee (problems 3.a and 3.b) affect your bank's income if the Smiths are unique? If they're not? Consider what it means if you charge the account fee on 10% of your accounts or if 5% of your accounts overdraw once in a year.

---

7. You should feel free to play around with an online credit card interest calculator to see the total cost of the financing depending on how much the Smiths pay on their card balance every month.

PART I

REGULATION

SECTION A

Regulation by Private Law

CHAPTER 2

REGULATION THROUGH CONTRACT AND TORT

I. TWO FLAVORS OF REGULATION THROUGH CONTRACT

Consumer finance is a business based in the first instance on contract. There are three important implications of contract as the basis for consumer finance.

A. Market Discipline

First, the fact that consumer finance is based on contract means that business-to-consumer relationships are subject to some measure of market discipline. Contract involves a "bilateral monopoly"—both parties to a contract must agree for there to be a contract. This means that consumers and businesses both ideally have the ability to say "no" when they are confronted with unsatisfactory terms of dealing. Furthermore, because many contractual consumer financial relationships are terminable at will by the consumer (*e.g.*, a consumer can close a bank account or prepay a loan), the consumer retains an important ability to exit from an unsatisfactory relationship and to withhold business in the future.

The contractual nature of many consumer finance relationships is a predicate for market discipline, and market discipline acts as the first line of regulation of the consumer finance industry. While much of this course will be about law, market discipline is a critical regulatory tool that does not operate through law, even though its strength is shaped by law. Market discipline is also one of the most common consumer finance tools, especially for the small-dollar transactions that make up the bulk of consumer financial relationships. If you are hit with a $30 charge by your bank that you think is unfair, are you likely to litigate? As Judge Posner observed, "only a lunatic or a fanatic sues for $30." *Carnegie* v. *Household Int'l, Inc.*, 376 F.3d 656, 661 (7th Cir. 2004). Instead, in most cases consumers either "lump it" or exit the relationship. Note, however, the inverse implication regarding large-dollar transactions like mortgage loans.

It is important not to overstate the role of market discipline, however. Its strength varies considerably by market. Businesses may not always care about market discipline if they are fly-by-night. This problem appears even among mainstream financial services firms. Thus, after Fairbanks Capital entered into a consent decree with the Federal Trade Commission for mortgage servicing abuses, *FTC v. Fairbanks Capital Corp. et al.*, No. 03-12219 (D. Mass. 2003), Fairbanks promptly rebranded itself as Select Portfolio Servicing. Only industry cognoscenti would have known it was the same company.

Similarly, even non-fly-by-night businesses can be subject to short-termist pressures on earnings from shareholders or can suffer from agency problems in terms of employee compensation in which their employees are incentivized to be short-termist. Indeed, a business that can make enough money in time period one might not care about time period two.

Likewise, market discipline is generally impaired by consumers' tendency toward privacy in financial matters, which means that consumers' finances are often externally opaque, in turn limiting signaling between consumers in the consumer finance market. Suppose you have a very financially savvy friend. You might think to free-ride on your friend's smarts and work by copying your friend's behavior. This isn't so easy, however. Do you know what bank issues your friend's credit card? You might learn this and try to get the same card, but do you know if you are receiving the same terms as your friend? Just because the cards look the same doesn't mean that they have the same contractual terms.

There is a market for third-party reviews of financial products and customized financial advice, such as that found through *Consumer Reports* magazine (and website) and Mint.com, but it is hard for consumers to know how reliable these recommendations are, much less whether the advisors are receiving referral fees for highlighting or steering consumers toward particular products. How useful, then, are third-party reviews of financial products?

Market discipline can also be undermined by the "sticky" nature of consumer financial relationships. Many consumer finance dealings are not one-off interactions, such as the cashing of a check by a check casher, but extended relationships. While a consumer might only get a mortgage loan or a car loan once from a particular lender, the consumer is likely to maintain those loans for a number of years. Similarly, the consumer is likely to maintain a bank account or a credit card for a substantial period of time with a single institution. In both situations, market discipline can be undermined because of the stickiness of relationships.

For example, consumers are reluctant to switch deposit accounts on a regular basis because of the lock-in effect of automatic bill pay and direct deposit, among other factors. Similarly, constantly switching credit cards can result in a consumer forfeiting the value accumulated in a credit card's rewards program. And there can be substantial transaction costs to switching, in terms of both search costs (because you have to find a better deal to make it worthwhile) and actually executing the transaction. For mortgage loans, in particular, closing costs of render a refinancing unprofitable for a consumer. The result of all of this is that consumers may suffer not just from the problem of poor initial choices, but also from the problem of failing to "switch horses" when they should. *See* Yoon-Ho Alex Lee & K. Jeremy Ko, *Consumer Mistakes in the Mortgage Market: Choosing Unwisely Versus Not Switching Wisely*, 14 U. Pa. J. Bus. L. 417 (2012). Market discipline is great if you can get it, but its strength is inconsistent within consumer financial transactions.

B. Contractual Terms and Tortious Overreaches

The second implication of the contractual basis for consumer financial relationships is that the terms of the contract itself function as regulation. A business's ability to charge a consumer arises, in most cases, solely from contract. Likewise, a consumer's ability to demand performance from a business also generally arises from contract. The flip side of this is that when a business or consumer takes value absent contractual assent, there is likely a tort. The combination of contract providing for the terms of a relationship and tort policing unconsented conduct provides a powerful layer of regulation in addition to market discipline.

The combination of contract and tort provides an important initial level of regulation of consumer finance relationships. The contract sets out the terms by which the parties will deal, and by implication, the terms by which they will not deal. Thus, to the extent that a contract authorizes a business to charge the consumer only certain charges, it is it does not authorize other charges. Accordingly, collection of those charges will be a tort.

Consider a pawn loan agreement. In a pawn loan transaction, a consumer gets a loan from a pawnshop in exchange for giving the pawnshop certain goods, say an engagement ring or an amplifier, as a pledge of collateral. As part of the loan agreement, the consumer expressly warrants that he or she has clear title to the items pledged. Pursuant to the agreement, the consumer has a fixed amount of time to repay the loan plus any authorized fees. If the consumer repays the loan in a timely fashion, the consumer gets the pledged goods back. (This is known as "redeeming" the goods.) If the consumer fails to timely redeem the goods, they become property of the pawnshop, which may then sell them, but the pawnshop may not otherwise attempt to collect from the consumer. Critically, the consumer is not obligated to redeem the goods. In other words, the consumer has a choice of whether to keep the loan proceeds or redeem the goods, and the amount of the pawn loan will reflect the pawnshop's estimate of what it can make selling the goods.

This entire lending relationship is contractual, although state law will generally regulate the fees that can be charged, provide for a minimum redemption period, and require certain disclosures. Additionally, federal law will mandate disclosure of credit terms, impose certain data privacy, anti-discrimination, and anti-money laundering requirements, and, in certain cases involving active duty military servicemembers, impose fee limitations. But the core of the transaction remains contractual.

To see how contract and tort operate to regulate the pawn relationship, suppose that the consumer attempts to redeem the goods in a timely fashion, but the pawnshop refuses to return the goods to the consumer (having already sold them). The consumer will have a contract claim against the pawnshop for refusing to perform on the redemption leg of the pawn contract. The consumer will also have a tort claim against the pawnshop for converting her property. The consumer may well have additional statutory claims against the pawnshop, and the elements of proof and remedies may be different than the common law claims, but the core basis of liability remains the same.

It's important to recognize that contract and tort cut both ways, protecting the business as well as the consumer. Suppose that the pledged goods had been stolen, and a police stolen goods unit recovers them from the pawnshop. The pawnshop now has a contract claim against the borrower for breach of warranty. And if the borrower knew the goods were stolen, the pawnshop also has a tort claim against the borrower for fraud. Whether the pawnshop will ever be able to collect on these claims is another matter, but in theory, at least, contract and tort give the pawnshop some protection.

Tort also obviously polices relationships that are not just outside the boundaries of contract, but in which there is no contract. A consumer who obtains a loan fraudulently has tort liability, just as a bank that opens up unauthorized consumer accounts has tort liability.

C. Negative Implications for Non-Contractual Consumer Relationships

While contract provides the basis for consumer financial relationships, there are many derivative relationships in which relationships are not contractual, at least from the consumer's perspective. While consumers generally are able to pick their lender, they are not able to pick their loan servicer, their credit reporting bureau, or their debt collector. Similarly, a consumer can choose whether to make a payment at a merchant and the method of payment, but it is the merchant, not the consumer, that picks the payment processor. Indeed, in some lending markets consumers do not get to meaningfully select their lenders; instead, consumer "leads" are auctioned off by a "lead generator," and the auction winner is the only lender the consumer gets to deal with. These non-contractual relationships often present particular problems because they are not subject to the same type of market discipline as contractual relationships. *See, e.g.*, Pew Charitable Trusts, *Payday Lending in America: Fraud and Abuse Online: Harmful Practices in Internet Payday Lending* (2014). The following remarks by Richard Cordray, the first Director of the Consumer Financial Protection Bureau, highlight the problems that can arise in these non-contractual "derivative" markets.

Prepared Remarks by Richard Cordray
Director of the Consumer Financial Protection Bureau

Consumer Advisory Board Meeting, Washington, D.C.
February 20, 2013

. . .

Another problem that consumers face on the pathway to opportunity is that in certain important markets—such as debt collection, loan servicing, and credit reporting—they are unable to choose their provider of financial products or services. When people cannot "vote with their feet," their clout is limited, even though these products and services can have a profound influence on their lives. When a market's central focus is on the nature of the financial relationship between two businesses, consumers can become collateral damage to the dynamics that actually drive the economics of such markets.

Take, for example, the market for debt collection. When a consumer does not pay back a debt, the creditor may decide to sell it to or contract with a debt collector to secure payment of what is still owed. Once this occurs, the paying business relationship has shifted; it now lies between the debt collector and the creditor, not the consumer and the creditor. This can lead to mistreatment of the consumer, who becomes, in effect, a kind of "bystander" to the new business relationship. In this situation, creditors may have little reason to ensure that debt collectors treat consumers fairly and appropriately or that they maintain and use accurate information. Given this dysfunctional dynamic, there is little wonder that debt collection has proven to be one of the most common sources of complaints in the realm of consumer finance.

The same phenomenon is found in other markets as well. Mortgage servicing involves a relationship between the owner of the mortgage—perhaps the original lender, or someone who later bought the loan rights, or even an investor in some form of security backed by the original loan—and a third party tasked with processing the payments and pay-outs made to administer the loan.

The servicer is hired by the mortgage holder, not by the borrower. As a result, the financial incentives governing the servicer's conduct and activities are once again outside the consumer's control. Unpleasant surprises, constant runarounds, and mistreatment stemming from a lack of investment in customer service are examples of unacceptable practices that have been harming consumers for almost a decade now.

The same problematic incentive structure can be found in student loan servicing or any loan servicing market, of course; mortgage servicing is simply the most well-known example. Many consumers seek to negotiate for a more affordable payment plan on their loan obligations, only to find themselves stymied, even when a modification would make sense for all concerned. We have seen the impact this has had for so many homeowners, and we are looking to take steps that may address the same kinds of problems for student loan borrowers.

The credit reporting industry is another market in which consumers can become largely incidental to a business relationship between others. Here, the paying business relationship lies between the credit reporting firm and a third party that is interested in evaluating the risks of offering credit to consumers. The credit reporting firm has to balance its clients' needs for accurate information with their desire to keep costs low. The levels and types of inaccuracies that the purchasers of credit reports are willing to tolerate get resolved in the marketplace.

What is quite clear, however, is that consumers have no real say in such decisions and their interests are an afterthought at best. From the perspective of the credit reporting firm and its clients, inaccurate reports may be no more than a statistic or an error rate. But for individual consumers whose reports are incorrect, the damage done to their lives can be severe and lasting.

Without consumer choice, a key element of market discipline is lacking. The result is to permit or even facilitate a distinct indifference to the interests of individual consumers. At the Bureau, we are taking on this problem by highlighting troublesome practices and working to fix them. . . .

II. MANDATORY CONTRACT TERMS: GOOD FAITH, FAIR DEALING, AND "CONSCIONABILITY"

While a contract consists primarily of the terms of the agreement, plus any gap-filler terms mandated by law, such as delivery terms when not specified, Uniform Commercial Code (UCC) § 2-308, it also includes certain implied duties, namely the implied covenants of good faith and fair dealing, and is subject to certain equitable doctrines, such as unconscionability, that can be invoked as defenses to enforcement of the contract. Hopefully you recall something about unconscionability from your first-year contracts course. As a refresher, recall that a transaction can be procedurally or substantively unconscionable, or both. As the California Supreme Court has explained:

> [P]rocedural unconscionability requires oppression or surprise. Oppression occurs where a contract involves lack of negotiation and meaningful choice, surprise where the allegedly unconscionable provision is hidden within a prolix printed form. Substantive unconscionability pertains to the fairness of an agreement's actual terms and to assessments of whether they are overly harsh or one-sided. A contract term is not substantively unconscionable when it merely gives one side a greater benefit; rather, the term must be so one-sided as to shock the conscience.

Pinnacle Museum Tower Ass'n v. Pincale Market Development (U.S.), LLC, 55 Cal.4th 223, 247 (Cal. 2012). There is some variation in state law, but generally both procedural and substantive unconscionability must be shown for a transaction to be avoided as unconscionable. (Typically unconscionability is a defense, rather than an affirmative cause of action, but it might provide the predicate for other affirmative grounds for suit.) This does not mean that the showing needs to be the same for each type of unconscionability. Thus, California law requires that while both procedural and substantive unconscionability must be shown, "they need not be present in the same degree" and are evaluated on a "sliding scale" such that the stronger the showing of procedural unconscionability, the lesser of a showing must be made regarding substantive unconscionability and vice versa. *Armendariz v. Foundation Health PsychCare Services, Inc.*, 24 Cal.4th 83, 114 (Cal. 2000). Critically, unconscionability is a doctrine that depends on the particular facts and circumstances of a case; in the abstract, parties cannot be sure if it will apply.

The doctrine of unconscionability is typically taught through the famous case of *Williams v. Walker-Thomas Furniture Company.* While a bright star in the contracts firmament, *Walker-Thomas* is also a consumer finance case, and it provides a useful starting point for considering the reach and limitations of contract law for regulating consumer financial transactions.

As you read the two reported decisions in the case (the first appeal and the appeal from that decision), consider which of the rationales for consumer financial regulation are shaping how the courts approach the case.

Also, when reading these cases, try to think about the issues involved from both the perspective of the consumer and the perspective of the financial services provider. What does the regulation do to the consumer? To the business? While this course is focused on the regulation of consumer finance, it is important to understand regulation, including regulation by contract, as a piece of the consumer finance business ecosystem. Regulation is a factor that shapes the products available to consumers; it largely defines the sphere of competition for consumer finance providers. An understanding of what is and is not possible within the existing regulatory system is important not just from a legal systems standpoint, but also from a business standpoint.

Ora Lee Williams v. Walker-Thomas Furniture Company

198 A.2d 914 (D.C. Ct. App. 1964)

QUINN, Associate Judge.

Appellant, a person of limited education separated from her husband, is maintaining herself and her seven children by means of public assistance. During the period 1957-1962 she had a continuous course of dealings with appellee from which she purchased many household articles on the installment plan. These included sheets, curtains, rugs, chairs, a chest of drawers, beds, mattresses, a washing machine, and a stereo set. In 1963 appellee filed a complaint in replevin for possession of all the items purchased by appellant, alleging that her payments were in default and that it retained title to the goods according to the sales contracts. By the writ of replevin appellee obtained a bed, chest of drawers, washing machine, and the stereo set. After hearing testimony and examining the contracts, the trial court entered judgment for appellee.

Appellant's principal contentions on appeal are (1) there was a lack of meeting of the minds, and (2) the contracts were against public policy.

Appellant signed fourteen contracts in all. They were approximately six inches in length and each contained a long paragraph in extremely fine print. One of the sentences in this paragraph provided that payments, after the first purchase, were to be prorated on all purchases then outstanding. Mathematically, this had the effect of keeping a balance due on all items until the time balance was completely eliminated. It meant that title to the first purchase, remained in appellee until the fourteenth purchase, made some five years later, was fully paid.

At trial appellant testified that she understood the agreements to mean that when payments on the running account were sufficient to balance the amount due on an individual item, the item became hers. She testified that most of the purchases were made at her home; that the contracts were signed in blank; that she did not read the instruments; and that she was not provided with a copy. She admitted, however, that she did not ask anyone to read or explain the contracts to her.

We have stated that "one who refrains from reading a contract and in conscious ignorance of its terms voluntarily assents thereto will not be relieved from his bad bargain." *Bob Wilson, Inc. v. Swann*, D.C. Mun. App., 168 A.2d 198, 199 (1961). "One who signs a contract has a duty to read it and is obligated according to its terms." *Hollywood Credit Clothing Co. v. Gibson*, D.C. App., 188 A.2d 348, 349 (1963). "It is as much the duty of a person who cannot read the language in which a contract is written to have someone read it to him before he signs it, as it is the duty of one who can read to peruse it himself before signing it." *Stern v. Moneyweight Scale Co.*, 42 App. D.C. 162, 165 (1914).

A careful review of the record shows that appellant's assent was not obtained "by fraud or even misrepresentation falling short of fraud." *Hollywood Credit Clothing Co. v. Gibson, supra.* This is not a case of mutual misunderstanding but a unilateral mistake. Under these circumstances, appellant's first contention is without merit.

Appellant's second argument presents a more serious question. The record reveals that prior to the last purchase appellant had reduced the balance in her account to $164. The last purchase, a stereo set, raised the balance due to $678. Significantly, at the time of this and the preceding purchases, appellee was aware of appellant's financial position. The reverse side of the stereo contract listed the name of appellant's social worker and her $218 monthly stipend from the government. Nevertheless, with full knowledge that appellant had to feed, clothe and support both herself and seven children on this amount, appellee sold her a $514 stereo set.

We cannot condemn too strongly appellee's conduct. It raises serious questions of sharp practice and irresponsible business dealings. A review of the legislation in the District of Columbia affecting retail sales and the pertinent decisions of the highest court in this jurisdiction disclose, however, no ground upon which this court can declare the contracts in question contrary to public policy. We note that were the Maryland Retail Installment Sales Act, Art. 83 §§ 128-153, or its equivalent, in force in the District of Columbia, we could grant appellant appropriate relief. We think Congress should consider corrective legislation to protect the public from such exploitive contracts as were utilized in the case at bar.

Affirmed.

Williams v. Walker-Thomas Furniture Company; Thorne et al. v. Walker-Thomas Furniture Company

350 F.2d 445 (D.C. Cir. 1965)

J. Skelly WRIGHT, Circuit Judge:

Appellee, Walker-Thomas Furniture Company, operates a retail furniture store in the District of Columbia. During the period from 1957 to 1962 each appellant in these cases purchased a number of household items from Walker-Thomas, for which payment was to be made in installments. The terms of each purchase were contained in a printed form contract which set forth the value of the purchased item and purported to lease the item to appellant for a stipulated monthly rent payment. The contract then provided, in substance, that title would remain in Walker-Thomas until the total of all the monthly payments made equaled the stated value of the item, at which time appellants could take title. In the event of a default in the payment of any monthly installment, Walker-Thomas could repossess the item.

The contract further provided that "the amount of each periodical installment payment to be made by [purchaser] to the Company under this present lease shall be inclusive of and not in addition to the amount of each installment payment to be made by [purchaser] under such prior leases, bills or accounts; *and all payments now and hereafter made by [purchaser] shall be credited pro rata on all outstanding leases, bills and accounts* due the Company by [purchaser] at the time each such payment is made." (Emphasis added.) The effect of this rather obscure provision was to keep a balance due on every item purchased until the balance due on all items, whenever purchased, was liquidated. As a result, the debt incurred at the time of purchase of each item was secured by the right to repossess all the items previously purchased by the same purchaser, and each new item purchased automatically became subject to a security interest arising out of the previous dealings.

On May 12, 1962, appellant Thorne purchased an item described as a Daveno, three tables, and two lamps, having total stated value of $391.10. Shortly thereafter, he defaulted on his monthly payments and appellee sought to replevy all the items purchased since the first transaction in 1958.* Similarly, on April 17, 1962, appellant Williams bought a stereo set of stated value of $514.95.[1] She too defaulted shortly thereafter, and appellee sought to replevy all the items purchased since December, 1957. The Court of General Sessions granted judgment for appellee. The District of Columbia Court of Appeals affirmed, and we granted appellants' motion for leave to appeal to this court.

Appellants' principal contention, rejected by both the trial and the appellate courts below, is that these contracts, or at least some of them, are unconscionable and, hence, not enforceable. In its opinion in *Williams v. Walker-Thomas Furniture Company*, 198 A.2d 914, 916 (1964), the District of Columbia Court of Appeals explained its rejection of this contention as [being based on its lack of power to refuse to enforce an unconscionable contract.]

We do not agree that the court lacked the power to refuse enforcement to contracts found to be unconscionable. In other jurisdictions, it has been held as a matter of common law that unconscionable contracts are not enforceable. While no decision of this court so holding has been found, the notion that an unconscionable bargain should not be given full enforcement is by no means novel. In *Scott v. United States*, 79 U.S. (12 Wall.) 443, 445 (1870), the Supreme Court stated:

> . . . If a contract be unreasonable and unconscionable, but not void for fraud, a court of law will give to the party who sues for its breach damages, not according to its letter, but only such as he is equitably entitled to. . . .

Since we have never adopted or rejected such a rule, the question here presented is actually one of first impression.

Congress has recently enacted the Uniform Commercial Code, which specifically provides that the court may refuse to enforce a contract which it finds to be unconscionable at the time it was made. 28 D.C. Code § 2-302 (Supp. IV 1965). The enactment of this section, which occurred subsequent to the contracts here in suit, does not mean that the common law of the District of Columbia was otherwise at the time of

---

* [Replevin is an action to recover one's wrongfully detained goods. —Ed.]

1. At the time of this purchase her account showed a balance of $164 still owing from her prior purchases. The total of all the purchases made over the years in question came to $1,800. The total payments amounted to $1,400.

enactment, nor does it preclude the court from adopting a similar rule in the exercise of its powers to develop the common law for the District of Columbia. In fact, in view of the absence of prior authority on the point, we consider the congressional adoption of § 2-302 persuasive authority for following the rationale of the cases from which the section is explicitly derived. Accordingly, we hold that where the element of unconscionability is present at the time a contract is made, the contract should not be enforced.

Unconscionability has generally been recognized to include an absence of meaningful choice on the part of one of the parties together with contract terms which are unreasonably favorable to the other party. Whether a meaningful choice is present in a particular case can only be determined by consideration of all the circumstances surrounding the transaction. In many cases the meaningfulness of the choice is negated by a gross inequality of bargaining power.[7] The manner in which the contract was entered is also relevant to this consideration. Did each party to the contract, considering his obvious education or lack of it, have a reasonable opportunity to understand the terms of the contract, or were the important terms hidden in a maze of fine print and minimized by deceptive sales practices? Ordinarily, one who signs an agreement without full knowledge of its terms might be held to assume the risk that he has entered a one-sided bargain.[8] But when a party of little bargaining power, and hence little real choice, signs a commercially unreasonable contract with little or no knowledge of its terms, it is hardly likely that his consent, or even an objective manifestation of his consent, was ever given to all the terms. In such a case the usual rule that the terms of the agreement are not to be questioned should be abandoned and the court should consider whether the terms of the contract are so unfair that enforcement should be withheld.

In determining reasonableness or fairness, the primary concern must be with the terms of the contract considered in light of the circumstances existing when the contract was made. The test is not simple, nor can it be mechanically applied. The terms are to be considered "in the light of the general commercial background and the commercial

---

7. . . . Inquiry into the relative bargaining power of the two parties is not an inquiry wholly divorced from the general question of unconscionability, since a one-sided bargain is itself evidence of the inequality of the bargaining parties. This fact was vaguely recognized in the common law doctrine of intrinsic fraud, that is, fraud which can be presumed from the grossly unfair nature of the terms of the contract. See the oft-quoted statement of Lord Hardwicke in *Earl of Chesterfield v. Janssen*, 28 Eng. Rep. 82, 100 (1751):

> . . . [Fraud] may be apparent from the intrinsic nature and subject of the bargain itself; such as no man in his senses and not under delusion would make. . . .

And *cf. Hume v. United States*, 132 U.S. [406, 413 (1889)], where the Court characterized the English cases as "cases in which one party took advantage of the other's ignorance of arithmetic to impose upon him, and the fraud was apparent from the face of the contracts.". . . .

8. *See* Restatement, Contracts § 70 (1932); *Note*, 63 Harv. L. Rev. 494 (1950). *See also Daley v. People's Building, Loan & Savings Ass'n*, 178 Mass. 13 (1901), in which Mr. Justice Holmes, while sitting on the Supreme Judicial Court of Massachusetts, made this observation:

> . . . Courts are less and less disposed to interfere with parties making such contracts as they choose, so long as they interfere with no one's welfare but their own. . . . It will be understood that we are speaking of parties standing in an equal position where neither has any oppressive advantage or power. . . .

needs of the particular trade or case."[11] Corbin suggests the test as being whether the terms are "so extreme as to appear unconscionable according to the mores and business practices of the time and place." 1 CORBIN, [CONTRACTS § 128 (1963)]. We think this formulation correctly states the test to be applied in those cases where no meaningful choice was exercised upon entering the contract.

Because the trial court and the appellate court did not feel that enforcement could be refused, no findings were made on the possible unconscionability of the contracts in these cases. Since the record is not sufficient for our deciding the issue as a matter of law, the cases must be remanded to the trial court for further proceedings.

So ordered.

DANAHER, Circuit Judge (dissenting):

The District of Columbia Court of Appeals obviously was as unhappy about the situation here presented as any of us can possibly be. Its opinion in the *Williams* case, quoted in the majority text, concludes: "We think Congress should consider corrective legislation to protect the public from such exploitive contracts as were utilized in the case at bar."

My view is thus summed up by an able court which made no finding that there had actually been sharp practice. Rather the appellant seems to have known precisely where she stood.

There are many aspects of public policy here involved. What is a luxury to some may seem an outright necessity to others. Is public oversight to be required of the expenditures of relief funds? A washing machine, e.g., in the hands of a relief client might become a fruitful source of income. Many relief clients may well need credit, and certain business establishments will take long chances on the sale of items, expecting their pricing policies will afford a degree of protection commensurate with the risk. Perhaps a remedy when necessary will be found within the provisions of the "Loan Shark" law, D.C. CODE §§ 26-601 *et seq.* (1961).

I mention such matters only to emphasize the desirability of a cautious approach to any such problem, particularly since the law for so long has allowed parties such great latitude in making their own contracts. I dare say there must annually be thousands upon thousands of installment credit transactions in this jurisdiction, and one can only speculate as to the effect the decision in these cases will have.

I join the District of Columbia Court of Appeals in its disposition of the issues.

Notes on *Williams v. Walker-Thomas Furniture Co.*

1. Judge Skelly Wright refers to Walker-Thomas Furniture taking a "security interest" in the items Ms. Williams purchased on credit. A security interest, sometimes called a mortgage or a lien, is a type of contingent property interest in particular property known as "collateral" that secures the repayment of a debt. The security interest is

11. Comment, Uniform Commercial Code § 2-307.

parasitic on the debt; without the debt, the security interest is meaningless. A security interest secures repayment of the debt by permitting the creditor to force the sale of the collateral if there is a default on the debt (with personalty, the creditor may also seize possession of the collateral prior to the sale). The debt is then repaid from the proceeds of the sale, with any surplus going back to the debtor. Until the sale is concluded, the debtor may "**redeem**" the collateral from the security interest by repaying the debt, but once the sale is completed the debtor's right to redeem is "foreclosed." Hence the sale is called a "**foreclosure sale.**" The foreclosure sale may be conducted privately or publicly depending on the jurisdiction and type of collateral involved.

2. Be sure you understand the transactional problem in *Williams v. Walker-Thomas Furniture*. The defendants made a series of purchases on retail credit under separate contracts. These contracts were all "**installment sales**" or "conditional sales" contracts, which provided that title would remain with the seller until the goods had been paid for in full, but the buyer would have possession and use of the goods in the interim. The "credit" component of the sales was that the goods did not have to be paid for upfront; no funds were ever disbursed from Walker-Thomas to the defendants. While Walker-Thomas did not take a formally documented security interest, the installment sales contract functioned much like a loan for the purchase price of the contract secured by a security interest in the goods sold.

3. Critically, the sales contracts provided that any payments made would be prorated among all the contracts, rather than applied to any specific contract. That meant that none of the contracts would be paid off until all of the contracts were paid off. Accordingly, upon a default, Walker-Thomas Furniture could repossess the goods purchased under any and all of the contracts. Without the payment proration clause, Walker-Thomas Furniture would have been allowed to repossess only the stereo from Ms. Williams, not the other items. Thus, Walker-Thomas Furniture understood itself as simply exercising its contractual rights when it repossessed the goods from Ms. Williams and the Thornes.

4. Procedurally, *Williams v. Walker-Thomas* is a relic. The law of the District of Columbia at the time permitted a creditor on a conditional sales agreement to repossess goods without any pre-seizure hearing. Instead, the creditor had to get a writ of replevin from the Court of General Sessions, which merely required the creditor to file a verified complaint and enter into an undertaking. The writ would then be given to the marshal for execution. Only subsequent to the seizure would there be an opportunity for a hearing, which typically resulted in a default judgment for the seller/lender.

5. Pre-hearing replevin with a bond was subsequently held to be unconstitutional by the Supreme Court. *Fuentes v. Shevin*, 407 U.S. 67 (1972). Replevin actions now require a hearing before the seizure. In contrast, self-help repossession (as long as there is no breach of the peace) is still permitted under the Uniform Commercial Code, UCC § 9-609(a), because it is not considered state action subject to the Fourteenth Amendment as no court and no law officer is involved. *See Flagg Bros., Inc. v. Brooks*, 436 U.S. 149 (1978) (upholding the constitutionality of UCC Article 7 self-help repossession for warehousemen). Walker-Thomas Furniture could not have engaged in self-help repossession under the UCC for two reasons. First, the District of Columbia had not yet adopted the UCC and second, Walker-Thomas Furniture did not formally have a security interest, even though the contract was designed to function as a secured loan. Also, as discussed below, Walker-Thomas could not, after 1985, legally take a non-possessory, non-purchase money security interest in household goods. 16 C.F.R. § 444.

6. In early drafts of the D.C. Circuit Court opinion, Judge Skelly Wright focused on the structural problems in the behavior of Walker-Thomas Furniture: selling used goods as new, at above-market prices, and selling goods to customers it knew were likely to default. These behaviors were not specific to Ms. Williams or the Thornes. Instead, as Professor Anne Fleming has observed, "Wright's draft suggested that these contracts might be unconscionable because of these terms and an ongoing pattern of conduct by the seller, rather than isolated defects in individual transactions." Anne Fleming, *The Rise and Fall of Unconscionability as the "Law of the Poor"*, 102 Geo. L.J. 1383, 1419 (2014). What was the effect of Wright changing the opinion to focus on the particular vulnerability of Ms. William and the Thornes?

7. The opinions leave out details from the evidence presented to the courts. For example, Ora Lee Williams was a single mother with an eighth-grade education, while William Thorne had a third-grade education and was only marginally literate. Likewise, the contracts did not include price terms, and the contracts were folded over by the door-to-door salesman so that only the signature line was visible to the consumers.

8. Ora Lee Williams couldn't afford to pay the $36 necessary to prevent repossession of her household goods. She was represented at trial and through two appeals by a legal aid organization, which spent some 210 hours of legal work on the case. Robert H. Skilton & Orrin L. Helstad, *Protection of the Installment Buyer of Goods Under the Uniform Commercial Code*, 65 Mich. L. Rev. 1465, 1480, n.38 (1967).

9. After *Walker-Thomas* was remanded to the trial court, it settled, with Walker-Thomas Furniture paying Williams $200 for the goods it had repossessed three years earlier.

III. REGULATION AS AN ALTERNATIVE TO CONTRACT DOCTRINE

The D.C. Circuit appeal in *Williams v. Walker-Thomas Furniture* was decided in 1965. At that time the federal government played a relatively limited role in consumer financial regulation. The federal government's real entrance into consumer financial regulation only occurred in 1968, with the enactment of the Consumer Credit Protection Act. Prior to 1968, however, the Federal Trade Commission (FTC) did have some authority to regulate consumer finance under section 5 of the Federal Trade Commission Act, which prohibits "unfair or deceptive acts or practices in or affecting commerce." 15 U.S.C. § 45(a)(1).

The FTC, however, was expressly denied "unfair or deceptive acts or practices" authority over "banks, savings and loan institutions . . . [and] Federal credit unions." 15 U.S.C. § 45(a)(2). This restriction was not as important originally as it is today. While the FTC did not have regulatory authority over most financial institutions under section 5 of the FTC Act, it did have authority over retail credit, that is credit issued directly by merchants, which was the major form of non-mortgage consumer credit well into the 1980s.

Banks, savings and loan institutions, and credit unions (collectively, "depositaries") were regulated by various bank regulators, some federal, some state. We will examine this system in a later chapter. Prior to 1975, they were not explicitly prohibited from engaging in "unfair or deceptive acts or practices." The terms on which they could do business and the products they could offer were, however, often highly regulated, and bank regulators held a great deal of informal sway over bank behavior.

In 1975, the FTC proposed its Credit Practices Rule, 16 C.F.R. Part 444, which was only finalized in 1984, becoming effective in 1985. Virtually identical rules were adopted by bank regulators in 1986, and until 2016 covered all lenders.[1] Unlike unconscionability, the FTC Credit Practices Rule is backed up by public enforcement; the FTC can bring suits for violations of the Credit Practices Rule. There is no private right of action under the FTC Act, however, or the rules thereunder.

The FTC Credit Practices Rule expressly forbids the taking of non-possessory security interests in household goods other than purchase money security interests. 16 C.F.R. § 444.2(a)(4). A purchase money security interest is a security interest given to secure a loan of money made specifically for the purchase of a good. Thus, if a consumer were to purchase a washing machine on store credit and give the store a security interest in the washing machine, that would be a purchase money security interest. But if the consumer were to try and subsequently borrow against the washing machine as collateral, it would not be allowed under the FTC Credit Practices Rule. Be aware that the scope of the FTC Credit Practices Rule is determined by its definition of "household goods," which excludes works of art and certain antiques, jewelry, and electronic entertainment equipment. 16 C.F.R. § 444.1(i). There are no reported cases interpreting this provision of the Credit Practices Rule.

The FTC Credit Practices Rule addresses the concern about forfeitures of personal property because of non-purchase money security interests. Was that the issue in *Walker-Thomas*, though? *Walker-Thomas* is about the intersection of a security interest (or something that operates like a security interest) with a scheme of payment application that is very favorable to the lender. Payment application issues continue to remain problematic in consumer finance: for example, if a credit card has balances accruing interest at different rates (perhaps a low-balance transfer rate and another, higher, cash-advance rate), to which balance should a payment be applied? Likewise, in what order should credits and debits be applied to a bank account? The ordering will determine how often a borrower overdrafts and thus

1. Technically, the bank regulators' rulemaking authority under section 5 of the FTC Act was revoked by in July 2010 by the Dodd-Frank Wall Street Reform and Consumer Protection Act, and bank regulators subsequently repealed their rules at various points between 2011 and 2016. The bank regulators and the Consumer Financial Protection Bureau issued joint guidance, however, stating their belief that the previously prohibited practices still remained prohibited (without specific enumeration) under section 5536 of the Dodd-Frank Act. Interagency Guidance Regarding Unfair and Deceptive Credit Practices, Aug. 22, 2014.

how many overdraft fees will be charged. We'll return to these payment application questions in later chapters.

The FTC Credit Practices Rule is part of a broader constellation of regulatory limitations on businesses' remedies against consumers. Pre-hearing garnishment and replevin were both held to be unconstitutional violations of due process by the Supreme Court. *Sniadich v. Family Finance Corp.*, 395 U.S. 337 (1969) (pre-hearing garnishment); *Fuentes v. Shevin*, 407 U.S. 67 (1972) (replevin). Federal law limits the amount of post-hearing wage garnishment, 15 U.S.C. § 1673, and state law further restricts it in some cases. State law also provides that certain property of debtors—which includes judgment debtors—is exempt from the levies of creditors. Federal regulation restricts state holder-in-due-course doctrine to protect consumer borrowers' rights against assignees of debts. 16 C.F.R. § 433.2. Federal law imposes a delayed foreclosure timetable on mortgages and requires mortgage servicers to engage in loss mitigation in some instances. 12 C.F.R. § 1024.41. And federal law limits consumer liability for unauthorized credit and debit card transactions. 15 U.S.C. § 1643; 12 C.F.R. § 1026.12(b); 15 U.S.C. § 1693g(a); 12 C.F.R. § 1005.6(b). These limitations are an important feature of the consumer finance regulatory regime. These regulations substantially narrow creditors' remedies. Do you think this is likely, in turn, to affect the terms on which consumers can obtain credit? If so, what do you think the political pressures are regarding these regulations?

While the general contours of unconscionability—oppression or surprise and lack of fairness in terms of overly harsh or one-sided contract terms—are well understood, unconscionability is a standard, not a rule. Various attempts have been made to codify unconscionability and related equitable concepts of good faith and fair dealing in both federal and state law and make them more rule-like. Typically these codifications do little to crystalize the standard. *See, e.g.*, Iowa Code § 537.5108 (Iowa Uniform Consumer Credit Code).

Contract and tort law provide a first-level set of regulation of the business-to-consumer relationship in consumer finance. To the extent that a practice does not comport with the express terms of a contract or violates a duty, the legal implications are clear. But there are many practices that might be seen by some as problematic that do not obviously violate contract or duty. Equitable doctrines such as unconscionability can address these situations, but the difficulty in defining such inequitable acts and practices makes equity an unreliable method of consumer protection and business regulation. Consumers cannot rely on equitable doctrines such as unconscionability to protect them from oppressive contracts, and businesses cannot rely on their behavior being upheld as legal. Appeal to contract or tort law is also a method of consumer protection dependent on ex post litigation, which most consumers can ill afford. Accordingly, state and federal law frequently expressly prohibit or authorize various consumer finance practices. Still, as we shall see, both state and federal law have maintained broad catchall prohibitions on "unfair," "deceptive," and "abusive" acts and practices, a set of terms that sounds in the same type of equity jurisprudence as unconscionability. Even though doctrines such as unconscionability are not always predictable in application, they have a flexibility that legislatures are loath to see depart from the regulatory system.

Problem Set 2

1. The contract in *Walker-Thomas Furniture* was not formally structured as a security interest, but as a retail installment sale, yet it functioned much as if Walker-Thomas Furniture had taken a security interest in the items Ms. Williams purchase.

- **a.** Why would Walker-Thomas Furniture want to take a security interest in Ms. Williams's "sheets, curtains, rugs, chairs, a chest of drawers, beds, mattresses, a washing machine, and a stereo set"?
- **b.** Why might Ms. Williams want to grant such a security interest?
- **c.** Is this a contract "such as no man in his senses and not under delusion would make on the one hand, and as no honest and fair man would accept on the other" as Lord Hardwicke famously formulated unconscionability in *Earl of Chesterfield v. Janssen*, 28 Eng. Rep. 82, 100 (Ch. 1750)?
- **d.** Given your answers to the previous parts of this question, what effect do you think the FTC Credit Practices has on consumers like Ms. Williams? 16 C.F.R. § 444.2(a)(4).

2. You are counsel to Ms. Williams in the *Walker-Thomas Furniture* litigation. Counsel for Walker-Thomas has argued that there was nothing unclear about the terms in the Walker-Thomas Furniture form contract, and that when there is full and clear disclosure, contracts should be enforced because competition and reputational consequences will drive bad actors and practices from the market. What's your response?

3. You are general counsel to Metropolitan Aspirational Furnishings, a competitor to Walker-Thomas. Metropolitan Aspirational Furnishings very much wants to comply with the law, but also to be able to keep serving the poor urban communities in which it operates. "We're good folks. We help people get the stuff they need, but we always want to follow the law. That's what we do," Metropolitan Aspirational's CEO says to you. What is the advice you give your client after the *Walker-Thomas* decision comes out? How about after the FTC Credit Practices Rule was promulgated? 16 C.F.R. § 444.2(a)(4).

4. You are general counsel to Urban Jungle Furniture, a competitor to Walker-Thomas. Urban Jungle follows the law . . . when it is economically beneficial to do so. "It's legal as long as you get away with it," Urban Jungle's CEO likes to say. What advice do you give to Urban Jungle after the *Walker-Thomas Furniture* decision? How about after the FTC Credit Practices Rule was promulgated? 16 C.F.R. § 444.2(a)(4).

5. It is 1966. You are counsel to the newly elected majority leader in the state legislature. She has just read about the transaction in *Williams v. Walker-Thomas*. She wants to know whether the equitable doctrine of unconscionability can be relied on to always prevent the application of oppressive terms to consumers like Ora Lee Williams. If not, is there a better legislative solution? Does that leave any space for equitable doctrines like unconscionability?

6. Gerry Rzewinski is an impecunious but brilliant Julliard-trained pianist, with a PhD in musicology from the University of Chicago. Gerry rents his apartment and doesn't have a car. The rebuilt 1911 Steinway model D concert grand piano named "Trudy" that Gerry inherited from his parents some years back is by far his most valuable possession and the centerpiece of his living room. Trudy would easily sell for $85,000 and has great sentimental value to Gerry, who says, "They just don't make 'em like this anymore." Gerry is very pleased that as part of Trudy's rebuild an electronic humidifier was attached underneath the piano.

Gerry's beloved Collie dog and close companion, Jennie, is ill and needs an expensive operation or she will die. Gerry doesn't have insurance for Jennie, and the animal hospital is demanding payment in advance.

Gerry has gone into LakeShore Bank to see about a $10,000 loan. You are the loan officer. Gerry explains that he makes about $50,000 annually from teaching and occasional performances, but that he cannot document most of this income, because it is largely in cash. Will you give him a loan? What if he offers to post Trudy as collateral? *See* 16 C.F.R. Part 444.

7. Suppose that in the previous problem, LakeShore Bank would not make Gerry Rzewinski a loan. How might Gerry still obtain credit to pay for Jennie's operation? Consider that Gerry lives in Illinois, which has a statutory 10-day minimum redemption period for pawnshops and an additional 30-day extension option for the borrower. 205 ILCS 510/10. Further extensions are allowed but require the agreement of both the pawnshop and the borrower. *Id.* Illinois also permits pawnshops to charge a monthly finance charge of up to 20% of the loan amount. 205 ILCS 501/2.

8. Metropolitan Aspirational Furniture has been considering some new business models. It wants to comply with the FTC Credit Practices Rule and has requested that you, as outside counsel, write an opinion letter about which of the following transactional structures would be acceptable under the Credit Practices Rule, 16 C.F.R. Part 444:

a. The consumer will make a series of separate purchases on credit, each under a separate loan contract. Each loan contract is secured by a purchase money security interest in the goods purchased, as well as by a security interest in any other goods previously purchased from MAF on which a balance is still owing on the purchase contract.

b. The consumer will make a series of separate purchases on credit, each under a separate loan contract. Each loan is secured by a purchase money security interest in the goods purchased. Each loan contract will contain a "cross-default" clause that provides that a default on one loan is a default on all of the other loans outstanding.

c. The consumer will make a series of separate purchases on credit, each under a separate loan contract. Each loan is secured by a purchase money security interest in the goods purchased. Each loan contract will contain a clause providing that any payments received by MAF will be pro-rated among all outstanding loan contracts.

d. The consumer will make a series of separate purchases on credit, each under a separate contract. Each contract will provide that title to the goods purchased will not transfer to the consumer until the entire balance is paid. Each loan contract will contain a clause providing that any payments received by MAF will be pro-rated among all outstanding loan contracts.

e. The consumer will rent the goods from MAF under a non-cancelable lease for a term slightly shorter than the expected useful economic life of the goods. Each lease contract will contain a clause providing that any payments received by MAF will be pro-rated among all outstanding leases.

f. The consumer will rent the goods from MAF under a lease for a term slightly shorter than the expected useful economic life of the goods. The consumer can cancel the lease at will and will have a purchase option exercisable at any time with a strike price equal to the sale price of the goods adjusted upward to reflect time value of money for the length of the lease. Any past payments under the lease will be credited to the purchase option. Each lease contract will contain a clause providing that any payments received by MAF will be pro-rated among all outstanding leases.

CHAPTER 3

PROCEDURAL LIMITS ON PRIVATE ENFORCEMENT: ARBITRATION AND CLASS ACTION WAIVERS

I. THE COST OF LITIGATION

Disputes inevitably arise between consumers and businesses. These disputes can run both ways. A consumer may believe that a business has failed to honor the terms of its contract, for example by changing the terms of a fixed-rate account. Or a business may believe that a consumer has failed to honor its contractual obligations, for example by failing to pay a bill on time. These disputes can sometimes be resolved informally, but often they result in litigation.

In the previous chapter we saw how contract and tort law form the first level of consumer finance regulation. Contract and tort law shape the consumer financial relationship, but critical to the operation of contract and tort as meaningful modes of regulation is the ability of parties to enforce the law.

Contract and tort law require private enforcement. That means consumers must take businesses to court and vice versa. Non-judicial remedies, as we have seen, are extremely limited. A secured creditor has a self-help right of repossession of collateral, but only if the repossession does not breach the peace. Given that non-possessory non-purchase money security interests are prohibited in most household goods, there is only a limited space for self-help repossession in consumer finance: vehicle lending and mortgage lending (in certain states). Otherwise, remedies for businesses and consumers run through the court.

In the previous chapter we also saw an important limitation on private enforcement: it's expensive. Litigation is expensive and time-consuming not just for consumers, but also for businesses. Attorneys cost money. There are court fees. And litigation can be distracting and eat up time. Executives lose days in depositions and testimony. Documents must be retained and produced. Moreover, the default rule in American courts is that parties pay their own costs.

The expense of litigation means that neither consumers nor businesses are likely to bring suit over small-dollar claims in most cases. In other words, small losses are written off. It isn't worthwhile for a business to sue a consumer over a $30 unpaid bill. Instead, it is far easier to either write off the bill or to sell the $30 account receivable along with the other uncollectible account receivables to a collection agency that might make some dunning calls, but is unlikely to go to court to collect such a small balance. Moreover, business plaintiffs can use the threat of credit reporting or of refusing future service to induce consumers to pay.

Instead, for business plaintiffs seeking to enforce their rights, the cost of bringing litigation or of writing off debts that are not economical to collect is a cost of doing business that might get passed back to consumers in the form of higher prices or reduced services. Thus, restriction of self-help remedies for creditors might well result in higher costs of credit or reduce credit availability.

Similarly, it isn't worthwhile for a consumer individually to sue a business over a $10 overcharge. It's easier just to "lump it." As Judge Richard Posner famously observed, "only a lunatic or a fanatic sues for $30." *Carnegie* v. *Household Int'l, Inc.*, 376 F.3d 656, 661 (7th Cir. 2004). To understand why, it's worth taking a deeper look into the economics of plaintiff-side litigation.

A. Plaintiffs' Litigation Economics

The costs of civil litigation vary extensively depending on the complexity of the case, the attorneys' fee rates and staffing, the extent of motion practice, the type of discovery and number of expert witnesses involved, and how far the litigation progresses before a resolution is reached. Recognizing the limitation on cost estimates, it is still possible to get a general sense of the cost of civil litigation. It will cost in the tens or hundreds of thousands of dollars for relatively simply civil cases. More complex cases, including class actions, can cost substantially more to litigate.

One survey-based study done by the National Center for State Courts estimates that the median contract case involves around 370 hours of attorney time to take all the way through trial: 37 hours on researching and filing the complaint and defending motions to dismiss, 88 hours on discovery, 25 hours on settlement discussions, 50 hours on pre-trial motions, 143 hours on trial, and 29 hours on post-trial work. Paula Hannaford-Agor & Nicole L. Waters, *Estimating the Cost of Civil Litigation*, Nat'l Center for State Courts, Caseload Highlights, Jan. 2013, at 1. Accordingly, based on a $250/hour average attorneys' fee rate, the median cost for a contract suit was around $91,000. *Id.* This does not include attorney expenses, such as travel and lodging.

For the purposes of seeing the economics of consumer finance litigation, let's posit that a typical consumer case costs $100,000 to litigate fully. There are not many consumers who are going to pay $100,000 to pursue a claim of $30 or $100 or even $1,000. Instead, if they are going to litigate, it will be on a contingency-fee basis. Indeed, for such small claims, the consumer is unlikely to be willing to even cover litigation expenses.

So let's assume that any litigation will be on a contingency-fee basis with the plaintiff's law firm paying all of the litigation expenses. Let's posit a 33% contingency arrangement, that plaintiff's counsel thinks there is a 50% chance of winning if the case is fully litigated, and that the plaintiff's firm needs to clear $100,000 in order to cover all of its expenses (e.g., associate salaries and rent) and make a reasonable profit for its partners. On these assumptions, in order for that plaintiff's firm to just break even, it would need the case to have an expected value of $600,000! Few individual consumer finance cases have actual damages anywhere near such a level.

To be sure, we could play with these numbers. Let's suppose that plaintiff's counsel only takes very strong cases, ones where it thinks it has a 75% chance of winning. If so, then it would only need the case to have an expected value of $400,000, still much higher than the actual damages in most consumer cases. To take it to the extreme, let's assume that there is no question that the plaintiff will win. It is a 100% certainty. With a 33% contingency, however, the litigation is not economically viable unless the damages awarded are at least $300,000, still much more than the individual damages in most consumer finance cases.

Of course, few cases are actually fully litigated. Many result in a dismissal or settlement prior to trial. Consumer cases are likely to settle only after summary judgment motions, so based on the time breakdown above, we might be looking at fees and expenses of more like $50,000. If so, then the break-even figures fall to $300,000 (with 50% chance of success), $200,000 (with 75% chance of success), and $150,000 (with 100% chance of success). These figures are still all substantially more than the typical actual damages incurred by an individual consumer in most consumer finance cases.

Obviously, in real life the calculations are more complex and plaintiffs' attorneys cannot readily gauge how strong a case is when they take it on; among other things, they have not yet done the necessary legal research or conducted discovery. The point that you should see here is that litigation is not cheap. In fact, it is typically far more expensive than the actual damages in consumer finance cases. Accordingly, absent legal provisions that change the economics of litigation, many consumer cases will not get brought, even if unquestionably meritorious. Based on actual damages alone, most consumer finance claims are, from the perspective of a plaintiff's attorney, negative value claims.

B. Procedural Devices to Change Plaintiffs' Litigation Economics

1. Fee-Shifting

Five procedural devices help change the economics of litigation to ensure that there is a greater likelihood of consumers being able to bring claims. First, many consumer finance statutes include fee-shifting provisions. While the standard "American Rule" is that each party pays its costs in litigation, many consumer laws have one-sided fee-shifting, such that if the consumer prevails, the consumer can recover reasonable attorneys' fees and expenses. *E.g.*, 15 U.S.C. § 1640(a)(3) (Truth in Lending Act); 15 U.S.C. § 1681n(3) (Fair Credit Reporting Act); 15 U.S.C. § 1691e(d) (Equal Credit Opportunity Act); 15 U.S.C. § 1692k(a)(3) (Fair Debt Collection Practices Act); 15 U.S.C. § 1693m(a)(3) (Electronic Fund Transfer Act); 15 U.S.C. § 1709(c) (Interstate Land Sales Act); 15 U.S.C. § 2310(d)(2) (Magnusson-Moss Warranty Act); Cal. Civ. Code § 1788.30(c) (California's Rosenthal Fair Debt Collection Practices Act).

It is important to note that this is not the "English Rule": under most fee-shifting statutes, if the consumer loses, the consumer is still not liable for the defendant's fees and expenses.[1] Some statutes will permit the defendant to recover fees, however, if the plaintiff filed in bad faith. *E.g.*, 15 U.S.C. § 1681n(c) (Fair Credit Reporting Act); 15 U.S.C. § 1693m(f) (Electronic Fund Transfer Act); Cal. Civ. Code § 1788.30(c) (California's Rosenthal Fair Debt Collection Practices Act).

Consider what fee-shifting does for plaintiffs' litigation economics. It renders the ultimate damages in the case irrelevant. Even if the plaintiff recovers only nominal damages (say $1), the plaintiff will also recover all legal costs. That eliminates the disincentive to pursue meritorious but low-damages cases that exist in a contingency-fee regime without fee-shifting. Fee-shifting does not mean that attorneys are likely to take long-shot cases, but it does facilitate the prosecution of sure bet cases with small damages.

Of course fee-shifting is not typically for all legal fees, but only for reasonable legal fees, which are typically evaluated on an hourly basis (plus expenses like expert witness fees) considering attorney experience, attorney skill, and the nature of the case. Still, fee-shifting is potentially transformative in terms of facilitating vindication of rights outside of a class context when only small amounts are at stake.

2. Statutory Damages

Second, some consumer finance statutes include minimum statutory damages. Even if the harm to a consumer is nominal, the consumer can still recover such statutory damages (assuming that there is not a constitutional standing issue). *E.g.*, 15 U.S.C. § 1640(a)(2) (Truth in Lending Act); 15 U.S.C. § 1681n(1)(B) (Fair Credit Reporting Act); 15 U.S.C. § 1692k(a)(2) (Fair Debt Collection Practices Act); 15 U.S.C. § 1693m(a)(2) (Electronic Fund Transfer Act); Cal. Civ. Code § 1788.30(b) (California's Rosenthal Fair Debt Collection Practices Act). The effect is to increase consumer plaintiffs' potential recoveries. Statutory damages tend to be relatively small, however—in the range of a few hundred to a few thousand dollars per violation—so they are seldom game changers in terms of the economics of individual consumer actions.[2]

3. Punitive Damages

Third, some consumer finance statutes authorize punitive damages. *E.g.*, 15 U.S.C. § 1681n(a)(2); 15 U.S.C. § 1691e(b) (Equal Credit Opportunity Act). Authorization of punitive damages can potentially substantially increase consumer plaintiffs' recoveries, but such authorization is the exception, not the rule, in consumer finance statutes.

---

1. Because the fee-shifting covers all attorneys' fees, not just those associated with the particular statutory claim, there is a strong incentive for consumers to bring suits that include claims under statutes that authorize fee-shifting.

2. Whether multiple violations result in multiple recoveries depends on the statute, but generally multiple violations result in a single statutory damage award. *E.g.*, 15 U.S.C. § 1640(g) (single recovery for multiple Truth in Lending Act violations); *Wright v. Finance Service of Norwalk*, 22 F.3d 647 (6th Cir. 1994) (single recovery for multiple Fair Debt Collection Practices Act violations).

4. Small Claims Courts

Every state has some sort of small claims court that has streamlined procedures and lower costs, but such fora are not necessarily available to consumers, particularly if they bring a federal statutory claim against the defendant, who can then remove to federal district court. Still, let's optimistically suppose that a small claims court reduces litigation costs to $2,500 or 10 hours of attorney time. With a 33% contingency arrangement, the recovery would still have to be $7,500, which exceeds the maximum recovery allowed in a majority of states' small claims courts. Perhaps the consumer can proceed pro se, but that might affect the likelihood of success, and the value of the consumer's own time has to be considered. Notably, most states require corporate entities to be represented by attorneys even in small claims court, so a small claims court action can impose costs on the defendant that are greater than the amount at stake.

Ironically, in many states, small claims courts are used heavily by debt collectors suing consumers because of the lower cost of litigation relative to that in courts of general jurisdiction.[3] *See* Peter A. Holland, *The One Hundred Billion Dollar Problem in Small Claims Court: Robo-Signing and Lack of Proof in Debt Buyer Cases*, 6 J. Bus. & Tech. L. 259 (2011); Lauren Goldberg, *Dealing in Debt: The High-Stakes World of Debt-Collection After FDCPA*, 79 S. Cal. L. Rev. 711, 729, 741-745 (2006). Given that many collection suits result in default judgments and that small claims courts do not generally require litigants to be represented by counsel, a creditor pursuing an unpaid debt can cheaply file an action in small claims court using a standard form and can then send a non-attorney employee to present the claim. In other words, small claims courts often facilitate attorney-free judicial debt collection.

5. Class Actions

Finally, and most importantly, the ability to pursue claims of multiple consumers jointly in a single litigation, as a class action, creates economies of scale for litigation. Class actions cost more to litigate—the class must be certified, for example, and settlements and attorneys' fees must be approved by the court. But the increase in cost is much smaller than the potential increase in recoveries. If an individual consumer's damages are only $30, but there are 1 million consumers in the class, then at a 33% contingency and a 50% chance of success, plaintiffs' attorneys would still break even as long as costs were less than $5 million. (Obviously, plaintiffs' attorneys would want to diversify their investments, which have delayed and unpredictable payout times, and they typically do so, by buying pieces of each other's suits.) Thus, while fee-shifting, statutory damages, and punitive damages can increase the viability of individual consumer finance litigation (and these are all still available

3. Some state small claims courts are not open for debt collector actions. *See* Okla. Stat. Ann. tit. 12 § 1751(B) ("No action may be brought under the small claims procedure by any collection agency, collection agent, or assignee of a claim. . . .").

for class litigation as well), what really changes the economics of litigation is the ability to pursue class actions.

Given the prevalence of small-dollar transactions (and harms) in consumer finance, the viability of class actions is critical to private enforcement. Class actions are not always available, however. They depend on the existence of systematic misbehavior, rather than one-off problems. Not surprisingly consumers with one-off problems generally have to "lump it" or vote with their pocketbook and take their business elsewhere.

C. Defendants' Litigation Economics

It's important not to lose sight of the fact that litigation imposes costs on defendants as well as plaintiffs. Litigation is also expensive for defendants. For consumer defendants this often means that litigation results in default judgments that reflect the relative economic strength of the parties, rather than the merits of the case.

For business defendants, the costs (as opposed to damages) of defending litigation are still substantial, although typically not prohibitive. These costs are not just the very-well-paid lawyers and expert witnesses, but also the distraction it can cause. Executives lose days in depositions and testimony. Documents must be retained and produced. Indeed, when a business is faced with an individual consumer plaintiff, the potential damages are often less than the cost of defending the case. But when a business is faced with a plaintiff class, there is the possibility of damages being awarded in a material amount, and this puts pressure on the business to settle, even if the claims are not meritorious. Of course if the costs of litigation are so high as to preclude plaintiffs from suing in the first place, then the fact that it would also be expensive for defendants is irrelevant, as those expenses will never be imposed because the litigation will never be brought in the first place.

II. ARBITRATION

Reducing the cost of litigation—of dispute resolution—helps increase contract enforcement and facilitates parties getting the true benefit of their bargain. Arbitration presents an alternative system of adjudication that is *potentially* cheaper and faster. The major argument for arbitration as opposed to judicial litigation is that it is a more efficient method of achieving justice and that its lower costs actually help consumers in three ways: (1) by making justice more accessible to them, (2) by enabling cost savings for businesses that can be passed through to consumers in the form of lower prices or better service, and (3) by easing the burden on the court system so that litigated cases can proceed more expeditiously.

At the same time, however, arbitration can also function as a procedural hurdle that impedes effective enforcement of contracts and torts, particularly by frustrating class actions. While arbitration might lower cost barriers to enforcement, it can also act as one of a number of procedural hurdles that impede consumer litigation.[4] This chapter first considers arbitration agreements and the arguments in favor of and against pre-dispute agreements for binding mandatory arbitration in the context of individual consumer claims before turning to the question of class actions and arbitration.

Arbitration is a consensual alternative to a judicial process; both parties must agree to arbitrate. While the agreement can be made post-dispute, agreements to arbitrate are often pre-dispute agreements included in consumer finance contracts. Arbitrations can take on a variety of forms, but typically both sides are able to conduct some discovery and present evidence and arguments to the arbitrators who then issue a ruling known as an award.

Arbitration requirements are quite common for many consumer financial products other than mortgages and federal student loans (where they are now prohibited). Such requirements are virtually always take-it-or-leave-it contracts of adhesion, drafted by the financial services firm. Arbitration clauses also appear in contracts across product groups, so consumers have little choice but to accept arbitration if they want to use a product from any provider. Arbitration requirements are standard in some products, like pre-paid cards, and appear in a majority of credit cardholder agreements. For credit cards and deposit accounts, the largest financial institutions are much more likely to require arbitration than smaller institutions, but because of market concentration, this means that many consumers still end up with arbitration clauses.

To enforce an arbitral award, it must be taken to a court, which then engages in a minimal review. Federal law has long favored enforcement of arbitral agreements. The Federal Arbitration Act of 1925 provides that in contracts involving interstate commerce (which includes virtually all consumer finance contracts), pre-dispute arbitration clauses are valid and enforceable to the extent that any other contract would be. 9 U.S.C. § 2.

The Federal Arbitration Act provides that courts determine in the first instance whether there was an agreement to arbitrate. 9 U.S.C. § 4. This means that courts must determine if there is a so-called "delegation clause" in the contract that commits the particular dispute to arbitration. The Supreme Court has held that there must be "clear and unmistakable" evidence of the agreement to arbitrate. *AT&T Technologies, Inc. v. Communications Workers*, 475 U.S. 643, 649 (1986).

4. Consider a pair of other examples. First, consumer fraud claims must be pled in particular under Federal Rule of Civil Procedure 9(b), which can sometimes be difficult to do absent discovery, which will not be granted if the pleading is insufficient. Second, the Federal Rule of Civil Procedure 12(b) pleading standards under *Bell Atlantic v. Twombly*, 50 U.S. 544 (2007), and *Ashcraft v. Iqbal*, 556 U.S. 662 (2009), under which a court must determine the plausibility of a complaint as part of its evaluation of a motion to dismiss, further raises the possibility of meritorious consumer claims being dismissed because a judge finds them implausible. Indeed, before September 2016, when a $185 million settlement of a government enforcement action was announced, how many judges would have found plausible an allegation that Wells Fargo, one of the largest banks in the United States, had fraudulently opened over two million bank accounts and credit card accounts for consumers without their consent? To some judges, such an allegation would surely have sounded outlandish and farfetched.

If there is a delegation clause that clearly and unmistakably commits a dispute to arbitration, there is still the question of whether the clause is enforceable. That is a distinct determination from the enforceability of the contract as a whole because arbitration clauses are, as a matter of substantive federal law, severable from the remainder of the contract. *Buckeye Check Cashing, Inc. v. Cardegna*, 546 U.S. 440, 445 (2006). Accordingly, only a challenge to the validity of the delegation clause may be heard by the court.[5]

This means that a party seeking to challenge the enforceability of an arbitration agreement must lodge an objection specifically to the delegation clause. *Rent-A-Center, West, Inc. v. Jackson*, 561 U.S. 63, 70-75 (2010). Such a challenge may, however, be based on the same arguments that are raised with respect to other provisions in the arbitration agreement if they necessarily implicate the enforceability of the delegation clause. *See, e.g., MacDonald v. CashCall, Inc.*, 2018 U.S. App. LEXIS 4795, at *10-*11 (3rd Cir. Feb. 27, 2018) (holding that a complaint alleging that because the arbitration procedure provided was illusory because no arbitral forum existed was a sufficient challenge to the delegation clause because a provision requiring the enforceability of the arbitration procedure through arbitration is also necessarily illusory). Thus, if the party seeking to avoid arbitration were to allege that there was never assent to a contract of any sort, it would necessarily be an allegation that there was never assent to the delegation clause, and therefore the matter would be heard by a court, not an arbitrator. The same would be true regarding a challenge to the contract as a whole based on mistake or duress. But if the challenge were based on the unenforceability of the contract as a whole on public policy grounds or unconscionability, then the delegation clause would not be specifically challenged, and the arbitrator would decide on the enforceability of the contract as a whole. *See Buckeye Check Cashing, Inc.*, 546 U.S. at 445 (arbitral tribunal to decide on whether payday loan agreement was void for alleged illegality).

If a challenge to arbitration is based on the delegation clause itself specifically being unconscionable, the matter is more fraught. The particular facts and circumstances of a delegation clause could render it unenforceable, but there cannot be a general presumption that certain features of arbitration, such as a class action mechanism or rules of discovery or evidence render it unconscionable. *See AT&T Mobility LLC v. Concepcion*, 563 U.S. 333, 341-44 (2011).

---

5. *Buckeye Check Cashing* assumes that the arbitration agreement itself did delegate determination of the validity of the contract to the arbitrator, but this is an assumption that may not always hold true. Because arbitration agreements are contracts, if the arbitration agreement does not delegate determination of validity of the contract as a whole to the arbitrator, then there are no grounds for sending it to the arbitrator for such a determination. While arbitration agreements may not themselves always contain direct language to that effect, they frequently incorporate the rules of arbitration associations by reference, and those rules will provide that the arbitrator has authority to determine the validity of the contract as a whole. For example, ADR Services Rule 8 provides that

> "Unless the issue of arbitrability has been previously determined by the court, the arbitrator shall have the power to rule on his or her own jurisdiction, including any objections with respect to the existence, scope or validity of the arbitration agreement. In addition, the arbitrator shall have the power to determine the existence or validity of a contract of which an arbitration clause forms a part."

Federal courts have generally held that incorporation by reference in an arbitration agreement expressly delegates to the arbitrator authority to decide the validity of the contract.

The Federal Arbitration Act also provides that interlocutory appeals may not be taken from orders compelling arbitration, so parties must go through arbitration before appealing the issue of arbitrability. 9 U.S.C. § 16.

The Federal Arbitration Act provides that arbitral rulings may be vacated in federal court only in limited circumstances. Section 10(a) of the Federal Arbitration Act enumerates four grounds for vacation of arbitral awards:

> (1) where the award was procured by corruption, fraud, or undue means;
> (2) where there was evident partiality or corruption in the arbitrators, or either of them;
> (3) where the arbitrators were guilty of misconduct in refusing to postpone the hearing, upon sufficient cause shown, or in refusing to hear evidence pertinent and material to the controversy; or of any other misbehavior by which the rights of any party have been prejudiced; or
> (4) where the arbitrators exceeded their powers, or so imperfectly executed them that a mutual, final, and definite award upon the subject matter submitted was not made.

9 U.S.C. § 10(a).

Additionally, some (but not all) federal circuit courts of appeals have recognized an additional ground for vacating arbitral awards, namely that the award was made in "manifest disregard of law." Manifest disregard of law is not mere error. Instead, it requires the arbitral tribunal to have willfully ignored a well-defined legal principle that is not open to different interpretations and that is controlling on a dispute and affects its outcome. In other words, a mere misinterpretation of the law will not suffice. Notably, the "manifest disregard of law" doctrine only applies to legal questions; there is no equivalent doctrine for arbitral tribunals' disregard of facts.

The vitality of the "manifest disregard of law" doctrine is unclear. In *Hall Street Associates, LLC v. Mattel, Inc.*, 552 U.S. 576 (2008), the Supreme Court held that parties could not *contractually* expand the grounds for overturning arbitral awards. This would seem to imply that non-statutory doctrines, such as the "manifest disregard of law" doctrine, are not a valid basis for overturning arbitral awards. (The parties in *Hall Street Associates* had contracted for vacation if the arbitrator's findings of fact were not supported by substantial evidence, or if the arbitrator's legal rulings were clearly erroneous.) Yet two years later, the Supreme Court assumed, without deciding, that the "manifest disregard" doctrine still applied. *Stolt-Nielsen S.A. v. AnimalFeeds Int'l Corp.*, 559 U.S. 662, 669-670, 672 n.3 (2010). As a result, circuit courts of appeals continue to be split on the continuing validity of the doctrine. Whatever the number of grounds for vacating arbitral awards, courts are generally quite deferential to arbitral decisions. *Oxford Health Plans LLC v. Sutter*, 569 U.S. ___ (2013).

If the court does not find grounds to vacate the award, the court then issues an order that confirms the award. This court order can then be executed.

The unspoken assumption of advocates of arbitration is that the lower-cost justice that arbitration provides is substantively equivalent to that of the courts. In other words, arbitration advocates claim arbitration does not compromise fairness for the sake of efficiency. Both the claims of efficiency and of substantive equivalency are the subject of debate.

A. Efficiency Claims

1. Cost

Empirical studies on consumer dispute arbitration costs compared with court costs present a mixed picture, depending on what costs are included. Searle Civil Justice Institute, *Consumer Arbitration Before the American Arbitration Association: Preliminary Report*, Mar. 2009, at 6-7. Courts charge a flat fee for access, while arbitration involves hourly fees for arbitrators, as well as fees for the arbitration service provider.

Yet this might not be the proper basis for comparison. To the extent that arbitration is quicker or involves fewer motions and less discovery and appeals, attorneys' fees and internal expenses in arbitration might be lower, as might the opportunity costs from litigating. Moreover, in many consumer arbitration cases, the share of arbitration costs for which consumers are responsible is capped and often zero.

Of course, it is not clear whether the proper baseline for comparison is litigating a case through judgment and appeals or the more common outcome of litigating a case up to a settlement. Additionally, any empirical study faces a recursivity problem—which cases actually get brought in either courts or arbitration are determined in part by fee structures. The different cost structure of consumer arbitrations may in fact encourage smaller-dollar or weaker claims to be brought, if the ratio of expected arbitration awards to arbitration costs is more favorable than the ratio of expected litigation awards to litigation costs.

To get a sense of arbitration costs, consider that the fee schedule for the American Arbitration Association (AAA), the predominant arbitration administrator for consumer financial product arbitration. The AAA caps consumer fees in b2c arbitrations at a $200 filing fee. The business party to such an arbitration must pay a filing fee of between $1,700 and $2,200, a $500 hearing fee (if there is a hearing), and the arbitrator's compensation of $1,500/hearing day per arbitrator or $750 per case if there is no hearing. Am. Arbitration Ass'n, *Consumer Arbitration Rules: Costs of Arbitration* (effective Jan. 1, 2016). The parties can, of course, contract for different fee allocation, but it would seem that an arbitration with a one-day hearing before a three-arbitrator panel would have costs of $7,400 in addition to the costs each party incurs in preparing and presenting its case.

These costs are worth considering in light of the size of arbitration claims. The CFPB undertook a study of AAA-arbitrated consumer financial product cases from 2010 to 2012. It found that 69% of the cases involved disputed debt amounts, while 60% of the cases had affirmative consumer claims (29% had both). *See* CFPB, *Arbitration Study*, Mar. 2015, at 31. In these cases, the median (mean) disputed debt was $10,996 ($15,705), *id.* at 26, while the median (mean) affirmative claim was for $11,500 ($17,008), *id.* at 23. Thus, the ratio of arbitration costs to amount in controversy is fairly high.

2. Speed

Arbitration speed is a factor in determining arbitration cost, but merits distinct consideration. Arbitration is generally believed to be faster than court litigation.

Searle Civil Justice Institute, *Consumer Arbitration Before the American Arbitration Association: Preliminary Report*, Mar. 2009, at 8. Arbitration involves less discovery, fewer motions, and fewer appellate opportunities. Moreover, arbitration usually involves shorter queues than litigation. Most litigation, however, results in settlement, rather than judgment. It is not clear whether consumer arbitration results in arbitral awards faster than litigation produces settlements.

The CFPB arbitration study found that the median arbitration resulting in a decision on the merits took 150 days in 2010-2011. CFPB, *Arbitration Study*, Mar. 2015, at 73. While this seems like a fairly fast resolution, it is not clear how long an equivalent set of cases would take to resolve in the judicial system or even if they would be brought.

3. Externalities

Consideration of the efficiency of arbitration vis-à-vis litigation must, of course, account for externalities. Litigation produces positive externalities in the form of precedent, which allows for business planning and reduces subsequent litigation, and claim and issue preclusion, which prevent having to re-litigate the same matters, potentially with inconsistent outcomes. Arbitration does not produce these externalities. Arbitration does not necessarily produce written opinions explaining awards, and one arbitral panel is not bound by the determinations of another. There is no claim or issue preclusion between arbitrations. It is not clear how these externalities should be valued, but the valuation uncertainty does not negate their existence as real efficiency considerations.

All of this is to say that the efficiency case for arbitration is uncertain. Depending on how one frames the efficiency inquiry, arbitration can appear more or less efficient than litigation.

B. Claims of Substantively Equivalent Outcomes

Even if arbitration were more cost efficient than litigation, that would only matter to the extent that arbitration provides substantively equivalent outcomes to litigation. Otherwise, it is simply providing a different type of justice at a different cost, rather than the same justice at a lower cost.

1. Win Rates and Award Sizes

Arbitral outcomes can be compared with those of courts both in terms of win rates and size of awards. It is hard to know what the appropriate win rate baseline is for comparison, however, particularly given the incidence of settlement in litigation and the difficulty in finding sufficiently comparable sets of cases. Existing studies have found very different results depending on whether consumers or businesses bring the arbitration case and the identity of the arbitral forum. Similarly, award sizes are difficult to compare without knowing the relative strength of cases. Still, a major attraction of arbitration to business defendants is that it avoids a jury trial. Businesses are often concerned about juries that sympathize with fellow consumers, produce runaway judgments, and award punitive damages. To be sure, most civil litigation never ends up in front of a jury, but this is in part because of the settlement incentives created by fear of unpredictable juries.

2. Repeat Player Bias?

Another concern about arbitration is that it may involve a repeat player bias because arbitrators or arbitration forums seeking to ensure future business are incentivized to treat repeat players favorably so that they will be selected to arbitrate future disputes. A related concern is that repeat players are able to influence the design of arbitration systems and do so in ways that systematically favor them. The available empirical evidence (mainly from employment dispute arbitration) indicates that there may be a repeat player bias. Searle Civil Justice Institute, *Consumer Arbitration Before the American Arbitration Association: Preliminary Report*, Mar. 2009, at 16. Unfortunately, it is hard to distinguish between repeat player bias and the fact that repeat players may be screening which cases they arbitrate based on their knowledge of which are likely to be successful in the arbitration system.

3. Quality of Adjudication and Due Process

Arbitration is clearly procedurally different from civil litigation, and that in and of itself raises concerns about fairness. Arbitration lacks some of the procedural protections of a judicial litigation. Rules of procedure and evidence do not necessarily apply, third-party interventions and amicus briefs are not necessarily accepted, arbitrators are not bound by precedent, arbitrations do not produce precedent (or even necessarily written opinions), and arbitration proceedings are not public. Hearings are private and often confidential with no transcript or often with no written decision, which makes it hard to review the arbitration for bias. Testimony need not be given under oath (in which case there would not be perjury liability). There is no jury in arbitrations, and exclusionary rules do not apply.[6] There is no right to discovery unless stipulated or awarded by the arbitrator. Appellate review of arbitral decisions is extremely limited, as we have seen. And, most importantly for our purposes (and discussed at length below), arbitration does not necessarily permit class actions, and arbitration agreements can specifically exclude class arbitration.

The differences in procedures shape the leverage that both consumers and businesses have in negotiating settlements. Business defendants can inundate consumer plaintiffs with discovery responses, while consumer plaintiffs can harass business defendants with "fishing expeditions" in discovery. It is not clear which way arbitration ultimately changes the balance of power. That said, arbitration appears

---

6. The rules of some arbitration associations require certain due process minimums in the arbitration agreements they arbitrate. For example, the Consumer Arbitration Rules of the American Arbitration Association (AAA) require consumer arbitration agreements to comply with the AAA's Consumer Due Process Protocol. AAA Consumer Arbitration Rule R-1(d). The AAA permits businesses to submit their arbitration agreements for a compliance review prior to a dispute arising, AAA Consumer Arbitration Rule R-12, and, if the arbitration clause is approved, it is then published in a clause registry. AAA can require waiver of specific noncompliant provisions in arbitration agreements without rejecting the entire agreement.

much more likely to result in rulings on the merits, as opposed to settlement, which would seem to improve substantive justice, all else equal.

Whether or not these procedural differences have any substantive justice impact, they indicate that arbitration provides a different sort of justice than a formal legal action does. Thus, while arbitration might be less expensive or quicker than a formal legal action, it also provides fewer protections procedurally. To the extent that procedure is understood to have substantive effects, this may matter.

4. Remedies

Arbitration is often limited in the remedies it can provide. Arbitrators cannot usually award injunctive relief, only damages, and generally cannot award punitive damages. The difference in remedies is among the most substantial differences between arbitration and judicial process.

5. Neutrality of the Adjudicator

One concern about arbitration is the neutrality of the arbitrator. There are a variety of methods for appointing arbitrators, but typically arbitrators are appointed by a national arbitration organization in accordance with pre-set procedures. The arbitrators may or may not have particular technical expertise in consumer finance; many are retired judges, law partners, or academics.

In 2007, Public Citizen published a report on arbitration of consumer credit card disputes that strongly implied that that arbitrations were biased against consumers. Public Citizen, *The Arbitration Trap: How Credit Card Companies Ensnare Consumers*, Sept. 2007, *at* http://www.citizen.org/documents/ArbitrationTrap.pdf. The report analyzed 33,948 California consumer credit card debt arbitrations handled by the National Arbitration Forum (NAF) between 2003 and 2007. NAF at the time handled over 50,000 consumer credit card arbitrations a year nationally. Almost all of these arbitrations were "collection" cases filed by the card issuer or credit card debt buyers, with the majority brought by MBNA, a large credit card issuer, or buyers of MBNA card debt. Only 118 of the 33,948 cases were brought by consumers. Most of the arbitrations were done by a handful of arbitrators, who were paid hourly but tended to receive work based on their speed. Twenty-eight arbitrators handled 90% of the cases, with one arbitrator handling as many as 68 cases in a single day.

The awards in the NAF California cases heavily favored card issuers. Ninety-four percent of rulings were for card issuers, a result similar with rulings in Alabama involving a single card issuer. The high percentage of cases ruling for card issuers or debt buyers coupled with the procedural nature of the arbitrations led Public Citizen to allege that the process was fundamentally corrupt.

The major national arbitration organizations—the American Arbitration Association, ADRS, JAMS, and NAF—generally permit each side to veto or strike a number of proposed arbitrators. A repeat player in the arbitration system, such as a credit card issuer, is likely to have knowledge about whether to strike an arbitrator that a one-time player, like a consumer, would lack. The result, the Public Citizen report indicates, is that the arbitrator pool ends up systematically biased against consumers. The Public Citizen report featured the story of Harvard Law School Professor Elizabeth Bartholet, who had served as an NAF arbitrator until she ruled against a card issuer:

> Elizabeth Bartholet's brief career as an NAF arbitrator ended abruptly after she ruled against a credit card company.
>
> A Harvard Law School professor and veteran arbitrator, Bartholet said in an interview that she was recruited by NAF. Beginning in 2003, she handled about 19 cases involving one credit card company in a 14-month period, as she testified in a sworn deposition in September 2006. She ruled for the company 18 times and the 19th case was dismissed. Then came the 20th case. After the company filed an arbitration claim, the debtor asserted a counterclaim. She awarded the debtor about $48,000.
>
> Subsequently, she said, NAF removed her from seven credit card cases she was scheduled to handle and told the debtors Bartholet could not handle them because she had a scheduling conflict, an assertion she denied. In addition, she testified that credit card companies voluntarily dismissed another four cases that had been on her agenda.
>
> Bartholet testified that she asked an NAF employee if "there could be any reason for them disqualifying me other than the fact that I ruled against them in Case Y" – the $48,000 award to the credit card holder. "She said no," Bartholet testified. "She basically agreed that that was the reason and in response to my concern about this misleading letter about my unavailability having been sent out, she said that it was a form letter that was simply regularly sent out in all of the cases."
>
> Bartholet resigned as an arbitrator in February 2005, citing concern for NAF ethics and "its apparent systematic bias in favor of the financial services industry."

Public Citizen, *The Arbitration Trap: How Credit Card Companies Ensnare Consumers*, Sept. 2007, at 29-30.

Public Citizen's 94% figure appears quite shocking, but what is the baseline for comparison? Many consumer arbitrations are collection actions commenced not by the consumer, but by a business creditor. Many of these arbitrations are uncontested, much like default judgments in courts. These are typically actions for money lent and not repaid, and there is usually no question that the consumer owes the money. This suggests that consumers would be unlikely to prevail in many arbitrations, even with neutral arbitrators. Indeed, the 94% figure could even be too *low*! Still, it underscores that arbitrations are not a forum in which consumers tend to prevail.

In 2009 the Minnesota Attorney General sued the NAF, alleging that it ran a biased arbitration process that favored credit card issuers and that NAF had conflicting connections with major collection law firms, including cross-ownership. NAF quickly settled and agreed to cease arbitrating consumer collection disputes for credit cards as well as health care, utilities, telecommunications, leases, and other loans. While NAF might have been an outlier, this case points to concerns about arbitrator neutrality that are less salient with a professional and transparent judiciary.

Businesses often agree to pay the costs of arbitration, which may on the surface appear to be a move that tilts arbitration toward consumers. But an arbitrator is unlikely to see a particular consumer more than once, while it is likely to see businesses repeatedly, which should raise concerns that arbitrators will be sensitive to the interests of those who are regularly paying their fees.

III. CLASS ACTIONS AND ARBITRATION

Even with a neutral arbitrator, agreements to arbitrate are almost always contracts of adhesion, meaning that the provision is not freely bargained for by the consumer. Instead, it is part of a take-it-or-leave-it bundle of contract terms. This suggests that consumers' consent to the arbitration may be less than complete. While the consumer is agreeing to the bundle of terms, the consumer is likely to undervalue the arbitral provision (or any adjudicative provision) ex ante, whereas the business will not. The consumer is unlikely to know the probability that there will be a dispute and that arbitration will be invoked, much less how this will hurt (or benefit) him or her. Furthermore, if the consumer believed that a dispute were likely, the consumer would probably avoid the underlying transaction altogether. The result is that the consumer will place little value on the arbitration provision ex ante (if the consumer even reads it and understands it).

In contrast, a business is often a repeat player. If so, it should have a reasonably good idea of the percentage of transactions or customers that will result in arbitral disputes. It also knows the value of arbitration relative to judicial litigation; indeed, if the business did not value the arbitration provision, it would not insist on it. In short, the business is likely to properly value arbitration ex ante. The result is that businesses contract for arbitration based on an informational advantage over consumers. This suggests that if arbitration agreements were separately bargained for, say, with consumers who accepted arbitration receiving a discount, it might encourage consumers to start pricing arbitration by making it more salient. Yet even in such circumstances, consumers are likely to always undervalue arbitration and other adjudicative provisions ex ante because of optimism about the transaction and lack of experience.

Class action waivers can be bundled with an agreement to arbitrate or even extend to a class arbitration waiver. These waivers have the same contract of adhesion and experience/optimism asymmetry problems as agreements to arbitrate, but they also raise a distinct concern, namely the problem of "**negative value claims**" that will not be litigated unless they can be joined in a class so that costs can be shared, even as probabilistic recoveries are increased, thereby making the litigation potentially net positive value for plaintiffs' attorneys, which is necessary for the litigation to be brought.

The bundling of class action waivers with arbitration agreements is critical for the enforceability of class action waivers. Absent such bundling, class action waivers would be vulnerable to being unenforceable as against public policy or unconscionable, etc. But when bundled with arbitration agreements, class action waivers are able to shelter the strong federal policy favoring enforcement of agreements to arbitrate. Indeed, the ability to use arbitration to effectuate a class action waiver is one of the major attractions of arbitration for consumer financial firms.

A. *AT&T Mobility LLC v. Concepcion*

In 2011, the Supreme Court held in *AT&T Mobility LLC v. Concepcion*, 563 U.S. 333 (2011), that the Federal Arbitration Act "prohibits States from conditioning the enforceability of certain arbitration agreements on the availability of classwide arbitration procedures." The case involved a dispute over a $30.22 sales tax charge that AT&T claimed from consumers on a "free phone" that came with a mobile phone contract. When the consumer brought a putative class action for false advertising and fraud in federal district court, AT&T moved to compel arbitration under the terms of its contract. The contract required the arbitration to be brought in the parties' "individual capacity, and not as a plaintiff or class member in any purported class or representative proceeding" and further provided that "the arbitrator may not consolidate more than one person's claims, and may not otherwise preside over any form of a representative or class proceeding."

The Ninth Circuit Court of Appeals refused to enforce arbitration because under a ruling of the California Supreme Court, which established a rule known as the *Discover Bank* rule, the arbitration provision was unconscionable "because AT&T had not shown that bilateral arbitration adequately substituted for the deterrent effects of class actions." The *Discover Bank* rule provided that a class action waiver was an unconscionable exculpation from liability if it was part of a contract of adhesion, it involved a suit with a predictably small amount of damages, and the party with superior bargaining power engaged in a scheme to deliberately cheat consumers. *See Discover Bank v. Superior Court*, 36 Cal.4th 148 (Cal. 2005).

In a 4-1-4 decision, the Supreme Court reversed, finding that California law was preempted by the Federal Arbitration Act. The Supreme Court noted that although California did not require class arbitration, it effectively gave parties a right to demand it ex post. The Supreme Court found that this interfered with federal law. Writing for a plurality, Justice Scalia noted that:

> First, the switch from bilateral to class arbitration sacrifices the principal advantage of arbitration—its informality—and makes the process slower, more costly, and more likely to generate procedural morass than final judgment. "In bilateral arbitration, parties forgo the procedural rigor and appellate review of the courts in order to realize the benefits of private dispute resolution: lower costs, greater efficiency and speed, and the ability to choose expert adjudicators to resolve specialized disputes." But before an arbitrator may decide the merits of a claim in classwide procedures, he must first decide, for example, whether the class itself may be certified, whether the named parties are sufficiently representative and typical, and how discovery for the class should be conducted. A cursory comparison of bilateral and class arbitration illustrates the difference. According to the American Arbitration Association (AAA), the average consumer arbitration between January and August 2007 resulted in a disposition on the merits in six months, four months if the arbitration was conducted by documents only. AAA, Analysis of the AAA's Consumer Arbitration Caseload, online at http://www.adr.org/si.asp?id=5027 (all Internet materials as visited Apr. 25, 2011, and available in Clerk of Court's case file). As of September 2009, the AAA had opened 283 class arbitrations. Of those, 121 remained active, and 162 had been settled, withdrawn, or dismissed. Not a single one, however, had resulted in a final

award on the merits. For those cases that were no longer active, the median time from filing to settlement, withdrawal, or dismissal—not judgment on the merits—was 583 days, and the mean was 630 days.

Second, class arbitration *requires* procedural formality. The AAA's rules governing class arbitrations mimic the Federal Rules of Civil Procedure for class litigation. Compare AAA, Supplementary Rules for Class Arbitrations (effective Oct. 8, 2003), online at http://www.adr.org/sp.asp?id=21936, with Fed. Rule Civ. Proc. 23. And while parties can alter those procedures by contract, an alternative is not obvious. If procedures are too informal, absent class members would not be bound by the arbitration. For a class-action money judgment to bind absentees in litigation, class representatives must at all times adequately represent absent class members, and absent members must be afforded notice, an opportunity to be heard, and a right to opt out of the class. At least this amount of process would presumably be required for absent parties to be bound by the results of arbitration.

. . .

Third, class arbitration greatly increases risks to defendants. Informal procedures do of course have a cost: The absence of multilayered review makes it more likely that errors will go uncorrected. Defendants are willing to accept the costs of these errors in arbitration, since their impact is limited to the size of individual disputes, and presumably outweighed by savings from avoiding the courts. But when damages allegedly owed to tens of thousands of potential claimants are aggregated and decided at once, the risk of an error will often become unacceptable. Faced with even a small chance of a devastating loss, defendants will be pressured into settling questionable claims. Other courts have noted the risk of "in terrorem" settlements that class actions entail, and class arbitration would be no different.

Arbitration is poorly suited to the higher stakes of class litigation. In litigation, a defendant may appeal a certification decision on an interlocutory basis and, if unsuccessful, may appeal from a final judgment as well. Questions of law are reviewed *de novo* and questions of fact for clear error. In contrast, 9 U.S.C. § 10 allows a court to vacate an arbitral award *only* where the award "was procured by corruption, fraud, or undue means"; "there was evident partiality or corruption in the arbitrators"; "the arbitrators were guilty of misconduct in refusing to postpone the hearing . . . or in refusing to hear evidence pertinent and material to the controversy[,] or of any other misbehavior by which the rights of any party have been prejudiced"; or if the "arbitrators exceeded their powers, or so imperfectly executed them that a mutual, final, and definite award . . . was not made." The AAA rules do authorize judicial review of certification decisions, but this review is unlikely to have much effect given these limitations; review under § 10 focuses on misconduct rather than mistake. And parties may not contractually expand the grounds or nature of judicial review. We find it hard to believe that defendants would bet the company with no effective means of review, and even harder to believe that Congress would have intended to allow state courts to force such a decision.

The Concepcions contend that because parties may and sometimes do agree to aggregation, class procedures are not necessarily incompatible with arbitration. But the same could be said about procedures that the Concepcions admit States may not superimpose on arbitration: Parties *could* agree to arbitrate pursuant to the Federal Rules of Civil Procedure, or pursuant to a discovery process rivaling that in litigation. Arbitration is a matter of contract, and the [Federal Arbitration Act or] FAA requires courts to honor parties' expectations. But what the parties in the aforementioned examples would have agreed to is not arbitration as envisioned by the FAA, lacks its benefits, and therefore may not be required by state law.

The dissent claims that class proceedings are necessary to prosecute small-dollar claims that might otherwise slip through the legal system. See *post*, at ___. But States cannot require a procedure that is inconsistent with the FAA, even if it is desirable for unrelated reasons. Moreover, the claim here was most unlikely to go unresolved. As noted earlier, the arbitration agreement provides that AT&T will pay claimants a minimum of $7,500 and twice their attorney's fees if they obtain an arbitration award greater than AT&T's last settlement offer. The District Court found this scheme sufficient to provide incentive for the individual prosecution of meritorious claims that are not immediately settled, and the Ninth Circuit admitted that aggrieved customers who filed claims would be "essentially guarantee[d]" to be made whole. Indeed, the District Court concluded that the Concepcions were *better off* under their arbitration agreement with AT&T than they would have been as participants in a class action, which "could take months, if not years, and which may merely yield an opportunity to submit a claim for recovery of a small percentage of a few dollars."

. . .

Because it "stands as an obstacle to the accomplishment and execution of the full purposes and objectives of Congress," California's *Discover Bank* rule is preempted by the FAA. The judgment of the Ninth Circuit is reversed, and the case is remanded for further proceedings consistent with this opinion.

Justice Thomas concurred in the judgment, but noted that he believed that:

the FAA requires that an agreement to arbitrate be enforced . . . unless a party successfully asserts a defense concerning the formation of the agreement to arbitrate, such as fraud, duress, or mutual mistake. . . . Contract defenses unrelated to the making of the agreement—such as public policy—could not be the basis for declining to enforce an arbitration clause.

Justice Thomas observed that the California law was based on a position that in certain contracts of adhesion, arbitration agreements function as exculpatory clauses, but that the California Supreme Court had never found that "operate to insulate a party from liability that would otherwise be imposed under California law" and "did not conclude that a customer would sign such an agreement only if under the influence of fraud, duress, or delusion."

Justices Breyer, Ginsburg, Sotomayor, and Kagan dissented. The dissent noted that:

The majority's contrary view (that *Discover Bank* stands as an "obstacle" to the accomplishment of the federal law's objective) rests primarily upon its claims that the *Discover Bank* rule increases the complexity of arbitration procedures, thereby discouraging parties from entering into arbitration agreements, and to that extent discriminating in practice against arbitration. These claims are not well founded.

For one thing, a state rule of law that would sometimes set aside as unconscionable a contract term that forbids class arbitration is not (as the majority claims) like a rule that would require "ultimate disposition by a jury" or "judicially monitored discovery" or use of "the Federal Rules of Evidence." Unlike the majority's examples, class arbitration is consistent with the use of arbitration. It is a form of arbitration that is well known in California and followed elsewhere. Indeed, the AAA has told us that it has found class arbitration to be "a fair, balanced, and efficient means of resolving class disputes." And unlike the majority's examples, the *Discover Bank* rule imposes equivalent limitations on litigation; hence it cannot fairly be characterized as a targeted attack on arbitration.

Where does the majority get its contrary idea—that individual, rather than class, arbitration is a "fundamental attribut[e]" of arbitration? The majority does not explain. And it is unlikely to be able to trace its present view to the history of the arbitration statute itself [because arbitration procedures were not fully developed at the time and typically involved disputes between merchants of roughly equivalent bargaining power].

For another thing, the majority's argument that the *Discover Bank* rule will discourage arbitration rests critically upon the wrong comparison. The majority compares the complexity of class arbitration with that of bilateral arbitration. And it finds the former more complex. But, if incentives are at issue, the *relevant* comparison is not "arbitration with arbitration" but a comparison between class arbitration and judicial class actions. After all, in respect to the relevant set of contracts, the *Discover Bank* rule similarly and equally sets aside clauses that forbid class procedures—whether arbitration procedures or ordinary judicial procedures are at issue.

Why would a typical defendant (say, a business) prefer a judicial class action to class arbitration? AAA statistics "suggest that class arbitration proceedings take more time than the average commercial arbitration, but may take *less time* than the average class action in court." Data from California courts confirm that class arbitrations can take considerably less time than in-court proceedings in which class certification is sought. And a single class proceeding is surely more efficient than thousands of separate proceedings for identical claims. Thus, if speedy resolution of disputes were all that mattered, then the *Discover Bank* rule would reinforce, not obstruct, that objective of the Act.

The majority's related claim that the *Discover Bank* rule will discourage the use of arbitration because "[a]rbitration is poorly suited to . . . higher stakes" lacks empirical support. *Ante*, at ___. Indeed, the majority provides no convincing reason to believe that parties are unwilling to submit high-stake disputes to arbitration. And there are numerous counterexamples. Loftus, *Rivals Resolve Dispute Over Drug*, WALL STREET JOURNAL, Apr. 16, 2011, p. B2 (discussing $500 million settlement in dispute submitted to arbitration); Ziobro, *Kraft Seeks Arbitration In Fight With Starbucks Over Distribution*, Wall Street Journal, Nov. 30, 2010, p. B10 (describing initiation of an arbitration in which the payout "could be higher" than $1.5 billion); Markoff, *Software Arbitration Ruling Gives I.B.M. $833 Million From Fujitsu*, N. Y. TIMES, Nov. 30, 1988, p. A1 (describing both companies as "pleased with the ruling" resolving a licensing dispute).

Further, even though contract defenses, *e.g.*, duress and unconscionability, slow down the dispute resolution process, federal arbitration law normally leaves such matters to the States. A provision in a contract of adhesion (for example, requiring a consumer to decide very quickly whether to pursue a claim) might increase the speed and efficiency of arbitrating a dispute, but the State can forbid it. [Citations omitted.] The *Discover Bank* rule amounts to a variation on this theme. California is free to define unconscionability as it sees fit, and its common law is of no federal concern so long as the State does not adopt a special rule that disfavors arbitration. Cf. *Doctor's Associates, supra*, at 687. See also *ante*, at ___, n., 179 L. Ed. 2d, at 761 (Thomas, J., concurring) (suggesting that, under certain circumstances, California might remain free to apply its unconscionability doctrine).

Because California applies the same legal principles to address the unconscionability of class arbitration waivers as it does to address the unconscionability of any other contractual provision, the merits of class proceedings should not factor into our decision. If California had applied its law of duress to void an arbitration agreement, would it matter if the procedures in the coerced agreement were efficient?

Regardless, the majority highlights the disadvantages of class arbitrations, as it sees them. . . . But class proceedings have countervailing advantages. In general agreements that forbid the consolidation of claims can lead small-dollar claimants to abandon their claims rather than to litigate. I suspect that it is true even here, for as the Court of Appeals recognized, AT&T can avoid the $7,500 payout (the payout that supposedly makes the Concepcions' arbitration worthwhile) simply by paying the claim's face value, such that "the maximum gain to a customer for the hassle of arbitrating a $30.22 dispute is still just $30.22."

What rational lawyer would have signed on to represent the Concepcions in litigation for the possibility of fees stemming from a $30.22 claim? See, *e.g.*, *Carnegie* v. *Household Int'l, Inc.*, 376 F.3d 656, 661 (CA7 2004) ("The *realistic* alternative to a class action is not 17 million individual suits, but zero individual suits, as only a lunatic or a fanatic sues for $30"). In California's perfectly rational view, nonclass arbitration over such sums will also sometimes have the effect of depriving claimants of their claims (say, for example, where claiming the $30.22 were to involve filling out many forms that require technical legal knowledge or waiting at great length while a call is placed on hold). *Discover Bank* sets forth circumstances in which the California courts believe that the terms of consumer contracts can be manipulated to insulate an agreement's author from liability for its own frauds by "deliberately cheat[ing] large numbers of consumers out of individually small sums of money." 36 Cal. 4th, at 162-163, 113 P. 3d, at 1110. Why is this kind of decision—weighing the pros and cons of all class proceedings alike—not California's to make?

* * *

B. State Courts Push Back Against *Concepcion*

How binding of a constraint is *Concepcion* on states to limit arbitration clauses on the basis of unconscionability? The Missouri Supreme Court ruled on the issue shortly after *Concepcion* was decided in a case involving auto title lending, a form of short-term, small-dollar lending in which the loan is secured by the pledge of the title to the borrower's used car. In *Brewer v. Missouri Title Loans*, 364 S.W.3d 486 (Mo. 2012) (en banc), the Missouri Supreme Court counted votes in *Concepcion* and noted that the four dissenters plus Justice Thomas's concurrence opened the door for courts to look at a loan agreement as a whole to determine the conscionability of the class arbitration waiver it contained. The Missouri Supreme Court found that the agreement as a whole was unconscionable because it was non-negotiable, difficult to understand, and one-sided, and because of the superior bargaining position of the lender. Unconscionability is a defense to contract formation, so the Missouri Supreme Court refused to enforce the arbitration clause. *Brewer* then reads *Concepcion* as still allowing for courts to refuse to enforce arbitration clauses if they find defenses to the underlying formation of the contract, including unconscionability, which may stem from the particulars of the arbitration clause itself.

Concepcion was not the Supreme Court's last word on class arbitration. In *American Express Company v. Italian Colors Restaurant*, 133 S. Ct. 2304 (2013), the Supreme Court again addressed class arbitration. This time the issue was not preemption of state law, but the enforceability under federal law of a class arbitration waiver, which the plaintiffs contended prevented them from effectively vindicating their federal law rights. The plaintiffs had brought an anti-trust suit against American Express alleging that American Express used its monopoly power to insist on a contract with a tying arrangement. The Supreme Court split 4-1-3 to hold that a contractual class waiver of class arbitration is enforceable under the FAA even "when the plaintiff's cost of individually arbitrating a federal statutory claim exceeds the potential recovery." The same four Justices who ruled for compelling arbitration in *AT&T v. Concepcion* found that *Concepcion* compelled the same result in *Italian Colors.* Justice Thomas concurred on the same grounds as in *Concepcion*. Justice Kagan in dissent noted the irony of "[t]he monopolist get[ting] to use its monopoly power to insist on a contract effectively depriving its victims of all legal recourse."

Subsequent to *Italian Colors*, the California Supreme Court has found room to void arbitration requirements. In *Sonic-Calabasas A, Inc. v. Moreno*, a case involving a claim for unpaid wages, the California Supreme Court noted that:

> *Italian Colors* does not alter the unconscionability analysis we set forth above. Where a state-law rule interferes with fundamental attributes of arbitration, the FAA preempts the state-law rule even if the rule is designed to facilitate prosecution of certain kinds of claims. *Concepcion* established this principle, *Italian Colors* reaffirmed it, and we apply it today to invalidate the categorical rule on waiving a [dispute resolution hearing required by California statute for employee wage recovery claims] that we [previously adopted].
>
> Yet a court, when faced with an unconscionability claim arising from an adhesive employment contract . . . must still determine whether the overall bargain was unreasonably one-sided. This unconscionability inquiry does not, in purpose or effect, express a preference for nonarbitral as opposed to arbitral forums. To the contrary, it promotes and encourages the use of conventional bilateral arbitration as a means of low-cost, efficient dispute resolution. Our unconscionability doctrine poses no obstacle to enforcement of arbitration agreements so long as the arbitral scheme, however designed, provides employees with an accessible, affordable process for resolving wage disputes that does not "effectively block[] every forum for the redress of [wage] disputes, including arbitration itself."

57 Cal. 4th 1109, 1157-1158 (Cal. 2013) (Liu, J.). In other words, while arbitration is not categorically unconscionable, it might be unconscionable in any particular set

of facts of circumstances, just like any other contract provision. California has also held that a pre-dispute arbitration agreement that waived the right to seek public injunctive relief in any forum is contrary to California public policy and therefore unenforceable. *McGill v. Citibank, N.A.*, 2017 Cal. LEXIS 2551 (Apr. 6, 2017). Because this is a generally applicable contract defense, the California Supreme Court has held that it is not preempted by the FAA, as interpreted by *Concepcion* and *Italian Colors. Id.*

IV. REGULATION OF ARBITRATION PROVISIONS

A. Mortgage Contracts

Arbitration agreements have always been rarer in mortgage loans. Mortgage loans are typically of much larger size than other consumer financial transactions, thereby changing the economics of litigation. More importantly, however, the quasi-governmental entities in the secondary mortgage market have refused to purchase mortgages with binding mandatory arbitration clauses because they were seen as unfriendly to consumers. In December 2003 Freddie Mac announced it would cease purchasing mortgages with binding mandatory arbitration clauses, while Fannie Mae made a similar announcement in October 2004. *See* Peter G. Miller, *A Better Approach to Mortgage Arbitration*, REALTY TIMES, Oct. 12, 2004.

Since June 2013, arbitration agreements have been prohibited in residential mortgage loans. The Dodd-Frank Act amended the Truth in Lending Act to prohibit mandatory pre-dispute arbitration clauses in residential mortgages and home equity lines of credit. 15 U.S.C. § 1639c(e)(1). Post-dispute agreements to arbitrate are still allowed, 15 U.S.C. § 1639c(e)(2), but the statute provides that statutory causes of action cannot be waived.[7]

B. Federal Student Loans

The majority of student loans are made by the federal government through eligible higher education institutions. Student loan borrowers can raise as a defense against repayment any state law claims they might have against the school (e.g., for fraud or breach of contract). On November 1, 2016, the Department of Education finalized regulations prohibiting schools from entering into pre-dispute arbitration agreements with borrowers that cover borrower defense claims, 34 C.F.R. § 685.300(f), or from using pre-dispute arbitration agreements to preclude students from bringing class actions against the school related to their borrower defense claims, 34 C.F.R. § 685.300(e). 81 Fed. Reg. 75926-76089. The regulations also required schools to submit to the Department of Education any records from any arbitration with students relating to borrower defense claims. 34 C.F.R. § 685.300(g). Nothing

7. Could the TILA prohibition on requiring "any other nonjudicial procedure" as a method for resolving any controversy be interpreted as a prohibition on non-judicial foreclosure? *See* 15 U.S.C. § 1639c(e)(2).

in the Department of Education's regulations precludes a school from post-dispute arbitration or from requiring pre-dispute arbitration for other types of disputes with students. In June 2017, before the rules became effective, the Department of Education delayed their effective date indefinitely. 82 Fed. Reg. 27621-22.

C. CFPB Regulatory Limits on Pre-Dispute Arbitration Agreements

The Consumer Financial Protection Bureau (CFPB) has the specific authority to restrict pre-dispute arbitration. 12 U.S.C. § 5518. In July 2017, the CFPB promulgated a final rule on pre-dispute arbitration. The rule would have allowed parties to agree to arbitration only as long as it did not preclude class actions.

In October 2017, the rule was overturned under the Congressional Review Act, 5 U.S.C. §§ 801 *et seq.*, with a tie vote in the Senate broken by Vice President Pence. All 48 Democrats and two Republicans in the Senate voted to uphold the rule. The effect of the Congressional Review Act resolution overturning the rulemaking is that the CFPB is precluded from promulgating any rulemaking on the subject that is "substantially the same" without express Congressional authorization. 5 U.S.C. § 801(b). What constitutes "substantially the same" is unclear. The Congressional Review Act prohibits judicial review, so it is also unclear how "substantially the same" would be defined. 5 U.S.C. § 805. At the very least, however, the Congressional Review Act overturn of the rulemaking represents a substantial setback for efforts to limit the use of arbitration to ban class actions.

Problem Set 3

1. After several years at a large law firm in the big city, you decided you wanted a change of pace and moved back to your smaller hometown where you've opened up a successful general litigation practice and taken on a couple of associates. A new client, Justin Barrett, has come through the door. Justin tells you about how his bank, Continental Express Bank, N.A., charged him ten unauthorized overdraft fees, totaling $350. Justin wants you to sue the bank to get his money back. What do you tell him?

2. First Bank of Springfield, Illinois, is a small community bank with only a couple of branches. First Bank strives hard to please its customers. "We want our customers to be happy. That's our business. That's how my grandfather got us through the Great Depression," says First Bank's president and owner, Melanie Miller, whose family has owned First Bank for three generations. Several other small community banks in Illinois have recently been sued by class action attorneys for not having the required physical signage about fees on their ATMs, even though there is full disclosure of the fee information on the ATM screen itself. The statute is a strict liability statute, and this has left the banks vulnerable to suit after vandals (who some suspect are in cahoots with the class action attorneys) pried off the physical signage from the ATMs. Miller is terrified of such a suit: "We don't have the resources to fight a class action suit. Even a settlement would seriously harm our ability to provide services to our customers." What might First Bank consider doing? *See AT&T Mobility LLC v. Concepcion*, 563 U.S. 333 (2011).

3. Famed real estate developer David Dennison has founded Dennison University, a non-accredited, for-profit educational organization that promises students that Dennison's "hand-picked" instructors will teach them the secrets of successful real estate investment. In fact, Dennison himself had no role whatsoever in selecting instructors, who were simply motivational speakers without any real estate investing expertise using badly edited PowerPoint presentations that were heavily cribbed from public sources. If Dennison University has a binding mandatory arbitration clause in its student contract, will it be able to defeat a class action suit? *See AT&T Mobility LLC v. Concepcion*, 563 U.S. 333 (2011); *Brewer v. Missouri Title Loans*, 364 S.W.3d 486 (Mo. 2012); *Sonic-Calabasas A, Inc. v. Moreno*, 57 Cal. 4th 1109 (Cal. 2013); *McGill v. Citibank, N.A.*, 2017 Cal. LEXIS 2551 (Apr. 6, 2017).

4. Galina Petrova, a California resident, has a credit card with Wells Fargo. One wintry day Galina was walking from work to a Starbucks for coffee. Her route took her down the sidewalk in front of a Wells Fargo branch. The sidewalk was covered with a slick sheet of ice, despite it not having rained or snowed for at least three days; Wells Fargo never bothered to salt or shovel the sidewalk next to the branch. Galina slipped on the ice and broke her hip.

- **a.** When Galina sues Wells Fargo for negligence, can Wells successfully compel arbitration of the suit? *See* Arbitration Provision from Wells Fargo Consumer Credit Card Customer Agreement & Disclosure Statement (2017) ("Wells Fargo Agreement"), ¶31(1).
- **b.** If Wells is successful in compelling arbitration, what are the consequences for Galina of having sued in court? *See* Wells Fargo Agreement, ¶31(1).
- **c.** Does the answer to (a) change if Galina brings suit in small claims court? (California small claims courts can give awards of up to $10,000 as of 2018.) *See* Wells Fargo Agreement, ¶31(1).
- **d.** Would the answer to (a) change if Galina had closed her Wells Fargo credit card three years ago? *See* Wells Fargo Agreement, ¶31(3).
- **e.** Would the answer to (a) change if Galina had never had a Wells Fargo account, but a Wells Fargo employee fraudulently opened up a new credit card account in her name without her knowledge? *See Buckeye Check Cashing, Inc. v. Cardegna*, 546 U.S. 440 (2006).
- **f.** Can Galina be included as a member of a class in a class action suit that someone else initiates about Wells's actions regarding the card accounts? *See* Wells Fargo Agreement, ¶31(2).

5. You are counsel to First Premier Bank, a subprime credit card issuer, that is, a bank that specializes in making credit card loans to consumers with very poor credit. First Premier cards are all initially issued with credit lines of $500. One of the bank's cardholders, Robert Enayati, has fallen six months behind on his payments. Enayati's current balance is $600. First Premier has already cut off Enayati's credit line and is now trying to collect.

- **a.** Does First Premier have to go to arbitration or can it go to court to collect from Enayati?
- **b.** If First Premier goes to court, and Enayati has a counterclaim based on a state unfair and deceptive acts or practices statute, does that counterclaim also get heard in court or must it go to arbitration?

6. Galina Petrova (from question 4) has been required to arbitrate her tort claim against Wells Fargo. After hearing both sides' presentations, the arbitrator took a coin and flipped it in the air, saying, "Heads—Galina, Tails—Wells." The coin landed on tails. Does Galina have any recourse? *See* 9 U.S.C. § 10(a); AAA Consumer Arbitration Rules R-43(b), R-49(c).

7. First Premier chose to arbitrate its claim against Robert Enayati (in problem 5), and the arbitrator awarded First Premier $2,500.

- **a.** Suppose that the arbitral award was made on both a clearly erroneous legal basis and incorrect factual conclusions. Can Robert get it overturned? *See* 9 U.S.C. § 10(a); Arbitration Agreement from First Premier Bank Credit Card Contract and Account Opening Disclosure Statement (2017) ("First Premier Agreement") ("The Arbitrator's Award" in the third column); AAA Consumer Arbitration Rule R-49(c); *Hall Street Associates, LLC v. Mattel, Inc.*, 552 U.S. 576 (2008).
- **b.** Now suppose that Robert believes that there was misconduct involved in the arbitral award. He believes that the son one of the three arbitrators works for a company that that relies on Wells Fargo for a substantial portion of its business. What can Robert do about this? *See* 9 U.S.C. § 10(a); AAA Consumer Arbitration Rules R-49(d)-(e).

Arbitration Provision from Wells Fargo Consumer Credit Card Customer Agreement & Disclosure Statement (2017)

Arbitration

(31) Dispute Resolution Program: Arbitration Agreement.

1. **Binding Arbitration.** You and Wells Fargo Bank, N.A. (the "Bank") agree that if a Dispute arises between you and the Bank, upon demand by either you or the Bank, the Dispute shall be resolved by the following arbitration process. The foregoing notwithstanding, the Bank shall not initiate an arbitration to collect a consumer debt, but reserves the right to arbitrate all other disputes with its consumer customers. A "Dispute" is any unresolved disagreement between you and the Bank. It includes any disagreement relating in any way to the Card or related services, Accounts, or matters; to your use of any of the Bank's banking locations or facilities; or to any means you may use to access the Bank. It includes claims based on broken promises or contracts, torts, or other wrongful actions. It also includes statutory, common law, and equitable claims. A Dispute also includes any disagreements about the meaning or application of this Arbitration Agreement. This Arbitration Agreement shall survive the payment or closure of your Account. **YOU UNDERSTAND AND AGREE THAT YOU AND THE BANK ARE WAIVING THE RIGHT TO A JURY TRIAL OR TRIAL BEFORE A JUDGE IN A PUBLIC COURT.** As the sole exception to this Arbitration Agreement, you and the Bank retain the right to pursue in small claims court any Dispute that is within that court's jurisdiction. If either you or the Bank fails to submit to binding arbitration following lawful demand, the party so failing bears all costs and expenses incurred by the other in compelling arbitration.

2. **Arbitration Procedure; Severability.** Either you or the Bank may submit a Dispute to binding arbitration at any time notwithstanding that a lawsuit or other proceeding has been previously commenced. **NEITHER YOU NOR THE BANK SHALL BE ENTITLED TO JOIN OR CONSOLIDATE DISPUTES BY OR AGAINST OTHERS IN ANY ARBITRATION, OR TO INCLUDE IN ANY ARBITRATION ANY DISPUTE AS A REPRESENTATIVE OR MEMBER OF A CLASS, OR TO ACT IN ANY ARBITRATION IN THE INTEREST OF THE GENERAL PUBLIC OR IN A PRIVATE ATTORNEY GENERAL CAPACITY.** Each arbitration, including the selection of the arbitrator(s), shall be administered by the American Arbitration Association (AAA), or such other administrator as you and the Bank may mutually agree to (the AAA or such other mutually agreeable administrator to be referred to hereinafter as the "Arbitration Administrator"), according to the Commercial Arbitration Rules and the Supplemental Procedures for Consumer Related Disputes ("AAA Rules"). To the extent that there is any variance between the AAA Rules and this Arbitration Agreement, this Arbitration Agreement shall control. Arbitrator(s) must be members of the state bar where the arbitration is held, with expertise in the substantive laws applicable to the subject matter of the Dispute. No arbitrator or other party to an arbitration proceeding may disclose the existence, content, or results thereof, except for disclosures of information by a party required in the ordinary course of its business or by applicable law or regulation. You and the Bank (the "Parties") agree that in this relationship: (1) The Parties are participating in transactions involving interstate commerce; and (2) This Arbitration Agreement and any resulting arbitration are governed by the provisions of the Federal Arbitration Act (Title 9 of the United States Code), and, to the extent any provision of that Act is inapplicable, unenforceable or invalid, the laws of the state of South Dakota. If any of the provisions of this Arbitration Agreement dealing with class action, class arbitration, private attorney general action, other representative action, joinder,

or consolidation is found to be illegal or unenforceable, that invalid provision shall not be severable and this entire Arbitration Agreement shall be unenforceable.

3. **Rights Preserved**. This Arbitration Agreement does not prohibit the Parties from exercising any lawful rights or using other available remedies to preserve, foreclose, or obtain possession of real or personal property; exercise self-help remedies, including setoff and repossession rights; or obtain provisional or ancillary remedies such as injunctive relief, attachment, garnishment, or the appointment of a receiver by a court of competent jurisdiction. Any statute of limitations applicable to any Dispute applies to any arbitration between the Parties. The provisions of this Arbitration Agreement shall survive termination, amendment, or expiration of the Card or any other relationship between you and the Bank.

4. **Fees and Expenses of Arbitration.** Arbitration fees shall be determined by the rules or procedures of the Arbitration Administrator, unless limited by applicable law. Please check with the Arbitration Administrator to determine the fees applicable to any arbitration you may file. If the applicable law of the state in which you opened your Account limits the amount of fees and expenses to be paid by you, then no allocation of fees and expenses to you shall exceed this limitation. Unless inconsistent with applicable law, each of us shall bear the expense of our own attorney, expert and witness fees, regardless of which of us prevails in the arbitration.

Arbitration Agreement from First Premier Bank Credit Card Contract and Account Opening Disclosure Statement (2017)

ARBITRATION AND LITIGATION

This Arbitration Provision ("Provision") facilitates the prompt and efficient resolution of any disputes that may arise between you and us. Arbitration is a form of private dispute-resolution in which persons with a dispute waive their rights to file a lawsuit, to proceed in court and to a jury trial, and instead submit their disputes to a neutral third person (an arbitrator) for a binding decision. You have the right to opt out of this Provision, which means you would retain your right to litigate your disputes in a court, either before a judge or jury. To exercise your right to opt out you must provide us with written notice no later than 30 days after your Credit Account is first opened. If we do not receive your written notice within that time frame, your rights to opt out will terminate, and you agree that the provisions of this section will apply.

PLEASE READ THIS PROVISION CAREFULLY. IT PROVIDES THAT ALL DISPUTES ARISING OUT OF OR CONNECTED TO THIS CONTRACT SHALL BE RESOLVED BY BINDING ARBITRATION. ARBITRATION REPLACES THE RIGHT TO GO TO COURT. IN THE ABSENCE OF THIS ARBITRATION AGREEMENT. YOU AND WE MAY OTHERWISE HAVE HAD A RIGHT OR OPPORTUNITY TO BRING CLAIMS IN A COURT, BEFORE A JUDGE OR JURY AND/OR TO PARTICIPATE IN OR BE REPRESENTED IN A CASE FILED IN COURT BY OTHERS (INCLUDING, BUT NOT LIMITED TO, CLASS ACTIONS). EXCEPT AS OTHERWISE PROVIDED, ENTERING INTO THIS AGREEMENT CONSTITUTES A WAIVER OF YOUR RIGHT TO LITIGATE CLAIMS AND ALL OPPORTUNITY TO BE HEARD BY A JUDGE OR JURY.

Parties and Matters Subject to Arbitration: For purposes of this Provision, "you" and "us" include the employees, parents, subsidiaries, affiliates, beneficiaries, agents and assigns of you and us. For purposes of this Provision, "Claim" means any claim, dispute or controversy by either you or us, arising out of or relating in any way to this Contract, this Provision (including claims regarding the applicability, enforceability or validity of this Provision), your Credit Account, any transaction on your Credit Account and our relationship. "Claim" also refers to any interaction or communication between you and us that occurred prior to or concurrent with entering into this Contract, including those now in existence, regardless of present knowledge. "Claim" shall refer to claims of every kind and nature, including, but not limited to, initial claims, counterclaims, cross-claims and third party claims. All Claims are subject to arbitration, regardless of legal theory and remedy sought, including, but not limited to, claims based in contract, tort (including negligence, intentional tort, fraud and fraud in the inducement), agency, statutory law (federal and state), administrative regulations or any other source of law (including equity).

Agreement to Arbitrate: Any Claim arising out of or relating to this Contract, or the breach of this Contract or your Credit Account, shall be resolved and settled exclusively and finally by binding arbitration, in accordance with this Provision. Binding arbitration shall not be required, however, for collection actions by us relating to your Credit Account. Furthermore, both you and we retain the right to pursue in a small claims court any Claim that within that court's jurisdiction, provided the Claim proceeds on an individual basis. However, only a court of law, not an arbitrator, shall determine the validity and effect of this Provision's prohibition of class arbitration. For any Claims covered by this Provision, a party who asserted a Claim in a lawsuit in court may elect arbitration with respect to any Claim subsequently asserted in that lawsuit by any other party.

Voluntary Waiver of the Right to a Jury Trial and Class Action Participation: As a result of this Provision, neither you nor we have the right to litigate any Claim in court or the right to a jury trial on any Claim, except as provided above. **YOU AGREE THAT YOU ARE VOLUNTARILY AND KNOWINGLY WAIVING ANY RIGHT YOU MAY HAVE TO GO TO COURT OR TO HAVE A JURY TRIAL. FURTHERMORE, NEITHER YOU NOR WE MAY SERVE AS A REPRESENTATIVE, A PRIVATE ATTORNEY GENERAL, OR IN ANY OTHER REPRESENTATIVE CAPACITY.**

SIMILARLY, NEITHER YOU NOR WE MAY PARTICIPATE AS A MEMBER OF A CLASS OF CLAIMANTS IN A LAWSUIT OF ANY CLAIM.

Prohibition of Class Arbitration: All Claims shall be resolved by binding arbitration on an individual basis. Claims made and remedies sought as part of a class action, private attorney general or other representative action are subject to arbitration on an individual (non-class, nonrepresentative) basis. Therefore, the arbitrator has no authority to conduct class-wide proceedings and will be restricted to resolving individual Claims. **UNDER THIS ARBITRATION PROVISION THERE IS NO RIGHT OR AUTHORITY FOR ANY CLAIMS TO BE ARBITRATED ON A CLASS BASIS.** Arbitration will only be conducted on an individual Claim basis and there is no right or authority to consolidate or join any of your Claims with any other Claims. **YOU AGREE THAT YOU ARE VOLUNTARILY AND KNOWINGLY WAIVING ANY RIGHT TO PARTICIPATE AS A REPRESENTATIVE OR MEMBER OF ANY CLASS OF CLAIMANTS PERTAINING TO ANY CLAIM SUBJECT TO ARBITRATION UNDER THIS PROVISION.**

Governing Law: This agreement to arbitrate is made pursuant to a transaction involving interstate commerce and shall be governed by the Federal Arbitration Act, 9 U.S.C. §§ 1-16, as it may be amended. If for any reason the Federal Arbitration Act does not apply, the substantive law of the State of South Dakota shall govern this Provision.

Arbitration Location and Procedure: Any arbitration hearing at which you wish to appear will take place at a location within the federal judicial district that includes your billing address at the time the Claim is filed. The party bringing the Claim may file its Claim at the American Arbitration Association ("AAA"), or an arbitration organization mutually agreed upon by the parties. The arbitration organization that is selected will administer the arbitration pursuant to its procedures in effect at the time of filing, subject to this Provision. If you do not agree to file your claim with AAA, and the parries cannot agree on an alternative arbitration organization, an arbitrator will be appointed by a court pursuant to the Federal Arbitration Act. In the event of a conflict or inconsistency between the respective organization's rules and this Provision, this Provision shall govern. The arbitration will be conducted before a single arbitrator, whose authority is limited solely to individual Claims between you and us. The arbitration will not be consolidated with any other arbitration proceeding. Any decision rendered in such arbitration proceeding will be final and binding on the parties and judgment maybe entered in a court of competent jurisdiction. The rules and forms of AAA may be obtained as follows: American Arbitration Association, (1-800-778-7879), 335 Madison Avenue, Floor 10, New York, NY 10017, website at www.adr.org.

Arbitrator's Authority: The arbitrator shall apply the applicable substantive law, consistent with the Federal Arbitration Act; shall apply statutes of limitation, and shall honor claims of privilege recognized at law. In conducting the arbitration proceeding, the arbitrator shall not apply any federal or state rules of civil procedure or evidence. **PURSUANT TO THIS ARBITRATION PROVISION, THERE IS NO RIGHT TO ENGAGE IN PREARBITRATION DISCOVERY EXCEPT AS PROVIDED FOR IN THE RULES AND PROCEDURES OF THE RESPECTIVE CHOSEN NATIONAL ARBITRAL ORGANIZATION.** Either party may, however, request to expand the scope of discovery. If a request is made, within 15 days of the requesting party's notice, the objecting party may submit objections to the arbitrator with a copy of the objections provided to the party requesting expansion. The grant or denial of a party's request will be in the sole discretion of the arbitrator, who shall notify the parties of the final decision within 20 days of the objecting party's submission.

The Arbitrator's Award: The arbitrator has the ability to award to the prevailing party all remedies available at common law, by statute or in equity, including injunctive relief, declaratory relief, arbitration costs and attorney fees. The arbitrator shall not, however, have authority to award any punitive damages. **YOU AND WE AGREE THAT PUNITIVE DAMAGES ARE NOT RECOVERABLE IN ANY ARBITRATION OR OTHER PROCEEDING UNDER THIS CONTRACT EXCEPT TO THE EXTENT PUNITIVE DAMAGES WOULD BE AVAILABLE IN LITIGATION.** For awards not in excess of $5,000.00, upon the timely request of any party, the arbitrator shall provide a brief written explanation of the basis for the award. In the event an award exceeds $5,000.00, or in which there is a request for equitable relief with a potential financial impact or value in excess of $5,000.00, the award of the arbitrator shall be in writing and shall specify the facts and the law on which it is based. In such case, the arbitrator's findings of fact must be supported by substantial evidence and the arbitrator's conclusions of law must not be based on legal error or be erroneous under the applicable substantive law. Further, in addition to the Federal Arbitration Act's grounds for vacation, modification or correction of the arbitrator's award, the parties shall have the right to judicial review of the arbitrator's award to determine whether the arbitrator's findings of fact are supported by substantial evidence and whether the arbitrator's conclusions of law are based on legal error or are erroneous under the applicable substantive law. Judgment upon the award rendered by the arbitrator may be entered in any court having jurisdiction thereof. However, if the award is in excess of $5,000.00, judgment may be entered only upon determination by the court that the award is supported by substantial evidence and is not erroneous or based on legal error.

Expenses: Regardless of who demands arbitration, we will pay all expenses of arbitration, including the filing, administrative, hearing and arbitrator's fees ("Arbitration Fees"), to the extent that the Arbitration Fees exceed the amounts you would be required to pay for filing a lawsuit in a court. Throughout the arbitration, each party shall bear his or her own attorney fees and expenses, such as witness and expert witness fees. If you prevail in the arbitration of any Claim against us, we will reimburse you for any fees you paid to the arbitration organization in connection with the arbitration.

Binding Effect and Survival: You and we agree that, except as specifically provided for above, the arbitrator's decision will be final and binding on all parties subject to this Provision. This Provision is binding upon you, us, and the heirs, successors, assigns and related third parties of you and us. This Provision shall survive termination of your account, whether it be through voluntary payment of the debt in full by you, a legal proceeding initiated by us to collect a debt that you owe, a bankruptcy by you or a sale of your Credit Account by us.

Severability: If any portion of this Provision is deemed invalid or unenforceable under any law or statute consistent with the FAA, such a finding shall not invalidate any remaining portion of this Provision, the Contract or any other agreement entered into by you with us. However, the prohibition on class arbitration is not severable from the remainder of this Provision. In the event that a court deems the prohibition on class arbitration to be invalid and unenforceable, any subsequent class action or representative proceeding shall be in a court of law and will not be subject to binding.

PART I

REGULATION

SECTION B

Regulation by Public Law

CHAPTER 4

STATE REGULATION AND UDAP

In addition to state common law of contracts and torts, states also regulate consumer finance in a number of ways. First, states control entry into parts of the consumer finance business through licensing requirements. Second, states may impose some types of prudential regulations on financial services businesses to ensure their solvency. These prudential requirements are typically combined with some form of active supervision of consumer finance businesses, such as periodic examinations of books and records. Third, states regulate the substantive conduct of consumer finance business through disclosure requirements and mandates and prohibitions on product terms, such as fee and interest rate caps. Fourth, every state has some form of a statute prohibiting Unfair and Deceptive Acts and Practices (UDAP, pronounced as YOU-dap). And finally, states engage in public enforcement of consumer finance laws.

I. LICENSING

Many types of consumer finance businesses require special licensing. States generally have licensing requirements for banks, non-bank lenders, mortgage brokers, mortgage servicers, check cashers, and money transmitters. While certain lines of business, particularly parties involved in lending and payments, are generally licensed, other types of consumer finance businesses, such as debt collectors, are not specially licensed.

Critically, banks and credit unions may receive their license (known as a charter) from either the federal government or state government, and federally chartered banks are entitled to operate in all states without state licensing. Non-bank consumer financial services businesses, however, must comply with state licensing requirements if applicable.

Licensing requirements are generally part of larger regulatory regimes that limit the type of business a licensee can engage in, as well as the terms under which the licensee can engage in that business.

The specific licensing requirements vary, but the process generally consists of the submission of an application for a license, including various financial statements and a surety bond, followed by an investigation by a state regulatory authority. The financial statements and surety bond are designed to give the state regulator confidence that if the license is granted the licensee will have the financial wherewithal to perform the contracts into which it enters.

Most state licensing regimes for non-banks involve a relatively pro forma process in which, if the licensee submits the proper paper work and obtains the necessary bond, the license will be granted unless there are red flags about the licensee's fitness of character, such as past criminal convictions or bankruptcies. The Michigan Money Transmission Services Act, found in the statutory supplement, is typical of such licensing statutes. The largely pro forma nature of state licensing for non-banks differs substantially from the bank chartering system in which bank regulators frequently seek to limit the extent of competition among banks in any geographic area lest they cannibalize each other's business.

In addition to licensing regimes specific to the financial services industry, some types of consumer finance service providers, such as accountants, attorneys, realtors, and tax preparers, are regulated as professionals by the states. The licensing for these professionals is a substantially different type of licensing, as it is not based on financial requirements, and looks not just at fitness of character, but also at some demonstrated mastery of certain knowledge (*e.g.*, the bar exam).

II. PRUDENTIAL REQUIREMENTS AND SUPERVISION

An important regulatory concern about consumer financial services businesses is that they might end up insolvent and unable to meet their obligations. For example, if a money transmitter were to file for bankruptcy, the funds consumers had entrusted to it for transmission might not be transmitted, while if a lender were to fail, it might have unmet obligations to consumers. Accordingly, state-licensed consumer finance businesses are often subject to capital requirements, as well as to periodic inspections by state regulators.

Consider again the Michigan Money Transmission Services Act, which regulates the "selling or issuing of payment instruments or stored value devices or receiving money or monetary value for transmission," MCL § 487.1003, and requires that any party engaged in such activities be licensed by the state. MCL § 487.1011. The Michigan Money Transmission Services Act contains a requirement that licensees maintain "permissible investments" with a market value of no less than "all of its outstanding payment instruments." MCL § 487.1031. It then specifies exactly what sort of investments are "permissible," but with some limitations on the amount of certain types of investments. MCL § 487.1032. If you have taken a banking regulation course, you may recognize these prudential requirements as looking like miniature versions of bank capital requirements.

Another important feature of prudential regulation is periodic examinations of the licensed business. Examiners from the state regulatory agency will descend (often unannounced) on the licensed business and demand to inspect books and records, review policies and procedures, interview management, observe operations, and inspect a sampling of transaction records to ensure compliance with the applicable regulatory requirements, both in terms of the licensees' safety and soundness and in terms of consumer protection laws. Regulators will often have examination manuals that specify the methodology for such examinations, but there is a substantial amount of discretion in how examinations are conducted.

III. TERM AND CONDUCT REGULATION

States prescribe substantive term and conduct requirements for consumer finance businesses. The particulars vary substantially by product and by state, but frequently there is some level of mandated disclosure of terms to consumers, as well as some limitations on practices or fees.

Term and conduct regulation takes on many forms. It is possible, however, to identify several broad categories of state term and conduct regulation:

1. *Disclosure regulations.* Disclosure is one of the most common methods of consumer finance regulation. It essentially mandates the terms of the transaction, namely the terms on which information must be conveyed by the financial service provider to the consumer. Disclosure comes in many forms and can occur at a range of times and cover both the terms of a product as well as developments relating to a relationship (such as a data breach).

   Note that disclosure regulations come in two basic flavors. One type (what we usually think of as disclosure) mandates the provision of specific information, often in a particular format and at a particular time. The other type is a more general prohibition on deception, which does not mandate any specific form or timing, but may require provision of all material information to the consumer. State regulation includes both affirmative disclosure requirements and negative anti-deception rules that bolster the affirmative disclosure requirements. We will examine disclosure regulations in much more depth later in the book.
2. *Price regulations.* Foremost among price regulation are usury laws, which we will examine in more depth later in the book, but price regulations also include limitations on the amount and types of fees that can be charged to consumers. Examples of the latter type at the state level are restrictions on fees associated with check cashing, pawnshop lending, payday loans, and credit report freeze fees.
3. *Quantity limitations.* State laws will sometimes restrict how many loans or transactions a consumer can make or limit the amount of loans. Examples of this are state restrictions on the amount of payday loans. On the federal level there are restrictions on the frequency of transfers from savings accounts.
4. *Transaction frequency and timing regulations.* This can involve mandatory "cooling-off periods" between transactions or limitations on how many times a loan can be refinanced by the same lender (when the loan is repaid using the proceeds of a new loan, thereby continuing the indebtedness). These features commonly appear in state regulation of payday loans—short-term, high-cost loans that the lender can collect by directly drawing on the borrower's bank

account without first obtaining a judgment. These loans are typically two-week loans but are often refinanced multiple times so that the borrower is indebted for months at a high cost.

Another type of timing regulation deals with the time before a consumer is locked into a transaction, such as a mandatory period during which a consumer can cancel or rescind a transaction. State mortgage regulation sometimes includes a delay window, and federal mortgage regulation includes a rescission right that can last for some time in certain cases. A third type of timing regulation deals with how fast consumer financial service providers must respond to certain inquiries or requests, such as investigating claims of error.

5. *Payment application rules.* The application of payments is sometimes regulated, both in terms of when payments or deposits must be credited to or debited from a consumer, and in terms of the order of the application among multiple obligations.
6. *Capacity regulations.* Regulations sometimes require the consumer to have a certain financial capacity or wherewithal in order to enter into a transaction. Ability-to-repay requirements fall squarely into this category, as do requirements for pre-transaction counseling, such as federal law mandates for some high-cost mortgages.

   Usury limitations can also be understood as a mechanism for capacity regulation—if the interest rate on loans is restricted, lenders are less likely to lend to riskier borrowers, creating an effect similar to an ability-to-repay requirement.

   Disclosure regulations can also be seen as a type of capacity regulation on the theory that, absent disclosure, consumers lack the capacity to make informed decisions about whether to use a financial product or service.

   Notably, consumer finance basically lacks equivalents to the investor sophistication requirements that appear in certain securities law exemptions. Why do you think this might be? Why would we enable more sophisticated investors to have different investment opportunities in securities markets, but not with regard to, say, credit or savings products?

   Do we see an equivalent to consumer capacity regulations in state licensing regimes for businesses?
7. *Anti-tying regulations.* State and federal regulations will sometimes restrict the tying of different consumer financial products. For example, an anti-tying regulation might prohibit a financial services firm from making opening a credit card a requirement of opening a deposit account. These anti-tying provisions are generally designed to preserve consumer choice in separate product markets and prevent firms with market power (even local market power) in one product market from leveraging it to expand into other markets in which they are not competitive.
8. *Anti-kickback rules.* Some consumer financial products operate through brokered or referral markets. Regulations sometimes restrict whether and how brokers can be compensated for their role. Examples of this are restrictions on

the compensation received by mortgage brokers and prohibitions on certain payments in real estate settlements.

9. *Privacy regulations.* Financial information can be very revealing both about a person's wealth and consumption decisions. By the same token, however, consumer financial data is also extremely valuable, both to legitimate merchants and to fraudsters. Regulations restricting the sharing of information or requiring that consumers be provided with information about how their data may be used are another (largely toothless) category of substantive consumer finance regulation.
10. *Anti-fraud and anti-money laundering regulations.* Money laundering is primarily addressed through federal law, but occasionally state regulation will impose some sort of customer identification requirement as an anti-fraud measure, particularly in the case of pawn transactions.
11. *Mandatory terms and procedures to facilitate consumer vindication of rights.* State law sometimes mandates terms and procedures that are designed to facilitate consumers' vindication of their rights. This can include mandatory dispute and error resolution procedures and small claims courts, but also statutory fee-shifting and statutory damages provisions.
12. *Mandatory terms and procedures to limit consumer liability.* Finally, state law often mandates terms and procedures to limit consumers' liability to creditors. These include restrictions on garnishment and property exemptions and the exercise of setoff rights, but also timetables for foreclosure actions.

What does this all look like on the ground? Consider two state regulatory regimes as examples: Mississippi's check-cashing regulation and Illinois's payday lending regulation.

Mississippi licenses and regulates check-cashing businesses. Check cashers essentially purchase checks payable to the consumer by paying the consumer the face amount of the check minus some discount. That discount is represented as a fee charged for the check cashing. Thus, a $100 check with a 2% discount would translate into a $2 fee for the $100 check, so the consumer would receive $98 in exchange for the check. As part of the transaction, the consumer endorses the check to the check casher (that is, signs over the check by writing on the back of the check), and the check casher then bears the risk of collecting on the check.

In Mississippi, licensed check cashers are prohibited by statute from directly or indirectly charging fees exceeding the greater of 3% or $5 for government checks, the greater of 10% or $5 for personal checks, and the greater of 5% or $5 for all other checks. Miss. Stat. Ann. § 75-67-517. In other words, Mississippi has enacted a price regulation regarding check cashing. Mississippi also requires that:

> Any fee charged by a licensee for cashing a check shall be posted conspicuously to the bearer of the check before cashing the check, and the fee shall be a service fee and not interest.

Miss. Stat. Ann. § 75-67-515(4). This is a disclosure regulation. (Treating the fee as a service fee, rather than interest, is an attempt to forestall the application of other federal and state statutory provisions.)

The Mississippi Banking Commission regulations further require licensed check cashers to:

> display a sign disclosing the maximum fees allowed to be charged for cashing checks. The sign must be at least 20"x 20" and the print must be large and bold in order to allow customers to easily read the information. Such sign must be displayed in a conspicuous place and in easy view of all persons who enter the place of business.

Miss. Check Casher Regulations, Rule 3.5, http://www.dbcf.state.ms.us/documents/cons_finance/checkchasherregs120112.pdf. Again, this is a disclosure regulation. The Mississippi Banking Commission also requires that consumers sign a receipt for funds received in a check-cashing transaction. *Id.*, Rule 3.4. The signing of a receipt is a regulation meant to clarify assent to the transaction, and thus to facilitate consumer (and check casher) vindication of rights.

Additionally, Mississippi check cashers are prohibited from cashing checks unless they have first obtained appropriate identification from the customer indicating authority of the casher to cash the check. Miss. Stat. Ann. § 75-67-515(7). This is an anti-fraud regulation.

What we see, then, in Mississippi's regulatory regime for check cashers consists of licensing, but also of a substantive term requirement in the form of a price cap as well as transactional practice requirements of disclosures and consumer signing of receipts, and an anti-fraud requirement of customer identification.

Check cashing is one of the most straightforward consumer financial transactions. It is a one-off sale of a check by the consumer for cash. Other consumer financial products involve extended relationships between the product provider and the consumer. More complicated products will have more complex substantive term requirements, but the basic idea is the same.

Thus, Illinois's Payday Lending Reform Act also has a licensing regime for payday lenders and imposes disclosure requirements and regulates the fees that may be charged to borrowers. The Illinois PLRA also limits the total dollar volume of payday loans a consumer may have from all lenders at any one time, restricts rollovers of loans (a rollover is a refinancing of a loan with a new loan), limits the total length of consecutive payday loan indebtedness among different lenders, and imposes "cooling-off periods" between loans in some instances. Finally, the PLRA requires that borrowers be offered a repayment plan if they are unable to repay according to the agreed-upon terms. 815 ILCS 122/2-40. These are much more extensive substantive term regulations than the Mississippi check-cashing statute provides.

We will return in much more depth to the substantive term and conduct regulations applicable to various payment, deposit, and credit products in the second half of the book, which examines specific products and their regulatory regimes.

State term and conduct regulation is often preempted as applied to federally chartered banks and credit unions. A fuller discussion of preemption issues may be found in Chapter 9.

IV. UDAP

Every state has some form of an unfair and deceptive acts and practices (UDAP) statute. These statutes always prohibit deceptive practices, and many states' statutes also prohibit unfair and unconscionable practices, over and above whatever equitable principles exist in state law. UDAP liability sounds in neither contract nor tort, but its own category of statutory liability. UDAP liability does not require a contractual relationship. An important implication of this is that UDAP claims are not subject to contract and tort defenses or rules such as the Statute of Frauds, assumption of risk, the economic loss rule, parol evidence rule, privity requirements, or limitations on remedies or waivers.

State UDAP statutes, which were generally adopted in the 1970s and 1980s, are not uniform in either their text or their interpretation, but they often mirror section 5 of the Federal Trade Commission Act, 15 U.S.C. § 45, which prohibits unfair and deceptive acts and practices. Thus, state UDAP statutes are sometimes known as mini-FTC Acts. State UDAP statutes are sometimes known as mini-FTC Acts.

Although state UDAP statutes are a major form of consumer protection, they are not a consumer-finance-specific mode of regulation. Instead, most state UDAP statutes apply generally to all commerce, with various types of commerce then carved out from the statute.

State UDAP statutes vary considerably in their coverage. Thus, some statutes (as interpreted by state courts) prohibit only deceptive, not unfair acts, while others prohibit only particular unfair *and* deceptive acts and practices. Significantly, some UDAP statutes exclude entire types of businesses, such as all regulated industries, or insurance companies, or lenders, or real estate.

Some statutes require that the plaintiff prove intent or show reliance or a public impact, while others do not. Some require proof of intent or knowledge for deception claims, while others do not. Some UDAP statutes create a private right of action for consumers, while others can only be enforced by the state attorney general. (Section 5 of the Federal Trade Commission Act similarly lacks a private right of action.) Some state UDAP statutes permit class actions; others do not. Some require the consumer to provide the business with pre-suit notification and an opportunity to settle; others do not have such requirements. Some UDAP statutes provide for restitution, some for civil monetary penalties (with major variation in the size of penalties authorized), and some for equitable relief. Some provide for awards of attorneys' fees, but others do not. And some UDAP statutes provide for rulemaking authority for state agencies, while others do not. Thus, the strength of UDAP statutes varies considerably among states, even if the basic legal concept of a statutory prohibition on unfairness and deception is broadly shared.

A. Deception

Deception under UDAP statutes is always broader than common law fraud. It looks to whether a representation is misleading. A statement can be misleading even when true, if it has deceptive implications. Similarly, a failure to disclose material information can be deceptive. Whether a representation is misleading is generally determined by whether the intended audience would be deceived if behaving reasonably for that audience in the circumstances. State UDAP statutes sometimes follow an older FTC standard, namely whether a practice has the tendency to mislead even a minority of consumers.

Critically, in most states (and for the FTC Act), deception does not require reliance, but there still must be causation between deception and any injury if damages are sought. While reliance and causation are related concepts, they are not identical. Thus, in a New York case involving a bank loan, a bank had promised that there would be no prepayment fee, but then assessed a fee when the consumer sought to prepay. The New York Court of Appeals held that the consumers did not need to show that they had relied on the bank's misrepresentation when entering the loan. It was sufficient to show causation that because of the deception they were forced to pay a charge for which they were not liable. *Stutman v. Chemical Bank*, 731 N.E. 2d 608 (N.Y. 2000).

Deception also requires that a misrepresentation be material; a false statement about the weather in the context of a home mortgage application would not constitute deception, as it is not material to the loan. Materiality is generally presumed if there is an express representation relating to the transaction, an intentionally implied representation, or if the business should have known that the consumer would need information that was withheld.

B. Unfairness

While most state UDAP statutes refer to unfairness, a substantial minority instead prohibit unconscionable acts and practices, and a couple states do not have any statutory prohibition on either unfairness or unconscionability. The definition of unfairness or unconscionability varies among state UDAP statutes. Most state courts interpret state UDAP statutes utilizing the so-called *Sperry & Hutchinson* standard for unfairness. *See FTC v. Sperry & Hutchinson Co.*, 405, U.S. 233, 244-45 (1972). The *Sperry & Hutchinson* emerged from a 1964 FTC rulemaking and was the standard followed by the FTC until 1980. The *Sperry & Hutchinson* standard considers:

> 1) whether the practice, without necessarily having been previously considered unlawful, offends public policy as it has been established by statutes, the common law, or otherwise—whether, in other words, it is within at least the penumbra of some common law, statutory, or other established concept of unfairness; (2) whether it is immoral, unethical, oppressive, or unscrupulous; (3) whether it causes substantial injury to consumers (or competitors or other businessmen).

Statement of Basis and Purpose of Trade Regulation Rule 408, Unfair or Deceptive Advertising and Labeling of Cigarettes in Relation to the Health Hazards of Smoking. 29 Fed. Reg. 8355 (1964). Under intense political pressure for perceived regulatory overreach, the FTC amended its definition of unfairness in 1980 through a policy statement, Policy Statement on Unfairness (Dec. 17, 1980), and that policy statement was codified in 1994 amendments to the FTC Act. The codified version defines unfair as requiring a likelihood of substantial injury to consumers that is not reasonably avoidable by consumers and not outweighed by countervailing benefits to consumers or competition. 15 U.S.C. § 45(n). A minority of states follow the current FTC Act in terms of defining unfairness.

The particular formulation of an unfairness standard may not especially matter, however, because unfairness is a question for the trier of fact—the jury or, in a bench trial, the judge. The trier of fact's overall impression of the particular facts and circumstances of a case is likely to be more important than the particular standard at issue. In other words, unfairness is likely to operate similarly to common law unconscionability.

C. The California Unfair Competition Law

California has one of the more powerful UDAP statutes, the California Unfair Competition Law (or UCL, also known as section 17200—"seventeen-two-hundred"). Section 17200 is a very powerful sword for plaintiffs. It creates a private right of action for any "unlawful" behavior, even if the unlawful behavior itself is the violation of a statute or regulation that lacks a private right of action and even if the statute itself bars private rights of action. *See Rose v. Bank of Am., N.A.*, 57 Cal.4th 390, 393 (2013); *Zhang v. Super. Ct. (Cal. Capital Ins. Co.)*, 57 Cal. 4th 364 (2013). This is hardly a unique feature to the California UDAP statute; several other states have similar provisions.

The California Unfair Competition Law does not provide for recovery of attorneys' fees, but a successful plaintiff may seek attorneys' fees pursuant to California Code of Civil Procedure section 1021.5; there is no corresponding right for a successful defendant to recover its fees.

California has another statute, the Consumer Legal Remedies Act, Cal. Civ. Code §§ 1750 *et seq.*, which provides for monetary damages and attorneys' fees, but the statute has been held not to apply to consumer financial services, but to be limited to sales and leases of goods and services. *Berry v. Am. Expr. Co.*, 147 Cal.App.4th 224, 233 (2007) (credit cards not covered by CLRA); *Fairbanks v. Superior Court*, 46 Cal.4th 56, 64-65 (2009) (ancillary services to insurance not covered by CLRA).

The following case, *Boschma v. Home Loan Center*, illustrates the application of the California Unfair Competition Law and the distinction between liability under the California Unfair Competition Law and common law causes of action, such as fraud. *Boschma* involves so-called payment-option adjustable-rate mortgages (payment-option ARMs). These are not intuitive products, so a brief explanation will help you understand the case.

Suppose you borrow $200,000 to purchase a home. The loan has a 30-year term, meaning it will be paid back over 30 years. You won't pay in one lump sum, but in monthly installments. Each monthly installment payment will be credited in part to the principal balance of the loan (the $200,000 you borrowed) and in part to the interest that has accrued on the outstanding principal balance. Eventually the principal balance will be reduced to zero and the loan will be paid off. The process of paying down the principal balance over time is called "**amortization**," and different amortization schedules—allocation of monthly payments to principal or interest—affect how much the borrower ends up paying in total because the longer the principal is outstanding, the more interest that will accrue and need to be repaid too. To the extent you pay back the principal more quickly (say in 15 years, rather than over 30), there will be a smaller balance on which interest accrues every month, so you will end up paying less interest and thus less in total. And vice versa.

We already saw an amortization issue lurking in *Walker-Thomas Furniture*—none of the loans amortized until they all amortized; instead, every new purchase extended the amortization period for all existing loans. We'll cover amortization in more detail in a later chapter, but for now the thing to understand about the loan in *Boschma* is that the consumers signed up for a loan with two interlinked features. First, the loan had an adjustable interest rate that would periodically change. The interest rate was initially a below-market "teaser" rate that would reset after a year to a higher rate, indicating a higher monthly payment going forward.

The second feature of the *Boschma* loan was that it gave the borrowers a choice about the size of monthly payment amount (a "pick-a-pay" option). Every month they could choose from a menu of payment options: (1) a payment based on having the loan amortize over a 15-year period; (2) a smaller payment based on a 30-year amortization (resulting in greater total payments); (3) an even smaller non-amortizing payment of just the interest that had accrued, so that the principal would not be reduced at all; and (4) a payment so small that it would not cover any principal or even all of the interest that had accrued that month. This last payment option would result in the additional interest that had accrued, but not been paid off, being added to the principal balance for the following month, producing "**negative amortization.**" Rather than the loan being paid down, the loan balance would *increase* if the negative amortization payment option were selected. The default option for the payment schedule given to the borrowers was a payment size based on the initial teaser interest rate, such that if the rate reset to a higher rate, that same payment amount would inevitably result in negative amortization.

Clarence E. Boschma v. Home Loan Center, Inc.

198 Cal.App.4th 230 (2011)

IKOLA, J.

The defining feature of an option adjustable rate mortgage loan (Option ARM) with a discounted initial interest rate (*i.e.*, a "teaser" rate) is, for a limited number of years, the borrower may (by paying the minimum amount required to avoid default on the loan) make a monthly payment that is insufficient to pay off *the interest* accruing on the loan principal. Rather than amortizing the loan with each minimum monthly payment (as occurs with a standard mortgage loan), "negative amortization" occurs—a borrower who elects to make only the scheduled payment during the initial years of the Option ARM owes more to the lender than he or she did on the date the loan was made. After an initial period of several years in which negative amortization can occur, a borrower's payment schedule then recasts to require a minimum monthly payment that amortizes the loan.

In this case, plaintiffs sued defendant Home Loan Center, Inc., for (1) fraudulent omissions and (2) violations of Business and Professions Code section 17200 *et seq*. (section 17200). Plaintiffs, individual borrowers who entered into Option ARM's with defendant, allege defendant's loan documents failed to adequately and accurately disclose the essential terms of the loans, namely that plaintiffs *would* suffer negative amortization if they made monthly payments according to the only payment schedule provided to them prior to the closing of the loan. The court sustained defendant's demurrer to the second amended complaint without leave to amend, reasoning that the loan documentation adequately described the nature of Option ARM's. We reverse the ensuing judgment. Plaintiffs adequately alleged fraud and section 17200 causes of action.

FACTS

. . . The Boschmas refinanced their existing home loan with defendant on or about February 1, 2006, utilizing an Option ARM. Robison agreed to an Option ARM with defendant on or about November 22, 2005; the operative complaint does not specify whether her loan was a purchase money loan or a refinancing of an existing loan. * * *

The Note

Plaintiffs executed nearly identical documents entitled "ADJUSTABLE RATE NOTE" (Note). The Note features a bold, capitalized disclaimer below its title and loan identification numbers: "THIS NOTE CONTAINS PROVISIONS THAT WILL CHANGE THE INTEREST RATE AND THE MONTHLY PAYMENT. THERE MAY BE A LIMIT ON THE AMOUNT THAT THE MONTHLY PAYMENT CAN INCREASE OR DECREASE. THE PRINCIPAL AMOUNT TO REPAY COULD BE GREATER THAN THE AMOUNT ORIGINALLY BORROWED, BUT NOT MORE THAN THE LIMIT STATED IN THIS NOTE." Following this disclaimer, the Note indicates the date of execution (Feb. 1, 2006, for the Boschmas, and Nov. 22, 2005, for Robison), the site of execution (Irvine, Cal.), and the address of the property that secures the loan for each party. The Note then lists 11 separate terms, which we quote in relevant part below.

[Other key terms of the note are detailed. They explain how the payment option feature works.]

Program Disclosure

Plaintiffs also received a three-page document entitled "ADJUSTABLE RATE MORTGAGE LOAN PROGRAM DISCLOSURE 12-MONTH AVERAGE OF MONTHLY 1-YR CONSTANT MATURITY INDEX PAYMENT-CAPPED NON-CONVERTIBLE ARM." This disclosure describes the features of the loan provided to plaintiffs. The middle of the first paragraph states in all capital letters: "THIS LOAN ALLOWS FOR NEGATIVE AMORTIZATION." The document uses bullet point explanations of the mechanics of the loan (on topics such as how interest rates are determined, how the interest rate can change, and how the payment can change), as well as examples showing the effect of interest rate fluctuations on payments made by a borrower. Our review of this material suggests it is consistent with the terms described in the Note. * * *

Plaintiffs received federal Truth-in-Lending Disclosure Statements (TILDS) that included payment schedules. The court observed that] it is *implicit* in plaintiffs' payment schedules that negative amortization will occur if plaintiffs were to remit only the monthly payment amounts set forth in the payment schedules.

Allegations in the Second Amended Complaint

The gravamen of plaintiffs' operative complaint is that defendant failed to disclose prior to plaintiffs entering into their Option ARM's: (1) "the loans were designed to cause negative amortization to occur"; (2) "the monthly payment amounts listed in the loan documents for the first two to five years of the loans were based entirely upon a low 'teaser' interest rate (though *not* disclosed as such by Defendants) which existed for only a single month and which was substantially lower than the actual interest rate that would be charged, such that these payment amounts would never be sufficient to pay the interest due each month"; and (3) "when [plaintiffs] followed the contractual payment schedule in the loan documents, negative amortization was *certain* to occur, resulting in a significant loss of equity in borrowers' homes, and making it much more difficult for borrowers to refinance the loans [because of the prepayment penalty included in the loan for paying off the loan within the first three years of the loan]; thus, as each month passed, the homeowners would actually owe more money than they did at the outset of the loan, with less time to repay it."

Plaintiffs allege that instead of clearly describing the consequences of making the scheduled payments set forth in the TILDS, the actual disclosures in the loan documents suggest only that negative amortization *could* occur and that payments *may* change from the original schedule based on future variability in interest rates. "Borrowers were *not* provided, before entering into the loans, with any other payment schedule or with any informed option to make payments different than those listed in the [TILDS] payment schedule." "[H]ad Defendant disclosed the payment amounts sufficient to avoid negative amortization from occurring [plaintiffs] would not have entered into the loans."

Plaintiffs allege this information was material to their decision to accept Option ARM's and they would not have entered into their Option ARM's had defendant made accurate disclosures. Plaintiffs allege defendant actively concealed and suppressed material facts from plaintiffs. "Defendants purposefully and intentionally devised this Option ARM loan scheme of flatly omitting material information and, in some cases, making partial representations while omitting material facts, in order to deceive consumers into believing that these loans would provide a low payment and corresponding interest rate for the first two to five years of the Note and that, if they made their payments according to the payment schedule provided by Defendants, this would be sufficient to pay both principal and interest." Plaintiffs allege damages consisting of loss of equity in their homes and other unspecified damages.

With regard to their section 17200 claim, plaintiffs allege defendant's practices (as described above) were unlawful, unfair, and fraudulent. Plaintiffs identify their "injury and lost money and property" as "the amount of negative amortization resulting from Defendant's scheme." . . .

It is important to demarcate the boundaries of this dispute. The following are *not* at issue in this case: (1) should it be legal to offer Option ARM's to typical mortgage borrowers and (2) should it be legal to utilize teaser (discounted) interest rates (here 1.25 percent for the first *month* of a 30-year loan), which bear no relation to the actual cost of credit? Our only concern in this case is whether plaintiffs stated a cause of action under state law based on defendant's allegedly misleading, incomplete, and/or inaccurate disclosures in the Option ARM documents provided to plaintiffs.

It does not appear California state courts have addressed this precise issue. . . .

Fraud

Actual fraud consists, among other things, of "[t]he suppression of that which is true, by one having knowledge or belief of the fact" or "[a]ny other act fitted to deceive." (Civ. Code, § 1572, subds. 3, 5; *see also* Civ. Code, § 1710, subd. 3 [definition of "deceit" includes "[t]he suppression of a fact, by one who is bound to disclose it, or who gives information of other facts which are likely to mislead for want of communication of that fact"]; *Vega v. Jones, Day, Reavis & Pogue* (2004) 121 Cal.App.4th 282, 292 (*Vega*) ["active concealment or suppression of facts . . . is the equivalent of a false representation"].)

"'[T]he elements of an action for fraud and deceit based on concealment are: (1) the defendant must have concealed or suppressed a material fact, (2) the defendant must have been under a duty to disclose the fact to the plaintiff, (3) the defendant must have intentionally concealed or suppressed the fact with the intent to defraud the plaintiff, (4) the plaintiff must have been unaware of the fact and would not have acted as he did if he had known of the concealed or suppressed fact, and (5) as a result of the concealment or suppression of the fact, the plaintiff must have sustained damage.'" (*Hahn v. Mirda* (2007) 147 Cal.App.4th 740, 748.) Fraud must be pleaded with specificity rather than with "'general and conclusory'" allegations.

First element: Did plaintiffs adequately plead concealed or suppressed material facts? We agree with *Jordan, supra,* 745 F.Supp.2d 1084, that, with regard to the alleged fraudulent omissions at issue, the enhanced pleading burden of a fraud claim is met by the attachment of the relevant Option ARM documents: "[P]laintiffs' evidence is the mortgage instrument, which provides the specific content of the allegedly false representations related to negative amortization, as well as the date and place of the alleged fraud. While the precise identities of the employees responsible . . . are not specified in the loan instrument, defendants possess the superior knowledge of who was responsible for crafting these loan documents." (*Id.* at p. 1096.)

The closer question is whether defendant can be deemed to have concealed or suppressed material facts even though at least some of these facts *can be* distilled from the loan documents through careful analysis of the Note and payment schedule. Defendant did not omit any mention of negative amortization. (*See, e.g., Vega, supra,* 121 Cal. App.4th at p. 292 [plaintiff states cause of action by alleging law firm "'sanitized'" acquisition disclosure by removing mention of "'toxic' stock"].) Instead, defendant did not clearly state in the loan documents that plaintiffs *were receiving* a discounted initial interest rate and that making the minimum payments according to the TILDS payment schedule *definitely would* result in negative amortization.

We restate some of the relevant terms from the Option ARM documents. The Note states, in relevant part: (1) Section 2(A)—"I will pay interest at a yearly rate of 1.250%. The interest rate I pay may change"; (2) Section 2(B)—"The interest rate I will pay may change on the first day of April 1, 2006, and on that day every month thereafter"; (3) Section 3(A)—"I will pay principal and interest by making payments every month"; (4) Section 3(B)—"Each of my initial monthly payments will be in the amount of $833.13. This amount may change"; (5) Section 3(C)—"My monthly payment may change . . . on the 1st day of April, 2007"; and (6) Section 3(E)—"My monthly payment could be less than the amount of the interest portion of the monthly payment. . . ." The program disclosure suggests that plaintiffs might have a discounted rate, or they might have a premium rate. The program disclosure explains that the Option ARM "ALLOWS FOR NEGATIVE AMORTIZATION." The program disclosure states: "Because the Interest Rate has the potential to increase each month but the payment changes are generally limited to once every twelve months, the monthly payment may be insufficient to pay the interest which is accruing. . . ."

Keeping in mind the procedural posture of this case, we conclude plaintiffs have adequately pleaded that material facts were concealed by inaccurate representations and half-truths. If plaintiffs can show defendant intentionally used its Option ARM forms to deceive borrowers, plaintiffs may be able to establish a fraud claim. Plaintiffs' actual interest rates and monthly payments sufficient to amortize the loan (or at least pay the accruing interest) were hidden in the complexity of the Option ARM contract terms. "'The fact that a false statement may be obviously false to those who are trained and experienced does not change its character, nor take away its power to deceive others less experienced. There is no duty resting upon a citizen to suspect the honesty of those with whom he [or she] transacts business. Laws are made to protect the trusting as well as the suspicious. [T]he rule of *caveat emptor* should not be relied upon to reward fraud and deception.'" (*Thompson v. 10,000 RV Sales, Inc.* (2005) 130 Cal.App.4th 950, 976.)

The root of the alleged deficiencies in defendant's disclosures is defendant's use of a significantly discounted teaser rate rather than an initial rate set near the rate that would result from the application of the variable rate formula in the Note (an index plus 3.5/3.25 percent). The teaser rate creates an artificially low (compared to the actual cost of credit) initial payment schedule and guarantees that the actual applicable interest rate (after the first month of the loan) will exceed the interest rate used to calculate the payment schedule for the initial years of the loan. If the initial interest rate were set using the Note's variable rate formula, it would actually be possible that interest rates would adjust downward (or stay the same) after the first payment and no negative amortization would occur. In other words, the disclosures' conditional language is accurate absent a significantly discounted rate. An Option ARM loan without a teaser rate would result in a higher initial interest rate, higher initial minimum payments pursuant to the payment schedule, and a much narrower gap (even if interest rates increased) between the borrower's payment "options." Of course, without a teaser rate, the surface attractiveness of Option ARM's would have been greatly diminished precisely because the stated (initial) interest rate and (initial) payment would be higher.

Second element: Did defendant have a duty to disclose the allegedly concealed material facts to plaintiffs? Defendant certainly had a legal duty under TILA to clearly and conspicuously describe the terms of the loan to plaintiffs. (*Ralston II, supra*, 2010 WL 3211931 at pp. *4-*5.) And, even ignoring TILA, defendant had a common law duty to avoid making partial, misleading representations that effectively concealed material facts. [Citations omitted.]

Third element: Did defendant conceal or suppress the truth about negative amortization with the intent to defraud plaintiffs? Taking plaintiffs' factual allegations to be true, defendant intentionally omitted a clear disclosure of the nature of plaintiffs' loans because giving a clear explanation of how the loans worked would have punctured the illusion of a low payment, low interest rate loan. An alternate explanation might be that defendant (apparently like many other mortgage lenders, as evidenced by the repetition of the same disclosures in cases discussed herein) utilized a set of forms for all Option ARM's. Perhaps these forms were selected in an effort to comply with TILA requirements regardless of the particular terms of an individual loan (*e.g.*, whether a discounted interest rate was used) rather than as a nefarious scheme to deceive consumers. But we will not weigh the likelihood of these competing narratives on demurrer.

Fourth element: Did plaintiffs plead reliance? Reliance can be proved in a fraudulent omission case by establishing that "had the omitted information been disclosed, [the plaintiff] would have been aware of it and behaved differently." (*Mirkin v. Wasserman* (1993) 5 Cal.4th 1082, 1093.) Plaintiffs have alleged this fact; it would be improper to adjudicate the factual question of plaintiffs' actual reliance at the demurrer stage.[11] Moreover, given our analysis of the loan documents, we reject the contention that the disclosures actually given to plaintiffs preclude reasonable reliance. (*Ralston II, supra*, 2010 WL 3211931 at pp. *5-*6 [rejecting argument that plaintiff could not prove reliance because of the contents of the loan documents]; *see also Alliance Mortgage Co. v. Rothwell* (1995) 10 Cal.4th 1226, 1239 [whether reliance is reasonable is usually a question of fact].)

Fifth element: Did plaintiffs suffer damages as a result of defendant's fraud? Plaintiffs' theory of damages (lost home equity) is problematic. Every month in which plaintiffs suffered negative amortization was a month in which they enjoyed payments lower than the amount needed to amortize the loan (or even to pay off the accruing interest). In exchange for gradually declining equity, plaintiffs retained liquid cash that they

11. Of course, the mere fact that borrowers took out Option ARM's does not necessarily prove they were misled by disclosures. Borrowers who understood the terms of the loan may still have agreed to the loan because it enabled them to buy now and pay later. Some borrowers may have speculated that real estate prices would continue to climb, enabling them to refinance after the initial low payment period ended. Others may have speculated that they would have more income in a few years and that they needed to buy a home before they were "priced out" of the market. And still others may have utilized Option ARM's to facilitate non-housing-related consumer spending or to finance small businesses. This highlights the difference between disclosure policy concerns (*i.e.*, does the consumer understand the credit product) and more paternalistic policy concerns as to whether consumers should be allowed to take on the risk of an Option ARM.

otherwise would have paid to defendant (or another lender). Viewed in this manner, plaintiffs' only "injury" is the psychological revelation (whenever it occurred) that they were not receiving a free lunch from defendant: plaintiffs could have low payments or pay off their loans, but not both at the same time. But plaintiffs' allegation of lost equity in their homes is sufficient at this stage of the proceedings to overrule defendant's demurrer. We construe plaintiffs' allegations (including the allegation that the prepayment penalty precluded refinancing into a better loan) broadly to encompass an assertion that they were misled into agreeing to Option ARM's, which led to lost equity in their homes because the terms of the Option ARM's put them in a worse economic position than they would have been had they utilized a different credit product (*i.e.*, by deciding not to refinance their previous loans or by taking out a more suitable loan).

Section 17200

California's UCL "does not proscribe specific activities, but broadly prohibits 'any unlawful, unfair or fraudulent business act or practice and unfair, deceptive, untrue or misleading advertising.' (§ 17200.) The UCL 'governs "anti-competitive business practices" as well as injuries to consumers and has as a major purpose "the preservation of fair business competition." [Citations omitted.] By proscribing "any unlawful" business practice, "section 17200 'borrows' violations of other laws and treats them as unlawful practices that the unfair competition law makes independently actionable. Because . . . section 17200 is written in the disjunctive, it establishes three varieties of unfair competition—acts or practices which are unlawful, or unfair, or fraudulent. In other words, a practice is prohibited as 'unfair' or 'deceptive' even if not 'unlawful' and vice versa." (*Puentes v. Wells Fargo Home Mortgage, Inc.* (2008) 160 Cal.App.4th 638, 643-644.)

"'[A] practice may be deemed unfair even if not specifically proscribed by some other law.'" (*Korea Supply Co. v. Lockheed Martin Corp.* (2003) 29 Cal.4th 1134, 1143.) According to some appellate courts, a business practice is "unfair" under the UCL if (1) the consumer injury is substantial; (2) the injury is not outweighed by any countervailing benefits to consumers or competition; and (3) the injury could not reasonably have been avoided by consumers themselves. (*Camacho v. Automobile Club of Southern California* (2006) 142 Cal.App.4th 1394, 1403-1405.) Other courts require "that the public policy which is a predicate to a consumer unfair competition action under the 'unfair' prong of the UCL . . . be tethered to specific constitutional, statutory, or regulatory provisions." (*Bardin v. DaimlerChrysler Corp.* (2006) 136 Cal.App.4th 1255, 1260-1261.) Still others assess whether the practice "is immoral, unethical, oppressive, unscrupulous or substantially injurious to consumers . . . [weighing] the utility of the defendant's conduct against the gravity of the harm to the alleged victim." (*Id.* at p. 1260.) And some courts, in reviewing a pleading, apply all three tests. (*Drum v. San Fernando Valley Bar Assn.* (2010) 182 Cal.App.4th 247, 256-257.)

"[A] fraudulent business practice is one that is likely to deceive members of the public." (*Morgan v. AT&T Wireless Services, Inc.* (2009) 177 Cal.App.4th 1235, 1255.) "A claim based upon the fraudulent business practice prong of the UCL is 'distinct from common law fraud. "A [common law] fraudulent deception must be actually false, known to be false by the perpetrator and reasonably relied upon by a victim who incurs damages. None of these elements are required to state a claim for . . . relief" under the UCL. [Citations omitted.] This distinction reflects the UCL's focus on the defendant's conduct, rather than the plaintiff's damages, in service of the statute's larger purpose of protecting the general public against unscrupulous business practices.' " (*Ibid.*) A fraudulent business practice "'"may be accurate on some level, but will nonetheless tend to mislead or deceive. . . . A perfectly true statement couched in such a manner that it is likely to mislead or deceive the consumer, such as by failure to disclose other relevant information, is actionable under"' the UCL." (*McKell v. Washington Mutual, Inc.* (2006) 142 Cal.App.4th 1457, 1471.)

With regard to their section 17200 claim, plaintiffs rely heavily on the concept of fraud. Although the second amended complaint alleges "unlawful" behavior, the only statutes specifically cited are Civil Code sections 1572 (actual fraud—omissions), 1573 (constructive fraud by omission), and 1710 (deceit). Based on our analysis of plaintiffs' common law fraud claim, we conclude plaintiffs have adequately pleaded a section 17200 claim under the unlawful and fraudulent prongs.[12]

Plaintiffs' "unfair" allegations also focus on the same material omissions/misleading disclosures in the loan documents. *Jordan, supra,* 745 F.Supp.2d at page 1100, found the plaintiffs adequately pleaded that Option ARM loans with conditional disclosures with regard to negative amortization were "unfair" under the UCL: "Plaintiffs have sufficiently alleged that they did not discover the certainty of negative amortization until they were 'locked in' with a harsh prepayment penalty under the terms of the agreement. They allege that the loan documents do not clearly specify the certainty of negative amortization. . . . Additionally, the payment schedule does not clearly indicate it is based upon the teaser rate rather than the APR listed on the top of the page. Thus, plaintiffs have sufficiently alleged that an ordinary consumer relying on the plain language of the loan agreement might not have been able to avoid the injury of negative amortization because they did not understand it was certain to occur."

We agree. As noted above in our discussion of damages, it may be difficult for plaintiffs to prove they could not have avoided *any* of the harm of negative amortization--they could have simply paid more each month once they discovered their required payment was not sufficient to pay off the interest accruing on the loan. But plaintiffs may show they were unable to avoid some substantial negative amortization. And we see no countervailing value in defendant's practice of providing general, byzantine descriptions of Option ARM's, with no clear disclosures explaining that, with regard to plaintiffs' particular loans, negative amortization would certainly occur if payments were made according to the payment schedule. To the contrary, a compelling argument can be made that lenders should be discouraged from competing by offering misleading teaser rates and low scheduled initial payments (rather than competing with regard to low effective interest rates, low fees, and economically sustainable payment schedules). Finally, to the extent an "unfair" claim must be "tethered" to specific statutory or

12. Plaintiffs' claim under the unlawful prong is, in a sense, duplicative of plaintiffs' common law fraud cause of action (unlike the "fraudulent" prong claim, which is easier to prove in the § 17200 context). But, of course, there are separate remedies for fraud and section 17200 claims. We see no reason to force plaintiffs to select between the two causes of action at this stage of the proceedings.

regulatory provisions, TILA and Regulation Z provide an adequate tether even though plaintiffs are not directly relying on federal law to make their claims. * * *

DISPOSITION

The judgment is reversed. The trial court is directed to overrule defendant's demurrer to the second amended complaint. Plaintiffs' request for judicial notice is granted. Plaintiffs shall recover costs incurred on appeal.

Rylaarsdam, Acting P. J., and O'Leary, J., concurred.

RYLAARSDAM, Acting P. J., Concurring.

I concur; plaintiffs stated facts sufficient to constitute causes of action. But I want to emphasize that, to prove they were damaged, plaintiffs must show more than the fact that, as a result of the negative amortization, their loan balances increased. This does not constitute damages. For every dollar by which the loan balances increased, they were able to keep a dollar to be saved or spent as they pleased. To prove the alleged damages plaintiffs will have to present evidence that, because of the structure of the loans, they suffered actual damages beyond their loss of equity.

Can an otherwise legal act be a UDAP violation? What if a firm's regulators have not objected? The following Massachusetts case addresses these questions.

Commonwealth v. Fremont Investment & Loan

452 Mass. 733 (2008)

BOTSFORD, J.

The Commonwealth, acting through the Attorney General, commenced this consumer protection enforcement action against the defendant Fremont Investment & Loan and its parent company, Fremont General Corporation (collectively, Fremont), claiming that Fremont, in originating and servicing certain "subprime"[3] mortgage loans between 2004 and 2007 in Massachusetts, acted unfairly and deceptively in violation of G. L. c. 93A, § 2. Fremont appeals from a preliminary injunction granted by a judge in the Superior Court in favor of the Attorney General that restricts, but does not remove, Fremont's ability to foreclose on loans with features that the judge described as "presumptively unfair." All of the loans at issue are secured by mortgages on the borrowers' homes.

Based on the record before him, the judge concluded that the Attorney General had established a likelihood of success on the merits of her claim that in originating home mortgage loans with four characteristics that made it almost certain the borrower

3. "Subprime" loans are loans made to borrowers who generally would not qualify for traditional loans offered at the generally prevailing rate of interest for conventional mortgages.

would not be able to make the necessary loan payments, leading to default and then foreclosure, Fremont had committed an unfair act or practice within the meaning of G. L. c. 93A, § 2. . . . We affirm the motion judge's grant of the preliminary injunction, as modified.

1. BACKGROUND.

Fremont is an industrial bank chartered by the State of California. Between January 2004, and March 2007, Fremont originated 14,578 loans to Massachusetts residents secured by mortgages on owner-occupied homes. Of the loans originated during that time period, roughly 3,000 remain active and roughly 2,500 continue to be owned or serviced* by Fremont.[6] An estimated fifty to sixty per cent of Fremont's loans in Massachusetts were subprime.[7] Because subprime borrowers present a greater risk to the lender, the interest rate charged for a subprime loan is typically higher than the rate charged for conventional or prime mortgages.[8] After funding the loan, Fremont generally sold it on the secondary market, which largely insulated Fremont from losses arising from borrower default.[9]

In originating loans, Fremont did not interact directly with the borrowers; rather, mortgage brokers acting as independent contractors would help a borrower select a mortgage product, and communicate with a Fremont account executive to request a selected product and provide the borrower's loan application and credit report. If approved by Fremont's underwriting department, the loan would proceed to closing and the broker would receive a broker's fee.

Fremont's subprime loan products offered a number of different features to cater to borrowers with low income. A large majority of Fremont's subprime loans were adjustable rate mortgage (ARM) loans, which bore a fixed interest rate for the first two or three years, and then adjusted every six months to a considerably higher variable rate for the remaining period of what was generally a thirty year loan. Thus, borrowers'

---

* Servicing refers to the daily management of loans—sending out billing statements, collecting payments, responding to borrower queries, and handling defaults.

6. As of July 2007, Fremont owned and serviced approximately 290 loans in Massachusetts, and serviced but no longer owned approximately 2,200 other Massachusetts loans, all covered by the preliminary injunction.

7. The judge made this estimate based on the fact that sixty-four per cent of all Fremont's loans were adjustable rate mortgage loans (ARM loans), and 38.4 per cent were "stated income" loans, in which the borrower provided no documentation of his or her income. The judge inferred, based on the limited record available at the preliminary injunction stage, that all of the stated income loans were subprime ARM loans, and a majority of the remaining ARM loans were also subprime.

8. It is not clear that the higher interest rates on Fremont's loans were always appropriate. Federal agencies have warned that the subprime lending market creates incentives to inflate interest rates unnecessarily. Board of Governors of the Federal Reserve System, Federal Deposit Insurance Corporation, Office of the Comptroller of the Currency, Office of Thrift Supervision, Interagency Guidance on Subprime Lending at 5 (Mar. 1, 1999). In 51.4 per cent of Fremont's loans generally, and seventy-three per cent of a sample of delinquent Fremont loans analyzed by the Attorney General, Fremont paid a "yield spread premium" to the broker as compensation for placing the borrower into a higher interest rate bracket than the one for which he or she would otherwise qualify.

9. Affidavits of former Fremont employees that are included in the preliminary injunction record support the view that Fremont's mortgage loan products and its underwriting policies were influenced by the interest of investors in purchasing the loans.

monthly mortgage payments would start out lower and then increase substantially after the introductory two-year or three-year period. To determine loan qualification, Fremont generally required that borrowers have a debt-to-income ratio of less than or equal to fifty per cent—that is, that the borrowers' monthly debt obligations, including the applied-for mortgage, not exceed one-half their income. However, in calculating the debt-to-income ratio, Fremont considered only the monthly payment required for the introductory rate period of the mortgage loan, not the payment that would ultimately be required at the substantially higher "fully indexed" interest rate.[11] As an additional feature to attract subprime borrowers, who typically had little or no savings, Fremont offered loans with no down payment. Instead of a down payment, Fremont would finance the full value of the property, resulting in a "loan-to-value ratio" approaching one hundred per cent. Most such financing was accomplished through the provision of a first mortgage providing eighty per cent financing and an additional "piggy-back loan" providing twenty per cent.[12]

As of the time the Attorney General initiated this case in 2007, a significant number of Fremont's loans were in default.[13] An analysis by the Attorney General of ninety-eight of those loans indicated that all were ARM loans with a substantial increase in payments required after the first two (or in a few cases, three) years, and that ninety per cent of the ninety-eight had a one hundred per cent loan-to-value ratio.

. . .

The judge granted a preliminary injunction in a memorandum of decision dated February 25, 2008. In his decision, the judge found no evidence in the preliminary injunction record that Fremont encouraged or condoned misrepresentation of borrowers' incomes on stated income loans, or that Fremont deceived borrowers by concealing or misrepresenting the terms of its loans. However, the judge determined that the Attorney General was likely to prevail on the claim that Fremont's loans featuring a combination of the following four characteristics qualified as "unfair" under G. L. c. 93A, § 2: (1) the loans were ARM loans with an introductory rate period of three years or less; (2) they featured an introductory rate for the initial period that was at least three per cent below the fully indexed rate; (3) they were made to borrowers for whom the debt-to-income ratio would have exceeded fifty per cent had Fremont measured the borrower's debt by the monthly payments that would be due at the fully indexed rate rather than under the introductory rate; and (4) the loan-to-value ratio was one hundred per cent, or the loan featured a substantial prepayment penalty (defined by the judge as

---

11. The "fully indexed" rate refers to the interest rate that represents the LIBOR rate at the time of the loan's inception plus the rate add specified in the loan documents. The judge noted that calculation of the debt-to-income ratio based on the fully indexed rate generally yields a ratio that exceeds fifty per cent.

12. Two other features bear mention, although they are not directly relevant to the preliminary injunction. . . . 38.4 per cent of all Fremont's loans were stated income loans without income documentation required. In addition, 12.2 per cent of Fremont's loans offered the borrower lower monthly payments based on a forty-year amortization schedule, with a balloon payment required at the end of thirty years; the usual amortization schedule was based on a thirty-year period.

13. As of January 15, 2008, Fremont had allegedly indicated to the Attorney General that it intended to foreclose on approximately twenty per cent of its loans. We take notice that the industry-wide delinquency rate has increased in the intervening months.

greater than the "conventional prepayment penalty" defined in G. L. c. 183C, § 2) or a prepayment penalty that extended beyond the introductory rate period.

The judge reasoned that Fremont as a lender should have recognized that loans with the first three characteristics just described were "doomed to foreclosure" unless the borrower could refinance the loan at or near the end of the introductory rate period, and obtain in the process a new and low introductory rate.[14] The fourth factor, however, would make it essentially impossible for subprime borrowers to refinance unless housing prices increased, because if housing prices remained steady or declined, a borrower with a mortgage loan having a loan-to-value ratio of one hundred per cent or a substantial prepayment penalty was not likely to have the necessary equity or financial capacity to obtain a new loan. The judge stated that, "[g]iven the fluctuations in the housing market and the inherent uncertainties as to how that market will fluctuate over time . . . it is unfair for a lender to issue a home mortgage loan secured by the borrower's principal dwelling that the lender reasonably expects will fall into default once the introductory period ends unless the fair market value of the home has increased at the close of the introductory period. To issue a home mortgage loan whose success relies on the hope that the fair market value of the home will increase during the introductory period is as unfair as issuing a home mortgage loan whose success depends on the hope that the borrower's income will increase during that same period."

The judge concluded that the balance of harms favored granting the preliminary injunction, and that the public interest would be served by doing so. The injunction he granted requires Fremont to do the following: (1) to give advance notice to the Attorney General of its intent to foreclose on any of its home mortgage loans; and (2) as to loans that possess each of the four characteristics of unfair loans just described and that are secured by the borrower's principal dwelling (referred to in the injunction as "presumptively unfair" loans), to work with the Attorney General to "resolve" their differences regarding foreclosure—presumably through a restructure or workout of the loan. If the loan cannot be worked out, Fremont is required to obtain approval for foreclosure from the court. The judge made clear that the injunction in no way relieved borrowers of their obligation ultimately to prove that a particular loan was unfair and foreclosure should not be permitted, or their obligation to repay the loans they had received.

. . .

3. DISCUSSION.

Fremont argues that the judge committed [a] "fundamental" error[] of law in concluding that the Attorney General was likely to prevail on the merits of her c. 93A claim: . . . the judge failed to recognize that under G. L. c. 93A, § 3, Fremont's loans are exempt from c. 93A because all of Fremont's challenged loan terms were permitted under the Federal and Massachusetts laws and regulatory standards governing mortgage lenders.

14. The judge's prognosis of doom followed from the fact that the interest payments required when the introductory rate period ended and the fully indexed rate came into play would be significantly greater than the payments called for under the introductory rate (so-called "payment shock"). As a result, the borrower's debt-to-income ratio would necessarily increase, probably and foreseeably beyond the borrower's breaking point.

Fremont also contends that the judge erred in determining that the public interest would be served by the preliminary injunction order. We address these arguments separately below. Before doing so, we consider a basic claim that lies underneath all of Fremont's legal challenges to the injunction.

a. Retroactive application of unfairness standards.

Fremont's basic contention is that, while the terms of its subprime loans may arguably seem "unfair" within the meaning of G. L. c. 93A, § 2, if judged by current standards applicable to the mortgage lending industry, they did not violate any established concept of unfairness at the time they were originated; the judge, in Fremont's view, applied new rules or standards for defining what is "unfair" in a retroactive or ex post facto fashion—a result that is not in accord with the proper interpretation of c. 93A, § 2, and also represents "bad policy," because (among other reasons) lenders cannot know what rules govern their conduct, which will reduce their willingness to extend credit, hurting Massachusetts consumers. We do not agree that the judge applied a new standard retroactively.

General Laws c. 93A, § 2 (*a*), makes unlawful any "unfair or deceptive acts or practices in the conduct of any trade or commerce." Chapter 93A creates new substantive rights, and in particular cases, "mak[es] conduct unlawful which was not unlawful under the common law or any prior statute." *Kattar v. Demoulas*, 433 Mass. 1, 12 (2000). The statute does not define unfairness, recognizing that "[t]here is no limit to human inventiveness in this field." *Kattar v. Demoulas, supra* at 13. What is significant is the particular circumstances and context in which the term is applied. See *Kerlinsky v. Fidelity & Deposit Co.*, 690 F. Supp. 1112, 1119 (D. Mass. 1987), aff'd, 843 F.2d 1383 (1st Cir. 1988). It is well established that a practice may be deemed unfair if it is "within at least the penumbra of some common-law, statutory, or other established concept of unfairness." *PMP Assocs., Inc. v. Globe Newspaper Co.*, 366 Mass. 593, 596 (1975).

Fremont highlights the judge's statement that at the time Fremont made the loans in question between 2004 and March of 2007, loans with the four characteristics the judge identified as unfair were not considered by the industry or more generally to be unfair; Fremont argues this acknowledgment by the judge is proof that the judge was creating a new definition or standard of unfairness. The argument lacks merit. First, the judge's statement that Fremont's combination of loan features were not recognized to be unfair does not mean the converse: that the loans were recognized to be fair. More to the point, at the core of the judge's decision is a determination that when Fremont chose to combine in a subprime loan the four characteristics the judge identified, *Fremont* knew or should have known that they would operate in concert essentially to guarantee that the borrower would be unable to pay and default would follow unless residential real estate values continued to rise indefinitely[16]—an assumption that, in the judge's view, logic and experience had already shown as of January, 2004, to be unreasonable. The

16. It would be necessary for housing values to continue to rise so that the borrower could refinance his or her loan at the end of the introductory rate period, before the (likely) unaffordable indexed rate came into play.

judge concluded that the Attorney General was likely to prove that Fremont's actions, in originating loans with terms that in combination would lead predictably to the consequence of the borrowers' default and foreclosure, were within established concepts of unfairness at the time the loans were made, and thus in violation of G. L. c. 93A, § 2. The record supports this conclusion.

Fremont correctly points out that as a bank in the business of mortgage lending, it is subject to State and Federal regulation by a variety of agencies.[17] Well before 2004, State and Federal regulatory guidance explicitly warned lending institutions making subprime loans that, even if they were in compliance with banking-specific laws and regulations and were "underwrit[ing] loans on a safe and sound basis, [their] policies could still be considered unfair and deceptive practices" under G. L. c. 93A. Consumer Affairs and Business Regulation Massachusetts Division of Banks, Subprime Lending (Dec. 10, 1997). More particularly, the principle had been clearly stated before 2004 that loans made to borrowers on terms that showed they would be unable to pay and therefore were likely to lead to default, were unsafe and unsound, and probably unfair. Thus, an interagency Federal guidance published January 31, 2001, jointly by the Office of the Comptroller of the Currency (OCC), the Board of Governors of the Federal Reserve System, the FDIC, and the Office of Thrift Supervision, stated: "Loans to borrowers who do not demonstrate the capacity to repay the loan, *as structured*, from sources other than the collateral pledged are generally considered unsafe and unsound" (emphasis supplied).[19] Expanded Guidance for Subprime Lending Programs at 11 (Jan. 31, 2001). On February 21, 2003, one year before the first of Fremont's loans at issue, the OCC warned that certain loans could be unfair to consumers:

> When a loan has been made based on the foreclosure value of the collateral, rather than on a determination that the borrower has the capacity to make the scheduled payments under the terms of the loan, based on the borrower's current and expected income, current obligations, employment status, and other relevant financial resources, the lender is effectively counting on its ability to seize the borrower's equity in the collateral to satisfy the obligation and to recover the typically high fees associated with such credit. Not surprisingly, such credits experience foreclosure rates higher than the norm.
>
> [S]uch disregard of basic principles of loan underwriting lies at the heart of predatory lending . . . .

OCC Advisory Letter, Guidelines for National Banks to Guard Against Predatory and Abusive Lending Practices, AL 2003-2 at 2 (Feb. 21, 2003).

---

17. State agencies regulating mortgage lending by banks such as Fremont and other lenders include the Massachusetts Division of Banks, and Federal agencies include the Office of the Comptroller of the Currency (OCC), the Board of Governors of the Federal Reserve System, the Federal Deposit Insurance Corporation (FDIC), and the Office of Thrift Supervision.

19. "Unsafe and unsound" refers to practices that carry too high a risk of financial harm to the lending institution, rather than to the consumer. Not all conduct that is institutionally unsafe and unsound is harmful to borrowers. However, when the lending institution's practices are deemed unsafe and unsound because they create too high a risk of default and foreclosure, the borrower, as the counterparty to the loan, obviously faces the same risk. Accordingly, such lending practices may indicate unfairness under G. L. c. 93A . . .

The record here suggests that Fremont made no effort to determine whether borrowers could "make the scheduled payments under the terms of the loan." Rather, as the judge determined, loans were made in the understanding that they would have to be refinanced before the end of the introductory period. Fremont suggested in oral argument that the loans were underwritten in the expectation, reasonable at the time, that housing prices would improve during the introductory loan term, and thus could be refinanced before the higher payments began. However, it was unreasonable, and unfair to the borrower, for Fremont to structure its loans on such unsupportable optimism. As a bank and mortgage lender, Fremont had been warned repeatedly before 2004 (in the context of guidance on loan safety and soundness) that it needed to consider the performance of its loans in declining markets. *See, e.g.,* Consumer Affairs and Business Regulation Massachusetts Division of Banks, Subprime Lending (Dec. 10, 1997) ("[M]ost subprime loans have been originated during robust economic conditions and have not been tested by a downturn in the economy. Management must ensure that the institution has adequate financial and operational strength to address these concerns effectively"). Fremont cannot now claim that it was taken by surprise by the effects of an economic decline, or that it should not be held responsible.

. . .

c. General Laws c. 93A, § 3.

Fremont argues that the Commonwealth's claim is barred by G. L. c. 93A, § 3, because Fremont's actions were permitted by the law as it existed at the time it originated the loans. We disagree.

General Laws c. 93A, § 3, provides:

> Nothing in this chapter shall apply to transactions or actions otherwise permitted under laws as administered by any regulatory board or officer acting under statutory authority of the commonwealth or of the United States.
>
> For the purpose of this section, the burden of proving exemptions from the provisions of this chapter shall be upon the person claiming the exemptions.

This provision must be read together with G. L. c. 93A, § 2. That section "'created new substantive rights,'" and thus "[t]he fact that particular conduct is permitted by statute or by common law principles should be considered, but it is not conclusive on the question of unfairness." *Schubach v. Household Fin. Corp.*, 375 Mass. 133, 137, 376 N.E.2d 140 (1978). See *Kattar v. Demoulas*, 433 Mass. 1, 13, 739 N.E.2d 246 (2000) ("Legality of underlying conduct is not necessarily a defense to a claim under c. 93A"). A defendant's burden in claiming the exemption is "a difficult one to meet. To sustain it, a defendant must show more than the mere existence of a related or even overlapping regulatory scheme that covers the transaction. Rather, a defendant must show that such scheme affirmatively *permits* the practice which is alleged to be unfair or deceptive" (emphasis in original). *Fleming v. National Union Fire Ins. Co.*, 445 Mass. 381, 390, 837 N.E.2d 1113 (2005).

The judge concluded, as have we, that the Attorney General is likely to succeed on her claim that Fremont's practice of originating loans bearing the particular combination of four features identified in the preliminary injunction was unfair. To carry its burden under G. L. c. 93A, § 3, of demonstrating that a regulatory scheme "affirmatively *permits* the practice which is alleged to be unfair," Fremont must show that some regulatory scheme affirmatively permitted the practice of combining all of those features. Fremont has not done so. Rather, it cites authority demonstrating, it asserts, that each of the four features was permitted by statute and regulatory authorities. Assuming, without deciding, that Fremont is correct that every feature was affirmatively permitted separately, it was Fremont's choice to combine them into a package that it should have known was "doomed to foreclosure"; the relevant question is whether some State or Federal authority permitted that combination. No authority did.

d. Public interest.

Because the Attorney General, in the name of the Commonwealth, brings this case to carry out her statutory mandate to enforce the Consumer Protection Act, it is necessary to consider whether the preliminary injunction order promotes the public interest. Fremont argues that it does not, primarily because in Fremont's view, the order imposes new standards on lending practices that were considered permissible and acceptable when the loans were made. The result, Fremont claims, will be an unwillingness on the part of lenders to extend credit to Massachusetts consumers because they will be unwilling to risk doing business in an environment where standards are uncertain and the rules may change after the fact.

Our previous discussion, and rejection, of Fremont's claim that the judge retroactively applied new unfairness standards disposes of Fremont's public interest argument; we do not accept the premise that, in concluding that Fremont is likely to be found to have violated established concepts of unfairness, the judge's order has created an environment of uncertainty that lenders will shun. The injunction order crafted by the judge strikes a balance between the interests of borrowers who face foreclosure and loss of their homes under home loan mortgage terms that are at least presumptively unfair, on the one hand; and the interest of the lender in recovering the value of its loans to borrowers who received the benefit of those loaned funds and continue to have a contractual obligation to repay, on the other. The order does not bar foreclosure as a remedy for the lender, nor does it relieve borrowers of their obligations ultimately to repay the loans. Rather, it requires, where the mortgage loan terms include all four features deemed presumptively unfair, that Fremont explore alternatives to foreclosure in the first instance (a step that Fremont has indicated its desire to take in any event), and then seek approval of the court. If the court does not approve the foreclosure, that decision merely leaves the preliminary injunction in place until the Commonwealth has an opportunity to try to prove that the particular loan at issue actually violated c. 93A—a burden that is never shifted to Fremont. We conclude the order serves the public interest.

4. CONCLUSION.

A judgment is to be entered affirming the grant of the preliminary injunction and remanding the case to the Superior Court for further proceedings.

Questions on *Fremont Investment and Loan*

Fremont was about a preliminary injunction against a lender (this information was omitted from the case but such injunction would also apply to any purchaser of the covered loans from the lender). Does *Fremont* announce a general legal rule in Massachusetts or does the injunctive relief nature of the case limit its application? If there's a general rule, what is that rule? That loans made without regard to ability to repay may not be foreclosed absent court approval? Does that effectively impose an ability-to-repay requirement for mortgages under the Massachusetts UDAP statute? And does anything in *Fremont* limit that rule to mortgages? What would you do if you were, say, an auto lender in Massachusetts, after seeing this ruling?

V. ENFORCEMENT

States also engage in enforcement of their various consumer finance laws. They also have authority to enforce certain federal consumer finance laws, as discussed in Chapters 8 and 9. State enforcement is sometimes handled by the state attorney general and sometimes by the relevant state financial regulatory authority; the precise contours of litigation authority vary by state.

The identity of the party with litigation authority may matter significantly. State attorneys general are elected officials who often have their eye on higher office. This cuts two ways. On the one hand, they may be eager to curry favor with regulated industries as a way of encouraging campaign donations. On the other hand, consumer financial protection litigation can be a popular and high-profile way of establishing populist bona fides. State financial regulatory authorities are usually headed by political appointees of the state governor. The same political considerations may affect enforcement, but the head of a state financial regulatory authority is often looking at the possibility of future employment in the financial services space, which adds another dynamic to enforcement actions.

State enforcement is freed from some of the constraints faced by consumer litigants. State enforcement actions are often subject to less onerous pleading requirements. For example, states often do not need to plead reliance in consumer fraud cases, whereas a consumer litigant would. Indeed, in some situations states do not even need to plead consumer harm. States can also obtain remedies for large groups of consumers without having to go through class certification requirements. States also do not suffer the same budgetary constraints as individual consumers. But state enforcement is nevertheless often resource-constrained, requiring states to pick and choose which enforcement actions they want to bring.

What we see then is that states are engaged in a wide range of regulatory activities affecting consumer finance. The particulars of regulation vary substantially between states, however. Some products, such as payday loans, are prohibited in some states, while allowed in others. Moreover, state regulation is subject to preemption by federal law in respect to federally chartered entities and for areas in which federal regulation is so pervasive as to occupy the field. The result is that while there is substantial state regulation of consumer finance, it is best described as a crazy quilt. While it may make sense as a regulatory regime within any particular state, when seen at a national level, it is confusing and inconsistent.

Problem Set 4

1. Fadi Al-Wir wants to open up a business in Dearborn, Michigan, that will provide international remittance services, specializing in wire transfers to the Middle East. Fadi, an American citizen who has worked as a lawyer for several years, has never been convicted of a crime. He has a personal net worth of $200,000, including $40,000 in cash. What will Fadi have to do to open his business, and what will it cost him? *See* MCL §§ 487.1011, 487.1013, 487.1014, 487.1042(3); 18 U.S.C. § 1960.

2. Ka-Pow! a Michigan-licensed money transmitter, had a very bad day. Due to a sticky key on a keyboard, Ka-Pow! accidentally misrouted over $3 million in wire transfers made on behalf of customers, and all of the funds were erroneously routed to the Moldovan bank account of Boris Levitin, who is unlikely to ever return the funds. The misrouted funds include $20,000 that Abul Hasani gave to Ka-Pow! to transmit to his family in Bangladesh. Those funds are his total savings from working as a gardener for five years in America.

At the time of the mistake, Ka-Pow! had $3.3 million in payment instruments sold and money in transmission. Ka-Pow! had $2.5 million in cash, $400,000 in U.S. Treasury bonds, and $100,000 in Apple common stock. Ka-Pow! also had an investment of $1.3 million in a very successful race horse named Model-T.

Ka-Pow! owes $1 million on a five-year balloon note to remodel its ten store fronts. That note, which is secured by Ka-Pow!'s real estate, fixtures, and equipment, will be coming due in next week. Ka-Pow! also owes $2 million on a bank line of credit, secured by its deposit accounts and investments in Treasury bonds and Apple common stock. How likely is it that Abul will be able to recover the $20,000 and, if so, when? *See* MCL §§ 487.1013, 487.1031, 487.1032.

3. SyncedUp, a professional networking website, wants to create a service that will allow its members to transmit funds to each other. SyncedUp thinking is that its members will often get together for drinks or lunch and that they can settle up bills between them through payments on the website. SyncedUp operates in all 50 states and the District of Columbia. How many money transmitter licenses will it need to get? What are the implications of this?

4. First Bank of Ojai, California, took a non-possessory non-purchase money security interest in Los Angeles resident Rebecca Tushnet's diamond-and-sapphire wedding ring to secure a $10,000 loan. When Rebecca defaulted on the loan, she lost the ring in the subsequent foreclosure sale. Rebecca has come to you for legal advice. Does Rebecca have any recourse? If so, will you take the case? *See* 16 C.F.R. § 444.2(a)(4); Cal. Civ. Code §§ 17200, 17203; Cal. Code Civ. Proc. § 1021.5.

5. Deepak Gupta, a resident of San Jose, California, doesn't have great credit. He was relieved therefore when Fast Lane Automotive, Inc. sold him a used Nissan Altima on credit. Deepak really needed the car in order to get to work; his old jalopy just wasn't sufficiently reliable anymore. Deepak filled out a credit application for a loan from Fast Lane, which he was told would be processed by Fast Lane's credit department. The financing manager told Deepak that "the credit department is a little backed up, but everything should be good; we'll let you know if there are any problems. You can drive the car home today if you'd like."

The sale included a trade-in of Deepak's old car. The Fast Lane salesman told Deepak that he could either have a $2,000 higher trade-in price or a 1% lower interest rate on the loan. Deepak chose to take a reduced interest rate, which ended up being 10% annually. After agreeing on the sale and trade-in pricing and financing terms, the salesman at Fast Lane handed Deepak the keys and let him drive off with the Altima, which he proudly showed off to his family and friends.

Several days later, however, Fast Lane called Deepak to tell him that he wasn't ultimately approved for the financing on the terms offered and that he had to sign a new loan agreement at a higher interest rate (13% annually) or else he would have to return the car, but that he would not be able to unwind the trade-in. When Deepak objected, Fast Lane told him, "That's a separate deal, and besides, we might have sold your old junker by now." Fast Lane also pointed out to Deepak that the used car sale agreement he signed includes a fine print clause that the sale is "subject to approval of financing."

Deepak agreed to the new loan terms, but felt he'd been treated pretty shabbily. He's come to you to see if he might have any legal recourse. Does Deepak have a potential common law fraud claim against Fast Lane Automotive? How about a claim under the California UCL? *See Boschma v. Home Loan Center,* 198 Cal.App.4th 230 (2011); Cal. Civ. Code §§ 17200, 17203.

CHAPTER 5

THE CFPB I: HISTORY AND POLICY

Since July 21, 2011, the central node of consumer finance regulation has been the Consumer Financial Protection Bureau, created by the Dodd-Frank Wall Street Reform and Consumer Protection Act of 2010. The CFPB is not the only government agency involved in consumer finance regulation, but it is the most important because of its national regulatory scope over almost all entities involved in consumer payments, credit, savings, and debt collection. The CFPB administers a large number of pre-existing, subject-matter-specific statutes, such as the Electronic Fund Transfer Act and the Truth in Lending Act, but it also has a critical catchall authority, the ability to prohibit "unfair, deceptive, and abusive acts and practices" (UDAAP) in consumer finance. Note that the CFPB's UDAAP (two "A"s) is in distinction to the UDAP (single "A") powers of the FTC and the states, which cover only "unfair" and "deceptive" acts and practices, not "abusive" ones.

Even if an act or practice is not prohibited by a specific statute, it might still be a UDAAP violation. The combination of UDAAP authority with broad jurisdiction makes the CFPB the key agency in consumer finance regulation. As we will see in subsequent chapters, however, the CFPB shares its authority with other federal and state agencies, and the jurisdictional interaction plays an important role in consumer finance regulation.

This chapter provides a background on the history and policy behind the creation of the CFPB. The following two chapters cover, respectively, the scope of CFPB jurisdiction and the specific powers and limitations on the CFPB.

I. HISTORY AND POLICY BEHIND THE CFPB

A. Consumer Financial Regulation Pre-2010

Prior to the New Deal, the consumer finance business was run almost entirely through state-law entities: individuals, state-chartered banks, thrifts, credit unions, finance companies, insurance companies, and retailers. The federal government played almost no role in consumer protection in the financial arena. Instead, consumer protection in general, including in financial services, was part of the general police power of the states.

Pre-New Deal state regulation of consumer finance took three main forms. First, state tort and contract law provided protections against fraud, misrepresentation, and other forms of unfair dealing. Second, every state had a usury statute that limited the maximum legal rate of interest for certain types of borrowing transactions. And third, state law often restricted the types of products that state-chartered financial institutions were permitted to offer. While these restrictions often had consumer-protection benefits, they were designed first and foremost to protect the solvency of financial institutions by limiting the types of risks they could assume. Enforcement of consumer finance regulation was primarily a private affair, although usury was sometimes a criminal matter.

The institutional and regulatory framework for consumer finance began to change during the New Deal and World War II, with the federal government assuming an increasingly important role. Federal charters became available for new types of financial institutions and the federal government got into the business of insuring or guaranteeing deposits and mortgage loans and then later the business of making or guaranteeing student loans. With chartering and insurance came federal regulation, sometimes preempting state regulation, sometimes co-existing with it. At first, this federal regulation was, like state financial institution regulation, aimed primarily at ensuring the solvency of federally chartered or insured institutions.

For example, restrictions on the rate of interest federally insured banks could pay on deposits was aimed at preventing bank failures. While bank failures harmed consumers, the main policy concern was not the plight of individual depositors so much as the systemic effect of bank failures because of contraction of the monetary supply. To be sure, deposit insurance also had an important collateral effect of consumer protection. Similarly, the federal government's intervention in housing finance was deliberately aimed at fostering the use of long-term, amortized mortgages because of their macroeconomic stability benefits. These stability benefits were the aggregate result of the individual consumer-protection benefits from these mortgages. Ultimately, though, the protection of individual consumers was not a feature of New Deal financial regulation.

World War II saw further federal involvement in the regulation of consumer credit. This was done explicitly for purposes of furthering the war effort. These regulations, which existed with minor interruptions until 1952, were aimed at reducing consumer demand so that war production would not have to compete with private consumption. While there were collateral consumer-protection benefits from reducing the availability of credit, the policy goal was otherwise.

Starting in 1938, the Federal Trade Commission began to have authority to proscribe "unfair or deceptive acts or practices" (UDAP, as distinct from UDAAP). The FTC's jurisdiction extended to retail and non-bank credit. Banks, however, were explicitly exempted from the FTC's new authority.

Historically the FTC's limited jurisdiction exception was not particularly important. Non-mortgage consumer credit was, prior to the 1980s, primarily from retailers and auto finance companies. Credit cards were not a widespread product until the 1980s, and other non-check consumer payment instruments were rarities. (Payday lending did not exist until the 1990s.) This meant that the FTC historically had a reach that covered much of the consumer credit market, with state regulators providing a further layer of rulemaking and enforcement. While banks were not subject to FTC regulation, federally chartered and federally insured financial institutions were, after 1975, subject to federal prohibitions on UDAP. In practice, however, federal bank regulators had a great deal of moral suasion power to affect federally chartered or insured banks' behavior, and federal bank regulators did have the power to take away federally chartered banks' charters. Moreover, starting in 1966, federal bank regulators had the power to order banks to cease and desist from "unsafe and unsound practices." In any event, prior to the 1980s, banks' role in consumer credit was primarily in the mortgage market, but the terms of mortgage loans were substantially controlled by public or quasi-public secondary market institutions—the Federal Housing Administration, Ginnie Mae, Fannie Mae, and Freddie Mac.

The federal government began to play an increasingly large role in the regulation of key areas of consumer finance starting with the landmark Consumer Credit Protection Act of 1968. Since then, the federal government has played a major or exclusive regulatory role for consumer payments, consumer lending, bank deposits, debt collection and credit reporting, consumer goods warranties, and various associated areas, such as certain types of insurance or interstate sales.

While the FTC had authority over non-bank entities in consumer finance, depository lenders were subject to a spider web of different regulators, with additional regulators dealing with the housing market and certain other areas of consumer finance. Federal jurisdiction expanded on a largely ad hoc basis, rather than as part of a conscious policy to federalize consumer financial protection. The result was that prior to the creation of the CFPB, federal responsibility for consumer financial protection was divided among a large number of regulatory agencies. Some of these agencies had the ability to promulgate regulations, some also exercised supervisory authority over financial institutions, and some only enforced existing regulations. Sometimes authority was over a class of institutions, and sometimes it was over a particular type of product.

Thus, as of 2010, responsibility for consumer protection was split among the:

- Office of the Comptroller of the Currency (national banks, federally chartered branches, agencies of foreign banks);
- Office of Thrift Supervision (federal thrifts and thrift holding companies);
- National Credit Union Administration (federal credit unions and federally insured state credit unions);
- Federal Reserve Board (bank holding companies, state-chartered member banks, non-bank subsidiaries of bank holding companies, branches and agencies of foreign banking organizations operating in the United States and their parent banks, and some aspects of checks and electronic payment systems);
- Federal Deposit Insurance Corporation (state-charted insured banks and insured branches of foreign banks);

- Federal Housing Finance Agency (the mortgage industry in general through Federal Home Loan Banks, Fannie Mae and Freddie Mac);
- The Department of Housing and Urban Development (real estate settlement procedures and FHA-insured mortgage loans);
- Veterans Administration (now the Department of Veterans Affairs) (VA-guaranteed mortgage loans);
- Internal Revenue Service (tax preparers);
- Federal Trade Commission (non-banks, including debt collectors);
- Department of Defense (payday lending to active duty military and their family members); and
- Department of Justice (residual anti-fraud authority).

This poorly coordinated federal regulatory mélange co-existed uneasily with state regulation, particularly of non-bank financial institutions, and enforcement by state attorneys general and state bank regulators, as well as private litigation. States, however, were increasingly excluded from consumer financial services regulation because of federal preemption of state regulation of national banks and federal thrifts, with the preempted state protections rarely replaced with equivalent federal protections.

By the 2000s, problems with the consumer financial protection regime were beginning to show. Consumer complaints about credit card and payday lenders were rampant; consumer bankruptcy filings, a barometer of household financial health, were steadily rising; and an alarming shift had occurred in mortgage finance toward riskier, exotic products. While federal regulators were well aware of these changes,[1] they did little to prevent them, even when directed to do so by Congress. To the contrary, some federal bank regulators engaged in an aggressive campaign to preempt state laws that would have restricted more aggressive forms of lending.[2] Thus, at a Congressional hearing in 2008, Representative Barney Frank, Chairman of the House Financial Services Committee, stated,

> When [Federal Reserve] Chairman Bernanke testified [before this Committee at a recent hearing] . . . he said something I hadn't heard in my 28 years in this body: a Chairman of the Federal Reserve Board uttering the words "consumer protection." It had not happened since 1981.[3]

---

1. *See, e.g.*, Remarks by Julie L. Williams, Acting Comptroller of the Currency, Before the BAI National Loan Review Conference, New Orleans, LA, Mar. 21.

2. *See, e.g.*, Arthur E. Wilmarth, Jr., *The OCC's Preemption Rules Exceed the Agency's Authority and Present a Serious Threat to the Dual Banking System and Consumer Protection*, 23 Ann. Rev. Banking & Fin. L. 225 (2004); Kathleen Engel & Patricia McCoy, *The Subprime Virus: Reckless Credit, Regulatory Failure, and Next Steps* 157-187 (2011) (detailing deregulation via preemption and lack of enforcement in housing market).

3. House Financial Services Committee, Subcommittee on Financial Institutions and Consumer Credit Hearing, The Credit Cardholders' Bill of Rights: Providing New Protections for Consumers, Mar. 13, 2008, at 6.

B. Problems with the Pre-2010 Regulatory Architecture

The pre-CFPB consumer financial protection regime had four major structural flaws:

1. consumer protection was an "orphan" mission, that is it had no regulatory "home" in any single agency;
2. consumer protection was often subordinated to regulatory concerns about bank profitability;
3. there was a lack of regulatory expertise in consumer financial issues; and
4. the diffusion of regulatory responsibility created regulatory arbitrage opportunities that fueled a race to the bottom.

1. Consumer Protection as an Orphan Mission

Pre-CFPB, the regulatory consumer financial protection role was fractured among multiple agencies on both the federal and state levels. There were several reasons for this. First, consumer financial products markets were historically quite different. Until the 1990s a great deal of credit was provided by retailers, and they were all under the authority of the FTC. Banks and credit unions were not under FTC authority, but they tended to retain the loans they originated and therefore had stronger reputational incentives to treat their customers well. Moreover, consumer protection was not the driving factor behind many regulatory regimes, which were assigned to different agencies based on various logics, with consumer-protection functions assigned as a tag-along afterthought.

The division of consumer financial protection responsibility created a number of regulatory problems. First, it made consumer protection an orphan mission. Because no agency had an exclusive role of consumer protection in financial services, there was a dangerous tendency for consumer protection to fall between the cracks. Only one agency, the Federal Trade Commission, had consumer protection as its primary role. The FTC, however, had very limited jurisdiction in financial services—it did not have authority over federally chartered or insured banks, thrifts, or credit unions. This left only bit players in financial services within the FTC's regulatory ken. Because consumer protection was everyone's responsibility, it became no one's responsibility, and accountability and performance suffered therewith.

2. Consumer Protection Subordinated to Regulatory Concerns About Bank Profitability

The leading entities in the consumer finance system are banks, frequently with federal charters. Federal banking regulators—the Federal Reserve Board, FDIC, NCUA, OCC, and OTS—all had consumer financial protection responsibilities for the particular types of entities they regulated. Consumer financial protection, however, was not their only or even primary mission. Instead, their primary mission was bank safety and soundness. There was a conflict between the safety-and-soundness mission and the consumer-protection mission. Safety and soundness ultimately means profitability because only profitable financial institutions can be safe and sound. Unfair, deceptive, and abusive practices, however, can be highly profitable; that is the only reason to engage in them. If they are only mildly profitable, the regulatory and reputational risk would make the practice not worthwhile. Placing the two missions together in a single agency ensured that one would trump the other. Consumer protection was routinely subordinated to bank profitability concerns, except when the most egregious practices were at stake.

The subordination of consumer protection to bank profitability may also have been the result of the "**capture**" of financial regulators by financial services industry interests. "Capture" refers to the situation in which a regulator acts in the interests of the industry it regulates, rather than in the public interest. Revolving door employment contributes to capture problems in bank regulation as in other areas of regulation. Federal bank regulators would often leave government employment to find employment at banks, as bank lobbyists, as bank consultants, or as bank lawyers. Regulators might then attempt to curry favor with future employers by adopting regulatory stances favorable to those future employers, such as lax consumer protection.

3. Regulators with Limited Expertise

Another effect of the fracturing of the consumer financial protection mission was that it limited agency expertise. No agency had the incentive to develop a deep expertise in the area in terms of data collection and analysis, consumer product testing, or litigation. Empirical analysis is crucial to setting consumer finance policy; theoretical economics cannot provide a guide in complex market situations. Empirical analysis, however, requires data, and as a general matter federal regulators collected surprisingly little information on consumer financial products. There was no federal statistic on the total volume of credit card debt, on checking account overdrafts, on payday loans, on refund anticipation loans, or on auto title loans, much less their terms and performance. For mortgages, there were no nationwide governmental measures of terms, performance, or foreclosures. At best, particular agencies collect data on some aspect of the businesses they regulated, but there was no coordination of the data to provide an economy-wide picture.

Not only did the pre-CFPB agencies lack data, but they also lacked dedicated teams of economists, statisticians, psychologists, and attorneys to analyze the data to understand how product design and legal regulation shape consumer finances and what optimal policies might be. For example, in 2009, only 12 of the Federal Reserve Board's 128 economists on its research and statistics staff listed consumer finance as a focus, even though consumer spending accounts for approximately 70% of GDP and a sizable share of bank lending.[4] Other federal financial regulators had far fewer staffers working full-time on consumer financial issues, and none of the bank regulators had sizable enforcement staffs. Again, in contrast, the FTC, which

---

4. Adam J. Levitin, *The Consumer Financial Protection Agency* 5 (Pew Financial Reform Project, Briefing Paper #3, 2009).

does have a wealth of consumer-protection litigation experience, lacks jurisdiction over banks.

4. Opportunities for Regulatory Arbitrage

The splintered regulatory authority environment created opportunities for financial institutions to engage in regulatory arbitrage, and this set off a race to the bottom among regulators competing for regulatory turf. Federal banking authorities competed with state regulators and with each other for the business of chartering banks. Banks can and do switch their charters from state to federal and vice versa, and prior to the Dodd-Frank Act also switched their type of federal charter, such as from a banking to a thrift charter.

Chartering is a crucial business for banking regulatory agencies for two reasons: these agencies' primary authority is largely coextensive with the extent of their chartering, and some federal and state banking regulators receive the majority of their budgets from their chartering fees, unlike other potential consumer-protection regulators. Because no single regulator had complete primary authority over the entire banking system, any single regulator moving by itself for more vigorous consumer-protection regulations or enforcement would have put the entities it regulated at a disadvantage relative to the entities regulated by other banking regulators. These relative costs would cause a flight of charters from the first-mover regulator, which would affect the regulator's budget. Similarly, a regulator that adopted a more lax consumer-protection stance would find itself receiving more chartering business and a greater budget. The result of chartering competition was, in the words of Arthur Burns, a former Chairman of the Federal Reserve Board, nothing less than "competition in laxity."[5]

An example of chartering competition creating a race to the bottom is the fate of state usury laws, which capped the maximum rate of interest on loans and thereby placed a limit on how much risk lenders—and borrowers—could take on loans. State usury laws were largely eviscerated following the Supreme Court's 1978 decision in *Marquette National Bank of Minneapolis v. First of Omaha Service Corp.*[6] *Marquette* held that the usury ceiling that applied to a federally chartered bank's lending operations was that of the state in which the bank is located, not the state of the borrower. This ruling meant that national banks could base themselves in states with high or nonexistent usury ceilings, like Delaware and South Dakota, and export the rate ceilings to other states.

Marquette set off a two-part regulatory race to the bottom, as banks began to switch to federal charters and look for states with high or no usury ceilings. Some states responded by eliminating or raising usury ceilings to keep national bank operations in their states. Other states adopted parity laws that would allow their state-chartered banks the same leeway as national banks.[7] Federal bank regulators

---

5. Howell E. Jackson & Edward L. Symons, Jr., *Regulation of Financial Institutions* 52 (1999) (quoting Chairman Burns).

6. 439 U.S. 299 (1978).

7. Adam J. Levitin, *Hydraulic Regulation: Regulating Credit Markets Upstream*, 26 Yale J. Reg. 143, 158 (2009).

subsequently pushed to expand the definition of interest to cover various bank fees and the thinly regulated subsidiaries of national banks.[8] The result was that usury laws and any ability of states to regulate financial services fees were effectively eviscerated, not as the result of a considered policy decision, but as a result of the Supreme Court's interpretation of passing language in the 1863 National Bank Act.

The combination of preemption and federal chartering significantly undermined the traditional state consumer-protection regime built on private law enforcement, usury statutes, and activities restrictions. Private law enforcement via tort and contract suits were always impractical methods of consumer protection because of the economics of litigation small-dollar, often "negative value" claims. Class actions address some of the litigation economics problem, but procedural limitations on class actions coupled with the expanded use of binding mandatory arbitration limit their effectiveness. Federal preemption often kept the states from undertaking public enforcement actions, and federal enforcement was rare prior to the CFPB. *Marquette* and subsequent case law largely eliminated the reach of state usury statutes. And the institutional shift from state entities to federally chartered entities meant that state activity restrictions no longer applied to many financial institutions, while federal regulation was more permissive, in part because of chartering competition.

An example of the effect of these factors can be found in the pre-2010 consumer-protection activities (or lack thereof) of the Office of Comptroller of the Currency (OCC), the primary regulator of national banks, which include the country's largest financial institutions. Thus, in 2005, only 3 of the OCC's 2,650 employees had investigating and resolving consumer complaints as their primary job.[9] This figure contrasts with the resident teams of perhaps 20 to 40 bank examiners at each of the largest national banks, engaged primarily, if not exclusively, in safety-and-soundness regulation.

Similarly, while in 2003 alone, state bank agencies brought 4,035 consumer enforcement actions, from 2000 to 2007, the OCC brought just 11 consumer enforcement actions. The biggest two actions involved cases that were initiated and investigated by state attorneys general and that the OCC initially tried to prevent from going forward.[10]

---

8. *See Smiley v. Citibank (South Dakota), N.A.*, 517 U.S. 735, 744-745 (1996) (deferring to the OCC's regulatory determination that the term "interest" in the National Bank Act encompasses credit card late-payment fees); *Watters v. Wachovia Bank, N.A.*, 550 U.S. 1, 22 (2007) (upholding OCC regulatory determination that federal preemption applies equally to state regulations of subsidiaries of national banks as it does to state regulations of the parent banks).

9. Stephanie Mencimer, *No Account*, The New Republic, Aug. 27, 2007, at 14.

10. *Id.; see also Credit Card Practices: Current Consumer and Regulatory Issues: Hearing Before the H. Subcomm. on Fin. Institutions and Consumer Credit of the H. Comm. on Fin. Servs.*, 110th Cong. 7 (2007) (statement of Arthur E. Wilmarth, Jr., Professor of Law, George Washington University Law School); Arthur E. Wilmarth Jr., *The OCC's Preemption Rules Exceed the Agency's Authority and Present a Serious Threat to the Dual Banking System and Consumer Protection*, 23 Ann. Rev. Banking & Fin. L. 225 (2004); Robert Berner & Brian Grow, *They Warned Us About the Mortgage Crisis*, BusinessWeek, Oct. 9, 2008, at 36 (stating that thirteen of 495 OCC enforcement actions were consumer-related and only one involved subprime mortgage lending).

Indeed, from 2000 to April 2009, the OCC levied a mere 73 fines, only 6 of which were for consumer-protection violations.[11] The others were for safety and soundness violations (46, almost all for failure to require flood insurance for mortgage loans against collateral in flood plains), money laundering violations (10), or violations that were unspecified in the stipulation and consent order (11). Of the consumer-protection violations, two related to payday lending, two related to discriminatory lending (including Home Mortgage Disclosure Act violations for failure to properly collect data on mortgage lending), one related to telemarketing, and one related to data security. The OCC's fines were generally miniscule, often no more than several hundred or several thousand dollars, only a small fraction compared to a bank's balance sheet. Only eight penalties topped a million dollars, and of those, only two were for consumer-protection violations; the others were for money-laundering violations. Prior to 2010, the OCC brought only one formal enforcement action on consumer-protection grounds against any of the top ten national banks (by 2008 sizes), which collectively held 76% of OCC-regulated assets.[12]

To be sure, formal enforcement actions and civil fines are not the full measure of OCC consumer-protection activities, but in light of the myriad complaints about mortgage, credit card, auto, payday, title, and refund anticipation lenders, the presence of only eleven formal consumer-protection actions and six consumer-protection-related fines (and only one against a major institution) over the past seven-plus years creates an extremely strong inference of enforcement apathy, if not outright disinclination.

The OCC has even thrown in its regulatory weight to attempt to protect national banks from consumer-protection regulation by other federal agencies. The Federal Trade Commission Act prohibits unfair and deceptive acts and practices ("UDAP") in interstate commerce[13] and gives the Federal Reserve Board the power to define those acts for national banks.[14] In July 2008, the Federal Reserve proposed an expansion of its UDAP regulations for national banks' credit card lending practices.[15] Parallel regulations were promulgated by the OTS and the NCUA for national thrifts and credit unions.[16]

The OCC's reaction to the proposed regulations, which many consumer advocates did not feel went far enough, was to write a letter to the Federal Reserve Board registering its opposition.[17] In its letter, the OCC argued (without adducing any evidence) that the proposed regulations would harm consumers because they would

11. Levitin, *supra* note 7, at 153.

12. The OCC reached a $144 million settlement in 2008 with Wachovia for deceptive marketing activities by third-party telemarketers enabled by the bank. *See* FDIC, Statistics on Depository Institutions.

13. 15 U.S.C. § 45(a).

14. 15 U.S.C. § 57a(f).

15. Regulation AA: Unfair and Deceptive Acts and Practices Regulations for the Federal Reserve System Board of Governors, 73 Fed. Reg. 28,904 (proposed May 19, 2008) (to be codified at 12 C.F.R. pt. 227).

16. Unfair and Deceptive Acts and Practices Regulations for the Department of Treasury, Office of Thrift Supervision, 73 Fed. Reg. 28,904 (proposed May 19, 2008) (to be codified at 12 C.F.R. pt. 535); Unfair and Deceptive Acts and Practices Regulations for the Federal Reserve System Board of Governors, 73 Fed. Reg. 28,904 (proposed May 19, 2008) (to be codified at 12 C.F.R. pt. 706).

17. Cheyenne Hopkins, *OCC Presses Fed to Alter Proposal on Card Reform*, Am. Banker, Aug. 21, 2008, at 1.

reduce available credit.[18] It is not clear what bearing an economic efficiency concern like the reduction in credit availability has on the essential fairness of a business practice—what a UDAP regulation aims to address. Regardless, the OCC's real concern was evident elsewhere in the letter—that the proposed UDAP regulations would reduce bank profitability, which would hurt bank safety and soundness, particularly in light of the weakened conditions of national banks because of the mortgage crisis. Left unstated is the OCC's assumption that it is acceptable for a national bank to engage in unfair and deceptive acts and practices if that is the only way for the national bank to make a profit. UDAP regulations are explicitly about consumer protection, but the OCC's letter to the Federal Reserve shows that the OCC believes that bank profitability trumps consumer protection.

The OCC's failure to engage in meaningful consumer-protection regulation and enforcement is symptomatic of larger structural problems in banking regulation. The OCC was hardly an isolated case; its now-defunct sister agency, the Office of Thrift Supervision (OTS), had an equally unimpressive track record on consumer protection. The pre-Dodd-Frank Act substantive shortcomings in consumer financial protection stemmed, in the first instance, from organizational architecture issues that made consumer protection an orphan mission and subordinated it to safety-and-soundness concerns about banks.

C. Creation of the CFPB

The flaws in the consumer financial protection system prompted then Harvard Law School Professor (and subsequently Senator) Elizabeth Warren to call for a Financial Product Safety Commission.[19] Professor Warren argued that consumers should be protected from dangerous financial products just as they are from dangerous consumer products, not only by tort law, but also by regulation. Just as it is not possible to buy a toaster with a one-in-five chance of exploding, so too it should not be possible to obtain a financial product with a one-in-five chance of causing serious harm to the consumer. In Professor Warren's view, too many consumers were ending up with mortgages or credit cards that were causing more harm than good. Professor Warren argued that the existing financial regulatory framework was incapable of meeting the challenge and called for a new regulatory agency made equal to the task. Professor Warren's original article calling for a new consumer finance regulatory agency is excerpted below.

---

18. *Id.*

19. Elizabeth Warren, *Unsafe at Any Rate*, Democracy: A Journal of Ideas, Summer 2007. Warren's article's title was a play on Ralph Nader's 1965 book *Unsafe at Any Speed* about the safety problems in the design of American automobiles, which contributed to the creation of the Consumer Product Safety Commission in 1972. *See also* Oren Bar-Gill & Elizabeth Warren, *Making Credit Safer*, 157 U. Pa. L. Rev. 1 (2008). Professor Heidi Manadanis Schooner had previously proposed expanding FTC authority to cover banks. Heidi Manadanis Schooner, *Consuming Debt: Structuring the Federal Response to Abuses in Consumer Credit*, 18 Loy. Consumer L. Rev. 43, 82 (2005).

Unsafe at Any Rate
Elizabeth Warren

5 DEMOCRACY: A JOURNAL OF IDEAS (Summer 2007)

IF IT'S GOOD ENOUGH FOR MICROWAVES, IT'S GOOD ENOUGH FOR MORTGAGES. WHY WE NEED A FINANCIAL PRODUCT SAFETY COMMISSION

It is impossible to buy a toaster that has a one-in-five chance of bursting into flames and burning down your house. But it is possible to refinance an existing home with a mortgage that has the same one-in-five chance of putting the family out on the street–and the mortgage won't even carry a disclosure of that fact to the homeowner. Similarly, it's impossible to change the price on a toaster once it has been purchased. But long after the papers have been signed, it is possible to triple the price of the credit used to finance the purchase of that appliance, even if the customer meets all the credit terms, in full and on time. Why are consumers safe when they purchase tangible consumer products with cash, but when they sign up for routine financial products like mortgages and credit cards they are left at the mercy of their creditors?

The difference between the two markets is regulation. Although considered an epithet in Washington since Ronald Reagan swept into the White House, the "R-word" supports a booming market in tangible consumer goods. Nearly every product sold in America has passed basic safety regulations well in advance of reaching store shelves. Credit products, by comparison, are regulated by a tattered patchwork of federal and state laws that have failed to adapt to changing markets. Moreover, thanks to effective regulation, innovation in the market for physical products has led to more safety and cutting-edge features. By comparison, innovation in financial products has produced incomprehensible terms and sharp practices that have left families at the mercy of those who write the contracts.

Sometimes consumer trust in a creditor is well-placed. Indeed, credit has provided real value for millions of households, permitting the purchase of homes that can add to family wealth accumulation and cars that can expand job opportunities. Credit can also provide a critical safety net and a chance for a family to borrow against a better tomorrow when they hit job layoffs, medical problems, or family break-ups today. Other financial products, such as life insurance and annuities, also can greatly enhance a family's security. Consumers might not spend hours pouring over the details of their credit card terms or understand every paper they signed at a real estate closing, but many of those financial products are offered on fair terms that benefit both seller and customer.

But for a growing number of families who are steered into over-priced credit products, risky subprime mortgages, and misleading insurance plans, trust in a creditor turns out to be costly. And for families who get tangled up with truly dangerous financial products, the result can be wiped-out savings, lost homes, higher costs for car insurance, denial of jobs, troubled marriages, bleak retirements, and broken lives.

Consumers can enter the market to buy physical products confident that they won't be tricked into buying exploding toasters and other unreasonably dangerous products.

They can concentrate their shopping efforts in other directions, helping to drive a competitive market that keeps costs low and encourages innovation in convenience, durability, and style. Consumers entering the market to buy financial products should enjoy the same protection. Just as the Consumer Product Safety Commission (CPSC) protects buyers of goods and supports a competitive market, we need the same for consumers of financial products–a new regulatory regime, and even a new regulatory body, to protect consumers who use credit cards, home mortgages, car loans, and a host of other products. The time has come to put scaremongering to rest and to recognize that regulation can often support and advance efficient and more dynamic markets.

* * *

The Financial Product Safety Commission

Clearly, it is time for a new model of financial regulation, one focused primarily on consumer safety rather than corporate profitability. Financial products should be subject to the same routine safety screening that now governs the sale of every toaster, washing machine, and child's car seat sold on the American market.

The model for such safety regulation is the U.S. Consumer Product Safety Commission (CPSC), an independent health and safety regulatory agency founded in 1972 by the Nixon Administration. The CPSC's mission is to protect the American public from risks of injury and death from products used in the home, school, and recreation. The agency has the authority to develop uniform safety standards, order the recall of unsafe products, and ban products that pose unreasonable risks. In establishing the Commission, Congress recognized that "the complexities of consumer products and the diverse nature and abilities of consumers using them frequently result in an inability of users to anticipate risks and to safeguard themselves adequately."

The evidence clearly shows that CPSC is a cost-effective agency. Since it was established, product-related death and injury rates in the United States have decreased substantially. The CPSC estimates that just three safety standards for three products alone–cigarette lighters, cribs, and baby walkers–save more than $2 billion annually. The annual estimated savings is more than CPSC's total cumulative budget since its inception.

So why not create a Financial Product Safety Commission (FPSC)? Like its counterpart for ordinary consumer products, this agency would be charged with responsibility to establish guidelines for consumer disclosure, collect and report data about the uses of different financial products, review new financial products for safety, and require modification of dangerous products before they can be marketed to the public. The agency could review mortgages, credit cards, car loans, and a number of other financial products, such as life insurance and annuity contracts. In effect, the FPSC would evaluate these products to eliminate the hidden tricks and traps that make some of them far more dangerous than others.

An FPSC would promote the benefits of free markets by assuring that consumers can enter credit markets with confidence that the products they purchase meet minimum safety standards. No one expects every customer to become an engineer to buy a toaster that doesn't burst into flames, or analyze complex diagrams to buy an infant car seat that doesn't collapse on impact. By the same reasoning, no customer should be forced to read the fine print in 30-plus-page credit card contracts to determine whether the company claims it can seize property paid for with the credit card or raise the interest rate by more than 20 points if the customer gets into a dispute with the water company.

Instead, an FPSC would develop precisely such expertise in consumer financial products. A commission would be able to collect data about which financial products are least understood, what kinds of disclosures are most effective, and which products are most likely to result in consumer default. Free of legislative micromanaging, it could develop nuanced regulatory responses; some terms might be banned altogether, while others might be permitted only with clearer disclosure. A Commission might promote uniform disclosures that make it easier to compare products from one issuer to another, and to discern conflicts of interest on the part of a mortgage broker or seller of a currently loosely regulated financial product. In the area of credit card regulation, for example, an FPSC might want to review the following terms that appear in some–but not all–credit card agreements: universal clauses; unlimited and unexplained fees; interest rate increases that exceed 10 percentage points; and an issuer's claim that it can change the terms of cards after money has been borrowed. It would also promote such market-enhancing practices as a simple, easy-to-read paragraph that explains all interest charges; clear explanations of when fees will be imposed; a requirement that the terms of a credit card remain the same until the card expires; no marketing targeted at college students or people under age 21; and a statement showing how long it will take to pay off the balance, as well as how much interest will be paid if the customer makes the minimum monthly payments on the outstanding balance on a credit card.

With every agency, the fear of regulatory capture is ever-present. But in a world in which there is little coherent, consumer-oriented regulation of any kind, an FPSC with power to act is far better than the available alternatives. Whether it is housed in a current agency like the CPSC or stands alone, the point is to concentrate the review of financial products in a single location, with a focus on the safety of the products as consumers use them. Companies that offer good products would have little to fear. Indeed, if they could conduct business without competing with companies whose business model involves misleading the customer, then the companies offering safer products would be more likely to flourish. Moreover, with an FPSC, consumer credit companies would be free to innovate on a level playing field within the boundaries of clearly disclosed terms and open competition–not hidden terms designed to mislead consumers.

The consumer financial services industry has grown to more than $3 trillion in annual business. Lenders employ thousands of lawyers, marketing agencies, statisticians, and business strategists to help them increase profits. In a rapidly changing market, customers need someone on their side to help make certain that the financial products they buy meet minimum safety standards. A Financial Product Safety Commission would be the consumers' ally.

A Well-Regulated Market

When markets work, they produce value for both buyers and sellers, both borrowers and lenders. But the basic premise of any free market is full information. When a lender can bury a sentence at the bottom of 47 lines of text saying it can change any term at any time for any reason, the market is broken.

Product safety standards will not fix every problem associated with consumer credit. It is possible to stuff a toaster with dirty socks and start a fire, and, even with safety standards, it will remain possible to get burned by credit products. Some people won't even have to try very hard. But safety standards can make a critical difference for millions of families. Families who are steered into higher-priced mortgages solely because the broker wanted a higher fee would have a greater chance of buying–and keeping–a home. A student who wanted a credit card with a firm credit limit–not an approval for thousands of dollars more of credit and higher fees and interest–could stay out of trouble. An older person who needed a little cash to make it until her Social Security check arrived would have a manageable loan, not one that would escalate into thousands of dollars in fees.

Industry practices would change as well. Corporate profit models based on marketing mortgages with a one-in-five chance of costing a family its home would stop. Credit card models that lure 18-year-olds with no income and no credit history into debt with promises of "no parental approval"–on the assumption that their parents will pay it off, rather than see their children begin their adult lives with ruined credit histories–would stop. Rollovers that can turn a simple loan into a mountain of debt would stop.

Personal responsibility will always play a critical role in dealing with credit cards, just as personal responsibility remains a central feature in the safe use of any other product. But a Financial Product Safety Commission could eliminate some of the most egregious tricks and traps in the credit industry. And for every family who avoids a trap or doesn't get caught by a trick, that's regulation that works.

While Professor Warren's proposal for a CFPB pre-dated the financial crisis of 2008, the crisis created the political opening for turning Professor Warren's proposal into law. Legislation to create a CFPB had been in the works in the summer of 2008 and was formally introduced in September 2008, at the height of the financial crisis.[20] This early legislation, based closely on Professor Warren's proposal, did not move, but when the Obama Administration presented its proposal for a major overhaul of the financial regulatory system,[21] a major plank was the creation of a consumer financial protection agency. The Obama Administration's draft proposal became the template for both the House and Senate versions of the legislation, albeit with important distinctions. The final version of the legislation, which created the CFPB, is the Consumer Financial Protection Act, which is title X of the Dodd-Frank Act.

The purpose of the CFPB is set forth in the Consumer Financial Protection Act. The CFPB is supposed to both "ensure that all consumers have access to markets for consumer financial products and services" and to ensure that "markets for

20. Consumer Credit Safety Commission Act of 2008, S. 3629, 110th Cong. (2008).
21. Dep't of the Treasury, Financial Regulatory Reform: A New Foundation 55-70 (2009).

consumer financial products and services are fair, transparent, and competitive." 12 U.S.C. § 5511(a). Thus, there is both an access mission, which includes fair lending enforcement, and a market fairness and transparency mission.

The Consumer Financial Protection Act also sets forth the CFPB's objectives, namely that with respect to consumer financial products and services:

> (1) consumers are provided with timely and understandable information to make responsible decisions about financial transactions;
> (2) consumers are protected from unfair, deceptive, or abusive acts and practices and from discrimination;
> (3) outdated, unnecessary, or unduly burdensome regulations are regularly identified and addressed in order to reduce unwarranted regulatory burdens;
> (4) Federal consumer financial law is enforced consistently, without regard to the status of a person as a depository institution, in order to promote fair competition; and
> (5) markets for consumer financial products and services operate transparently and efficiently to facilitate access and innovation.

12 U.S.C. § 5511(b). Notice the different strands of consumer finance regulatory theory represented: both information provision and education to facilitate markets *and* protection against sharp or discriminatory practices. At the same time, the objectives include the mission of reducing "unwarranted regulatory burdens" and ensuring equal treatment of different types of financial institutions.

Finally, the Consumer Financial Protection Act enumerates the "primary functions" of the CFPB. These "primary functions" provide a good overview of the types of activities the CFPB does:

> (1) conducting financial education programs;
> (2) collecting, investigating, and responding to consumer complaints;
> (3) collecting, researching, monitoring, and publishing information relevant to the functioning of markets for consumer financial products and services to identify risks to consumers and the proper functioning of such markets;
> (4) subject to sections 5514 through 5516 of this title, supervising covered persons for compliance with Federal consumer financial law, and taking appropriate enforcement action to address violations of Federal consumer financial law;
> (5) issuing rules, orders, and guidance implementing Federal consumer financial law; and
> (6) performing such support activities as may be necessary or useful to facilitate the other functions of the Bureau.

12 U.S.C. § 5511(c). While our focus in this book will be on the CFPB's activities in terms of the fourth and fifth functions—covering supervision, enforcement, and rulemaking—these functions are supported by the CFPB's research and consumer complaint investigation functions and complemented by its financial education initiatives.

Problem Set 5

1. Elizabeth Warren's idea for a consumer financial protection agency is based on the analogy that mortgages are like toasters: just as we don't allow exploding toasters on the market, we shouldn't allow exploding financial products to be on the market. What do you think of this analogy? Are mortgages like toasters? What does this say about the similarities between a consumer product safety regime and a consumer financial protection regime?

2. Consider a different product safety regulation regime: drug safety. Prescription drugs cannot be sold without pre-approval by the Food and Drug Administration. Pre-approval for drugs typically requires a drug to have gone through three phases of clinical testing, which test for safety, safe dosage range, side effects, and efficacy. Would a drug safety analogy make more sense? What would be the costs and benefits of a pre-approval regime? What would testing consist of?

3. Does state regulation of consumer finance make sense in an era of national markets? Prior to 1994, banks were restricted in their ability to engage in interstate branching, but today many large banks operate branches in multiple states, and the Internet has enabled lenders to achieve a national reach without a physical presence. What are the costs and benefits of having states play a role in consumer finance regulation either by rulemaking or through enforcement? Does your view on overlapping federal and state regulation depend on which political party is in office?

4. The CFPB's mission includes "ensuring that all consumers have access to markets for consumer financial products and services." 12 U.S.C. § 5511(a). Is this a charge to take steps to facilitate the availability of credit generally (that is, emphasis is on *access*)? Or is it an anti-discrimination charge (emphasis on *all consumers*)? How might this reading affect how the CFPB conducts itself? Why might the CFPB prefer one reading over another?

CHAPTER 6

THE CFPB II: RULEMAKING

The CFPB has rulemaking, enforcement, and supervision authority over various parts of the consumer finance industry. Rulemaking and enforcement are likely activities that are familiar to you.

Rulemaking involves the process of promulgating rules under the various statutes administered by the CFPB. The CFPB administers two sets of statutes. First, it administers a set of eighteen statutes that pre-dated the CFPB's creation. These statutes are known as the "**enumerated consumer laws.**" Second, the CFPB administers its own organic statute, the Consumer Financial Protection Act, which includes authority for UDAAP rulemaking, authority for mandating disclosures for consumer financial products, as well as rulemaking restricting binding mandatory arbitration.

Enforcement involves bringing litigation to enforce the applicable statutes and rules thereunder. Supervision may be less familiar, but is no less important. Supervision involves undertaking examinations of the books, records, and practices of regulated firms. The CFPB employs a large number of "**examiners,**" who periodically show up at regulated firms and inspect the firms for compliance with federal consumer financial protection laws.

Rulemaking, enforcement, and supervision are not the sum total of the CFPB's activities. The CFPB also engages in a substantial program of consumer education and market facilitation. These activities range from providing comparison-shopping tools on the CFPB's website to providing educational outreach services to seniors and armed servicemembers. While these activities are an important part of what the CFPB does, they are not covered in this book as they are not part of the traditional set of regulatory tools and their impact on the consumer finance market is hard to gauge.

The respective extent of CFPB jurisdiction for rulemaking, enforcement, and supervision is not identical. The CFPB's rulemaking authority is broader than its supervision authority and substantially broader than its enforcement authority. This chapter and the following two chapters cover the scope of the CFPB's jurisdiction for each of these areas of regulation.

The CFPB is authorized to engage in rulemaking under "Federal consumer financial law." 12 U.S.C. § 5512(a). "**Federal consumer financial law**" is defined to include two distinct sets of authority: (1) the CFPB's "**organic**" authority under the Consumer Financial Protection Act (Title X of Dodd-Frank), and (2) authority under certain pre-existing federal laws that has been transferred to the CFPB. 12 U.S.C. § 5481(14).

The CFPB's organic rulemaking authority is limited to defining certain acts and practices as unfair, deceptive, or abusive (UDAAP), 12 U.S.C. § 5531, mandating disclosures, 12 U.S.C. § 5532, requiring registration of certain non-banks, 12 U.S.C. § 5512(b)(7), and restricting pre-dispute arbitration, 12 U.S.C. § 5518. The organic powers are separate from and cumulative to the CFPB's authority under the transferred federal statutes, which are referred to as "**enumerated consumer laws.**" 12 U.S.C. § 5481(12).

I. THE ENUMERATED CONSUMER LAWS

The "enumerated consumer laws" cover some eighteen different statutes, including the:

- **Consumer Leasing Act** (governing consumer leases);
- **Electronic Fund Transfer Act** (governing ATMs, debit cards, ACH, prepaid, and remittance payments, inter alia);
- **Equal Credit Opportunity Act** (anti-discriminatory lending);
- **Fair Credit Billing Act** (governing consumers' rights regarding bills for repayment of consumer credit);
- **Fair Credit Reporting Act** (governing reporting about consumers to credit reporting agencies);
- **Fair Debt Collection Practices Act** (governing debt collection);
- Parts of the **Gramm-Leach-Bliley Act** (consumer financial privacy provisions, but not data security provisions);
- **Home Mortgage Disclosure Act** (data collection on mortgage lending for fair lending purposes)
- **Home Owners Protection Act** (governing private mortgage insurance);
- **Home Ownership and Equity Protection Act** (governing certain high-cost mortgage loans);
- **Interstate Land Sales Act** (governing certain interstate sales of real estate);
- **Omnibus Appropriations Act of 2009, Section 626** (governing unfair and deceptive acts in mortgage lending, mortgage modification services, and foreclosure rescue services);
- **SAFE Mortgage Licensing Act** (governing the licensing of mortgage loan officers);
- **Real Estate Settlement Procedures Act** (governing real estate closings and mortgage servicing);

- **Truth in Lending Act** (governing disclosure of the cost of consumer credit and prohibiting certain credit terms); and
- **Truth in Savings Act** (governing disclosure regulation of savings accounts).[1]

The enumerated consumer laws are topic-area specific; the CFPB may have jurisdiction over certain entities only for the purposes of a particular enumerated consumer law without having general rulemaking authority over it under the Consumer Financial Protection Act. We will return to a consideration of some of the enumerated consumer laws in Part II of the book, which covers particular consumer product markets. For now you should be aware that the CFPB can undertake rulemakings in a particular product market either under the rulemaking power delegated to it under an enumerated consumer law or under its organic powers or under both; the lack of specific authority under an enumerated consumer law does not preclude use of the broader organic power as the organic power is from a later-enacted statute and is thus not bound by the limitations of the earlier-enacted enumerated consumer law.

II. ORGANIC POWERS UNDER THE CONSUMER FINANCIAL PROTECTION ACT

The scope of the CFPB's jurisdiction for rulemaking under the Consumer Financial Protection Act is limited to "covered persons" and "service providers."[2] Therefore, to understand the scope of the CFPB's supervision and organic rulemaking authority, we must turn to the definitions of "covered persons" and "service providers," which requires a tour through the definitional section of the Consumer Financial Protection Act, 12 U.S.C. § 5481.

A. Covered Persons

The Consumer Financial Protection Act defines "**covered person**" as "any person that engaged in offering or providing a consumer financial product or service" or any affiliate of such a person if the affiliate acts as a service provider to the covered person. 12 U.S.C. § 5481(6). A "**consumer financial product or service**" is then defined as "any financial product or service" (itself a defined term), 12 U.S.C.

---

1. The CFPB is also separately authorized by section 1097 of the Consumer Financial Protection Act, codified at 15 U.S.C. § 1638 note, to prescribe rules regarding unfair and deceptive acts and practices (UDAP) regarding mortgage loans, including loan modification and foreclosure rescue services. Violations of such a rule are treated as violations of both the Consumer Financial Protection Act's prohibition on UDAAP (12 U.S.C. § 5536) and violations of rules under the Federal Trade Commission Act (15 U.S.C. § 57a). One implication of this separate font of authority is that the CFPB need not comply with the requirements for rulemaking under 12 U.S.C. § 5531 (UDAAP) or 5 U.S.C. § 45 (FTC Act UDAP).

2. 12 U.S.C. §§ 5531 (UDAAP rulemaking authority for covered persons and service providers); 5532 (disclosure power limited to "consumer financial products and services"); 5536 (prohibited acts for covered persons and service providers). The CFPB's disclosure power is not explicitly limited to covered persons, only to "consumer financial products and services," 12 U.S.C. § 5532(a), but a "covered person" is one who "offers or providers a consumer financial product or service." 12 U.S.C. § 5481(6).

§ 5481(15), that "is offered or provided for use by consumers primarily for personal, family, or household purposes" or certain ancillary services provided in connection with the offering or provision of a consumer financial product. 12 U.S.C. § 5481(5).

The Consumer Financial Protection Act contains an extensive definition of "**financial product or service.**" 12 U.S.C. § 5481(15). For a product to be a "consumer financial product" it must not only be in the statutory list of product lines, but also be offered or provided for use by consumers primarily for personal, family, or household purposes. 12 U.S.C. § 5481(5), (15). The Act defines "financial product or service" as covering:

- extensions, servicing, brokerage, and sales of credit;
- certain finance leases;
- real estate settlement services other than appraisals and insurance;
- deposit taking;
- transmission and exchanging of funds;
- sale or provision of stored value or payment instruments;
- check cashing, collection, and guarantee services;
- provision of payments or financial data processing products by technological means;
- financial advisory services;
- collecting, analyzing, maintaining, or providing consumer report or account information for use in offering or providing other consumer financial products or services, except to the extent it is to be used in-house or by an affiliate;
- debt collection.

12 U.S.C. § 5481(15). The CFPB is also authorized to expand the definition of "financial product or service" to prevent evasion or to ensure that all consumer products offered by banks are covered. 12 U.S.C. § 5481(15)(A)(x). Most of the terms used in the 12 U.S.C. § 5481(15) definition of "financial product or service" are not themselves defined in the Consumer Financial Protection Act. Some of these terms are defined in other laws, such as the Uniform Commercial Code (regarding finance leases), or the Fair Credit Reporting Act (regarding the definition of a "consumer report"). Presumably the Consumer Financial Protection Act's definitions will be interpreted with reference to these other laws, but the statute lacks cross-references.

The effect of the Consumer Financial Protection Act's definition of "financial product or service" is to give the CFPB authority over several major functions of consumer finance: deposits and safekeeping; payments; credit and leases; debt collection; and advisory services. Excluded are non-deposit investments (including money market mutual funds, but not money market deposit accounts) and insurance. 12 U.S.C. § 5481(15)(C).

Critically, the CFPB's authority under enumerated consumer laws covers some entities that are not providing "consumer financial products or services," particularly insurers. The CFPB has authority under the Home Owners Protection Act to regulate some aspects of private mortgage insurance, which would likely not be considered a "consumer financial product or service" because of the insurance exclusion. Private mortgage insurers may also have liability under the Real Estate

Settlement Procedures Act.[3] Similarly, the Interstate Land Sales Act covers certain pure sale activities not considered "consumer financial products or services."

Just who might be a "covered person" might surprise you. Consider the following excerpt from a CFPB complaint that with a companion action resulted in settlements that produced $120 million in consumer refunds and $38 million in fines.

Complaint
CFPB v. Cellco Partnership d/b/a Verizon Wireless

No. 3:15-cv-03268-PGS-LHG (D.N.J. May 12, 2015)

The Consumer Financial Protection Bureau . . . brings this action against Cellco Partnership d/b/a Verizon Wireless ("Verizon") and alleges as follows:

. . .

2. Until at least January 2014, Verizon included third-party charges on its customers' wireless-telephone bills. Many of these third-party charges were never authorized by consumers and, as a result, wrongfully cost Verizon's customers millons of dollars each year.

3. Verizon unfairly charged its customers by creating a billing and payment-processing system that gave third parties virtually unfettered access to its cusomers' accounts. This access allowed third parties to "cram" unauthorized charges onto wireless bills.

4. Verizon automatically enrolled customers in its third-party billing system without their knowledge or consent. Many customers were therefore unaware of the unauthorized charges.

. . .

6. Verizon profited from this system because it shifted the risk to its customers, who had to pay all charges under the company's terms and conditions of service. . . .While its customers suffered losses, Verizon retained 30% or more of the gross revenue it collected for third-party charges, totaling hundreds of millions of dollars.

. . .

10. Verizon extends credit to, and processes payments for, consumers in connection with third-party goods. Verizon is therefore a "covered person" under the CFPA. 12 U.S.C. § 5481(6), 15(A)(i) & (vii).

B. Service Providers

In addition to rulemaking jurisdiction over covered persons, the CFPB can also exercise its organic rulemaking authority over "**service providers**," a term defined by the Act. 12 U.S.C. § 5481(26). A "service provider" is a person that provides a "material service to a covered person in connection with the offering or provision by such covered person of a consumer financial product or service." 12 U.S.C. § 5481(26)(A).

3. 12 U.S.C. § 2607(a) (prohibiting the giving or accepting of kickbacks in real estate settlements).

It includes a person who "participates in designing, operating, or maintaining the consumer financial product or service" or one who "processes transactions relating to the consumer financial product or service (other than unknowingly or incidentally transmitting or processing financial data in a manner that such data is undifferentiated from other types of data of the same form as the person transmits or processes)." 12 U.S.C. § 5481(26)(A)(i)-(ii). Excluded from the definition are general ministerial support services and the provision of advertising time or space. 12 U.S.C. § 5481(26)(B).

The following case provides a consideration of whether a firm that does not directly deal with consumers is nonetheless a "service provider" and subject to CFPB jurisdiction. The case arises in an enforcement, rather than a rulemaking context, but the analysis is the same, as the CFPB's enforcement jurisdiction for unfair, deceptive, and abusive acts and practices is limited to covered persons and service providers.

Order Denying Motion to Dismiss CFPB v. Universal Debt & Payment Solutions, LLC

No. 1:15-CV-00859-RWS (N.D. Ga. Sept. 1, 2015)

STORY, J.

This case comes before the Court on Defendant Pathfinder Payment Solutions, Inc.'s Motion to Dismiss, Defendant Global Payments, Inc.'s Motion to Dismiss, and Defendant Frontline Processing Corp.'s Motion to Dismiss. . . .

BACKGROUND

The Consumer Financial Protection Bureau ("CFPB") brings this action against numerous individuals and entities in connection with a massive debt-collection scheme. The CFPB alleges violations of the Fair Debt Collection Practices Act ("FDCPA"), 15 U.S.C. §§ 1692–1692p, and the Consumer Financial Protection Act ("CFPA"), 12 U.S.C. §§ 5531, 5536(a). According to the CFPB, several individuals [including Defendant Mohan Bagga] created limited liability companies in Georgia and New York ["Debt Collectors"] to perpetrate a debt-collection scheme targeting millions of consumers.

I. The Debt-Collection Scheme

The Debt Collectors made millions of collection calls to consumers in attempts to collect debts the Debt Collectors were not in fact owed. The Debt Collectors threatened litigation and told consumers they needed to settle the debt to avoid a restraining order or criminal prosecution. When asked for information about the purported debts, the Debt Collectors refused to identify the lenders but, by reciting the consumers' personal information, including Social Security number, date of birth, and place of employment, convinced consumers the debts were legitimate and were owed to them. The Debt Collectors purchased that identifying information from debt and data brokers. When consumers provided their payment information, the Debt Collectors used payment processors to withdraw funds from the consumers' accounts.

Defendant Global Payments, Inc. ("Global Payments" or "Global") is a payment processor that processed transactions for the Debt Collectors. Payment processors "enable merchants to accept check, card, and electronic payments at a point of sale." During a transaction, the card information is captured by a point-of-sale terminal card reader and transmitted to a payment network. (Payment processors are sponsored by an acquiring bank that is registered with one or more card associations, such as Visa or MasterCard. They are also subject to the rules and credit risk policies of the card associations.)

Two other companies, Defendants Pathfinder Payment Solutions, Inc. ("Pathfinder") and Frontline Processing Corp. ("Frontline") are independent sales organizations ("ISOs") that entered into merchant services agreements with a Global Payments subsidiary to market Global Payments' processing services to merchants. Pathfinder also agreed to review potential merchants' creditworthiness, to underwrite the merchants, to monitor processing activity to detect fraud and risk, and to advise Global Payments accordingly. Frontline agreed to prescreen merchants for compliance with Global Payments' credit criteria.

The CFPB accuses Global Payments, Pathfinder, and Frontline (collectively, "Payment Processors") . . . of engaging in unfair acts or practices (Count IX). The CFPB asserts that the Payment Processors "enabled [the Debt Collectors] to efficiently accept payments and convince consumers that they were credible merchants." Moreover, these Defendants were required to follow policies and procedures to evaluate merchant creditworthiness and identify fraud. This is because payment processors face credit exposure given that merchants are paid quickly, while consumers' payments are provisional and may be reversed if a consumer disputes a charge, resulting in a "chargeback." If a merchant is unwilling or unable to fund the reversed transaction, the payment processor is responsible for the chargeback.

Global Payments' credit policy, like the card networks' policies, identifies collection agencies as "prohibited merchants" that the ISOs were not to solicit and which required Global Payments' approval. Global Payments also prohibited "Aggregators," which are merchants who use their processing account to process payments for other merchants—a practice called "factoring." Defendants considered collection agencies to be high-risk merchants because they processed only "card-not-present" transactions. Thus, Global Payments' policies required more scrutiny of card-not-present merchants. The CFPB alleges, however, that Global Payments, Pathfinder, and Frontline all failed to monitor the Debt Collectors' accounts for signs of unlawful conduct and . . . that this conduct amounted to unfair acts or practices. 12 U.S.C. §§ 5531(a), (c)(1), 5536(a)(1)(B). . . .

Global Payments and the ISOs move for dismissal of both claims against them pursuant to Federal Rule of Civil Procedure 12(b)(6), asserting that the Complaint fails to state a claim upon which relief can be granted.

. . .

III. Count IX: Unfair Acts or Practices

The CFPB alleges the Payment Processors' independent violations of the CFPA for engaging in unfair acts or practices as the next basis for liability. Under the CFPA, it is unlawful for "any covered person or service provider . . . to engage in any unfair, deceptive, or abusive act or practice." 12 U.S.C. § 5536(a)(1)(B). Pathfinder and Frontline deny they are either covered persons or service providers under the statute. Global Payments denies it is a covered person but does not dispute that it is a service provider. All assert they did not engage in unfair acts or practices.

The CFPB responds that the Payment Processors committed primary violations of the CFPA because they are covered persons or service providers, and they "committed unfair acts or practices by ignoring clear signs of illegal conduct while collecting consumers' payments for the Debt Collectors."

A. Covered Persons

Each Payment Processor argues it is not a covered person. A covered person includes:

> **(A)** any person that engages in offering or providing a consumer financial product or service; and
> **(B)** any affiliate of a person described in subparagraph (A) if such affiliate acts as a service provider to such person.

12 U.S.C. § 5481(6). The statute in turn defines a "consumer financial product or service" as a financial product or service that "is offered or provided for use by consumers primarily for personal, family, or household purposes." Id. § 5481(5). The statute defines a financial product or service by listing eleven categories of services, one of which is "providing payments or other financial data processing products or services to a consumer by any technological means, including . . . through any payments systems or network used for processing payments data." Id. § 5481(15) (emphasis added).

The Payment Processors contend they did not offer their services to consumers but to merchants (and/or to Global, in the case of the ISOs). Nor are they affiliates of covered persons. In the paragraphs of the Complaint where the CFPB alleges Global Payments is a covered person and a service provider, it does not allege Global provides financial services to consumers, only to the Debt Collectors. The same is true for Pathfinder and Frontline. But, even if the Payment Processors are not covered persons, they could still be subject to liability for unfair acts or practices if they are service providers. See 12 U.S.C. § 5536(a). As explained below, they are.

B. Service Providers

The CFPA defines a "service provider" as:

> any person that provides a material service to a covered person in connection with the offering or provision by such covered person of a consumer financial product or service, including a person that—
>
> > **(i)** participates in designing, operating, or maintaining the consumer financial product or service; or
> > **(ii)** processes transactions relating to the consumer financial product or service (other than unknowingly or incidentally transmitting or processing financial data in a manner that such data is undifferentiated from other types of data of the same form as the person transmits or processes).

12 U.S.C. § 5481(26)(A). Global Payments does not argue that it is not a service provider. Pathfinder contends that it meets express exceptions to the definition, while Frontline disputes that it provided material services to the Debt Collectors.

1. Pathfinder

One of the exceptions to the definition of "service provider" is as follows:

> The term "service provider" does not include a person solely by virtue of such person offering or providing to a covered person–
>
> **(i)** a support service of a type provided to businesses generally or a similar ministerial service . . . .

12 U.S.C. § 5481(26)(B). Pathfinder states it is exempt because it unknowingly or incidentally transmitted financial data and provided a ministerial support service to merchants, the covered persons under the statute. First, the main definition of "service provider" includes a person that "processes transactions relating to the consumer financial product or service (other than knowingly or incidentally transmitting or processing financial data in a manner that such data is undifferentiated from other types of data of the same form as the person transmits or processes)." 12 U.S.C. § 5481(26)(A). Pathfinder bases one of its exception arguments on this caveat. But the CFPB alleges that Pathfinder provided services other than processing transactions, such as underwriting merchants, approving applications, and monitoring for risk. Therefore the statutory language does not exempt Pathfinder.

Pathfinder's second argument is that it fits into the exemption under 12 U.S.C. § 5481(26)(B) as "a support service of a type provided to businesses generally or a similar ministerial service." Yet while ISOs (and payment processors) provide services to many types of businesses, an ISO's services are not ministerial. The plain meaning of the term "ministerial" describes "an act that involves obedience to instructions or laws instead of discretion, judgment, or skill." Ministerial, Black's Law Dictionary 1086 (9th ed. 2009). Pathfinder performed underwriting and screening services and was supposed to monitor for risk after Pathfinder and Global approved merchant accounts. Pathfinder's duties involved discretion, judgment, and skill because it had to evaluate creditworthiness and make judgments about merchants' risk levels.

The Court finds that Pathfinder is not covered by the exemptions it identifies. Furthermore, the Court finds that the allegations adequately state Pathfinder is a service provider. Pathfinder processed the Debt Collectors' applications and enabled them to obtain accounts with Global Payments. Without the ability to obtain payment processing accounts, the Debt Collectors could not have succeeded in their scheme. Thus, Pathfinder provided material services to the Debt Collectors. Because the Payment Processors do not challenge that the Debt Collectors are covered persons, Pathfinder provided material services to a covered person and is a service provider as defined in § 5481(26).

2. Frontline

Frontline similarly disputes that it provided material services, and it asserts that it provided services for the benefit of Global, not the Debt Collectors. Although Frontline may have contracted with Global to serve as an ISO, the Court finds that the CFPB plausibly alleges Frontline provided services to the Debt Collectors by processing their applications and assisting them in obtaining payment processing accounts. Again, these services were material because the Debt Collectors could not have processed consumer credit cards without a Global account. Even though Global had final approval, as an ISO Frontline provided a screening function the merchants had to pass before obtaining a payment processing account. The Court finds that the Complaint adequately alleges that Frontline provided material services to a covered person and consequently is a service provider.

C. Procedural Limitations on Rulemakings

The CFPB is subject to a number of constraints on its rulemaking authority. First, like that of all federal agencies, CFPB rulemaking is subject to the Administrative Procedure Act. 5 U.S.C. §§ 500 *et seq*. This means that the CFPB rulemaking must proceed with public notice of the proposed rulemaking, provision of an opportunity for the public to comment on the proposal, and publication of the final rule before its effective date.

Second, the CFPB is one of only three federal agencies (the others being the EPA and OSHA) that is required to comply with additional procedural steps for rulemakings under the Small Business Regulatory Enforcement Fairness Act of 1996. 5 U.S.C. § 553 (2006). SBREFA essentially requires the CFPB to get advance comments on certain proposed rulemakings from a panel of small businesses and representatives of certain government agencies.

Third, the CFPB is required to undertake a cost-benefit analysis of the rulemaking, including consideration of "the potential reduction of access by consumers to consumer financial products and services," and the impact on small depositaries and rural consumers. 12 U.S.C. § 5512(b)(2)(A).[4]

Fourth, the CFPB is required to undertake a subsequent review of every "significant" rule or order within at least five years of its issuance. 12 U.S.C. § 5512(d). The term "significant" is not defined by statute, but the review of these "significant" rules or orders is mandatory.

Fifth, the CFPB's rulemakings, alone among all federal agencies, are subject to a veto by the Financial Stability Oversight Council, a college of federal financial regulators. 12 U.S.C. § 5513.

And finally, CFPB rulemakings are subject to being voided during a limited window following promulgation under the Congressional Review Act, 5 U.S.C. §§ 801-808, by a simple majority vote of both houses of Congress (not subject to the filibuster) with presidential signature. If a regulation is so voided, the agency

4. This cost-benefit analysis requirement is distinct from the one that applies by executive order to certain other agencies. *See* Exec. Order No. 12,866, 3 C.F.R. §§ 638 (1993).

is thereafter precluded from issuing a rule that is "substantially the same" absent express authorization, but what this means is unclear and the Congressional Review Act forbids any judicial review. The CFPB's arbitration rule was voided under the Congressional Review Act, as was its Guidance on Indirect Auto Lending.

Beyond these procedural limitations, the CFPB is also subject to certain jurisdictional limits on its rulemakings. A number of categories of entities are excluded from its rulemaking authority (as well as from supervision and enforcement authority). We will examine these exclusions in more detail in a subsequent chapter.

Problem Set 6

1. Which of the following are entities are subject to the CFPB's rulemaking authority to prohibit unfair, deceptive, and abusive acts and practices in regard to the specified activities? *See* 12 U.S.C. §§ 5481(5), 5481(6), 5531(b).

a. Fidelity Fiduciary Bank, where Anna Gelpern maintains both a checking and a savings account. *See* 12 U.S.C. § 5481(8); 12 U.S.C. § (15)(A)(iv).

b. Ka-Pow!, a company that transmits the remittances that Jorge Granados, a small construction contractor in Maryland, sends every month to his family in El Salvador. *See* 12 U.S.C. §§ 5481(15)(A)(iv)-(v), 5481(18), 5481(29).

c. QuickiCash, which cashed Bill Burn's Social Security Disability Insurance Check for a fee of 3% of the face amount of the check. *See* 12 U.S.C. § 5481(15)(A)(vi).

d. Usurious George Ltd., a Cook Islands corporation that offers payday loans—short-term, small-dollar loans that it can collect via a direct debit of the borrower's bank account—over the Internet. *See* 12 U.S.C. § 5481(15)(A)(i).

e. American Mortgage Servicing Corp., a firm that manages home mortgage loans, including collecting payments, on behalf of various investment firms that own the mortgage loans. American Mortgage Servicing Corp. did not originate the mortgage loans. *See* 12 U.S.C. § 5481(15)(A)(i).

f. Bonnie Lewis, a realtor (real estate broker), who helps prospective homebuyers find home and prospective home sellers sell their homes. *See* 12 U.S.C. § 5481(15)(A).

g. Fast Times Automotive Acceptance Corp., which originated the three-year non-operating lease for hotshot attorney Dan Mullens's Lexus sedan. Dan frequently uses the Lexus for transportation to work. *See* 12 U.S.C. §§ 5481(5), 5481(15)(A)(ii).

h. Somerset Title Company, a title insurer that provides title insurance, property appraisal, and real estate settlement services. *See* 12 U.S.C. §§ 5481(3), 5481(15)(A)(iii), 5481(15)(C)(i).

i. Panopticon Inc., a credit reporting bureau that collects information on consumers' bill payment history and sells such information to prospective creditors, insurers, and employers. *See* 12 U.S.C. §§ 5481(15)(A)(ix), 15 U.S.C. § 1681a(d).

j. RoundUp LLC, a firm that buys delinquent debts from doctors' offices and attempts to collect the debts. *See* 12 U.S.C. § 5481(5); 12 U.S.C. § 5481(7); 12 U.S.C. §§ 5481(15)(A)(i), (x).

k. Penelope Weiss, an accountant who provides tax preparation services to consumers. *See* 12 U.S.C. § 5481(15)(viii).
l. The American Arbitration Association, a firm that provides for-fee arbitration services (including arbitrators) to both consumers and financial services businesses. *See* 12 U.S.C. § 5481(15)(x); 5481(26).

2. Saule Omarova purchased a Visa brand prepaid card (balance $50) at a SpeedyMart convenience store as a Christmas present for her dear friend Bob Hockett. The card was issued by Continental Express Bank, N.A. and operates on the Visa payment network. It can be used at any merchant that accepts Visa brand payments. Continental Express Bank designed and operates the card; SpeedyMart merely acts as the sales agent, while Visa process the payment between Continental Express Bank and merchants who accept the card for payment. Bob was extremely touched by the thoughtful and personal nature of the gift. If the CFPB undertakes a rulemaking regarding unfair acts and practices with gift cards, will it apply to:
a. SpeedyMart? *See* 12 U.S.C. §§ 5481(8), 5481(15)(A)(v), 5481(26), 5481(28).
b. Continental Express Bank? *See* 12 U.S.C. §§ 5481(8), 5481(15)(A)(iv), 5481(15)(A)(v), 5481(15)(A)(vii), 5481(28).
c. Visa? *See* 12 U.S.C. §§ 5481(11), 5481(15)(A)(vii), 5481(15)(C)(ii), 5481(26).

3. You have been tasked with overseeing a CFPB rulemaking on a small-dollar credit product. What factors do you need to consider in the rulemaking and how will you do this? *See* 12 U.S.C. § 5512(b)(2).

CHAPTER 7

THE CFPB III: SUPERVISION

I. WHAT IS SUPERVISION?

The CFPB has supervisory authority over certain entities. This means that the CFPB has the authority to send in teams of examiners to look at the entity's books and records and inquire about its operations with an eye toward establishing whether the entity is in compliance with federal consumer financial protection laws. Supervision is essentially a non-public compliance audit undertaken by a regulator.

The CFPB has established examination procedures; these procedures vary by the type of entity involved, particularly by the types of consumer financial products and services in which it deals, but generally, a CFPB examination will typically commence with an initial conference with management, a request for records, and a review of the entity's compliance management system. Based on this initial review, the CFPB will determine whether to do a more in-depth on-site examination.

An on-site examination is a lengthier process that requires assistance from the regulated entity's staff. An on-site examination might last for several or even a dozen weeks. Examiners will interview senior managers, loan officers, compliance officers, and account personnel; inspect the firm's written policies and procedures (including compliance management systems) to ensure their adequacy; observe operations, such as at call centers and branches; compare the firm's formal policies and procedures to actual practices through a review of a sample of transactions; review samples of loan applications, servicing records, and collection call recordings; and review how the firm deals with complaints and maintains records.

No advanced notice of an examination is required, but the CFPB typically sends supervised entities an examination Information Request (IR) prior to commencing an examination, usually with at least 60 days' advance notice. The IR will contain a list of information and documents that the supervised entity is requested to provide to the CFPB either for off-site review or to make available to examiners onsite.

The purpose of the examination is to form a picture of the firm's compliance both for communicating to the firm areas in which it might need improvement and for identifying potential areas for either enforcement actions or rulemakings. What the CFPB learns during its examinations is confidential; the information can be used by the CFPB, but it cannot be shared with private parties. 12 C.F.R. § 1070. The examination process is a critical way for the CFPB to gather intelligence about market practices and to learn where regulatory problems lie and informally communicate concerns to regulated entities.[1]

The supervision process also provides a channel for non-public enforcement. If an examination results in findings of potential violations of federal consumer financial law, the CFPB may send a Potential Action and Request for Response (PARR) letter. A PARR letter, which is not public, provides notice of preliminary findings of violations and advises the supervised entity that the CFPB may take a public enforcement action based on the findings. Supervised entities are invited to respond to PARR letters, but the entire PARR process is informal and discretionary. Additionally, an examination might result in the CFPB designating certain "Matters Requiring Attention" (MRAs), that is, alleged violations of law or compliance management weaknesses. The CFPB will often request a written response to the designation of an MRA that indicates how the matter will be addressed. A regulated firm is under no formal duty to address matters designated in an MRA, but often regulated firms will voluntarily remediate the issues identified by the CFPB during the examination process, in which case the CFPB will generally not bring an enforcement action.

The CFPB reports on these non-public supervisory actions in general terms (without identifying the firm involved) in its periodic Supervisory Highlights, but otherwise they are invisible to the public. For example, consider this description the CFPB provided of a set of parallel supervisory actions:

> Supervision cited the unfair practice of [certain unnamed mortgage servicers of] requiring all borrowers, regardless of individual circumstance, to enter into across-the-board waivers of existing claims in order to obtain a forbearance or loan modification agreement. As these servicers presented these clauses in a "take it or leave it" fashion in the ordinary course of offering loss mitigation agreements, rather than in the context of resolution of a contested claim or another individualized analysis of the servicer's risks and the consumer's potential claims, Supervision determined that these servicers had engaged in unfair practices. As a result, Supervision directed these servicers to cease using broad waiver clauses like those identified in these examinations in loss mitigation agreements in the ordinary course of business, without regard to individual circumstances. Supervision also directed them to cease enforcing the existing unfair waiver clauses and to provide notice to the borrowers that it would not enforce these waivers in the future.

CFPB, *Winter 2013 Supervisory Highlights*, 6-7. Supervision, then, can function as a type of informal enforcement. Does this fit into any administrative law paradigm you've ever seen? Informal policy-making through supervision is a basic tool in financial regulation, and it lies entirely outside of the administrative law framework because it is all formally voluntary: regulators make (very pointed) suggestions, with an implied threat of public enforcement actions and harsher terms for

---

1. Relatedly, the CFPB has established complaint registries, which provide another source of intelligence about market practices.

settlement if there is non-compliance, and regulated firms voluntarily comply, at least insofar as they are not formally compelled to do so. It is extremely rare for a firm to challenge supervisory findings or fail to heed supervisory suggestions.

What are the benefits of such non-public enforcement to the CFPB? To regulated firms? Are there any downsides? How can other firms learn what is expected of them absent a public record? What about the lack of reputational consequences that might follow from public enforcement actions?

II. SCOPE OF SUPERVISION AUTHORITY

The scope of the CFPB's supervision authority is more limited than that of its rulemaking authority. Whereas CFPB rulemaking authority applies to all covered persons and service providers (unless subject to a carve-out) as well as extending to persons subject to rules under the enumerated consumer laws, supervision authority applies only to a subset of covered persons and service providers. That is, supervision authority does not track with coverage of the enumerated consumer laws, and it does not even include all covered persons and service providers. Among covered persons and service providers, supervision authority depends, in the first instance, on whether an entity is a bank or not, and then to the size of the bank. To understand the division of supervisory authority for banks, it is necessary to understand something of the general structure of U.S. bank regulatory authority, which is a crazy quilt produced by the federal structure of the regulatory system.

A. Banks and the Dual Banking System

A banking charter is required to operate a bank. Unlike a general corporate charter, modern banking charters are not readily granted to anyone who meets the statutory requirements and pays the requisite fee (such a system of "wild cat" banking did exist in the early nineteenth century, often with disastrous results for depositors and noteholders). Instead, bank chartering is limited.

The United States has a "**dual banking system**," meaning that banks may be chartered by either federal or state government. All banks have at least one **prudential regulator**, meaning a regulator tasked with ensuring that the bank is safe and sound, meaning that the bank is not engaged in unduly risky practices and is not likely to fail. Prudential regulation is, at core, solvency regulation. Prudential regulators generally have authority to enforce consumer finance laws, and in some cases they are the only party with such authority over an institution. Yet consumer financial protection is not prudential regulators' primary task, and their solvency mission can conflict with their secondary consumer financial protection mission because predatory practices can be profitable and improve a bank's bottom line.

In many cases there is a primary prudential regulator, while other regulators have secondary authority over the institution. Primary prudential regulatory authority over banks depends on (1) whether a bank has a federal or state charter, (2) the type of charter (bank, savings association, credit union), (3) whether the bank has federal deposit insurance, and (4) whether the bank is a member of the Federal Reserve System.

Some financial institutions are federally chartered, meaning that their corporate charter comes from the federal government. There are three types of federally chartered institutions: national banks, federal savings associations, and federal credit unions. The different types of charters grant different powers to the institutions: federal savings associations and federal credit unions are more limited than national banks in the types of business they can undertake. National banks can always be identified because they will either have the word "national" in their name or the initials "N.A." (National Association) following their name. Other banks are not permitted to use "national" in their names. Thus, the State National Bank of Georgia would be a federally chartered bank. Likewise, federal savings associations and credit unions are readily identifiable as such because they have the word "federal" in their names or the initials "FSB" (federal savings bank) or "FCU" (federal credit union) after their names.

All federally chartered institutions have federal deposit or share insurance. National banks and federal savings associations have FDIC deposit insurance, while federal credit unions have NCUA share insurance. For national banks and federal savings unions the primary regulator is the Office of the Comptroller of the Currency (the OCC), a bureau of the Treasury Department.[2]

Although the OCC and OTS are part of the Treasury Department, they are autonomous, and the Treasury Secretary lacks authority to force the Comptroller of the Currency (or, previously, the Director of the OTS) to promulgate any rule.[3] Additionally, an independent agency, the National Credit Union Administration (NCUA), has authority over federal credit unions. State credit unions that lack federal credit union insurance are solely state regulated.

Other types of financial institutions are state-chartered, meaning that they have a corporate charter granted by a particular state. These institutions include state banks, state savings associations, and state credit unions. Nearly all state-chartered banks and savings associations have federal deposit insurance through the FDIC. Some of those insured banks and savings associations are also members of the Federal Reserve System. Those that are Federal Reserve member banks have the Federal Reserve Board as their primary prudential regulator, while insured, non-member banks have the FDIC as their primary prudential

2. Prior to the Dodd-Frank Act, another Treasury office, the Office of Thrift Supervision (the OTS, and before it, the Federal Home Loan Bank Board) had authority over federal savings associations. The OTS has since been folded into the OCC as part of the Dodd-Frank Act.

3. 12 U.S.C. §§ 1 (OCC), 1462a(b) (OTS).

regulator. There are virtually no uninsured state-chartered banks because lack of federal deposit insurance is such a major competitive disadvantage. State-chartered credit unions have NCUA share insurance, but there are many that do not. The primary regulator for those with share insurance is the NCUA, while uninsured state-chartered credit unions have a state regulator as their primary regulator.

Although the primary regulator for almost all state-chartered banks is a federal regulatory agency, state regulators still have secondary authority over state-chartered institutions. This includes visitorial authority, meaning that state regulators can show up in person and demand access to the banks' books, records, facilities, and employees for inspection.

Banking operations are often supported by subsidiary "bank service companies," by affiliated (but not subsidiary) service companies, and by third-party service companies and agents. Bank operating subsidiaries (which have state-issued corporate charters and are limited to engaging in functions in which national banks may themselves engage), financial subsidiaries (which are state-chartered and may engage in functions not authorized under the National Bank Act (NBA)), and independent bank and thrift service companies are subject to the same regulatory oversight as the parent institution or the institution they service.[4] Additionally, bank and thrift holding companies and financial holding companies are regulated by the Federal Reserve.[5] (Formerly, thrift holding companies were regulated by the OTS. 12 U.S.C. § 1467a (2006)). Other various non-banking affiliates of federal financial institutions may or may not fall under primary federal or state regulators, depending on their activities. Other lending institutions, like state-chartered finance companies (operating with a general corporate charter, rather than a banking charter), are not subject to federal banking regulations at all, except to the extent that they are bank service companies.

The role of states in regulating the banking industry has declined considerably in the past few decades. Non-insured, non-member banks make up only a small, unimportant corner in the consumer credit economy; consumer lending is now dominated by federally chartered institutions, especially national banks. For example, the ten largest credit card issuers, which account for around 90% of the card market in terms of total card debt outstanding, all have federal banking or thrift charters. Nilson Rep., Issue 895, at 10-11 (2008). The banks that conduct the overwhelming majority of consumer lending now have a federal agency as their primary regulator.

Table 7.1 summarizes the division of primary prudential regulatory authority.

4. *Watters v. Wachovia Bank, N.A.*, 550 U.S. 1, 6-8 (2007) (bank operating subsidiaries); 12 U.S.C. §§ 24(g)(3) (financial subsidiaries), 1867(a) (bank service companies), 1464(d)(7)(A) (thrift service companies).

5. 12 U.S.C. § 1844(b) (bank holding companies); 12 U.S.C. §§ 1841(p), 1843(l)(1), 1844(b) (2006) (financial holding companies).

Table 7.1 Division of Primary Prudential Regulatory Authority

Institution	Regulator
National bank	OCC
Federal savings association	OCC
State bank, member, insured	Federal Reserve Board
State bank, non-member, insured	FDIC
State bank, non-member, non-insured	State regulator
State savings association, member, insured	Federal Reserve Board
State savings association, non-member, insured	FDIC
State savings association, non-insured	State regulator
Federal credit union	NCUA
State credit union, insured	NCUA
State credit union, uninsured	State regulator
Operating subsidiary	Same as parent

B. Division of Bank Supervision Authority Between CFPB and Federal Prudential Regulators

Prior to the Dodd-Frank Act, consumer protection responsibility generally also fell on the relevant prudential regulator. Today, the CFPB has supervisory authority over only the largest depository institutions, namely federally insured banks, savings associations, and credit unions and their affiliates if the *depository* has total assets of over $10 billion ("**very large banks**"). 12 U.S.C. § 5515.[6]

The $10 billion threshold is not inflation adjusted, so the scope of CFPB authority will expand over time. As of the beginning of 2017, only 115 banks and thrifts and 6 credit unions, out of nearly 16,000 depositories nationwide, fell within the scope of CFPB supervisory authority. While the majority of depositories are not subject to CFPB supervision, it is worth noting that those that are subject to CFPB supervision hold 82% of the assets in the banking system.

Smaller financial institutions are subject to supervision only by their primary prudential regulator—the Office of Comptroller of the Currency, Federal Deposit Insurance Corporation, Federal Reserve Board, or National Credit Union

6. Unlike other $10 billion thresholds that are used elsewhere in federal financial regulation, *e.g.*, 15 U.S.C. § 1693o-2(a)(6)(A); 12 U.S.C. § 5365(h)-(i), this $10 billion is not calculated based on the depository's consolidated group, nor is it a net figure that accounts for liabilities. Instead, it is simply a question of whether the depository itself has $10 billion in assets. If so, then the depository and its affiliates that offer consumer financial products or services are subject to CFPB examination authority.

Administration. 12 U.S.C. § 5516. The CFPB can, however, obtain reports from them on a sampling basis, and the CFPB and prudential regulators can and do share information, generally under formal memoranda of understanding.

The CFPB also has supervisory authority over service providers to very large banks. 12 U.S.C. § 5515(d). Service providers to smaller banks are not subject to CFPB supervisory authority, unless they are a service provider to "a substantial number of smaller banks." 12 U.S.C. § 5516(e).

The division of supervision authority based on bank size is a politically driven decision. The United States had roughly 12,000 banks and credit unions as of the end of 2017, but the majority of assets in the banking system were held by a limited number of large institutions. Despite this disparity in economic size, small institutions tend, as a group, to have outsized political power due to their geographic dispersion and importance in local economies. The Dodd-Frank Act's choice to exempt smaller institutions from CFPB supervision appears to be a purely political choice, particularly as smaller institutions were not seen as being responsible for the 2008 financial crisis and thus in need of different supervision.

C. Supervision of Non-Banks

Prior to the creation of the CFPB, there was no federal supervisory system for non-bank covered persons. Instead, these non-bank entities were subject to state supervision, if any.

The CFPB has supervisory authority only over a subset of non-bank "covered persons," namely those covered persons who are:

- parties offering or providing residential mortgage loan origination, brokerage, or servicing;
- parties offering loan modification or foreclosure relief services;
- payday lenders;
- private student lenders;
- "larger participants" in a market for other consumer financial products or service;
- any party the CFPB has reasonable cause to determine is engaged in conduct that poses risks to consumers with regard to the offering or provision of consumer financial products or services.

12 U.S.C. § 5514(a)(1).

The CFPB has done five "larger participant" definition rulemakings to date: on debt collection, credit reporting, auto lending, student loan servicing, and international money transfers.

For debt collection, the CFPB defines "**larger participant**" as any entity that, with its affiliates, collects more than $10 million annually in receipts, 12 C.F.R. § 1090.105, while for consumer credit reporting, the threshold for being a larger participant is $7 million in annual receipts from consumer credit reporting activities. 12 C.F.R. § 1090.104. The debt collection rule, when enacted, covered 175 firms (only 4% of the total number of collection firms) that collectively have 64% of the annual receipts in the market. The credit reporting rule covered around 30 firms that had 94% of the annual receipts in the market. For auto lending, the CFPB has defined "larger participant" as any non-bank auto finance company that makes, acquires, or refinances 10,000 or more auto loans or leases annually. 12 C.F.R. § 1090.108. This covered roughly 34 firms, which accounted for around 90% of the non-bank auto loan and lease market.

Non-bank student loan servicers are larger participants if they and their affiliates serviced over 1 million accounts at the end of the previous year, with separate loans treated as separate accounts. 12 C.F.R. § 1090.106. The larger participant rule covers around seven non-bank student loan servicers. These include servicers of both federal student loans and private student loans. And non-bank international money transfer firms are treated as larger participants if they and their affiliates performed over 1 million transfers in the previous year. 12 C.F.R. § 1090.107. Roughly 25 non-bank money transfer firms are covered by the rule.

In addition, the CFPB has supervisory authority over service providers to non-banks that are subject to its supervisory authority. 12 U.S.C. § 5514(e).

All told, then, then CFPB has supervisory authority over a handful of very large financial institutions, as well as payday lenders, private student lenders, mortgage lenders and servicers, and certain large debt collectors, credit reporting agencies, and non-bank auto lenders.

Who's left out, then, from CFPB supervision? Smaller depositories, service providers that are not also covered persons, check cashers, pawn brokers, auto title lenders, credit counselors, money transmitters, payment processors, and consumer lessors, among others. Some of these entities, such as the smaller depositories, are supervised by other federal financial regulators, while other entities may be subject to state supervisory regimes.

D. Market Surveillance

The CFPB is specifically charged with monitoring consumer financial markets for risks posed to consumers in the offering or provision of financial services. Such monitoring is meant to support CFPB rulemaking, as well as enforcement. 12 U.S.C. § 5512(c). This is an important charge of active market surveillance, meaning that the CFPB is not merely supposed to be reactive to complaints brought to it or uncovered during its supervision process, but actively monitoring consumer finance markets as a whole beyond the scope of its supervision authority. The CFPB is required to publish a report at least annually about the findings from its monitoring. 12 U.S.C. § 5512(c)(4)(B)(ii).

The monitoring authority includes authority to collect data on "the organization, business conduct, markets, and activities of covered persons and service providers," including from examination reports (including from other regulators), consumer complaints, voluntary surveys and interviews, and commercial databases. 12 U.S.C. § 5512(c)(4). The CFPB can also compel covered persons and service provides to file reports on their activities, under oath if need be. Such reports can also be required to assess whether a non-depository is a covered person. 12 U.S.C.

§ 5512(c)(5). Additionally, the CFPB can prescribe registration requirements for non-depositories. 12 U.S.C. § 5512(c)(7). Exactly what such registration requirements could entail is unclear. Could the CFPB, for example, impose a registration requirement conditioned on a minimum net worth or on other terms? Could it impose a fee that it would collect?

Problem Set 7

1. You're the general counsel at Mastodon National Bank ($40 billion total assets). The CFPB just conducted an examination. At the conclusion of the examination, the head of the examination team told you that the CFPB "expects that Mastodon National Bank will cease offering depositors advances against their pension payments unless the interest rate on the advances is under 36% APR." The pension advance product has been quite profitable for your bank, and customers seem to appreciate it, even at its current pricing of 72% APR. Do you have to comply with the CFPB? 12 U.S.C. §§ 5515(b), 5517(o).

2. Which agency has supervisory authority over each of the following depository and affiliated entities?

- **a.** Continental Express Bank, N.A., a national bank with $110 billion in total assets that takes deposits, makes loans, and offers various payment services. 12 U.S.C. §§ 5481(5)-(6), 5481(15)(A)(i), 5481(15)(A)(iv)-(v), 5515(a)(1), (b).
- **b.** Metropolitan Bancorp, an FDIC-insured state-chartered non-member bank with $100 million in total assets that takes deposits, makes loans, and offers various payment services. 12 U.S.C. §§ 5481(5)-(6), 5481(15)(A)(i), 5481(15)(A)(iv)-(v), 5515(b), 5516.
- **c.** Somerset Moms' Credit Union, a Maryland-chartered credit union with $2 million in total assets and without federal insurance. Somerset Moms' takes deposits, makes loans, and offers various payment services. 12 U.S.C. §§ 5481(5)-(6), 5481(15)(A)(i), 5481(15)(A)(iv)-(v), 5515(b), 5516.
- **d.** ConEx Service Corp., a state-chartered corporate subsidiary of Continental Express Bank, N.A. from part (a). ConEx Service Corp. has total assets of $3 million. 12 U.S.C. § 5515(a)(1).
- **e.** CX Loan Service Corp., a state-chartered firm that provides document custody and lien release processing services for Continental Express Bank, N.A., from part (a). CX, which is not a corporate affiliate of Continental Express Bank, N.A., has total assets of $5 million. 12 U.S.C. §§ 5481(26), 5515(d).
- **f.** Peninsula Financial, a state-chartered firm that helps small community banks with less than $100 million in total assets design deposit account overdraft programs. 12 U.S.C. §§ 5481(26)(A)(i), 5516(e).

3. Which agency, if any, has supervisory authority over each of the following non-depositories?

- **a.** Old Northwest Loans, a non-bank mortgage lender and servicer with $25 billion in net assets. 12 U.S.C. §§ 5481(5)-(6), 5481(15)(A)(i), 5514(a)(1)(A).
- **b.** Sir-Lend-a-Lot, a payday lender with $1 million total assets. 12 U.S.C. §§ 5481(5)-(6), 5481(15)(A)(i), 5514(a)(1)(E).

c. FlyPaper LLC, a lead generation website that advertises payday loans and auctions the "leads" from interested consumers to payday lenders who then attempt to close the deal with the consumer. 12 U.S.C. §§ 5481(5)-(6), 5481(15)(A)(i), 5481(26)(A)(ii), 5514(e).
d. The Fast and the Usurious, Inc., a vehicle title lender that makes loans against vehicle titles, rather than purchase money loans for vehicles. 12 U.S.C. §§ 5481(5)-(6), 5481(15)(A)(i), 5514(a)(1).
e. MegaloMart, a large retailer that allows consumers to make purchases of appliances on store credit. 12 U.S.C. §§ 5481(5)-(6), 5481(15)(A)(i), 5514(a).
f. PayUp, a debt collection firm that collect debts on behalf of third parties. Last year PayUp collected over $25 million on behalf of its clients. 12 U.S.C. §§ 5481(5)-(6), 5481(15)(A)(x), 5514(a)(1)(B); 12 C.F.R. § 1090.105.
g. Valedictorian Finance LLC, a firm that makes and services student loans. 12 U.S.C. §§ 5481(5)-(6), 5481(15)(A)(i), 5514(B), 5514(D); 12 C.F.R. § 1090.106.

4. You've been tasked with designing the CFPB's examination procedures for private student lenders. What sort of information are you interested in obtaining as part of an examination and why?

CHAPTER 8

THE CFPB IV: ENFORCEMENT AND JURISDICTIONAL LIMITS

I. ENFORCEMENT

A. Scope of Enforcement Jurisdiction

The CFPB has its own enforcement power, meaning that it can bring either administrative proceedings before a CFPB administrative law judge or lawsuits in federal district courts.[1] The CFPB's enforcement authority is limited to bringing actions to enforce "**Federal consumer financial law**," 12 U.S.C. § 5564(a), and certain rules promulgated by the Federal Trade Commission under statutes not administered by the CFPB, most notably the Telemarketing Sales Rule.[2] "Federal consumer financial law" covers violations of the Consumer Financial Protection Act itself and rulemakings thereunder—UDAAP (unfair, deceptive, and abusive acts and practices),[3] disclosures, registration, and limitations of pre-dispute arbitration—as well as the enumerated consumer laws and rulemakings thereunder. 12 U.S.C. § 5481(14).

The CFPB's enforcement jurisdiction generally covers six categories of persons:

- Covered persons;
- Related persons of non-depository entities;
- Service providers;
- Parties subject to specific enumerated consumer laws;

1. Appeals from administrative proceedings are heard first by the CFPB Director and then by the Circuit Court of Appeals for the D.C. Circuit. The CFPB has its own litigation authority at all levels except for the Supreme Court, where it must receive permission to litigate from the Attorney General 12 U.S.C. § 5564(e).

2. 12 U.S.C. § 5583(i); 76 Fed. Reg. 31222 (May 31, 2011). The CFPB has enforcement authority for the FTC's regulations under the Telemarketing Sales Rule (16 C.F.R. Part 310); Rule for Use of Prenotification Negative Option Plans (16 C.F.R. Part 425); Rule Concerning Cooling-Off Period for Sales Made at Homes or at Certain Other Locations (16 C.F.R. Part 429); Rule for Preservation of Consumers' Claims and Defenses (16 C.F.R. Part 433); Credit Practices Rule (16 C.F.R. Part 444); Mail or Telephone Order Merchandise Rule (16 C.F.R. Part 435); Disclosure Requirements and Prohibitions Concerning Franchising (16 C.F.R. Part 436); Disclosure Requirements and Prohibitions Concerning Business Opportunities (16 C.F.R. Part 437).

3. Curiously, the statutory language of the Consumer Financial Protection Act does not require UDAAP violations to relate to consumer financial products, merely that the violator be a covered person or service provider. Thus, it would seem that the UDAAP violation could, in theory, be in an unrelated line of business. *Cf.* 12 U.S.C. §§ 5536(a)(1)(A), 5536(a)(1)(B). Even if this is a correct statutory reading, it is unlikely that the CFPB would ever interpret the statute to extend so far.

- Parties subject to certain specified FTC rules;
- Parties that provide "substantial assistance" to UDAAP violations.

The categories of covered persons and service providers are already familiar to you from the previous chapter regarding the scope of CFPB rulemaking jurisdiction. The parties subject to specific enumerated consumer laws or FTC rules are subject-matter specific and need not concern us here; many will overlap with covered persons and service providers. The novel category here are "related parties" and parties that provide "substantial assistance" to UDAAP violations.

B. Related Persons of Non-Depository Institutions

"Related persons" of non-depository institutions are deemed to be "covered persons" for the purposes of the Consumer Financial Protection Act, 12 U.S.C. § 5481(25)(b), and are therefore subject to CFPB enforcement (and rulemakings). Such related persons of non-depository institutions include officers, directors, and managerial employees.

Related person liability means that limited liability through corporate form is not a defense against CFPB actions. Owners, directors, and officers are themselves *personally* liable for violations of federal consumer financial law (both UDAAP and the enumerated consumer laws) if they are involved in a violation. Related person liability vastly increases the CFPB's enforcement power, as it creates liability for actual people, not just corporate entities.

The category of "related persons" also includes "any independent contractor (including any attorney, appraiser, or accountant) who knowingly or recklessly participates" in a violation of a law or breach of fiduciary duty. 12 U.S.C. § 5481(25)(c). Such independent contractors are subject to a scienter requirement that does not exist for other related persons, who have a strict liability standard.

Thus, an attorney for a bank, whether in-house or outside counsel, could not be a related person because related person excludes persons connected with depositories. Accordingly, the bank's attorney could not be a covered person. An in-house attorney for a non-bank payment processor, however, might well be an "officer" of a covered person, and therefore a "related person" and thus herself a covered person. An outside counsel to a non-bank payment processor would have to knowingly or recklessly participate in a legal violation in order to be a related person and thus a covered person.

C. Substantial Assistance

The CFPB's enforcement authority extends to violations of "Federal consumer financial law," which includes the Consumer Financial Protection Act, which in turn includes a provision making it unlawful for "any person to knowingly or recklessly provide substantial assistance to a covered person or service provider" in a UDAAP violation. 12 U.S.C. § 5536(a)(3). Substantial assistance liability is essentially a flavor of aiding and abetting liability.

Two distinct types of defendants potentially face substantial assistance liability. First there are insiders—owners and managers. Many of them may also qualify as "related persons," but recall that "related person" status does not apply to depository institutions. A person might not be a related person because the covered person is a depository, but might still have substantial assistance liability. Second, there are counterparties to covered persons that might not qualify as service providers, but that might still provide substantial assistance in a UDAAP violation. Substantial assistance not only overrides jurisdictional limitation on related persons and service providers, but it also enables the CFPB to expand its jurisdiction to industries not otherwise within its regulatory bailiwick, as shown in the *ACICS* case below.

There are two important limitations on substantial assistance claims. First, substantial assistance claims require a predicate UDAAP violation by a covered person or service provider; they cannot be brought based on violations of the enumerated consumer laws. This limitation is less constraining than it might seem, however. Some acts or practices that violate an enumerated consumer law can also be cast as UDAAP violations.

Second, as with independent contractor "related persons," there is a scienter requirement, namely that the assistance be provided "knowingly or recklessly." The CFPB has argued that this requirement is satisfied by turning a willing blind eye to red flags of fraud, but it remains uncertain whether one can be reckless absent a duty to investigate.

In Chapter 6 you read part of the order denying the motion to dismiss in *CFPB v. Universal Debt & Payment Solutions, LLC*. That part of the order dealt with the CFPB's claim that the payment processors that handled the payments in a fraudulent debt collection scheme were "service providers" and thus committed UDAAP violations. The CFPB also alleged on the same facts that the payment processors provided "substantial assistance" to the other parties in the debt collection scheme, liability that does not depend on the payment processors being "service providers." This part of the order is reproduced below.

Order Denying Motion to Dismiss CFPB v. Universal Debt & Payment Solutions, LLC

No. 1:15-CV-00859-RWS (N.D. Ga. Sept. 1, 2015)

STORY, J.

This case comes before the Court on Defendant Pathfinder Payment Solutions, Inc.'s Motion to Dismiss, Defendant Global Payments, Inc.'s Motion to Dismiss, and Defendant Frontline Processing Corp.'s Motion to Dismiss. . . .

BACKGROUND

. . .

I. The Debt-Collection Scheme

The Debt Collectors made millions of collection calls to consumers in attempts to collect debts the Debt Collectors were not in fact owed. The Debt Collectors threatened litigation and told consumers they needed to settle the debt to avoid a restraining order or criminal prosecution. When asked for information about the purported debts, the Debt Collectors refused to identify the lenders but, by reciting the consumers' personal information, including Social Security number, date of birth, and place of employment, convinced consumers the debts were legitimate and were owed to them. The Debt Collectors purchased that identifying information from debt and data brokers. When consumers provided their payment information, the Debt Collectors used payment processors to withdraw funds from the consumers' accounts.

Defendant Global Payments, Inc. ("Global Payments" or "Global") is a payment processor that processed transactions for the Debt Collectors. Payment processors "enable merchants to accept check, card, and electronic payments at a point of sale." During a transaction, the card information is captured by a point-of-sale terminal card reader and transmitted to a payment network. (Payment processors are sponsored by an acquiring bank that is registered with one or more card associations, such as Visa or MasterCard. They are also subject to the rules and credit risk policies of the card associations.)

Two other companies, Defendants Pathfinder Payment Solutions, Inc. ("Pathfinder") and Frontline Processing Corp. ("Frontline") are independent sales organizations ("ISOs") that entered into merchant services agreements with a Global Payments subsidiary to market Global Payments' processing services to merchants. Pathfinder also agreed to review potential merchants' creditworthiness, to underwrite the merchants, to monitor processing activity to detect fraud and risk, and to advise Global Payments accordingly. Frontline agreed to prescreen merchants for compliance with Global Payments' credit criteria.

The CFPB accuses Global Payments, Pathfinder, and Frontline (collectively, "Payment Processors") of providing substantial assistance to the Debt Collectors' unfair or deceptive conduct (Count VIII). . . . The CFPB asserts that the Payment Processors "enabled [the Debt Collectors] to efficiently accept payments and convince consumers that they were credible merchants." Moreover, these Defendants were required to follow policies and procedures to evaluate merchant creditworthiness and identify fraud. This is because payment processors face credit exposure given that merchants are paid quickly, while consumers' payments are provisional and may be reversed if a consumer disputes a charge, resulting in a "chargeback." If a merchant is unwilling or unable to fund the reversed transaction, the payment processor is responsible for the chargeback.

Global Payments' credit policy, like the card networks' policies, identifies collection agencies as "prohibited merchants" that the ISOs were not to solicit and which required Global Payments' approval. Global Payments also prohibited "Aggregators," which are merchants who use their processing account to process payments for other merchants—a practice called "factoring." Defendants considered collection agencies to be high-risk merchants because they processed only "card-not-present" transactions. Thus, Global Payments' policies required more scrutiny of card-not-present merchants. The CFPB alleges, however, that Global Payments, Pathfinder, and Frontline all failed to monitor the Debt Collectors' accounts for signs of unlawful conduct and thus "knowingly or recklessly provided substantial assistance" to the Debt Collectors' scheme. 12 U.S.C. § 5536(a)(3). . . .

Global Payments and the ISOs move for dismissal of both claims against them pursuant to Federal Rule of Civil Procedure 12(b)(6), asserting that the Complaint fails to state a claim upon which relief can be granted.

. . .

B. Substantial Assistance

The Payment Processors contend that even if they acted knowingly or recklessly, they still did not provide substantial assistance under the allegations in the Complaint. The CFPB alleges the Payment Processors provided substantial assistance "by enabling them to accept payment by credit and debit card, legitimizing the Debt Collectors' business, making transactions easy for consumers and the Debt Collectors, enabling the Debt Collectors to accept payment from consumers with insufficient cash, and facilitating the Debt Collectors' efficient collection of consumers' funds."

Global Payments argues that it merely provided payment processing services to the Debt Collectors and that there are no allegations plausibly showing that there is a substantial causal connection between Global's conduct and harm to consumers. Pathfinder too asserts it cannot be held liable for substantial assistance because it provided services to the Debt Collectors in the routine course of business just like any other business would. Frontline insists that it only had a limited screening function before forwarding potential merchant applications to Global, that it did not have the responsibility to monitor for risk, and that in any event Global had already been processing transactions for UDPS and Credit Power for over a year before Frontline submitted their applications.

[The court rejected the argument that proximate cause is required for a substantial assistance claim, and adopted the standard that the CFPB must plead that the defendant "in some sort associated himself with the venture, that the defendant participated in it as in something that he wished to bring about, and that he sought by his action to make it succeed." *SEC v. Apuzzo*, 689 F.3d 204, 212 (2d Cir. 2012). The court also noted that a greater degree of scienter reduces the burden in showing substantial assistance and vice versa.]

1. Global Payments

Global emphasizes its limited and routine role as a payment processor: "Global simply provided a technology platform to process payments," and the processing of payments was simply "'the daily grist of the mill' for payment processors like Global."

Considering Global's conduct within the framework of the language in *Apuzzo*, the Court finds that the CFPB has adequately alleged that Global did in some sort associate itself with the venture, participate in it as something it wished to bring about, and seek to make it succeed by approving the Debt Collectors' applications and processing payments. While payment processing is in many ways routine, the processing of consumer bank cards was far from an incidental part of the Debt Collectors' scheme. The entire purpose of the abusive phone calls was to bully and harass consumers into turning over their bank card information, a scheme made possible only by the approval of a payment processing account that enabled the Debt Collectors to process card-not-present transactions.

Global cites *Woods v. Barnett Bank of Ft. Lauderdale*, which stated that "knowing assistance can be inferred from atypical business actions." 765 F.2d at 1012. According to Global, nothing about processing payments is atypical. But *Woods* further explained that a common practice for a bank, such as writing a reference for one of its customers, "can hardly be regarded as 'the daily grist of the mill'" in the context of a securities fraud case when the letter "contain[s] statements of which the writer has no knowledge, [and is issued] without even minimal investigation to determine whether its contents are accurate, solely for the purpose of 'currying favor' with a good client." *Id. Woods* therefore suggests that common business practices could nevertheless substantially assist unlawful conduct if there are "atypical" factors involved in the common practice. Here, the CFPB alleges the warning signs of fraud—like high rates of chargebacks containing alarming consumer narratives, along with MATCH alerts and deficient applications—demonstrate that Global's payment processing was not merely the typical grist of the mill.[8]

Global Payments expresses its concern that holding it liable would "impose on Global a strict liability standard for every transaction it processes" and consequently upend the entire payments industry. The Court notes that the elements of substantial assistance "cannot be considered in isolation from one another." *Apuzzo*, 689 F.3d at 214. So, innocuous business practices in one context could amount to substantial assistance to unfair, deceptive, and abusive practices in another, as long as the aider or abettor knows of or is reckless to the risk of the primary violation. Taking the extensive allegations of warning signs that the Debt Collectors were defrauding consumers along with Global Payments' own credit policy requiring that it approve collection agencies (and thus more closely scrutinize them), at this stage the Court finds that the CFPB alleges facts that plausibly support a finding that Global Payments knowingly or recklessly provided substantial assistance to the Debt Collectors.

2. Pathfinder

Pathfinder similarly argues that it cannot be liable for substantial assistance based on such routine business practices. It analogizes its services to those any business needs to operate, like cleaning services, business checking accounts, mail services, and internet access. For many of the same reasons stated above, the Court rejects Pathfinder's argument. Pathfinder's alleged assistance was substantial in this context because UDPS and Credit Power had to apply to ISOs like Pathfinder to obtain an account with Global Payments. Once approved, Pathfinder was responsible for risk monitoring and received numerous warning signs of suspicious debt-collection practices, including

8. Another case Global Payments cites, *Perfect 10, Inc. v. Visa Int'l Serv. Ass'n*, 494 F.3d 788, 796 (9th Cir. 2007), found that "credit card companies cannot be said to materially contribute to [copyright] infringement . . . because they have no direct connection to that infringement." That case is distinguishable from this one because the court went on to observe that in contrast to websites like Amazon.com and services like Napster or Grokster, "the services provided by the credit card companies do not help locate and are not used to distribute the infringing images." *Id.* By contrast, Global Payments *did* help the Debt Collectors obtain money they were not owed by processing consumer's bank card numbers.

high chargeback rates, Visa and Discover's termination of the Debt Collectors, and the like. But Pathfinder did not take action to investigate that activity, thus allowing the Debt Collectors to continue their scheme. Even though Pathfinder itself did not process payments, it approved deficient applications of high-risk merchants and subsequently failed to act in the face of obvious warning signs of a debt-collection scheme. For that reason, it is plausible that Pathfinder associated itself with the venture, participated in it as something it wished to bring about, and sought by its action to make it succeed.

3. Frontline

For its part, Frontline says it "only received, prescreened, and forwarded potential merchant applications to Global for Global's acceptance or rejection. Frontline clearly maintains no authority over the approval of a merchant for processing." Moreover, these activities cannot amount to substantial assistance because Global had been processing transactions for the Debt Collectors for more than a year by the time Frontline processed the applications. And in any event, Frontline states that any substantial assistance it provided was to Global, not the Debt Collectors.

Based on the allegations in the Complaint, however, it is plausible that Frontline provided substantial assistance to the Debt Collectors. While Frontline may not have had final authority to approve merchants for payment processing accounts, Global contracted with Frontline to serve as an ISO, and Frontline had the responsibility of underwriting merchants—certainly a crucial step for the Debt Collectors in ultimately securing payment processing accounts. Moreover, even if Frontline's contract was with Global Payments, its approval of merchant applications benefitted merchants because it enabled them to process bank card transactions. In addition, as for Frontline's argument that Global was already processing the Debt Collectors' transactions when they applied to Frontline, the Complaint nonetheless alleges Frontline screened the applications and consequently had the opportunity to recognize and investigate signs the Debt Collectors were illegitimate. By approving the Debt Collectors' applications and failing to investigate obvious red flags, Frontline did in some way associate itself with the scheme and help to make it succeed. Consequently, at this stage the CFPB plausibly alleges substantial assistance against Frontline.

D. Limitation on Enforcement Against Smaller Depositories

There is an important limitation on CFPB enforcement jurisdiction. The CFPB is prohibited from bringing enforcement actions against smaller (<$10 billion total assets) depositories. 12 U.S.C. § 5516(d). Instead, enforcement in such cases is the province of the appropriate prudential regulator—the Office of Comptroller of the Currency, Federal Deposit Insurance Corporation, Federal Reserve Board, or National Credit Union Administration.

For large banks, the Bureau has primary but non-exclusive enforcement authority along with prudential regulators, 12 U.S.C. § 5515(c), while for non-depositories, the CFPB shares enforcement authority with the FTC according to a memorandum of understanding. 12 U.S.C. § 5514(c)(3). Thus, while the CFPB makes rules that apply to all depositories, it has enforcement authority over only a subset of large depositories. As of the third quarter of 2017, CFPB enforcement authority over depositories extended to 119 banks and thrifts and 6 credit unions. Another 32 affiliates of these depositories and credit unions are subject to CFPB supervision and enforcement.

Recall that the CFPB's statutorily defined mission includes enforcing "Federal consumer financial law consistently" and "ensuring that . . . federal consumer financial law is enforced consistently, without regard to the status of a person as a depository institution." 12 U.S.C. § 5511(a), 5511(b)(4). Is it possible for the CFPB to ensure consistent enforcement when it has enforcement authority over only a subset of the financial services industry? If the OCC or Federal Reserve Board were to take a different interpretation of the law than the CFPB, say, a different interpretation of the scienter requirement for substantial assistance, would there be consistent enforcement?

E. Shared Enforcement Power with State Attorneys General

While the Consumer Financial Protection Act created a powerful new federal consumer financial regulator, it also took care to preserve a significant state role in consumer financial protection. The preservation of the states' role in consumer financial protection was a conscious step to protect against the possibility of the federal agency becoming "captured" by consumer financial industry interests.[4]

Critically, state attorneys general retain broad enforcement authority under both state and federal law, albeit with certain limitations. The Consumer Financial Protection Act provides that state attorneys general have the authority to enforce the Act and regulations issued thereunder. 12 U.S.C. § 5552. The effect of this provision is that the Consumer Financial Protection Act not only preserves existing state enforcement authority, but actually expands it.

State attorneys general and state regulators may bring actions under their own state laws (if not preempted, as discussed in Chapter 9) against any type of financial institution. 12 U.S.C. § 5552(d)(1). For state-chartered covered persons, they may also bring actions under the Consumer Financial Protection Act or under CFPB regulations promulgated under the Consumer Financial Protection Act.[5] Because the enumerated consumer laws are incorporated into the Consumer Financial Protection Act—violations of an enumerated consumer law are violations of 12 U.S.C. § 5536(a)(1)(A)—this provision not only lets the states enforce the organic provisions of the Consumer

4. The Consumer Financial Protection Act provides that the CFPA is not to be construed as affecting state law except where there is an inconsistency, with greater state protections for consumers not being considered inconsistencies. 12 U.S.C. § 5551. In other words, the Act is not meant to displace state law. The CFPA also creates a mechanism by which a majority of states can petition the CFPB to undertake a rulemaking. While it is unclear whether this device will ever be used, it deliberately creates a "shaming" mechanism to force CFPB action in the event that the agency ever adopts an anti-regulatory stance.

5. In some cases this may be an expansion of the litigation authority of state attorneys general or bank regulators, as sometimes only one or the other has enforcement authority; the CFP Act arguably grants state actors authority that they may not have under state law.

Financial Protection Act, such as the UDAAP provision, but also all of the enumerated consumer laws and regulations thereunder.

For national banks and federal savings associations, however, states may only bring suits to enforce rules promulgated by the CFPB under the Consumer Financial Protection Act, not the provisions of the Act itself. Before doing so, however, the state must give the CFPB and the OCC notice, after which the CFPB may intervene in the matter, including on appeal. *See* 12 U.S.C. § 5552(a)(3).[6]

It might seem odd at first blush that the states could enforce CFPB rulemakings, but not the enabling statute itself or the enumerated consumer laws themselves against national banks and federal savings associations. This arrangement seems designed particularly with the Consumer Financial Protection Act's Unfair, Deceptive, and Abusive Acts and Practices (UDAAP) provision in mind. The states may not bring suits against national banks or federal savings associations under the federal UDAAP statute itself. That is to say, the states cannot decide what is an unfair or deceptive or abusive act or practice *under federal law* as applied to a national bank or federal thrift. They can only bring UDAAP suits against federally chartered banks and thrifts if the CFPB has undertaken a UDAAP rulemaking and the federally chartered bank or thrift has violated the rule. Thus, states are constrained in their ability to use UDAAP against federal banks and thrifts.

The negative implication from this provision is that states are free to bring suits under the federal UDAAP *statute* as well as under CFPB regulations against all state-chartered entities and federal credit unions. *See also* 12 U.S.C. § 5552(a)(1). In other words, state attorneys general have been deputized to enforce a very potent federal statute. State attorneys general need not go through their own notice-and-comment rulemaking processes to bring enforcement actions under the federal UDAAP statute. Instead, their actions will be judged against the statute itself—if cases actually go to trial. Given how common settlements are, the ability to use the federal UDAAP statute appears to have given state attorneys general a powerful litigation tool.

The result is that states' UDAP (one "A") powers are vastly expanded. Whatever limitations exist on state UDAP statutes—having only the ability to prosecute "deceptive" acts, not "unfair" ones, statutes of limitations, damages caps, etc.—would not seem to apply to a state moving under the federal UDAAP statute. At the same time, states would not be subject to federal pleading standards, even if they proceeded under UDAAP. Thus, the Consumer Financial Protection Act has given states an extremely powerful new enforcement tool when dealing with consumer financial product providers other than national banks and federal savings associations. Several states have already eagerly used the federal UDAAP power in consumer financial enforcement matters, and the jurisdictional limits on CFPB UDAAP enforcement under 12 U.S.C. §§ 5517 (retailers, purchase money lenders,

---

6. Curiously, the status of federal credit unions is unaddressed. States are not specifically prohibited from bringing suit under the Consumer Financial Protection Act or regulations thereunder against federal credit unions.

practice of law, etc.) and 5519 (auto dealers) do not by their own terms apply to state attorneys general.

There is a flip side to this dual enforcement authority to consider—a covered person or service provider or material assister that settles with the CFPB may still have freestanding, independent liability to one or more state attorneys general and vice versa. While this should prevent the CFPB from entering into lowball settlements, it also means that defendants may in fact *want* states to file suit so as to incorporate them into global settlements.

F. Administrative or Judicial Adjudication

If the CFPB believes that a party is violating federal consumer financial law, the agency may proceed in one of two ways: it may commence litigation in a federal district court, 12 U.S.C. §§ 5564(a), 5564(f), or it may conduct an administrative adjudication before an administrative law judge under the Administrative Procedure Act, 12 U.S.C. § 5563 (applying 5 U.S.C. §§ 554 and 556). Any orders from an administrative hearing must be taken to a federal district court for enforcement. 12 U.S.C § 5563(d). Appeals of an administrative law judge's rulings are heard by the CFPB Director, 5 U.S.C. § 556(b), and appeals from the Director's rulings go to either the Circuit Court of Appeals for the District of Columbia or the court of appeals in which the appellant's principal office is located. 12 U.S.C. § 5563(b)(4).

G. Relief Available

The relief that the CFPB can obtain in an enforcement action is wide-ranging. It includes rescission or reformation of contracts; refunds or returns of money or real property; restitution; disgorgement or compensation for unjust enrichment; payment of damages; civil monetary penalties; and injunctive relief. 12 U.S.C. § 5565(a)(2). Civil monetary penalties are limited by statute, 12 U.S.C. § 5565(c), and complement any relief available under the enumerated consumer laws. A simple violation has civil monetary penalties of a maximum of $5,000/day, but if the violation is reckless, then penalties increase to a maximum of $25,000/day, and for knowing violations, the penalties rise to $1 million/day per violation. The penalties are not inflation-adjusted. 12 U.S.C. § 5565(c).

These civil monetary policies give the CFPB tremendous leverage when litigating enforcement actions. Every transaction with each consumer that violates a statute is a separate violation, so even if the civil monetary penalties are below the statutory caps, the CFPB still has the ability to credibly threaten to bankrupt firms that choose to litigate and lose. This creates a strong incentive for firms to settle with the CFPB.

In the aid of enforcement actions, the CFPB has substantial authority to undertake investigations, including issuing subpoenas and civil investigative demands. 12 U.S.C. § 5562(b)-(c). These subpoenas and civil investigative demands need not be limited to "covered persons" or "service providers" or even persons who are providing "substantial assistance." Instead, they cover "any person" whom the CFPB has reason to believe "may be in possession, custody, or control of any documentary material or tangible things, or may have any information, relevant to a violation."

The CFPB can compel document production, answers to interrogatories, and testimony through a civil investigative demand. 12 U.S.C. § 5562(c). Thus, even though a person or firm may not itself have liability to the CFPB, it can still be compelled to produce documents or testimony in response to a request from the CFPB. The following case considers how far this authority reaches.

CFPB v. Accrediting Council for Independent Colleges & Schools

2016 U.S. Dist. LEXIS 53644 (D.D.C. April 21, 2016)

Richard J. LEON, J.

On October 29, 2015, the Consumer Financial Protection Bureau ("CFPB" or "petitioner") filed a petition in this Court, seeking an order requiring the Accrediting Council for Independent Colleges and Schools ("ACICS" or "respondent") to comply with a Civil Investigative Demand the CFPB issued to it on August 25, 2015. Because the CFPB did not have authority to issue this Civil Investigative Demand, the petitioner's request is DENIED and this case is DISMISSED.

BACKGROUND

On August 25, 2015, the CFPB issued to ACICS, an accreditor of for-profit colleges, a Civil Investigative Demand ("CID") with the stated purpose of "determin[ing] whether any entity or person has engaged or is engaging in unlawful acts and practices in connection with accrediting for-profit colleges." The CID required ACICS to designate a company representative to appear and give oral testimony regarding ACICS's policies, procedures, and practices relating to the accreditation of seven particular schools, and to respond to two interrogatories: (1) to identify all post-secondary educational institutions that ACICS has accredited since January 2010 and (2) to identify all individuals affiliated with ACICS who conducted any accreditation reviews since January 1, 2010 specific to twenty-one particular schools. According to the CFPB, this CID was issued following a CFPB investigation of "for-profit colleges for deceptive practices tied to their private student-lending activities."

. . . To date ACICS has not complied with the CID and opposes the CFPB's petition on the ground that it "concerns an investigation that is well outside the scope of the agency's authority." For the following reasons, I agree.

LEGAL STANDARD

In determining whether to enforce a CID, a court must consider (1) whether the agency has the authority to make the inquiry, (2) whether the information sought is reasonably relevant, and (3) whether the demand is not too indefinite. *See United States v, Morton Salt Co.*, 338 U.S. 632, 652 (1950); *FTC v. Texaco, Inc.*, 555 F.2d 862, 872 (D.C. Cir. 1977); *CFTC v. Ekasala*, 62 F. Supp. 3d 88, 93 (D.D.C. 2014). If these three requirements are met, a court should enforce the petition unless it is unduly burdensome. *See, e.g., Texaco*, 555 F.2d at 882. Although a court's role at this stage is "neither minor nor ministerial" it is "a strictly limited one," designed to further the "important governmental interest in the expeditious investigation of possible unlawful activity." *Id.*

at 871-72. In short, the Court is not "to determine whether the [targeted entity's] activities [are] covered by the statute," but rather whether the information sought is relevant to an investigation for "a lawfully authorized purpose." *Id.* at 872 (discussing *Endicott Johnson v. Perkins*, 317 U.S. 501 (1943)). Moreover, agencies are generally accorded broad deference both their interpretation of the scope of their authority and their estimation of the relevance of requested records. *See FTC v. Ken Roberts Co.*, 276 F.3d 583, 586-87 (D.C. Cir. 2001) ("[W]e have held that enforcement of an agency's investigatory subpoena will be denied only when there is 'a patent lack of jurisdiction' in an agency to regulate or to investigate."); *Dir., Office of Thrift Supervision v. Vinson & Elkins, LLP*, 124 F.3d 1304, 1307 (D.C. Cir. 1997) ("We give the agency a wide berth as to relevance because it need establish only that the information is relevant to its investigation not to a hypothetical adjudication, and as we have explained, the boundary of an investigation need only, indeed can only, be defined in general terms."). Nevertheless, where it is clear that an agency either lacks the authority to investigate or is seeking information irrelevant to a lawful investigatory purpose, a court must set such inquiry aside. *See Morton Salt*, 338 U.S. at 652 ("[A] governmental investigation . . . may be of such a sweeping nature and so unrelated to the matter properly under inquiry as to exceed the investigatory power.").

ANALYSIS

In the final analysis this case boils down to the answer to one question: Did the CFPB have the statutory authority to issue the CID in question? Unfortunately for the CFPB, the answer is no. How so?

The CFPB was established on July 21, 2010 by Title X of the Dodd-Frank Wall Street Reform and Consumer Protection Act, which tasked the CFPB with "regulat[ing] the offering and provision of consumer financial products or services under the Federal consumer financial laws." 12 U.S.C. § 5491(a). As such, the CFPB is authorized, *inter alia*, to take action "to prevent a covered person or service provider from committing or engaging in an unfair, deceptive, or abusive act or practice under Federal law in connection with any transaction with a consumer for a consumer financial product or service, or the offering of a consumer financial product or service." *Id.* § 5531(a). To facilitate this purpose, the CFPB may issue CIDs to "any person [believed to] be in possession, custody, or control of any documentary material or tangible things, or may have any information, relevant to a violation" of the federal consumer financial laws. *Id.* § 5562(c)(1). These CIDs must "state the nature of the conduct constituting the alleged violation which is under investigation and the provision of law applicable to such violation." *Id.* § 5562(c)(2).

Purportedly acting pursuant to this authority, the CFPB issued a CID to ACICS, which contained the following statement of purpose:

> The purpose of this investigation is to determine whether any entity or person has engaged or is engaging in unlawful acts and practices *in connection with accrediting for-profit colleges*, in violation of sections 1031 and 1036 of the Consumer Financial Protection Act of 2010, 12 U.S.C. §§ 5531, 5536, or any other Federal consumer financial protection law. The purpose of this investigation is also to determine whether Bureau action to obtain legal or equitable relief would be in the public interest.

ACICS argues that this language demonstrates the CFPB is attempting to conduct an investigation outside its statutory authority—that is, an investigation into the accreditation process of for-profit schools.[2] As previously discussed, the CFPB investigative authority is limited to inquiries to determine whether there has been a violation of any consumer financial laws. *See* 12 U.S.C. §§ 5561(1), (5). As respondent points out, and the CFPB does not deny, none of these laws address, regulate, or even tangentially implicate the accrediting process of for-profit colleges. Thus, at first blush, the CID's statement of purpose appears to concern a subject matter that is *not* within the statutory jurisdiction of the CFPB. *See Ken Roberts*, 276 F.3d at 586-87 (finding that a court asked to enforce a CID must ensure that "the subject matter of the investigation is within the statutory jurisdiction of the subpoena-issuing agency" (internal quotation marks omitted)).

Realizing the absence of a clear nexus between the consumer financial laws it is tasked with enforcing and its purported investigation into accreditation of for-profit schools, the CFPB argues that because it indisputably "has authority to investigate for-profit schools in relation to their lending and financial-advisory services," it also has authority to investigate whether any entity has engaged in any unlawful acts relating to the accreditation of those schools. Put simply, this post-hoc justification is a bridge too far! As ACICS has repeatedly and accurately explained, the accreditation process simply has no connection to a school's private student lending practices. Moreover, ACICS is *not* involved in the financial aid decisions of the schools it accredits, which means that it plays no part in deciding whether to make or fund a student loan.

The CFPB objects that it "is not obligated to accept at face value ACICS's generalized description of its interaction with the schools it accredits, or what aspects of those schools' activities it 'touches,'" but rather it has the right to investigate and determine for itself whether these assertions are true.[3] Please. Although it may be that the CFPB is entitled to learn whether ACICS is connected in any way to potential violations of the consumer financial laws by the schools it accredits, the statement of purpose and the CFPB's actual requests belie any notion that its inquiry is limited in this way. Indeed, the statement of purpose says nothing about an investigation into the lending or financial-advisory practices of for-profit schools. Moreover, the CFPB's requests—for a list of *all schools* ACICS has accredited since 2010, for a list of *all individuals involved in the*

---

2. ACICS also spends much of its opposition discussing why it is not subject to the Consumer Financial Protection Act. Heeding our Circuit Court's instructions, however, I must agree with petitioner that this preliminary stage it is not the appropriate forum to adjudicate whether ACICS's activities are covered by any consumer financial law. *See Texaco*, 555 F.2d at 872 (cautioning courts considering petitions to enforce administrate subpoenas that they are not consider the ultimate question of "whether the [targeted entity's] activities [are] covered by the statute" at this preliminary stage). I have no doubt that if the CFPB pursues a case against ACICS in the future these significant threshold questions will be at the center of the litigation.

3. Indeed, in its Notice of Supplemental Filing the CFPB argues that ACICS's Accreditation Criteria suggest the opposite, noting provisions that seemingly require ACICS to ensure that "[a]ll institutionally financed loans [be] collected in accordance with sound and aggressive business practices for the collection of student loans" and that schools "avoid false, misleading, or exaggerated statements" about institutional loans offered. ACICS, however, reaffirmed that it "does not evaluate debt collection, and its activities are not connected to the provision of a financial service or product," and explained that while it confirms that the schools it accredits have policies in place to meet certain standards, it does not evaluate the content of those policies.

accreditation of twenty-one enumerated schools, and for representatives to attest to the *overall approach* to accrediting seven enumerated schools—clearly reveal its investigation targets the accreditation process generally. This the CFPB was never empowered to do. *See Morton Salt,* 338 U.S. at 652. And the fact that the CFPB is also investigating for-profit schools for suspected violations of the consumer financial laws in connection with their lending and financial-advisory services does nothing to change this.[4]

CONCLUSION

Although it is understandable that new agencies like the CFPB will struggle to establish the exact parameters of their authority, they must be especially prudent before choosing to plow head long into fields not clearly ceded to them by Congress. *See Texaco,* 555 F.2d at 874. Thus, having concluded that the CFPB lacks authority to investigate the process for accrediting for-profit schools, I am compelled to DENY its Petition to Enforce Civil Investigative Demand.

Note on *CFPB v. ACICS*

Judge Leon's refusal to enforce the CID against ACICS was affirmed by the D.C. Circuit on the narrow ground that the CFPB had failed to comply with the requirements of 12 U.S.C. § 5562(c)(2) because it did not "state the nature of the conduct constituting the alleged violation which is under investigation and the provision of law applicable to such violation" with sufficient specificity *CFPB v. ACICS,* 854 F.3d 683 (D.C. Cir. 2017). The D.C. Circuit expressed no opinion on whether the CFPB could enforce a proper CID against ACICS. While the CFPB was denied the Civil Investigative Demand, the Department of Education stripped ACICS of its recognition as an accrediting agency. Decision of the Sec., *In re* Accrediting Council for Indep. Colleges & Schools, Dept. of Ed. No. 16-44-O, Dec. 12, 2016.

H. Enforcement *Qua* Rulemaking

The CFPB has been frequently accused of using enforcement in lieu of rulemaking. Notice-and-comment rulemaking is an arduous process and subject to litigation challenges. In contrast, enforcement actions can be brought more quickly, and given the potential relief the CFPB can obtain, frequently result in settlements in the form of consent orders. These settlements must be approved by federal courts,

4. Even if the CFPB had put forward an investigatory purpose within the scope of its authority, for example, the lending practices of for-profit schools, the requested information may, nevertheless, be beyond reach as not reasonably relevant to that purpose. *See Texaco,* 555 F.2d at 874 ("[T]he relevance of the agency's subpoena requests may be measured only against the general purposes of the investigation."). As ACICS has aptly explained, the accreditation process does not touch the schools' lending or financial-advisory practices.

but the consent orders receive less exacting judicial review and are not subject to a true adversarial proceeding. By targeting firms within an industry for enforcement actions, the CFPB is able to effectively set standards for that industry without engaging in rulemaking, as firms in the industry will react to the consent order by adjusting their practices so as to avoid being the subject of enforcement actions themselves. Moreover, CFPB examiners' understanding of permissible practices is likely to reflect the standards set through consent orders, creating a self-reinforcing feedback loop. It is important to emphasize that the issue with rulemaking through enforcement is a policy issue, rather than a legal issue. Enforcement actions do not formally affect non-parties' rights, so there is no formal prejudicial effect and thus no due process issue, even if, practically, past enforcement actions shape expectations of both industry and the CFPB.

II. GENERAL EXCLUSIONS FROM CFPB AUTHORITY

Certain entities are entirely excluded from CFPB authority rulemaking, supervision, and enforcement. The exclusions, however, are not absolute, and the section of the Consumer Financial Protection Act detailing them is among the Act's most complicated.

A. Non-Financial Goods or Service Providers

The major exclusion is for "merchants, retailers, and other sellers of non-financial goods or services." 12 U.S.C. § 5517(a). The CFPB is prohibited from regulating anyone selling or brokering non-financial goods or services, "except to the extent that such person is engaged in offering or providing any consumer financial product or service, or is otherwise subject to any enumerated consumer law." 12 U.S.C. § 5517(a)(1). In other words, if a retailer, such as a convenience store, also offers remittance services, the CFPB can regulate the financing, but not the retailer's sales practices.

This prohibition is essentially a restatement of the positive limitations on the CFPB's authority. The CFPB's rulemaking authority is limited to "covered persons," 12 U.S.C. § 5481(6), namely those who offer or provide "consumer financial products or services," 12 U.S.C. § 5481(5), and rulemaking authority under the enumerated consumer laws. The CFPB's supervision authority is limited to "covered persons," 12 U.S.C. § 5481(6), while the CFPB's enforcement authority is limited to prosecuting violations of "Federal consumer financial law," 12 U.S.C. § 5481(14), which comprises the enumerated consumer laws and the organic powers in the Consumer Financial Protection Act, which are in turn limited to "covered persons."

B. Purchase Money Financing

Certain financial transactions related to the sale of non-financial goods and services are also exempted from CFPB jurisdiction. Specifically, the CFPB lacks jurisdiction over "a merchant, retailer, or seller of nonfinancial goods or services," when that merchant offers or provides purchase money financing or undertakes the collection or sale of defaulted purchase money debts. 12 U.S.C. § 5517(a)(2)(A).

This purchase money carve-out is limited, however. It does not apply when the sale of non-financial good or service is essentially a subterfuge, such as when the value of the purchase money credit "significantly exceed[s] the market value of the nonfinancial good or service provided," 12 U.S.C. § 5517(a)(2)(B)(ii). Additionally, the carve-out does not apply if the merchant is "significantly engaged" in offering consumer financial products or services. 12 U.S.C. § 5517(a)(2)(C). What constitutes "significant engagement" is unclear.

The carve-out also does not apply if the merchant regularly extends credit subject to a finance charge. Thus, if the merchant regularly offers free purchase money credit for six months, there is no CFPB jurisdiction on the basis of that purchase money credit, but if the merchant regularly offers delayed payment and charges a finance charge for service, there is jurisdiction. 12 U.S.C. § 5517(a)(2)(B)(iii). Even if the merchant does charge a finance charge, if it is a "small business," it is still exempt from CFPB regulation. 12 U.S.C. § 5517(a)(2)(D)(ii). In other words, the CFPB has jurisdiction over large retailers that offer financing if there is a charge for the financing, but the jurisdiction is limited to issues relating to the financing. There is no jurisdiction over small retailers unless they are offering other consumer financial products or services.

Perhaps most importantly, the carve-out does not apply if the merchant sells the purchase money obligation prior to default. In other words, if the merchant is originating and selling non-defaulted loans (including to an affiliate, it would seem), the merchant will be under CFPB jurisdiction. Even if the carve-out applies, the merchant is still subject to the enumerated consumer laws. State attorney general enforcement jurisdiction under section 5552 is limited to CFPB jurisdiction under section 5517. 12 U.S.C. § 5517(a)(2)(E). There may be other grounds, however, for state enforcement.

C. Jurisdictional Carve-Outs

Excluded from the scope of all CFPB authority are realtors, retailers of manufactured homes and modular homes (also known as mobile homes), and tax preparers and accountants, except to the extent that they are engaged in offering or providing consumer financial products or services, particularly the extension of credit, or would already be covered by an enumerated consumer law. 12 U.S.C. §§ 5517(b)-(d).

Attorneys are also exempted from CFPB authority, but only for supervision and enforcement, and then only to the extent of the practice of law, and never from the enumerated consumer laws. 12 U.S.C. § 5517(e). Thus, an attorney who is engaged in debt collection (other than through litigation) might well be subject to CFPB enforcement under an enumerated consumer law. The CFPB is further prohibited from regulating entities regulated by the SEC, CFTC, IRS (as charities), Farm Credit Administration, state securities regulators, state insurance regulators, as well as employee benefit and compensation plans, except to the extent that these entities offer or provide consumer financial products or services or are otherwise subject to the enumerated consumer laws. 12 U.S.C. §§ 5517(f)-(l).

D. Clawback of the Jurisdictional Carve-Outs

Significantly, despite the carve-outs from CFPB authority for these various groups, there is a statutory clawback of authority. The Consumer Financial Protection Act provides that, notwithstanding the carve-outs, the entities excluded from CFPB authority:

> (1) may be a service provider; and
> (2) may be subject to requests from, or requirements imposed by, the Bureau regarding information in order to carry out the responsibilities and functions of the Bureau.

12 U.S.C. § 5517(n).

This clawback provision appears to provide that otherwise carved-out persons may nonetheless be as "service providers" and therefore subject to CFPB UDAAP rulemaking and UDAAP enforcement (whether by the CFPB, FTC, or attorneys general), both of which specifically apply to "service providers" in addition to "covered persons."

Moreover, if the clawback does make the carved-out persons potentially service providers, then they may also be "covered persons," because the definition of "covered person" includes a service provider that is affiliated with another covered person, meaning under the control of that other covered person. 12 U.S.C. §§ 5481(1), 5481(6). Control is not defined in the statute. Control might not be restricted to ownership; it might also include agency relationships. If control is defined in terms of agency, rather than ownership, then a law firm or accounting firm that "participates in designing, operating, or maintaining the consumer financial product or service," at the direction of a covered person, 12 U.S.C. § 5481(26)(A)(i), might be treated as an affiliate of that covered person and thus subject to regulation as a covered person. In that case, the full panoply of the Bureau's rulemaking, supervision, and enforcement powers would apply, notwithstanding the existence of a carve-out.[7]

E. Auto Dealers' Carve-Out

After intense lobbying efforts during the passage of the Dodd-Frank Act, auto and boat dealers won their own special exemption from all CFPB authority. 12 U.S.C. § 5519. The CFPB is generally prohibited from exercising any rulemaking, supervision, or enforcement authority with regard to auto and boat dealers, both under its organic powers and under the enumerated consumer laws. Instead, the FTC retains authority over auto and boat dealers, 12 U.S.C. § 5519(d), which is basically the FTC's own UDAP authority plus enforcement of certain enumerated consumer laws, most notably the Truth in Lending Act. The FTC also has UDAP rulemaking power (under Administrative Procedure Act process) for auto dealers not subject to CFPB jurisdiction. 12 U.S.C. § 1029(d). This means that the FTC does not have the authority

7. While the statutory structure of carve-out, clawback, and definitions may seem unnecessarily complex and opaque, the drafting might well have been a deliberate attempt to obfuscate the true extent of CFPB jurisdiction in order to facilitate passage of the Consumer Financial Protection Act.

to proscribe any act or practice by an auto dealer as "abusive." Significantly, the auto dealer carve-out is not an exemption from coverage under the Consumer Financial Protection Act, only from the CFPB's exercise of authority. This would appear to mean that auto dealers are still subject to enforcement of the statutory UDAAP prohibition by state attorneys general. *See* 12 U.S.C. § 5552.

The auto dealer carve-out does not, in any event, deprive the CFPB of all authority regarding auto dealers. The CFPB retains regulatory authority over auto and boat dealers to the extent that they offer financing (including leases) directly to consumers and do not routinely assign the loan or lease to an unaffiliated third party. (In other words, the CFPB cannot regulate auto and boat dealers when they are merely serving as loan/lease origination conduits—basically as brokers. 12 U.S.C. § 5519(b). In practical terms, this means that the CFPB has regulatory authority over "buy here, pay here" auto dealers, which are a subset of used car dealers that retain the loans they make. Unless the buy here, pay here dealer has done over 10,000 originations annually—a figure few if any dealers meet—it is not subject to CFPB supervision, only rulemaking and enforcement. The Bureau generally lacks regulatory authority over new car dealers because they typically sell their loans to unaffiliated third parties. The CFPB also has retains regulatory authority if an auto or boat dealer provides services related to real property transactions or offers any other consumer financial product or service not related to the sale or servicing of vehicles. *Id.* Additionally, the CFPB is entitled to obtain information from auto dealers in order to determine if they are subject to its authority. 12 U.S.C. § 5512(c)(5).

You might notice that there is a strange relationship between sections 5517(a) and 5519. Auto dealers are not subject to CFPB regulation if they routinely sell their loans, while retailers are subject to CFPB regulation if they sell performing purchase money loans. Why are auto dealers seen as a regulatory concern when they retain their loans, but retailers only when they sell their loans? Perhaps the answer is that if a retailer retains its loans, it is more likely to be subject to reputational sanctions, whereas reputational sanctions are thought to have less purchase with (used) car dealers. In any event, the interaction between sections 5517(a) and 5519 is far from clear. Isn't an auto dealer also a retailer? If so, which section applies?

The CFPB does, of course, have regulatory authority over non-dealer financing of motor vehicles. The CFPB also has full regulatory authority over indirect auto lenders—the third parties that purchase loans from auto dealers. These indirect auto lenders are engaged in offering a consumer financial product or service by virtue of purchasing loans. 12 U.S.C. § 5481(15)(A)(i). Notably, the service provider clawback does not apply to auto and boat dealers; their exclusion from CFPB regulatory authority is more complete.

III. WHAT THE CFPB CANNOT DO

Taking in what we've seen in this chapter and the preceding one, the CFPB has substantial rulemaking, supervision, and enforcement powers, but as we have seen there are numerous limitations and checks on these powers. It is also worthwhile emphasizing what the CFPB *cannot* do in substantive terms:

- The CFPB cannot force financial institutions to extend credit.
- The CFPB cannot mandate the offering of any financial product, including requiring financial institutions to offer "standard" or "plain vanilla" products if they offer "alternative" products.
- The CFPB cannot require consumers to purchase financial products.
- The CFPB cannot create private rights of action.
- The CFPB cannot promulgate a usury regulation.

12 U.S.C. § 5517(o).

At most, then, the CFPB can use rulemaking and enforcement to curtail the offering of certain financial products. The CFPB's toolkit is one of restriction, not facilitation, other than by way of exemption from liability. 12 U.S.C. § 5512(b)(3).

Problem Set 8

1. Which governmental agencies can bring enforcement actions against the following depositories and associated entities for unfair, deceptive, and abusive acts and practices in violation of 12 U.S.C. § 5536(a)(1)(B) or in violation of 12 U.S.C. § 5536(a)(1)(A) of an implementing rule enacted under 12 U.S.C. § 5531?

a. Continental Express Bank, N.A., a national bank with $110 billion in total assets that takes deposits, makes loans, and offers various payment services. *See* 12 U.S.C. §§ 5481(5)-(6), 5481(15)(A)(i), 5481(15)(A)(iv)-(v), 5515(c), 5552(a)(1)-(2).

b. Metropolitan Bancorp, an FDIC-insured state-chartered non-member bank with $100 million in total assets that takes deposits, makes loans, and offers various payment services. *See* 12 U.S.C. §§ 5481(5)-(6), 5481(15)(A)(i), 5481(15)(A)(iv)-(v), 5516(d), 5552(a)(1).

c. CX Loan Service Corp., a state-chartered firm that provides handles the paperwork for lien releases on mortgage loans made by Continental Express Bank, N.A. (from part (a)). CX Loan Service Corporation is not a corporate affiliate of Continental Express Bank. *See* 12 U.S.C. §§ 5481(26), 5515(d), 5552(a)(2).

2. Which governmental agencies can bring enforcement actions against the following non-depository entities for unfair, deceptive, and abusive acts and practices in violation of 12 U.S.C. § 5536?

a. Sir-Lend-a-Lot, a Missouri-licensed payday lender with $1 million of total assets. *See* 12 U.S.C. §§ 5481(5)-(6), 5481(15)(A)(i), 5514(c), 5552(a)(1).

b. The Fast and the Usurious, Inc., a vehicle title lender that makes loans against vehicle titles, rather than purchase money loans for vehicles. *See* 12 U.S.C. §§ 5481(5)-(6), 5481(15)(A)(i), 5514(c), 5552(a)(1).

c. MegaloMart, a large retailer that allows consumers to make purchases of appliances on store credit. MegaloMart only sells debts when they are in default. *See* 12 U.S.C. §§ 5481(5)-(6), 5481(15)(A)(i), 5514(c), 5517(a)(2), 5552(a)(1).

d. AquaManatee, a Florida Jet Ski dealership that offers dealer financing on its Jet Skis. AquaManatee retains the loans unless they go into default, when it sells them to unaffiliated debt buyers. *See* 12 U.S.C. §§ 5481(15)(A)(i), 5514(c), 5517(a)(2), 5519.

e. CollectCall, a debt collection firm that collects debts on behalf of third parties. Last year CollectCall collected $2 million on behalf of its clients. *See* 12 U.S.C. §§ 5481(5)-(6), 5481(15)(A)(x), 5514(c); 12 C.F.R. § 1090.105 (*see* Chapter 7).

f. Katherine Porter, a consumer bankruptcy attorney who represents consumers in Chapter 7 and Chapter 13 bankruptcies. *See* 12 U.S.C. §§ 5481(5)-(6), 5481 (15)(A)(viii), 5514(c), 5517(e), 5517(n), 5552(a)(1).

g. The City of Chicago, Illinois, which collects various debts owed to the city, including unpaid taxes and parking tickets. *See* 12 U.S.C. §§ 5481(5)-(6), 5481(15)(A)(x), 5552(a)(1).

3. FlyPaper LLC is a lead generator for payday loans. FlyPaper runs a website that advertises payday loans. Prospective borrowers submit their information through the website, and FlyPaper then auctions it off in almost real time to various payday lenders. The winning lender gets the borrower "lead" and the exclusive ability to deal with the borrower. Some of the payday loans made through leads generated by FlyPaper are from lenders that violate state laws prohibiting "rollovers" of the loans, that is refinancing a loan with a new one so that the borrower's indebtedness is extended. FlyPaper is aware of complaints about rollovers, but has never investigated and has taken no steps to restrict the terms on which it sells leads.

a. Can the CFPB bring an enforcement action against FlyPaper? *See* 12 U.S.C. §§ 5481(26)(A), 5481(26)(B)(ii), 5531, 5536(a)(1), 5536(a)(3).

b. FlyPaper is wholly owned by Ted Janger, who lets his nephew Johnny Pottow run the business on a day-to-day basis. Do either Janger or Pottow face any personal liability? *See* 12 U.S.C. § 5481(25)(C).

c. Does Susan Block-Lieb, the general counsel of FlyPaper, face any liability? 12 U.S.C. §§ 5481(25)(C), 5481(26), 5517(e), 5517(n).

d. Does Erik Gerding, the independent contractor who does the web design for FlyPaper, face any liability? *See* 12 U.S.C. §§ 5481(25)(C)(iii), 5481(26).

4. A 2017 Treasury Department Report on the Dodd-Frank Act criticized "the CFPB's habit of effectively announcing new prohibitions through enforcement actions. This practice forecloses the opportunity for public comment and deprives regulated parties of fair notice concerning the rules to which they must conform their conduct." Dept. of the Treasury, *A Financial System that Creates Economic Opportunities: Banks and Credit Unions*, June 2017, at 82. Why do you think the CFPB might use enforcement actions in lieu of rulemaking? What are the trade-offs of trying to set policy through enforcement actions versus rulemaking?

CHAPTER 9

FEDERALISM AND PREEMPTION

The CFPB's jurisdiction borders on and sometimes overlaps with that of state regulators. Moreover, other federal financial regulators' authority sometimes intersects with that of the states. This chapter explores the boundaries of these various agencies' jurisdictions. While at first glance the state-federal regulatory division may not seem particularly noteworthy, the experience of regulatory arbitrage and competition in the decades before the Dodd-Frank Act suggests that it is absolutely critical to determining the substance of consumer financial regulation both in terms of rulemaking and enforcement. Different regulators are subject to different political pressures and are thus more or less inclined to regulate (or deregulate). For example, while a Republican-appointed CFPB Director might be less aggressive in enforcement actions than a Democratic-appointed CFPB Director, to the extent that there are Democratic state attorneys general (especially those with their eye on governorships or senate seats), those state attorneys general might pick up some of the enforcement slack.

A final regulatory jurisdictional boundary is between federal bank regulators and the states. While the CFPB has authority over federal consumer financial laws, states are allowed to regulate beyond and in addition to the CFPB. These state regulations may be preempted by federal law.

I. TYPES OF PREEMPTION

The Supremacy Clause of the Constitution subordinates state law to federal law. U.S. Const. art. VI, cl. 2. Thus, when state law conflicts with federal law, state law must yield. State law can be preempted by federal law in three ways. First, the state law can be expressly preempted by statute or regulation. This is known as **express preemption**. For example, the Home Owners Loan Act (which governs federal savings associations) expressly preempts state usury laws as applied to federal savings associations. 12 U.S.C. § 1463(g). Second, there can be a conflict between state and federal law, either when it is impossible to comply with both federal and state law or when state law poses a sufficient obstacle to the objectives of federal law. This is known as **conflict preemption**. And third, there is **field preemption**, which occurs when there is a sufficiently pervasive federal regulatory scheme that the federal government is said to "occupy the field" such as to leave no room for supplemental state regulation.

II. FEDERAL PREEMPTION BEFORE THE DODD-FRANK ACT

Prior to the Dodd-Frank Act, federal preemption was a major obstacle for states seeking to regulate federally chartered financial institutions. When challenged on preemption grounds, state laws regulating financial institutions were nearly all invalidated as applied to national banks and thrifts, and preemption risk chilled other potential state attempts to regulate financial institutions.

Pre-Dodd-Frank Act preemption jurisprudence differed for national banks and federal savings associations because of different statutory bases. National banks' powers are governed by the National Bank Act; national thrifts' powers are governed by the Home Owners Loan Act, and federal credit unions are governed by the Federal Credit Union Act. The Office of Thrift Supervision (which regulated federal savings associations) claimed that there was field preemption for federal savings associations. Some lower courts agreed,[1] even though the Supreme Court pointedly declined to make such a finding,[2] instead finding instances of conflict preemption in addition to certain provisions involving express preemption. For national banks, however, federal courts never declared that any federal statute so completely occupies the field of banking regulation that it left no room for state regulation, but instead found express preemption based on specific federal statutes[3] and regulations[4] or conflict preemption.[5]

Starting in the 1990s, the Office of Comptroller of the Currency (OCC) and the Office of Thrift Supervision (OTS) waged a concerted campaign to preempt state consumer protection laws as applied to national banks and federal thrifts. The OCC/OTS preemption campaign culminated in the 2004 issuance by the OCC of preemption regulations.[6] The OCC preemption regulations declared that state laws were preempted if they "obstruct, impair, or condition a national bank's ability to fully

---

1. *E.g., Silvas v. E*Trade Mortg. Corp.*, 514 F.3d 1001, 1004 (9th Cir. 2008); *First Fed. Sav. & Loan Ass'n v. Greenwald*, 591 F.2d 417, 425-426 (1st Cir. 1979); *Kupiec v. Rep. Fed. Sav. & Loan Ass'n*, 512 F.2d 147, 150-152 (7th Cir. 1975).

2. *Fidelity Fed. Sav. & Loan Ass'n v. De la Cuesta*, 458 U.S. 141, 159 n.14 (1982) ("Because we find an actual conflict between federal and state law, we need not decide whether the HOLA or the [FHLBB's] regulations occupy the field of due-on-sale law or the entire field of federal savings and loan regulation."); *id.* at 171-172 (O'Connor, J., concurring) ("I join in the Court's opinion but write separately to emphasize that the authority of the Federal Home Loan Bank Board to pre-empt state laws is not limitless.").

3. *E.g.*, 12 U.S.C. §§ 707, 1735f-7 (explicit preemption of state laws governing interest rates on residential first mortgage loans); 12 U.S.C. § 3803(c) (explicit preemption of state laws restricting exotic mortgage structures).

4. *De la Cuesta*, 458 U.S. at 153 ("Federal regulations have no less pre-emptive effect than federal statutes.").

5. *Watters v. Wachovia Bank, N.A.*, 550 U.S. 1 (2007).

6. Bank Activities and Operations; Real Estate Lending and Appraisals, 69 Fed. Reg. 1904 (Jan. 7, 2004) (to be codified at 12 C.F.R. pts. 7, 34). These regulations were issued in proposed form at 68 Fed. Reg. 46,119 (proposed Aug. 5, 2003).

exercise" its powers, either directly or through operating subsidiaries.[7] Other regulations specifically preempted state laws on interest and usury, non-interest fees and charges, ATMs, deposit taking, non-real estate lending, and real-estate lending. While the statutory authority for passing the preemption regulation was unclear (in contrast to the specific language in the Home Owners Loan Act authorizing the OTS preemption regulations), the OCC interpreted this regulation broadly to preempt most state consumer protection laws, creating something effectively close to field preemption. At least prior to 2010, courts generally upheld the OCC preemption, even if not always in reference to the 2004 regulations.[8]

The goal of the OCC/OTS preemption campaign was to make federal bank/thrift charters more attractive by reducing the regulatory constraints under which federal banking entities had to operate. Increasing the share of the banking industry with federal charters increased the budgets and importance of the OCC and OTS and encouraged the complete federalization of banking regulation, an unstated but often assumed policy goal of federal bank regulators. Preemption alone, however, was not sufficient to increase the relative attractiveness of federal charters. Instead, preemption of state laws had to be combined with the failure to provide equivalent federal regulations. Thus, preemption not only resulted in *uniform* regulation of national banks and federal thrifts across states, but also in their *deregulation*.

Note that deregulation by preemption is a very different way of deregulating than by direct congressional action as with legislation like the Depositary Institutions Deregulation and Monetary Control Act of 1980 (DIDMCA) and the Alternative Mortgage Transactions Parity Act (AMTPA) of 1982. Instead of having the deregulatory process exposed to the political process, deregulation by preemption meant that most constituencies—including consumers—were effectively frozen out of the decision-making process, as the OCC and OTS had only financial institution constituencies and had their own interests at stake in terms of budgets and power.

Preemption, then, may not simply be an issue of whether regulation will be done by states or by the federal government, but it is also about the strength of consumer financial protection regulation. In the pre-CFPB universe, preemption meant weaker consumer financial protection regulation, as the federal bank regulators had very different motivations regarding consumer financial protection than electively responsive state attorneys general.

As the mortgage bubble formed in the 2000s, states attempted to enforce their consumer protection laws to limit the most aggressive predatory lending, but found themselves stymied by OCC and OTS preemption. While it was clear that states were preempted from most regulation of national banks and federal savings associations, a good deal of subprime lending was done by non-bank affiliates of national banks and federal savings associations. Whether state attempts to regulate these entities were also preempted was the issue in the first of two major preemption decisions in the 2000s. The first was *Watters v. Wachovia Bank, N.A.*, 550 U.S. 1 (2007).

7. 69 Fed. Reg. 1904, 1911–13 (Jan. 13, 2004) (codified at 12 C.F.R. pts. 7, 34 (2011).

8. *See, e.g., Am. Bankers Ass'n v. Lockyer*, 239 F. Supp. 2d 1000 (E.D. Cal. 2002) (preemption of California state credit card minimum payment warning requirement).

In that case, the Supreme Court held that Michigan's attempt to require licensing, reporting, and supervision of a state-chartered operating subsidiary of a national bank was preempted by the National Bank Act.

Two years after *Watters,* the Supreme Court ruled on *Cuomo v. The Clearing House Ass'n, LLC,* 557 U.S. 519 (2009), another preemption decision involving an attempt of a state to regulate a national bank itself, rather than a subsidiary. In *Cuomo,* a state attorney general had sent letters to several national banks requesting, "in lieu of [a non-judicial investigatory] subpoena," non-public information about their lending practices to ascertain whether the banks had violated state fair lending laws. The issue before the court was whether OCC preemption regulations claiming to preempt state law enforcement were a reasonable interpretation of the National Bank Act. The Court held that they were not because when a state brings suit it is acting as a "law-enforcer" rather than as a "supervisor." Yet *Cuomo* still placed limits on state regulation of national banks. Under *Cuomo,* states can bring suit against national banks, but they cannot force national banks to provide information for investigations other than through the normal discovery process in litigation; states have no supervisory authority over national banks. To the extent that a state attorney general has non-judicial investigatory subpoena power, that cannot be exercised against a national bank. Under *Watters,* this meant that states could not engage in regular examinations or non-litigation regulation of national bank operating subsidiaries as of National Bank Act preemption extended to national bank operating subsidiaries. This was the state of National Bank Act preemption law prior to the Dodd-Frank Wall Street Reform and Consumer Financial Protection Act of 2010.

III. THE DODD-FRANK ACT AND PREEMPTION

The deregulatory effect of preemption was a major complaint from consumer advocates, state bank supervisors, and attorneys general, and in the aftermath of the financial crisis in 2008, deregulation by preemption was often identified as a factor contributing to the decline in mortgage underwriting standards.

Not surprisingly, the Consumer Financial Protection Act (title X of the Dodd-Frank Act) rebalanced the relationship between federal and state authorities in consumer financial protection. Section 1044 of the Act (codified at 12 U.S.C. § 25b) was expressly titled a clarification of preemption standards: "State Law Preemption Standards for National Banks and Subsidiaries Clarified." The provision limits preemption solely to national banks; it does not extend to their non-national bank subsidiaries or affiliates. The Consumer Financial Protection Act directly rejects *Watters v. Wachovia Bank, N.A.,* as it provides that:

> a State consumer financial law shall apply to a subsidiary or affiliate of a national bank (other than a subsidiary or affiliate that is chartered as a national bank) to the same extent that the State consumer financial law applies to any person, corporation, or other entity subject to such State law.

12 U.S.C. § 25b(e). For good measure the Consumer Financial Protection Act further states that nothing in the National Bank Act shall be construed as "preempting,

annulling, or affecting the applicability of State law to any subsidiary, affiliate, or agent of a national bank." 12 U.S.C. § 25b(h)(2).

For national banks and federal thrifts, the Consumer Financial Protection Act limits preemption to three specific instances:

(1) When a state law would have a discriminatory effect on national banks relative to state-chartered banks.
(2) When "in accordance with the legal standard for preemption in the decision of the Supreme Court of the United States in *Barnett Bank of Marion County, N.A. v. Nelson, Florida Insurance Commissioner*, 517 U.S. 25 (1996), the State consumer financial law prevents or significantly interferes with the exercise by the national bank of its powers;" or
(3) When the state law is preempted by a provision of federal law other than the National Bank Act.

12 U.S.C. § 25b(b). In other words, there is no express preemption for national banks, no field preemption for national banks. A new category of "**discrimination preemption**" is created, and the category of conflict preemption is preserved, but it is limited to instances when there is a finding based on "substantial evidence" that the state law "prevents or significantly interferes with the exercise" of the national bank's powers. *See Baptista v. JPMorgan Chase Bank, N.A.*, 640 F.3d 1194, 1197 (11th Cir. 2011) ("Thus it is clear that under the Dodd-Frank Act, the proper preemption test asks whether there is a significant conflict between the state and federal statutes—that is, the test for conflict preemption."). The "significant interference" standard, with the unusual direction to apply the standard in an older Supreme Court ruling, is much narrower than the standard in the OCC's pre-Dodd-Frank Act 2004 preemption regulations, namely that a state law must merely "obstruct, impair, or condition a national bank's ability to fully exercise" its powers.

The Dodd-Frank Act authorizes the OCC to preempt state laws by regulation, but requires that such preemption be "on a case-by-case basis," which requires a "determination . . . concerning the impact of a particular State consumer financial law on any national bank that is subject to the law, or the law of any other State with substantively equivalent terms." 12 U.S.C. § 25b(b)(3). The Dodd-Frank Act further imposes a higher burden of proof for OCC preemption rulings; the Comptroller's preemption determinations must be supported by "substantial evidence" that the state law in question prevents or significantly interferes with the exercise of national bank powers. 12 U.S.C. § 25b(c).

Preemption still remains the order of the day, however, in regard to usury laws, which are addressed by a different statutory provision and covered in more detail in Chapter 23. The Consumer Financial Protection Act continues preemption of state usury laws in an oblique fashion: 12 U.S.C. § 25b(f) provides for the "preservation of powers related to charging interest" under section 85 of the National Bank Act. 12 U.S.C. § 85. While section 85 does not itself expressly preempt state laws in all circumstances, the Supreme Court has interpreted it broadly in *Marquette National Bank of Minneapolis v. First of Omaha Service Corp.*, 439 U.S. 299 (1978), to subject national banks only to the interest rate limitations of their headquarters state, irrespective of where they do business. National banks are thus allowed to export their home state's usury laws. The *Marquette* decision is well-known and much denounced; Congress's "preservation of the powers related to charging interest" would appear to be an awkward endorsement of the ruling.[9]

While the Consumer Financial Protection Act rejects *Watters*, it endorses *Cuomo v. Clearing House Ass'n LLC*, providing that:

> In accordance with the decision of the Supreme Court of the United States in *Cuomo v. Clearing House Assn., L.L.C.* (129 S. Ct. 2710 (2009)), no provision of [the National Bank Act] which relates to visitorial powers or otherwise limits or restricts the visitorial authority to which any national bank is subject shall be construed as limiting or restricting the authority of any attorney general (or other chief law enforcement officer) of any State to bring an action against a national bank in a court of appropriate jurisdiction to enforce an applicable law and to seek relief as authorized by such law.

12 U.S.C. § 25b(i)(1). In other words, the Consumer Financial Protection Act does not authorize states to have visitorial powers, but lack of visitorial powers does not preclude state enforcement actions against national banks. And because *Watters* was overturned legislatively, 12 U.S.C. § 25b(e), states *do* have the ability to compel national bank operating subsidiaries to turn over information pursuant to non-judicial investigatory subpoenas or the equivalent.

The Consumer Financial Protection Act further specifies that the OCC publish and update quarterly a list of preemption determinations and requires that preemption rulings must be reviewed at least every five years through a notice and public comment process. 12 U.S.C. §§ 25b(d)(1), 25b(g).

A similar provision exists for federal savings associations, including a clear statement that federal law governing savings associations "does not occupy the field in any area of State law." 12 U.S.C. § 1465. This is an express rejection of the OTS's earlier claims of field preemption under the Home Owners Loan Act.[10]

Beyond circumscribing National Bank Act and Home Owners Loan Act preemption, the Consumer Financial Protection Act also makes clear that it does not itself preempt state law "except to the extent that any such provision of law is inconsistent with the provisions of [the Act] and then only to the extent of the inconsistency" with greater protection not being inconsistent. 12 U.S.C. § 5551(a). The Home Owners Loan Act (HOLA) has been amended to state that HOLA preemption tracks National Bank Act preemption and that there is no field preemption for federal savings associations. 12 U.S.C. § 1465.

As preemption is based under *Barnett Bank* on prevention or significant interference with a national bank's exercise of its powers, it is necessary to understand first what those powers are. Section 24 of the National Bank Act contains the basic authorization provision for national bank activities, while section 371 separately authorizes real estate lending.

---

9. A parallel statutory provision, 12 U.S.C. § 1831d, applies to state-chartered banks, while yet another statutory provision preempts state usury laws for mortgage loans, irrespective of the institutional nature of the lender. 12 U.S.C. 6 1735f-7.

10. *See* former 12 C.F.R. § 560.2(a)(2008) (". . . .OTS hereby occupies the entire field of lending regulation for federal savings associations. . . .").

National banks, then, are restricted to powers incidental to the business of banking, as well as real estate lending (and a few other powers specifically granted in other provisions of the National Bank Act). But what is the "business of banking"? And what falls within the scope of "incidental powers"? The business of banking covers the core modern banking troika of taking deposits, making payments, and lending funds. But critically, the business of banking is not limited to the five specific activities listed in section 24(Seventh) of the National Bank Act. *Nationsbank of N.C., N.A. v. Variable Annuity Life Ins. Co.*, 513 U.S. 251, 258 n.2 (1995). Instead, the incidental powers of national banks can extend beyond the enumerated powers in section 24(Seventh). While the extent of national bank powers is a controversial issue, it is not one that particularly implicates the payment and lending functions of consumer finance.

IV. NEW OCC PREEMPTION REGULATIONS

Following the enactment of the Dodd-Frank Act, the OCC promulgated a new rule regarding preemption. The rule clarified that "visitorial powers" included direct investigations of national banks, including documents and testimony required from the banks, but excluded suits by states' attorneys general per *Cuomo*. The rule jettisoned the OCC's preemption standard of whether the activity "obstructs, impairs, or conditions" the exercise of powers of a national bank or federal savings association.

The OCC, however, adopted a controversial interpretation of the *Barnett Bank of Marion County, N.A. v. Nelson, Florida Insurance Commissioner*, 517 U.S. 25 (1996) decision referenced in the Dodd-Frank Act's preemption standards.[11] In *Barnett*, the Supreme Court had ruled that a state law prohibiting national banks from selling insurance in certain locations was preempted by a 1916 federal statute authorizing such actions because the state law was an "obstacle to the accomplishment and execution of the full purposes and objectives of Congress" that "prevent[s] or significantly interfere[s] with the national bank's exercise of its powers."

The OCC's post-Dodd-Frank preemption regulation concluded that "prevents or significantly interferes" is not the actual preemption standard itself. Instead, the OCC's position is that the "prevents or significantly interferes" standard has to be interpreted in light of the underlying reasoning in the *Barnett Bank* decision, which the OCC contends is "conflict preemption. . . which includes, but is but not bounded by the 'prevent or significantly interfere' formulation." 76 Fed. Reg. 43549, 43555-56, July 21, 2011. On this basis, the OCC concluded that "precedents consistent with that analysis—which may include regulations adopted consistent with such a conflict preemption justification—are also preserved." *Id.*

It is important to recognize that the OCC does not determine preemption. OCC preemption regulations are the OCC's interpretation of the National Bank Act. But pursuant to section 25b(b)(5)(A) of the National Bank Act (as amended by

11. The Treasury Department's General Counsel even took the unprecedented step of submitting a public comment in opposition to the rulemaking. *See* Kate Davidson, *Treasury Sharply Criticizes OCC's Preemption Proposal*, Am. Banker, June 28, 2011.

Dodd-Frank), the OCC does not receive *Chevron* deference in terms of its preemption determinations. Instead, courts are charged with assessing the merits of the OCC's reasoning and any other factors the court thinks are relevant.

V. THE CURRENT STATUS OF NATIONAL BANK ACT PREEMPTION

The following decision shows that even under the Consumer Financial Protection Act's new preemption standards, preemption is not a dead doctrine.

Parks v. MBNA America Bank, N.A.

54 Cal. 4th 376 (Cal. 2012)

Liu, J.

We granted review to address whether the National Bank Act of 1864 (13 Stat. 99) (NBA) preempts Civil Code section 1748.9, a California law requiring that certain disclosures accompany preprinted checks that a credit card issuer provides to its cardholders for use as credit. The NBA contains no such requirement with respect to the issuance of so-called "convenience checks" to credit customers. Instead, it broadly grants to national banks "all such incidental power as shall be necessary to carry on the business of banking . . . by [among other powers] loaning money on personal security." (12 U.S.C. § 24, par. Seventh.) We conclude that the NBA preempts Civil Code section 1748.9 because the state law stands as an obstacle to the broad grant of power given by the NBA to national banks to conduct the business of banking. Accordingly, we reverse the Court of Appeal's judgment and remand the matter to that court for further proceedings consistent with our opinion.

. . . In 2003, MBNA [now FIA Card Services, N.A., a subsidiary of Bank of America, N.A.] issued a credit card to plaintiff Allan Parks. Later that year, as part of its service to cardholders, MBNA extended credit to plaintiff by sending him preprinted drafts, commonly referred to as "convenience checks." (See *Rose v. Chase Bank U.S.A., N.A.* (9th Cir. 2008) 513 F.3d 1032, 1034 (*Rose*).) Plaintiff used several of these convenience checks to purchase holiday gifts and pay bills, and he incurred finance charges in excess of those he would have incurred had he used his credit card for similar transactions. The convenience checks that MBNA sent to Parks did not include disclosures required by Civil Code section 1748.9. That statute says: "A credit card issuer that extends credit to a cardholder through the use of a preprinted check or draft shall disclose on the front of an attachment that is affixed by perforation or other means to the preprinted check or draft, in clear and conspicuous language, all of the following information: (1) That 'use of the attached check or draft will constitute a charge against your credit account.' (2) The annual percentage rate and the calculation of finance charges, as required by Section 226.16 of Regulation Z of the Code of Federal Regulations, associated with the use of the attached check or draft. (3) Whether the finance charges are triggered immediately upon the use of the check or draft." (Civ. Code, § 1748.9, subd. (a) (paragraphing omitted) (hereafter section 1748.9).)

In 2004, plaintiff sued MBNA on behalf of himself and similarly situated MBNA customers, alleging that the bank engaged in unfair competition in violation of Business and Professions Code section 17200 *et seq*. by failing to make the disclosures mandated by section 1748.9. Plaintiff sought both monetary and injunctive relief. MBNA took the position that the NBA and a now-superseded federal regulation, title 12 Code of Federal Regulations part 7.4008(d) (2004) (hereafter former regulation 7.4008(d)), preempt the state disclosure law. (Former regulation 7.4008(d) was superseded by a 2010 amendment to 12 C.F.R. section 7.4008 promulgated after Congress enacted the Dodd-Frank Wall Street Reform and Consumer Protection Act (Pub. L. No. 111-203 (July 21, 2010) 124 Stat. 1376) (hereafter Dodd-Frank Act).)

. . . [T]he main dispute in this case . . . is, whether section 1748.9 stands as an obstacle to the accomplishment and execution of the NBA's purposes.

. . . [W]e conclude that the NBA preempts section 1748.9. . . . [T]he NBA broadly authorizes national banks to exercise "all such incidental power as shall be necessary to carry on the business of banking." (12 U.S.C. § 24, par. Seventh.) This broad power expressly includes "loaning money on personal security." (*Ibid.*) The disclosure requirements in section 1748.9 impose a condition on the federally authorized power of national banks to loan money on personal security. Those requirements say that national banks like MBNA may offer credit in the form of convenience checks so long as the checks contain specific disclosures. But here, as in *Barnett Bank*, the federal statute does not grant national banks a "*limited* permission, that is, permission to [loan money on personal security] *to the extent that state law also grants permission to do so.*" (*Barnett Bank of Marion County, N.A. v. Nelson* (1996) 517 U.S. 25, 31 (*Barnett Bank*).) Instead, federal law authorizes national banks to loan money on personal security with "no 'indication' that Congress intended to subject that power to local restriction." (*Id.* at p. 35, quoting *Franklin Nat. Bank of Franklin Square v. New York* (1954) 347 U.S. 373, 378 (*Franklin*).

The specific disclosure obligations imposed by section 1748.9 exceed any requirements in federal law. The requirement in section 1748.9 that disclosures appear "on the front of an attachment that is affixed by perforation or other means to the preprinted check or draft" has no counterpart in federal law. The same is true of section 1748.9's requirement that precise language ("use of the attached check or draft will constitute a charge against your credit account") appear on each check. (§ 1748.9, subd. (a)(1).) In addition, although federal regulations require certain disclosures when the terms of using a convenience check differ from the terms of the customer's credit account (12 C.F.R. § [10]26.9(b)(1), (2)), they do not mandate that every convenience check disclose "[w]hether the finance charges are triggered immediately upon use of the check," as section 1748.9, subdivision (a)(3) requires. Furthermore, although section 1748.9, subdivision (a)(2) mandates disclosure of interest rates and finance charges "as required by Section [10]26.16 of Regulation Z of the Code of Federal Regulations," that federal regulation pertains to "advertising" (see 12 C.F.R. § [10]26.16) and arguably does not apply to convenience check offers.

In characterizing the disclosure requirements of section 1748.9, the Court of Appeal said that the statute "does not *forbid* the exercise of a banking power authorized by the NBA. Section 1748.9 does not bar national banks from loaning money on personal security through convenience checks." It is true that section 1748.9, unlike the state law in *Barnett Bank* that prohibited national banks from selling insurance in small towns, does not outlaw a category of banking activity. However, to say that MBNA *may* offer convenience checks *so long as* it complies with section 1748.9 is equivalent to saying that MBNA *may not* offer convenience checks *unless* it complies with section 1748.9. Whether phrased as a conditional permission or as a contingent prohibition, the effect of section 1748.9 is to forbid national banks from offering credit in the form of convenience checks unless they comply with state law. As demonstrated by the instant lawsuit brought under California's unfair competition law (Bus. & Prof. Code, § 17200 et seq.), a national bank may be subject to monetary liability, and its convenience check offers may be enjoined, if it does not comply.

Requiring compliance with section 1748.9 as a condition of "loaning money on personal security" (12 U.S.C. § 24, par. Seventh) through convenience checks "significantly impair[s] the exercise of authority" granted to national banks by the NBA (*Watters, supra*, 550 U.S. at p. 12). Section 1748.9 prescribes the *content* of the disclosures by specifying what must be disclosed on each convenience check. Section 1748.9 prescribes specific *language* that a credit card issuer must use ("use of the attached check or draft will constitute a charge against your credit account"). (§ 1748.9, subd. (a)(1).) In addition, section 1748.9 prescribes the *manner* and *format* of the disclosures: the disclosures must appear "on the front of an attachment," the attachment must be "affixed by perforation or other means to the preprinted check," and the disclosures must appear "in clear and conspicuous language." These requirements as to the content, language, manner, and format of disclosures seem no less prescriptive than the New York law in *Franklin* that prohibited banks other than the state's own chartered savings institutions from using the word "saving" or "savings" in their advertisements or business. (See *Franklin, supra*, 347 U.S. at p. 374 fn. 1, citing N.Y. stat.) The New York law did not bar national banks from receiving deposits or soliciting deposits through advertisements. It simply required national banks operating in New York to use other words to entice people to deposit their money for safe-keeping and to describe the business of protecting, growing, and lending those deposits. (See *Franklin*, at p. 378 ["'[The state] does not object to national banks taking savings deposits or even to their advertising that fact so long as they do not use the word 'savings.'"].) Nevertheless, the high court held that the state law impermissibly interfered with the federally authorized business of national banks. (See *id.* at pp. 377-378.)

Moreover, even if California's disclosure requirements by themselves do not seem particularly onerous, the high court in *Watters* made clear that our preemption analysis must consider the burden of disclosure "regimes imposed not just by [California], but by all States in which the banks operate." (*Watters, supra*, 550 U.S. at p. 13.) If disclosure requirements such as those in section 1748.9 were allowed to stand, national banks operating in multiple states would face the prospect of "'limitations and restrictions as various and as numerous as the States.' [Citation omitted.]" (*Id.* at p. 14.) National banks would have to monitor requirements as to the content, language, manner, and format of disclosures for each of the 50 states (and possibly municipalities as well), and continually adjust their convenience check offers to comply with the prescriptions of each local jurisdiction. Such "[d]iverse and duplicative [regulation] of national banks' engagement in the business of banking . . . is precisely what the NBA was designed to prevent." (*Id.* at pp. 13-14.) Congress intended national banks to have broad power to engage in the "business of banking" by "loaning money on personal security" (12 U.S.C. § 24, par. Seventh), and that power would be significantly impaired if national banks had to comply with a diverse or duplicative patchwork of local disclosure requirements.

. . . Concluding that "[s]ection 1748.9 does not, on its face, significantly impair federally authorized powers under the NBA," the Court of Appeal held that "national banks claiming preemption must make a factual showing that the disclosure requirement significantly impairs the exercise of the relevant power or powers." After stating this requirement of factual proof, the Court of Appeal said "[w]e need not elucidate a precise 'yardstick for measuring when a state law "significantly interferes with" . . . the exercise of national banks' powers.' [Citation omitted.]" We believe the Court of Appeal's approach is unsupported by preemption case law and unworkable in practice.

In *Franklin, supra,* 347 U.S. 373, the court did not examine record evidence before concluding that the state prohibition on using the word "savings" significantly impaired the ability of national banks to advertise. And in *Watters, supra,* 550 U.S. 1, the court did not undertake an evidentiary inquiry before concluding that the state registration and supervision regime significantly impaired the real estate lending powers of national banks and their operating subsidiaries. (See *Watters* [*v. Wachovia Bank, N.A.* (2007)] 550 U.S. [1,] 35 (dis. opn. of Stevens, J.) ["There is no evidence . . . that compliance with the Michigan statutes imposed any special burdens on Wachovia Mortgage's activities . . . ."].) The Court of Appeal cited our decision in *Perdue,* where we held on the pleadings that the state law survived preemption and then said that "*conceivably* information not contained in the pleadings *might* lead to a different conclusion." (*Perdue v. Crocker Nat'l Bank,* 38 Cal.3d 913, 943 (1985), italics added; see *id.* at pp. 943-944 ["We cannot presume, without evidence, that prohibiting a national bank from setting unreasonable prices or enforcing an unconscionable contract will render that bank less efficient, less competitive or less able to fulfill its function in a national banking system."].) But *Perdue*'s speculative statement was dicta, and we know of no case decided by our court or by the United States Supreme Court in which the issue of preemption turned on whether a national bank made an adequate factual showing that state law significantly impaired its federally authorized powers.

That the Court of Appeal declined to "elucidate a precise 'yardstick for measuring'" significant impairment suggests the impracticality of this approach. As *amici curiae* American Bankers Association and California Bankers Association explain:

> If the yardstick consists of a cost threshold for the specific state law, the law might be preempted as applied to some banks but not others, as banks with more expansive convenience-check activities are able to evidence higher costs. If, in contrast, the yardstick focuses on costs in proportion to the size of the bank, the law might be preempted as to smaller banks but not larger banks. In fact, preemption outcomes might change over time for a specific bank, as it expands its operations. Preemption rulings based on 'factual evidence' for a particular defendant bank therefore will have little value—even for a single bank—much less for many or all national banks.

> Additionally, the new evidentiary requirement will make it very difficult for national banks to predict, in advance, with which state laws they must comply. Even where one national bank has litigated the applicability of the precise state law at issue, other national banks will not be able to rely on the outcome of that litigation because the inquiry will vary depending on the particular operations of the bank and the factual showing made. A national bank that believes it has been subjected to a preempted law will be forced to initiate a lawsuit and submit its *own* evidence, to prove significant impairment of its *own* operations. Otherwise, absent such a lawsuit, the bank would have to monitor, analyze, and comply with state laws that may in fact be preempted. . . .

Here, we conclude as a matter of law that the NBA preempts the disclosure requirements in section 1748.9.

Because we find section 1748.9 preempted by the NBA, we express no view on whether section 1748.9 is also preempted by former regulation 7.4008(d).

. . . The judgment of the Court of Appeal is reversed and the matter remanded for further proceedings.

Questions and Notes on *Parks v. MBNA*

1. Does *Parks* mean that there is National Bank Act preemption whenever there is variation in state law?

2. Should the fact that California is the only state with convenience check disclosure requirements affect the application of *Parks'* interpretation of the "significant interference" standard?

3. Exactly how is "significant interference" to be measured after *Parks* if not on an "as applied" basis with the evidentiary burden on specific institutions?

To summarize, then, state power in consumer financial regulation after the Consumer Financial Protection Act coexists with federal authority. States can still regulate consumer financial products; state statutes, regulations, orders, and interpretations are preempted only in regard to national banks and federal savings associations themselves and then only in limited circumstances, most notably usury laws and laws that "prevent or significantly interfere" with national banks' and federal savings associations' powers. States still lack visitorial powers over national banks and federal savings associations. Yet, state enforcement authority is greater than before the Consumer Financial Protection Act, both in terms of the entities states can bring actions against and in terms of the types of actions they can bring, producing a belt-and-suspenders enforcement in tandem with the CFPB.

VI. TRUE LENDER CASES AND PREEMPTION

Whatever the current standard for National Bank Act preemption, there is a separate question regarding which institutions can shelter in that preemption or in other related statutory preemption, such as the Federal Deposit Insurance Act's preemption of state interest rate limits on federally insured, state-chartered banks. 12 U.S.C. 1831d(a).

For the National Bank Act, national banks are themselves obviously beneficiaries of preemption, and *Watters v. Wachovia Bank, N.A* extended preemption to state-chartered subsidiaries of national banks, but it was rolled back by the Dodd-Frank Act. But how much further does preemption under any of the banking statutes extend? Does it only cover banks? Their subsidiaries and corporate affiliates? Does it cover debt collection firms that purchase bad debts from national banks? Securitization trusts created and serviced by national banks? The following case addresses how far National Bank Act preemption stretches: is it a privilege that is specific to certain entities, or does it travel with receivables created by an entity?

Madden v. Midland Funding, LLC

786 F.3d 246 (2d Cir. 2015)

STRAUB, *Circuit Judge*:

This putative class action alleges violations of the Fair Debt Collection Practices Act ("FDCPA") and New York's usury law. The proposed class representative, Saliha Madden, alleges that the defendants violated the FDCPA by charging and attempting to collect interest at a rate higher than that permitted under the law of her home state, which is New York. The defendants contend that Madden's claims fail as a matter of law [because the] state law usury claims and FDCPA claims predicated on state-law violations against a national bank's assignees, such as the defendants here, are preempted by the National Bank Act ("NBA"). . . .

The District Court entered judgment for the defendants. Because neither defendant is a national bank nor a subsidiary or agent of a national bank, or is otherwise acting on behalf of a national bank, and because application of the state law on which Madden's claims rely would not significantly interfere with any national bank's ability to exercise its powers under the NBA, we reverse the District Court's holding that the NBA preempts Madden's claims and accordingly vacate the judgment of the District Court.. . .

BACKGROUND

A. Madden's Credit Card Debt, the Sale of Her Account, and the Defendants' Collection Efforts

In 2005, Saliha Madden, a resident of New York, opened a Bank of America ("BoA") credit card account. BoA is a national bank. The account was governed by a document she received from BoA titled "Cardholder Agreement." The following year, BoA's credit card program was consolidated into another national bank, FIA Card Services, N.A. ("FIA"). Contemporaneously with the transfer to FIA, the account's terms and conditions were amended upon receipt by Madden of a document titled "Change In Terms," which contained a Delaware choice-of-law clause.

Madden owed approximately $5,000 on her credit card account and in 2008, FIA "charged-off" her account (*i.e.*, wrote off her debt as uncollectable). FIA then sold Madden's debt to Defendant-Appellee Midland Funding, LLC ("Midland Funding"), a debt purchaser. Midland Credit Management, Inc. ("Midland Credit"), the other defendant in this case, is an affiliate of Midland Funding that services Midland Funding's consumer debt accounts. Neither defendant is a national bank. Upon Midland Funding's acquisition of Madden's debt, neither FIA nor BoA possessed any further interest in the account.

In November 2010, Midland Credit sent Madden a letter seeking to collect payment on her debt and stating that an interest rate of 27% per year applied.

B. Procedural History

A year later, Madden filed suit against the defendants—on behalf of herself and a putative class—alleging that they had engaged in abusive and unfair debt collection practices in violation of the FDCPA, 15 U.S.C. §§ 1692e, 1692f, and had charged a usurious rate of interest in violation of New York law, N.Y. Gen. Bus. Law § 349; N.Y. Gen. Oblig. Law § 5-501; N.Y. Penal Law § 190.40 (proscribing interest from being charged at a rate exceeding 25% per year).

. . .

DISCUSSION

Madden argues on appeal that the District Court erred in holding that NBA preemption bars her state-law usury claims. We agree. Because neither defendant is a national bank nor a subsidiary or agent of a national bank, or is otherwise acting on behalf of a national bank, and because application of the state law on which Madden's claims rely would not significantly interfere with any national bank's ability to exercise its powers under the NBA, we reverse the District Court's holding that the NBA preempts Madden's claims and accordingly vacate the judgment of the District Court. We also vacate the District Court's judgment as to Madden's FDCPA claim and the denial of class certification because those rulings were predicated on the same flawed preemption analysis.

. . .

I. National Bank Act Preemption

The federal preemption doctrine derives from the Supremacy Clause of the United States Constitution, which provides that "the Laws of the United States which shall be made in Pursuance" of the Constitution "shall be the supreme Law of the Land." U.S. Const. art. VI, cl. 2. According to the Supreme Court, "[t]he phrase 'Laws of the United States' encompasses both federal statutes themselves and federal regulations that are properly adopted in accordance with statutory authorization." *City of New York v. FCC*, 486 U.S. 57, 63 (1988).

"Preemption can generally occur in three ways: where Congress has expressly preempted state law, where Congress has legislated so comprehensively that federal law occupies an entire field of regulation and leaves no room for state law, or where federal law conflicts with state law." *Wachovia Bank, N.A. v. Burke*, 414 F.3d 305, 313 (2d Cir. 2005). The defendants appear to suggest that this case involves "conflict preemption," which "occurs when compliance with both state and federal law is impossible, or when the state law stands as an obstacle to the accomplishment and execution of the full purposes and objective of Congress." *United States v. Locke*, 529 U.S. 89, 109 (2000).

The National Bank Act expressly permits national banks to "charge on any loan . . . interest at the rate allowed by the laws of the State, Territory, or District where the bank is located." 12 U.S.C. § 85. It also "provide[s] the exclusive cause of action" for usury claims against national banks, *Beneficial Nat'l Bank v. Anderson*, 539 U.S. 1, 11 (2003), and "therefore completely preempt[s] analogous state-law usury claims," *Sullivan v. Am. Airlines, Inc.*, 424 F.3d 267, 275 (2d Cir. 2005). Thus, there is "no such thing as a state-law claim of usury against a national bank." *Beneficial Nat'l Bank*, 539 U.S. at 11; *see also Pac. Capital Bank, N.A. v. Connecticut*, 542 F.3d 341, 352 (2d Cir. 2008) ("[A] state in which a national bank makes a loan may not permissibly require the bank to charge an interest rate lower than that allowed by its home state."). Accordingly, because FIA is incorporated in Delaware, which permits banks to charge interest rates that would be usurious under New York law, FIA's collection at those rates in New York does not violate the NBA and is not subject to New York's stricter usury laws, which the NBA preempts.

The defendants argue that, as assignees of a national bank, they too are allowed under the NBA to charge interest at the rate permitted by the state where the assignor national bank is located—here, Delaware. We disagree. In certain circumstances, NBA preemption can be extended to non-national bank entities. To apply NBA preemption to an action taken by a non-national bank entity, application of state law to that action must significantly interfere with a national bank's ability to exercise its power under the NBA. *See Barnett Bank of Marion Cnty., N.A. v. Nelson*, 517 U.S. 25, 33 (1996); *Pac. Capital Bank*, 542 F.3d at 353.

The Supreme Court has suggested that NBA preemption may extend to entities beyond a national bank itself, such as non-national banks acting as the "equivalent to national banks with respect to powers exercised under federal law." *Watters v. Wachovia Bank, N.A.*, 550 U.S. 1, 18 (2007). For example, the Supreme Court has held that operating subsidiaries of national banks may benefit from NBA preemption. *Id.; see also Burke*, 414 F.3d at 309 (deferring to reasonable regulation that operating subsidiaries of national banks receive the same preemptive benefit as the parent bank). This Court has also held that agents of national banks can benefit from NBA preemption. *Pac. Capital Bank*, 542 F.3d at 353-54 (holding that a third-party tax preparer who facilitated the processing of refund anticipation loans for a national bank was not subject to Connecticut law regulating such loans); *see also SPGGC, LLC v. Ayotte*, 488 F.3d 525, 532 (1st Cir. 2007) ("The National Bank Act explicitly states that a national bank may use 'duly authorized officers or agents' to exercise its incidental powers.").

The Office of the Comptroller of the Currency ("OCC"), "a federal agency that charters, regulates, and supervises all national banks," *Town of Babylon v. Fed. Hous. Fin. Agency*, 699 F.3d 221, 224 n.2 (2d Cir. 2012), has made clear that third-party debt buyers are distinct from agents or subsidiaries of a national bank, *see* OCC Bulletin

2014-37, Risk Management Guidance (Aug. 4, 2014), *available at* http://www.occ.gov/news-issuances/bulletins/2014/bulletin-2014-37.html ("Banks may pursue collection of delinquent accounts by (1) handling the collections internally, (2) using third parties as agents in collecting the debt, or (3) selling the debt to debt buyers for a fee."). In fact, it is precisely because national banks do not exercise control over third-party debt buyers that the OCC issued guidance regarding how national banks should manage the risk associated with selling consumer debt to third parties. *See id.*

In most cases in which NBA preemption has been applied to a non-national bank entity, the entity has exercised the powers of a national bank—*i.e.*, has acted on behalf of a national bank in carrying out the national bank's business. This is not the case here. The defendants did not act on behalf of BoA or FIA in attempting to collect on Madden's debt. The defendants acted solely on their own behalves, as the owners of the debt.

No other mechanism appears on these facts by which applying state usury laws to the third-party debt buyers would significantly interfere with either national bank's ability to exercise its powers under the NBA. *See Barnett Bank*, 517 U.S. at 33. Rather, such application would "limit[] only activities of the third party which are otherwise subject to state control," *SPGGC, LLC v. Blumenthal*, 505 F.3d 183, 191 (2d Cir. 2007), and which are not protected by federal banking law or subject to OCC oversight.

. . .

Furthermore, extension of NBA preemption to third-party debt collectors such as the defendants would be an overly broad application of the NBA. Although national banks' agents and subsidiaries exercise national banks' powers and receive protection under the NBA when doing so, extending those protections to third parties would create an end-run around usury laws for non-national bank entities that are not acting on behalf of a national bank.

. . .

We REVERSE the District Court's holding as to National Bank Act preemption. . . .

Madden dealt with a bank selling defaulted loans to a debt collector. But sometimes non-bank lenders agree to purchase most or all receivables from a national bank's lending program in an arrangement known as **rent-a-bank** lending. In a typical rent-a-bank operation, the national bank is the formal lender, but that will be the extent of its meaningful involvement in the loan: the non-bank will design a lending program, including underwriting criteria itself, and will handle virtually all operations in the program, such as sales and marketing and servicing. The non-bank will also purchase all or almost all of the receivables generated by the national bank pursuant to the lending program almost immediately after they are created. The sole purpose of rent-a-bank lending is for the non-bank lender to shelter in National Bank Act preemption; the national bank is essentially selling its preemption rights. Bank regulators have indicated concern about risks arising from rent-a-bank relationships, particularly in regard to money laundering violations, but they have not prohibited them. *See* FDIC Financial Institutions Letter 52-2015 (Nov. 16, 2015).

West Virginia v. CashCall, Inc.

605 F. Supp. 2d 781 (S.D.W.V. 2009)

Joseph R. Goodwin, Chief Judge.

Pending before the court is Defendant CashCall's Motion to Dismiss, and the plaintiff's Motion to Remand For the reasons herein, the plaintiff's Motion is GRANTED and Defendant CashCall's Motion is DENIED as moot.

I. BACKGROUND

On October 8, 2008, the State of West Virginia ("the State") filed a Complaint against the defendants, CashCall, Inc. ("CashCall"), and J. Paul Reddam, in the Circuit Court of Kanawha County, West Virginia. In that Complaint, the State alleges, among other things, that CashCall participated in an alleged "rent-a-bank" or "rent-a-charter" scheme designed to avoid West Virginia usury laws. The so-called "scheme" entailed CashCall's entry into a Marketing Agreement (the "Agreement") with a bank chartered in South Dakota, the First Bank and Trust of Milbank ("the Bank"). The Agreement provided that CashCall would market loans to consumers as an agent of the Bank. The Bank would then approve and directly fund the loans. Three business days later, CashCall would, pursuant to the Agreement, purchase the loan from the Bank and become the owner of the loan. The State argues that CashCall's overall involvement with those loans rendered it the de facto lender of the loans and that the interest rates charged on those loans exceed the amount allowed by West Virginia usury laws.

On November 17, 2008, CashCall removed this action to federal court and the State subsequently filed a Motion to Remand. CashCall has also filed a Motion to Dismiss [under Federal Rule of Civil Procedure 12(b)(6)]. . . .

II. MOTION TO REMAND

In its Notice of Removal, CashCall asserts that this court has federal question jurisdiction over this matter by virtue of the complete preemption doctrine. Specifically, CashCall argues that the Bank is the real party in interest with respect to the State's claims, "each and every [one of which] concerns consumer loans made in West Virginia *by the Bank*." (emphasis in the original). Because the Bank is the real lender, CashCall argues, the State's usury law claim is completely preempted by § 27 of the Federal Deposit Insurance Act ("FDIA"), 12 U.S.C. § 1831d. The State responds that its Complaint only raises state law claims against CashCall, which is not a bank. Therefore, the State argues, the claims do not raise a federal question establishing federal subject matter jurisdiction and removal of this case to federal court was improper. I FIND that because the State only asserts state law claims against CashCall, a non-bank entity, the claims do not implicate the FDIA, the FDIA does not completely preempt the state-law claims, and there are no federal questions on the face of the Complaint. Accordingly, the State's Motion to Remand is GRANTED.

A. Complete Preemption Doctrine

A defendant may remove to federal court any case filed in state court over which federal courts have original jurisdiction. 28 U.S.C. § 1441. Federal courts have original jurisdiction over all civil actions arising under the laws of the United States. 28 U.S.C. § 1331. An action arises under the laws of the United States if a federal claim or question appears on the face of a well-pleaded complaint. *Caterpillar, Inc. v. Williams,* 482 U.S. 386, 392 (1987).

The well-pleaded complaint rule limits a defendant's ability to remove a case involving federal questions because it allows removal only if "the *plaintiff's* complaint establishes that the case 'arises under' federal law." *Franchise Tax Bd. of Cal. v. Constr. Laborers Vacation Trust for S. Cal.,* 463 U.S. 1, 10 (1983) (emphasis in original). In other words, "a right or immunity created by the Constitution or laws of the United States must be an element, and an essential one, of the plaintiff's cause of action" before removal can occur. *Id.* at 10-11. Further, an action cannot be removed to federal court based upon "a federal defense, including the defense of preemption, even if the defense is anticipated in the plaintiff's complaint, and even if both parties admit that the defense is the only question truly at issue in the case." *Id.* at 14; *see also Caterpillar,* 482 U.S. at 393.

The complete preemption doctrine is an "independent corollary of the well-pleaded complaint rule." *Caterpillar,* 482 U.S. at 393. As explained by the United States Supreme Court, the doctrine of complete preemption applies when the preemptive force of a federal statute is so "extraordinary" that it converts a complaint solely asserting state law claims into one raising a federal question and satisfying the well-pleaded complaint rule. *Id.* Thus, "[o]nce an area of state law has been completely pre-empted, any claim purportedly based on that pre-empted state law is considered, from its inception, a federal claim, and therefore arises under federal law." *Id.*

B. The State's Usury Law Claim Against CashCall Is Not Completely Preempted

The complete preemption question in this case involves § 27 of the FDIA. Section 27 allows a state-chartered bank to charge interest rates permitted in its home state on loans made outside of its home state, even if the interest rate would be illegal in the state where the loan is made. 12 U.S.C. § 1831d(a). Therefore, state usury laws establishing maximum permissible interest rates do not apply to loans made by out-of-state banks. *Id.* In *Discover Bank et al. v. Vaden,* 489 F.3d 594, 603-04 (4th Cir. 2007), *rev'd on other grounds,* 556 U.S. 49, (2009), the Fourth Circuit held that § 27 of the FDIA completely preempts state usury law claims against state-chartered banks.

In this case, the State asserts a usury law claim against CashCall, a non-bank entity. The State alleges that "[t]he relationship between CashCall and the Bank was a sham intended to circumvent the usury and consumer protection laws of West Virginia," and that "CashCall made 'usurious loans,' in violation of [West Virginia law]." *(Id.,* Ex. A PP 82, 84). The FDIA does not apply to non-bank entities. *Vaden,* 489 F.3d at 601 n.6. Thus, on its face, the Complaint does not state any usury law claims against a state-chartered bank that would implicate the FDIA and be completely preempted.

Nevertheless, courts addressing the complete preemption question with respect to state usury law claims have found it necessary to determine whether the claims were actually directed against a federally or state-chartered bank. *See In re Cmty. Bank of N. Va. et al.,* 418 F.3d 277, 296 (3d Cir. 2005) ("[W]e must examine the . . . complaint to determine if it alleged state law claims of unlawful interest by a nationally or state chartered bank"); *Krispin v. May Dep't Stores Co.,* 218 F.3d 919, 924 (8th Cir. 2000) ("[T]he question of complete preemption in this case turns on whether appellants' suit against the [non-bank] store actually amounted, at least in part, to a state usury claim against the bank."). Courts evaluating the removal of state usury law claims similar to those in this case have found that the claims were directed only against the non-bank entity, rather than the bank, and that the claims were not completely preempted. For example, in *Colorado ex rel. Salazar v. Ace Cash Express, Inc.,* 188 F. Supp. 2d 1282 (D. Colo. 2002), the plaintiff alleged that the defendant was an unlicensed supervised lender charging excessive and improper fees in violation of state law. *Id.* at 1284. The defendant removed the action on the grounds that it operated as an agent for a national bank and therefore the claims were completely preempted by the National Bank Act ("NBA"), 12 U.S.C. § 85. *Id.* The district court found that removal was improper because the defendant was a separate entity from the bank and the plaintiff alleged no claims against the bank. *Id.* at 1285.

. . . [T]he State has only asserted state claims against a non-bank entity—CashCall. Further, CashCall and the Bank are completely separate entities. . . .The presence of th[ose] factors in this case support a conclusion that the usury law claim is directed only against CashCall.

The Complaint as a whole provides further support that the usury claim is directed against CashCall, rather than the Bank. The ten causes of action in the Complaint allege that CashCall violated a large number of West Virginia consumer protection laws. The totality of the Complaint shows that the State's suit is directed against a single, specific entity violating a host of state laws including the usury law—that entity is CashCall, not the Bank.

. . . The claims in this case are limited to CashCall's conduct and do not implicate the Bank's rights under the FDIA. The State does not dispute that the Bank, as a South Dakota-chartered bank, may make loans in West Virginia and charge interest rates permitted in South Dakota. Further, the Complaint does not target such loans and charges by the Bank. The Complaint does target, however, loans and interest charges allegedly made by CashCall. If CashCall is found to be a de facto lender, then CashCall may be liable under West Virginia usury laws. A contrary determination that CashCall is not a real lender will not result in the Bank's liability or regulation under state laws, but will merely relieve CashCall of liability under those laws. Thus, an adjudication of the usury claim in this matter will not affect the Bank's rights to make loans and charge FDIA-permitted interest rates in West Virginia.

CashCall mistakenly argues that the complete preemption of § 27 necessarily applies to the State's usury law claim because the Bank is the real lender in the relationship. It is true that in some cases, courts have found that state usury law claims nominally directed against a non-bank entity were actually directed against a related bank and thus were completely preempted by the FDIA or NBA. *See Vaden,* 489 F.3d at 603;

Krispin, 218 F.3d at 924. But those cases are distinguishable from this one. First, there was no question in *Vaden* and *Krispin* that the state-banks controlled the allegedly usurious charges. *See Vaden,* 489 F.3d at 603 (emphasizing the fact that the bank set the interest rates being challenged); *Krispin,* 218 F.3d at 924 (finding that the bank set the fees being challenged). In this case, the State alleges that CashCall is the de facto lender and there is a factual question as to the identity of the true lender.[9] Second, the state-banks and agents in *Vaden* and *Krispin* were related either through an indemnity agreement or through their corporate structure. *See Vaden,* 489 F.3d at 602-03 (explaining that the bank agreed to indemnify the agent from damages caused by the bank, including its violation of state and federal laws); *Krispin,* 218 F.3d at 923 (explaining that the bank was a wholly-owned subsidiary of the servicing agent). In contrast, CashCall and the Bank are completely separate entities.

Finally, the character of the complaints in *Vaden* and *Krispin* contrast sharply with the complaint in this case. The plaintiffs in the former cases were seeking damages caused by usurious fees. In such cases, the fact that a state-chartered bank may be the true lender of the loans may bear some weight in the complete preemption analysis because monetary recovery is sought from the responsible entity, which may be the bank. In this case, however, the attorney general of the State of West Virginia is seeking relief from the harmful conduct of a *specific entity*—CashCall. This broad objective is evident in the Complaint. Where, as here, a lawsuit is directed at the usurious conduct of a *specific non-bank entity* that does not benefit from the privileges conferred by the FDIA, the fact that a state-chartered bank might be the true lender responsible for allegedly usurious loans is less significant. This is because the bank is not the targeted entity and cannot provide the sought relief even if it turns out to be the real lender; the non-bank entity would remain the target.

Ultimately, as expressed in *Salazar,* CashCall "confuses what this case *is* and is *not* about. The Complaint *strictly* is about a non-bank's violation of *state* law. It alleges *no* claims against a *[state-chartered] bank* under the *[FDIA]." Salazar,* 188 F. Supp. 2d at 1285 (emphasis in the original). I FIND that the State's usury law claim is directed against CashCall, which is not a bank, and therefore, the claim does not invoke and cannot be completely preempted by the FDIA. Accordingly, I FIND that the State's Complaint does not raise any federal questions on its face and that this court does not have subject matter jurisdiction over this case.

III. CONCLUSION

As discussed above, this court does not have subject matter jurisdiction over the instant matter. Accordingly, I GRANT the State's Motion to Remand and ORDER this case remanded to the Circuit Court of Kanawha County, West Virginia. Further, I DENY as moot CashCall's Motion to Dismiss.

---

9. I cannot determine which entity is the true lender based on the record before the court. Therefore, even assuming that the Bank's definite status as the true lender would be dispositive of the complete preemption question, CashCall has not sustained its burden of establishing that fact.

VII. TRIBAL LENDING

A variation on the rent-a-bank lending structure is the rent-a-tribe structure. Rent-a-tribe lending uses a Native American tribal entity (or sometimes just a non-tribal entity owned by a Native American tribe member) as the formal lender, with a non-tribal entity designing the lending program, providing the funding for the loans, and handling most or all of the marketing, servicing, and collections, as well as purchasing all or almost all of the receivables from the tribal entity.

The reason some lenders do rent-a-tribe arrangements is the belief that tribal sovereign immunity will shield them not only from state regulation, but also from federal regulation by the CFPB. This reasoning is questionable. It is clear that while a tribe itself may have immunity, individual tribal members and employees do not. *Santa Clara Pueblo v. Martinez*, 436 U.S. 49, 59 (1978). Moreover, the loans made by a tribal entity outside of tribal territory are subject to state and federal law. As the Supreme Court noted in the context of off-reservation gambling under the auspices of a tribal casino, "[A] State lacks the ability to sue a tribe for illegal gaming when that activity occurs off the reservation. But a State, on its own lands, has many other powers over tribal gaming that it does not possess (absent consent) in Indian territory. Unless federal law provides differently, 'Indians going beyond reservation boundaries' are subject to any generally applicable state law." *Michigan v. Bay Mills Indian Cmty.*, 134 S. Ct. 2024 (2014). *See also, e.g., Consumer Fin. Prot. Bureau v. Great Plains Lending, LLC*, 846 F.3d 1049 (9th Cir. 2017) (affirming ruling to compel tribal compliance with CFPB civil investigatory demand); *Consumer Fin. Prot. Bureau v. CashCall, Inc.*, 2016 U.S. Dist. LEXIS 130584 (C.D. Cal. Aug. 31, 2016) (granting partial summary judgment to CFPB on deceptiveness claim and holding that non-tribal entities were the "true lender"—part of the complaint in this case is included in Chapter 11); *Otoe-Missouria Tribe of Indians v. N.Y. State Dep't of Fin. Servs.*, 769 F.3d 105 (2d Cir. 2014) (denying plaintiff tribe's preliminary injunction against the New York State Department of Financial Services from interfering with the tribe's consumer lending business). Thus, it appears that whatever immunity a tribal entity itself may have, such immunity does not necessarily transfer to other persons or entities involved in the lending operation. These other entities may still be liable for state UDAP or federal UDAAP or substantial assistance violations, and even potentially liable under state criminal law. The continued viability of rent-a-tribe lending is questionable in light of recent legal developments.

VIII. OFFSHORE LENDING

Another jurisdictional twist is to use offshore entities as the consumer financial product service provider. The contract with the consumer will then provide for a foreign choice of law. For example, the Massachusetts attorney general shut down a vehicle title lender that charged rates as high as 619% APR was run as a Cook Islands corporation. The contract purported to be governed by New Zealand law (which has no usury cap) and required all disputes to be mediated in New

Zealand. The apparent purpose of this was to circumvent Massachusetts's 36% APR usury rate. *Commonwealth v. Liquidation LLC*, no. 1684-cv-00688 (Mass. Sup. Ct. Suffolk County 2016). The result was an injunction against the title lender operating in Massachusetts.

The CFPB has also brought suit against a Malta-based Internet payday lender for various UDAAP violations. *CFPB v. NDG Financial Corp.*, no. 1:15-cv-05211-CM (S.D.N.Y. 2015). The lender included a Malta choice-of-law provision, which, if applicable, would exempt it from U.S. states' usury laws. The lender has also claimed that it is not subject to U.S. jurisdiction because it has no physical presence in the United States. The case remains pending as of the writing of this book.

Problem Set 9

1. The New York Attorney General has heard ugly reports about discriminatory auto lending by Gotham National Bank that, if true, would be in violation of both state and federal law. An initial investigation by the Attorney General has failed to reveal a single borrower of color from Gotham National Bank, but numerous would-be borrowers of color whose loan applications were denied despite sterling credit. Is the New York Attorney General likely to file suit? If so, how is the suit likely to fare? *See Cuomo v. The Clearing House Ass'n.*

2. Oregon has passed a statute that requires all institutions that accept deposits, on a daily basis, to post credits to bank accounts before debits and to post the smallest debits before the largest ones, unless the customer explicitly agrees otherwise using a form prescribed by the state banking commission. Violations subject the bank to private civil liability as well as fines by the state banking regulator. The purpose of the statute is to reduce the number of overdrafts that are likely to occur. Mastodon National Bank has brought suit challenging the Oregon statute. Is the suit likely to succeed? *See* 12 U.S.C. § 25b; 12 C.F.R. § 7.4007; *Parks v. MBNA Nat'l Bank.*

3. New Mexico's Home Loan Protection Act prohibits home mortgage refinancings that do not provide a reasonable, tangible net benefit to the borrower. By its own terms, the law applies to all home mortgage refinancings by any "creditor," which is in turn defined as "a person who regularly offers or makes a home loan." The express purpose of the prohibition is to address "abusive mortgage lending." N.M. Stat. Ann. § 58-21A-2. Would such a statute likely be preempted as applied to a loan made by a national bank? *See* 12 U.S.C. §§ 24(Seventh), 25b; 12 C.F.R. §§ 34.3(a), 34.4(a)(4), 34.4(a)(10), 34.4(b)(9).

4. Mohammed Vakil is a self-employed chiropractor in Wisconsin. He financed the purchase of a custom motorcycle from Laverna National Bank and Trust, and promptly defaulted on the loan. Vakil has sued Laverna National Bank and Trust for violations of the Wisconsin Fair Debt Collection Act based on some 400 collection calls Laverna made to Vakil and his business over the course of six months, including to his employees, who learned the terrible secret of his indebtedness. The Wisconsin Fair Debt Collection Act applies to all "debt collectors" and "creditors" and forbids "abusive collection calls" and "disclosure of indebtedness at a borrower's place of work." Laverna National Bank and Trust has moved to dismiss Vakil's suit as preempted by the National Bank Act. Will it succeed? *See* 12 U.S.C. § 25b; 12 C.F.R. § 7.4008(e)(4).

5. DigiCredit is a Georgia corporation that has designed a lending program with Bank of the East, N.A. in which Bank of the East will issue Visa brand credit cards to a target market of consumers with poor credit scores. DigiCredit has designed the entire lending program, including the underwriting criteria, and handles all of the marketing and servicing of the credit card accounts. DigiCredit also buys all of the receivables generated from the accounts after they have aged for 24 hours, with a carve-out for $1 million receivables. Bank of the East retains ownership of the account, but is prohibited from transferring such ownership without DigiCredit's consent. The interest rate on the DigiCredit cards is 144% APR, far higher than the usury rates that would be applicable to a non-bank lender in several of the states in which DigiCredit's cardholders reside. When Tewanna Wilkinson, a cardholder from Colorado, which has a usury rate of 21% APR, raises usury as a defense to DigiCredit's collection lawsuit against her, will she prevail, assuming that the Colorado usury rate is the one applicable to her card? *See West Virginia v. CashCall Inc.*, 605 F. Supp. 2d 781 (S.D.W.V. 2009); *Madden v. Midland Funding*, 786 F.3d 246 (2d Cir. 2015); 12 C.F.R. § 7.4001.

6. Banco Merica makes subprime auto loans. Banco Merica securitizes the loans, meaning that the receivables, but not the accounts, are sold to a specially created trust, in exchange for securities representing beneficial interests in the trust, which Banco Merica's securities affiliate then sells to capital market investors. Banco Merica services the loans via a contract with the trust. Banco Merica also maintains a 10% stake in the trust and provides various forms of credit support to the trust, such that if the borrowers don't pay on their loans Banco Merica will be liable to the trust to a limited amount. Some of the auto loans have interest rates that exceed Illinois's usury laws.

- **a.** When the Illinois Attorney General brings suit against Banco Merica for violation of the state's usury laws, who will prevail? 12 U.S.C. § 1831d(a).
- **b.** When the Illinois Attorney General brings suit against the trust for violation of state usury laws who will prevail? *See Madden v. Midland Funding*, 786 F.3d 246 (2d Cir. 2015); 12 U.S.C. § 25b(e); 12 C.F.R. §§ 7.4001(b), 7.4008(d)(10).
- **c.** What about when the Illinois Attorney General also sues Banco Merica for debt collection violations relating to collecting debts that are not owed because they are usurious?

CHAPTER 10

UDAAP I: UNFAIR AND DECEPTIVE ACTS AND PRACTICES

The CFPB's furthest reaching—and most controversial—power is its authority to prohibit unfair, deceptive or abusive acts and practices (UDAAP). The CFPB has authority to undertake rulemakings that identify UDAAP or to bring enforcement actions on the basis of UDAAP. State attorneys general and federal banking regulators may also bring enforcement actions under the UDAAP power.

The UDAAP power is found in two statutory provisions. Section 1036 of the Dodd-Frank Act (12 U.S.C. § 5536) provides that UDAAPs are unlawful, as is provision of substantial assistance in the commission of a UDAAP. Section 1031 of the Dodd-Frank Act (12 U.S.C. § 5531) then authorizes the CFPB to undertake enforcement actions or rulemakings in regard to UDAAP and provides definitions of "unfairness" and "abusive," but not deception.

This chapter covers unfairness and deception; the following chapter covers abusiveness. As you will see, unfairness and deception under the Consumer Financial Protection Act are substantially similar to those concepts under the Federal Trade Commission Act. Abusiveness is a new category of liability, but UDAAP, like UDAP, is still a function of statute, so it is never subject to contract and tort rules and defenses.

I. UNFAIR ACTS AND PRACTICES

Unfairness is defined under the Consumer Financial Protection Act. 12 U.S.C. § 5531(c)(1). The definition, which is almost a verbatim copy of the definition in section 5 of the FTC Act, 15 U.S.C. § 45(n), involves three elements. First, the act or practice must "cause or be likely to cause substantial injury to consumers." 12 U.S.C. § 5531(c)(1)(A). Second, the injury must not be "reasonably avoidable by consumers." 12 U.S.C. § 5531(c)(1)(A). And third, the injury must not be "outweighed by countervailing benefits to consumers or competition." 12 U.S.C. § 5531(c)(1)(B).

The CFPB's own interpretation of unfairness, as reflected in its Supervision and Examination Manual (v.2, Oct. 2012), a document that provides internal guidance to CFPB supervisory staff, draws heavily on the FTC's Policy Statement on Unfairness (Dec. 17, 1980).

CFPB Supervision and Examination Manual—UDAAP v.2 (Oct. 2012)

. . .

- ***The act or practice must cause or be likely to cause substantial injury to consumers.***
  Substantial injury usually involves monetary harm. Monetary harm includes, for example, costs or fees paid by consumers as a result of an unfair practice. An act or practice that causes a small amount of harm to a large number of people may be deemed to cause substantial injury.
  Actual injury is not required in every case. A significant risk of concrete harm is also sufficient. However, trivial or merely speculative harms are typically insufficient for a finding of substantial injury. Emotional impact and other more subjective types of harm also will not ordinarily amount to substantial injury. Nevertheless, in certain circumstances, such as unreasonable debt collection harassment, emotional impacts may amount to or contribute to substantial injury.
- ***Consumers must not be reasonably able to avoid the injury.***
  An act or practice is not considered unfair if consumers may reasonably avoid injury. Consumers cannot reasonably avoid injury if the act or practice interferes with their ability to effectively make decisions or to take action to avoid injury. Normally the marketplace is self-correcting; it is governed by consumer choice and the ability of individual consumers to make their own private decisions without regulatory intervention. If material information about a product, such as pricing, is modified after, or withheld until after, the consumer has committed to purchasing the product; however, the consumer cannot reasonably avoid the injury. Moreover, consumers cannot avoid injury if they are coerced into purchasing unwanted products or services or if a transaction occurs without their knowledge or consent.
  A key question is *not* whether a consumer could have made a better choice. Rather, the question is whether an act or practice hinders a consumer's decision-making. For example, not having access to important information could prevent consumers from comparing available alternatives, choosing those that are most desirable to them, and avoiding those that are inadequate or unsatisfactory. In addition, if almost all market participants engage in a practice, a consumer's incentive to search elsewhere for better terms is reduced, and the practice may not be reasonably avoidable.
  The actions that a consumer is expected to take to avoid injury must be reasonable. While a consumer might avoid harm by hiring independent experts to test products in advance or by bringing legal claims for damages in every case of harm, these actions generally would be too expensive to be practical for individual consumers and, therefore, are not reasonable.
- ***The injury must not be outweighed by countervailing benefits to consumers or competition.***

> To be unfair, the act or practice must be injurious in its net effects — that is, the injury must not be outweighed by any offsetting consumer or competitive benefits that also are produced by the act or practice. Offsetting consumer or competitive benefits of an act or practice may include lower prices to the consumer or a wider availability of products and services resulting from competition.
>
> Costs that would be incurred for measures to prevent the injury also are taken into account in determining whether an act or practice is unfair. These costs may include the costs to the institution in taking preventive measures and the costs to society as a whole of any increased burden and similar matters.

Note that the second element, reasonable avoidability, seems to incorporate something similar to the "absence of meaningful choice" analysis for unconscionability. *Williams v. Walker-Thomas Furniture Co.*, 350 F.2d 445, 449 (D.C. Cir. 1965). Indeed, in the context of the FTC Act, the FTC has noted that if a particular contract term is widespread in an industry, it reduces the incentive to search for better terms:

> If 80 percent of creditors include a certain clause in their contracts, for example, even the consumer who examines contracts from three different sellers has less than even chance of finding a contract without the clause. In such circumstances, relatively few consumers are likely to find the effort worthwhile. . . .

FTC, Trade Regulation Rule; Credit Practices, 49 Fed. Reg. 7740, 7746 (Mar. 1, 1984). Likewise, to the extent that a practice is of the type that a reasonable consumer—not a perfect consumer—would be unlikely to pay attention to, then the practice is not reasonably avoidable. Thus, the FTC, in its rulemaking for the Credit Practices Rule observed that "Because remedies [such as repossession] are relevant only in the event of default, and default is relatively infrequent, consumers reasonably concentrate their search on such factors as interest rates and payment terms." *Id.* Reasonable avoidability may also differ depending on the marketplace for a product. Characteristics of a product's target market—English ability, age, infirmity, financial distress—may all affect what is reasonably avoidable.

The final element of unfairness involves a type of cost-benefit analysis involving weighing the consumer harm against consumer or competitive benefits. While the statute prescribes a weighing of the injuries caused by a practice versus the benefits from a practice, it provides no guidance on how to conduct such a balancing. The legislative history of the FTC Act indicates that the cost-benefit analysis need not be a quantitative one, but could instead be qualitative. Sen. Rep. No. 130, 103d Cong. 2d Sess. 12 (1994), *reprinted in* 1994 U.S.C.C.AN. 1787-1788. In some cases, the balancing presents no problem—there are some practices that provide no obvious benefit to consumers, such billing for services not provided. In other cases, however, the analysis will necessarily be more complex. Thus, a practice might possibly benefit one group of consumers and harm another, such as a pricing structure that has one group of consumers subsidizing others. The resolution of such situations is entirely fact-dependent.

The CFPB has invoked unfairness in only one proposed rulemaking so far, that for payment, vehicle title, and other high-cost installment loans, a situation in which there are some countervailing benefits to be considered, and that the proposed rule attempts to preserve while excising the most problematic features of these products. A discussion of the CFPB's interpretation of unfairness in this context appears in a subsequent chapter on small-dollar lending.

In enforcement actions, the CFPB has thus far generally eschewed situations in which the cost-benefit analysis is less than clear cut. Consider how the CFPB has applied unfairness in the following consent orders. Is there much question about countervailing benefits to consumers or competition?

Consent Order
In the Matter of RBS Citizens Financial Group, Inc. (n/k/a Citizens Financial Group, Inc.), RBS Citizens, N.A (n/k/a Citizens Bank, N.A), and Citizens Bank of Pennsylvania

Administrative Proceeding No. 2015-CFPB-0020 (Aug. 11, 2015)

The Consumer Financial Protection Bureau ("Bureau") has reviewed the deposit processing practices of RES Citizens Financial Group, Inc. (now known as Citizens Financial Group, Inc.), RES Citizens, N.A. (now known as Citizens Bank, N.A.), and Citizens Bank of Pennsylvania (collectively, the "Respondents" as defined below) and has determined: (1) the Respondents processed deposits such that certain customers did not receive credit for the full amount of deposited funds, which is an unfair act or practice in violation of 12 U.S.C. §§ 5531, 5536. . . . Under Sections 1053 and 1055 of the Consumer Financial Protection Act of 2010 ("CFPA" as defined below), 12 U.S.C. §§ 5563, 5565, the Bureau issues this Order.

Each Respondent has executed a "Stipulation and Consent to the Issuance of a Consent Order," ("Stipulations"), each of which is incorporated by reference and accepted by the Bureau. By these Stipulations, Respondents consented to the issuance of this Order by the Bureau under Sections 1053 and 1055 of the CFPA, 12 U.S.C. §§ 5563 and 5565, without admitting or denying any of the findings of fact or conclusions of law, except that Respondents admit the facts necessary to establish the Bureau's jurisdiction over Respondents and the subject matter of this action.

DEFINITIONS

3. The following definitions apply to this Order:

. . .

h. . . . "Deposit Discrepancy" means a deposit transaction where the total deposit amount the Banks read on the deposit slip differed from the total of the amounts read from the checks, cash deposited, and/or other deposit items.

. . .

BUREAU FINDINGS AND CONCLUSIONS

The Bureau finds the following:

4. Citizens Holding Company is a commercial bank holding company with $136 billion in total assets. Citizens and CBP are separately chartered banks that are subsidiaries of Citizens Holding Company.

5. Citizens is an insured depository institution with $106 billion in assets as of March 31, 2015. CBP is an insured depository institution with $34 billion in assets as of March 31, 2015. Therefore, both Citizens and CBP are insured depository institutions with assets greater than $10 billion within the meaning of 12 U.S.C. § 5515(a). They are also covered persons as that term is defined by 12 U.S.C. § 5481(6).

6. Citizens Holding Company performed centralized compliance management for both Banks, including in relation to the consumer communications and deposit processing practices that are the subject of this Order. Citizens Holding Company, therefore, acted as a Service Provider to its banking subsidiaries Citizens and CBP.

FINDINGS AND CONCLUSIONS AS TO UNFAIR PRACTICES IN CONNECTION WITH DEPOSIT PROCESSING

7. During the Relevant Period, the Banks used an Enterprise Transaction System ("ETS") for processing deposits.

8. The Banks generally required consumers making a deposit to present (i) the deposit items (*e.g.*, checks, cash); and (ii) a deposit slip on which the customer indicated the total amount of funds being deposited. Having received those documents, Citizens or CBP then provided the consumer with a receipt for the transaction reflecting the amount stated on the deposit slip.

9. Each branch then assembled the deposit items and deposit slips into batches, and sent those batches to one of several centralized processing facilities shared by the Banks.

10. ETS flagged for the Banks' attention deposit transactions where the total deposit amount the Banks read on the deposit slip appeared to differ from the total of the amounts read from the checks, cash deposited, and/or other deposit items (a Deposit Discrepancy as defined above).

11. Deposit Discrepancies indicated to the Banks that a question existed as to the amount the customer deposited.

12. For transactions where the Deposit Discrepancy was above a defined threshold ($50.00 prior to September 2012 and $25.00 thereafter), it was the Banks' practice to review the underlying documents (*e.g.*, checks) to determine the actual deposit amount, and then make any adjustments necessary to correct the amount the consumer was credited.

13. Where, however, a Deposit Discrepancy fell below those levels, the Banks followed a different practice: rather than attempting to ascertain the actual deposit amount, they credited the consumer's account with the amount read on the deposit slip, even where the Banks knew the items the consumer deposited indicated a different amount.

14. In most cases of Deposit Discrepancies, the amount read on the deposit slip was incorrect. As a result, the Banks' customers received credit for a deposit amount that was likely inaccurate.

15. Because ETS would not accept a transaction in which the amount credited to a customer's account did not match the funds deposited with the Bank, the Banks created "substitution tickets" which credited or debited the Banks' general ledger account with the difference between the amounts credited to the customer's account and funds deposited with the Banks.

16. The Banks' practice harmed consumers when the amount scanned on the deposit slip was less than the amount of the deposit items associated with the deposit. In such cases, the Banks did not give consumers full credit for their deposits.

17. When the amount scanned on the deposit slip was more than the amount of the deposit items associated with the deposit, consumers were credited for more than their actual deposit amount.

18. During the Relevant Period, the Banks under-credited consumers by approximately $12.3 million.

19. The Banks' practices with respect to Deposit Discrepancies (as described above) did not comply with their own policy. The Banks' policy was to perform a limited review of the underlying documents when the Deposit Discrepancy fell within an intermediate range (most recently, between $5.00 and $25.00; prior to February 2011, between $23.00 and $50.00); and to provide no review when the Deposit Discrepancy fell beneath the intermediate range. Contrary to the Banks' policy, in most cases they did not perform the limited review for Deposit Discrepancies in the intermediate range; and, as described above, credited consumers with the amount on the deposit slip.

20. Respondents failed to detect this compliance failure due to weaknesses in the Banks' compliance management system and oversight failures.

21. In November 2013, the Banks fully implemented technological and practice changes to their deposit processing system, and transitioned away from ETS.

22. Section 1036(a)(1)(B) of the CFPA prohibits "unfair, deceptive, or abusive" acts or practices. 12 U.S.C. § 5536(a)(1)(B). An act or practice is unfair if it causes or is likely to cause consumers substantial injury that is not reasonably avoidable and if the substantial injury is not outweighed by countervailing benefits to consumers or to competition.

23. The Banks' practice for resolving Deposit Discrepancies resulted in consumers receiving less than full credit for their deposits and caused substantial injury to consumers. This injury was not reasonably avoidable or outweighed by any countervailing benefit to consumers or to competition.

24. Thus, the Banks engaged in unfair acts and practices in violation of Sections 1036(a)(1)(B) and 1031(c)(1) of the CFPA. 12 U.S.C. §§ 5536(a)(1)(B) and 5531(c)(1).

Notes on *RBS Citizens Financial*

1. The CFPB also brought a "deception" claim against Citizens for expressly and impliedly representing that all deposits were subject to verification when in many instances Citizens did not verify or correct the deposit inaccuracies identified by ETS.

2. Citizens agreed to pay $11 million to reimburse the affected consumers, as well as a $7.5 million civil monetary penalty.

Consent Order
In the Matter of Wells Fargo Bank, N.A.

Administrative Proceeding 2016-CFPB-0015 (Sept. 4, 2016)

The Consumer Financial Protection Bureau (Bureau) has reviewed the sales practices of Wells Fargo Bank, N.A. (Respondent, as defined below) and determined that it has engaged in the following acts and practices: (1) opened unauthorized deposit accounts for existing customers and transferred funds to those accounts from their owners' other accounts, all without their customers' knowledge or consent; (2) submitted applications for credit cards in consumers' names using consumers' information without their knowledge or consent; (3) enrolled consumers in online-banking services that they did not request; and (4) ordered and activated debit cards using consumers' information without their knowledge or consent. The Bureau has concluded that such acts violate §§ 1031 and 1036(a)(1)(B) of the Consumer Financial Protection Act of 2010 (CFPA), 12 U.S.C. §§ 5531 and 5536(a)(1)(B). Under §§ 1053 and 1055 of CFPA, 12 U.S.C. §§ 5563, 5565, the Bureau issues this Consent Order (Consent Order).

BUREAU FINDINGS AND CONCLUSIONS

The Bureau finds the following:

1. Respondent is a national bank headquartered in Sioux Falls, South Dakota. Respondent is an insured depository institution with assets greater than $10 billion within the meaning of 12 U.S.C. § 5515(a).

2. Respondent is a "covered person" under 12 U.S.C. § 5481(6).

3. During the Relevant Period, Respondent offered a broad array of consumer financial products and services, including mortgages, savings and checking accounts, credit cards, debit and ATM cards, and online-banking services.

4. Respondent sought to distinguish itself in the marketplace as a leader in "cross-selling" banking products and services to its existing customers.

5. Respondent set sales goals and implemented sales incentives, including an incentive-compensation program, in part to increase the number of banking products and services that its employees sold to its customers.

6. Thousands of Respondent's employees engaged in Improper Sales Practices to satisfy sales goals and earn financial rewards under Respondent's incentive-compensation program. During the Relevant Period, Respondent terminated roughly 5,300 employees for engaging in Improper Sales Practices.

7. Respondent's employees engaged in "simulated funding." To qualify for incentives that rewarded bankers for opening new accounts that were funded shortly after opening, Respondent's employees opened deposit accounts without consumers' knowledge or consent and then transferred funds from consumers' authorized accounts to temporarily fund the unauthorized accounts in a manner sufficient for the employee to obtain credit under the incentive-compensation program.

8. Respondent's employees submitted applications for and obtained credit cards for consumers without the consumers' knowledge or consent.

9. Respondent's employees used email addresses not belonging to consumers to enroll consumers in online-banking services without their knowledge or consent.

10. Respondent's employees requested debit cards and created personal identification numbers (PINs) to activate them without the consumer's knowledge or consent.

11. During the Relevant Period, Respondent's employees opened hundreds of thousands of unauthorized deposit accounts and applied for tens of thousands of credit cards for consumers without consumers' knowledge or consent.

12. Respondent has performed an analysis to assess the scope of Improper Sales Practices that occurred between May 2011 and July 2015, including the number of potential instances of such practices.

FINDINGS AND CONCLUSIONS AS TO UNAUTHORIZED DEPOSIT ACCOUNTS & SIMULATED FUNDING

13. Respondent's analysis concluded that its employees opened 1,534,280 deposit accounts that may not have been authorized and that may have been funded through simulated funding, or transferring funds from consumers' existing accounts without their knowledge or consent. That analysis determined that roughly 85,000 of those accounts incurred about $2 million in fees, which Respondent is in the process of refunding. The fees included overdraft fees on linked accounts the consumers already had, monthly service fees imposed for failure to keep a minimum balance in the unauthorized account, and other fees.

14. Section 1036(a)(1)(B) of the CFPA prohibits "unfair" acts or practices. 12 U.S.C. § 5536(a)(1)(B). An act or practice is unfair if it causes or is likely to cause consumers substantial injury that is not reasonably avoidable and is not outweighed by countervailing benefits to consumers or to competition. 12 U.S.C. § 5531(c)(1).

15. By opening unauthorized deposit accounts and engaging in acts of simulated funding, Respondent caused and was likely to cause substantial injury to consumers that was not reasonably avoidable, because it occurred without consumers' knowledge, and was not outweighed by countervailing benefits to consumers or to competition.

. . .

19. Therefore, Respondent engaged in "unfair" . . . acts or practices that violate §§ 1031(c)(1) . . . and 1036(a)(1)(B) of the CFPA. 12 U.S.C. §§ 5531(c)(1) . . . 5536(a)(1)(B).

FINDINGS AND CONCLUSIONS AS TO UNAUTHORIZED CREDIT CARDS

20. Respondent's analysis concluded that its employees submitted applications for 565,443 credit-card accounts that may not have been authorized by using consumers' information without their knowledge or consent. That analysis determined that roughly 14,000 of those accounts incurred $403,145 in fees, which Respondent is in the process of refunding. Fees incurred by consumers on such accounts included annual fees and overdraft-protection fees, as well as associated finance or interest charges and other late fees.

21. Section 1036(a)(1)(B) of the CFPA prohibits "unfair" acts or practices. 12 U.S.C. § 5536(a)(1)(B). An act or practice is unfair if it causes or is likely to cause consumers substantial injury that is not reasonably avoidable and is not outweighed by countervailing benefits to consumers or to competition. 12 U.S.C. § 5531(c)(1).

22. By applying for and opening credit-card accounts using consumers' information without their knowledge or consent, Respondent caused and was likely to cause substantial injury that was not reasonably avoidable, because it occurred without consumers' knowledge, and was not outweighed by countervailing benefits to consumers or competition.

. . .

26. Therefore, Respondent engaged in "unfair" . . . acts or practices that violate §§ 1031(c)(1) . . . and 1036(a)(1)(B) of the CFPA. 12 U.S.C. §§ 5531(c)(1) . . . 5536(a)(1)(B).

Notes on *Wells Fargo Bank*

1. As part of the consent order Wells Fargo agreed to pay a $100 million fine, the largest imposed by the CFPB to date. Wells Fargo also agreed to pay an additional $35 million to the Office of the Comptroller of the Currency and $50 million to the City and County of Los Angeles.

2. The CFPB also brought "abusive" claims against Wells Fargo based in part on the same facts.

3. Consumer claims against Wells Fargo faced the problem of arbitration clauses. Go back and look at the Wells Fargo arbitration agreement in Chapter 3. Do you think it covers fake account openings?

4. The CFPB's consent order resulted in high profile Congressional hearings on the fake accounts, and eventually the resignation of Wells Fargo's chairman and CEO, John Stumpf. In 2018 the Federal Reserve Board forbade Wells Fargo from making acquisitions and ordered divestment of certain assets. Also in 2018, Wells Fargo was fined an additional $1 billion by the CFPB and OCC in light of further legal violations regarding consumers.

5. The problem of unauthorized account creation is not limited to Wells Fargo. It was an issue also in the CFPB's enforcement action against PayPal and Bill Me Later, part of which appears in the next chapter (regarding a different issue). Similarly, the CFPB's PayPal/Bill Me Later action alleged failure to post payments to accounts, much like the situation in Citizens Bank.

II. DECEPTIVE ACTS AND PRACTICES

The Consumer Financial Protection Act prohibits deceptive acts and practices by covered persons and service providers, but it does not define the term "deceptive." The CFPB has not issued an official interpretation of the term, but the CFPB Supervision and Examination Manual (v.2, Oct. 2012) provides that:

A representation, omission, act, or practice is deceptive when:

(1) the representation, omission, act, or practice misleads or is likely to mislead the consumer;
(2) the consumer's interpretation of the representation, omission, act, or practice is reasonable under the circumstances; and
(3) the misleading representation, omission, act, or practice is material.

The Supervision and Examination Manual further provides that a representation or omission is material "if it is likely to affect a consumer's choice of, or conduct regarding, the product or service." Significantly, actual harm to a consumer is not necessary under this interpretation. Deception, then, involves a material representation, omission, or practice that is likely to mislead a reasonable consumer.

The CFPB's internal definition of deception tracks the FTC's Policy Statement on Deception under the Federal Trade Commission Act's unfair and deceptive acts and practices provisions (15 U.S.C. § 45(a)). Indeed, both the Supervision and Examination Manual and CFPB Bulletin 2012-16 (July 18, 2012) state that the CFPB's understanding of deception is "informed by the FTC's standard for deception." *See* CFPB Examination Manual (v.2, Oct. 2012), at 5, n. 10.

The FTC Act's prohibition against deceptive acts and practices seems to have been originally aimed at misleading advertisement. Thus, critically, deception requires some sort of representation or omission; products themselves are unlikely to be deceptive. Instead, it is their marketing and presentation that might be. Unlike fraud, however, deception does not require intent; instead, it is focused on the effect on the reasonable consumer:

> The definition is broad enough to cover every form of advertisement deception over which it would be humanly practicable to exercise governmental control. It covers every case of imposition on a purchaser for which there could be a practical remedy. It reaches every case from that of inadvertent or uninformed advertising to that of the most subtle as well as the most vicious types of advertisement.[1]

As the FTC refined the concept, deception requires a material representation or omission that is likely to mislead a reasonable consumer.[2] Thus, a statement could in fact be true, but it might still be misleading.

It is important to note that subsequent disclosures cannot correct early deceptive claims. For example, disclosures made at the point of sale cannot undo the deception in general media advertisement. Likewise, small print in a document cannot save a misleading misrepresentation elsewhere in the document. And, even if proper disclosures are made in a writing, if a contemporary oral sales presentation effectively obscures the meaning of the written disclosures, then the total effect is deceptive. (Remember that there is no parol evidence rule for UDAP, so a merger clause or disclaimers in the contract will not keep out oral representations!)

---

1. H.R. Rep. No. 1613, at 4 (1937).

2. Letter from James C. Miller Michael, Chairman, Fed. Trade Comm'n, to John D. Dingell, Chairman, Comm. on Energy & Commerce, FTC Policy Statement on Deception (Oct. 14. 1983), appended to Cliffdale Associates, Inc., 103 F.T.C. 110, 174 (1984).

Thus, one example of an activity the FTC found to be deceptive were television advertisements for vehicle leasing companies that represented that the vehicles could be leased for "$0 down," but a "blur" of "unreadable fine print" on flashed on the screen at the end of the advertisement in fact disclosed that there were costs of at least $1,000.[3] Another example was a mortgage broker's advertisement of loan refinancings at "3.5% fixed payment 30-year loan" or "3.5% fixed payment for 30 years," implying a 30-year loan with an interest rate fixed at 3.5%, when in fact the broker was offering payment-option adjustable rate mortgages that could negatively amortize.[4]

Critically, deception need not necessarily involve a false statement, although a material false statement is likely to be deceptive. To date the CFPB has brought more deception actions than any other sort of action. Consider the deceptive behavior in the following two cases.

Consent Order
In the Matter of Dwolla, Inc.

CFPB Administrative Proceeding, No. 2016-CFPB-0007 (Feb. 27, 2016)

The Consumer Financial Protection Bureau (Bureau) has reviewed certain acts and practices of Dwolla, Inc. (Respondent, as defined below) and has identified the following law violations: deceptive acts and practices relating to false representations regarding Respondent's data-security practices in violation of Sections 1031(a) and 1036(a)(1) of the Consumer Financial Protection Act of 2010 (CFPA), 12 U.S.C. §§ 5531(a), 5536(a)(1). Under Sections 1053 and 1055 of the CFPA, 12 U.S.C. §§ 5563, 5565, the Bureau issues this Consent Order (Consent Order).

. . .

1. Respondent launched services in Iowa on December 1, 2009; in California on April 5, 2010; and nationally on December 1, 2010.

2. Respondent's payment network allows a consumer to become a Member by registering for a Dwolla account at Dwolla.com. A Member can then access his or her Dwolla account through the Dwolla website or through individual applications. Members can direct Respondent to effect a transfer of funds to the Dwolla account of another consumer or merchant. The funds for the transfer can come either from funds stored in the consumer's Dwolla account or a personal bank account linked to the consumer's Dwolla account.

3. In order to open a Dwolla account, consumers must submit their name, address, date of birth, telephone number, and Social Security number.

---

3. Complaint, *In the Matter of General Motors Corporation*, FTC Docket No. C-3710 (Feb. 11, 1997); Complaint, *In the Matter of American Honda Motor Company, Inc.*, FTC Docket No. C-3711 (Feb. 11, 1997); Complaint, *In the Matter of American Isuzu Motors, Inc.*, FTC Docket No C-3712 (Feb. 11, 1997); Complaint, *In the Matter of Mitsubishi Sales of America, Inc.*, FTC Docket No. C-3713 (Feb. 11, 1997); Complaint, *In the Matter of Mazda Motor of America, Inc.*, FTC Docket No. C-3714 (Feb. 11, 1997). The cases all concluded in consent decrees.

4. FTC v. Chase Financial Funding, Inc., No. SACV04-549 (C.D. Cal. 2004), Stipulated Preliminary Injunction.

4. In order to link a bank account to a Dwolla account, consumers must submit a bank account number and routing number.

5. In order to transfer funds using a Dwolla account, consumers must enter a username, password, and a unique 4-digit PIN.

6. Respondent stores consumers' sensitive personal information, including the information supplied to Respondent described in Paragraphs 8-10.

7. Respondent holds consumers' funds in a single, pooled account at Veridian Credit Union, an Iowa-chartered, federally-insured credit union, or Compass Bank, a federally-insured bank.

8. Respondent has been collecting and storing consumers' sensitive personal information and providing a platform for financial transactions since December 1, 2009.

9. As of May 2015, Respondent had approximately 653,000 Members and had transferred as much as $5,000,000 per day.

FINDINGS AND CONCLUSIONS AS TO DECEPTIVE DATA-SECURITY REPRESENTATIONS

10. From January 2011 to March 2014, Respondent represented, or caused to be represented, expressly or by implication, to consumers that Respondent employs reasonable and appropriate measures to protect data obtained from consumers from unauthorized access, as detailed below.

11. Respondent represented to consumers that its network and transactions were "safe" and "secure."

12. On its website, Respondent represented that "Dwolla empowers anyone with an internet connection to safely send money to friends or businesses."

13. Respondent's website stated that Dwolla transactions were "safer [than credit cards] and less of a liability for both consumers and merchants."

14. On its website or in direct communications with consumers, Respondent made the following representations indicating that its data-security practices met or exceeded industry standards:

a. Dwolla's data-security practices "exceed industry standards," or "surpass industry security standards";
b. Dwolla "sets a new precedent for the industry for safety and security";
c. Dwolla stores consumer information "in a bank-level hosting and security environment"; and
d. Dwolla encrypts data "utilizing the same standards required by the federal government."

15. On its website or in direct communications with consumers, Respondent made the following representations regarding its encryption and data-security measures:

a. "All information is securely encrypted and stored";
b. "100% of your info is encrypted and stored securely";
c. Dwolla encrypts "all sensitive information that exists on its servers";
d. Dwolla uses "industry standard encryption technology";
e. Dwolla "encrypt[s] data in transit and at rest";

f. "Dwolla's website, mobile applications, connection to financial institutions, back end, and even APIs use the latest encryption and secure connections"; and

g. Dwolla is "PCI compliant".

16. The Payment Card Industry (PCI) Security Standards Council is an open global forum that issues the data-security compliance standards for cardholder data adopted by some of the world's largest payment card networks, including American Express, MasterCard, and Visa.

17. Respondent represented to consumers that its transactions, servers, and data centers were compliant with the standards set forth by the PCI Security Standards Council.

18. In fact, Respondent failed to employ reasonable and appropriate measures to protect data obtained from consumers from unauthorized access.

19. In fact, Respondent's data-security practices did not "surpass" or "exceed" industry standards.

20. In fact, Respondent did not encrypt all sensitive consumer information in its possession at rest.

21. In fact, Respondent's transactions, servers, and data centers were not PCI compliant.

22. In particular, Dwolla failed to:

a. adopt and implement data-security policies and procedures reasonable and appropriate for the organization;

b. use appropriate measures to identify reasonably foreseeable security risks;

c. ensure that employees who have access to or handle consumer information received adequate training and guidance about security risks;

d. use encryption technologies to properly safeguard sensitive consumer information; and

e. practice secure software development, particularly with regard to consumer-facing applications developed at an affiliated website, Dwollalabs.

DATA SECURITY POLICIES AND PROCEDURES

23. From its launch until at least September 2012, Respondent did not adopt or implement reasonable and appropriate data-security policies and procedures governing the collection, maintenance, or storage of consumers' personal information.

24. From its launch until at least October 2013, Respondent did not adopt or implement a written data-security plan to govern the collection, maintenance, or storage of consumers' personal information.

RISK ASSESSMENTS

30. Respondent also failed to conduct adequate, regular risk assessments to identify reasonably foreseeable internal and external risks to consumers' personal information, or to assess the safeguards in place to control those risks.

31. Respondent conducted its first comprehensive risk assessment in mid-2014.

EMPLOYEE TRAINING

32. Until at least December 2012, Respondent's employees received little to no data-security training on their responsibilities for handling and protecting the security of consumers' personal information.

33. Respondent did not hold its first mandatory employee training on data security until mid-2014.

34. In December 2012, Respondent hired a third party auditor to perform the first penetration test of Dwolla.com. In that test, a phishing e-mail attack was distributed to Respondent's employees that contained a suspicious URL link. Nearly half of Respondent's employees opened the e-mail, and of those, 62% of employees clicked on the URL link. Of those that clicked the link, 25% of employees further attempted to register on the phishing site and provided a username and password.

35. Dwolla failed to address the results of this test or educate its personnel about the dangers of phishing.

36. Dwolla did not conduct its first mandatory employee data-security training until mid-2014.

ENCRYPTION

37. Relevant industry standards require encryption of sensitive data.

38. In numerous instances, Respondent stored, transmitted, or caused to be transmitted the following consumer personal information without encrypting that data:

a. first and last names;
b. mailing addresses;
c. Dwolla 4-digit PINS;
d. Social Security numbers;
e. Bank account information; and
f. digital images of driver's licenses, Social Security cards and utility bills.

39. Dwolla also encouraged consumers to submit sensitive information via e-mail in clear text, including Social Security numbers and scans of driver's licenses, utility bills, and passports, in order to expedite the registration process for new users.

TESTING SOFTWARE

40. In July 2012, Respondent hired a software development manager in Iowa who began to establish and implement secure software development practices to govern Respondent's software development operations.

41. At the same time, Respondent operated an alternative software development operation, Dwollalabs.com (Dwollalabs).

42. The software developer leading Dwollalabs software development had no data-security training.

43. The software development that occurred at Dwollalabs did not comply with the security practices that Respondent had implemented to govern the company's software development operations.

44. Respondent created applications through this software developer and released those applications to the public on Dwollalabs.com.

45. Sensitive consumer data was stored on Dwollalabs.com and on its apps.

46. Respondent failed to test the security of the apps on Dwollalabs.com prior to releasing the apps to the public to ensure that consumers' information was protected.

47. These apps included #Dwolla, MassPay, Dwolla IOS app, and Dwolla for Windows.

48. Respondent did not conduct risk assessments or penetration tests on Dwollalabs.com.

49. Respondent's representations regarding its data-security practices, as described in Paragraphs 15-22, were likely to mislead a reasonable consumer into believing that Dwolla had incorporated reasonable and appropriate data-security practices when it had not.

50. Respondent's representations were material because they were likely to affect a consumer's choice or conduct regarding whether to become a member of Dwolla's network.

51. Thus, Dwolla's practices, as described in Paragraphs 15-22, constitute deceptive acts or practices in violation of the CFPA, 12 U.S.C. §§ 5531(a) and 5536(a)(1)(B).

In the Matter of Discover Bank, Greenwood, Delaware Joint Consent Order, Order for Restitution, and Order to Pay Civil Monetary Penalty

Docket No. FDIC-11-548b; FDIC-11-55k; 2021-CFPB-0005 (Sept. 24, 2012)

. . .

The [Federal Deposit Insurance Corporation ("FDIC")] and CFPB have determined that Discover has engaged in deceptive acts and practices in or affecting commerce, in violation of section 5 of the Federal Trade Commission Act ("Section 5"), 15 U.S.C. § 45(a)(l), and in deceptive acts and practices in violation of sections 1031 and 1036 of the CFP Act (together "Section 1036"), 12 U.S.C. §§ 5531,5536, in connection with the marketing, sales, and operation of Discover's Payment Protection, Identity Theft Protection, Wallet Protection and Credit Score Tracker products, as well as any related predecessor products (each a "Product" and, collectively, the "Products") that were offered and sold to individual holders of Discover consumer credit card accounts (each a "Cardmember") by Discover. . . .

The FDIC and CFPB find, and Discover neither admits nor denies, the following facts:

1. Discover marketed and sold the Products to Cardmembers during the Period December 1, 2007 through August 31, 2011 (the "relevant time period"). During this time, Discover sold one or more Products to approximately 4.7 million Cardmembers.

2. During the relevant time period, Discover telemarketed the Products to Cardmembers through both outbound sales calls and inbound customer service

calls. Discover contracted with telemarketing vendors to conduct outbound sales calls. Additionally, Discover's in-house telemarketers marketed the Products when Cardmembers called to active their Discover credit cards or placed other types of customer service calls.

3. Discover developed numerous versions of telemarketing scripts that were used to market each Product. Discover required its in-house and third-party telemarketers to adhere to these scripts. The scripts led telemarketers through the introduction and sales of the products and the outbound telemarketing scripts also typically provided the telemarketers with specific responses to questions that Cardmembers might raise during a telemarketing call.

4. Discover's inbound and outbound telemarketing scripts contained material misrepresentations and omissions related to the Products. These misrepresentations and omissions were likely to mislead reasonable consumers about whether they were purchasing a Product during a telemarketing sales call. Examples of these misrepresentations and omissions include, but are not limited to, the following:

a. Introductory statements contained in the outbound telemarketing scripts that disguised the purpose of an outbound sales call by indicating to Cardmembers that Discover was placing a courtesy call and misleadingly implied that a Product was a free "benefit" rather than a program for which Discover charged an additional fee.

b. Language in telemarketing scripts that frequently asked Cardmembers if they agreed to "be enrolled" in or "become a member" of a Product program but omitted the material fact that enrollment or membership constituted an agreement to purchase the Product.

c. Language in telemarketing scripts that frequently solicited Cardmembers' interest in "enrolling" in a Product program before providing the Product's price or material terms and conditions.

d. Statements in telemarketing scripts that typically stated that Cardmembers would receive a letter describing the Payment Protection Product's material terms and conditions before Cardmembers were required to pay for that Product, implying that Cardmembers had not purchased the Product before receipt of the letter. In fact, Discover sent its Cardmembers this letter only after Cardmembers had been enrolled in the Payment Protection Product program.

e. Suggested rebuttal responses in outbound telemarketing scripts that implied that Cardmembers could comparison shop by reviewing a comprehensive list of Product terms and conditions before they were enrolled in a Product program. In fact, Cardmembers were required to first purchase a Product before receiving a comprehensive list of Product terms and conditions.

5. Frequently, Discover's telemarketers spoke more rapidly during the mandatory disclosure portion of the sales call, which included a statement of the Product's price and some—but not all—material terms and conditions of the Product. Discover's telemarketers also frequently downplayed this mandatory disclosure during their telemarketing sales presentation, implying to Cardmembers that the mandatory disclosure was

not important, even though it was designed to alert Cardmembers to the Product's price and certain terms and conditions.

6. The impact of Discover's deceptive telemarketing scripts and presentations was compounded by the fact that Discover did not need to ask Cardmembers for their credit card numbers in order to bill them for the Products because it had access to Cardmembers' credit card numbers and could (and did) directly bill the cost of the Products to Cardmembers' Discover accounts.

7. Discover's telemarketing scripts for the Payment Protection Product also typically failed to disclose material terms and conditions of the Payment Protection Product. For example, these scripts failed to state that individuals who are self-employed, unemployed, employed part-time, or suffering from a pre-existing medical condition cannot obtain certain Payment Protection Product benefits.

Notes and Questions about *Discover*

1. Discover was the CFPB's second enforcement action. The first was a very similar case against Capital One. Discover settled for restitution of $200 million to three and a half million customers plus a $14 million penalty and injunctive relief. Approximately two million of the consumers received full restitution. Capital One settled for restitution of $140 million to two million customers plus a $25 million penalty and injunctive relief. Subsequent cases were brought against American Express, Bank of America, and JPMorgan Chase, resulting in a total of $1.5 billion in consumer restitution.

2. In January 2015, the UK Financial Conduct Authority ordered 11 UK banks, including a Capital One affiliate, to make restitution of hundreds of millions of pounds to consumers for "mis-selling" unnecessary "card security" insurance the duplicates existing legal protections. Press Release, Financial Conduct Authority, *Compensation Agreed for Consumers Sold Card Security Products*, Jan. 27, 2015.

3. What exactly was it that was deceptive in the Discover case? Was it the add-on products (payment protection plans, identity theft protection, and credit monitoring) themselves? Or was it the manner in which these products were marketed?

4. Does the CFPB ever express an opinion about the value of the add-on products? Do you think the CFPB would have brought the enforcement action if it believed that the add-on products were valuable to consumers? If these products were so valuable, would Discover need to push them on consumers?

5. Do you think the CFPB would have brought the enforcement action if the authorization process had more frictions, such as the consumer having to give Discover his or her credit card number (*see* ¶6)?

6. The CFPB alleged that cardholders had to purchase a product before they could receive a comprehensive list of terms of conditions (*see* ¶4(e)). Is that materially different than the infamous shrink wrap contracts cases such as *ProCD, Inc. v. Zeidenberg*, 86 F.3d 1447 (7th Cir. 1996), and *Hill v. Gateway 2000*, 105 F.3d 1147 (7th Cir. 1997), which upheld enforcement of terms that were included in the product box that was shipped following purchase?

Problem Set 10

1. Slaab Motor Corporation leases its high-end Scandinavian-designed cars to consumers. Slaab ran a set of television advertisements with a well-known actor telling consumers that under Slaab's "No Money Down Program" they could lease vehicles for "$0 down and just a low monthly lease payment." The end of the commercials featured a blur of fine print briefly flashed on the screen that disclosed, as required by Regulation M (governing consumer leases), additional mandatory upfront fees for paperwork processing, etc., of at least $1,000. These additional costs are also disclosed to consumers as part of the paperwork when they are signing a lease. When the CFPB sues Slaab for deception, what is the likely outcome? *See* 12 U.S.C. § 5531.

2. The Sloppy Jalopy, LLC, is a used car dealership owned by Johnny Cartilage. The Sloppy Jalopy offers financing to its customers. When The Sloppy Jalopy makes a loan, it does not bother to verify the borrower's income or assets or even obtain a credit score for the borrower. Instead, The Sloppy Jalopy assures itself of repayment through the repossession value of the car and then by pursuing defaulted consumers for any deficiency. "Yeah, we sometimes aren't able to collect," says Cartilage, "but it'd be a helluva lot more expensive to have to verify incomes and actually underwrite the loans based on ability to repay. We probably wouldn't be able to help so many customers with that cost structure. It's easier for us to just charge higher interest rates and accept higher charge-offs. Our customers don't have good credit, so they're willing to accept high interest rates. Most don't really care about the rate, only the monthly payment, so we can always find a car and loan structure that fits the customer's budget."

Nearly a quarter of The Sloppy Jalopy's customers default before their loans reach maturity. A typical situation is that of Rachel Benson, a single mother and bartender. Rachel needs a car to get to work at her new, better-paying job on the far side of town and to take her toddler to childcare. Rachel had been turned down by a couple of used car dealers because of the difficulty in verifying her heavily tip-based income when she came to The Sloppy Jalopy. The salesman at The Sloppy Jalopy asked Rachel how much she could afford to pay a month. She said, "Around $150, I think." "Great, then we have the car for you," said the salesman, who pointed her to a 2010 Chevy Impala with 80,000 miles on it. When Rachel mentioned that she didn't have good credit, the salesman said, "Don't you worry about that, now. The Sloppy Jalopy guarantees that it will find a loan to make it work for you."

Rachel bought the Impala for $500 down with a $7,500 loan at 20% annually from The Sloppy Jalopy. She was supposed to make monthly payments of $145 for ten years. The loan terms were all clearly disclosed. The car had significant mechanical trouble, and with the repair costs Rachel was unable to make her loan payments and defaulted a year into the loan. The Sloppy Jalopy repossessed the car (after it was repaired) and sold it for $3,000. It then proceeded to garnish Rachel paychecks for the remaining balance on the loan.

The CFPB has brought suit against The Sloppy Jalopy alleging that it is engaged in an unfair act or practice because it is making loans without regard to borrowers' ability to repay. What is the likely outcome of the litigation? *See* 12 U.S.C. § 5531(c).

3. Metropolitan Bancorp decided to change the method it uses for ordering the crediting and debiting of payments to its consumers' accounts. Under the old method, payments were credited chronologically as they were received by the bank. Under the new method, all payments made on any day are credited or debited in order from largest to smallest. This increases the number of overdrafts (and thus fees), but it also means that the consumers' largest payments (such as mortgage, rent, and car loans) are more likely to clear and not be denied for insufficient funds. Metropolitan charges only $10 per overdraft and charges only one overdraft fee per day, with a maximum of four days of charges.

- **a.** Assume Metropolitan notified its account holders of the change with a clear and prominent notice. Is the transaction-ordering practice unfair? *See* 12 U.S.C. § 5531(c); CFPB Supervision and Examination Manual—UDAAP v. 2 (Oct. 2012).
- **b.** Now assume that Metropolitan did not send a specific notice to account holders, but included on their periodic account statements a fine print sentence noting that "Terms and conditions of your deposit account may have changed. See Account Terms and Conditions on our website for further information," and included a URL. The URL linked to the revised Terms and Conditions, a 50-page document, and did not specify what, if anything, had been changed. Does this change the unfairness analysis? *See* 12 U.S.C. § 5531(c); CFPB Supervision and Examination Manual—UDAAP v. 2 (Oct. 2012).
- **c.** Assuming the same facts as in part (b), is the transaction-ordering practice deceptive? *See* 12 U.S.C. § 5531.

4. Old Northwest Loans, a non-bank mortgage lender, refinanced Patricia McCoy's 30-year 10% APR fixed-rate mortgage into a 30-year adjustable-rate mortgage with a two-year initial 6% fixed-rate period, followed by annual adjustments based on a spread of 8% above the 30-year Treasury bond rate. The new loan has a five-year prepayment penalty of 5% of the unpaid principal balance of the loan. Has Old Northwest Loans engaged in an unfair act or practice? *See* 12 U.S.C. § 5531(c); CFPB Supervision and Examination Manual—UDAAP v. 2 (Oct. 2012).

5. You are General Counsel and Chief Compliance Officer for Continental Express Bank, N.A., a large credit card issuer. Continental Express offers a number of add-on services similar to the ones offered by Discover Bank. These add-on services are hugely profitable. Having read the *Discover* consent order, what is your advice about what Continental Express should do in the future?

CHAPTER 11

UDAAP II: ABUSIVE ACTS AND PRACTICES

I. ABUSIVE ACTS AND PRACTICES

The power to prohibit "abusive" acts and practices is easily the CFPB's most controversial power. It is controversial because the category of "abusive" is a new addition to the traditional prohibition on unfair and deceptive acts and practices and thus raises questions about precisely what sorts of acts and practices might be "abusive."

The Dodd-Frank Act does not directly define "abusive." Instead, it provides that "[t]he Bureau shall have no authority under this section to declare an act or practice abusive in connection with the provision of a consumer financial product or service, unless the act or practice" meets one of four descriptions. 12 U.S.C. § 5531. This means that CFPB rulemaking and enforcement on "abusive" acts and practices must meet one or more of the four enumerated categories. It does not literally bind other parties with enforcement authority under the Consumer Financial Protection Act, such as state attorneys general, 12 U.S.C. § 5552(a)(1), or federal banking regulators, 12 U.S.C. § 5516(d)(1), even if that is likely to be the practical effect.

As codified, there are four separate types of acts or practices that may be abusive.

1. Acts or practices that materially interfere with the ability of a consumer to understand terms or conditions of the product or service.
2. Acts or practices that take unreasonable advantage of the consumer's lack of understanding of the product or service's risks, costs, or conditions.
3. Acts and practices that take unreasonable advantage of the consumer's inability to protect his or her own interests when choosing or using a product or service.
4. Acts and practices that take unreasonable advantage of the consumer's reliance on a covered person to act in the consumer's interests.

12 U.S.C. § 5531(d). It is possible for a fact pattern to be covered by more than one prong of the abusive definition.

The limited legislative history of the "abusive" provision is not especially illuminating, but it appears that the provision is meant to be a catchall that covers situations that do not neatly fall into "unfair" or "deceptive," something like a codified unconscionability standard. Because of the controversial nature of the power, the CFPB has been reluctant to invoke it. The CFPB has invoked the "abusive" standard only once in rulemaking. In enforcement matters, too, the CFPB has used "abusive" sparingly. As of the start of 2018, the CFPB had brought 200 enforcement actions. While many of these actions invoked unfairness or deception as well as violations of the enumerated consumer laws, only 27 (13.5% of the total) had "abusive" counts. Every one of these cases also involved counts of unfairness or deception, and many also involved counts under other statutes. As far as the author can determine, only a single case, All American Check Cashing, Inc., presented below, has had an abusive count that was based on an activity that did not also generate a deception or unfairness count. A few of the abusive cases resulted in consent orders, but none of these cases have yet resulted in a published opinion based on a contested interpretation of the term or its application.

To date, there has been no court ruling interpreting "abusive." Instead, clues to interpretation lie in complaints in CFPB enforcement actions and in the CFPB's sole rulemaking undertaken with the abusive power. Materials on each of the four categories of "abusive" are presented in turn below.

A. Material Interference with the Ability of a Consumer to Understand Terms and Conditions of a Consumer Financial Product or Service

Complaint
CFPB v. All American Check Cashing, Inc.

No. 3:16-cv-00356-WHB-JCG (S.D. Miss. May 11, 2016)

. . .

AACC'S CHECK CASHING BUSINESS

9. [Defendant All American Check Cashing ("AACC")] began offering check cashing services in Mississippi in March 1999, in Louisiana in July 2012, and in Alabama in October 2013.

10. AACC charges consumers a fee to cash their checks. In Mississippi and Alabama, AACC's policy is to charge consumers 3% of the amount of the check to cash government-issued checks, and 5% of the amount of the check to cash other checks. In Louisiana, AACC's policy is to charge consumers 2% of the amount of the check to cash government-issued checks, and 5% of the amount of the check to cash other checks. In addition, in all states, AACC's policy is to charge a minimum fee of $5. There are businesses and financial institutions located near AACC stores that charge consumers lower fees to cash a check.

11. AACC's check cashing business has been lucrative. In recent years, AACC has cashed about 12,000 to 17,000 checks and collected more than approximately $1 million in check cashing fees, annually.

AACC'S POLICY AND PRACTICE OF REFUSING TO DISCLOSE THE CHECK CASHING FEE TO CONSUMERS

12. Because the check cashing fees are fixed, when a consumer presents a check to AACC to cash, the AACC employee knows the fee structure (*e.g.*, 3% or 5%). To determine the particular fee percentage a consumer will pay, the only information the AACC employee needs to know is whether or not the check is a government check, which the employee can almost always determine by looking at the face of the check. In addition, if the employee calculates the fee or knows that the $5 minimum applies, the employee also knows the dollar amount of the fee.

13. AACC prohibits employees from orally disclosing to consumers the fee structure (e.g. 3% or 5%), the fee percentage that applies to a transaction (e.g. 3%), or the dollar amount of the fee, at any point during a check cashing transaction, even when a consumer asks the employee what the fee is.

14. AACC's policy and training documents instruct employees to "[n]ever tell the customer the fee" and "[n]ever quote the fee or the percentage to the customer[.]"

15. AACC regularly trains and monitors its employees to ensure that they adhere to this prohibition. For example, AACC provides a training presentation to new· employees instructing them to "NEVER TELL THE CUSTOMER THE FEE."

16. In a January 5, 2013 email, Mr. Gray [the president and owner of AACC] listed the check cashing methods and systems he created, including: "NEVER spout off the fee in dollars or in percent."

. . .

18. When a consumer asks how much it costs to cash a check, AACC requires employees to deflect the question long enough to verify and process the check. For example, AACC instructs employees to say that the employees are not sure what the fee is and need to take additional steps to determine the fee, such as putting information in the store's computer, processing the check, or verifying the check. AACC also trains employees to falsely state "I will let you know [the fee] in just a moment," or state that the fee depends on the company that issued the check.

19. In both Mississippi and Louisiana, two of the jurisdictions within which AACC operates, the law provides for certain disclosures related to fees for check cashing services. At all times relevant to the allegations in this Complaint, AACC and Gray formulated and carried out a program aimed at subverting these consumer protections.

20. Mississippi law requires that consumers sign an acknowledgment of the fees charged when cashing a check. The receipt that AACC provides to consumers to sign at the end of the transaction lists the fee charged, but AACC requires employees to "[c]ount money out over receipt" to block the consumer's view of the fee. Employees sometimes use other items to cover the fee, such as small giveaways. AACC also instructs employees to minimize the amount of time that the consumer can see the receipt before signing it. AACC instructs its employees to "keep [the] receipt away from customer as much as possible," "keep the [receipt] for [the consumer] to sign on the counter for only a second," and "remove [the] receipt and check as quickly as possible." One former supervisor

stated, "Employees at the stores I supervised asked customers to sign the receipt after the money was counted out over the receipt, so customers would not have a clear view of the fees listed on the receipt before signing it." Even if the consumer sees the fee on the receipt, the receipt lists the "Fee Charged" and the "Date Cashed" in the past tense, indicating that the transaction has been completed and the fee already charged.

21. In both Mississippi and Louisiana, AACC is required to display a sign listing the fee percentages that AACC charges to cash checks. AACC does not permit employees to direct a consumer's attention to the sign, even if the consumer asks about the amount of the fee. In fact, AACC seeks to prevent consumers from seeing the sign. In AACC stores, the sign is placed under the counter. Per company policy, AACC employees must direct consumers to a seat in the lobby while their check is being verified and processed, and ensure that the consumer's time at the counter is as minimal as possible. The information on the sign can be difficult to read from the lobby. One former employee stated that he was told by a store manager to keep the consumer's time at the counter as short as possible "to minimize the chance that the customer would see the fees listed on the sign under the counter[.]"

22. AACC also trains employees to distract consumers from finding out the fee by engaging in small talk, providing consumers with information not relevant to the transaction, showing them the cash, and providing small, free gifts. During one training, AACC instructed employees to ensure "[c]onstant information [is] given to customer" so that "they are overwhelmed with info." AACC's goal is to distract consumers as much as possible so that transactions can be completed without consumers learning the fee.

23. One consumer described AACC's failure to disclose its check cashing fee as follows:

> I went into All American Check Cashing . . . to cash my tax refund check which was roughly $4100. Upon asking how much the fee would be I was told that it wouldnt be expensive. There were no signs in the . . . building telling customers how much their services were. So, once my check was cashed, the guy . . . brung me my money. While he was counting the money, I kept asking how much did yall charge because he kept my ID over the amount charged and everytime I would move the ID he would grab it back so I wouldnt see the fee. I was charged $200+!!!!! Im very upset that I was overcharged . . . On top of that, they provided no paperwork. Something has got to be done.

AACC'S POLICY AND PRACTICE OF MAKING IT DIFFICULT FOR CONSUMERS TO CANCEL OR REVERSE A CHECK CASHING TRANSACTION

24. AACC compounds its obfuscation of check cashing fees by making it difficult or impossible for consumers to cancel or reverse a check cashing transaction if and when they do learn the fee. AACC does this by, among other things, making misrepresentations about the consumer's ability to cancel or reverse a transaction, and taking steps during processing that make it difficult or impossible for the consumer to cash a check elsewhere.

25. According to one former supervisor, "the only time you ever have the transaction voided . . . is if the customer is pretty much kicking and screaming, fussing, cussing[.]"

26. In some cases, AACC makes false or misleading representations to discourage consumers from cancelling or reversing a transaction. For example, employees sometimes falsely say that because of steps taken by AACC during processing, the consumer cannot reverse the transaction and cash the check elsewhere, even when the consumer could, in fact, reverse the transaction and cash the check elsewhere. Employees also foster the misimpression that if the check is taken to a bank, then the bank will hold the check for a long period of time—further delaying consumers' access to their funds—when the AACC employees do not know whether or not this is true. Employees also tell consumers that it will take a long time to void or reverse a transaction, when this is not true.

27. In some instances, the steps AACC takes while processing a check actually do make it difficult or impossible for the consumer to cash the check elsewhere, and thus AACC locks the consumer into the transaction. For example, when processing a check, employees sometimes apply a stamp to the back of the check—such as, "FOR DEPOSIT ONLY: ALL AMERICAN CHECK CASHING INC"—that prevents or interferes with the consumer's ability to cash the check elsewhere. Some employees stamp a consumer's check and then, if the consumer becomes upset about fee, tell the consumer that the consumer cannot cash that check elsewhere.

28. AACC also uses physical custody of the check to control consumers and to compel consumers to pay the fee even if they object. Training documents instruct employees to "[a]lways keep the check" because doing so "[k]eeps [the employee] in control of the situation" so the "[c]ustomer can't just walk out and leave without talking to you."

. . .

ABUSIVE ACTS AND PRACTICES IN CHECK CASHING

Count I

. . .

67. In numerous instances, in connection with offering and providing check cashing to consumers, Defendants have materially interfered with the ability of consumers to understand a term or condition of their check cashing services by having a policy to never tell the consumer the fee—even when the consumer asks, blocking the fee amount listed on the receipt, minimizing the amount of time the consumer has to see the receipt, interfering with the consumer's ability to see the sign listing fee percentages, making false or misleading statements to consumers about the availability of information about the fee, and making false or misleading statements to consumers about their ability to cancel or reverse the transaction or to cash their check elsewhere.

68. Defendants' acts and practices in connection with check cashing constitute abusive acts or practices in violation of Sections 1031 and 1036 of the CFPA. 12 U.S.C. §§ 5531(a) and (d)(1), 5536(a)(1)(B).

Count II

. . .

70. In numerous instances, in connection with offering and providing check cashing to consumers, Defendants have taken unreasonable advantage of the inability of

consumers to protect their interests in selecting or using Defendants' check cashing services by pressuring or coercing consumers to cash their checks at AACC, including by retaining custody of the check to prevent consumers from leaving, processing the check without the consumer's consent, applying an AACC stamp to the back of the check during processing to impair the consumer's ability to cash the check elsewhere, and making misrepresentations about the consumer's ability to cancel or reverse the transaction or cash the check elsewhere.

71. Defendants' acts and practices in connection with check cashing constitute abusive acts or practices in violation of Sections 1031 and 1036 of the CFPA. 12 U.S.C. §§ 5531(a) and (d)(2)(B), 5536(a)(1)(B).

Notes

1. The material interference alleged in *All American Check Cashing* was supposedly deliberate. Does the material interference standard seem to require that such interference be deliberate, or could it be inadvertent? For example, would a store's inadvertent failure to display up-to-date pricing on its website constitute material interference if done by a covered person or service provider in connection with a consumer financial product or service?

2. Much of the material interference alleged in *All American Check Cashing* is rather crass physical interference (covering up the receipt, positioning the signage in a way that is hard to see). Would it be material interference to bury key terms in fine print? Isn't that akin to what All American allegedly did? What about disclosures that highlight the terms that are favorable to the consumer, such as rewards programs, but that disclose fees without emphasizing them?

B. Taking Unreasonable Advantage of Consumers' Lack of Understanding of Material Risks, Costs, or Conditions

First Amended Complaint
CFPB v. CashCall, Inc.

No. 1:13-cv-13167 (GAO) (D. Mass. Mar. 21, 2014)

INTRODUCTION

The Consumer Financial Protection Bureau brings this action against Defendants CashCall, Inc., WS Funding, LLC, Delbert Services Corporation, and J. Paul Reddam under the Consumer Financial Protection Act of 2010 (CFPA), 12 U.S.C. §§ 5531(a), 5536(a), 5564(a). Defendants purchased, serviced, and collected consumer-installment loans that state laws rendered void or limited the consumer's obligation to repay. As a result, Defendants took money from consumers that those consumers did not owe and typically could ill-afford to lose.

. . .

STATE LAWS PROTECTING CONSUMERS WHO TAKE OUT SMALL-DOLLAR LOANS

9. Many states have enacted laws that govern the terms of small-dollar consumer loans, including laws that restrict which entities may engage in these transactions, require lenders to be licensed or otherwise subject to state regulation, and impose civil and criminal usury limits.

10. Those laws reflect the states' strong public policies that loans breaching those restrictions pose significant harm to state residents.

Interest-Rate Caps

11. To deter violations of such laws and redress consumer harm, several states have adopted laws that render small-dollar loans void if they exceed the usury limit. If a lender makes a covered loan that exceeds the usury limit in these states, the lender has no legal right to collect money from consumers in repayment of the loan. [A list of state usury laws follows.]

. . .

Licensing Requirements

13. Many states, including Alabama, Arizona, Colorado, Illinois, Indiana, Kentucky, Massachusetts, Minnesota, Montana, New Hampshire, New Jersey, New Mexico, New York, North Carolina, and Ohio, also have implemented licensing regimes that include measures aimed at preventing and penalizing harmful consumer-lending practices. Those state-licensing regimes reflect substantive consumer-protection concerns by, for instance:

a. Ensuring that licensees possess the requisite character, fitness, financial responsibility, or experience, [citations omitted]

b. Ensuring compliance with loan-term and disclosure regulations by providing for compliance oversight by state regulators and requiring recordkeeping and annual reports, [citations omitted].

14. These state-licensing statutes reflect the states' strong public policy that entities seeking to engage in the consumer-lending business with state residents must be vetted and subject to oversight by regulators to ensure that they adhere to consumer-protection and other laws.

15. To incentivize licensure and redress consumer harm, several states have adopted laws that render small-dollar loans void if they are made without a license. If a covered loan is made without a license in these states, the entity has no right to collect from consumers, or the consumers have no obligation to pay money in repayment of the loan. [State-specific examples omitted.]

. . .

SMALL-DOLLAR LOANS MADE TO CONSUMERS IN THE SUBJECT STATES

Description of the Loans

19. Western Sky Financial, LLC is an online lender. It is owned by a member of the Cheyenne River Sioux Indian Reservation, but is not owned or operated by a tribe or tribal entity. Western Sky is a limited-liability company organized under South Dakota law. It purports that loans made in its name are subject only to the laws of the Cheyenne River Sioux Indian Reservation.

20. Beginning in late 2009, CashCall and its wholly owned subsidiary, WS Funding, entered into a series of agreements with Western Sky to secure high-cost, consumer-installment loans that – purportedly – did not have to comply with state law (WS Loans).

21. Under these agreements, WS Loans were made in Western Sky's name, but were marketed by CashCall, financed by WS Funding, almost immediately sold and assigned to WS Funding, and then serviced and collected by CashCall, Delbert, or both.

22. Between early 2010 and late 2013, hundreds of thousands of WS Loans were made to consumers nationwide, including to consumers in the Subject States.

23. WS Loans ranged from $850 to $10,000. They carried upfront fees, lengthy repayment terms, and annual percentage rates (APRs) ranging from 89.68% to 342.86%. The precise terms evolved over the life of the program and varied based on the amount of the loan.

. . .

Violations of Interest-Rate Caps in Certain Subject States

26. The usury laws of the Subject States applied to WS Loans, and the WS Loans made to consumers in those states violated those interest-rate caps. The loans made to consumers in Arkansas, Minnesota, New Hampshire, and New York violated applicable usury restrictions and were thus void. . . . Neither Western Sky nor Defendants had a legal right to collect money from consumers in repayment of WS Loans made to consumers in these states.

. . .

Violations of Licensing Requirements in Certain Subject States

28. The licensing laws of the Subject States applied to WS Loans, and the WS Loans made to consumers in those states violated those laws. Western Sky, which did not a hold a consumer-lending license in any state, made WS Loans to consumers in Alabama, Arizona, Colorado, Illinois, Indiana, Kentucky, Massachusetts, Minnesota, Montana, New Hampshire, New Jersey, New Mexico, New York, North Carolina, and Ohio, each of which required Western Sky to obtain a license before making WS Loans to their residents.

29. Likewise, neither CashCall nor WS Funding held the requisite license when acquiring WS Loans made to consumers in Massachusetts, Montana, North Carolina, or Colorado.

30. As a result, many WS Loans made to consumers in Alabama, Arizona, Indiana, Illinois, Kentucky, Massachusetts, Minnesota, Montana, New Hampshire, New Jersey, New Mexico, New York, North Carolina, and Ohio were void. Neither Western Sky, nor Defendants, had a legal right to collect money from consumers in those states in repayment of such loans.. . .

. . .

COUNT THREE

Abusiveness Related to Collecting Loan Payments that Consumers Did Not Owe

. . .

68. Section 1036(a)(1)(B) of the CFPA prohibits "abusive" acts or practices. 12 U.S.C. § 5536(a)(1)(B). An act or practice is abusive if it "takes unreasonable advantage of . . . a lack of understanding on the part of the consumer of the material risks, costs, or conditions of the product or service." 12 U.S.C. § 5531(d)(2)(A).

69. Consumers generally do not know or understand the impact that the above-cited usury and licensing laws of the Subject States have on their loans. Consumers who obtained WS Loans in the Subject States, where usury laws or consumer-licensing regimes rendered those loans void, or otherwise limited the consumer's obligation to repay them, typically lacked an understanding that those state laws vitiated Defendants' collection rights on all or part of the consumers' repayment obligations.

70. By nevertheless taking, or attempting to take, the full loan balance from those consumers, Defendants took unreasonable advantage of consumers' lack of understanding about the impact of applicable state laws on the parties' rights and obligations regarding WS Loans.

71. Therefore, Defendants have engaged in "abusive" acts or practices that violate sections 1031(a) and 1036(a)(1)(B) of the CFPA, 12 U.S.C. §§ 5531(a), 5536(a)(1)(B).

Question and Notes on *CashCall*

1. You've previously seen the "true lender" problem regarding preemption. Is Western Sky Financial, LLC the true lender on these loans? Recall that the loans are "almost immediately sold and assigned to WS Funding [a CashCall subsidiary], and then serviced and collected by CashCall, Delbert, or both."

2. The CFPB won summary judgment against CashCall and Delbert on the basis of a deception claim under the Consumer Financial Protection Act. Accordingly, the court did not address the unfairness or abusiveness claims in the complaint because the remedy would be the same. *CFPB v. CashCall, Inc.*, 2016 U.S. Dist. Lexis 130584 (C.D. Cal. Aug. 31, 2016).

The CFPB's Payday Rule is the only rulemaking to date that invokes the abusive standard. Below is an excerpt from the initial proposed rulemaking discussing the application of 12 U.S.C. § 5531(d)(2)(A). By way of background, a payday loan is a short loan (2 weeks or 1 month typically, matched to the borrower's payday) for a relatively small amount of money ($200-$500), with fees often in the range of $10-$20 for every $100 borrowed. Repayment of the loan is secured by the borrower giving the lender a post-dated check for the loan amount plus fees that the lender can then use to draw on the borrower's bank account if the borrower does not repay on time. Payday borrowers tend to be lower income and often in financial distress. Vehicle title loans are also short-term loans (usually for larger amounts than a payday loan) secured by the borrower's title to a vehicle. Vehicle title loans have similar costs to payday loans and a similarly financially distressed borrower base.

CFPB, Proposed Rule
Payday, Vehicle Title, and Certain High-Cost Installment Loans

81 Fed. Reg. 47864, 47935-47936 (July 22, 2016)

CONSUMERS LACK AN UNDERSTANDING OF MATERIAL RISKS AND COSTS

. . . [S]hort-term payday and vehicle title loans can and frequently do lead to a number of negative consequences for consumers, which range from extensive reborrowing to defaulting to being unable to pay other obligations or basic living expenses as a result of making an unaffordable payment. All of these—including the direct costs that may be payable to lenders and the collateral consequences that may flow from the loans—are risks or costs of these loans, as the Bureau understands and reasonably interprets that phrase.

The Bureau recognizes that consumers who take out a payday, vehicle title, or other short-term loan understand that they are incurring a debt which must be repaid within a prescribed period of time and that if they are unable to do so, they will either have to make other arrangements or suffer adverse consequences. The Bureau does not believe, however, that such a generalized understanding suffices to establish that consumers understand the material costs and risks of these products. Rather, the Bureau believes that it is reasonable to interpret "understanding" in this context to mean more than a mere awareness that it is within the realm of possibility that a particular negative consequence may follow or cost may be incurred as a result of using the product. For example, consumers may not understand that a risk is very likely to materialize or that—though relatively rare—the impact of a particular risk would be severe.

. . . [T]he single largest risk to a consumer of taking out a payday, vehicle title, or similar short-term loan is that the initial loan will lead to an extended cycle of indebtedness. This occurs in large part because the structure of the loan usually requires the consumer to make a lump-sum payment within a short period of time, typically two weeks, or a month, which would absorb such a large share of the consumer's disposable income as to leave the consumer unable to pay the consumer's major financial obligations and basic living expenses. Additionally, in States where it is permitted, lenders often offer borrowers the enticing, but ultimately costly, alternative of paying a smaller fee (such as 15 percent of the principal) and rolling over the loan or making back-to-back repayment and reborrowing transactions rather than repaying the loan in full—and many borrowers choose this option. Alternatively, borrowers may repay the loan in full when due but find it necessary to take out another loan a short time later, because the large amount of cash needed to repay the first loan relative to their income leaves them without sufficient funds to meet their other obligations and expenses. This cycle of indebtedness affects a large segment of borrowers: . . . 50 percent of storefront payday loan sequences contain at least four loans. One-third contain seven loans or more, by which point consumers will have paid charges equal to 100 percent of the amount borrowed and still owe the full amount of the principal. Almost one-quarter of loan sequences contain at least 10 loans in a row. And looking just at loans made to borrowers who are paid weekly, biweekly, or semi-monthly, 21 percent of loans are in sequences consisting of at least 20 loans. For loans made to borrowers who are paid monthly, 46 percent of loans are in sequences consisting of at least 10 loans.

The evidence . . . also shows that consumers who take out these loans typically appear not to understand when they first take out a loan how long they are likely to remain in debt and how costly that will be for them. Payday borrowers tend to overestimate their likelihood of repaying without reborrowing and underestimate the likelihood that they will end up in an extended loan sequence. . . . Thus, many consumers who expected to be in debt only a short amount of time can find themselves in a months-long cycle of indebtedness, paying hundreds of dollars in fees above what they expected while struggling to repay the original loan amount.

The Bureau has observed similar outcomes for borrowers of single-payment vehicle title loans. For example, 83 percent of vehicle title loans being reborrowed on the same day that a previous loan was due, and 85 percent of vehicle title loans are reborrowed within 30 days of a previous vehicle title loan. Fifty-six percent of vehicle title loan sequences consist of more than three loans, 36 percent consist of at least seven loans, and almost one quarter—23 percent—consist of more than 10 loans. . . .

Consumers are also exposed to other material risks and costs in connection with covered short-term loans. . . . [T]he unaffordability of the payments for many consumers creates a substantial risk of default. Indeed, 20 percent of payday loan sequences and 33 percent of title loan sequences end in default. And 69 percent of payday loan defaults occur in loan sequences in which the consumer reborrows at least once. For a payday borrower, the cost of default generally includes the cost of at least one, and often multiple, NSF [Non-Sufficient Funds or Bounce] fees assessed by the borrower's bank when the lender attempts to cash the borrower's postdated check or debit the consumer's account via ACH transfer and the attempt fails. NSFs are associated with a high rate of bank account closures. Defaults also often expose consumers to aggressive debt collection activities by the lender or a third-party debt collector. The consequences of default can be even more dire for a vehicle title borrower, including the loss of the consumer's vehicle—which is the result in 20 percent of single-payment vehicle title loan sequences.

The Bureau does not believe that many consumers who take out payday, vehicle title, or other short-term loans understand the magnitude of these additional risks—for example, that they have at least a one in five (or for auto title borrowers a one in three) chance of defaulting. Nor are payday borrowers likely to factor into their decision on whether to take out the loan the many collateral consequences of default, including expensive bank fees, aggressive collections, or the costs of having to get to work or otherwise from place to place if their vehicle is repossessed.

. . . [S]everal factors can impede consumers' understanding of the material risks and costs of payday, vehicle title, and other short-term loans. To begin with, there is a mismatch between how these loans are structured and how they operate in practice. Although the loans are presented as standalone short-term products, only a minority of payday loans are repaid without any reborrowing. These loans often instead produce lengthy cycles of rollovers or new loans taken out shortly after the prior loans are repaid. Empirical evidence shows that consumers are not able to accurately predict how many times they will reborrow, and thus are not able to tell when they take out the first loan how long their cycles will last and how much they will ultimately pay for the initial disbursement of loan proceeds. Even consumers who believe they will be unable to repay the loan immediately and therefore expect some amount of reborrowing are generally unable to predict accurately how many times they will reborrow and at what cost. This is especially true for consumers who reborrow many times.

In addition, consumers in extreme financial distress tend to focus on their immediate liquidity needs rather than potential future costs in a way that makes them particularly susceptible to lender marketing, and payday and vehicle title lenders often emphasize the speed with which the lender will provide funds to the consumer. In fact, numerous lenders select company names that emphasize rapid loan funding. But there is a substantial disparity between how these loans are marketed by lenders and how they are actually experienced by many consumers. While covered short-term loans are marketed as short-duration loans intended for short-term or emergency use only, a substantial percentage of consumers do not repay the loan quickly and thus either default, or, in a majority of the cases, reborrow—often many times. Moreover, consumers who take out covered short-term loans may be overly optimistic about their future cash flow. Such incorrect expectations may lead consumers to misunderstand whether they will have the ability to repay the loan, or to expect that they will be able to repay it after reborrowing only a few times. These consumers may find themselves caught in a cycle of reborrowing that is both very costly and very difficult to escape.

C. Taking Unreasonable Advantage of the Inability of the Consumer to Protect His Interests

---

Complaint, CFPB v. PayPal, Inc. and Bill Me Later, Inc.

No. 1:15-cv-01426 (D. Md. May 19, 2015)

The Consumer Financial Protection Bureau (Bureau) brings this action against PayPal, Inc. (PayPal) and Bill Me Later, Inc. (BML [a wholly owned subsidiary of PayPal]). The Bureau brings this action under the Consumer Financial Protection Act of 2010 (CFPA), 12 U.S.C. §§ 5531, 5536(a), 5564, 5565, and alleges as follows.

. . .

FACTUAL BACKGROUND

9. PayPal provides an online-payments system that enables consumers to make digital payments and money transfers through a PayPal Wallet with linked bank, credit-card, and PayPal-held funds.

10. From 2008 and through the present, Defendants have marketed a line of credit once called Bill Me Later, and now called PayPal Credit, that is offered to consumers making purchases from eBay and thousands of online merchants. Defendants handle consumer interactions with PayPal Credit, operate its electronic platform, and receive payments associated with the consumers' lines of credit. Bill Me Later and PayPal Credit are referred to collectively as PayPal Credit in this Complaint.

. . .

DEFENDANTS DEFERRED-INTEREST PRACTICES

34. Where consumers used PayPal Credit for multiple transactions, they frequently received deferred-interest offers applicable to those transactions. The deferred-interest periods for the transactions would expire on different dates, depending on the date of the initial transaction. Consumers thus could have multiple deferred-interest balances as well as a balance for standard purchases for the same account.

35. Defendants did not provide consumers with adequate information to allow them to understand how Defendants applied payments to various balances and how much consumers needed to pay to avoid deferred interest. Many consumers with multiple deferred-interest promotional balances did not understand how the Defendants allocated payments. Numerous consumers believed they made a payment large enough to pay off purchases with expiring promotions, but the Defendants allocated payments in a way that resulted in the consumer incurring deferred interest.

36. Before early 2013, Defendants' practice was to apply payments in excess of the minimum payment proportionally to all deferred-interest promotional balances with the same rate, most of which were 19.99%, regardless of expiration date, unless a promotion was expiring within two billing cycles, in which case excess payments would be applied to that promotion.

37. Defendants represented that consumers could contact Defendants' customer-service representatives if they wanted more information about the product, including payment allocation and how much they would need to pay to avoid interest.

38. Additionally, Defendants represented that consumers could contact Defendants' customer-service representatives to request that payments be allocated to specific balances in a way different than Defendants' default method for allocating payments. Notwithstanding this representation, many consumers could not reach a customer-service agent at all, or Defendants ignored such re-allocation requests, or allocated payments differently than consumers requested.

39. In the first quarter of 2013, Defendants implemented a new payment-allocation hierarchy and began applying payments in excess of the minimum amount due to deferred-interest promotions in order of expiration date. Also, if a consumer had a balance on any deferred-interest promotions expiring in the following two billing cycles, Defendants began allocating even minimum payments to promotional balances before revolving balances. Defendants updated their billing statements to include the payment amount needed to avoid interest charges in a Payment Summary box located at the top of the billing statement.

. . .

COUNT V (ABUSIVE DEFERRED-INTEREST ACTS OR PRACTICES)

. . .

71. An act or practice is abusive under the CFPA if it "takes unreasonable advantage of . . . the inability of the consumer to protect the interests of the consumer in selecting or using a consumer financial product or service." 12 U.S.C. § 5531(d)(2)(B).

72. Before 2013, Defendants provided little information to consumers about how it allocated payments to and among standard and multiple deferred-interest balances. Nor

did Defendants explain that PayPal Credit's practice was to apply amounts in excess of the minimum payment proportionally to most, or all, promotional balances.

73. Defendants purported to allow consumers to control the allocation of payments by requesting that their payments be allocated to specific balances, but consumers seeking to make such requests often could not reach a customer-service representative. When consumers contacted Defendants' customer-service department for more information about the Defendants' payment-allocation methods or the amount they needed to pay to avoid interest, consumers were often given misinformation. When consumers made specific allocation requests, Defendants often ignored such requests or allocated payments differently than consumers requested.

74. As a result, consumers could not clearly understand how payments were applied to deferred-interest promotions and Defendants allocated payments in a way that consumers would not have chosen. Thus, consumers could not protect their interests in selecting and using Defendants' product.

75. Therefore, Defendants engaged in abusive acts or practices in violation of the CFPA, 12 U.S.C. § 5531(d)(2)(B).

Questions and Notes on *PayPal*

1. In *PayPal,* the CFPB alleged that an inadequately disclosed default payment allocation method that favored the creditor combined with poor customer service that made it difficult for consumers to change their payment allocation was an abusive act or practice.

- **a.** Would the practice still be abusive if it were adequately disclosed?
- **b.** Would the practice still be abusive if it were easy for consumers to change the payment allocation?
- **c.** Would the practice still be abusive if the default payment allocation were not unfavorable to consumers?
- **d.** Would the practice still be abusive if it were a mandatory payment allocation, but fully disclosed?

2. In 2009 Congress prohibited similar payment allocation methods for credit cards as part of the Credit CARD Act. Credit card issuers are required to apply payments that exceed minimums to higher interest rate balances first. 15 U.S.C. § 1666c(b).

3. Have you seen a payment allocation problem previously in this book? Where? Does that inform your answer to the first question here, about whether an unfavorable payment allocation method alone is abusive, even if disclosed? What if it is simply a default that can be changed?

4. Could the CFPB have brought an unfairness claim against PayPal on the same facts? Why do you think it didn't?

5. Does the "inability to protect their interests" part of abusive sound like procedural unconscionability, which can arise when a consumer lacks a meaningful choice? That is, would a monopolist firm inherently be engaged in an abusive practice under the "inability to protect their interests" definition? Is this a substantially different situation than one in which consumers have a choice between products but have trouble properly differentiating the products or the risks involved (as in the previous question)?

The CFPB has even used the "inability of the consumer to protect his or her interests" to go after behavior that is seemingly permitted by contract law. Reach back to your 1L contract class. There is a good chance you read a case called *Carnival Cruise Lines v. Shute*. In that case, the Supreme Court, sitting in admiralty jurisdiction, found that a forum selection clause printed on the back of a cruise ship ticket was "fundamentally fair" insofar as the cruise line had a particular interest and connection with the forum selected and consumers had the ability to return the ticket and demand a refund. 499 U.S. 585 (1991). The Court believed (without any support in the record whatsoever) that if the cruise company could insist on the forum of its choice, it would reduce the cruise company's costs, which would benefit consumers in the form of lower ticket prices. Is the following complaint consistent with *Shute* on either its unfairness counts or its abusiveness counts?

Complaint
CFPB; State of North Carolina; and Commonwealth of Virginia v. Freedom Stores, Inc.

No. 2:14-cv-643 (E.D. Va. Dec. 18, 2014)

. . .

GOODS AND SERVICES PROVIDED TO CONSUMERS BY FREEDOM, FAC, AND MCS

13. Freedom [Stores Inc.] is a nationwide retailer of consumer goods, including household appliances, jewelry, furniture, electronics, airline tickets, and stereo equipment. The company sells merchandise online at http://www.shopfreedom.com and at its fourteen retail stores, which are all located near military bases, including in North Carolina and Virginia.

14. From January 1, 2010, to November 1, 2013, Freedom financed its customers' retail purchases through retail-installment contracts, which established monthly payments that were typically due on the second of each month. Many of the consumers who obtained credit from Freedom were current or former members of the United States military or their family members.

15. Freedom immediately assigned the retail-installment contracts it issued to FAC, which was responsible for servicing and collecting consumers' Freedom-related debts.

16. From January 1, 2010, to November 1, 2013, MCS extended credit to consumers who purchased retail goods at over 300 independent retailers ("MCS Dealers") within MCS's dealer network, some of which were located in North Carolina and Virginia.

17. MCS's credit contracts were revolving-credit agreements. . . .

. . .

COMPANIES' PRACTICE OF FILING COLLECTION SUITS IN A DISTANT FORUM

50. FAC and MCS filed debt-collection lawsuits against consumers when their accounts fell behind by 60 days. Staff members in the "legal department" of FAC's and MCS's collections unit prepared warrant-in-debt actions to be filed in Virginia courts.

51. The FAC and MCS credit contracts contained a non-negotiable, venue-selection clause that designated the state or federal courts of Virginia.

. . .

54. From January 1, 2010, through November 1, 2013, FAC and MCS filed all of their debt-collection lawsuits in Norfolk General District Court, even against consumers who lived far away from Norfolk, Virginia, at the time of the suit, rather than in a judicial district where the consumers lived or where the consumers were physically present when they executed the financing contracts. FAC, MCS, Freedom, and the MCS Dealers did not require their staff to inform consumers, at the time of contract, that they would be sued in Virginia if they became delinquent.

55. Many consumers were sued in Virginia without actual knowledge of the lawsuit.

56. Whether or not they had actual notice of the lawsuit, consumers who lived far away from Norfolk, Virginia, found it difficult or impossible to travel to defend FAC's and MCS's actions.

57. From July 21, 2011 to December 31, 2013, FAC and MCS filed over 3,500 lawsuits in Norfolk, Virginia, against consumers who lived in distant venues and who were not physically present in Norfolk, Virginia, when they executed the underlying financing contract; almost all of the lawsuits resulted in a default judgment.

58. Upon obtaining those default judgments, FAC and MCS attempted to garnish consumers' wages or impose liens on their bank accounts.

59. Certain consumers did not learn they had been sued until they unsuccessfully attempted to withdraw cash from their bank accounts, which had been garnished.

COUNT ONE

(VIOLATIONS OF THE CONSUMER FINANCIAL PROTECTION ACT) DISTANT FORUM UNFAIRNESS CLAIM-ASSERTED BY THE BUREAU, NORTH CAROLINA, AND VIRGINIA AGAINST FAC AND MCS

62. The allegations in paragraphs 1-61 are incorporated here by reference.

63. Section 1036(a)(1)(B) of the CFP A prohibits "unfair, deceptive, or abusive acts or practices." 12 U.S.C. § 5536(a)(1)(B). An act or practice is unfair if it "causes or is likely to cause substantial injury to consumers" that "is not reasonably avoidable by consumers[] and . . . is not outweighed by countervailing benefits to consumers or to competition." 12 U.S.C. § 553l(c)(1).

64. In the course of extending credit and collecting on credit contracts from July 21, 2011, to November 1, 2013, FAC and MCS filed debt-collection lawsuits in Norfolk, Virginia, against consumers who (i) had signed contracts far away from Norfolk, Virginia, and (ii) resided far away from Norfolk, Virginia, when the lawsuits were commenced.

65. Many consumers were unaware that the credit contracts contained a venue-selection clause; they had little opportunity to review the credit contracts at the time of signing.

66. Even if the consumers read and understood the venue-selection clause, there was no opportunity to bargain for its removal because the clause was non-negotiable.

67. The practice of filing debt-collection lawsuits in a distant forum when the consumer does not live in that forum and was not physically present in that forum when the contract was executed is likely to cause substantial injury that is not reasonably avoidable by consumers and is not outweighed by any countervailing benefit.

68. FAC's and MCS's practice of filing debt-collection lawsuits in a distant forum when the consumers did not live in that forum and were not physically present in that forum when they executed the financing contract is unfair. Because FAC and MCS are "covered persons," their conduct is unlawful under sections 1031 and 1036(a)(1)(B) of the CFPA, 12 U.S.C. §§ 5531, 5536(a)(1)(B).

. . .

COUNT THREE
(VIOLATIONS OF THE CONSUMER FINANCIAL PROTECTION ACT)
DISTANT FORUM ABUSIVENESS CLAIM-ASSERTED BY THE BUREAU, NORTH CAROLINA, AND VIRGINIA AGAINST FAC AND MCS

72. The allegations in paragraphs 1-61 are incorporated here by reference.

73. Section 1036(a)(1)(B) of the CFP A prohibits "unfair, deceptive, or abusive acts or practices." 12 U.S.C. § 5536(a)(1)(B). An act or practice is abusive if it "takes unreasonable advantage of . . . the inability of the consumer to protect the interests of the consumer in selecting or using a consumer financial product or service." 12 U.S.C. § 5531(d)(2)(B).

74. In the course of extending credit and collecting on credit contracts from July 21, 2011, to November 1, 2013, FAC and MCS filed debt-collection lawsuits in Virginia courts against consumers who (i) had signed contracts far away from Norfolk, Virginia, and (ii) resided far away from Norfolk, Virginia, when the lawsuits were commenced.

75. Many consumers were unaware that the credit contracts contained a venue-selection clause; they had little opportunity to review the credit contracts at the time of signing.

76. Even if consumers read and understood the venue-selection clause, there was no opportunity to bargain for its removal because the clause was non-negotiable.

77. The practice of filing debt-collection lawsuits based on the venue-selection clause at issue was almost certain to produce default judgments and lead to garnishments against consumers who were unable to appear and assert a defense. This practice took unreasonable advantage of the inability of consumers to protect their interests while using or choosing credit agreements.

78. FAC's and MCS's practice of filing debt-collection suits in a distant forum is abusive. Because FAC and MCS are "covered persons," their conduct is unlawful under sections 1031 and 1036(a)(1)(B) of the CFPA, 12 U.S.C. §§ 5531, 5536(a)(1)(B).

Questions and Notes on *Freedom Stores*

1. Can the CFPB's complaint against Freedom Stores be squared with the Supreme Court's decision in *Carnival Cruise Lines v. Shute*? For the unfairness count? For the abusiveness count? Does it matter for purposes of UDAAP whether a provision would be enforceable as a matter of contract law?

2. Does the CFPB seem to believe that there are *any* offsetting consumer benefits from the forum selection provision? Why wouldn't the Supreme Court's logic in *Carnival Cruise Lines v. Shute* that a forum selection clause that facilitates debt collection also dictate a conclusion that it must result in consumer benefit through lower credit prices?

3. Suppose the Supreme Court was right about the forum selection clause in *Carnival Cruise Lines v. Shute* saving the cruise line money. Does it necessarily follow that those savings result in lower prices for consumers? Who else might benefit from the savings?

4. How far can the *Freedom Stores* complaint be read? Is it limited to forum selection clauses, or does it also extend to arbitration agreements (basically a flavor of forum selection clause)? Is it limited to litigation forum issues, or does it extend to all contracts of adhesion? Does anything in the complaint indicate a limitation?

5. The complaint against Freedom Stores also alleged various unfair debt collection practices aimed at the clientele served by Freedom Stores—military servicemembers and their families. Freedom Stores settled the case for $2.5 million in restitution and a $100,000 fine. Suppose that this settlement is also as good of one as could reasonably be obtained in class action litigation that might take several years with class certification issues and motion practice. Also suppose that class counsel can get a 33% contingency fee approved by the court. Do you think it would be easy to get reputable counsel to take on a class action against Freedom Stores? What does this say about the importance of public enforcement? Is it more critical for public enforcement agencies to focus resources on big cases or small ones?

The CFPB's Payday Rule was promulgated not just under 12 U.S.C. § 5531(d)(2)(A), but also under section 5531(d)(2)(B). What follows is the discussion of the application of this provision in the proposed rulemaking.

CFPB, Proposed Rule
Payday, Vehicle Title, and Certain High-Cost Installment Loans

81 Fed. Reg. 47864, 47934-47935 (July 22, 2016)

CONSUMER INABILITY TO PROTECT INTERESTS

. . . [I]t is reasonable to also conclude from the structure of [12 U.S.C. § 5531(d)], which separately declares it abusive to take unreasonable advantage of consumer lack of understanding or of consumers' inability to protect their interests in using or selecting a product or service that, in some circumstances, consumers may understand the risks and costs of a product, but nonetheless be unable to protect their interests in selecting or using the product. The Bureau believes that consumers who take out an initial payday loan, vehicle title loan, or other short-term loan may be unable to protect their interests in selecting or using such loans, given their immediate need for credit and their inability in the moment to search out or develop alternatives that would either enable them to avoid the need to borrow or to borrow on terms that are within their ability to repay.

. . . [C]onsumers who take out payday or short-term vehicle title loans typically have exhausted other sources of credit such as their credit card(s). In the months leading up to their liquidity shortfall, they typically have tried and failed to obtain other forms of credit. Their need is immediate. Moreover, consumers facing an immediate liquidity shortfall may believe that a short-term loan is their only choice; one study found that 37 percent of borrowers say they have been in such a difficult financial situation that they would take a payday loan on any terms offered. They may not have the time or other resources to seek out, develop, or take advantage of alternatives. These factors may place consumers in such a vulnerable position when seeking out and taking these loans that they are potentially unable to protect their interests.

The Bureau also believes that once consumers have commenced a loan sequence they may be unable to protect their interests in the selection or use of subsequent loans. After the initial loan in a sequence has been consummated, the consumer is legally obligated to repay the debt. Consumers who do not have the ability to repay that initial loan are faced with making a choice among three bad options: they can either default on the loan, skip or delay payments on major financial obligations or living expenses in order to repay the loan, or, as is most often the case, take out another loan and soon face the same predicament again. At that point, at least some consumers may gain a fuller awareness of the risks and costs of this type of loan, but by then it may be too late for the consumer to be able to protect her interests. Each of these choices results in increased costs to consumers—often very high and unexpected costs—which harm consumers' interests. An unaffordable first loan can thus ensnare consumers in a cycle of debt from which consumers have no reasonable means to extricate themselves, rendering them unable to protect their interests in selecting or using covered short-term loans.

PRACTICE TAKES UNREASONABLE ADVANTAGE OF CONSUMER VULNERABILITIES

Under [12 U.S.C. § 5531(d)(2)], a practice is abusive if it takes unreasonable advantage of consumers' lack of understanding or inability to protect their interests. The Bureau believes that the lender practice of making covered short-term loans without determining that the consumer has the ability to repay may take unreasonable advantage both of consumers' lack of understanding of the material risks, costs, and conditions of such loans, and consumers' inability to protect their interests in selecting or using the loans.

The Bureau recognizes that in any transaction involving a consumer financial product or service there is likely to be some information asymmetry between the consumer and the financial institution. Often, the financial institution will have superior bargaining power as well. [12 U.S.C. § 5531(d)(2)] does not prohibit financial institutions from taking advantage of their superior knowledge or bargaining power to maximize their profit. Indeed, in a market economy, market participants with such advantages generally pursue their self-interests. However, [12 U.S.C. § 5531(d)(2)] makes plain that there comes a point at which a financial institution's conduct in leveraging its superior information or bargaining power becomes unreasonable advantage-taking and thus is abusive.

The Dodd-Frank Act delegates to the Bureau the responsibility for determining when that line has been crossed. The Bureau believes that such determinations are best made with respect to any particular act or practice by taking into account all of the facts and circumstances that are relevant to assessing whether such an act or practice takes unreasonable advantage of consumers' lack of understanding or of consumers' inability to protect their interests. Several interrelated considerations lead the Bureau to believe that the practice of making payday, vehicle title, and other short-term loans without regard to the consumer's ability to repay may cross the line and take unreasonable advantage of consumers' lack of understanding and inability to protect their interests.

The Bureau first notes that the practice of making loans without regard to the consumer's ability to repay stands in stark contrast to the practice of lenders in virtually every other credit market, and upends traditional notions of responsible lending enshrined in safety-and-soundness principles as well as in a number of other laws. The general presupposition of credit markets is that the interests of lenders and borrowers are closely aligned: lenders succeed (*i.e.*, profit) only when consumers succeed (*i.e.*, repay their loan according to its terms). For example, lenders in other markets, including other subprime lenders, typically do not make loans without first making an assessment that consumers have the capacity to repay the loan according to the loan terms. Indeed, "capacity" is one of the traditional three "Cs" of lending* and is often embodied in tests that look at debt as a proportion of the consumer's income or at the consumer's residual income after repaying the debt.

In the markets for payday, vehicle title, and similar short-term loans, however, lenders have built a business model that—unbeknownst to borrowers—depends upon the consumer's lack of capacity to repay such loans without needing to reborrow. As explained above, the costs of maintaining business operations (which include customer acquisition costs and overhead expenses) often exceed the revenue that could be generated from making individual short-term loans that are repaid without reborrowing. Thus, lenders' business model depends upon a substantial percentage of consumers not being able to repay their loans when due and, instead, taking out multiple additional loans in quick succession. Indeed, upwards of half of all payday and single-payment vehicle title loans are made to—and an even higher percentage of revenue is derived from—borrowers in a sequence of ten loans or more. This dependency on revenue from long-term debt cycles has been acknowledged by industry stakeholders. For example . . . an attorney for a national trade association representing storefront payday lenders asserted in a letter to the Bureau that, "[i]n any large, mature payday loan portfolio, loans to

---

* The three "Cs" are credit score, capacity to pay, and collateral.—Ed.

repeat borrowers generally constitute between 70 and 90 percent of the portfolio, and for some lenders, even more."

Also relevant in assessing whether the practice at issue here involves unreasonable advantage-taking is the vulnerability of the consumers seeking these types of loans. . . . [P]ayday and vehicle title borrowers—and by extension borrowers of similar short-term loans—generally have modest incomes, little or no savings, and have tried and failed to obtain other forms of credit. They generally turn to these products in times of need as a "last resort," and when the loan comes due and threatens to take a large portion of their income, their situation becomes, if anything, even more desperate.

In addition, the evidence . . . suggests that lenders engage in practices that further exacerbate the risks and costs to the interests of consumers. Lenders market these loans as being for use "until next payday" or to "tide over" consumers until they receive income, thus encouraging overly optimistic thinking about how the consumer is likely to use the product. Lender advertising also focuses on immediacy and speed, which may increase consumers' existing sense of urgency. Lenders make an initial short-term loan and then roll over or make new loans to consumers in close proximity to the prior loan, compounding the consumer's initial inability to repay. Lenders make this reborrowing option easy and salient to consumers in comparison to repayment of the full loan principal. Moreover, lenders do not appear to encourage borrowers to reduce the outstanding principal over the course of a loan sequence, which would help consumers extricate themselves from the cycle of indebtedness more quickly and reduce their costs from reborrowing. Storefront lenders in particular encourage loan sequences because they encourage or require consumers to repay in person in an effort to frame the consumer's experience in a way to encourage reborrowing. Lenders often give financial incentives to employees to reward maximizing loan volume.

By not determining that consumers have the ability to repay their loans, lenders potentially take unreasonable advantage of a lack of understanding on the part of the consumer of the material risks of those loans and of the inability of the consumer to protect the interests of the consumer in selecting or using those loans.

D. Taking Unreasonable Advantage of Consumers' Reasonable Reliance on a Covered Person to Act in the Consumer's Interest

Complaint
CFPB & Attorney General of Florida v. College Education Services LLC

No. 8:14-cv-3078 (M.D. Fla. Dec. 11, 2014).

1. The Consumer Financial Protection Bureau [and Florida Attorney General bring this suit in connection with] Defendants' marketing and sale of student-loan debt-relief services. . .

. . .

FACTUAL BACKGROUND

11. From on or about September 2010 through February 2013, Defendants marketed and advertised debt-relief services to financially distressed student-loan borrowers whose loans were in default or garnishment.

12. CES targeted these consumers through expensive Google AdWords online marketing campaigns. When consumers conducted Google searches using phrases such as "defaulted student loan," "student loan garnishment," "student loan forgiveness," and "paying student loan tough," CES ads making the following types of claims would be displayed on their screens:

Default of Student Loan
Call 877-730-5368
Money Back Guaranteed
Get Out 4-8 weeks!
Stop Wage Garnishment

Guaranteed-Stop Wage Garnishment
With a Minimum Monthly Payment
Student Loan Forgiveness

Apply Now To Get Your
Student Loan Forgiveness,
Friendly Staff Waiting

Student Loan Relief
Cut Your Student Loan Monthly
Payment Up to 50% – Save Today!

12. The ads directed consumers to one of CES's websites, including CollegeDefaultedStudentLoan.com or HelpStudentLoanDefault.com. On those websites, CES asserted that "[w]e can help you fix your student loans" and encouraged consumers to "[l]et us find the best Solution to all of Your Federal Student Loan Troubles!"

13. CES's websites further claimed that the company's services would enable distressed student loan debtors to:

> Join thousands of college graduates who've already:
>
> Cut their monthly payments by as [sic] 50 percent! Removed wage garnishment and monetary judgments against them!
>
> Consolidated countless loans into just one streamlined monthly payment! Dramatically improved their credit rating and score!

14. CES portrayed its mission as "help[ing] individual [sic] and families, regardless of circumstance, end financial crisis and solve money management problems caused by outstanding student loans." CES promised to "establish custom-tailored programs and plans for your specific individual needs."

15. CES's websites listed a toll-free number and instructed consumers either to call or input their contact information into a form on the website.

16. For consumers who submitted contact information through a website, a CES telemarketer called them back within five minutes. If the telemarketers could not reach a consumer, they would call twice a day for up to 10 days to get the consumer on the phone.

17. When speaking with consumers, CES's telemarketers introduced themselves as student loan "counselors" or "advisors." CES telemarketers claimed they had the knowledge and expertise necessary to "custom-tailor[] programs and plans" to meet each consumer's "individual needs" and free consumers from "financial misfortune."

18. CES's loan "counselors" pledged to assist consumers in "securing a new Federally-backed consolidated loan," which they claimed would result in, among other things, lower monthly payments, freedom from default or garnishment in eight weeks or less, and improved credit scores.

19. CES instructed its loan "counselors" to emphasize the following in its initial calls with borrowers in default:

> This program will have you out of default in 4-6 weeks. The benefits of getting out of default are significant to people in default (GIVE 4-5 EXAMPLES THAT ARE RELEVENT [sic] TO THE CALLER'S SITUATION).
>
> 1. Prevent or Stop Wage Garnishment
> 2. Prevent or Stop IRS Tax Seizures
> 3. Improve your Credit Score-will show that defaulted loans are now paid in full and you will have a new loan with a new lender showing in good standing. (FYI-Info is not erased)
> 4. Avoid suspension, Revocation or Non-Renewal of Professional Licenses
> 5. Prevent Litigation and Judgment Costs
> 6. Become Eligible for Unlimited Forbearances & Deferments
> 7. Stop the Harassing phone calls from Bill Collectors
> 8. Obtain your Diploma & Transcripts
> 9. Become Eligible for Financial Aid (Federal Student Loans & Pell Grants).

20. Regardless of the borrower's student-loan issues or particular circumstances, CES telemarketers assured the borrower that "from looking at your loans and situation, you do qualify for our program and services."

21. CES's telemarketers exploited consumers' financial distress, pressuring consumers into paying significant advance fees by repeatedly promising that CES could resolve all their student-loan woes.

22. CES charged consumers between $195 and $2,500 based on the amount of student-loan debt at issue, with the average fee being about $500. CES required all or a substantial portion of its fee to be paid before it would perform any debt-relief services on the consumer's behalf.

23. CES collected millions in advance fees from consumers seeking student-loan debt-relief services.

24. After receiving payment details, the telemarketers would thank the consumers for "trusting CES with providing a solution to your Student Loan situation" and again promised that "the result [was] . . . 100% guaranteed."

CES FAILED TO PROVIDE THE GUARANTEED SERVICES

25. Despite its promise of "guaranteed" results, CES could not and did not resolve all of the student-loan issues faced by the consumers who paid for its services.

26. CES often failed to (1) provide any services to borrowers, (2) deliver the "guaranteed" lower monthly payments, relief from default or garnishment, loan forgiveness, or improved credit scores, or (3) obtain relief in less than six or eight weeks as promised. Indeed, CES exacerbated the student-loan difficulties of some of the financially distressed consumers it promised to help.

27. CES did not perform the promised individualized assessments of consumers' student-loan situations to determine the best debt-relief options. To the extent CES provided any debt-relief services, they consisted nearly exclusively of applying for student-loan consolidation and subsequent repayment plans.

28. As purported experts, CES knew or should have known that loan consolidation was not an option for every student-loan borrower, and even when available, could not resolve all the student-loan issues CES's customers faced or provide the relief CES "guaranteed" in every instance.

29. CES did not explain to consumers the requirements for loan consolidation or the relative benefits and risks of different consolidation options. Specifically, CES did not advise consumers that: (1) certain federal and private loans could not be consolidated; (2) certain consolidation-repayment plans could result in higher monthly payments or other negative consequences; (3) consolidation might lead to other unfavorable results, such as the loss of grace periods; (4) loans in default often could not be consolidated until after the successful completion of months-long trial-repayment plans; and (5) other debt-relief strategies or options might better meet the customer's needs.

30. In fact, in a number of cases, CES did not even assess whether the consumer had loans that were eligible for consolidation before taking advance fees.

31. Further, for some consumers who qualified for loan consolidation, CES selected monthly repayment plans that increased their monthly payments—the exact opposite of what those borrowers expected and desired when they engaged CES's debt-relief services.

32. CES also misled consumers about its ability to obtain loan forgiveness. CES could not "guarantee" loan forgiveness; all it could do was, at most, assist certain consumers in establishing eligibility for such relief.

33. Further, CES had no basis to assert that its services would lead to improved credit scores. CES did not check consumers' credit scores before or after the company performed debt-relief services on their behalf, and had no way of knowing how, or to what extent, even a successful loan consolidation would impact a consumer's credit score.

34. Thus, through false promises and "guarantees," CES raked in millions in advance fees from consumers while leaving many of them in the same or a worse student-loan predicament than before.

COUNT IV
ABUSIVENESS

. . .

55. An act or practice is abusive under the CFPA if it "takes unreasonable advantage of . . . the reasonable reliance by the consumer on a covered person to act in the interests of the consumer." 12 U.S.C. § 5531(d)(2)(C).

56. In numerous instances, in connection with the offering or providing of student-loan debt-relief services, CES targeted financially distressed consumers by using sophisticated and expensive Internet-marketing campaigns aimed at attracting consumers whose student loans were in default or garnishment or whose monthly payments were otherwise unaffordable.

57. CES's telemarketers held themselves out as loan counselors and advisors with the expertise to establish custom-tailored programs to address each student-loan debtor's specific needs. CES created the illusion of expertise and individualized advice to induce consumers to reasonably rely on the company to act in their interests in seeking and selecting student loan debt-relief plans.

58. CES did not undertake the promised individualized assessment of each consumer's student-loan situation. Instead, to the extent CES provided services, it primarily sought to consolidate its customers' student loans.

59. CES took unreasonable advantage of the reasonable reliance of consumers by enrolling and taking fees from consumers whose loans were ineligible for consolidation or who did not otherwise qualify for the relief the company promised.

60. For example, CES took advance fees to consolidate private loans that were not eligible for consolidation with federal loans. CES also took upfront fees to enroll some consumers in income-based repayment plans or loan forgiveness programs for which they were not eligible. In addition, CES placed some consumers in repayment plans that increased their monthly student-loan payments, leaving those consumers in a more financially precarious position than before.

61. Therefore, the acts and practices set forth in paragraphs 56 to 60 constitute abusive acts or practices in violation of the CFPA, 12 U.S.C. § 5536(a)(1)(B).

Notes on *College Educational Services*

1. As used by the CFPB thus far, the fourth prong of "abusive," 12 U.S.C. § 5531(d)(2)(C), taking "unreasonable advantage of . . . the reasonable reliance by the consumer on a covered person to act in the interests of the consumer," has been to address quasi-agency situations in which a party is offering to perform a service for the consumer, such as helping adjust the consumer's debts with a third party or to broker a loan from a third party.

2. Is it possible to read the fourth prong of the "abusive" definition, 12 U.S.C. § 5531(d)(2)(C), to cover traditional debtor-creditor relationships, or is it limited to when there is an implication that a covered party is actually the consumer's agent? That is, do debtors have a reasonable expectation that creditors will only extend them credit that they can be reasonably expected to handle? In other words, can the fourth prong be read to imply an ability-to-repay requirement for all lending? There are already statutory ability-to-repay requirements for mortgages and credit cards; the fourth prong of the "abusive" definition may open the door to a broader set of consumer repayment capacity requirements.

Problem Set 11

1. Review problem 1 in Problem Set 10. What would the result be if the CFPB brought suit against Slaab Motor Corporation alleging that it is engaged in an abusive act or practice based on its advertisement of zero-down leases, when it is impossible to lease a car without paying at least $1,000 in upfront fees? *See* 12 U.S.C. §§ 5531(d)(1), 5531(d)(2)(A).

2. Review problem 2 in from Problem Set 10. What would the result be if the CFPB brought suit against The Sloppy Jalopy alleging that it is engaged in an abusive act or practice because it is making loans without regard to borrowers' ability to repay? *See* 12 U.S.C. § 5531(d)(2)(A)-(C).

3. Review problem 3 in Problem Set 10. What would the result be if the CFPB brought suit against Metropolitan Bancorp alleging that its new overdraft policy is an abusive act or practice? Does the outcome depend on the form of notice given to consumers of the change in the policy? *See* 12 U.S.C. § 5531(d)(2)(A)-(B).

4. Valedictorian Finance Corp. makes student loans. Valedictorian Finance's loan contract includes a provision providing that its attorneys' fees for collecting on unpaid loans plus a 10% markup will be added to the principal balance of the loan. The provision is not negotiable. When Valedictorian Finance adds attorneys' fees and the markup to loan balances, is it engaged in an abusive act or practice? *See* 12 U.S.C. § 5531(d)(2)(B); *CFPB v. Freedom Stores, Inc.*, Complaint ¶76.

5. Golden Years Mortgage Company specializes in making reverse mortgages—a type of mortgage loan made to individuals age 62 and older, that provides funds to the consumer, the repayment of which is secured by the home and not due until the consumer either moves or deceases. The reverse mortgage product thus lets older consumer borrow against their home equity without immediate repayment obligations. The Golden Years loan forms include several pages of fine print (nine-point san serif font with reduced kerning to be precise) regarding the terms and conditions of the loan. Is this an abusive act or practice? *See* 12 U.S.C. §§ 5531(d)(1), 5531(d)(2)(A); *CFPB v. All American Check Cashing, Inc.*, Complaint, ¶67.

6. Sir-Lend-a-Lot, a payday lender, operates in Texas, a state in which 19% of the population lacks basic prose literacy skills in English, and only 78% of residents over age 25 have a high school diploma. Sir-Lend-a-Lot's term disclosures are written at a twelfth-grade level and are only in English despite many of its borrowers being native Spanish speakers. Is this an abusive act or practice? *See* 12 U.S.C. §§ 5531(d)(1), 5531(d)(2)(A); *CFPB v. All American Check Cashing, Inc.*, Complaint, ¶67.

PART I

REGULATION

SECTION C

Disclosure Regulation and Consumer Rationality

CHAPTER 12

DISCLOSURE REGULATION

I. DISCLOSURE, DISCLOSURE EVERYWHERE, AND NARY A THING DISCLOSED?

Mandatory disclosure is a major mode of consumer financial regulation. While some consumer financial regulations prohibit or require particular product terms, the bulk of consumer financial regulation consists of requirements for information to be disclosed. Virtually all of the federal "enumerated consumer laws" now administered by the CFPB have major disclosure components: the Truth in Lending Act, the Truth in Savings Act, the Electronic Fund Transfer Act, the Real Estate Settlement Procedures Act, the Gramm-Leach-Bliley Act privacy provisions, the Consumer Leasing Act, the Interstate Land Sales Act, the Homeowners Protection Act, and the Home Ownership and Equity Protection Act. The disclosure requirements in these statutes vary on several dimensions. In every case, we must ask who has a duty to disclose what to whom, when, how, and why? We also need to ask whether disclosure is effective.

Disclosures can take on a range of forms. They can be printed information, which might be on a product itself (*e.g.*, a toothpaste tube or juice container), or might be on a separate sheet of paper, or both (prescription drugs), or on the web. The disclosure might be in long-form text, but it might also be in a shorthand code (*e.g.*, movie ratings or safety star ratings for vehicles), a symbol (various kashrut symbols or an Underwriters Laboratory symbol), or a picture (*e.g.*, a death's-head). It might also be auditory (the backup beep on trucks or talking crosswalks), visual (colored signs and lights at a railroad crossing), tactile (rumble strips and speed bumps), or even olfactory (the sulfur smell required to be added to methane gas) or gustatory (bittering agents added to toxic products). The point here is that there are a lot of different ways information can be conveyed, and not all are likely to be equally effective. An olfactory disclosure about a gas leak is very effective at indicating danger even to a consumer who isn't paying attention, but it conveys only a very limited amount of information. Conversely, a long-form text disclosure might give a consumer a lot of information, but might not be very effective as a form of communication because it requires the consumer to read and think about the text.

While consumer finance disclosures are typically made in print and involve pages of fine print, they are occasionally verbal (such as counseling requirements), and in some cases cannot be in fine print. For example, the Truth in Lending Act requires disclosures for reverse mortgages—a product typically used by older Americans to extract equity value from their homes—to be "in conspicuous type." 15 U.S.C. § 1648(a).

II. WHY DO DISCLOSURE?

There are numerous regulatory techniques that appear in consumer finance. Sometimes the market is relied on to self-regulate. Sometimes regulation involves mandating or prohibiting particular products or product terms or practices. Sometimes regulation involves the licensing of product providers. Sometimes regulation involves the ongoing supervision of product providers. Sometimes regulation involves the regulatory pre-approval of new products. Sometimes regulation requires the offering of particular options or products. Sometimes the regulation creates greater potential liability for the provider of certain types of products as a way of encouraging the provision of other types of products. But by far the most common regulatory technique in consumer finance is mandatory disclosure.

The roots of disclosure lie in contract doctrine. Contract law is founded on parties agreeing to an exchange. If the parties do not understand and agree on the terms of the exchange, there has not been a meeting of the minds, and absent that consensus, there is no contract. From a contract doctrine perspective the meeting of the minds is important because it is necessary for consent to a creation of private law. Whereas some law, like tort law, implies duties on everyone, contract law involves a private creation of liability. Thus, consent is important for principles of fairness to the parties involved and because of the involvement of the state through contract enforcement in the courts.

A meeting of the minds is also important from an economic perspective. Markets require information to function. A fundamental principle of economics is the price theory of demand—that levels of demand for a product relate to the price of a product. Parties will only enter into an exchange if they believe it to be welfare-enhancing. Thus, Elizabeth will sell her watch to Adam for $100 only if she values the $100 more than the watch, and vice versa for Adam. By agreeing to the exchange, Elizabeth and Adam have revealed their preferences as to what they believe will maximize their welfare. But what if Elizabeth thought she were selling the watch for $100, but the sales contract (drafted by Adam and not read by Elizabeth) actually said $90? If so, we can't be sure that the transaction was in fact expressing Elizabeth's preferences or that there was consent. Elizabeth might have been willing to sell the watch for $90, but perhaps she wouldn't part with it for anything less than $100.

The price theory of demand is predicated on price information existing. Absent *accurate* price information, there will not be efficient levels of demand for a product. Accurate information necessarily means information about the total price of the product. If information is inaccurate—or perceived inaccurately—then it can result in the use of the wrong type of product, the over- or underuse of a type of product, or the use of the wrong product within a type. Thus, ensuring that there is sufficient and accurate information is important both from the perspective of individual consumer welfare and from the perspective of aggregate supply and demand in the economy.

Contract law has doctrines like mistake and misrepresentation to allow contracts to be rescinded if they turn out to be based on incorrect information about existing facts. Yet contract doctrine itself does not impose a general duty to disclose, beyond that which is contained in more general concepts of good faith and fair dealing. *See Laidlaw v. Organ*, 15 U.S. 178 (1817) (establishing *caveat emptor* rule in American law, but noting a good faith exception). Instead, the baseline rule of contracts is *caveat emptor.*[1] Active concealment may cross the line into torts of concealment, misrepresentation, and fraud.

Consider, though, how *caveat emptor* applies to a credit product, for instance. The failure to disclose an interest rate or a fee would seem to go to the heart of the bargain and thus enable contract rescission. But not all disclosures are created equal. Exactly what must be disclosed, and how? How must the interest rate be disclosed? If the lender discloses a "12% interest rate," what does that mean? Consider some of the possibilities: it could be a daily, weekly, monthly, or annual rate. It could be an annual rate based on a 360-day year or on a 365-day year. It could be disclosed not as a rate, but simply as the total amount of interest charged.

From a contract-law perspective, the particular form of the disclosure does not matter; instead, it is the fact that there has been a disclosure. But contract law is mainly concerned with simple bilateral relationships. It is not concerned with ensuring greater market-wide efficiencies or with consumer welfare in a broad sense.

Yet from these macro perspectives, the form in which information is disclosed is just as important as the fact of disclosure. Having standardized disclosure metrics, for example requiring interest rates to be quoted as annual rates, rather than based on whatever time period the lender desires, enables an easier apples-to-apples comparison for the consumer.

The price theory of demand basis for mandating disclosure goes to the question of whether the consumer should use a product at all: whether to take a loan or make a purchase. But disclosure also facilitates a second level of consumer decision-making: comparative consumption choices. If a consumer decides that it's a good idea to get a loan, there might be multiple lending options, whether from one or multiple lenders. Disclosure gives the consumer the information necessary to choose among these options. Thus, by helping consumers make welfare-maximizing decisions about whether to consume and which consumption option to choose, disclosure plays a key consumer-protection function. Likewise, disclosure helps consumers decide not only whether to transact and with whom to transact, but also whether to remain in a transactional relationship. Should a consumer refinance a loan or switch banking relationships? Disclosures facilitate that decision too.

---

1. There are, of course, numerous exceptions, most notably the implied warranty of merchantability for sales of goods. UCC § 2-314.

Facilitating comparisons among consumption options has an important collateral effect: it creates competitive pressure on businesses to offer better terms. Competitive pressure can both drive sharp practices from the market and push down even fairly structured prices. This competitive pressure is yet another important consumer-protection function of disclosure.

A final consumer-protection benefit of disclosure is that it prevents bait-and-switch sales tactics. Disclosure can establish a set of terms to which a consumer can then insist that a business adhere. Disclosure forces businesses to commit to the terms on which they transact. This certainty is essential for markets to function. If consumers cannot rely on getting the terms they are offered, they will eschew the marketplace.

Consider the preamble to the Truth in Lending Act of 1968, the "crown jewel" of federal disclosure regulations:

> The Congress finds that economic stabilization would be enhanced and the competition among the various financial institutions and other firms engaged in the extension of consumer credit would be strengthened by the informed use of credit. The informed use of credit results from an awareness of the cost thereof by consumers. It is the purpose of this subchapter to assure a meaningful disclosure of credit terms so that the consumer will be able to compare more readily the various credit terms available to him and avoid the uninformed use of credit, and to protect the consumer against inaccurate and unfair credit billing and credit card practices.

15 U.S.C. § 1601(a). Which rationale(s) for disclosure is(are) articulated in the preamble? Which are not? Keep this in mind as we examine the disclosure regimes for particular products in future chapters. Do the disclosure regimes all match the TILA rationale(s)?

Disclosure obligations in consumer finance are not limited to disclosure as part of the contracting process ("contractual disclosure"). While contractual disclosure is mainly aimed at ensuring that consumers have the information necessary to make an informed decision about entering a contract, contractual disclosures can also affect post-transaction behavior. William C. Whitford, *The Functions of Disclosure Regulation in Consumer Transactions*, 1973 Wis. L. Rev. 400, 405 (noting in the context of warranty disclosure); Yoon-Ho Alex Lee & K. Jeremy Ko, *Consumer Mistakes in the Mortgage Market: Choosing Unwisely Versus Not Switching Wisely*, 14 U. Pa. J. Bus. L. 417 (2012) (noting failures to refinance). A consumer's decision of whether to pre-pay or refinance a loan or whether to draw on a line of credit are all decisions subsequent to the initial contract, yet they are shaped by disclosures as well.

In addition to contractual disclosures there are also sometimes regulations of consumer finance advertising and solicitations or what in contract jargon might be called invitations to deal ("pre-contractual disclosure"). The concern in these situations is about deceptive advertisement that lures in consumers by advertising what looks like a good deal only to then surprise the consumer subsequently with less favorable terms, hoping to take advantage of the consumer's sunk search costs. Consumer finance disclosure requirements also often include requirements about monthly billing or account statements and transaction receipts ("post-contractual disclosure"). These post-contractual disclosure requirements are designed to ensure that the consumer can verify whether transactions have been done correctly and to enable the consumer to dispute erroneous transactions.

Of course, simply requiring information to be disclosed does not guarantee that it will be used. Whether disclosure regulation reflects predictive models of consumer behavior or normative aspirations for how consumers should act is very much an open question. William C. Whitford, *The Functions of Disclosure Regulation in Consumer Transactions*, 1973 Wis. L. Rev. 400, 436-437 (suggesting that disclosure regulation is driven by normative views of consumer behavior). Moreover, mandating disclosure may be a politically convenient way for legislators and regulators to satisfy the demand for consumer-protection regulation in a way that faces relatively less opposition from the financial services industry than substantive term regulation, particularly if disclosure is unlikely to affect consumer behavior. *See id.* From a financial services industry perspective mandatory disclosure may be viewed as an acceptable second best to non-regulation.

III. DOES DISCLOSURE WORK?

Does disclosure work for consumer financial products? The evidence is mixed and seems to vary depending on the type of transaction involved, and also about what disclosure is meant to accomplish.

After the enactment of the Truth in Lending Act, the centerpiece of consumer finance disclosures, several empirical studies attempted to gauge its impact.[2] These studies indicated that after TILA became effective, few consumers were able to report the interest rates on their contracts with complete accuracy, but the reported rates tended to be closer to the actual rates after TILA than before TILA. This finding is consistent both with TILA being moderately effective, but also with TILA merely improving consumer awareness of the prevailing level of interest rates, rather than the specific rate in their contract. A more recent study about the impact of changes to TILA suggests that the statute is ineffective beyond a general sorting.[3] Other studies show that TILA and Real Estate Settlement Procedures Act mortgage credit disclosures appear to be utterly ineffective.[4]

---

2. *See, e.g.*, Board of Governors of the Federal Reserve System, Annual Report to Congress on Truth in Lending for the Year 1969, appendix B (1970); Board of Governors of the Federal Reserve System, Annual Report to Congress on Truth in Lending for the Year 1970, appendix B (1971); G. Day & W. Brandt, *A Study of Consumer Credit Decisions: Implications for Present and Prospective Legislation* (1972); Robert P. Shay & Milton W. Schober, *Consumer Awareness of Annual Percentage Rates of Charge in Consumer Installment Credit: Before and After Truth in Lending Became Effective* (1971); Lewis Mandell, *Consumer Perception of Incurred Interest Rates: An Empirical Test of the Efficacy of the Truth-in-Lending Law*, 26 J. Fin. 1143 (1971); Comment, *The Impact of Truth in Lending on Automobile Financing-An Empirical Study*, 4 U. Cal. Davis L. Rev. 179 (1971); Thomas A. Durkin, *Consumer Awareness of Credit Terms: Review and New Evidence*, 48 J. Bus. 253 (1975).

3. Sherrill Shaffer, *The Competitive Impact of Disclosure Requirements in the Credit Card Industry*, 15 J. Reg. Econ. 183 (1999).

4. Brian K. Bucks & Karen M. Pence, *Do Borrowers Know Their Mortgage Terms?* 64 J. Urban Econ. (2008); James M. Lacko & Janis K. Pappalardo, *The Failure and Promise of Mandated Consumer Mortgage Disclosures: Evidence from Qualitative Interviews and a Controlled Experiment with Mortgage Borrowers*, 100 Am. Econ. Rev. 516 (2010).

How is disclosure working for you? Do you know the interest rates and fees that apply to your credit cards? What your bank will charge for an overdraft? What will trigger those fees?

A. Australian ATM Fees

There are relatively few real-world consumer finance disclosure experiments. Instead, most are done in controlled environments. But it is clear that mandatory disclosure has a major effect on consumer behavior in very simple transactional contexts.

Consider an example from Australia. Consumers in Australia can either use their own bank's ATMs ("home" ATMs) or another bank's ATMs ("foreign" ATMs) to withdraw cash. Foreign ATMs typically charge an AU$2 fee for withdrawals; home banks will also occasionally apply a fee for use of a foreign ATM. Prior to March 2009, ATM fees were not required to be disclosed to consumers prior to transacting, and they seldom were. Instead, ATM fees were disclosed only on the consumer's monthly bank statement. Starting in March 2009, however, Australia required foreign ATM fees and the possibility of additional home bank fees to be disclosed on the ATM screen to the consumer before an ATM transaction was consummated. The result was a notable shift in consumer behavior. Consumers began to use foreign ATMs for a notably smaller percentage of ATM transactions in terms of both number and dollar withdrawals involved (Figures 12.1 and 12.2, respectively), and

Figure 12.1 Percentage of Australian ATM Transactions at Home and Foreign ATMs

Figure 12.2 Percentage of Dollars Withdrawn in Australian ATM Transactions at Home and Foreign ATMs

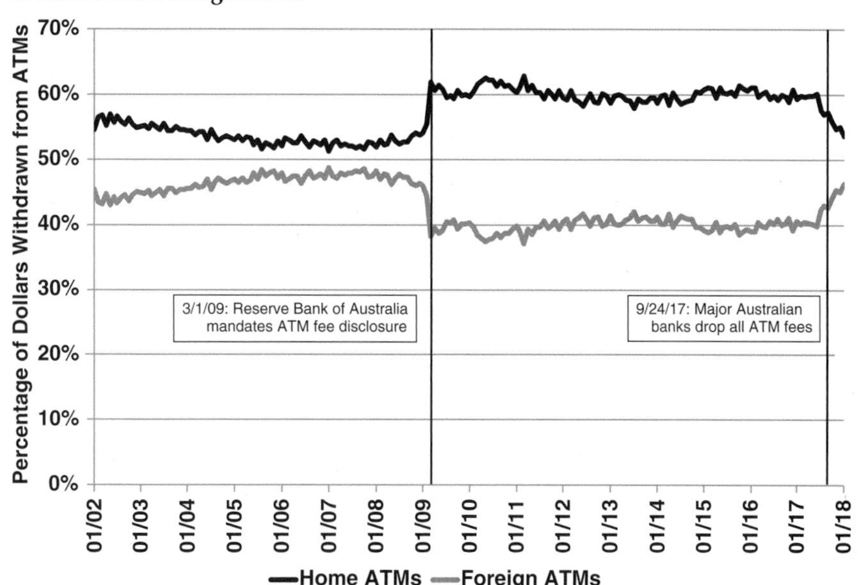

began to take larger amounts out of foreign ATMs when used (Figure 12.3) in order to minimize the number of fees. Clearly, consumers reacted to the disclosure of the ATM fees, and they reacted exactly as one would expect.[5]

ATM withdrawals, however, are very simple transactions. The consumer is getting cash immediately from his or her own funds. The disclosure happens *immediately* before the transaction occurs; there is no intervening time. The transaction is a one-shot deal; no balances are carried, etc., and the transaction is usually a standalone transaction—it is not bundled with a purchase or with other transactions. It is just about money now in exchange for a fee now. Few consumer financial transactions are so simple.

B. More Complex Transactions and Products

As noted above, for more complex products, like credit cards and mortgage loans, the data on disclosure's effectiveness is less encouraging. Indeed, it should not be surprising. More complex products require disclosure of more information, which is harder for consumers to process because of fundamental cognitive limitations. To some extent consumers respond by simply ignoring disclosures. Other times they focus on particular salient terms in the disclosure or rely on various heuristics to navigate through the information.

5. At the end of September 2017, the major Australian banks all announced that they were dropping their ATM fees entirely. The result, not surprisingly, has been an increased use of foreign ATMs relative to home ATMs (*see* Figures 12.1 and 12.2).

Figure 12.3 Average Australian ATM Withdrawal Amount ($AUS)

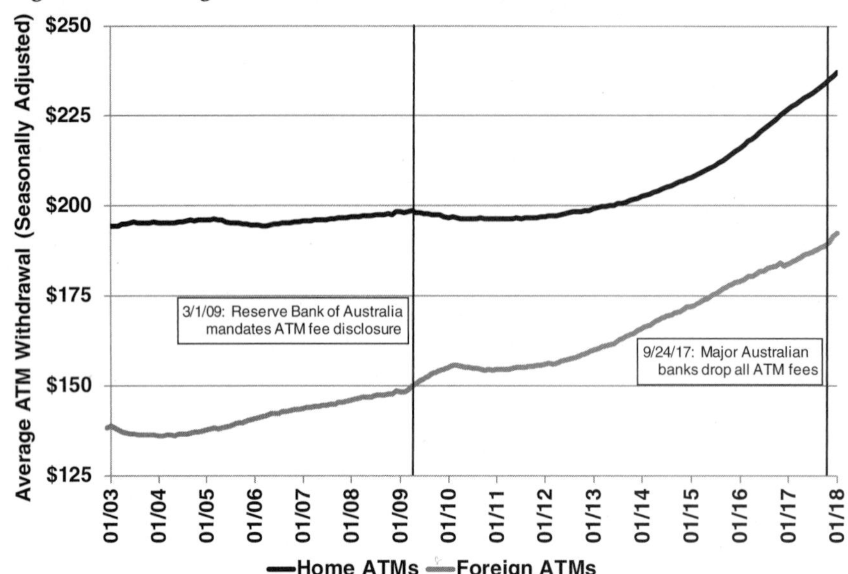

C. Product Standardization as a Remedy for Complexity

While complexity poses an obstacle for the effectiveness of disclosure, it also points to a partial remedy: product standardization. To the extent that product options differ on fewer dimensions, the focus of a consumer's inquiry is narrower, so search costs and information overload are reduced and comparisons facilitated. At its most extreme, standardized products are commodities, varying solely in price term. To be sure, product standardization is more helpful when a consumer is trying to choose among similar products than when trying to decide whether to consume at all. And product standardization reduces the range of consumer choice—which may not be desirable for all consumers.

There are two important implications from effects of product standardization. The first is that standardization will often be resisted by sellers—financial services firms in the consumer finance marketplace. Standardization facilitates price competition and therefore reduces product margins for all firms. Accordingly, firms will often attempt to differentiate fundamentally similar products through add-on features or through pricing schemes that frustrate comparisons, such as splintering the price among multiple fees to create a constellation of fees unique to the product.

The second implication is that if regulators want to facilitate disclosure, they may at times need to regulate for product standardization. Disclosure is often a "soft" remedy—as regulation goes it is a light touch that preserves choices while providing greater information. It doesn't require paternalistic judgments about what products should look like. Who could object to that?

But that is precisely the point. To the extent that a disclosure regime is ineffective, it is unlikely to be opposed by regulated firms. Legislators and regulators can declare "mission accomplished," and say that they have cleaned up a problematic industry by requiring more disclosures, and regulated firms can keep on doing essentially what they have been doing if the disclosures are not effective.

But imagine that the goal is not just the appearance of effective regulation, but actually regulations that facilitate efficient markets (with the idea that truly efficient markets will drive out bad products). If so, then for disclosure to work, it may, at times, need to be accompanied by "hard" fiat regulation that prohibits or mandates particular product terms in order to produce product standardization. There are light touch ways of applying such "hard" regulation—for example, instead of having mandatory rules, creating default rules and safe harbors for products that comply with the default rules. Likewise, simply requiring disclosures that use a particular form can have the effect of encouraging product standardization. If a product does not fit with the categories on the form it will make proper disclosure difficult for the seller and thus potentially create liability for the seller, which creates an incentive for the seller to conform its product to the disclosure form's categories.

There are lots of ways of achieving results that are similar to that of fiat regulation, but the ultimate point still stands: effective disclosure may in some circumstances require a pairing with substantive term regulation. Disclosure is most effective when products are simple; standardization reduces complexity and increases price competition; and firms are incentivized to avoid standardization: therefore absent substantive term regulation aimed at product standardization, disclosure may simply be ineffective. But how should regulators go about deciding what the standard terms of a product should be? This is a vexing question as regulators do not like to second-guess consumer preferences.

D. Format Matters: Evidence from Grocery Store Unit Pricing

Some states require unit pricing to be disclosed in grocery stores. Thus, apple juice would be priced according to a standard unit, such as a fluid ounce, rather than separate prices for 2-gallon, 1-gallon, and quart containers. The unit pricing means that one can compare how much a standard unit costs without regard to the number of units contained in a package, enabling an apple-juice-to-apple-juice comparison.

Typically, unit pricing must be disclosed on the item's display. So if there are five types of apple juice, there are five different unit price display stickers on different store shelves. Consumers are generally aware of such unit pricing,[6] but often do not

6. Monroe P. Friedman, *Dual-Price Labels: Usage Patterns and Potential Benefits for Shoppers in Inner-City and Suburban Supermarkets*, Cong. Record E3086-E3102 (Apr. 15, 1971); David T. McCullough & Daniel I. Padberg, *United Pricing in Supermarkets: Alternatives, Costs, and Consumer Reaction*, 1 Search: Agriculture 1 (1971); Lawrence M. Lamont *et al. Unit Pricing: A Positive Response to Consumerism*, 6 Euro. J. of Marketing 223 (1972); James M. Carman, *A Summary of Empirical Research in Unit Pricing*, 48 J. Retailing 63 (1972-1973); Charlene C. Price, *Consumer Awareness and Use of Unit Pricing*, Nat'l Econ. Analysis Division, Economics, Statistics, and Cooperatives Service, U.S. Dept. of Agriculture, ESCS-30 (Aug. 1978); Bruce F. McElroy & David A. Aaker, *Unit Pricing Six Years After Introduction*, 3 J. Retailing 44 (1979); David A. Aaker & Gary T. Ford, *Unit Pricing Ten Years Later: A Replication*, 47 J. Marketing 118 (1983).

use it or do not purchase the lowest-cost-per-unit products.[7] However, a couple of states require unit prices to be displayed as a list for all products in a category, rather than as disaggregated unit price tags. For example, a list might be:

Able Brand Apple Juice (1 gallon):	$0.1059/ounce
Baker Brand Apple Juice (2 gallon):	$0.1700/ounce
Charlie Brand Organic Apple Juice (½ gallon):	$0.2800/ounce

When a list of unit prices is required to be disclosed, unit pricing does affect consumer behavior; consumers will shift their purchases toward the cheapest unit priced product.[8] This suggests that disclosure efficacy very much depends on the way in which information is presented to consumers. It also suggests that to the extent disclosure is intended to facilitate comparison-shopping, it is unlikely to be effective absent the provision to consumers of a readily comparable compilation of disclosures for competing products.

The article excerpted below, by Professors Omri Ben-Shahar and Carl E. Schneider, explains the shortcomings of mandatory disclosure in more detail. It also suggests why it might be such a common form of regulation: it is a politically palatable way to regulate a product without actually restricting the terms of the product. Disclosure requirements thus often represent a political compromise, but if they are ineffective, is it a sensible one?

Omri Ben-Shahar & Carl E. Schneider
The Failure of Mandated Disclosure

159 U. Pa. L. Rev. 647 (2011)

. . .

Mandated disclosure . . . rests on a plausible assumption: that when it comes to decisionmaking, more information is better than less. More information helps people make better decisions, thus bolstering their autonomy. Since people can no longer customize most transactions, disclosure helps restore some individual control. It may also induce enterprises to behave more efficiently.

. . .

A. THE OVERLOAD EFFECT

. . . When mandates are too detailed, both disclosers and disclosees have trouble. Forms become so long and elaborate that disclosers have problems assembling and

---

7. McCollough & Padberg, *supra* note 6; William E. Kilbourne, *A Factorial Experiment on the Impact of Unit Pricing on Low-Income Consumers*, 11 J. Marketing Research 453 (1974); *but see* Hans R. Isakson & Alex R. Maurizi, *The Consumer Economics of Unit Pricing*, 10 J. Marketing Research 277 (1973).

8. Edward J. Russo *et al.*, *An Effective Display of Unit Price Information*, 39 J. Marketing 11 (1975); Edward J. Russo, *The Value of Unit Price Information*, 14 J. Marketing Research 193 (1977); Valarie A. Zeithaml, *Consumer Response to In-Store Information Environments*, 8 J. Consumer Research 347 (1982).

organizing the information, and disclosees do not read them and cannot understand, assimilate, and analyze the avalanche of information.

The classic overload statement is Miller's "magical number seven"—seven being roughly the number of items people can keep in short-term memory. This number is often thought too high, but many typical disclosures easily exceed it. For example, *Miranda* warnings average 96 words and range up to 408 words. Rogers invokes Miller's number and concludes that even with "verbal chunking" (combining data into a single item for easier storage) "the upper limit of information processing for Miranda warnings is likely less than 75 words....Even when cued, participants with less than a 12th grade education recalled only 55.8% of the verbal material." And this still overstates understanding, since "many suspects have cognitive deficits and are further impaired by highly stressful circumstances," and since "the mere recitation of concepts cannot be equated with genuine understanding."

. . .

B. THE ACCUMULATION PROBLEM

The overload effect pervades the Disclosure Republic, but it is at least well known in the literature and by lawmakers. However, they hardly notice the "accumulation" problem. Lawmakers evaluate disclosure mandates issue-by-issue, but in disclosees' lives, each disclosure competes for their time and attention with other disclosures, with their investigations into unmandated knowledge, and with everything they do besides collecting information and making decisions (like working, playing, and living with their families). One disclosure by itself may seem trivial, but en masse disclosures are overwhelming.

Even if disclosees wanted to read all the disclosures relevant to their decisions, they could not do so proficiently, and practically they could not do so at all. They soon learn their lesson and give up any inclination they may have had to devote their lives to disclosures.

Lawmakers are shielded from the accumulation problem. They deal with trouble stories and the social problems they symbolize one at a time, in specialized agencies or committees, or in courts confronted with a particular case or controversy. In those contexts, nothing draws their attention to the accumulation problem; nor would raising it be a politically attractive maneuver. And even if the literature eventually recognized the accumulation problem, even if the literature informed lawmakers, and even if lawmakers wanted to thin the disclosure landscape by selecting only a few critical disclosures, the lawmakers would not have the competence, incentives, or opportunity for doing so. Furthermore, the American system of overlapping jurisdictions permits one lawmaker to act even if other lawmakers with concurrent jurisdiction believe action is unnecessary, undesirable, or even unsafe.

. . .

The standard response to illiteracy and innumeracy is to demand simpler forms. But for decades experts have labored intelligently and earnestly to present complex information accessibly, and it is now clear that only modest progress is possible. For example, one sophisticated attempt at a simple guide for prostate-cancer patients aimed for a seventh-grade reading level, which would exclude roughly half the population. A recent study of mutual-fund disclosures is to like effect. Unfortunately, complexity cannot be explained simply. Sophisticated vocabularies and professional languages encapsulate complex thoughts. If only simple words may be used, everything must be spelled out. This returns us to the overload problem. Many words make forms repellently long and cognitively overwhelming.

. . .

We have already said that providing complex information in large quantities makes it hard for disclosees to acquire and understand disclosures. The problem worsens when they try to use such information. People can keep only a few factors in mind when analyzing a problem. A "large body of empirical work suggest[s] that the integration of different types of information and values into a decision is a very difficult cognitive process. Evidence shows that people can process and use only a limited number of variables." In fact, information may *decrease* the reliability of decisions: "When individuals had more information, their ability to use it 'consistently' declined."

One study, for instance, asked expert handicappers to predict horse races. The more information the handicappers had, the more confident they were, but their "predictive ability was as good with 5 variables as with 10, 20, or 40." Worse, "reliability of the choices *decreased* as more information was made available."

It will come as no surprise, then, that consumers borrow more than is rational. The calculations required to borrow shrewdly are numerous and knotty: Consumers must compare relative costs of credit and cash, compare different financial products (such as short- versus long-term or secured versus unsecured), set the proper level of saving versus consumption, factor in the time value of money and how it might evolve, and assign each factor a weight. Faced with all this, it is hard not to overweight a few simple, easily understood factors like low present interest rates.

People often simplify decisions by pruning away factors, and at the extreme they consult a single factor. Making trade-offs to integrate conflicting dimensions into an overall choice is such a complex cognitive task that people tend to use heuristic shortcuts that may not produce optimal decisions. These simplified strategies include selecting only one dimension and ignoring others or focusing on concrete, easy to understand concepts such as cost rather than more complicated and less precise factors such as quality indicators.

The more overwhelming a decision, the more appealing radical shortcuts become. Indeed, confronted with disclosures containing many items, people consider only the simplified shortcut—some bottom line. Loan shoppers, for example, when given more information about subcomponents of the loan price, were less likely to choose the cheaper loan than shoppers who saw only the bottom-line price.

So (perhaps because of the anchoring heuristic) the rule for borrowing seems to be, *can I afford the monthly payment?* This requires minimal calculation, but it distorts the cost of credit. It obscures comparisons between competing credit offers and between the cost of credit and the cost of paying for a household purchase out of savings. Most importantly, it renders disclosure of APR and related credit terms interesting but irrelevant.

Problem Set 12

1. Which of the following issues would better disclosure requirements have prevented? What does this tell you about the importance of disclosure in consumer finance? What sort of problems are not addressed by disclosure?

a. Walker-Thomas Furniture's cross-collateralized installment sale to Ora Lee Williams of various household items. *See* Chapter 2.

b. RBS Citizens Bank's practice of resolving deposit "discrepancies" in its favor. *See* Chapter 10.

c. Wells Fargo's practice of opening up fake accounts without consumer authorization. *See* Chapters 10 and 11.

d. Dwolla's misrepresentations regarding its data security measures. *See* Chapter 10.

2. Consider the "Credit Card Safety Star Act of 2007" proposal described in the press release below. Do you think such a proposal would be effective at helping promote fairer credit card practices?

Wyden, Obama Introduce "Credit Card Safety Star Act of 2007"
5-Star Safety Rating System Brings Transparency to Credit Card Agreements

Press Release, Dec. 5, 2007

Washington, D.C. - Working to give consumers the tools to make informed choices about complex credit card agreements, U.S. Senators Ron Wyden (D-OR) and Barack Obama (D-IL) today introduced the "Credit Card Safety Star Act of 2007." The legislation creates a five-star safety rating system for credit cards in order to increase the transparency of credit card agreements and encourage issuers to abandon abusive practices by offering consumers fair terms they can understand.

"This legislation will help people understand if they can expect their card issuer to treat them fairly, or kick them when they are down," said Wyden. "With the financial future of so many Americans dependent upon unreadable jargon in credit card documents, arming consumers with usable information is more critical than ever."

"Consumers need some way to know which credit cards are safe and which ones are most likely to get them into financial trouble with fees, penalties, and charges," Senator Obama said. "A Safety Star system is an innovative approach to require credit card companies to increase transparency and hold them accountable for any hidden charges or changes. This bill will give consumers a powerful tool to protect themselves, while giving credit card companies an incentive to improve their practices."

Much like the five-star crash test rating system for new cars, the "Credit Card Safety Star Act of 2007" will give consumers a window into the safety of their credit cards. Under the legislation, every credit card, billing statement, agreement, application, and piece of marketing material will be required to carry the credit card's safety star rating, which will range anywhere from one to five stars, with five stars representing the safest cards.

Cards will be awarded stars based on a points system, with cards earning points for consumer friendly terms and losing them for terms designed to get consumers into trouble. For example, card issuers that can change the terms of an agreement at any time for any reason would receive a one-star safety rating.; while credit cards that give 90 days notice before the issuer intends to change terms, or cards that write their agreements at an accessible reading level would get more stars.

Under the Credit Card Safety Star rating system it is expected that most of the cards available on today's market will rate an average of one or two stars. Similarly, when the five-star crash rating system for new cars first came into existence, no car received more than two stars in any of its crash ratings. Today, however, many cars receive five-star ratings. The Credit Card Safety Star program is designed to have a similar effect on the credit industry by forcing card issuers to compete on the basis of providing a consumer-friendly product. Consumers prefer credit cards with fair terms, so they are more likely to choose cards with higher star ratings. Therefore, card issuers will have to improve their practices in order to attract and keep customers.

The Credit Card Safety Star program would be administered by the Federal Reserve and periodically reevaluated and updated based on market innovations and the program's effectiveness. Because some issuers may refuse to abandon some of their worst practices despite market competition, the program is designed to accommodate the possibility of further legislation or regulations eliminating such practices.

. . .

---

3. Bank account term disclosures frequently run to 100+ pages. Account disclosures are also frequently not available online and require a consumer to make an in-person inquiry at a bank branch.

- **a.** Given this, how easy is it to compare bank accounts terms?
- **b.** The Pew Charitable Trusts designed a model bank account term disclosure form that was meant to fit on two pages. A number of banks adopted the model form, but few, if any, used Pew's precise formatting. The banks added in their own logos and color schemes and fonts, such that page breaks are not the same between the different bank's adoptions or even the same number of pages. How effective do you expect these model forms will be at increasing competition for deposit accounts? Why do you think banks might have adopted these model forms?

4. As the Associate Director for Research and Markets at the CFPB, you've been tasked with figuring out a way to improve credit card account opening disclosures. How do you go about figuring out what will be effective at alerting consumers to the differences between cards?

CHAPTER 13

BEHAVIORAL ECONOMICS

I. CLASSICAL VS. BEHAVIORAL ECONOMICS

Classical economics is based on the assumption of revealed preferences—that the choices that economic actors make indicate their preferences. These choices are understood to indicate what the individual believes will maximize some objective function (typically the utility or welfare function) under the constraints faced by the individual.

Classical economics assumes that a consumer will compare the opportunity cost of various decisions and then pursue an activity until the marginal benefit equals the marginal cost. Thus, if I choose to eat ice cream instead of broccoli, this decision reveals that I believe the consumption of ice cream to be maximizing my welfare function. Similarly, I will keep eating ice cream until the marginal benefit of its deliciousness is outweighed by the its various marginal costs to my welfare.

Critically, while classical economics assumes rational behavior, it is able to account for consumer error. Thus, if an individual is faced with uncertainty, classical economics assumes that the individual maximizes his or her expected utility by assigning probabilities to different states of the world.

For example, if I don't like wearing a seatbelt in the car, my decisions of whether to wear one depends on my estimation of the likelihood of being in a car accident where wearing a seatbelt would protect me from injury. It is completely rational to evaluate whether I should wear a seatbelt in this fashion, but it is also entirely possible that I miscalculate the likelihood of that accident, which is something that I might try to account for in my calculation.

Behavioral economics incorporates insights from psychology to question the fundamental assumption of classical economics, namely that a party's choices reveal its actual preferences. Instead, behavioral economics emphasizes that consumers exhibit biased, non-random deviations from purely rational behavior, which makes it impossible to assume that choices do in fact reveal true preferences.

Behavioral economics has three fundamental insights about human behavior. First, it recognizes that human beings process information imperfectly. There are many reasons for this, including imperfect cognitive faculties and the cost of acquiring and processing information, and it leads people to rely on shortcuts—rules of thumb or heuristics—for evaluating problems.

The second fundamental insight is that the manner in which information is presented affects how it is understood. This means that the format of information, the timing at which information is presented, the contents of the information, both in terms of what is included and what is not included, the source of the information, and the context in which the information is presented all affect how the information is perceived. For an extreme example, the disclosure of information made by a small print sign at a checkout counter to a parent coping with a bevy of impatient toddlers is likely to have a different impact than the same disclosure made orally to that parent by the President of the United States in a quiet conversation in the Oval Office.

Consider a small sampling of the ways in which consumers' perceptions of prices can be affected through relatively simple changes in presentation. You've probably noticed that many merchants advertise prices ending with 99¢. Why? Because of the left-digit pricing effect: consumers perceive $19.99 as materially different from $20.00 because of an anchoring effect based on the leftmost digit.[1] Other types of anchoring that affect analytical framing can be through presentation of daily equivalence, comparison with petty cash expenses such as the cost of a cup of coffee, and use of installment payment structures (that create a smaller reference payment).[2]

Likewise, consumers perceive prices with fewer syllables to be cheaper, perhaps because the brain subconsciously encodes an auditory version of the text that is read.[3] Thus, $27.82 is perceived as larger than $28.16. Phonetic length may also explain why prices without commas are perceived of as smaller than those with: $1000 vs. $1,000.[4] Similarly, font sizes matter. Smaller (or larger) visual magnitudes reinforce smaller (or larger) numerical magnitudes, just as words associated with small (or large) magnitude reinforce numerical magnitudes, such as "low maintenance" or "high performance."[5]

Even things like removing a currency symbol from a price can make it seem cheaper to consumers,[6] while selective use of different colors (particularly red for men) seem to focus attention on particular terms.[7]

---

1. Manoj Thomas & Vicki Morwitz, *Penny Wise and Pound Foolish: The Left-Digit Effect in Price Cognition,* 32 J. Consumer Research 54 (2005).

2. Tridib Mazumdar et al., *Reference Price Research: Review and Propositions,* 69 J. Mktg. 84 (2005); John T. Gourville, *Pennies-a-Day: The Effect of Temporal Reframing on Transaction Evaluation,* 24 J. Consumer Research 395 (1998); John T. Gourville, *The Effect of Implicit Versus Explicit Comparisons on Temporal Pricing Claims,* 10 Mktg. Letters 113 (1999).

3. Keith S. Coulter et al., *Comma n' cents in Pricing: The Effects of Auditory Representation Encoding on Price Magnitude Perceptions,* 22 J. Consumer Psych. 395 (2012); Stanislas Dehaene, *Varieties of Numerical Abilities,* 44 Cognition 1 (1992).

4. Keith S. Coulter et al., *Comma n' cents in Pricing: The Effects of Auditory Representation Encoding on Price Magnitude Perceptions,* 22 J. Consumer Psych. 395 (2012).

5. Keith S. Coulter & Robin A. Coulter, *Size Does Matter: The Effects of Magnitude Representation Congruency on Price Perceptions and Purchase Likelihood,* 15 J. Consumer Psych. 64 (2005).

6. Sybil S. Yang et al., *Menu Price Presentation Influences Consumer Purchase Behavior in Restaurants,* 28 Int'l J. Hosp. Mgmt. 157 (2009).

7. Nancy M. Puccinelli et al., *Are Men Seduced by Red? The Effect of Red Versus Black Prices on Price Perceptions,* 89 J. Retailing 115 (2013).

Perhaps most relevant to consumer finance is the use of "**partitioned pricing**" (also known as "drip pricing").[8] This means splitting the price into smaller component units, rather than a bundled, all-in price. Consumers encounter this all the time, with shipping and handling costs separated out from the base price, as well as with sales taxes being separated out from the advertised price. A price for a loan can be split into an interest rate and multiple fees, for example. The result can be that none of the price points seems especially large, and it can be difficult for the consumer to engage in an apples-to-apples comparison with other products because pricing structures might not be quite the same, and an all-in cost can be hard to compute (never overestimate consumer numeracy).

Similarly, delayed pricing, where the consumer is not confronted with the cost of the transaction at the time of the transaction, reduces the salience of the pricing for the consumer and may result in the consumer misestimating the price. For example, a consumer might overdraw a bank account at time 1, but not actually be presented with the overdraft fee until time 2. The fee, even if known to the consumer, is much less salient at time 1, when the transaction decision is made, than at time 2.

The third fundamental insight of behavioral economics is that human beings often make mistakes in predictable, systematic ways. We have numerous categories of bounded rationality, bounded willpower, and bounded self-interest. For example, people often engage in hyperbolic discounting or exhibit irrational anchoring effects, loss aversion, endowment effects, status quo bias, time-inconsistent choices, or over- or underestimation biases.

Behavioral economics, then, is about questioning the revealed preference assumption that underlies classical economics. It is important to emphasize that behavioral economics is not about imperfect information or information asymmetries per se. Information asymmetries or incomplete or imperfect information is perfectly compatible with classical economics. Likewise, agency problems are not a behavioral economics issue per se.

Behavioral economics is about the *processing* of information, not about the presence or lack of information or about incentive structures. Information and agency problems can, however, trigger biased cognitive responses. For example, when faced with an information asymmetry and high costs of gathering and processing enough information to overcome the asymmetry, consumers are likely to rely on a heuristic as a shortcut, and that opens the door to cognitive biases.

II. BEHAVIORAL ECONOMICS AND CONSUMER FINANCE

A. Thimblerig

Behavioral economics problems in consumer finance can be analogized to the situation depicted in Hieronymus Bosch's famous painting of the *Conjurer*, which

8. *See* Johannes Voester *et al.*, *Partitioned Pricing: Review of the Literature and Directions for Further Research*, 10 Rev. Managerial Sci. 1 (2016).

shows a game of thimblerig. Thimblerig, also known as the shell game or, when played with cards, as three-card monte, involves a pea or ball being placed under one of three thimbles or small cups. The dealer then shifts the thimbles around. The player tries to guess which cup is covering the pea. If the player is right, the player gets the amount of the bet from the dealer; if the player is wrong, the dealer gets the money from the player.

When played cleanly, thimblerig is simply a game about whether the player is able to follow the dealer's sleights of hand in shuffling the thimbles. The dealer's goal is to distract the player and make the player focus on the wrong thimble. The idea is to draw the player's attention away from the thimble containing the pea.

Thimblerig, however, is usually not played cleanly. Instead, the dealer—often with shills who are pretending to be onlookers or other players—will employ various ruses to ensure that the player never wins and is simply parted with his money. These ruses frequently involve distracting the player if the player is on to the right thimble, so the dealer can move the thimbles again.

Or, as shown in Hieronymus Bosch's painting (below), the game itself might be a distraction from the real action. On the far left of the picture, the player's pocket is being picked by a man in the garb of a Dominican friar while the player concentrates

Figure 13.1 Hieronymus Bosch's *The Conjurer*

on the game. Indeed, in Bosch's picture, everything is laid out to distract the viewer from the theft; the very design of the picture is a riff on thimblerig: the viewer's attention is focused on shell game on the table in the center of the picture; the mark's gaze leads away from his purse. Even the Dominican's skyward gaze distracts the viewer from the theft in progress. Bosch himself is playing the thimblerig dealer, and in any variation, the dealer's goal in thimblerig is to distract the player so that the player does not focus on where the real action is, be it the pea or his purse.

No less a personage than Laura Ingalls Wilder recognized the perils of thimblerig in *Farmer Boy*, part of the *Little House on the Prairie* series. In this novel, young Almanzo Wilder (Laura's future husband) sees a game of thimblerig at the county fair. Almanzo's sure that he knows where the pea is, and tells his father so. His father counsels him to just wait and watch. Another man bets on the game and selects the very thimble that Almanzo thinks contains the pea. Of course is it empty. As Wilder relates:

> Almanzo couldn't understand it. He had seen the pea under that shell, and then it wasn't there. He asked Father how the man had done it.
>
> "I don't know, Almanzo," Father said. "But he knows. It's his game. Never bet your money on another man's game."

Laura Ingalls Wilder, *Farmer Boy* 255-256 (1953 rev. ed.).

B. Cognitive Thimblerig

Consumer finance products often employ a type of thimblerigging that exploits cognitive biases as the basis for distraction. Consumer financial products typically have multiple terms—different interest rates and fees and bundled products. These terms are all part of the price of the product, as are other contractual terms such as dispute resolution rights and liability limitations. Each one of these terms is like a thimble. The pea, however, is the total cost of the product. The more thimbles into which the total cost is splintered, however, the harder it is for consumers to see the pea and thus compare the product with another. Instead, in the context of fractured pricing, consumers are likely to focus on the most salient terms, and weight those terms more heavily than others.

The saliency of terms is a combination of the consumer's idiosyncratic concerns and those terms emphasized by the financial product's provider. The ability to emphasize certain terms (and in so doing deemphasize others) lets financial product providers play thimblerig, as consumers' attention can be directed toward less important terms and away from the real cost of the product, with the result being that consumers underestimate the cost of using the product, so they will overconsume the product. The result is that the transaction is not what the consumer really bargained for. There is no real *consensus ad idem*; the proverbial meeting of the minds never occurs. Instead, we have a behavioral trick being used to deceive the consumer.

Note that this is overconsumption relative to what the consumer would consume if the total cost were transparent. In other words, the overconsumption measure here is being determined in reference to revealed preferences, not in reference to a paternalistically derived consumption level.

Is there anything inherently wrong with cognitive thimblerig? Arguably, the answer is no. To be sure, the consumer isn't getting the deal that he thought he was getting, and if he understood the deal he was getting, he might not have entered into it. But that's not the business's fault. Full information is, after all, available for the consumer. It can hardly be the business's fault if the consumer fails to process the information correctly.

On the other hand, what if the business knows (or should know) that many consumers are unlikely to understand the product? What if the disclosures are in fine-point font and made to a population of seniors? (Federal law requires that disclosures for reverse mortgages, a product targeted at seniors, be "conspicuous.") What if the disclosures are in legalese and made to an immigrant population or a population with an eighth-grade reading level? That is, are disclosures to be made to an objective, generic consumer or tailored, if not to the individual, to the demographics likely to be served? These are not *behavioral* issues. They are simply comprehension issues.

But what if the business chose to design the product in a way that makes it less likely that a consumer would understand? For example, what if a credit card issuer tested several formats for its periodic statements and found that one that emphasized the minimum payment amount relative to the total balance resulted in more consumers making just the minimum payment and adopted that disclosure form? This raises serious questions about good faith and fair dealing and unconscionability.

III. BEHAVIORALLY INFORMED REGULATION

It is one thing to identify how cognitive biases may explain both product design and consumer usage patterns. It is another thing to translate that into regulation. Assuming that regulation is in fact merited, what should this regulation look like?

A. Behavioral Economics' Limited Guidance on Regulation

One complication is that while behavioral economics has made great headway in undermining the rational actor/revealed preference model of classical economics, it has not succeeded in supplanting it with an alternative model because it does not provide a predictive model of human behavior, only a picture of complication. While behavioral economics is very good at telling us that rational actor models may not work when applied to consumers (the question of its application to organizational behavior is more complex), it does not provide an alternative set of predictions. In part this is because most behavioral biases can be paired with an offsetting bias, and the netting remains uncertain in any given application.

The inability of behavioral economics to provide an alternative generic predictive model also stems from variations in cognitive biases. Not everyone suffers from the same cognitive biases equally, just as we all use different heuristics based, in part, on our individualized experiences. Moreover, there is the possibility of what Richard Epstein has termed "second-order rationality," rational responses to cognitive biases. Richard A. Epstein, *Behavioral Economics: Human Errors and Market Corrections*, 73 U. Chi. L. Rev. 111 (2006). A consumer who fears falling prey to the siren song of a cognitive bias can invoke various devices such as those that bound Ulysses to the mast. Thus, consumers rely on specialists and intermediaries who might be less prone to such biases. Similarly, cognitive mistakes often seem to dissipate in markets with competition, learning (particularly in markets with standardized products), and specialization.

All of this is to say that behavioral economics teaches us to be sensitive to various forms of non-rational behavior among consumers, but it does not tell us how to determine what consumers' actual preferences are, and therefore does not lay out a path for achieving those preferences. Instead, the prescriptive response of behavioral economics to cognitive biases is to find mechanisms that "debias" consumers, such as default settings (requiring opt-outs rather than opt-ins, for example). Debiasing, however, presumes that the debiased outcome, rather than the biased outcome, is the preferable one for consumers. And this is directly contrary to revealed preference theory. In fact, it often means disregarding the revealed preference of the consumer in favor of what the debiaser believes to be the true preference.

This substitution of the judgment of another party for the consumer's has fostered a major philosophical objection to behavioral economics, namely that it begets paternalism and disregards consumer choice and will.

Irrespective of one's views on paternalism, businesses are well aware of consumers' cognitive biases. They know that even if not all consumers exhibit the same biases to the same degree, a large number will make predictable mistakes in information processing. A profit-maximizing business will exploit these mistakes. The exploitative side of behavioral economics has been largely ignored in the legal literature, but it plays a critical role in the design and marketing of financial products. The problem, then, is not that consumers make mistakes, but that financial institutions deliberately exploit these mistakes to produce transactions that are not mutually beneficial or at least siphon off some of the consumer's benefit from the transaction for the financial institution. Put differently, in consumer finance, behavioral economics is often used by businesses as a sword against consumers, rather than as a shield by regulators.

B. Reactive Regulation to Behavioral Problems

On the one hand, behaviorally informed regulation could simply identify when product structure takes advantage of consumer cognitive biases, and, if appropriate, require changes in product structure, such as banning product terms. This is sharp-elbowed, traditional regulation. It does not try to craft a behavioral response so much as eliminate product features that take advantage of behavioral biases.

C. Behavioral Regulation

Behavioral economics can be used not just diagnostically to identify problems to address through traditional regulatory tools, but also to expand the regulatory tool kit. One idea that has been popularized in this regard is the idea of "nudges"—use of legal rules to encourage debiasing without actually mandating any particular behavior.

For example, if consumers fail to save adequately for retirement, they could be defaulted into automatic enrollment in 401(k) plans, rather than having to take affirmative steps to enroll in 401(k)s. Likewise, if consumers consume too much in the way of sweets and not enough vegetables, making vegetables more prominent and accessible in cafeterias relative to sweets may change consumption. *See* Richard H. Thaler & Cass R. Sunstein, *Nudge: Improving Decisions About Health, Wealth, and Happiness* (2009). This concept of using opt-outs rather than opt-ins and changing framing of information in order to foster non-mandatory defaults is termed "libertarian paternalism"—the idea being that liberty is preserved within a soft paternalist context, such that those who really don't want to be in a 401(k) or who really want sweets instead of vegetables can still exercise their preferences. Yet merely having a default setting, such as requiring consumers to affirmatively opt-in to for-fee overdraft protection services, may be insufficient if the opt-in process is controlled by regulated entities that can manipulate it. *See* Lauren E. Willis, *When Nudges Fail: Slippery Defaults*, 80 Chicago L. Rev. 1155 (2013).

How behavioral economics will affect consumer finance regulation is an open question. It remains to be seen exactly what role behavioral economics will play in setting policy at the CFPB and how it will interact with the CFPB's legal framework.

IV. CRITICISMS OF BEHAVIORAL ECONOMICS

A. Are Behavioral Claims Empirically Supported?

Behavioral economics is ultimately founded on a set of empirical claims about consumer behavior, namely that consumers, as an empirical matter, do not conform to the rational choice model posited by classical economics. Are these empirical claims borne out? Four issues arise in this regard: whether there is evidence for cognitive biases in the first place; whether the biases are mitigated by learning; whether the market will self-correct via market-driven education; and how pervasive biases are.

One question about behavioral economics is whether there is evidence for cognitive biases in the first place. Sometimes whether consumers are making irrational decisions is a matter of degree and thus perspective. For example, is it irrational for consumers not to switch from a high interest rate credit card to a lower-rate card? This depends on the costs to the consumer of switching and whether the consumer can rely on retaining the low rate on the new card. In other words, to determine if this decision is rational, one needs to know a great deal of information. Professor Wright suggests that the evidence is more complex than behavioralists contend.

Joshua D. Wright

Behavioral Law and Economics, Paternalism, and Consumer Contracts: An Empirical Perspective

2 N.Y.U. J.L. & LIBERTY 470 (2007)

A. ARE CREDIT CARD USERS RATIONAL AFTER ALL?

There are a number of empirical studies examining actual consumer behavior in the credit card market. A comprehensive and recent study by Tom Brown and Lacey Plache tests the hypotheses of the behavioral model using a survey of consumer financial behavior commissioned by Visa U.S.A. known as the Payment System Panel Study ("PSPS"). Brown and Plache conclude that hyperbolic discounting "does not explain the behavior of credit card issuers and their customers."

Specifically, Brown and Plache are able to directly test the following predictions of the behavioral models of borrowing behavior:

> (1) Consumers with revolving balances should carry cards with higher long-term interest rates, lower annual fees, and higher short-term benefits such as rewards relative to consumers who do not carry balances on their cards every month;
>
> (2) Consumers with revolving balances will not substitute away from the use of credit cards when a new "pay-now" alternative, such as a debit card, is introduced.

Brown and Plache examine the first of these predictions by comparing the credit card features selected by non-revolvers and revolvers. If the behavioral predictions of debtor behavior are correct, one would expect to see consumers who revolve debt carrying cards with no annual fees and higher interest rates than the non-revolving cohort. Brown and Plache, however, find that more non-revolvers than revolvers carry cards with average minimum APRs of greater than 10 percent and note that "this result does not support the hypothesis that hyperbolic discounting results in consumers bearing credit card debt at high interest rates." Brown and Plache also find that while most cardholders do not carry cards with annual fees, the majority of those that do are revolvers rather than non-revolvers. Again, the authors note that this result is inconsistent with the behavioral account of consumer "seduction" by short term features. Finally, Brown and Plache also find that cardholders carrying cards without annual fees or with rewards programs are less likely to revolve balances than cardholders as a group.

Sumit Agrawal, Souphala Chomsisengphet, Chunlin Liu, and Nicholas Souleles ("ACLS") exploit a natural experiment involving credit card offers from a large U.S. bank to over 150,000 account-holders to test [] credit card consumers' ability to select the optimal credit contract. ACLS examine consumers' selection between two credit card contracts, one with an annual fee but a lower interest rate and a second with no annual fee and a higher interest rate. The authors then examine post-contract borrowing behavior in order to assess whether consumers have selected the optimal credit card contract for their borrowing patterns, defined by minimizing ex post costs. Importantly, ACLS are also able to measure the magnitude of any ex post losses flowing from the choice of a sub-optimal contract. Consistent with Brown and Plache, ACLS find that the majority of consumers (about 60%) select the optimal credit card contract. Although a substantial minority of consumers initially select the "wrong" contract and incur avoidable interest charges, the authors find that these errors are bounded in magnitude by the level of the annual fee (typically around $25). Further, consistent with standard economic theory, the probability of selecting the sub-optimal credit card contract [] decreases with the cost of the error and increases with repeated consumer error, suggesting that learning may mitigate the relevant biases.

While these studies do not completely refute the possibility that behavioral biases cause some consumers to make sub-optimal decisions, the findings pose a challenge to behavioral scholars. Both the frequency and magnitude of sub-optimal credit card contract decisions appear to be less severe than is assumed in the behavioral law and economics literature. Further, it is difficult to reconcile models of irrational consumer behavior with the collective findings that consumers largely select the right contracts and err less often when the costs of doing so are higher. The best evidence of at least some consumer irrationality in this context is that a small minority of consumers make repeated errors. However, given that the magnitude of error costs are typically small, and perhaps greater than the effort costs of switching cards ex post, the failure of the some consumers to correct sub-optimal decisions may also be consistent with rational consumer behavior.

This empirical evidence is in tension with the simple behavioral theories relied upon in the legal literature, and contradicts the behavioral predictions that consumers are not sensitive to changes in contract terms. When coupled with the fact that the majority of consumers appear not to carry balances at all, this evidence suggests that the magnitude of the effects of behavioral biases may be overstated in the behavioral law and economics literature. Further, because paternalistic regulation of consumers may reduce incentives to learn (and thus, opportunities to mitigate biases at lower cost), the wisdom of implementing such regulations is unclear.

A second prediction of the behavioral account of borrowing is that consumers who carry revolving debt will not substitute away from credit cards when a new "pay-now" payment method emerges. Brown and Plache describe the hypothesis as follows:

> If people really do not expect to end up in debt when they use their credit cards, then there is no reason to expect them to substitute away from credit cards that typically offer a thirty-day float period in addition to other benefits to a new pay-now payment method that offers some of the benefits of credit cards, such as universal acceptance and no (or negative) marginal cost, without incurring debt, but requires immediate payment.

Brown and Plache show that revolvers responded to the introduction of the general purpose debit card by shifting spending away from credit cards.

There is also evidence suggesting that consumer borrowing behaviors, and particular substitution patterns, respond to the relative prices of alternative forms of debt. Specifically, Todd Zywicki shows that the increase in consumer debt has occurred along with a corresponding decrease in installment debt burdens, suggesting a shift in the composition of consumer debt away from less attractive forms of debt such as pawn shops, check-cashers, and rent-to-owns. The evidence that consumer substitution patterns are sensitive to relative prices not only suggests rational behavior, but also indicates that at least some portion of the increase in consumer credit card debt is a function of consumer preferences for credit card debt over installment debt. To the extent that consumers are exhibiting rational switching behavior away from more burdensome forms of debt, it is difficult to understand how the introduction of this additional choice for consumers decreases welfare.

B. Learning

Are such biases inherent and immalleable, or are they correctable through learning? In some circumstances, consumers seem to exhibit "once burned, twice shy" behavior—after having a problem with a product or service that is sufficiently costly, consumers are more attentive to the risks involved going forward. Similarly, professionals and repeat players are less likely to exhibit an endowment effect than novices, as a real-world experiment involving baseball card collectors shows. Novices exhibited evidence of endowment effects—valuing cards they owned more than what they were offered—whereas dealers and experienced non-dealers did not. John A. List, *Does Market Experience Eliminate Market Anomalies?*, 118 Q. J. Econ. 41 (2003). This may be evidence of an endowment effect due to sentimental factors versus a purely monetary calculation, but it also points to learning affecting behavior.

Evidence of learning has also been found in consumer credit markets. One paper has found that consumers who pay a credit card fee one month are 40% less likely to pay a fee the next month, and that monthly fee payments fell by 75% over the first three years of an account. Sumit Agarwal, John C. Driscoll, Xavier Gabaix & David Laibson, *Learning in the Credit Card Market* (NBER Working Paper No. 13822, Feb. 2008). This same paper, however, found that the learning has only a short-term effect and its benefits deteriorate completely after around ten months. In other words, learning may be dependent on the recency of experience. *Id.*

Learning may mitigate cognitive biases, although the problem of rookie mistakes still remains, and the permanency of learning is uncertain.

C. Competition and Seller Education

Won't competition encourage sellers to attempt to debias consumers and to price at cost, irrespective of consumer biases? Richard Epstein has argued that markets will:

> shut down unless something is done to correct the consumer misperception. [T]he only complication is to identify which of the sellers of the identical product will undertake the cost of correcting consumers' misperception. One possibility is that

> none will do it, because any such seller's action will benefit others who expend no resources on correction. But this conclusion only illustrates the hopeless artificiality of any example that presupposes universal ignorance of the value of any standard commodity. One firm may well try to individuate its product by branding, so that it can capture the gains of correction. More likely, some curious consumer will figure out that the common perception is incorrect and spread the word to his friends. Remember, all consumers will not, in any real-world setting, have identical valuations, so one is likely to uncover this ostensible mistake of unknown origin. There is no incentive on the part of any consumer to disregard the truthful information once it is acquired, for this case is not one where there is a future probability of some uncertain event, where various consumers have to decide the extent of their risk aversion. These are all cases where the values are certain, but unknown. It seems quite improbable that no one will be able to work out the mistakes. In practice, it will not be an interesting case.

Richard A. Epstein, *Behavioral Economics: Human Errors and Market Corrections*, 73 U. Chi. L. Rev. 111, 121-122 (2006). Does this claim hold true in markets with partitioned pricing or only in markets with single price points? Are firms incentivized to adopt more complicated partitioned pricing as a result?

D. Distribution of Cognitive Biases in the Population

A final criticism of behavioral regulation relates to how pervasive cognitive biases are. Even if some consumers exhibit particular cognitive biases, not all consumers do and not all to the same degree. Thus, one study of payday loan borrower indicates that about 60% of borrowers accurately predict how long it will take them to pay off their loans, suggesting that an optimism bias about time to pay off exists in only part of the borrower population. Ronald Mann, *Assessing the Optimism of Payday Loan Borrowers*, (Columbia Law and Economics Working Paper No. 443, Mar. 2013).

If biases are exhibited by only part of the population it suggests that policies intended to account for cognitive biases may at times be overly broad and impose costs on those without cognitive biases in order to protect those with them. *See* Richard A. Epstein, *Behavioral Economics: Human Errors and Market Corrections*, 73 Chi. L. Rev. 111, 121-122 (2006). As such, the regulatory calculus is more complex. Consider how the "unfair" standard applies when part of a consumer population is affected negatively and part is affected positively by an act or practice. It makes the balancing test in the regulation much more complicated.

The heterogeneity of consumer behavior has implications for class actions as well. To the extent that a proposed class is defined as a group of consumers whose understanding of a product was unfairly exploited, the proposed class members' variation in cognitive understanding might be a ground for attacking objecting to class certification.

Problem Set 13

1. Given what you've read about behavioral economics, would you expect consumers to spend more when paying with cash or with a debit card? Why? How does your explanation apply to contactless (tap-to-pay) technologies?

2. Continental Express Bank, N.A. has employed a team of consumer psychologists to help it maximize returns on its credit card lending portfolio. The psychologists first suggested that Continental Express change its product structures to eliminate annual fees for most cards and increase late fees to twice the level of competitors' offerings. The psychologists then suggested that Continental Express emphasize "no annual fee" in its advertising and its credit card rewards program while not mentioning the late fees. Is this a UDAAP violation? *See* 12 U.S.C. § 5536.

3. Continental Express's psychology team has suggested that in lieu of the annual fee the bank charge a monthly "network security fee" equal to one-twelfth of the previous annual fee. Is this a UDAAP violation? *See* 12 U.S.C. § 5536.

4. Following the advice of its psychology team, Continental Express has now changed the format of its periodic billing statements. As always, the statements state both the total amount due and the minimum payment due. But the new format emphasizes the minimum payment amount relative to the total amount due. Specifically, the minimum payment is listed in bold font that is several points larger than the total amount due. It is also placed to the right of the total amount due next to a box where the consumer can write in the amount of payment remitted. Is this a UDAAP violation? *See* 12 U.S.C. §§ 5531(d)(1), 5531(d)(2)(A), 5536; *CFPB v. All American Check Cashing*, Complaint, ¶ 67.

5. In early versions of the legislation that became the Consumer Financial Protection Act, there was a so-called "plain vanilla" provision that would have required the CFPB designate certain financial products as "standard products" and would require that covered persons offering "alternative products" also offer consumers a "standard product" option. The idea behind plain vanilla was to debias consumers by presenting them with a baseline for comparing other products so they could identify which might be a "Rocky Road." Do you think this would have been a good idea?

PART II

MARKETS

SECTION A

Payments

CHAPTER 14

DEPOSIT ACCOUNTS

I. OVERVIEW

A. How to Protect Value?

Consumers don't usually consume all of their assets at once. Some assets are saved for later. Holding on to an asset, however, creates risks. First, the asset could be lost. It could be stolen or destroyed or damaged. Second, the asset could lose value. It could depreciate or otherwise deteriorate.

Imagine a farmer. The farmer harvests his wheat crop in the fall and perhaps sells some to purchase items he immediately needs. But he also keeps some to feed his family during the winter and for seed in the spring. What does the farmer do with that retained harvest? He wants to put it somewhere safe, where it won't be stolen, either by people or animals, and where it will not be damaged by the elements. That necessitates a granary. He also wants to store it in a place where it will not rot and thus lose value. That necessitates certain conditions for the granary. It must have a certain level of ventilation and humidity and light.

The same kind of concerns exist for a consumer whose assets are not the harvest from the fields, but rather cash. How can a consumer make sure that the cash will be protected against theft and destruction? And how can a consumer make sure that the cash will not lose value?

B. The Safekeeping Problem

There are lots of ways to protect the cash against theft or destruction. It can be carried and guarded on the consumer's person or in property the consumer controls, such as in a safe or, in the case of the author's uncle John, under a mattress. But most consumers are not expert at protecting cash. Too much cash in a wallet is inconvenient and possibly uncomfortable and unsightly and makes the loss or theft of the wallet a real risk. A lot of people may have access to a consumer's home or other property, and thus the ability to pilfer. It's usually easier to entrust the cash to a third party that is more expert in guarding it.

Historically, this role was played by goldsmiths, but for some time that role has been played by banks. In its simplest form, this is simply the safe deposit box, whereby a consumer places assets (cash or other assets) into a double locked box with the depositor having one key and the bank a second one. The bank will not open the box absent proper identification of the depositor, who must also have a key to the box.

What if the safe deposit box were destroyed or burgled? This is a common enough problem with natural disasters, such as hurricanes, and over a thousand safe deposit boxes at 5 World Trade Center were destroyed on September 11, 2001. The law governing safe deposit boxes varies by state, usually treating the relationship as either a bailment (requiring reasonable care by the bailee) or a lease (not requiring any particular level of care), but also allowing contractual limitations of the liability. *See* Joseph A. Oliva & Timothy E. Markey, *Safe Deposit Box Losses Under the Financial Institution Bond,* 13 Fidelity L. Assoc. J. 113, 114-119 (2007). Thus, the simple safe deposit box is not an absolute solution to the safekeeping problem. It may make the assets safer, but there are still risks.

The solution to these risks comes in the form of the bank deposit. Whereas a safe deposit box depositor is entitled to recover specific, identifiable assets from the safe deposit box, a depositor of cash with a bank is not entitled to those specific dollar bills back, just to the total amount of the deposit (plus any interest). In other words, the bank deposit relies on the fungibility of the asset entrusted to the bank. The bank deposit is a general unsecured liability of the bank, whereas the safe deposit box contents are a specific quasi-secured liability.

Because the bank deposit is a general unsecured liability, its repayment is guaranteed by nothing more than the bank's equity value; there are no specific assets pledged for the repayment of the deposit. In the world of limited liability entities (that is where equityholders have no liability for corporate debts), this means that the equity of the bank (rather than assets of the equityholders of the bank) must be exhausted before the depositors take a loss.

The history of banking in the United States prior to 1933, however, was one littered with bank failures; a bank's equity was no guarantee that depositors would ultimately be able to get their money back. Hence the creation of federal deposit insurance in 1933, as a second-loss position guaranteeing repayment of certain deposits after the bank's equity had been exhausted. So we have devised a form of absolute safekeeping for fungible cash assets—the federally insured bank deposit.

C. The Depreciation Problem

What about the second problem, namely, depreciation? Storage on one's own person or property means that the cash can always depreciate because of inflation. The only way that the cash will not lose value via depreciation in an inflationary economy is if it is earning money (and even then, it might still be depreciating, just not as fast). Banks can potentially solve the depreciation problem as well. A bank deposit is a loan made from the depositor to the bank. This means that the depositor is a creditor of the bank, and the interest rate on the deposit is the interest rate on the loan. That interest helps deal with the depreciation problem. Thus, a federally insured bank deposit solves both the safekeeping problem and the depreciation problem simultaneously.

D. Bank Deposits

Banks need to get the money to make loans from somewhere. Deposits are one source. Banks like deposits. Compared to other places banks might look for money, deposits are a cheap source of funding, as they often pay little or no interest. Banks can then make a tidy profit by borrowing cheaply from depositors and re-lending the money at a higher rate to bank borrowers. The different between the rate at which banks borrow from depositors and the rate at which they lend is known as the interest rate spread or interest rate margin.

Consumer also like deposits. Aside from cash, bank accounts are the most widely held consumer financial product. As of 2016, 98% of households had some sort of deposit account at a financial institution.[1]

The terms of bank deposits are regulated by federal law, by state law, and by the contract—the account agreement—between the bank and the depositor. Federal law governs the disclosure of account terms,[2] the availability to the depositor of funds deposited into the account,[3] and the terms under which funds can be withdrawn.[4] Historically, federal law (Reg Q) also regulated the payment of interest on deposits.[5] Federal law also provides for insurance on deposits,[6] provides for disclosure of insured or non-insured status,[7] and regulates the amount of reserves—liquid cash assets—that a bank must maintain.[8] For accounts that can make or receive electronic transfers—such as any account linked to a debit card—federal law also governs periodic statements.[9] Transfers to and from accounts—payments—are governed by a combination of uniform state law and federal law, but are a distinct topic that we will examine in a later chapter.

The federal laws dealing with bank deposits are administered by a number of agencies. The CFPB administers the Truth in Savings Act, dealing with disclosure of account terms, and the parts of the Federal Deposit Insurance Act dealing with disclosure of non-insured depository status, as well as the periodic-statement requirements of the Electronic Fund Transfer Act (EFTA). Deposit insurance is itself administered by the Federal Deposit Insurance Corporation, while funds availability and withdrawal limitations are governed by Federal Reserve Board regulations.

---

1. Jesse Bricker et al., *Changes in U.S. Family Finances from 2013 to 2016: Evidence from the Survey of Consumer Finances*, 103 Fed. Reserve Bull. 1, 18 (2017).
2. Truth in Savings Act, 12 U.S.C. § 4301 *et seq.* Regulation DD, 12 C.F.R. Pt. 230.
3. Expedited Funds Availability Act, 12 U.S.C. §§ 4001-4010; Check Clearing for the 21st Century Act (Check21 Act), 12 U.S.C. §§ 5001-5018; Regulation CC, 12 C.F.R. Pt. 229.
4. Regulation D, 12 C.F.R. Pt. 204.
5. 12 C.F.R. Pt. 217 (repealed).
6. Federal Deposit Insurance Act, 12 U.S.C. § 1801 *et seq.*; 12 C.F.R. Pt. 330.
7. 12 U.S.C. § 1831t.
8. 12 C.F.R. § 204.5.
9. 15 U.S.C. § 1693d.

Federal Reserve Board regulations (many of which have since transferred to the CFPB) bear alphabetical labels: Regulation A, Regulation B, etc. They are commonly referred to simply as "Reg A," "Reg B," etc.

II. TYPES OF BANK ACCOUNTS

While there is tremendous variation in the terms of bank accounts, legally, bank accounts fall into two basic categories based on their treatment under federal law. There are **transaction accounts** and **time deposit accounts.**

A. Transaction Accounts

Federal Reserve Board regulations define transaction accounts as accounts:

> from which the depositor or account holder is permitted to make transfers or withdrawals by negotiable or transferable instrument, payment order of withdrawal, telephone transfer, or other similar device for the purpose of making payments or transfers to third persons or others or from which the depositor may make third party payments at an automated teller machine (ATM) or a remote service unit, or other electronic device, including by debit card . . .

12 C.F.R. § 204.2(e). An account that requires withdrawals or transfers to be made in person is not a transaction account. Transaction accounts include **demand deposits**—accounts for which the depositor may withdraw funds without a penalty with less than seven days' notice to the bank. 12 C.F.R. § 204.2(e)(1). Demand deposits include **checking accounts**, 12 C.F.R. § 204.2(b)(1).

A check is a type of **negotiable instrument.** UCC § 3-104. This means, among other things, that the check can be transferred through **negotiation**: physical delivery of the check plus **indorsement**, which means that the payee on the check signs over the check to the transferee. The signature is placed on the back of the check (*in dorso* means "on the back" in Latin), hence the term **indorsement.** We'll learn more about checks in a later chapter, but for now the critical thing to understand is that a check is an order from a depositor to a bank directing the bank to pay someone.

The term "checking account" is not a legally significant term. Instead, it is merely a type of demand deposit account; the name is a historical vestige from a time when there were more distinctions regarding the types of transfers or withdrawals that could be made from accounts. Indeed, today a consumer can have a "checking account" and never actually write a check or even have a checkbook. There is no regulation of the issuance of checkbooks, and the form of a check is simply a matter of contract between a bank and its customer.

B. Time Deposits & Certificates of Deposit

Transaction accounts are defined to exclude time deposits. Time deposits are accounts for which at least seven days' notice is needed for withdrawal without penalty. Some time deposits have a particular **maturity date**, before which the funds cannot be withdrawn (or cannot be without penalty). The most common type of time deposit with a maturity date is a **certificate of deposit** or CD. A CD is defined by the state-law Uniform Commercial Code as a negotiable instrument "containing an acknowledgment by a bank that a sum of money has been received by the bank and a promise by the bank to repay the sum of money. A certificate of deposit is a note of the bank." UCC § 3-104(j). A note is a promise to pay money, as contrasted with a direction to pay, like a check. The foregoing definition does not mean, however, that something that is called a "certificate of deposit" must conform with the UCC's definition, including its negotiability requirement. A CD that does conform with the UCC, however, benefits from the UCC's six-year statute of limitations for enforcement of a CD. UCC § 3-118.

CDs will pay depositors an interest rate, which may be fixed, step, or variable. Larger CDs and longer-maturity CDs typically pay higher rates. CDs also have a maturity date on which the interest is paid. CDs typically have an early withdrawal penalty, as the bank wants to be certain of its funding costs for the duration of the CD. A depositor must give a bank instructions about payment of the CD before it matures (or sometimes within a short post-maturity grace period) or the CD will usually automatically roll over for another equal maturity period at the same rate.

Some CDs are "**callable**," meaning that the issuing bank has the right to terminate the CD. A bank may want to do this if interest rates fall and it can obtain funding at a cheaper rate than it is paying for the deposit. Callable CDs will have a "**call period**." The call period is not the same as the maturity. Thus, a "one-year noncallable CD" means that the CD is not callable within the first year, but the maturity date could easily be ten years in the future.

C. Other Savings Accounts

Some time deposits do not have a particular maturity date. These are known as savings accounts. Time deposits take a variety of forms. Some are called **passbook savings accounts**. These involve the issuance to the depositor of a passbook, a small booklet in which a depositor's deposits and withdrawals are recorded, as well as any interest that has accrued at the time of the presentment of the passbook. With a passbook savings account, the depositor does not receive periodic statements; instead, the passbook serves as the record of transactions. 15 U.S.C. § 1693d(d). Other time deposits are in the form of statement savings accounts, which involve the issuance of periodic account statements to the depositor.

D. Money Market Deposit Account (MMDA)

Another type of time deposit is the **Money Market Deposit Account** (MMDA). An MMDA is an interest-earning savings account with limited transaction/withdrawal privileges. They were originally created as a way of avoiding the now defunct prohibition on the payment of interest on demand deposit accounts. An MMDA pays interest based on the current rates in money markets—markets for short-term, high-quality liabilities. MMDAs typically offer slightly higher yields than other types of savings accounts, but banks also typically require minimum account balances.

E. Money Market Mutual Funds (MMMF)

An MMDA is distinct from a **money market mutual fund** (MMMF) or money fund. MMMF are conservative investment vehicles that compete with CDs and other bank-based savings vehicles but are structured differently and are subject to a different regulatory regime. Whereas a depositor is a creditor of an MMDA, a shareholder in an MMMF is an equity investor. An MMDA pays interest, whereas an MMMF pays dividends. Whereas bank-deposit-based savings vehicles like MMDAs are regulated by prudential bank regulators and the CFPB, MMMF are regulated by the SEC. And unlike an MMDA, an MMMF is not insured by the FDIC, although the bailout of MMMFs in 2008 may lead some to conclude that all MMMFs are implicitly guaranteed by the U.S. government. Yet despite these differences, MMMFs are direct competitors with bank-based savings vehicles for investors looking for short-term, highly liquid, extremely safe investments. Many banks offer or broker MMMFs as well as offer MMDAs, but they are distinct products, run through different units within a bank.

A consumer invests in an MMMF by buying shares—fractional interests—in the fund. The fund has no debt (or virtually no)—the shares in the fund are an equity interest. The SEC requires that money market funds invest solely in short-term debt securities—those that mature in 13 months or less, that the weighted average maturity of a money market fund's investments be less than 60 days, and that the weighted average life of the fund's investments be less than 120 days. 17 C.F.R. § 270.2a-7(c)(2). There are also limitations on the quality and liquidity of the fund's investments. 17 C.F.R. § 270.2a-7(c)(3)-(5).

MMMFs aim to maintain a $1.00 per share net asset value (NAV). Earnings on the shares are paid to shareholders as dividends (either reinvested in more shares or in cash), and it should be the dividends, not the NAV per share, that fluctuates. Even so, it is possible for the share price of an MMMF to drop below $1.00, which is known as "breaking the buck." This can happen if the value of the MMMF's assets declines sufficiently so that the value paid into the fund is less than the value of its assets. This has happened twice since 1970. When this happens, MMMF investors that redeem their funds receive back less than 100% of the funds they invested.

The dividend yield on money market funds is typically quoted as a seven-day yield rather than an annual percentage yield, as on a savings account. Money market funds charge account fees and account expenses to pay the fund manager and its expenses. This decreases the yield of a money market fund.

Some MMMF (and also stock brokerage accounts) permit consumers to write checks against the accounts. These accounts, however, are not considered bank accounts and are not regulated as such.

III. DISCLOSURE OF ACCOUNT TERMS

The major federal regulation of consumer deposit accounts is the Truth in Savings Act (TISA). TISA is a disclosure regime that applies to all consumer deposit accounts at federally insured depositories. 12 U.S.C. § 4313(1).

The TISA disclosure regime deals with three different types of disclosures: solicitations and advertisements; account opening disclosures; and periodic account statements. TISA requires that all solicitations, announcements, and advertisements of accounts by banks or deposit brokers, excluding those made on on-premises displays, must disclose certain content; the form of the disclosure is left up to the depository. 12 U.S.C. § 4302(a). There is a safe harbor, however, for disclosures that use model forms published by the CFPB. 12 U.S.C. § 4308. TISA requires that solicitations and the like disclose as applicable: the **annual percentage yield (APY)** and period for the APY, as well any minimum balances, initial deposit or length of deposit necessary to earn the APY, a statement that other fees and conditions might reduce the APY, and a statement about penalties for early withdrawal. 12 U.S.C. § 4302(a).

The APY is a standardized unit measurement of interest rates. If a bank merely advertised a 12% interest rate, it would be unclear if 12% meant 12% per year, per month, per week, etc. It would also be unclear whether that 12% reflected any compounding of interest or not—that is, does interest accrue on interest? The APY avoids any such confusion. The APY is calculated by taking the total amount of interest that would be paid on a $100 deposit in the course of a 365-day year (including any compounding) and dividing that amount by $100. 12 U.S.C. § 4313(2). Thus, if a $100 deposit resulted in $6 in interest in the course of a year, the APY would be 6% (=$6/$100). It is important to note that the APY is merely a measure of interest rates. It does not indicate the actual return on an account because it does not reflect any fees that the depositor might pay. Such a measure, accounting for fees, would be called the "effective APY."

TISA also requires solicitations to disclose minimum balance and other requirements to receive the APY; and minimum initial deposit amount, regular fees, and any early withdrawal penalty. On-premises displays must merely display the APY and a statement that further information is available from bank employees. 12 U.S.C. § 4302(c). "On-premises" is not defined by statute.

Additionally, TISA also places limits on what may be called "free" or "no-fee" accounts. 12 U.S.C. § 4302(d). If those terms are used, the account must have no regular fees, no maximum number of transactions, and no minimum balance requirement. Misleading or inaccurate advertisements are also expressly prohibited. 12 U.S.C. § 4302(e).

TISA requires that insured depositories maintain "**account schedules**." 12 U.S.C. § 4303. These schedules must be made available to depositors upon the opening of an account and at the depositor's request. 12 U.S.C. § 4305. A TISA account schedule must list *for all accounts* all fees and the APY and its calculation and relevant term and minimum balance requirements. It must also be in "clear and plain language" and "in a format designed to allow consumers to readily understand the terms." 12 U.S.C. § 4303(e). Whereas the TISA solicitation disclosure requirement is about advertisements of particular accounts, the TISA account schedule requirement encompasses all types of accounts offered by the depository.

Finally, TISA requires certain content to be in periodic account statements. 12 U.S.C. § 4307. Significantly, TISA does not require periodic account statements. *See* 12 CFR § 230.6(a) ("*If* a depository institution mails or delivers a periodic statement . . .") (emphasis added). That requirement, as we shall see, comes from elsewhere in federal law, and applies only to accounts that can be accessed through electronic fund transfers, such as ATM card and debit card transactions. 15 U.S.C. § 1693d(c). If a periodic statement is issued, however, it must contain the APY, any fees charged, any interest earned, and the number of days in the period. 12 U.S.C. § 4307. Almost all accounts today allow for electronic fund transfers, and thus require periodic statements, so the TISA periodic-statement requirements generally apply.

TISA also contains some substantive term regulation relating to the payment of interest. 12 U.S.C. § 4306. TISA requires interest to be calculated on the full amount of principal and to be applied from the business day on which the bank itself receives provisional credit for funds deposited into the account. 12 U.S.C. § 4306(a), (c). TISA does not, however, require any particular method for the calculation of interest. 12 U.S.C. § 4306(b).

Regulation DD, administered by the CFPB, implements TISA. Reg DD contains model disclosure forms, and details about the APY calculation and accuracy tolerances, but adds little substantively to the statute other than in regard to overdraft fees, which we will consider in a later chapter.

There is no private right of action in the current version of the TISA statute. The original version of the statute had a private right of action (section 271, codified at 12 U.S.C. § 4310), but it was repealed in 1996 as part of an omnibus appropriations bill. Section 271 had imposed civil liability for violations of TISA, with statutory minimum damages of $100 and maximums of $1,000 per violation in addition to actual damages, but with a cap in class actions of the lesser of $500,000 or 1% of the depository's net worth. It also had a safe harbor for clerical, computer, and other bona fide errors. Today, public enforcement is limited to the CFPB and appropriate prudential regulator. A TISA violation may, however, be a predicate for a state-law UDAP violation in some cases, effectively creating a private right of action.

TISA does not have its own liability provision. Instead, TISA provides that a violation is to be treated as a violation of the Federal Deposit Insurance Act (FDIA) or subtitle E of the Consumer Financial Protection Act, depending on whether an action is brought by a prudential regulator or the CFPB. 12 U.S.C. § 4309(b). If a prudential regulator brings an action, the general liability provision of the FDIA, 12 U.S.C. § 1818, applies. This provision permits a range of actions from cease-and-desist orders to termination of FDIC insurance to civil monetary penalties. Monetary penalties are tiered depending on the type of violation, starting at $5,000/day, going then to $25,000/day and then to $1,000,000/day. Subtitle E of the Consumer Financial Protection Act provides for a range of relief including rescission, refund, restitution, disgorgement, damages, activity limitations, and civil monetary penalties that match the FDIA's. 12 U.S.C. § 5565(a)(2), (c).

IV. PERIODIC STATEMENTS

There is no generic right to receive a periodic bank statement. Recall that the Truth in Savings Act required various disclosures in a periodic statement, but that it did not require periodic statements. 12 U.S.C. § 4307. Instead, the right to a periodic statement only exists for particular types of accounts, namely those "to or from which electronic fund transfers can be made." 15 U.S.C. § 1693d(c); 12 C.F.R. § 205.9(b). The Electronic Fund Transfers Act and Regulation E thereunder mandate that financial institutions send consumers "a periodic statement for each monthly cycle in which an electronic fund transfer has occurred; and shall send a periodic statement at least quarterly if no transfer has occurred." 12 C.F.R. § 205.9(b). *See also* 15 U.S.C. § 1693d(c). An "electronic fund transfer" is a "transfer of funds, other than a transaction originated by check, draft, or similar paper instrument, which is initiated through an electronic terminal, telephonic instrument, or computer or magnetic tape so as to order, instruct, or authorize a financial institution to debit or credit an account." 15 U.S.C. § 1693a(7). An "electronic fund transfer" includes "point-of-sale transfers, automated teller machine transactions, direct deposits or withdrawals of funds, and transfers initiated by telephone," but excludes wire transfers, 15 U.S.C. § 1693a(7)(B), transfers to purchase or sell securities or commodities, 15 U.S.C. § 1693a(7)(C), such as to a linked brokerage account, and linked overdraft overage between savings and demand deposit accounts, 15 U.S.C. § 1693a(7)(D).

The periodic-statement requirement does not apply to passbook accounts that may be accessed only by preauthorized credits (such as direct deposit) if the passbook is updated upon presentation to reflect transactions since the last presentation. 12 U.S.C. § 1693d(d); 12 C.F.R. § 1005.9(c)(1). Intra-institutional transfers need only be documented on a periodic statement for one account. 12 C.F.R. § 1005.9(c)(2).

The EFTA/Reg E require that the periodic statement must indicate the account number, the account's opening and closing balance in the period, and any fees assessed. 12 C.F.R. § 1005.9(b)(2)-(4). Additionally, for every "electronic fund transfer," the periodic statement must indicate the amount and date of the transfer, the type of the transfer and type of account(s) involved, the location of any ATM used in a transfer, and the name of any third-party transferor or transferee. 12 C.F.R. § 1005.9(b)(1). Finally, addresses and telephone numbers for inquiries must be provided. 12 C.F.R. § 1005.9(b)(5)-(6). In addition, the Truth in Savings Act requires the statement to contain the applicable APY, any fees charged, any interest earned, and the number of days in the statement period. 12 U.S.C. § 4307.

Why is a periodic statement important? It allows a consumer to see what activity has been happening with his or her account. This is important if the consumer is to detect mistakes or fraud. The statement also helps the consumer with household budgeting and staying apprised of his or her finances generally.

Why does the right to a periodic statement exist only for accounts that can be accessed by electronic fund transfers and not for accounts accessible only by "check, draft, or similar paper instrument"? The answer seems to be because paper leaves a trail. When a consumer writes a check, the check can be duplicated or otherwise recorded by the consumer. An electronic payment does not inherently create such a record for the consumer. Yet, it is far from clear that other accounts will in fact create "paper trails." Consider, however, what rights a consumer has with an account that can only be accessed by "check, draft, or similar paper instrument." Federal law is silent on the issue. State law—primarily Article 4 of the Uniform Commercial Code (UCC)—has some provisions that address the right to account statements or canceled checks.

UCC Article 4 does not require banks to provide consumers with statements. UCC § 4-406, official cmt. 1. But if a bank does do so, then it must either (1) return or make available paid checks ("items" in UCC parlance) or (2) provide a sufficient account statement to enable the consumer to identify the checks paid, meaning check number, amount, and date of payment. UCC § 4-406(a). In other words, the bank does not have to track payees. Moreover, the deposit account agreement may contractually vary or opt out of this requirement. UCC § 4-103(a). Banks are incentivized, however, to provide statements or make paid checks available because if they do, then the consumer has a duty to "exercise reasonable promptness in examining the statement or the items" to determine if there are unauthorized payments. If the consumer fails to do so, then the bank may not be liable for unauthorized transaction(s). UCC §§ 4-406(c)-(e).

Some states have additional, non-uniform requirements. For example, New York requires canceled checks to be returned with an account statement, N.Y. Banking Law § 9-m, while Massachusetts requires canceled checks to be returned free of charge upon request. Mass. Gen. Laws ch. 167D, § 27. The federal Check21 Act, 12 U.S.C. §§ 5001 *et seq.*, which permits, but does not require, image exchange of checks, rather than physical paper exchange, would appear to preempt these statutes, at least in the case of checks cleared through image exchange.

V. FUNDS AVAILABILITY

When a consumer transfers funds into a deposit account, not all of the funds may be immediately available for the consumer to use. Some transfers take time to clear, meaning that it takes time before the bank has actually received the funds. To the extent that the bank permits the consumer to withdraw or otherwise transfer funds that haven't yet cleared, the bank is essentially extending credit to the consumer and thereby incurring a risk that it will not be repaid. This problem is particularly acute when a consumer transfers funds into a bank account via check. This is because there is a lag between the time when a check is deposited at a bank and when the bank is able to collect funds on the check.

A check payment involves at least four parties: the **drawer** or maker of the check; the **payee** or recipient of the payment; the **depositary bank** in which the check is deposited (depositary is spelled with an "a" in UCC parlance); and the **payor bank** on which the check is drawn. The drawer tenders the check to the payee who deposits the check in the depositary bank. The depositary bank provisionally credits the payment to the payee's account, pending collection of the check. The depositary bank then presents the check to the payor's bank for payment. At this point the payor bank has a choice of whether to honor or dishonor the check. If the payor bank honors the check, it pays the depositary bank and debits the drawer's account. If the payor bank dishonors the check, however, it must notify the depositary bank, which will unwind the provisional credit to the payee's account.

An important point to observe here is that the drawer's account is not debited until the check is settled by the payor bank. There can be a substantial gap between when a check is written and when the funds are debited from the drawer's account. This time gap is known as "**float**." It is essentially a form of credit for the drawer provided by the banking system. Part of the float period includes a double crediting of funds—the payee's account is provisionally credited upon deposit, but the drawer's account is not yet debited.

The rules of how this works are provided by Article 4 of the Uniform Commercial Code, supplemented by Federal Reserve Board regulations and operating circulars as well as by the rules of check clearinghouses. The technical details need not concern us in this chapter beyond one critical point: the payor bank has a time window in which to decide whether it will honor the check or not. During this time window, the depositary bank assumes a credit risk for any funds it makes available to the payee for withdrawal or transfer.

Some consumers deliberately take advantage of the free credit offered in the form of float to write checks before they have the funds in their account to pay the check. This is called "**playing the float**," and the consumer intends to have the account funded by the time the check is presented for payment. Others, however, take advantage of float without intending to have the account funded at the time of presentment. This is a criminal activity known as "**check kiting**" or "**paper hanging**." The check kiter typically exploits float by writing a check on one bank for greater value than the account balance and then writing a check from another insufficiently funded account in another bank. If the checks are timed correctly, then the funds from each check serve to cover the other, allowing the kiter to inflate the balance of the accounts. This allows other checks to be written in payment for real goods and services or for funds to be withdrawn by the kiter, who then absconds.

While check kiting fraud is often small, it can also result in surprisingly large frauds. In 2013, Saquib Khan, the "deli king of Staten Island" was arrested for an $82 million check-kiting fraud, writing hundreds of checks to himself from banks across New York City and racing around the city to deposit them in accounts under his name or those of his businesses in order to finance his business with float. *See* Sam Dolnick, *Deli King's Downfall: $82 Million Check-Kiting Case*, N.Y. Times, Feb. 22, 2013.

An easy solution to the check-kiting risk would be for the depositary bank to refuse to make any funds available to the payee until it was sure that the check would be honored. Consumers, however, want to have funds available to them when they make deposits. They do not want to have to wait for items to clear, a complex and opaque process over which they have no control. The Regulation CC funds availability rules promulgated by the Federal Reserve Board present a compromise. The rules are somewhat complex, and all of the details need not concern us. Table 14.1 summarizes minimum availability rules—banks are free to make more funds available sooner. Critically, availability is keyed off of terms of "business day" and "banking day." A "business day" is a weekday, excluding federal holidays as observed (i.e., January 2 is a federal holiday if January 1 falls on a Sunday). 12 C.F.R. § 229.2(g). "Banking day" refers to the part of any business day when a bank is open to the public for substantially all banking functions. 12 C.F.R. § 229.2(f). Note that while funds may not be immediately available, interest must begin to accrue in interest-bearing accounts on the business day after the banking day of the deposit. 12 C.F.R. § 229.14. *See also* 12 U.S.C. § 4306(c).

Reg CC also requires disclosure of funds availability policies. Banks must disclose their funds availability policy prior to the opening of a new account. 12 C.F.R. § 229.16. More general disclosures indicating that not all funds deposited may be immediately available must also be made on deposit slips, at deposit-taking branches, and on ATMs. 12 C.F.R. § 229.18. Table 14.1, below, summarizes the funds availability rules.

Table 14.1 Regulation CC Funds Availability Rules Summary

Type of Deposit	Date of Availability After Banking Day of Deposit
In-Person Deposit to Payee's Account	
• Cash • Postal money orders • Federal Reserve checks • State and local gov't checks • Cashier's checks • Certified checks • Teller's checks • On-us checks (written from an account at the same depositary bank)	1st business day ("next-day availability").
In-Person Deposit to Payee's Account	
• Other checks	$200 on 1st business day, rest on 2d business day. If deposit is a check, cash withdrawal availability is limited to $200 on 1st business day, $400 on 2d business day, and remainder on 3d business day.
Deposit Not In-Person or Indorsed to 3d Party	
• All types of deposits	$200 on 1st business day, rest on 2d business day. If deposit is a check, cash withdrawal availability is limited to $200 on 1st business day, $400 on 2d business day, and remainder on 3d business day.
Electronic Payments	
• Wire transfer, ACH	1st business day after funds actually collected.
Deposits at Non-Proprietary ATMs	
• All types of deposits, irrespective of other rules	5th business day. If deposit is a check, cash withdrawal availability is limited to $400 on 5th business day, and remainder on 6th business day.

There are a number of exceptions to funds availability rules. Banks in Alaska, Hawaii, Puerto Rico, and the Virgin Islands can add an extra day to the availability schedule for most deposits other than cash, electronic, or government checks. Additionally, exceptions exist for new accounts (where kiting risk is greatest), large deposits (aggregating over $5,000 in a day), redeposited checks, customers with repeated overdrafts, and where there is reasonable cause to doubt collectability (which must be based on the specific facts of a check). 12 C.F.R. § 229.13. Reg CC is, of course, simply a floor for funds availability. Banks may always choose to make funds available sooner for their customers, and they often do so for seasoned accounts.

Check processing has undergone major changes in the past decade, with the result that most checks are processed quite fast. Prior to 2001, checks were cleared physically. This meant that checks were physically transferred around the country by plane, train, and automobile. A check written by a Maine resident to a San Diego resident had to first be delivered from Maine to San Diego, and then physically returned to the Maine resident's bank for presentment. If the check were dishonored, it would have to travel back the same route to San Diego, in reverse.

This physical transportation system for checks was slow and costly. It was also dependent on air transportation being available nationally. The September 11, 2011 terrorist attacks exposed the vulnerability of the check-payment system to serious disruption because of the closure of air space nationally for nearly a week. Congress responded to this problem by passing the Check Clearing for the 21st Century Act (known as the Check21 Act),[10] which permits, but does not require, banks to clear checks via electronic image exchange, rather than the exchange of physical paper checks. It took several years for image exchange to catch on, but by 2010, over 99% of checks deposited for clearing through the Federal Reserve were deposited electronically.[11] Not only has the legal and technological background for check payment changed since 2001, but at the same time, checks have been steadily supplanted by debit cards for many payments. Between the changes in check processing and the declining use of checks, float has largely disappeared, as Figure 14.1 shows. This means that consumers no longer have access to an informal source of free credit provided by inefficiencies in the payment system.

10. Public Law 108–100, 117 Stat. 1177, codified at 12 U.S.C. 5001 *et seq.*

11. Proposed Rulemaking, Availability of Funds and Collection of Checks, 76 Fed. Reg. 16862, Mar. 25, 2011. Prior to Check21, a fifth to a quarter of checks were presented electronically, mainly through Magnetic Character Ink Recognition (MICR) programs, rather than image exchange. A somewhat lower percentage of returned checks are handled electronically. *Id.* at 16862-16863.

Figure 14.1 Items in the Process of Collection at Federal Reserve Banks[12]

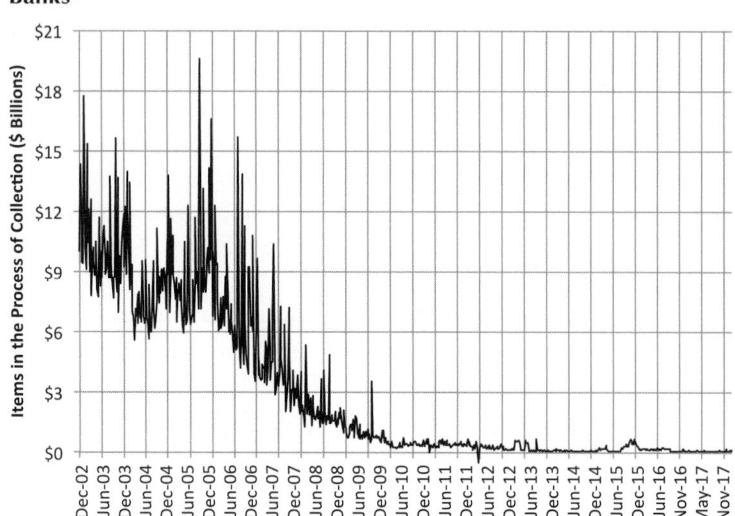

VI. RESERVE REQUIREMENTS AND WITHDRAWAL/ TRANSFER RESTRICTIONS

Federal law places restrictions on withdrawals and transfers from "**savings accounts.**" Regulation D under the Federal Reserve Act governs the reserve requirements of depositories. Depositories are required to maintain a certain level of "reserves," meaning cash in the vault or on deposit at a Federal Reserve Bank or at certain other financial institutions. 12 C.F.R. § 204.5. Reserve requirements are set in relation to the net amount of funds on deposit in "**transaction accounts**" at a bank. 12 C.F.R. § 204.4. Reserve requirements are currently $2.013 million plus 10% of the net transaction amount over $79.5 million. *Id.* Reserve requirements are periodically re-calculated. *Id.*

The purpose of reserve requirements is to ensure that the bank has enough ready liquidity to meet withdrawal demands. Note that banks are not required to keep 100 cents on the dollar available in ready cash for every deposit. Instead, only a fraction of the deposit must be kept on hand. This is because depositors are unlikely to all simultaneously attempt to withdraw their funds. Unless, of course, there is a bank run.

The classic Christmas movie *It's a Wonderful Life* provides the best illustration of this. George Bailey (played by Jimmy Stewart) owns the Bailey Building & Loan, a small bank, and faces a depositor run. As the depositors clamor for their money bank, Bailey explains why it isn't possible—the deposited funds have been loaned out to bank borrowers, and aren't sitting in a vault:

12. Federal Reserve Statistical Release H.4.1.

> You're thinking of this place all wrong, as if I had the money back in the safe. The money's not here. Your money's in Joe's house, that's right next to yours. And in the Kennedy house and Mrs. Macklin's house and a hundred others. Why, you're lending them the money to build, and then they're going to pay it back to you as best they can.

The practice of maintaining only a fraction of deposits in ready cash is called **fractional reserve banking**. By requiring only fractional reserves, banks are thus freed from being mere bailees of funds, and can instead re-loan the funds deposited to them, minus the fractional reserve required. The re-loaned funds are typically deposited into other banks, which can then re-loan them again, minus the fractional reserve. Thus, for $100 deposited in one bank, the bank can loan out $90. The $90 will then be deposited by the borrower in its own bank, which can re-loan $81, and so on. Thus, with a 10% reserve requirement, $100 of bank deposits generates as much as $1,000 worth of financing in the economy. Thus, for a $100 deposit with a 10% reserve requirement, the monetary supply expansion is $1,000.

The importance of the multiplier effect of fractional reserve banking is that it allows the monetary supply to grow to a multiple beyond the monetary base created by a central bank. The impact of this is perhaps clearer in an economy in which the monetary base relates to something tangible, like a gold supply, than it is in an economy with a fiat currency like the United States currently has. It also means that changing reserve requirements are one tool the Federal Reserve Board has for expanding or contracting the monetary supply—and hence the level of economic activity—in the economy. The trade-off involved in fractional reserve banking is the gaining of the multiplier effect, which encourages economic growth, against the risk of bank runs.

For reserve requirements to be meaningful, bank regulators need to be able to accurately determine the amount of funds against which a bank must hold reserves. Reserves are only required for transaction accounts, meaning accounts from which a depositor can readily withdraw funds, such as demand deposits accounts. 12 C.F.R. § 204.2(e)(1)-(2). Deposits that cannot be quickly withdrawn do not present the same type of liquidity concerns that necessitate reserving.[13]

Accordingly, a transaction account is defined to exclude a "time account" or a "savings account." 12 C.F.R. § 204.2(e). A time account is an account from which the depositor may not make withdrawals for at least six days after making the deposit unless subject to an early withdrawal penalty. 12 C.F.R. § 204.2(c)(1)(i). A time account includes deposits that are payable on a specified date or after the expiration of a specified amount of time at least a week after the deposit, 12 C.F.R. § 204.2(c)(1)(i)(A)-(B), as well as those without a specific date payable, a subset of time accounts, which are known as "savings accounts" or "savings deposits." 12 C.F.R. §§ 204.2(c)(1)(ii), (d)(1). Thus, a "certificate of deposit" or "CD" is a type of time account represented by a certificate with a defined maturity date on which it is payable. *See* 12 C.F.R. § 204.2(c)(2). To qualify as a "savings deposit," an account must not be payable on a certain date,

13. The exception would be if a large volume of time deposits matured simultaneously, but the expectation is that maturities will be reasonably staggered.

12 C.F.R. § 204.2(d)(1), and must either require that the depositor give the bank at least a week's notice prior to withdrawal, 12 C.F.R. § 204.2(d)(1), or permit no more than six withdrawals or transfers in a single monthly statement cycle to the depositor's other accounts or third-party accounts. (Transfers to the bank itself are not counted.) 12 C.F.R. § 204.2(d)(2). Thus, regular share accounts at credit unions and regular accounts at savings and loan associations are savings deposits, 12 C.F.R. § 204.2(d)(1), as are passbook and statement savings accounts and money market deposit accounts with monthly transfer/withdrawal limitations, 12 C.F.R. § 204.2(d)(2).

Thus, for certain types of accounts, a consumer's ability to transfer or withdraw funds is limited to six transactions per month or statement cycle by federal banking regulations aimed at ensuring that banks have sufficient cash on hand to pay their potentially short-maturity obligations and to provide macroeconomic control over the economy. Withdrawal and transfer limitations are an example of a consumer financial regulation that has very little to do with consumers directly.

VII. DEPOSIT INSURANCE

Bank deposits may be insured by the Federal Deposit Insurance Corporation (FDIC). The FDIC is a government agency in corporate form. It is run by a five-member board that includes the Comptroller of the Currency and the CFPB Director. The FDIC maintains a mutual insurance fund for insured banks. Insured banks are charged premiums based on their deposit base. If an insured bank fails, the FDIC takes over the bank and pays the insured depositors out of its deposit insurance fund. The insurance covers up to $250,000 per insured account ownership category per insured institution. 12 C.F.R. § 330.1(o). Deposit insurance is the cornerstone of modern consumer banking because it largely eliminates the risk of depositor runs.

A consumer can have more than one insured account by virtue of qualifying under multiple ownership categories, but accounts within an ownership category are aggregated. There are several account ownership categories, but the two most important ones for most consumers are individual accounts and joint accounts. An individual account is owned by one person, while a joint account is owned by two or more persons. Individual accounts are insured up to $250,000 in aggregate per owner. The form of the individual account—demand deposit, savings, CD, money market demand account, etc., does not matter for determining the total amount of funds in individual accounts. Thus, if a single depositor has three individual accounts of $100,000 each at the same institution, $250,000 is of the total insured, and $50,000 is uninsured. If those three accounts were spread around to multiple institutions, however, each would be fully insured.

Joint accounts (Adam or Eve; Adam and Eve; Adam and Eve and Seth, etc.) are insured up to $250,000 per co-owner. Thus, a joint account with two co-owners would be insured up $500,000 total. If a depositor has multiple joint accounts, the allocation of insurance becomes a bit more complex, but the basic principle is still $250,000 per depositor within an account ownership category. Thus, if Adam and Eve have a joint account with a $150,000 balance, Adam and Seth have a joint account with a

$200,000 balance, and Adam, Eve, and Seth have a joint account with a $375,000 balance, Adam's combined ownership interest in the joint accounts would be $300,000 (= $75,000 + $100,000 + $125,000), of which only the first $250,000 would be insured. Eve's interest would be $200,000 (= $75,000 +$125,000) and would be fully insured, while Seth's interest would be $225,000 (= $100,000 + $125,000) and would also be fully insured. 12 C.F.R. § 330.9(b).

Remember that coverage is $250,000 per individual per ownership category at an insured institution. Thus, a husband and wife could each have an account in their own name as well as a joint account at a single bank. Together, they could have up to $1,000,000 in insured deposits among the three accounts. Certain retirement and trust accounts are also covered for beneficiaries, which could increase our happy couple's insured coverage even further. If, however, there were $300,000 in the husband's individual account, only $250,000 would be insured, even if there were only $400,000 in the joint account (enabling another $50,000 in coverage for both husband and wife in the joint account). Coverage limits cannot be transferred across ownership categories.

High-net-worth depositors can easily go over the FDIC insurance cap. This has led to a brokered deposit market for excess deposits over the FDIC insurance limits. Deposit brokers will help high-net-worth individuals spread out their cash holdings among financial institutions, and banks actively compete for these brokered deposits, which usually take the form of certificates of deposit. Deposit brokerage is unregulated, although FDIC insurance assessments are adjusted based on the extent that banks rely on brokered deposits, and banks that are not well-capitalized are prohibited from accepting brokered deposits. 12 U.S.C. § 1831f(a); 12 C.F.R. § 337.6.

Depository institutions lacking federal deposit insurance are required to "include conspicuously in all periodic statements of account, on each signature card, and on each passbook, certificate of deposit, or share certificate a notice that the institution is not federally insured, and that if the institution fails, the Federal Government does not guarantee that depositors will get back their money." 12 U.S.C. § 1831t(b)(1). Uninsured depositories are also required to provide notice of their uninsured status in all advertising containing information beyond the name, logo, and contact information of the institution, as well as at teller windows, branches, and websites. 12 U.S.C. § 1831t(b)(2). Depositors must sign a written acknowledgement of the lack of federal insurance and its potential consequences if the depository fails. 12 U.S.C. § 1831t(b)(3). The disclosure and consent requirements are subject to enforcement by the CFPB, the FTC, and state banking supervisors. 12 U.S.C. § 1831t(f).

The disclosure requirements for uninsured depositories have little practical importance today, as almost no depositories lack FDIC insurance (perhaps in part because of the negative disclosures that uninsured banks must make). Yet, as we shall see in a future chapter, prepaid debit cards can function as ersatz bank accounts and generally lack FDIC insurance. The disclosure requirements relating to lack of federal deposit insurance apply to "depository institutions," which are defined to mean "bank or savings association[s]." 12 U.S.C. § 1813(c). Because the cards are not a "bank" or "savings association," the uninsured disclosure requirement does not apply to them.

Problem Set 14

1. You're working in the compliance department of Mastodon National Bank. The head of the compliance department has asked you to review the following advertisements and communications for TISA compliance:

   a. Mastodon National offers a checking account that pays 4.99% APY if the account holder remains enrolled at an accredited higher education institution. Otherwise, there will be a monthly account fee of $15, unless there is a minimum balance maintained of $1,000. Can Mastodon National Bank put posters on public buses and trains and in train stations that tout the "Mastodon National Bank no-fee, high-yield, 4.99% APY student checking account"? If so, what will TISA require its advertisements to contain? *See* 12 U.S.C. §§ 4302(a)-(b), 4302(d)-(e); 12 C.F.R. § 1030.8.

   b. Mastodon National Bank's website states: "Open a Mastodon High-Yield Checking Account Today! Amazing 4.09% APY. Further information available by calling our toll-free number." Is Mastodon National Bank violating TISA? *See* 12 U.S.C. §§ 4302(a), 4302(c), 4302(e).

   c. Mastodon National Bank has a multipage website. The information required for TISA account schedules is all found on the Mastodon National website, but it is not all on a single page (one URL). Instead, it is dispersed among several pages. Is Goliath National TISA compliant? *See* 12 U.S.C. § 4302(a), 4302(e), 4303(a), 4303(e).

2. Rachel Jackson has a passbook savings account at Metropolitan Bancorp. Rachel hasn't received a periodic statement for her account. Rachel also has an interest-bearing checking account at Banco Merica that she accesses with an ATM card.

   a. Suppose that Rachel hasn't received periodic statements from either bank. Can she successfully bring suit against either bank for failure to provide periodic statements? *See* 15 U.S.C. § 1693d(c)-(d); UCC §§ 4-103(a), 4-406(a); UCC § 4-406 official cmt. 1, Cal. Bus. & Prof. Code §§ 17200, 17203.

   b. Now suppose that Rachel's been receiving periodic statements from Banco Merica, but the statements do not indicate the APY. Instead, they only state how much she has earned in interest in dollars and cents. Can she successfully bring suit over the periodic statements? *See* 12 U.S.C. §§ 4301(b), 4307; 15 U.S.C. § 1693d(c)-(d); UCC §§ 4-103(a), Cal. Bus. & Prof. Code §§ 17200, 17203.

   c. Now suppose that Rachel is being audited by the IRS and needs to find records of various transactions for which she took tax deductions. In particular, Rachel needs to be able to show the IRS that she made payments to particular parties for specified services. Will she be able to obtain her transaction records from three years ago, and will they be sufficient to indicate what she paid to whom? What if Rachel no longer banks at Banco Merica? *See* UCC §§ 4-104(5), 4-406(a)-(b).

3. On Friday the 1st, David Min had a bank account balance of $5,000. That morning, he deposited a $2,000 personal check in a Mastodon National Bank ATM. On

Monday the 4th, he received a direct deposit via ACH of $1,000. On Tuesday the 5th, he deposited a $500 personal check and $300 cash to his Mastodon National Bank account using an Metropolitan Bancorp ATM. On Wednesday the 6th, David deposited a $700 state tax refund check, $400 cash, and a $600 check made out to his daughter that she had indorsed to him at the teller window of his local Mastodon National Bank branch. On Thursday the 7th, he tried to deposit a $200 municipal tax refund check at the teller window of his local Mastodon National branch but was told by the teller to use the bank's ATM instead, which he did.

a. What is the "available balance" in David's Mastodon National Bank account on each day between Friday the 1st and Friday the 15th?

b. Suppose that on Friday the 1st, David decided he wanted to withdraw $5,300 in cash. How soon could he do so? What if he wanted to withdraw $6,000 in cash? Would the answer be different if he were to write a check?

4. Melissa Jacoby has $50,000 in a Mastodon National Bank checking account in her name alone, $100,000 in a Mastodon National Bank savings account in her name alone, $40,000 in a Mastodon National Bank Money Market Deposit Account, $150,000 in a Mastodon National Bank CD payable to her alone, and $600,000 in a Mastodon National Bank joint account with her friend Mark. She also has $200,000 in a CD from Behemoth Bancorp, N.A., an affiliate of Mastodon National Bank with a common holding company, and $1,000,000 in a money market mutual fund run by Leviathan Financial, another affiliate of Mastodon National Bank. Mastodon National Bank has run into financial trouble and has been seized by the FDIC. What is the effect on Melissa?

5. Mastodon National Bank wants to attract very large deposits from extremely wealthy individuals but is having trouble competing with money market mutual funds. Marv Youngerman, the CEO of Mastodon National Bank, explains, "wealthy depositors really want absolute safety for their money, but because their FDIC insurance coverage is capped, the choose to put their money in money market mutual funds because they have higher yield than our bank accounts."

a. Youngerman is thinking that if Mastodon National can offer higher yields, it will be able to compete with money market mutual funds. What could Mastodon National do to try to boost its yields? How is the FDIC likely to feel about this?

b. Youngerman's been approached by banking consultant Peninsula Financial, which has suggested that Mastodon National could take large deposits and (through Peninsula's brokerage) purchase CDs at other FDIC-insured institutions, which would, in turn purchase matched CDs at Mastodon National Bank. Thus, with a $2 million deposit, Mastodon National Bank would purchase seven CDs for $250,000 at seven other banks, which would, in turn, each purchase a matched CD from Mastodon National, which will hold the CDs in trust for the original depositor. Mastodon National Bank will still have $2 million in deposits, but it will all be FDIC-insured. Will this transaction solve Mastodon National's problem in terms of attracting large deposits? What concerns might the FDIC have?

CHAPTER 15

OVERDRAFT AND THE UNBANKED

I. DEPOSIT ACCOUNT ECONOMICS

Deposit accounts are costly for a bank to maintain. Cost accounting for bank accounts is not precise. There are some costs directly associated with individual accounts, such as regulatory compliance costs (account opening customer identification verification; disclosure of account schedules; periodic statements), interest payments, fraud losses, and federal deposit insurance premiums.

Many costs, however, are not associated with individual accounts. Technology systems are needed to enable transfers in and out of the account and to calculate balances and funds availability. There are marketing expenses in prospecting for new customers. There are overhead expenses for call centers and brick and mortar branches: purchasing and paying taxes on or leasing the real estate; utilities (the lights have to stay on); security; personnel (salaries and benefits for everyone from tellers to the CEO); office supplies and equipment and supporting technology systems; regulatory compliance costs not associated with individual accounts. These overhead costs do not change with the marginal increase in the number of accounts, but they are instead "lumpy," and may change with certain aggregate numbers of accounts. While these costs are not associated with individual accounts, banks often treat them for cost accounting purposes as associated with maintaining deposit accounts.

Not surprisingly, there is a great range in the estimates of the cost of opening and maintaining a deposit account. One source estimates the cost of opening an account is between $150 and $200 and the cost of maintaining an account is estimated at $250-$300 per year.[1] Other, older sources, however, put the price of account maintenance significantly lower, between $48 and $145 per year.[2] What is clear from all the estimates is that there are significant costs to a bank to maintaining a deposit account.

1. American Bankers Association, *Cost of a Checking Account*, http://www.aba.com/Press/Documents/e7a636cc2d244ec998d2ed16c23d1955CostofCheckingAccountsOnePageronJusttheCostsofAcco.pdf.

2. Fed. Reserve Bd., Functional Cost & Profit Analysis 129 (1997) (cost of a fully loaded account is $145). *See* Ralph Haberfeld, *Cognitive Dissonance, Microeconomics, and Checking Accounts*, BANKSTOCKS.COM (Mar. 4, 2002), http://www.bankstocks.com/article.asp?id=517 (estimating variable costs at $48).

Banks need to be able to pay for the provision of accounts. The revenues associated with a bank account are no more precise than the costs. Banks make money in two ways: spread and fees. Spread is the difference between a bank's own cost of funds and its return on investments. A core part of the business of banking is intermediating between borrowers and investors. When you deposit your money in the bank, you are making a loan to the bank. It might be an interest-free loan (or with fees included, a negative interest loan), but it is a loan nonetheless. You are the bank's creditor. The bank then takes the money you've deposited and loans it out to someone else or otherwise invests the funds. The bank is looking to get a greater return on its investments than it has to pay you in interest plus its various operating costs. This is the so-called 3-6-3 model of banking: borrow funds at 3%, loan them out at 6%, and be on the golf course by 3 P.M.

Banks also make money from fees. Sometimes fees are closely related to an account and sometimes less so. Some fees are for provision of particular products or services associated with an account or accessing the account. For example, there are account maintenance fees, fees for checkbooks, fees for ATM usage, fees for wire transfers, insufficient funds (bounce) fees, etc. Sometimes, however, fees are hard to differentiate from spread. Bank overdraft fees, for example, are economically interchangeable with interest, and payment card interchange fees (charged to merchants on credit or debit card transactions) were originally designed as a way to circumvent usury restrictions. Both types of fees involve the bank extending some amount of credit and hoping for a return greater than their costs of funds. Other fees are less closely associated with an account. The deposit account is a consumer's foundational financial relationship, and that relationship gives the bank the opportunity to "cross-sell" other financial products, such as credit products (credit cards, mortgages, auto loans), insurance, and investments. The revenue from these cross-sold products can be, but often is not, credited to the "gateway" product of the deposit account.

A. The Shift to Fee-Based Revenue

Historically, the lion's share of bank revenue came from interest spreads. But interest spreads have tightened, and banks have shifted to fee-based income to compensate. These fees take a variety of forms, such as monthly account fees ("subscription fees") and fees for particular services. Monthly fees are often applied to accounts that fail to maintain a certain minimum balance. "Free" or "No-fee" checking accounts have become more common over the past decade, as banks have recruited depositors by replacing set, up-front fees with behaviorally contingent back-end fees.

The shift from up-front to back-end, contingent fees in deposit accounts is a revenue model, found in other areas of consumer finance such as credit cards (where late fees, over-limit fees, and interest rate increases replaced annual fees during the 1990s), and short-term loans, such as payday and auto title loans (where a large share of revenue is built into rollover fees), takes advantage of consumers' optimism bias: consumers underestimate the likelihood that they will incur behaviorally contingent fees and therefore value them less than fixed, up-front subscription fees.

Figure 15.1 Increase in Bank Fee Income[3]

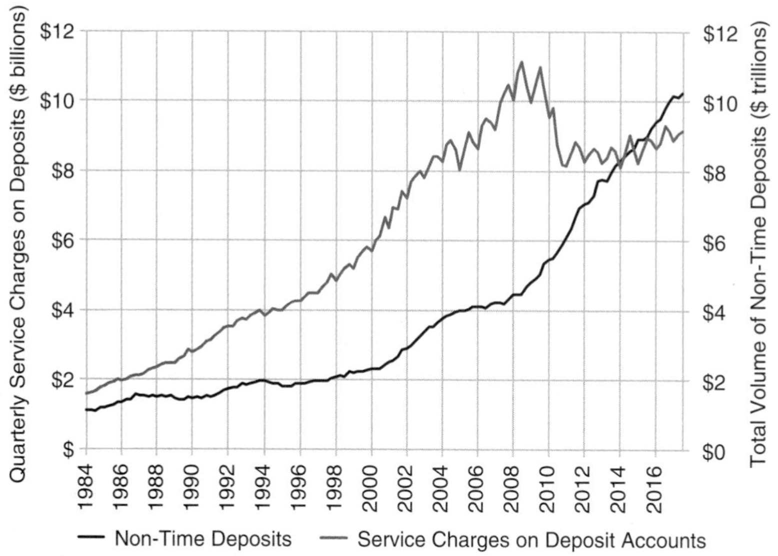

B. Overdraft Fees

In deposit accounts, the major back-end, behaviorally contingent fee is the overdraft fee. Table 15.1, below, shows the average fee amounts for consumer checking accounts between 2010 and mid-2012. Overdraft fees are by far the largest share, representing over half of total average fees for all accounts, and a much higher share of fees for those accounts that have opted into optional overdraft protection for certain types of transactions.

Table 15.1 Monthly Net Checking Account Fees Per Account (2010-2012)[4]

Fee Type	Overall	Accounts Opted into Overdraft Coverage	Accounts Not Opted into Overdraft Coverage
ATM and Account Usage Fees	$1.66	$2.08	$1.61
Maintenance Fees	$1.28	$1.53	$1.24
Transfer Fees	$0.54	$0.85	$0.50
Other Fees	$1.18	$3.02	$0.93
Overdraft and NSF Fees	$5.21	$21.61	$2.98
Total Fees	**$9.87**	**$29.09**	**$7.26**

3. FDIC Quarterly Banking Profile.
4. CFPB, CFPB Data Point: Checking Account Overdraft (2014), at 9.

Since 2000, overdraft fees have become a major source of bank income, driven by the massive growth in non-cash payments (a 53% increase from 2000 to 2011), which has increased the opportunities for overdrafts.

As of 2012, roughly a fifth of bank revenue derived from overdraft fees, with small banks and credit unions, in particular, often heavily dependent on overdraft.[5] (*See* Figure 15.2.) A large number of small financial institutions would have negative income absent overdraft.[6] In 2015, bank overdraft fees were estimated to total $32.5 billion, nearly three times what they were in the early 1990s. (*See* Figure 15.3.)

An overdraft occurs when a consumer runs a negative deposit account balance. Recall that a deposit account is a loan from the consumer to the bank. An overdraft reverses this relationship. Overdraft originated as a discretionary accommodation banks made to trusted customers from time to time. Prior to the era of electronic fund transfers, funds moved in and out of bank accounts primarily by check and cash withdrawals from a teller. As we learned in the last chapter, the timing of check clearance was hard to predict. A consumer could not know when a check given in payment of an obligation would be deposited or how long a deposit would take to clear. As a result, a consumer might find funds withdrawn from an account before she or he expected them to be and account balances to be depleted at a hard to predict rate.

Figure 15.2 Bank Deposit Account Revenue by Sources (2012)[7]

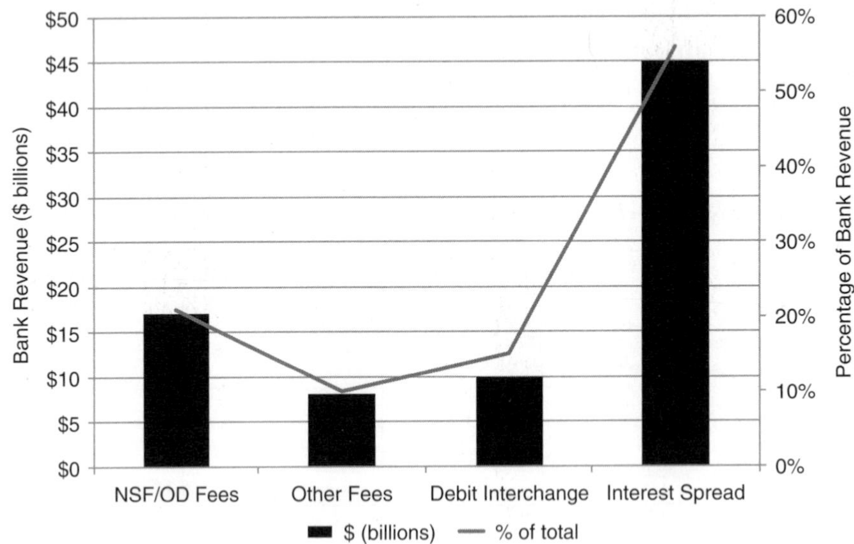

5. *See* Adam J. Levitin, *Overdraft Regulation: Is There a Silver Lining for Credit Unions?* Filene Research Institute Research Brief No. 211 (July 2010).

6. *Id.*

7. FDIC, author's estimate.

Figure 15.3 Total Overdraft and NSF Fee Revenue[8]

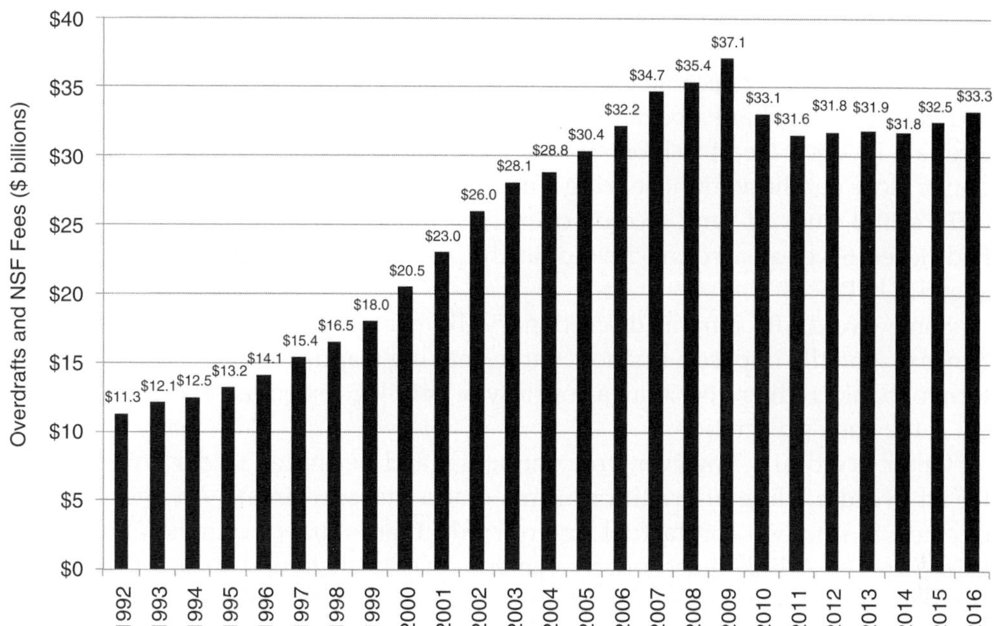

If a consumer wrote a check that was presented for payment at a time when the account balance was too low, the check would be dishonored for insufficient funds ("NSF") and would "bounce."[9] A bounced check could be costly and embarrassing to the consumer. The consumer's bank (the payor bank) might charge the consumer a NSF fee, and the depositary bank might charge the payee a bounce fee as well, which the payee might charge to the consumer. Likewise, the payee of the bounced check might charge a late fee or interest because of lack of timely payment. In some cases, as with utility companies, a bounced check might result in the utility being disconnected, resulting in a fee being required to reconnect it. Bouncing a check imposes a set of costs on consumers, and no clear benefit. (Notably, however, while banks generally charge NSF fees for bounced checks and ACH transactions, they do not for debit inquiries at merchants or ATMs.)

Therefore, for trusted customers, banks would allow accounts to run short-term negative balances, based on the expectation that funds would be quickly replenished. The ability to overdraw offers a potential benefit for consumers in that it can help them smooth out liquidity hiccups and thereby avoid NSF fees, bounce fees, and late penalty fees or interest charges from merchants or billers.

8. Huffington Post; Moebs Services.

9. Whereas a check can only be presented a single time and thus result in a single NSF fee, ACH items may be re-presented two times after the initial denial for insufficient funds, and thus result in as many as three NSF fees. NACHA Rules § 2.12.4 (Reinitiation of Returned Entries).

Because discretionary overdraft was a privilege or courtesy, not a contractual right, regulators did not consider it to be credit and thus subject to Truth in Lending Act disclosure requirements, fair lending laws, or state usury statutes.

As check clearing became more highly automated and electronic fund transfers began to be used, banks began to start charging fees for overdrafting. The bank, after all, incurs a credit risk on an overdraft, as the consumer might simply abandon or close out the account, leaving a negative balance. This is not an idle risk—the CFPB's 2013 study of bank account overdrafts found that in 2011, banks on average had closed 6% of all accounts involuntarily, presumably most because of sustained negative balances.

Some overdrafts remain discretionary. By charging fees on these overdrafts, banks essentially impose a finance charge, making it appear more like a contractual form of bank credit, rather than a courtesy or privilege extended to certain customers at the bank's discretion.

Other overdrafts, however, are contractual and permitted under an agreement for an **overdraft line of credit** or a **linked account agreement**. An overdraft line of credit is simply a contractual line of credit that is drawn on when an account is overdrawn. A linked account agreement permits customers to cover overdrafts from one account with funds in another account. For example, an overdraft on a checking account might be covered with funds in a savings account. Regulation D's reserve requirements limit the number of withdrawals from a savings account in a month. 12 C.F.R. § 204.2.

Related to overdrafting are "**deposit advance**" programs. These products are short-term, open-ended lines of credit provided to depositors with recurring direct deposits. Thus, a consumer with a regular bi-weekly payroll deposit could borrow against the anticipated deposit by drawing on the deposit advance line of credit. Deposit advance is essentially a form of payday lending by banks and is addressed in more detail in Chapter 30.

C. Overdraft Pricing

Overdrafts do not reflect competitive market pricing. Depositors are essentially a captive market for overdraft. There is not a market for account-linked, third-party overdraft lines of credit. Instead, if a consumer is permitted to overdraw, it is on the bank's terms. The consumer has no ability to shop based on price or other terms.

Overdraft fees, however, are not structured to correlate with risk; fees are rarely correlated with the size or length of banks' exposure and never based on the risk posed by an individual consumer. Nor do fees appear to be designed to be punitive and thus a deterrent against overdrafting, as the method for determining when fees apply (discussed in the next section) is usually opaque to the consumer, frustrating planning and learning. Instead, they appear to reflect monopolistic and opportunistic pricing. As fee arrangements have evolved, a fee is typically applied for each transaction that overdraws. Some banks vary fees by the size of the overdraft and some by the length of the overdraft, but most will charge multiple overdraft fees—one for every transaction that occurs that creates or increases a negative balance.

Moreover, some banks have **sustained negative balance fees** for extended periods of being overdrawn. These fees may be in addition to the fee for any particular overdraft.

D. Calculation of Account Balances

Banks also began to experiment with the method for processing transactions, in particular, the order in which credits and debits to the account would be made, and the method for calculating account balances. Banks found that they could significantly increase overdraft fee revenue by their choice of balance calculation rules. There is considerable variation in balance calculation methods, and the opacity and manipulation of balance calculations has been one of the major criticisms of overdraft.

There is substantial variation in how banks process transactions, with several variables. Some banks process transactions in nightly batches for each day, while others process transactions periodically intra-day. Some banks post credits before debits or vice versa. Among debits different orders are used, sometimes by transaction size, sometimes by transaction type (check, ATM, ACH, etc.), sometimes involving chronological order or serial ordering (for ATM transactions or checks). Additionally, funds availability calculations and debit card holds (which make certain funds temporarily unavailable) can affect the overdraft calculation.

Typically the account balance calculation is done on a per account basis, rather than a per customer basis as with FDIC insurance coverage (other than with linked-account overdraft protection). Thus, if a consumer has two accounts at the same bank and overdraws one, it will not matter that there is available balance in the other in terms of determining that there has been an overdraft.

To illustrate the complexity in balance calculation, consider the series of decisions a bank has to make about how an account balance is to be calculated from any given starting balance. First, it is necessary to determine what will be included in the calculation of a balance. Is it simply the ledger amount, or should holds and authorizations be taken into account? For example, when a debit card is used to make a purchase at a gas station, the transaction will typically be pre-authorized for $100. The consumer might only purchase $30 worth of gas, but there will be a hold on the account for $100—for which the bank is potentially liable—for up to three days. Should the bank calculate the balance based on $100 or on $30? The difference might result in an overdraft or overdrafts.

Next, the bank must determine how transactions are to be posted to the account. This involves initially deciding whether credits (transactions adding funds to the account) or debits (transactions removing funds from the account) will be applied first to the balance or whether they will be applied based on when the bank is notified or whether they will be applied in buckets based on the type of transfer (*e.g.,* check versus ACH). Applying debits before credits will increase the likelihood of an overdraft.

The next issue is whether transactions will be posted in chronological order, serial number order (for checks), high to low by transaction amount, or low to high by transaction amount. Again, this can be done for all transactions or differently for different buckets of transactions. The ordering of transaction posting will determine whether an account ever runs a negative balance, and, if so, how many transactions are there once it has a negative balance.

Finally, there is the question of when overdraft fees will be applied. Are they applied only at the end of a day, or when overdrafts occur, thereby further decreasing balances and making more overdrafts likely? There isn't a neutral position here, but rather a set of choices for a bank to make.

Overdraft fees are generally charged per overdraft, irrespective of the size of the overdraft. There can be multiple overdrafts on an account. Thus, if an account had an opening balance of $100, and then had debits of $60, $30, $20, $10, and $10, in that order, the final three debits would each result in an overdraft. Posting transactions from smallest to largest is likely to minimize the number of overdrafts. Thus, in the transaction example above, a smallest to largest posting would result in one overdraft. In contrast, a largest to smallest posting will maximize the number of overdrafts, in this case three. If there is a $35 per overdraft fee, the difference in the posting orders is $70 in fees. The following case excerpt explains in more detail how a largest to smallest posting order can maximize overdrafts.

Gutierrez v. Wells Fargo Bank, N.A.

704 F.3d 712 (9th Cir. 2012)

MCKEOWN, Circuit Judge:

. . . "Posting" is the procedure banks use to process debit items presented for payment against accounts. During the wee hours after midnight, the posting process takes all debit items presented for payment during the preceding business day and subtracts them from the account balance. These items are typically debit-card transactions and checks. If the account balance is sufficient to cover all items presented for payment, there will be no overdrafts, regardless of the bookkeeping method used. If, however, the account balance is insufficient to cover every debit item, then the account will be overdrawn. When an account is overdrawn, the posting sequence can have a dramatic effect on the *number* of overdrafts incurred by the account (even though the total *sum* overdrawn will be exactly the same). The *number* of overdrafts drives the amount of overdraft fees.

Before April 2001, Wells Fargo used a low-to-high posting order. Under this system, the bank posted settlement items from lowest-to-highest dollar amount. Low-to-high posting paid as many items as the account balance could cover and thus *minimized* the number of overdrafts. Beginning in April of 2001, Wells Fargo did an about-face in California and began posting debit-card purchases in order of highest-to-lowest dollar amount. This system had the immediate effect of *maximizing* the number of overdrafts. The customer's account was now depleted more rapidly than would be the case if the bank posted transactions in low-to-high order or, in some cases, chronological order.

As an illustration, consider a customer with $100 in his account who uses his debit-card to buy ten small items totaling $99, followed by one large item for $100, all of which are presented to the bank for payment on the same day. Under chronological posting or low-to-high posting, only one overdraft would occur because the ten small items totaling $99 would post first, leaving $1 in the account. The $100 charge would then post, causing the sole overdraft. Using high-to-low sequencing, however, these purchases would lead to ten overdraft events because the largest item, $100, would be posted first—depleting the entire account balance—followed by the ten transactions totaling $99. Overdraft fees are based on the number of withdrawals that exceed the balance in the account, not on the amount of the overdraft. When high-to-low sequencing is used, the fees charged by the bank for the overdrafts can dramatically exceed the amount by which the account was actually overdrawn. For example, Gutierrez incurred $143 in overdraft fees as a consequence of a $49 overdraft, and Erin Walker incurred $506 in overdraft fees for exceeding her account balance by $120.

Gutierrez claims that Wells Fargo made the switch to high-to-low processing in order to increase the amount of overdraft fees by maximizing the number of overdrafts. The bank amplified the effect of its fee maximization plan, which it named "Balance Sheet Engineering," through several related practices that are not at issue here.

Wells Fargo was ultimately found liable to the tune of $203 million, not for its choice of posting order, but for misrepresentations about its posting order. High-to-low posting is permitted. Whether it is inherently bad for consumers is less clear. Some commentators have noted that the largest transactions are quite possibly the most important ones for a consumer, and that a consumer would want those to be processed first so as to be sure there are funds and the transaction will not be denied.[10] This observation does not mean, however, that a largest-to-smallest posting order necessarily benefits consumers. If the bank is willing to cover the overdrafts (and charge a fee), then the consumer has not benefitted from the largest and most important transactions not being denied. Instead, the consumer has simply paid more for credit that would likely have been extended with a smallest-to-largest transaction processing order.

The manipulation of posting orders—and non-disclosure of posting procedures—resulted in major class action suits against banks, with over $1 billion in settlements.

E. Who Overdrafts?

Overdrafts are fairly common. A CFPB study found that in 2011, 27% of accounts incurred an overdraft fee. Yet, while the occasional overdraft is common enough, most overdrafts are the result of serial overdrafting by a more discrete set of consumers. The same CFPB study found that roughly three-fourths of overdraft fees were charged to around 8% of accounts, which have over ten overdrafts per year.

---

10. *See, e.g.,* Todd J. Zywicki & Nick Tuszynski, *The Economics and Regulation of Bank Overdraft Protection,* 9 Engage (2008).

(*See* Table 15.2.) While the average account incurring overdraft fees paid $225 in fees in 2011, these frequent overdrafters pay on average nearly $400/year in overdraft fees. This comports with an FDIC study from 2008 that found that three-quarters of accounts studied did not overdraft in a year. Instead 84% of overdrafts came from just 9% of accounts, and 68% from just 5% of accounts that had 20 or more overdrafts in a year. (*See* Table 15.3.)

To be sure, a consumer can in the course of a day easily accumulate multiple overdrafts without being aware of it, but it appears that there is a small segment of the depositor base that uses overdraft as a regular source of small-dollar credit. It is not clear the extent to which overdraft is substituting for other small-dollar credit sources, such as credit cards, payday loans, and auto title loans.

Table 15.2 Distribution of Accounts and Gross Overdraft Fees by Overdraft Frequency (2010-2012)[11]

Annualized Number of Overdrafts	Accounts	Overdraft Fees	Annualized Overdraft Fees Paid
0	69.8%	0.0%	$0.00
1-3	12.5%	8.6%	$29.62
4-10	9.4%	17.7%	$81.67
>10	8.3%	73.7%	$380.40

Table 15.3 Distribution of Overdrafts Among Accounts (2008)[12]

No. of Overdrafts per Account	% of Accounts	% of NSF or Overdrafts	Average Cost to Account
0	75%	n/a	n/a
1-4	12%	7%	$64
5-9	5%	9%	$215
10-19	4%	16%	$451
20+	5%	68%	$610

II. REGULATION OF OVERDRAFTS

A. State Law and Overdrafts

Overdrafts are sometimes regulated by state law. The Uniform Commercial Code permits overdrafts for "items" that are "properly payable." UCC § 4-401. An "item"

11. CFPB, *CFPB Data Point: Checking Account Overdraft* (2014), at 12.
12. FDIC (2008).

is an "instrument," such as a check, or a signed, written promise or order to pay money, but it does not include wire transfers, credit, or debit card payments. UCC § 4-104(9). An item is only properly payable if it was authorized by the customer (such as through a signature) pursuant to the account agreement. UCC § 4-401. The UCC permits banks to dishonor an item that would create an overdraft absent agreement to pay the overdraft. UCC § 4-402(a). The UCC gives banks significant leeway in when and how to make the determination of an account balance for purposes of determining if there is an overdraft. UCC § 4-402(c).

While every state has adopted Article 4 of the UCC, some states have additional laws relating to overdrafts that cover not just checks, but also overdrafts resulting from other types of payments. These laws have been held to be preempted to the extent they dictate a particular posting order of credits and debits, *Gutierrez v. Wells Fargo Bank, N.A.*, 704 F.3d 712 (9th Cir. 2012), but banks still face liability if they are misleading regarding their posting order. *Id.*

B. Federal Overdraft Regulations

While overdraft operates as credit, it is not regulated as credit. Regulation Z under the Truth in Lending Act excludes from the definition of a "finance charge" any "[c]harges imposed by a financial institution for paying items that overdraw an account, unless the payment of such items and the imposition of the charge were previously agreed upon in writing." 12 C.F.R. § 1026.4(c)(3). Similarly, even formal, non-discretionary overdraft lines of credit tied to accounts that are accessible by debit card are not subject to TILA solicitation and application disclosures. 12 C.F.R. § 1026.5a(a)(5)(ii).

Instead, federal law regulates overdraft as a type of electronic fund transfer under Regulation E under the Electronic Fund Transfers Acts. Reg E requires consumers to affirmatively opt in to having for-fee overdraft protection for overdrafts made using non-recurring point-of-sale debit and ATM transactions. 12 C.F.R. § 1005.17(b)(1). Both Reg E and Reg DD under the Truth in Savings Act were subsequently transferred to CFPB administration.

The Reg E opt-in requirement does not apply to overdrafts on checks or regularly scheduled transactions (such as automatic bill pay). *Id.* The types of transactions to which the opt-in requirement applies are ones on which the bank itself incurs no fee for a denial of a transaction for insufficient funds. Banks are prohibited from coercing consumers into accepting for-fee overdraft protection by applying different pricing and terms to consumers who to do not accept for-fee overdraft services or conditioning payment of other types of overdraft on consumer opt-in. 12 C.F.R. § 1005.17(b)(2)-(3). Reg E restricts the content of the opt-in notice, 12 C.F.R. § 1005.17(d), but this restriction does not limit banks' ability to communicate with consumers about overdraft in other forms. This means that banks have substantial control over the opt-in process, and are thus able to influence whether a consumer is likely to opt-in to for-fee overdraft coverage. *See* Lauren E. Willis, *When Nudges Fail: Slippery Defaults*, 80 Chicago L. Rev. 1155 (2013). Consumers can freely revoke their consent to the opt-in, but there is no expiration date for the consent provided. 12 C.F.R. §§ 1005.17(f)-(g).

Reg DD requires banks to make certain disclosures when advertising overdraft services, including disclosure of the fee amount, but this requirement does not apply to broadcast or electronic media advertising or outdoor advertising like billboards. 12 C.F.R. § 1030.11(b)(1)-(4). Its main application is to literature the bank hands out to prospective consumers. Reg DD also requires banks to disclose possible fees, including overdraft fees, in initial account schedules that are provided upon the opening of an account. 12 C.F.R. § 1030.4(b)(4). Changes in account terms must be disclosed too, usually at least 30 days in advance of the change. 12 C.F.R. § 1030.5(a). Thus, if a bank were to change the terms of its overdraft program, it would have to disclose such change. Presumably the bank would have to resolicit consents to for-fee overdraft services if there were a change in terms in the overdraft program, but nothing in Reg E or Reg DD directly says so, and a bank might argue that once initial consent had been provided, consent to subsequent changes of terms could be implied if the consumer were duly notified. In other words, after an initial opt-in, the rule would change to opt-out. This would seem to be, at the very least, against the spirit of the opt-in requirement, but it would otherwise impose substantial resolicitation costs on banks that might be undertaking minor changes in terms that might in fact benefit consumers (for example, a reduction in overdraft fees).

Reg DD generally requires banks to disclose fees actually assessed in periodic statements, although such disclosure may be for aggregate fees by category. 12 C.F.R. § 1030.6(a)(3). Reg DD separately requires that banks provide in each periodic account statement the total amount of overdraft and insufficient fund (NSF) fees for the period covered by the statement, as well as the year to date. 12 C.F.R. § 1030.11(a). Thus, aggregate disclosure of overdraft fees and of NSF fees would satisfy Reg DD. Consider whether this is helpful to a consumer who might want to identify and challenge a particular overdraft. (The EFTA/Reg E error resolution process, discussed in Chapter 20, might provide a solution for the consumer if individual fees are not itemized, but it would require additional effort from the consumer.)

Notably, federal regulations do not specifically address the order in which transactions are posted to an account. Funds availability rules deal with the day on which funds must be available but do not specify the posting order within the day. All overdraft practices, including opt-in solicitations, are of course covered by the federal UDAAP statute, 12 U.S.C. §§ 5531, 5536.

C. Other Overdraft Guidance

In addition to Regulations E and DD, federal bank regulators have provided some non-binding guidance regarding overdraft fees. The FDIC has issued regulatory guidance to insured banks that indicated that the FDIC expects them to:

- Give consumers the opportunity to affirmatively choose the overdraft payment product that overall best meets their needs;
- Monitor accounts and take meaningful and effective action to limit use by customers as a form of short-term, high-cost credit, including, for example, giving customers who overdraw their accounts on more than six occasions where a fee is charged in a

rolling twelve-month period a reasonable opportunity to choose a less costly alternative and decide whether to continue with fee-based overdraft coverage;

- Institute appropriate daily limits on overdraft fees;
- Consider eliminating overdraft fees for transactions that overdraw an account by a de minimis amount
- Not process transactions in a manner designed to maximize the cost to consumers.[13]

Moreover, if a fee is charged for a *de minimis* overdraft, the FDIC expects it to be "reasonable and proportional to the amount of the original transaction."[14] What this means in real terms is unclear. The FDIC guidance is not formally binding and there is no right of action under the FDIC's guidance.

D. Effect of Overdraft Regulation

The Reg E opt-in requirement was proposed in 2008, finalized at the end of 2009, and became effective in July 2010. It appears to have had a substantial effect on overdrafting. Total bank service fees on deposit accounts, over half of which are for overdraft, fell by 27% in the year after the rule was proposed, and have remained largely flat since the regulations came into effect. (*See* Figure 15.4.)

Figure 15.4 Total Bank Service Charges on Deposit Accounts

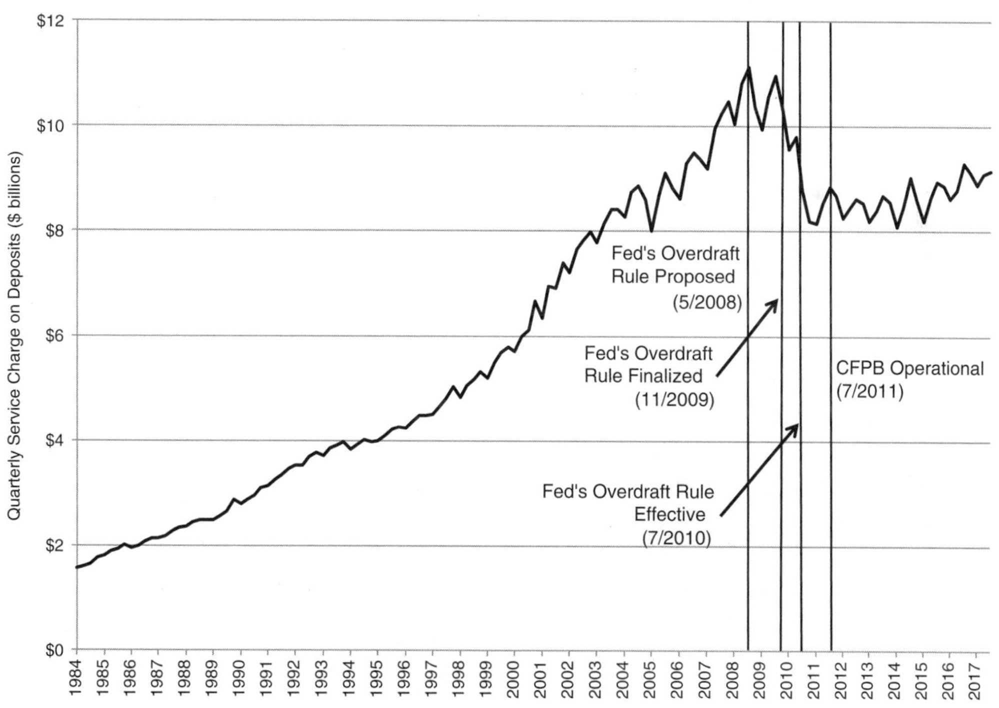

13. FDIC Financial Institutions Letters, FIL-81-2010, Nov. 24, 2010, at 1.
14. *Id.* at 4 n.5. The OCC proposed guidance, 76 Fed. Reg. 33409, June 8, 2010, but subsequently withdrew it.

Reg E seems to be reducing overdrafts in part because of relatively low opt-in rates. Not all banks even offer overdraft, but for those that do, the opt-in rates were 16.1% overall in a CFPB study.[15] The opt-in rate seems to vary considerably by bank, however. It is also higher for new accounts, suggesting that banks are able to use the accounting opening interaction to encourage opting-in.[16]

Opt-in rates also vary considerably based on consumers' past overdraft history. Consumers who overdrafted heavily in the past tend to opt in at substantially higher rates, as shown by Table 15.4. Notably, accounts that did not opt in saw a 45% drop in fees paid in the next six months in the CFPB's study, while opt-in accounts saw total fees paid increase by 9%. Those heavy users who did not opt in saw substantial reduction in overdraft and NSF fees—their total fees paid dropped by 63% or over $450 per account on average over six months.

Some banks have experimented with technological solutions to help consumers manage overdrafts. For example, some banks allow consumers to set up text message alerts when balances fall beneath a certain threshold. Anecdotal evidence is that such alerts do not have much effect on the number of overdrafts. Indeed, one would only expect an effect if overdrafts were because of carelessness, rather than because of true liquidity problems.

Table 15.4 Overdraft Coverage Opt-In Percentage (2010)[17]

Overdrafts per Year	Opt-In Rate
0	11.3%
1-3	27.1%
4-10	34.6%
10+	44.7%
All Accounts	15.2%

III. THE UNBANKED

Seven percent of US households—constituting 9 million households with 15.6 million adults and 7.6 million children—are "unbanked," meaning that they lack a transaction account at a financial institution.[18] Another 19.9% of households (24.5 million households with 51.5 million adults and 16.3 million children) are "underbanked," meaning that they have a transaction account at a depository institution, but also use "fringe" financial products, such as non-bank money orders, check-cashing services, payday loans (which require having a bank account), rent-to-own

15. CFPB, *CFPB Study of Overdraft Programs, A White Paper of Initial Data Findings* (June 2013), at 29.
16. *Id.* at 30.
17. *Id.* at 31.
18. FDIC, *FDIC National Survey of Unbanked and Underbanked Households* 1 (Oct. 20, 2016).

arrangements, pawn shops, or refund anticipation loans.[19] (To these categories, we might add the "unhappily banked"—those with banking relationships that do not satisfy their needs at a reasonable cost.) The unbanked and the underbanked are disproportionately minority, headed by single parents, younger, less educated, Southern, and lower income. Some of the unbanked have never been in the banking system, while others have dropped out of it or been kicked out of it because of repeat extended overdrafts.

Being unbanked or underbanked is not in and of itself a problem. Instead, it raises concerns for two reasons. Lack of or limited access to traditional financial services may indicate limited access overall to financial services or that a higher price is paid for financial services, both of which may interfere with household wealth formation. Access to the banking system is a critical part of being able to participate in the modern commercial world, and those without access to financial services are not able to engage in the same sort of transactions as others. For example, it is difficult to rent a car or book airline tickets or a hotel room without a credit card. Similarly, a credit card of some sort is frequently necessary for making purchases over the Internet. Absence of a deposit account complicates the ability to keep funds safe for future use, and access to traditional credit sources, such as mortgage, auto, and credit card lenders often depends on having a bank account.

The unbanked/underbanked population presents both a challenge and an opportunity to the mainstream financial services industry. There are serious obstacles to banking the unbanked from both the financial institution and consumer sides. Yet there is also an enormous untapped potential customer base.

A. Financial Institution-Side Obstacles to Accessing Banking Services

The economics of deposit accounts explain some of the unbanked phenomenon. Poorer consumers—who are likely to have small account balances—are unlikely to be profitable bank depositors, absent overdraft fees. Recall that estimates of the cost of maintaining a deposit account are in the $200 range, annually. A small balance account simply does not generate enough interest spread income to be profitable absent fees.

To illustrate, let's imagine that a bank can make a 3% annual net interest margin. In order to generate $200 of interest income at this rate, a deposit account would have to have an annual average balance of $6,666. Even with a 6% net interest margin, the account would have to have a balance of $3,333 to generate $200 in annual interest income. And this amount of income might not even make the account a break-even proposition for the bank.

In 2016, the median transaction account had a balance of $4,500. Jesse Bricker *et al., Changes in U.S. Family Finances from 2013 to 2016: Evidence from the Survey of Consumer Finances*, 103 Fed. Reserve Bull. 1, 18, (2017). The poor are likely to have far

19. *Id.*

lower balances. This means that absent a willingness to cross-subsidize small balance accounts with the income from high-balance accounts, small balance accounts just aren't worthwhile for banks. Moreover, in times of low prevailing interest rates—often when the economy is performing poorly—small balance accounts are relatively less attractive. The only way low-balance accounts can be profitable on their own is with high fees, and those fees make the accounts unattractive to low-balance depositors. As Figure 15.5 shows, low balance accounts are money losers for banks . . . unless the balances are so low that they generate overdraft fees.

Figure 15.5 assumes annual average account balances. The financial affairs of low-income consumers, however, are frequently unstable. This means that account lives tend to be shorter than for higher-income consumers. Shorter account lives increase the risk of a financial institution not recouping any sunk costs involved in the account. Overdrawn accounts may be closed and not repaid. Thus, the profitability of offering mainstream deposit-account-based financial services to the poor is at best a questionable proposition for financial institutions.[21]

Figure 15.5 Average Revenue per Deposit Account (2012)[20]

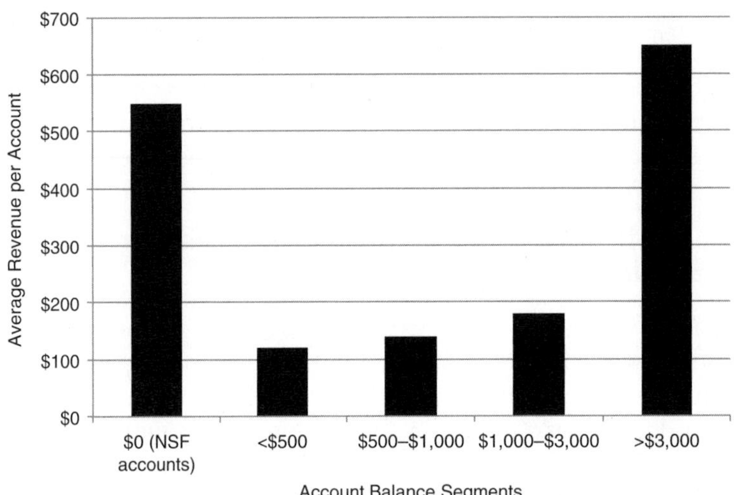

B. Consumer-Side Obstacles to Accessing Banking Services

On the consumer side, too, there are obstacles to banking the unbanked. The economics of traditional checking accounts do not make sense for the poor because of minimum balance requirements or monthly fees and bounced check fees.[22] Other

20. Oliver Wyman, FDIC.

21. Michael S. Barr, *Banking the Poor,* 21 Yale J. Reg. 121, 177 (2004) (noting that financial institutions' perception that low-income consumers are not profitable contributes to their lack of service to low-income consumers).

22. *Id.*

low-income consumers have past credit problems, including histories of bounced checks, that keep them out of the banking system, as banks do not want to assume high-risk checking account customers.[23]

Other problems are sociological. Some consumers simply don't trust banks.[24] This can be out of lack of familiarity or personal idiosyncrasies. (For example, my dear uncle (by marriage) John, a former college professor, still keeps his money under his mattress . . . or so I'm told.) For consumers who are not used to dealing with banks, the experience can be daunting. Banks are often fairly formal places and there is no obvious guide for a consumer who has no experience in dealing with them. For many Americans, likely including anyone reading this text, going to a bank is second nature; we have been going with our parents to make deposits since we were children. But for a novice, particularly a poor one, the experience can be intimidating.

The poor also frequently lack access to convenient banking services.[25] Convenience plays an important role in consumer decisions about use of financial institutions. Lower-income neighborhoods are less well served by mainstream financial institutions, making it harder geographically to connect the poor with banks. Rural populations face similar challenges. Internet banking has started to overcome geographic limitations. The poor, however, are less likely to have Internet access and thus the ability to do Internet banking. The growing prevalence of smartphones may change this, but the poor often use prepaid smartphones, so exhausting a supply of prepaid data can also mean being cut off from a financial service provider.

Finally, some of the unbanked are illegal immigrants. Know Your Customer (KYC) rules designed to prevent money laundering and terrorism financing mandate identification documentation when opening bank accounts. (These rules are addressed in Chapter 17.) Undocumented immigrants understandably shy away from mainstream financial institutions and rely on a shadow consumer finance system, particularly for remittances to families in their countries of origin.

The following chapter addresses prepaid cards, which have emerged as one of the major developments in banking the unbanked; prepaid cards can function as ersatz bank accounts, without the overhead expense of running brick and mortar branches. They come with their own set of issues, however.

---

23. *Id.* at 181-182.

24. A large percentage of unbanked respondents to surveys reported that they were not "comfortable" dealing with banks. *See* John P. Caskey, *Lower Income Americans, Higher Cost Financial Services* 20 (1997) (17.6% of respondents); Arthur B. Kennickell *et al.*, *Recent Changes in U.S. Family Finances: Evidence from the 1998 and 2001 Survey of Consumer Finances, 89* Fed. Res. Bull. 1, 10 (2003) (noting that 22.6% of unbanked respondents "do not like dealing with a bank"); Sherrie Rhine *et al.*, *The Role of Alternative Financial Service Providers in Serving LMI Neighborhoods, in* Changing Financial Markets and Community Development: A Federal Reserve System Community Affairs Conference 59 (Jackson L. Blanton *et al.*, eds., 2001) (reporting that 30% of respondents cited distrust of banks, an aversion to dealing with banks, and privacy concerns).

25. Barr, *supra* note 21, at 182-183.

Problem Set 15

1. Rep. David "The Hammer" Whelan has been redistricted and his district now includes a substantial poor urban population, many of whom are unbanked. The Hammer is up for reelection next year and he wants to be able to propose legislative changes that will help his unbanked constituency. He's particularly concerned that it might not be economically feasible for banks to offer accounts to his constituents. What sort of changes might reduce the cost of offering checkable demand-deposit accounts to low-income consumers?

2. Senator Prudence Dogood has called for the US Postal Service to offer basic banking services to consumers: accepting demand deposits and time deposits, enabling payments via check, debit card, and ACH, and making small-dollar loans (maximum size of $300). You're legislative counsel to another senator who is uncommitted on the proposal, but concerned about the large number of unbanked and underbanked consumers in her state. The senator has asked you for your evaluation of Senator Dogood's proposal: What benefits and risks do you see in it?

3. Josh Kaufman opted into for-fee overdraft protection from his bank. He subsequently purchased a Venti Caramel Macchiato at Starbucks with his debit card for $4.75. When he got his bank statement, he found that the transaction cost him a $35 overdraft fee. When Josh complained to the bank, he was told that he opted into overdraft coverage when he opened his account three years ago.

- **a.** Does Josh have any recourse against the bank? *See* 12 C.F.R. § 1005.17(d)(2)-(3); *Williams v. Walker-Thomas Furniture Co.*, 350 F.2d 445 (D.C. Cir. 1965) (in Chapter 2).
- **b.** Josh would like to be able to receive a notice before he transacts warning him if the transaction is an overdraft. "That way I won't be buying $40 lattes," he says. Why doesn't Josh get such a notice?

4. Josh Kaufman (from problem 3) banks at Bank of America. An excerpt from his Bank of America deposit agreement may be found after this problem set.

- **a.** On Friday, Josh wrote three checks from his account with check numbers 104, 105, and 106. He also purchased another Caramel Macchiato at Starbucks with his debit card, used his debit card to pay for a half tank of gas, took $200 out of the ATM, and paid his regular Netflix subscription payment via automatic bill payment. Friday was also payday. Josh has direct deposit from his employer, but he also received a reimbursement check from a co-worker, which he deposited to his account at 5 P.M. that Friday at a Bank of America ATM. Can you tell Josh in what order his transactions will be processed? How confident are you? *See* 12 C.F.R. §§ 229.10(b), 229.10(c)(vii), 229.12(b).
- **b.** Can Josh determine if Bank of America is complying with the deposit agreement?
- **c.** Why do you think Bank of America groups transactions into categories and processes categories separately? (Hint: why does Bank of America process checks and scheduled electronic debits after point-of-sale debits?)

5. Mastodon National Bank wants to encourage consumers to opt in to its overdraft protection service. Would any of the following strategies be problematic?

a. Charging a NSF fee that is greater than its overdraft fee and informing consumers of the relationship between the fees. *See* 12 U.S.C. §§ 5531, 5536; 12 C.F.R. § 1005.17(b)(2).
b. Offering a $15 account credit to consumers who opt in to overdraft protection. *See* 12 U.S.C. §§ 5531, 5536; 12 C.F.R. § 1005.17(b)(3).
c. Not charging overdraft fees, but instituting a $20/month account fee, which it waives when an account is not overdrawn. *See* 12 C.F.R. § 1005.17(b)(2)-(3).

6. Mastodon National Bank wants to calculate account balances for overdraft and NSF purposes by applying debits before credits and with debits applied from largest to smallest. You are outside counsel to Mastodon National Bank. What advice do you have about this plan? *See Gutierrez v. Wells Fargo Bank, N.A.*, 704 F.3d 712 (9th Cir. 2012); 12 U.S.C. §§ 5531, 5536.

Bank of America, Deposit Agreement and Disclosures

Effective November 10, 2017[26]

PROCESSING AND POSTING ORDERS

Processing Transactions and Posting Orders

Posting transactions to your account impacts your account balance. Posting a credit increases your balance. Posting a debit or hold reduces your balance. Credits include teller deposits, direct deposits and credits we make. Holds include deposit holds, debit card authorizations, and holds related to cash withdrawals and electronic transfers. Debits include withdrawals, transfers, payments, checks, one-time and recurring debit card transactions, and fees.

We use automated systems to process transactions and then to post transactions to accounts. When we process multiple transactions for your account on the same day, you agree that we may in our discretion determine our posting orders for the transactions and that we may credit, authorize, accept, pay, decline or return credits, debits and holds in any order at our option.

Posting Orders

This section summarizes how we generally post some common transactions to your account.

We group the different types of transactions into categories. We use several different categories for holds, credits, and debits. Most categories include more than one transaction type.

After the end of the business day, our automated systems assign each transaction received for that day to a category. We generally post all transactions within a category, using the posting order or orders that apply to that category, before we post any transactions assigned to the next category.

---

26. https://www.bankofamerica.com/deposits/resources/deposit-agreements.go.

We start with the balance in your account at the beginning of the business day, subtract holds from your balance, and make any adjustments from prior days. Next, we generally add credits to your balance and then subtract debits from your balance. Some, but not all, of our categories are shown below. For each debit category shown below, we list some common types of debits that we assign to the category and summarize how we generally post them within the category.

- We add deposits and other credits to your balance.
- Then, we subtract from your balance in date and time order the types of debits listed in this paragraph, when our systems receive date and time information. If our systems do not receive date and time information, then we subtract the remaining debits in this category from your balance in order from the highest to lowest dollar amount.
  Common debits in this category include:
  - one-time and recurring debit card transactions;
  - withdrawals made at our tellers and ATMs;
  - one-time transfers made at ATMs, through our tellers, by telephone, and through Online Banking and Mobile Banking;
  - checks you wrote that are cashed at our tellers; and
  - wire transfers.
- Then, for other checks you wrote, we subtract from your balance checks with check numbers sequentially in check number order when our systems can read the check number.

  Next, checks without a check number that our systems can read are subtracted in order from highest to lowest dollar amount.
  As an example, on the same business day we receive five checks that you wrote and were not cashed at a teller. Our systems can read three of the check numbers, which are #105, #112, and #115. The other two checks do not have check numbers that our systems can read. We subtract check #105 first, then #112, and then #115. Then, we subtract the two remaining checks in order from the highest to lowest dollar amount.

- Then, we subtract from your balance many other types of electronic debits in order from the highest to lowest dollar amount. These debits include: scheduled transfers, preauthorized or automatic payments that use your deposit account number (generally referred to as automated clearing house (ACH) debits), and Online Banking and Mobile Banking bill payments.
- Then, we subtract from your balance most fees (such as monthly maintenance fees, overdraft item fees, returned item fees, and ATM fees) in order from highest to lowest dollar amount. Some fees may show as "processing" until the next day.

Changing Posting Orders

You agree that we may determine in our discretion the orders in which we post transactions to your account.

You agree that we may determine in our discretion the categories, the transactions within a category, the order among categories, and the posting orders within a category. We sometimes add or delete categories, change posting orders within categories and move transaction types among categories. You agree that we may in our discretion make these changes at any time without notice to you.

Posting Orders Determined at End of Day

We receive credits, debits and holds throughout the day. Regardless of when during the day we receive transactions for your account, you agree that we may treat them as if we received all transactions at the same time at the end of the business day.

During the day, we show some transactions as processing. As an example, we show some transactions as processing on the Account Details screen in Online Banking. Please note that transactions shown as processing have not been posted yet. The posting order for these transactions is determined at the end of the day, with the other transactions we receive for that day.

You should note that often we do not receive debits on the same day that you conduct them. As an example, when you use your debit card to pay for a purchase at a merchant and sign for the transaction, we usually receive an authorization request from the merchant the same day, but we might not receive the final debit card transaction for payment and posting until several days later.

We generally post credits and debits to your account, and report them on your statement, in a different order than the order in which you conduct them or we receive them.

Overdraft Fees

We generally determine at the time we post a debit to your account whether it creates an overdraft and whether an overdraft or returned item fee applies. You should note that sometimes we authorize a transaction at a time when you have enough available funds to cover it, but because other transactions post before it and reduce your balance, the transaction creates an overdraft when we post it to your account. You can avoid fees for overdrafts and returned items by making sure that your account always contains enough available funds to cover all of your transactions. When your account balance includes some funds that are subject to a hold, dispute or legal process, you should note that those funds are not available to cover your transactions.

We offer services to help you manage and keep track of your finances, such as Online Banking and Online Alerts. Please see "How to Get Started" at the beginning of this agreement.

Our posting orders can impact the number of overdraft fees we charge you when you do not have enough available funds to cover all of your transactions. When several debits arrive the same business day for payment from your account and you do not have enough available funds in your account to cover all of the debits we receive for that day, you understand that some posting orders can result in more overdrafts, and more fees for overdraft items and returned items, than if we had used other posting orders. You agree that we may in our discretion choose our posting orders, and also change them from time to time, regardless of whether additional fees may result.

When your account balance includes some funds that are not available at the time that we post a debit, and you do not have enough available funds in your account to cover the debit, the debit results in an overdraft and we generally charge you an overdraft item fee or returned item fee for the debit. You should note that we do not show holds, or distinguish between available and unavailable funds in your account balance, on your statement so when you review your statement later, it might appear that you had enough available funds in your account to cover a debit for which we charged you a fee.

Certain Transactions Made After Business Day Ends

During processing, we generally include in your account balance some transactions that you make after the business day cut-off, but before the end of the calendar day. These transactions are described below. This can impact fees that apply to your account. The credits can help you avoid overdrafts, returned items, and related fees. However, the debits can cause you to incur overdrafts, returned items, and related fees. You should note that we show these transactions on your statement as posting to your account on our next business day.

Credits. We generally add to your account balance the following credits, when the transaction occurs after the cutoff time for the business day, but during the same calendar day:

- Cash deposited at one of our ATMs or financial centers, and
- Transfers to your account from another deposit account with us made at one of our ATMs or financial centers, through Online Banking, Mobile Banking, or by calling customer service.

Debits. We generally subtract from your account balance the following debits, when the transaction occurs after the cutoff time for the business day, but during the same calendar day:

- Cash withdrawals made at one of our ATMs or financial centers, and
- Transfers from your account made at one of our ATMs or financial centers, through Online Banking, Mobile Banking, or by calling customer service.

CHAPTER 16

PREPAID CARDS

I. WHAT IS A PREPAID CARD?

We have previously seen that bank accounts offer consumers a bundle of services: safekeeping/investment and payments through checks and debit cards. That combination of services is particularly valuable to consumers as it allows them to simultaneously protect and access their funds. Yet, a relationship with a bank is hardly necessary for a consumer to obtain a similar bundle of safekeeping and payments. Instead, the consumer can use a "**prepaid card**" that functions like an ersatz bank account without having any banking relationship whatsoever.

Prepaid cards (sometimes referred to as "prepaid debit cards") are often called "**stored value cards**," and it is this stored value function that is the feature that distinguishes them from regular debit cards. A regular debit card is just an access device used to order money to be drawn from the cardholder's deposit account. There's nothing magical about a debit card being a 2.125" x 3.325" rectangle of plastic with a magnetic stripe on one side (and possibly a microchip inside). The physical form is largely irrelevant; it only matters to the extent that it is necessary to interface with particular card reading equipment, but a card can be used without a reader. What is important is not the physical form of the card, but the data on the card (on both the magnetic stripe on the back of the card and the printed or embossed information on the front and back of the card) that indicate the source of funds that it is used to access.

A normal debit card pulls money out of a deposit account at a bank.[1] A prepaid card, in contrast, does not access the cardholder's bank account. Instead, the value is drawn from the bank account of the card provider rather than that of the cardholder. The value might be tracked on the card itself or it might simply serve as an access device to an account that is tracked elsewhere, but in either case the real value doesn't actually reside on the card. It is ultimately sitting in a bank account, just the prepaid card issuer's bank account, rather than the consumer's bank account.

Moreover, prepaid cards that operate on the Visa and MasterCard payment networks—that is, those prepaid cards that can be used for payment at most merchants rather than at only a single merchant or small consortium of merchants—are required by Visa and MasterCard to have an FDIC-insured bank as the issuer of the

1. The regular debit card need not even be issued by the bank that holds the account. These products, known as "**decoupled debit**," have not caught on despite attempts by Capital One and HSBC, but they represent an important division of the deposit/payment relationship.

card. That issuer bank might play a minimal role in the actual design and administration of the prepaid card program, but it is nonetheless an essential party because it holds the keys to accessing the payment system. Banks are never truly disintermediated from the financial system; innovations like prepaid cards merely impose institutional superstructures on top of the banking system.

This distinction is important for a couple of reasons. First, it changes the cost structure of the product. A traditional bank account requires the whole brick and mortar apparatus of a bank branch to acquire and maintain the account. That's expensive, even if the costs can be spread out over myriad accounts. A prepaid card is likely to offer much more limited service to a consumer than a traditional bank account, so its operational costs should be lower. Second, prepaid cards are not subject to the same regulatory apparatus as bank accounts. While this too affects the cost structure, it also affects the level of protections consumers have when using prepaid cards.

Prepaid cards have become an increasingly popular means of accessing financial services for both poor and younger consumers. A particular type of prepaid card, known as an **electronic benefit transfer** or **EBT** card, is also widely used for the disbursement of government welfare benefits. In 2016, American consumers undertook some 6.75 billion transactions on non-EBT prepaid cards for a dollar volume of $256.36 billion, or $38 per average transaction.[2] Another 2.41 billion transactions for $65.55 billion were undertaken on EBT cards.[3] As we will see, however, there are is a huge variety of prepaid cards, and they have very different functions, so that aggregate transaction volumes and counts do not tell the whole story of the use of prepaid cards. Figures 16.1 and 16.2 illustrate the growth in the dollar volume and number of prepaid and EBT transactions.

Figure 16.1 Prepaid and EBT Transaction Volume[4]

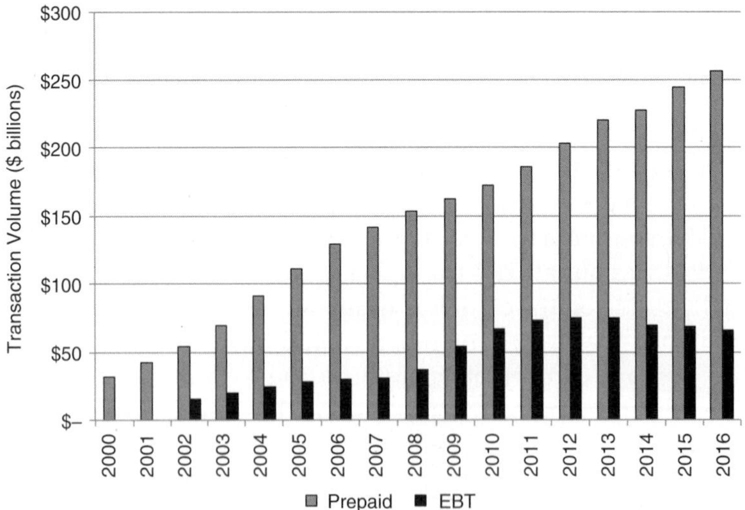

2. Nilson Report No. 1122, at 10 (Dec. 2017).
3. *Id.*
4. Nilson Reports, Nos. 847, 869, 890, 915, 939, 962, 1100, 1122.

Figure 16.2 Number of Prepaid and EBT Transactions[5]

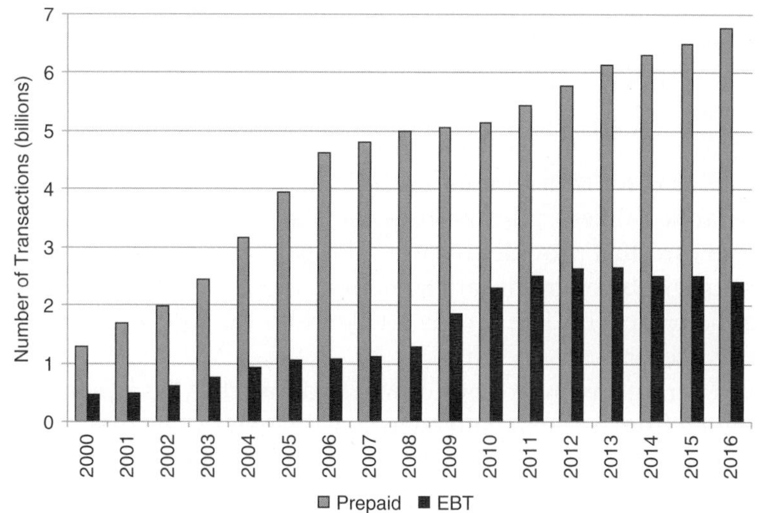

A. Prepaid Cards Are Everywhere

There are a wide variety of prepaid products with different features and that are used for different purposes.

1. Alternative to Transaction Accounts

Some prepaid cards serve as alternatives to transaction accounts. The cards enable consumers to store funds received by cash, check, or direct deposits as well as pay bills at point of sale or online. A prepaid card can be an attractive alternative to a transaction account for consumers who do not want to incur bank account maintenance fees or minimum balance requirements. For other consumers, a prepaid card might actually offer greater convenience than a bank account in terms of locations at which the card can be reloaded, or money withdrawn. They can be used to make payments at locations that won't take cash, including, sometimes, online, and can be used to accept direct deposit and set up for automatic bill payment. This allows consumers to avoid check-cashing outlets and having to pay for money orders, as well as avoid bank fees and overdrafts. Prepaid cards also offer potentially greater security than cash—at least if they require use of a PIN number. Some prepaid cards give the ability to track spending. Some cards even suggest that they may help build creditworthiness.

Some consumers simply cannot get a bank account because of their poor credit profile. Prepaid cards do not generally require a credit check. Moreover, the casual observer cannot distinguish between a prepaid card and a regular debit or credit card, so the user of a prepaid card is, at least in the choice of payment instrument,

5. *Id.*

indistinguishable from a traditional middle-class consumer with a bank account and a credit or debit card. Thus, a prepaid card may also offer its holder that great intangible "respect." Russell Simmons lends his name to the RushCard line of prepaid cards issued by The Bancorp Bank (Visa requires that its cards be issued by FDIC-insurance-eligible entities, but this does not mean that the funds on the cards are themselves insured deposits), including the Baby Phat card (complete with phat cat logo), the KLS card (with Kimora) or the Dynasty Card (with then third baseman for the New York Yankees, Alex Rodriguez). The RushCard website notes that it is "[t]he prepaid card that provides respect."[6] Prepaid cards give consumers who cannot get a regular debit or credit card something close to transactional equality with their better-heeled peers. The card is a ticket into the modern commercial world, albeit one for a second-class berth.

Is prepaid part of an upward or a downward trajectory? Is it being used by those who are moving from being unbanked to quasi-banked, or by those who are banked but are being pushed out of the system by bank fees? It could well be both. We don't know, but this has important implications for how we view the growth of prepaid.

2. Government Benefit Disbursement

Other prepaid cards are used for disbursement of government benefits—what is known as "electronic benefit transfers" or "EBT." The consumer is issued a card by the government (which contracts with a bank to act as its administrative agent), and the card is periodically reloaded not by the consumer, but by the government, whenever benefits are disbursed.

Federal and state governments use prepaid cards for disbursement of welfare (Temporary Aid for Needy Families or TANF), food stamps (Supplemental Nutritional Assistance Program or SNAP), state unemployment benefits, court-ordered payments, and prison disbursements. Since 2013, Social Security or Supplemental Security Income payments have been made electronically for most recipients instead of by paper check.[7] Some state benefit programs remain paper-based, however.

Although separate cards are used for different programs, the shift from paper to EBT cards has saved the federal government money, enabled faster and more reliable access to benefits, and eliminated the risk of checks stolen in the mail. For consumers with deposit accounts, the benefits can be sent as an automated clearinghouse item (direct deposit). The federal government has also partnered with financial institutions to encourage the provision of affordable Electronic Transfer Accounts, but is also enabling the use of a prepaid debit card called a Direct Express card. Direct Express cards, however, are only reloadable by the federal government; the consumer cannot add other funds to a Direct Express card.

---

6. http://www.rushcard.com/whyrushcard/respect.aspx.

7. The federal government has indicated that it will keep making check payments to those individuals who have not set up a method for receiving electronic transfers, but new benefit recipients must set up an electronic transfer method.

Federal regulations limit the ability of other prepaid cards to qualify for direct deposit of government benefits, as the funds on those cards must be FDIC-insured, and subject to the Electronic Fund Transfer Act, 31 C.F.R. § 210.5(b)(5), although certain cards are exempt from various EFTA provisions. While there are cards that meet both requirements, the cost of FDIC insurance and EFTA compliance raises the costs of providing the card, and federal regulations cap a significant revenue source for prepaid cards that can be used for things other than for physical, in-person transactions, such as online bill pay.[8] The result is that federal benefit disbursements to prepaid cards have remained limited to Direct Express cards.

3. Check Cashing Alternative

Still other cards are used primarily as an alternative to check cashing. Consumers without transaction accounts historically had to rely on check-cashing outlets in order to accept check payments, such as paychecks and government benefits. Check cashers also frequently offer payment services, such as money orders, to enable bill payment and remittances from consumers without checking accounts.

Check-cashing fees are not insignificant, however, and use of a check-cashing outlet may make a consumer a target for street crime, as a consumer leaving a check casher is likely to be carrying cash. Some prepaid card issuers accept check deposits to prepaid card accounts via ATM or bank branch without a fee. The card can then be used to access cash or to make payments. Thus, the card functions as an alternative (and potentially cheaper) check casher.

4. Transportation Payment

One of the most widespread uses of prepaid cards is for public transit fares. Many public transit systems use plastic and/or paper prepaid cards as a means of payment of fares. The use of these cards benefits the transit systems by enabling the separation of fare purchases from the use of trains and buses and avoids the problems of fraudulent tokens. It is expensive and cumbersome to have conductors collect fares from riders. Either dedicated personnel must be used or all passengers must be funneled through a limited number of entrances to a train or bus where they will pay. This slows down departures from stations and stops, thereby making transit systems less efficient. The use of prepaid card kiosks, machines, and third-party vendors enables consumers to purchase their fares separately from boarding or riding on public transit, and that enables more efficient provision of the transportation itself.

---

8. A federal law, known as the Durbin Amendment, regulates debit card swipe fees (also known as interchange fees, covered in more depth in the Chapter 18). Swipe fees are functionally (if not formally) paid by merchants that accept card payments to card issuers. Debit card swipe fees are regulated and capped, but an exclusion exists for certain prepaid cards. The exclusion, however, is limited to prepaid cards that can be used only to access government benefits, 15 U.S.C. § 1693o-2(a)(7)(A)(i), 12 C.F.R. § 235.5(b), and for prepaid cards that can be used only for physical, in-person transactions. 15 U.S.C. § 1693o-2(a)(7)(A)(ii) (exempting only transactions made using the card); 12 C.F.R. § 235.5(c)(1)(iii) (interpreting the exemption to exist only if the card is the "only means of access to the underlying funds").

Some prepaid transit card systems require the scanning of a magnetic stripe on a card. Others, however, have begun to use **near field communication (NFC)**, which involves the use of a card with a small **radio frequency identification (RFID)** chip inside and RFID scanners. NFC cards are simply tapped or waved near a scanner rather than having a card swiped or inserted into a reader. The use of NFC can speed up payment—an important consideration when dealing with boarding trains and buses—as NFC cards can—depending on the sensitivity of the reader—be used without taking a card out of a wallet or purse.

NFC cards also show up in another way, namely payment of tolls. Devices like E-ZPass and Fast Lane use RFID for payment of tolls. These devices are linked to accounts that are prepaid from credit cards, but they could just as easily be prepaid in other ways.

Transit cards can raise particular privacy concerns, as they enable transit systems—and law enforcement—to track the use of the card and thus the travel of the card user. This can sometimes be beneficial to consumers, in terms of both enabling law enforcement to protect them and to catch card thieves, but can also be invasive. For example, a transit system's records might show the travel habits of a philandering spouse, especially for entry-and-exit presentment systems like that of the Washington, D.C., Metro.

5. Payroll and Flexible Spending Account Cards

Some employers pay their employees using ACH transfers to payroll cards. These cards can then be used at ATMs to access cash or for point-of-sale (POS) debit purchases. Payroll cards are attractive to employers with many unbanked employees, such as fast food restaurants. With deposit accounts, the employees are unable to be paid by direct deposit. Using payroll cards helps employers reduce check printing and distribution costs. The cost of printing and distributing a payroll check is between $1.00 and $2.50 per check, whereas the cost of paying an employee who has a payroll card is about $0.10 per payment (in addition to the upfront cost of the card). Mark Furletti, Fed. Reserve Bank of Phila., *Prepaid Cards: How Do They Function? How Are They Regulated? Conference Summary, June 3-4, 2004*, at 10. Employees may also see these cards as a boon, because they help avoid the trip to a check-cashing outlet with its attendant fees and theft risks.

Prepaid cards are also used for Flexible Spending Accounts (FSAs), which are employer-maintained accounts into which an employee can place a portion of pre-tax earnings for subsequent use for certain types of tax-free spending, such as health care, dependent care, or transportation. FSAs are governed by IRS regulations. Prepaid FSA cards ensure that funds are spent directly out of FSAs, rather than spent out of pocket with reimbursement to then be sought for an FSA. No claim forms need to be filled out when using a prepaid FSA card, as opposed to seeking reimbursement from a non-card FSA. Employers often like prepaid FSA cards because they help encourage the use of FSAs, and to the extent that an employee designates income to be placed in an FSA, the employer is not obligated to pay the nearly employer contribution to Social Security and Medicare under the Federal

Insurance Contribution Act (FICA). The employer contribution is currently 7.65% of the salary/wages paid to the employee, with a cap on the Social Security component.

6. Budget Discipline

Yet other prepaid cards are used for budget discipline purposes. Consumers might give their children prepaid cards as a way of enabling independent spending, within a limit. A child with a credit card or debit card could end up spending far more than the parent would like, whereas a child with a prepaid card can only do limited damage. The budget discipline function is not limited to children, however. Adults will also use prepaid cards as a means of policing their own budgets. For example, a consumer might put $25 on a Starbucks prepaid card. That will be the consumer's coffee allowance for the month. To be sure, nothing prevents the consumer from also using another payment method to satisfy cravings for caffeine and calories, but the separate source of funds provides a payment discipline.

Other consumers will use multiple prepaid cards with different cards being used for payment of different obligations: one card for utilities, another for groceries, another for transportation, etc. Again, this is a form of budget disciplining. Additionally, overdrafting is not possible on most prepaid cards, so they provide a means of avoiding overdraft fees and instilling spending discipline. (Some cards, however, have a credit function and others have NSF fees.)

7. Gifts

Still other prepaid cards are used as gifts, replacing the paper gift certificate. Cash gifts are sometimes thought of as gauche, but not everyone wants to receive a bright red reindeer sweater with fuzzy antlers for a holiday present. A prepaid card can solve the dilemma and help steer between the vulgar Scylla of cash and the tacky Charybdis of ugly sweaters. A prepaid card provides a way of transferring a very generic form of value that leaves the consumption decision in the hands of the recipient, rather than the giver of the gift.

Some prepaid gift cards are issued directly by merchants, creating a form of store credit for the cardholder. Others are issued by consortia of merchants or by shopping malls for use at all stores in the malls. Yet others are general use or "branded" gift cards that carry the logo of a national payment system network such as MasterCard, Visa, or American Express.

8. Loyalty Programs

Some prepaid cards enable loyalty and reward programs from merchants. Prepaid cards can be integrated into systems that track purchases and repeat use can be encouraged and rewarded through various types of coupons. For example, making ten purchases at a coffee shop with the shop's prepaid card might entitle the consumer to a free cup of coffee. The coffee shop is hoping that the consumer will keep coming back in order to use the card to get the free cup of coffee, and that the consumer might make other purchases beside the coffee.

9. Scrip

Certain prepaid cards can only be used to make purchases at a limited number of merchants. Transportation cards are one particular type of scrip card. Others are issued by businesses to employees or universities to students to enable purchases only from the employer or the university or nearby establishments. These cards are primarily used as a way to enable employers and schools to simplify their cash handling. For example, a university could have photocopies in libraries that take cash and coins, but that necessitates collecting the cash and coins from all of the photocopiers on a regular basis. It is easier to have a handful of loading kiosks that issue prepaid cards that can then be used with the photocopiers. Scrip has also started to emerge with digital content, such as for purchases of ring tones, games, and digital media.

10. Phone Cards

A long-standing type of prepaid card is a prepaid phone card, in which a consumer buys a certain number of minutes or telecommunication value. Prepaid cards are used to pay for both long-distance and mobile services. The typical consumer telecom contract involves the carrier extending phone time to the consumer upfront, with payment to follow later. In other words, the carrier extends phone time to the consumer on credit. Prepaid cards reverse the relationship. Mobile telecom carriers typically require a credit check before providing service to a consumer. Consumers who have poor credit can still get a mobile phone by using a prepaid card (which might be merged into the phone itself), such as through Cricket. Prepaid phone cards (or phones) are also attractive to consumers who do not want a long-term contract, want to know all possible fees upfront, or want call-time budgeting (such as phones provided by parents for children). Other utilities and gas stations also make use of prepaid cards, albeit less frequently.

11. Anonymous Purchases and Money Laundering

Not all uses of prepaid cards are so benign. Some prepaid cards also enable anonymous transfers of value. Cash, precious metals, and gemstones still remain the classic ways of transferring value anonymously, either to make embarrassing purchases (e.g., adult materials), to launder the proceeds of criminal activities (e.g., drug dealing or prostitution), or to fund illegal enterprises (including terrorism). Prepaid cards have advantages over their other modes of value transfer. Prepaid cards can be anonymous. Not everyone wishes for his or her financial institution or spouse to know about a purchase at a sex shop. Such a purchase would show up on a credit card or account statement that a spouse might see. Anecdotal evidence suggests that a surprising amount of prepaid card usage is to facilitate anonymous (if legal) purchases.

Prepaid cards are also are discrete and compact. A suitcase full of cash will set off alarm bells; a piece of plastic will not. Moreover, cash, precious metals, and gemstones need to be moved around physically. A prepaid card can be used to transfer funds physically, simply by tendering the card, but it can also be used to make transfers remotely in some cases. It can sometimes be used for making online and telephone purchases, something cash, precious metals, and gemstones cannot be used for. Thus, prepaid cards are of particular interest for money launderers or those who wish to live on life on the lam and not show up "on the grid" as happens to Benjamin Franklin Gates (played by Nicholas Cage) in the film *National Treasure* (2004) when he uses a Visa credit card to pay for a copy of the Declaration of Independence at the National Archives.

B. How Prepaid Cards Function

Despite their variety of uses, prepaid cards vary functionally along only a few dimensions. First, some cards are **reloadable**, while others (such as many gift cards) are not. Reloadable cards are often personalized, with the user's name embossed on the card. The difference matters from a regulatory perspective in terms of the application of anti-money laundering rules. Reloadable cards require cardholder identification verification similar to that required for new bank account holders. Most cards also require activation, which requires the cardholder to provide personal identification information that is verified using a third-party authentication system such as those provided by credit reporting agencies or LexisNexis and enables screening against the Treasury Department's Office of Foreign Asset Control's list of Specially Designated Nationals whose assets are blocked and are prohibited from doing business in the United States because of their involvement with terrorism, narcotics, or human rights abuses. Some reloadable cards, like Treasury's Direct Express card, can only be reloaded via government direct deposit. Others can be reloaded from multiple sources.

A second major distinction among prepaid cards is where they can be used. Some cards are **general-purpose cards** (also known as **open-loop** cards) and others are **limited-purpose cards** (also known as **closed-loop cards**). A general-purpose card will carry the logo or "**bug**" of a payment card network like MasterCard, Visa, or American Express on the front. These cards can be used at any merchant that accepts the particular networks' cards. A limited-purpose card doesn't bear a network "bug" and can only be used at a single merchant or at a set of merchants associated together in a shopping mall or sometimes at a limited number of geographically related merchants. For example, a bus card or a subway card (whether plastic or paper) issued by a public transportation system is a closed-loop debit card.

Similarly, university ID cards that allow funds to be stored on the card are limited-purpose stored value cards. Sometimes these university ID cards can be used not just at the university, but also at nearby establishments. This kind of closed-loop card is sometimes called a hybrid loop card. For example, Georgetown's GOCard and Harvard's Crimson Cash can be used both on- and off-campus, but are hardly general-purpose cards. (There is a separate question about whether universities are engaged in unauthorized banking.) Starbucks cards or gift cards from a store are also stored value products; these types of cards are just plastic version of the rapidly disappearing paper gift certificate.

A third distinction among cards is whether they are **online** or **offline** cards. An online card provides direct access to a database for obtaining authorization for payment. An offline card, in contrast, allows the merchant to capture data at point of sale and subsequently transmit it to a database for authorization.

The fourth functional distinction among prepaid cards is whether they are **accountable** or **unaccountable.** The difference is whether there is any record of the value associated with the card other than the card itself. An unaccountable card is like cash—if you lose it, it's lost, and you lose access to the value associated with the card. A paper subway card is an example of an unaccountable stored value card. An accountable or host-based card has its information also stored on a remote computer system and the card's data can be linked to the owner's identity, like a credit card. This means that, like a credit card, if the card is lost, it can be deactivated and a new card issued. Whether or not a card is accountable can have a major effect regarding what regulations apply to the card.

Some cards can be either accountable or unaccountable. For example, the Washington Metropolitan Transit Authority issues a plastic Metro card called SmarTrip, in addition to paper tickets. The SmarTrip card is a host-based, accountable system, but the cardholder has to register the card online for its accountable features to be useful by registering ownership. In contrast, the Massachusetts Bay Transit Authority's CharlieCard is an unaccountable plastic card. Losing a CharlieCard is no different than losing a paper CharlieTicket.

The online/offline and accountable/unaccountable distinctions are related. An offline unaccountable card would maintain the funds balance solely on the card. An offline accountable card, however, would record the available funds balance on the card, enabling payment authorization without contacting a central database, but also maintain a central data facility elsewhere. Online systems are presumably all accountable, as payment authorization requires contacting a remote facility, although conceivably balance information could be stored on the card and the authorization could consist of security checks unrelated to the balance.

Significantly, a single prepaid card can be used to access funds from multiple sources. Thus, the Georgetown University GOCard can also serve as a student ID card, a stored value card for use on the Georgetown campus and at some nearby merchants, and as a DC Metro card. The funds put on the GOCard are separate from the funds accessible for use of the Metro.

Likewise, some cards have both stored value and credit functions and permit overdrafting. The same idea extends beyond small rectangular plastic cards to electronic devices. If the card is just an access device carrying account and authorization data, that data can be carried in other forms, such as a smartphone or other mobile device.

II. PREPAID CARD PRICING AND FEES

A major way that prepaid cards differ from traditional bank account-linked debit cards is in their pricing. The traditional debit card is part of a suite of retail banking products based around the deposit account. Fee income for the retail banking product suite is generally based on the deposit account or on the use of particular non-standard services, rather than associated with the use of the debit card to access funds from the deposit account. Indeed, the bank wants to encourage the use of the debit card as it is paid swipe or interchange fees by merchants when the card is used to make purchases.

As with a bank account, the issuer of a prepaid card makes spread income on the funds placed on the card. To the extent that funds are not used, that means greater spread income for the card issuer. Indeed, if funds are never used, they may be forfeited to the card issuer; card issuers for gift cards typically count on a certain amount of "breakage," meaning paid, but unclaimed cards. Prepaid card issuers also receive swipe fees from the use of prepaid cards. Prepaid cards, however, do not have an associated retail product suite; all fee revenue on prepaid cards comes from fees on the card themselves, and there is no overdraft fee revenue on prepaid cards.

Prepaid cards boast an enormous variety of fees. The precise constellation (and names) of fees varies by card, making comparison shopping difficult; there is no standard format for disclosure of prepaid card fees. A hardly exhaustive list of fee types includes: fees to buy the card; activation fees; monthly charge or "maintenance fees"; cash withdrawal fees (ATMs, etc.); balance inquiry fees; "convenience fee"—for using a PIN number, rather than a signature to authorize a transaction (card issuers receive lower swipe fee income from PIN transactions); reloading fees; inactivity fees; expiry dates and loss of any unused funds; plan change fees; cancellation fees; paper statements fees; currency conversion fees; bill payment enrollment fees; bill payment fees; replacement card fees; and denied transaction or NSF fees.

These fees can add up. The short-lived Kardashian Kard was estimated to cost $99.95 in fees for a year's use. Hip-hop impresario Russell Simmons's "RushCard" has a pay-as-you-go program that could cost a typical user more than $43 in fees in the first month. (Another RushCard payment plan costs a more modest $17 per month). Recently, a number of low-fee prepaid card options have begun to emerge, such as Bluebird from American Express and WalMart, the WalMart MasterCard brand MoneyCard (offered by a consortium of WalMart, GE Capital, and Green Dot Corp.), and Liquid, a prepaid Visa brand product from Chase. As new institutions enter the prepaid space, it is unclear whether products like the Kardashian Kard and the RushCard will be able to continue to maintain their fee structures.

Even with clear, upfront disclosure of fees, it is far from clear that the disclosure is meaningful, as many of the fees are contingent on consumer usage patterns. For the fee disclosures to enable meaningful comparison shopping, a cardholder would have to be able to predict his or her financial behavior well into the future. Given that prepaid card users are often consumers with more limited means, this may be particularly complicated, as the poor often have volatile and unpredictable financial lives. Accordingly, fee disclosure, even if done punctiliously, may be next to meaningless in terms of ensuring an efficient market and optimal decision making by consumers.

III. REGULATION OF PREPAID CARDS

Prepaid cards raise several regulatory issues. First, there is the question of what regulatory regime applies. Private law remains the major source of prepaid card regulation. Some cards, however, are subject to the Electronic Fund Transfer Act (EFTA) and Regulation E (commonly known as "Reg E"). The application of EFTA/Reg E determines the content and requirement of various disclosures, unauthorized transaction liability rules, error resolution procedures, right to periodic statements and receipts, and, in some cases, what fees may be charged. Because cardholders are creditors of the card issuer, the possibility of card issuer insolvency is a risk for consumers. Some cards are covered by federal deposit insurance, while some, but not all, others are covered by state money transmitter law. Finally, prepaid cards raise a variety of issues for anti-money laundering rules.

A. Private Law

The core regulation of prepaid cards is contract. The cardholder agreement for a prepaid card is the basic document that sets forth the rights of the cardholder and the duties of the card issuer.

Federal and state law sometimes provide mandatory terms for prepaid cards, but many cards are not subject to any formal regulation. In addition, for general-purpose cards, card network rules of American Express, MasterCard, and Visa may govern the terms of the cards. In particular, card networks often have so-called zero-liability policies. It is not clear, however, whether consumers have privity to enforce these "zero-liability" policies for unauthorized cards, which sometimes come with fine print exceptions, and for unaccountable cards, zero liability policies have little meaning.

B. Electronic Fund Transfer Act/Regulation E

Some prepaid cards are regulated by the EFTA and Reg E thereunder, which is administered by the CFPB. Products covered by EFTA/Reg E are subject to a set of rules requiring: initial disclosures of about the terms of the covered transactions, 12 C.F.R. § 1005.7; notification of changes in terms, 12 C.F.R. § 1005.8(a); periodic account statements, 12 C.F.R. § 1005.9(b); transaction receipts for transactions at electronic terminals, such as point-of-sale (POS) terminals and ATMs, 12 C.F.R. § 1005.9(a); limitations on liability for unauthorized transactions, 12 C.F.R. § 1005.6, error resolution processes requiring investigation and written explanations if the financial institution denies there was an error, 12 C.F.R. § 1005.11; and annual error resolution procedure notices, 12 C.F.R. § 1005.8(b). Notably, EFTA disclosures do not mandate the use of a particular format.

Compliance with these provisions is costly for financial institutions. Periodic statements and annual error resolution procedure notice necessitate frequent mailings, which involve costs of paper, printing, and postage. POS and ATM receipt requirements create further costs (some of which might be shifted to other parties by contract). Error resolution investigations and explanations likewise add manpower and paper, printing, and postage costs. Mandatory consumer liability limitations for unauthorized transactions mean that financial institutions bear the risk of most fraud losses. On top of all of this, there are compliance costs. In short, if a prepaid card is subject to EFTA/Reg E, it is a much more expensive product for a financial institution to offer. Unless greater revenue attaches to the card, it will be less profitable that an otherwise identical card not subject to EFTA/Reg E.

The EFTA and Reg E applies only to transfers of funds "initiated through an electronic terminal, telephonic instrument, or computer or magnetic tape so as to order, instruct, or authorize a financial institution to debit or credit an account." 15 U.S.C. § 1693a(6); 12 C.F.R. § 1005.3. This means that there has to be an account controlled by a financial institution. If there is no account at a financial institution involved, then EFTA/Reg E does not apply.

A "financial institution" is a "State or National bank, a State or Federal savings and loan association, a mutual savings bank, a State or Federal credit union, or any other person who, directly or indirectly, holds an account belonging to a consumer." 15 U.S.C. § 1693(a)(9); 12 C.F.R. § 1005.2(i). Thus, everything turns on the definition of "account."

The EFTA defines "account" as "a demand deposit, savings deposit, or other asset account . . . established primarily for personal, family, or household purposes." 15 U.S.C. § 1693a(2). It also expressly includes payroll cards in its definition, although payroll cards are exempt from certain requirements, such as the provision of periodic statements. 12 C.F.R. §§ 1005.2(b)(2), 1005.18(b). Different initial disclosure, liability, and error resolutions rules also apply to payroll cards. 12 C.F.R. § 1005.18(c).

1. Prepaid Cards

In 2016 the CFPB finalized a prepaid card rule, due to go into effect on April 1, 2019.[9] The basic move in the rulemaking is to apply Reg E protection to most prepaid cards by changing the Reg E definition of "account" to include prepaid cards. Specifically, the definition of "account" will be expanded to include a "prepaid account." 12 C.F.R. § 1005.2(b)(3). "Prepaid account" is in turn defined as including payroll accounts, government benefit accounts, accounts marketed or labeled as "prepaid" and redeemable at multiple, unaffiliated merchants or usable at ATMs, and accounts other than checkable accounts that are capable of being loaded with funds subsequent to issuance and can be used for transactions with multiple unaffiliated merchants. 12 C.F.R. § 1005.2(b)(3)(i)(A)-(d). The definition of "prepaid account" expressly excludes health savings accounts, flexible spending arrangements, and transit and parking cards, as well as needs-tested welfare distribution cards,[10] gift cards and certificates, and loyalty program cards. 12 C.F.R. § 1005.2(b)(3)(ii).

9. The CFPB's prepaid rule, 81 Fed. Reg. 84325 (Nov. 22, 2016) will go effective on April 1, 2019, 83 Fed. Reg. 6364 (Feb. 13, 2018).

10. Electronic benefit transfers (EBT) for needs-based government benefits programs like TANF and SNAP (food stamps) are expressly excluded from EFTA. 15 U.S.C. § 1693b(d)(2).

Prepaid cards are generally subject to EFTA requirements, including now standardized account opening disclosures that facilitate comparison shopping, but have modified rules regarding error resolution and liability limitations and the provision of periodic statements. Specifically, in lieu of periodic statements, prepaid card providers may make available to cardholders telephonically or over the Internet balance and transaction history information, including summary totals of fees on a monthly and annual basis. Error resolution and liability rules for lost cards and unauthorized transactions (discussed in Chapter 20) are generally the same, but there is no requirement of provisional account credit for errors with unverified accounts, meaning where the cardholder has not registered ownership.

2. Gift Cards

While "gift cards" are excluded from the definition of "prepaid account," since 2009 some gift cards have been covered by certain provisions of the EFTA/Reg E. These provisions of the EFTA do not depend on there being an "electronic fund transfer." Instead, they are freestanding statutory requirements. 15 U.S.C. § 1693l-1. These requirements apply only to "general-use prepaid cards," "gift certificates," and "store gift cards." Excluded from the definitions of these items are reloadable cards not marketed or labeled as a "gift card" or "gift certificate," prepaid phone cards, promotional, loyalty, and award cards, and all paper gift certificates. 15 U.S.C. § 1693l-1(a)(2)(D).

For gift cards covered by the EFTA, dormancy, inactivity, and service fees (other than an initial charge) are prohibited unless the card has not be used for a year, and the fee and the terms under which it may be assessed have been clearly and conspicuously disclosed on the card itself and the purchaser has been informed of such fee at the before the purchase. 15 U.S.C. § 1693l-1(b)(1)-(3). Only one such fee may be charged in a month. 15 U.S.C. § 1693l-1(b)(2)(C). Expiry dates are also prohibited for gift cards unless the expiry date is more than five years from the date of issue or last load and the expiration terms are clearly and conspicuously stated on the card. 15 U.S.C. § 1693l-1(c).

C. Insolvency Risks

Prepaid cardholders are the creditors of the issuer of the card. If the card issuer becomes insolvent, the cardholders may find that merchants are unwilling to accept their cards for payment or that they cannot access the funds.

If the card issuer is a retailer that files for bankruptcy, the cardholders' situation is unclear. Arguably, the prepaid funds are held in trust for the cardholders and thus not part of the retailer's bankruptcy estate. This would mean that the cardholders would recover all their funds. Some state laws impose such a trust, but they do not require segregation of funds and retailers do not generally segregate the proceeds from the sale of prepaid cards in separate accounts, so it is unclear how a federal bankruptcy court would treat such a case.

Alternatively, the prepaid funds might be part of the issuer's bankruptcy estate, but consumers might have a priority claim under 11 U.S.C. § 507(a)(7) up to a statutory dollar cap for deposits for personal goods not delivered. *See In re WW Warehouse*, 313 B.R. 588 (Bankr. D. Del. 2004) (granting priority treatment to gift certificate holders). Priority status guarantees (non-timely) repayment in full a chapter 11 reorganization, but not in a liquidation. In any case, prepaid cards do not clearly fit into the statutory language, which is designed to protect consumer down payments for household goods. If the trust and priority theories are rejected, then the cardholders would have a general unsecured claim, meaning they will likely have little or no recovery.

If the card issuer is a depository institution, there is a question of whether the prepaid funds are covered by FDIC insurance. Generally, the FDIC arranges for all assets of a failed depository to be transferred to another bank, which will honor the cards, but there is no legal requirement that this occur. If it does not, then absent FDIC insurance coverage, the cardholders will lose their prepaid funds.

The FDIC has issued a General Counsel's opinion indicating that most prepaid cards, including payroll and government benefits cards, would likely be covered by FDIC insurance, but coverage depends on the details of how the card is structured. FDIC insurance will only apply if the card is issued by a depository, which holds the funds in a custodial relationship (it does not matter in whose name the account is formally held), the card is accountable and the owner is identifiable, and the funds are legally owned by the cardholder. If so, the FDIC treats the funds like any other consumer account for purposes of calculating the deposit insurance cap. FDIC General Counsel Opinion No. 8, *Insurability of Funds Underlying Stored Value Cards and Other Nontraditional Access Mechanisms*, 73 Fed. Reg. 67155 (Nov. 13, 2008).

D. State Law

Prepaid cards may be subject to state regulation in several ways. Card issuers may be subject to state money transmitter laws, some states have their own gift card regulation, and state abandoned property laws may apply to unclaimed funds on prepaid cards.

1. State Money Transmitter Laws

Prepaid card issuers may be subject to state money transmitter laws. Forty-five states have non-identical money transmitter laws. Fifteen of the statutes explicitly cover prepaid products. For example, California's Money Transmission Act defines "[m]oney transmission" as including "selling or issuing stored value." Cal. Fin. Code § 2003(o).

State money transmitter laws are primarily safety-and-soundness regulations, including a licensing process with net worth and bonding requirements, criminal background checks for officers and directors, and various ongoing auditing and reporting requirements. State money transmitter laws also typically require that funds deposited with the money transmitter be invested in secure investments and that funds given by a consumer to an agent of a money transmitter be remitted to the transmitter itself within a specified period of time.

Typically depositories and their agents are exempt from licensing, either by statute or because of federal preemption. Issuers of closed-loop cards or cards redeemable only for goods and services, not for cash, are also frequently exempt from state money transmitter licensing. Some states' exemptions are explicit within the money transmitter statute, while others have exemptions pursuant to opinion letters from state banking regulators. For example, Pennsylvania's Department of Banking and Securities has issued opinion letters that exempt payroll debit cards and retailer closed-loop gift cards from the Pennsylvania Money Transmitter Act, 7 P.S. § 6101 *et seq*. *See* Opinion Letter, May 13, 2005 ("Gift Cards Issued by Retail Stores"); Opinion Letter, September 2, 2005 ("Payroll Debit Cards").

Operating without a license may be a crime under state law. *E.g.*, 7 P.S. § 6116. It may also be a federal crime. 18 U.S.C. § 1690 criminalizes unlicensed money transmitting, meaning "transferring funds on behalf of the public by any and all means," if operating without a license is a criminal offense under state law.

2. State Gift Card Laws

State law may impose additional regulations on gift cards, such as limiting fees, expirations, and requiring that funds paid for the cards be held in trust for the cardholders (none, however, currently require segregation of funds). Some of these laws predate the Credit CARD Act's gift card provisions, while others have been updated to track the CARD Act. The extent to which these statutes might be preempted is always an open question when dealing with federally chartered financial institutions.

3. State Abandoned Property Statutes

Every state has an abandoned property statute that provides that such property escheats to the state. (To which state property is escheat is a separate and somewhat complicated issue.) Property is considered abandoned after it has not been used or claimed for a certain period of time and its owner cannot be located. For prepaid cards, these statutes may require unused funds on cards to be turned over to the state after a dormancy period, typically three to five years, if the owner cannot be located. For an anonymous gift card, dormancy alone is sufficient for an escheat, as owners cannot be identified.

Many state statutes, however, exempt prepaid products and gift certificates because the issuer's ability to retain the unused funds or "breakage" is critical to the economics of the card issuance. As long as the issuer retains the funds, it earns interest on them, and if the card expires and the funds are not escheated to the state, they become the issuer's. Anonymous gift cards are typically issued by special purpose gift card companies established in states with favorable escheat laws, while non-anonymous cards are typically designed to have service fees debited such that the card balance will be zero by the time an escheat would occur.

Problem Set 16

1. Trader Bob's Grocery Store sells Bob's Great Gift Cards, a closed-loop, unaccountable, offline prepaid card. Trader Bob's also offers the Bob-O-Link Card, a closed-loop, accountable, online prepaid grocery card. Does Trader Bob's have to provide cardholders with periodic statements for either type of card? *See* 15 U.S.C. §§ 1693a, 1693d(c)-(e); 12 C.F.R. § 1005.2(b).

2. Trader Bob's wants to put a three-year expiry date on Bob's Great Gift Cards. Can Trader Bob's do this? *See* 15 U.S.C. § 1693l-1.

3. You are general counsel at Bindi, a new prepaid card issuer. The folks on the business side of the company would like to avoid the EFTA's restrictions on dormancy fees and forfeitures due to expiry terms because they believe there is a lot of money to be made from such fees, particularly from cards given as gifts during the holiday season that get misplaced by distracted consumers. The business folks have proposed selling a card that is labeled "Gratitude by Bindi" and bears a picture of a Christmas tree in the upper right of the card. The card will be sold at displays that state "Show your Gratitude this holiday season with a Bindi card." *See* 15 U.S.C. § 1693l-1(a)(2)(D).

4. Bindi (from problem 3) is also contemplating charging a one-time "network security fee" to cover its anti-money laundering compliance costs prorated by the number of cards it has issued. Is it permitted to do so? *See* 15 U.S.C. §§ 1693l-1(a)(3), (b); 12 C.F.R. § 1005.20(a)(6).

5. Darth Vaper, a chain of smokeless tobacco stores, has been paying its employees through payroll cards. On payday (every two weeks), Darth Vaper transfers funds from its master account at Banco Merica to the accounts for individual employees' cards.

   a. When Darth Vaper files for bankruptcy because of a tort judgment related to the health effects of its vapes, who owns the balances on employees' payroll cards?

   b. What would the impact be on Darth Vaper employees with balances on their payroll cards if Banco Merica were to fail?

CHAPTER 17

ANTI-MONEY LAUNDERING REGULATIONS

I. MONEY LAUNDERING AND CRIME

Money laundering is the process of making the proceeds of illegal activities appear to be legal. Federal (and state) statutes provide for the forfeiture of criminal proceeds. *See* 18 U.S.C. §§ 982, 1963; 21 U.S.C. § 853. Moreover, some types of criminal proceeds can potentially be traced and therefore result in the criminal's apprehension. Accordingly, criminal enterprises have a strong interest in making dirty money appear to be clean and usable like any other funds. Hence the term money "laundering."

Related to making dirty money appear clean is the process of transferring funds among actors within a criminal enterprise undetected. For example, domestic U.S. supporters of an illegal foreign terrorist organization may wish to transfer funds to that terrorist organization, or members of that terrorist organization may wish to transfer funds to other members. The parties to these transfers do not want their transfers to be traceable to law enforcement or national security agencies. While the funds being transferred may have perfectly legal origins, the transfers to or between criminal actors are also called money laundering. Although these two types of money laundering are distinct, they both share a goal of making funds hard to trace, and, to that end, involve a common three-stage process of placement, layering, and integration.

Placement is the movement of funds away from direct association with the crime. For example, a drug dealer may control a merchant, Aunt Dottie's Ice Cream Parlor, that has a bank account with Fidelity Fiduciary Bank (FFB). The drug dealer will mix in the cash proceeds from drug sales with cash proceeds from ice cream sales to deposit at FFB. At this point the dirty money has been placed into the financial system and disassociated with the drugs.

Layering involves further transfers to make the funds hard to trace. Layering often involves transfers through offshore accounts and sham transactions between shell companies to make it appear as if there are legitimate business transactions occurring. Thus, our drug dealer might have funds moved via wire transfer from the ice cream parlor's account at FFB to an offshore account at Bank of the Caymans (BoC) held in the name of a shell company, Acme, Ltd. Acme, Ltd. will use the funds to make a loan to a second shell company, Emca, Ltd. that is supposedly an ice cream supplier. Emca, Ltd. will then use the funds to pay a false invoice from Cool Beans, with the payment being deposited back at FFB. The money has made a global round trip right back to FFB, but it now appears to have absolutely no association with the drug dealing.

The final step then is **integration**—making the cleansed funds available again to the criminal. This part is easy. The drug dealer who controls Aunt Dottie's Ice Cream Parlor dividends or loans himself funds from the deposit account at FFB, which he uses to buy a yacht, a jet ski, a Ferrari, a race horse, a small office building, and various investments for his 401(k). QED.

If the criminal wants to move the funds internationally, it can be done through a set of wash financial transactions between an account controlled by the criminal in one country and an account controlled by the same criminal in another country. The criminal might enter into a set of matched swap agreements with FFB, one swap agreement being domestic and the other with an account at FFB that was opened by the criminal in a different country. The swap will be such that the domestic account will surely end up paying out on it to the foreign account. Other than the transaction costs involved, the effect of the swap will be a wash from the criminal's perspective, but the money can be shifted internationally while appearing to be moved through legitimate transactions.

II. THE ANTI-MONEY LAUNDERING SYSTEM

Anti-money laundering (AML) laws are a key part of criminal law enforcement and anti-terrorism activities. The problem law enforcement faces is that there is an overwhelming volume of transactions occurring in the United States on a daily basis. Even in an age of supercomputers, it is not possible for law enforcement to analyze every one of those transactions. Moreover, most transactions are informationally limited at least in terms of what a financial institution can see. A bank can see the names and general locations of merchants at which a consumer makes a credit or debit card purchase and the general nature of the merchant's business, but not the specific items purchased (or even how many), much less whether the purchase was actually a sham and no goods or services were rendered. Likewise, with a check, a payor bank can see the supposed name of the payee, but the only thing the payor bank really knows is the account and routing number on the check. There is no way to tell what the check was written for. ACH and wire transfers present the same type of limited information. What this means is that even with adequate computing power, there's no easy way to tell through automation if a transaction is a money-laundering transaction or not; some further human investigation is necessary.

Privacy concerns, however, counsel against allowing the government to simply examine all financial transactions, and a statute called the Right to Financial Privacy Act, 12 U.S.C. §§ 3401-3422, limits the federal government's ability to obtain consumer financial records absent a warrant or subpoena. Given this constraint, the basic design of AML laws is to deputize (or dragoon) financial institutions into doing a first cut of identifying potential money-laundering transactions and reporting these suspicious transactions to the government. The government then has a much more limited set of transactions to investigate using its finite human resources.

The legislative hook for this deputization is the Bank Secrecy Act, 31 U.S.C. § 5311 *et seq.* and the Treasury Department regulations thereunder, 31 C.F.R. Chapter X. The Bank Secrecy Act authorizes various reporting and record keeping requirements (implemented by regulation) and sets forth penalties for noncompliance.

A wide range of financial institutions are subject to AML regulations: banks, thrifts, and credit unions and the operators of credit card networks, but also casinos, commodities and securities brokers and dealers, mutual funds, and a category of entities known as "money services businesses" (MSBs). MSBs include coin dealers, check cashers, sellers of travelers' checks and money orders, the U.S. Postal Service, money transmitters, and various parties involved in the issuance and sale of prepaid cards. 31 C.F.R. § 1010.100(ff). Strangely excluded from the definition are payments processors—non-bank parties that connect merchants to payment networks such as MasterCard and Visa. 31 C.F.R. § 1010.100(ff)(5)(ii)(B).

Several consequences flow from having an AML system that relies on financial institutions to identify potential money-laundering transactions. First, financial institutions need to have in place systems for identifying suspicious transactions. This requires them to have AML compliance programs. *See, e.g.*, 31 C.F.R. § 1020.210 (AML programs for depositories); 31 C.F.R. § 1022.210 (AML programs for money services businesses).

The components of an AML program differ by institution type. For depositories, it involves having a set of internal procedures and controls to conduct customer due diligence and identify suspicious transactions as required by regulation, having appropriate training for personnel, having a designated AML point person, and undertaking compliance testing. 31 C.F.R. § 1022.210(b). For other financial institutions the requirements differ, but still include having procedures in place to identify suspicious transactions, employee training, and a point person for AML compliance.

A second consequence of financial institutions being deputized as the first level of AML screening is that financial institutions need to be able to identify their customers. This is necessary not just because of the off chance that a customer is a wanted individual or on a government sanctions list, but because of the use of shell companies and mules in money-laundering transactions. If financial institutions can identify their customers, it enables law enforcement to subsequently piece together transactional relationships. As a result, bank AML compliance programs include so-called **know your customer (KYC)** rules, requiring the implementation of a **Customer Identification Program (CIP)** for verifying the identity of a person opening an account at a depository, 31 C.F.R. § 1020.220, and for verifying the identity of a person engaging in a transaction that trips the AML threshold. 31 C.F.R. § 1010.312.

CIP requirements do not exist for all types of institutions subject to AML regulations. Instead, they exist for depositories and credit unions, as well as for broker-dealers, mutual funds, and commodities futures merchants. In other words, there are no CIP requirements for MSBs or for third-party loan or finance companies (non-bank finance companies that do not make residential mortgage loans are not covered by AML regulations at all).

CIP requirements apply to anyone opening an "account" at a bank. That includes deposit accounts, credit cards, and other bank loans, but also reloadable prepaid cards. When opening an account, the bank must obtain sufficient identifying information about the consumer's name, date of birth (if an individual), address, and an identification number (Social Security number, taxpayer identification number, or, for foreigners, a passport number). 31 C.F.R. § 1020.220(2)(i)(A). Such identifying information may be obtained from a third party for credit card accounts. 31 C.F.R. § 1020.220(2)(i)(C).

Information verification under a CIP may be done through either documentary or non-documentary sources, but documentary sources are preferred and, for individuals, should include a non-expired government identification with a photograph. 31 C.F.R. § 1020.220(2)(ii)(A). Non-documentary sources can include comparison of information provided by the consumer with information from a consumer reporting agency or public database or by checking references with other financial institutions. 31 C.F.R. § 1020.220(2)(ii)(B). If a bank account is opened in a corporate name, the bank must be able to identify the ultimate beneficial owner(s) of the account. 31 C.F.R. § 1010.620(b)(1). Given the layering of corporate ownership, where one entity can own another and yet another, and the possibility of minority interests in entities, etc., this can be a substantial challenge.

The third consequence of financial institutions being pressed into the AML system is that financial institutions need to maintain records of transactions, including of customer identification, so law enforcement can later examine those records if the need arises. Financial institutions are required to maintain for five years records of transactions over the reporting threshold. 31 C.F.R. §§ 1010.410, 1022.400. Non-bank financial institutions are further required to keep records of funds transmittals over $3,000. 31 C.F.R. §§ 1010.410(e), 1022.400.

The fourth consequence of the use of financial institutions as screeners in the AML system is that financial institutions are required to report certain transactions to law enforcement authorities.

Two types of transactions trigger the reporting requirement. First are "deposit, withdrawal, exchange of currency or other payment or transfer" of more than $10,000 in a single day. 31 C.F.R. §§ 1010.311, 1010.313. The bright-line $10,000 reporting rule by itself would invite easy evasion by **"structuring"** transactions to evade detection, particularly by splitting them into smaller component transactions, a practice known as **"smurfing."** Attempting to evade AML requirements via transaction structuring or providing assistance in such structuring is itself illegal. 31 U.S.C. § 5324; 31 C.F.R. § 1010.314. Financial institutions are supposed to keep an eye out for structured transactions and other suspicious transaction patterns. Thus, the second type of transaction that triggers a reporting requirement is simply a "suspicious transaction."

The definition of "suspicious transaction" is somewhat different for banks and for money services businesses. For banks, a suspicious transaction is a transaction that "involves or aggregates at least $5,000," and for which the financial institution "knows, suspects, or has reason to suspect," that

> (i) The transaction involves funds derived from illegal activities or is intended or conducted in order to hide or disguise funds or assets derived from illegal activities (including, without limitation, the ownership, nature, source, location, or control of such funds or assets) as part of a plan to violate or evade any Federal law or regulation or to avoid any transaction reporting requirement under Federal law or regulation;
> (ii) The transaction is designed to evade any requirements of this chapter or of any other regulations promulgated under the Bank Secrecy Act; or
> (iii) The transaction has no business or apparent lawful purpose or is not the sort in which the particular customer would normally be expected to engage, and the bank knows of no reasonable explanation for the transaction after examining the available facts, including the background and possible purpose of the transaction.

31 C.F.R. § 1020.320(a)(2). For money services businesses, the trigger amount is $2,000 and, in addition to the three additional factors for banks to consider, there is a factor of the money services business knowing or suspecting that the transaction "involves the use of the money services business to facilitate criminal activity." 31 C.F.R. § 1022.320(a)(2).

Financial institutions are required to file **Suspicious Activity Reports** or **SARs** on all such transactions regardless of dollar amount. 31 C.F.R. §§ 1010.320, 1022.320. The reports must be filed within 30 days of the transaction with the **Financial Crimes Enforcement Network (FinCEN)**, a bureau in the Treasury Department, which is the primary agency tasked with combatting money laundering. 31 C.F.R. § 1010.320(b).

Finally, buttressing the entire financial institution-based AML system are strict penalties not just for money laundering, 18 U.S.C. §§ 1956-57, but for financial institutions that fail to have adequate AML compliance programs, 12 U.S.C. § 1818; 31 U.S.C. §§ 5321-22. These penalties are needed because financial institutions themselves gain nothing directly from AML compliance. Instead, their only incentive to have AML compliance programs is to avoid penalties. Given that the AML system depends on financial institution participation, regulators—and here it includes criminal law enforcement authorities—tend to take a sterner view of AML violations than on consumer protection violations.

III. PREPAID CARDS AND MONEY LAUNDERING

A key part of money laundering is getting funds into the formal financial system in order to take advantage of the payment system, which is by far the easiest way to move value between parties. Some forms of value, such a gems and gold (and once upon a time before they were banned in the United States, bearer bonds) are hard to trace, but they are not the most readily liquid assets, particularly when dealing with large values. Cash is, of course, liquid, and unless bills are marked or serial numbers noted, it is hard to trace, but cash is bulky for large-value transfers. It is easy enough to carry $10,000 in a suitcase, but $10 million is another matter.

Prepaid cards offer a solution to this problem in money laundering. Because of their convenience and potential anonymity, prepaid cards have become a recent favorite of money launderers. Prepaid cards can be used in each stage of money laundering. Illegal funds can be used to purchase and load prepaid cards. Funds can then be layered through transfers between prepaid cards or with ATM withdrawals for cash that is then used to purchase and load further prepaid cards. Finally, prepaid cards can be used to integrate the funds by providing the medium for purchases of other assets or for cash withdrawals or overseas remittances.

Prepaid cards raise special AML issues. Recall that AML rules apply to "**money services businesses**" (MSBs), which is defined to include providers and sellers of prepaid cards (referred to in the regulations as "prepaid access") and also money transmitters. 31 C.F.R. § 1010.100(ff)(4), (5), (7). MSBs are subject to somewhat different AML requirements than banks. We've already seen that MSBs have a different definition of "suspicious activity" for which a SAR must be filed—most notably a $2,000 rather than a $5,000 threshold.

Additionally, MSBs are required to register with FinCEN. 31 C.F.R. § 1022.380. There is an exception, however for "sellers of prepaid access" as well as one for entities that are MSBs solely on account of being agents of MSBs. 31 C.F.R. § 1022.380. The registration requirement is backed up by criminal penalties that are separate from and additional to a requirement that any MSB that is a "money transmitter" be licensed. 18 U.S.C. § 1960. Special CIP requirements and record-keeping requirements also apply to providers and sellers of prepaid access. 31 C.F.R. §§ 1022.210(d)(iv), 1022.420.

IV. CREDIT CARD LAUNDERING

The Telemarketing Sales Rule, 16 C.F.R. Part 310, under the Telemarketing and Consumer Fraud and Abuse Prevention Act, 15 U.S.C. §§ 6101-6108, prohibits deceptive acts and practices in telemarketing. While telemarketing regulation primarily involves sales issues, it does have some consumer finance angles as well. Among the provisions of the Telemarketing Sales Rules is a prohibition against "credit card laundering" (also known as "factoring"), which is the practice of one merchant submitting another merchant's credit card sales drafts to its bank for processing as if they were its own. Thus, a consumer might give its card information to one merchant, which lacks a credit card processing relationship, and that merchant will give the information to another merchant to submit as if the transaction were performed with the second merchant. The second merchant will presumably take a payment from the first merchant for this, probably in the form of a discounted remission when it is paid on the transaction.

Credit card laundering is typically done to mask consumer fraud: the first merchant might be a fraudulent telemarketer that accepts payments for goods that are never shipped. The telemarketer is unable to get a credit card merchant account with a bank because it is too risky: the telemarketer will owe too many refunds to defrauded consumers and might abscond without paying them. Under credit card network rules, the telemarketer's bank would be left on the hook for the refunds. The second merchant participates based on either sympathy with a concocted story by the first merchant (*e.g.*, "I'm a new business that needs help because I'm not established enough yet to get a merchant account.") or a promise of "guaranteed" easy income in the form of a cut of the first merchant's receipts.

While the Telemarketing Sales Rule is generally limited to telemarketing transactions, the credit card laundering prohibition is drafted to apply to "any person" who obtains "access to the credit card system through the use of a business relationship or affiliation with a merchant, when such access is not authorized by the merchant agreement or the applicable credit card system." 16 C.F.R. § 301.3(c)(3). The prohibition applies not only to the first merchant—that is, the one that obtains access to the credit card system improperly—but also to any party that knowingly (or with conscious avoidance of knowledge) "provides substantial assistance or support." 16 C.F.R. § 301.3(b). Thus, the merchant that submits the receipts is potentially liable for a Telemarketing Sales Rule violation as well.

The substantial assistance provision is not limited to the second merchant, however. It also covers payment processors and banks that knowingly (or with conscious avoidance of knowledge) permit credit card laundering. Thus, a payment processor that turns a deliberate blind eye to red flags of fraud, such as excessive **chargeback** (transaction reversal) rates, or patterns of short-term usage (designed to avoid notice, much like smurfing) has potentially violated the Telemarketing Sales Rule.

The FTC and CFPB both enforce the Telemarketing Sales Rule, but the prohibition on credit card laundering applies only to, well, credit cards. It does not apply to other payment methods, such as debit cards or ACH. Instead, laundering and assistance to laundering in those contexts are covered by the Bank Secrecy Act reporting and record-keeping requirements, 31 U.S.C. § 5311 *et seq.*, and by federal statutes covering wire fraud, mail fraud, and bank fraud and the Anti-Fraud Injunction Act, 18 U.S.C. §§ 1341-1345. For banks that assist in such schemes, civil liability is increased by the Financial Institutions Reform, Recovery, and Enforcement Act (FIRREA), 12 U.S.C. § 1833a, upon a predicate violation of the bank fraud statute, 18 U.S.C. § 1344.

V. AML AND CONSUMER FRAUD: OPERATION CHOKE POINT

In 2013, the Department of Justice announced an initiative called "Operation Choke Point," aimed at prosecuting AML violations by payment processors relating to consumer fraud. The Department of Justice has wide-ranging authority to investigate fraud, including wire fraud "affecting a federally insured financial institution,"[1] and a Bank Secrecy Act violation can constitute the predicate illegal activity for wire fraud, which in turn can trigger FIRREA civil liability. The Department of Justice's strategy is explained in the speech excerpted below.

1. 12 U.S.C. § 1833a(a), (c), (g); 18 U.S.C. § 1343 (wire fraud).

Remarks of Michael J. Bresnick, Executive Director, Financial Fraud Enforcement Task Force, at the Exchequer Club of Washington, DC, Mar. 20, 2013

. . .

[The federal-state Financial Fraud Enforcement Task Force's Consumer Protection Working Group is] investigating the businesses that process payments on behalf of the fraudulent merchants—financial intermediaries referred to as third-party payment processors. It's this third priority that I'd like to discuss in a little more detail.

The reason that we are focused on financial institutions and payment processors is because they are the so-called bottlenecks, or choke-points, in the fraud committed by so many merchants that victimize consumers and launder their illegal proceeds. For example, third-party payment processors are frequently the means by which fraudulent merchants are able to get paid.[2] They provide the scammers with access to the national banking system and facilitate the movement of money from the victim of the fraud to the scam artist. And financial institutions through which these fraudulent proceeds flow, we have seen, are not always blind to the fraud. In fact, we have observed that some financial institutions actually have been complicit in these schemes, ignoring their BSA/AML obligations, and either know about—or are willfully blind to— the fraudulent proceeds flowing through their institutions.

Our prioritization of this issue is based on this principle: If we can eliminate the mass-marketing fraudsters' access to the U.S. financial system—that is, if we can stop the scammers from accessing consumers' bank accounts—then we can protect the consumers and starve the scammers. This will significantly reduce the frequency of and harm caused by this type of fraud. We hope to close the access to the banking system that mass marketing fraudsters enjoy—effectively putting a chokehold on it—and put a stop to this billion dollar problem that has harmed so many American consumers, including many of our senior citizens.

Sadly, what we've seen is that too many banks allow payment processors to continue to maintain accounts within their institutions, despite the presence of glaring red flags

---

2. Some ACH transactions involve a Third-Party Payment Processor (TPPP). A TPPP serves as an agent for the Originator. The Originator will transmit the transaction information to the TPPP, which will in turn transmit the information to the ODFI. In some cases, TPPP are allowed to have direct access to the ACH Operator for debit transactions. NACHA Rule 8.2.2.8.

There are legitimate uses of TPPP, which have specialization and technical capacities many Originators lack. The use of TPPPs began in the context of payroll management firms that were making ACH *credit* transactions (direct deposit), where funds were being transferred *to* consumers' accounts. ACH debit involves transfers *from* consumers' accounts and raises concerns about whether the transactions are authorized.

NACHA Rules aim to ensure the integrity of the ACH payment system and the trust and confidence of its users. Accordingly, NACHA Rules require ODFIs to monitor Originators' or TPPP's return rates for unauthorized transactions. NACHA Rules currently have a 1% threshold for unauthorized transaction return rates; a pending proposal would lower the threshold to 0.5%. NACHA Rules 2.17.2.1, 10.2.1.

indicative of fraud, such as high return rates on the processors' accounts.* High return rates trigger a duty by the bank and the third-party payment processor to inquire into the reasons for the high rate of returns, in particular whether the merchant is engaged in fraud.

Nevertheless, we have actually seen instances where the return rates on processors' accounts have exceeded 30%, 40%, 50%, and, even 85%. Just to put this in perspective, the industry average return rate for ACH transactions is less than 1.5%, and the industry average for all bank checks processed through the check clearing system is less than one-half of one percent. Return rates at the levels we have seen are more than red flags. They are ambulance sirens, screaming out for attention.

A perfect example of the type of activity I'm talking about is the recent complaint against the First Bank of Delaware filed by the Department in the Eastern District of Pennsylvania, in Philadelphia. There, investigators found that in just an eleven-month period from 2010 to 2011, the First Bank of Delaware permitted four payment processors to process more than $123 million in transactions. Amazingly, more than half of the withdrawal transactions that the bank originated during this time were rejected, either because the consumer complained that the transaction was unauthorized, there were insufficient funds to complete the transaction, or the account was closed, each of which may indicate potential fraud and trigger the need for further inquiry. But the bank did nothing. Nothing, but continue to collect its fees per transaction, while consumers continued to get gouged by unscrupulous scam artists. Ultimately, the government alleged that the bank was engaged in a scheme to defraud under the Financial Institutions Reform, Recovery, and Enforcement Act and the bank agreed to pay a civil money penalty before surrendering its charter and closing its doors.

Underscoring the importance of this case, in the press release announcing a parallel action with the Financial Crimes Enforcement Network, the Acting Chairman of the FDIC, Martin Gruenberg, said, "Effective Bank Secrecy Act and anti-money laundering programs that are commensurate with the risk profile of the institution are vital to protecting our financial system." He added that "[t]he significant penalty assessed in this case emphasizes the importance of having strong internal controls to assure compliance with anti-money laundering regulations and to detect and report potential money laundering or other illicit financial activities."

So, the First Bank of Delaware is a model of irresponsible behavior by a bank.

Of course, this conduct is completely unacceptable. And it is receiving significant attention from the Department of Justice. In fact, right now within the Civil Division there are attorneys and investigators who are investigating similar unlawful conduct,

* ["Return" is ACH parlance for "bounce," but it may be triggered both by insufficient funds for payment or by the payor contesting the payment's authorization. In an ACH debit transaction, the payee's bank places a payment request with the payor's bank and in the process warrants that the transaction was authorized, that the transaction complies with NACHA Rules, including that the ACH entries do not "violate the laws of the United States." The payee's bank also indemnifies the payor's bank for any costs arising from an unauthorized transaction. NACHA Rules 2.4.1 (ODFI warranties to RDFI); 2.4.4 (ODFI indemnification of RDFI). This means that the payee's bank will be on the hook for any funds in an ACH return. It will have the right to recover them from the payee, but if the payee is out of business or insolvent, the payee's bank will bear the loss. The important point to see here is that the payee's bank is vouching for the transaction and may be liable for it. —ED.]

and they will not hesitate to act when they see evidence of wrongdoing. Our message to banks is this: Maintaining robust BSA/AML policies and procedures is not merely optional or a polite suggestion. It is absolutely necessary, and required by law. Failure to do so can result in significant civil, or even criminal, penalties under the Bank Secrecy Act, FIRREA, and other statutes.

Consequently, banks should endeavor not only to know their customers, but also to know their customers' customers. Before they agree to do business with a third-party payment processor, banks should strive to learn more about the processors' merchant-clients, including the names of the principals, the location of the business, and the products being sold, among other things. If they are going to allow their institutions to be used by others as a gateway to access the bank accounts of our nation's consumers, banks need to know for whom they are processing payments. Because if they don't, they might be allowing some unscrupulous scam artist to be taking the last dollars of a senior citizen who fell prey to another fraud scheme, and hundreds of millions of dollars of additional proceeds of fraud to flow through their institutions. And in that case, they might later find themselves in the unfortunate position of the First Bank of Delaware.

In addition, as part of our focus on the role of financial institutions and third-party payment processors in mass-marketing fraud schemes, we naturally also are examining banks' relationship with the payday lending industry, known widely as a subprime and high-risk business. We are aware, for instance, that some payday lending businesses operating on the Internet have been making loans to consumers in violation of the state laws where the borrowers reside. And, as discussed earlier, these payday lending companies are able to take the consumers' money primarily because banks are originating debit transactions against consumers' bank accounts. This practice raises some questions.

As you know, the Bank Secrecy Act demands that banks have effective compliance programs to prevent illegal use of the banking system by the banks' clients. Bank regulatory guidance exhorts banks to collect information sufficient to determine whether a client poses a threat of criminal or other unlawful conduct.

Banks, therefore, should consider whether originating debit transactions on behalf of Internet payday lenders—particularly where the loans may violate state laws—is consistent with their BSA obligations.

Understandably, it may not be so simple a task for a bank to determine whether the loans being processed through it are in violation of the state law where the borrower resides. The ACH routing information, for example, may not indicate to the bank in which state the consumer lives, and variations in state laws could preclude blanket conclusions. Yet, at a minimum, banks might consider determining the states where the payday lender makes loans, as well as what types of loans it offers, the APR of the loans, and whether it make loans to consumers in violation of state, as well as federal, laws. By asking these questions, a bank may become aware of certain red flags, inviting further scrutiny and further action. The bury-your-head-in-the-sand approach, to the contrary, is certain to result in no action, even where some might be warranted, and is fraught with danger to consumers.

It comes down to this: When a bank allows its customers, and even its customers' customers, access to the national banking system, it should endeavor to understand the true nature of the business that it will allow to access the payment system, and the risks posed to consumers and society regarding criminal or other unlawful conduct.

Operation Choke Point resulted in only a handful of prosecutions but proved highly controversial. While the Department of Justice did not bring many actions under Operation Choke Point before it was terminated, it seems to have prompted banks to reexamine their Bank Secrecy Act/Anti-Money Laundering compliance, as well as their NACHA Rules compliance. In some case this might have resulted in banks deciding it was more cost effective to terminate business relationships than to undertake the necessary steps to ensure that the relationship was in compliance with the necessary legal requirements. The result was that some high-risk businesses, such as gun dealers, pornographers, sellers of drug paraphernalia, coin dealers, online gambling websites, and payday lenders, found their access to the ACH system—and to the banking system as a whole—cut off. Critics of Operation Choke Point alleged that it was undertaken to quash disfavored industries, as opposed to industries with high incidence of consumer fraud. In any event, Operation Choke Point illustrates that markets can be regulated (intentionally or not) through indirect regulation of their service providers. It also illustrates the far-ranging effects of AML regulations.

Problem Set 17

1. A-B-Pharma-C sells Visa Vanilla prepaid gift cards. These are open-loop, anonymous, accountable, online prepaid cards. The balance on a card can be checked, but the cardholder remains anonymous. Does this program require A-B-Pharma-C to register with FinCEN? To maintain an anti-money laundering compliance program? Retain records of consumers' card transactions? *See* 31 C.F.R. § 1010.100(ff)(4)(iii), 1010.100(ff)(5)(2)(e), 1010.100(ff)(7), 1022.380(a)(1), 1022.210, 1010.410.

2. Trader Bob's Grocery Store is offering the Bob-O-Link Card, a closed-loop, accountable, online prepaid grocery card as a means of helping families manage their food budgets. Consumers have to register with Trader Bob's when they open the card. The Trader Bob's card has a load limit of $1,000 per month. Does Trader Bob's have to verify the identification of the purchaser of the cards? *See* 31 C.F.R. § 1010.312.

3. Does Trader Bob's have to register with FinCEN on the basis of the Bob-O-Link card? Does it have an anti-money laundering compliance program on the basis of Bob-O-Link card program? Retain records of consumers' card transactions? *See* 31 C.F.R. § 1010.100(ff)(4)(iii), 1010.100(ff)(5)(2)(e), 1010.100(ff)(7), 1022.380(a)(1), 1022.210, 1010.410.

4. Trader Bob's also sells Bob's Great Gift Cards, a closed-loop, unaccountable, offline prepaid card. Does this program require Trader Bob's to register with FinCEN? To maintain an anti-money laundering compliance program? Retain records of consumers' card transactions? If so, for how long? *See* 31 C.F.R. § 1010.100(ff)(4)(iii), 1010.100(ff)(5)(2)(e), 1010.100(ff)(7), 1022.380(a)(1), 1022.210, 1010.410, 1022.420.

5. You found yourself talking with your new neighbor, Mrs. Gates. It turns out that her son Billy and his friend Steve-O are the wunderkind programmers who have designed an amazingly addictive iOS app called Brainrot. In order to advance in Brainrot, virtually any player will have to make purchases of lives, energy, ammunition, gold, and gems. These items will not be used immediately but will instead be stored and available for the player's use. If a player were to somehow pull away from the game and return to the human society for a week, the lives, energy, etc. would be waiting for him on his return. The game can be accessed anywhere; the player's information is stored in the cloud. Brainrot is a multiplayer game, and players can share their in-game purchases with each other. In fact, a common practice is for player to chip in and give each other's avatars birthday presents in the form of in-game purchases. Is there anything you think of mentioning to Mrs. Gates?

6. Jimmy Cravolliton, a creepy permanent associate in your firm's tax department, has dropped by your office late one evening when few people are still at the firm. Jimmy tells you that he knows that you're the firm's AML guru and that he's got to go on a long trip and it is *very* important that no one can track his whereabouts, including through his payments. Having watched Nicholas Cage in *National Treasure*, he's worried that using his credit card will be a dead giveaway of his location. You get the feeling that it wouldn't be wise to blow him off or steer him wrong. What do you say to Jimmy? *See* Model Rules of Professional Conduct 1.2(d), 1.4(a)(5), 1.6(a)-(b), 8.3, 8.4.

7. You are the Chief Compliance Officer at Cashex, a third-party payment processor that processes credit card payments on behalf of its merchant clients.

   a. One of Cashex's clients, Aunt Dottie's Ice Cream Parlor, has had a very high rate of chargebacks—over 60% of its aggregate dollar volume. Virtually all of the chargebacks relate, however, to just 1% of its transactions—those for more than $1,000. What are you worried about? *See* 16 C.F.R. § 310.3(b); 18 U.S.C. §§ 1343, 1344, 1349. What obligations do you have? *See* 31 C.F.R. § 1010.100(ff)(5)(ii)(B). Would you have concerns if there were no chargebacks, but a steady stream of $1,000 or larger transactions?

   b. Upon instruction from its merchant clients, Cashex creates a payment device known as remotely created check (RCC, also called a demand draft or a remotely created payment order) in the name of a consumer, drawn on the consumer's bank account (complete with bank routing number and account number). The RCC looks like a regular check, but it is not signed by the payor, but rather by Cashex, asserting authority to sign on behalf of the payor. Cashex then deposits the RCC at its bank, Metropolitan Bancorp, which in turn presents the check to the consumer's bank for payment. Last year, on behalf of five merchant-clients, Cashex deposited at Metropolitan Bancorp over 1.3 million RCCs, with a face amount of $45 million. Over half of the RCCs were returned unpaid by the consumers' banks on the grounds that the consumers had not authorized the checks or that the merchant had breached a warranty. Does Cashex face any liability? *See* 18 U.S.C. §§ 1341-1345. How about Metropolitan Bancorp? *See* 12 U.S.C. § 1833a; 31 C.F.R. §§ 1010.320, 1022.320.

CHAPTER 18

PAYMENT SYSTEMS I: PAPER PAYMENTS

I. PAYMENTS IN SOCIETY

Payments are the most basic and critical function of consumer finance. While it is easy to take payment systems for granted, they are the core infrastructure of all commerce. Payment systems provide a means of transferring value in the present in a monetary medium. Absent payment systems, we would be reduced to barter.

To see just how important payments are, imagine how you would purchase a computer in a world of barter. What do you have that Apple would be willing to barter for? Indeed, how would Apple pay its employees and suppliers in a barter economy? It could give them computers, of course, but what if Apple had to pay someone for less than the value of a full computer? Could it give them a lot of keyboards and mice? Barter puts serious constraints on economic activity by making the units of exchange lumpy, which potentially frustrates transactions.

Accordingly, one of the great advances in commerce was the development of money. Money can take any number of forms—paper, specie, wampum, beaver pelts, camels and cattle, and electronic credits—but it always represents a medium of value. Money is only valuable, however, to the extent that it is accepted as a medium of value. If I refuse to accept the form of money you offer as payment, your money is of less value. Indeed, the nature of money is that it has huge **network effects** or **network externalities**. If you are the only person who accepts dollars as money, the dollars have no value. If I also accept the dollars as money, they have some value, however. The value of dollars to both you and me increases with each additional person who accepts them as currency. Thus, there is a positive externality from acceptance of currency. Thus, a U.S. dollar is more useful than a Swedish kröner (unless, perhaps, if you are in Sweden). Put another way, the value of money depends on whether it is accepted.

Some forms of money have some inherent consumption value: cattle and camels can be consumed or milked, pelts can be transformed into clothing, but generally there is a trade-off between forms of money with consumption value and forms with greater convenience and durability. While cattle can be consumed, they aren't easy to move around, require care and resources to maintain, and have limited life-spans (although they can also reproduce). On the other hand a currency like wampum (shells) or paper money can be easily transported, does not require care to maintain, and has a life-span potentially longer than a person's.

Figures 18.1 through 18.4 present some basic statistical information about U.S. payment systems. Figures 18.1 and 18.2 show consumer payment system market share over time by number of transactions and by dollar volume. A few big trends are apparent. First, checks have been steadily declining as a payment system in both number and volume. Cash has been declining in terms of number of transactions but has maintained a steady share of dollar volume. Replacing check transactions have been first and foremost debit card transactions, but also other payment systems, primarily **automated clearing house (ACH)** transactions.

Figure 18.1 U.S. Consumer Payments Market Share by Number of Transactions[1]

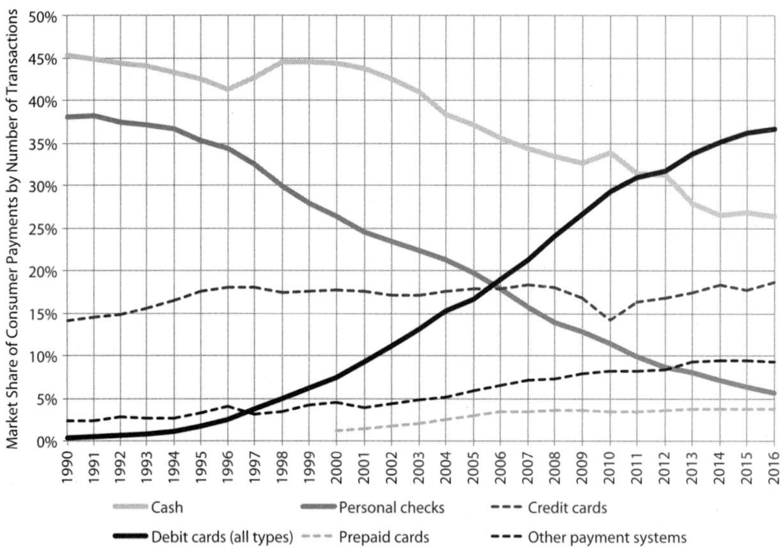

Figure 18.2 U.S. Consumer Payments Market Share by Dollar Volume[2]

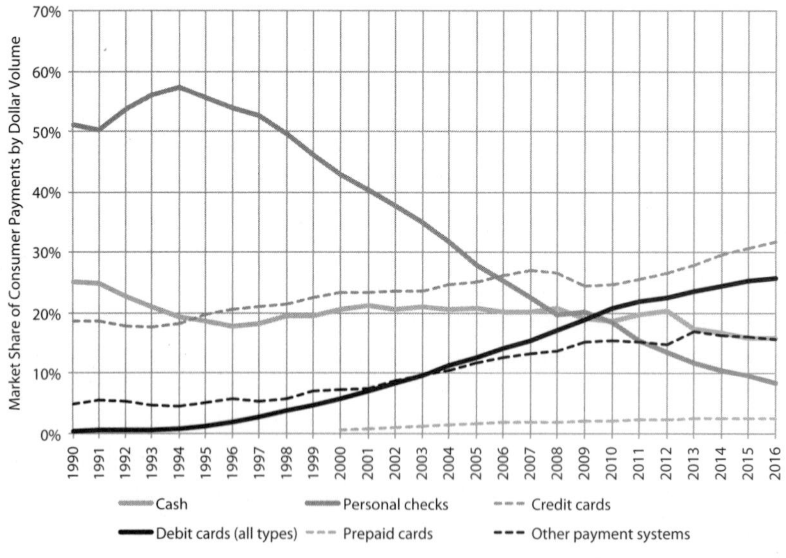

1. Nilson Reports.
2. Nilson Reports.

Figure 18.3 shows the average transaction amount by payment system type in 2012. It shows that consumer check and credit card and ACH transactions tend to be much larger than cash and debit card transactions, reflecting, in part, that checks and credit cards and ACH are often used for larger-dollar transactions, such as payment of rent, mortgage, and utility bills and purchase of large-ticket items. ACH transactions may either be pre-authorized, such as automated bill payment, or "remote" ACH transactions involving the conversion of checks into ACH items. Cash and debit cards (including prepaid cards) are more frequently used for casual consumer spending, such as transactions for transportation and dining.

Figure 18.4 provides a more granular breakdown of transaction volume by payment system type, but it does not break out consumer and business transactions. This

Figure 18.3 Avg. U.S. Consumer Transaction Amount by Type, 2016[3]

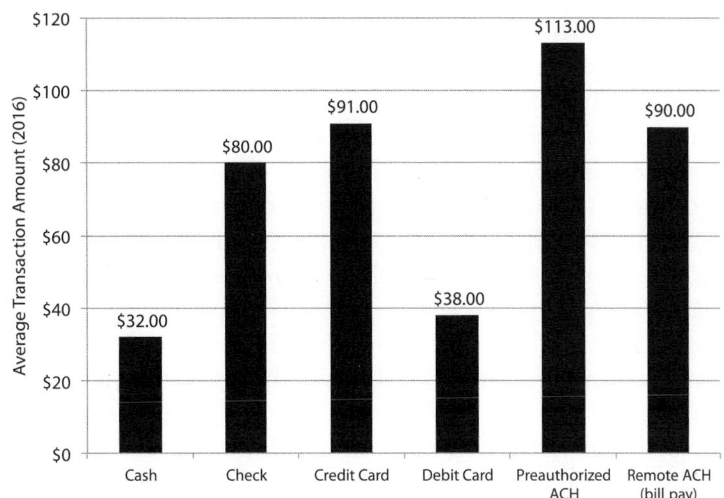

Figure 18.4 2016 U.S. Transaction Volume by Type[4]

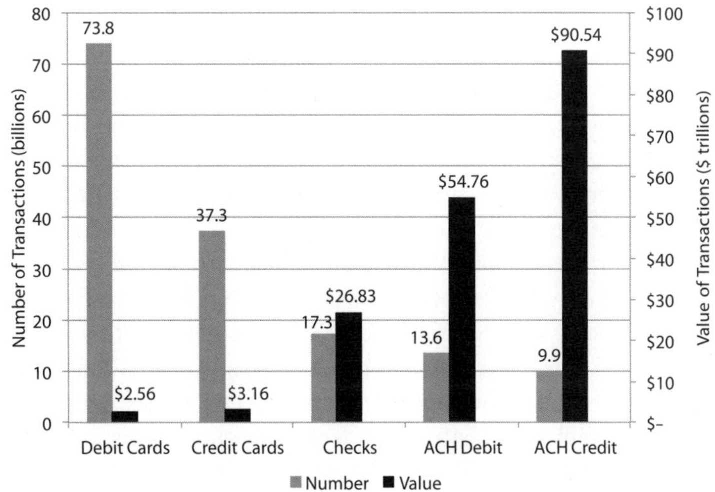

3. Nilson Report, No. 1122 (Dec. 2017), at 10.
4. Federal Reserve Payment Study, 2017 Annual Supplement.

underscores an important point—in many cases the same law governs both business and consumer transactions. What Figure 18.4 shows is that businesses are much heavier users of ACH than consumers, and that businesses are, not surprisingly, undertaking larger transaction volumes, particularly for ACH and check transactions.

II. CASH

A. The Cost of Cash

As a payment system, cash (including both paper currency and coinage) is a beautifully simple way of transferring value. Value is transferred through a change in physical possession of the cash. While agency relationships can be intertwined, typically cash payment is direct between the parties to a payment transaction.

Every payment system, though, has costs, and cash is no different. Wampum shells need to be collected and strung; beavers need to be trapped, skinned, cured, and stored; camels and cattle need to be domesticated, fed, and herded. So to with paper currency and coins. Someone has to spend the money to print and distribute the currency. That someone is, in the first instance, the United States government. The workings of the system are different for paper currency and coins.

U.S. paper currency today consists almost entirely of Federal Reserve notes. These Federal Reserve notes are *notes*—that is, promises to pay. Historically, notes were redeemable in gold or silver, and the promise to pay was a promise to redeem the note at a set rate of exchange. Today, however, Federal Reserve notes are fiat currency that are not redeemable for specie. Indeed, the legal structure of U.S. currency is quite convoluted.

Federal Reserve notes are "obligations of the United States." 12 U.S.C. § 411. The notes are issued by the Board of Governors of the Federal Reserve System, an independent federal regulatory agency. The notes are issued in response to demand from one of the 12 regional Federal Reserve Banks, which are private entities owned by their member banks. The regional Reserve Banks' demand is based on demand for currency from their member banks, which in turn supply currency to other banks and to consumers and businesses. A significant amount of United States currency—perhaps between half and two-thirds of the value in circulation—is held abroad, where it is used as a store of value and as a medium of exchange.

The regional Reserve Banks must post collateral with the Board of Governors equal to the face amount of the notes issued. 12 U.S.C. § 412. (The notes bear a letter and serial number identifying the regional Reserve Bank to which the note was issued.) The collateral can consist of any of the regional Reserve Banks' assets. Most is in the form of Treasury securities and gold certificates, but it can also include checks indorsed by Federal Reserve member banks. The use of a check as collateral is useful for illustrating how the collateral system works: when a $100 check is deposited at a bank, that bank can indorse the check over to the regional Federal Reserve Bank in exchange for $100 in cash, which the regional Federal Reserve Bank obtains by providing that $100 check, indorsed by its member bank (which makes the member bank liable on the check).

Thus, while Federal Reserve notes are formally "obligations of the United States," they are effectively guaranteed by the entire U.S. banking system, or, more precisely, the payment obligation is first on the U.S. banking system, and only then on the United States government. Federal Reserve notes are liabilities of the regional Reserve Banks in that if they are given notes by their member banks, they must redeem them for account credit. But given that Federal Reserve notes are not redeemable for specie, it is not clear what it means for the notes to be an obligation of the United States government. Instead, the requirement that currency be collateralized essentially ties the amount of currency in circulation to real economy demand.

While the Federal Reserve is the issuance authority for paper currency, the currency is made by the Treasury Department's Bureau of Engraving and Printing, which charges the Federal Reserve Board for the cost of producing the currency, rather than selling it at face value. The cost of producing a bill varies by the particular bill, but it is under 15 cents for all bills and around 5 cents for very small denomination bills, which lack some of the anti-counterfeiting security features of the larger denomination bills. The cost to the Federal Reserve Board of printing, transporting, and destroying mutilated paper currency was $660 million in 2016. It cost the Federal Reserve Board another $530 million for "processing, paying, receiving, verification, destruction, transportation, and non-standard packaging of currency" in 2016.

Coin issuance is determined separately by the United States Mint. The Mint sells circulating coins only to the Federal Reserve Banks. The sales are at face value. (The Mint also sells bullion coins and numismatic coins and medals to collectors but does so as a fiscally separate program.) The Reserve Banks then supply the coins to their member banks, which supply them to other banks and to merchants and consumers. While the Mint is the issuance authority for coinage, its issuance is functionally determined by the level of demand from its sole customer, the Federal Reserve Banks, which place monthly orders and provide the Mint with a 12-month rolling order forecast. The volume of coin issuance has ranged from around $500 million to nearly $1.1 billion during the 2009-2016 period. U.S. Mint, 2016 Annual Report.

The "profit" the Mint makes on circulating coin issuance is known as **seigniorage**. Thus, if it costs the Mint 11.14 cents to produce a quarter, which it sells to a Federal Reserve Bank for 25 cents, the Mint's seigniorage is 13.86 cents. To the extent the Mint has revenue exceeding a statutory amount, it is remitted to the Treasury Department's General Fund. 31 U.S.C. § 5136. While the costs of producing coins depend on both the price of the unfinished metals and the efficiency of the Mint's operations, the Mint has for some time sold pennies and nickels at a loss, while making a profit on sales of dimes, quarters, and dollar coins. In 2016, the Mint lost 50 cents for each dollar of pennies produced and 26.4 cents for each dollar of nickels produced. U.S. Mint 2016 Annual Report.

While there are direct production and distribution costs to the government for cash, the biggest cost to the government is a hidden one—uncollected tax revenue on cash transactions. Uncollected cash transaction tax revenue is estimated to be at least $100 billion annually, making non-taxation by far the biggest cost of cash, or, put another way, the largest informal subsidy of the cash system. Bhaskar Chakravorti & Benjamin D. Mazzotta, *The Cost of Cash in the United States*, Institute for Business in the Global Economy, 2013.

Cash has costs for businesses and consumers, too. Cash is estimated to cost businesses (including banks) some $55 billion annually for ATM operations, new branch costs, bank robberies, retail theft, security, cash registers, and armored cars. Most of this ($40 billion) is from cash theft losses.

Cash is estimated to cost households $43 billion annually for theft ($500 million), time spent obtaining cash ($34 billion), account fees ($460 million), and ATM fees ($8 billion). Time spent, although not a monetary cost necessarily, is by far the largest component of this, as consumers spend 28 minutes per month on average traveling to the point where they access cash.

All in all, cash is estimated to cost the economy $200 billion annually. Bhaskar Chakravorti & Benjamin D. Mazzotta, *The Cost of Cash in the United States*, Institute for Business in the Global Economy, 2013. This estimate, however, is a problematic figure, as not all of this is deadweight loss. Much is value that is simply redistributed within the economy: uncollected taxes and theft losses. Only consumer time spent on obtaining cash is a clear deadweight loss.

III. CHECKS

Until recently, checks were the leading non-cash consumer payment system in the United States. Even as the use of checks has declined, there are still a lot of checks written and paid every year. In 2015 there were 19.4 billion checks written for $27.34 trillion. (By comparison in 2003, there were 37.3 billion checks written for $41.21 trillion.) Of these checks, 8.8 billion were consumer-to-business payments, 5.3 billion were business-to-business payments, 3.4 billion were business-to-consumer payments (primarily payroll), and 1.8 billion were consumer-to-consumer payments. 2016 Federal Reserve Payment Study. Figure 18.5 shows that the rough contours of

Figure 18.5 Billions of Checks Written Annually, Select Years[5]

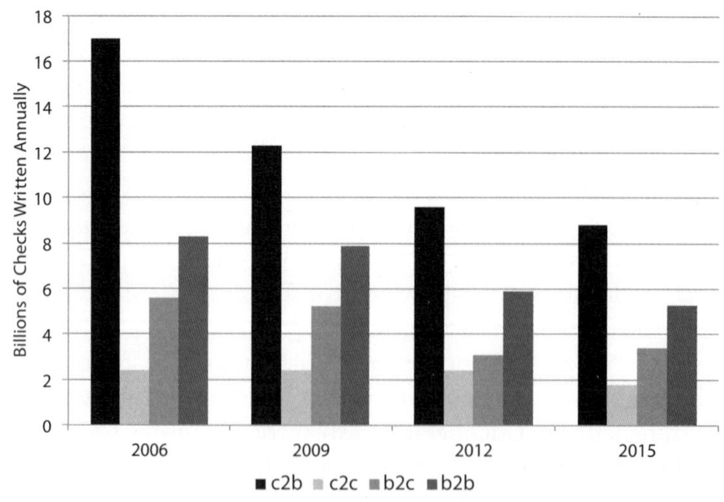

5. 2016 Federal Reserve Payments Study, at 27-28.

who is writing checks to whom has remained steady for several years, but that there has been a notable decline in checks written by consumers to businesses, as online bill payment via ACH has replaced checks. Business-to-consumer check payments have also declined, although not as steeply, as direct deposit has replaced checks.

What exactly *is* a check though? A check is an instruction to bank from a depositor directing the bank to make a payment from a specified account. In the parlance of the Uniform Commercial Code, a check is a bank "draft," which is a type of an "order." UCC § 3-104(f).[6] Article 3 of the Uniform Commercial Code provides certain requirements for a check to qualify as a negotiable instrument and therefore be subject to Article 3, but there are no general legal requirements for the physical *form* of a check; a payment order branded into the side of a cow would suffice to meet the legal definition of a check. Such a bovine check would be unlikely to be accepted for deposit, however, as banks are not required to accept deposits, except to the extent they have agreed to do so. Thus, most deposit account agreements will specify the terms on which checks will be accepted for deposit. Critically, however, a check does not have to be written on a check from the maker's checkbook. It is possible for the maker to authorize a third party to create a check on its behalf; this is sometimes done in telephone order transactions using what are known as **remotely created checks**.[7]

A. The Checking System

A check transaction usually involves at least four parties:

1. the **drawer**, who writes the check;
2. the **payee**, to whom the check is written
3. the **depositary bank**, which is the bank at which the check is deposited;
4. the **payor bank**, which is the drawee of the check.

Thus, the drawer writes a check and gives the physical paper check to the payee. The check is a written order to the payor bank to pay money to the payee. The payee then deposits the check at the depositary bank (or cashes it). The depositary bank presents the check for payment to the payor bank. The payor bank then must decide whether to honor (pay) the check or dishonor it. If the payor bank honors the check, the payor bank will then debit the drawer's account.

The payor bank has until midnight on the banking day following the banking day of presentment to decide whether it will honor the check. UCC §§ 4-104(3), 4-104(10), 4-301. This is known as the **midnight deadline**. If dishonor is not indicated by the midnight deadline, the payor bank must honor the check and hope it can collect from the payor for the funds. UCC § 4-302. The midnight deadline is keyed

6. UCC Article 3 defines "check" as "(i) a draft, other than a documentary draft, payable on demand and drawn on a bank or (ii) a cashier's check or teller's check. An instrument may be a check even though it is described on its face by another term, such as "money order." UCC § 3-104(f).

7. There is a special transfer and presentment warranty for remotely created checks that the check was authorized to be issued in the stated amount by the person on whose account the item is drawn. UCC §§ 3-416(a)(6), 4-208(a)(4).

off of **banking days**. A banking day is not a regular day. Instead, it is "the part of a day on which a bank is open to the public for carrying on substantially all of its banking functions." UCC § 4-104(3). As the Official Comments to the UCC explain, "Under this definition, that part of a business day when a bank is open only for limited functions, e.g., to receive deposits and cash checks, but with loan, bookkeeping and other departments closed, is not part of a banking day." UCC § 4-104, Official Comment 2. In other words, depending on how the bank operates, a weekend or holiday may well not be a banking day. Moreover, if a bank only offers substantially all services for a limited number of hours a day, say from 9 A.M. to 2 P.M., the banking day would cease at 2 P.M., so a presentment at 3 P.M. would be treated as having occurred on the next banking day (which might not be the following calendar date).

If the payor bank dishonors the check, it must return it to the depositary bank, which will give the check back to the payee, who can then sue on the check. Federal Reserve Bank regulations require the return to be in an expeditious manner, 12 C.F.R. § 229.31(b)(1), and, if the check is for $5,000 or more, for the payor bank also must provide a notice of non-payment that, among other things, includes the reason for non-payment. 12 C.F.R. § 229.31(c)(2).

Only a very small percentage of checks are returned, but given the large number of checks total, the number of returned items is still substantial. In 2012 only 0.35% of checks were returned unpaid, but this amounted to 64 million returned checks out of 18.3 billion processed.[8]

There is no generic legal limit on the number of times a bounced check can be represented, but functionally such a check is likely to be presented only once or possibly twice *as a check*. (It is possible to convert a check into an ACH item as we will see later in this chapter.) This is because a Federal Reserve Bank Operating Circular provides that the Federal Reserve System will not handle checks that have bounced twice in any form. Federal Reserve Operating Circular No. 3, § 3.1(a), July 23, 2015.

In some cases, the payor bank and the depositary bank are the same institution. In such case, the check is called an "**on-us**" check and merely involves shifting money around between accounts at the payor/depositary bank. Figure 18.6, below, illustrates the movement of the payment order (the check) and money in a simple check transaction.

While a check transaction only needs to involve four parties, often it involves additional parties. These additional parties can appear in two places within the chain, either between the drawer and the payee or between the depositary bank and the payor bank.

First, a check may be transferred by the payee prior to deposit at a bank. Such transfers are not especially common, but they are possible, and are typically done by "indorsement," meaning that the payee signs his or her name on the back of the check (*in dorso* is Latin for "on the back"). An indorsement can be "**in blank**" or "**special**" or "**restrictive**." An indorsement in blank involves nothing more than the signing of a name on the back of the check. Such an indorsement transforms

8. 2013 Federal Reserve Payments Study, at 30.

Figure 18.6. Simple Check Transaction

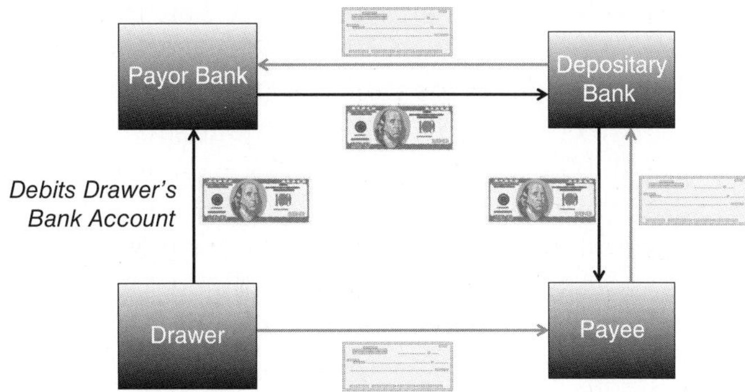

the check into **bearer paper**, which can be deposited (enforced) by anyone who obtains physical possession of the check. UCC § 3-205. If the check contains a special indorsement, such as "pay to Adam Levitin" or "pay to the order of Adam Levitin," then the check can only be paid to Adam Levitin (in the first case) or to Adam Levitin or his subsequent indorsee (in the second case). If the check contains a restrictive indorsement, such as "for deposit only" or "for deposit only in the account of Adam Levitin," then the check can only be paid pursuant to the terms of the restrictive indorsement. A special indorsement is a type of restrictive indorsement. UCC §§ 3-205, 3-206.

In theory, a check can be indorsed and transferred innumerable times before it is deposited; if there is insufficient room for additional signatures, another piece of paper, called an allonge, can be affixed to the check. Notably, however, a bank is never obligated to accept a check for deposit, and a check accompanied by an allonge is unlikely to be accepted. Figure 18.7, below, shows a check transaction with multiple indorsements before deposit.

Figure 18.7 Check Transaction with Multiple Indorsements

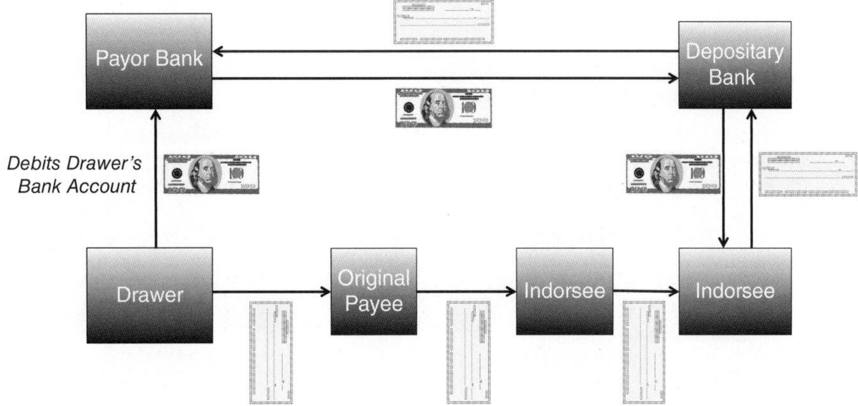

The second place where additional parties may appear in a check transaction is between the depositary bank and the payor bank. Whereas multiple indorsements are rare, the presence of intermediate "**collecting banks**" is quite common. Recall that there are nearly 7,000 banks in the United States and a similar number of credit unions. Most of these banks and credit unions are quite small and local and unlikely to have direct relationships with most other banks and credit unions. Instead, they are likely to have direct relationships only with a few local institutions.

While any bank could, in theory, send a check for collection to another bank, banks tend to send checks for collection through more centralized routes. Local banks usually have a correspondent relationship with a larger bank, which will in turn have relationships with other larger banks. Additionally, checks may get processed through clearinghouses, which are essentially centralized nodes for exchanging checks and value. The regional Federal Reserve Banks (which are banks for banks) and corporate credit unions (which are credit unions for credit unions), as well as some other private entities, operate clearinghouses.

Clearinghouses usually have netting rules that allow all transactions between any two parties in the clearinghouse system on a particular day to be netted out, so only one payment must be made between clearinghouse members, rather than a payment on each individual check. While this system of netting creates huge efficiencies, it also means that clearinghouse members can potentially owe the clearinghouse large sums during the course of any particular day. These sums are called **daylight overdrafts**. They are not to be confused with consumer overdrafts, and they must be settled at the end of the day, but if a clearinghouse member institution were to be taken into receivership during the middle of the day, the clearinghouse could, in theory, be stuck with a large unpaid liability. Most clearinghouses have rules that allow for loss spreading among clearinghouse members, as well as callable capital. Figure 18.8, below, illustrates a check transaction with both multiple indorsements and multiple collecting banks.

Figure 18.8 Check Transaction with Multiple Indorsements and Multiple Collecting Banks

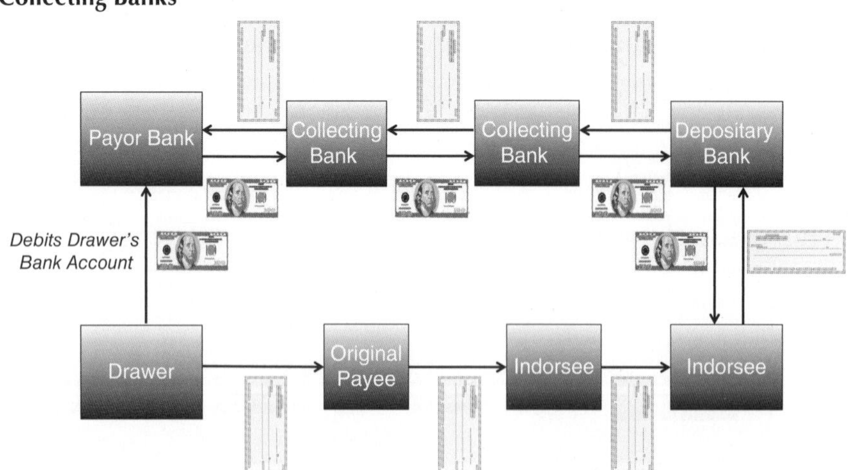

B. Regulation of Checks

Checks are governed by a combination of state and federal law. Article 3 of the Uniform Commercial Code governs the rights of a drawer of a check vis-à-vis anyone who attempts to enforce the check and obtain payment from the drawer's bank. This means that Article 3 governs the rights of the drawer both against anyone who deposits or cashes the check, but also against any bank that pays on the check.

Article 4 of the Uniform Commercial Code governs the rights of banks within the check-clearing system. (In Article 4 parlance, a check is an "item.") It also governs the rights of a payor bank vis-à-vis the drawer, including when the payor bank may charge the drawer's account, the payor bank's liability for wrongful dishonor, stop payment rights, and the duty of the drawer to discover and report unauthorized signatures or alterations. Most importantly, Article 4 permits variation by agreement, UCC § 4-103, which means that the bank account agreement is typically the "law" that governs checks, albeit with a backdrop of good faith, fair dealing, and UDAP and UDAAP principles.

Federal law also governs parts of the checking system, including funds availability, collection of checks by Federal Reserve Banks, and "check truncation," discussed below. Finally, perhaps the most important federal regulation of the checking system is the requirement that every Federal Reserve Bank honor checks at par. 12 U.S.C. § 360. **Par clearance** means that a deposit of a $100 check results in a $100 account credit, rather than a discounted credit. Prior to the creation of the Federal Reserve system, banks would discount checks payable from each other to account for the risk of dishonor: if a bank paid out $100 on a $100 check deposit only to find that the check was dishonored, the bank could be out the $100. To account for the risk of dishonor, banks would often pay less than the face amount of the check, depending, in part, on their familiarity with the bank on which the check was drawn and the customer. The result was tremendous deadweight loss in the checking system because discounting was not done efficiently due to limited information.

Only Federal Reserve banks are required to accept checks at par, but the Fed attempted in the 1920s to use its market power to coerce nationwide par check clearance. These attempts were defeated in a series of Supreme Court rulings. *Am. Bank & Trust Co. v. Federal Reserve Bank of Atlanta*, 256 U.S. 350 (1921); *American Bank & Trust Co. v. Federal Reserve Bank of Atlanta*, 262 U.S. 643 (1923); *Farmers & Merchants Bank v. Federal Reserve Bank of Richmond*, 262 U.S. 649 (1923). Nonetheless, because of the Fed's persistence, by the 1980s the par clearance of checks had become a nationwide reality to the point that par clearance is taken for granted. As we will see, not all payment systems involve par clearance, and the mixture of par clearance and discounting has created major anti-trust issues for credit and debit card systems.

A check can be used to make a gratuitous payment or to make a payment in satisfaction of an **underlying debt obligation**. When a check is given to pay for an underlying obligation the underlying obligation is "suspended" until the check is paid or dishonored. UCC § 3-310(b). If the check is dishonored, the person to whom the underlying obligation is owed can bring suit either to enforce the check or on the underlying obligation. UCC § 3-310(b)(3). A suit on the check is much easier to bring because the underlying obligation need not be proven or even be legally enforceable. All that must be shown is that a check was written and dishonored.

C. The Technology Revolution in Checking

Technological changes have revolutionized the world of checking in two key ways. First, in the late 1950s and early 1960s, the account and routing numbers on checks began to be encoded in magnetic ink, which enabled **Magnetic Ink Character Recognition (MICR)** or machine-readable checks. MICR does not, of course, capture the *amount* of the check, but it does enable much more efficient routing of checks. Optical character reading technology, however, enables banks to accept most checks without a human being ever looking at the check.

Second, in 2003, Congress passed the Check Clearing for the 21st Century Act, better known as the **Check21 Act**, which permits (but does not require) electronic conversion of checks, known as "**check truncation**." Prior to Check21, all checking transactions required the physical movement of paper at every stage of the transaction. A check written by a Tampa, Florida resident to a Las Vegas resident had to first be delivered from Tampa to Las Vegas, let's say by the U.S. Postal Service. After the payee deposited the check in Las Vegas, the check would be physically returned to the drawer's bank in Tampa for presentment. This would likely have meant an armored car ride from Los Vegas to Los Angeles, a flight from Los Angeles to Cincinnati and then another flight from Cincinnati to Miami, followed by an armored car ride from Miami to Tampa. If the check were dishonored, it would have to travel back the same route, in reverse.

The result was an incredibly inefficient system of planes, trains, automobiles, and numerous check sorting centers to move around pieces of paper. Figure 18.9, below, shows the Federal Reserve's air transportation routes, which look like the routes of a major national air carrier. Further connections (e.g., Las Vegas to Los Angeles) were handled by ground transportation. Yet for all of this, the system functioned surprisingly well, handling billions of checks per year with relatively few problems.

The terrorist attacks of September 11, 2001, revealed just how vulnerable the nation's payment systems were to disruption, however. The Federal Reserve Bank of New York was temporarily closed because of the attacks, which took place nearby in lower Manhattan, and air space nationwide was shut down for nearly a week, preventing air transit of checks. As a result the nation's major payment system ground to a halt. This meant that business and consumer payments simply could not happen. Payrolls could be made, rent and utilities payments could not be processed, etc. The Federal Reserve System temporarily guaranteed collection of all checks in the system until airspace could be reopened. When airspace was reopened, the first planes in the air were planes out of Tetterboro airport in northern New Jersey, carrying checks processed by the Federal Reserve Bank of New York.

Congress recognized the huge vulnerability posed by physical check delivery requirements, and passed the Check Clearing for the 21st Century Act (known as the Check21 Act), which allows (but does not require) for **check truncation** and the creation of **substitute checks**. Check truncation involves conversion of the

Figure 18.9 Federal Reserve Check Relay Air Transportation Network, circa 2001.

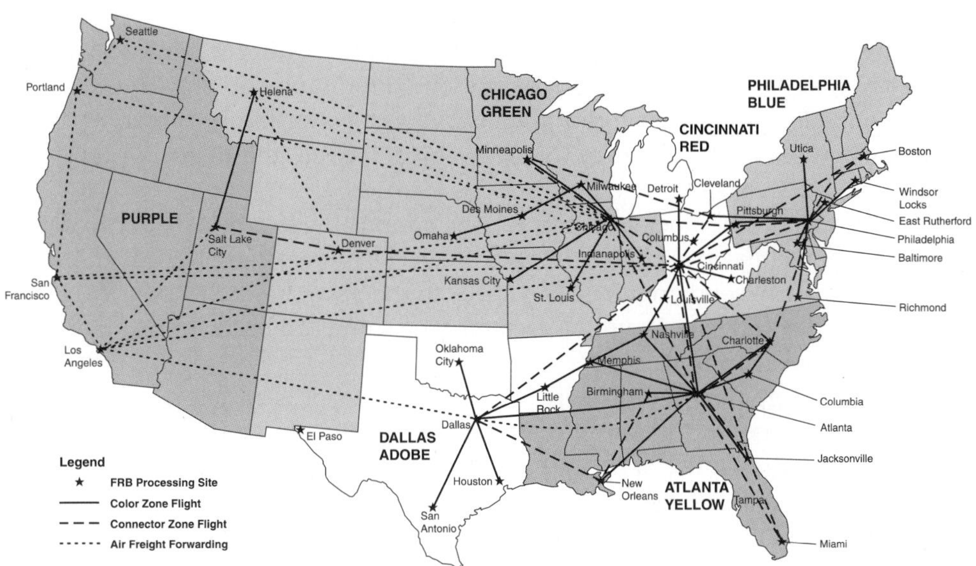

information on a paper check to an electronic format (be it data or an image). Such data or an image can then be transmitted electronically and then transformed back into a substitute check, that is, a physical paper check that reproduces the original paper check.

The Check21 Act provides that "[a] substitute check shall be the legal equivalent of the original check for all purposes," and that:

> A person may deposit, present, or send for collection or return a substitute check without an agreement with the recipient, so long as a bank has [made the requisite Check21 warranties].

12 U.S.C. §§ 5003(a)-(b), 5004. Thus, Check21 permits use of substitute checks only if a bank that transfers, presents, or returns the substitute check is willing to make a pair of special warranties about the substitute check. The first warranty is that "the substitute check meets all the requirements for legal equivalence" to a paper check, namely that the substitute check:

> (1) accurately represents all of the information on the front and back of the original check as of the time the original check was truncated; and
> (2) bears the legend: "This is a legal copy of your check. You can use it the same way you would use the original check."

12 U.S.C. § 5003(b), 5004(1). The second warranty is that:

> no depositary bank, drawee, drawer, or endorser will receive presentment or return of the substitute check, the original check, or a copy or other paper or electronic version of the substitute check or original check such that the bank, drawee, drawer, or

> endorser will be asked to make a payment based on a check that the bank, drawee, drawer, or endorser has already paid.

12 U.S.C. § 5004(2). In other words, check truncation requires a bank to warrant that the original paper check will not be presented for payment. The Check21 warranties are made "to the transferee, any subsequent collecting or returning bank, the depositary bank, the drawee, the drawer, the payee, the depositor, and any endorser." 12 U.S.C. § 5004.

Check21 opened the door to a pair of innovations. First, Check21 allowed (but did not require) banks to exchange images of checks rather than physical checks. A depositary bank can send an image of a check to the payor bank. If a physical check is needed, a substitute check will be created. The same can occur in reverse, if the check is dishonored and returned.

Image exchange caught on slowly at first, but today it is widely used with side result of greatly speeding up the check collection system and eliminating float. As a result of the increased use of image exchange, many fewer planes, trains, automobiles, and check-processing centers are needed.

Second, Check21 enabled the deposit via transmission of electronic information, rather than of physical paper. Check21 provides that "A person may deposit . . . a substitute check," and this enabled a new technology called **remote deposit capture (RDC)** that came into use in late 2005. All that is required for RDC is submission of a photograph of the check to the bank along with certain account information.

RDC offers depositors several advantages over traditional methods of making deposits: sending an employee to the bank with the daily deposits; contracting with an armored car service or courier to deliver the deposits; or having customers directly remit checks to the bank through a lockbox operation.

For a business doing any volume of deposits, RDC may be cheaper than other depositing methods. RDC vitiates the need to physically send checks to a bank during business hours. Not only does this reduce burdens on employee time, paperwork, and theft risk, but it can also accelerate funds availability. Some banks offer a later cut-off time for crediting RDC deposits and speed up funds availability schedules. Because of quicker clearing time, the RDC process also reveals bounced checks sooner.

RDC also allows businesses to consolidate their banking relationships. If a business has offices in multiple states, it might not be able to use the same bank for making physical deposits from all of its locations. Using RDC, however, all the deposits can be made at a single institution.

For banks, RDC presents three key benefits. First, it lowers their costs for check processing. According to National Automated Clearing House Association, the cost of processing a paper check ranges from 75 cents to $3, and averages around $1.22, whereas an electronic check costs between 32 and 70 cents to process.[9] Moreover, RDC frees up teller time from check capture for other services.

---

9. NACHA—The Electronic Payments Association, *at* http://www.electronicpayments.org/financial/fi.check-conversion.benefits.php.

Second, RDC creates a new fee-for-services product for banks. Banks generally charge merchants a monthly fee and a per-transaction or per-check fee for RDC. Third, RDC can benefit a financial institution because it creates a "sticky" relationship with the depositor. The sunk costs of customized RDC hardware and software are likely to increase RDC customer retention.

RDC greatly speeds up the check-clearance process. It potentially allows a check to be cashed and cleared electronically on the same day. By allowing for float to be eliminated, RDC makes checks much more like debit cards or ACH economically, albeit with a different set of public and private legal protections.

Because RDC is a check-depositing method, it poses the usual fraud risks with checks, as well as the risk of errors from the scanning process and of duplicate presentment, either from fraud or by mistake.

RDC, however, poses two additional fraud issues. First, RDC makes it more difficult for banks to detect fraud because they may not be able to access the original physical check. Banks' fraud units are used to working with original checks and being able to examine watermarks and the original paper in order to detect alterations. With RDC, the original physical check may have been destroyed or, if not, will not be accessible to the bank in a timely manner. Instead, banks will have to rely solely on electronic images, where image quality limitations may pose fraud detection challenges.

Second, RDC creates a unique risk of duplicate presentment and payment. Because an image of the check is used for the deposit, the physical check can still be deposited. This presents a risk for the check's maker of its account being duplicatively debited, for the paying bank of paying twice on the same check, and for depositary banks of breaching the Check21 Act warranty of single payment. 12 U.S.C. § 5004(2). If there were a duplicative presentment, the paying bank could pay twice, and then sue *either* depositary bank for breach of its Check21 warranty of single payment.

Federal Reserve Board regulations provide that a bank that accepts a deposit via RDC indemnifies any bank that receives a later deposit of the original paper check against the risk of a duplicative deposit, unless second bank accepted the original check with a restrictive indorsement that is inconsistent with the means of deposit. 12 C.F.R. § 229.34(f)(1)-(2). This means that a bank that takes RDC can require depositors to indorse checks with "for mobile deposit only" as part of the RDC process, so if the check is then accepted for physical deposit by another bank, the other bank will not be indemnified. 12 C.F.R. § 229.34(f)(3).

RDC creates not only a risk of both an electronic and a physical presentment, but also of multiple electronic presentments. A check's image can be deposited at multiple banks or multiple accounts at the same bank. In such a situation, the paying bank would still be able to sue any and all of the depositary banks for breach of their Check21 single payment warranty, but there would be no indemnification requirement as between those banks. The indemnification requirement is only from RDC to paper, not RDC to RDC.

The Check21 warranty of single payment applies only to banks, not to depositors. The depositary bank's liability for duplicate presentment, however, is generally shifted to the depositor by contract. Because of the risks involved with RDC, many banks have offered the service only to their existing clients or have additional underwriting criteria for it.

RDC is only possible if a bank is willing to make the warranties required by the Check21 Act for substitute checks. Therefore, banks can choose whether they are willing to accept RDC. RDC is now widely offered, but banks are still cautious with the technology because RDC poses potential multiple deposit problems—the same check can be deposited at multiple banks via image as well as the physical check being deposited, but to date, fraud problems with RDC have been limited.

RDC is about the payee-depositary bank relationship, whereas image exchange is about the depositary bank-payor bank relationship. It is possible to have RDC without image exchange and vice versa. Thus, a depositary bank could accept a deposit via an image, but then convert the image to a substitute check and present that physical substitute check for payment to the payor bank. It is, of course, possible to combine RDC and image capture in a transaction, so that no physical paper ever moves in the checking system other than from the drawer to the payee.

In 2015, 62% of check deposits were paper deposits. 2016 Federal Reserve Payments Study. The rest were image deposits. The majority of these deposits were interbank transfers in correspondent banking regulations, but RDC by consumers constituted only 3% of deposits (with another 13% being RDC from businesses). *Id.*

Additionally, a physical check or remotely deposited check can be converted to an automated clearing house (ACH) entry and presented for payment through the ACH system rather than through the checking system. (A payment can also begin life as an ACH entry.) Different law applies to transactions processed through the ACH system, and not all checks are eligible for **ACH conversion**. As Figure 18.10 illustrates, a deposit may be made either by paper or as a truncated check via RDC, and separately a check may be presented for payment by the depositary bank using the original paper (if the original paper check was deposited), using a substitute check (a paper reproduction of the original), using a truncated check (electronic image exchange), or as an ACH entry. The fact that a check begins life with physical paper does not guarantee that it will remain as paper throughout its processing. Of the 19.4 billion checks written in 2015, 2.1 billion (11%) were converted to ACH entries.[10]

D. Check Cashing

Although checks can be transferred via negotiation, negotiated transfers outside of the banking system are rare. Instead, most negotiation occurs when a consumer signs a check over to his bank or when the bank then signs the check over to the payor bank. Likewise, checks are typically deposited in the payee's bank account by the payee.

10. 2013 Federal Reserve Payments Study, at 25.

Figure 18.10 Check21 Act Deposit and Presentment Options

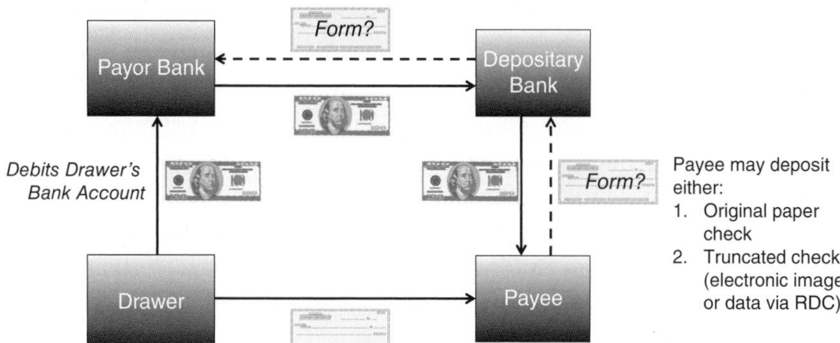

Sometimes, however, consumers will sell a check to a check casher, which then attempts to collect on the check. In a check-cashing transaction, the consumer indorses the check over to the casher and receives a cash payment of the face amount of the check minus a fee, which might be a percentage of the face amount or a flat dollar fee. Fees tend to range between 1% to 5% of the face amount. The fee covers the check casher's costs, including collection risk, and profit margin. Check cashers assume a collection risk on the check—the check might be subject to a stop payment order, might be forged, or might be written by an insolvent entity.

The business of check cashing is generally regulated by states, which typically require certain fee disclosures and also often impose fees caps. Some states also have licensing regimes for check cashers. Check cashers are never obligated to accept checks. Many have limits on the size of checks they will accept, and cashers will generally decline checks that bear indicia of fraud. This means, among other things, that check cashers will rarely accept checks that bear an indorsement, as they have no way of determining whether the indorsement is legitimate.

Why do consumers use check cashers? For some consumers it is a matter of lack of alternatives. Unbanked consumers have few options for converting a check into cash except using a check casher. But many, if not a majority, of the users of check cashers actually have bank accounts. Given that banks usually cash their depositors' checks for free, why would these consumers want to pay a check casher?

Perhaps the most important reason is speed of funds availability. Check cashers make a lump sum of most of the face amount of the check immediately available in cash; banks are only obligated to follow the Reg CC funds availability rules. Some consumers, then, are willing to pay a premium for immediate liquidity. A second reason consumers use check cashers is convenience. Many urban neighborhoods have limited banking options, and banks generally have limited business hours. Check cashers, in contrast, tend to serve poorer neighborhoods and have extended business hours. Again, this is about immediate liquidity. Finally, some consumers want to use check cashers to avoid garnishments or income reporting.

Problem Set 18

1. Meredith Richards received a $200 check from her mom for her birthday, as well as $100 in cash from her grandmother. Meredith immediately put the cash and check away in her wallet, which she promptly forgot on the table at a restaurant, where it was picked up by the busboy, Ben Brown.

   a. Is Ben Brown able to go and spend the cash?

   b. Is Ben Brown able to cash the check? *See* UCC §§ 1-201(21), 3-301.

2. Now suppose that before putting the check in her wallet Meredith had written one of the following indorsements on the check. Would either change Ben Brown's ability to cash the check?

   a. "For deposit only in the account of Meredith Richards." *See* UCC § 3-206.

   b. "Meredith Richards." *See* UCC §§ 3-204, 3-205.

3. On Monday, June 1, Frederick McFrodd deposited at the Nome branch of State National Bank of Alaska a $3,000 check payable from the account of one Sean Ferguson at the Bank of West Palm Beach, Florida. McFrodd had opened up an account at State National Bank of Alaska the week prior. The State National Bank of Alaska presented the check through the mail to Bank of West Palm Beach, Florida for payment at 4 P.M. on Thursday, June 4. The Bank of West Palm Beach, Florida, conducts business Monday through Friday between 9 A.M. and 3 P.M.

   a. How long does the Bank of West Palm Beach, Florida have to decide whether to pay the check? *See* UCC §§ 4-104(3), 4-104(10), 4-301, 4-302.

   b. How much money might State National Bank of Alaska have to make available to Frederick McFrodd before it learns if the check is dishonored? *See* Reg CC Funds Availability Rules in Chapter 14, Table 14.1.

   c. Is there any way for State National Bank of Alaska to mitigate the check-kiting risk it faces?

4. First Bank of Springfield is considering accepting deposits through remote deposit capture and the bank's president and owner, Andy Chen, has come to you, the bank's longtime outside counsel, to get your advice. Andy tells you that the bank has been handling checks through image exchange for the last few years and that it's worked out really well. "We've been able to really reduce float on checks, as a result, and with no increase in our fraud rate." Andy wants to know if he can expect the same outcome via remote deposit capture, and if not, what the bank can do to minimize its risks. What do you tell him?

CHAPTER 19

PAYMENT SYSTEMS II: ELECTRONIC PAYMENTS

I. DEBIT AND CREDIT CARDS

As we saw in the previous chapter, a check is nothing more than a piece of paper ordering a bank to make a payment from a deposit account. All that is needed for such an order is (1) information identifying the bank and account, (2) information identifying the payee, (3) information about the payment amount, and (4) an authorization of the payment. The bank's routing number and account number are MICR encoded, the payee and payment amount are written on the face of the check, and the drawer's signature is the authorization of the payment. These same four elements can be assembled electronically as well. One way to do this is a debit or credit card.

As payment systems, debit and credit cards function identically. The only difference is that a debit card draws funds from a consumer's deposit account, whereas a credit card draws funds from a consumer's line of credit. While this results in important regulatory differences, there is little functional difference. We will worry about the credit function of credit cards later. For now, we will consider them solely as a payment system along with debit cards.

A payment card (debit or credit) is a device that satisfies points (1) and (4) via electronic transmission of account information and authorization. The card itself has account information encoded on it. It may also require a signature or personal identification number (PIN) for authorization. When the card is used the payee's identity (2) and the payment amount information (3) is also transmitted electronically (although this information is separate from the information on the card).

All of this is to say that the form factor of a debit or credit card is basically irrelevant but for the fact that much of the equipment set up to transmit debit transaction information requires a particular form factor of a card that is 3³/₈ inches by 2¹/₈ inches, with a magnetically encoded stripe on its back, and typically with various information embossed on the front and possibly also listed on the back. The string of digits embossed on the front and coded on the magnetic stripe indicate the category of card issuer, network, an issuer identification number (six digits total); an account number (up to twelve digits), and final single check digit that is used to verify the other digits on the card according to an algorithm known as a Luhn algorithm. These digits play much the same function as the MICR-encoded data on a check. Separate from these embossed digits are issue and expiration dates and various security codes that are sometimes used for authorization verification. As a general matter, however, there is nothing magical about the fact that a debit or credit card is a card. While we tend to focus on the tangible form factor of the card, the nature of the payment card payment system is not in fact dependent on there being a card.

While debit and credit cards have little functional difference beyond their source of funds, they have somewhat different histories.

A. Brief History of Credit and Debit Cards

The first mass use credit cards debuted in 1950 with the Diners Club card. This card was a **charge card**, meaning that the balance on the card had to be repaid in full each month, rather than only repaid in part like a true credit card. The Diners Club card was not issued by a bank, and it was used mainly for travel and entertainment purposes, as was American Express's offering, which debuted in 1958. (American Express introduced the first plastic card in 1959—previous cards were made of cardboard or celluloid.) Like Diners Club, American Express was not a bank. Instead, it was a money transfer firm that specialized in money orders and travelers checks; it did not take deposits.

Banks did not enter the credit card business until the 1960s because of restrictions on interstate branch banking. Prior to 1994, federal law prohibited banks from operating branches in multiple states. Among other effects, this prohibition inhibited the development of a national bank-based payment system because consumer interaction with banks at this time was largely in-person at bank branches, rather than via phone or mail. (Remember, no Internet, no Web!) Thus, while a bank could create an in-state system, such a system was of limited use. In 1958, Bank of America (then California-based) created a credit card program called BankAmericard for use in California. The program was successful, and in 1965, Bank of America began licensing the BankAmericard system to other banks outside of California. In 1970, BankAmericard converted to a membership organization with reciprocal card acceptance. If a cardholder showed up at a merchant with a banking relationship with one of the members, the card would be accepted. In 1976, BankAmericard began to use Visa as its brand name. Visa became a public company in 2008 in response to anti-trust concerns, although banks still control a special class of its stock.

At nearly the same time, in 1966, a group of other credit card issuing banks in California, including Wells Fargo and Bank of California, joined together to create a membership organization known as the InterBank Card Association that provided for reciprocal card acceptance among members. The InterBank Card's name was changed to MasterCard in 1969, as a number of large New York banks joined the association, and in 1979, the name was changed to MasterCard. In 2006, MasterCard became a publicly traded corporation in response to anti-trust concerns, although banks and a charitable foundation still control two special classes of its stock.

Debit cards can be used both at point of sale (POS) and at automated teller machines (ATMs). The basic technology is the same. Debit cards began to be used in the 1960s, first only for ATM transactions, but by the mid-1970s POS sale terminals for debit cards began to appear. A court ruling in 1985 held that ATMs were not "bank branches," and thus not subject to the restrictions on interstate branch banking at the time. *Independent Bankers Ass'n v. Marine Midland Bank, N.A.*, 757 F.2d 453 (2d Cir. 1985). This ruling encouraged the development of interstate electronic fund transfer (EFT) networks. While EFT networks were solely regional at first, regional networks would enter reciprocity agreements with each other, and by the early 1990s national EFT networks emerged. POS use of debit cards remained quite limited until the mid-1990s, when debit terminals became more common at merchants to the point that they are now ubiquitous.

B. Structure of Credit and Debit Card Payment Systems

Almost all payment card payments are consumer-to-business payments. Thus, in a debit card transaction, there are always at least five parties involved:

- The consumer;
- The merchant;
- The card **issuer** (the bank the issued the debit card);
- The **acquirer** bank (the merchant's bank); and
- The card **network**.

Whereas a check transaction involved a consumer and a merchant and their respective banks, a debit card transaction involves an additional party, the card network, that provides the connection between the consumer's and merchant's banks. For debit (and credit) cards, the consumer's bank is called the **issuer bank**, as it issues the card. For debit cards, the issuer bank is almost always the bank at which the consumer has a deposit account. **Decoupled debit**, in which the card is issued by a different bank than the one at which the deposit account is located, is theoretically possible, but faces regulatory obstacles and has met little success as a business.

The merchant's bank is known as the **acquirer bank**. The reason for this is that the merchant's bank is essentially acquiring from the merchant the right to be paid by the consumer and then collecting on this payment obligation itself. The acquiring market is extremely concentrated, but very competitive on price. It is a low-margin, high-volume business, and acquirers have high turnover rates in their portfolios. Often the relationship between a merchant and its acquirer is intermediated by other entities such as **third-party payment processors** and **independent service organizations (ISOs)** and technology vendors. Typically, acquiring banks enter into contracts with payment processors to manage the banks' merchant processing program. The processors in turn will contract with multiple ISOs to sign up merchants for accounts. The ISOs may themselves use various sub-ISOs or sales agents. While the ISOs recruit merchants, the merchants must still be underwritten to the acquirer bank and processor's underwriting criteria as the processor and acquirer assume the risk of non-performance by the merchant on transactions, which can result in a **chargeback**—a reversal of the transaction, resulting in the acquirer (and then the processor and then ultimately the merchant) having to refund money to the issuer bank and ultimately to the consumer. If the merchant is insolvent, the loss will fall on the acquirer and/or processor.

The card network will be either an EFT network or an offline debit card network. The consumer does not have contractual privity with the network, but the network

Figure 19.1 Parties to MasterCard and Visa and EFT Networks

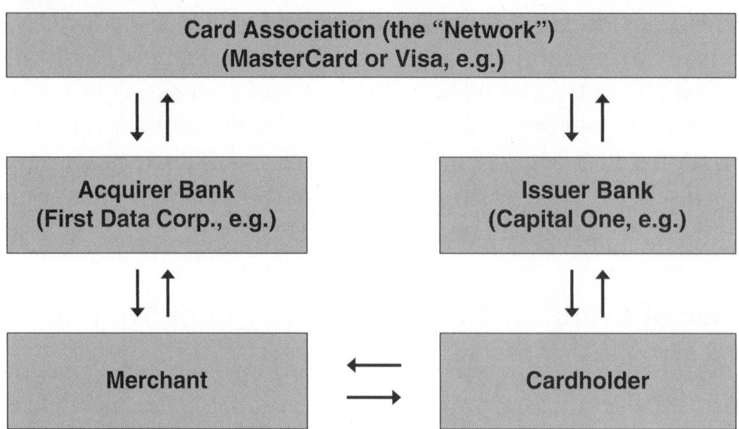

appears in the form of the logo or "bug" on the debit card (e.g., Visa, Interlink, Star). The bug might be on the front or the back of the card, and sometimes it does not appear at all. All cards are capable of operating on at least two unaffiliated networks. Figure 19.1 illustrates a basic debit or credit card transaction structure for MasterCard and Visa and EFT networks.

This five-party structure is the design of MasterCard, Visa, and EFT networks. American Express and Discover Cards can involve a slightly different arrangement. Amex and Discover are always the network, but they may also be the issuer and acquirer. In such cases, there are only three parties to the credit card transaction—consumer, merchant, and issuer/acquirer/network. Both Amex and Discover also have some third-party issuers, such as a Citibank American Express card. In such situations, Amex and Discover are still the network and acquirer. (*See* Figure 19.2.)

Whereas credit card transactions are almost always authorized with a signature (when done in person), debit transactions can be authorized with either a

Figure 19.2 Parties to American Express and Discover Networks

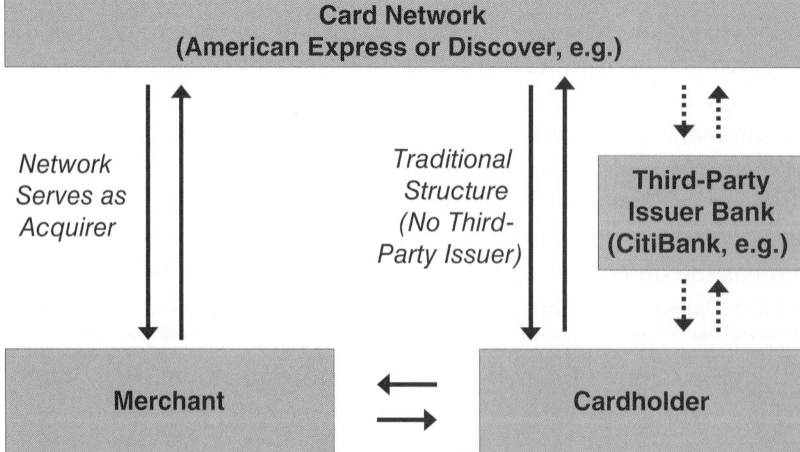

signature or a PIN. Signature debit is also known as "offline debit," while PIN debit is known as "online debit." Signature debit transactions are processed using the MasterCard and Visa credit card network structure. That's why you are sometimes asked to press "credit" on the PIN pad at point of sale when you use a debit card. Pressing credit routes the transaction over the credit card network. PIN debit transactions are processed over local electronic fund transfer (EFT) networks that also do ATM transactions. The same physical debit card will always be able to operate on at least two unaffiliated networks, one of which will be a signature and one a PIN network, typically. While the signature networks are nationwide, the EFT networks tend to be regional, but with reciprocity agreements. Thus, when you use your debit card, you often cannot be sure who is processing the transaction.

Sometimes there is no signature or PIN required for a credit or debit transaction. This is because some card network rules will allow merchants to waive the signature or PIN if the merchant agrees to assume all losses on unauthorized transactions. For all "card-not-present" transactions, such as Internet and telephone transactions—there is no signature or PIN used and the merchant bears all fraud loss. Some "card-present" transactions are also signatureless. These signatureless programs are limited to relatively small-dollar purchases (under $50 typically), and are usually found only at merchants with high register traffic, such as grocery stores, where speed benefits outweigh the fraud risk.

For both signature and PIN transactions, there are three steps in processing the transaction: **authorization, clearance, and settlement** (ACS). The transaction is always first authorized, meaning that the network and the issuer are contacted to see if the transaction may go forward. Note that authorization does not necessarily happen in real time, so a merchant may have parted with goods and services before knowing if the transaction was authorized. If the transaction is authorized, it is then cleared by the network. Clearing means the transfer of funds from the issuer to the acquirer. After the funds have been cleared, they are settled into merchant's account and debited from the consumer's account.

C. Regulation of Consumer-Issuer Relations for Debit and Credit Cards

The consumer-issuer bank relationship in debit and credit cards is regulated primarily by federal law, although there is a backdrop of common law contracts and torts. For debit cards, the consumer-issuer relationship is regulated by the Electronic Fund Transfer Act (EFTA) and Regulation E thereunder, as well as by Regulation CC relating to funds availability. For credit cards, the consumer-issuer relationship is regulated by the Truth in Lending Act (TILA) and Regulation Z thereunder. These statutes provide rules relating to liability for unauthorized transactions and error and dispute resolution, which are covered in Chapter 20. These statutes also contain various disclosure requirements and, in the case of credit cards and "gift cards," certain substantive term restrictions that are covered in other chapters.

D. Interchange Fees and the Merchant Side of Payment Cards

Like all other payment systems, there is a cost to operating debit and credit card payments. Debit cards are somewhat complicated in terms of costs because they are not stand-alone products (excluding decoupled debit). They are part of a retail product suite offered by banks that includes deposit accounts. Thus, it is difficult to cost out debit cards separately from the other retail banking offerings. For example, should branch overhead be a cost attributed to debit cards?

Putting aside account fees, etc., there are some fees specific to payment cards paid by merchants, banks, and consumers. If you go and buy $100 worth of groceries with your debit or credit card, the merchant notifies its acquirer, which notifies the card network, which notifies the issuer. If the transaction is authorized, the issuer forwards funds to the network, which sends them to the acquirer, which then settles them into the merchant's account. While $100 is then debited from your bank account (if a debit card) or from your line of credit (if a credit card), the merchant does not receive $100.00. Instead, the merchant might only be credited with $97.00 by its acquirer bank. This is because the acquirer bank takes out a cut known as the **merchant discount fee**. The merchant discount fee is a bank fee to merchants. It is individually negotiated between the acquirer and the merchant.

The acquirer holds back some of the funds because of the risk that the consumer will claim that the transaction was unauthorized or that the goods and services sold were defective or were not delivered. The acquirer holds some risk on the underlying transaction. For example, imagine that the merchant is an airline. The airline sells tickets months or weeks before flights. This means that the airline gets paid well before it delivers services. The airline might file for bankruptcy after it has sold tickets, but before it has delivered the services. In such a case, the consumers would demand their money back from the issuer. The issuer would, in turn, be entitled to get the money back from the acquirer, which would leave the acquirer holding the bag as an unsecured creditor of the airline in the bankruptcy trying to get the money back. Not surprisingly, merchant discount fees are extremely high in certain industries with high rates of customer disputes. Adult websites often have merchant discount fees of 15% or more: "I didn't subscribe to that porn site! I'm a happily married man!"

The acquirer does not keep the entire merchant discount fee. The acquirer must pay a **switch fee** to the card network for its services. The acquirer must also pay an **interchange fee** to the issuer, which bears the risk of reimbursing the consumer from its own funds if the acquirer goes bankrupt. These fees are deducted from the funds cleared to the acquirer. The network fee is very small—the networks make money on volume. Historically, however, the interchange fee was substantial, often a flat fee of 5 cents to 10 cents plus 2%-3% of the transaction for credit card transactions. Thus, of the $100 credit card transaction, the issuer might receive $2.50, the network would get 10 cents, and the acquirer would get 40 cents. For signature debit cards, interchange fees were historically only slightly lower, but with the same fee structure. For PIN debit cards, however, interchange fees tended to be limited to flat fees of around 19 cents to 22 cents irrespective of transaction size. In addition to the

Figure 19.3 Fee Division in Network Illustrated with a $100 Credit Card Purchase with a 2% Merchant Discount Rate and a 1.6% Interchange Rate

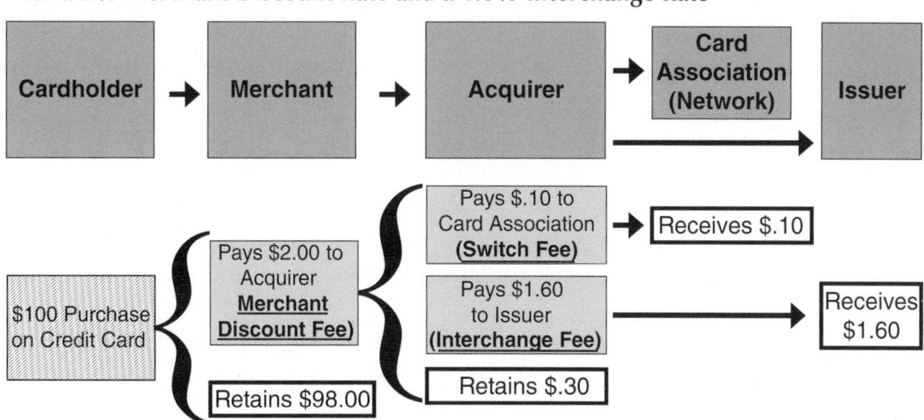

merchant discount fee, merchants must also pay other fees for returns (known as chargebacks), and data security non-compliance.

The interchange fee is specific to the Visa/MasterCard/EFT model. In the Amex/Discover model (other than when there is a third-party issuer) there is no interchange fee. Instead, there is solely a merchant discount fee.

While the interchange fee is an interbank fee, it gets passed on to the merchant, just like the network fee, as part of the merchant discount fee. Indeed, merchant discount fees are often structured as "interchange plus." Confusingly, sometimes the merchant discount fee is called (incorrectly) the interchange fee. These fees (both merchant discount and interchange) are also referred to as **swipe fees**; that term is probably best used for the merchant discount fee.

In theory the issuer and the acquirer could negotiate the interchange fee directly. But with thousands of banks in the country, thousands of bilateral negotiations each year or so would be a mess. Instead, the interchange fee is set by the card network. The fees are the same for all banks. They vary, however, based on the merchant's industry, the type of debit card (consumer versus business, *e.g.*), and on the level of rewards on the debit card. In other words, the interchange fee, while officially an interbank fee, is not set to compensate issuers for the bankruptcy risk of the acquirer, but instead is based on the characteristics of the merchant and the consumer.

To understand why, one needs to recognize that all forms of payments exhibit network effects: the value of the payment system depends on the number of users. Payment systems, however, have two types of users: those paying and those accepting payment. For our purposes, let's oversimplify and call those paying "consumers" and those accepting payment "merchants." If merchants aren't willing to take a form of payment, then that payment system isn't valuable to consumers and vice versa.

This phenomenon is known as a **two-sided network**. It is not exclusive to payments—auction houses, brokerages, newspapers, and heterosexual dating services are all two-sided networks. This creates a chicken-and-egg problem when creating a new payment system: how do you get enough consumers and merchants simultaneously using the system so that it is appealing to both? And then how do you maintain the balance between them?

The answer is to adjust the costs of using the payment system so as to put more of the costs on the party most willing to pay. This is known as maximizing price elasticities. Maximization of price elasticities can be observed in night clubs that want to get a particular mix of men and women. (Another two-sided network.) Clubs sometimes host "ladies' nights," when discounts are given to women, who are presumed to be less willing than men to pay for the social network services of the club. Similarly, dating services will frequently charge men a different rate to participate than women.

The same goes for payments. If merchants are willing to pay more for a payment system than consumers, then the payment system will put more of the cost on merchants. Interchange fees are the mechanism for allocating costs with the debit card system. Although interchange fees formally shift costs between acquirer and issuers, they function to shift costs between the end users: merchants and consumers. Interchange fees affect merchants' costs because they set a floor for the merchant discount fee. Higher interchange fees mean higher merchant discount fees. Interchange fees also affect consumers' costs because they are used to fund issuers' rewards programs and to subsidize other costs of offering retail banking services. Historically, issuers accounted for rewards programs as reductions in interchange income. Rewards programs are estimated to account for only around 45% of the value of interchange, meaning that interchange is not a pure pass through from merchants to consumers.

In recent years interchange fees have been a particular point of content between merchants and banks, both for debit cards and credit cards (discussed below). Merchants have seen the cost of accepting payment card transactions steadily rise without any new benefits to card acceptance. While there are numerous benefits to card acceptance for merchants—payment guarantee, speed of payment, and security being foremost among them—merchants do not benefit from subsidizing rewards programs unless those rewards create loyalty to the specific merchant. The local dry cleaner does not benefit from funding consumers' frequent flyer miles. No one will get an extra shirt cleaned because of some miles.

The problem that merchants face is that payment card networks have rules that prohibit merchants from passing on the costs of accepting payments to consumers. Thus, there is discounting between the issuer and acquirer (interchange) and between the acquirer and the merchant (merchant discount fee), but restrictions on discounting debit (and credit) payments between the merchant and consumer. The merchant cannot say, "If you pay me with your debit card for $100 worth of goods, you'll have to pay $105." (Meaning that the payment would be discounted by $5 in terms of the good given.) For a payment card network, preventing such reallocation between merchants and consumers is critical to maximizing price elasticities and maximizing revenue. But consider how this kind of reallocation works in other two-sided networks. At ladies' night, a woman can always buy a man a drink. And there can be all sorts of reallocations outside of the club. The club cannot control the relationships among it various patrons. But that is what payment card networks do.

E. Merchant Restraint Rules

Merchants who accept payment cards agree in their contracts with their acquirer banks to be bound by the card networks' rules, although the rules are available to merchants only in abridged form, if at all. The networks employ a number of rules (sometimes called "**merchant restraints**") to increase card usage at the expense of other payment systems and to limit price competition within the credit card industry in order to maintain higher interchange rates. Each network has its own set of rules, but all are substantially similar. Additionally, state law in 11 states (with 40% of the U.S. population) prohibit surcharging for credit card transactions.[1]

Merchant restraints can be classified into two broad categories of interconnected rules. The first category consists of rules that restrict the way in which merchants can price credit cards. There are three rules in this category: **no-surcharge rules**, non-differentiation rules (also known as the all-products rule), and non-discrimination rules. No-surcharge rules forbid merchants to impose a surcharge for the use of credit (or debit) cards, thus linking the price consumers are charged for using credit cards with the price charged for using other payment systems. In effect this means that consumers almost never see an explicit price for using a particular payment system. Instead, the price of payment is bundled with that of the goods or services being purchased.

Whereas no-surcharge rules link credit card prices with other payment systems' prices, non-differentiation rules link the prices of different types of credit cards within a brand. Non-differentiation rules prohibit merchants from charging different prices for particular types of cards within a brand, even though costs to merchants vary significantly within brands. Consumers pay the same price to transact with all types of MasterCards, Visa cards, American Express cards, and Discover cards. Likewise, transactions on rewards cards and corporate cards do not cost cardholders more than transactions on regular consumer cards, even though they can cost merchants twice as much.

As a catchall, merchants are forbidden from discriminating against the card association's cards in any way. Thus, merchants may not use discourage the use of brands' cards through non-pricing methods. No-surcharge rules, non-differentiation rules, and non-discrimination rules prevent merchants from passing on the marginal cost of a consumer's choice of payment system to that consumer. Thus, consumers are not forced to internalize the full costs of their choice of payment system. Instead, at point of sale, all payment systems, as well as all card brands and all card types within card brands, have the same costs to consumers. Therefore, consumers choose among payment systems without factoring in point-of-sale costs.

---

1. The Supreme Court held that New York's no-surcharge statute was a regulation of speech because it restricted how merchants were able to communicate pricing and remanded for a determination of whether it constituted a First Amendment violation. Expressions Hair Design v. Schneiderman, 581 U.S. __ (2017). On remand, the case was certified to the New York Court of Appeals for clarification of the statute. *Expressions Hair Design v.* Schneiderman, 877 F.3d. 99 (2d Cir. 2017). California and Florida's no-surcharge laws have been held to be unconstitutional. *Italian Colors Restaurant v. Becerra*, 878 F.3d 1165 (9th Cir. 2018); Dana's R.R. Supply v. Attorney General, 807 F.3d 1235 (11th Cir. 2015).

The second category of merchant restraints consists of rules that restrict merchants' ability to selectively accept particular credit cards or to selectively accept credit cards for particular transactions. These rules are the honor-all-cards rule (also known as the all-banks or all-issuers rule), the all-outlets rule, and the no-minimum- and no-maximum-amount rule. The honor-all-cards rule requires merchants to accept all credit cards bearing the card association's brand, while the all-outlets rule requires merchants to accept cards at all their locations (all-outlets rule), regardless of different business models (*e.g.,* Internet store, mainline retail, discount outlet).

The no-minimum- and no-maximum-amount rule forbids merchants from imposing either a minimum or maximum charge amount, although this rule is widely flouted. The no-minimum- and no-maximum-amount rule prevent merchants from steering transactions on which card payments are particularly costly to non-card payment systems. Small transactions are less profitable for merchants when paid on a bank payment card because the flat fee part of the interchange fee schedule. On a small transaction, the flat fee amount can consume a significant amount of a merchant's profit margin.

Honor-all-cards, all-outlets, and no-minimum- and no-maximum-amount rules prevent merchants from picking and choosing what sort of cards they will to accept within a card brand and for which transactions they will accept credit cards. Card acceptance is an all-or-none proposition within a brand, even though the costs to merchants of card acceptance vary enormously among cards within a brand and by transaction size.

The net effects of the card associations' rules are: (1) to force merchants to charge the same price for goods or services, regardless of a consumer's payment method; (2) to prevent merchants from steering consumers to cheaper payment options; and (3) to increase the number of credit card transactions and thus interchange and ultimately interest income for issuers.

Merchant restraints also prevent consumers from accounting for the cost of payment systems when deciding which one to use. Instead, consumers decide based solely on factors such as convenience, bundled rewards, image, and float. These factors tend to favor credit card transactions over other payment systems. Higher purchase volume increases issuers' income on the front end in terms of interchange fees and on the back end in terms of more interest, late fees, and penalties.

Merchant restraint rules have a profound, if hidden effect on consumers. The cost of accepting payment cards is typically higher than the cost of accepting other forms of payment. Yet merchants are unable to force cost internalization on those consumers who use higher-cost forms of payment because of merchant restraints. The result is that all consumers pay the same price for goods and services, irrespective of their method of payment. So who absorbs the cost of the higher-costing payment systems? The answer depends on how competitive the merchant's industry is, but the cost will be either absorbed by the merchant in the form of reduced profit margins or by consumers in the form of higher prices and less service. To the extent that the cost of payment cards is passed on to consumers, it means that consumers with lower-cost payment systems, such as cash or non-rewards cards, are subsidizing those with higher-cost payment systems, like rewards cards. This is likely a regressive cross-subsidy from lower-income cash consumers to higher-income credit card consumers. It also incentivizes greater use of the most expensive payment system—credit cards—by funding rewards, which make the cost *to a consumer* of using a credit card just as a transacting device lower and possibly negative. By the law of large numbers, if more consumers are using credit cards for payments, more of them will end up—unintentionally—using credit cards to revolve a balance and paying interest and fees for the privilege.

Merchant restraints have been a sore point for merchants, who have pursued both anti-trust litigation and legislative initiatives to try to either lower the cost of accepting payments or at least enable the costs to be passed on to consumers (which would presumably make card payments less desirable and therefore end up forcing lower costs to merchants). For debit cards, merchants' legislative campaign was successful and debit card interchange fees have been regulated by federal law since 2010 under a provision of the Dodd-Frank Act known as the Durbin Interchange Amendment.

F. Durbin Amendment and Regulation of Debit Interchange Fees

The Durbin Amendment has two main requirements: a debit interchange fee price cap provision and then a set of provisions aimed at fostering price competition beneath the price cap. First, the Durbin Amendment requires that interchange fees on all electronic debit transactions must be "reasonable and proportional to the cost incurred by the issuer with respect to the transaction." 15 U.S.C. § 1693o-2(a). This provision applies solely to interchange fees received by banks and credit unions with total consolidated assets of at least $10 billion—roughly 100 of the over 14,000 banks and credit unions in the United States. 15 U.S.C. § 1693o-2(a)(6). Also exempted are government-administered electronic benefit cards and reloadable prepaid cards that are not "gift cards." 15 U.S.C. § 1693o-2(a)(7).

"Reasonable and proportional to the cost" is defined by Federal Reserve Board regulation. The Federal Reserve has defined a safe harbor for debit interchange fees at 21 cents per transaction plus a 1 cent per transaction issuer-specific variance above the incremental cost for a transaction for fraud prevention costs, provided that the issuer complies with certain fraud prevention standards.

The Durbin Amendment also attempts to foster competition beneath the price cap among payment card networks for debit card transactions. To this end, the Durbin Amendment prohibits various payment card network rules that have limited price competition among networks. 15 U.S.C. § 1693o-2(b). The cost to a merchant of an electronic debit transaction is not just the interchange fee. It also includes any network fees and the acquirer's spread. Most merchants pay a merchant discount fee that is explicitly priced as "interchange plus," meaning that the merchant pays a fee that is equal to the interchange rate plus network fees plus the acquirer's spread. As acquirers' spread is generally the same irrespective of the network over which a transaction is routed, the distinction in pricing between networks typically depends on the sum of interchange and network fees.

It is the total pricing bundle of interchange and network fees, not the breakdown therein, that is relevant to merchants. Whereas the Durbin Amendment price cap addresses only interchange fees, the other provisions are aimed at affecting the total pricing bundle (interchange plus other fees) that merchants face for electronic debit transactions. In other words, while the first part of the Durbin Amendment involves regulatory price capping, the second part of the Durbin Amendment relies on market competition to control prices.

The key provision is of the second part of the Amendment is the so-called **multi-homing** provision. Multi-homing refers to the ability to route a payment card transaction over multiple networks.[2] When multi-homing is possible, the transaction can find its way "home" through multiple routings. 15 U.S.C. § 1693o-2(b)(1)(A). The Amendment further provides that neither card issuers nor networks may restrict the ability of merchants to direct the routing of the transaction. 15 U.S.C. § 1693o-2(b)(1)(B).

The effect of the Durbin Amendment has been to significantly lower interchange fees at non-exempt issuers: fees fell from 43 cents per transaction in 2009 to 23 cents per transaction in 2016, with fees virtually equal for signature debit and PIN debit, meaning that because of the regulation, signature debit fees have fallen to PIN debit fee levels. In contrast, exempt issuers' fees in 2016 remained at 42 cents, which broke down to an average of 51 cents per transaction for signature debit and 26 cents per transaction for PIN debit, meaning that without regulation signature debit remains more expensive than PIN debit. Federal Reserve Board, Average Debit Card Interchange Fee by Payment Card Network.

G. The Durbin Amendment and Merchant Restraints

The Durbin Amendment also has a set of provisions that apply not just to debit cards, but to all payment cards. The Durbin Amendment prohibits restrictions on the offering of discounts for the use of a particular form of payment. Federal law had previously authorized cash discounts, but the Durbin Amendment expands this and provides that merchants may always offer a discount or in-kind incentive for payment in any form. The Durbin Amendment does not authorize surcharging, although mathematically a surcharge and a discount are indistinguishable. (Behaviorally, however, they are not—consumers have mild positive reactions to discounts, but strongly negative reactions to surcharges.)

The Durbin Amendment also limits payment card networks from setting minimum and maximum transaction amounts. Payment card networks may not prohibit minimum transaction amounts, so long as the minimum transaction amount is no more than $10. Thus, unless state law prohibits a minimum amount, a merchant may state that payment cards are not accepted for transactions of less than $10. Federal agencies (like the IRS) and higher education institutions may also impose maximum transaction amounts. 15 U.S.C. § 1693o-2(b)(3). These provisions

2. *See* Jean-Charles Rochet & Jean Tirole, *Platform Competition in Two-Sided Markets*, 1 J. Eur. Econ. Ass'n 990, 995 (2003) (adopting the Internet protocol term "multi-homing" and applying it payment card network context in which "a fraction of end users on one or the two sides connect to several platforms").

pare back some of the merchant restraint rules, but they do not allow merchants to discriminate among debit cards or among credit cards based on the issuer. 15 U.S.C. § 1693o-2(b)(4). Whether a merchant could discriminate among cards on other grounds would depend on card network and state law.

II. AUTOMATED CLEARINGHOUSE (ACH)

The automated clearinghouse or ACH is an electronic payment method for moving funds between accounts at depository institutions. ACH is one of the largest payment methods for business and consumer transactions. In 2017, there were over 21.5 billion ACH transactions for nearly $47 trillion performed in the United States.[3] Despite the volume of ACH payments, ACH remains one of the least familiar payment systems to consumers, at least in name, because it does not have a distinctive retail façade as ACH transactions do not require a special access device like a check or payment card. Instead, an ACH transaction merely requires transmission of a bank account and bank routing number, which can be done orally, in print, or electronically.

A. Parties to an ACH Transaction

Structurally, an ACH transaction looks much like a debit card or credit card transaction, with a network operator that intermediates between the payor and the payee's financial institutions. An ACH transaction involves (at least) five roles:[4] an Originator, a Receiver, an Originator's depository financial institution (ODFI), a Receiver's depository financial institution (RDFI), and an ACH Operator. Sometimes there will also be a Third-Party Payment Processor (TPPP) involved as well, which serves as an agent for the Originator.

Both the ODFI and RDFI are always banks. The Originator (or TPPP, if one is involved in the transaction) has a bank account at the ODFI, while the Receiver has a bank account at the RDFI. The ODFI and RDFI each have accounts with the ACH Operator. There are only two ACH Operators in the United States: the Federal Reserve System's FedACH and the Clearing House's Electronic Payments Network.

B. How an ACH Transaction Works

In an ACH transaction, the Originator instructs the ODFI to submit a debit or credit instruction to the ACH Operator, which is the clearinghouse. The flow of funds and the applicable NACHA rules depend on whether an ACH transaction is an **"ACH credit"** or **"ACH debit"** transaction. The difference between an ACH credit and an ACH debit transaction is whether the *Receiver's* account is credited or debited. NACHA 2013 Operating Guide at OG2. Obviously a debit to the Receiver's

---

3. NACHA, ACH Network Statistics 2017.

4. It is possible that the ODFI and RDFI are the same institution in an "on-us" ACH transaction. Also, sometimes more than one ACH Operator will be involved in a transaction.

account should be matched by a credit to an Originator's account or vice versa, so the terminology is confusing.

Irrespective of whether the Receiver's account is credited or debited, data flows are the same in all ACH transactions and explain the ACH system's terminology: data flows always start with the Originator and end with the Receiver. In an ACH credit transaction, the data and funds move the same direction, from Originator to Receiver, while in an ACH debit transaction, the data flows from Originator to Receiver, but the funds flow the opposite direction. Thus, an ACH credit transaction is a "push" of funds by the payor, whereas an ACH debit is a "pull" of funds from the payor.

C. ACH Credit Transactions

In an ACH credit transaction, such as direct deposit, the Originator (e.g., an employer) directs its ODFI to transfer funds to the Receiver (e.g., an employee). The ODFI will transmit both an electronic ACH file and funds to the ACH Operator, which will then transmit the ACH file to the RDFI and credit the RDFI's account. The RDFI will then settle the funds into the Receiver's account. Note that in order to do this sort of transaction, the Originator needs the Receiver's bank account and routing numbers. Also note that the information flow (the movement of the ACH file) goes in the same direction as the funds. Additionally note that there is no paper moving in an ACH transaction; all flows of information are processed electronically. Figure 4, below, illustrates an ACH credit transaction.

Figure 19.4 ACH Credit Transaction

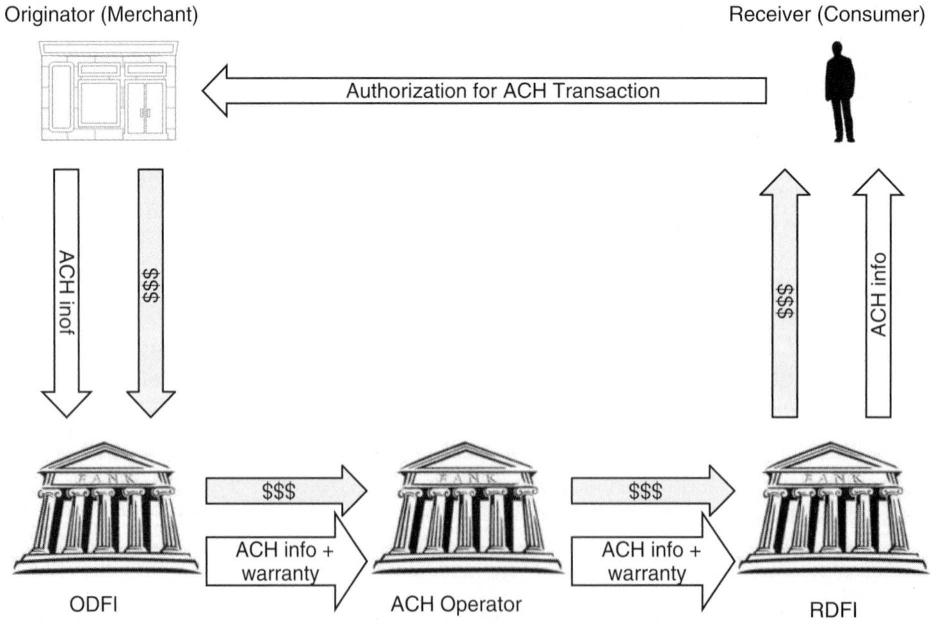

D. ACH Debit Transactions

In an ACH debit transaction, such as a recurring monthly debit of an account by a mortgage lender per the borrower's authorization, the Originator (the mortgage lender) directs the ODFI to request that the RDFI transfer funds from the account of the Receiver (the borrower) at the RDFI. In order to do so, the Receiver must have authorized the transaction. The pre-authorization might be written (as in a recurring bill payment arrangement), oral (for telephone transactions), or electronic (for Internet or card-based transactions). The pre-authorization might precede the transaction by only a nanosecond.

After obtaining the Receiver's authorization, the Originator transmits the transaction information, including the Receiver's bank routing and account number, to the ODFI. The ODFI then formats this information into an electronic file (an ACH file). The ODFI will then transmit the ACH file to the ACH Operator, which will transmit it to the RDFI, which, if there is money in the account of the Receiver (the borrower), will debit the account and transmit the funds to the ACH Operator, which will credit the ODFI's account, with the ODFI then settling the funds into the account of the Originator (the mortgage lender) at the ODFI.[5] Figure 5, below, illustrates an ACH debit transaction.

Figure 19.5 ACH Debit Transaction

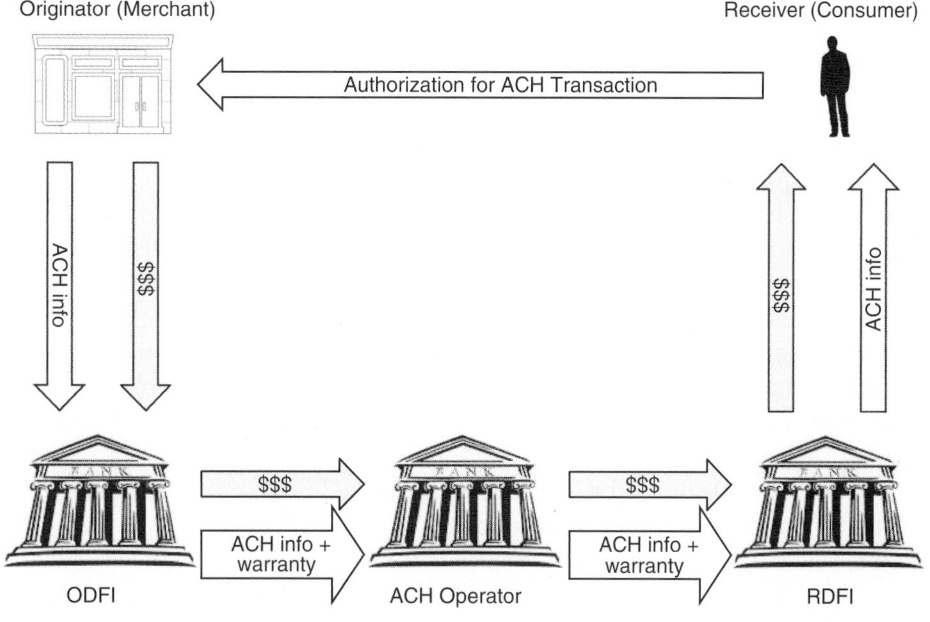

5. ACH is a batch processing system, which means that individual transactions are not processed in real time. Instead, the ODFI accumulates ACH transactions and sorts them by destination for electronic transmission to the ACH Operator at a predetermined time. NACHA Operating Guide 2017, at OG1. The transactions batched in a particular time period are netted out by the ACH Operator among the various ODFIs and RDFIs in the system. The batch processing creates economies of scale as compared to the alternative of real time gross settlement such as is used in FedWire wire transfers (the continuous settlement of individual funds transfers on an order-by-order basis without netting).

In an ACH debit transaction, the information flow is opposite the funds flow. In an ACH debit transaction, the Originator initiates the transaction, but is somewhat confusingly the payee. The distinction between ACH debit and ACH credit matters in terms of different settlement speed rules.

E. ACH Processing

ACH is a **batch processing system**, meaning that ACH transactions are not processed in real time, but in batches. The ODFI accumulates ACH transactions (known as ACH "entries") and sorts them by destination for electronic transmission to the ACH Operator at a predetermined time. NACHA Operating Guide 2017, at OG1. The entries batched in a particular time period are netted out by the ACH Operator among the various ODFIs and RDFIs in the system. The batch processing creates economies of scale as compared to the alternative of real time gross settlement such as is used in FedWire wire transfers (the continuous settlement of individual funds transfers on an order-by-order basis without netting).

The ACH Operator nets out the ACH transactions among the various ODFIs and RDFIs within a time period and credits and debits the ODFIs' and RDFIs' accounts with the Operator, while transmitting the information about which recipient's account to credit or debit to the RDFIs, which then settle the transferred funds into the recipient's account at the RDFI.

F. Basic Rules for ACH Transactions

Different rules govern consumer and business ACH transactions. ACH transactions involving consumers are governed by a combination of the Electronic Fund Transfer Act and Regulation E thereunder and the rules of the National Automated Clearing House Association (NACHA), a not-for-profit membership association of banks that sets the standards for ACH operations in the United States.[6] Business-to-business ACH transactions are governed by NACHA rules and contract law. NACHA rules differ in some cases for business-to-business and consumer transactions.

The EFTA and Reg E apply only to transfers by financial institutions to/from "accounts," which are defined as having "a demand deposit (checking), savings, or other consumer asset account . . . held directly or indirectly by a financial institution and established primarily for personal, family, or household purposes." 12 C.F.R. §§ 1005.2(b)(1), 1005.2(b)(7); 15 U.S.C. § 1693a(2). Accordingly, the EFTA and Reg E apply only to consumer transactions.

Reg E sets a baseline for ACH consumer transactions, with NACHA rules providing additional consumer protections in some cases. Reg E error resolution and unauthorized transaction liability rules (covered in Chapter 18) apply to ACH

6. NACHA Rules are a private set of industry self-regulatory rules, adopted by either a three-fourths vote of NACHA members by number or a two-thirds vote by weighted transaction volume. In other words, NACHA Rules are rules that banks themselves think are necessary.

transactions, but NACHA rules create some additional consumer rights and business risks.

NACHA rules create a set of mandatory warranties from ODFIs to RDFIs, including that the transaction complies with NACHA rules, which incorporate a broad provision that the ACH entries do not "violate the laws of the United States," thereby making the ODFI essentially vouch for the legality of the transaction.[7] These warranties are backed up with indemnification of the RDFI by the ODFI.[8]

The most critical of all NACHA rules incorporated into the ODFI warranties is that an Originator must receive authorization for an ACH transaction from the Receiver. NACHA Operating Rule 2.3.1. This applies to ACH credit and ACH debit transactions. Authorization is not just for the transaction with the particular Originator, but also for the amount and the timing of the transaction. NACHA Operating Rule 3.12.1. Authorization is waived for person-to-person credits, and may be oral only for business-to-consumer credits. NACHA Operating Rule 2.3.2.1. Authorization of debits from a consumer's account must be in writing or "similarly authenticated." NACHA Operating Rule 2.3.2.2. For debits, the Originator must provide the Receiver with an electronic or hard copy of the authorization, which the Receiver must retain for two years. NACHA Operating Rule 2.3.2.5. Thus, not only is the ODFI vouching for the legality of the transaction, it is also vouching for the authorization of the transaction through its NACHA warranties to the RDFI.

G. ACH Conversion of Checks

Some ACH transactions involve the conversion of checks into ACH items. Recall that to perform an ACH transaction what is needed is authorization plus the Receiver's bank account and routing number. A check contains the bank account and routing number, so it can easily be converted into an ACH entry. This can be done by a business or by a bank on behalf of a business or consumer. For example, remote deposit of checks involves either conversion of the check to an ACH entry by the depositor itself or for the depositor to transmit a picture of the check to the depository bank, which will convert the account and routing number into an ACH entry. Depending on where the conversion is done, it is treated as a different type of ACH entry, but in all cases authorization is still needed to be provided by the Receiver to the Originator. Thus, NACHA rules require language similar to the following to authorize ACH conversion:

> When you provide a check as payment, you authorize us either to use information from your check to make a one-time electronic fund transfer from your account or to process the payment as a check transaction.

Conversion of physical items to electronic creates a potential problem of multiple payments. When physical checks are converted into ACH entries, the physical check is supposed to be destroyed after the ACH entry is processed. This does not always

7. NACHA Rule 2.4.1 (ODFI warranties to RDFI).
8. NACHA Rule 2.4.4 (ODFI indemnification of RDFI).

happen, however, and sometimes the physical check is presented for payment subsequently, which can result in a double debit against the payor's account.

H. Funds Availability

Regulation D creates the baseline rule for ACH funds availability. Regulation D provides that a bank must make funds available on the business day following the banking day on which it "actually and finally collected funds" from an electronic payment. 12 C.F.R. § 229.10(b)(1). NACHA Rules provide additional requirements. NACHA requires that a Receiver's account may not be debited prior to the settlement date—when the DFI is credited or debited by the ACH Operator, and that an ACH credit entry must be made available to the Receiver no later than the settlement date. NACHA Operating Rules 3.3.1.1, 3.3.2. A special rule applies to ACH transactions for direct deposit of payroll. These transactions are known by a three-letter Standard Entry Code (SEC) indicating type of ACH transaction PPD (Prearranged Payment and Deposit). If the ACH Operator makes it available to the RFDI by 5:00 p.m. on the banking day before the settlement day, then the RDFI must make funds available at the start of the settlement day (generally 9:00 a.m. local time). This ensures that payroll funds are available at the earliest possible time for employees.

I. Stop Payments

ACH enables stop payments. An RDFI is generally obligated to honor a stop payment request from a Receiver with three business days before a scheduled debit. NACHA Operating Rule 3.7.1. The request may be written or oral. *Id.* Within the three-business-day window, the RDFI may honor the stop payment request at its discretion. For a single entry (one-time payment), the RDFI must honor the stop payment if made within an unspecified reasonable time period. NACHA Operating Rule 3.7.1.2. The RDFI may require written confirmation of an oral stop instruction. If so, the oral stop instruction terminates within 14 days. Once an ACH file is transmitted to the ACH Operator, however, it cannot be stopped. NACHA Rule 2.7. The transaction can be reversed, however, if it is for the wrong dollar amount, made to the wrong account, or a duplicate transaction. NACHA Operating Rule 2.9.1. Reversals must be undertaken within 24 hours of discovery of the error and in all cases within five banking days of the original entry. NACHA Operating Rule 2.8.3. If the payee's account is overdrawn or closed, however, the bank that has received the payment is under no obligation to reverse the debit. In other words, the bank that received the payment is not required to incur any credit risk itself because of an error.

J. ACH Returns

ACH transactions may be denied or, in ACH parlance, "returned." An ACH "return" item is separate and distinct from a return of merchandise paid for via

ACH. Thus, a firm like Zappos, which sells shoes and other merchandise online, has a high rate of *merchandise* returns, but this does not mean that Zappos has a high *ACH* return rate. If a customer pays for shoes from Zappos via ACH and then returns shoes to Zappos, there is not normally an ACH return. Instead, Zappos would return the funds via an offsetting ACH credit.

ACH returns may happen for insufficient funds or for lack of authorization. ACH credit transactions will not happen if there are insufficient funds absent an overdraft, which is a matter between the Originator and the ODFI. The ODFI will not transmit the ACH file absent sufficient funds.

ACH debit transactions, however, can be presented for payment when there are insufficient funds in the account of the Receiver (payee) at the RDFI. ACH debit transactions can be represented for payment twice (for a total of three presentments, the so-called **three-bites-at-the-apple** rule) within 180 days. NACHA Rule 2.12.4.

Under NACHA rules, if the Receiver has insufficient funds at the RDFI, the RDFI must return the ACH debit. (The RDFI may, by contract, pass the costs on to the Receiver as an overdraft.) The return must be transmitted by the RFDI by the opening of business on the second banking day after the settlement date. NACHA Operating Rule 3.8. Otherwise, the payment becomes the RDFI's own liability. As settlement may occur on the day following the ACH transaction, an Originator of an ACH debit item might not be sure that it would be paid for a couple of days. Accordingly, ACH debit creates a risk for merchants in point-of-sale transactions because they will have parted with goods before being assured of payment.

NACHA rules also require that if the Receiver did not in fact authorize the ACH debit, the RDFI return the ACH (entitling it to reimbursement for any funds it has transmitted) within 60 days of posting the debit to the Receiver's account. NACHA Operating Rule 3.13.1(b). The RDFI must also re-credit the Receiver's account. NACHA Operating Rule 3.11. RDFI must accept a written statement from a Receiver that a transaction was unauthorized. NACHA Operating Rule 3.12.4.

The return time limit for unauthorized ACH transactions raises a potential problem for RDFI because under Regulation E, a consumer has 60 days from notification to dispute a transaction under Regulation E. The consumer might receive notification via a bank statement 30 days after settlement. This means that the 60-day ACH return period could expire before the consumer's 60-day dispute right expires. In other words, the RDFI is protected for days 1-60, but the consumer's dispute right could run from days 30-90, leaving the RDFI on the hook for any unauthorized transactions that are not disputed until days 61-90.

ACH debit returns present a risk for ODFIs too. Most directly, ODFIs are assessed an "unauthorized entry fee" of $4.50 per return (paid to the RDFI) if the return is due to an authorization issue.[9] Additionally, there is a risk to ODFIs of originator insolvency that is similar to the risk an acquirer bank assumes in a credit card or debit card transaction. Suppose a consumer contends that she did not authorize an ACH debit and timely notifies her bank (the RDFI) after the funds have been

9. NACHA, *Improving ACH Network Quality—Unauthorized Entry Fee, at* https://www.nacha.org/rules/improving-ach-network-quality-unauthorized-entry-fee.

debited but before 60 days from the debiting have lapsed. In such a situation, RDFI will "return" the ACH debit item and look to be reimbursed by the lender's bank (the ODFI) for the funds that were improperly debited from the consumer's bank account. The RDFI will have a right to the funds from the ODFI because the ODFI has violated its warranty that the transaction was authorized and indemnified the RDFI for any costs arising from an unauthorized transaction.[10] The ODFI bank will be on the hook for these funds; it will have the right to recover them from the lender, but if the lender is out of business or insolvent, the ODFI will bear the loss. The important point to see here is that the ODFI is vouching for the transaction and may be liable for it.

K. Third-Party Payment Processors

Some ACH transactions involve a Third-Party Payment Processor (TPPP). A TPPP serves as an agent for the Originator. The Originator will transmit the transaction information to the TPPP, which will in turn transmit the information to the ODFI. In some cases, TPPP are allowed to have direct access to the ACH Operator for debit transactions.[11] Figure 19.6, below, illustrates an ACH debit transaction involving a TPPP.

There are legitimate uses of TPPP, which have specialization and technical capacities that many Originators lack. The use of TPPPs began in the context of payroll

Figure 19.6 ACH Debit Transaction with Third-Party Payment Processor

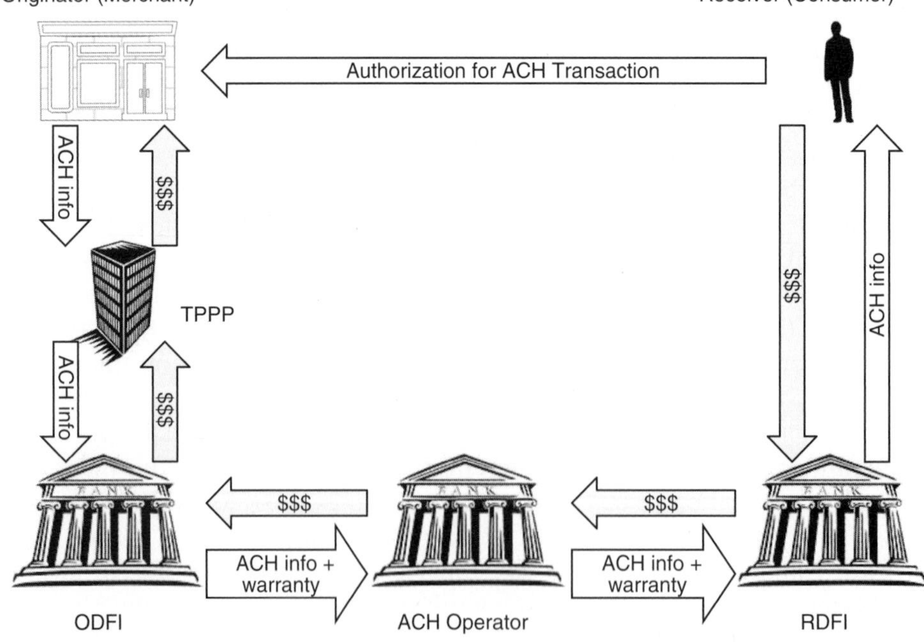

10. NACHA Rules 2.4.1 (ODFI warranties to RDFI); 2.4.4 (ODFI indemnification of RDFI).
11. NACHA Rule 2.2.2.2.

management firms that were making ACH *credit* transactions (direct deposit), where funds were being transferred *to* consumers' accounts. ACH debit, however, involves transfers *from* consumers' accounts and is therefore more likely to raise concerns about whether the transactions are authorized.

NACHA Rules aim to ensure the integrity of the ACH payment system and the trust and confidence of its users. Accordingly, NACHA Rules require ODFIs to monitor Originators' or TPPP's return rates for unauthorized ACH debit transactions. NACHA Rules currently have a 0.5% threshold for unauthorized debit transaction return rates.[12] The average NACHA unauthorized debit transaction return rate in 2013 was 0.03%.[13] NACHA also has a 3.0% threshold for debit returns for administrative or account data errors and a 15% threshold for all debit returns for any reason (excluding ACH conversions of previously bounced checks). Figure 19.6 below illustrates an ACH debit transaction with a third-party payment processor.

If an unauthorized transaction return rate exceeds 0.5%, then within 10 banking days the ODFI must submit to NACHA various information about the Originator or TPPP, submit a plan for reducing the return rate to no more than 0.5% within thirty days, and must in fact achieve such a reduction and maintain it for an additional 180 days.[14] If the ODFI fails to do so, it is subject to fines or suspension by NACHA.[15] NACHA fines and NACHA suspension, in particular, present a material risk for ODFIs. As a result, ODFIs will often simply terminate their business relationship with Originators whose unauthorized transaction return rates exceed the 0.5% threshold.

Because Originators with high unauthorized return rates for ACH debit risk being cut out of the ACH system, they often seek to use TPPPs to mask their return rates. TPPPs typically serve multiple Originators. Because the return rate for a TPPP with multiple Originators is the transaction weighted average return rate of all of its Originators, an Originator that uses a TPPP can have an unauthorized transaction return rate that exceeds the NACHA threshold if the TPPP also serves Originators with low return rates. Thus, the use of TPPPs enables Originators with high unauthorized transaction return rates to maintain access to the ACH system. NACHA has recognized this risk and since July 18, 2010 has required that ODFI's contracts with TPPPs include provisions that give the ODFI the right to terminate or suspect the contract or to terminate or suspend any Originator of the TPPP.

L. ACH Compared with Other Payment Systems

ACH differs from checks operationally in several key ways. First, ACH is an entirely electronic payment system. No paper is involved. Second, ACH can involve

12. NACHA Rules 2.17.2.1, 8.1.1.3, 10.2.1.

13. NACHA, *ACH Network Risk and Enforcement Topics*, *at* https://www.nacha.org/rules/ach-network-risk-and-enforcement-topics.

14. NACHA Rules 2.17.2.1, 2.17.2.2, 8.1.1.3.

15. NACHA Rule 10.2.2.

both credit and debit transactions, whereas checks are solely debit.[16] And third, excluding on-us transactions, ACH transactions all go through clearinghouses; there are no bilateral ACH exchanges.

ACH differs from debit card and credit card payments in a few ways as well.[17] First, ACH is not a guaranteed payment. Neither ACH nor debit card and credit card payments are real time payments, but debit and credit card payments made over a payment card network are guaranteed by the card network (but paid by the card issuer, unless the issuer fails, in which case the loss is borne by the network). Therefore, the seller of goods in a point-of-sale transaction can be confident that it will be paid, be it by the consumer, issuer, or network. In an ACH debit transaction, there is no guarantee of payment. If the Originator's account at the ODFI does not have sufficient funds, the transaction will not go through. The seller of goods at point of sale will not know this, however, for at least 48 hours. Therefore, ACH point-of-sale debit has been slow to catch on relative to other ACH debit transactions, such as bill payment.

Second, ACH does not require either the payor (known as the Originator) or the payee (known as the recipient) to have a relationship with a particular clearinghouse. Debit and credit card payments require that the payor be a cardholder, meaning that the payor holds a card issued by a financial institution that is a member of a payment card network (which operates as the clearinghouse for the payments). The payee must also have an account with a bank that is a member of the same payment card network. While neither the payor nor the payee usually has contractual dealings with the network, they are bound by the network rules, as we have seen in the previous chapter. A consumer with a MasterCard cannot use the card to pay a merchant that only takes Visa. ACH is different. Anyone with a bank account can make or receive an ACH payment to or from anyone with a bank account. There is not requirement that each party deal with a bank that is a member of the same ACH network.

Beyond this, the major differences between ACH and debit and credit card payments are who controls the "rails" over which the transactions are processed, the particular network rules, and the costs involved. ACH transactions are incredibly cheap. FedACH's 2018 fees are volume-based, but range from $0.0002-$0.0035 per transaction for ODFIs (with a minimum of $50/month) and from $0.0017 to $0.0035 per transaction for RDFIs (with a minimum of $40/month). ODFIs are charged a surcharge of $0.0010 per item for same-day ACH service. FedACH Services 2018 Fee Schedule. In addition, NACHA charges financial institutions using ACH $216 annually and plus $0.000162 per transaction, irrespective of transaction size. NACHA

16. Technically, checks are orders for payment, which seem like ACH credit, but the presentation structure, in which the payee presents the check for payment, is more like a debit pulling funds from the payor's account.

17. There are ACH debit cards. These cards are primarily merchant-issued, although Capital One and HSBC both had experiments in "decoupled debit" products, which involved cards issued by Capital One or HSBC that could be used for ACH transactions drawing on deposit accounts at other banks. The idea was that the payment device relationship need not be linked to the deposit account relationship. The Federal Reserve Board's Durbin Interchange Amendment rulemaking has made decoupled debit a financially impracticable product.

Network Administration Fees, 2017 Schedule of Fees. The low cost of ACH transactions makes them very attractive to businesses that are looking to make or receive payments, but less attractive to financial institutions, which do not have an obvious method of profiting from ACH.

Problem Set 19

1. Justin Horton is contemplating signing a landscaping and lawn care contract with Elaine Ellis Lawn Services. Ellis is charging $5,000 annually for the services, to be billed monthly at the start of each month, but is offering a 3% discount for prepayment by check. Horton is debating whether to prepay given that his rewards card pays only 1% cash back on the transaction. Why is Ellis offering the discount and what should Horton do?

2. Ja Rule Productions LLC was promoting Fyre Festival, an ultra-exclusive music festival in the Bahamas. Hundreds of incurably hip, affluent individuals paid Ja Rule Productions LLC $1,200 or more in advance on their credit cards for various festival packages of admission, food, drinks, and lodging. Unfortunately, the Fyre Festival was unable to deliver on its promise of music, food, drinks, lodging, and proximity to the rich and famous, and Ja Rule Productions LLC lacks the funds to refund the festival packages because it had spent the money on organizing the festival. Who bears the loss in such a situation, and how could it be minimized?

3. Burger Urger, a regional fast-food chain restaurant has been paying its employees in cash. In order to make this work, at the end of every Thursday the Burger Urger's corporate treasury transfers payroll funds from Burger Urger's general corporate bank account to an armored car company for delivery to various Burger Urger's locations during the day on Friday.

This system has some problems. Sometimes the armored cars get stuck in traffic and are late, so employees have to stick around waiting to get paid, which causes particular problems for those employees with child-care obligations, who need the cash to make payments due by the close of business on Friday, or who have other obligations on Fridays. The cash payment system also requires employees who do not work on Friday to show up at the restaurants to get paid, but the time at which the money will arrive is unpredictable. There's also an occasional theft risk—the armored cars have been robbed on occasion. While the funds are guarantied by the armored car company, the robberies further delay payroll. Additionally, there's been a spate of robberies of employees on Fridays after payroll is delivered.

Burger Urger's has asked your advice on what it can do it improve its payroll system. It wants to find the cheapest system possible, but also to do right by its employees and enable them to get paid in full for the hard work they've done.

4. QuickiCash is a small storefront payday lender that makes short-term cash advances to customers against their future paychecks or government benefit checks. Quickicash requires its customers to provide both a note promising repayment and a post-dated personal check, dated to the maturity date of the loan. If the customer fails to repay the loan at maturity, QuickiCash will cash the check. Chris Peterson, the owner

of QuickiCash, is frustrated that often customers fail to repay *and* the post-dated checks bounce, resulting in QuickiCash getting hit with bounce fees from its bank, Banco Merica.

a. Chris's heard that some payday lenders are using ACH rather than the checking system to collect from customers and is interested in learning more. He's come to your law office to learn what benefits and risks there are to him from using ACH. What do you tell him?

b. Now suppose that your client is the Banco Merica. What risks does the bank assume with ACH, and how do you minimize them? *See* NACHA Rules 2.4.1, 2.4.4; 31 C.F.R. § 1020.320(a)(2) (*see* Chapter 17).

5. Meglomart, a major big-box retailer that operates in all 50 states, wants to encourage its customers to make payments with the cheapest possible payment methods, ideally ACH, but if not ACH, then PIN debit. Meglomart also recognizes that some customers lack the readily available funds to make large purchases (such as for flat-screen TVs) and will need to make such purchases on credit cards. Meglomart's business model is based on high sales volume and low profit margins, and it famously squeezes all of its suppliers to keep down prices. What can Meglomart do to encourage consumers to use ACH and/or PIN debit, or, if paying with credit card, to use lower-cost credit card options?

CHAPTER 20

PAYMENT LIABILITY RULES

I. LIABILITY RULES FOR PAYMENTS

Payments law has five major issues: speed, costs, authorization, errors, and finality. The five major payments issues are, of course, not completely separable. The Durbin Amendment adjusts debit card fee caps based on fraud losses, which are an authorization issue. Fraud losses in turn can relate to speed of transactions, as we saw with check kiting. And errors are linked to finality—if a mistake is made, can it be unwound? Nonetheless, conceptually it is helpful to distinguish between these issues.

As it happens we have already covered some of these issues. We saw some aspects of speed issues in Chapter 12, when dealing with funds availability. We covered costs issues in Chapters 16 and 17. In this chapter, we address the three remaining issues—authorization, errors, and finality.

A. Authorization

Absent authorization of the payor (or court order), funds cannot legally be taken out of a consumer's deposit account, prepaid card, or line of credit. Yet unauthorized transactions happen all the time because of fraud. In the typical payments fraud scenario, the consumer has authorized no payment whatsoever, but a fraudster directs a payment from the consumer's account. In other situations, the consumer might have authorized a payment, but the fraudster will redirect it or will change the payment amount.

Different payment systems have different authorization methods, but they are all vulnerable to various types of fraud, be it family fraud (*e.g.*, a child using a parent's credit card without authorization) or stranger fraud (*e.g.*, my hacker cousin Boris stealing your credit card information and using it to make purchases in your name). Different types of payment systems allocate fraud liability in different ways. Ideally, the fraudster is liable for the loss. But often there's no recovery to be had from the fraudster, at least not immediately. Who is liable, then, for the loss on the fraud? Non-cash payments involve financial institutions acting as agents for consumers and businesses that are making and receiving payments. Agents need authority to act. If a payment has not been authorized, the agent lacks authority to make the transaction and may therefore be liable for the transaction itself. Does the loss fall on the consumer, the consumer's financial institution, the financial institution of the payment's recipient (which might be the fraudster's bank or might be the bank of a merchant), or a third party that parted with goods or services in exchange for the unauthorized payment? What incentives will such liability rules create? Should parties' negligence affect the liability allocations? As we will see, the loss-allocation rules stem from different federal and state laws as well as from contract and are not consistent across payment systems. Query whether that comports with consumers' expectations.

B. Errors

To err is human, and payments are no exception. People make mistakes with payment instructions, either indicating an incorrect transferee or an incorrect payment amount or time. Even if error rates are low, the frequency of payment transactions—the most common type of transaction there is—means that as an absolute number, there will be numerous errors in any payment system. Financial institutions can also make mistakes with payments, crediting or debiting the wrong account or for the wrong amount or at the wrong time. As payments have become increasingly automated, however, financial institution error rates have likely fallen (although there is no industry-wide data). Instead, the financial institution is likely to simply execute the instructions given by the consumer, irrespective of whether they contain an error.

Errors are costly, and that cost must be borne by someone. Who has the liability for errors in payment? Different systems have different rules, as we shall see, but generally the principle that governs error liability in payments is a tort principle of putting the liability on the least-cost avoider of the error.

C. Finality

Different payment systems operate at different speeds. This means that some slower systems offer chances to stop or unwind transactions before they are final. The ability to stop a transaction enables some errors to be corrected, but this comes at the expense of certainty within the system. As we have seen with check kiting, this is no small matter as financial institutions are required to make some funds (and often make more funds than required) available to customers before a transaction is final.

This chapter proceeds to consider authorization, errors, and finality, in the context of cash, checks, debit cards, ACH transactions, and credit cards.

II. CASH

It might seem strange to think about the law of cash. We use cash from childhood and give it very little thought, although legally and economically it is a fascinating concept. We need not concern ourselves with the issues of fiat currency here, but one of the remarkable features about cash is it that it is bearer paper, transferred by possession. If I want to pay you in cash, I need to physically hand over the cash to you with the intent of it being a permanent transfer (as opposed to a temporary bailment). This is both a boon and a limitation for cash. It enables very simple transactions, but it also means that cash poses lots of risks because possession is functionally (even if not legally) ownership.

While cash payment is easy, not every transaction can be performed with cash. Cash is famously "legal tender for all debts, public and private." *See* 31 U.S.C. § 5103. That does not create a right to payment in cash. If I am purchasing groceries at the supermarket, there is no debt, so there is no right to cash payment. If the supermarket permits me to purchase on credit, I may settle my debt by tendering cash payment. Consider restaurants—if you pay after eating, do you have a right to pay in cash?

The formal law of cash is quite different from the reality of cash. Formally, if you have a $10 bill in your wallet, that particular bill is your property. If you are robbed and the police catch the robber and recover the $10 bill plus some other $10 bills from the robber, you have a right to get back your particular $10 bill. Realistically, though, you are unlikely to care which $10 bill you get back. Absent some idiosyncratic value you attach to a particular bill (*e.g.*, the first $10 bill you earned) or something else that makes the bill intrinsically more valuable than $10 (*e.g.*, it bears a mistake in the engraving of Alexander Hamilton or is splattered with John Lennon's blood), every single piece of cash is fungible with others of the same denomination (yes, maybe a really ratty bill isn't worth as much as a crisp one because it can't be used in vending machines . . .).

While you formally own cash, it is bearer paper, so possession is more than nine-tenths of the law. Suppose that Darwin gives Millicent $1,000. Whose money is it? Darwin claims that the money was a bailment—he wanted Millicent to hold onto the money for him, say for safekeeping. Millicent claims that it was a gift. Absent evidence of Darwin's intent, Millicent will likely prevail.

Similarly, consider the problem of found cash. If you find a $20 on the sidewalk, whose money is it? Your title to cash, as it were, only comes from possession, so you cannot prove absolute rights in cash. What if I say the $20 is mine? At best you can prove that you have superior title to me, but you cannot prove absolute title. *See Armory v. Delamirie* (1722) 1 Strange 505. Therefore, if you lose cash, it is functionally lost forever. And if cash is stolen, you are not likely to be able to reclaim the bill if you later spot it and can identify the serial number, if it is in the possession of a good-faith taker from the thief.

Another implication of the bearer paper nature of cash is that cash transactions are immediately final absent some other legal right to unwind the transaction. (Such as those provided by Article 2 of the UCC for certain sales.) There is no generic right to "backsies" or to unwind cash transactions.

Two types of errors arise with cash. The first is that someone hands over more cash than intended. For example, I give you a $10 bill as payment, thinking it was a $1 bill. If so, you have no right to the extra $9. If you knowingly take the $10 and don't alert me, you have converted my property, and I have a potential action for conversion or trover or replevin or unjust enrichment against you.

Realistically, however, matters like this involving cash are not decided by courts. Instead, they are worked out informally between the parties. If you want me to do business with you again, you might give me back the $9 overpayment. If we are in a one-time dealing, you might deny overpayment and keep the money. And if the overpayment was not to you, but to your agent (say, a cashier), then the agent might look to keep the overpayment himself.

The second type of cash error is payment in cash to the wrong person. This situation might arise if cash is tendered to a person believed to be a store employee, but who in fact is not. Again, legally, that person has no right to the cash and as a formal matter can be compelled to return it. But realistically, the person is likely to abscond and even if located never be compelled to repay.

Cash is a payment system that is virtually free from the problem of unauthorized transactions. The authorization question only arises in the context of an agent using a principal's cash without the principal's authorization. The principal has a conversion claim against the agent, but the party with whom the agent transacted should be able to keep the cash absent knowledge that the agent acted without authority. Compare this to the case of a purchaser of stolen goods. The purchaser may be deprived of the goods, even if a good-faith purchaser, because the thief did not have the ability to impart good title. (Note that there are situations in which a bailee can sell a bailment without authority and transfer good title to a good-faith purchaser. *See* UCC § 2-403.) But cash is different than goods, as title is functionally a matter of possession. To the extent that the party that transacted with the agent knows about the unauthorized use of the cash, it is essentially a conspirator in the conversion, rather than an arm's-length party. But absent knowledge, the transaction is final and the lack of authorization is only a matter between the principal and the agent. The payment itself cannot be challenged.

III. CHECKS

In Chapter 11, we covered the basic mechanics of a check transaction: the maker gives the check to the payee, who deposits the check in the depository bank. The depository bank then presents the check to the payor bank (directly or through various intermediaries) for payment. If the payor bank does not timely dishonor the check and refuse payment, then the payor bank is on the hook for the check, irrespective of whether there are funds in the maker's account. The depository bank bears risk too in that it is required by Regulation CC to make some funds immediately available to the payee, and may make additional funds available before it knows whether a check has been dishonored.

Traditionally, the checking system involved moving physical checks across the country for presentment and for return if dishonored. The Check21 Act has allowed for banks to instead exchange images of checks, which can be done electronically. This not only saves the costs of physically transporting checks, but also greatly reduced the time between deposit and presentment. The result has been the reduction of float in the banking system and a decrease in check-kiting risk for banks.

A. Unauthorized Transactions

While check-kiting risk has been reduced (although hardly eliminated), there is still the risk of other types of fraud in the checking system. Authorization for a check comes in the form of the payor's signature. Signatures, however, can readily be forged and applied to forged or stolen checks. The Uniform Commercial Code provides the liability rules for unauthorized check transactions. It provides that only a person who actually signed a check is liable on the check. UCC § 3-401(a). Thus, on a forged check, only the forger has signer liability, but not the putative payor. UCC § 3-403(a). The check is not properly payable by the putative payor's bank, so it has no right to debit the putative payor's bank account. UCC § 4-401(a). If the bank pays the check, the bank may attempt to recover the payment from the payee. UCC § 3-418. Note, though, that signer liability is not the only way a putative payor might be liable on a check.

Even legitimately signed checks can still be altered, meaning that the names of payees or the amounts of payments can be changed. A legitimately signed check might be altered or completed (if incomplete) by the payee or by a thief who obtains the check. If a check is altered, the payor bank may still pay it from the payor's account according to its original terms, and if the check was completed without authorization, the payor bank may pay it according to its completed terms. UCC § 3-407(c). In other words, the payor is liable for unauthorized completions of checks. This is essentially a deemed negligence rule, as the situation would only arise when the payor had signed a check but left either the payee's name or amount of payment incomplete, meaning that the payor would be the least-cost avoider of the completion fraud.

While UCC § 3-407(c) conclusively presumes negligence by the payor, the UCC otherwise has a contributory negligence regime regarding for forged signatures and alterations. UCC § 3-406. This liability is distinct from signer liability. Signer liability is based on having signed an instrument, not on deviation from a standard of care. Therefore, even if a consumer did not sign an instrument, the consumer could still be liable for losses incurred by a bank due to forgery or alternation if the consumer failed to take proper care. For example, in *Marx v. Whitney Bank*, 713 So. 2d 1142 (La. 1998), the court held that there was a question of fact for the jury to determine regarding whether there was negligence when a grandfather knew that his grandson had access to his checkbook during visits, resulting in $10,000 in unauthorized checks.

The UCC accomplishes this by precluding payors "whose failure to exercise ordinary care substantially contributes to" an alternation or forged signature, from raising the alteration or forgery as a defense against the payor's bank. UCC § 3-406(a). If, however, the bank also failed to exercise ordinary care, then losses are allocated according to the degree of contributory negligence. UCC § 3-406(b).

Typically a consumer will not learn of a forgery or alteration on a check he has made until after the check has been paid by his bank. The UCC's contributory negligence rules impose a duty on the consumer to examine bank statements; failure to do so in a timely fashion and report unauthorized transactions can result in the consumer losing the ability to assert the unauthorized signature or alteration against the bank, UCC § 4-406(c)-(d), if the bank suffered a loss because of the consumer's negligence, unless the bank has also been negligent, in which case a proportional negligence regime applies. UCC § 4-406(e). Likewise, if the consumer does not raise the unauthorized transactions within a year, the consumer loses any ability to recover the payments from the bank. UCC § 4-406(f). This provision functions like a statute of limitations on claims of unauthorized payments.

It's easy enough to imagine ways in which a consumer might be negligent. A consumer might leave signed checks in a checkbook that is readily accessible to others, or might simply have forgotten to fill in a line on the check that is tendered to a payee. Likewise, a consumer might fail to look at her bank statements and thus not notice unauthorized transactions. But what about banks? How might a bank be negligent with paying a check? Recall that the payor bank has a limited time during which to decide if it is going to pay a check. UCC § 4-301 (deadline of midnight on the next banking day after the banking day on which check is received). If the payor bank does not decline to pay by that deadline, it is liable to the depositary bank for payment of the amount of the check. At the same time, however, if the payor bank improperly declines to pay a properly payable item, it is liable to the payor for the actual damages caused by wrongful dishonor and any consequential damages that can be proven. UCC § 4-402(a)-(b).

The possibility of consequential damages for wrongful dishonor liability creates an incentive for banks to lean toward payment of checks when in doubt. Given that the check processing system is highly automated, banks rarely examine check signatures against specimen signatures they have on file. This means that there is a built-in level of negligence on the bank side, but one that banks have decided is an acceptable risk given the cost savings of not actually comparing signatures (which is of questionable value in the first place). Likewise, a bank might be negligent if it paid despite the presence of a stop payment order (discussed below).

One other form of fraud can arise with checks. Once a check has been received by the payee it can become bearer paper if it has been indorsed (meaning it has been signed on the back—*in dorso*) "in blank," meaning that the payee has signed his name, but without any restrictive language, such as "for deposit only," with the indorsement. Once the check is bearer paper, anyone with possession becomes a person entitled to enforce it. UCC § 3-301. There is still conversion liability for the thief, assuming he can be caught. UCC § 3-320.

B. Error

The problem of error does not really exist as such in the checking system. A bank is entitled to rely on whatever information is given to it on a check because of the existence of presentment and encoding warranties. UCC §§ 4-208-209. As checks are written to persons, not account numbers, there is not usually a problem of the wrong person being listed as the payee, and mistakes regarding the amount of the payment indicated on the check are the maker's liability. (If the bank overpays, that is a different matter; the bank is liable for any overpayment beyond what was authorized by the check. *See* UCC § 4-401(a).)

C. Finality

The "finality" of a check payment operates in two ways. First, once a consumer pays with a check, that check can be presented for payment. A check can be "backdated," meaning that the date written on the check will be at some point in the future, but backdating has no legal effect on whether a check is properly payable, unless the consumer notifies his bank about the backdating, UCC § 4-401(c), or there is some additional agreement between the consumer payor and her bank, UCC § 4-103(a). Because backdating does not, standing alone, have any effect on payability, a consumer cannot control the timing of presentment once a check is given in payment. The consumer can agree with the payee about when the check will be deposited, but the breach of such an agreement has no effect on whether the check is properly payable by the consumer's bank; the consumer's only remedy is against the payee for breach of contract.

Although consumers cannot control when a check will be paid, absent additional steps, consumers do have a right to stop payment of checks under UCC § 4-403. The stop payment instruction must "describe[] the item or account with reasonable certainty [and be] received at a time and in a manner that affords the bank a reasonable opportunity to act on it." UCC § 4-403(a). The stop payment order is good for six months. Banks are not obligated to pay checks that are more than six months old, but are permitted to do so, and given that banks do not generally look at check dates (hence UCC § 4-401(c) allowing for payment of backdated checks), this provision is not likely to do much to help a consumer with an expired stop payment order. UCC § 4-404. If the stop payment order is given orally, it must be confirmed in writing within 14 days or it will lapse. Stop payment orders may be renewed. UCC § 4-403(b).

IV. DEBIT CARDS

In the previous chapter we reviewed the workings of a debit card transaction: the cardholder presents the card (or card data) to the merchant, who transmits the data for authorization. If the transaction is authorized, then the funds will be removed from the cardholder's account at the issuer bank and transmitted through the card network to the merchant's acquirer bank, which will settle the funds into the merchant's account.

In this system, there may be a lag in some circumstances between the time of authorization and the time a final amount is submitted for payment. For example, gas stations, rental cars, hotel rooms, and restaurants all involve transactions where there is likely to be authorization before the final purchase amount is known. In such cases, issuers authorize the transaction for a set amount that might be much higher than the actual amount. The authorized amount is treated as on hold and is not accessible to the cardholder for use for other transactions. This can result in other transactions not clearing for insufficient funds (and bounce fees) or overdrafts. These holds sometimes last up to three days.

Although debit card transactions do not clear in real time, they cannot generally be stopped once initiated, so there is effective finality to all transactions, although they can be unwound in a separate transaction.

A. Unauthorized Transactions

There are a few scenarios in which an unauthorized debit card transaction could occur. It is worthwhile understanding them because the main law addressing consumer liability for unauthorized transactions was written with only one of the situations in mind, even though it may no longer be the typical unauthorized transaction situation. The traditional unauthorized transaction situation involves a thief who purloins a physical debit card from a consumer and then uses that same physical debit card to make transactions. But an unauthorized debit card could also occur if a fraudster were to obtain the payment authorization information on the debit card. This might occur by simply "skimming" the information using a card reader or it might occur through a data breach of a merchant or financial institution. Neither case requires the fraudster to obtain possession of the physical card. Once the fraudster has acquired the payment authorization information, the fraudster can code it onto a new physical card, thereby creating a cloned card (the information programed onto the card is what is used to authorize the transaction in most instances, and it need not correspond with the physical information embossed on the card). Alternatively, the fraudster could simply use the payment authorization digits themselves, such as in an Internet transaction. Recognizing these three different scenarios is helpful for parsing through the law governing unauthorized debit card (and also credit card) transactions.

Most commentary on consumer liability for unauthorized debit card transactions makes two assumptions. First the commentary assumes that the Electronic Fund Transfers Act and Regulation E thereunder are the sole applicable law. And second, the commentary assumes that the EFTA/Reg E liability rules apply to all debit card transactions. Both assumptions are wrong. The EFTA/Reg E is supplemented by common law, and the EFTA/Reg E rules on unauthorized transactions apply solely to transactions undertaken with "accepted access devices," where there is a means of identifying the cardholder. These requirements exclude certain debit transactions.

The EFTA and Reg E provide detailed rules about unauthorized debit card transaction, but they are not the sole source of law, nor do they cover all possible unauthorized electronic fund transfers. While state law is often preempted regarding electronic fund transfers, EFTA/Reg E allows states to further limit cardholder liability for unauthorized transactions. 15 U.S.C. § 1693g(d); 12 C.F.R. § 1005.6(b)(6). Thus, the EFTA/Reg E is a floor, not a ceiling in terms of cardholder liability, that may be exceeded by any "applicable law," which would, presumably include the common law, not just statute and contract.

Moreover, situations not expressly covered by the EFTA/Reg E remain governed by common law, which will start with the deposit account agreement and add on tort principles to the extent that contract does not govern. The basic principle at common law is that a consumer is not liable for an unauthorized transaction—the bank is the consumer's agent in the transaction, and without authorization, the agent may not transact for the principal—the consumer. To the extent that funds are moved out of the consumer's account without authorization, the bank would be liable for breach of contract or, if the situation is not covered by contract, conversion.[1] Payment card network rules round out the picture as they may create additional protections for consumers.

The starting point for understanding the EFTA/Reg E coverage is the definition of "electronic fund transfer." An electronic fund transfer is a "transfer of funds that is initiated through an electronic terminal, telephone, computer, or magnetic tape for the purpose of ordering, instructing, or authorizing a financial institution to debit or credit a consumer's account." 15 U.S.C. § 1693a(7); 12 C.F.R. § 1005.3. In other words, for there to be an electronic fund transfer, there must be (1) a transfer of funds, (2) initiated through some sort of electronic device, (3) that directs a financial institution to (4) make a payment to/from (5) an account. An "account" is defined as being a deposit account held "directly or indirectly by a financial institution," and established for personal, family, or household use. 15 U.S.C. § 1693a(2); 12 C.F.R. § 1005.2(b)(1). Thus, an "electronic fund transfer" includes debit card transactions at point of sale, but also ATM transactions, direct deposits and automatic bill payments via ACH, and telephonically initiated transfers. 15 U.S.C. § 1693a(7); 12 C.F.R. § 1005.2(b)(1).

The definition of "electronic fund transfer" is key to understanding the authorization rules of Reg E because Reg E defines an "unauthorized electronic fund transfer" to be an "electronic fund transfer initiated by a person other than the consumer without actual authority to initiate the transfer and from which the consumer receives no benefit." 15 U.S.C. § 1693a(12); 12 C.F.R. § 1005.2(m). Reg E excludes from this definition electronic fund transfers that are initiated by someone to whom the consumer gave the "access device"—meaning the debit card—as well as so-called first-party fraud, that is, fraud by the consumer. 15 U.S.C. § 1693a(12); 12 C.F.R. § 1005.2(m)(1)-(2). Also excluded are transfers initiated by the financial institution or its employees, so involuntary debits, such as account fees, are not unauthorized electronic fund transfers under Reg E. 12 C.F.R. § 1005.2(m)(3). If the bank wants to argue that the transaction was in fact authorized, the bank bears the burden of proof. 15 U.S.C. § 1693g(b).

The basic rule in the EFTA/Reg E is that a consumer has no liability whatsoever on any unauthorized electronic funds transfer unless (1) the card or other access device was an "accepted access device," and (2) the bank that issued the card or other access device provided means for identifying the consumer. 15 U.S.C. § 1693g(a); 12 C.F.R. § 1005.6(a). Unless both of these criteria are met, the EFTA/Reg E absolve the consumer of any liability.

1. To the extent that liability is determined by tort law, a consumer's contributory negligence would be a factor, but to the extent that contract law controls, then contributory negligence is irrelevant.

1. Accepted Access Devices

An "accepted access device" is one that the consumer has actually requested and received. 12 C.F.R. § 1005.2(a)(2). Therefore, if a debit card were stolen in the mail by a fraudster, the consumer would have no liability whatsoever for the fraudulent transactions. Indeed, the EFTA/Reg E would not even require that the consumer notify the bank that the card had not been received.

The EFTA provision limiting liability to accepted access devices was written in response to the concern about card issuing mailing out "live" or "hot" cards that could be used without activation by the account holders. Thus, any mail thief would be able to start making payments from a consumer's account without the consumer even knowing that the card had been intercepted in the mail.

The "accepted access device," requirement may in fact limit cardholders' liability in other situations as well. Suppose a card is cloned, meaning that the payment authorization data is copied off of a card that is an accepted access device and used to create a new physical card. Is that cloned card an "accepted access device" because the original card was? Similarly, suppose a fraudster simply copies the payment authorization digits off of a debit card and uses them to transact online. Is that an "accepted access device"? In both situations, it is hard to see why it would be. The whole point of the liability limitation for accepted access devices is so that consumers will not be liable for transactions made using access devices for which they have not accepted responsibility. The consumer has accepted responsibility for a particular card, not for other cards or for the payment authorization digits themselves, any more than if the card issuer had mailed out two cards and only one was accepted by the consumer. Thus, liability under the EFTA/Reg E should be limited only to transactions made using stolen debit cards that had previously been accepted by the cardholder; the consumer should have no liability under the EFTA/Reg E for transactions undertaken with cloned cards or with the authorization digits taken from a debit card. Why "should"? Because there isn't any case or guidance clearly stating this, but it is hard to read the existing statute or regulation otherwise.

2. Means of Identifying the Consumer

The EFTA/Reg E further provide that consumer liability is limited to situations in which "the issuer of such card, code, or other means of access has provided a means whereby the user of such card, code, or other means of access can be identified as the person authorized to use it, such as by signature, photograph, or fingerprint or by electronic or mechanical confirmation." 15 U.S.C. § 1693g(a); 12 C.F.R. § 1005.6(a). In other words, if a merchant lacks the means to confirm the consumer's identity, then the consumer cannot be liable for use of the card. Note that some of these means of identification—a signature or picture—are of questionable value. Unclear is whether a debit card that has a signature block, but which lacks an actual signature, would satisfy the requirement; while consumers are supposed to sign their cards, cards are still functional without the signature. Likewise, the status of a PIN as an identification is unclear. A PIN number does not inherently identify the authorized user. The reference to "code" in the EFTA unauthorized transaction liability provision is to a code as an access device, not as an identification measure.

Nonetheless, the CFPB's Official Interpretation of this provision is that a PIN is a means of identification. Official Interpretation to 12 C.F.R. § 1005.6(a). It remains unclear if the mere fact that a card has a PIN is sufficient if the unauthorized transaction was performed without a PIN, such as online. It would seem to be akin to the card with the unsigned signature block and the consumer should not be liability at all under the EFTA/Reg E for the transaction.

It would also seem that identification requirement, which applies to the *issuer* of the card, would preclude any consumer liability under the EFTA/Reg E for cloned cards or lifted card payment authorization digits. Lifted digits would not have any means for consumer identification. A cloned card might have means of identifying a consumer (that is, the fraudster), but those means would not be provided by "the issuer or such card," but by the fraudster.

3. Liability for Past Unauthorized Transactions

For unauthorized transactions on an accepted access device where the consumer's identity can be verified, the EFTA and Reg E provides two tiers of liability that work as a type of contributory negligence regime. It is not based on negligence generally, but solely on negligence in terms of notifying the bank of the loss of the card. The consumer is always liable for up to $50, irrespective of the consumer's level of care or the nature of the unauthorized transaction (stolen card vs. cloned vs. ACH transfer). If the card is lost or stolen, however, a different rule applies. If the consumer notifies the bank within two business days of learning that a debit card is lost or stolen, then the consumer's liability will remain capped at $50. 15 U.S.C. § 1693g(a)(1); 12 C.F.R. § 1005.6(b)(1). If the consumer does not give notice within two business days, however, the consumer's liability cap rises to $500, but only for losses that the bank can show would not have occurred had the consumer given timely notice of the "loss or theft" of the access device. 15 U.S.C. § 1693g(a)(2); 12 C.F.R. § 1005.6(b)(2). The EFTA/Reg E liability limitations for past unauthorized transactions apply for each individual unauthorized transfer or series of related unauthorized transfers. Thus, if there were two separate, unrelated unauthorized transfers, the liability caps would be applied to each separately.

If the unauthorized transaction is not due to a card being lost or stolen, only the $50 cap applies. It is unclear whether a cloned card or a transaction using stolen payment authorization digits involves the "loss or theft" of the card. Given that the cardholder would still have the original card—and quite likely no reason to know of the *data* theft—this provision should not apply, so the consumer's liability should be limited to $50 if such a transaction were deemed to be on an accepted card with means to identify the cardholder.

Note that these liability cap amounts are not inflation adjusted. $50 in 1978, when the EFTA was adopted, is $198 in 2018 dollars, and $500 in 1978 dollars would be $1,983 in 2018 dollars. The EFTA's one-year statute of limitations, however, effectively limits a consumer's ability to enforce the liability cap if the consumer waits too long to act. 15 U.S.C. § 1693m(g).

4. Liability for Future Unauthorized Transactions

Separately from the two tiers of liability for past unauthorized transactions on a lost or stolen card, if a consumer fails to report an unauthorized *transaction* (as opposed to a lost or stolen debit *card*) that appears on a periodic account statement within 60 days of the transmittal of the statement, then the consumer incurs unlimited liability for all unauthorized transactions that occur between the end of those 60 days and provision of notice to the issuer, provided that the issuer can show that the transactions would not have occurred had there been timely notice. 15 U.S.C. § 1693g(a)(2); 12 C.F.R. § 1005.6(b)(3). If notice is never provided, there is no cap to liability whatsoever. The 60-day limit can be extended for extenuating circumstances. 15 U.S.C. § 1693g(a)(2); 12 C.F.R. § 1005.6(b)(4).

It is important to recognize that this provision deals solely with future unauthorized transactions; it does not address the consumer's liability on the unauthorized transaction(s) that appeared on the periodic statement. If those transactions were made with an accepted access device, then the $50/$500 cap would apply, while if they were made without an accepted access device (*e.g.*, with a cloned card or with stolen bank account/routing numbers used for an ACH transaction), then the liability would be determined by common law (plus card network or ACH network rules).

Notice that this structure results in a strange gap: the consumer has limited liability for the original unauthorized transactions under EFTA/Reg E. The consumer also has unlimited liability for unauthorized transactions after 60 days from the transmittal of the statement. But for the intermediate period, once the statement has been transmitted, but before 60 days have run, the EFTA/Reg E are silent regarding consumer liability, which takes us back to common law, and, unless the parties have contracted otherwise, that means that the consumer has no liability. Indeed, for the EFTA/Reg E 60-day notice window to be meaningful, this has to be the rule.

5. Consequential Damages

The EFTA/Reg E liability limits apply only to unauthorized transactions themselves. They do not appear to cover consequential damages from unauthorized transactions. Other statutes, particularly UCC § 4-402, providing for consequential damages from wrongful dishonor of checks, and contract law principles in general may provide a route to recovering consequential damages from an unauthorized transaction.

6. Payment Card Network Liability Policies

Some payment card networks have "zero liability" policies. For example, Visa has a "Zero Liability Policy" that covers both debit and credit cards. It requires cardholders to review their monthly statement and immediately report unauthorized transactions to their card issuer. Issuers are supposed to re-credit accounts for unauthorized debits within five business days of notification. But the policy also states that:

> Replacement funds are provided on a provisional basis and may be withheld, delayed, limited, or rescinded by your issuer based on the following: Gross negligence or fraud; Delay in reporting unauthorized use; Investigation and verification of claim; Account standing and history.[2]

---

2. Visa, Zero Liability, *at* https://www.visa.com/chip/personal/security/zero-liability.jsp.

What exactly, then, is the scope of this policy? Consumers are directed to their card issuers for details, but the fine print of contains exclusions like those listed above that render the "policy" an illusory promise, one that is fulfilled solely at the discretion of the issuer (or Visa). In any event, given that the consumer lacks contractual privity with Visa, it is not clear whether such a policy is actionable. What then is the point of such a policy? At the very least it increases consumers' confidence in the Visa system.[3]

B. Error Resolution

The EFTA and Regulation E also provide for an error resolution system. "Error" is defined quite broadly by Reg E. It includes unauthorized transactions as well as incorrect transactions. 12 C.F.R. § 1005.11(a)(1)(i)-(ii). It also includes omission of transactions from periodic statements, incorrect receipts for transactions, other deficiencies with periodic statements and receipts, and any request by the consumer for clarification or additional information regarding the transaction. 12 C.F.R. § 1005.11(a)(iii)-(vii). Thus, an error (*i.e.*, a request for clarification) may be triggered by a response to another error (such as a claim of an incorrect transaction).

This broad definition is important because the EFTA and Reg E create a set of rights that follow from there being an "error." If a financial institution receives adequate notice of an error from the consumer—oral or written notice made within 60 days of the transmittal of the periodic statement that first reflects the error and which enables the bank to identify the consumer's name and account number and indicates what the consumer believes to be in error (other than requests for more information)—then the bank must undertake certain steps. 12 C.F.R. § 1005.11(b).

Once a bank is notified of an error, then it is required to undertake and complete an investigation within ten business days, to report to the consumer within three business days from completion of the investigation, and correct any error it determines exists within one business day. 12 C.F.R. § 1005.11(c)(1). The investigation undertaken by the bank is only one of its own records. 12 C.F.R. § 1005.11(c)(4). If the bank is unable to complete the investigation within ten business days, then it may take up to 45 days total, but it must provisionally re-credit the consumer's account (but may withhold $50 for unauthorized transactions), giving the consumer full use of the funds in the interim. This means the consumer could withdraw the funds and the close out the account.

If the bank concludes that no error has occurred (or that a different error has occurred), the bank is required to provide a written explanation to the consumer and to provide the documentation that is relied on if requested by the consumer. 12 C.F.R. § 1005.11(d)(1). Any provisional credits may be reversed, but the bank must honor checks and pre-authorized transfers for five days as if the credit had not been reversed. 12 C.F.R. § 1005.11(d)(2). If the consumer is still not satisfied, the consumer

3. Query whether there is a UDAAP violation lurking in advertising an illusory "zero liability policy."

is left to pursue its remedies in court; the bank has fulfilled its EFTA/Reg E error resolution duties.

The EFTA/Reg E error resolution process is a mandatory dispute resolution process for financial institutions. Bank interactions with account holders are largely automated—the bank will automatically generate periodic statements that will be sent to consumers without any human review. The EFTA/Reg E error resolution process forces human intervention. It effectively makes financial institutions "listen" to consumer complaints and explain what is going on to the consumer.

The EFTA/Reg E error resolution system is not a mandatory process for consumers. A consumer could always forgo the error resolution process and bring litigation to obtain relief; few consumers are likely to want to proceed that way, however. The reason the error resolution process is mandatory for financial institutions is because absent the requirement, they might well say, "see you in court," knowing that for small-dollar errors no one will actually litigate. Financial institutions are incentivized to comply with the error resolution process through the threat of treble damages (from the threshold of the usual EFTA damages). 15 U.S.C. § 1693f(e).

What does the process really get consumers, though? It gets them what is hopefully a good-faith investigation and explanation, which might be useful for subsequent litigation, but there is no guarantee of relief.

V. AUTOMATED CLEARINGHOUSE (ACH)

Almost all ACH transactions are subject to the EFTA and Regulation E. *See* 12 C.F.R. § 1005.2(b)(2). The only ACH transactions not covered by the EFTA are represented check (RCK) transactions—checks that were presented for payment as paper instruments and bounced and were subsequently converted into ACH entries for re-presentment. These are covered by Reg E. The Official Interpretation to Reg E explains that:

> The electronic re-presentment of a returned check is not covered by Regulation E because the transaction originated by check. Regulation E does apply, however, to any fee debited via an EFT from a consumer's account by the payee because the check was returned for insufficient or uncollected funds. The person debiting the fee electronically must obtain the consumer's authorization.

Supplement I to 12 C.F.R. Part 1005, Official Interpretation 3(c)(1). In other words, electronic debits of bounce fees are covered by Regulation, 12 C.F.R. § 1005.2(b)(3), but the ACH re-presentment of the check itself is not. There were some 2.21 million represented check transactions in 2017, so this gap in Reg E coverage is meaningful.

ACH transactions are, therefore, generally subject to the EFTA and Reg E's rules on unauthorized transactions and error liability. Regulation E, however, places some additional authorization requirements on ACH conversions of checks and bounce fees processed through ACH. ACH check conversions and bounce fees require certain advance notice to the consumer of the right to convert or collect the fees electronically. 12 C.F.R. § 1005.2(b)(2)-(3).

The EFTA also has a special rule for pre-authorized electronic fund transfers that applies primarily to ACH (and not to debit cards). These are transactions that arise in the context of recurring bill payments, which is generally done through ACH. In the case of a pre-authorized transfer, there must be a written authorization of the transfer (a debit card swipe alone would not suffice, therefore). 15 U.S.C. § 1693e; 12 C.F.R. § 1005.10(b). With pre-authorized transfers, consumers have a stop payment right. 15 U.S.C. § 1693e; 12 C.F.R. § 1005.10(c). The stop payment right applies only to future pre-authorized transfers; in other words, the transfer authorization may be revoked. The stop payment right is only effective upon three business days' notice.

Beyond the EFTA and Regulation E, ACH transactions are also subject to National Automated Clearing House Association (NACHA) Rules. NACHA Rules provide some additional consumer protections, and for represented check transactions, they provide the only set of consumer protections.

NACHA has two relevant rules beyond what the EFTA and Reg E provide. First, NACHA Rules require authorization for all ACH transactions. NACHA Operating Rule 2.3.1. The particular form of authorization required varies by ACH transaction, but it can exceed that which is required by EFTA/Reg E, which has specific requirements only for electronic conversions of checks and bounce fees. If an ACH transaction is not authorized, there is no consumer liability to the bank.

Second, NACHA Rules create a stop payment right. NACHA Operating Rule 3.7.1.2. For an ACH debit transaction (where money is pulled from the consumer's account), the right may be exercised through either a verbal or written communication to the RDFI (the consumer's bank) that gives the RDFI a reasonable opportunity to act. The NACHA stop payment right is not particularly meaningful, however, as ACH transactions tend to be processed quickly, often on the same day or next day. The result is that the NACHA stop payment right adds little to the EFTA/Reg E stop payment right for pre-authorized transactions.

NACHA Rules present a possible problem for consumers, however: lack of privity. Nonetheless, consumers seem to be able to assert claims based on NACHA Rules. The particular theory by which lack of privity is overcome varies: third-party beneficiary status, *see Sec. First Network Bank v. C.A.P.S., Inc.*, 2002 WL 485352, at *6, n.7 (N.D. Ill. Mar. 29, 2002); incorporation in deposit and debit card agreements; or state UDAP laws (the argument being that it is an unfair or deceptive act or practice for a financial institution not to abide by NACHA Rules).

VI. CREDIT CARDS

We saw the basic structure and economics of credit card transactions in Chapter 16: when a consumer presents a card for payment, the payment is authorized and then funds are moved from the issuer through the network to the acquirer, which settles the funds into the merchant's account. The issuer will then bill the consumer for the payment at the end of the billing period and will charge interest if the consumer does not pay off the account balance in full and on time. If the account is over-limit, the transaction may be denied by the issuer.

Authorization issues and error resolution are both governed by the Truth in Lending Act and Regulation Z, in addition to credit card network rules and cardholder agreements. There is no stop payment right per se on a credit card. TILA and Reg Z do, however, provide a mechanism for a consumer to withhold payment to the card issuer in certain circumstances when the consumer has a dispute with a merchant, either about the merchandise or the charge amount. While TILA and Reg Z address the same issues as the EFTA and Reg E, there are surprising differences in both substance and drafting between the regulatory schemes.

The starting point for understanding TILA and Reg Z's rules dealing with unauthorized credit card transactions and errors on credit card transactions is the definition of "credit card." A "credit card" transaction is a transaction undertaken using a card or other device that allows for repeat use payment from a line of credit. 12 C.F.R. § 1026.2(a)(15) 15 U.S.C. § 1602(l). The term includes charge cards, on which balances must be repaid in full each billing cycle. Significantly, the definition of "credit card" excludes the use of landline and mobile phone bills for third-party billing. These arrangements are functionally a line of credit—phone service is extended in advance of payment—but there is no formal credit agreement or even credit limit involved. This is not to say that one could not argue that phone billing is de facto a line of credit and covered by TILA/Reg Z, but thus far the industry has avoided TILA/Reg Z coverage.

A. Unauthorized Transactions

Reg Z defines "unauthorized use" to mean "the use of a credit card by a person, other than the cardholder, who does not have actual, implied, or apparent authority for such use, and from which the cardholder receives no benefit." 12 C.F.R. § 1016.12(b)(i). *See also* 15 U.S.C. § 1602(p). In other words, unauthorized use is determined in reference to principles of agency law and is narrower than the definition for an "unauthorized electronic fund transfer," which is any transfer for which there is not "actual authority." Implied or apparent authority is insufficient to authorize an electronic fund transfer, but it is for a credit card. The Official Interpretation of this provision explains that:

> If a cardholder furnishes a credit card and grants authority to make credit transactions to a person (such as a family member or coworker) who exceeds the authority given, the cardholder is liable for the transaction(s) unless the cardholder has notified the creditor that use of the credit card by that person is no longer authorized.

Supplement I to 12 C.F.R. Part 1026, Official Interpretation 12(b)(1)(ii). As with the EFTA and Reg E, if the card issuer wants to argue that the transaction was in fact authorized, the issuer bears the burden of proof. 15 U.S.C. § 1643(b).

1. Accepted Credit Cards

As the EFTA/Reg E provide for debit cards, consumers are liable under TILA/Reg Z only for credit card transactions undertaken on "accepted credit cards," 15 U.S.C.

§ 1643(a)(1)(C); 12 C.F.R. § 1026.12(b)(2)(i). An "accepted credit card" is a card that the consumer has actually requested and received. 15 U.S.C. § 1602(m). Therefore, if a credit card were stolen in the mail by a fraudster, the consumer would have no liability for the fraudulent transactions. Likewise, the issues with cloned card or lifted card digits that arise under the EFTA/Reg E for debit cards would apply with equal force to credit cards.

2. Means of Identifying the Consumer

Also as the EFTA/Reg E provide for debit cards, TILA and Reg Z impose an additional important restriction on consumer liability, namely that it only attaches if "[t]he card issuer has provided a means to identify the cardholder on the account or the authorized user of the card." 12 C.F.R. § 1026.12(b)(ii)(3); 15 U.S.C. § 1643(a)(1)(F). Such a means of identification can include a photograph, signature, fingerprint, or biometric. Supplement I to 12 C.F.R. Part 1026, Official Interpretation 12(b)(2)(iii). The little-known implication of this is that credit cardholders have zero liability for unauthorized transactions in all card-not-present situations, such as telephonic or Internet transactions. *Id.*

3. Single Tier of Liability

In card-present situations, however, for unauthorized transactions on an accepted credit card, the consumer's liability is capped at $50. 15 U.S.C. §§ 1643(a), 1643(d); 12 C.F.R. § 1026.12(b). This figure is not inflation adjusted and has not changed since TILA was adopted. Fifty dollars in 1970, when the TILA provision was adopted, is $328 in 2018 dollars. Thus, under TILA and Reg Z, a consumer's liability for unauthorized transactions is $50 for card-present and $0 for card-not-present transactions. It is unclear if the TILA/Reg Z liability cap applies separately to individual unauthorized transfers. It seems to apply to all related unauthorized transfers, but nothing in the regulatory language directly addresses this issue.

TILA/Reg Z do not have even a limited contributory negligence regime like EFTA/Reg E, and, indeed, there is no requirement that the consumer timely notify the issuer of unauthorized transactions. The only function that notice serves in the TILA/Reg Z system is to potentially further cap the consumer's liability *under* the $50 maximum unauthorized transaction liability ceiling for card-present transactions. The $50 liability limit is for all transactions prior to notification. Thus, with prompt notification, a consumer's liability could well be less than $50. (The same is true with the $50/$500 EFTA/Reg E debit card liability limits.) As with EFTA/Reg E, there is no provision addressing consequential damages of unauthorized transactions under TILA/Reg Z; common law rules instead govern. Note, however, that TILA's one-year statute of limitations effectively limits a consumer's ability to enforce the liability cap, at least in regard to TILA. 15 U.S.C. § 1640(e).

In addition to TILA/Reg Z, card networks' policies may further limit liability in the manner discussed above for debit cards. 15 U.S.C. § 1643(c); 12 C.F.R. § 1026.12(b)(4). Notice that in the credit card context these zero liability policies do much less work than in the debit card context.

4. Coverage Extends to Business Credit Cards

While TILA/Reg Z generally apply only to natural person consumers, unauthorized transaction liability rules are an exception. The liability rules apply to "cardholders," which are defined in 12 C.F.R. § 1026.2(a)(8) as being natural persons using cards for "consumer credit," meaning "personal, family, or household purposes," 12 C.F.R. § 1026.2(a)(12), but for the limited purpose of liability rules "cardholder" is defined to cover all entities and cards issued for all purposes. *See* 15 U.S.C. § 1602(n). In other words, business cards are covered by the liability rules.

Yet there is a carve-out. 12 C.F.R. § 1026.12(b)(5) allows card issuers to contract around the Reg Z liability rules for corporate liability in situations where more than ten cards are issued to a business for its employees. The liability of individual employees always remains circumscribed by the Reg Z liability rules, however. 12 C.F.R. § 1026.12(b)(5).

Table 20.1 Consumer Liability for Unauthorized Transactions

	Credit Cards (Card Present)	Credit Cards (Card Not Present)	Debit Cards	Checks	ACH
Not an Accepted Access Device	$0	$0	$0	$0	$0
Access Device Lacks Means to Identify Consumer	$0	$0	$0	$0	$0
Unauthorized Transaction Promptly Reported on Accepted Access Device with Means to Identify Consumer	$50	$0	$50	$0, unless contributory negligence	$0
Unauthorized Transaction Not Reported Within Two Business Days of Loss or Theft of Accepted Access Device with Means to Identify Consumer	$50	$0	$500	$0, unless contributory negligence	$0
Unauthorized Transaction Not Reported Within 60 Days of Transmittal of Periodic Statement	$50	$0	Unlimited future liability; past liability determined by other rules	Unlimited future liability; $0 past liability	$0

B. Error Resolution

Like EFTA/Reg E, TILA/Reg Z create an error resolution system that forces card issuers to listen to consumer complaints and explain what is going on or correct the problem. TILA/Reg Z define the scope of the system in terms of "billing errors," which are defined to include actual errors—wrong amounts, failure to credit payments, calculation errors, etc., 15 U.S.C. § 1666(b)(1), 1666(b)(4), 1666(b)(5); 12 C.F.R. § 1026.13(a)(4)-(5)—but also billing for goods and services not accepted by the consumer (returns), 15 U.S.C. § 1666(b)(3); 12 C.F.R. § 1026.13(a)(3), unauthorized transactions, 15 U.S.C. § 1666(b)(1); 12 C.F.R. § 1026.13(a)(1); failure to comply with TILA billing statement disclosure requirements, 15 U.S.C. § 1666(b)(6); 12 C.F.R. § 1026.13(a)(2), 1026.13(a)(8), and consumer requests for clarification of items on the periodic statement, 15 U.S.C. § 1666(b)(2); 12 C.F.R. § 1026.13(a)(7).

As with EFTA/Reg E, an appropriate written notice to a creditor of a TILA/Reg Z billing error, delivered within 60 days of the transmittal of the periodic statement at issue, triggers a duty to investigate. 15 U.S.C. § 1666(a); 12 C.F.R. § 1026.13(b). Creditors have the shorter of two billing cycles or 90 days to investigate and notify the consumer of the resolution. 15 U.S.C. § 1666(a)(3); 12 C.F.R. § 1026.13(c)(2), 1026.13(e)-(f). If the creditor does not complete its investigation and provide notice to the consumer within 30 days, the creditor must instead send an acknowledgement of receipt of the billing error notice to the consumer. 15 U.S.C. § 1666(a)(3); 12 C.F.R. § 1026.13(c)(1). Once the creditor has completed its investigation and either rectified the billing error or explained why there was not an error, its obligations are fulfilled, and the account returns to normal status.

While the billing error notice remains pending, the consumer may withhold the disputed amount and the card issuer may not attempt to collect it, accelerate the debt or restrict the account, or engage in credit reporting on the amount. 15 U.S.C. §§ 1666(c)-(d), 1666a(a); 12 C.F.R. § 1026.13(d)(1)-(3). The creditor may do all of these things for other amounts owed, however. 15 U.S.C. §§ 1666(c); 12 C.F.R. § 1026.13(d)(4).

As with EFTA/Reg E, the TILA/Reg Z billing error regime is mandatory for card issuers, but not for consumers. Whereas the EFTA/Reg E billing error regime was enforced against banks with treble damages, the TILA/Reg Z regime is enforced through a forfeiture of the right to collect the amount of the billing error and any finance charges thereon, but this forfeiture is capped at $50. 15 U.S.C. § 1666(e).

C. Raising Claims and Defenses to Merchants Against Issuers

At common law, an assignee is subject to any defenses that could be raised against the assignor.[4] *See* Restatement (Second) of Contracts § 336(2). The assignee is

4. An important exception exists for holders in due course of negotiable instruments, UCC §§ 3-305, 3-306, but credit card sale receipts are not negotiable instruments. *See* UCC § 3-104. As Professor Ronald Mann has observed, there's nothing that prevents credit card receipts from being negotiable, but the industry doesn't value the negotiability so it doesn't bother meeting the requirements of UCC § 3-104. *See* Ronald J. Mann, *Searching for Negotiability in Credit and Payment Systems*, 44 UCLA L. Rev. 951, 964-965 (1997). This is also why the FTC's Holder in Due Course Rule, discussed in Chapter 32, does not apply to credit cards—there is no need. 16 C.F.R. § 433.1.

also, at common law, subject to all claims in recoupment that could be raised against its assignor.[5] An assignee is not, however, at common law, subject to affirmative claims that could be made against the assignor.

The Truth in Lending Act provides a reaffirmation and extension of common law in regard to credit cards. The card issuer is, recall, functionally the assignee of the merchant. The merchant sells the transaction to its acquirer, which resells it to the issuer bank, which then seeks to collect from the consumer. TILA provides that card issuers are subject not only to all defenses and claims in recoupment that a consumer could raise against a merchant when a credit card is used for payment, but also to all affirmative claims (other than tort claims) that the cardholder could raise against the merchant. 15 U.S.C. § 1666i. Thus, if the goods purchased did not conform to spec or did not comply with the warranty of merchantability or the merchant committed fraud, the consumer could raise those issues as a defense against the card issuer. More significantly, though, if the consumer had a UDAP or other statutory claim against the merchant, the consumer could raise it against the card issuer. If the consumer were successful with the claim or defense, the card issuer would be left to try and recover from the merchant as its subrogee.

The TILA right to raise claims and defenses as to a merchant against the card issuer is subject to certain restrictions, including that:

- the disputed amount is greater than $50;
- the cardholder has to attempt to resolve the dispute with the merchant in good faith (unless the merchant has filed for bankruptcy);
- the place where the initial transaction occurred was in the same state as the mailing address previously provided by the cardholder or was within 100 miles from such address (which might sometimes be in a non-contiguous state);
- and the claims or defenses asserted are limited to the "amount of credit outstanding with respect to such transaction at the time the cardholder first notifies the card issuer or the person honoring the credit card of such claim or defense."[6] 15 U.S.C. § 1666i(b).

In such situations, Reg Z provides that the consumer may also withhold payment from the *card issuer* while the dispute with the *merchant* is outstanding, and not incur finance charges or negative credit reporting on the withheld amount. 12 C.F.R. § 1026.12(c)(1)-(2). Moreover, even if the cardholder has paid down the balance, the cardholder can still dispute it using the TILA error resolution mechanism, Official Comment to 12 C.F.R. § 1026.13, which allows the consumer to withhold the disputed amount and prevents credit reporting or other retaliation while the billing error process remains.

---

5. A claim in recoupment is an offsetting claim from the same transaction. If *X* owed *Y* on a contract, and *Y* owed *X* on the same contract, the offset between the obligations would be a claim in recoupment.

6. TILA provides a method for applying payment to determine if the particular transaction has been paid down: payments are applied first to late fees, then finance charges, and then to debits in their order of posting. 15 U.S.C. § 1666i(b).

At first glance, section 1666i seems to separate consumers into lucky and unlucky ones based on geography, namely those who live near "the place the initial transaction occurred" and those who don't, a rather strange dividing line in the age of Internet commerce. (Notice that TILA provides no guidance where the transaction occurred, which is no small matter in an Internet or phone transaction—where is a third-party Amazon seller "located"?) For geographically "lucky" consumers, section 1666i says that they can raise any claims or defenses they would have against the merchant against the card issuer. In other words, if there is a contract defense of non-delivery or a claim for unjust enrichment, etc., against the merchant, that can be raised against the card issuer. If the consumer is successful, the card issuer will be subrogated to the consumer's rights when it then turns around and pursues the merchant for repayment.

Here's the irony: the geographically "unlucky" cardholders are actually in a position that is almost as good as the geographically "lucky" ones' position. This is because 15 U.S.C. § 1666i does nothing in terms of defenses, only claims. Recall that TILA sits as a superstructure on top of common law contract principles. Absent section 1666i, cardholders would be able to raise defenses and claims in recoupment they have against the merchant against the card issuer as a matter of basic contract law. This means that without section 1666i, cardholders could always have raised the claims and defenses they have against the merchant against the card issuer *absent a waiver of those claims and defenses.*

Section 1666i was adopted as part of the 1974 amendments to TILA. The legislative history of the amendments indicates that prior to the amendments, cardholder agreements typically contained waivers of claims and defenses. Senate Report No. 93-278 (June 28, 1973), at 9-11. Thus, TILA section 1666i was an override of those contractual waivers, but only for local-ish commerce, out of fear that merchants would refuse to accept non-local cards rather than risk out-of-state disputes.

What section 1666i does, then, is it creates a new right to bring affirmative non-tort claims against the card issuer that could be brought against the merchant, and it restores the right to raise defenses and claims in recoupment. The section 1666i rights are subject to geographic limitations, but if the consumer has not waived his common law right to raise defenses and claims in recoupment against the card issuer, then the section 1666i geographic limitations would apply solely to affirmative claims. The continuing viability of common law assignee defenses often eludes litigants and courts who assume that TILA defines the extent of the right. The other important addition from section 1666i is the Reg Z provision allowing a consumer who qualifies for the section 1666i rights to withhold payment from the card issuer without adverse credit reporting. If a consumer raises section 1666i against a card issuer, the card issuer can turn around and seek to recover from the merchant, but the consumer is spared having to pay the card issuer and then having to try and recover from the merchant.

Problem Set 20

1. Fenya the Thief enjoys robbing people at gunpoint.

   a. When Fenya makes off with your wallet (containing $500 in cash), what is your liability?

   b. What happens if Fenya's caught with the money?

   c. What if in the interim Fenya robbed someone else of $250 and also spent $150 of the money, which he had shuffled before placing into his wallet?

2. Frankie the Forger has intercepted the new checkbook you ordered in the mail and has been writing checks on your account. You notify your bank as soon as you discover that your account, which had held $2,500, has been drained. What's your maximum liability? Your bank's? The banks at which the checks were deposited? *See* UCC §§ 3-401, 3-403, 4-401(a).

3. Let's admit it: you aren't always the most careful person. You left your checkbook sitting on the table in the law school cafeteria with some pre-signed checks inside, and your ethically challenged classmate, "Bar Exam" Barry, helped himself to a check that she wrote out to "CASH" for $249 (just under the felony grand larceny threshold).

   a. What's your liability, assuming that Barry is judgment proof? *See* UCC §§ 3-401, 3-406, 3-407(c), 4-401(a), 4-401(d), 4-406.

   b. Now suppose that you had a signed check in the book made out to your cousin Larry, but Barry added some loops to the "L" in Larry to make it read "Barry" and then cashed the check. What's your liability, assuming that Barry is judgment proof? *See* UCC §§ 3-103, 3-401, 3-406, 3-407(c), 4-401, 4-406.

4. You were going out of town and knew that you'd have a rental payment due while you were away, so you gave your landlord a backdated check and asked her not to deposit it until the date written on the check. Your landlord forgot and deposited the check a week early, so it resulted in an overdraft that your bank covered, but that cost you $40. Do you have the ability to get the overdraft unwound? *See* UCC § 4-401(a)-(c).

5. You were very excited about a great painting you saw in a gallery and wrote the gallery a check for $20,000, with the understanding that you'd pick the painting up next week after the check had cleared. The next day you read in the newspaper that the gallery owner had been charged with trafficking in forgeries. Is there anything you can do to stop the transaction? *See* UCC § 4-403.

6. Oh no! Boris Levitin, the infamous hacker, has stolen your Visa debit card information from a poorly protected server at a merchant, made a physical counterfeit card, and gone on a $20,000 shopping spree at the Apple Store! You only learn of this a month later when you look at your bank account statement. The statement had been sitting on your desk for two weeks. You immediately telephone the bank to report the problem.

   a. What's your liability? *See* 15 U.S.C. § 1693g(a); 12 C.F.R. §§ 1005.2, 1005.3, 1005.6(a)-(b); Visa Zero Liability Policy.

   b. What if Boris had instead stolen your physical credit card and used it to purchase a flatscreen TV at Best Buy for $3,000? *See* 15 U.S.C. §§ 1602(m), 1643(a); 12 C.F.R. § 1026.2(a), 1026.12(b); Visa Zero Liability Policy.

   c. Does your answer to part (c) change if you didn't call your card issuer for 120 days? *See* 15 U.S.C. §§ 1602(m), 1643(a).

d. What if Boris had instead used your stolen card information to make a counterfeit card that he used to purchase the flatscreen TV at Best Buy for $3,000? *See* 15 U.S.C. §§ 1602(m), 1643(a); 12 C.F.R. § 1026.2(a), 1026.12(b); Visa Zero Liability Policy.

e. What if Boris had stolen your credit card information, but not the physical card, and used the information to make $5,000 in purchases online at Amazon.com? *See* 15 U.S.C. §§ 1602(m), 1643(a); 12 C.F.R. § 1026.12(b)(2)(iii); Visa Zero Liability Policy.

7. Mallory the Mailthief has intercepted your newly issued credit card in the mail and managed to activate it. He's since gone on a spending binge at art galleries around town. What's your liability? *See* 15 U.S.C. §§ 1602(g), 1643(a); 12 C.F.R. §§ 1026.12(b)(2)(i).

8. You've been very proud to establish your own successful 30-lawyer law firm. The firm has a Continental Express Bank, N.A., corporate card account, and all partners and associates are issued cards that they can use to charge business expenses. One of your associates, Abby Absconder, rang up a huge purchase of personalized luxury goods and then skipped town. What is your firm's liability for Abby's purchases? *See* 15 U.S.C. § 1643(b); 12 C.F.R. §§ 1026.2(a)(8), 1026.2(a)(12), 1026.12(b)(1)(i), 1026.12(b)(5); Supplement I to 12 C.F.R. Part 1026, Official Interpretation 12(b)(1)(ii).

9. After Sandy Choi's $1,250 rent check bounced, she made the unpleasant discovery that someone had stolen her debit card, which she rarely uses. The thief took out the entire $4,000 that was in her bank account. As a result, her rent check bounced. Her landlord now says she owes a $50 bounce fee per her rental contract. Sandy has also discovered that the thief kept using the card after the account was cleared out, resulting in ten overdrafts, totaling $1,000, for which her bank charged her $35/overdraft. Additionally, Sandy's bank honored a $100 check Sandy wrote, even though it caused an overdraft, and charged her $35 for it. Sandy has not specifically opted into overdraft protection, but she immediately contacted her bank after realizing that her debit card was stolen. The theft must have occurred recently because there were no unauthorized transactions on Sandy's most recent bank statement.

a. What is Sandy's liability? *See* 12 C.F.R. §§ 1005.2, 1005.3, 1005.6(a)-(b); UCC § 4-402; Visa Zero Liability Policy.

b. Would Sandy's liability be different if the stolen debit card were a PIN debit card and because she has trouble keeping track of all of her PINs and passwords, she had written in Sharpie on the back of her card: "PIN: 4118"? *See* 12 C.F.R. § 1005.6(b).

10. Infamous hacker Boris Levitin's girlfriend, Natasha, was spying over your shoulder when you were writing a check, copied down your account and routing info, and has initiated an ACH debit transaction from your account, directing payment to herself. What is your maximum liability? *See* 12 C.F.R. § 1005.6(b); NACHA Rule 2.3.1.

11. There's a charge for $30 that you don't recognize on your credit card bill; you aren't sure if it was a purchase you made while on a trip or if it is an unauthorized transaction. How can you find out? *See* 12 C.F.R. 1026.13.

12. Anne Fleming used the Santa Barbara, California-based Oenosmile Wine Club to run an impressive scam. Anne lured high-rolling oenophile (wine fanatic) club members to pay upfront in $10,000 increments for large shipments of rare future vintages to be delivered in a year or more. The wine always seemed to be arriving soon, but never actually arrived, until one day Fleming absconded with all of the Club's funds and disappeared into a life of luxury in the South Pacific. A subsequent investigation revealed that Fleming, a teetotaler, never ordered any wine in the first place. Oenosmile Wine Club members paid for future wine shipments via credit card, and, because Oenosmile only took Continental Express cards, Club members were collectively owed some $36 million in undelivered wine shipments for which they had already paid Continental Express. Among the Oenosmile Wine Club members are Chris Brummer, a resident of Sacramento, California, and Don Langevoort, a resident of McLean, Virginia.

a. In the case of both Brummer and Langevoort, who is going to be stuck with the losses? *See* 15 U.S.C. §§ 1666i; 12 C.F.R. § 1026.12(c).

b. Suppose that Brummer and Langevoort had only joined the Oenosmile Wine Club two weeks before Fleming absconded. Neither has yet received a billing statement reflecting the charges to the Oenosmile Wine Club. Does this change things for Brummer and Langevoort? *See* 12 C.F.R. § 1026.12(c).

CHAPTER 21

EMERGING PAYMENT SYSTEMS

The Internet era has produced impressive technological developments in payment systems. The developments have occurred in three basic areas: digital wallets, cryptocurrencies, and the development of payment intermediaries known as aggregators. While this technology has transformed the musty old world of payments into a cool kid, the consumer and merchant interfaces have not fundamentally changed the legal framework for payments. The technological changes, however, have created a different set of risks for merchants and consumers, as the excerpts below explain.

I. DIGITAL WALLETS

A. What's a Digital Wallet?

Adam J. Levitin

Pandora's Digital Box: The Promise and Perils of Digital Wallets

167 U. PA. L. REV. 305 (2018)

. . .

Digital wallets build on the traditional payment card network structure. Digital wallets do not change the fundamental transaction structure, but instead may change the method and nature of the data communicated between consumers and merchants.

A digital wallet is a computer software application that stores and transmits payment authorization data for one or more credit or deposit accounts. Once a consumer loads her payment account data into a digital wallet, the digital wallet can then be used as a payment device for that account, transmitting the data to merchants to authorize payment.

1. Types of Digital Wallets

The term "digital wallet" encompasses a broad range of products. These products vary in four dimensions: acceptance, funding, pass-through versus staged status, and form factor. The Acceptance, the first dimension of variation, refers to where the wallet can be used to make payments. Some wallets are "general purpose wallets" that can be used for payments at any merchant, while others are "business wallets" that can be used only at a single merchant or group of associated merchants, much like a private label credit card. ApplePay, AndroidPay, SamsungPay, and PayPal all offer general purpose wallets. Retailers like Starbucks (which offers the most widely used mobile wallet by far), Walmart, and Amazon.com offer single-business wallets, as do online retailers that store consumers' payment information.

Second, how the wallet is funded varies. Some digital wallets are either "open wallets" that can be linked to any payment source (credit, debit, or ACH with any payment network brand or bank). Others are "limited open wallets" that can be linked to a limited number of payment sources. Still other digital wallets are "bank-open wallets" that can be linked to payment source offered by a specific bank, or "brand-open wallets" that can be linked to any payment source offered by a particular payment network. (In some cases, the wallet is both brand- and bank- specific.) And finally, wallets can be "closed wallets" that can be linked only to a single payment source from a single bank or brand. Thus far, all major single business and multi-business wallets have been open wallets or limited open wallets. . . .

Third, digital wallets are either "pass-through" wallets or "staged" wallets. In a pass-through wallet, the digital device merely substitutes for a plastic card: instead of the payment authorization being stored on a card, it is stored on a phone or some other device. AndroidPay, ApplePay, and SamsungPay are all pass-through wallets.

Other wallets, however, such as Google Wallet, PayPal, Square Cash, and Venmo, are staged wallets. A payment from a consumer to a merchant with a staged wallet is divided into two distinct legs. First, there is a funding leg, in which the consumer makes funds available to the digital wallet. The funding comes from whatever source the consumer selects—a bank account, a credit card, a line of credit from the staged wallet provider, or a payment balance on the staged wallet. The second leg moves the funds from the staged wallet to the merchant. This second leg may involve a different payment method than the first leg: the staged wallet might be funded through a credit card, but the payment to the merchant might be through ACH, thereby enabling the staged wallet provider to arbitrage the difference between its funding and its payment costs.

The staged wallet provider serves as an intermediary between the consumer and the merchant, accepting payment from the consumer and then relaying payment to the merchant through a method of its own choosing.[18] Because the staged wallet provider stands between the consumer and the merchant, the merchant may receive different transaction information than if it transacted directly with the consumer. Similarly, the financial institutions involved in the funding leg see only the transfer to the staged wallet; they have no visibility into the identity of the ultimate merchant recipient. Because of the two transactional legs in a staged wallet transaction, there is also the possibility

18. A similar intermediation role is played on the merchant side by merchant aggregators such as Square, Etsy, iZettle, WyzAnt, and Stripe. Some digital wallet providers, such as PayPal and Amazon are also merchant aggregators. The consumer essentially makes the payment to the merchant aggregator, which then relays the payment to the merchant. The merchant aggregator business model is based on the merchant aggregator having a lower cost of receiving payments than the merchants themselves and arbitraging that spread.

of the consumer having a payment balance on the wallet—funds held by the wallet provider for the consumer, much like a bank deposit. Such payment balances are not possible on pass-through wallets.

Fourth, digital wallets vary by form factor. Form factor variation is a major functional distinction between traditional plastic cards and digital wallets. While all digital wallets are software based, some are accessed through web browsers, others through mobile device apps, and some through both. Web-based wallets store the consumer's payment data in the cloud and can be accessed by any device with a web browser, whether a desktop or a mobile device. Some web-based digital wallets, such as PayPal and Google Wallet, are general-purpose wallets, which are not specific to any particular merchant. Most web-based digital wallets, however, are single-business-wallets. And any merchant that stores consumer payment information in a way that it can be used for future transactions is offering a type of digital wallet. Thus many airlines, rental car companies, and Internet retailers offer digital wallets. Likewise, Amazon.com offers a multi-business wallet that can be used for payments to all Amazon.com sellers.

2. Mobile Wallets

Other digital wallets are "mobile wallets" that run on mobile devices, including smartphones, tablets, wearables, key fobs, and dongles. Some, such as AndroidPay, ApplePay, and SamsungPay, are specific to the particular combination of software and hardware on certain devices. Others, such as the Starbucks app or PayPal, are apps that can run on multiple operating systems. Web-based wallets can of course be accessed from mobile devices, even if they do not have a specific mobile app (although some, like PayPal, do). Mobile wallets utilize a range of communications technologies for transmitting payment data from the device to merchants, including magnetic stripe emulation, Near Field Communication (NFC), Quick Recognition (QR) Code, Bluetooth, Bluetooth Low Energy (BLE), instant messaging (SMS), and the Internet.

Confusingly, some digital wallets have both web-based and app-based versions. Likewise, the same device, such as a smartphone, can host multiple digital wallets, which may utilize different communications technologies. For example, an iPhone user could use both ApplePay and a free-standing digital wallet application that would make payments over the Internet. Even more confusingly, some digital wallets are able to be included in other digital wallets. Thus, Capital One Pay can be used as a free-standing digital wallet or included inside an ApplePay wallet. At the same time, however, Apple does not make the NFC chip in iPhones available to third-party apps. Thus, the only NFC-based digital wallet that can run on an iPhone is ApplePay, even though other digital wallets that do not use NFC can be used on an iPhone. In contrast, the NFC chip on Android devices is available to third-party developers.

C. WHAT DIGITAL WALLETS CHANGE

For payments processed through credit and debit Card Networks, digital wallets do not change the fundamental design of the five-party payment card system set up. Nor do they necessarily change the basic fee structure in the credit or debit card system, although they may reallocate some of the value in the system and possibly increase costs. To the extent that digital wallets provide the possibility of ACH payments, however, the fee structure is altered because in an ACH transition there are no interbank fees, only a small per transaction fee paid to the ACH operator.

What digital wallets do change, irrespective of how the payments are processed, is the possible range of communication technologies for transmitting payment authorization from consumers to merchants and, more importantly, the format of the payment authorization data. These changes are significant because they may affect the flow and control of consumer data. Finally, digital wallets potentially change payments from being an isolated one-way data flow to being part of a richer, two-way communications environment that encompasses the entire retail experience from advertising and search to purchase, shipping, returns, and customer loyalty.

1. The Method of Transmission of Payment Authorization Data from Consumers to Merchants

Digital wallets enable payments to be made from credit and demand deposit accounts using devices other than plastic credit and debit cards. In so doing, they expand the possible range of technologies used to transmit payment authorization from consumers to merchants. Transmission of the payment data in the rest of the payment network system (credit, debit, or ACH) remains unaffected by this change; ultimately, the consumer's bank will only authorize the transaction if the authorization data comes to it through a payment network in which it participates.

The traditional plastic payment card is merely an access device for an account, be it a demand deposit account or a line of credit account. Accessing such an account requires transmission of proper authorization information to the bank that holds the account—the issuer. Access does not require a plastic card. Demand deposit accounts, for instance, do not require a plastic card for access; they may also be accessed by checks or by the account and routing number for ACH transactions. Likewise, even with a credit card account, authorization information can be transmitted in numerous forms by the consumer to the merchant, who then relays it to the issuer through a payment Card Network. For example, with a traditional card, the authorization data—the information on the front (and possibly the back) of the card—can be transmitted by swiping the card's magnetic stripe through a magnetic stripe reader, by oral transmission to the merchant (such as in telephonic transactions), or by manual input (such as entry of the card information in a website), or, in recent years, through "contactless" transactions using NFC.

Digital wallets potentially increase the possible methods for transmitting payment authorization data from a consumer to a merchant. Thus, a digital wallet might use NFC technology, the Internet, text messaging, or magnetic stripe emulation for transmission of payment data. The use of different data transmission technologies can potentially increase the risks faced by a merchant when accepting payments. . . .

2. The Nature of Payment Authorization Data

Digital wallets may also affect the format and nature of the information being transmitted from the consumer to the merchant, as well as from the merchant to the payment

Figure 2 Payment Card Transaction with Digital Wallet

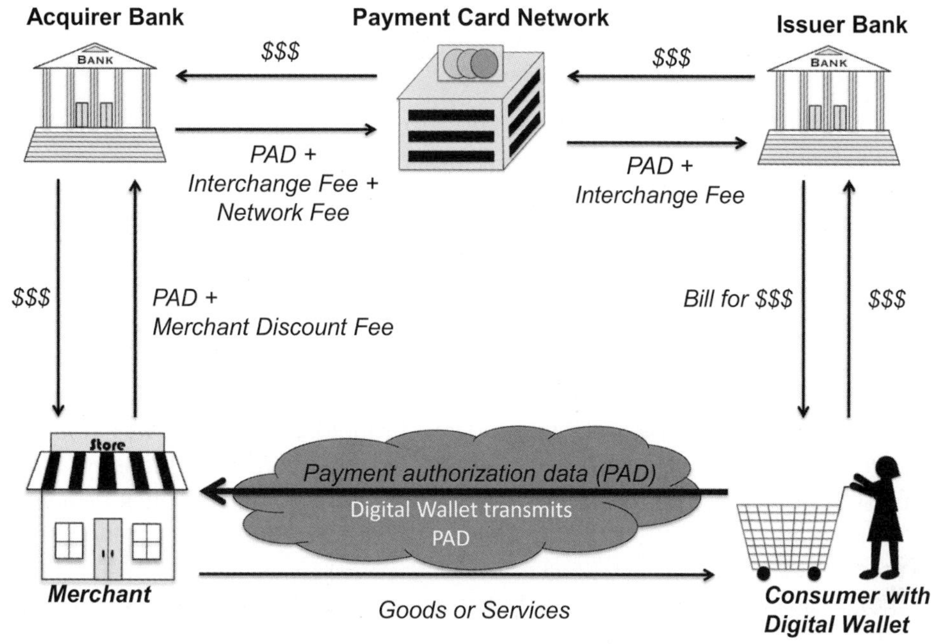

network. By altering the format and nature of the information transmitted, digital wallets may mask a cardholder's PAN and thereby deprive the merchant of the informational value of the transaction.

In a traditional credit or debit card transaction, the consumer transmits his unencrypted PAN as well as a static card verification value (either the CVV1 that is encoded on a magnetic stripe or the CVV2 digits written on the back of the card) to the merchant.[23] The merchant then relays the PAN and verification code information to its acquirer and thence to the network and, ultimately, the issuer for authorization. If a fraudster were to intercept or steal unencrypted payment authorization data either from the consumer or from any of the parties in the transmission chain, the fraudster could use it to create counterfeit physical cards or in fraudulent card-not-present transactions.

The Card Networks have encouraged adoption of security measures to address this fraud risk, although the particular measures encouraged have been questioned in terms of their effectiveness and distributional implications for participants in the payment card network systems. The two primary security responses to the risk of theft of payment data are (a) to reduce data retention by merchants and acquirers; and (b) to render payment data harder for thieves to use. Reducing data retention means that there is simply less

23. The precise terminology for the card verification value or card verification code varies by card network. In this Article for consistency, I refer to CVV1 (static, magnetic stripe data), CVV2 (static, back of card), and CVV3 (dynamic, EMV chip generated).

payment authorization data sitting around for thieves to steal. Rendering data harder to use makes it less valuable and therefore less tempting to would-be thieves.

a. *PCI-DSS Mandated Encryption*

The mechanism for enforcing these security measures is the mandate of compliance with the Payment Card Industry Data Security Standard (PCI-DSS). PCI-DSS is promulgated by the Payment Card Industry Security Standards Council, an entity created and controlled by American Express, Discover, JCB International, MasterCard, and Visa. The Card Networks require that the acquirer banks to ensure that their merchants comply with PCI-DSS (and hold the acquirers liable for assessments upon noncompliance), so acquirers require their merchants to attest that they are in compliance with PCI-DSS.

A recent update to the PCI-DSS restricts data retention, providing that "[t]he only cardholder data that may be stored after authorization is the primary account number or PAN (rendered unreadable), expiration date, cardholder name, and service code."[26] Under PCI-DSS, "sensitive authentication data," such as card verification codes (the unembossed numbers on the back of cards), PIN numbers, and Full Track data (which contains all of the preceding data fields) may not be stored after authorization, even if encrypted.

PCI-DSS also requires that any data that is retained be rendered less valuable for thieves through various methods of obfuscating data. In particular, PCI-DSS requires that the PAN (but not the cardholder's name, expiration date, or service code) be rendered unreadable anywhere it is stored by encryption, hashing, or truncation methods. PCI-DSS also requires that sensitive information be encrypted for transmission over open, public networks, like the Internet. Therefore, once a merchant receives cardholder data, the portion of that data that is deemed "sensitive authentication data" should never be stored post-authorization, PANs should always be stored in encrypted form, and all sensitive data should only be transmitted in encrypted form. While this is not quite the same as mandating end-to-end encryption of all data, it achieves something similar.

PCI-DSS compliance is supposed to address the security vulnerability of cardholder data that a merchant has captured and retained, as well as the security vulnerabilities of transmission through open networks of cardholder data. Notably, however, PCI-DSS does not require that payment data be transmitted to the merchant in an encrypted form, unless it is transmitted over an open, public network, like the Internet. Transmission over in-house, private networks may still be done "in the clear" (*i.e.*, unencrypted).

b. *EMV Chip Cards*

PCI-DSS relies on encryption as its primary security method. Encryption involves using a mathematical algorithm to scramble data in such a way that only someone who has the decoding key can read the data. Another, distinct security technology is the integrated circuit card (ICC), also known as the "Chip" or EMV card. A Chip card contains a microchip that is used with a special card reader to communication with

26. PCI Security Standards Council, PCI-DSS 36 (Version 3.1 2015).

the microchip to verify that the card is a genuine card. The communications channel in a Chip card payment flows through the contact between the reader and the chip on the card. Chip cards, however, can also be "hybrid" cards capable of transmitting data via traditional magnetic stripe or NFC contactless technology, as well as through the chip.

When a Chip card is inserted in a Chip card reader, the microchip on the card generates a unique card verification code (CVV3) for each transaction based on a challenge-and-response interaction with the Chip card reader. The transaction-specific CVV3 and the PAN are transmitted to the merchant in the transaction and sent ultimately to the issuing bank, which then uses them to authorize (or decline) the transaction. The PAN and transaction-specific CVV3 are still transmitted "in the clear"—that is unencrypted—from the Chip card to the merchant's terminal. Because Chip cards transmit unencrypted payment data to the merchant, PCI-DSS–mandated encryption is the main bulwark of defense against theft of payment authorization data from merchants.

It is often wrongly assumed that Chip technology prevents the creation of counterfeit cards. Although Chip technology makes it more difficult to counterfeit cards because the dynamic CVV3 on a Chip card can be used for only a single transaction, it does not prevent all counterfeit fraud. Creating a fully functional counterfeit Chip card for an account would not be cost-effective: the cost of cracking the security would exceed the credit limit on almost any account. But the effectiveness of Chip technology as a security measure is reduced by the lack of a universal adoption mandate, the coexistence of the magnetic stripe authorization channel, the lack of domain specificity for PAN data, and the varying levels of card data verification used by issuers. The existence of multiple authorization channels that use data that is largely non-specific to any particular channel enables fraudsters to arbitrage the differences in security measures for each channel.

For example, in a type of "milking" attack, a CVV3 and other authorization data could be lifted from a Chip card without a transaction being performed through a fake or altered terminal or RFID reader. That milked data could then be encoded on a magnetic stripe card and used at a non-Chip terminal or at a Chip terminal that reverts to a magnetic strip transaction when presented with a non-functional Chip card (a feature known as the "fallback function"). Indeed, it is even possible to encode the magnetic stripe such that the card appears to the reader to be "Chip-less", and thus that the reader will not instruct the consumer to insert the card into the Chip reader slot. While a diligent issuer should still catch such arbitrages based on differences in the service code for Chip and magnetic stripe transactions, issuers' verification procedures are not standardized.

Moreover, even if a valid CVV3 cannot be captured, the PAN skimmed from a Chip card can be used in those card-not-present transactions that do not require a CVV2 because there is no domain specificity for PAN. Thus one likely effect of the adoption of Chip technology will be the migration of fraud (or at least fraud attempts) from card-present transactions to card-not-present transactions, as well as to card-present merchants that do not accept Chip transactions. So a more accurate statement of Chip technology's effect is that while it makes it not cost-effective to counterfeit a fully functional Chip card, it does not prevent all forms of card counterfeiting because Chip card data can be used for magnetic stripe and card-not-present transactions.

All Chip cards and readers are made to conform to specifications from EMVCo, LLC. EMV is an acronym for the names of the venture's original partners, Europay International, MasterCard International, and Visa International. The current members of EMVCo, LLC are American Express, JCB, Discover, MasterCard (which purchased Europay), UnionPay, and Visa—significantly, not the U.S. PIN-debit networks or ACH operators.

The use of Chip cards and readers is not mandated in the United States, but it is encouraged by a change in the Card Networks' rules regarding liability for unauthorized transactions. In the United States, as of October 2015, American Express, Discover, MasterCard, and Visa (but not the PIN-debit networks because they are not co-owners of EMVCo) instituted a change in their rules that allocate liability for unauthorized card-present transactions.

Historically, for card-present transactions (which include contactless transactions), the card issuer was liable for unauthorized transactions provided that the merchant followed the requisite security procedures. Otherwise the acquirer would be liable for the unauthorized transaction, but would contractually transfer the liability to the merchant. In contrast, merchants have always been liable for all unauthorized transactions in card-not-present situations, although they can, by contract, shift the liability to other parties, such as the Card Networks for card-not-present authentication services.

Under the revised rules, called the "EMV liability shift," if a consumer presents a Chip card in a card-present situation, liability for counterfeit card transactions shifts to the acquirer (and thence to the merchant), unless the merchant properly uses a Chip card reader, in which case the liability shifts back to the issuer. The old rule that issuers are liable for counterfeit card-present transactions remains in place if the card presented is not a Chip card, as well as for unauthorized transactions not involving counterfeit cards. By issuing EMV cards, issuers are thus able to shift the fraud risk for counterfeit cards to merchants. Although EMV cards cost more to issue than traditional magnetic stripe-only cards, most issuers appear to have determined that the savings from the liability rule shift outweigh the issuance cost, especially when reissuance is done as part of the normal card replacement cycle.

Despite the EMV liability shift, magnetic stripe technology is still widely used in the United States, even though it will presumably be phased out at some point in the future. For the time being, however, the Chip and magnetic stripe technologies operate side-by-side. Many cardholders still have magnetic stripe-only cards. Issuers are replacing magnetic-stripe–only cards with hybrid cards that can be used for both magnetic stripe and Chip transactions, but the replacement appears to be part of the normal card replacement cycle. Even with hybrid cards, however, many merchants have not installed or activated EMV card readers because of the high cost of the equipment and the subsequent PCI-DSS and EMV-compliance certifications relative to the merchant's anti-fraud benefits.

Another reason for limited adoption of Chip acceptance is that part of the benefit from a merchant's use of Chip technology is the protection it provides to *other* merchants by reducing the likelihood that a data breach at the merchant will be used for fraud at those other merchants. In this regard, adoption of Chip technology is analogous to vaccination, in that it not only protects the vaccinated individual, but it creates positive externalities for other unvaccinated individuals in that the vaccinated individual cannot infect them. Merchants, however, are unlikely to account for this positive externality when making their decisions about accepting Chip transactions, and neither merchants nor issuers are mandated to use Chip technology. The lack of universal adoption combined with the continued use of magnetic stripe technology undercuts the potential effectiveness of Chip technology by creating opportunities to arbitrage security measures between authorization channels. Still, as Chip transactions become more common, fraudsters are likely to concentrate their attention on merchants that do not accept Chip transactions, thereby increasing the value to merchants of accepting Chip transactions.

The adoption of Chip technology does not affect merchants' ability to use PANs for anti-fraud, customer loyalty, advertising, and returns. Although the card verification code on a Chip transaction is dynamic, the cardholder's PAN is not, and is unencrypted when transmitted to the merchant. This means that with Chip transactions, the merchant can correlate different transactions made with the same PAN, which facilitates anti-fraud, customer loyalty, and returns.

Digital wallets can, but need not perform Chip transactions. Some mobile wallets like ApplePay use a chip in the mobile device as the EMV chip for card present transactions, where the consumer is face-to-face with the merchants. The ability for a mobile wallet to do a Chip transaction, however, depends on the communications channel used by the wallet; web-based wallets, for example, cannot do Chip transactions.

c. Tokenization

Another security measure is "tokenization" that is the replacement of payment card data—the PAN and the card verification code—with randomly generated substitute data known as a "token". The token looks like a PAN and card verification code, in that it contains the same number of digits, but it is in fact a random number that does not match any actual PAN, so it cannot itself be used for a subsequent transaction.

Unlike encryption, tokenization does not scramble data using algorithmic transformations. Instead, tokenization replaces the original data with randomly generated substitute data. The match between the random token value and the original data is recorded in a secure codebook (called a "vault") retained by the issuer. Tokenization, according to Visa's CEO, is "the single biggest change that's been made in the payment networks easily over the past 15 or 20 years and maybe longer."[50]

Tokenization is not a necessary feature of digital wallets, but it appears to be an increasingly standard security measure. By the same token, tokenization is not specific to digital wallets; it can be used by a merchant for any transaction as part of a layered security approach. For example, a merchant can transmit encrypted payment data to its acquirer. The acquirer will forward the encrypted PAN and card verification code to the Card Network and the issuer for authorization, but will itself (or through a vendor)

50. *See VISA CEO Confirms Tokens as New Network Revenue Stream*, PYMNTS.com, Nov. 13, 2014 (quoting Charles Scharf, CEO of Visa).

tokenize the data and return only a token to the merchant. The merchant will retain the tokenized data, rather than the original encrypted PAN and card verification code. This tokenized data is useless not only to the hackers, but also to the merchant. Digital wallets potentially mask PANs by facilitating data "tokenization" before the data is even transmitted to the merchant.

It is possible, however, to use a "multi-pay" token that is unique to both a PAN and a merchant. A multi-pay token is essentially a merchant-specific ersatz PAN. Such a multi-pay token can be used for subsequent transactions, including refunds and credits, but only at a single merchant. This is a solution that is often deployed by eCommerce merchants that store payment information in online digital wallets. After the initial transaction, the token will be linked with a description such as the card brand and the last four digits of a PAN. When the consumer selects the card with that particular description, the merchant will transmit the corresponding token to the acquirer, which will decode the token and transmit the original PAN and card verification code to the issuer for authorization. Digital wallets offered by eCommerce merchants thus frequently use multi-pay tokenization. A multi-pay token also enables merchants to track a consumer's transactions for anti-fraud purposes, and—if the merchant can correlate customer address or other identification information with the token— advertising, and loyalty program purposes.

Tokenization is also used by offline digital wallets. The particular application of tokenization varies by digital wallet, but its use in the ApplePay digital wallet is instructive. When a consumer loads a card on the ApplePay digital wallet, the consumer first enters her card information in the ApplePay application on an iOS device. When the consumer does so, the iOS device communicates with Apple, indicating from which bank Apple should request a token and card verification code algorithm. In response to a request from Apple, the bank transmits the token and card verification code algorithm to Apple, which then re-transmits the token and card verification code algorithm to the iOS device. The token and card verification code algorithm are then stored by the iOS device on a special, dedicated microchip known as a "secure element" that cannot be accessed by iOS applications other than ApplePay. Only the token and the card verification code algorithm are stored on the iOS device; the cardholder's PAN is not stored on the iOS device.

When a consumer authorizes a transaction—for example, through a fingerprint scan or entry of a PIN in ApplePay—the secure element is prompted to take the token and encrypt it using the card verification code algorithm. Although the token is itself static, the card verification code algorithm uses it to produce a unique cryptogram for every transaction, just as with a regular "Chip" card. ApplePay transmits the encrypted token to the merchant either through NFC or through a web browser.

Tokenization plus encryption means that there are effectively two levels of data obfuscation between the cardholder's PAN and the cryptogram that is transmitted to the merchant. The cryptogram received by the merchant is an encrypted token, with an algorithmic relationship between the cryptogram and the unencrypted token, and a random relationship between the token and the PAN.

After ApplePay transmits the cryptogram to the merchant, the merchant (through its acquirer) retransmits it to the payment Card Network. The network will apply the card verification code algorithm to unencrypt the cryptogram, which, if the cryptogram is authentic, will produce the token. If the cryptogram is authentic, then the network will pass the unencrypted token along to the issuer, which will decode the token, producing the PAN of the cardholder attempting the transaction. Once the issuer determines that the token is authentic and that a transaction is authorized for the associated account, the issuer will authorize the transaction. All of this takes place in a matter of seconds.

The basic mechanics of a tokenized transaction are similar to that of a regular magnetic stripe or Chip card transaction, but in a tokenized transaction, the merchant never sees the cardholder's PAN. Instead, the merchant has access to only a dynamically encrypted token. Thus, the merchant is not able to track transactions from the same consumer, thereby frustrating anti-fraud measures, advertising and customer loyalty programs, and potentially even returns. Figure 3 shows how a token-generating digital wallet fits in a payment Card Network.

3. The Economics of Payment Card Transactions

a. Fees

Digital wallets may also affect the economics of payment card transactions because they represent another mouth to feed in the transactional ecosystem. Services such as tokenization are not free. The parties that provide the digital wallet expect to be compensated, and their compensation will either come out of the pockets of acquirers, issuers, and the payment Card Networks, or will be passed on to merchants or to consumers.

Figure 3 Payment Card Transaction with Token-Generating Digital Wallet

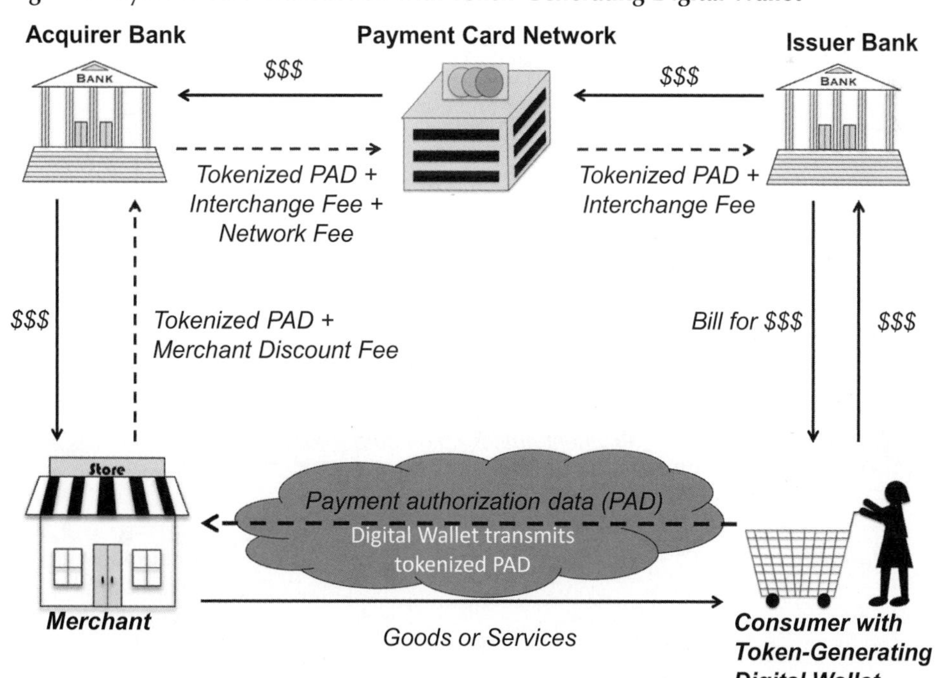

For example, on every ApplePay transaction, the card issuer reportedly pays Apple fifteen basis points (0.15%) on the transaction volume. Those fifteen basis points eat into the issuer's bottom line. As the volume of ApplePay transactions increases, issuers will surely look to recoup those fifteen basis points elsewhere. Similarly, the Card Networks themselves have indicated that they see digital wallets as a potential revenue source.[58]

To the extent issuers or networks have increased expenses or seek to increase their own revenue, the result will likely be higher costs for acquirers. Demand for network services appears to be greater for acquirers (and thus merchants) than for issuers (and thus consumers) given that fees currently flow from acquirers to issuers in almost all payment card systems. Therefore, it seems likely that the costs of digital wallets will fall on acquirers in the first instance. To the extent that the costs of digital wallets fall on acquirers, the acquirers will, in turn, likely pass along the increased costs to merchants in the merchant discount fee, which is often structured as an express pass-through of the fees paid by the acquirer plus an additional mark-up percentage. Figures 4 and 5, respectively, show the fee structure for a traditional payment card transaction and for a digital wallet transaction.

b. Monetizable Data

Digital wallets affect payment card economics in ways beyond fees, however. They also affect the flow of data in payment card transactions. Consumer data is a hugely

Figure 4 Traditional Payment Card Transaction Economics

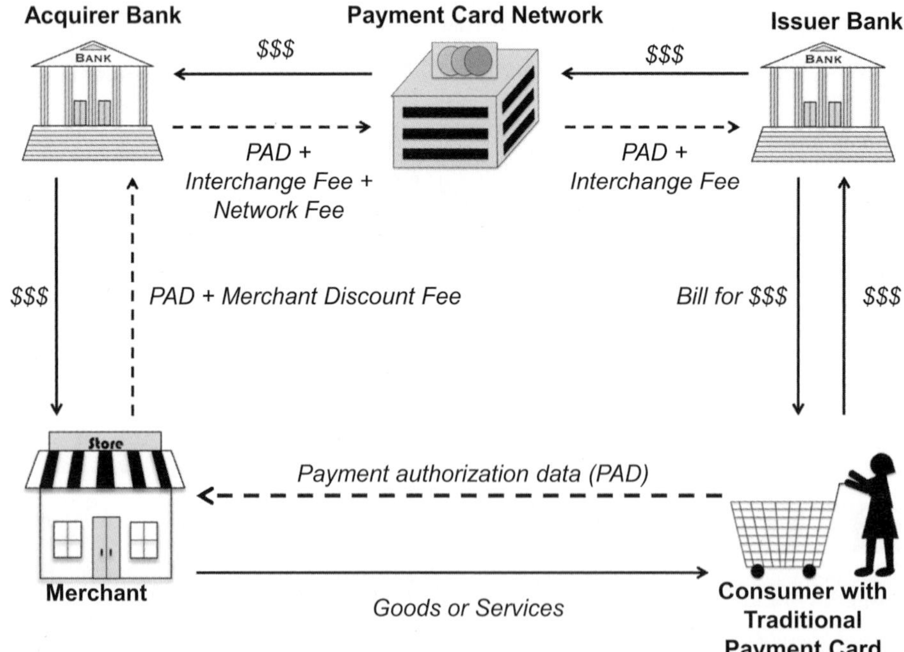

58. *See supra* note 50.

Figure 5. Payment Card Transaction Economics with Digital Wallets

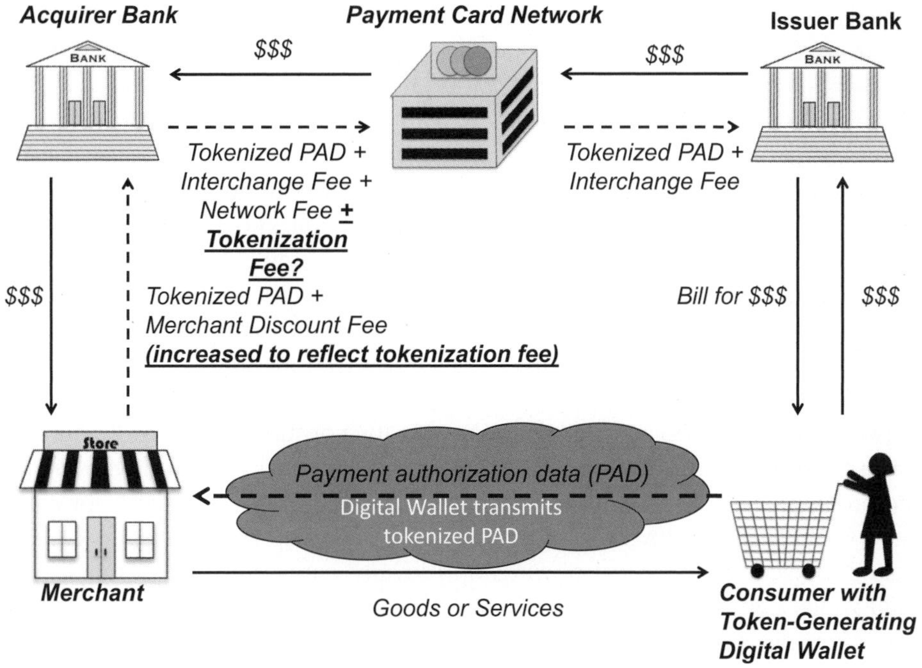

valuable by-product of payment transactions. It can be analyzed for marketing purposes, as payment data tells about what a consumer has been interested in purchasing and what they are willing to pay for it. This data that can be utilized by a wide range of merchants, including those that generate the data, their competitors, and even merchants in other sectors, including financial institutions. Yet if general consumer information is digital gold, payment information is digital platinum: It is information about how consumers actually spend, and past spending is often indicative of future spending. It is data already linked with monetization.

In a traditional plastic card transaction, most of the valuable consumer data—what particular items were purchased and at what price—is retained by the merchant and not shared with the Card Network or the Issuer bank. Instead, the financial institutions involved in the transaction see only an aggregate level of spending, the name of the merchant, and a general category label for the merchant. Absent a merchant's agreement, they cannot see item-level data (also known as stock-keeping unit (SKU)-level data or Level 3 data). Digital wallets can potentially reallocate that valuable data from the merchant to either the Card Network or the issuer. . . .

. . .

A. CONSUMER BENEFITS AND RISKS

1. Consumer Benefits from Digital Wallets

Digital wallets hold out important benefits to consumers: the possibility of faster and more convenient payments; improved record-keeping; and the integration of payments with loyalty and rewards programs; and helpful, targeted advertising and promotions.

Digital wallet payments can *potentially* be faster than traditional card payment. In particular, for EMV transactions, digital wallet payments made via NFC are faster than those made with a chip card using an EMV terminal.

Digital wallets can also help consumers with their recordkeeping and accounting. By storing a record of consumer transactions, digital wallets can facilitate consumer returns, exchanges, and reimbursements, as well as assist with tax keeping and personal financial planning. Paper receipts are bulky, require organization, and are easy to lose. A digital wallet can keep all of a consumer's receipts in one place, permit search and sorting, and takes up no additional space. Digital wallets can also provide data transfers to other software applications, such as personal finance applications like Quicken, that can be used for keeping track of a consumer's finances both generally and specifically for tax preparation.

Convenience (and coolness) is also a benefit for consumers. Rather than carrying around a bulky wallet full of store loyalty cards or a key chain covered with miniature reward program tags that are easy to forget to use, a digital wallet can store information for multiple rewards and loyalty programs without taking up any more physical space. And although separate physical rewards and loyalty cards are easy to forget to use, a digital wallet can automatically apply rewards and loyalty programs with payment. Another convenience is that some digital wallet apps allow a customer to "order ahead" so that the order is ready when the customer arrives at the merchant's store.

Digital wallets also facilitate targeted promotions and advertising, which can benefit consumers. These promotions can be integrated with payments so that they are automatically applied when transacting, and targeted advertising can help consumers find products they might be interested in. Likewise, consumers can benefit from advertising and promotions because merchants are able to focus their promotions on the consumers most likely to use their products and to tailor their promotions toward those consumers' interests.

2. Consumer Risks from Digital Wallets

Digital wallets are not without their risks for consumers. Though many of the risks apply generally to all payment systems, the subsection highlights additional risks specific to digital wallets.

a. *Varying Legal Regimes*

One of the risks related to digital wallets is the possibility of a shift of the governing legal regime. Different payment methods are subject to different legal regimes. The Truth in Lending Act (TILA) and Regulation Z thereunder govern credit cards, while the Electronic Fund Transfers Act (EFTA) and Regulation E thereunder govern debit cards, and ACH transactions are governed by the private rules of National Automated Clearinghouse Association (NACHA) and potentially the EFTA/Regulation E, depending on the particular transactional details. These statutes and regulations provide a legal framework for disclosure requirements, liability for unauthorized transactions, and resolution of errors and system malfunctions. The TILA/Regulation Z rules for credit cards vary somewhat from the EFTA/Regulation E rules for debit cards and NACHA Rules. For example, consumers' unauthorized transaction liability for credit cards is capped at $50, while for debit cards it varies between $50, $500, and unlimited liability, depending on the consumer's negligence, and under NACHA rules there is no consumer liability for unauthorized transactions.

Presumably, the application of TILA/Regulation Z or EFTA/Regulation E does not change based on the form factor of the payment device used, at least for pass-through wallets like ApplePay, where the digital device merely substitutes for the plastic card. TILA defines credit card as "any card, plate, coupon book or other credit device existing for the purpose of obtaining money, property, labor, or services on credit."[70] Thus, as the Fourth Circuit has observed, the "core element of a 'credit card' is the account number, not the piece of plastic."[71]

Similarly, while the application of the EFTA is keyed to the use of an "accepted card or other means of access," and Regulation E is keyed to the use of an "access device"[72] The Official CFPB Staff Interpretation of "access device", the two have identical definitions: "a card, code, or other means of access to a consumer's account."[73] The official CFPB interpretation of "access device" includes "debit cards, personal identification numbers (PINs), telephone transfer and telephone bill payment codes, and other means that may be used by a consumer to initiate an electronic fund transfer."[74]

While it would appear from these observations that TILA/Regulation Z and EFTA/Regulation E apply to digital wallets depending on the funding source of the payment, there is no case law yet on that point. Digital wallets do not affect the application of NACHA Rules because ACH is not a device-specific payment system. And even if these legal rules do not change for pass-through wallets, they can still be a source of consumer confusion, because a digital wallet might default a consumer's payment choice to a particular payment method, thereby selecting an applicable legal regime without the consumer realizing. For example, if a digital wallet contains both credit and debit cards, but the digital wallet defaults to the use of the debit card, the consumer's liability for unauthorized transactions increases, even though the consumer may not have deliberately selected a debit card in the same way as when the consumer chooses which card to take out of a physical wallet. There is no possibility of default payment selection with physical wallets.

Staged wallets (such as PayPal) present an additional source of confusion in terms of the applicable legal regime. Recall that in a staged wallet there are two coupled transactions: a funding transaction and a payment transaction. The different stages of the transaction may well be subject to different legal regimes, something consumers are unlikely to know or understand. Suppose that the funding for a staged wallet transaction

---

70. 15 U.S.C. § 1602(k).

71. United States v. Bice-Bey, 701 F.2d 1086, 1092 (4th Cir. 1983) (use of credit card account number over telephone qualified as a "credit card" for TILA criminal fraud liability).

72. 12 C.F.R. § 1005.6.

73. 12 U.S.C. § 1693a(1); 12 C.F.R. § 1005.2(a)(1).

74. Official Interpretation to 12 C.F.R. § 1005.2(a).

is from a debit card, while the payment transaction is through ACH. The funding transaction would be subject to the EFTA/Regulation E. The payment transaction, however, would most likely to be subject to NACHA Rules, but it is also possible to characterize it as a prepaid debit card transaction, which is not expressly subject to EFTA/Regulation E.

The point here is that there may be some shift or confusion about which legal regime applies, and depending on the particular design of a digital wallet, there may also be a transformation in the applicable legal regime, which can impact consumers' rights in terms of disclosure requirements, unauthorized transaction liability, and error resolution. Consumers may well be unaware of these issues, and this bespeaks a need to consider greater uniformity in the regulation of different types of consumer payment systems, as well as a need to give consumers clear control over their default choice of payment source.

b. Security Measures and Fraud Risk

Digital wallets vary in terms of security measures: the consumer action needed to authorize the transaction, the sort of data stored, the sort of encryption or tokenization used, the applications that can access the consumer's data, and the ability to remotely disable or "wipe" the device with a "kill" switch. Moreover, some wallets are more easily hacked than others. As a result, there are different fraud risk profiles for different devices.

Consumers' direct pecuniary exposure to fraud risk is limited, however, for traditional plastic credit and debit cards, and as noted in the previous subsection, those same legal regimes would seemingly apply to credit and debit payments via digital wallet. There are, however, important indirect pecuniary and non-pecuniary costs for consumers when dealing with fraud, such as the hassle involved of notifying card issuers, getting cards reissued, and resetting automatic bill payments. Thus there are still fraud risks to consumers from digital wallets. Indeed, to the extent that digital wallets store other consumer information, the impact of fraud can be greater—a fraudster might not only access the consumer's funds, but adding insult to injury, he might use the consumer's coupons, too.

Even within a particular digital wallet, there are security differences based on the type of payment made: for instance, a credit card or signature-debit card versus a PIN-debit card. Debit cards are legally required to "multihome," meaning be capable of processing transactions on more than one unaffiliated network. Whether the consumer is defaulted by the Application Identifier (AID)—software on the merchant's point-of-sale terminal—to using a particular network (and thus a particular authorization technology) and whether the consumer understands the choice involved both have implications for the fraud risk, because there is a much greater fraud risk for single-factor authenticated signature-debit than for two-factor authenticated PIN-debit payments. It is much easier for fraudsters to copy a card's magnetic strip than to copy a PIN and the one-time data from a chip, for example.

The number of parties involved in digital-wallet transactions might exacerbate fraud problems for consumers due to confusion about the proper party to contact when fraud is suspected. Consumers have little ability to sensibly evaluate the security measures on different devices, so they cannot protect their interests with any type of security measure; their main protection is the federal limits on direct pecuniary liability for unauthorized transactions.

c. *Error Resolution*

An important part of the federal regulation of credit and debit cards are the regimes for addressing error resolution. Card issuers are obligated to investigate consumer claims of error in a timely fashion, and consumers can withhold payment while such investigation is pending.

With a traditional plastic card, it is very clear whom the consumer should contact regarding an error. With a digital wallet, it is less clear. For example, would a consumer who had an error claim from a Chase Visa transaction using ApplePay know to contact Chase directly, rather than Apple or Visa? The problem is not the transformation of error resolution rights, but rather confusion because it can lead to delay in contacting the proper party. This confusion can result in delay (which changes legal liability regarding unauthorized debit card transactions) or the consumer simply giving up, effectively depriving the consumer of her error resolution rights.

d. *Wallet Provider Insolvency*

Staged digital wallets such as PayPal, Venmo, and Google Wallet, allow consumers to maintain balances their respective digital accounts. The funds in these accounts are not FDIC-insured; they are simply unsecured claims against the wallet-provider. Thus, in the event of PayPal, Venmo, or Google Wallet's bankruptcy, there might be no recovery for consumers with account balances.

Wallet-provider insolvency presents a risk even with pass-through wallets as well. Even if the wallet provider does not hold funds for the consumer, it still holds consumer data. If a wallet provider were to become insolvent and cease operations, consumers would be cut off from any data stored in the cloud. This could include receipts for purchases and transaction histories, which would frustrate consumer attempts at product returns or accounting.

e. *Loss of Privacy*

Perhaps the most important difference in risks for consumers between traditional plastic cards and digital wallets is privacy. A consumer's spending habits are extremely revealing, conveying information about a consumer's interests and problems. As a saying often attributed to Martin Luther goes, "Show me where a man spends his time and money, and I'll show you his god." Unsurprisingly, then, survey data indicates that privacy concerns are quite salient for consumers with mobile wallets.

Traditional plastic cards do not offer the high level of anonymity of cash transactions. Nonetheless, they offer a reasonable degree of privacy insofar as they do not enable other parties to see the entire picture of a consumer's transacting behavior. A transaction with a traditional plastic card transmits only data about that particular transaction undertaken with that particular card. It does not transmit data about other transactions on that card or on other cards, much less about the consumer's other behavior, such as the consumer's web browsing history.

A merchant to whom a traditional plastic card payment is made receives substantial information about that particular transaction. The merchant will know exactly what the consumer purchased (known as the "stock keeping unit" or SKU-level, or Level 3 data), for what price, and when. But the merchant is limited in its ability to aggregate information from multiple transactions. At most, the merchant can aggregate other transactions the consumer has made using that particular card with that particular merchant. The merchant has no visibility into the consumer's other transactions at other merchants or using other payment cards, and the merchant will have no window into the consumer's payment history and account balances. And if the merchant is a brick-and-mortar retailer, it will also not have any visibility into consumers' web browsing and search history.

Conversely, with traditional plastic cards, financial institutions have much greater ability to aggregate information from transactions made at multiple merchants, even on multiple cards. But that information is still much more limited than what is available to merchants. With traditional plastic card transactions, neither the Card Network nor the consumer's bank ever sees the SKU data. Instead, these institutions can identify all of the various merchants used by the consumer by whatever name the merchant uses: the merchant's industry by broad category (*e.g.*, "Hardware Equipment and Supplies" or "Supermarkets"); and the manner in which the transaction was authorized (card-present or card-not-present), which provides some information about the consumer's past location (assuming the consumer was the one who actually used the card).

To be sure, merchant category data can, in some cases, be quite revealing about the consumer. Consider categories such as "Wig and Toupee Stores," "Massage Parlors," "Counseling Services–Debt, Marriage, or Personal," or "Bail and Bond Payments". One does not need to know the detailed services purchased to get an impression of the consumer; some credit card issuers allegedly have used such information in their pricing algorithms.[90] But the level of consumer information revealed through merchant categories is also quite limited in many cases, such as with "Supermarkets" and "Book Stores." For example, a Card Network or card issuer would not be able to tell if a consumer's grocery store purchase was an ethnic food product (*e.g.*, a Manischewitz or Goya brand product), if a consumer's pharmacy purchase was a contraceptive, or if a purchase under the merchant category of "miscellaneous general merchandise" was a sex toy. All that to say, with traditional plastic cards specific consumption information remains obfuscated from the Card Networks and card issuers.

The result of this situation is that traditional plastic cards do not provide a comprehensive view of a consumer's purchasing habits. Instead, the consumer's transactional habits are divided into distinct silos. Although the consumer does not have privacy

90. *See* Complaint, FTC v. CompuCredit Corp. and Jefferson Capital Systems, LLC, No. 1:08-cv-1976, ¶ 75 (N.D. Ga., June 10, 2008). The FTC and CompuCredit settled the case for an estimated $114 in consumer restitution plus injunctive relief. Press Release, FTC, Subprime Credit Card Marketer to Provide At Least $114 Million in Consumer Redress to Settle FTC Charges of Deceptive Conduct, Dec. 19, 2008, *at* https://www.ftc.gov/news-events/press-releases/2008/12/subprime-credit-card-marketer-provide-least-114-million-consumer.

over particular transactions, she retains a certain level of privacy because no one has a detailed overview of her entire transactional life.

It is, of course, possible for the data from individual transactions to be aggregated, but such aggregation is unlikely in the traditional plastic card context. Merchants are loath to share their data with other merchants or financial institutions, and card issuers are loath to share their cardholders' information with other issuers.

Digital wallets potentially change this privacy picture. A digital wallet can aggregate data on payments at multiple merchants using multiple payment accounts because all the data is stored in one place. It can also combine this data with data on the consumer's past web browsing and geolocation. Digital wallets can even potentially add SKU-level data for transactions if the consumer uses a web- or app-based shopping cart, or if the merchant provides a digital receipt. Not all digital wallets collect or combine such information, but the possibility of such wide-reaching data collection substantially changes consumer privacy in commercial transactions. A much fuller picture of the consumer's search, location, and purchasing habits is potentially available through a digital wallet than through a traditional plastic card. The level of privacy that traditional plastic cards preserved through information siloing is thus readily lost with digital wallets.

Further, the integrated portrait of a consumer's transactional life is not the consumer's to control. It can be shared or sold with virtually any entity, and unlike merchants and card issuers, digital wallet providers can only readily monetize the data they collect through sales to third parties.

The data aggregation facilitated by digital wallets enables much more targeted advertising and rewards, which is a boon to some consumers. Not all consumers, however, want to part with their privacy or want targeted advertising and rewards, and the degree of control a consumer has over his or her privacy is likely to be limited and opaquely disclosed through general disclosures regarding the collection and sharing of data. Digital wallets thus pose a privacy risk to consumers. Consumers might be willing to part with some or all of their privacy, but by using a digital wallet, the consumer can easily lose control of her privacy to a degree that she may not anticipate or fully understand.

. . .

B. MERCHANT BENEFITS AND RISKS FROM DIGITAL WALLETS

1. Merchant Benefits from Digital Wallets

For retailers, digital wallets offer some attractions as payment devices—in particular, potentially greater tender speed—but the real attraction of digital wallets goes beyond payments: digital wallets are the potential lynchpin for an integrated suite of retailing services covering the entire retail experience from advertising and consumer search functions to payment and shipping, returns, and loyalty programs.

In twentieth-century commerce, these various retailing services were splintered on multiple platforms. The consumer obtained information about products through a variety of channels, ranging from store windows to advertisements to Internet searches. The advertising and search functions were completely delinked from the payment process, and the payment process was not connected with tracking of shipping, the processing of returns, or customer loyalty programs. Thus in twentieth-century commerce, each retailing function was essentially siloed.

This siloing limited retailers' ability to exploit consumer data because no one in the purchasing chain had a complete informational picture. For example, a traditional brick-and-mortar retailer generally knows only about the sales it has made, not about consumers' unsuccessful searches. Moreover, even though that retailer is able to match the consumer's credit card purchases made using the same card by using the consumer's name and card number, the retailer is not able to match transactions made by the same consumer using different payment methods because consumer names are not unique. This is why some merchants use loyalty cards that provide a unique identifier for the consumer that can be used for all transactions, irrespective of payment method.

Twenty-first-century retailing involves the integration of these different functions into a single platform that provides search, payment, and relationship management functions. This integrated retail platform gives merchants greater ability to attract and retain customers. The integration of payments and communications can be very beneficial for both consumers and merchants, although it does raise important consumer privacy concerns.

Integrated retail platforms already exist for many eCommerce merchants. Amazon, for example, already provides a well-integrated platform for these services within its universe. Amazon provides advertising and a search function, it stores payment information in its own digital wallet, and it enables tracking of shipments and return processing on the same platform. In contrast, traditional retailers lack information about unsuccessful searches, repeat searches and purchases, items saved for later in digital shopping carts, and even how long consumers spend looking at particular products or placing their mouse on a particular product's portion of a display. Twenty-first century commerce creates an incredible wealth of consumer information for merchants, and that information can be analyzed and monetized. Amazon has pursued this twenty-first-century retailing model within a single firm that sells nearly everything.

A successful integrated digital retail platform requires two-way communications. The consumer needs to be able to transmit a range of information to the merchant, and the merchant needs to be able to transmit a range of information to the consumer. This is not possible with a traditional "dumb" payment card. The traditional plastic card is a one-way communication device that transmits payment authorization data and nothing more. It is, by definition, not integrated into a larger retail platform. Putting such a card into a digital wallet, however, makes it possible to integrate payments into an all-encompassing retail services suite. Digital wallets promise to bring the online integrated retail experience into brick-and-mortar commerce through mobile devices.

While it is possible to offer many of the other services separately from payments, integrating payments into the retail suite makes the transaction more seamless for the consumer. This is important for retailers because the more seamless a transaction is, the less likely it is that the consumer will become distracted or have second thoughts and not go through with the purchase. For online retailers in particular, "abandoned carts" are a major problem—one index has found abandonment rates of 78%—and most often at the payment stage. One of the causes of abandonment is issues with payments—including excessive security checks and declines—that would not occur with a digital wallet. Avoiding these issues by integrating payments into a retail platform should ultimately then result in more completed sales. Digital wallets thus affect not just payments, but the very model of retailing.

2. Merchant Risks from Digital Wallets

a. Control Over Customer Data

The single most important concern for merchants regarding digital wallets is the loss of control over customer data. Digital wallets are an informationally rich environment as compared to traditional plastic cards. A digital wallet can potentially tie together information about a consumer's web searches, transactions (on multiple cards), physical locations (current and past), and contact information (such as email address and phone number). The collection of this linked information enables advanced consumer behavior analytics. It also creates a channel for real-time marketing communications. The consumer behavior data and communications channel can be combined, in turn, to produce very targeted advertising and offers for consumers.

The problem digital wallets present for merchants is that although merchants sow the seeds for the informational crop, they are not the ones who reap its harvest. The additional information about a consumer generated by a digital wallet is controlled neither by the merchant nor by the consumer. Instead, it is controlled by the digital wallet provider and/or the payment Card Network. Indeed, because of tokenization, digital wallets can result in an informational diminution for merchants (as discussed in the following subsections). So, despite the greater informational wealth created by digital wallets, merchants come out worse—not only does all of the additional value go to other parties, but digital wallet payments may produce less informational value for merchants than traditional card payments.

The problem merchants face, however, is not simply that other parties are the ones who can harvest and harness the additional data generated by digital wallet transactions, but that nothing prevents digital wallet providers or the Card Networks from selling the data to third parties, including the merchant's competitors, who can then use it to poach the merchant's customer relationships. The merchants interviewed for this Article—all Fortune 500 firms—unanimously described this concern as among their most pressing.

For example, hypothetical fast food restaurant Tast-i-Fast could enter into a deal with a digital wallet provider under which Tast-i-Fast obtains information on all of the digital wallet transactions at its competitor Quick-i-Serve. This is hardly what Quick-i-Serve wants—why should it be generating data for its competitor's benefit?

The possibility of the Card Networks selling data on a merchant's transactions to a competitor of the merchant already exists with traditional plastic cards, though that information is of limited use. If Tast-i-Fast purchased traditional plastic card information from a network, it would generally not be able to link purchases made on different cards to the same consumer. Nor would it be able to link the information to either the consumer's web searches or physical location. These factors limit the analytical value of the information. Even if Tast-i-Fast could generate a compelling insight from its information to attract consumers away from Quick-i-Serve, it could not communicate that offer to the consumers in real time. At best, it could use targeted advertising and hope that the advertising's message would not decay between the time of its receipt and the time of a purchase.

These limitations on linking and utilizing information disappear with a digital wallet. A digital wallet provider can sell a much richer selection of consumer data and real-time communication access to the consumer. Consider this scenario: Meg has used her smart-phone-based digital wallet to purchase baby supplies and baby furniture. Meg now goes shopping at The Store, a large retailer. As soon as she enters The Store's parking lot, she receives this text message from her digital wallet provider: "Hi Meg! We see you're in The Store's parking lot. We wanted to let you know that TheWeb.com is offering diapers at ten percent less than The Store, and with free shipping, but only if you purchase in the next hour (through this link)." Not one to turn down a good deal, Meg selects the link, purchases the diapers online, and drives out of The Store's parking lot without even getting out of her car. The Store has lost her business to TheWeb.com.

How did this happen? Meg's digital wallet provider knows her general type of purchases and is able to determine the stores she frequents, though perhaps not the exact items she purchases. It is also able to see her web searches, and because of a geolocation sensor in the smartphone, it can determine where Meg has gone and when. That allows the digital wallet provider to guess the types of items Meg might be interested in purchasing, and to identify when she is on the cusp of a potential purchase. That data can then be sold to a merchant, such as TheWeb.com, which can swoop in with a better offer for Meg (with access to Meg's device again provided by the digital wallet provider).

For Meg this might be a great deal; she has gotten cheaper diapers, and saved some time. But it is a bad deal for The Store, which loses lost a sale of diapers, any potential impulse buys Meg might make, and any revenue that would result if Meg had paid for the purchase with The Store's private-label or co-brand payment card. The Store is getting scooped on these transactions because it has lost control over customer information because of the digital wallet.

Now consider the possibility that the digital wallet provider could itself be a large online retailer. The scenario above would allow such a retailer to scoop business away from brick-and-mortar retailers. Brick-and-mortar retailers' fear over being scooped by online competitors is hardly a far-fetched scenario: Walmart is sufficiently concerned about Amazon obtaining data on its sales that it forbids its vendors from using Amazon cloud computing services.

The Honor All Wallets rules [a card network rule that requires retailers to accept payments from all devices that utilize any technology through which the retailer accepts the network's payments] prevents the brick-and-mortar retailer from taking steps to protect its business from this sort of poaching via mobile devices. If the brick-and-mortar retailer accepts Visa payments through NFC, it must accept them from all Visa NFC devices, ranging from NFC-enabled plastic cards to NFC digital wallets, including digital wallets offered by its competitors. Thus if Amazon were to offer an NFC-based digital wallet (to which it could potentially migrate the 150 million or so payment accounts it already has in its web-based digital wallet), brick-and-mortar retailers that take NFC payments would have to accept it and give Amazon access to their customer information.

Payment companies that employ co-branded cards (e.g., a United Airlines Visa) already have insight into customer behavior, but a smartphone digital wallet is a real-time communications channel with geolocation, enabling timely and targeted offers, advertisements, and coupons in a way that a co-branded card does not. Moreover, with a co-branded card, the consumer must sign up (and qualify) for the card. Providing a digital wallet is much simpler; the consumer has already signed up and qualified for the card(s) and just has to put it in the wallet. Subsequently, the wallet provider or Card Network can gain a window into the transacting on all of the cards on the wallet.

Digital wallets thus present a material change in the terms under which a merchant transacts. When merchants transact with a digital wallet, they surrender data that might be used to poach their future sales. Every digital wallet transaction carries a set of competitive risks that traditional plastic cards do not. These risks are not necessarily identical for all digital wallets. Merchants, however, are forced to accept them all if they take any using a particular technology. Thus merchants receive materially less value with digital wallet transactions than with traditional plastic cards.

For some merchants, device-based digital wallets present an additional competitive threat. Some merchants already provide their own web-based digital wallets that store payment card authorization data. These merchants have made a major investment to get consumer data and now face the prospect of disintermediation and loss of control over the data. For instance, while airlines are primarily card-not-present merchants, but they do some business in card-present settings at ticket counters and on planes. Many airlines offer their own web-based digital wallets. If customers use competing digital wallets for card-not-present ticket purchases from a specific airline, the informational value of the airline's own digital wallet diminishes.

b. Customer Relationship Management

Digital wallets can also interfere with merchants' ability to manage customer relationships. If a consumer is having difficulty transacting with a digital wallet, a merchant's sales associate is unlikely to be able to assist because the sales associate may not be familiar with that particular wallet. The customer, however, might still hold the merchant responsible for his or her inability to transact and be reluctant to patronize the merchant again.

When digital wallets tokenize payments, further customer relationship management issues may emerge. With a tokenized payment, the merchant sees only the token, not the PAN. Merchants use PANs for a variety of purposes including returns, chargebacks, product safety recalls, loyalty programs, fraud prevention, and anti-money laundering law compliance. Tokenization interferes with these applications of the PAN. For example, if a husband and wife are both on a credit card account, their plastic cards will both have the same PAN. Therefore, if the husband mistakenly purchases the wrong item, the wife can return the item with a receipt and her credit card because her card's PAN will match that on the receipt; the PANs for multiple cards on the same account are the same. With tokenization, however, the husband and wife will each have separate and unassociated tokens, and the wife will be unable to return her husband's misguided purchase. Indeed, some manufacturers, like Apple, have device-specific tokens, meaning that a receipt from an ApplePay purchase using an iPad would not correspond to an ApplePay purchase made with an iPhone. Likewise, some token service providers (such as American Express) provide domain-specific tokens, so an NFC payment would have a different token than a Chip transaction. While some merchants have work-arounds, such as additional loyalty card data that can provide an alternative method of identifying the customer, not all do, and maintaining such a program can be costly.

Likewise, the ability to see PANs lets merchants track customers' purchase histories. This can be used for advertising and loyalty programs, as well as for product safety recalls, fraud prevention, and anti-money laundering compliance. If a merchant sees that a customer has been purchasing baby products, for example, the merchant may want to send the customer targeted advertisements about other baby products or coupons for such products. By creating a transactional history trail, payment card transactions provide merchants with a form of value that cash transactions do not. Similarly, if a merchant sees an attempted purchase that is inconsistent with a past transaction history in terms of location, amount, or item, it may raise red flags about potential fraud. And the ability to track multiple purchases enables merchants to spot suspicious purchase patterns (such as repeat mass purchases of stored value cards) for which anti-money laundering law requires suspicious activity reports (SARs).

EMVCo has developed a specification for a Payment Account Reference (PAR), a twenty-nine digit alphanumeric sequence that would be consistent for an account regardless of form factor, but which could not itself be used to authorize payment. Use of PARs, however, is potentially expensive. First, merchants must adapt their systems to handle these twenty-nine digit sequences. This can involve reprogramming thousands of point-of-sale terminals, which can, in turn, necessitate recertification of those terminals. Moreover, the PAR would be supplied by the token service provider—Visa, MasterCard, or AmEx. The U.S. PIN-debit networks are not certified as token providers by EMV and thus cannot provide PARs. Token service provider control over the PARs means that the providers could charge for PARs, thereby increasing merchants' cost of accepting payments. Ironically, then, while tokenization might decrease payment fraud rates, it could result in *higher* costs to merchants.

c. *Tender Choice and Payment Routing*

Digital wallets can affect both tender choice and payment routing. Tender choice refers to the type of payment the consumer chooses to use, such as credit, debit, or ACH. To the extent that digital wallets affect tender choice, it could result in a generational shift in tender overall given millennials' high use of mobile devices.

Tender choice is often determined by the very setup of a digital wallet. Some digital wallets, such as those offered directly by individual banks, allow only that bank's cards to be used. Thus Capital One Wallet (using Android host-card emulation) and ChasePay (using QR codes) allow the use of only Capital One and Chase cards, respectively.

Other digital wallets are open to cards from multiple financial institutions, but that does not necessarily translate to a diversity of cards in the wallet, much less active competition for transactions. While consumers might carry multiple cards in a physical wallet, they will frequently load only a single card onto a digital wallet. The "top of the wallet" card is often the only card on a digital wallet. In this sense, digital wallets are often less "wallets" than simply digital versions of a single plastic card.

Because many consumers load only a single card onto a digital wallet, to the extent that consumers can be steered to loading a particular card onto the wallet, it effectively steers the consumer's choice of tender. Some digital wallets, like ApplePay and SamsungPay were rolled out initially with participation by only credit card issuers. As a result, the first cards loaded on these wallets—and therefore the default card for the payments from the wallet absent additional consumer action—were credit cards. The result is a tender shift, toward credit, and away from debit, at least for early adopters of these wallets.

Intellectual property rights may also affect tender and routing steering for digital wallets. For example, mobile wallets based on smartphones, like ApplePay and SamsungPay, offer consumers the option to authorize individual payments using biometrics—specifically, fingerprint scans. The use of a biometric for authorization is (in theory) quicker, easier, and more secure than having to enter a PIN number. Biometric authorization, however, is available only for credit and signature-debit cards; it is not available for PIN-debit cards. This is because when EMVCo, the joint venture between the major credit Card Networks, licensed the Common Payment Application—EMV's chip card specification—to U.S. debit Card Networks, the license did not include biometric Customer Verification Method (CVM). Thus ApplePay's default biometric CVM is not enabled for PIN debit networks. This discourages use of PIN debit and encourages use of credit or signature-debit.

Digital wallets may also affect routing choices. Routing refers to the processing of a transaction, and it can have a major effect on cost. A debit transaction that is routed through a signature-debit network is much more expensive for a merchant than if it were routed through a PIN-debit network.

Additionally, there is differential ease of use for different types of payments with digital wallets. The differential ease of use can result either from the economic deals of digital wallet providers or from intellectual property rights limitations. Digital wallet providers can have an incentive to steer payment toward certain payment Card Networks' products or even toward certain banks' cards as part of their own economic deals, although to date this has not manifested itself.

The combination of digital wallets and Chip technology also facilitates issuer steering of routing choices for debit card transactions. The Durbin Amendment requires that all debit cards have the possibility of being routed over two unaffiliated networks, and that merchants be allowed to determine the routing of the transaction. For magnetic stripe transactions, merchants are able to choose the routing based on the bank identification number (BIN) on the card. For domestic Chip transactions, the routing selection is done through the AID software on the merchant's point-of-sale Chip terminal. The AID selects between different routing applications on the Chip card's chip. Not all routing applications contain the same routing choices. For example, MasterCard and Visa each have a "Common AID" for U.S. domestic transactions that contains all domestic PIN- and signature-debit networks. Additionally, MasterCard and Visa have their own AIDs, that contain, respectively, only MasterCard (and its Maestro PIN-debit subsidiary) and Visa (and its Interlink PIN-debit subsidiary) networks.

The use of a mobile wallet potentially enables the cardholder to override of use of the Common AID in favor of the MasterCard AID or Visa AID (which do not contain PIN-debit networks), thereby undermining merchants' ability to choose the transaction routing. The override would work similar to the traditional magnetic stripe debit routing choice of pressing "credit" (for signature-debit) or "debit" (for PIN-debit). The cardholder can, in turn, be encouraged by an issuer or Card Network to exercise the override either by direct financial incentives, such as rewards for transactions run over particular network or by more subtle cues, such as the placement of AID choices on the device screen or the names assigned to the choices.

For example, a mobile wallet might ask the consumer if she wants to pay with "Visa debit" or "U.S. debit". The consumer knows that she has a Visa card because of the Visa logo on the front of the card. She likely does not know that her Visa card is also a card capable of running on one or more unaffiliated PIN-debit networks. At best, these networks' logos will appear on the back of the card, but none are called "U.S. debit", which is a generic moniker for PIN-debit networks. When faced with the choice between the known brand and the unknown brand, the consumer is likely to choose the known brand, resulting in the payment being routed as a more expensive Visa signature-debit transaction.

This issue has already appeared on Chip terminals at point-of-sale, where a screen appears for the cardholder to "select payment." Merchants can reprogram their Chip terminals to turn off this selection screen, but doing so may necessitate EMV compliance recertification and leave the merchant exposed to counterfeit fraud liability under the EMV liability shift rule in the interim. Only the very largest and most sophisticated merchants are likely to attempt to reprogram their Chip terminals. With a mobile wallet, however, reprogramming is not an option for the merchant. The routing override may well be a violation of the Durbin Amendment and rules thereunder, but to the extent it occurs on mobile wallets, it will be more difficult for merchants to identify and address.

d. Fraud and Data Security

Digital wallets pose fraud and data-security breach risks for merchants. Payment card fraud and data security breaches are injurious to merchants in numerous ways. First, merchants lose the value of the goods and services they part with to the fraudster. Second, they lose the costs of restocking and of dealing with the fraud administratively. Third, they may suffer reputational damage vis-à-vis the consumers whose accounts were used for unauthorized transactions. Fourth, merchants may face liability to consumers related to the fraud. Fifth, if a breach results in fraud at *other* merchants, the breached merchant might be liable for the losses. And sixth, merchants pay merchant discount fees even on the fraudulent transactions. Merchant discount fees are sometimes refunded in certain cases with unauthorized transactions involving mobile wallets, but the inability to identify which transactions were undertaken with which form-factor means that merchants are unable to verify that they have been properly credited with reversals of merchant discount fees.

Different technologies present different security risks, and even within a technology, different form factors or devices may pose different security risks. Some digital wallets may be more vulnerable to use by fraudsters, who will load fake or unauthorized accounts onto digital wallets. This was a significant problem with ApplePay's initial rollout. Moreover, the security of communications between a digital wallet and a merchant may vary by device. To the extent that there is a data security breach in the communications process, the stolen data can itself be used for unauthorized transactions. Even if the unauthorized transactions occur at other merchants, there can still be serious reputational harm to the breached merchants, which might also have liability to other merchants and consumers.

The Honor All Wallets rules and lack of ability to identify devices means that merchants cannot protect themselves either proactively or reactively by declining to accept certain devices or by limiting the types of purchases they will allow on a device. For example, even if a merchant were to believe that communications via certain NFC wearables were compromisable, the merchant could not refuse to accept NFC payments from those wearables.

Likewise, if a security problem were to emerge with specific wallets, allowing them to be used for fraudulent transactions, merchants could not protect themselves reactively by limiting purchases of open-loop gift cards (a favorite purchase for fraudsters) or of high-value items with ApplePay. The Honor All Wallets rules prevent merchants from refusing to accept or from discriminating against less secure devices despite the risks they pose to merchants.

e. *Intellectual Property Liability*

Patent trolls are a fact of modern business life. Patent trolls are firms that purchase patents for the purpose of bringing litigation against alleged infringers of the patents. As a result, patent trolls will often sue indiscriminately any party that has had any interaction with a patent.

Mobile wallets involve new (and changing) technologies that can implicate a range of patents. As a result, they are a fertile ground for patent trolling. While merchants are generally involved in mobile wallets only as recipients of payments (or potentially as users in the case of chargebacks and returns), large merchants make tempting targets for patent trolls. Indeed, some of the merchants interviewed for this Article have been sued for patent infringement on the basis of their acceptance of contactless payments.

Because merchants have no ability to determine exactly what technology—and thus what patents—are implicated by a particular payment's communication medium, they have little ability to protect themselves against potential patent infringement liability other than by negotiating for indemnification from their acquirer banks. The acquirer banks themselves, however, themselves do not have control over which technologies are allowed to access a payment Card Network. That decision is controlled solely by the Card Network itself.

Standard law-and-economics theory dictates that liability should be placed on the party with the lowest cost to avoid a harm, the so-called "least-cost avoider." In the case of patent liability for mobile wallets, the only party with the ability to avoid the harm of patent infringement is the Card Network because it is the party that makes the decision whether to allow technology to access the network. Placing the liability on the least-cost avoider would suggest that the Card Networks should completely indemnify merchants for any patent infringement liability caused by accepting a device approved by the network. The fact that merchants are not completely indemnified by the Card Networks means that the Card Networks do not internalize the full cost of patent infringement, so they are not incentivized to take the optimal level of care when approving technologies for accessing the network. Accordingly, accepting payments from mobile wallets creates a risk of patent infringement liability for merchants.

f. Cost of Accepting Payments

Beyond tender and routing choices, digital wallets raise the possibility of potential increases in the costs of accepting payment. The addition of digital wallet providers into the payment ecosystem means that there are additional mouths at the table. Digital wallet providers expect to be compensated for their services, and this compensation must come from somewhere. Apple, for example, reportedly receives fifteen basis points on every ApplePay transaction. These fifteen basis points are paid by the card issuer, which reduces the issuer's profits. As ApplePay's transaction volume grows, these fifteen basis points will become increasingly significant to issuers, who will be incentivized to recover them from other parties, such as by pressuring the Card Networks to increase interchange fees.

The Card Networks too, may look at digital wallets as a revenue source. Thus, Visa created a "tokenization" fee, reportedly seven cents per token and two cents per decline, which it waived for the first year, before later suspending the fee for issuers that do their processing through Visa. It would not be surprising if Visa were to reinstitute the fees once issuers have sufficiently committed to—and become locked into—tokenization of transactions.

Similarly, MasterCard has created "digital enablement fees" for both issuers and acquirers. Issuers are subject to a fifty cent "digitization" fee for the provision of a token and a "Digital Enablement Service Lifecycle Management" fee of ten cents per month for tokenized PAN, as well as a fee of two and a half cents for calls to its "alternate network application programming interface". Acquirers are charged one basis point on select card-not-present transaction volumes.

Additionally. . . the networks are likely to charge for PAR numbers that stand in for a PAN with a tokenized payment in order to facilitate fraud detection, returns, and loyalty programs. The PAR is necessary only because of tokenization, which many merchants do not want; through tokenization, the Card Networks are in a position to charge merchants more for a less valuable product.

When considering all of the risks posed by digital wallets, it is not clear if there is a compelling general value proposition for their acceptance by merchants. On the one hand, digital wallets offer the possibility of better data security and integration of loyalty programs with payments. On the other hand, they pose the specter of loss of data through tokenization, loss of control over customer data and the customer relationship, undifferentiated security risks, greater liability, and higher costs of payment acceptance both because of tender and routing shifts and because of additional fees. The tradeoffs may vary by merchant and by digital wallet; it may well be that in some cases it makes sense for a merchant to accept a digital wallet. Because of the Honor All Wallets rules, however, merchants are not able to select which digital wallets they wish to accept and on what terms. The result is to preclude merchants from protecting their own interest or from seeking out favorable deals with individual digital wallet providers. Thus it does not even matter how compelling a business proposition a particular digital wallet offers to a merchant; the merchant will have to accept that digital wallet on the same terms as all other digital wallets if it accepts any payments that use that wallet's communications technology.

B. Peer-to-Peer Payments

A subset of digital wallets are apps such as Venmo and Zelle that can be used for peer-to-peer payments, meaning payments made directly from one consumer to another. These apps are not materially different from digital wallets in general, but they differ substantially from each other. Venmo, like PayPal, which owns it, is a staged wallet that can be funded from a number of sources. It uses same-day ACH clearance, so the funding leg might be through a credit card, but the payment leg is always through ACH. Zelle, in contrast, is not a staged wallet; one cannot maintain a Zelle account balance. Zelle is funded solely from bank accounts. Zelle also uses same-day ACH clearance, but Zelle transactions result in faster funds availability because the banks that participate in Zelle front the funds before they have cleared through the ACH system.

Beyond differences in funding source and payment speed, Venmo and Zelle differ most notably in the type of contractual protections they provide users. Venmo provides a limited purchaser protection policy, such that it will, in some circumstances, reimburse a buyer who pays with Venmo and receives non-conforming goods or does not receive any goods at all. In contrast, there is no purchaser protection policy for Zelle; once funds have been sent, the risk is entirely on the buyer, just as with a cash transaction.

II. CRYPTOCURRENCIES

One of the major developments in payments in recent years has been the use of so-called **cryptocurrencies** or **virtual currencies**—privately issued digital currencies, such as Bitcoin and Ethereum. All of these virtual currencies involve a digital medium that captures a record of ownership of some notional unit of value. While such digital value media are colloquially called currencies, they have one critical distinction from traditional currencies—they are not legal tender (primarily because they are not issued directly by or under license of the state). This means that they cannot be used to pay obligations to the government (taxes, customs duties, fees) and that, absent a counterparty's consent, they cannot be used to satisfy a private obligation. Although not recognized as legal tender, cryptocurrencies still function as a medium of exchange and as a store of value, but in this regard they are not different from any other tradable store of value, such as cigarettes, Tide detergent, gold bullion, airline miles, wampum, etc. *See* Lee A. Sheppard, *Busting the Bitcoin Myth,* 142 Tax Notes 896 (Mar. 3, 2014).

Cryptocurrencies have appeared for a number of reasons. In some instances they may hold out at least the impression of greater privacy or anonymity, which may be particularly desirable for money laundering or illicit payments. They may also offer the possibility of more predictable and controlled inflation than fiat currencies, particularly in unstable, developing economies. And they hold out the promise of a currency free from government manipulation, which has particular political appeal to some.

Bitcoin is the classic and perhaps paradigmatic cryptocurrency. It operates using a technology known as the block chain, as the article below explains. The precise operations of other cryptocurrencies may vary, but most utilize block chain technology to maintain a distributed ledger of ownership of the cryptocurrency.

Adam J. Levitin

Bitcoin in 5 Pages or Less or Your Money Back: A Bitcoin Primer

(2016)

While most national currencies exist in a cash form, more recent private currencies or **scrip** exist in solely digital media. In particular, Bitcoin represents a new cashless digital currency. Bitcoin is a currency and peer-to-peer payment system created in 2009 by a mysterious and pseudonymous developer known as Satoshi Nakamoto. (As a currency, the lower-case "bitcoin" is used, while the upper-case "Bitcoin" refers to the entire system.) Bitcoin operates on a decentralized peer-to-peer network, meaning that there is no central Bitcoin server and no firm managing the system. Instead, the entire Bitcoin system consists of versions of the Bitcoin software that users download and operate on their own devices. The software is entirely open-source. An entity called The Bitcoin Foundation appears to be the lead developer, but is teetering on insolvency.

The lack of a central authority is a fundamental feature of Bitcoin. Its entire design is based around decentralization. While decentralization makes it harder to control the system, it does not preclude manipulation of the system, as Bitcoin is functionally a democracy based on computing power, rather than individual voting. A majority of computing power determines who is considered to "own" a bitcoin. In other words, property rights in bitcoins are determined by the majority of computing power in the system.

Bitcoins are held in **Bitcoin wallets**. This is a digital wallet comprised of software installed on a computer or mobile device or on a webserver. Typically wallets are provided on a for-fee basis by third-party providers; the precise details of how wallet holdings operate varies with providers, which also often serve as Bitcoin exchanges. Each wallet can hold bitcoins for multiple Bitcoin addresses; it is not possible to hold bitcoins without a Bitcoin address. Bitcoin transfers occur between Bitcoin addresses. To make a Bitcoin transfer, one generates a Bitcoin address using the wallet.

Every time a new Bitcoin address is created, a pair of cryptographic keys—unique alphanumeric sequences—are also generated. The keys consist of a public key and a private key. The private key is used with a mathematical algorithm to produce a Bitcoin **signature**. The key remains private to the owner of the Bitcoin wallet, but the signature is publicly viewable and can be used with the public key to verify that the owner of the wallet has authorized the transfer of the Bitcoins.

Bitcoin is a **push**, rather than a **pull** transfer system, meaning that transactions are initiated by the party sending the bitcoins, rather than by the recipient. Because Bitcoin is a decentralized system, transfers are direct between end-users; they are not routed through a central system. This sets up one of Bitcoin's key challenges: verifying payments so as to prevent a **double-spend** problem similar to check-kiting that is a potential bane for all non-real time payments.

To wit: Let's say Adam has 50 Satoshi (that's the subunit of a bitcoin) associated with an address in a bitcoin wallet. If Adam pays Boris 50 Satoshi (that's the subunit of a bitcoin), what prevents Adam from then paying Carl with the same 50 Satoshi? How does anyone know who actually has the right to those 50 Satoshi? (This double payment problem also appears with a new checking technology, called Remote Deposit Capture, in which checks are deposited through image transmission, rather than the transfer of the physical check.) Because Bitcoin lacks a central authority through which all transactions are run, a more complex solution is necessary to verify which transaction was the original spend (and hence which would be the later and unsuccessful spend): the Bitcoin mining process, which is also the process through which new bitcoins are created.

Here's how verification through mining works. When Adam wants to send bitcoins to Boris, he needs to get Boris's address, which includes a public key. Adam then creates a message signed with his private key that attaches Boris's public key to that amount of bitcoins. When Adam sends the message to Boris is also broadcast to the entire Bitcoin network; a transfer of bitcoins is not simply a private affair between the parties to the transfer. The broadcasting of the transfer is done to enable anyone in the network (including, presumably the parties to the transfer) to verify this transaction by solving the associated algorithms.

The verification process is costly and involves the application of a tremendous amount of computing power to check that the keys match. When successful, the transaction is **confirmed**. This verification process produces a **block**, which is then distributed within the network as part of an ever-growing **block chain** that is stored with every Bitcoin wallet. (When a wallet is downloaded, it also includes the block chain as it exists up to that point.) The block chain is a public record of all transactions in bitcoin history. It is essentially a public ownership ledger. (The block chain can be used for tracking ownership of all types of property, but that is a different application of the technology.)

This verification should show that Adam sent the bitcoins to Boris before Adam sent the same coins to Carl, so that only Boris's ownership of that 50 Satoshi is verified. The public nature of the block chain ledger makes it difficult for Adam to double-spend.

The creation and constant expansion of the block chain also means that all Bitcoin transactions are recorded and therefore traceable to some degree, although the record contains only the information about the IP addresses and transaction amount involved, not the identity of the owner of the addresses or who actually did the transaction. Bitcoin is pseudonymous, not anonymous.

The process of verification through block production is known as Bitcoin **mining**. Absent mining, Bitcoin does not work because there is no verification of the block chain. Mining involves the application of tremendous computing power to search for possible solutions to a complex mathematical algorithm. (Think of this as somewhat like searching for prime numbers, which become rarer and rarer as numbers get larger and larger.)

Mining is done by private parties—participants in the Bitcoin network—but not every Bitcoin user is a miner. Mining takes a lot of computing power, which requires equipment and electricity. In other words, mining has costs. (At this point, the block chain is so large, that it cannot be downloaded on a regular personal computer.) So while there isn't a central verification party that has to be paid, there are decentralized verification parties that have to be incentivized to conduct verification through mining.

There are two incentives to mine: successful miners receive a bounty of newly created bitcoins and they may also receive a transaction fee for the verification service, if offered by the party whose transaction they are verifying. Bitcoin is designed to making mining difficult and to adjust the difficulty of the mining to the success. Mining is supposed to produce roughly one block every ten minutes, which means that it takes about 10 minutes for a transaction to be verified.

The mining process also means that bitcoin is currently an inflationary currency, with the value of a bitcoin decreasing with each additional coin mined. Offsetting this inflationary trend, however, is the growth in demand for bitcoins. At a certain point, however, there will be few, if any new bitcoins mined, as the cost of mining will exceed the likely return as successful mining becomes rare due to the nature of the bitcoin algorithm. Unlike most payment systems, where there is a flat marginal cost for the additional transaction, bitcoin has an increasing cost for the marginal transaction, at least in terms of algorithmic complexity. This increasing cost of algorithmic complexity necessitates more computing power and electricity. To the extent that computing power and electricity become cheaper, the marginal cost of an additional transaction may in fact decrease, but the possibility of increasing marginal costs for additional transactions distinguishes bitcoin from traditional payment systems.

At most there can be 21 million bitcoins. As of the date of writing, there are between 12 and 13 million, but with new mining successful every ten minutes it should take around 100 years before the system cap is reached. At that point, the value of bitcoins will fluctuate solely based on demand for them, rather than changes in both supply and demand. Currently, most bitcoins do not circulate, but are instead held for investment.

Currently no one is offering transaction fees for Bitcoin mining. The sole incentive is the creation of new Bitcoins. At some point, however, either all bitcoins will have been created or the cost of mining will be prohibitive relative to the reward of new bitcoins. Whenever this does occur, transaction fees will emerge in the Bitcoin system. Moreover, use of Bitcoin requires a digital wallet, which typically involves additional fees. In other words, Bitcoin is not really a cost-free system.

Currently Bitcoin's operating costs are largely invisible to Bitcoin users because they occur through inflation, which is an incredibly non-salient type of cost. Every successful mining creates new bitcoins, which reduces the value of *all* existing bitcoins, not just those of the users' whose transaction was verified. This inflation would be hard to notice in the first place, but it is further masked by the offsetting deflation caused by the growth in demand for bitcoins.

Once no more bitcoins are being "minted," however, then transaction fees will kick in. Transaction fees will be much more salient, as they will be paid by the parties to a transaction directly, and at the time of the transaction. (It's not quite clear how those transaction fees will get set, as transactions would proceed with by bids without knowing if the bids will be accepted. In other words, Adam will pay Boris before Adam and Boris know if the transaction fee offered is high enough to incentivize anyone to verify their transaction. They might be able to subsequently increase their offer, but in the meantime, Adam might have also paid Carl and offered enough to have that transaction verified, leaving the transaction with Boris ineffective, to Boris's chagrin.) Because Bitcoin has a structure that makes its costs extremely non-salient until the network is fully grown, it lowers one of the barriers to entry for a new payment system, namely the transaction costs of the system. (Note, however, that while Bitcoin does not have transaction fees built into the system, the providers of Bitcoin wallets and Bitcoin exchanges do charge fees for their services, and these costs can make Bitcoin an unattractive proposition for consumers.)

Notably, while a bitcoin can be transferred between Bitcoin wallets, Bitcoin wallets (and their private keys) can be transferred outside of the Bitcoin network. Likewise, however secure transactions are *within* the Bitcoin network, there are risks from outside the network. A Bitcoin wallet can be hacked. It can also be lost with a computer failure or loss of a mobile device. Likewise, it can be lost if passwords are lost. These risks are not particularly different from those for cash, which can be stolen or lost. Similarly, like cash, the value of bitcoins can fluctuate relative to other currencies; there is always exchange rate risk on bitcoins.

A unique risk for Bitcoin is the possibility of manipulation of the block chain. It is possible for the block chain to "fork" meaning that there are two conflicting block paths. In such an event, the miners decide which chain is valid by continuing to add blocks to it and not the other. The longest block chain is presumed to be the valid one, but this situation means that if a user controls the majority of the computational power in the mining network he can manipulate the block chain to his advantage by creating a fork, with one chain sending bitcoins to his own wallet, and another selling bitcoins to a buyer. The majority miner would then add to the first block chain, which would invalidate the chain that purchased the bitcoins, while keeping the money from the second transaction. This is a so-called ">50%" or "51%" attack. Such a 51% attack would take enormous computing power, but is conceivably within the scope of some nation's national security resources.

Finally, Bitcoin does not entirely eliminate the double-spend problem. Block chain verification is fast, but not real time (which would require substantially more computing power). A scenario known as the "race attack," takes advantage of the small time window for verification of blocks. Two near simultaneous transactions could enable a double-spend by creating a fork in the block chain, with the party whose transaction is recorded in the invalid fork losing out.

At this stage, Bitcoin is more a curiosity and speculative medium than a real value transference medium or payment system, but it points to the possibility of non-dollar payment systems in the United States in the future. Whether regulators will cede the economic control that comes with a national currency to a private payment medium remains uncertain, however.

III. AGGREGATORS

Another emerging area of payments is less about technology than about a new business model, that of the aggregator. Aggregators, such as PayPal and Square, aggregate payments from small merchants and then serve as the merchant of record for credit and debit card networks. The basic idea is to arbitrage the high interchange rates small merchants would pay with the lower interchange rate that the aggregator pays by virtue of its volume. What this means is that when a consumer makes a payment to a merchant via PayPal, the consumer is actually making a payment to PayPal. This payment is processed as credit, debit, or ACH, depending on what the consumer chooses. Once PayPal is paid via the credit, debit, or ACH system, it then credits the merchant's account at PayPal for the payment (minus a cut). If the merchant wishes to withdraw funds, PayPal will transfer the funds via ACH to the merchant's deposit account at a financial institution. In other words, on a PayPal transaction there are actually *two* payments, one to PayPal and one from PayPal to the merchant. The following excerpt explains the basic business model of PayPal and other aggregators.

Adam J. Levitin

Payment Wars: The Merchant-Bank Struggle for Control of Payment Systems

12 STAN. J. L., BUS. & FIN. 425 (2007)

1. THE CASE OF PAYPAL: ADDING VALUE AS A MIDDLEMAN

The Internet has been the locus of the most exciting developments in payments technology and business models. In particular, PayPal has played a major role in solidifying the use of credit cards networks to process Internet auction payments. This is a market that the card networks and member banks might have otherwise had difficulty reaching.

PayPal is an e-Bay subsidiary. It is not a bank, so it does not have the high regulatory costs of a bank, although it is subject to the Electronic Fund Transfer Act. It began as an on-line payment service that allowed consumers to make transactions using either pre-funded or credit-funded PayPal accounts. Thus, merchants were accepting PayPal's credit risk, not the consumers'. Moreover, merchants did not need to be equipped to accept payment cards to accept PayPal payments.

PayPal has since expanded to offer a full array of merchant payment services, from lines of credit (through GE Money Bank) to accounting, for both Internet and brick-and-mortar merchants. Its essential service to merchants, however, is factoring. When a consumer makes a purchase from a PayPal serviced merchant, the consumer actually pays PayPal, which then relays the payment on the merchant for a fee. Although PayPal functions like an acquirer, it is not an acquirer. Rather, it operates like a factor, purchasing receivables and collecting them itself, through acquirer banks. Unlike many factoring arrangements, though, PayPal commits to purchase the receivables as an outputs contract.

Transactions on PayPal can be made in a number of forms, including payment cards. The consumer never sees that PayPal is involved, unless payment is made with a PayPal account, and the merchant never sees the consumer's payment information. PayPal's intermediary status creates a level of financial privacy and security that are attractive to many consumers. Merchants are willing to use the service because PayPal's fees are lower than those they would pay in a traditional acquirer relationship.

By allowing PayPal to stand between them and payment card networks, merchants are also able to hedge the costs of high and low cost payment systems and of premium and regular payment cards. Merchants pay PayPal the same rate for all cards (and for all forms of payment). In this manner, PayPal enables merchants to circumvent the impact of the card associations' honor-all-cards and all-outlets rules.

PayPal is a credit and payment cost arbitrage operation. PayPal presents a lower credit risk than the merchants its services. PayPal has an extensive credit history, low fraud rates in the industry and an enormous sales volume. PayPal's low credit risk allows its primary acquirer, Wells Fargo, to offer it a much better discount rate than a small merchant could receive. PayPal arbitrages its own credit risk to offer high credit risk merchants, such as eBay sellers, lower discount rates than they could otherwise obtain. PayPal keeps the spread between its own discount rate and what it charges the merchants.

PayPal also arbitrages its funding mix. PayPal lets consumers use a wide array of payment methods, some of which have very low costs to PayPal and some of which have high costs. PayPal, however, charges merchants the same fee regardless of the means of transaction. PayPal thus assumes the risk (and benefit) of payment costs. PayPal's funding mix allows it to accept lower profit margins on credit card transactions because of the higher profit margins on ACH and bank account transactions.

PayPal has made tentative moves into brick-and-mortar processing, although its core business still comes from eBay sellers. PayPal offers an option for merchants to receive non-Internet payments via a virtual terminal, for which it charges a small monthly fee. PayPal is probably better suited for e-commerce solutions for small businesses than for the general market place.

Thus far, the bank networks have been tolerant of PayPal because PayPal does not compete with the bank networks; rather it extends their reach. To the extent that either PayPal attempts to expand its brick-and-mortar presence or the banks eye the small business e-commerce market for themselves, PayPal will come into more direct competition with banks. Even if PayPal is unable to expand effectively beyond e-commerce payments, it has extended the bank networks to a developing sector of the payments economy by offering small Internet merchants a payments solution at lower cost than traditional acquirer relationships. PayPal illustrates how non-banks are using technology to offer an improved package of services for both consumer and merchant at lower cost than traditional banks.

PayPal is a middleman, but it is a middleman that actually adds value by reducing transaction costs. The merchant-bank struggle over control is ultimately about cost, and PayPal demonstrates that there is room for restructuring payments costs in a way that pleases all parties through credit risk arbitrage like factoring and other innovative financial/technological structures.

Because aggregators such as PayPal serve as the merchant of record, their presence in a transaction complicates error and dispute resolution and rights in the event of an unauthorized transaction. Payment intermediaries typically have their own error and dispute resolution rules. The application of the Electronic Fund Transfer Act and the Truth in Lending Act to aggregators is also murky and may depend on the specifics of a transaction.

While the aggregator business model is primarily about arbitraging merchant discount fees, there can be a technological component as well. PayPal operates entirely through a web-based interface: the consumer enters his payment data on a website and never presents a physical card to the merchant even if the PayPal transaction is funded from a credit card or debit card. In contrast, some aggregators, such as Square, offer a physical magnetic stripe interface. In a Square transaction, the consumer swipes his physical card through a small (square-shaped) magnetic stripe reader that is connected to the phone jack on the merchant's mobile device and that interfaces with an app on the device. Square is thus both providing the point-of-sale technology and serving as an aggregator for the transaction. Square thus enables very small merchants and merchants that lack a permanent storefront to accept card payments using the relatively fast magnetic stripe to transfer data electronically without investing in expensive point-of-sale equipment.

Problem Set 21

1. Hotshot attorney Dan Mullens loves his new iPhone. As soon as he got the iPhone, he loaded his Continental Express Bank, N.A. Magenta Card credit card data into ApplePay, and he's been using it gleefully ever since to make all kinds of purchases. The details of how all of this works are described in the first article excerpt in this chapter. Dan also recently loaded in his Fidelity Fiduciary Bank debit card, which he uses to make peer-to-peer payments to friends using ApplePay's pay-by-text-message function. This lets Dan and his buddies easily settle up bills for meals. Apple is able to see all of

Dan's transactions and has been collecting data on them. Dan's been wondering, however, what would happen if something went wrong with ApplePay. If a payment isn't received or Dan gets double billed for the same payment, to whom should he turn for recourse? *See* 15 U.S.C. §§ 1666, 1666i, 1693a(9), 1693f, 1693g, 1693h.

2. Based on the operations described above, is Apple subject to CFPB UDAAP rulemaking or enforcement? *See* 12 U.S.C. §§ 5481(5), 5481(6), 5481(15)(iv), 5481(15)(v), 5481(15)(vii), 5481(15)(ix), 5481(18), 5481(26), 5531(a)-(b); 15 U.S.C. § 1681a(d).

3. Stella Ndinge opened a Hemispheros staged digital wallet account to make online purchases with merchants. She did so by giving Hemispheros her credit card information. When Stella pays with Hemispheros, Hemispheros charges her credit card and then turns around and pays the merchant using ACH. Hemispheros user agreement states that "Your liability for unauthorized transactions will be determined in accordance with applicable federal law." Stella's seen a $40 charge on her latest credit card billing statement that she doesn't recognize. What are her rights in these circumstances? *See* 15 U.S.C. §§ 1643, 1693g, NACHA Operating Rule 2.3.1.

4. Your college acquaintance Jeb Mulvaney was always a vocal libertarian. You ran into him at a party, and he started pitching you on how important Bitcoin is for Americans' freedom. Jeb explains, "With Bitcoin we are freed from the ability of the Federal Reserve to manipulate the currency. It's the free market that makes all the decisions, the way it should be. And best of all, there are none of those pesky interchange fees on Bitcoin, so it's great for small businesses like me." Is Jeb right?

PART II

MARKETS

SECTION B

Credit

CHAPTER 22

CREDIT BASICS

Remember the Smiths, our median-income family from Chapter 1? They're interested in purchasing a car. The Smiths currently drive a late-model Honda Civic, but would like to get an SUV to accommodate their children, Patty and John, and their pet Dachshund, Johnny Squeaky, as well as any of their children's friends who might be with them. The SUV the Smiths have their eye on, a Honda CR-V, sells for around $24,000. The Smiths only have $6,000 in cash saved up, so they are looking for an $18,000 loan (or possibly more to cover taxes, fees, etc.) to finance their car purchase.

I. SOURCES OF REPAYMENT

Suppose you are a lender approached by the Smiths. How do you go about evaluating their loan request? The first question you are probably going to ask is how the Smiths will repay the loan.

There are four possible ways. First, they could pay off the loan out of the assets they currently possess. That is, they could go and sell their stuff and use the proceeds to pay for the loan. That's not a very appealing repayment source for a lender because it requires the lender to first go and value the Smiths' stuff and then to ensure that they keep the stuff and don't give it away or sell it and divert the proceeds to something else.

Second, the Smiths could pay off the loan from the car itself. If the car were to be sold, the sale proceeds could be applied to the loan balance. That will only work as a source of repayment, however, if the value of the car exceeds the loan balance. Valuation will be easier if the lender is the seller—it should know exactly how much the car is worth, and even if not, cars are a relatively easy item to value (think the Kelley Blue Book). That necessitates the Smiths maintaining the car and having the car insured against casualty. It also means that the lender needs to have first dibs on the proceeds of the car.

A third possible source of repayment would be Jim and Mary's future earnings. That's great . . . if Jim and Mary have an income source that is adequate to pay the debt and the Smiths' other expenses. That means that the lender will want to verify the Smiths' income source in some way: old paystubs or tax forms or contacting their employers. Of course, past income is no guaranty of future income. If Jim or

Mary loses a job, repayment might be a problem. The lender will also likely want to know something about the Smiths' other expenses and whether the Smiths are the type of people who repay their debts. The lender will likely turn to a credit report for this information. The credit report will list (most of) the Smiths' other financial debts, as well as their payment history on those debts. It will also likely come with a credit score that rates the Smiths' propensity for repayment relative to other consumers. The credit report obviously won't list all of the Smiths' obligations, much less their daily expenses like groceries, but it will provide the lender with further information that it can analyze above some baseline assumptions about the Smiths' regular expenses.

The fourth possibility is that the Smiths won't be the ultimate source for repayment. If they have a co-signor or guarantor, then their own ability to repay is less critical.

The next thing the lender is likely to do is to try to figure out the terms of a loan that will work for the Smiths. There are numerous potential variables to a loan. It's worthwhile to understand the most common ones.

II. LOAN TERMS

A. Balance

First, the loan will have a specified **balance**. This is the amount the borrower owes at any point in time. The balance will be divided between **principal** and everything else. Principal (always with an "a") is the balance on which the loan will accrue interest. The initial principal balance will be the initial amount of the loan, but the principal balance may decrease or increase going forward depending on the interest rate, fees, and repayment of the loan.

B. Maturity and Prepayment

Second, the loan will either be a **term loan** or a **revolving loan**. A term loan, also known as a **closed-end** loan, is a loan made for a set period; the entire loan must be repaid by some specified date. Car loans and most home mortgages are term loans. In contrast, a loan might be a revolving loan, also known as a line of credit or a revolver or a revolving line of credit, which does not have a date for repayment in full. Instead, the borrower can repeatedly borrow and repay up to some specified limit. Credit cards are the most common example of this—repayment in full is not required in any given month—but home equity lines of credit, revolving loans secured by the borrower's house, are also common.

If the loan is a term loan, it will have a **term** or length. Sometimes this is called a "tenor" or "maturity." That term might be measured in days, weeks, months, or years. With an auto loan, it is likely measured in months: 48 months, 60 months, 72 months, etc. The term of the loan is determined by its start date (either when the money is disbursed or when the borrower becomes legally obligated) and the

maturity date—the final due date for the loan. Term loans may be single-payment loans or they may be **installment loans**, for which the borrower will make multiple periodic payments before the final maturity date. Auto loans and mortgage loans are common installment loans, while most payday loans are single-payment loans.

If the loan is a revolving loan, also known as **open-end** credit, it may have periodic due dates, such as with credit cards. Alternatively, it might have a final maturity date at which point the entire loan must be repaid, but with interim payment timing at the borrower's discretion.

Loans can sometimes be prepaid in part or in full, meaning that the borrower can pay down or pay off the loan early. Doing so will reduce the amount of interest that will accrue on the loan because there will be a smaller balance outstanding on which interest will accrue. Moreover, a borrower may wish to prepay a loan by refinancing. If market interest rates drop or a borrower's own creditworthiness improves, the borrower may save substantially by refinancing into a loan with a lower interest rate. Conversely, prepayment means that the lender is deprived of a loan on which it has been earning an above-market return. The lender will get repaid, but will have to reinvest in a less favorable environment.

Contrary to general expectation, American law did not traditionally allow prepayment. Lenders did not have to accept early payments absent contractual agreement to the contrary. Dale A. Whitman, *An Introduction to the Law of Prepayment* (2007). That said, when consumer lenders wish to restrict prepayment they usually do so explicitly. Outright prohibitions on prepayment are rare in consumer lending. Instead, loans will have prepayment penalties or yield maintenance clauses that compensate the lender for early repayment.

C. Interest Rates, Points, and Fees

Third, the loan may have an **interest rate**. This is the rate at which interest accrues on the principal balance. Interest is the basic cost of the loan—the price of money. Lenders charge interest to reflect the cost of making a loan, including the opportunity cost of not being able to invest the funds elsewhere, as well as to compensate them for the risk of non-payment on the loan. Some loans will have only a single interest rate, while others will have multiple rates that will accrue on different types of balances or based on whether the loan is in default or not.

There are numerous ways of expressing interest rates. Most commonly interest rates are expressed as a percentage for a specified period of time, such as 10% per year, or 2% per month. Other times the rate might be expressed as a fee relative to a balance, such as $10 every year for every $100 of balance. Less frequently, rates might be expressed in basis points. A basis point is 1/100th of a percent, or .0001. Thus, 100 basis points or 100 bps is equal to 1%. Basis points are a standard way of expressing interest for business loans, but not for consumer loans. The use of basis points helps avoid the confusion that can result if someone said that the interest rate increased by 1%. That could mean that a 4% rate loan is now a 5% loan, or it could mean that it is now a 4.04% loan. In contrast, if one said that the interest rate increased by 100 basis points, it would be clear that the 4% (or 400 bps) rate had increased to 5% (500 bps).

The interest may be simple interest or compounding interest. **Simple interest** is applied to the principal balance every specified period, but does not become part of the principal balance. Thus, a $100 balance at 20% simple interest would result in a $120 balance at the end of a year, but during the second year interest would still accrue only on the $100 principal balance, not on the total of principal plus the first year's interest ($120), so after two years, the borrower would owe $140 (= $100 + $20 +$20). In other words, there is no interest on interest when a simple interest rate is used.

In contrast, **compound interest** includes interest on interest. With 20% interest, compound annually, the borrower would still owe $120 after one year, but after two years, the borrower would owe $144: $100 of principal plus $20 in interest from year 1 and $24 in interest from year 2 (= 20% of $120). The difference can be significant if there are numerous compounding periods. Let's play these loans out over ten years. With 10% simple interest, the borrower will owe $200 at the end of ten years, but with compound interest, the borrower will owe $619.17. That's a substantial difference. As Albert Einstein is reputed to have said, "Compound interest is the strongest force known to man!"

To calculate the total amount of compound interest that will accrue the easiest thing is to use a compound interest calculator that can be found on the Web. But if you insist on doing things old school, the formula is as follows:

$$\text{Compound Interest} = P \times [(1+i)^n\text{-}1]$$

(Where P = principal, i = annual interest rate as a percentage, and n = number of compounding periods.)

As this formula shows, the difference between simple and compound interest also depends on the frequency of compounding. Let's use the same numbers, but have interest compounded not annually, but monthly. The balance will be $726.83. More frequent compounding means that more interest will accrue over the life of the loan. This means that compounding affects the price of a loan. To see, consider two loans, both for $10,000 for ten years. One has a 5% interest rate, compounded annually. It will result in $6,288.95 in interest over the life of the loan. The other loan has an interest rate of only 4.879345%, but is compounded daily. It too will result in interest of $6,288.95 over the life of the loan. So if the borrower were simply to choose based on interest rates, the borrower would of course take the second loan, even though there is no difference in the cost of the loans.

In a subsequent chapter we will see that there is a particular measure of the cost of a loan, known as the Annual Percentage Rate or APR, that attempts to capture the cost of a loan in a standard unit. The APR is not the same as the interest rate—it is an annualization of the interest rate that will reflect any compounding during the year, but not annual compounding.

Interest rates are sometimes **fixed rates**, meaning that they are a constant rate that does not change over time. Other times, however, interest rates can change. There are two types of changeable rate. The first are called **variable rates** or **adjustable rates**. Variable rates tend to change periodically based on some independently verifiable index, such as the yield on a U.S. government security or the Federal Funds rate (a rate at which banks can borrow from the Federal Reserve) that provides a base rate. These variable rates will be represented as the base rate plus a **margin** over the base rate, such as FF + 2.25%. To figure out the rate that would be applied at any point in time one would have to look up the Federal Funds for the applicable date and then add 2.25% to it. Variable rates can differ on the frequency of the adjustment period; some loans might adjust rates every month or six months, while others might adjust annually. Variable rates are sometimes subject to rate caps, either ceilings, floors, or collars (a ceiling and a floor).

The other type of changeable rate is a **step up rate**, meaning that the rates increase (or for a **step down** loan, decrease) over time according to a pre-set schedule, rather than according to the movement of an independent index rate. Thus, a loan might be at 4% for the first two years, and then step up to 6% for the remaining three years. A variation of this is for a loan to step up (or down) from a fixed rate to a variable rate (or less frequently, vice versa). Thus, a loan might have a three-year fixed rate period and then a 27-year adjustable rate period. (Such a loan is often designated a 3/27. Confusingly, a 5/1 has a five-year fixed rate period followed by an adjustable rate period of varying lengths with annual adjustments.)

Sometimes borrowers will prepay interest, meaning that they will make a larger payment upfront. Such prepaid interest is known as **points.** One point equals 1% of the loan balance, so on an $18,000 loan, 1 point would be $180. Why would someone every prepay interest rather than just take out a smaller loan? That is, why would someone take a loan for $18,000 and immediately repay $180, rather than just take out a loan for $17,820 and have interest accrue on a smaller balance? The answer is that the lender will decrease the interest rate on the loan in exchange for the points. There is no fixed exchange rate—it is entirely a matter for the parties' bargaining. What is going on is that the lender and the borrower are betting on the likelihood of the borrower prepaying the loan before some break-even point. Because points result in lower interest rates, if the borrower stays in the loan long enough, the borrower will reap the savings of the lower effective interest rate.

To calculate the break-even period for points, divide the cost of the points as a dollar amount by the monthly interest savings from paying points. The quotient is the number of payment periods necessary for the loan to be outstanding for the borrower to break even with points. If the borrower stays in the loan for longer, the borrower will save money because of the points.

Points, then, make sense if the borrower is betting that he will not prepay the loan before the break-even point, while for a lender, they are a way of protecting against the borrower's prepayment. Prepayment is an important risk lenders face—if the borrower repays the loan before maturity, the lender will have to go and reinvest the funds. Market interest rates may well be lower than the rate on the loan (indeed, this is the major incentive for borrowers to prepay, often by **refinancing** the loan with the proceeds of a new loan), so prepayment deprives the lender of the benefit of its above-market rate loan. Points give the lender some protection because if the borrower prepays, the lender will not receive unaccrued interest, but will still get to retain all accrued interest and the points as prepaid interest.

Not all loans are prepayable. Lenders will sometimes impose prepayment restrictions on loans. These can come in the form of prepayment penalties, yield maintenance clauses (requiring compensation of the lender for unaccrued interest based on the reinvestment environment), or simple prohibitions on prepayment.

In addition to interest, loans frequently entail various types of **fees**. These fees may be fixed fees, charged periodically, such as an annual fee of some sort, but they may also be initial (and unavoidable) fees that get rolled into the loan balance, such as a loan documentation fee, or contingent fees that are only charged based on the borrower's behavior. Examples of this would be late fees, over-limit fees, inactivity fees, and balance statement fees. Fees are sometimes expressed as flat amounts, and sometimes as percentages of the balance. Fixed or periodic fees can be viewed as equivalent to interest in some circumstances.

D. Amortization

Fourth, loans vary by **amortization** structure. Amortization refers to the repayment of the principal balance of the loan. Some loans are not amortized at all. These are called bullet or balloon or interest-only or I/O loans. With an interest-only loan, the borrower makes periodic payments of interest, but not of principal. The entire principal is instead repaid in a lump sum—known as a bullet or balloon—at the loan's maturity.

Other loans are fully amortized, meaning that the borrower makes periodic payments of principal throughout the life of the loan, so that the principal balance of the loan is constantly decreasing, and with it the interest that would accrue on that principal. Fully amortized loans do not all have the same amortization schedule, meaning the same rate at which principal is repaid.

Some loans use **equal principal payment amortization**, which means that the amount of principal repaid in each periodic installment remains constant, while the amount of interest (and hence the total payment) varies. Let's return to the Smiths' loan to illustrate. Let's assume that they borrow $18,000 at 3% for 60 months, compounded monthly. With such a loan, there would be a principal payment of $300 every month, but the interest payments would change as the balance declined. Thus, in month 1, there would be $45 in interest for a total payment of $345. In month 2, the principal balance would be $17,700, so the interest would be only $44.25, for a total payment of $344.25. By month 60, the principal balance would be $300.75, so the interest would only be $0.75. The total interest paid with this method would be $1,372.50.

More commonly, however, loans use **constant payment amortization,** also known as the **actuarial method**. This method of amortization keeps periodic payment level even as the makeup of principal and interest changes. With constant payment amortization the initial payments are primarily interest, with very little reduction of principal, while the later payments include much more principal. Thus, using the Smiths' $18,000 loan for 60 months at 3% annual interest, the monthly payments for the entire term of the loan would be $323.44, but the composition of that payment would change over time. In month 1, it would consist of $278.44 in principal and $45.00 in interest, while in month 2 it would consist of $279.14 in principal and $44.30 in interest. In month 60 there would be a balance of $322.40, so the final payment would be $321.59 in principal and $0.81 in interest. In other words, the component of the payment that is principal increases over time, while the interest component decreases over time. The total interest payments on this loan will be $1,406.17, or nearly 2.5% more than for the equal principal payments amortization method.

So how did we figure out the monthly payment and the allocation of principal and interest? First we have to determine the monthly payment. To do that we need to know the number of periodic payments and the *periodic* interest rate, that is, the interest rate per period, rather than annually (unless payments are annual). In our case we have 60 payments and the periodic interest rate is 0.25% (= 3.0%/12). We also need to calculate the discount factor. This is more complicated. Where n is the number of periodic payments and i is the periodic interest rate, the discount factor is

$$\frac{(1 + i)^n - 1}{i(1 + i)^n}$$

In our case, this is:

$$\frac{(1 + .0025)^{60} - 1}{.0025(1 + .0025)^{60}} = 55.6523577$$

Once we have the discount factor, we take the loan amount, $18,000, and divide it by the discount factor (55.6525377) = $323.44 (rounded up).

Now that we know our monthly payment, we have to determine the allocation of principal and interest. We start by taking the *periodic* interest rate and applying it to the principal balance at the beginning of the loan: 0.25% × $18,000 = $45.00. That is the amount of interest for the first month of the loan. Because the total payment is $323.44, the amount of principal in that payment is $278.44. We then turn to month two. The principal balance is now $17,721.56, so the periodic interest is $44.30. That means that of the $323.44 monthly payment in month two, the $279.14 is principal. We repeat this laborious process until we get to the end of the loan. Using a spreadsheet or an online amortization schedule calculator is much easier, but now at least you know what the mechanics are.

While calculating a constant payment amortization is clearly *much* more complex than calculating a equal principal repayment amortization, consumers are never the ones who actually calculate the amortization schedule (can you imagine!), so it is perhaps simpler from a consumer perspective because the monthly payment remains constant. (Obviously, if a loan has a variable rate, the amortization schedule needs to be recalculated whenever an interest rate adjustment is made.) The following amortization table shows a constant payment amortization of the Smiths' $18,000 auto loan at a 3% interest rate.

Figure 22.1 Constant Payment Amortization of the Smiths' Auto Loan

Month	Principal Amount Outstanding	Monthly Loan Paymemt	Interest Paid	Principal Paid
1	$18,000.00	$323.44	$45.00	$278.44
2	$17,721.56	$323.44	$44.30	$279.14
3	$17,442.42	$323.44	$43.61	$279.83
4	$17,162.59	$323.44	$42.91	$280.53
5	$16,882.06	$323.44	$42.21	$281.23
6	$16,600.82	$323.44	$41.50	$281.94
7	$16,318.88	$323.44	$40.80	$282.64
8	$16,036.24	$323.44	$40.09	$283.35
9	$15,752.89	$323.44	$39.38	$284.06
10	$15,468.83	$323.44	$38.67	$284.77
11	$15,184.07	$323.44	$37.96	$285.48
12	$14,898.59	$323.44	$37.25	$286.19
13	$14,612.39	$323.44	$36.53	$286.91
14	$14,325.48	$323.44	$35.81	$287.63
15	$14,037.86	$323.44	$35.09	$288.35
16	$13,749.51	$323.44	$34.37	$289.07
17	$13,460.45	$323.44	$33.65	$289.79
18	$13,170.66	$323.44	$32.93	$290.51
19	$12,880.14	$323.44	$32.20	$291.24
20	$12,588.90	$323.44	$31.47	$291.97
21	$12,296.94	$323.44	$30.74	$292.70
22	$12,004.24	$323.44	$30.01	$293.43
23	$11,710.81	$323.44	$29.28	$294.16
24	$11,416.65	$323.44	$28.54	$294.90
25	$11,121.75	$323.44	$27.80	$295.64
26	$10,826.11	$323.44	$27.07	$296.37
27	$10,529.74	$323.44	$26.32	$297.12
28	$10,232.62	$323.44	$25.58	$297.86
29	$9,934.76	$323.44	$24.84	$298.60
30	$9,636.16	$323.44	$24.09	$299.35
31	$9,336.81	$323.44	$23.34	$300.10
32	$9,036.71	$323.44	$22.59	$300.85
33	$8,735.86	$323.44	$21.84	$301.60
34	$8,434.26	$323.44	$21.09	$302.35
35	$8,131.91	$323.44	$20.33	$303.11
36	$7,828.80	$323.44	$19.57	$303.87
37	$7,524.93	$323.44	$18.81	$304.63
38	$7,220.30	$323.44	$18.05	$305.39
39	$6,914.91	$323.44	$17.29	$306.15
40	$6,608.76	$323.44	$16.52	$306.92
41	$6,301.84	$323.44	$15.75	$307.69
42	$5,994.16	$323.44	$14.99	$308.45
43	$5,685.70	$323.44	$14.21	$309.23
44	$5,376.48	$323.44	$13.44	$310.00
45	$5,066.48	$323.44	$12.67	$310.77
46	$4,755.71	$323.44	$11.89	$311.55
47	$4,444.15	$323.44	$11.11	$312.33
48	$4,131.82	$323.44	$10.33	$313.11
49	$3,818.71	$323.44	$9.55	$313.89
50	$3,504.82	$323.44	$8.76	$314.68
51	$3,190.14	$323.44	$7.98	$315.46
52	$2,874.68	$323.44	$7.19	$316.25
53	$2,558.43	$323.44	$6.40	$317.04
54	$2,241.38	$323.44	$5.60	$317.84
55	$1,923.54	$323.44	$4.81	$318.63
56	$1,604.91	$323.44	$4.01	$319.43
57	$1,285.49	$323.44	$3.21	$320.23
58	$965.26	$323.44	$2.41	$321.03
59	$644.23	$323.44	$1.61	$321.83
60	$322.40	$323.40	$0.81	$322.59

A variation on constant payment amortization is the **Rule of 78s**, also known as **sum-of-the-digits** method. The Rule of 78s is prohibited for consumer loans with a term of over 61 months because prepayment is more likely on longer-term loans (as is the cost of the Rule of 78s). 15 U.S.C. § 1615(b). The Rule of 78s still gets some use in auto lending, however.

Under the Rule of 78s, periodic payments are constant, but the amount of interest in any particular periodic payment is computed with a different method. Under the Rule of 78s, the total monthly payment is calculated as above. But the interest allocation (and hence the principal allocation) is based on a percentage relating to the *summation* (remember that sigma (Σ)that stands for summation from math class?) of the total number of periods. Specifically, the repayment periods are numbered consecutively and those numbers are then summed. Thus, for a 12-month period, the periods would be numbered 1 through 12, and the sum (1+2+3+ . . . 10+11+12) would be 78 (hence the name of the method). The total interest charges over the life of the loan would then be allocated by period in inverse order: 12/78ths of the total charges to the first month, 11/78ths to the second month, 10/78ths to the third month, etc. For a 60-month loan, the denominator would be 1830 ($=\Sigma_1^{60}n$) and the first month would get 60/1830ths of the interest, while the second month getting 59/1830ths, etc. What should be apparent is that the Rule of 78s first, is totally non-intuitive to consumers and, second, it substantially weights interest charges to the beginning of the loan.

Thus, with the Smiths' $18,000 60-month auto loan at 3% annual interest, the Rule of 78s would still have monthly payments of $323.44 and total interest of $1,406.40 (basically the same as with constant payment amortization), but the first month's payment would consist of $277.33 in principal and $46.11 in interest, while the second month's payment would be $278.10 in principal and $45.34 in interest, and the last month would be $322.67 in principal and $0.77 in interest. In other words, the Rule of 78s front-loads interest more than constant payment amortization. The result is to penalize borrowers who prepay, as they get less interest savings than under constant payment amortization.

Amortization gets trickier yet. Some loans are only **partially amortized**. An example of this would be a loan with a 30-year maturity, but a 40-year amortization period. The principal would be paid down as if over a 40-year schedule, but because the maturity date comes at year 30, there would still be the final ten years of principal amortization that had not yet occurred. The outstanding principal would be due, meaning that there would be a **balloon payment** due, just not a balloon for the entire principal amount. The usual assumption with loans with balloon payments is that the loan will be refinanced prior to the balloon payment coming due. If the loan isn't or can't be refinanced, however, the balloon payment requirement substantially raises the risk of default.

Some loans allow for **negative amortization**, meaning that the borrower can allow the loan balance to *grow* over the term of the loan. This would happen if the borrower made payments that were insufficient to even pay off the interest that had accrued on the loan. Thus, if $100 in interest accrued on a loan every month, but the borrower paid only $80, the total loan balance would be *increasing*. Conversely, some loans have minimum payment amounts to ensure positive amortization (even if it is minimal).

Maturities and amortization schedules can substantially change the affordability of a loan to a borrower. Let's suppose that the Smiths have $300/month that they can spend on a car. Let's also suppose that the Smiths can get a 3% interest rate from their lender. If the Smiths have to finance their $18,000 loan over five years, their monthly payment will be $323.44, over their budget, and they will end up having to repay a total of $19,406 using a constant payment amortization. If the Smiths instead take a seven-year loan, their total monthly payment will decline to $238, but the total amount they will repay will increase to $19,979.

Likewise, consider the difference for the Smiths between a five-year fully amortized loan (with constant payment amortization) and a five-year interest-only loan. With the fully amortized loan, their monthly payment with be $323.44 and they will repay a total of $19,406. With an interest-only loan without compounding, their monthly payment will be just $90, but they will pay a total of $23,400, including a final balloon payment of $18,090. Such a loan has short-term affordability, but a much higher price in the end, and creates a real repayment risk unless the Smiths can save up $18,090 (the original principal plus one month of interest) by the maturity date.

Now let's see the most extreme scenario, a negative amortization loan. Let's assume that the Smiths only pay $50 per month, instead of the full $90 of interest that would accrue. Now compounding will come into play. With the previous examples, the Smiths paid all interest when it was due, so it didn't matter that the interest compounded. But if they don't pay all of the interest when it comes due, then they face compounding. They will end up paying $27,737.12 for this loan. Again, this loan is even more affordable on a monthly basis, but there will be a balloon of $20,787.12 (more than the original principal plus one month of interest) due in the final month.

E. Collateral and Down Payment

Repayment for some loans is secured by a pledge of **collateral**. Collateral is property that the borrower has promised that the lender may forcibly sell if the borrower defaults, with the proceeds of the sale being applied to the loan balance. When a lender takes a pledge of collateral it has a **security interest** or **lien** on the collateral, which is a type of contingent property interest in the collateral.

Several types of common consumer loans are formally collateralized: home mortgages, vehicle purchase loans, vehicle title loans, and certain household appliance and furnishing loans. In all of these situations, the borrower retains control of the collateral during the course of the loan; the lender has a **non-possessory security interest** in the property. Some loans, however, involve the lender taking a **possessory security interest** in the property during the course of the loan: pawn loans and secured credit cards, a product aimed at consumers with very poor credit in which the credit card borrowing is collateralized by a cash deposit with the lender.

Beyond this, however, other types of consumer loans are functionally collateralized. Bank account overdrafts are functionally collateralized by the bank's right to set off future deposits against the overdraft. Payday loans are functionally collateralized by the lender's right to draw on the borrower's bank account. As we saw in Chapter 2, the FTC's Credit Practices Rule generally prohibits non-possessory non-purchase money security interests in household goods.

Lenders take security interests for a few reasons. First, the collateral may itself be valuable as a source of repayment. A house or a car will often have substantial value when sold. To the extent collateral has value, the borrower's ability to repay from other sources is less important. Second, the collateral might be much more valuable to the borrower than the lender, and the threat of its forcible sale can create an *in terrorem* incentive for repayment. We saw this dynamic at work in Chapter 2 in *Williams v. Walker-Thomas Furniture*, where there was little resale value in bed linens and a shower curtain, but some *in terrorem* value. And third, the pledge of collateral is a way for the borrower to signal intent to repay when creditworthiness cannot easily be otherwise gauged.

When a loan is collateralized, it may be either **recourse** or **non-recourse**. If a loan is non-recourse, then the lender may look solely to the collateral as a source of repayment; the lender has no right to pursue the borrower's other assets. If a loan is recourse, the lender may choose whether to pursue the collateral or the borrower's other assets (or both, but with only a single total recovery allowed). Most consumer loans are formally recourse, although an important subset of home mortgage loans are non-recourse.

Now recall that the Honda CR-V the Smiths are eyeing retails for $24,000. The Smiths could try to get a loan for this amount, but instead, they are hoping to borrow only $18,000 or so. This means that they will pay for $6,000 of the sale price from their own current funds. This is their **down payment**. The down payment is the part of the purchase price that is not borrowed. It constitutes the borrower's immediate equity interest in the property purchased.

Not all loans have down payments; a down payment only appears when a loan is used to finance the purchase of a particular good or home. You might think that a lender would be indifferent to the amount of a down payment; all it would affect is the loan size, right? But in fact a down payment is a type of a buy-in for the borrower that is particularly important if the loan is collateralized and non-recourse. The down payment means that the borrower has some skin in the game. That means the borrower will take better care of the collateral property and be less likely to default if the property value has declined because the borrower may lose part of its down payment.

A down payment should be distinguished from an **earnest money deposit**. Earnest money deposits are generally used solely in home purchase transactions. When a buyer makes an offer on a home, the buyer might include a check with the offer of 1% or 2% of the offer amount. If the offer is accepted and the buyer refuses to consummate the sale for any reason not permitted in the purchase contract (typical contingencies being the borrower obtaining financing and the property passing an inspection), then the seller may keep the earnest money deposit. The purpose of such a deposit is to show that the buyer is serious about going through with the transaction so that the seller does not turn down other offers only to end up with no sale.

F. Payment Allocation

Another variation among loans is how payments are applied. Some loans have separate sub-balances that accrue interest at different rates, such as credit cards that have a "purchase" balance and a "cash advance" balance and perhaps also a promotional balance transfer balance. When a borrower remits a payment, to which balance should the payment be applied? Obviously it is more favorable to the borrower to apply payments to higher interest rate balances first, and vice versa for the lender. The CARD Act has addressed this for credit cards, 15 U.S.C. § 1666c(b)(1), by requiring payments above the minimum payment to be allocated first to the highest rate balance and then to each successive balance in order of interest rate, but it still arises in other contexts, such as in the *CFPB v. PayPal* complaint in Chapter 8. Likewise, as we saw in *Williams v. Walker-Thomas Furniture* in Chapter 2, different payment application rules can result in sub-balances remaining outstanding for an extended period or getting paid off.

III. UNDERWRITING

Recall that we started by asking how the Smiths would be able to repay their loan. Even if the Smiths have a possible source of repayment, that doesn't mean that the loan is without risk. Lenders need to price for risk. The process by which lenders determine the pricing on a loan given the risk presented by a particular borrower is known as **underwriting**.

It's important to recognize that not all loans are underwritten, in the sense that pricing varies by borrower characteristics. Some loans have one-size-fits-all pricing, in that borrowers either qualify for the loan or do not, but if they do, they all get the same terms. Examples of this are public student loans (engineering majors pay the same as English majors), many payday loans, bank account overdrafts, and overdraft lines of credit. There are several reasons why a lender might not underwrite a loan: cost (especially relative to loan size), the availability of enhanced collection rights that obviate the need for a borrower-specific risk premium, and political constraints (for public student loans).

Those loans that are underwritten have some form of **risk-based pricing**, but this term can be quite misleading. Even if there is risk-based pricing on a loan, that does not mean that most of the price of the loan reflects the borrower's risk profile. Instead, it means that the *marginal* price of the loan varies by the borrower's risk profile, but much of the loan price might be based on the lender's own cost structure, such as its overhead and cost of funds and costs of acquiring borrower leads.

The precise underwriting process varies by lender, but there are a number of common basic features for consumer credit.[1] First, most lenders will pull a credit report on the borrower. Credit reports indicate what obligations the borrower currently has and the borrower's history of repayment on various obligations, as well as indicators of whether the borrower has previously filed for bankruptcy or been

1. Commercial lending is often to finance income-generating projects, so the income-generating potential of a project is an additional factor considered in commercial lending.

the subject of a foreclosure or judgment. Not all obligations appear on credit reports, but most institutional financial debt does (home rental payments often do not, however). Additionally a credit report can come with a credit score, a numerical representation of the borrower's credit risk. There are multiple credit scoring models in use, but they all tend to be based on the borrower's repayment history, number and amount of obligations outstanding, and use of credit lines. Lenders typically use a borrower's credit score as a heuristic for evaluating borrowers' overall creditworthiness and likelihood of future repayment.

Many lenders also look to verify the borrower's current income and/or assets. This can take the form of verifying employment, looking at past tax documents (such as form W-2s from employers), or looking at bank statements. The combination of information about borrowers' income and borrowers' obligations enables lenders to create a ratio called a **debt-to-income (DTI) ratio**. There are two types of DTI ratios. One is a **front-end DTI ratio** that is the ratio of the periodic payment obligation on the loan to the borrower's income over the same period. The other is a **back-end DTI ratio** that is the ratio of all of the borrower's various periodic payment obligations to the borrower's income over the same period. The front-end ratio only looks at the affordability of the loan in a vacuum, whereas the back-end ratio looks at the affordability in the context of all of the borrower's obligations. DTI ratios are often used for underwriting decisions.

Underwriting necessarily requires that the lender have information about the borrower. A problem lenders frequently face is that an informational asymmetry in which the borrower knows more about his or her likelihood of repayment than the lender (although this can be reversed given borrower optimism biases). Moreover, because of incomplete information, lenders may not be able to distinguish adequately between borrowers in terms of risk. This can potentially lead to credit rationing. Economists Joseph Stiglitz and Andrew Weiss showed that when lenders cannot distinguish among borrowers in terms of risk, a lender that raises its prices (charges a higher interest rate) may suffer adverse selection because only riskier borrowers would be willing to borrow at such a rate. Joseph Stiglitz & Andrew Weiss, *Credit Rationing in Markets with Imperfect Information*, 71 Am. Econ. Rev. 393 (1981). Moreover, higher interest rates may result in a moral hazard, as borrowers may engage in riskier borrower behavior (more a problem with business borrowers) in order to generate higher returns to service the loan. Accordingly, instead of raising prices until excess demand for credit is exhausted, lenders might choose to limit the quantity of lending—that is, engage in credit rationing.

Collateral requirements and enhanced collection rights provide a method by which lenders can mitigate adverse selection problems in some situations.[2] If the collateral

2. Stiglitz and Weiss show that collateral requirements can in fact result in adverse selection, but only in very particularized conditions, which are unlikely to be generically true in consumer finance. First, they show that there will be an adverse selection problem when smaller projects are riskier than large projects. 71 Am. Econ. Rev. 393, 402. Second, they show that there will be an adverse selection problem when borrowers' willingness to accept risk varies materially by their wealth, with wealthier borrowers being more willing to assume risk because of the decreasing marginal value of money to them. *Id.* But this point is true of wealthier borrowers irrespective of collateral.

is sufficient to guarantee repayment, the lender may not be concerned with the borrower's likelihood of default. Of course, when collateral is involved with a loan, the lender will also want to have an appraisal of the collateral because the lender will not want to lend beyond a specified **loan-to-value** (LTV) ratio. This is because the lender wants to be sure that if there is a default it will be able to seize and sell the collateral for repayment of the loan, a collection approach that works only if the collateral resale value is greater than the loan balance, so lenders will generally seek to have a borrower equity cushion in the collateral in the form of a LTV of less than 100%.

Note that with an amortized loan, the LTV will decrease over time with the borrower's payments *if the collateral value remains steady or rises*. Some types of collateral, such as homes, may well appreciate, but other type of collateral, such as vehicles and home appliances, will inevitably depreciate, and likely faster than the loan amortizes, meaning that the LTV may increase over the life of the loan, even as the balance decreases.

How do lenders use all of this information in underwriting? Typically lenders have pricing "buckets," such that pricing goes up in steps, rather than along a smooth spectrum. A lender might offer one set of terms to borrowers with a credit score between 660 and 700 who have no bankruptcies, who have a back-end DTI below 45%, and who are looking to borrow at no more than 80% LTV, while borrowers with a credit score of 700-720 and the same features will get a different set of terms, and borrowers with the 660-700 credit score but a bankruptcy in the past three years will get yet another set of terms. The particular formula used by lenders is never public and may well contain more variables than just these, such as the existence of other relationships with the lender (such as a deposit account or other loan).

IV. LOAN VERSUS LEASE

A loan is one way that the Smiths might get a car, but another way is a lease. Let's assume that the expected useful life of a Honda CR-V is seven years. The Smiths could get a seven-year loan for $18,000 at 3% and pay $238/month with a total payment of $19,979. Alternatively, the Smiths could lease the car. If they paid $6,000 down (leases can have down payments too), their lease payments at 3% over 7 years should be exactly the same as their loan payments. The lease functions like a collateral arrangement—if the borrower fails to pay on time, the lessor can repossess the leased car, which is its property.

While it is possible to conceive of periodic lease payments as reflecting an interest rate, lessors are not allowed to express lease payments in such terms, in part because leases often have additional non-periodic payments that could render a periodic rate misleading. *See* 12 C.F.R. § 1013.4(s). Lessors will internally refer to the lease cost in terms of a "**lease factor**" or "**money factor**" or "**factor**." The factor is equal to 1/2,400 of an equivalent APR (assuming that there are only the periodic payment on the lease). Thus, a money factor of .00325 would translate to an APR of 7.8%. Money factors are often quoted as if multiplied by 1,000: hence a .00325 money factor would be 3.25. While money factors are not generally disclosed to consumers, when they are they can be misleading because they look like a very low APR (especially when multiplied by 1,000) but are in fact equivalent to APRs that are 2.4 times as large.

While the monthly payments, in the above scenario, are the same, there is a critical difference. At the end of the lease the car would revert back to the lessor, while with the loan, the Smiths would have clean title to the car. If the car is in better-than-anticipated shape at the end of seven years that upside value would go the Smiths with a loan, but not with a lease.

The loan versus lease trade-off is seldom as clean as in the example above. Car leases often have annual mileage restrictions and extra charges for overage miles. They may also have early termination restrictions, which is similar to a prepayment penalty on a loan. The lease might also have a purchase option. Moreover, the lease term might well be shorter than the loan term. On the one hand this means that the Smiths won't be locked in to continuing to use that same vehicle, but on the other it means that they will be exposed to market risk when they want to get a new lease—if market rates are higher, they'll pay more. The same is true regarding their own credit. If they're less creditworthy, they'll pay more.

The loan versus lease choice exists, of course, for other financed purchases, such as housing, where a consumer can either rent or buy. Given that most housing leases are for one or perhaps two years, it means that renters are exposed not just to general market conditions and changes in their own credit, but also to the gentrification of their neighborhood. If the neighborhood improves, rents will go up; owners who have financed their home with a mortgage are not exposed to gentrification this way, but, depending on the terms of the lease, the owners may have additional costs and risks regarding the upkeep of the property.

The loan versus lease distinction matters for a number of legal issues. Secured loans are governed by UCC Article 9, while leases of personalty are governed by UCC Article 2A, and leases of realty fall under common law. Moreover, federal regulations vary—the disclosure regime for leases is different than that for loans—and leased property is treated differently if the borrower or lessor files for bankruptcy. Be aware that whether a transaction is a loan or a lease does not depend on how it is titled, but on its economic realities. *See* UCC §§ 1-203, 2A-102, 9-109(a)(1).

Problem Set 22

1. Kimberly Adkins just got hired as a professor at Springfield University. She's looking for a place to live. She's trying to decide between buying and renting. Explain the trade-offs in terms of risks and benefits.

2. Kimberly (from problem 1) decided to rent initially, but now that she's gotten tenure, she wants to buy a house. She doesn't have the funds to purchase outright, so she'll need to take out a mortgage loan. Explain the trade-offs she faces in terms of getting:

   a. A 15-year mortgage versus a 30-year mortgage.
   b. A fixed-rate mortgage versus an adjustable rate mortgage.
   c. A fully amortized mortgage versus a balloon mortgage.

3. Kimberly has decided on a $200,000 30-year fixed-rate, fully amortized mortgage from the First Bank of Springfield. The Bank has offered her a 5.00% rate on the loan with no points or a 4.59% rate on the loan with two points.

   a. How long does Kimberly need to stay in the mortgage for the points to be a good deal? [You will need an online amortization calculator and a spreadsheet to answer this question.]
   b. What effect will the loan terms have on Kimberly's mobility or her likelihood of refinancing if market rates drop or her credit improves?
   c. Why might First Bank of Springfield offer Kimberly a loan with points?

4. First Bank of Springfield wants to expand its mortgage lending business, but it just can't find more borrowers who qualify for a traditional 30-year fixed-rate, fully amortized mortgage. What could First Bank of Springfield offer to make its mortgage products more affordable to borrowers, at least on a monthly payment basis?

5. Stuart Zuckerman is trying to compare a 15- and a 30-year fixed-rate mortgage for a home purchase. Both would be for $400,000; he would pay 20% down on the property. The 15-year mortgage would be at 3% and the 30-year mortgage at 3.75%. Both have constant payment amortization. Stuart knows there is a good chance he will move after seven years in his property.

   a. How much equity will he have built up in the property by the end of seven years with each mortgage, assuming no property appreciation?
   b. How much total interest will he pay with each loan, assuming annual compounding?

[You will need an amortization calculator to assist you with this problem.]

CHAPTER 23

USURY

I. INTRODUCTION

Usury laws are the most ancient type of consumer finance regulation. Usury laws prohibit lending on interest either as an absolute matter or at a certain rate. Usury laws are thus a public policy restriction on borrowers' and lenders' ability to contract that limits the supply of credit. The effect is to limit consumers' ability to finance their current consumption from future income.

Usury laws are highly controversial. From one perspective they are the paradigm of prudent paternalism to protect borrowers and society from the decisions of unwise or overly optimistic borrowers and the predations of rapacious lenders. From another perspective they are heavy-handed distortionary interventions in credit markets that merely restrict legitimate credit for those who need it most, possibly driving them to illegal sources of credit or income.

Today almost every state has a usury limit of some sort on its books. Yet usury laws are largely inapplicable to many consumer lenders because of the numerous exceptions in the laws and federal preemption. Nonetheless, understanding how and when usury laws operate and why they have largely been rendered ineffective is critical for understanding the history and current workings of consumer finance regulation. To the extent that usury laws are not providing safeguards for consumers against becoming overleveraged and entering into ill-advised contracts, it places a greater burden on other regulatory tools.

Usury law is deeply tied to religious and moral tradition. Usury prohibitions of varying severity can be found in the Jewish, Christian, and Muslim traditions.[1] These historical religious prohibitions were against lending money on interest at all. Indeed, usury was once seen as so deplorable that Dante's *Inferno* consigned usurers to the seventh circle of hell, along with murderers, those who committed suicide, blasphemers, and Sodomites.[2] Four centuries later, William Noy, the attorney general for James I of England, declared that "usurers are well ranked with murderers."[3]

Both the Jewish and Christian prohibitions on usury only applied to loans made to co-religionists. Jews were excluded from most professions in medieval Europe, but moneylending was an area open to them, and the prohibition on usury resulted

1. *See, e.g.*, Exodus 22:24; Leviticus 25:36-37; Deuteronomy 23:20-21; Ezekiel 18:17; Psalm 15:5; Matthew 25:27; Luke 19:22-23; Al-Baqarah 2:275-280; Al-'Imran 3:130; Al-Nisa 4:161; Ar-Rum 30:39. Other prescriptions are to be found in Vedic and Buddhist texts. The interpretation of these verses is a matter unto itself.

2. Dante Alighieri, *Divine Comedy—Inferno*, Canto XI, XVII.

3. Calvin Elliot, *Usury: A Scriptural, Ethical, and Economic View* 264 (1902).

in Jews becoming synonymous with moneylending, a situation captured in the plays of Marlow (*The Jew of Malta*) and Shakespeare (*Shylock or the Merchant of Venice*).

With the expulsion of the Jews from England and Wales in 1290, moneylending shifted to Christians, frequently foreigners (often called Lombards, irrespective of their geographic origin being northern Italy or elsewhere, hence Lombard Street, the English Wall Street). Lending money on interest remained illegal (and at times a capital offense!) in England until 1545, when Henry VIII, freed from the authority of the Roman Catholic Church, legalized lending on interest of no more than 10%.[4] His successors repealed the statute, but it was reenacted by Elizabeth I,[5] with subsequent statutes merely changing the legal maximum rate. After Elizabeth I, usury laws became a matter of price, not principle. Such it is today in the United States, where usury statutes now refer to caps on interest rates, rather than outright prohibitions on charging any interest on loans.

II. STATE USURY LAWS

Usury laws are mainly state laws. They vary considerably by state and have changed significantly over time. Sometimes usury is a complete or partial defense to a contract suit, sometimes it is a freestanding civil cause of action, and sometimes it is even a criminal provision. The remedies vary from voiding interest over the usury rate to voiding the entire debt (principal and interest) to permitting offset of usurious interest against the debt (thereby reducing the principal) to statutory damages.

In most states, usury laws exist by statute, but Arkansas has a constitutional usury provision.[6] Sometimes usury provisions involve a fixed maximum rate; other times they involve a rate that floats in reference to an independently verifiable market rate. Usury laws are also often filled with exceptions. Typically, certain classes of loans are excluded from usury laws (or alternatively, the laws only apply to specific types of loans). Sometimes different rate caps apply to different types of loans. In some states, the resulting statutes become quite complicated.

Moreover, as discussed more below, states often have "parity laws" that permit certain lenders to make loans at the rate permitted in *other* states so as not to put the state's domestic institutions at a competitive disadvantage. In addition, there are definitional questions of what constitutes a "loan," what constitutes "interest," and how interest is calculated.

For example, is a sale and repurchase agreement a loan? If I contract to sell you 100 shares of IBM stock for $10,000 today and to repurchase them for $10,100 tomorrow, it is equivalent economically to me making you a loan of $10,000 at a 365% annual interest rate (1% interest per day), secured by the IBM stock. The $100 difference between the sale price and the repurchase price is equivalent to interest. $100

4. 37 Hen.viii c. 9. (1545). A 1540 Hapsburg statute permitted interest on commercial loans of up to 12% in the Austrian Netherlands. *See* MM. J. Lameere & H. Simont, eds., *Recueil des ordonnances des Pays Bas*, deuxième série, 1506-1700, Commission Royale d'Histoire, 6 vols., Vol. IV: jan. 1536 – dec. 1543 232-238 (Brussels: J. Goemaere, 1907).

5. 13 Eliz. c. 8.

6. Ark. Const. amend. 89 (2011) (17% usury limit).

of interest on $10,000 for one day translates into $36,500 in interest on the $10,000 over a 365-day year. Hence, the annual interest rate would be 365%.

This kind of sale and repurchase transaction is called a "repo," not to be confused with "repo" in the sense of "repossession" of collateral. Would such a repo be covered under a state usury statute? How about transaction forms used in Islamic banking, which prohibits interest in the narrow sense, but permits functional equivalents? Similarly, are fees or "points" on a loan to be treated as "interest" for the purposes of a usury statute? Their treatment under state usury law may not match their treatment under federal law for the purpose of calculating the "Annual Percentage Rate," the form in which federal law requires "finance charges" (which include interest and some fees) to be expressed for Truth in Lending Act disclosures.

The result is that usury laws, rather than being simple blunt prohibitions, are often quite complex. In addition, as we will see below, selective federal preemption of state usury laws and state legislative responses have added further complications. Most of these complications have the effect of limiting the application of state usury laws, which are today best characterized as Swiss cheese, such that a well-counseled lender can usually avoid their application.

III. FEDERAL USURY LAWS

Federal law also has some usury provisions that interface with state law; different laws apply to different types of financial institutions: national banks, federal savings associations, and federal credit unions. 12 U.S.C. §§ 85-86, 1463(g), 1757(5)(a)(vi). National banks and federal savings associations are generally permitted to charge the greater of (1) the maximum interest rate "fixed by the laws" of the state in which they are located and (2) the greater of 7% or 1% over their local Federal Reserve Bank's 90-day commercial paper discount rate. 12 U.S.C. § 85. When a state by statute expressly permits interest at a contractually agreed upon rate, that is a rate "fixed by law." *Daggs v. Phoenix Nat'l Bank*, 177 U.S. 549 (1900). As we will see in a moment, federally chartered financial institutions that lend across state lines have been effectively exempted from the borrower's state usury laws without being subjected meaningful federal replacement usury limits.

Since 1987, the NCUA has permitted federal credit unions to charge an additional 3% in interest rates, for an 18% rate ceiling.[7] The 18% is interpreted by the NCUA as covering an effective rate, rather than a stated rate,[8] but the NCUA does not consider late charges to be finance charges for usury cap purposes.[9] Accordingly, federal credit unions generally price their higher-rate products, like credit cards, just up to the 18% limit or slightly below to leave room for the adjustment from stated to effective rates.

7. Statement of The Honorable Joann M. Johnson, Chairman, National Credit Union Administration, "Regulation Z and Credit Card Disclosure Revisions" before the Subcommittee on Financial Institutions and Consumer Credit, U.S. House of Representatives, June 7, 2007, at 14; NCUA Letter to Federal Credit Unions, Apr. 2011, Letter No. 11-FCU-04 (authorizing 18% cap for 2012).

8. NCUA Letter 09-FCU-05 (July 2009); NCUA OCG Opinion Letter 00-1217, Jan. 25, 2001

9. NCUA OGC Opinion Letter Nos. 91-0412.

A. Mortgages (National Housing Act)

Various provisions of federal law specifically preempt state usury laws regarding many types of mortgage loans. One provision, a National Housing Act provision dating from 1934, preempts state usury laws for FHA-insured mortgages. 12 U.S.C. §§ 1735f-7. This provision was necessary to ensure a national market in FHA-eligible mortgages. Adam Gordon, Note, *The Creation of Homeownership: How New Deal Changes in Banking Regulation Simultaneously Made Homeownership Accessible to Whites and Out of Reach for Blacks*, 115 Yale L.J. 186, 188-189, 194-195, 224 tbl.1 (2005). The National Housing Act was not expressing Congressional opposition to usury laws. Instead, it was concerned with uniformity of usury laws when the federal government was involved. Thus, Congress also provided that the HUD Secretary could set a maximum interest rate for FHA-insurance eligible loans. 12 U.S.C. § 1701L. In other words, the National Housing Act changed usury laws for a class of mortgages from state law to federal, with the usury limit set by regulation and the penalty for violation being ineligibility for FHA insurance, as opposed to a defense to enforcement of part or all of the loan.

Prior to 1980, the usury rate on FHA-insured mortgages was generally 5%. As interest rates rose in the 1970s, there was significant pressure to allow lending at higher rates; lenders would not lend at rates lower than their own cost of funds. Thus, in 1980, the FHA removed its usury limit. *See* Cathy Lesser Mansfield, *The Road to Subprime "HEL" Was Paved with Good Congressional Intentions: Usury Deregulation and the Subprime Home Equity Market*, 51 S.C. L. Rev. 473, 484-492 (2000).

Another federal statutory provision, section 501 of the Depositary Institutions Deregulation and Monetary Control Act of 1980 (DIDMCA) preempts any state law, including state constitutional provisions, that limits mortgage interest, discount points, and finance or other charges. 12 U.S.C. § 1735f-7a(a). The DIDMCA preemption applies to any "federally related mortgage loan," a term that includes mortgages that are federally insured, made by a FDIC-insured institution, made by a federally regulated institution (aren't all institutions federally regulated on some level?), eligible for purchase by Fannie Mae and Freddie Mac (government-sponsored secondary-market entities), or made by an individual who regularly extends more than $1 million annually in residential real estate loans. 12 U.S.C. § 1735f-5(b). In other words, DIDMCA preemption covers virtually all mortgage loans not made by individuals (*e.g.*, by rich uncle Scrooge). The DIDMCA provision permitted states to opt out of preemption in a limited time window. 12 U.S.C. § 1735f-7a(b). Fifteen states opted out, so their usury laws are only preempted by DIDMCA in regard to FHA-insured mortgages, which are a relatively small part of the market. Preemption for other mortgages may still be possible based on other laws or regulations.

The OCC and OTS passed regulations implementing DIDMCA preemption. 12 C.F.R. §§ 190.1, 590.1. While largely restating the statutory provisions, the preemption regulations note that "[t]he purpose of this permanent preemption of state interest-rate ceilings applicable to Federally-related residential mortgage loans is to ensure that the availability of such loans is not impeded in states having restrictive interest limitations." *Id.* The regulations also interpret the federal statute as preempting not just civil usury laws for mortgages, but also criminal usury provisions. 12 C.F.R. §§ 190.101, 590.101.

B. Consumer Financial Protection Bureau (Dodd-Frank Act)

Concerns about an overzealous CFPB restricting the availability of credit resulted in the Dodd-Frank Act explicitly prohibiting the CFPB from enacting a "usury limit." 12 U.S.C. § 5517(o). What exactly is a usury limit, though? The state usury statutes excerpted in the statutory supplement show that usury provisions can vary greatly. Did Congress merely prohibit a rate cap? Does this provision mean that the CFPB cannot cap fees, thereby forcing a higher proportion of costs to interest rates? What about establishing safe harbors for loans under a certain rate? Or, conversely, what if the CFPB created regulatory burdens for loans over a certain rate? Would a cap on total costs, such as an *in duplum* rule (discussed in the box below) be prohibited?

Comparative Usury Law: South Africa

While this is not a book on comparative consumer finance law, it is instructive to consider other ways usury laws or their equivalents could be constructed. South Africa restricts unpaid and accrued interest and fees on loans to no more than the principal amount of the loan.[10] This is a Roman law principle known as *in duplum*.[11] The rule exists in South African common law as well as in the South African National Credit Act.

The *in duplum* rule does not prescribe a particular rate of interest. Instead, it prescribes a relationship between the rate of interest and the duration of the loan and repayment of the loan.

Consider a $100 fixed-term balloon loan under the *in duplum* rule. All principal and interest is repaid in a single payment at the end of the loan's term. The South African *in duplum* rule would limit interest to $100 on that loan. If that interest were all accrued in one year, then the *in duplum* rule would have capped the loan at 100% interest. But if the interest were accrued in two years, then the *in duplum* rule would act as a 50% rate cap. In other words, *in duplum* permits higher rates for shorter-term loans. Are interest rates in the U.S. higher for short-term loans like payday and auto title loans or long-term loans like mortgages and student loans?

---

10. National Credit Act, 34 of 2005 § 103(5), 102(2)(c). The rule also exists in South African common law. Stroebel v. Stroebel 1973 (2) SA 137 (T); Commercial Bank of Zimbabwe Ltd v. MM Builders & Suppliers (Pty) Ltd and Others and Three Similar Cases 1997 (2) SA 375 (W) at 303C-E; Standard Bank of South Africa Ltd. v. Oneanate Investments (Pty) Ltd. (in Liquidation) 1998 (1) SA 811 (SCA); F & I Advisors (Edms) Bpk en 'n Ander v. Eerste Nasionale Bank van Suidelike Afrika Bpk 1999 (1) SA 515 (SCA); Georgias and Another v. Standard Chartered Finance Zimbabwe Ltd 2000 (1) SA 126 (ZS); Sanlam Life Insurance Ltd v. South African Breweries Ltd. 2000 (2) SA 647 (W); Commissioner, South African Revenue Service v. Woulidge 2002 (1) SA 68 (SCA); Meyer v. Catwalk Investments 354 (Pty) Ltd. en Andere 2004 (6) SA 107 (T); Verulam Medicentre (Pty) Ltd. V. Ethekweni Municipality 2005 (2) SA 451 (D).

11. *See* Michelle Kelly-Louw, *Better Consumer Protection Under the Statutory In Duplum Rule*, 11 J. Cons. & Comm. L. 20 (2007).

In duplum works differently for revolving loans like credit cards. If there were $100 outstanding on the loan, interest and fees would be capped at $100. If the borrower than repaid $40 and that were all credited to repayment of interest, then the lender could charge another $40 in interest under the *in duplum rule*. Likewise, if $30 of the repayment was credited to interest and $10 to principal, then the lender could only charge another $20 in interest (so that the outstanding interest would be $90, as would be the outstanding principal).[12] Thus, as long as repayments are credited first to interest and second to principal, *in duplum* does not truly limit the amount of interest that can be paid on a revolving loan *if the borrower makes payments*. It does, however, protect the borrower from interest piling up beyond a certain level if the borrower does not make payments.

Does this arrangement make sense? The law limits the liability of a borrower who makes no payments, while a borrower who does make payments could end up being liable for significantly more. Does that discourage payment?

In addition to the *in duplum* rule, South Africa authorizes the Cabinet Minister responsible for consumer credit to set a traditional usury rate.[13] The Minister is required, however to set the rate after considering:

- "the need to make credit available to" "(i) historically disadvantaged persons; (ii) low income persons and communities; and (iii) remote, isolated or low density populations and communities";
- "the conditions prevailing in the credit market, including the cost of credit and the optimal functioning of the consumer credit market," and
- "the social impact on low income customers."[14]

The statute provides no guidance on how these factors are to be considered, but it is notable for a very different approach than in the US, where usury rates are generally the province of the legislature. (Historically, the FHA did set a regulatory usury rate for mortgages it would insure.) What advantages or disadvantages do you see to a regulatory usury cap?

IV. FEDERAL PREEMPTION AND PARITY LAWS

Have you ever wondered why so many credit cards are issued by banks based in Delaware or South Dakota? Consider the Delaware usury statute after reading the Supreme Court's *Marquette* decision below.

12. Commercial Bank of Zimbabwe Ltd v. MM Builders & Suppliers (Pty) Ltd and Others and Three Similar Cases 1997 (2) SA 375 (W) at 303C-E; LTA Construction Bpk v. Administrateur, Transvaal 1992 (1) SA 473 (A) at 482C; Margo v. Gardner, (564/09) [2010] ZASCA 110 (Sept. 17, 2010).

13. National Credit Act, 34 of 2005 § 105(1).

14. National Credit Act, 34 of 2005 §§ 105(2), 13(a).

Marquette National Bank of Minneapolis v. First of Omaha Service Corp.

439 U.S. 299 (1978)

Mr. Justice BRENNAN delivered the opinion of the Court.

The question for decision is whether the National Bank Act, 12 U.S.C. § 85,[1] authorizes a national bank based in one State to charge its out-of-state credit-card customers an interest rate on unpaid balances allowed by its home State, when that rate is greater than that permitted by the State of the bank's nonresident customers. The Minnesota Supreme Court held that the bank is allowed by § 85 to charge the higher rate. We affirm.

I

The First National Bank of Omaha (Omaha Bank) is a national banking association with its charter address in Omaha, Neb.[2] Omaha Bank is a card-issuing member in the BankAmericard plan. This plan enables cardholders to purchase goods and services from participating merchants and to obtain cash advances from participating banks throughout the United States and the world. Omaha Bank has systematically sought to enroll in its BankAmericard program the residents, merchants, and banks of the nearby State of Minnesota. The solicitation of Minnesota merchants and banks is carried on by respondent First of Omaha Service Corp. (Omaha Service Corp.), a wholly owned subsidiary of Omaha Bank.

Minnesota residents are obligated to pay Omaha Bank interest on the outstanding balances of their BankAmericards. Nebraska law permits Omaha Bank to charge interest on the unpaid balances of cardholder accounts at a rate of 18% per year on the first $999.99, and 12% per year on amounts of $1,000 and over. Minnesota law, however, fixes the permissible annual interest on such accounts at 12%. To compensate for the reduced interest, Minnesota law permits banks to charge annual fees of up to $15 for the privilege of using a bank credit card.

The instant case began when petitioner Marquette National Bank of Minneapolis (Marquette), itself a national banking association enrolled in the BankAmericard plan, brought suit in the District Court of Hennepin County, Minn., to enjoin Omaha Bank and Omaha Service Corp. from soliciting in Minnesota for Omaha Bank's BankAmericard program until such time as that program complied with Minnesota law. Marquette claimed to be losing customers to Omaha Bank because, unlike the Nebraska bank,

1. Section 85 states in pertinent part:

"Any association may take, receive, reserve, and charge on any loan or discount made, or upon any notes, bills of exchange, or other evidences of debt, interest at the rate allowed by the laws of the State, Territory, or District where the bank is located, or at a rate of 1 per centum in excess of the discount rate on ninety-day commercial paper in effect at the Federal reserve bank in the Federal reserve district where the bank is located, or in the case of business or agricultural loans in the amount of $25,000 or more, at a rate of 5 per centum in excess of the discount rate on ninety-day commercial paper in effect at the Federal Reserve bank in the Federal Reserve district where the bank is located, whichever may be the greater, and no more, except that where by the laws of any State a different rate is limited for banks organized under State laws, the rate so limited shall be allowed for associations organized or existing in any such State under this chapter."

Marquette was forced by the low rate of interest permissible under Minnesota law to charge a $10 annual fee for the use of its credit cards.

Marquette named as defendants Omaha Bank, Omaha Service Corp., which is organized under the laws of Nebraska but qualified to do business and doing business in Minnesota, and the Credit Bureau of St. Paul, Inc., a corporation organized under the laws of Minnesota having its principal office in St. Paul, Minn. Omaha Service Corp. participates in Omaha Bank's BankAmericard program by entering into agreements with banks and merchants necessary to the operation of the BankAmericard scheme. At the time Marquette filed its complaint, Omaha Service Corp. had not yet entered into any such agreements in Minnesota, although it intended to do so. For its services, Omaha Service Corp. receives a fee from Omaha Bank, but it does not itself extend credit or receive interest. It was alleged that the Credit Bureau of St. Paul, Inc., solicited prospective cardholders for Omaha Bank's BankAmericard program in Minnesota.

[Procedural history of case omitted. The Minnesota Attorney General intervened as a plaintiff seeking a permanent injunction against Omaha Bank.]

II

. . .

Omaha Bank is a national bank; it is an "[instrumentality] of the Federal government, created for a public purpose, and as such necessarily subject to the paramount authority of the United States." The interest rate that Omaha Bank may charge in its BankAmericard program is thus governed by federal law. The provision of § 85 called into question states:

> Any association may take, receive, reserve, and charge on any loan or discount made, or upon any notes, bills of exchange, or other evidences of debt, interest at the rate allowed by the laws of the State, Territory, or District *where the bank is located,* . . . and no more, except that where by the laws of any State a different rate is limited for banks organized under State laws, the rate so limited shall be allowed for associations organized or existing in any such State under this chapter. (Emphasis supplied.)

Section 85 thus plainly provides that a national bank may charge interest "on any loan" at the rate allowed by the laws of the State in which the bank is "located." The question before us is therefore narrowed to whether Omaha Bank and its BankAmericard program are "located" in Nebraska and for that reason entitled to charge its Minnesota customers the rate of interest authorized by Nebraska law.

There is no question but that Omaha Bank itself, apart from its BankAmericard program, is located in Nebraska. Petitioners concede as much. The National Bank Act requires a national bank to state in its organization certificate "[the] place where its operations of discount and deposit are to be carried on, designating the State, Territory, or district, and the particular county and city, town, or village." 12 U.S.C. § 22. The

2. The National Bank Act, 12 U.S.C. § 22, provides that a national bank must create an "organization certificate" which specifically states "[the] place where its operations of discount and deposit are to be carried on, designating the State, Territory, or District, and the particular county and city, town, or village."

charter address of Omaha Bank is in Omaha, Douglas County, Neb. The bank operates no branch banks in Minnesota, nor apparently could it under federal law.

The State of Minnesota, however, contends that this conclusion must be altered if Omaha Bank's BankAmericard program is considered: "In the context of a national bank which systematically solicits Minnesota residents for credit cards to be used in transactions with Minnesota merchants the bank must be deemed to be 'located' in Minnesota for purposes of this credit card program."

We disagree. Section 85 was originally enacted as § 30 of the National Bank Act of 1864.* The congressional debates surrounding the enactment of § 30 were conducted on the assumption that a national bank was "located" for purposes of the section in the State named in its organization certificate. Omaha Bank cannot be deprived of this location merely because it is extending credit to residents of a foreign State. Minnesota residents were always free to visit Nebraska and receive loans in that State. It has not been suggested that Minnesota usury laws would apply to such transactions. Although the convenience of modern mail permits Minnesota residents holding Omaha Bank's BankAmericards to receive loans without visiting Nebraska, credit on the use of their cards is nevertheless similarly extended by Omaha Bank in Nebraska by the bank's honoring of the sales drafts of participating Minnesota merchants and banks. Finance charges on the unpaid balances of cardholders are assessed by the bank in Omaha, Neb., and all payments on unpaid balances are remitted to the bank in Omaha, Neb. Furthermore, the bank issues its BankAmericards in Omaha, Neb., after credit assessments made by the bank in that city.

Nor can the fact that Omaha Bank's BankAmericards are used "in transactions with Minnesota merchants" be determinative of the bank's location for purposes of § 85. The bank's BankAmericard enables its holder "to purchase goods and services from participating merchants and obtain cash advances from participating banks throughout the United States and the world." Minnesota residents can thus use their Omaha Bank BankAmericards to purchase services in the State of New York or mail-order goods from the State of Michigan. If the location of the bank were to depend on the whereabouts of each credit card transaction, the meaning of the term "located" would be so stretched as to throw into confusion the complex system of modern interstate banking. A national bank could never be certain whether its contacts with residents of foreign States were sufficient to alter its location for purposes of § 85. We do not choose to invite these difficulties by rendering so elastic the term "located." The mere fact that Omaha Bank has enrolled Minnesota residents, merchants, and banks in its BankAmericard program thus does not suffice to "locate" that bank in Minnesota for purposes of 12 U.S.C. § 85.

---

* [The National Bank Act provision at issue is from an 1864 statute designed to finance the Civil War. National banks were created to foster demand for U.S. government debt. National banks were required to have a substantial portion of their capital in U.S. government debt and were given the privilege of issuing national bank notes (the predecessor to today's Federal Reserve notes, which we call "dollars"), but could only issue them in relation to their holdings of Treasury debt. As it turned out, this financing scheme wasn't especially successful.—ED.]

III

Since Omaha Bank and its BankAmericard program are "located" in Nebraska, the plain language of § 85 provides that the bank may charge "on any loan" the rate "allowed" by the State of Nebraska. Petitioners contend, however, that this reading of the statute violates the basic legislative intent of the National Bank Act. At the time Congress enacted § 30 of the National Bank Act of 1864, so petitioners' argument runs, it intended "to insure competitive equality between state and national banks in the charging of interest." This policy could best be effectuated by limiting national banks to the rate of interest allowed by the States in which the banks were located. Since Congress in 1864 was addressing a financial system in which incorporated banks were "local institutions," it did not "contemplate a national bank soliciting customers and entering loan agreements outside of the state in which it was established." Therefore to interpret § 85 to apply to interstate loans such as those involved in this case would not only enlarge impermissibly the original intent of Congress, but would also undercut the basic policy foundations of the statute by upsetting the competitive equality now existing between state and national banks.

We cannot accept petitioners' argument. Whatever policy of "competitive equality" has been discerned in other sections of the National Bank Act, § 30 and its descendants have been interpreted for over a century to give "advantages to National banks over their State competitors." "National banks," it was said in *Tiffany*, "have been National favorites." The policy of competitive equality between state and national banks, however, is not truly at the core of this case. Instead, we are confronted by the inequalities that occur when a national bank applies the interest rates of its home State in its dealing with residents of a foreign State. These inequalities affect both national and state banks in the foreign State. Indeed, in the instant case Marquette is a national bank claiming to be injured by the unequal interest rates charged by another national bank. Whether the inequalities which thus occur when the interest rates of one State are "exported" into another violate the intent of Congress in enacting § 30 in part depends on whether Congress in 1864 was aware of the existence of a system of interstate banking in which such inequalities would seem a necessary part.

Close examination of the National Bank Act of 1864, its legislative history, and its historical context makes clear that, contrary to the suggestion of petitioners, Congress intended to facilitate what Representative Hooper termed a "national banking system." . . .

We cannot assume that Congress was oblivious to the existence of such common commercial transactions [involving interstate loans]. We find it implausible to conclude, therefore, that Congress meant through its silence to exempt interstate loans from the reach of § 30. We would certainly be exceedingly reluctant to read such a hiatus into the regulatory scheme of § 30 in the absence of evidence of specific congressional intent. Petitioners have adduced no such evidence.

Petitioners' final argument is that the "exportation" of interest rates, such as occurred in this case, will significantly impair the ability of States to enact effective usury laws. This impairment, however, has always been implicit in the structure of the National Bank Act, since citizens of one State were free to visit a neighboring State to receive credit at foreign interest rates.[31] This impairment may in fact be accentuated by the ease with which interstate credit is available by mail through the use of modern credit cards. But the protection of state usury laws is an issue of legislative policy, and any plea to alter § 85 to further that end is better addressed to the wisdom of Congress than to the judgment of this Court.[31]

Affirmed.

Notes and Questions on *Marquette*

1. On what basis did the Supreme Court determine the interest rate that the First National Bank of Omaha could charge? Is it a policy argument or a statutory interpretation argument?

2. Does it strike you as odd that the *Marquette* issue never arose in the 114 years prior that the National Bank Act was on the books? Why did it only emerge in the late 1970s?

3. In 1864 there was no interstate banking, although there was limited interstate lending by non-banks. State-chartered banks were confined to operating in a single state (and often with one branch) and national banks were required to abide by the laws of the state in which they were headquartered. Does that change your view of the case? Can Congress really have intended the result in *Marquette*? Irrespective, what implication should be drawn from Congress's lack of response to *Marquette*?

4. Is the "except that where by the laws" language in section 85 of the National Bank Act permissive or restrictive? That is, is it permitting a higher rate of interest than the alternatives mentioned above or placing a lower boundary on the rate of interest?

5. Imagine how the world would look without *Marquette*. *Marquette* goes a long way toward creating a national credit market. But for *Marquette* there would be interstate banking, but interest rates and credit availability would vary by state. The credit availability in Texarkana, Arkansas, might be different than in Texarkana, Texas. Is this a bad outcome from a social perspective? What about its impact on compliance and operating costs for a bank offering products in multiple states?

---

31. When the National Bank Act of 1864 originally passed the House, it imposed a uniform maximum rate of interest of 7% on all national banks. Such a provision, of course, would have eliminated interstate inequalities among national banks resulting from differing state usury rates.

The present § 85 provides that national banks may charge interest:

> at the rate allowed by the laws of the State . . . where the bank is located, or at a rate of 1 per centum in excess of the discount rate on ninety-day commercial paper in effect at the Federal reserve bank in the Federal reserve district where the bank is located, or in the case of business or agricultural loans in the amount of $25,000 or more, at a rate of 5 per centum in excess of the discount rate on ninety-day commercial paper in effect at the Federal Reserve bank in the Federal Reserve district where the bank is located, whichever may be the greater, and no more. . . .

To the extent the enumerated federal rates of interest are greater than permissible state rates, state usury laws must, of course, give way to the federal statute.

A. Parity Laws

The *Marquette* decision did not itself void state usury laws. Rather, it allowed for the exportation of a national bank's home state's usury laws to other states where the national bank did business. *Marquette* was, on some level, a choice of law decision. Yet *Marquette* set off a chain of legislative responses that had the effect of enabling banks to avoid usury laws altogether if they wished.

In the wake of *Marquette* both federal and state laws were passed to ensure competitive equality for state-chartered banks. These laws are called "parity" laws. State parity laws permitted state banks to charge the maximum rate that could be charged by a national bank doing business in the state. Thus, if one state's law had a 10% usury cap, but a national bank based in another state was subject to a 30% cap, the state-chartered banks in the first state could charge 30% interest.

In 1980, Congress passed the Depositary Institutions Deregulation and Monetary Control Act (DIDMCA), the first major piece of post-New Deal financial deregulation legislation. Section 521 of DIDMCA amended the National Bank Act by adding section 27, a state bank parity provision that gave parity to all state banks, effectively gutting all usury laws for banks. 12 U.S.C. § 1831d.[15]

Can the DIDMCA provision be read as an implicit endorsement of the *Marquette* decision? Congress certainly didn't reverse *Marquette*. But DIDMCA is hardly a ringing endorsement of a preemption policy.

If the purpose of preemption is to create a national market, why leave state usury laws intact? Indeed, why not make all bank regulation national? Why leave some state consumer protection laws in place as applied to national banks or banks in general?

The DIDMCA provision allows state-chartered, FDIC-insured banks to charge the greater of the maximum rate allowed in the state in which the bank is located or 1% above the Federal Reserve 90-day commercial paper discount rate for the applicable Federal Reserve District. In other words, this provision allowed state-chartered, FDIC-insured banks to export their home states' interest rates, just as *Marquette* permitted national banks to do.

What the statute did not do, however, was permit state-chartered insured banks to charge out-of-state rates in their home state. To wit, if Illinois had an 8% usury limit, an Illinois chartered state bank could charge 8% in Illinois or in Michigan, even if Michigan had a 6% usury rate. But a national bank based in Indiana, which has a 12% usury limit, could charge 12% in either Illinois or Michigan as well as in Indiana. Thus, the Illinois bank would remain at a competitive disadvantage to the Indiana bank absent a change to Illinois law.

Not surprisingly, national banks with major credit card lending operations began to relocate to states with no or liberal usury laws to take advantage of the *Marquette* decision. As related by Robin Stein's *The Ascendancy of the Credit Card Industry*,[16] in 1980, Citibank's credit card operations were in deep trouble. It had already lost over

---

15. 12 U.S.C. § 1831u(f) separately addresses usury caps in state constitutions. (Note that DIDMCA was passed with Democrats controlling the White House, and both houses of Congress.)

16. http://www.pbs.org/wgbh/pages/frontline/shows/credit/more/rise.html.

$1 billion in its initial foray into card lending, and was faced with inflation rates that exceeded the maximum rate it could charge under New York usury laws.

Citibank offered South Dakota—itself economically hard-pressed due to wheat prices—a deal it couldn't refuse. If South Dakota would pass the requisite legislation, Citibank would move its credit card operations to the state, bringing South Dakota hundreds of high-paying white-collar jobs. Citibank promised 400 jobs for South Dakota if it quickly passed a bill inviting Citibank to the state, and promised to open only a "limited" bank (a national bank subsidiary of the main national bank) in an inconvenient location for customers with unfavorable in-state interest rates so as not to compete with local banks. Citibank drafted the legislation and it was introduced and passed through the legislature in a single day. Soon South Dakota had the highest usury limit in the country: 25%. Citibank more than delivered on its jobs promise, bringing 3,000 jobs to South Dakota and paving the way for deals for other banks as well. Quickly First Premier (a major subprime card issuer) and Wells Fargo moved their operations to South Dakota as well.

In February 1981, Delaware enacted a new statute that eliminated usury rates for bank credit card lenders. In 1982 Maryland National Bank created a Delaware-based national bank subsidiary, Maryland Bank, N.A., later called MBNA. MBNA became the country's largest credit card issuer before its 2005 acquisition by Bank of America, effective in 2006. Bank of America changed MBNA's name to FIA Card Services, N.A. Banks also began to switch from state to federal charters in order to take advantage of *Marquette.*

Marquette thus sparked a race among states to relax their usury laws in order to retain their domestic banking business. Illinois, like virtually every other state, passed a parity statute that permitted Illinois banks to charge the maximum rate permitted to out-of-state banks. Thus, an Illinois-chartered bank can now charge whatever rate a state or national bank in another state can charge. The usury law has accordingly become a matter of the lowest common denominator.

By 1988, 18 states had removed interest rate ceilings, and the supply of credit card loans expanded rapidly over the subsequent 20 years. This increase in supply was concentrated most among high-risk borrowers because the interest rate ceilings restrict credit most among that segment of the market.

The impact of state parity laws was expanded by a subsequent Supreme Court decision. In 1996, in a case captioned *Smiley v. Citibank (South Dakota), N.A.*, 517 U.S. 735, the Supreme Court, deferring to an OCC interpretation, held that the term "interest" in the National Bank Act encompassed late fees. As a result, state laws that purported to restrict national banks' ability to charge fees were preempted, and state parity laws then meant that states lost control over the fees charged by their own banks.

The *Smiley* decision, according to Duncan A. MacDonald, the former general counsel for Citibank's credit card division, "took the lid off" late fees in the card industry. "The late fees that were common across the industry, up until [the Supreme Court ruling], were in the $5 and the $10 range. And the economic thinking was that there had to be flexibility to allow up to $15." The fees shot up quickly to as high as $39 after the decision.[17]

---

17. Robin Stein, *The Ascendancy of the Credit Card Industry*, http://www.pbs.org/wgbh/pages/frontline/shows/credit/more/rise.html.

It is important to recognize that the impact of *Marquette* was limited to banks. *Marquette* did not void state usury laws, but created a hole in them for banks. Nonbanks such as payday lenders and pawn shops continue to be subject to state usury laws. What this means is that the major impact of *Marquette* was on the credit card market. Most types of standard bank loan products—mortgages, auto loans, and student loans, have lower interest rates than credit cards, such that usury caps would rarely be an issue except in periods of extremely high market interest rates. But even when market rates are low, credit card interest rates frequently exceed states' general usury caps. Thus, it is questionable whether the credit card market would have expanded as rapidly as it did in the 1980s and 1990s but for the *Marquette* decision. Instead, without *Marquette,* the United States consumer credit system might look more like that of many European countries where debit cards combined with bank overdraft are the dominant payment/credit instrument.

V. THE INSTITUTIONALIZATION OF CONSUMER FINANCE

It's very easy to forget that the institutional shape of the financial world has changed considerably over the past century. In 1952, the first year for which the Federal Reserve has data, 51% of the mortgage loans outstanding by dollar amount were held by non-institutional entities—households or wealthy individuals or relatives.[18] Credit cards did not exist on any scale until the 1960s, and they were not a mass-market product until the 1980s. In part this was because of the limited credit reporting system presented an obstacle for non-local lending, as lenders lacked adequate information about potential borrowers. In part it was also because of geographic restrictions on banking. Banks were geographically confined by branch banking statutes well into the 1990s. Most banks operated in only one state and frequently had only one branch. As late as 1994, when the Riegle-Neal Interstate Banking and Branching Act was passed, there were only ten multistate banks in the country. As a result, banks were considerably smaller; there were large money-center institutions, but there was a limit to the deposit base available for these banks. Prior to the 1980s, a great deal of consumer credit was provided either by merchants or by non-bank finance companies. If you wanted to buy a sofa (perhaps a Daveno?), you would get your financing from the furniture store (such as Walker-Thomas Furniture Co.). If you were making a purchase at Marshall Fields or Gimbels, you would get credit from the store. Today, seller financing is primarily the realm of furniture, home improvement, and electronics stores and car dealerships, although some of the remaining department stores continue the tradition by offering store credit cards.

The different treatment of banks and non-banks under usury laws was undoubtedly a factor in the institutionalization of consumer finance. The FHA usury cap only affected institutional lenders because the FHA would only insure loans made

18. Federal Reserve Statistical Release Z.1 (Flow of Funds), table L.217.

by institutional lenders given its concerns about recourse to lenders in certain circumstances. This made it much easier for institutional actors (who already had diversification benefits over private parties) to make mortgage loans, as the credit risk was on the government on FHA-insured loans. The advent of FHA insurance (and subsequent policies of Fannie Mae and Freddie Mac) squeezed non-institutional lenders out of the mortgage market. The non-institutional lenders were gone by the time the FHA usury cap disappeared. Similarly, *Marquette* and parity laws exempted banks from state usury laws. A handful of commercial parties managed to acquire industrial loan companies (ILCs),[19] but by-and-large they were unable to compete for the lending business with national banks as interest rates rose in the late 1970s and early 1980s. In some states only bank lenders could profitably make unsecured loans in the early 1980s without violating usury laws.

Today the institutional versus non-institutional issue has reemerged in a different guise with various attempts to crowd-fund loans or person-to-person lending platforms. These platforms are more likely to be subject to usury laws than banks. Given that crowd-funded or person-to-person loans are likely to be riskier and thus higher-interest-rate loans, there may be parts of the market that these new financing channels cannot access because of usury limits, and their inability reach the entire market may limit their development.

VI. MAKING SENSE OF USURY LAWS

To start to make sense of usury laws, perhaps the best place to start is to understand the arguments against them, as the rationales for usury laws are best understood as exceptions to the general propositions argued against usury as a restriction on the freedom of contract.

A. Arguments Against Usury Laws

The main arguments against usury laws are that they are paternalistic interferences with freedom of contract; that they can unduly restrict credit, particularly if base rates rise high enough; and that they only curtail legitimate credit, and therefore shunt demand for credit into illegal and sometimes violent markets. There is no question that usury laws are paternalistic. But paternalism is sometimes justified, particularly when there are externalities present or a party is unable to adequately protect itself in the market. As we will see, usury rationales tend to focus on one of these issues.

A flat, fixed usury rate is a clunky regulatory measure without question. In the late 1970s and early 1980s, the then 10% rate cap in the Arkansas state constitution,

19. An industrial loan company is a type of limited-power bank. An ILC can accept a full range of deposits from consumers and nonprofits, but is prohibited from accepting demand deposits from commercial customers. ILCs are eligible for FDIC insurance, but their corporate owner(s) are not subject to Bank Holding Company Act regulation. *See* 12 U.S.C. § 1841(c)(2)(H).

for example, was disastrous when the rate on Treasury bonds (considered the paradigm "risk-free" investment) went up to 21% in the early 1980s.[20] If a risk-free investment was paying 21%, no other loans could be made at 10%. A usury law, however, need not be a flat, fixed rate. Instead, it can be varied by product type, and it can be a variable rate linked to some sort of "risk-free" index.

Concern about substitution of illegal credit for legal credit is another prominent argument against usury laws. If restrictions on legal credit do not reduce the demand for credit, then they would only force borrowers excluded from the legal market into the illegal market and thus expose them to rapacious loan sharks.[21]

It is not clear as an empirical matter whether the substitution hypothesis holds up or if consumers would in fact do without or turn to other legitimate sources of credit such as family and friends. Even if they do turn to loan sharks, however, as Professor Robert Mayer has observed, there are two distinct types of loan sharks—violent and non-violent. Robert Mayer, *Loan Sharks, Interest-Rate Caps, and Deregulation*, 69 Wash. & Lee L. Rev. 807 (2012). Violent loan sharking has been far rarer than non-violent loan sharking and is a phenomenon that was primarily associated with organized crime in large cities during the first half of the twentieth century. The democratization of credit enabled by risk-based underwriting and the federal criminalization of violent loan sharking (or "extortionate credit" in federal criminal law lingo) as part of the Truth in Lending Act in 1968, Pub. L. 90-321, 82 Stat. 146, 159-62, May 29, 1968, codified at 18 U.S.C. § 891-896. Thus, the extent to which usury laws would really end up encouraging violent loan sharking is unclear.

B. Arguments for Usury Laws

There are several arguments that have been proposed for usury laws. They can be grouped into three distinct types of rationales. First, there are mystery rationales, which take usury prescriptions either as apodictic divine commandment or as a type of Hayekian social learning that may not be well-understood, but that society jettisons at its peril. Not much need be said about these rationales, as they are a basically a "take it on faith" approach, and might suggest not permitting interest at all, which does no work in answering the question of what interest is.

The other rationales for usury laws either relate to the limitation of risk—be it to consumers, lenders, the economy, or third parties and the public fisc—or relate to concerns about contractual fairness. Both the risk and the fairness rationales provide justifications for paternalistic interference with contracting. The risk rationales focus on externalities created by high-cost lending, while the fairness rationales question whether there is truly free contracting occurring with high-cost loans.

20. *See* Kenneth E. Galchus *et al.*, *A History of Usury Law in Arkansas: 1836-1990*, 12 U. Ark. Little Rock L. Rev. 695 (1990).

21. *See, e.g.*, Justice David Baker & MacKenzie Breitenstein, *History Repeats Itself: Why Interest Rate Caps Pave the Way for the Return of the Loan Sharks*, 127 Banking L.J. 581 (2010); Todd Zywicki, *Consumer Use and Government Regulation of Title Pledge Lending*, 22 Loy. Consumer L. Rev. 425, 457 (2010).

The risk and fairness rationales are hard to disentangle because it is often difficult to distinguish between risk premia and supracompetitive pricing. To see why, it helps to start with contract basics.

The loan contract is an exchange of money now for more money later. Standard contract law does not inquire about the adequacy of consideration—a peppercorn or even the recital of a promise is enough to uphold most contracts. A major exception would be a swap of identical currency or commodities, such as $100 for $1,000 (at least in identical denominations) or one bushel of wheat for three bushels of wheat. These contracts are almost never made (why would they be?) and therefore are never litigated. As long as there is some difference in the objects being traded, we do not generally inquire about adequacy of consideration. Thus, there is no question about the validity of a contract swapping dollars for pesos—although both are money, there are different risks involved with each type of currency.

A loan contract is a contract of money for money, but there are different risks involved because of the timing of the payments. The interest rate includes a time-value component, a risk adjustment component, and a profit component. Fixed-rate usury limits do not distinguish between the components, but the existence of variable-rate usury limits indicates that the real target of usury laws is the risk-adjusted and/or profit components. Time value is much better understood in modern financial economies than in the ancient or medieval world.

Identifying the risk-adjusted and/or profit component of loans as the real target of usury laws helps pinpoint the concern about usury. It is either about borrowers taking on more risk than they should or about borrowers being exploited by creditors with some sort of market power that allows them to extract supracompetitive rents. These are very different rationales. One focuses on borrowers' lack of self-control or self-knowledge, while the other focuses on lenders' overreaching. To the extent that a borrower either does not understand the loan terms and credit costs or is misguidedly optimistic about his ability to repay a loan quickly (and therefore not be saddled with extensive interest payments), the focus on the concern is on the borrower. Thus, as Lord Mansfield famously wrote, "Usury was made to protect men who act with their eyes open; to protect them against themselves." *Lowe v. Waller*, 2 Dougl. 738 (1781). But to the extent that a borrower ends up in a high-cost loan because of financial duress or lack of bargaining power or misleading disclosure of credit costs, the focus is on the lender taking advantage of the consumer. As Mansfield explained, usury laws exist because it is "well known that a borrower in distress would agree to any terms." *Id.*

To the extent that usury laws are targeted at high-risk premia, the concern is variously a concern for the borrowers, a concern about the incentives high-cost debt creates for the borrowers' other behavior, and a concern about the externalities that can occur from overly risky borrowing. The higher the interest rate on a loan, the more pressure there is on the borrower to find an investment strategy that will pay off the loan. In other words, high-interest-rate debt may encourage risky borrower behavior.

To the extent the borrower is engaged in high-risk behavior, it also puts the lender at risk. If the borrower's strategy to pay off the loan fails, the borrower will default on the loan. The high interest rate will not help the lender unless it has a sufficiently diversified portfolio of loans *and* has priced correctly for risk across the portfolio. Thus, even if the fate of the borrower were of no concern, high-cost lending can create greater risk for lenders and, because of the interconnected nature of financial institutions, there is a negative systemic risk externality from high-cost lending. Moreover, lenders that lend at high rates may face an adverse selection problem: the only consumers who would be willing to borrow at such rates (rationally) are those who pose an even greater risk than the rates reflect. If consumers have greater information about their risk than lenders, adverse selection is likely to prevail.

Additionally, by lending at high rates, lenders can find themselves in an unwitting common pool problem—the high interest rates from multiple lenders might overwhelm a consumer's capacity to repay and might ultimately result in greater losses for all lenders. While modern credit reporting makes it possible for lenders to see the current balance outstanding on consumers' obligations, the interest rates on obligations do not appear on credit reports.

All else being equal, the risk of default increases as the cost of a loan increases. Defaults can be socially costly. If a consumer is unable to repay his debts, he may end up on the public dole. Indeed, the existence of the social safety net itself may encourage greater risk taking, which in turn drives up the costs to the social safety net. Thus, Professor Eric Posner has argued that usury laws may play a role in protecting the public fisc from having to pick up the tab for overextended debtors. Eric A. Posner, *Contract Law in the Welfare State: A Defense of the Unconscionability Doctrine, Usury Laws, and Related Limitations on the Freedom to Contract*, 24 J. Leg. Stud. 283 (1995).

To the extent that usury laws are targeted at supracompetitive profits, the concern is about lenders taking advantage of a less than perfect market. This is ultimately a market efficiency concern in which the problem is not loan default as much as loan performance, as the lender only gets its supracompetitive rents if the loan performs. While usury laws are not specific to banks, it is notable that banking is an area with an inherent market competition problem—entry into the field is limited. Not everyone with capital can obtain a banking charter. Thus, usury laws can be seen as a way to counterbalance the restrictions on competition in banking. This explanation is hard to reconcile, however, with the current situation, in which usury laws apply primarily to non-banks. Still, usury laws can be seen as a type of anti-trust provision that imply that there are certain contract terms that should not attain in a competitive market.

The problem with supracompetitive rents is that they are diverting the borrower's consumption power from other types of consumption. Consider a family. The money the family spends paying down credit card debt is money that cannot be spent on other purchases. Thus, the shift in consumption deprives other market participants of business. It is important to recognize that the lender will use the money it makes from the family to either buy new assets (including making new loans), pay its employees and vendors, or to pay dividends to its shareholders. The money does not disappear. But the money may shift distributionally and geographically, including overseas.

That shift in consumption can create externalities, by depriving the debtor's dependents of consumption. Thus, every dollar the family spends on paying credit card interest is a dollar he cannot spend on piano lessons, braces, or winter clothes. Of course, the family may have incurred the credit card debt to get the car fixed so the parents could get to work and not lose their jobs, because without income, there is no possibility of piano lessons, braces, or winter clothes.

The concern about externalities may explain why usury laws are often limited to personal loans. But the limitation to personal loans may also point to a concern about borrower sophistication, raising the question of whether usury is really a form of unconscionability.

If one accepts that there is a good rationale for usury laws, what should the usury limit be? Should it vary by product type? High rates on small loans are less likely to cause financial distress than with larger loans. By lender or by borrower? Do market power rationales play out differently depending on the identity of parties?

It is much easier to make an argument for usury limits in general than to stake out a particular limit. Consider, however, whether there might be some empirical thresholds. For example, we could imagine an omniscient regulator plotting default rates against interest rates on loans. There might be some clear cut-off points at which default rates jump significantly, suggesting that the marginal benefits of permitting lending above that particular rate are lower. Alternatively, it might be possible to determine that once default rates pass a certain threshold, the social benefits from lending at that rate are outweighed by the costs. Doing so, however, would require quantifying the social costs and benefits of loan default and loan performance. In the end, it is all conjecture; no empirical justification of usury provisions has been attempted.

Another way to see usury laws is as a type of presumptive unconscionability statute—that if someone borrows at above a certain rate of interest there must be some sort of duress or misunderstanding or unfairness involved. In other words, the substantive outcome is an indicator of procedural problems in contracting.

Having such a presumption has several benefits. It creates a level of certainty and fairness for lenders that comes from a bright-line rule, rather than from a fuzzy standard like unconscionability. It also makes judicial administration much easier; there is no need to take into account the totality of the circumstances. Instead, there is simply the question of whether a loan was at a particular rate.

If usury is a type of presumptive unconscionability doctrine, then it would make sense for usury limits to be set relatively high—beyond the point at which there would be serious questions about the fairness of the loan. If so, then the particular usury limit is not so much at issue—it need only be sufficiently high so as to avoid implicating loans that may or may not be unfair given their terms. It might also make sense to have tiered presumptions—rebuttable if rates were above a certain level and conclusive if they were higher still.

Problem Set 23

1. When you saw your Aunt Lolly over the holidays she was very upset to have just read an article in Costco magazine about consumer debt problems. She says, "I can't believe that banks are allowed to charge 36% interest or more. I thought there were usury laws. Can't that new consumer agency Elizabeth Warren created do something about it?" What do you tell her? *See Marquette Nat'l Bank of Minneapolis v. First of Omaha Serv. Corp.*, 439 U.S. 299 (1978); 12 U.S.C. § 5517(o).

2. Jacqueline Gulbachesi has been running a very successful pawn shop in Chicago, and she would like to turn her store into a nationwide chain. In Chicago, she charges 7% monthly interest on pawn loans. Will she be able to operate on those terms in:

a. Arkansas? *See* Ark. Const. amend. 89.
b. Colorado? *See* Colo. Rev. Stat. §§ 5-1-202; 12-56-101(2)(b).
c. Delaware? *See* 24 Del. Code § 2316.
d. New York? *See* N.Y. Gen. Bus. L. § 5-46.

3. What is the maximum rate of interest a bank may charge on:

a. A credit card in Delaware? *See* 5 Del. Code §§ 943, 953; 12 U.S.C. §§ 85, 1831d(1); *Marquette Nat'l Bank of Minneapolis v. First of Omaha Serv. Corp.*, 439 U.S. 299 (1978).
b. A credit card loan in Colorado? *See* Colo. Rev. Stat. §§ 5-1-301, 5-2-201.
c. A credit card loan in Arkansas? *See* Ark. Const. amend. 89; 12 U.S.C. § 1831u(f)(1)(A).
d. A mortgage loan in New York, which did not opt out of DIDMCA? *See* 12 U.S.C. § 1735f-7A(a).
e. A mortgage loan in Colorado, which is a DIDMCA opt-out state? *See* Colo. Rev. Stat. §§ 5-1-301, 5-2-201.

4. Rocky Mountain Finance, a non-bank finance company based in Denver, Colorado, has come to you for legal advice. They want to know:

a. Are points on a mortgage—prepaid interest—counted toward the Colorado usury cap? *See* Colo. Rev. Stat. §§ 5-1-301, 5-2-201.
b. Does Colorado's usury rate refer to the rate of simple interest or compounded interest? *See* Colo. Rev. Stat. §§ 5-1-301, 5-2-201.
c. Will they violate the Colorado usury law by having a 21% interest rate on loans that use the Rule of 78s to allocate payments? *See* Colo. Rev. Stat. §§ 5-1-301, 5-2-201.

5. J. Wright & Co. made Larissa LaRue a $10,000 signature loan at a usurious rate. Larissa has paid $2,000 when she sues Wright for usury and also files a complaint with the state attorney general. What are the potential consequences for Wright in:

a. Colorado? *See* Colo. Rev. Stat. §§ 5-5-201, 5-5-301, 18-15-104.
b. Delaware? *See* 6 Del. Code § 2304.
c. New York? *See* N.Y. Gen. Oblig. L. §§ 5-511, 5-513; N.Y. Penal L. § 45.

6. Dark-horse presidential candidate Senator Maury Glass (I-AK) has called for a national usury law, limiting interest rates at 36%. Your friend, the editorial page editor of a major national newspaper, is intrigued by the proposal and is wondering if her newspaper should endorse the position. Knowing of your expertise in consumer finance, she's curious for your opinion. What do you tell her?

CHAPTER 24

FAIR LENDING

I. FAIR LENDING

Access to financial services is not been shared equally by all Americans. Historically there has often been overt and sometimes legally sanctioned discrimination in financial services against various groups including women, people of color, ethnic and religious minorities, and older Americans. Discrimination has not ended, even if it is usually less overt, and there are still major structural differences in wealth among groups based in large part on historical conditions.

The moral and legal problems with discrimination generally are well known. There are two reasons, however, why discrimination in consumer credit finance is especially problematic.

First, access to financial services is critical for building household wealth and transferring it between generations. For example, home equity is a major form of household wealth. It can be transmitted intergenerationally and is tax advantaged, as the tax basis of an heir is the market value of a property at the time of inheritance. 26 U.S.C. § 1014(a). Absent access to financial services, achieving home ownership is difficult and takes longer. The result is that racial wealth disparities (which translate indirectly into disparities in educational and employment opportunity, health, and political power) are exacerbated intergenerationally.

For example, there are substantial differences among races in terms of wealth. Census data indicate that the median net worth for a white family is over $132,000 and over $112,000 for Asian families, but only around $12,000 for Hispanic families and around $9,000 for black families. U.S. Census, *Median Value of Assets for Households, by Type of Asset Owned and Selected Characteristics: 2013.* Homeownership—the home being the largest single asset for many households—also differs substantially by race. As of the fourth quarter of 2017, 73% of whites, 58% of Asians, 47% of Hispanics, and 42% of blacks were homeowners. U.S. Census, Quarterly Residential Vacancies and Home Ownership, Fourth Quarter 2017, Release CB18-08.

Minority groups still often struggle to obtain credit. A 2018 study by the Center for Investigative Reporting found that people of color were significantly more likely to be denied a conventional home purchase loan than their white counterparts, even after controlling for income. In Philadelphia, for example, the study found that a black family was 2.7 times more likely to be denied a mortgage than a white family with equivalent income.[1]

Even when minority groups obtain credit, they tend to pay more. A recent study found that black mortgage borrowers on average pay 29 basis points (0.29%) more than comparable white borrowers, even controlling for observed mortgage features, borrower characteristics, consumer shopping behaviors, and types of lending institution. Ping Cheng *et al.*, *Racial Discrepancy in Mortgage Interest Rates*, 51 J. R.E. Fin. Econ. 101, 118 (2015). The study also found that for borrowers paying above median rates, black women paid 57.36 basis points (0.5736%) more than their white counterparts, compared to 19.30 basis points (0.1930%) for black men. *Id.* at 117. An additional 57.36 basis points added to a $250,000 30-year mortgage at 4% annual interest translates to $84 more in monthly payments or $30,240 over the life of the loan. The extra cost of credit will of course leave these women even more financial vulnerable in the long run.

Second, discrimination segments markets. If there is a white housing market and a black housing market, for example, each segregated is, by definition, smaller than an integrated national housing market. The smaller market size may hurt market efficiency, by eliminating potential economies of scale and reducing competition in each part of the market. In this sense, discrimination hurts not just minorities but the entire market. Note that while this argument has some parallels to arguments related to the benefits of diversity for majority groups in settings such as higher education, this is not an argument about the benefits of interaction. Instead, it is simply the observation that a bigger market is more liquid and that the liquidity benefits accrue to all participants (majority and minority) in the market. Note also that a larger share of the liquidity benefit in an integrated market is likely to be captured by minority participants simply because the segregated minority market would necessarily be smaller; the liquidity difference between integrated and segregated markets is larger for minorities.

This chapter considers some of the theoretical and historical background of discrimination in consumer financial services before turning to the three major pieces of federal regulation dealing with discriminatory lending: the Fair Housing Act; the Equal Credit Opportunity Act and Regulation B; and the Community Reinvestment Act and other duties to serve. Be aware, however, that other civil rights laws, such as sections 1981 and 1982 of the Federal Civil Rights Act and the Americans with Disabilities Act may also have application with lending discrimination.

A. Why Discriminate? Economic Theories of Discrimination

As a starting point, it's worth asking why lenders would ever discriminate. What's in it for lenders? There are numerous possible answers. There might be overt bias or unconscious bias (such that the lender does not even realize) that motivate the discrimination. Alternatively, there might not be any bias at all, but just outright opportunistic exploitation (although one has to ask why such opportunism would be more focused on certain groups). The economics literature has developed two basic models of discriminatory lending.

1. The study did not, however, control for things such as credit scores, loan-to-value ratios, and debt-to-income ratios.

The first model posits that lenders are in fact prejudiced and have a "taste for discrimination." This model, pioneered by economist Gary Becker, explains why discrimination exists in a market with rational, profit-maximizing lenders. *See* Gary S. Becker, *The Economics of Discrimination* (1957). Lenders with a taste for discrimination suffer a non-pecuniary disutility from doing business with a disliked individual. Discriminatory lenders therefore maximize their utility by charging higher rates to disliked individuals in order to offset the non-pecuniary disutility.

In Becker's model, competition should, in the long run, eliminate discrimination, as lenders with a taste for discrimination will be outperformed by lenders without a taste for discrimination because the latter will lend to the disliked group at more reasonable rates and therefore capture their business, enabling non-discriminating lenders to expand, while the market for discriminating lenders would contract. This outcome, however, assumes a fully competitive market and that consumers do not themselves have a taste for discrimination. As we have seen there are numerous regulatory barriers to entry to the financial services market that make it unlikely to be a perfectly competitive market.

A second theory is that discrimination is the result of informational problems, rather than prejudices or intention to discriminate. In one version of this theory, lenders face incomplete information about credit applicants and use their preexisting beliefs about group characteristics as a heuristic to fill in informational gaps. *See* Kenneth J. Arrow, *Some Mathematical Models of Race Discrimination in the Labor Market, in Racial Discrimination in Economic Life* (Anthony J. Pascal, ed., 1972); Edmund S. Phelps, *The Statistical Theory of Racism and Sexism,* 62 Am. Econ. Rev. 659 (1972). In other words, a lender might find it cheaper to use the characteristics of a loan applicant's group to estimate the applicant's creditworthiness than to investigate the particular applicant. Depending on whether the preexisting beliefs about group characteristic are positive or negative, the reliance on group characteristics could result in greater or lesser credit availability or higher or lower credit pricing.

A later version of an information-based theory of discrimination is that it may be more costly for lenders to evaluate applicants with whom they do not share a common "cultural affinity" or background. The different informational cost structure results in less credit availability and/or higher costs of credit for outsiders.[2] Charles W. Calomiris *et al., Housing-Finance Intervention and Private Incentives: Helping Minorities and the Poor,* 26 J. Money, Credit, & Banking 634 (1994); Stanley D. Longhofer, *Cultural Affinity and Mortgage Discrimination,* Fed. Reserve Bank of Cleveland Econ. Rev. 2 (3d Quarter 1996).

B. Discrimination in Consumer Financial Services

Discrimination in consumer financial services has two distinct lineages. One deals with discrimination based on race, ethnicity, national origin, religion, and sexual orientation. The other deals with discrimination based on gender, family status, and age.

---

2. This model would seem to imply not only that majority group lenders would discriminate against minority borrowers, but also that minority lenders would discriminate against majority group members.

Discrimination in financial services based on race, ethnicity, national origin, or religion is a reflection of larger prejudices. It takes two forms. One is simply a refusal to deal with members of the disfavored group. This is self-reinforcing; members of minority groups do not attempt to access majority-offered financial services because of an assumption that they will be denied service due to prejudice.

The other form is a willingness to deal with minority groups, but by offering different products and services. We've seen this previously in *Williams v. Walker-Thomas Furniture Co.*, but other examples abound, including in literature. William Faulkner has an African-American mill worker relate that, "[Old Man Snopes] lent me five dollars over two years ago and all I does, every Saturday night I goes to the store and pays him a dime. He aint even mentioned that five dollars." William Faulkner, *The Hamlet*, Book 1, ch. 3. A dime a week every year for two years is $10.40 interest paid on a $5 loan or 104% APR. To some extent the differences in the type and terms of credit reflect the different socioeconomic status of minority groups, which tend to be poorer and thus perhaps less creditworthy, but it too is often self-reinforcing, as higher-cost financial products inhibited wealth accumulation.

Housing is a particular area of discrimination. In many cases sellers historically (and even today) refused to sell to people of color and religious and ethnic minorities. Some neighborhoods had racially restrictive deed covenants. Such covenants were ruled unenforceable in court as a violation of the Fourteenth Amendment's Equal Protection Clause in *Shelley v. Kramer*, 334 U.S. 1 (1948). Nevertheless, housing discrimination remained widespread as a matter of practice, and housing stock (and therefore schools) remained segregated; realtors would not show properties in white neighborhoods to African-American buyers; white sellers would not sell to African-American buyers; and banks would not provide financing for African-American buyers, particularly if they were buying in a white neighborhood. While some of this was motivated by outright racial animus, there was also a potential economic calculus; a bank that financed African-American buyers in white neighborhoods jeopardized its business from its white clientele. Moreover, if the neighborhood "changed" from white to black, prevailing economic realities might mean that the bank risked a decline in the value of its collateral. Thus, even if financial institutions bore no racial animus, they might still discriminate. Prohibiting discrimination on racial grounds changed the economic calculus of discrimination.

The problems of housing discrimination were most pronounced on racial lines, but hardly so limited. Hispanics and Jews, among others, also frequently encountered discrimination in housing markets. *See, e.g.*, Antero Pietila, *Not in My Neighborhood: How Bigotry Shaped a Great American City* (2010) (describing discrimination against blacks and Jews in the Baltimore housing market). Within minority and immigrant neighborhoods, renting was and is more common than home ownership. In part this is because of wealth disparities, but it is also because of the limited availability of credit for home purchases; historically, when minorities and immigrants purchased homes it was in cash, not on credit.

The lack of availability of credit was partly due to prejudiced denial of service due, but part was more fundamental: mainstream providers of credit simply did not operate in minority or immigrant neighborhoods, whether because of prejudice, doubts about profitability, or reputational concerns vis-à-vis prejudiced clientele. Instead, an informal credit economy developed, with immigrant savings banks, beneficial associations, and lending circles, as well as extortionate loan sharking.

In the twentieth century a particular form of discrimination in financial services emerged that was known as "redlining"—the practice of not lending or insuring within particular geographic areas of high minority concentration. Redlining was different from previous refusals to serve people of color or other minority groups because it applied to entire geographic areas, not simply to members of minority communities in those areas, but the areas were selected because of their concentration of minorities.

The origins of redlining are with the Home Owners Loan Corporation, a New Deal-era government corporation that purchased and restructured distressed mortgages. While the HOLC played a critical role in stabilizing the U.S. housing market during the Depression, one of its legacies was maps of major metropolitan areas in which it color-indicated different levels of "residential security"—indicating the quality of housing stock as well as the racial and immigrant composition of the neighborhood as measures of the likelihood of properties to maintain their values. The supposedly riskiest (generally African-American) neighborhoods were marked with a red line and were eschewed by HOLC (and subsequently FHA).

While federal fair lending laws and changes in industry practice have sharply reduced traditional redlining, a new type of redlining has emerged in the past decades. This new type of redlining, known as "**reverse redlining**," refers to the targeting of minority neighborhoods for predatory lending. Instead of the lack of lending that marked traditional redlining, reverse redlining features lending, but with different product structures and costs than in non-minority neighborhoods.

The second discrimination lineage derives from the historical patriarchal structure of the household economy, which privileged adult men. Historically, in Anglo-American law, a child did not have a distinct legal personhood until his or her majority, and women lost their distinct legal existence upon marriage. Children were part of the legal persona of their parents (or apprentices of their masters). Married women were subsumed into the legal identity of their husbands under the principle of *coverture*, with a married woman known as a *feme covert* under the legal protection of her husband.

Among the implications of coverture was that a married woman could not contract for debt independently of her husband. This was both a limitation and protection on married women (and children), as it meant they had to have their husband's (father's) permission to contract for an enforceable debt, but also shielded them from the enforcement of debts contracted without the husband's (father's) assent. *See* Claudia Zaher, *When a Woman's Marital Status Determined Her Legal Status: A Research Guide on the Common Law Doctrine of Coverture*, 94 L. Library J. 459 (2002). Coverture laws were steadily eroded starting in the second half of the nineteenth century as every U.S. jurisdiction passed a Married

Women's Property Act in order to facilitate stable intergenerational wealth transfers. *See* Reva B. Siegel, *The Modernization of Marital Status Law: Adjudicating Wives' Rights to Earnings, 1860–1930*, 82 Geo. L.J. 2127, 2135-2136 (1994). Similarly, ages of contractual majority began to become more standardized and younger, liberating youths from their parents.

Despite coverture disappearing from the formal legal landscape, prior to the 1970s, single, divorced, or widowed women frequently could not obtain large loans, such as mortgages, without a male relative co-signing. Likewise, women's earnings were often discounted in loan underwriting, and a change in marital status could constitute a default on a loan.

The historic legacy of discrimination in credit markets is one of structural inequality—minority communities are poorer today in part because they were denied credit in the past and that makes it harder for them to qualify for credit today, much less on equal terms. Historical discrimination is self-reinforcing, but it is compounded by ongoing discrimination in credit markets.

Justice Department Reaches $335 Million Settlement to Resolve Allegations of Lending Discrimination by Countrywide Financial Corporation

Department of Justice, Office of Public Affairs
Dec. 21, 2011

. . .

The United States also alleges that Countrywide discriminated by steering thousands of African-American and Hispanic borrowers into subprime mortgages when non-Hispanic white borrowers with similar credit profiles received prime loans. All the borrowers who were discriminated against were qualified for Countrywide mortgage loans according to Countrywide's own underwriting criteria.

. . .

The United States' complaint alleges that African-American and Hispanic borrowers paid more than non-Hispanic white borrowers, not based on borrower risk, but because of their race or national origin. Countrywide's business practice allowed its loan officers and mortgage brokers to vary a loan's interest rate and other fees from the price it set based on the borrower's objective credit-related factors. This subjective and unguided pricing discretion resulted in African American and Hispanic borrowers paying more. The complaint further alleges that Countrywide was aware the fees and interest rates it was charging discriminated against African-American and Hispanic borrowers, but failed to impose meaningful limits or guidelines to stop it.

. . .

The United States' complaint also alleges that, as a result of Countrywide's policies and practices, qualified African-American and Hispanic borrowers were placed in subprime loans rather than prime loans even when similarly-qualified non-Hispanic white borrowers were placed in prime loans. The discriminatory placement of borrowers in subprime loans, also known as "steering," occurred because it was Countrywide's business practice to allow mortgage brokers and employees to place a loan applicant in a subprime loan even when the applicant qualified for a prime loan. In addition, Countrywide gave mortgage brokers discretion to request exceptions to the underwriting guidelines, and Countrywide's employees had discretion to grant these exceptions.

This is the first time that the Justice Department has alleged and obtained relief for borrowers who were steered into loans based on race or national origin, a practice that systematically placed borrowers of color into subprime mortgage loan products while placing non-Hispanic white borrowers with similar creditworthiness in prime loans. By steering borrowers into subprime loans from 2004 to 2007, the complaint alleges, Countrywide harmed those qualified African-American and Hispanic borrowers. Subprime loans generally carried higher-cost terms, such as prepayment penalties and exploding adjustable interest rates that increased suddenly after two or three years, making the payments unaffordable and leaving the borrowers at a much higher risk of foreclosure.

The settlement also resolves the department's claim that Countrywide violated the Equal Credit Opportunity Act by discriminating on the basis of marital status against non-applicant spouses of borrowers by encouraging them to sign away their home ownership rights. The law allows married individuals to apply for credit either in their own name or jointly with their spouse, even when the property is owned by both spouses. For applications made by married individuals applying solely in their own name between 2004 and 2008, Countrywide encouraged non-applicant spouses to sign quitclaim deeds or other documents transferring their legal rights and interests in jointly-held property to the borrowing spouse. Non-applicant spouses who execute a quitclaim deed risk substantial uncertainty and financial loss by losing all their rights and interests in the property securing the loan. . . .

Both federal and state laws attempt to address the problem of discrimination in financial services. The response has been twofold. First, there are specific federal and state statutes that prohibit various types of discrimination in financial services. Anti-discrimination laws, however, do little to unwind the structural effects of past discrimination. Second, the federal government has various duties to serve for certain types of financial institutions that are meant to encourage provision of service to minority and low-to-moderate-income (LTMI) communities. While these duties to serve are meant to reverse structural discrimination, their effects are questionable, not least because the nature of discrimination in financial services has changed. Whereas historically discrimination meant complete denial of service, it now often means provision of service, but on worse terms, such that financial products can end up eroding rather than enhancing communities' wealth.

II. FAIR HOUSING ACT

Federal law has prohibited racial discrimination in housing since the Civil Rights Act of 1866. The 1866 statute, however, required evidence of intentional discrimination, limiting its effectiveness as an anti-discrimination tool. The Fair Housing Act of 1968 (Title VIII of the Civil Rights Act of 1968) created a more robust anti-discrimination regime for real estate transactions: sales, leases, and real estate financing. The goal of the Fair Housing Act was to create a unitary national housing market. Prior (and indeed subsequent) to the Fair Housing Act, there were separate white and black housing markets, as well as religious and ethnic segregation. Discrimination in housing affects potentially every aspect of people's lives. It affects where people live and that in turn affects who they associate with, where children go to school, employment opportunities and commutes, the accessibility of public amenities and retail shopping facilities, and even health. Because of the extensive effects of housing on the fabric of people's lives, it has been a particular focus of anti-discrimination efforts.

The Fair Housing Act originally prohibited discrimination in housing on the basis of race, color, religion, and national origin. In 1974, sex was added as a protected category, and since 1988 the Fair Housing Act has also prohibited discrimination on the basis of disability ("handicap" in Fair Housing Act parlance), and family status.[3]

"Familial status" is defined as the domicile of a person under the age of 18, as well as any person who is pregnant or in the process of securing legal custody of a person under age 18. 42 U.S.C. § 3602(k); 24 C.F.R. § 100.2. Thus, property rules that expressly discriminate against children under 18 are disparate treatment violations of the Fair Housing Act. The familial status limits do not apply to housing for older persons, meaning housing intended for and occupied solely by persons 62 and older or 55 and older if at least 80% of the occupied units have at least one occupant who is 55 or older. 42 U.S.C. § 3607(b).

The Fair Housing Act also prohibits discrimination in sale or rental of a dwelling, including in the terms of the sale or rental, on the basis of a handicap of the buyer or renter, a person who will reside in the dwelling, or any person associated with the buyer or renter. 42 U.S.C. § 3604(f). "Handicap" is defined as "(1) a physical or mental impairment which substantially limits one or more of such person's major life activities, (2) a record of having such an impairment, or (3) being regarded as having such an impairment." The definition excludes current use or addiction to illegal substances. 42 U.S.C. § 3602(h); 24 C.F.R. § 100.201. Discrimination includes refusing to permit a handicapped person to make reasonable modifications of the premises that are necessary to afford full enjoyment at his or her own expense. Landlords may condition permission of modification on restoration of the property. 42 U.S.C. § 3604(f)(3). The Fair Housing Act does not require, however, that "a dwelling be made available to an individual whose tenancy would constitute a direct

---

3. Similar prohibitions exist specifically for Fannie Mae, Freddie Mac, and the Federal Home Loan Banks. 12 U.S.C. § 4545.

threat to the health or safety of other individuals or whose tenancy would result in substantial physical damage to the property of others." 42 U.S.C. § 3604(f)(9).

Additionally, the Fair Housing Act prohibits discrimination by any person or entity engaged in residential-real-estate-related transactions—financing, selling, brokering or appraising residential real property—to discriminate on the basis of race, color, religion, sex, handicap, familial status, or national origin. 42 U.S.C. § 3605.

The Fair Housing Act has a number of exceptions. Other than the prohibition on discriminatory advertisements, none of the provisions of the Act apply to single-family houses sold or rented by the owner, as long as the owner does not own more than three such houses at a time and the sale or rental does not involve a broker, agent, or salesman. 42 U.S.C. § 3603(b)(1). The Fair Housing Act also does not apply to the sale or rental of units in properties with no more than four units if one is owner-occupied. 42 U.S.C. § 3603(b)(2). The Act permits religious organizations to give preference to co-religionists for housing they operate, supervise, or control. 42 U.S.C. § 3607(a). The Fair Housing Act also permits private clubs to give preference to its members for incidental non-commercial lodgings. 42 U.S.C. § 3607(a).

The Fair Housing Act may be enforced by private parties, by the HUD Secretary, or by the Attorney General (when there is a pattern of violations). 42 U.S.C. §§ 3610 (HUD), 3612 (HUD), 3613 (private parties), 3614 (Attorney General). Private parties may also file a complaint with HUD, which then undertakes an investigation and decides if it wishes to bring a charge. 42 U.S.C. § 3610. HUD has rulemaking authority under the Fair Housing Act, 42 U.S.C. § 3614a. Notably, the CFPB does not have rulemaking or enforcement authority for the Fair Housing Act.

The statutes of limitations and remedies under the Fair Housing Act vary depending on who brings the action. The Fair Housing Act has a two-year statute of limitations for private actions. 42 U.S.C. § 3613(a)(1). It allows for private plaintiffs to recover actual and punitive damages and attorneys' fees, and obtain injunctive relief. 42 U.S.C. § 3613(b). Enforcement by the Department of Justice has an 18-month statute of limitations. 42 U.S.C. § 3614(b). The Department of Justice can obtain injunctive relief, monetary compensation for aggrieved persons, and civil monetary penalties of $50,000 for the first violation and $100,000 for subsequent violations. 42 U.S.C. § 3614(d). HUD is required to bring a complaint within one year of the violation, 42 U.S.C. § 3610(a). HUD can recover actual damages, attorneys fees (for the aggrieved person), obtain injunctive relief, and civil monetary penalties of $10,000 if there were no prior violations and up to $50,000 if there have been multiple prior violations.

Enforcement of the Fair Housing Act is facilitated by the **Home Mortgage Disclosure Act (HMDA) of 1975.** HMDA originally required depository lenders and their subsidiaries to report lending volumes by Census tract (which can then be cross-referenced against Census race data) but was amended in 1989 by the Financial Institutions Reform, Recovery, and Enforcement Act (FIRREA) to require loan-level reporting of mortgage applications and originations. The Housing and Economic Recovery Act (HERA) of 2008 requires further data fields about loan characteristics, such as loan-to-value ratio, credit score, and debt-to-income ratio, to be reported as part of HMDA. The Home Owners Equity Protection Act (HOEPA) of 1994 requires certain higher-cost loans to be separately reported in HMDA data. HMDA currently applies to all but the smallest mortgage lenders irrespective of institution type and remains a key tool in policing discriminatory mortgage lending.

A distinct federal statutory provision prohibits discrimination on account of sex in mortgage lending for loans secured by one-to-four-family residences made by institutional lenders or those doing at least $1 million in mortgage lending annually. 12 U.S.C. § 1735f-5. The provision also requires that the "combined income of both husband and wife" shall be considered for the purpose of extending mortgage credit "to a married couple or either member thereof."

The reach of the Fair Housing Act might surprise you. The City of Miami, Florida, successfully sued a number of major banks for:

> discriminatorily impos[ing] more onerous, and indeed "predatory," conditions on loans made to minority [black and Hispanic] borrowers than to similarly situated nonminority borrowers. Those "predatory" practices included, among others, excessively high interest rates, unjustified fees, teaser low-rate loans that overstated refinancing opportunities, large prepayment penalties, and—when default loomed—unjustified refusals to refinance or modify the loans. Due to the discriminatory nature of the Banks' practices, default and foreclosure rates among minority borrowers were higher than among otherwise similar white borrowers and were concentrated in minority neighborhoods. Higher foreclosure rates lowered property values and diminished property-tax revenue. Higher foreclosure rates—especially when accompanied by vacancies—also increased demand for municipal services, such as police, fire, and building and code enforcement services, all needed "to remedy blight and unsafe and dangerous conditions" that the foreclosures and vacancies generate.

Bank of Am. Corp. v. City of Miami, 137 S. Ct. 1296 (2017). Municipalities, then, have been able to wield the Fair Housing Act to bring suits for lending practices that indirectly affect municipal finances.

III. EQUAL CREDIT OPPORTUNITY ACT

The Fair Housing Act applies only to housing (including rental housing) and housing-related credit. The Equal Credit Opportunity Act of 1974 extended anti-discrimination provisions to all forms of credit. The original version of the Equal Credit Opportunity Act prohibited discrimination only on the basis of sex and marital status. This version, which emerged from the Senate version of the bill, is perhaps best understood as a product of the women's movement, in contrast to the Fair Housing Act, the enactment of which was driven by first and foremost concerns of racial discrimination. In 1976, however, ECOA was amended to extend protected class status to race, ethnicity, age, and reliance on public assistance, a definition that tracked the original House version of the bill.

While the Fair Housing Act justly targets housing discrimination as a particularly invidious form of discrimination because of the broad effects of housing on peoples' lives, credit discrimination generally has broad effects, too. The ability to purchase a home depends, for most individuals, on access to credit, as does the ability to purchase a car, to obtain post-secondary education, or to start a business. Indeed, Internet commerce has made access to credit cards essential for being able to fully participate in modern commercial life. ECOA is aimed at addressing discrimination not just in consumer credit markets, but in all credit markets.

ECOA prohibits:

> any creditor to discriminate against any applicant, with respect to any aspect of a credit transaction—
>
> (1) on the basis of race, color, religion, national origin, sex or marital status, or age (provided the applicant has the capacity to contract);
>
> (2) because all or part of the applicant's income derives from any public assistance program; or
>
> (3) because the applicant has in good faith exercised any right under this chapter.

15 U.S.C. § 1691(a).

ECOA's prohibitions only partially overlap with those of the Fair Housing Act. While both statutes apply to mortgage loans, only the Fair Housing Act applies to home sales or rentals or ancillary services. Moreover, the protected classes are not identical. Both prohibit discrimination based on race, color, religion, national origin, or sex. Only the Fair Housing Act covers disabilities (including mental conditions), however, while only ECOA covers age or public assistance income. ECOA prohibits discrimination on the basis of marital status, whereas the Fair Housing Act covers "familial status," which would appear to be a broader category. Lastly, the Fair Housing Act deals only with residential real estate, but covers both sales and rentals. ECOA, in contrast, covers only credit transactions but is not limited to consumer transactions. ECOA also covers extensions of credit for business purposes because its scope is not in reference to a "consumer credit transaction," but merely to a "credit transaction." 15 U.S.C. § 1691(a).

ECOA is implemented through Regulation B, originally administered by the Federal Reserve Board and now by the CFPB. (ECOA/Reg B is the only CFPB-administered statute regulating business-to-business conduct.) Reg B goes substantially beyond the limited text of ECOA in terms of what it prohibits. Reg B has two central prohibitions, the second of which goes beyond the explicit language of ECOA:

> (a) **Discrimination.** A creditor shall not discriminate against an applicant on a prohibited basis regarding any aspect of a credit transaction.
>
> (b) **Discouragement.** A creditor shall not make any oral or written statement, in advertising or otherwise, to applicants or prospective applicants that would discourage, on a prohibited basis, a reasonable person from making or pursuing an application.

12 C.F.R. § 1002.4. This means that the anti-discrimination prohibition extends to the entire life cycle of lending: advertising, underwriting, and the terms of credit.

ECOA does not define "credit transaction," but it does define "credit" and "creditor," 15 U.S.C. § 1691a(d)-(e), and Reg B expands that definition. Under Reg B, the term "creditor" covers any person who "regularly participates in a credit decision, including setting the terms of the credit." That means that "creditor" is not limited to the actual lender—the funder of the loan, but also extends to any third parties that are involved in the credit-granting decision. 12 C.F.R. § 1002.2(l). Reg B also includes under the definition of "creditor" any assignee of the original creditor that participates in the credit granting decision, as well as persons who refer consumers to creditors or creditors to consumers. Thus, a loan broker that steers borrowers to particular lenders based on a protected class would be in violation of ECOA.

Reg B significantly expands the scope of ECOA's prohibitions. Reg B has three general categories of activity it regulates: lenders' requests for information from borrowers; lenders' evaluation of borrowers' loan applications; and the actual terms on which lenders extend credit.

A. Information Requests

ECOA itself does not prohibit inquiries regarding protected classes. Instead, it specifically provides that certain inquiries are not discriminatory. 15 U.S.C. § 1691(b). Reg B imputes a negative inference to this and prohibits inquiries regarding protected classes:

> A creditor shall not inquire about the race, color, religion, national origin, or sex of an applicant or any other person in connection with a credit transaction [other than pursuant to limited exceptions].

12 C.F.R. § 1002.5(b). This prohibition is tempered by exceptions for self-testing to ensure ECOA compliance, 12 C.F.R. § 1002.5(b)(1), title requests (*i.e.*, Mr., Mrs., Ms., Miss.), 12 C.F.R. § 1002.5(b)(2), and for spousal information in certain circumstances, namely that the spouse will be liable on the loan or will be providing income or collateral for repayment of the loan. 12 C.F.R. § 1002.5(c)-(d). For home mortgage transactions, however, creditors are *required* to request certain protected class information about the borrower. 12 C.F.R. § 1002.13. This is data required by the Home Mortgage Disclosure Act for the purpose of ensuring creditors' compliance with the Fair Housing Act and ECOA, and this must be explained with the request for information. Borrowers may, of course, refuse to provide the data. A data collection requirement exists for loans made to women-owned, minority-owned, or small businesses. 15 U.S.C. § 1691c-2.

B. Application Evaluation

Reg B specifically prohibits creditors from considering certain information, such as age, public assistance, childbearing capacity, and childrearing, in underwriting, even though that information might well be informative about an applicant's risk. 12 C.F.R. § 1002.6.

C. Terms of Extension of Credit

Reg B also imposes restrictions on the terms of extensions of credit. Specifically Reg B limits creditors' ability to require spousal signature (if the spouse is not on the loan or the loan is not secured by joint property) or demand that a married name be used. 12 C.F.R. § 1002.7(b), (d).

D. ECOA Procedural Requirements

In addition to its broad prohibition on discrimination in credit transactions, ECOA contains a set of procedural requirements that can trigger liability even if there is no discrimination. These procedural requirements are generally designed to facilitate enforcement of ECOA's anti-discrimination provision by requiring creditors to provide certain notices to borrowers and to maintain records of their interactions.

ECOA requires that a lender must notify a loan applicant of any action it takes in regard to the application within 30 days of receipt of the application. 12 C.F.R. § 1002.9(a)(1). That notice may be an approval of the application, notice of an incomplete application, or notice of an adverse action. No particular type of notice is required for loan approval; implicit notice, such as sending the consumer a credit card, would suffice. For incomplete application notices, the creditor must send a written notice explaining the additional information required. 12 C.F.R. § 1002.9(c)(2). For adverse actions, however, there are more specific requirements. 12 C.F.R. § 1002.9(a)(2).

An **adverse action** is defined by ECOA as a denial or revocation of credit, a change in terms on an account, or refusal to grant credit in substantially the amount or on substantially the terms requested. 15 U.S.C. § 1691(d)(6). Reg B, however, narrows that definition by providing that if a creditor makes a counteroffer to the applicant's request and that counteroffer is accepted that there is no adverse action. 12 C.F.R. § 1002.2(c). (Query whether the regulation is vulnerable to an APA challenge on this point.) A counteroffer that is not accepted is an adverse action, but questions remain about the exact distinction between counteroffers and adverse actions. A creditor may also choose to reject an incomplete loan application and treat the rejection as an adverse action rather than as an incomplete application. 12 C.F.R. § 1002.9(c)(1).

If there is an adverse action, then the creditor must within 30 days notify the consumer in writing of the adverse action, and provide: (1) the name and address of the creditor; (2) a statement of the ECOA anti-discrimination provision; (3) the name and address of the federal agency administering ECOA for the creditor; and (4) either a statement of the specific reasons for the adverse action or a disclosure of the applicant's right to a statement of specific reasons if requested within 60 days of the notice. 12 C.F.R. § 1002.9(a)(2). The specificity requirement means that a generic statement that the adverse action was based on the creditor's internal policies or failure to have a sufficient credit score are insufficient. Instead, for a credit score, the notice must give some explanation of why the borrower failed to achieve a sufficient credit score. The purpose of the ECOA adverse action notice is to force the creditor to explain the adverse action, so that if the explanation does not seem true, the consumer can pursue his or her ECOA rights.

The Fair Credit Reporting Act, covered in chapter 35, also has a requirement for consumer notification upon an adverse action (defined more broadly) that is based upon information in a consumer's credit report. FCRA and ECOA adverse action notices may be combined.

ECOA additionally requires creditors to maintain records of applicants for 25 months after any ECOA notice is sent out. 12 C.F.R. § 1002.12. The 25 months corresponded to two-year statute of limitations on ECOA prior to the Dodd-Frank Act. Dodd-Frank, however, expanded ECOA's statute of limitations to five years, 15 U.S.C. § 1691e(f), but Reg B has not been amended to reflect this. As a result, ECOA suits brought outside of 25 months after an ECOA notice is sent may face an evidentiary problem.

E. ECOA Liability

ECOA is enforced by both the CFPB and prudential regulators (for small banks) and has a private right of action. Liability under ECOA and the Fair Housing Act is not cumulative for the same acts. 15 U.S.C. § 1691e(i). ECOA permits recovery of actual damages and costs as well as equitable relief and punitive damages of up to $10,000 for individual plaintiffs or the lesser of $500,000 or 1% of the defendant's net worth for a class. 15 U.S.C. § 1691e(a)-(d).

F. ECOA Compliance

Many lenders engage in what is referred to as **self-evaluation** for ECOA compliance. Self-evaluation is a generic name for processes by which institutions evaluate their own fair lending compliance. Common self-evaluation techniques include undertaking second-look reviews of denied loan applications, undertaking comparative analyses of loan files, analyzing Home Mortgage Disclosure Act Data for disparities in lending by the institution, and examining cases in which exceptions are made to the institution's lending policies to ensure that the exceptions are not being done in a discriminatory fashion.

Self-evaluation is distinct from **self-testing**, a unique legal feature of ECOA. 15 U.S.C. § 1691c-1. An ECOA self-test is "any program, practice, or study designed and used specifically to determine the extent or effectiveness of a creditor's compliance with" ECOA or Reg B and that "creates information that is not available and cannot be derived from files/records related to credit transactions." 12 C.F.R. § 1002.15(b)(1). In other words, a self-test is a self-evaluation that creates new information beyond an analysis of loan files. Common types of self-testing are the use of mystery shoppers to identify discrimination prior to loan applications and surveys of loan applicants after the lending decision. The benefit of a self-test is that its results are privileged, but only if the lender takes appropriate corrective actions. Self-testing and correction does not affect private or public liability for past ECOA violations, but it is considered as an important mitigating factor by regulatory agencies when considering enforcement actions for disparate impact discrimination.

Lucas Rosa v. Park West Bank & Trust Co.

214 F.3d 213 (1st Cir. 2000)

LYNCH, *Circuit Judge*. Lucas Rosa sued the Park West Bank & Trust Co. under the Equal Credit Opportunity Act (ECOA), 15 U.S.C. §§ 1691-1691f, and various state laws. He alleged that the Bank refused to provide him with a loan application because he did not come dressed in masculine attire and that the Bank's refusal amounted to sex discrimination under the Act. The district court granted the Bank's motion to dismiss the ECOA claim, Fed. R. Civ. P. 12(b)(6); concurrently, the court dismissed Rosa's pendent state law claims for lack of subject matter jurisdiction. Rosa appeals and, given the standards for dismissing a case under Rule 12(b)(6), we reverse.

I.

According to the complaint, which we take to be true for the purpose of this appeal, *see Duckworth v. Pratt & Whitney, Inc.*, 152 F.3d 1, 3 (1st Cir. 1998), on July 21, 1998, Rosa came to the Bank to apply for a loan. A biological male, he was dressed in traditionally feminine attire. He requested a loan application from Norma Brunelle, a bank employee. Brunelle asked Rosa for identification. Rosa produced three forms of photo identification: (1) a Massachusetts Department of Public Welfare Card; (2) a Massachusetts Identification Card; and (3) a Money Stop Check Cashing ID Card. Brunelle looked at the identification cards and told Rosa that she would not provide him with a loan application until he "went home and changed." She said that he had to be dressed like one of the identification cards in which he appeared in more traditionally male attire before she would provide him with a loan application and process his loan request.

II.

Rosa sued the Bank for violations of the ECOA and various Massachusetts antidiscrimination statutes, *see* Mass. Gen. Laws ch. 272, §§ 92A, 98; *id.* ch. 151B, § 4(14). Rosa charged that "by requiring [him] to conform to sex stereotypes before proceeding with the credit transaction, [the Bank] unlawfully discriminated against [him] with respect to an aspect of a credit transaction on the basis of sex." He claims to have suffered emotional distress, including anxiety, depression, humiliation, and extreme embarrassment. Rosa seeks damages, attorney's fees, and injunctive relief.

Without filing an answer to the complaint, the Bank moved to dismiss pursuant to Federal Rule of Civil Procedure 12(b)(6). The district court granted the Bank's motion. The court stated:

> The issue in this case is not [Rosa's] sex, but rather how he chose to dress when applying for a loan. Because the Act does not prohibit discrimination based on the manner in which someone dresses, Park West's requirement that Rosa change his clothes does not give rise to claims of illegal discrimination. Further, even if Park West's statement or action were based upon Rosa's sexual orientation or perceived sexual orientation, the Act does not prohibit such discrimination.

Price Waterhouse v. Hopkins, 490 U.S. 228 (1988), which Rosa relied on, was not to the contrary, according to the district court, because that case "neither holds, nor even suggests, that discrimination based merely on a person's attire is impermissible."

On appeal, Rosa says that the district court "fundamentally misconceived the law as applicable to the Plaintiff's claim by concluding that there may be no relationship, as a matter of law, between telling a bank customer what to wear and sex discrimination." Rosa also says that the district court misapplied Rule 12(b)(6) when it, allegedly, resolved factual questions.

The Bank says that Rosa loses for two reasons. First, citing cases pertaining to gays and transsexuals, it says that the ECOA does not apply to crossdressers. Second, the Bank says that its employee genuinely could not identify Rosa, which is why she asked him to go home and change.

III.

We review a motion to dismiss de novo. *See Duckworth*, 152 F.3d at 3. In interpreting the ECOA, this court looks to Title VII case law, that is, to federal employment discrimination law. *See Mercado-Garcia v. Ponce Fed. Bank*, 979 F.2d 890, 893 (1st Cir. 1992) (applying the Title VII burden-shifting regime to ECOA); *see also, e.g., Lewis v. ACB Bus. Servs. Inc.*, 135 F.3d 389, 406 (6th Cir. 1998) (same). *But see Latimore v. Citibank Fed. Sav. Bank*, 151 F.3d 712, 713-15 (7th Cir. 1998) (rejecting the Title VII burden-shifting model for ECOA). The Bank itself refers us to Title VII case law to interpret the ECOA.

The ECOA prohibits discrimination, "with respect to any aspect of a credit transaction[,] on the basis of race, color, religion, national origin, sex or marital status, or age." 15 U.S.C. § 1691(a). Thus to prevail, the alleged discrimination against Rosa must have been "on the basis of . . . sex." *See Oncale v. Sundowner Offshore Servs., Inc.*, 523 U.S. 75, 78 (1998). The ECOA's sex discrimination prohibition "protects men as well as women." *Id.*

While the district court was correct in saying that the prohibited bases of discrimination under the ECOA do not include style of dress or sexual orientation, that is not the discrimination alleged. It is alleged that the Bank's actions were taken, in whole or in part, "on the basis of . . . [the appellant's] sex." The Bank, by seeking dismissal under Rule 12(b)(6), subjected itself to rigorous standards. We may affirm dismissal "only if it is clear that no relief could be granted under any set of facts that could be proved consistent with the allegations." *Hishon v. King & Spalding*, 467 U.S. 69, 73 (1984). Whatever facts emerge, and they may turn out to have nothing to do with sex-based discrimination, we cannot say at this point that the plaintiff has no viable theory of sex discrimination consistent with the facts alleged.

The evidence is not yet developed, and thus it is not yet clear why Brunelle told Rosa to go home and change. It may be that this case involves an instance of disparate treatment based on sex in the denial of credit. *See International Bhd. of Teamsters v. United States*, 431 U.S. 324, 335 n.15 (1977) ("'Disparate treatment' . . . is the most easily understood type of discrimination. The employer simply treats some people less favorably than others because of their . . . sex."); *Gerdom v. Continental Airlines, Inc.*, 692 F.2d 602, 610 (9th Cir. 1982) (en banc), *cert. denied*, 460 U.S. 1074 (1983) (invalidating airline's policy of weight limitations for female "flight hostesses" but not for similarly situated male "directors of passenger services" as impermissible disparate treatment); *Carroll v. Talman Fed. Sav. & Loan Assoc.*, 604 F.2d 1028, 1033 (7th Cir. 1979), *cert. denied*, 445 U.S. 929 (1980) (invalidating policy that female employees wear uniforms but that similarly situated male employees need wear only business dress as impermissible disparate treatment); *Allen v. Lovejoy*, 553 F.2d 522, 524 (6th Cir. 1977) (invalidating rule requiring abandonment upon marriage of surname that was applied to women, but not to men). It is reasonable to infer that Brunelle told Rosa to go home and change because she thought that Rosa's attire did not accord with his male gender: in other words, that Rosa did not receive the loan application because he was a man, whereas a similarly situated woman would have received the loan application. That is, the Bank may treat, for credit purposes, a woman who dresses like a man differently than a man who dresses like a woman. If so, the Bank concedes, Rosa may have a claim. Indeed, under *Price Waterhouse*, "stereotyped remarks [including statements about dressing more 'femininely'] can certainly be *evidence* that gender played a part." *Price Waterhouse*, 490 U.S. at 251. It is also reasonable to infer, though, that Brunelle refused to give Rosa the loan application because she thought he was gay, confusing sexual orientation with cross-dressing.[1] If so, Rosa concedes, our precedents dictate that he would have no recourse under the federal Act. *See Higgins v. New Balance Athletic Shoe, Inc.*, 194 F.3d 252, 259 (1st Cir. 1999). It is reasonable to infer, as well, that Brunelle simply could not ascertain whether the person shown in the identification card photographs was the same person that appeared before her that day. If this were the case, Rosa again would be out of luck. It is reasonable to infer, finally, that Brunelle may have had mixed motives, some of which fall into the prohibited category.

It is too early to say what the facts will show; it is apparent, however, that, under some set of facts within the bounds of the allegations and non-conclusory facts in the complaint, Rosa may be able to prove a claim under the ECOA. *See Conley v. Gibson*, 355 U.S. 41, 47-48 (1957) (stating that the notice pleading permitted by the federal rules requires only "'a short and plain statement of the claim' that will give the defendant fair notice of what the plaintiff's claim is and the grounds upon which it rests"); *Langadinos v. American Airlines, Inc.*, 199 F.3d 68, 72-73 (1st Cir. 2000); FED. R. CIV. P. 8(a).

We *reverse* and remand for further proceedings in accordance with this opinion.

The CFPB has stated that it interprets ECOA to apply to discrimination on the basis of gender identity and sexual orientation under the rubric of discrimination based on "sex" and analogy to EEOC rulings. CFPB Letter to Mr. Michael Adams,

1. Massachusetts law, the subject of the pendent state-law claims, does prohibit discrimination based on sexual orientation. *See* Mass. Gen. Laws ch. 272, §§ 92A, 98; *id.* ch. 151B, § 4(14).

CEO, Services & Advocacy for GLBT Elders (SAGE), Aug. 30, 2016. The CFPB's interpretation was not promulgated through a notice-and-comment rulemaking, and it is unclear whether it would be legally enforceable. The interpretation is also readily reversible by a future CFPB Director.

IV. DISPARATE IMPACT UNDER FEDERAL FAIR LENDING LAWS

The Fair Housing Act and ECOA clearly prohibit intentional discrimination or **disparate treatment** of protected classes. But what about a facially neutral practice that has a **disparate impact**? Is that a fair lending violation? What if there is no evidence of discriminatory intent?

These questions are particularly salient due to changes in credit markets. The major legal structure of fair lending laws dates from the 1960s and 1970s. Credit markets have changed since then. They are increasingly automated and data-driven. This may reduce the opportunity for deliberate human prejudice (although it could be programmed in, of course), but it raises the importance of disparate impacts relating to statistical correlations that might appear to have a good business justification.

In 2015 the Supreme Court held that disparate impact claims can be brought under the Fair Housing Act. *Tex. Dep't of Hous. & Cmty. Affairs v. Inclusive Cmtys. Project, Inc.*, 135 S. Ct. 2507 (2015). It remains unresolved whether disparate impact claims may be brought under ECOA. The CFPB, however, has indicated that it intends to apply a disparate impact "**effects test**" in its ECOA examinations and enforcement practices. CFPB Bulletin 2012-04, from April 18, 2012. Regulation B, which the CFPB inherited from the Federal Reserve Board, has an explicit "effects test," 12 C.F.R. § 1002.6(a), as do HUD regulations under the Fair Housing Act, 24 C.F.R. § 100.500.

The "effects test" derives from the employment discrimination cases of *Griggs v. Duke Power Co.*, 401 U.S. 424 (1971), and *Albemarle Paper Co. v. Moody*, 422 U.S. 405 (1975). It provides that irrespective of discriminatory intent, there can still be a Fair Housing Act or ECOA violation if a practice has a disparate effect or impact on members of a protected class, unless the financial service provider demonstrates that there is a legitimate business objective justifying the practice. The justification "must be manifest and may be neither hypothetical nor speculative." Interagency Fair Lending Examination Procedures, August 2009, *at* http://www.ffiec.gov/pdf/fairlend.pdf.

Relevant factors in such a justification are typically related to cost, profitability, soundness, or other measurable objectives. Even if there is a business justification, the practice may still be a Fair Housing Act or ECOA violation if there is an available alternative practice with a less discriminatory effect. 24 C.F.R. § 100.500. In litigation, the burden of showing such an alternative practice is usually on the challenger of a practice. The following case explains how disparate impact litigation works under the Fair Housing Act.

Tex. Dep't of Housing & Community Affairs v. Inclusive Communities Project, Inc.

135 S. Ct. 2507 (2015)

Justice KENNEDY delivered the opinion of the Court.

The underlying dispute in this case concerns where housing for low-income persons should be constructed in Dallas, Texas—that is, whether the housing should be built in the inner city or in the suburbs. [Plaintiff nonprofit housing corporation alleged that the Texas Department of Housing and Community Affairs had allocated too many housing tax credits for construction of low-income housing to predominantly black inner-city areas and not enough to predominantly white suburban neighborhoods with the result of continuing segregated housing patterns and discouraging housing for low-income blacks in the suburbs.] This dispute comes to the Court on a disparate-impact theory of liability. In contrast to a disparate-treatment case, where a "plaintiff must establish that the defendant had a discriminatory intent or motive," a plaintiff bringing a disparate-impact claim challenges practices that have a "disproportionately adverse effect on minorities" and are otherwise unjustified by a legitimate rationale. *Ricci* v. *DeStefano*, 557 U.S. 557, 577 (2009). The question presented for the Court's determination is whether disparate-impact claims are cognizable under the Fair Housing Act (or FHA), 82 Stat. 81, as amended, 42 U.S.C. §§ 3601 *et seq.*

. . .

II

The issue here is whether, under a proper interpretation of the FHA, housing decisions with a disparate impact are prohibited. . . .

Recognition of disparate-impact claims is consistent with the FHA's central purpose. The FHA . . . was enacted to eradicate discriminatory practices within a sector of our Nation's economy. *See* 42 U.S.C. § 3601 ("It is the policy of the United States to provide, within constitutional limitations, for fair housing throughout the United States"); H. R. Rep., at 15 (explaining the FHA "provides a clear national policy against discrimination in housing").

These unlawful practices include zoning laws and other housing restrictions that function unfairly to exclude minorities from certain neighborhoods without any sufficient justification. Suits targeting such practices reside at the heartland of disparate-impact liability. *See, e.g., Huntington*, 488 U.S., at 16-18 (invalidating zoning law preventing construction of multifamily rental units); *Black Jack*, 508 F. 2d, at 1182-1188 (invalidating ordinance prohibiting construction of new multifamily dwellings); *Greater New Orleans Fair Housing Action Center v. St. Bernard Parish*, 641 F. Supp. 2d 563, 569, 577-578 (E.D. La. 2009) (invalidating post-Hurricane Katrina ordinance restricting the rental of housing units to only "'blood relative[s]'" in an area of the city that was 88.3% white and 7.6% black). The availability of disparate-impact liability, furthermore, has allowed private developers to vindicate the FHA's objectives and to protect their property rights by stopping municipalities from enforcing arbitrary and, in practice, discriminatory ordinances barring the construction of certain types of housing units. Recognition of disparate-impact liability under the FHA also plays a role in uncovering discriminatory intent: It permits plaintiffs to counteract unconscious prejudices and disguised animus that escape easy classification as disparate treatment. In this way disparate-impact liability may prevent segregated housing patterns that might otherwise result from covert and illicit stereotyping.

But disparate-impact liability has always been properly limited in key respects that avoid the serious constitutional questions that might arise under the FHA, for instance, if such liability were imposed based solely on a showing of a statistical disparity. Disparate-impact liability mandates the "removal of artificial, arbitrary, and unnecessary barriers," not the displacement of valid governmental policies. *Griggs, supra,* at 431. The FHA is not an instrument to force housing authorities to reorder their priorities. Rather, the FHA aims to ensure that those priorities can be achieved without arbitrarily creating discriminatory effects or perpetuating segregation.

. . .

It would be paradoxical to construe the FHA to impose onerous costs on actors who encourage revitalizing dilapidated housing in our Nation's cities merely because some other priority might seem preferable. Entrepreneurs must be given latitude to consider market factors. Zoning officials, moreover, must often make decisions based on a mix of factors, both objective (such as cost and traffic patterns) and, at least to some extent, subjective (such as preserving historic architecture). These factors contribute to a community's quality of life and are legitimate concerns for housing authorities. The FHA does not decree a particular vision of urban development; and it does not put housing authorities and private developers in a double bind of liability, subject to suit whether they choose to rejuvenate a city core or to promote new low-income housing in suburban communities. As HUD itself recognized in its recent rulemaking, disparate-impact liability "does not mandate that affordable housing be located in neighborhoods with any particular characteristic." 78 Fed. Reg. 11476.

In a similar vein, a disparate-impact claim that relies on a statistical disparity must fail if the plaintiff cannot point to a defendant's policy or policies causing that disparity. A robust causality requirement ensures that "[r]acial imbalance . . . does not, without more, establish a prima facie case of disparate impact" and thus protects defendants from being held liable for racial disparities they did not create. *Wards Cove Packing Co.* v. *Atonio*, 490 U.S. 642, 653 (1989), superseded by statute on other grounds, 42 U.S.C. § 2000e-2(k). Without adequate safeguards at the prima facie stage, disparate-impact liability might cause race to be used and considered in a pervasive way and "would almost inexorably lead" governmental or private entities to use "numerical quotas," and serious constitutional questions then could arise. 490 U.S., at 653.

The litigation at issue here provides an example. From the standpoint of determining advantage or disadvantage to racial minorities, it seems difficult to say as a general matter that a decision to build low-income housing in a blighted inner-city neighborhood instead of a suburb is discriminatory, or vice versa. If those sorts of judgments are subject to challenge without adequate safeguards, then there is a danger that potential defendants may adopt racial quotas—a circumstance that itself raises serious constitutional concerns.

Courts must therefore examine with care whether a plaintiff has made out a prima facie case of disparate impact and prompt resolution of these cases is important. A plaintiff who fails to allege facts at the pleading stage or produce statistical evidence demonstrating a causal connection cannot make out a prima facie case of disparate impact. For instance, a plaintiff challenging the decision of a private developer to construct a new building in one location rather than another will not easily be able to show this is a policy causing a disparate impact because such a one-time decision may not be a policy at all. It may also be difficult to establish causation because of the multiple factors that go into investment decisions about where to construct or renovate housing units. And as Judge Jones observed below, if the ICP cannot show a causal connection between the Department's policy and a disparate impact—for instance, because federal law substantially limits the Department's discretion—that should result in dismissal of this case. 747 F. 3d, at 283-284 (specially concurring opinion).

The FHA imposes a command with respect to disparate-impact liability. Here, that command goes to a state entity. In other cases, the command will go to a private person or entity. Governmental or private policies are not contrary to the disparate-impact requirement unless they are "artificial, arbitrary, and unnecessary barriers." *Griggs*, 401 U.S., at 431. Difficult questions might arise if disparate-impact liability under the FHA caused race to be used and considered in a pervasive and explicit manner to justify governmental or private actions that, in fact, tend to perpetuate race-based considerations rather than move beyond them. Courts should avoid interpreting disparate-impact liability to be so expansive as to inject racial considerations into every housing decision.

The limitations on disparate-impact liability discussed here are also necessary to protect potential defendants against abusive disparate-impact claims. If the specter of disparate-impact litigation causes private developers to no longer construct or renovate housing units for low-income individuals, then the FHA would have undermined its own purpose as well as the free-market system. And as to governmental entities, they must not be prevented from achieving legitimate objectives, such as ensuring compliance with health and safety codes. . . .

Were standards for proceeding with disparate-impact suits not to incorporate at least the safeguards discussed here, then disparate-impact liability might displace valid governmental and private priorities, rather than solely "remov[ing] . . . artificial, arbitrary, and unnecessary barriers." *Griggs*, 401 U.S., at 431. And that, in turn, would set our Nation back in its quest to reduce the salience of race in our social and economic system.

It must be noted further that, even when courts do find liability under a disparate-impact theory, their remedial orders must be consistent with the Constitution. Remedial orders in disparate-impact cases should concentrate on the elimination of the offending practice that "arbitrar[ily] . . . operate[s] invidiously to discriminate on the basis of rac[e]." *Ibid.* If additional measures are adopted, courts should strive to design them to eliminate racial disparities through race-neutral means. See *Richmond* v. *J. A. Croson Co.*, 488 U.S. 469, 510 (1989) (plurality opinion) ("[T]he city has at its disposal a whole array of race-neutral devices to increase the accessibility of city contracting opportunities to small entrepreneurs of all races"). Remedial orders that impose racial targets or quotas might raise more difficult constitutional questions.

While the automatic or pervasive injection of race into public and private transactions covered by the FHA has special dangers, it is also true that race may be considered in certain circumstances and in a proper fashion. *Cf. Parents Involved in Community Schools* v. *Seattle School Dist. No. 1*, 551 U.S. 701, 789 (2007) (Kennedy, J., concurring in part and concurring in judgment) ("School boards may pursue the goal of bringing together students of diverse backgrounds and races through other means, including strategic site selection of new schools; [and] drawing attendance zones with general recognition of the demographics of neighborhoods"). Just as this Court has not "question[ed] an employer's affirmative efforts to ensure that all groups have a fair opportunity to apply for promotions and to participate in the [promotion] process," *Ricci*, 557 U.S., at 585, it likewise does not impugn housing authorities' race-neutral efforts to encourage revitalization of communities that have long suffered the harsh consequences of segregated housing patterns. When setting their larger goals, local housing authorities may choose to foster diversity and combat racial isolation with race-neutral tools, and mere awareness of race in attempting to solve the problems facing inner cities does not doom that endeavor at the outset.

The Court holds that disparate-impact claims are cognizable under the Fair Housing Act. . . .

[The Chief Justice and Justices Alito, Scalia, and Thomas dissented.]

Note

On remand, the District Court held that the plantiff Inclusive Communities Project, Inc. had failed to identify a "specific, facially neutral policy that purportedly causes a racially disparate impact." While the plaintiff had pointed to the "cumulative effects' of the defendant's decision-making process, the court held that such a "generalized policy of discretion was insufficient to prove disparate impact." Inclusive Cmtys. Project, Inc. v. Tex. Dep't of Hous. & Cmty. Affairs, 2016 U.S. Dist. Lexis 114562, *20, 2016 WL 4494322 (N.D. Tex. Aug. 26, 2016). The district court further noted that being able to identify a particular policy was essential for crafting a remedy, as the plaintiff was not asking for defendants' discretion to be curtailed but for it to be directed towards a specific policy of desegregated housing. *Id.* at *20-*22. The court also found that the plaintiff had not shown that defendants' policy in allowing discretion in how it allocated tax credits caused a statistically significant racial disparity. *Id.* at *25-*26.

Disparate impact issues have been prominent not just in housing markets, but also in auto lending, a $1.2 trillion dollar market with some 110 million loans. In March 2013, the CFPB issued a Bulletin putting indirect auto lenders on notice that it would be taking a close look at dealer markups on financing arrangements in which the dealer essentially serves as a broker. CFPB Bulletin 2013-02 (Mar. 21, 2013).

Consumers often obtain their auto loans from the car dealer, but the dealer will not lend unless it has arranged to sell the loan to an indirect lender. Indirect lenders compete not for consumers, but for dealer business. They do so by paying dealers more for more expensive loans—the dealer is allowed to "mark up" the loan above the minimum rate at which the indirect lender will purchase the loan, and the dealer gets compensated for that markup with a payment called the "dealer reserve." The dealer is thus incentivized to steer borrowers into higher-rate loans, and that steering might have a discriminatory impact against protected classes. (All of this is covered in more detail in Chapter 26.) Given that there is historically substantial evidence of discriminatory vehicle pricing by dealers, it would hardly be surprising if there were discriminatory credit pricing by dealers too. *See* Ian Ayres, *Fair Driving: Gender and Race Discrimination in Retail Car Negotiations*, 104 Harv. L. Rev. 817 (1991) (reporting result of study using mystery shoppers to document discriminatory vehicle pricing). The following CFPB Bulletin on indirect auto lending was voided by a Congressional Review Act resolution in 2018, but nonetheless gives a sense of the concerns of the CFPB. Recall as you read this that Reg B defines "creditor" to include assignees if the assignee is involved in the credit-granting decision. Is this Bulletin actually stating any new law?

CFPB Bulletin 2013-02

Date: March 21, 2013

SUBJECT: INDIRECT AUTO LENDING AND COMPLIANCE WITH THE EQUAL CREDIT OPPORTUNITY ACT

This bulletin provides guidance about compliance with the fair lending requirements of the Equal Credit Opportunity Act (ECOA) and its implementing regulation, Regulation B, for indirect auto lenders that permit dealers to increase consumer interest rates and that compensate dealers with a share of the increased interest revenues. This guidance applies to all indirect auto lenders within the jurisdiction of the Consumer Financial Protection Bureau (CFPB), including both depository institutions and nonbank institutions.

BACKGROUND

While consumers may seek financing for automobile purchases directly from a financial institution, many seek financing from the auto dealer. The auto dealer may provide that financing directly or it may facilitate indirect financing by a third party such as a depository institution, a nonbank affiliate of a depository institution, an independent nonbank, or a "captive" nonbank (an auto lender whose primary business is to finance the purchase of a specific manufacturer's automobiles).

In indirect auto financing, the dealer usually collects basic information regarding the applicant and uses an automated system to forward that information to several prospective indirect auto lenders. After evaluating the applicant, indirect auto lenders may choose not to become involved in the transaction or they may choose to provide the dealer with a risk-based "buy rate" that establishes a minimum interest rate at which the lender is willing to purchase the retail installment sales contract executed by the consumer for the purchase of the automobile. In some circumstances, the indirect auto lender may exercise discretion in adjusting the buy rate, making underwriting exceptions, or modifying other terms and conditions of the financing as a result of additional negotiation between the indirect auto lender and the dealer.

The indirect auto lender may also have a policy that allows the dealer to mark up the interest rate above the indirect auto lender's buy rate. In the event that the dealer charges the consumer an interest rate that is higher than the lender's buy rate, the lender may pay the dealer what is typically referred to as "reserve" (or "participation"), compensation based upon the difference in interest revenues between the buy rate and the actual note rate charged to the consumer in the retail installment contract executed with the dealer. Dealer reserve is one method lenders use to compensate dealers for the value they add by originating loans and finding financing sources.

The exact computation of compensation based on dealer markup varies across lenders and may vary between programs at the same lender. After the deal is consummated with the consumer, the retail installment contract may then be sold to the lender, which has already indicated its willingness to extend credit to the applicant.

The supervisory experience of the CFPB confirms that some indirect auto lenders have policies that allow auto dealers to mark up lender-established buy rates and that compensate dealers for those markups in the form of reserve (collectively, "markup and compensation policies"). Because of the incentives these policies create, and the discretion they permit, there is a significant risk that they will result in pricing disparities on the basis of race, national origin, and potentially other prohibited bases.

INDIRECT AUTO LENDERS AS CREDITORS UNDER THE ECOA

The ECOA makes it illegal for a "creditor" to discriminate in any aspect of a credit transaction because of race, color, religion, national origin, sex, marital status, age, receipt of income from any public assistance program, or the exercise, in good faith, of a right under the Consumer Credit Protection Act.

The ECOA defines a "creditor" to include not only "any person who regularly extends, renews, or continues credit," but also "any assignee of an original creditor who participates in the decision to extend, renew, or continue credit." Regulation B further provides that "creditor" means "a person, who, in the ordinary course of business, regularly participates in the decision of whether or not to extend credit" and expressly includes an "assignee, transferee, or subrogee who so participates."

The Commentary to Regulation B makes clear that an assignee is considered a "creditor" when the assignee participates in the credit decision. The Commentary provides that a "creditor" "includes all persons participating in the credit decision" and that "[t]his may include an assignee or a potential purchaser of the obligation who influences the credit decision by indicating whether or not it will purchase the obligation if the transaction is consummated."

Even as assignees of the installment contract, indirect auto lenders are creditors under the ECOA and Regulation B if, in the ordinary course of business, they regularly participate in a credit decision. The CFPB recognizes that there is a continuum of indirect lender participation in credit decisions, ranging from no participation to being the sole decision maker with respect to a particular transaction, and that a lender's practices and conduct may place it at various points along this continuum. The CFPB also recognizes that credit transactions in indirect auto lending take many forms. However, information gathered by the CFPB suggests that the standard practices of indirect auto lenders likely constitute participation in a credit decision under the ECOA and Regulation B.

For example, an indirect auto lender is likely a creditor under the ECOA when it evaluates an applicant's information, establishes a buy rate, and then communicates that buy rate to the dealer, indicating that it will purchase the obligation at the designated buy rate if the transaction is consummated. In addition, when a lender provides rate sheets to a dealer establishing buy rates and allows the dealer to mark up those buy rates, the lender may be a creditor under the ECOA when it later purchases a contract from such a dealer. These two examples are illustrative of common industry practices; indirect auto lenders may also be creditors under other circumstances.

THE LIABILITY OF INDIRECT AUTO LENDERS FOR DISCRIMINATION RESULTING FROM MARKUP AND COMPENSATION POLICIES

An additional consideration for auto lenders covered as creditors under the ECOA is whether and under what circumstances they are liable for pricing disparities on a prohibited basis. When such disparities exist within an indirect auto lender's portfolio, lenders may be liable under the legal doctrines of both disparate treatment and disparate impact.

An indirect auto lender's markup and compensation policies may alone be sufficient to trigger liability under the ECOA if the lender regularly participates in a credit decision and its policies result in discrimination. The disparities triggering liability could arise either within a particular dealer's transactions or across different dealers within the lender's portfolio. Thus, an indirect auto lender that permits dealer markup and compensates dealers on that basis may be liable for these policies and practices if they result in disparities on a prohibited basis.

Some indirect auto lenders may be operating under the incorrect assumption that they are not liable under the ECOA for pricing disparities caused by markup and compensation policies because Regulation B provides that "[a] person is not a creditor regarding any violation of the [ECOA] or [Regulation B] committed by another creditor unless the person knew or had reasonable notice of the act, policy, or practice that constituted the violation before becoming involved in the credit transaction."

This provision limits a creditor's liability for another creditor's ECOA violations under certain circumstances. But it does not limit a creditor's liability for its own violations—including, for example, disparities on a prohibited basis that result from the creditor's own markup and compensation policies. Additionally, an indirect auto lender further may have known or had reasonable notice of a dealer's discriminatory conduct, depending on the facts and circumstances.

LIMITING FAIR LENDING RISK IN INDIRECT AUTO LENDING

Institutions subject to CFPB jurisdiction, including indirect auto lenders, should take steps to ensure that they are operating in compliance with the ECOA and Regulation B as applied to dealer markup and compensation policies. These steps may include, but are not limited to:

- imposing controls on dealer markup and compensation policies, or otherwise revising dealer markup and compensation policies, and also monitoring and addressing the effects of those policies in the manner described below, so as to address unexplained pricing disparities on prohibited bases; or
- eliminating dealer discretion to mark up buy rates and fairly compensating dealers using another mechanism, such as a flat fee per transaction, that does not result in discrimination.

Another important tool for limiting fair lending risk in indirect auto lending is developing a robust fair lending compliance management program. The CFPB recognizes that the appropriate program will vary among financial institutions. In our most recent Supervisory Highlights, we set out the following features of a strong fair lending compliance program, which are applicable in the indirect auto lending context:

- an up-to-date fair lending policy statement;
- regular fair lending training for all employees involved with any aspect of the institution's credit transactions, as well as all officers and Board members;
- ongoing monitoring for compliance with fair lending policies and procedures;
- ongoing monitoring for compliance with other policies and procedures that are intended to reduce fair lending risk (such as controls on dealer discretion);
- review of lending policies for potential fair lending violations, including potential disparate impact;
- depending on the size and complexity of the financial institution, regular analysis of loan data in all product areas for potential disparities on a prohibited basis in pricing, underwriting, or other aspects of the credit transaction;
- regular assessment of the marketing of loan products; and
- meaningful oversight of fair lending compliance by management and, where appropriate, the financial institution's board of directors.

For some lenders, additional compliance-management components may be necessary to address significant fair lending risks. For example, indirect auto lenders that retain dealer markup and compensation policies may wish to address the fair lending risks of such policies by implementing systems for monitoring and corrective action by:

- sending communications to all participating dealers explaining the ECOA, stating the lender's expectations with respect to ECOA compliance, and articulating the dealer's obligation to mark up interest rates in a non-discriminatory manner in instances where such markups are permitted;
- conducting regular analyses of both dealer-specific and portfolio-wide loan pricing data for potential disparities on a prohibited basis resulting from dealer markup and compensation policies;
- commencing prompt corrective action against dealers, including restricting or eliminating their use of dealer markup and compensation policies or excluding dealers from future transactions, when analysis identifies unexplained disparities on a prohibited basis; and

- promptly remunerating affected consumers when unexplained disparities on a prohibited basis are identified either within an individual dealer's transactions or across the indirect lender's portfolio.

The CFPB will continue to closely review the operations of both depository and non-depository indirect auto lenders, utilizing all appropriate regulatory tools to assess whether supervisory, enforcement, or other actions may be necessary to ensure that the market for auto lending provides fair, equitable, and nondiscriminatory access to credit for consumers.

The practice of dealer financing markups bears certain resemblances to the yield-spread premiums received by mortgage brokers prior to their prohibition in 2010 by the Dodd-Frank Act. 15 U.S.C. § 1639b(c). Yield spread premiums were additional compensation mortgage brokers received from banks for brokering higher-cost loans. Yield-spread premiums thus incentivized brokers to steer consumers into higher-cost loans, particularly when dealing with consumers of color. Howell E. Jackson & Laurie Burlingame, *Kickbacks or Compensation: The Case of Yield Spread Premiums*, 12 Stan. J. L. Bus. & Fin. 289 (2007).

V. STATE FAIR LENDING LAWS

In addition to federal fair lending laws, individual states also have fair lending laws. The scope of these laws varies by state, but sometimes they are broader than federal law in terms of identification of protected classes. For example, some California law covers discrimination based on the "race, color, religion, sex, gender, gender identity, gender expression, sexual orientation, marital status, national origin, ancestry, familial status, source of income, disability, or genetic information" of a person. Cal. Gov. Code § 12955; Cal. Health & Safety Code § 35811; Cal. Bus. & Prof. Code § 16721.5; Cal. Civ. Code § 51. Likewise, New York's statute covers not only "race, creed, color, national origin, sexual orientation, military status, age, sex, marital status, childbearing potential, disability, or familial status," but also forbids inquiries about fertility, use or advocacy of birth control, and use of a different surname than a spouse. N.Y. Exec. L. § 296-a. A fair lending violation may also be a state UDAP violation.

VI. DUTIES TO SERVE: THE COMMUNITY REINVESTMENT ACT

In addition to anti-discrimination laws, there are also federal laws creating various duties to serve or affirmative obligations on certain financial institutions. The most prominent is the Community Reinvestment Act of 1977, although separate obligations exist for the government-sponsored enterprises Fannie Mae and Freddie

Mac and the Federal Home Loan Banks, which have explicit public purposes in their charters, including "provid[ing] ongoing assistance to the secondary market for residential mortgages (including activities relating to mortgages on housing for low- and moderate-income families involving a reasonable economic return that may be less than the return earned on other activities). . ." and "promot[ing] access to mortgage credit throughout the Nation (including central cities, rural areas, and underserved areas) . . ." 12 U.S.C. § 1716(3)-(4).

The Community Reinvestment Act (CRA) imposes a continuing and affirmative obligation on federally insured depositories to "help meet the credit needs of the local communities in which they are chartered consistent with the safe and sound operation of such institutions." 12 U.S.C. § 2901. The CRA only applies to the activities of a depository, not its non-depository affiliates or holding company, unless the depository elects to have them included in its evaluation. 12 U.S.C. § 2902(2); 12 C.F.R. § 228.42(d) (Regulation BB). Thus, non-bank financial firms are not subject to CRA obligations.

The statute itself is bare-bones, merely directing regulators to assess a depository's record of meeting the credit needs of its community, "consistent with the safe and sound operation of such institution." Most of the details are provided by regulations passed by prudential bank regulators. (The Federal Reserve regulation is Regulation BB.) Among factors prudential regulators have considered are a history of UDAAP violations.

The CRA was a response in part to frustration that fair lending laws alone were not ensuring the provision of credit to formerly redlined communities. CRA regulations require prudential regulators to evaluate how depositories serve their communities based on three separate lending, investment, and service tests that are applied to a bank's geographic assessment area, which is generally the counties in which a depository institution has offices or deposit-taking ATMs. Regulators are supposed to grade depositories on how they meet community needs with consideration of lending and provision of other financial services to low-to-moderate income households and small businesses. Regulators are required to consider an institution's CRA performance when reviewing applications for mergers, and for such activities as opening and closing branch banks. How to weigh CRA performance is largely left to the regulators' discretion. Since 1990, only 0.34% of exams have resulted in a failing grade, while over 96% earned satisfactory or higher.[4]

The CRA is primarily a hortatory tool. It does not require banks to actually make any loans. There is no private right of action or even a public right of action under the statute. Instead, the only real tool for enforcement is merger and branch opening/closing denial by regulators. This means that if a bank is not looking to merge or open/close branches, the CRA has little bite. While the CRA appears to have changed institutional culture, it does not appear to have had a major impact on

4. https://www.ffiec.gov/craratings/. From 1990 through 2017, out of 77,189 ratings, there were 264 of "substantial noncompliance," many to the same institution for different exam periods. There were 2,655 "needs to improve" ratings.

ensuring credit availability to LTMI or minority communities. Adam J. Levitin & Janneke H. Ratcliffe, *Rethinking Duties to Serve in Housing Finance*, in *Homeownership Built to Last: Balancing Access, Affordability, and Risk after the Housing Crisis* 317 (Eric Belsky *et al.*, eds. 2014). Moreover, because the CRA only applies to depositories, it does not cover all financial services firms. And perhaps most importantly, the CRA does not consider the terms on which financial services are extended. This leaves hanging, then, the question of what steps government can take to undo the structural legacy of historical credit discrimination.

Problem Set 24

1. Your cousin Dan "The Man" Tanz owns some investment properties near the state college campus. He generally rents them to visiting faculty members, but he has been approached by members of the ΣKT (the "Skats"), a notorious fraternity. They offer to pay the rent up-front and in cash, as well as to post the standard security deposit. Dan is nervous about renting to the Skats. "I'll never get the smell and the stains out," he moans. Dan is worried, however, that the Skats will sue him if he declines to rent to them. One of them mentioned that his Dad was a big-time lawyer (and former Skat brother), so they'd have no trouble paying. What advice do you give Dan? *See* 42 U.S.C. §§ 3603(b)(1), 3604(a)-(b).

2. Bonnie Lewis is a realtor. She is showing properties to Avram and Shoshanna Levine. The Levines have indicated that they are observant Jews and would like to live in a community with similar individuals, as it would facilitate friendships and religious observance; observant Jews require ten adult males for prayer and will not drive on the Sabbath or holidays, so location is of paramount importance to their religious observance. What should Bonnie do? *See* 42 U.S.C. §§ 3604(a)-(b), 3604(e), 3605, 3607(a).

3. You've just joined the board of the Halcyon Condominium Association. After some unfortunate incidents last summer, the board is considering adopting a rule regarding children's use of the pool. Specifically, the board is considering the following proposals:

- **a.** "No children under age 3 allowed in the pool."
- **b.** "Only toilet-trained children allowed in the pool."
- **c.** "Children under age 6 must use the kiddie pool."
- **d.** "Children under the age of 18 are not allowed in the pool or pool area at any time unless accompanied by their parents or legal guardian."
- **e.** "Children are not permitted to use the pool during Adult Swim times or to use the lap lanes."
- **f.** "No running, no diving, and no horseplay."

Do you have any concerns about these proposals? See 42 U.S.C. §§ 3604(b), 3604(f); 24 C.F.R. §§ 100.20, 100.50, 100.65, 100.201, 100.500.

4. The Alliance for the Mentally Ill (AMI) helps semi-functional individuals with mental illness rent apartments in order to deinstitutionalize them. AMI guarantees the rental payments of the tenant and posts the security deposit. AMI is helping Joanna Martin, a young woman struggling with schizophrenia, rent an apartment. Joanna has been holding a retail job at a Lululemon yoga shop for the past four months. Joanna, assisted by an AMI counselor, has responded to a rental ad you placed in the newspaper.

- **a.** Assuming that Joanna qualifies financially for the apartment, can you decline to rent the apartment to her? *See* 42 U.S.C. §§ 3602(h), 3604(f).
- **b.** Joanna has applied for a credit card at her local bank branch. When she filled out the application, she mentioned her mental health history to the bank officer. Can the bank consider her schizophrenia in its lending decision? *See* 15 U.S.C. § 1691.

5. Bobby and Kristin Lopez live in Illinois, one of roughly 26 states that permits property acquired by married people to be held as a tenancy by the entirety, meaning that neither spouse can commit an interest in the property without the agreement (and signature) of the other.

- **a.** Can the lender inquire if Kristin is married? *See* 15 U.S.C. § 1691(b)(1).
- **b.** Can Kristin get a mortgage without Bobby signing the loan? *See* 15 U.S.C. § 1691d(a).
- **c.** Would the answer to (b) be different if they moved to Connecticut, which does not have tenancy by the entirety? *See* 15 U.S.C. §§ 1691(a)-(b).

6. Simona Taschini has just applied for an auto loan from your bank. Simona is currently employed as a third-grade teacher at the local public elementary school. In the course of her loan application, she mentions to the loan officer that she's four months pregnant. Should the loan officer account for that in the underwriting decision? *See* 15 U.S.C. § 1691(a); 12 C.F.R. §§ 1002.5(d), 1002.6(b)(3).

7. Kathleen Engel responded to an ad from Deuce Ransome's Slaab dealership of 2% APR financing for well-qualified creditors, zero money down. When Kathleen applied for a loan to purchase a Slaab Centurion minivan, Deuce's finance manager collected her credit information, including a consumer report and credit score. The finance manager then told her that she qualified for the 2% APR rate, but would have to make a 20% down payment to get that rate, otherwise she would have to pay 5% APR. Frustrated, Kathleen stormed out of the dealership muttering something about "bait and switch." Kathleen's come to see you about whether she has any recourse against Deuce's. 15 U.S.C. § 1691(d); 12 C.F.R. §§ 1002.2(c), 1002.9(a)-(d).

8. On June 1, Alan White applied for a car loan from Deuce Ransome's Slaab dealership. The application stated that the applicant "seeks credit at the lowest available rate." Deuce Ransome's sent out the application for bids to various auto finance companies and banks based on their pre-set lending guidelines. Banco Merica had the winning bid, which was for a 3% APR loan, but which allowed Deuce's to mark up the loan by an additional 300 basis points. Slaab Motor Finance Corp. had placed a bid for a 2.5% APR loan, but with a markup of only 250 basis points allowed. Both bids required a 10% down payment. Alan accepted the loan at 6% APR, signed the paper work, and drove off with a stylish Slaab Albatross convertible.

- **a.** It's now August 1. Does Alan have any claim against Deuce Ransome's Slaab? 15 U.S.C. § 1691(d); 12 C.F.R. §§ 1002.2(c), 1002.2(l), 1002.9(a)-(d).
- **b.** It's still August 1. Does Alan have any claim against Banco Merica? 15 U.S.C. § 1691(d); 12 C.F.R. §§ 1002.2(c), 1002.2(l), 1002.9(a)-(d).

9. You are working in the general counsel's office of Continental Express Bank, N.A., a major credit card lender.

- **a.** ConEx has discovered that there is a high correlation between credit default risk on credit cards and ZIP code. ConEx business people want to update the underwriting guidelines for the firm to simply prohibit lending in those ZIP codes in which credit default risk is high. What do you advise? *See* 12 C.F.R. § 1002.6(a).
- **b.** ConEx's business team now wants to use choice of college major as an underwriting factor, such that it will extend credit on more favorable terms to computer science and organic chemistry majors. As general counsel, what do you advise? *See* 12 C.F.R. § 1002.6(a).

10. You are an Assistant U.S. Attorney for the District of Mississippi. The U.S. Attorney for the District has made clear that she wants to prioritize fair lending enforcement. She mentions to you that Magnolia State Bank has a policy of not making mortgage loans of under $500,000. It does business in Mississippi, where the median home price is well under $500,000 in all but one of the state's counties. Carroll County median home prices are $624,000. Carroll County is 65% white, whereas Mississippi as a whole is 60% white. What are your thoughts on what you would want to know about whether there is a fair lending case here?

11. You are the Chief Compliance Officer at Fast Times Automotive Acceptance Corporation, a non-bank finance company that specializes in making indirect auto loans. Having read CFPB Bulletin 2013-02, will you continue to permit dealer markups? If so, what steps will you take to ensure ECOA compliance? To protect yourself from liability? *See* 15 U.S.C. § 1691c-1; 12 C.F.R. § 1002.15.

CHAPTER 25

TRUTH IN LENDING

I. THE TRUTH IN LENDING ACT

Mandatory disclosure of consumer finance contract terms began to appear with state retail installment sales acts, the first of which was enacted in 1935. A decade before the enactment of the federal Truth in Lending Act of 1968 (TILA), at least 31 states had state-level disclosure regulations for some types of consumer finance. Joseph P. Jordan & James H. Yagla, *Retail Installment Sales: History and Development of Regulation*, 45 Marquette L. Rev. 555, 566 (1962). TILA was Title I of the Consumer Credit Protection Act of 1968 (CCPA). The CCPA was the federal government's first deliberate foray into consumer protection regulation qua consumer protection regulation.[1] TILA was originally paired in the CCPA with two other titles that contained clear substantive term prohibitions, one criminalizing "extortionate credit" (violent loan sharking), and another imposing a federal cap on wage garnishments. In 1976, TILA was amended to include coverage of leases of consumer goods. Today, the CCPA also includes ECOA and the EFTA as well as provisions on credit repair organizations, credit reporting agencies, and debt collection.

TILA itself has evolved from a statute consisting of primarily disclosure requirements to a mix of disclosure requirements and substantive term and process regulations and remedies for violations. Our focus in this chapter is solely the disclosure requirements, but the boundaries between disclosure and substantive term and process regulation can be blurry. A requirement to disclose a particular term means that a product has to have a particular term. And the timing and form of the provision of disclosures shapes the lending process.

TILA's core disclosure requirement is for "creditors" to disclose the cost of credit using a pair of standard metrics: the "finance charge" and the "annual percentage rate" (APR). The logic behind this is explained in TILA's declaration of purpose:

> The informed use of credit results from an awareness of the cost thereof by consumers. It is the purpose of this subchapter to assure a meaningful disclosure of credit terms so that the consumer will be able to compare more readily the various credit terms available to him and avoid the uninformed use of credit. . . .

---

1. Prior regulations relating to the safety and soundness of financial institutions and to military preparedness had collateral consumer protection benefits, but these regulations were never cast as consumer protection regulations.

15 U.S.C. § 1601(a). The standardized metrics of the finance charge and APR facilitate comparison shopping by allowing an apples-to-apples comparison of the costs of credit, at least for similarly structured products.

While disclosure of the finance charge and APR are the core TILA disclosures, TILA disclosures are hardly so limited. TILA generally requires detailed disclosure of all the material terms of extensions of credit. Exactly what has to be disclosed depends on the product. TILA has different rules for two broad categories of credit: **open-end credit plans** (revolving lines of credit, including credit cards), 15 U.S.C. § 1637, and **closed-end credit** (term loans, such as mortgages, auto loans, and payday loans), 15 U.S.C. § 1638. TILA also has additional disclosure provisions applicable specifically to credit cards, home equity lines of credit, 15 U.S.C. § 1637a, high-cost mortgages, 15 U.S.C. § 1639, and reverse mortgages, 15 U.S.C. § 1648.

In this chapter we will not attempt to delve into the full details of each of these product-specific disclosure regimes; these will be addressed in subsequent product-specific chapters. Instead, the focus will be on the core TILA disclosure of the finance charge and the APR. Nonetheless, it is useful to have a general sense of what must be disclosed and when.

A. TILA Disclosures

TILA disclosure requirements apply at three points in time: advertising for credit; when an account is opened; and in periodic billing statements for open-end credit.

For open-end credit plans, creditors are prohibited from advertising any of the terms of the plan unless they also disclose any finance charges and, where applicable, the APR, while for closed-end credit, if a finance charge is expressed as a rate, the APR must be disclosed. 15 U.S.C. §§ 1663-1664.

For both closed-end and open-end credit, there is a more extensive a set of disclosures that must be made before an account is opened or a loan is made. 12 C.F.R. §§ 1026.6, 1026.18.

For closed-end credit the disclosure requirements include: the amount financed; an itemization of the amount financed; the finance charge; the APR; the terms under which the interest rate may vary and any limits thereon if it is a variable rate loan; the payment schedule; the total payments to be made; the total sale price for credit sales (the sum of the cash price plus the finance charge); prepayment charges and rebates; late fees; and any security interest taken. 12 C.F.R. § 1026.18(b).

For open-end credit, the disclosure laundry list is somewhat different. It includes: the APR and whatever various applicable rates exist for different balances or teaser rates; variable-rate information (if applicable); penalty rate information; annual or periodic fees; minimum fees; transaction charges; balance computation method; fees for cash advances, late payments, over-limit transactions, balance transfers, and returned payments; required credit insurance coverage; any available line of credit; and any security interests. 12 C.F.R. § 1026.6(b).

For open-end credit there is also a requirement of periodic statements that include certain additional disclosures that allow the consumer to identify transactions, balances, periodic rates applicable, and the balances to which those rates apply, as well as an itemization of charges imposed. 12 C.F.R. § 1026.7(b). There is no general periodic statement requirement for closed-end credit; such statements are required for mortgages, but do not require disclosures of finance charges or the APR. 12 C.F.R. § 1026.41.

B. Who Is a Creditor?

TILA's disclosure obligations apply to a "creditor," which is a defined term. A creditor must regularly extend credit, meaning that the debtor has a right to deferred payment, *in exchange for a finance charge.* 15 U.S.C. § 1602(g). If the debt is payable in more than four installments, however, a finance charge will be conclusively presumed. *Id.* (This is known as the "**Four Installments Rule.**") This presumption is to prevent merchants from "burying" the cost of credit in the price of the goods sold as a means of evading TILA disclosure. As the Supreme Court has noted,

> For example, two merchants might buy watches at wholesale for $20 [that] normally sell at retail for $40. Both might sell immediately to a consumer who agreed to pay $1 per week for 52 weeks. In one case, the merchant might claim that the price of the watch was $40 and that the remaining $12 constituted a charge for extending credit to the consumer. From the consumer's point of view, the credit charge represents the cost [that] he must pay for the privilege of deferring payment of the debt he has incurred. From the creditor's point of view, much simplified, the charge may represent the return [that] he might have earned had he been able to invest the proceeds from the sale of the watch from the date of the sale until the date of payment. The second merchant might claim that the price of the watch was $52 and that credit was free. The second merchant, like the first, has forgone the profits [that] he might have achieved by investing the sale proceeds from the day of the sale on. The second merchant may be said to have "buried" this cost in the price of the item sold. By whatever name, the $12 differential between the total payments and the price at which the merchandise could have been acquired is the cost of deferring payment.

Mourning v. Family Pub. Svc., Inc., 411 U.S. 356, 366 n.26 (1973). The Four Installments Rule assumes that if a creditor permits payment in more than four installments, that there is a finance charge baked into the purchase price.

In the 1960s and 1970s, when retail credit was still a major component of consumer credit, this was an issue of critical importance. Today, retail credit is less common, and it is usually relatively clear when there has been an extension of credit.

C. What Is a Finance Charge?

The TILA disclosure obligation rests on creditors, but that is only the beginning of the inquiry. Recall at the definition of "creditor" is a party that regularly extends consumer credit that is repayable *either* in more than four installments or "for which the payment of a finance charge is or may be required." 15 U.S.C. § 1602(g). While the number of installments is easy enough to determine, what is a "finance charge"? Both TILA and state-law disclosure requirements as well as many state usury laws key off of the TILA definition of the finance charge, so determining whether a charge is a "finance charge" is critical for determining compliance with these laws.

TILA provides a definition of "finance charge" as "the sum of all charges, payable directly or indirectly by the person to whom the credit is extended, and imposed directly or indirectly by the creditor as an incident to the extension of credit." 15 U.S.C. § 1605(a). Reg Z explains that this means that the finance charge is "the cost of consumer credit as a dollar amount." 12 C.F.R. § 1026.4. Excluded from the finance charge are charges payable in a comparable cash transaction. The finance charge also excludes third-party fees that would not be payable in a comparable cash transaction, unless the creditor either (1) requires the use of a third party (even if the consumer can choose the particular third party) or (2) retains the third-party fee (to the extent retained). 15 U.S.C. § 1605(a); 12 C.F.R. § 1026.4(a)(1). Fees charged by a mortgage broker, however, are always part of the finance charge. 12 C.F.R. § 1026(a)(3).

While this is the general rule, TILA and Reg Z provide a whole set of more specific applications and exceptions. The general idea with the finance charge, however, is to create a single all-in dollar figure for the cost of credit, so that a consumer can know how much he is paying for making a purchase on credit, relative to a cash purchase. This all-in figure means that distinctions between interest and fees disappear. Partitioned pricing is unwound by the finance charge. The result is a single figure that enables comparison pricing.

There are drawbacks to the finance charge as a means of comparing pricing. The finance charge only captures fees that are known at the time of the loan. Thus, a late fee is not generally part of the finance charge, even if there is a high probability that a consumer will pay a late fee. Similarly, with a variable rate loan, it is not possible to know at the time a loan is consummated what the total interest payments—and hence the finance charge—will be. TILA allows the creditor to use the current rate, as long as the estimated nature of the disclosure is itself disclosed. But this means that finance charges are inherently speculative for variable rate loans.

Another limitation to the finance charge is that it does not account for time—that is, it does not account for *when* a fee must be paid. A fee that is payable at the opening of a ten-year loan is treated the same for finance charge purposes as a monthly interest payment that is due in two years or a fee payable at the end of the loan. There is no attempt to take into account the time value of money or the differences in loan terms. Two loans might each have a $10 monthly finance charge, but if one loan is for six months and the other is for a year, the second loan's finance charge will be twice that of the first, even though they cost the same per month.

The following case considers what might be a finance charge and in what circumstances, and why it matters.

Gibson v. Bob Watson Chevrolet-Geo, Inc.

112 F.3d 283 (7th Cir. 1997)

POSNER, *Chief Judge.*

We have consolidated the appeals from the decisions dismissing on the pleadings three class action suits against Chicago-area automobile dealers for violation of the Truth in Lending Act, 15 U.S.C. §§ 1601 *et seq*. These suits are among some fifteen almost identical class actions filed by the same law firm against such dealers. For unexplained reasons the cases, having initially been randomly assigned to different district judges in the Northern District of Illinois, were *not* reassigned to a single judge, as authorized by N.D. Ill. R. 2.31, but remained with the original judges, eleven of whom have ruled on motions to dismiss the complaint or to grant summary judgment for the defendant. Six have denied such motions and five, including the three whose rulings are brought to us by these consolidated appeals, have granted them.

The facts are very simple, and can be illustrated by Gibson's case. She bought a used car from Bob Watson Chevrolet on credit. The dealer gave her a statement captioned "Itemization of Amount Financed." The statement contains a category referred to as "Amounts Paid to Others on Your Behalf," under which appears an entry that reads: "To North American for Extended Warranty $800.00." The dealer admits that a substantial though at present unknown amount of the $800 was retained by him rather than paid over to the company that issued the warranty (North American). The question is whether the failure to disclose this retention violates the Truth in Lending Act.

There are two possible violations. First, when the dealer sells cars for cash rather than on credit, it marks up the warranty less (according to the plaintiffs), and hence retains a smaller amount of the warranty charge. Because the charge by the issuer of the warranty is presumably unaffected by the amount of the dealer's mark-up, the dealer is levying an additional charge on its credit customers that plaintiffs call a "finance charge," which must be disclosed to the customer. 15 U.S.C. §§ 1605(a), 1638(a)(3); 12 C.F.R. § [10]26.18(d) and Pt. [10]26, Supp. I § 4(a); *Cowen v. Bank United of Texas*, FSB, 70 F.3d 937, 940 (7th Cir. 1995).

Second, the Act requires the lender or creditor to provide "a written itemization of the amount financed," including "each amount that is or will be paid to third persons by the creditor [the dealer here] on the consumer's behalf, together with an identification of or reference to the third person." 15 U.S.C. § 1638(a)(2)(B)(iii). The argument that Bob Watson Chevrolet (as before, we're using Gibson's case as typical of all three cases) violated this provision is straightforward, and let us start with it. The amount to be paid to North American on Gibson's behalf is not stated correctly in the written itemization of the amount financed that Gibson received. It is true that the consumer is not entitled to the statement unless he makes a written request for it, § 1638(a)(2)(B); 12 C.F.R. § [10]26.18(c)(2), and there is no indication that Gibson did. But the creditor is allowed to skip this stage and simply provide the itemization of the amount financed without being asked for it. 12 C.F.R. Pt. [10]26, Supp. I § 18(c)(1). That appears to be what Bob Watson Chevrolet did. In any event, it furnished the itemization, and the itemization contains a false representation.

The defendants emphasize quite properly that the Act is not a general prohibition of fraud in consumer transactions or even in consumer credit transactions. Its limited office is to protect consumers from being misled about the cost of credit. If the dealer retains the same amount of the warranty charge on credit purchases as he does on cash purchases, he is not misleading the consumer about the cost of buying on credit. But it is a contested issue whether the retention (mark-up) is the same; and even if it is, this is not a defense to the claim of inaccurate itemization, the second violation charged. Section 1638(a)(2)(B)(iii) is free-standing. It requires disclosure—meaning, we do not understand the defendants to deny, *accurate* disclosure, *Fairley v. Turan-Foley Imports, Inc.*, 65 F.3d 475, 479 (5th Cir. 1995)—of amounts paid to third persons by the creditor on the consumer's behalf, whether or not cash customers pay less. Bob Watson Chevrolet did not accurately disclose the amount that it paid North American for the extended warranty on the car that Gibson purchased. It said it paid $800; in fact it paid less.

The defendants argue that the Federal Reserve Board, the oracle of the Truth in Lending Act, 15 U.S.C. § 1604(a); *Anderson Bros. Ford v. Valencia*, 452 U.S. 205, 219 (1981); *Ford Motor Credit Co. v. Milhollin*, 444 U.S. 555, 565-69 (1980); *McGee v. Kerr-Hickman Chrysler Plymouth, Inc.*, 93 F.3d 380, 383 (7th Cir. 1996); *Cowen v. Bank United of Texas, FSB, supra*, 70 F.3d at 943, has issued an Official Staff Commentary that authorizes the dealers to do what they did here. The commentary (a part of the Federal Reserve Board's Regulation Z) addresses the situation in which the creditor retains a portion of the fee charged to a customer for a service provided by a third party, such as an extended warranty. It provides that "the creditor in such cases may reflect that the creditor has retained a portion of the amount paid to others. For example, the creditor could add to the category 'amount paid to others' language such as '(we may be retaining a portion of this amount).'" 12 C.F.R. Pt. [10]26, Supp. I § 18(c)(1)(iii)(2). The commentary, being limited to the case in which the fee "is payable in the same amount in comparable cash and credit transactions," *id.*, has no bearing on the claim that the dealers in these cases are hiding a finance charge. But as to the other possible violation, the failure to itemize accurately, the defendants contend that the words "may" and "could" show that they can if they want disclose that they are retaining some of the fee but that they are not required to do so. In other words, they read the commentary to say: "You may conceal the fact that you are pocketing part of the fee that is ostensibly for a third party, but if you are a commercial saint and would *prefer* to tell the truth, you may do that too." So interpreted, however, the commentary not only would be preposterous; it would contradict the statute. The only sensible reading of the commentary is as authorizing the dealer to disclose only the fact that he is retaining a portion of the charge, rather than the exact amount of the retention. Even this is a considerable stretch of the statute; and it is as far as, if not farther than, the statute will stretch.

The defendants' only other argument is that they have a safe harbor in form H-3 (another part of Regulation Z), 12 C.F.R. Pt. [10]26, App. H-3. A disclosure that complies with the form is not actionable. 15 U.S.C. §§ 1604(b), 1640(f); 12 C.F.R. Pt. [10]26, Supp. I Introduction P 1. Captioned "Amount Financed Itemization Model Form," the form contains a line for "Amounts paid to others on your behalf," and underneath it a line which reads "$____to (other)." Compliance with the form in Gibson's case would have required Bob Watson Chevrolet to list next to North American's name the actual amount paid to North American for the extended warranty. So the H-3 defense fails too—and for the further and independent reason that the safe harbor is unavailable to disclosures required to be given numerically, such as disclosure of the *amount* financed. 15 U.S.C. § 1604(b).

Two observations, one procedural, the other substantive, remain to be made about the issue of the undisclosed markup as a finance charge, the first alleged violation. In only one of our three cases (Hernandez's) was it actually pressed as a separate violation. In the others it was folded in with the failure-to-itemize claim, perhaps because the latter is a stronger claim but doesn't permit as large an award of damages. 15 U.S.C. § 1640(a). But since we must reverse all three cases with respect to the second violation, so that further proceedings in the district court are necessary in any event, and since the other two cases were dismissed on the pleadings, we do not think that the claim of a hidden finance charge can be deemed waived in those cases by not having been made more perspicuously in the complaints. But, coming to our substantive observation, we emphasize that the claim has merit only if the dealer's markup on third-party charges is *systematically* higher on sales to credit customers than on sales to cash customers. If a dealer merely charges what the traffic will bear, the fact that a *particular* credit customer may be paying a higher mark-up than a *particular* cash customer would not transform the difference in mark-ups into a finance charge; it would have in fact no causal relation to the extension of credit. We cannot find a case that holds this, but it seems clear as a matter of principle; and it may very well describe this case—but the plaintiffs are entitled to an opportunity to show that it does not.

It wouldn't surprise us if the district judges in these three cases, and the judges in the similar cases that have been dismissed, thought that the plaintiffs' law firm is harassing Chicago-area automobile dealers with complaints about purely technical violations of a highly technical and much-criticized statute. Yet it is far from clear that the alleged violations should be regarded as entirely technical, even the violation of the requirement of accurate itemization of third-party charges. The consumer would have a greater incentive to shop around for an extended warranty, rather than take the one offered by the dealer, if he realized that the dealer was charging what the defendants' lawyer described as a "commission," and apparently a very sizable one, for its efforts in procuring the warranty from a third party. Or the consumer might be more prone to haggle than if he thought that the entire fee had been levied by a third party and so was outside the dealer's direct control. Or he might go to another dealer in search of lower mark-ups on third-party charges.

It is true that exposing this little fraud is a benefit only tenuously related to the objectives of the Truth in Lending Act, on which see 15 U.S.C. § 1601 (declaration of purpose). It is almost as great a fraud on cash purchasers as on credit purchasers; yet its exposure will benefit only the latter. (The relation that we are describing as tenuous lies in the fact that the size of the dealer's "commission" may be a clue to the presence of a hidden finance charge.) But statutes often outrun their rationales. We do not know why the drafters wanted third-party transactions listed separately, and by both amount and payee. There may have been a concern that nominal third-party payees might turn out to be affiliates of the creditor, or a desire to help consumers separate credit charges from other charges; the latter goal in particular would tie the requirement a little more securely to the underlying purposes of the statute. But we are just guessing.

The claim that what the dealers were doing here is concealing a finance charge has a closer connection to the Act's purposes. If the amount retained of the fee for an extended warranty or other third-party service is greater in credit transactions than in cash transactions, then in deciding whether to pay cash or buy on credit the consumer will assume that if he pays cash he will have to pay the same additional fee to get the extended warranty; if the facts are as the plaintiffs claim, he would not. The purchaser thinks he'll have to pay $800 for an extended warranty whether he pays cash or buys on credit, whereas if the retention really is smaller on cash purchases than on credit purchases and the third party's fee net of the retention is the same, the customer will not have to pay $800 if he pays cash for the car. This is a type of fraud that goes to the heart of the concerns that actuate the Truth in Lending Act. Cf. *Mourning v. Family Publications Service, Inc.*, 411 U.S. 356, 366-68 (1973).

Anyway the issue is not whether these violations are technical, or whether technical violations should be actionable, or whether consumer class actions should be discouraged, but whether the complaints in these cases state a claim. And since they do, the dismissal of the plaintiffs' state-law fraud claims on the ground that disclosures that comply with the Truth in Lending Act do not violate the Illinois consumer protection laws, 815 ILCS 375/5(4), 505/2, which confer immunity for acts "specifically authorized" by a federal or state agency, 815 ILCS 505/10b(1); *Lanier v. Associates Finance, Inc.*, 114 Ill. 2d 1 (Ill. 1986), was erroneous too. The judgments are therefore reversed with instructions to reinstate the lawsuits. We hope it's not too late for the district court to reassign all the identical Truth in Lending auto dealer class actions to one judge.

REVERSED AND REMANDED.

D. The Annual Percentage Rate

Interest rates are a common way of pricing credit, but it's easy for a creditor to manipulate the interest rate. A creditor can partition the pricing and have the finance charge be part in the way of a fee (or fees) and part in the way of an interest rate. Doing so makes the interest rate look lower. For example, Bob Lawless, a scofflaw used car dealer, might try to sell me a late model Toyota 86 for $10,000, financed by a one-year loan from Lawless Toyota at 10% annual interest, so that over a year I would pay $1,000 in interest on the loan. Alternatively, Lawless could charge 9% interest, but also have a "dealer transfer fee" of $100. I'll end up paying the same amount over a year: $900 interest plus the $100 fee; but if I were comparing financing offers with a straight 10% interest rate, the 9% rate would look cheaper.

Likewise, Lawless might say "10% interest," but then calculate that annual interest using a 300-day year, rather than a 365-day year. That means that the interest that would accrue on a daily basis would be 0.03333%, rather than 0.02739%. The result would be that over a year I would pay $1,216.67 in interest, rather than $1,000 in interest if I made no periodic payments. Alternatively, suppose it is a six-month loan. Lawless might state that there is a 10% interest rate, but that rate means 10% over six months, not 10% over a year. In other words, the annual interest rate would actually be 20% (or higher with compounding)!

Lawless's crafty tricks don't end there. Lawless might play around with interest compounding. **Compounding**, you'll recall from Chapter 22, refers to interest accruing on interest and contrasts with **simple interest**. Simple interest means that interest is applied only to the original loan balance, and not to accrued interest. A $10,000 loan at a 10% simple interest annually and no periodic payments by the borrower will produce interest charges of $1,000 over a year.

But now suppose that the loan compounds on a monthly basis. This means that interest will be calculated every month and added to the loan balance on which interest will accrue the next month. Thus, in the first month, there will be $83.33 of interest, which is $10,000 at the *monthly* rate of 10% ÷ 12. That means that for the second month, interest will accrue on a balance of $10,083.33, again at a monthly rate of 10% ÷ 12, resulting in $84.03 in interest. Thus, in the third month interest will now accrue on a balance of $10,167.36, etc. After a year, there will be total interest charges of $1,047.13 with monthly compounding, as compared to $1,000 with simple interest. The equivalent simple interest rate would be 10.4713%. And if the compounding were done daily on a 365-day year, there would be interest charges of $1,051.56. The equivalent simple interest rate would be 10.5156%. Compounding increases interest charges without increasing the way in which one states the "rate."

Lawless could also mess around with the balance on which interest accrues. For example, he might charge 10% annual interest on a 365-day year, but apply that 10% to a balance that is different (and larger) than the actual balance. For example, assume you pay down the loan by $500 every month, so that the loan will be paid off in 20 months. After one month, the loan balance is $9,500, and after two months the balance is $9,000, etc. Lawless, however, might charge interest not on the new, declining balance, but on the original balance of $10,000 until the loan is paid off. If you paid interest only on your actual balances, you would pay $875 in interest. But with Lawless's method, you would pay $1,666.67 in interest.

If the idea of toying with the balance on which interest accrues seems farfetched to you, consider a technique used by most credit card lenders—computing interest on an "average daily balance." Unlike with a car loan, the balance on a credit card loan will fluctuate during the month. Thus, for a 30-day billing period, there might be a balance of $1,000 for the first ten days, then a balance of $1,500 for the next ten days, then a balance of $2,000 for the last ten days, after which the consumer gets a billing statement. If the consumer does not pay the bill in full during the grace period (a "short pay"), then interest will accrue and appear as part of the balance on the next monthly billing statement.

Let's say that the consumer pays down $1,800 of the $2,000 balance, so that only $200 remains outstanding, and that the consumer makes no purchases the following month. What is the bill going to be the next month? The consumer might think that because the outstanding balance is $200, that is the balance on which interest would accrue. If interest were at 12% annually, that would be $2 for a month. In fact, however, under an "average daily balance" calculation, interest would accrue on the average daily balance during the month prior to that first billing statement. That average daily balance for that month was $1,500, so there would be $15 in interest accruing, not $2.

The point here is that there are lots of ways for a creditor to manipulate interest rates because the mere statement of an "interest rate" doesn't actually tell the whole story. It doesn't account for fees, it doesn't say the time period over which the rate is computed, it doesn't say how the balance to which the rate is applied is computed, and it doesn't say anything about compounding.

TILA's solution to this problem is a standardized all-in measure of credit costs called the "**annual percentage rate**" or "APR." The APR is a standard unit price for a finance charge. It is "a measure of the cost of credit, expressed as a yearly rate, that relates the amount and timing of value received by the consumer to the amount and timing of payments made." 12 C.F.R. § 1026.22(a). While the APR is expressed as a rate, it is almost always different (and higher than) from the interest rate on a credit product because the APR accounts for certain fees and other finance charges and for the compounding of interest. In other words, the APR is an attempt to measure the effective, rather than the nominal, cost of credit.[2] TILA requires disclosure of the APR in advertising and marketing materials that state the cost of credit, as well as in disclosures made when opening a creditor-debtor relationship and in any periodic billing statements.

The APR is computed slightly differently for open-end and closed-end credit. For open-end credit, such as credit cards and home equity lines of credit, as well as for balloon payment products such as most payday loans, the APR is calculated by taking the finance charge (*F*) for a period (*P*) (expressed as a number of days), dividing it by the balance (*B*) on which the finance charge was levied, and then multiplying that by the number of periods in a year:

$$APR = \frac{(F)}{(B)} \times \frac{365}{(P)}$$

Thus, if a two-week loan of \$100 had a finance charge of \$8, the APR would be (\$8/\$100) × (365/14) = 209%. Similarly, a \$1,000 per month finance charge on a \$100,000 30-year loan would be 12%.

Let's return, now, to the Lawless loan. (Ignore for the time being that it is a closed-end loan, not an open-end loan.) What is the APR? Our first challenge will be figuring out what the finance charge is. Because the APR is keyed to the finance charge, the definition of the finance charge is critical for the calculation of the APR. Let's suppose that Lawless is charging 10% interest on a one-year loan, compounded daily *and* also a \$100 dealer transfer fee that is charged only on credit transactions. Let's also assume that the Lawless loan is a balloon loan, with no periodic payments (that's the assumption that will let us use the open-end formula successfully). That means that there would be a finance charge on the loan of \$1,151.56: \$1,056.56 in interest charges plus the \$100 transfer fee. Plugging that into our equation, we get an APR of 11.5156%:

2. Confusingly, the term "APR" is often used in a non-technical way to mean "simple annual interest rate," as opposed to an "effective APR," which means something more like the legal APR under TILA—a rate that accounts for fees and compounding. Adding to the terminological confusion, we might speak of an "effective APR" that is different from the actual legal APR, namely a retrospective measure of the cost of credit that would include fees that are not included in the APR, such as late fees. While such a term has no legal significance, it is a potentially useful way of comparing all-in costs of credit.

$$APR = 11.5156\% = \frac{(1{,}151.56)}{(10{,}000.00)} \times \frac{365}{(365)}$$

Now let's complicate this a bit. Suppose that our loan is now a three-year balloon loan for $10,000, with 10% interest compounded daily, and also a $100 dealer transfer fee. Total interest over three years would be $3,498.03, and the fee is still $100, so the finance charge is $3,598.03. Our annualization factor is different now too. It's 365/1095 because the loan is over three years. Thus, we get an APR of 11.9934%, with the compound interest driving the increase.

$$APR = 11.9934\% = \frac{(3598.03)}{(10{,}000.00)} \times \frac{365}{(1095)}$$

Because the APR is based on the finance charge, it will automatically reflect any type of compounding used. Similarly, days of the year are not an issue for the APR because the calculation uses the actual days in the year (or allows for use of a stylized 360-day year, the difference of which is minimal relative to a 365- or 366-day year).

The APR is an annualization of the finance charge as a percentage of the original loan balance. The second part of the equation, 365/(*P*) or 360/(*P*), is an annualization factor. Because the APR is an annualized rate, short-term extensions of credit have a larger annualization factor. Assuming a 364-day year, a one-week extension of credit has an annualization factor of 52, while a two-week extension of credit has a factor of 26, and with a 360-day year, a one-month (assumed to be 30 days) extension has an annualization factor of 12. This means that the APR is a very good measure for comparing the costs of extensions of credit with similar durations, but a poor measure for comparing the costs of short-term versus long-term credit because the differences in the APR for credit of substantially different terms will be driven heavily by the annualization factor.

Note that the APR formula depends not just on the calculation of the finance charge as an absolute amount and on the period of the extension of credit, but also on the calculation of the balance on which the finance charge may be applied. While the calculation of the balance is often straightforward, creditors have significant flexibility to specify the balance that is to be used for APR calculation purposes. Such a balance need not be the actual balance owed on the loan. For example, a creditor could use an average two-month running balance as the basis for determining the balance to which a finance charge is applied. While this is prohibited for credit cards, it is permitted for other types of credit. 15 U.S.C. § 1637(j)(1).

APR calculation on closed-end credit is a lot more complicated. To see why it would be, consider the Lawless car loan again. It's a closed-end loan, and there are, presumably, required periodic loan payments. So the periodic payments are decreasing the loan balance, while interest is still compounding. Accounting for the periodic payment is tricky because one has to figure out how they are applied in terms of amortization. Are they going to principal, interest or both? And this is where things get quite mathy. The following paragraphs explain how the calculation works, but here's the thing: no human being ever actually performs the calculation on closed-end credit because it's so darn complicated. If you understand the calculation of the APR on open-end credit, you understand both the benefits of the APR and its shortcomings, and that's enough for our purposes. But if you're really dying to know how the calculation works on closed-end credit, here goes.

TILA requires the use of the "actuarial method of allocating payments made on a debt between the amount financed and the amount of the finance charge, pursuant to which a payment is applied first to the accumulated finance charge and the balance is applied to the unpaid amount financed" or other methods permitted by regulation. 15 U.S.C. § 1606(a)(1). Regulation Z, which implements TILA, permits both the "actuarial" method and what is called the "United States Rule" or "U.S. Rule method."[3] The major differences between the methods are:

(1) the U.S. Rule does not capitalize (compound) interest during the amortization of the loan, while the actuarial method does. This means that the U.S. Rule will produce higher APRs because the finance charge is being divided by a smaller balance quotient that does not include interest.
(2) the U.S. Rule does not permit for negative amortization, while the actuarial method does.
(3) The actuarial method counts the time unit using a special calendar (the "Federal calendar") in Appendix J to Regulation Z. Depending on the frequency of payments, a 360- or 365-day year is used. The U.S. Rule does not specify the calendar method used.

What this means is that the APR will frequently not match the interest rate. If the actuarial method is used, the APR will almost never match the interest rate, not least because it will frequently not correspond with the way a lender actually computes loan payments. The U.S. Rule can produce an APR that matches the interest rate if there are no finance charges other than interest, but this requires the lender to use the same calendar method for calculating the APR and the interest rate.

There are four commonly used calendar methods: actual/actual; actual/365; 30/360; and actual/360. The first annualizes by dividing the number of days in a period by the number of days in a year, adjusting for leap years as necessary. The second method assumes a 365-day year, irrespective of leap years. The third method, the 30/360 method, used for corporate bonds, U.S. Agency bonds, and mortgage-backed securities, assumes that all months are 30 days and then uses a 360-day year for ease of calculation. The final method annualizes by dividing the actual number of days in a period by a 360-day year. The lower denominator results in a rate calculation that benefits the lender by producing a lower APR (because of a lower annualization factor) and a higher yield on the loan because an actual year's worth of borrowing results in over a year's worth of interest.

3. The U.S. Rule derives from *Story v. Livingston*, 38 U.S. 359 (1839).

Appendix J to Regulation Z explains both the U.S. Rule and the actuarial method. There is one paragraph explaining the U.S. Rule and 15 pages of the Code of Federal Regulations detailing the complex formulas for the actuarial method, as well as extensive staff commentary. In addition, the Office of the Comptroller of the Currency has designed a computer program called APRWIN that is the standard method for APR validation. APRWIN uses only the actuarial method.

All of this is to say that calculating the APR on a closed-end loan is not a simple matter and involves technical details beyond the scope of this text. For our purposes, it is only necessary to know that compliance issues with APR disclosure for closed-end loans are surprisingly complicated and that APRs on closed-end loans may not be truly comparable with each other.

E. TILA Liability

At the end of the day, what's the importance of compliance with TILA and Reg Z's technical rules? It's a liability question.

There is a private right of action under TILA, but it does not extend to TILA advertising violations. 15 U.S.C. § 1640 (private right of action does not cover Part C of subchapter I of Chapter 41 of Title 15). Other disclosure problems are actionable, although TILA recognizes the complexity of the calculation and forgives "small" errors made in good faith. *E.g.*, 12 CFR §§ 1026(a)(2), 1026(a)(4).

TILA general liability for individual plaintiffs is the sum of the actual damages caused by the violation, statutory damages of twice the finance charge, and costs and attorney's fees. 15 U.S.C. § 1640(a). TILA statutory damages vary by type of credit. TILA also imposes minimum and maximum limits on the statutory damages that vary by type of credit. For open-end credit plans not secured by real property, the statutory damages are set at a minimum of $500 or maximum of $5,000 for unless there is a pattern of violations established, in which case the cap does not bind. For other credit transactions—closed-end or open-end and secured by real property—the minimum and maximum are $400 and $4,000 respectively.

For class actions, TILA again gives actual damages, statutory damages, and costs and attorney's fees, but imposes a cap on statutory damages of the lesser of $1 million or 1% of the net worth of the creditor.

TILA's *general* remedial provisions are rather weak. (We will see that there are some specific provisions for certain transactions that have somewhat stronger remedies.) Actual damages from a disclosure violation are likely to be small, and the statutory damages are capped. The real bite is likely to be from costs and attorney's fees. Remember, however, that a TILA violation might also be a predicate for other causes of action—state UDAP suits or even possibly a civil RICO suit, which brings with it treble damages.

A final thing to keep in mind about TILA. A TILA violation does not void a contract. TILA and Reg Z do not affect the validity or enforceability of contracts under state and federal law. 15 U.S.C. § 1610(d). A contract term that is never disclosed and is not imputed by statute is unlikely to be enforceable—because the parties never agreed on it. But it is possible for terms to be disclosed, just not in the locations and formats mandated by TILA and Reg Z. Such terms would presumably be enforceable, but would create a TILA cause of action.

Problem Set 25

1. "Slick" Jimmy Feinerman has opened up a new Slaab auto dealership and plans to offer dealer financing to buyers. He knows that to comply with the Truth in Lending Act he will have to disclose finance charges to borrowers. He's come to you to consult about exactly what is included in the finance charge he must disclose. What do you tell him regarding the following types of charges?

- **a.** Jimmy plans to charge interest on the loans. *See* 15 U.S.C. § 1605(a)(1); 12 C.F.R. § 1026.4(b)(1).
- **b.** Jimmy plans to charge consumers if he obtains a credit report on them before deciding to extend credit. *See* 15 U.S.C. § 1605(a)(4); 12 C.F.R. § 1026.4(b)(4).
- **c.** Jimmy wants to offer his customers single-payment credit life insurance—in exchange for paying an up-front premium, the debt they owe on the car loan will be forgiven in the event of their death. *See* 15 U.S.C. § 1605(a)(5); 12 C.F.R. §§ 1026.4(b)(7), 1026.4(d)(1).
- **d.** Jimmy intends to charge a $30 fee for recording the lien on the car, although the recording office only charges him $20. *See* 12 C.F.R. §§ 1026.4(b)(4), 1026.4(e)(1).
- **e.** If the consumer is late on a payment, Jimmy will charge a $35 late fee. *See* 12 C.F.R. § 1026.4(c)(2).
- **f.** Jimmy mentions that he offers a discount of 3% on the purchase price of the car if the down payment is made in cash or by check. *See* 12 C.F.R. §§ 1026.4(b)(9), 1026.4(c)(8).
- **g.** Jimmy charges a "dealer excess reserve," a markup of 5% on all cars on which he does not provide the financing. *See Gibson v. Bob Watson Chevrolet-Geo.*

2. Slick Jimmy (from problem 1) also plans to offer financing through the International Automotive Acceptance Corp. The loans will be made directly by IAAC, with Jimmy serving as a broker. Which of the following have to be disclosed per TILA?

- **a.** The brokerage fee of $50 for IAAC loans, $40 of which is retained by Jimmy and $10 of which goes to IAAC. *See* 12 C.F.R. § 1026.4(a)(1).
- **b.** Jimmy's "processing fee" of $20 for IAAC loans. *See* 12 C.F.R. §§ 1026.4(a)(1)-(2).

3. Slick Jimmy (from problems 1 and 2) thinks he has a trick for getting more consumers to come to his Slaab dealership. He gets relatively few cash buyers; most of his customers need financing. Deuce thinks he can lure more in by offering them a choice of 0% financing or a rebate against the purchase price of a car. "We'll offset the lower financing costs with higher sticker prices, and the consumers won't ever see those until they show up at the dealership," he says. "Anyone who asks for a price quote in advance will just happen to find that we no longer have that particular vehicle in stock when they show up." For example, Jimmy tells you a late model Slaab sells for $20,000 with a standard loan being at 3% for 5 years. Jimmy's planning on raising the sticker price to $23,000 but then offering 0% APR financing or a $3,000 rebate (with the loan at 3%). Will Jimmy's trick fly under TILA? 12 C.F.R. § 1026.4(a).

4. Eric Yee is refinancing the mortgage on his house. It is a $200,000, 30-year fully amortized mortgage with a 5% fixed interest rate with two points paid. Eric paid a $1,000 mortgage broker's fee as part of the refinancing as well as the following closing costs: appraisal ($300), credit report ($30), closing fee ($220), title search fee ($250), flood determination ($30), processing fee ($700), attorney's fees ($600), state refinancing taxes ($500), homeowner's insurance (first year required by lender) ($400), and two months' escrow deposit for property taxes and mortgage insurance ($400). What is the finance charge on Eric's loan? *See* 12 C.F.R. § 1026.4.

5. Amy Kurtz has a credit card from Mastodon National Bank. Revolved a balance of $1,000 last month. Her finance charge for the month was $20. What is her APR? *See* 15 U.S.C. § 1606; 12 C.F.R. § 1026.14.

6. QuikiCash is a small-dollar lender that offers its customers a product called a "Revolving Credit Plan," a revolving line of credit of $500 with a biweekly billing cycle date. Loans under the Revolving Credit Plan are made in $50 increments. The Revolving Credit Plan has two main elements to its pricing:

- an interest rate disclosed as 26% APR, assessed on average daily balances during a billing cycle;
- a "Required Account Protection Fee," a mandatory fee of $10 for every $50 in principal balance outstanding that is charged once every billing cycle date. The RAPF is described in the transaction documents as follows:

> Required Account Protection Fee: If you [the borrower] become unemployed due to a lay-off or reduction in force ("lay-off") by your employer, for the period of time you are unemployed, you will not be charged the Account Protection Fee or interest from the date that you provide written confirmation of your lay-off from the employer or governmental unemployment office for a period not to exceed 12 consecutive months. To be eligible to receive the suspension of payment under the Account Protection provision, you must pay all past due and current billing statement charges including minimum payment due for the current Billing Statement, which will be due on the next Payment Due Date. If your account is past due or you don't make your minimum payment for the charges due on your current billing statement by the Due Date, your account will continue to accrue interest and be charged all the fees due until you pay all past due and current Billing Statement amounts. When either you become employed again or the 12-consecutive-month period expires, i) interest will accrue in accordance with the terms of this Agreement starting from the new employment date, and ii) you will be charged an Account Protection Fee if you have a balance at the end of the business day preceding your next billing cycle date as set forth in in this Agreement. . . . If your loan was approved based upon your receipt of retirement or social security payments and your retirement or social security payments are suspended, Lender will suspend your interest payments and Account Protection Fee for the period of such suspension not to exceed 12 consecutive months upon receipt of written verification. If you fail to provide sufficient verification of your unemployment status or suspension of retirement or social security benefits,

> Lender reserves the right to assess the Account Protection Fee and interest from the date such charges were suspended.

The CFPB has received a large number of complaints by QuikiCash's borrowers and has commenced an investigation of QuikiCash. You are an enforcement attorney for the CFPB working on the investigation. What potential issues do you see with the QuikiCash Revolving Credit Plan? *See* 15 U.S.C. §§ 1605, 1606(a)(2), 1631, 1637(a)-(b).

CHAPTER 26

AUTO LENDING

Americans need cars. Most housing and places of business in the United States are built on an assumption of automotive transportation. As a result, 90% of Americans drive to work.

Cars, however, are expensive. Cars are one of the largest single purchases most households make other than home purchases. The average new car sold in 2017 for $34,670, or more than half of the median family's annual pre-tax income.[1] Even used cars aren't cheap. The average used car sales price in 2017 was $20,009.[2] Accordingly, most Americans do not purchase their vehicles in cash. Instead, they finance them. Eighty-five percent of new car sales and 54% of used car sales were financed in 2017.[3] Most of the financing is in the form of loans, but over a quarter of financing for new cars is in the form of leases.[4] (Leases are rare for used cars.) As of the end of 2017 there were around 110 million auto loans outstanding, with a total balance of $1.2 trillion.[5]

A car purchase is a complicated transaction that has several different components. Our concern in this chapter is solely is on the financing of the vehicle. It is important, however, to understand that the financing is not entirely separable from the rest of the transaction. In terms of the transaction, there is first the vehicle purchase itself and potentially a trade-in (sale) of another vehicle, financing for the purchase, and the purchase of various warranties, insurance products, and service contracts. While each of these items is a separate and negotiable transaction, the pricing of one is often linked to the pricing of another. Thus, a cheaper sales price might be linked to taking financing from a particular source or a particular trade-in value.

In recent years it has become possible to obtain information about vehicle pricing (including dealer price quotes) over the Internet, but that information is of limited use for consumers in shopping for cars because a consumer's concern is the all-in cost of a purchase (car, trade-in, financing, add-ons), rather than the cost of any particular component. Such all-in pricing is virtually impossible to obtain absent substantial transaction costs, namely appearing at a dealership in person and negotiating the transaction with a salesperson. In particular, auto loan pricing is based

1. National Association of Auto Dealers, NADA Data 2017 at 23.
2. *Id.* at 27.
3. *Id.* at 36.
4. *Id.*
5. N.Y. Federal Reserve Bank Quarterly Report on Household Debt and Credit.

Figure 26.1 Finance and Insurance Department and Service Department Contributions to Dealer Profits[6]

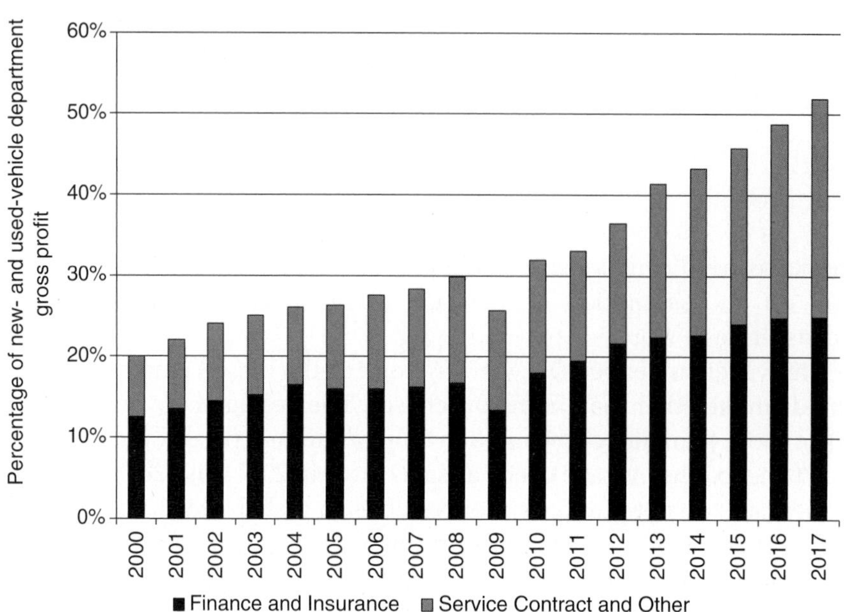

in part on individual consumer risk, so the only way for a consumer to compare financing prices is to go through the loan application process with multiple lenders. For dealer financing, this means that the consumer must complete almost the entire sales and financing process: picking a vehicle, negotiating the price, negotiating a trade-in value, and then and only then submitting a financing application at the dealer's financing and insurance (F&I) office. The huge transaction costs in this process mean that consumers are often rationally unwilling to shop around for better financing prices.

The increased availability of vehicle pricing information has decreased dealers' margins on vehicle sales by enabling consumers to negotiate better sales prices. This in turn has put pressure on dealers to generate more profits from financing and insurance and service contract products, making the F&I office an increasingly significant profit source for dealers. (*See* Figure 26.1.)

I. STRUCTURE OF THE AUTO LOAN MARKET

Dealers play an unusually important role in auto transactions. There are nearly 17,000 new auto dealers nationwide, although many dealers are parts of chains; there are nearly 8,000 individual owners of dealerships, with some chains having over 50 dealerships.[7] A typical dealer employs around 70 employees,[8] so no individual

6. National Association of Auto Dealers.
7. National Association of Auto Dealers, NADA Data 2017 at 17-18.
8. *Id.* at 33.

dealership is a particularly large business in terms of employees. The average dealership sells just over 900 new cars and 700 used cars per year, so there are relatively few sales on any given day.

State laws prohibit virtually all direct sales of vehicles by manufacturers; instead vehicles must be sold through third-party dealers. Dealers will frequently offer financing for vehicles, although in many cases the dealer is essentially an origination agent for an institutional lender that will purchase the loan from the dealer, rather than the ultimate lender itself.

There are three main types of dealers: franchises, independents, and buy-here-pay-here dealers. **Franchise dealers** have the exclusive franchise to sell or lease a particular brand of new vehicle. They will frequently also sell used vehicles and have a service department in order to perform warranty and recall service. Franchise dealers will generally sell the loans that they make to unaffiliated third parties shortly after making the transaction.

Independent dealers are not affiliated with particular manufacturers and are limited to selling used cars. Some also operate service departments. When independent dealers make loans they too generally sell them to unaffiliated third parties.

Buy-here-pay-here dealers sell older, high-mileage used cars to consumers with poor credit. Buy-here-pay-here dealers generally retain the loans they make (hence, "pay here") or transfer them to an affiliated buy-here-pay-here finance company. Buy-here-pay-here loans typically have very short terms and very high repossession rates.

The dealer is the original creditor in almost all auto finance transactions. When the dealer makes and retains the loan, the dealer is known as a **direct auto lender**. (The same would be true for financing provided directly to the consumer by a third-party source.) Dealers, however, are generally incentivized to sell the loans they make because they do not want to have to deal with the loan servicing and because of the funding costs of the loans. Dealers themselves have to borrow funds to purchase the cars in their inventory (known as "floor plan financing"). Dealers look to repay their floor plan lender from their vehicle sales, but if the dealer is itself providing the funds for the consumer to purchase the vehicle, it cannot repay the floor plan lender. Therefore, dealers sell the loan to a third-party lender. A third-party loan purchaser is known as an **indirect auto lender**.

There are several sources of indirect financing for auto loans. The market is somewhat different for new and used car loans. For new car loans, 29% of financing in 2017 came from banks. Another 52% of new car financing comes from **captive lenders**. A captive is a financing company (which may in fact be a bank), that is wholly owned by the car manufacturers (**original equipment manufacturers** or **OEMs**), such as Ford Motor Credit or American Honda Finance Company. By providing financing to purchasers of the associated manufacturer's cars, captives help facilitate manufacturers' sales. Credit unions do a surprisingly brisk business in auto lending; it is one of their mainstay businesses. They account for 13% of new car loans. Independent finance companies handle another 5% of new car loans. (See Figure 26.2.)

Figure 26.2 Market Share for New Car Financing in 2017[9]

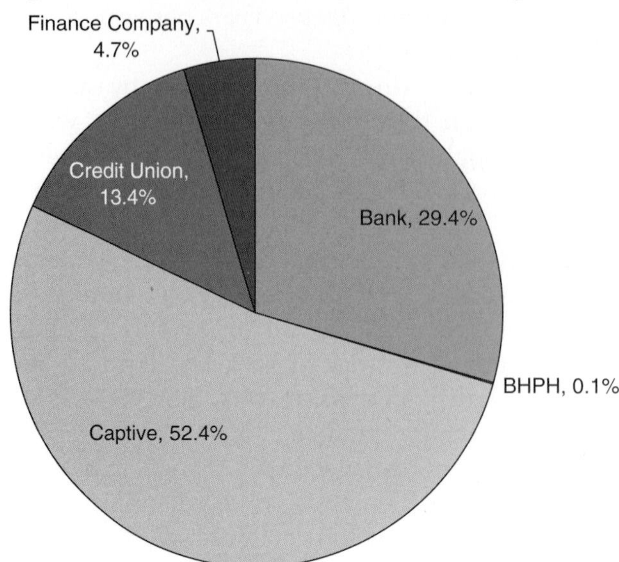

The used car market has different financing sources. Captives play only a small role in the market, which is dominated by banks and credit unions. Finance companies play a larger role here than in the new car market, and BHPH dealers also have a notable market share. (See Figure 26.3.) Shares of the overall auto financing market are shown in Figure 26.4.

Figure 26.3 Market Share for Used Car Financing in 2017[10]

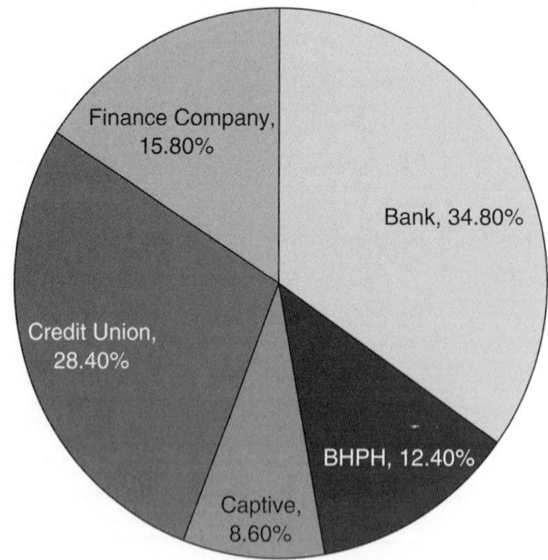

9. National Association of Auto Dealers, NADA Data 2017 at 37.
10. Experian, State of the Automotive Finance Markets Q4 2017, at 13.

Figure 26.4 Total Market Share for Auto Financing in 2017[11]

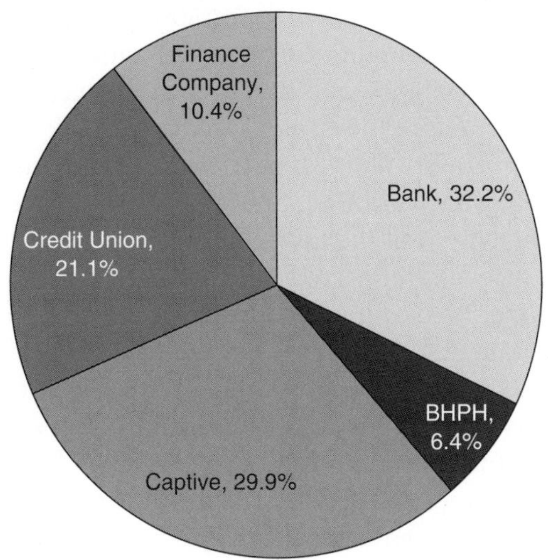

The auto finance market overall is not very concentrated. The top 20 lenders in 2015 accounted for 48% of all financing (75% of new and 38% of used), with no single lender having more than around 6% of the market.[12]

II. AUTO LOAN FINANCING PROCESS

There are three basic processes by which a consumer gets financing for an auto loan. First, the consumer can simply apply and get pre-approved for a loan separate and apart from the vehicle purchase. Thus, the consumer might first pre-apply for a loan from a bank or finance company that advertises over the Internet. The consumer will submit various information and authorize the lender to pull a credit report, after which the lender will decide whether to approve the consumer for a loan, how large of a loan, and on what terms. The consumer is not obligated to actually take the loan, and having that loan offer in hand gives the consumer substantial bargaining leverage if the consumer chooses to explore the other financing processes.

The second financing process is for the consumer to apply for a loan from the dealer in a direct lending situation, while the third is to apply for a loan from the dealer in an indirect lending situation. Direct lending is not available with most dealers, but the initial process is the same for both direct and indirect lending. Dealers will generally not discuss financing with the borrower until the borrower has selected a vehicle and any optional equipment and trade-ins. This means that the consumer must first meet and negotiate with a salesperson.

---

11. *Id.*
12. Experian, State of the Automotive Finance Market, Fourth Quarter 2015, at 15.

After the terms of the vehicle purchase and trade-in have been worked out, the consumer is transferred to another dealer employee in the F&I office (sometimes called the business office), to complete the purchase paperwork and to negotiate any financing and insurance, warranty, and service contract products.

In a direct lending situation, the dealer will simply take the consumer's credit application, pull a credit report and possibly income verification, and underwrite the loan itself, accounting for various manufacturer incentives, the amount of the down payment, and the length of the loan contract.

Dealers generally use standardized information system platforms, such as Dealer Track, Route One, or CUDL, to collect credit application information in a single data file. That data file can then be routed to one or more potential indirect lenders, which will respond with offers to purchase the loan based on their own underwriting. This enables the dealer to match the consumer with an indirect lender that is willing to purchase the loan.

The indirect lenders' offers will specify the minimum interest rate (the **buy rate**) and other terms the loan must have for the indirect lender to purchase. The dealer, however, is free to mark up the loan above the buy rate. That is, if the lender's buy rate is 3.00%, the dealer might charge 4.25%. This 1.25% difference is known as a **dealer markup** or a **dealer reserve** or **dealer participation**. The indirect lender generally allows the dealer to retain some or all of the markup (paid over time out of loan payments or as an up-front flat fee). Indirect lenders will sometimes cap dealer markups because higher dealer markups increase the riskiness of the loan; higher markups correlate with higher rates of default and repossession.

It's important to recognize the psychological pressures of an auto financing purchase. The consumer has already engaged in a lengthy sales process that has resulted in the consumer choosing a car that he wants, including a test drive. On average a consumer has already spent over an hour and a half at the dealership at this point.[13] The consumer is now psychologically invested in getting that car. Only after the showroom process and sales negotiation about price and trade-in, etc., is the consumer taken to the F&I office, where standard practice is to present the consumer with all products for which he qualifies. This means that the consumer will be presented with dozens of insurance, extended warranty, "protection," and service plan products, all *before* the loan terms are discussed.

The consumer has little, if any, basis for evaluating these add-on products on the spot. Extended warranties, for example, might have dozens of pages of disclosures detailing exactly what is covered and on what terms. The consumer is, therefore, likely to be susceptible to advice from the F&I representative, and not to ask too many questions because the consumer is, at this point, anxious to complete the transaction and drive off with his new car.

At last, into this dynamic, when the consumer just wants to be done with the transaction, comes the consumer's loan offer. Unless the consumer has another offer in hand, the consumer is stuck with the offers produced by the dealer through its

13. *See 2009 F&I Statistics*, F&I Magazine 26 (Dec. 2008).

indirect lending relationships. Those offers will be the indirect lenders' buy rates plus the dealer markup. The dealer is not looking to get the consumer into the cheapest loan, but into the loan with the largest dealer markup, which may or may not be the cheapest loan.

If the consumer balks, the dealer might lower its markup, but there is no competition among the indirect lenders for the consumer. Instead, the indirect lenders are competing for the dealer's business, and they compete by offering the dealer larger markups or more flexibility on underwriting the loan to approve deals faster. Herein lies the key problem in the auto financing market: competition in indirect auto lending is generally not for consumers, but for dealers. The nature of the dealer-centric sale-and-financing process means that there is little competition on financing unless the consumer has the savvy to get preapproved for a loan prior to shopping for the car.

Ultimately, if the consumer wants the car, the consumer will have to take the loan terms, and given the sunk transaction costs of searching and negotiating for the car and going through the F&I process, the consumer is likely to take the loan. The result is that consumers end up paying supracompetitive rates on auto loans: consumers who purchased cars in 2009 paid an extra $26 billion in interest due to dealer markups that averaged 101 basis points for new cars and 291 basis points for used cars.[14] Most consumers are unaware that dealers are even allowed to mark up loan rates: hence the use of the opaque terminology of "dealer reserve" and "dealer participation," rather than "markup."

III. BUY-HERE-PAY-HERE FINANCING

Borrowers with poor credit scores are known as "subprime" borrowers, whereas borrowers with good credit scores are known as "prime" borrowers. A specialized market has arisen to serve borrowers with poor credit. These are so-called buy-here-pay-here (BHPH) dealers—used car dealers that provide the financing themselves (or through a dealer-affiliated finance company).[15] Given the poor credit quality of the borrowers, it should be no surprise that BHPH companies charge higher rates for financing (25% APR is typical), that they require high down payments, and that the cars they finance tend to be older, high-mileage cars that are sold at a substantial markup (around 70% more than the dealer paid for the car).

This pricing is necessitated because BHPH dealers tend to have very high default rates. Around a quarter of BHPH loans default, often after only a few months. Contrast this with default rates of around 2%-3% for indirect loans and 1%-2% for direct loans on new cars. Therefore, BHPH dealers put a premium on being able to repossess the car quickly upon a payment default. As a result, most BHPH dealers will equip vehicles with tracking systems and starter kill switches in order to locate

14. Center for Responsible Lending.
15. There are some BHPH finance companies that serve multiple dealers, but these are the exception.

and disable the car for easier repossession. Once repossessed, the same car can be sold to another consumer, as long as the car still runs.

A typical BHPH dealer does not post prices on cars on the lot. Instead, when a consumer comes into the dealership, the question the salesperson has is how much the consumer can afford in terms of a weekly or biweekly payment. Once the consumer indicates his price range, then the salesperson will show the consumer the cars that will work in that price range. The consumer, then, is never really negotiating either purchase price or loan terms. Instead, the consumer is expressing a willingness to pay and allowing the dealer to maximize on that willingness to pay. In such a situation there is no competition or market discipline protecting the consumer.

IV. AUTO LOAN TERMS

Given all of the complications in the structure of the auto financing market, the terms of auto loans fortunately tend to be straightforward. Auto loans are virtually always term loans. The maturity tends to be between two and seven years, with most being between four and six years. The average loan term in 2017 was 67 months for a new car and 61 months for a used car.[16] In recent years, a trend has been emerging toward longer-term loans, particularly for borrowers with lower credit scores. CFPB, *Growth in Longer-Term Auto Loans,* Nov. 2017. The longer term reduces the monthly payment but increases the total cost of the loan. Auto loans generally are fully amortizing loans and are freely prepayable. Both fixed-rate and variable-rate loans are common for auto loans. Auto loans will also often have an initial low-interest-rate period after which the full rate will kick in.

The size of auto loans varies based on whether a vehicle is new or used. New vehicle loans tend to be for over $25,000, with used car loans being somewhat smaller, perhaps $17,000. One of the unusual features of auto finance is that the loan-to-value ratio (LTV) is almost always greater than 100% when the loan is made. That is, the loan is for more than the value of the car. LTVs on new cars tend to be around 110%, while those on used cars tend to be around 120%.

LTVs above 100% are exceedingly rare in other areas of asset-backed lending, such as mortgages. The reason for the high LTVs in auto finance is simple: the loan is not just financing the purchase of the car, but also financing a number of "add-on" products, and the value of the car drops substantially as soon as the consumer drives it off the lot.

The add-on products covered include not only additional pieces of equipment: racing stripes, wheel locks, etc., but also things such as LoJack systems, anti-theft devices, paint protection, extended warranties (additional warranties that extend beyond the manufacturer's warranty in either coverage or duration), and **Guaranteed Auto Protection (GAP) insurance.**

---

16. Federal Reserve Economic Data, Average Maturity of Used Car Loans at Finance Companies; Federal Reserve Economic Data, Average Maturity of New Car Loans at Finance Companies.

GAP insurance is an insurance policy that covers the amount on a financing obligation between the car's value and the insurance coverage on another policy. Thus, if there is a total vehicle loss and the consumer's regular car insurance only covers part of the value of the car, the GAP insurance will cover the deficiency on the car loan. For example, if the car is worth $20,000 and is totaled when the borrower owes $24,000, and the borrower's insurance covers only $18,000, the GAP insurance will kick in the $6,000 deficiency. GAP insurance, in other words, is limited credit insurance coverage only for catastrophic losses of the collateral vehicle. GAP "penetration"—meaning the percentage of consumers who purchase it—is quite high. In 2011, 34.9% of auto purchases on credit had GAP coverage.[17] Dealers particularly like selling GAP coverage because it means that in the event a vehicle is totaled, the consumer will be back in the market for a new car.

V. AUTO LEASING

Nearly a third of new cars are financed by lease. Economically the transactions are quite similar, as discussed in Chapter 22. The use of a "money factor," discussed in Chapter 22, to express lease rates is also generally limited to auto leasing. The CFPB's Examination Manual for Auto Finance provides a concise overview of auto leasing.

CFPB, Examination Procedures, Auto Finance

(June 2015)

Auto Leasing

Depository institutions have long engaged in auto leasing activities, and nonbank entities are a major player in the leasing sector. It is an important and growing part of the auto financing market for consumers. While the auto financing market is largely made up of purchase loans, in recent years, consumers have begun to migrate more towards leasing agreements.

Unlike the purchase of a vehicle, the consumer does not actually own the vehicle with a lien against a title. Instead, the consumer makes payments for the lease term. Auto leases are typically 12 months to 48 months in length, and include a "money factor" rather than an annual percentage rate (APR). An APR can be calculated by dividing the money factor by 2400.

At the end of the lease term, a consumer has the option to purchase the vehicle for a prenegotiated balloon payment that is based on the residual value. The residual value is the dollar amount the consumer's leased vehicle is estimated to be worth at the end of the lease. The lender bears the risk that it has estimated the residual value correctly.

17. Gregory Arroyo, *Tracking F&I Performance*, F&I and Showroom, (Jan. 2012).

For consumers, leasing a vehicle requires an application process and an ongoing contractual obligation that are both financial in nature and similar to entering into a financial arrangement to purchase a vehicle. Like a consumer seeking to qualify for a loan to purchase a vehicle, a consumer seeking to lease a vehicle must provide basic financial information such as income and credit history. Though a consumer who leases an automobile need not finance the entire cost of the vehicle, the consumer still undertakes a major financial obligation in the form of a commitment to make a stream of payments over a significant period of time. The consumer must consider how much cash to use, if any, for a capitalized cost reduction (similar to a down payment), the preferred lease term, and the affordability of monthly payments and other costs, including maintenance, insurance, and state registration fees.

. . .

Why would a consumer choose to lease over buy? First, the down payment and monthly payments may well be lower. Second, the leased car will always be relatively new. Third, there is no concern about what to do with the car once it gets old; there is no trade-in to negotiate on the next purchase. Instead, the consumer just returns the car at the end of the lease. And fourth, consumers rarely lease cars beyond the manufacturer's warranty, so there are fewer long-term maintenance concerns. (If the car is used for business purposes, there may also be tax advantages to leasing.)

On the other hand, with a car purchase, the consumer will ultimately own the car free-and-clear and will not have to make any more car payments; a lessee is always making a rental payment. Additionally, leases can often have additional costs beyond the base terms: extra charges for mileage above limitations specified in the lease, early cancellation penalties, and charges if the car is returned in less-than-top condition.

The point you should see here is simply that a lease is another way of financing a car, with the main difference being who will get the residual value of the car after the financing is complete. With a lease, the value returns to the lessor. With a loan, it goes to the borrower.

VI. DEFAULT AND REPOSSESSION

Auto loans are secured by a lien on the car. Although the consumer owns the car, the consumer's ownership interest is subject to the lender's contingent interest via the lien. If the borrower defaults on the loan, the lender has the right to repossess the car and sell the car, with the sale proceeds applied to the loan balance.

Auto repossession is governed by Article 9 of the Uniform Commercial Code. The UCC allows for "self-help" repossession, meaning that no law enforcement officer is involved in the process, just private agents ("repo men") of the lender, who find the car and either disable it or tow it away. UCC § 9-609(b)(2). The main rule governing repo men's behavior is that they are not allowed to "break the peace." If you've ever watched a reality TV show that follows a repo crew around (there have been several of these), you'll see that "breaking the peace" seems to rule out physical violence, but little else in terms of tricks, knavery, or even implicit threats.

The sale process is also handled privately. The general UCC rule is that the same must be "commercially reasonable," a capacious standard. UCC § 9-610(a). State law controls whether the lender is able to obtain a deficiency judgment if the proceeds of the sale are insufficient to cover the loan. Until the sale is completed, the car is still technically the property of the borrower, so it can be redeemed by paying off the loan, until the right of redemption is "foreclosed" by the completion of the sale. UCC § 9-623.

Auto loan repossession is a relatively fast process. Most lenders start the repossession process when a loan is 60-90 days' delinquent (contrast this with the 120 days mandated by federal regulation for home mortgage foreclosures). The time to find and sell the car generally takes a few weeks. In contrast, a home mortgage foreclosure can easily take a year, and in some states, up to three years.

When a car is leased, the car is technically the property of the lessor, with the lessee having only a temporary estate in the car. Car leases are governed by Article 2A of the UCC. Article 2A allows for self-help repossession by lessors, again with the limitation of no breaking of the peace. UCC § 2A-525. A lessor may always go to court, however, and replevy its property (like Walker-Thomas Furniture in *Williams v. Walker-Thomas Furniture*).

VII. REGULATION OF AUTO LENDING AND LEASING

A. Applicable Statutes

Two key federal statutes govern auto finance: the Truth-in-Lending Act (for loans) and the Consumer Leasing Act (for leases). These statutes are not unique in any way in their application to auto lending markets; TILA disclosures for auto loans are the same as for any closed-end loan.

Disclosure of auto lease terms are governed by the Consumer Leasing Act, 15 U.S.C. §§ 1667 *et seq*. It requires that prior to lease signing the consumer be given a detailed written statement (similar to a TILA disclosure) that itemizes everything the consumer has to pay or may have to pay, including all fees and taxes, the term of the lease, number and amount and due dates of lease payments, and total cost of the lease. The CLA also requires disclosure of any requirements for the lease, such as insurance requirements, disclosure of warranty terms and who is responsible for servicing the vehicle, disclosure of termination and lessee purchase options and charges, and the possibility of excessive mileage charges. 15 U.S.C. § 1667a. Lease disclosures may not use an annual percentage rate. 12 C.F.R. § 1013.4(s).

The CLA also imposes a substantive requirement on the terms of auto loans or leases: when a lessee's liability upon maturity of a lease is based on the residual value of the property, the liability must be based on a "reasonable approximation of the anticipated actual fair market value of the property on lease expiration." Thus, if the lease has a balloon payment that is supposed to reflect post-lease trade-in value on the vehicle (the residual value of the vehicle), it must be based on a reasonable approximation of what that value will be.

CLA has a pair of rebuttable presumptions about the estimated residual value. The CLA presumes that the estimated residual value is not reasonable or in good faith if it exceeds the actual residual value plus three times the regular monthly lease payment. 15 U.S.C. § 1667b. Importantly, however, the CLA presumptions do not apply to the extent that the difference between the estimated and actual residual value is due to physical damage to the car beyond normal wear and tear. *Id.; see also Wilson v. Omni Leasing*, 540 So. 2d 713 (Ala. 1989) (excluding damage to vehicle from calculation in CLA presumption). This provision effectively works to restrict lease balloon payments minus the residual value to three times the regular monthly lease payment, with an exception for additional wear-and-tear charges reflecting actual damage to the vehicle.

Beyond TILA and CLA, the federal statutes that affect auto financing include the Fair Credit Reporting Act, the Fair Debt Collection Practices Act, and the Magnusson-Moss Warranty Act (covering warranties' terms and rights of action).

Auto lending is governed not only by federal law, but also by state law, especially as many of the entities involved are state-chartered entities (such as dealerships). Virtually every state has some sort of auto finance and sales statute that may impose additional disclosure, term, or process requirements. For example, California's requires a set of disclosures in addition to TILA regarding itemization of amounts financed. Cal. Civ. Code § 2982.

Of particular note are two California statutes. First, California mandates that all buy-here-pay-here dealers provide at least a 1,000-mile/30-day warranty on all cars they offer for sale, without exception. Cal. Civ. Code §§ 1795.51; Cal. Vehicle Code §§ 241, 241.1. Even cars sold "as is" are deemed to come with this warranty. BHPH dealers are also prohibited from using electronic vehicle tracking and starter interrupters without notifying the consumer and obtaining consumer consent to tracking. Cal. Civ. Code § 2983.37.

Second, California also requires BHPH dealers to disclose the "reasonable market value" of each used car they offer for sale, in writing, posted on the vehicle itself. Cal. Vehicle Code § 11950. The value must be determined from a nationally recognized pricing guide, such as the Kelley Blue Book, the Black Book, or the National Automobile Dealers' Association Guide. *Id.* The purpose of the law is to force provision of pricing information to buyers who are not likely to shop around and could be price gouged.

Additionally, auto lenders (including dealers who are the original lenders in most instances) are subject to the UDAP prohibition of section 5 of the Federal Trade Commission Act and to the UDAAP prohibition of the Consumer Financial Protection Act. Neither of these statutes has a private right of action, however. Enforcement, therefore, depends on jurisdictional questions, which are somewhat complex for auto lending.

B. Regulatory Jurisdiction

The CFPB has only limited authority over the auto lending market. As you may recall from Chapter 8, the CFPB generally has no regulatory authority over auto dealers that are "predominantly engaged in the sale and servicing of motor vehicles, the leasing and servicing of motor vehicles, or both," unless those dealers either (1) offer financial services and products unrelated to vehicles, or (2) make loans and leases that are not routinely assigned to unaffiliated third parties. 12 U.S.C. § 5519. ("Servicing" here means servicing the car, not servicing the loan!) This means that the CFPB has no rulemaking, supervision, or enforcement authority over dealers in indirect auto lending arrangements if the dealer conducts both "sale *and* servicing" or "leasing *and* servicing." It is unclear if "and" really means "or" here: is a dealer that only offers sales or leases and does not have a servicing department subject to CFPB jurisdiction even if it routinely assigns all loans and leases to unaffiliated third parties? A plain language reading of the text would suggest so, although that would likely surprise such dealers.

The CFPB does have jurisdiction over buy-here-pay-here dealers, although it only exercises supervision authority over "larger participants," which it has defined as non-bank covered persons engaged in auto financing that have at least 10,000 aggregate annual originations (including refinancings and leases). The CFPB's larger participant rule expressly excludes motor vehicle dealers that are predominantly engaged in the sale and servicing or leasing and servicing of motor vehicles. Therefore, a typical BHPH dealer would be excluded from the larger participant rule, but a BHPH finance company could be covered by the rule if it had sufficient annual originations.

It is important to recognize that the auto dealer carve-out in section 5519 is *not* an exclusion from the definition of "covered person" or "service provider," the gateways to liability under the Consumer Financial Protection Act. Instead, it is an exemption from the *CFPB* exercising authority over the dealers. The exemption does not prevent state attorneys general from enforcing the UDAAP provision of the Consumer Financial Protection Act against all auto dealers, irrespective of the scope of CFPB authority. 12 U.S.C. § 5552(a)(1). These attorneys general can, of course, always bring state-law actions against dealers and indirect lenders. The following excerpt from a settlement agreement between a state attorney general and an indirect lender illustrates how attorneys general have recognized that regulation of the largest indirect lenders is likely to be a more effective route to regulating the auto lending market than attempting to directly regulate thousands of dealers, as the indirect lenders can essentially be dragooned into imposing requirements on all of the dealers with which they transact. The CFPB has similarly used settlements with indirect lenders in the fair lending context to press for changes in dealer behavior in regard to fair lending. *See generally* Adam J. Levitin, *Hydraulic Regulation: Regulating Credit Markets Upstream*, 26 Yale J. Reg. 143 (2009).

The following consent decree illustrates how litigation against indirect lenders can affect dealer practices. Here, the Massachusetts Attorney General has advanced a cutting-edge interpretation of "unfairness" as including lending without regard to the consumer's ability to repay. Why would it be unfair to lend to a consumer who lacks the ability repay? Consider the consequences to the consumer if the consumer cannot repay the loan: lost down payment, damaged credit score, the shame and hassle of debt collection, and ultimately the burden of having to repay the loan, which, if the consumer cannot afford it, implies serious reductions in the consumer's consumption levels, which can in turn impact the consumer's dependents, such as children.

Assurance of Discontinuance Pursuant to M.G.L. Chapter 93A, § 5 In the Matter of Santander Consumer USA Holdings, Inc.

No. 17-0946E (Mass. Super. Ct., Suffolk Co. Mar. 28, 2017)

I. INTRODUCTION

1. The Commonwealth of Massachusetts ("Commonwealth"), through the Office of Attorney General Maura Healey ("AGO"), and Santander Consumer USA Holdings Inc. (together with its subsidiaries, "SC") enter into this Assurance of Discontinuance ("AOD") pursuant to M.G.L. c. 93A, § 5.

2. SC is a Delaware corporation that is a holding company for Santander Consumer USA Inc. and subsidiaries, a specialized consumer finance company focused on vehicle finance as well as unsecured consumer lending products.

3. Pursuant to M.G.L. c. 93A, § 6, the AGO is conducting an ongoing investigation into the financing and securitization of non-prime (or subprime) automobile loans originated in Massachusetts ("Massachusetts Loans"). As part of this review, the AGO reviewed SC's business practices in Massachusetts.

4. Based on the AGO's review of SC's activities, the AGO alleges that SC facilitated the origination of certain Massachusetts loans that SC knew or should have known were unfair in violation of Chapter 93A. Certain of these loans were sold to third parties.

5. In lieu of litigation and in recognition of SC's assistance and cooperation throughout the investigation, the AGO agrees to accept this AOD on the terms and conditions contained herein, pursuant to the Massachusetts Consumer Protection Act, M.G.L. c. 93A, § 5. The AGO and SC both voluntarily enter into this AOD.

6. This AOD does not constitute an admission by SC of any fact or noncompliance with any state or federal law, rule, or regulation. SC enters into this AOD for settlement purposes only and neither admits nor denies the AGO's allegations. This AOD is made without any trial or adjudication of any issue of fact or law.

II. ALLEGATIONS

7. The Attorney General alleges the following:

BACKGROUND

8. SC is engaged in the business of indirect auto lending. In indirect auto lending, the consumer seeking an auto loan first enters a Retail Installment Contract ("RIC")

with the dealer. The dealer then sells the RIC to a finance company like SC, or to a bank or other lender. SC purchased numerous auto loans from Massachusetts auto dealers during a period that includes 2009-2014. SC acquired most of such Massachusetts loans from auto dealers in the form of RICs.

9. During the RIC sale process, SC typically has no direct contact with the borrower. SC approves and authorizes the terms of any particular loan based upon information on the credit application, which the dealers generally submit electronically to SC. At the time a dealer enters a RIC with a customer, the dealer expects to sell it to a particular finance company such as SC. The loans are on the dealers' books for only a short time before being transferred to SC.

10. A significant portion of SC's loans are in the category known as subprime (or nonprime). Obligors of this type of loan do not qualify for conventional motor vehicle financing as a result of, among other things, a lack of or adverse credit history, low income levels and/or the inability to provide adequate down payments.

11. For subprime loans acquired from certain Massachusetts auto dealers, SC predicts, based upon previous experience, that more than half of the loans will default.

12. SC funds its subprime auto loan business in part by selling some of the loans it purchases to third parties. As of the most recent data provided by SC, more than 78% of its loans originated through Massachusetts auto dealers were sold to third parties.

13. The sale of loans to third parties typically provides SC with capital to be used to purchase more loans.

DEALER REVIEWS

14. SC's dealer monitoring systems were inadequate to prevent the purchase of loans that were unfair under Chapter 93A during a period that includes 2009-2014.

15. In 2008, SC conducted an internal audit that found that SC's oversight of dealer originations was inadequate.

16. SC later developed a process for identifying and managing dealers with higher levels of delinquency, default and other issues. Dealers identified through this process were included on a list that was initially known as the "High Risk Dealer" or "HRD" list and is currently referred to as the "Dealer Performance Management" or "DPM" list.[1]

17. SC could subject dealers on the DPM list to greater scrutiny of their origination practices and also to greater stipulations (which are requirements that applicants document certain origination data—proof of income is one example of a stipulation).

18. SC examines the accuracy of income information on loan applications provided by certain dealers by conducting targeted dealer audits.[2] At times, these audits have included dealers on the DPM list. In the course of these audits, SC may seek to verify the borrower's income by consulting a third-party database containing employment and salary information, contacting the employer, and/or contacting the consumer. Where a borrower's verified income information is substantially lower than the income

1. We use the terms "HRD" and "DPM" interchangeably hereafter.

2. Similar reviews are sometimes known as performance reviews or quality reviews. We use the term "dealer audit" to refer to all of these types of reviews.

information on the application, SC, depending on the circumstances, considers the income "inflated" or "overinflated." These targeted dealer audits gave SC insight into the accuracy of the data reported by certain dealers in Massachusetts.

19. Loans from DPM list dealers perform worse both on early delinquency and gross credit losses than other loans.

20. SC also had a group of dealers that it referred to informally as the "fraud dealers," which described a subset of dealers for a certain car manufacturer ("Car Manufacturer A") that SC identified as having unusually high rates of early payment defaults ("EPDs"), primarily between 2013 and 2014. SC employees suspected that many of these dealers were engaging in fraud against SC by submitting loan applications reflecting inflated borrower income, thereby inducing SC to purchase loans it might not otherwise have purchased.

21. The issues for these dealers principally occurred during the early stages of an agreement between SC and Car Manufacturer A under which SC became the preferred provider of Car Manufacturer A loans.

22. In response, SC took some measures, such as increasing stipulations (including income stipulations) on loans purchased from dealers showing high levels of EPDs. SC also demanded that the dealers repurchase certain loans that defaulted on the first payment and look into and address the performance issues.

23. In a November 2013 email, a VP of Sales recognized that the high rate of early payment defaults at these dealers was likely the result of dealer efforts to inflate borrower income.

24. Ultimately, however, SC's follow up on findings concerning dealers with problematic activity was inadequate. SC did not focus sufficient attention on income inflation at dealers where fewer than half of the verified loans in a dealer audit indicated income inflation. While SC noted that a reason for this is that the higher the ratio, the more likely it is that the dealer is involved in the false submissions, the practice had the effect of not focusing attention on other dealers that also had instances of income inflation.

25. Moreover, SC audits had a threshold for counting individual loans with income inflation, and only considered them in audit reviews when the inflation was at least $500 or $1,000 per month.

26. Further, in its dealer audits, SC was able to verify a significant percentage, approximately 40%, of income inflation loans by asking the borrowers about their income. Where borrowers self-identified that their reported incomes were false, this was an indication that the false information derived from the dealer.

27. Nonetheless, SC continued to purchase loans from dealers even when income inflation rates at a particular dealership were high.

MASSACHUSETTS LOAN ORIGINATIONS

28. SC predicts that approximately 42% of the subprime loans originated by Massachusetts dealers on the DPM list during the period 2009-2014 have defaulted or are expected to default. For certain Massachusetts DPM list dealers, the expected default rate exceeded 50 percent.

29. There were also other issues beyond default rates with certain dealers on the DPM list. For example, with one Massachusetts dealer group ("Dealer A"), SC identified "power booking" in 2010. Power booking refers to stating that a vehicle, which serves as collateral for a loan, has additional equipment that it does not have so that the reported car value increases, which supports a higher loan amount.

30. Among other consequences, power booking allows a dealer to add more ancillary products (such as service contracts) to a loan without eclipsing maximum loan-to-value ratios. Dealers make money from ancillary product sales. When done improperly, adding ancillary products is known as "packing."

31. In a 2010 email, a SC Fraud/Risk Manager wrote of Dealer A: ". . . it looks like this dealer is power booking every deal."

32. SC confirmed power booking on nine loans from Dealer A and took certain steps to address it.

33. Dealer A has been by far the largest Massachusetts loan producer for SC of dealers on the DPM lists. Dealer A's SC loans continued to default at high rates.

34. SC audited Dealer A again in May 2013. SC reviewed 11 loans from Dealer A. Of those loans, one income was verified correct, seven were verified inflated, and three were not able to be verified. The smallest income overstatement in the verified inflated loans in the review was $45,324/year. There was also an allegation that the dealer "packed" a warranty. Moreover, the incomes the dealer reported contained a highly unlikely number of sevens, which SC called an "income trend." These findings were provided to SC's former CEO directly. SC continued to purchase hundreds of new loans from Dealer A. Those loans continued to default at a high rate, consistent with Dealer A's earlier loans. The anticipated default rate for Dealer A's subprime loans is over 50%.

35. SC also sometimes waived proof of income requirements for Massachusetts dealers that had been on the DPM list. During a period that includes 2009-2014, for Massachusetts dealers that at some point were on the DPM list, SC waived proof of income on approximately 10% of the loans that were supposed to require POI.

36. SC conducted audits of only a small percentage of DPM dealers in Massachusetts.

37. Despite the information known and available to SC regarding problematic activity and loan performance at certain dealers, SC continued to purchase loans from these dealers. In some instances, borrowers were not likely to be able to repay the loans that SC purchased, in part because the income data provided by the dealers was overstated. SC was thus reckless with respect to the unfairness under Chapter 93A of certain loans it purchased from certain Massachusetts dealers.

SC'S RESPONSE TO FINDINGS OF ISSUES

38. Loans from SC's dealers with problematic activity, in the aggregate, made up a significant portion of SC's total volume of loans.

39. Over time, SC has taken steps to improve its dealer monitoring processes and how it addresses dealers with problematic activity. Generally speaking, at various junctures SC has applied stipulations to those dealers, including proof of income stipulations. It has also demanded that the dealers repurchase some problem loans. In late 2014, SC created a group called the Dealer Council, comprised of SC personnel, to review dealer conduct and consider actions to be taken with respect to problem dealers.

40. SC believes that requiring proof of income often puts it at a competitive disadvantage and, therefore, will result in it acquiring fewer loans. SC explained that as a general matter, requiring proof of income decreased the number of acquired or "captured" loans, and therefore volume.

41. When SC demanded that a dealer repurchase loans, it was often limited to loans with early payment defaults and excluded loans with income inflation. If the borrower was making payments on a loan, SC would generally not seek to have the dealer repurchase that loan. Until relatively recently, SC would continue funding dealers' loans as long as dealers agreed to repurchase loans from SC.

42. For example, SC discovered power booking at stores from Dealer B, a Massachusetts dealer group. Dealer B agreed to make payments to SC with respect to certain of its stores but refused with respect to one store. SC's recommendation at its Dealer Council was to cut off only the store that refused to pay.

43. Around the 2013-2014 period, dealers whose loans SC purchased asked to be subjected to tougher requirements. In November 2013, for instance, SC's Pricing and Credit Risk Oversight Committee learned that certain dealership owners asked SC to require stipulations for lower credit loans because they did not trust some of their Finance and Insurance employees responsible for originating loans.

44. Ultimately, SC's dealers requested stipulations on all business in SC's riskiest credit tier.

45. The AGO's position is that SC's limited requests for income documentation, waivers of a number of those requests when made, failure to fully address dealers with problematic activity identified in its dealer audits as well as SC's purchasing loans with excessive predicted default rates (in some cases over 50%), resulted in SC recklessly causing the origination of unfair Massachusetts loans, including certain loans that the borrowers are not likely to be able to repay. Certain of these loans were sold to third parties and/or securitized.

. . .

Notes on *Santander Consumer USA Holdings*

1. The Santander investigation resulted in a settlement in which Santander paid $16.3 million in borrower relief and agreed to develop procedures to require proof of income or proof of book out (meaning proof that add-ons have in fact been installed in the car) when there appears to be income inflation or power booking at the dealer, and to have screens to prevent the sale to third parties of loans not in compliance with Massachusetts law, including borrower inability to repay the loan according to its terms.

2. Recall the *Fremont* case in Chapter 4, *Commonwealth v. Fremont Inv. & Loan*, 452 Mass. 733 (2008). In that case, Fremont Mortgage was found to have violated Massachusetts's UDAP statute by virtue of foreclosing on mortgage loans that were made (by third-party originators) without regard for consumers' ability to repay. Between *Fremont* and *Santander* can one read Massachusetts UDAP law to impose a general ability-to-repay requirement on all consumer lending?

As discussed in Chapter 25, the CFPB has also indicated that it will hold indirect auto lenders liable for discriminatory lending by dealers to the extent that the indirect lenders facilitate such discrimination with their markup policies. The CFPB has entered into settlements with several indirect auto lenders over discriminatory lending claims. It has also issued guidance about its expectations for indirect lenders in terms of Equal Credit Opportunity Act compliance. That guidance was voided in 2018 by a Congressional Review Act resolution, but the basic point of the guidance remains—under ECOA/Reg B the assignee of a loan that participates in the loan underwriting is a "creditor" and thus subject to ECOA's prohibitions.

For dealers not subject to CFPB jurisdiction, there is Federal Trade Commission jurisdiction. While the FTC lacks supervisory authority, it can bring enforcement actions, and it also has specific authorization to engage in UDAP rulemakings using an Administrative Procedures Act process (as opposed to the more cumbersome FTC Act process). The basic division of authority, then, is CFPB jurisdiction over dealers that provide the ultimate financing, and FTC jurisdiction over dealers in indirect lending, with the CFPB also having jurisdiction over the indirect lenders, and state attorneys general having enforcement jurisdiction over all parties.

VIII. AUTO LENDING SCAMS

Auto lending is sadly infamous for "scams" and the all-too-familiar stereotype of the sleazy used car dealer. It is far from clear how pervasive bad practices are in auto lending, but there are certainly well-identified patterns by which consumers' financing costs are inflated or manipulated. Sometimes these scams are meant as ways to extract additional money from the borrower; other times they are designed to get the borrower's loan approved from an indirect lender (such as with the "power booking" in the *Santander Consumer USA Holdings* case). This section is not meant to be an exclusive litany of scams, but to identify a number of common areas of regulatory concern. As a general matter, these scams tend to fall within the rubric of "deception," although some might also fall under "abusive" or constitute TILA or state auto finance law violations.

A. Yo-Yo Scams

Consumers are often eager to complete the transaction and leave the dealer lot with their car. While you might think that a dealer would not let a consumer drive off until and unless the car had been paid for, meaning that all financing was complete and in place, dealers instead allow "spot delivery," meaning that the consumer is allowed to take possession of the car before financing is finalized.

This practice leaves consumers vulnerable to so-called yo-yo scams. In a yo-yo scam, the consumer drives off with the car before financing is finalized, often with the dealer's assurances that everything will be fine and it's just waiting for some paperwork from the lender. A few days later the dealer then contacts the consumer and tells the consumer that the loan was not approved and the consumer will have to return the car . . . unless the consumer will agree to different and more onerous loan terms. Sometimes this is because the original loan was not in fact approved by the lender, but it can also simply be an opportunity for the dealer to increase its markup and hold up the consumer who is already invested in the car (and may have no other transportation options because of a trade-in that was done with the sale, and that trade-in vehicle has, of course, already been sold to someone else). If the consumer decides to return the car rather than take out a different loan, the dealer may sometimes (illegally, *see* Cal. Civ. Code § 2982.7(a)) refuse to return the down payment or charge wear-and-tear fees on the vehicle, which puts greater pressure on the consumer to accept the new loan terms. Alternatively, if the consumer refuses to return the car or take out a new loan, the dealer might threaten the consumer with prosecution for theft.

B. Loan Packing

Another problem in auto financing is **loan packing**. This is the practice of upselling the consumer on various add-on products: service contracts, GAP insurance, credit life insurance, disability insurance, dealer-installed vehicle upgrades, theft deterrent systems, "dealer prep" (*i.e.*, delivery of the car to the consumer), and, of course, rust proofing. Consumers don't purchase these products as stand-alone products; they would only ever consider them in the context of a vehicle purchase. These products are sold at a significant markup over their wholesale cost so they tend to be high-profit-margin products for dealers. Add-on products tend to be sold as bundled packages, which disguises individual items' actual cost and makes comparison shopping impossible. (Remember that the consumer is only offered these products once in the F&I office, so there is no comparison shopping really possible even in the first place.) Moreover, add-on products tend to be offered in terms of monthly payments, rather than total cost. This type of price partitioning makes the cost of the products seem smaller and separate from the total cost of the deal.

Loan packing is not inherently illegal, but loan packing can also happen through deception, in which case it is a different matter. Sometimes finance managers will falsely represent to consumers that certain add-on products must be purchased as a condition of the loan or that the cost of the financing will go up if an add-on is not purchased, when in fact the buy rate is unrelated to the purchase of the add-on and the dealer has already maxed out its allowed markup. Other times, if the consumer is focused on the monthly payment amount, the finance manager will quote a monthly payment amount that is larger than the amount actually due on the loan. Thus, a $25,000 loan at 3% for 60 months should have monthly payment of $449. But if the borrower is quoted $499/month, what else is included? Likely some sort of add-ons have been included without the consumer having actually selected them. Yet another version of loan packing involves the dealer telling the consumer that the "extended warranty is included," which it is, but for an additional cost; the consumer could purchase the vehicle for less without the extended warranty.

C. Trade-In Scams and Rolling Negative Equity

Trade-ins can also cause issues with financing. Consumers will often owe money on their old car. The old loan will need to be paid off as part of a trade-in. If everything goes right, the dealer gets the payoff amount from the old lender and pays off the loan, with the payoff amount deducted from the trade-in value.

Things can go wrong, however. The dealer can be late in making the payoff payment, resulting in an extra interest charge or late fee that is owed by the consumer. And if the dealership never pays off the loan, the consumer might be subject to suit by its lender. Payoffs are also susceptible to fraud. For example, a dealer might claim a higher payoff amounts than actually owed: the dealer claims a $10,000 payoff when only $9,500 is owed. The dealer pays off the $9,500 and just keeps the extra $500. Alternatively, a dealer will include the next month's interest on the old loan in the payoff amount, but take the trade-in today and only pay off the loan in a month. The dealer has gotten a month-long interest-free loan for the trade-in value from the consumer. (A related problem can exist with a dealer assumption of an old lease.)

Sometimes the consumer owes more on the old car than the vehicle is worth. In such a situation, when the car has "**negative equity**" or is "**upside down**," the dealer is simply refinancing the old loan with the new loan—the amount of negative equity should be rolled into the new loan and reflected in the loan disclosures as a refinancing of the old debt ("**rolling negative equity**"). Dealers will, however, sometimes inflate the purchase price of the car, rather than itemizing the loan for the additional amount as a refinancing of the original loan. This raises a number a TILA issues because it changes the cash vs. credit price of the car. The newly inflated price is really part of the credit price of the car, not the cash price, so it is a finance charge that must be disclosed as such. 15 U.S.C. § 1605(a). While the consumer pays the same irrespective of the itemization, there is still a TILA violation, presumably on the theory that the consumer could have refinanced the negative equity separately somehow and has been deprived of that opportunity.

Problem Set 26

1. After getting the runaround on a new car purchase, Congressman David "the Hammer" Whelan fed up with the auto finance industry, and he wants a Congressional hearing on problems in the industry. In particular, he wants to know what regulators are doing to prevent problems like the one he experienced. The Hammer wants to know which regulators should be on the hot seat for problems with different players in the auto finance industry. What do you, his legislative counsel, tell him for each of the following entities?

    a. Van Goghs Slaab, a franchisee-owned Slaab dealership that sells and services only Slaab Centurion minivans and makes loans and leases that it routinely assigns to the unaffiliated Slaab Motor Credit. *See* 12 U.S.C. §§ 5519, 5552(a)(1).

b. Auto von Bismarck's, a small, independent used-car dealer without a service department that routinely assigns its loans to unaffiliated finance companies and banks. *See* 12 U.S.C. §§ 5519, 5552(a)(1).

c. The Sloppy Jalopy, an independent used-car dealership that makes loans that it routinely sells to its affiliate, Auto-da-Fé Finance Corp. *See* 12 U.S.C. §§ 5519, 5552(a)(1).

d. Slaab Motor Credit, a captive finance company of Slaab Motor Corporation. *See* 12 U.S.C. §§ 5519, 5552(a)(1).

e. Continental Express Bank, N.A., a bank with over $10 billion in total assets that makes direct auto loans and purchases loans from auto dealers. *See* 12 U.S.C. §§ 5515, 5519, 5552(a)(2).

2. Deuce Ransome owns a Slaab Motors dealership in Bakersfield, California. Deuce's been advertising: "Come trade in your old car for credit for a new one. It doesn't matter if you still owe money on your car loan. Deuce will pay off your trade no matter what you owe. . . . Even if you're upside down, Deuce will pay off your trade." Yvonne d'Carlotte brought in her old Slaab Olympian, which was worth $6,000. Yvonne still owed $10,000 on the 3.5% purchase money loan she took out to buy the Olympian. Deuce credited Yvonne with $6,000 for the trade-in, which she applied to her purchase of a stylish new $30,000 Slaab Albatross (including all add-ons), which she financed through Deuce with an $8,000 down payment (including trade-in value) and a 4% APR. Deuce promptly sold the loan to Slaab Motor Credit. Yvonne just got her first monthly bill from Slaab Motor Credit, and was surprised to see that her loan balance was for $32,000. "I thought I only borrowed $22,000," she says. Yvonne is upset and wants to get her purchase rescinded. Does she have any recourse? *See* 12 U.S.C. § 5536; 15 U.S.C. § 45(a); Cal. Bus. & Professions Code §§ 17200, 17203.

3. Your neighbor's daughter, Suzy Jospin, was thrilled to be purchasing her first car, a cherry-red Slaab Epiphany. Suzy had worked all summer saving up money for a down payment so she could have the car when she went back to college. She had already selected the car and was in the dealer's finance office when the finance manager, Bill O'Sales, told her that she'd have to purchase a $2,500 extended warranty "because the bank requires it. Without the warranty, they won't make the loan." Suzy goes ahead and buys the warranty and takes the car.

Your neighbor has consulted with a lawyer who said that Suzy didn't have a great case because, "It's just her word against Bill O'Sales's, and he's going to say that she misunderstood whether the warranty was required." Your neighbor happens to be your state representative and is wondering if you, as a consumer finance expert, have any advice on a legislative fix that would address this problem. What do you say?

4. The CFPB has proposed a rule prohibiting as an abusive act or practice buy-here-pay-here dealers (that is, dealers subject to CFPB rulemaking jurisdiction) from making loans without first verifying the borrower's ability to repay the loan according to its original terms. This ability-to-repay requirement requires the lender to account for the borrower's other debt obligations as well as any housing rental and insurance costs. You represent a trade association of buy-here-pay-here auto dealers. What are your best arguments against the rulemaking? What do you anticipate the CFPB's responses to be?

CHAPTER 27

CREDIT CARDS

I. CREDIT CARDS GENERALLY

Credit cards are ubiquitous in modern American life. They are one of the primary methods by which consumers transact. In 2016, over $3.2 *trillion* was paid on 34.6 billion transactions using credit and charge cards in the United States.[1] Credit cards provide an enormous amount of short-term liquidity to consumers and are *the* primary source of general-purpose consumer credit. At the end of 2017, there was roughly $1 trillion in revolving consumer credit outstanding.[2] Of that $1 trillion, over 90%, or over $900 billion, is credit card debt. The rest is other forms of revolving, non-mortgage credit, like overdraft.

A. Credit Card Products

While most of the products known as "credit cards" are revolving lines of credit that do not have to be repaid in full every billing cycle, a subset are "charge cards" that require that the entire balance be paid off in full at the end of the month. Charge cards do not typically charge interest; instead, they usually have high annual fees. All credit card networks offer charge cards of some sort.

Some cards are "general purpose" cards that can be used at most merchants. These are cards that carry the Visa, MasterCard, American Express, or Discover logo. A subset of these cards are "co-branded" or "affinity" cards that are issued by a financial institution in a partnership with a merchant. For example, an airline and a bank might co-brand a card, such as a Chase United Airlines Visa card. The rewards program on the card will be connected to the merchant, which gets loyalty benefits in exchange for subsidizing the rewards program. A co-brand card is a general purpose card and should not be confused with a "private label" card, which is a card issued by a merchant rather than financial institution and is usable only at the merchant, rather than as a general purpose card. An example of this is the Target REDcard. The Target REDcard can be used only at Target. Target also, however, offers a Target Visa card (issued by Target's banking affiliate). The Target Visa can be used at any merchant that accepts Visa cards.

1. Nilson Report, #11022 (Dec. 2017), at 10.
2. Federal Reserve Statistical Release G.19.

B. The Card Industry

As we saw in Chapter 19 the major players in the credit card industry are issuers, acquirers, and card networks. Only issuers have direct relationships with consumers (or in the case of American Express and Discover, the issuer is often the network), and only issuers are involved in the credit-granting decision. Thus, to the extent that credit cards are considered a credit product rather than a payment product, the focus is on the card issuer.

The credit and payment functions of credit cards are never completely delinked, of course. Convenience users of credit cards—those who pay their bills in full and on time—still use the card as a credit product. It provides them with short-term liquidity, as they need not have funds in hand or in a bank account in order to make a purchase with a card. Instead, the card gives the cash management flexibility. They also benefit from the dispute resolution protections of credit cards, where the defenses against a merchant may be raised against the issuer, which is a feature available solely because the payment is made via credit, with the card issuer functionally acquiring the merchant's right to payment from the consumer.

Hundreds of financial institutions issue credit cards, although ten large banks account for around 90% of all credit card balances outstanding in the U.S. This contrasts with debit cards, where the top ten banks' market share is only about half as large. Many smaller financial institutions do not issue credit cards, in part because they are unable to capitalize on the economies of scale that exist for cards.

1. Card Issuer Revenue

Not all card issuers have the same business model. Some target particular market segments, such as ultra-prime, prime, and subprime borrowers, while others have different products aimed at different market segments. As a result, not all card issuers rely on the same types of revenue sources to the same degree or have the same expenses. Card issuers have four basic revenue sources: interest, interchange fees, consumer fees (annual fees, late fees, etc.) and add-on products (credit insurance, *e.g.*). Interest is by far the largest segment of most issuers' revenue, traditionally representing around two-thirds of revenue, followed by interchange at around 20%.

Notice that the distribution of card issuer revenues depends on the payment behavior patterns of card users. Users who pay their balances in full every billing period do not generate interest or late fee revenue. They might produce annual fees, however, and they produce interchange fees with every purchase. What this means is that the most profitable card users are likely to be those who regularly revolve a balance, as they produce not only interchange and annual fees, but also interest and late fee revenue.

Roughly two-thirds of cardholders on general purpose cards revolve their balances in any quarterly period with one-third using their cards just for transacting.

CFPB, *The Consumer Credit Card Market*, Dec. 2015. The division between transactor and revolver is not absolute—many transactors are "sloppy payers" who occasionally revolve a balance simply out of inadvertence, and some habitual revolvers repay their balances in full from time to time. Not surprisingly, consumers with worse credit quality are much more likely to revolve balances.

Consumer payment patterns also vary. In any particular month around 15% of accounts are likely to pay just the minimum payment required, with another 19% paying near the minimum. Around a quarter of accounts pay in full, with the remainder making some sort of intermediate payment. The importance of this variation is that consumers who regularly make only minimum or near-minimum payments are likely to have balances outstanding for significant periods of time, meaning interest will normally be accruing on the account.

2. Card Issuer Expenses

Card issuer expenses are primarily credit losses (charge-offs), operations and marketing (particularly direct mailings and rewards), costs of funds, and fraud. Traditionally, charge-offs and operations and marketing are the major expense; fraud has historically been a negligible percentage of costs.

Bank regulatory accounting rules require card issuers to "charge off" card debt that is 180 days past due or if the consumer files for bankruptcy. Federal Financial Institutions Examination Council, *Uniform Retail Credit Classification and Account Management Policy*. A "charged off" debt is not forgiven. It is simply an accounting term, meaning that the bank may not carry the debt on its books as an asset. A reduction in assets also reduces a bank's equity and thereby decreases the bank's leverage ratio: the ratio of equity to assets. This is can present a problem because banks are required to maintain a minimum equity-to-asset ratio. Note that charge-offs are a distinct accounting issue from loss reserving (allowance for loan and lease losses or ALLL) or troubled debt restructuring (TDR).

Because charge-offs are simply an accounting issue, charge-off status is not informative about ultimate recoveries on a loan. Not all charge-offs are actually losses in the end. Card issuers routinely recover a percentage of charged off debt, although often this is through the sale of the charged off debt to third-party collectors and brokers, generally at 10-15 cents on the dollar.

As Figure 27.1 shows, credit card charge-offs have traditionally been substantially higher than other types of bank-issued consumer credit (mortgages, car loans). But, as Figure 27.2 shows, card delinquency rates, while traditionally higher than other forms of bank-issued consumer credit, lagged behind mortgage delinquencies in the aftermath of the 2008 financial crisis. Why? It's possible to make a relatively small minimum payment on a credit card and keep the account current; mortgage lenders do not generally accept partial payments.

Figure 27.1 Bank Loan Charge-Off Rates[3]

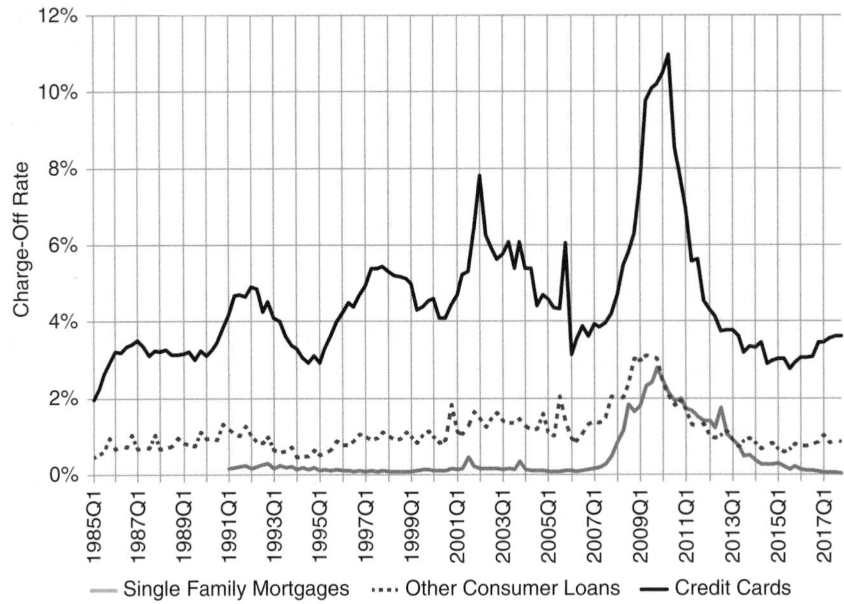

Figure 27.2 Bank Loan Delinquency Rates[4]

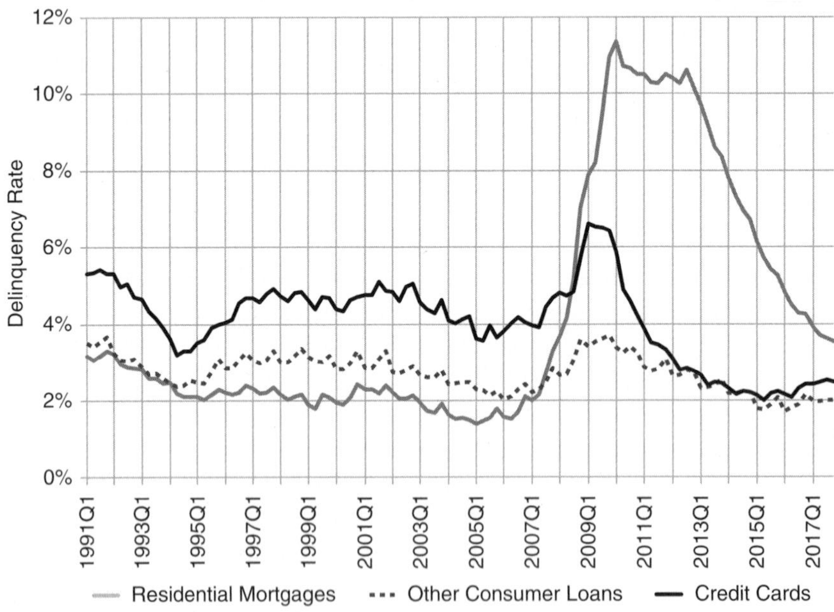

3. Federal Reserve, at http://www.federalreserve.gov/releases/chargeoff/.

A surprisingly large part of card issuers' costs comes from marketing through direct mailing. Card issuers sent out around 6 billion direct mailings in 2015. The average direct mail item cost slightly under $8. The response rate on these direct mailings is incredibly low compared to other types of direct mailing campaigns: often around half a percent. Direct mailing represent a large share of credit card issuer expenses, despite being a grossly inefficient way of acquiring customers.

C. A Very Brief History of Credit Cards and Their Regulation

Credit cards are so deeply ingrained in consumer behavior patterns that it is easy to forget what a recent development they are. While there have been types of card-based credit systems since the first half of the twentieth century, credit cards really emerged as a product only in the 1960s. Even then, however, they remained a niche product, used only by the well-to-do. The lines of credit accessed by cards are generally unsecured, and underwriting data and technology in the 1960s was still quite limited, so credit cards were provided only to very low-risk consumers. This began to change in the 1980s. The combination of interest rate deregulation and improvements in computing and credit scoring resulted in a "democratization of credit," and cards ceased to be the purview of the well-to-do. Instead, cards became a symbol of middle-class consumptive life.

Credit cards have been subject to the Truth in Lending Act (and Regulation Z) since the Act was adopted in 1968. Until 2009, most credit card regulation dealt with disclosure requirements and the billing error rights we saw in chapter 20 although there were also anti-tying rules and rules prohibiting card issuers from engaging in setoff against deposit accounts. 12 C.F.R. § 1026.12(d) (prohibiting setoff).

The typical credit card of the 1980s had an annual fee and a fixed interest rate and late fee, but relatively few other fees. Monthly minimum payment requirements were relatively high, perhaps 10% of the balance, meaning that balances would be paid off reasonably fast without further purchases.

As credit card debt grew during the 1980s, Congress reacted by amending the Truth in Lending Act in 1988 to require disclosure of credit card pricing in a tabular form that is known as the Schumer Box after then-Representative (now Senator) Charles Schumer of New York. Fair Credit and Charge Card Disclosure Act of 1988, Pub. L. 100-583, 102 Stat. 2960. The Schumer Box should be familiar to you as the standard format for credit card pricing disclosures. The Federal Reserve, however, only implemented the Schumer Box in 2000, twelve years later!

In the 1990s, however, card issuers started to become more creative in their product structuring, and cards became more complex products. In 1999, the average credit card solicitation had 13 numbers in it. By 2009, the average credit card solicitation had 33 numbers. Joshua M. Frank, *Numbers Game: The True Cost of Credit Card Mail Offers*, Center for Responsible Lending Research Report, Oct. 2010. Thus, even as Congress mandated greater disclosure, card issuers responded with a flood

4. Federal Reserve, at http://www.federalreserve.gov/releases/chargeoff/.

of information that made it nearly impossible to determine in advance the cost of revolving a balance for a given period of time (not least because the time when payments would be credited was in card issuers' control).

Cards did not simply become complex, however. They also began to experiment with behaviorally based pricing techniques. Starting with Providian Financial, card issuers began to eliminate annual fees and offer promotional or "teaser" rates, lower monthly payments, and rewards programs.

The genius of these strategies was that they lowered barriers to initial use of credit cards. Consumers were more willing to get cards if they did not face an unavoidable annual fee or interest rate and had more payment flexibility. Rewards programs (financed by interchange fees as we have seen) and 0% teaser rates made card usage more appealing by functionally lowering the cost of card purchases (and often lowering their perceived cost more than their real cost because of consumer overvaluation of rewards).

This strategy only worked, however, because of the existence of "sloppy payers"—consumers who are relatively good credit risks, but will often pay late and thus incur interest and fees. The increase in interest and fees would offset the lower annual fees and promotional rates.

Changes in card pricing structures went even further, however. Card issuers also started including terms in cardholder agreements that allowed them to change interest rates "at any time and for any reason," or "universal cross-default" clauses in which a default on one card (or any obligation) by the consumer would trigger a default interest rate's application on the card. These changes were sometimes even applied retroactively, to existing balances. In other words, the purchase would be made with the consumer thinking that it was at a 10% APR, and the card issuer could subsequently unilaterally declare that the APR would be 20%, applied retroactively to existing balances. Other examples of tricks and traps were applying payments to low APR balances before applying them to high APR balances (similar to the transaction posting issues we have seen with overdraft), or calculating the balances to which finance charges were applied to include funds that had been paid off on time.

II. PRICING AND COMPETITION IN THE CARD MARKET

Why didn't competition weed out the bad actors in the credit card market? That is, why did tricks and traps become common practices in the card industry? The card issuance market is not lacking for competition, as the deluge of direct mail indicates.

A. Sticky Relationships

One (nonexclusive) possibility is that the issuer-cardholder relationship is suboptimally sticky. There are costs to switching cards—the search costs plus the actual transaction costs of switching. When a consumer switches cards, the consumer may lose rewards points and will have to update any automatic billing arrangements. The closure of one line of credit and the opening of another may also harm the consumer's credit score. These costs alone discourage consumers from switching over small harms.

Relatedly, switching does not bring the consumer any guaranteed improvement. There is little transparency regarding issuer billing practices, such as forgiveness of fees or a propensity to increase rates or apply rate increases retroactively. Therefore a consumer is faced with certain costs and uncertain benefit from switching cards. In such a situation there is a degree of consumer lock-in, such that the consumer will not readily switch cards over small issues. A card issuer can exploit this lock-in by changing terms on consumers and hitting the consumer with supracompetitive fees and interest rates or through billing practices that have the effect of raising the cost of using a card.

B. Shrouded Pricing and the Curse of Debiasing

Another possibility is suggested by a seminal work on consumer markets by economists Xavier Gabaix and David Laibson, *Shrouded Attributes, Consumer Myopia, and Information Suppression in Competitive Markets*, 121 Q. J. Econ. 505 (2006). Gabaix and Laibson set forth a theory under which in competitive equilibrium firms have no incentive to make their prices transparent, and actually are incentivized to engage in billing tricks and traps. That is, in markets like the one Gabaix and Laibson describe, competition will not protect consumers unless the dynamics of competition are changed. Gaibaix and Laibson argue that firms are incentivized to exploit consumer mistakes by partitioning pricing between more salient and less salient prices, often "shrouding" parts of the pricing in fine print to make to make them less salient, such that a consumer will focus only on the unshrouded part of the price.

For example, a firm selling printers will sell the printer and ink separately (partitioning the pricing) and then shift much of the cost from the fixed, up-front cost of the printer to the contingent, future cost of the ink, which is less salient to the consumer at the time of the initial purchase. This means that if there are two competing firms, both of which charge the same total cost, but one of which partitions and shrouds its price and one of which doesn't, the one with shrouded pricing will be better able to attract business. Thus, if one firm charges $1,000 for a printer and a lifetime supply of ink, it will be at a disadvantage to a firm that charges $300 for the printer but then $100 per ink cartridge (if consumers tend to use more than seven over the life of the printer). Because consumers have difficulty predicting their future ink usage, they will focus on the cost of the printer, even if it is overall the worse deal. Similar situations can be found with cellphones that are sold bundled with data plans and airline seats and baggage fees (think Spirit Air).

Consider this in the consumer finance context. Suppose that Transparent Bank, which charges an all-in cost of a deposit account of $100/month, will have trouble competing with Shrouded Bank, which charges a fixed fee of $10/month and various overdraft, balance transfer, balance inquiry, and ATM fees. The total fees a consumer incurs may well be higher with Shrouded Bank, but because the pricing is partitioned, behaviorally contingent, and shrouded in fine print disclosures, the consumer is likely to perceive Transparent Bank as being more expensive.

Gabaix and Laibson argue that Transparent Bank could advertise to try to "debias" consumers about Shrouded Bank's pricing by alerting them to the presence of various fees, but it will run into "the curse of debiasing"—the debiasing campaign will make consumers more savvy about how they use the product, such that they will continue to patronize Shrouded Bank, but will simply be more careful to avoid the various fees. In other words, the debiasing effort will not generate more business for Transparent Bank, but will reduce some of Shrouded Bank's revenue. In light of this situation the competitive equilibrium is for Transparent Bank to adopt Shrouded Bank's pricing model. Transparency loses to shrouding. *See also* FTC, Trade Regulation Rule; Credit Practices, 49 Fed. Reg. 7740, 7746 (Mar. 1, 1984) ("Individual creditors have little incentive to provide better terms and explain their benefits to consumers, because a costly education effort would be required with all creditors sharing the benefits. Moreover, such a campaign might differentially attract relatively high risk borrowers.").

Consider how well Gabaix and Laibson's description fits the credit card market. In particular, consider what you see in card issuer advertising. Are you seeing "lowest total cost" advertised? Or are you seeing particular features, such as promotional rates or "no annual fees" advertised? Do you ever see debiasing advertisements that draw attention to competitors' hidden fees?

C. Are Lender and Borrower Interests Aligned?

If Gabaix and Laibson's model applies to credit cards (at least before 2009), a question remains: wouldn't too much unintended consumer debt drive up default rates and reduce lender profits? In other words, the trade off between, say, late fees and annual fees on a credit card is materially different than the trade off between the price of ink and the price of a printer. The printer/ink company does not have the collection problem that the card issuer faces. Given the increase in default risk, what lender would aggressively pursue a shrouded pricing model?

To understand why, it is necessary to question a traditional assumption about lending, namely that the borrower and the lender are partners and are both interested in the borrower's success: the lender wants the borrower to succeed, as that is how the lender will be repaid. Accordingly, the lender will not squeeze the borrower too hard because that may result in a default that will harm both of them.

Whether this assumption holds true in all markets, however, is less clear. First, if the management of a loan is divided from the economic interest in the loan, such as through securitization, the interests of the party managing the loan may not align with the borrower's, even if the interests of the party with the economic interest still do.

Second, there may be agency problems that interfere with the lender-borrower relationship. The lender acts through agents—loan officers—and those loan officers' incentives may not align with the lender. Depending on how the loan officers are compensated, they may be more interested in increasing lending volume than in ensuring that the loans that are made are sustainable.

Third, if there are other financial product relationships between a borrower and a lender, the lender might be willing to take a loss on one product if it will be more than offset by revenue from another product. A product like "free" checking may in fact be a loss leader for other products like overdraft credit or for the ability to readily market credit cards, car loans, mortgage loans, and annuities and other investment products to the consumer.

Fourth, for some financial products, default is more profitable than performance for the lender. Defaults can general additional revenue opportunities—penalty interest, late fees, and for collateralized loans, property inspection and preservation fees. If default becomes a profit center for a lender, it encourages the lender to make riskier, non-sustainable loans with an eye toward maximizing the number of defaults and thus default-related revenue.

And fifth, a borrower who pays interest and fees for a long enough period might still be a profitable borrower even if the borrower ultimately defaults. Ronald J. Mann, *Bankruptcy Reform and the "Sweat Box" of Credit Card Debt*, 2007 U. Ill. L. Rev. 101, 112-120. The concept of "**sweat box lending**" originated in a political economy theory attempting to explain the support of credit card issuers for a bankruptcy law reform that made it harder to file for bankruptcy. Yet it is possible to apply more broadly the basic insight: a loan with high fees and interest rates need not perform to maturity in order to be profitable for the lender. Sweat box lending describes some credit card issuers' business models, but it also can apply to other types of credit with relatively high fees and/or interest rates.

Suppose, for example, an amortizing $2,000 loan with a 60-month term at 90% annual interest, compounded monthly. By month 15, the consumer will have already paid over $2,081 in interest and will have also repaid $128 in principal. Thus, if the consumer defaults after month 15, the lender will have recovered $2,128—all of its principal and then some. To be sure, the lender might still be taking a loss given its cost of funds and operating expenses, but let's fast forward to month 20. At that time the lender will have recovered $2,888 on the loan, which is equivalent to having received a 27% annual return on the $2,000, which would surely cover the lender's cost of funds and other expenses and include a profit. Thus, even if the borrower only makes it a third of the way through the loan prior to defaulting, the borrower might be a profitable borrower.

The lender will, of course, make more money the longer any individual borrower performs prior to default. But in aggregate, the lender might prefer to have more borrowers who default sooner (than fewer borrowers who default later). To illustrate, if a borrower pays off the loan in full, the lender will receive payments totaling $9,119 on a loan of $2,000 principal over 60 months. But that would require stricter underwriting standards than a loan that only needs to make it to month 20. The borrower who pays in full on this loan returns 8x more revenue ($7,199 beyond recovery of principal) than the one who defaults after 20 months ($888 in revenue beyond recovery of principal). But the lender could make three 20-month loans over the same period as the 60-month loan, so the difference in profitability is really more like 2.67x. If the lender thinks that lower underwriting standards (guarantying only 20 months payment on average) will result in three times as many borrowers as underwriting for repayment in full (meaning three loans that default at 20 months, repeated three times with the same principal during a 60-month period, rather than one loan that performs to maturity), then the lower underwriting standards will be what a profit-maximizing lender will pursue. Higher interest rates, high up-front fees, and lack of amortization all increase the effectiveness of sweat box lending.

All in all, then, there is good reason to question the assumption that lenders—even lenders that hold loans on their own balance sheets—are consistently incentivized to lend prudently based on borrowers' repayment capacity.

III. THE CARD ACT

Following the financial crisis of 2008, the credit card market underwent a seismic regulatory shift. Legislation responding to the problems that had emerged in the credit card market in the 1990s and 2000s had gotten hearings in Congress but was languishing until the financial crisis. When the crisis broke, however, the political pressure to regulate the banking industry became much more intense, even if the crisis was driven by mortgages, not by credit card lending The credit card reform legislation was the only ready-to-go consumer financial litigation sitting on the shelf, and so, in 2009, Congress enacted the Credit Card Accountability, Disclosure, and Responsibility Act of 2009 (the CARD Act), the first post-crisis financial reform legislation.

The CARD Act contains two sets of provisions. One set regulates access to credit cards, including an ability-to-repay requirement. The other set regulates the terms of cards and their application, specifically regulation of interest rates, fees, and payment application. The CARD Act's provisions sit on top of the preexisting TILA/Reg Z provisions that cover account solicitations and account opening requirements, periodic disclosure requirements, and terms and conditions of credit and billing practices.

A. Regulation of Access to Credit Cards

1. Ability to Repay

The CARD Act imposes a number of restrictions on who can get a credit card. Most importantly, cards may not be issued to consumers absent the card issuer's consideration of the consumer's ability to repay. 15 U.S.C. § 1665e. This striking provision is a centerpiece of the CARD Act. The statutory provision itself is quite terse, leaving a great deal of room for regulatory interpretation. It does not even explicitly require that the consumer be able to repay, merely that the card issuer must consider the ability to make the required payments.

What are the required payments? Not the balance in full. Just the minimum payments. 12 C.F.R. § 1026.51(a)(2). Minimum payments are typically the greater of $10 or the sum of the finance charge + fees + 2% of the balance (or sometimes just fees + 2% of the balance). Thus, with a $10,000 balance, the minimum payment would only be $200 in a month. Accordingly, the ability-to-repay standard is not especially demanding.

Moreover, the CFPB's Official Interpretation of Reg Z permits card issuers to consider a consumer's income and assets based on information provided by the consumer or information from empirical models, including reasonably expected future income. Official Interpretation to § 1026.51(4)(i). Information about the consumer's assets may also be based on the consumer's self-reporting, Official Interpretation to § 1026.51(4)(iii), and debt information may rely on a credit report without assuming that lines of credit are fully utilized. Official Interpretation to § 1026.51(5). If the Federal Reserve's Official Staff Interpretation is taken seriously, how much force does the ability-to-repay requirement have?

2. Young Consumers and College Students

The CARD Act prohibits issuance of credit cards to consumers under age 21, unless the consumer has a co-signor who is over age 21 or can show independent means of repayment. 15 U.S.C. § 1637(c)(8). This means that college students are often not able to get credit cards of their own. They are still able to get other types of credit independently.

The credit card age of majority of 21 is a somewhat jarring contrast to the majority age for contracting in general and for other things such as voting, military service, driving, consensual sexual relations, and criminal liability. Indeed, only credit cards and consumption of alcohol require a majority age of 21.

The CARD Act restriction on card issuance to under-21-year olds is obviously a paternalistic regulatory approach. Why was Congress so concerned about 18-20-year olds with credit cards? Congress's decision to make a majority age of 21 for card issuance (absent financial independence) is a reflection of concern that many 18-20-year olds are not financially savvy. 18-20-year olds have in most cases been under the financial care of their parents. In their first years of living independently, they may need some time to learn out to manage their own basic finances before being given an independent line of credit.

Does this logic strike you as compelling? Is the problem the youth and inexperience of 18-20-year olds or is it something else? And if it is something else, is it a factor restricted or especially pronounced in 18-20-year olds? Does a requirement of demonstrating an independent ability to repay for 18-20-year-olds mean very much when that requirement only means being able to make the required minimum payments—in the range of 2% of the balance generally—on a card? A student working a few hours a week can generally show sufficient income to qualify independently for a card with a relatively small line.

The CARD Act also imposes restrictions on credit card marketing to college students. Card issuers may not offer tangible inducements such as free T-shirts for college students to open up cards with them if they are soliciting or near campus or at college-sponsored or related events. 15 U.S.C. § 1650(f)(2). Higher educational institutions and their affiliated alumni associations must also disclose their arrangements with card issuers. 15 U.S.C. § 1650(f)(1); 12 C.F.R. § 1026.57(a), (d) (defining a college card agreement to include alumni association affiliates' agreements). Colleges stand *in loco parentis* for some purposes. Does it make sense to limit their ability to permit colleges' card issuer partners to market to the college's students? If so, do these particular limitations in the CARD Act make sense?

B. Regulation of Interest Rates and Fees

Under the CARD Act, credit card pricing is heavily regulated, more so than any other type of consumer financial product, including mortgages. Interest rates are not capped per se—there is no federal usury statute for credit cards—but card issuers' ability to change rates unilaterally is highly constrained. Prior to the CARD Act, card issuers routinely reserved the right to change terms "at any time, for any reason" in their sole discretion. Sometimes a dispute on another card or line of credit would trigger a rate increase on a credit card. Sometimes a particular type of purchase (tire retreading, marriage counseling, massage parlor, *e.g.*) would trigger a rate increase. These rate increases would often apply not just prospectively but also to existing balances.

The CARD Act was a response to a variety of perceived abuses and overreaching by card issuers. It significantly restricted card issuers' ability to dynamically adjust their prices, either to respond to changes in risk or to take advantage of consumers' lock-in due to the transaction costs in switching cards. Under the CARD Act, card issuers are held to the deal that they reached with the consumer prior to the consumer's use of the card, and if the card issuer wishes to change the terms of the relationship, the consumer is given the opportunity to exit from the relationship in a way that avoids any coercion to remain and accept the changed terms.

1. Prospective Changes in Terms for New Balances

Under the CARD Act, a card issuer is generally prohibited from changing the terms of the card account during the first year of the account. 15 U.S.C. § 1666i-2(a). There are four exceptions to this prohibition, however. The card issuer may increase interest rates and fees:

1. Upon the expiration of promotional rate. 15 U.S.C. § 1666i-1(b)(1). Promotional rates are required to last for at least six months. 15 U.S.C. § 1666i-2(b).
2. If the card has a variable interest rate linked to a publicly available index and that index rate increases. 15 U.S.C. § 1666i-1(b)(2).
3. Following the termination of a workout or temporary hardship arrangement that had produced a temporarily reduce interest rate. 15 U.S.C. § 1666i-1(b)(3).
4. If the cardholder has failed to make a required minimum payment for 60 days past its due date. 15 U.S.C. § 1666i-1(b)(4). Recall that the 60 days past due are likely stacked on top of 21 days after the close of a billing cycle for the due date, so it might be closer to 90 days after a billing cycle closes before a card issuer can prospectively reprice the account.

After the first year of the account, the card issuer may generally change the prospective terms of an existing card account whenever it chooses for any reason:

market conditions, its own financial situation, a change in the consumer's risk profile, etc.

For all term changes, the card issuer must provide 45 days' advance notice of the change and give the consumer an opportunity to close the account. 15 U.S.C. § 1637(i)(1)-(3); 12 C.F.R. § 1026.9(c), (g).[5]

If the consumer closes the account, the card issuer cannot demand immediate repayment in full. Instead, the card issuer must allow payment over time, and card issuer cannot increase minimum payment requirements, for example, except to require the balance to be paid off within five years or to double the part of the minimum payment that is based on a percentage of the balance. 15 U.S.C. §§ 1637(i)(4), 1666i-1(c)(2).[6] While this provision protects consumers from payment shock and thus from being coerced into accepting changed terms, it also means that a card issuer that increases its interest rates in response to a change in the consumer's risk profile may find itself instead stuck with the repayment risk on existing balances on existing terms for up to five years. To be sure, the card issuer had already extended that credit, but as long as the consumer continues to make minimum payments required for a five-year amortization, the card issuer cannot recoup its funds any faster.

2. Changes in Terms on Existing Balances

At any point during an account's life, the interest rates and fees on existing balances may be increased only in the same four circumstances when a rate may be increased prospectively during the first year of an account. 15 U.S.C. § 1666i-1(a)-(b). 45 days' notice is also required for changes of terms on existing balances. 12 C.F.R. § 1026.9(c), (g). Likewise, the consumer may opt to close the account and will have the same time to pay off the balance as with a prospective term change. 15 U.S.C. §§ 1637(i)(4), 1666-1(c)(2).

You might reasonably ask how a card issuer could *ever* change terms on an existing balance. Isn't that a done deal? If the borrower borrowed at 10%, how can the card issuer now, after the fact, increasing the rate to 20%? Doesn't the ability to make such a change render the contract illusory?

There are three theories of why as a matter of contract law a card issuer should be able to change the terms on existing balances. The first is that the contract—the cardholder agreement—specifically allows them to do so, subject to the restrictions imposed by the CARD Act. Given the limited scenarios in which an account may be repriced, perhaps there isn't so much discretion given to the card issuer as to make the contract illusory. (Query whether such contracts were illusory prior to the

---

5. It is not clear whether the 45 days' notice can be provided prior to a periodic payment running 60 days delinquent; nothing in TILA or Reg Z addresses this. If not, then delinquency repricing cannot be done until an account is actually 105 days delinquent, minimum.

6. Minimum payments are typically structured as covering the greater of a fixed dollar figure, perhaps $10, or the total of all interest and fees that accrue in a billing cycle plus a small percentage of principal, usually around 2%. Thus, such a minimum payment could be increased to the greater of $10 or all interest and fees plus 4%. For small balances (less than $1,000), the doubling of a 2% minimum will result in a faster amortization than five years because the $10 fee level will eventually kick in, but in most cases the consumer will have at least five years to pay off the balance (although no new purchases can be made).

CARD Act.) The second theory is that if the consumer continues to use the card—or at least does not close the account—that the consumer has agreed to a modification of the contract. Any change or terms or modification of the contract would have to be undertaken in good faith, of course, which would not allow for the issuer to raise rates after-the-fact without good cause. The third theory is that in a number of states there are statutes specifically authorizing credit card change-in-terms, including on existing balances. *See, e.g.*, Ala. Code § 5-20-5; 5 Del. Code Ann. § 952; Ga. Code Ann. §§ 7-5-1, *et seq.*, Nev. Rev. Stat. § 97A.140(4); N.J.S.A. 17:3B-41; Ohio Rev. Stat. § 1109.20(D); S.D. Codified L. § 54-11-10; Utah Code § 70C-4-102. While these statutes are preempted to the extent they conflict with the CARD Act, it is not clear whether there is field preemption post-CARD Act or whether states still have some ability to regulate in the space. This point should remind you that even with the extensive federal regulation of credit cards, there is still an underlying contract that provides an important further level of regulation.

3. Unwinding Rate Increases

Card issuers are required under the CARD Act to conduct a review of accounts on which they have increased interest rates or fees at least once every six months after repricing to determine whether the conditions that lead to the rate increase still apply. 15 U.S.C. § 1665c; 12 C.F.R. §§ 1026.59(a), (c). This covers both repricing because of consumer-specific risk and repricing because of market conditions. Official Interpretation to 12 C.F.R. § 1026.59(a), #1. It also covers rate increases on both existing balances and prospectively. 12 C.F.R. § 1026.59(a)(2)(ii)(A).

If the conditions that led to the repricing no longer hold, the card issuer must restore the original rate within 45 days. 12 C.F.R. § 1026.59(a)(2)(ii)(B). Thus, if a consumer was 60 days late on a payment, but has cured that delinquent payment and has not subsequently run 60 days past due, the original interest rate on the account must be restored, even if every subsequent payment is delinquent (but not 60 days delinquent).

Additionally, if a cardholder who has run 60 days delinquent makes six consecutive minimum payments on time, the card issuer must restore the original account rate as to transactions that occurred within 14 days before or after the 12 C.F.R. § 1026.9(c) or (g) repricing notice. 12 C.F.R. § 1026.55(b)(4)(ii).

Thus, there are two separate off-ramps for rate increases due to delinquency. The 12 C.F.R. § 1026.55 off-ramp requires six consecutive timely minimum payments, but no cure, while the 12 C.F.R. § 1026.59 off-ramp requires cure, but not six consecutive timely minimum payments. The 12 C.F.R. § 1026.55 off-ramp is more limited in terms of the operation of the rate restoration, however, as it does not require the card issuer to restore rates to charges made more than 14 days, but less than 46 days, after the repricing notes. Official Interpretation to 12 C.F.R. § 1026.55(b)(4), #3(iv)(A).

4. Payment Application

The CARD Act also mandates the application of payments received by a card issuer if there are different balances accruing interest at different rates. 15 U.S.C.

§ 1666c. For example, there might be a balance at a promotional balance transfer APR, a balance at a purchase APR, and a balance at a cash advance APR. In such a case, the card issuer may apply the minimum payment as it wishes, but any payment in excess of the minimum must be applied to the highest APR balance until it is exhausted, and then to the next highest APR balance, etc. *Id.* The effect of this is to ensure that to the extent the consumer pays more than the minimum, the highest APR balances will be paid down faster, which is the most favorable payment allocation for a consumer.[7]

5. Payment Timing

The Truth in Lending Act regulates payment timing. Due dates for accounts must be the same each month. 15 U.S.C. § 1637(o)(1). This may be either the same numerical date or the last day of the month, even if it is not numerically the same. Official Interpretation to 12 C.F.R. § 1026.7(b)(11), #6. Thus, it is impossible to have a credit card account with a fixed due date of the 29th, 30th, or 31st. A billing cycle may be longer than a month, however, as long as the payment dates are the same. Official Interpretation to 12 C.F.R. § 1026.7(b)(11), #8.

The CARD Act further provides that a payment may not be considered as late unless the card issuer has adopted reasonable procedures to ensure that the periodic statement (which includes the payment invoice) is "mailed or delivered to the consumer not later than 21 days before the payment due date." 15 U.S.C. § 1666b(a); 12 C.F.R. § 1026.5(b)(2)(ii)(A). This provision limits when the card issuer may assess a late payment fee or credit report on an account as delinquent, as well as when the clock for an interest-rate increase due to 60-day delinquency may start to run. Effectively, this provision means that consumers have at least 21 days between when a bill is sent to them and payment is due.

The CARD Act further provides that if the card issuer offers a "grace period" for interest-free repayment, it must be at least 21-days long. 15 U.S.C. § 1666b(b); 12 C.F.R. § 1026.5(b)(2)(ii)(B). This does not mean that consumers automatically get at least 21 days of float on credit cards. Instead, it means that there are at least 21 days of float *if* the card issuer allows a finance-charge-free grace period of any sort. Given that billing cycles can be 31-days long, there can be as much as 52 days of float on a purchase made at the beginning of a billing cycle—the 31 days of float in the billing cycle and 21 days thereafter before payment is due—on a credit card purchase. Thus, cards provide consumers significant and possibly free liquidity.

While grace periods are common for credit cards, they are typically subject to limitations. Generally grace periods only apply if a balance is repaid in full and on time. Additionally, many issuers provide a grace period only if the *previous* billing cycle's balance was also repaid in full and on time. Some issuers even require the two previous billing cycles to have been paid in full for the cardholder to be eligible

7. If issues about application of payment to balances accruing at different rates sounds familiar, you've seen it before in the *Bill Me Later* case in chapter 11. Complaint, *CFPB v. PayPal, Inc. and Bill Me Later, Inc.*, No. 1:15-cv-01426 (D. Md. May 19, 2015). You've also seen another type of payment application case in Chapter 2 in *Williams v. Walker-Thomas Furniture Co.*, 350 F.2d 445 (D.C. Cir. 1965).

for a grace period. For example, consider this language from a Bank of America cardholder agreement:

> We will not charge you any interest on Purchases if you always pay your entire New Balance Total by the Payment Due Date. Specifically, you will not pay interest for an entire billing cycle on Purchases if you Paid in Full the two previous New Balance Totals on your account by their respective Payment Due Dates; otherwise, each Purchase begins to accrue interest on its transaction date or the first day of the billing cycle, whichever date is later.

To see how this applies, suppose that Alyssa's credit card has billing cycles that start on the first day of the month and close on the last day of the month and that Alyssa gets the statement for a billing cycle on the 5th day of the following month. The due date for the payments is on the 27th of that following month, but Alyssa always makes her payments on the 16th. Let's also suppose that Alyssa's card issuer offers a grace period only if both the current and the previous billing cycle are repaid in full and on time. Thus, on September 5th, Alyssa receives her card statement for the August billing cycle. She pays it on time and in full on September 16th. On October 5th she then gets her statement for the September billing cycle. It shows that she has $1,000 balance based on purchases she made in September. If Alyssa pays off that full $1,000 by the October 27th due date, no interest will accrue on the balance because she paid both the current billing cycle (the October 5th bill) and the previous one (the September 5th bill) in full and on time.

Now suppose that instead Alyssa did not pay off the September 5th billing statement in full. She gets her October 5th billing statement, which shows she has a balance of $1,200 (the balance on the September 5th bill plus interest on it plus new charges made during September). Alyssa pays off the entire $1,200 balance on October 16th, before the October 27th due date. Despite the on-time payment, however, she will still be assessed interest on this payment because she lost her grace period for September by virtue of having not paid her bill in full in August. That interest will most likely be calculated as running from September 1st until October 16th (when payment is received). The interest will show up on the billing statement she receives on November 5th. Because Alyssa's paid the October 5th billing statement in full, however, she will once again be eligible for a grace period for payment of the November 5th billing statement if she pays that bill on time and in full.

6. Limitations on Finance Charges

Perhaps the trickiest issue with credit cards is the calculation of interest. Calculating interest on credit cards is tricky because of the difficulties in determining the balance on which interest will be assessed. Recall from Chapter 25 that the APR is a standardized measure of the cost of credit relative to any particular balance. The APR does not regulate how a balance is to be calculated, however. By increasing the balance on which an APR is applied, total finance charges on an account may be increased without any change in how the APR is disclosed.

The balance on a card account may fluctuate during a billing cycle. To account for such fluctuations, card issuers generally determine balances using an "**average daily**

balance" method. This means that the card issuer calculates the daily balances for each day in the billing cycle and then takes their average and uses that as the balance to which interest is applied (at least in the first instance). To illustrate, suppose that Alyssa charged $300 on September 1, $200 on September 11, and $500 on September 26. Alyssa's average daily balance for her September billing cycle would then be $600: the average of $300 for ten days, $500 for twenty days, plus $1,000 for five days.

Consider, then, two scenarios. In scenario #1, Alyssa has no grace period on her card, but she repays in full and on time. Specifically, she pays back $1,000 on October 16th. Because there is no grace period, she will be charged interest, even though she paid on time. She will be charged interest on an average daily balance of $600 for 30 days (September 1st to September 30th) and on an average daily balance of $1,000 for 15 days (October 1st to October 15th). If we posit 14.6% annual simple interest (let's not get into compounding here), then Alyssa will be charged $13.20 in interest in all ($7.20 for September plus $6.00 for half of October).

In scenario #2, Alyssa again has no grace period on her card, but this time she pays back only $800 on October 16th. She will then be charged interest on an average daily balance of $600 for 30 days (September 1st to September 30th) and on an average daily balance of $1,000 for 15 days (October 1st to October 15th) and on an average daily balance of $200 for 16 days (October 16th to October 31st).

It's important to recognize what's going on here—without a grace period, Alyssa will pay interest even on funds that she has repaid on time. The $800 she repays on time will be included in the calculation of the average daily balance in September and in October until payment is received. So, if we again posit 14.6% annual simple interest, Alyssa will be charged $14.28 in interest ($7.20 for September and $6.00 for half of October and $1.28 for the remainder of October). Keep these two scenarios in mind as a baseline for understanding what the CARD Act does.

The CARD Act imposes some limitations on when finance charges may be assessed. Obviously finance charges cannot be assessed if a balance is subject to a grace period. But the CARD Act requires that even if a cardholder loses a grace period, the card issuer is still forbidden from imposing finance charges on either (1) the balance during the days of the previous billing cycle or (2) any amounts repaid on time in the current billing cycle. 15 U.S.C. § 1637(j); 12 C.F.R. § 1026.54(a)(1).

Again, to illustrate, imagine that Alyssa pays her September 5th billing statement in full and on time, so she is eligible for a grace period on her October 5th billing statement provided that she pay it in full and on time. On October 5th she then gets her statement that shows a $1,000 balance based on purchases she made in September. (Assume that this $1,000 balance was a result of the purchases detailed above that resulted in a $600 average daily balance for September.)

If Alyssa repays only $800 of her balance before the October 27th due date, she would lose her grace period on the October 5th statement. The CARD Act, however, provides that even if she does, she may still not be charged interest on her September purchases for the period from September 1st to September 30th. 15 U.S.C. § 1637(j)(1)(A); 12 C.F.R. § 1026.54(a)(1)(i). She may, however, be charged interest on those purchases from October 1st until payment is received. Additionally, Alyssa may not be charged interest on the $800 she repaid on time. 15 U.S.C. § 1637(j)(1)(B);

12 C.F.R. § 1026.54(a)(1)(ii). She may not be charged interest on this $800 for either the September 1st to September 30th period or for the October 1st to October 16th period.

What this means is that even though Alyssa has lost her grace period she may be assessed interest (appearing on her November 5th statement) only on the $200 balance that she revolves and only for the period from October 1st until October 31st (when her billing cycle closes). Thus, at a 14.6% simple annual rate, Alyssa would pay only $2.40 in interest, as opposed to the $14.28 in scenario #2.

Alternatively, however, if Alyssa did not pay her September 5th billing statement in full and on time, she would not be eligible for a grace period on her October 5th billing statement, *even though she paid that statement in full and on time*. Therefore, the CARD Act limitations on finance charges upon loss of a grace period would not apply. Official Interpretation to 12 C.F.R. § 1026.54(a)(1), #1.i.B.[8] This means that the card issuer could charge a finance charge on the September purchases from September 1st until payment is received in October. The result will be the same as scenario #1. The situation this produces is called "**trailing interest**," wherein a cardholder pays off a bill in full and on time only to find an interest charge on the following billing statement, as there was no grace period because of failure to pay a *prior* balance in full and on time.[9]

Likewise, if Alyssa did not pay her September 5th billing statement in full and on time, and also paid only $800 of her $1000 balance on her October 5th billing statement, the card issuer could charge her interest (compounded daily) on the September purchases from September 1st until October 31st, including on the $800 that was repaid on time. The result will be the same as scenario #2.

These particular twists in calculating the balance on which interest may be applied are hardly intuitive. This method of calculating interest is all fully disclosed in cardholder agreements, but it might well surprise a reasonable consumer, who would expect to be charged interest only on the revolving balance. The CARD Act and card industry practice pre-date the UDAAP provision in the Consumer Financial Protection Act. Consider, though, how the calculation of the finance charge looks from a UDAAP perspective. Does it take unreasonable advantage of a lack of consumer understanding of product terms and conditions, particularly in regard to trailing interest?

7. Fees

Fees are also regulated. Late, over-limit, or penalty fees must be "reasonable and proportional to such omission or violation." 15 U.S.C. § 1665d(a). As implemented by Regulation Z, the reasonable and proportionate requirement is not in relation to

---

8. It is not clear why this is the Official Interpretation's position, given that the statutory language does not seem to distinguish between reasons for loss of a grace period. The Official Interpretation enables substantially more trailing interest than otherwise.

9. Depending on how a card issuer crafts its application of trailing interest, however, it is possible to end up with a type of Xeno's paradox whereby the borrower can never fully pay down the balance without either overpaying or getting a payoff calculation for a specific date.

the actual transaction but to "the total costs incurred by the card issuer as a result of that type of violation." 12 C.F.R. § 1026.52(b)(1)(i). Card issuers must reevaluate their costs at least annually. *Id.*

A safe harbor exists for the reasonable and proportionate requirement. If the fee is no more than $25.00 for a first violation or $35.00 for a second violation of the same type in the same or next six billing cycles. 12 C.F.R. § 1026.52(b)(1)(ii)(A)-(B). These numbers are inflation adjusted annually. 12 C.F.R. § 1026.52(b)(1)(ii)(D). In no case, however, may the fee exceed the dollar amount associated with the violation. 12 C.F.R. § 1026.52(b)(2)(i). For charge cards, a fee of 3% of the delinquent balance is deemed reasonable and proportionate if the payment is more than two billing cycles late, which means 49-52 days late, as we shall see. 12 C.F.R. § 1026.52(b)(1)(ii)(C).

Additional restrictions apply to over-limit fees. Consumers must opt in to over-limit fees. 15 U.S.C. § 1637(k). Over-limit fees are limited to one per billing cycle and can only be re-imposed for the same over-limit violation in three consecutive billing cycles. 15 U.S.C. § 1637(k)(7). Other types of fees, such as for account closings, inactivity, or declined authorizations, may not be imposed. 12 C.F.R. § 1026.52(b)(2)(i)(B). Only one fee may be imposed for each type of violation. 12 C.F.R. § 1026.52(b)(2)(ii).

8. "Fee-Harvester" Cards

Special regulations apply to so-called subprime fee-harvester cards. 15 U.S.C. § 1637(n). These cards have very low credit limits—often $300 or less—and high up-front and recurring fees and interest rates. Prior to the CARD Act of 2009, fee-harvester cards often had up-front fees of $150, which were put on the card, meaning that the consumer paid $150 to have another $150 of credit line available. The CARD Act caps fees at account opening at 25% of the available line. 15 U.S.C. § 1637(n); 12 C.F.R. § 1026.52(a).

Fee-harvester cards are marketed to consumers with poor credit; they are often pitched as a way for a consumer to rebuild damaged credit that does not involve a "secured credit card"—a card for which repayment is secured by a cash deposit made at a bank. While Reg Z prohibits setoffs of deposit accounts against credit card debt, it explicitly excepts consensual security interests. 12 C.F.R. § 1026.12(d). With a secured card, a consumer might deposit $500 at a bank and get a $500 or $600 line of credit. In other words, very little actual credit is provided by the card. Instead, a secured credit card is largely making the consumer's own funds available to the consumer.

IV. IMPACT OF THE CARD ACT

Congress required the CFPB to do a study on the impact of the CARD Act. The CFPB found that the CARD Act had significantly reshaped the consumer credit card market and had been spectacularly successful in terms of simplifying credit card products. One study found that the average number of figures in card disclosures dropping from 33 in 2009 to 26 in 2010. Joshua M. Frank, *Numbers Game: The*

True Cost of Credit Card Mail Offers, Center for Responsible Lending Research Report, Oct. 2010. But that is hardly all, as the CFPB's initial CARD Act study, from 2013, excerpted below, makes clear.

CFPB, CARD Act Report:

A Review of the Impact of the CARD Act on the Consumer Credit Card Market, Oct. 1, 2013, at 5-6

. . .

COST OF CREDIT

The CARD Act has impacted the way that consumers pay for credit in the credit card marketplace and has significantly enhanced transparency for consumers. Overlimit fees and repricing actions have been largely eliminated; those effects can be directly traced to the Act. The dollar amount of late fees is down as well, and the CARD Act directly caused this reduction.

The end result is a market in which shopping for a credit card and comparing costs is far more straightforward than it was prior to enactment of the Act. Many credit card agreements have become shorter and easier to understand, though it is not clear how much of these changes can be attributed directly to the CARD Act since it did not explicitly mandate changes to the length and form of credit card agreements. Limitations on "back-end" fees, along with restrictions on an issuer's ability to raise interest rates, have simplified a consumer's cost calculations. Credit card costs are now more closely related to the clearly disclosed annual fees and interest rates. This greater transparency means a consumer deciding whether to charge a purchase can now make that decision with far more confidence that costs will be a function of the current interest rate rather than some yet-to-be determined interest rate that could be reassessed at any time and for any reason by the issuer.

Consistent with the shift towards more transparency as a result of upfront pricing, we find that, beginning in early 2009 and continuing through February 2010, when many provisions of the Act went into effect, the interest rate on credit card accounts increased, while back-end fees decreased or were eliminated. While some of this increase was likely intended to offset other changes in pricing affected by the CARD Act, we make no judgment on the extent to which the CARD Act, as distinguished from other factors such as the impact of the Great Recession, contributed to these increases.

However, we do find that among the card issuers represented in the Bureau's credit card database (representing between 85% and 90% of credit card industry balances), the total cost of credit – *i.e.* the annualized sum of all amounts paid by consumers (including both interest charges and fees) divided by the average of outstanding balances – *declined* by 194 basis points from Q4 2008 to Q4 2012. Again, it is unclear how much of that change is attributable to the CARD Act.

. . .

According to the Bureau's data, total credit line (whether used or unused) was $200 billion lower at the end of 2012 than when many provisions of the CARD Act took effect in February 2010. This decline disproportionately occurred in the subprime credit space. The industry contraction that we observe began before the enactment of the CARD Act and has continued through 2012, though at a slower pace than during the peak of the Great Recession. Even so, consumers still possessed $1.9 trillion in unused credit line at the end of 2012.

The evidence suggests that the CARD Act had a discernible impact on credit availability in three discrete respects. First, there has been a substantial decrease in the number of credit card accounts originated among students and other consumers under the age of 21. Second, the issuers contacted in preparing this report stated that a small but discernible percentage of applicants that they deemed otherwise creditworthy are being declined as a result of insufficient income to satisfy the Act's ability-to-pay requirement. Third, and relatedly, there has been a marked decline in the percentage of consumers receiving unsolicited credit line increases (also referred to as "proactive line increases") on their accounts. At least some of these limitations on access to credit appear to be intended consequences of the CARD Act's stated objective of creating fair and transparent practices with respect to open-end credit.

In a follow-up report from 2015, the CFPB noted that:

> The shift towards upfront pricing in the wake of the CARD Act remains resilient. Fees remain lower relative to balances than they did before implementation of the Act, again both overall and for consumers in different risk tiers. Had fees impacted by CARD Act rules continued at pre-CARD Act levels, consumers would have paid an additional $16 billion in such fees from the beginning of 2011 through the end of 2014.

CFPB, *The Consumer Credit Card Market*, Dec. 2015, at 10. The CARD Act, then, appears to be one of the most successful pieces of consumer financial regulation, resulting in a simplification and "de-shrouding" of card issuer pricing that shifted price most from back-end, behaviorally contingent pricing that consumers often underestimated to more salient up-front pricing that is subject to stronger price competition among issuers.

V. REMAINING CREDIT CARD REGULATION ISSUES

While the CARD Act substantially reformed the credit card market, a number of issues remain outstanding. The CFPB's CARD Act reports explain these issues.

CFPB, CARD Act Report:

A Review of the Impact of the CARD Act on the Consumer Credit Card Market

Oct. 1, 2013, at 5-6

REMAINING CONCERNS

. . .

There remain, however, some possible areas of concern—practices that may pose risks to consumers and may warrant further scrutiny by the Bureau. Based on the work that supports this report and our other activities, we identify six examples of such practices:

1. ADD-ON PRODUCTS: Credit card issuers market various "add-on" products to card users, including debt protection, identity theft protection, credit score monitoring, and other products that are supplementary to the actual extension of credit. The Bureau has found through its supervisory work that these products are frequently sold in a manner that harms consumers. The Bureau has engaged in enforcement actions and issued a bulletin that provides industry guidance on the marketing of these products. The Bureau will continue to closely review the sale of add-on products by card issuers and their service providers to determine whether additional actions are warranted.

2. FEE HARVESTER CARDS: Some card issuers charge upfront fees that exceed 25% of a card's initial credit limit, but those practices have been held not to be covered by the CARD Act because a portion of the fees are paid prior to account opening. The Bureau will continue to monitor the use of application fees in connection with account opening to determine if it should take action under its available authorities.

3. DEFERRED INTEREST PRODUCTS: In the private label credit card market, it is common to offer ["deferred interest"] promotional financing for purchases. These offers retroactively assess and charge interest if the balance is not paid in full by a specific date. [These programs offer "0% interest if paid in full" during a defined promotional period, which is generally six or 12 months. Consumers who repay the full promotional purchase in this window obtain free financing on what is often a large purchase. Those consumers who do not fully pay off the promotional balance by the end of the promotion, however, are subject to the same interest rate they would have paid in the absence of the promotion. Given that the interest rate on these cards is generally around 25%, the magnitude of the interest charge—if and when it is assessed—can be substantial.[10]]. . .

4. Many consumers are offered and accept "deferred interest" promotional financing on private label cards.

5. TRANSPARENCY ISSUES

a. ONLINE DISCLOSURES: The CARD Act mandated that certain disclosures be included on monthly billing statements, including warnings related to late fees and the cost to the consumer of making only the minimum payment due. Regulation Z adds other requirements for these statements. However, consumers who pay their bills electronically may not access their monthly statement and instead may use online portals which are not required to contain these disclosures. This reflects a more general challenge of translating regulations related to disclosures largely written for a paper-and-pencil world into the modern electronic world. The Bureau will observe closely how card issuers ensure that consumers receive disclosures in different channels.

b. REWARDS PRODUCTS: For certain consumers, comparison shopping for new credit cards frequently revolves around considering different rewards programs. Rewards offers can be highly complex, with detailed rules regarding the eligibility for sign-on bonuses, the value of earned points, the rate at which they are earned,

10. From CFPB, *The Consumer Credit Card Market*, Dec. 2015.

and the rules governing their forfeiture. In the course of its consumer research and market monitoring activities, the Bureau will review whether rewards disclosures are being made in a clear and transparent manner, as well as assess whether additional action is warranted.

c. GRACE PERIODS: For consumers who do not pay their balance in full each month, a key determinant of their cost of credit is the grace period. It is unclear whether consumers understand that once they carry a balance into a new month, interest will be assessed on the unpaid balance from the start of the prior month. Until the consumer qualifies for the grace period again, interest is assessed on all purchases from the date of purchase. It is likewise unclear whether consumers understand that even after they pay the full amount shown on their bill, they may still owe "trailing interest" for the period from the time the bill was issued until the time the payment was received. As with rewards products, the Bureau will review whether grace period limitations are being disclosed in a clear and transparent manner.

CFPB, The Consumer Credit Card Market

Dec. 2015, at 16-17

There remain, however, areas of concern for consumers. This report addresses a number of these, but three stand out:

- Deferred interest products are popular and provide many consumers with valuable interest-free loans on larger purchases, but they remain the most glaring exception to the general post-CARD Act trend towards upfront credit card pricing. Consumers with worse credit scores generally pay more for these products than consumers with higher scores. But they do so at the "back-end" of the transaction, and not pursuant to upfront transparent pricing differences. As we describe, moreover, there are significant indications that the lack of transparency in this market contributes to avoidable consumer costs. These costs can be substantial—and may have longer-term consequences;
- Subprime specialist credit card issuers offer products significantly more expensive than their mass market counterparts. Fees and interest assessed to their consumers exceeded 40% of those consumers' year-end balances in 2013 and 2014. In addition, given that these issuers place much greater reliance on origination and maintenance fees, and that these fees are charged against relatively small lines, their products create the risk that a significant share of consumer monthly payments go to cover fees and interest on fees—and not to paying off the principal balance created by spending on the card. These issuers tend to solicit applications using targeted direct mail. Despite offering longer and more complex credit card terms than mass market issuers, they send those mailings disproportionally to consumers with lower levels of formal education; and
- Most credit cards now have variable interest rates. These credit card rates will rise—even on existing balances—when background interest rates in the economy increase. This is not an argument against variable rate pricing. Such pricing is

> the norm for open-end products where the consumer can continue to draw on a credit line and borrow for an indefinite period of time so long as the account remains open and the full line has not been utilized. The concern here is that, in the wake of a historical long period of stable and low interest rates, consumers may be accumulating and revolving balances without an understanding that the price of doing so—even on existing balances—may well increase in the future. Given CARD Act restrictions on most other retroactive rate increases, consumers may not be expecting any increase on the rates they pay to borrow on credit cards.
>
> . . .

Problem Set 27

1. Sally Ramsey, a stay-at-home mother of two, wants to get a credit card. She does not want to have her husband as a co-signor on the card: "It's none of his business what I buy," says Sally. Sally's got a solid credit score, based in part on the auto loan and mortgage for which she and her husband are co-signors and a co-signed credit card she previously had. Can Sally get a card herself? *See* 15 U.S.C. § 1665e; 12 C.F.R. § 1026.51(a); Official Interpretation to 12 C.F.R. § 1026.51(a)(1)(i) #4.ii-iii, #6.

2. Alexander "Ace" Takeuchi is a brilliant Massachusetts Technical University computer science major set to graduate in the spring. He's been hard at work on a project he calls "SocioPathfinder" that he thinks will transform human relations. Ace is so engrossed in SocioPathfinder that he's been neglecting his studies. Ace needs capital if he's going to take Social SocioPathfinder further. He's decided to apply for a card from Continental Express Bank, N.A. Ace is a full-time student on financial aid, with $100,000 in student loan debt, and few assets other than his IP rights in SocioPathfinder (which are challenged by the Andover triplets).

   a. Can ConEx issue Ace a card? *See* 15 U.S.C. §§ 1637(c)(8), 1665e; 12 C.F.R. § 1026.51(a)-(b).

   b. What if it has data showing that the average post-graduation earnings of a Massachusetts Technical University computer science major are well over $100,000? *See* Official Interpretation to 12 C.F.R. § 1026.51(a)(1)(i) #5(iv).

3. Your college classmate, Grant McQueen, was recently laid off from his job at Eli's Tire Emporium. He's neglected to pay his credit card bill for the last three months. He finally looked at his credit card statement and saw that his interest rate had been increased from Prime + 12% to Prime + 24%. Grant knows that you've studied credit cards in law school. He says, "I thought they couldn't do that after that Credit Card Act. What gives? Is there any way to get my rate back down?" He shows you his cardholder agreement with Bank of America, which says:

> We may increase the APRs on new transactions up to the Penalty APR, based on your creditworthiness, each time a Total Minimum Payment Due is not received by its applicable Payment Due Date. We may elect to set your APRs for Purchases, Balance Transfers, Direct Deposit and Check Cash Advances, and Bank Cash Advances to different Penalty APRs. We will provide you with a minimum of 45 days advance notice. An increased Penalty APR will remain in effect indefinitely.

What do you tell Grant? *See* 15 U.S.C. §§ 1665c, 1666i-1; 12 C.F.R. §§ 1026.9(g)(2); 1026.55(a)-(b), 1026.59(e).

4. You've just joined the general counsel's office at Continental Express and are excited to get your first assignment. The GC has asked that you review a new card plan pricing proposal from the business team. They're suggesting that the new ConEx Magenta Card have a 0% teaser rate for 3 months, charging a $35 late fee, a $5 monthly line availability fee, and a $10 monthly "network security fee." They're also proposing that finance charges be applied to the average daily balance based on the last three billing cycles. They argue that this will help smooth out consumers' monthly payments, particularly during the holiday season, because monthly payments must include all finance charges + fees + 2.5% of the balance. What are your thoughts on this proposal? *See* 15 U.S.C. §§ 1637(j), 1637(n), 1665d, 1666i-2; 12 C.F.R. §§ 1026.52(b), 1026.54, 1026.55(b).

5. Duncan Lamprey has less-than-stellar credit and is chronically short on cash, but he'd like to get a credit card. He's seen advertisements for secured credit cards, like one from Capital One that has a 24.99% APR, a $300 credit limit, and requires that he grant the bank a security interest in a special security deposit account containing $300. He's also seen an advertisement for an unsecured card from a bank called First Premier. The First Premier product has a fixed-rate 36% APR, a one-time $29 processing fee, a $79 annual fee, and a $12 monthly fee (reduced to $8 for the first year) and offers a $300 credit limit. What are the trade-offs between these products for Duncan? *See* 15 U.S.C. § 1637(n); 12 C.F.R. § 1026.52(a).

6. Which of the three market diagnoses does the CARD Act seem to respond to, and how: the sticky relationship diagnosis, the shrouded pricing diagnosis, or the sweatbox diagnosis?

7. Consider the CARD Act's ability-to-repay requirement, 15 U.S.C. § 1665e, in connection with usury laws and with *Williams v. Walker-Thomas Furniture Co.*, 350 F.2d 445 (D.C. Cir. 1965) (in chapter 2). To what degree do these approaches to consumer finance regulation overlap? What are the trade-offs among the approaches? Do you think different sized institutions would prefer a particular approach?

CHAPTER 28

MORTGAGES I: MORTGAGE BASICS

I. WHAT'S A MORTGAGE?

A. Shelter and Investment

People need a place to live. They need housing. Housing, however, is expensive, and modern housing with indoor plumbing and electricity and HVAC certainly is. Relatively few consumers have the financial capacity to purchase housing outright, particularly in desirable locations, where limited housing stock (due to geographic and zoning constraints) and population growth have pushed up housing prices.

Because most consumers cannot purchase housing of a quality and location that they desire outright, most consumers either rent or purchase on credit. According to the Census's 2015 American Housing Survey, of the approximately 134 million year-round housing units in the United States, 118 million are occupied and 13 million are vacant (this includes properties for rent or sale).

Of the occupied properties, 74 million (63%) are owner-occupied and 44 million (37%) are rental. Of the owner-occupied properties, 30 million are owned "free and clear," without a mortgage on the property. The remaining 44 million have at least one mortgage on the property, with 4.4 million of the mortgaged properties encumbered with multiple mortgages. Thus, around 26% of households own their homes outright, 37% have mortgages on their homes, and 37% are renters. Figure 28.1 shows the breakdown of tenure and financing for American housing, while Figure 28.2 shows U.S. homeownership rates since the 1960s. (Homeownership rates were substantially lower—in the mid-40% rate—prior to the end of World War II and then jumped substantially between 1945 and 1960.)

Mortgages are not simply a means of financing housing consumption, however. A house is more than shelter. It is also a financial investment. Houses are long-term durable assets that may appreciate (or depreciate) depending on care and market supply and demand conditions. Purchasing a home is an investment in real estate. As a financial investment, homes are unusual. Not only are homes consumable, unlike, say, gold or corporate stock, but like the burning bush, they are nearly indefinitely consumable; the median U.S. home is a 40-year-old structure.

Figure 28.1 Tenure & Financing of American Housing, 2015[1]

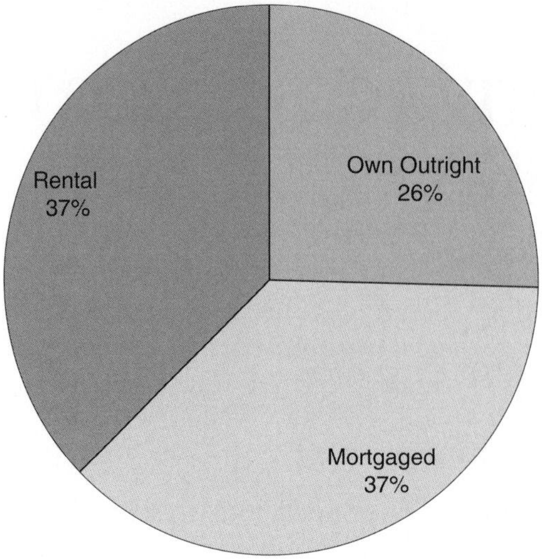

Rental 37%

Own Outright 26%

Mortgaged 37%

Figure 28.2 U.S. Homeownership Rates, 1960-2017[2]

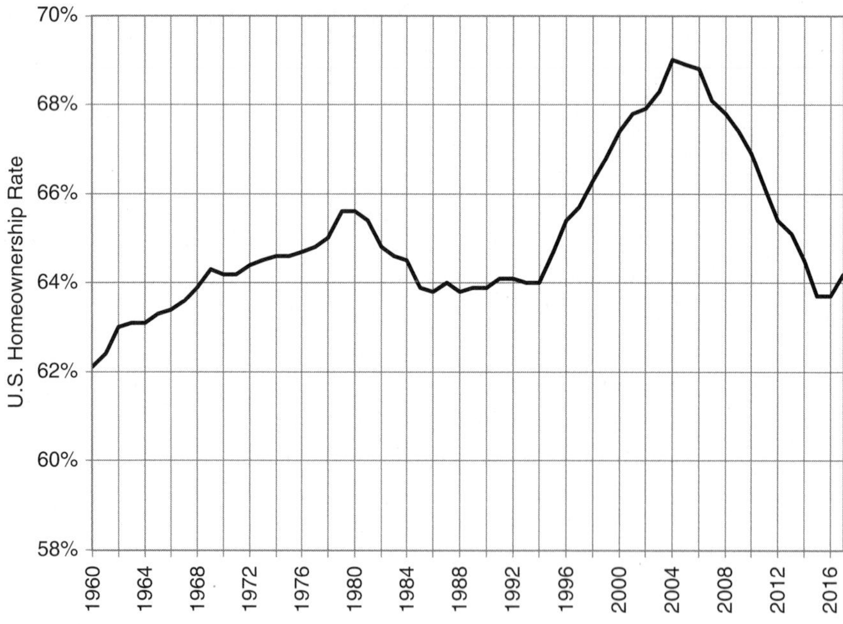

1. U.S. Census Bureau, 2015 American Housing Survey.
2. U.S. Census Bureau.

A home is not just a potentially appreciating investment. It is also an inflation hedge. When there is inflation, rental prices rise. A homeowner does not incur a similar increase in his or her cost of housing, however.[3] (If the home is financed with an adjustable-rate mortgage, that is another matter . . .)

A mortgage is a way to make a leveraged housing investment, meaning that the housing investment is purchased on credit. The leverage allows the consumer to telescope future income into today's purchasing power, thus enabling the consumer to buy more house than if purchasing in cash. Yet it also exposes the consumer to repayment risk. If the consumer's income does not remain at anticipated levels, the consumer may be unable to service the mortgage debt. If so, the consumer will have to sell the house (and use the sale proceeds to pay off the mortgage) or the lender will foreclose on the house and forcibly sell it (and apply the proceeds to the mortgage debt).

B. Mortgage Instruments

The financial product colloquially known as a "mortgage" is in fact typically composed of two separate financial instruments: a **note** and a **security instrument**. The note contains the promise to repay the debt. The security instrument (called a **mortgage** or **deed of trust**) pledges the house as collateral securing the repayment of the note. The note, then, is the trigger for the rights granted in the security instrument. If the note is not repaid, then the secured party may exercise its rights under the security instrument; without the note, the security instrument by itself is meaningless.

The terminology of a mortgage transaction is somewhat counterintuitive because of the colloquial use of the term: people talk about "getting a mortgage" from a lender. In fact, the consumer gets a loan from the lender and *gives* the lender a mortgage. Thus, the consumer is the mortgagor, while the lender is the mortgagee; the consumer has mortgaged the property.

The legal operation and understanding of a mortgage transaction varies by state, and is governed by state real property and commercial law. In some states, a mortgage is understood as a lien on the property. A lien is a contingent property right; the party holding the lien (the mortgagee) does not have title to the property, only a right to force a sale following a default on the note. States that understand mortgages in this way are called "lien theory" states.

Other states understand a mortgage as a sale and repurchase agreement: the borrower sells the house to the lender and has a right to repurchase it by repaying the loan. In a title theory state, the lender formally holds title to the house. (And this means that a mortgage in a title theory state is a transfer of real property, not just a financing, so it must comply with the Statute of Frauds, etc.)

Roughly half of U.S. states are lien theory states and half are title theory states. The lien theory/title theory distinction roughly tracks the name used for the security

3. To be sure, inflation will likely also result in nominal home price appreciation, and hence higher property tax assessments.

instrument. Lien theory states tend to use "mortgages," while title theory states tend to use "deeds of trust" or DOT. To see why there would be this rough correlation, the concept behind a DOT is that the borrower places the deed to the property in trust for the lender. The borrower (the "trustor") gives title to the property to the DOT trustee, who holds it on behalf of the lender (the DOT "beneficiary"). The DOT trustee is typically a title company or a local attorney. The DOT trustee is charged with releasing the deed to the trustor if the loan is paid off or with foreclosing if the trustor defaults. In the standard DOT arrangement, when the homeowner defaults, the beneficiary will appoint a substitute trustee, often an affiliate, to handle foreclosure. There is relatively little law on the precise duties of DOT trustees, which may be a potential issue in foreclosures. For the purposes of this chapter, we will use the term mortgage colloquially, except when a distinction is necessary.

C. Recordation

As a type of interest in real property, a mortgage may be recorded in the local land records. Every county or parish in the United States has a real estate recordation system.[4] Recordation is not required in most states for a mortgage (here meaning the security instrument) to be enforceable against the mortgagor. But recordation can vest the mortgagee with greater rights against the mortgagor and with rights against third parties. In some states, non-judicial foreclosure—usually a faster and cheaper procedure than judicial foreclosure—is only available for recorded mortgages.[5]

Moreover, recordation establishes the **priority** of the mortgage: the mortgagee's "dibs" on the collateral. Multiple loans can be secured by the same property. State law provides rules to sort out the priority of those claims. Lack of recording makes a mortgagee vulnerable to becoming subordinated to a subsequent recorded mortgage, thereby reducing the value of the unrecorded mortgage. Moreover, lack of recording makes a mortgagee vulnerable to having the its security interest voided because a subsequent bona fide purchaser will take the property without being subject to the unrecorded security interest. Lack of recording also makes a mortgage vulnerable to being avoided by a trustee in the mortgagor's bankruptcy. 11 U.S.C. § 544(a).

The majority of mortgages are currently recorded using a private recordation utility known as the Mortgage Electronic Registration System (MERS). When MERS is used, MERS is listed in county property records as the mortgagee; MERS private registry tracks the identity of the servicing agent of the lender. The idea behind

4. Several states also have additional, non-mandatory Torrens registration systems, usually at the state level, which register actual title, rather than recording documentary evidence of title. R.G. Patton, *The Torrens System of Land Title Registration*, 19 Minn. L. Rev. 519 (1934). In a Torrens system, the state investigates title. If satisfied, the state registers title. Registered owners have indefeasible title. The state provides indemnification for any legitimate claimant to superior title, but only monetary relief is possible; the property remains with the registered owner. Thomas J. Miceli & C.F. Sirmans, *The Economics of Land Transfer and Title Insurance*, 10 J. R.E. Fin. & Econ. 81 (1995). In a Torrens system, transfer of title is effective only upon registration of the transfer.

5. *See, e.g.*, Cal. Civ. Code § 2932.5 (West); Ga. Code Ann. § 44-14-162(b); Nev. Rev. Stat. § 106.210(1); Ore. Rev. Stat. § 86.735.

MERS is to immobilize title to mortgages so as to avoid payment of county recordation fees and enable faster transfers of mortgages. The model for MERS is the Depository Trust Corporation (DTC), which holds legal title to most equity securities issued in the United States, with trades in beneficial ownership being tracked in the DTC's book-entry system. The DTC is authorized by Article 8 of the UCC and by federal securities laws; no similar authority exists for MERS, which has been at the center of significant ongoing legal controversy, as MERS recordation system is neither transparent nor accurate.

D. Foreclosure and Recourse

If a homeowner defaults on a mortgage, the lender may accelerate the debt and commence foreclosure. Foreclosure is mainly a matter of state law. Recent CFPB regulations create additional legal obligations, and some lenders are subject to consent orders and settlements that impose further obligations.

Some states require **judicial foreclosure**, meaning through a lawsuit to determine the right to foreclose and a subsequent sale conducted by the sheriff, while others permit **non-judicial foreclosure**, meaning that the property is advertised and sold privately, without any judicial process. Yet other states, such as Massachusetts, have hybrid processes, requiring some judicial involvement, but a private sale. The precise procedures necessary to foreclose—and the length of time it takes—vary considerably by state.

A foreclosure sale technically forecloses the borrower's right to cure the default on the mortgage. In some states, however, the borrower has a post-foreclosure **right of redemption**. This means that in some states, the borrower may redeem the mortgage and retain the house by paying the purchase price paid by the foreclosure sale purchaser. The right of redemption is essentially a right to a matching bid at the auction, but it can be exercised only for a limited post-sale period. Borrowers often contractually waive the right to redeem.

Because a property belongs to a borrower up until the completion of a foreclosure sale, there is no right for foreclosure sale buyers to inspect the property on which they are bidding. This has the effect of depressing foreclosure sale prices, although savvy purchasers sometimes find workarounds. Lenders are permitted to **credit bid** at foreclosure sales by bidding in the amount owed on the mortgage. Credit bidding helps lenders ensure against lowball collusive bids by friends and family of the debtor and lets the lender take title to the property and subsequently sell it through a normal private sale with right of inspection. Note that a foreclosure is not the same as an eviction; if the borrower remains in the property after the foreclosure, then the foreclosure sale purchaser can go to court to get an eviction order.

A foreclosure sale only extinguishes the *lien* of the foreclosing creditor and any junior liens on the property. It does not extinguish senior liens. Foreclosure sale proceeds are paid to the lienholder conducting the sale and then to junior lienholder and then to the borrower; the senior lienholder does not recover. Accordingly, senior liens remain on the property after the foreclosure sale; the debt secured by the senior lien(s), however, is still owed by the original borrower. Thus, if the original borrower does not continue paying the mortgage on a house s/he no longer possesses, the senior lienholder may foreclose and take the house from the winner of the foreclosure sale on the junior lien. Accordingly, foreclosure sale borrowers will discount their purchase price by the amount of any senior liens outstanding. The result is that foreclosure sales are rarely brought by junior lienholders. They functionally have tagalong rights for the senior lienholder's foreclosure sale, rather than meaningful rights to foreclose themselves.

A foreclosure sale also does not discharge *debt* except to the extent the lender is repaid from the sale proceeds. If there is a **surplus** in a foreclosure sale—not a common occurrence after the foreclosing lender and all junior lienholders have been paid—it is paid to the borrower. If there is a **deficiency**, however, the treatment of the deficiency will vary by state and by the terms of the loan. Some loans are explicitly **non-recourse**, meaning that the lender can only recover from the proceeds of the property if the borrower does not pay willingly; the lender cannot pursue the borrower's other assets. Most mortgage loans, however, are formally **recourse**. State law, however, may provide that certain types of mortgages may be non-recourse or that a lender may not obtain a deficiency judgment if it chooses to foreclose using a particular method (such as non-judicial foreclosure). In other states the right to a deficiency judgment is discretionary to the judge. Infamously, prior to 2013, California law provided that purchase money mortgages were non-recourse, but refinancings were recourse. (The old law still applies to mortgages made before 2013.)

If a mortgage is recourse, and the foreclosure sale proceeds do not satisfy the balance owed on the mortgage, then the lender may obtain a deficiency judgment and attempt to collect it from the borrower. The deficiency judgment is just a regular unsecured debt that can be discharged in bankruptcy absent unusual circumstances. This means it is difficult to collect in most cases, particularly in states that restrict wage garnishment. The value of a deficiency judgment would appear to be primarily as a threat to induce payment rather than as a collection method.

II. MORTGAGE FEATURES

A. Interest Rates

Mortgage notes have several key features. Perhaps most important is the interest rate. The interest rate will usually either be fixed or variable.[6] If it is fixed, the mortgage is known as a fixed-rate mortgage (FRMs), while if it varies based on an index, it is called an adjustable-rate mortgage (ARM, pronounced either *ay-are-em* or *arm*). ARMs generally reset rates on an annual basis.

Some mortgages combine fixed and adjustable rate features. These are so-called hybrid ARMs will typically have an initial fixed-rate period and thereafter adjust

6. A small number of mortgages have graduated payments, in which payments increase or decrease based on a pre-set schedule, rather than an index.

their rates periodically. Hybrid ARMs will have their structure indicated in short hand with a fraction. The numerator is the fixed rate period, while the denominator is either the frequency of rate resets or the remaining term of the loan. Thus, a 5/1 ARM has a five-year fixed rate period and then adjusts the rate annually after five years for the duration of the mortgage, whereas a 2/28 would have a two-year fixed period, with 28 years of adjustable rates.

As of 2015, 94% of mortgages outstanding in the United States were FRMs, with most of the rest being ARMs. 2015 American Housing Survey. Among ARMs, 5/1s are the most common product, with 3/27s and 7/1s also being common. *Id.*

The structure of a mortgage's interest rates allocates interest rate risk between the borrower and the lender. If market interest rates rise, the monthly payments owed by an ARM borrower increase, while if rates fall, the monthly payments decrease. Thus, an ARM borrower bears the risk of changes in interest rates and is exposed to inflation, just like a renter.

For FRM borrowers, the allocation of interest rate risk is different. If market interest rates rise, a FRM borrower's payments do not increase. The FRM borrower thus has a hedge against inflation. The FRM lender, however, ends up with an asset providing a below-market return if interest rates rise. If interest rates fall, a FRM borrower's payments do not decrease. The FRM borrower can refinance and prepay, however, at the new, lower market rate. The borrower thus has a "put option" baked into the loan structure if the loan is prepayable. Even if there is a prepayment penalty, all it does is raise the "strike price" of the put option on the loan.

Thus, the FRM lender faces risk if rates rise or fall—either it will have a below-market investment or it will lose its above-market investment and have to reinvest in a less favorable rate climate. Interest rate risk is accordingly one of the major risks faced by a mortgage lender. The prepayable FRM structure is quite favorable to the borrower, particularly when combined with a long loan term. Why would the market have evolved to be so favorable to the borrower?

Part of the answer is regulatory intervention, part is consumer tastes, and part might be the result of efficient allocations of risk. The long-term, prepayable FRM is a distinctly American product; most of the world uses short-term or non-prepayable FRMs or ARMs. Long-term prepayable FRMs are a product that basically did not exist prior to the New Deal. During the Depression, the private housing finance system collapsed. The federal government programs and agencies that emerged between 1932 and 1944 were intensely focused on encouraging fixed-rate mortgages. Fixed rates help shield consumers from inflation and payment shocks, and thus created more stability for the household balance sheet; the fixed-rate mortgage was a major monthly expense around which a family could plan its budget. Not surprisingly, consumers have a strong taste for a fixed-rate mortgage, even with option-adjusted pricing (adjusting to account for the put option). 92% of first-lien mortgages in 2011 were fixed-rate obligations. Three percent were regular ARMs, and four percent involved some sort of hybrid. Lastly, it would seem that financial institutions are better positioned to bear interest rate risk than consumers are; consumers have few tools to hedge against inflation. Accordingly, allocating rate risk to financial institution lenders may be more efficient than allocating it to consumers.

B. Maturity Dates and Amortization

A mortgage loan has a maturity date or term, meaning a date by which they must be repaid. Closely related to term is the loan's amortization period. Amortization refers to the time period over which the loan's principal will be repaid. A loan may be fully amortized, partially amortized, or unamortized.

If a loan is fully amortized, that means that every month the borrower is paying down some of the loan's principal. There are different amortization schedules possible, but typically a borrower pays down very little principal in the first years of a loan, and instead pays off the principal toward the end of the loan.

If a loan is partially amortized, that means there is some principal repaid before maturity, but that there is still a balloon of principal due on the maturity date. If a loan is unamortized, no principal is due until the maturity date. Such a loan is called an interest-only loan or a balloon loan. The borrower makes monthly interest payments prior to the maturity date, and then pays all of the principal in a balloon payment at maturity. Such a loan structure reduces monthly payments, but means that the borrower must come up with the funds to make the balloon payment. Often the borrower relies on refinancing the loan prior to the maturity date and using the proceeds from the refinancing to pay off the loan.

Some loans—so-called payment-option mortgages—let borrowers choose their payment in any given month based on a menu of amortization schedules. Sometimes this menu includes the choice of negative amortization, meaning that the monthly payment is insufficient to pay down accrued interest, much less principal, so the loan balance *increases*. This sort of loan may make sense for some niche borrowers with seasonably varied income, but became a mass-market product during the housing bubble.

Thirty years is the most standard term for a mortgage in the United States. Sixty-eight percent of mortgage loans outstanding in 2015 had 30-year terms. 2015 American Housing Survey. The next most common term, fifteen years, accounted for only 12% of all mortgages. *Id.* Yet the average borrower remains in occupancy in a dwelling for far less time. From 2001 to 2008, the average tenure in a house was just six years; since then it has increased to nine years, but it is still much shorter than the average mortgage term. Why?

All else equal, a longer-term loan is riskier for a lender because there is more time during which things can go wrong. Yet for a borrower, a longer term means paying more interest, as there will be more time over which interest accrues, but if the loan is amortized, a longer loan term means lower monthly payments. So a longer-term loan is more expensive in the long run, but cheaper on a monthly basis, which is how most households budget. A longer-term loan also gives a borrower greater optionality. The borrower is not under a crunch to pay off the loan or refinance it. This means that the borrower is not at the mercy of markets—if the market is frozen for some reason, the borrower has flexibility. And given the prevalence of fixed-rate mortgages, a longer-term loan lets the borrower capitalize on the interest rate risk allocation.

Note that term and amortization need not match. A loan can have a 30-year term and a 40-year amortization, meaning that monthly payments are based off of a 40-year payment schedule. When the loan matures in year 30, the remaining principal—ten years of the amortization schedule—are due as a balloon. This sort of loan is called a 30/40.

C. Loan Size, Loan-to-Value Ratio, and Priority

The size of the loan is a critical feature for determining the lender's **credit risk.** Mortgage lending involves two primary risks: credit risk and interest rate risk. We have already seen rate risk. Credit risk goes to the question of whether the lender will be repaid on time. Mortgage lenders have two main possible sources of repayment: the borrower's income and the property itself. To the extent that the loan amount exceeds the property value, the lender cannot count on the property to provide a full recovery.

Lenders typically think of loan size in relation to property values. The ratio is called the **loan to value ratio** or **LTV ratio.** If an LTV is over 100%, that means the property is "**underwater**" or "**upside down**"—the homeowner has negative equity in the property. When LTV is in the 95%-100% range, it is called "**near negative equity,**" as the lender might not recover the full loan amount in a foreclosure given foreclosure sale costs and valuation uncertainties.

The borrower's ability to repay the loan either through voluntary cash payments or by surrendering the house gives the borrower something like a put option on the house, particularly if the loan is non-recourse (or functionally non-recourse). If the house is upside down, then the put option is in the money. If the borrower has the possibility of obtaining alternative housing at a more favorable monthly payment rate, then it may make sense for the borrower to strategically exercise the put option. Of course, homes are not simply financial instruments—they are also loci of family life and sentiments. Thus, lenders have a strong interest in reducing the attractiveness of the put option by ensuring that a borrower actually lives in the house: a borrower is much less likely to exercise the put option on an owner-occupied house than on an investment property, all else being equal. But this also means that lenders face a risk of asset substitution as part of their credit risk: what was originally an owner-occupied house can easily become an investment property.

LTVs can be measured for a single loan or for multiple loans cumulatively. The **combined LTV** or **cumulative LTV ratio (CLTV ratio)** measures the total leverage on the property as a ratio. Borrowers often have multiple mortgages on a property. These mortgages have a priority: first lien, second lien, etc. A mortgage lien only gives the lender the right to priority of repayment *in a foreclosure*. It does not give the lender priority in terms of which loan a borrower chooses to repay and when, much less payment priority over non-mortgage lenders, such as credit cards.

As we will see in the next chapter, federal law prohibits lenders from preventing borrowers from obtaining junior mortgages on their properties. Thus, while a lender with a first priority lien can control its own LTV, it cannot control the CLTV for the property, and the borrower's financial condition and behavioral incentives may be determined by CLTV, rather than the first lien mortgage's LTV.

In 2015, the median mortgage outstanding was $120,000, and the median LTV on first mortgages was 64%. U.S. Census, American Housing Survey (2015). This median figure, however, is based on mortgages outstanding, so it includes mortgages that might be 30 years old. Newer mortgages are generally larger and have higher LTVs, although in the past few years few loans have been made at more than 90% LTV other than those insured by FHA. Figure 28.3 shows the distribution of LTV ratios among U.S. mortgages in 2015.

D. Monthly Payment

Mortgage loans are repaid over time, with monthly payment of interest or principal and interest due from the borrower. If the borrower fails to make monthly payments, the lender may accelerate the entire principal of the loan. This means that it is critical that monthly payments be within a borrower's financial wherewithal. Monthly payments need to cover more than principal and interest, however. They also have to cover taxes and insurance. Taxing authorities can sometimes obtain liens that have priority over mortgage lenders. No mortgage lender wants that, as it can affect the lender's recovery in a foreclosure (and failure to pay taxes is a good indication that the borrower is in financial distress). Similarly, mortgage lenders want to be sure that their collateral is protected. Thus, they require

Figure 28.3 LTV Ratios by Cohort, U.S. Mortgages Outstanding in 2015[7]

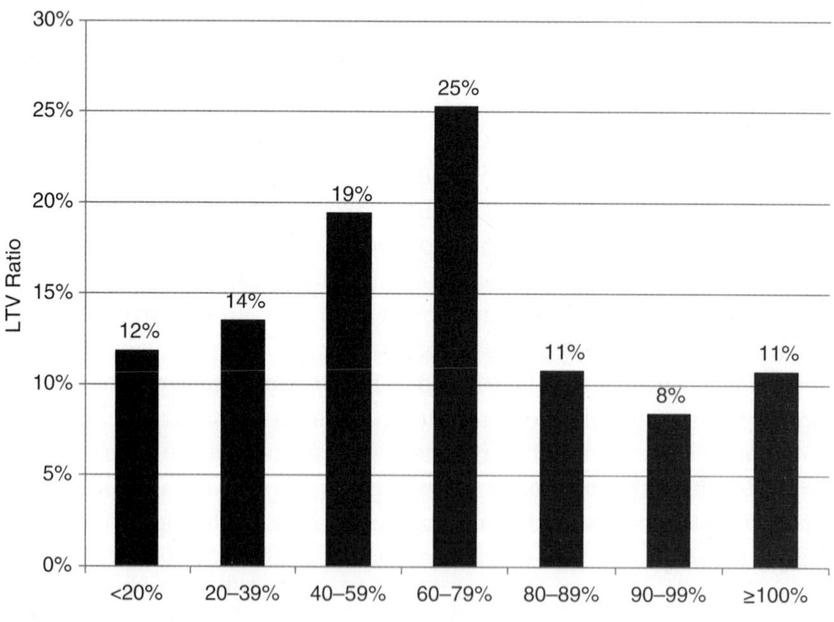

7. U.S. Census, American Housing Survey—Mortgage Characteristics (2015).

insurance of the property. (This is separate from title and mortgage insurance.) Mortgage payments are thus typically measured for affordability calculations as PITI: principal, interest, taxes, and insurance.

There is also another ratio commonly used in thinking about the affordability of monthly payments, the **debt-to-income ratio** or **DTI ratio.** DTI actually comes in two flavors, and it is important to distinguish between them. There is front-end DTI, which is the ratio of the borrower's monthly mortgage payment (usually measured as PITI) to the borrower's monthly income. And then there is the back-end DTI, which is the ratio of all (or of a subset) of the borrower's monthly debt service obligations to the borrower's monthly income. Front-end DTI looks simply to see if the mortgage payment is too high for the borrower in isolation, while back-end DTI looks to see how the mortgage payment fits into the borrower's existing set of financial obligations. While a mortgage might be affordable in isolation, the mortgage payment is competing with other creditors for a borrower's limited cash flow. This makes back-end DTI the more relevant calculation. Front-end DTI, however, is more commonly used, simply because the data is more readily available. To calculate back-end DTI, a credit report can be utilized, but not all payment obligations will show up on a credit report. Different lenders utilize different rules of thumb regarding DTI, but DTI and LTV ratios along with FICO scores are three of the critical elements in any mortgage loan underwriting.

Figure 28.5 shows the distribution of monthly first mortgage payments among the mortgaged population. Median monthly first mortgage payment was $1,030 in 2015.

Figure 28.4 Distribution of Monthly First Mortgage Payment, 2015[8]

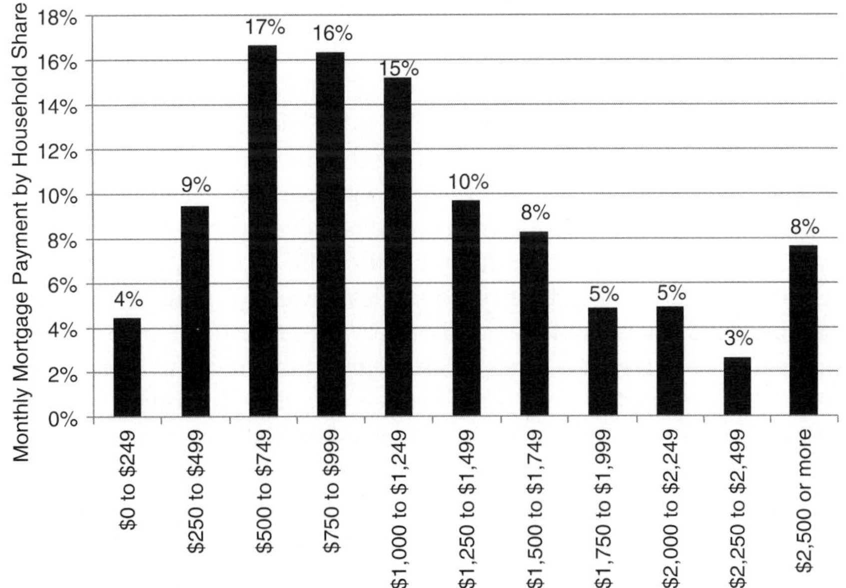

8. U.S. Census, American Housing Survey—Additional Mortgage Characteristics (2015).

III. TYPES OF MORTGAGES

A. Conventional Versus Insured

Beyond specific loan terms, mortgages come in a variety of flavors. First, a mortgage can be either **conventional** or **insured.** A conventional mortgage is a mortgage that is not insured or guaranteed by a government agency. A conventional mortgage may or may not be insured by a private mortgage insurer, with the lender as the loss payee. This means that if the homeowner defaults on the mortgage, the lender will cover the lender's losses up to an insured limit (usually 35% of the amount of the loan). Conventional mortgages do not require **private mortgage insurance** (PMI), but Fannie Mae and Freddie Mac—the major secondary market purchases of mortgages—are generally prohibited from purchasing mortgages with over 80% LTV absent private mortgage insurance. *See* 12 U.S.C. § 1454(a)(2) (Freddie Mac). Accordingly, lenders will often require PMI on loans with LTV > 80% so they will have the option of selling the mortgage in the secondary market.

An insured mortgage is one insured by the Federal Housing Administration, the Department of Veterans Affairs, or the Department of Agriculture's Rural Housing Service. Insured mortgages generally require lower down payments than conventional mortgages, making credit more easily obtainable by homeowners with limited asset accumulation, but the monthly payments are usually more expensive as a result: the borrower is paying for both the mortgage and an insurance premium. Private mortgage insurance also adds to the cost of a conventional loan, but private mortgage insurance terminates automatically in most cases once the LTV ratio reaches 78%, and may be canceled at the borrower's initiation when the LTV reaches 80%. Home Owners Protection Act (HOPA), 12 U.S.C. §§ 4901-4902.

Do not confuse PMI with title insurance. Mortgage lenders will generally require the borrower to purchase title insurance with the lender as the loss payee. Whereas PMI covers losses in the result of a default on the mortgage, title insurance covers losses due to defect in title, thereby ensuring that the lender always has some form of collateral even if the borrower's title to the property is invalid or unmarketable. The real value to a lender of title insurance, however, comes in the very fact that a policy is written. Before a title insurer will write a policy, it will undertake an investigation of title to the property, so the issuance of a policy provides a lender with assurance that there is likely good title. What's more, title insurance also commits the insurer to defending title, which means financing any litigation over title, an expense that can readily exceed the property's value. Borrowers will sometimes obtain title insurance for themselves, but its standard use is as lender-required insurance.

Different rules and regulations apply to insured mortgages than to conventional mortgages. The FHA, VA, and RHS all have their own particular requirements for mortgage underwriting and for mortgage servicing. We will generally not be examining these particular regulatory systems, but it is important to be aware that additional or different rules may apply to these types of mortgages.

B. Conforming Versus Jumbo

A second distinction in the mortgage market is between **conforming** and **jumbo** loans. This distinction refers to the size of the loan. A conforming loan is one that conforms to the statutory loan size limits for purchases by Fannie Mae and Freddie Mac. A conforming loan is not necessarily ever sold to Fannie or Freddie, but a conforming loan is eligible for purchase by Fannie and Freddie. Larger loans are known as jumbos. There is a private secondary market for jumbos.

C. Purchase Money Versus Refinancing

A third distinction in the mortgage market is between purchase money and refinance mortgages. A purchase mortgage is used to finance the acquisition of a property, while a refinancing uses the proceeds of a new mortgage to pay off the old mortgage. In 2015, 53% of mortgages were the original purchase money loan, with refinancing accounting for virtually all other mortgages.[9]

Some refinancing is called "cash-out refinancing." In such a refinancing, the homeowner borrows a greater amount than on the former mortgage and uses the extra financing for purposes other than paying off the old mortgage: home improvement and furnishings, paying off other higher interest rate debts, financing education, or other types of personal consumption. A cash-out refinancing allows a homeowner to turn home equity into cash. This means that all things being equal, a cash-out refinancing raises the LTV ratio on a property; typically, however, a cash-out refinancing follows an increase in property values, which would have lowered the LTV ratio.

D. Term Versus Line of Credit

A fourth distinction is whether a mortgage is a regular term loan or a revolving line of credit, the advances on which are secured by the house. If the loan is a revolving line of credit, it is known as a **home equity line of credit** or HELOC. With a HELOC, the homeowner can draw down on the line of credit to make finance purchases, much like a consumer can with a credit card. The difference, however, is that a consumer is unlikely to lose his or her house over a credit card default, whereas that is a risk with a HELOC. But because of the collateral pledge, a HELOC may be less expensive than a credit card. A HELOC is distinguished from a **home equity loan** or HEL, which is a term loan, frequently a junior mortgage.

E. Reverse Mortgages

Another product distinction is whether a mortgage is a regular mortgage or a **reverse mortgage**. In a regular mortgage, the lender advances funds to the

9. U.S. Census, American Housing Survey—Mortgage Characteristics (2015). There are a small number of "assumed" mortgages—where the buyer takes over the seller's mortgage, and wraparound mortgages, where the seller provides the buyer with a junior mortgage in addition to other financing.

borrower, who repays the funds over time. The monthly payment stream goes from the borrower to the lender. In a reverse mortgage, the payments go the other way: the lender makes monthly payments to the borrower. The borrower does not have to repay the mortgage so long as s/he lives in the home (a **tenure reverse mortgage**) or until the expiration of a particular time period (a **term reverse mortgage**). This means that the amount owed on a reverse mortgage increases over time as the borrower receives monthly payments and interest accrues. (Origination and servicing fees may also be applied, but payment is not due until the termination of the loan.) For both term and tenure reverse mortgages, the entire loan becomes due and owing if the borrower dies or sells the home or ceases to use it as a primary residence.

Reverse mortgages enable a borrower to cash out existing home equity. This is often particularly attractive to elderly borrowers who have accumulated equity in their home over the years and need retirement income or to pay for long-term care. A reverse mortgage may be particularly attractive because the payments are generally tax-free, as they are not income, but loan proceeds. Accordingly, reverse mortgages do not generally affect Social Security or Medicare benefits. While a reverse mortgage will reduce a borrower's ability to devise the property, this may not be of much concern to all borrowers, particularly those without children.

Reverse mortgages reflect a different type of risk arrangement than a regular mortgage. Most reverse mortgages are variable-rate, so the lender is not assuming rate risk. The lender is also not assuming the credit risk on the borrower. A reverse mortgage loan is based solely on the borrower's home equity and life expectancy; the borrower's income is usually irrelevant to a reverse mortgage lender, as it is not the expected source of repayment, unlike with a regular mortgage. Accordingly, the lender's primary risk on a reverse mortgage is that the LTV ratio will pass 100%. This can happen either because of a failure of the property to appreciate as anticipated or because the total of the payments to the borrower eventually exceeds the property value. Thus, a decline in property values is particularly devastating to a reverse mortgage lender.

Also recall that a reverse mortgage may be tenure-based, meaning that the lender keeps making annuity-like payments to the borrower as long as the borrower remains in the house. If the borrower outlives his or her expected lifespan, the lender may end up making advances beyond the value of the property. As a result, prior to the 1990s, most lenders would not make tenure-based reverse mortgages, only term-based reverse mortgages.

A reverse mortgage lender, then, is gambling on property values and life expectancies. In other words, a reverse mortgage is a bit like an annuity combined with real estate speculation. Who would make such a loan? As it turns out, the federal government.

Reverse mortgages are still a fairly niche product: there are approximately 357,000 of them outstanding as of 2015. 2015 American Housing Survey. Most reverse mortgages currently made are insured by FHA under its Home Equity Conversion Mortgage (HECM) program. This means that the federal government currently bears the credit risk on most reverse mortgages. HECMs are limited to borrowers aged 62 and older. 24 C.F.R. § 206.33. The age limitation helps reduce some of FHA's actuarial risk, but the decline in property values since 2006 has resulted in significant losses in the HECM program.

The amount a consumer can borrow on a reverse mortgage is based on an actuarial calculation of the consumer's life expectancy. Thus, an older consumer can get a larger reverse mortgage than a younger one. This has set up a particular problem for spouses of different ages. If both spouses hold title to the property, the reverse mortgage will be underwritten based on the actuarial life expectancy of the *younger* spouse.

A solution for borrowers and lenders wishing to obtain a larger mortgage is to have the younger spouse (frequently the wife) removed from the title to the property and then to have the older spouse borrow alone. The younger spouse needs to be removed from title to the property because if there is joint tenancy, tenancy by the entirety, or tenancy in common, the lender could not foreclose on the property and gain marketable title: the surviving spouse's right to occupancy would remain unaffected. The problem with this arrangement is that once the younger spouse (who may in fact be elderly) has been removed from the title to the property, that younger spouse loses the ability to remain in the property after the death of the older spouse. To the extent that the borrower does not understand this risk, reverse mortgage transactions that are preceded by removal of the younger spouse from the property title raise serious consumer protection concerns. In part because of this concern, FHA requires that HECM borrowers receive pre-closing counseling from a HUD-approved housing counselor. 24 C.F.R. § 206.41.

F. Prime, Subprime, Alt-A

A final distinction in mortgage products relates to the credit risk category of the borrower. A fully documented loan made to a borrower with good credit is called a **prime** loan. If the borrower's income and assets are less than fully documented or the borrower's credit record doesn't quite map onto a traditional prime loan, the loan is called an **Alt-A** loan. This is short for alternative A. Mortgages are categorized on an A through D grading scale based on the credit quality of the borrower. A prime loan is an A, while an Alt-A might be a loan made to a borrower with a prime credit score, but underwritten based on alternative factors. B, C, and D loans are loans made to borrowers with **subprime** credit.

The terminology in this area is imprecise and sometimes confusing. There is no generally accepted meaning of prime, Alt-A, or subprime. The terms can be used to refer to the borrower (as above) or to the loan's features, or to a lending strategy. When the term is applied to the borrower, credit scores (such as a FICO score) are usually the touchstone for categorization, but even then, there is not general agreement on whether subprime means a FICO of, say, below 660 or below 620. (Nor is it clear that a 620 FICO in the year 2000 was the same as a 620 FICO in the year 2010.)

When the terms are used to refer to products, prime means a traditional loan structure and reasonable pricing, while subprime refers to nontraditional loan structures and high pricing. This usage is both reinforced and made distinguishable by the separate federal regulatory regime known as the Home Owners Equity

Protection Act (HOEPA), applicable to high-cost mortgage loans. A HOEPA loan is often used as a synonym for a subprime loan, but not all subprime loans (even in terms of cost) are HOEPA loans; many loans are priced just below the HOEPA threshold.

When used to refer to a lending strategy, prime lending is income-based lending (looking to the borrower's income as the primary source of repayment), while subprime lending is asset-based lending (looking to the borrower's property as the primary source of repayment—that is, expecting foreclosure). Note that the application of these terms to both borrowers and loan products means that a subprime loan may be made to a prime borrower (or vice versa).

IV. THE MORTGAGE CONTRACT

Now that you have been introduced to the basic terminology and structuring concepts regarding mortgage loans, it makes sense to turn to the most fundamental part of the mortgage itself: the note and security instrument. There is an extensive federal and state regulatory apparatus for mortgages. It is truly a cradle-to-grave regulation system, and it is easy to be overwhelmed by its details. It is important, therefore, not to lose sight of the role of contract law in regulating mortgage lending. The mortgage is first and foremost a contract, and the rights of the borrower and lender are defined by that contract. To the extent that the lender is entitled to charge the borrower anything, the authority to do so stems from either the note or the mortgage.

Nearly all mortgage loans made in the United States use standardized documentation: the Fannie/Freddie Uniform Notes and the Fannie/Freddie Uniform Security Instruments. The Uniform Notes and Uniform Security Instruments are developed by Fannie Mae and Freddie Mac, the major secondary market purchasers of mortgages. Most mortgage loans are sold to Fannie and Freddie, and in most circumstances, Fannie and Freddie will purchase only loans that use the Uniform Notes and Security Instruments. Even lenders that do not contemplate selling their loans to Fannie Mae and Freddie Mac use the Uniform Notes and Security Instruments both because of the enhanced liquidity of the loans and because they have greater confidence in the drafting than with non-standardized documentation.[10]

Despite their name, the Uniform Notes and Uniform Security Instruments are not entirely uniform. There are, in fact, several different Uniform Notes for loans of different interest rate structures and, for eleven states, state-specific notes. There are also different Uniform Security Instruments for every jurisdiction. Nonetheless, while all of the Uniform Notes are fairly standardized, the Uniform Security Instruments contain a set of uniform covenants and then a few non-uniform, jurisdictionally specific covenants, generally relating to foreclosure. The discussion here references the Multistate Fixed-Rate Note (the "note") and the Deed of Trust for the District of Columbia. As you read the discussion below, consider carefully why

10. Julia Patterson Forrester, *Fannie Mae/Freddie Mac Uniform Mortgage Instruments: The Forgotten Benefit to Homeowners*, 72 Univ. Missouri L. Rev. 1077, 1085 (2007).

different provisions exist and what they do in terms of allocation of risks between borrower and lender.

A. The Note

The note contains a set of promises from the borrower relating to repayment. The most basic is the promise to repay the principal amount borrowed (Note ¶1). The note contains a recital of the money borrowed and a promise to repay in United States dollars (not in Australian or Canadian!). The note also states the rate at which interest will be charged on the principal and when it will be charged (Note ¶2). Additionally, the note contains terms relating to the schedule of payments and the maturity date of the loan (Note ¶3). The note also sets forth the borrower's right to prepay—if any—and whether there will be a penalty for prepayment (Note ¶4). The prepayment term also specifies how the prepayment will be applied—to accrued and unpaid interest or principal. The final promises related to payments relate to late fee and attorney's fee. If the borrower fails to make timely periodic payments, a specified late charge (typically 5% of the monthly payment) will be charged (Note ¶6(A)). Similarly, if the note holder accelerates repayment of the entire principal and accrued interest, then the note holder will have the right to be repaid for its collection expenses, including reasonable attorney's fees (Note ¶6(D)).

The note also specifies what constitutes a "**default**" (Note ¶6(B)). Normally a "default" is a failure to make the monthly payment and nothing more. This is distinct from events of default in the security instrument. The note does not require notice of default, nor does it require acceleration upon default. Indeed, the language of the note does not literally authorize acceleration. Instead it says that the note holder may send a notice of default and that the notice may informing the borrower that the note holder "may require" immediate repayment of the full amount of the principal and all accrued interest (Note ¶6(C)). If there is a default, the note holder has the right to accelerate the debt.

Four final note provisions are, um, noteworthy. First, the note contains a waiver of the borrower's rights of Presentment and Notice of Dishonor (Note ¶9). This means that the note holder does not have to make formal demand for payment in order to collection, as is required (but waivable) under Article 3 of the UCC. UCC § 3-504(a)-(b). Second, the note contains a savings clause (Note ¶5) stating that if some of the fees and charges exceed legally permitted limits (such as usury laws), then they will not be collected or if they are collected they will be refunded. This is to protect the lender against a defense to the entire note on the basis of the contract being illegal. (The lender would still have a claim for unjust enrichment for the money given, but it would lose its contractual protections if the contract were unenforceable because of illegality.) Third, the note expressly provides that anyone who signs, guarantees, or provides surety for the note is subject to its obligations and that there is joint liability among the parties to the note (Note ¶8).

Lastly, the note contains a reference to a "security instrument" (Note ¶10). This particular note provision does not literally have any effect other than notifying the borrower of the security instrument and some of its terms, but its inclusions might arguably incorporate those terms into the note, which would render the note non-negotiable. The chief importance of this would be that the note would not be governed by Article 3 of the UCC (arguably other provisions of the note render it non-negotiable in any case). If so, then there would be limitations on the enforcement of a lost note and no possibility of a "holder in due course"—the physical holder of a note who has taken it for value and without notice of certain defects and who therefore takes the note free of certain competing claims to ownership and defenses to enforcement.

The Uniform Multistate, Fixed-Rate Note is only three pages long. The security instrument is significantly longer—16 pages in the case of the Deed of Trust for the District of Columbia. There is no requirement that the note and the security instrument be separate instruments, but this is convention. Most of the provisions are identical to that in a mortgage, but there are a few differences.

B. The Security Instrument

The deed of trust opens with a definitions section, much like a typical loan agreement. Among the definitions are those of the three parties to the instrument: the "borrower," the "lender," and the "trustee." It also defines the "note" and the "loan," thereby linking the deed of trust to the particular note. Without the reference to a particular note, the deed of trust would be meaningless.

Following the definition section, the deed of trust contains the language that makes it operable. It explains that the purpose of the security instrument is to secure repayment of the loan evidenced by the note and the performance of the borrower's covenants and agreements under the security instrument and the note. "For this purpose, Borrower irrevocably grants and conveys to Trustee, in trust, with power of sale, the following described property. . . ." Thus, in a deed of trust, the borrower actually conveys legal title of the property—along with all improvements, easements, appurtenances, fixtures, replacements, and additions—to the deed of trust trustee. The property is held in trust for the deed of trust beneficiary, which is the lender. (*See* the definition of "Lender" in the deed of trust.) If the borrower repays on time, the deed of trust trustee is to re-convey the property to the borrower. Otherwise, the trustee is to use its "power of sale" to foreclose and sell the property for the lender.

The deed of trust contains a number of **covenants**. Covenants are agreements to do or refrain from doing something. Strangely, the first covenant in the deed of trust is not in fact a covenant—it is a representation. The "Borrower covenants that Borrower is lawfully seised of the estate hereby conveyed and has the right to grant and convey the Property and that the Property is unencumbered, except for encumbrances of record." This is not a promise to do something or refrain from doing something. Instead, it is a statement about the current state of the world, that is, a representation. In this case, the representation is that the borrower has sufficient rights in the property to enter into the deed of trust and also that there are no unrecorded liens on the property. Oddly, "encumbrances of record" is not a defined term, raising potential questions about exactly what is being represented.

The following sentence provides that the "Borrower warrants and will defend generally the title to the Property against all claims and demands, subject to any encumbrances of records." This indicates that the borrower is promising that as an ongoing matter s/he will keep the property free of competing claims other than preexisting liens and other encumbrances and will take the actions necessary to do so.

Following these "covenants" are a set of 21 numbered uniform covenants and then a set of three numbered non-uniform covenants. The uniform covenants are the same in all Fannie Mae/Freddie Mac uniform instruments, irrespective of the state. The non-uniform covenants vary by state. These covenants are meant to set forth the rights and duties of the borrower and the lender (via the trustee) under the security instrument. Some of these covenants are not in fact covenants, while others contain multiple unconnected covenants under the same number. Nonetheless, for clarity of reference, we will refer to them by their numbering.

The first covenant is that of the borrower to pay all amounts due under the note, as well as any escrow requirements in the security instrument. The covenant contains a number of fairly mundane details about payment, but also reserves the right for the lender to reject any partial payment, while providing that acceptance of a partial payment shall not be deemed a modification of the loan. The twelfth covenant (skipping ahead) further clarifies that forbearance by the lender in the form of an extension of time for payment or reamortization of the loan is not a release.

The second covenant provides for the application of payments, including prepayments, by the lender in terms of principal and interest, while the third covenant is a requirement that the borrower pay into an escrow account held by the lender for certain taxes and insurance premiums. The function of the escrow is to ensure that taxes and insurance premiums get paid. This is because some unpaid taxes can result in a tax lien with priority over the deed of trust. The insurance escrows are important for the lender because the lender is often the beneficiary of the insurance policies: if insurance on the property or on the mortgage is not paid, it will lapse, leaving the lender unsecured. The escrow is waivable by the lender, but the waiver is retractable. Relatedly, the fourth covenant requires the borrower to pay off all taxes, assessments, charges, fines, etc. that can obtain priority over the deed of trust so that the deed of trust maintains its priority.

The fifth covenant requires the borrower to maintain property insurance in the amounts (including deductible levels) and for the periods required by the lender. "All insurance policies required by Lender . . . shall name Lender . . . as an additional loss payee." The fifth covenant also permits the lender to obtain insurance coverage for the property itself at the borrower's expense if the borrower fails to maintain the required insurance. This is known as **force-placed insurance** and is often quite expensive as many lenders will obtain a policy from their captive insurance affiliate at a non-competitive rate. (Whether this is a violation of the Real Estate Settlement Procedures Act is another matter, taken up in the follow chapter.) To the extent that there is force-placed insurance, the premiums become part of the principal of the loan and bear interest per the terms of the note.

The tenth covenant (skipping ahead) covers more specific provisions for mortgage insurance, which is not necessarily required, while the eleventh covenant assigns all "Miscellaneous Proceeds" to the lender, ensuring that the lender can recover any compensation, settlement, damages, or proceeds paid by third parties for damage, destruction, or condemnation of the property or misrepresentations regarding the value or condition of the property. In other words, any proceeds from litigation regarding the property go to the lender.

The sixth covenant requires that the borrower use the property as his or her principal residence for at least one year. The seventh covenant commits the borrower to maintain and not damage the property and undertake repairs to it. The twenty-first covenant (skipping ahead) similarly requires the borrower not to permit the presence, release, disposal, or storage of hazardous substances on the property. These covenants are meant to ensure adequate care for the property that is serving as the lender's collateral. No lender wants their collateral to be a SuperFund site, and the covenant very deliberately states "Nothing herein shall create any obligation on Lender for an Environmental Cleanup."

The eighth covenant is really not a covenant, but a representation that all information the borrower gave during the loan application process was accurate and not materially misleading or false. This "covenant" also provides that it is a default on the loan if the borrower provided inaccurate information during the loan application process. Note that absent this "covenant," a materially false statement in the loan application process would not be a default under the security instrument. Instead, it would just be the predicate for a fraud suit that would have to be prosecuted in the courts, rather than entitling the lender to foreclose.

The ninth covenant provides an important, but limited protection for lenders. It provides that the lender may undertake actions "reasonable or appropriate" for protecting its interest in the property including paying off senior liens, appearing in litigation, securing and repairing the property, and paying "reasonable attorneys' fees" to protect its rights should the borrower breach its covenants or be in litigation regarding the property. The lender's expenditures under the ninth covenant are capitalized into the debt and bear interest per the note. The limitation of "reasonable and appropriate" is an important protect for borrowers, as without it lenders would have carte blanche to charge additional fees to distressed borrowers.

Relatedly, the first paragraph of the fourteenth covenant states that the lender may charge the borrower for "services performed in connection with" a default, including "attorneys' fees, property inspection and valuation fees." This covenant is not a freestanding authorization of fees and other charges. There are direct authorizations for various fees and charges in uniform covenants five and nine as well as in the non-uniform covenants (which cover attorney's fees and title fees for foreclosure). Instead, it is a "savings clause," to protect the loan from falling afoul of usury laws because of charges authorized under the security instrument. The reiteration of the fees that are authorized elsewhere in the security instrument is done to bring those fees within the scope of the savings clause. Were the fourteenth covenant a freestanding authorization of fees and charges, it would undermine the limitations on those fees and charges that exist in other covenants, such as requirements that those fees and charges be "reasonable or appropriate" or "necessary."

The eighteenth covenant contains a "due on sale" clause. This provides that if the property is sold, the entire loan accelerates and becomes due and owing. This clause prevents the loan from being "assumable" by a third party. This is important to a lender because if the borrower could be substituted without its consent, the loan might not be properly priced for the risks posed by the borrower or for the interest rate environment. While there are state law restricting with due on sale clauses, a federal statute, the Garn-St. Germain Act, preempts many of these state laws, and instead substitutes its own restrictions. In particular, lenders are prohibited from exercising due-on-sale clauses upon the creation of a junior lien, upon the death or divorce of a borrower or transfer of the property to the children or spouse of the borrower, or upon the granting of a leasehold interest of no more than three years without a purchase option. 12 U.S.C. § 1701j-3. This means that lenders are unable to prevent the creation of junior mortgage liens, and thus to control the combined loan-to-value ratio on the property. *See* Adam J. Levitin & Susan M. Wachter, *Second Liens and the Leverage Option*, 68 Vand. L. Rev. 1243 (2015).

The nineteenth covenant provides that the borrower has a right to reinstate the loan after acceleration, meaning to de-accelerate the loan. To do so, the borrower must cure any defaults and pay all attorney's fees and provide whatever reasonable assurances the lender requires prior to the earliest of five days before the foreclosure sale or entry of a judgment enforcing the security instrument. Note that this a wholly contractual provision—it is not required by statute.

The twentieth covenant provides that the note and the beneficiary status of the security instrument may be sold without prior notice to the borrower. The covenant also includes a waiver of both the borrower's and lender's right to litigate without notice to the other party of a breach of the agreement and provision of a reasonable time to correct the breach.

Of the non-uniform covenants, the first provides for acceleration of the loan upon default and for the lender to invoke the power of sale under the deed of trust and force a foreclosure. The lender must give notice to the borrower of breach prior to acceleration and provide at least 30 days to cure the default. The lender must also send appropriate notices regarding its invocation of the power of sale, which is governed by local law and Regulation X under the Real Estate Settlement Procedures Act.

If there is a foreclosure sale, the trustee is to deliver the deed to the property to the purchaser at the sale but without any covenants or warranties. The trustee's fee for the sale is provided by the covenant. If, on the other hand, the borrower repays the entire loan, then the trustee is to release the security instrument per the second non-uniform covenant, which would involve re-conveying the property to the borrower.

Finally, the third non-uniform covenant permits the lender, at its sole option, to remove the trustee and appoint a successor substitute trustee. The law of deed of trust trustees varies by jurisdiction, but as a general matter, they are not equivalent to donative trustees with broad fiduciary responsibilities. Instead, they generally have limited contractual duties (including good faith and fair dealing) plus normal duties of care. Frequently the lender will substitute the trustee when it is foreclosing, with the substitute trustee being an affiliate of the lender. If this use of a "trustee" that is not a fiduciary and is not a neutral party seems confusing, well, that's because it is.

Were the instrument a mortgage, rather than a deed of trust, it would not have the conveyance language as a faux covenant, nor would it have any of the provisions regarding the trustee, but otherwise it would be substantially the same. You may also have noticed that not all of the numbered covenants have been discussed here, nor have all of the provisions of the numbered ones. The omissions are simply because the provisions are not of particular interest for our purposes, but it bears emphasis that this is merely a partial summary of the actual provisions.

Problem Set 28

To answer this problem set, you'll want to download the Uniform Note and Uniform Security Instrument for the jurisdiction your professor specifies; citations here to non-uniform covenants in the Security Instrument cite to the Deed of Trust for the District of Columbia. The Uniform Notes are available at: https://www.fanniemae.com/single-family/notes and The Uniform Security Instruments are available at: https://www.fanniemae.com/singlefamily/security-instruments.

1. Gena Haugen took out a $400,000 mortgage with an 8% annual fixed interest rate in 2007 from Continental Express Bank, N.A. Interest rates have dropped and Gena could refinance into a 4.5% fixed-rate mortgage.

- **a.** What will be the effect on ConEx if Gena refinances? If interest rates are falling, what is the effect on the value of Gena's mortgage to ConEx?
- **b.** What if rates are rising? What could ConEx do to prevent Gena from refinancing?
- **c.** How would that affect the value of Gena's mortgage for ConEx?

2. When Gena (from problem 1) applied for the ConEx mortgage she stated that she planned to use the property as her principal residence. In fact, Gena was really planning on using the house as a rental property. What impact do you think the misstatement of residency had on the interest rate Gena pays on her mortgage? Why? *See* Security Instrument Covenant 6.

3. ConEx discovered that Gena misstated her intended residency on the mortgage application, but Gena is current on the mortgage. Is there anything ConEx can do? Are there any risks for ConEx in pursuing its rights? *See* Security Instrument Covenants 6, 8, 9, 14, 22 (non-uniform).

4. ConEx has also learned that Gena took out a second mortgage for $100,000 on the property two days after closing the ConEx loan. The ConEx loan had a loan-to-value ratio of 80%. Does the second mortgage affect ConEx in any way? If so, is there anything ConEx can do? Is there anything ConEx could have done? *See* Security Instrument, lawful seisin covenant, and warranty of title (two paragraphs before uniform covenants begin); Security Instrument Covenant 4; 12 U.S.C. § 1701j-3(d)(1).

5. Gena's ConEx loan was co-signed by her husband, but now they have gotten divorced, and Gena, the primary earner in the family, has moved out, and the house transferred to her husband as part of the divorce settlement. Does this affect ConEx in any way? If so, is there anything ConEx can do? What if the husband was not a co-signor? *See* Security Instrument Covenant 18; 12 U.S.C. § 1701j-3(d)(7).

6. Interest rates have risen to 12%, but Gena still has the 8% rate on her mortgage. Gena has decided to sell her house. The buyer, Houston Shaner, is interested in taking on the mortgage as well. Can he do so? Would ConEx like him to or not? *See* Security Instrument Covenant 18; 12 U.S.C. § 1701j-3(d).

7. Gena failed to make her monthly payment to ConEx last month and has also let her property and flood insurance lapse. As far as ConEx can tell, she has also apparently abandoned the house. What can ConEx do about this, and when? Does ConEx need to go to court for a remedy? *See* Security Instrument Covenants 1, 5, 9, 22 (non-uniform).

8. Following Gena's alleged default ConEx substituted its subsidiary ReConEx as trustee, notified ReConEx of the default, and requested that ReConEx exercise its power of sale and foreclose on the property. Gena's property is in a non-judicial foreclosure jurisdiction. Is there any way Gena can stop the non-judicial foreclosure? How much is it going to cost her to try? Where is the money going to come from? *See* Security Instrument Covenant 24 (non-uniform).

9. Gena has decided not to contest the foreclosure, but she sees that among the costs that ConEx believes it is entitled to recover is an $875 charge for winterizing the property and a $250 charge for two lawn mowings. Gena knows that the property can be winterized for under $100 and in any case, it's located in an area with mild winters. Gena used to have the husky, awkward teenager across the street mow her lawn for $10/mow. When Gena inquired about the charges, ConEx told her "We're just passing along the charges we get from Securital, our property preservation vendor."

- **a.** Should Gena try and fight these charges? *See* Security Instrument Covenants 9 and 14.
- **b.** Would your answer be any different if Gena learned that Securital is actually a wholly owned subsidiary of ConEx? If it is actually a division of ConEx? A joint venture between ConEx and a third party?

CHAPTER 29

MORTGAGES II: FEDERAL REGULATION

I. OVERVIEW OF MORTGAGE MARKET REGULATION

The mortgage market is heavily regulated on the federal and state level. Several different statutory schemes come into play for a cradle-to-grave regulatory system that cover mortgages from their origination to their termination. These schemes are incredibly detailed—far beyond the level we can cover in this course. Instead, we will look at the overall regulatory structure and at a few key features.

Federal mortgage regulations kick in even before a loan is made, as federal law mandates a system of regulation for mortgage originators. Beyond this, federal law regulates mortgage disclosures, mortgage terms, mortgage underwriting, mortgage settlement (closings), and mortgage servicing, including foreclosures to some degree.

States also regulate mortgages. While many state regulations are preempted, not all are, particularly regulations relating to non-depositor actors in the mortgage space: realtors, brokers, and servicers. State regulation of mortgages varies tremendously, ranging from complete laissez-faire to surprisingly intensive, and often not tracking states' political cultures: you might be surprised to learn that Texas has some of the strictest mortgage lending regulations in the nation.

Because of the high level of variation at the state level, however, this chapter covers only federal regulation of mortgages. It focuses on generally applicable federal mortgage regulatory regimes found in the Truth in Lending Act (TILA) and Real Estate Settlement Procedures Act (RESPA). It does not cover the particular regulatory regimes governing FHA, VA, U.S. Department of Agriculture, and Rural Housing Service mortgages or the regulation of the government-sponsored enterprises. Nor does it address the mortgage-related provisions of the Servicemembers' Civil Relief Act. You should be aware, however, that there might be numerous layers of law that can apply to any given mortgage; TILA and RESPA are only the first level of federal mortgage regulation.

II. MORTGAGE DISCLOSURE REGULATION

A. TILA & RESPA Disclosures

Disclosure regulations relating to mortgages are governed by two statutes, the Truth in Lending Act (and sub-statutes interpolated into TILA) and Regulation Z thereunder, and the Real Estate Settlement Procedures Act (RESPA) and Regulation X thereunder. TILA addresses the terms of the mortgage loan itself, while RESPA deals with the closing of the mortgage transaction and subsequent servicing of the loan.

TILA and RESPA each have a distinct set of disclosure requirements. The RESPA requirements do not apply to most mortgages; instead, as part of the **TILA-RESPA Integrated Disclosure** (or **TRID**), the CFPB has designed a set of disclosures housed in Regulation Z that suffice for both TILA and RESPA purposes. *See* 12 C.F.R. §§ 1024.5(d), 1026.19(e), 1026.37, 1026.38. The TRID applies to most closed-end consumer mortgages. Home equity lines of credit, reverse mortgages, mobile home mortgages, and mortgages simply on land (not on dwellings) use separate TILA and RESPA disclosures.

The TRID requires two separate disclosure documents, a "**Loan Estimate**" and a "**Closing Disclosure**." The Loan Estimate is a three-page form that must be delivered or mailed by the lender to the consumer no later than three business days after the receipt of a complete loan application, and at least seven business days before the consummation of the transaction. *See* 12 C.F.R. § 1026.19(e)(1)(iii). Receipt of a "loan application" is the trigger for providing a Loan Estimate, and a "loan application" is defined as consisting of just six pieces of information: the borrower's name, income, Social Security number (for a credit report), property address, estimated property value, and the desired loan amount. 12 C.F.R. § 1026.2(a)(3)(ii). Once a creditor has this information—none of which need be verified—it triggers the requirement of providing a Loan Estimate, even if the creditor wants more information before making a loan.

The Loan Estimate must remain valid for ten business days unless there is a changed circumstance regarding the consumer's eligibility, the closing costs, or the applicable interest rate, or a change requested by the consumer. 12 C.F.R. § 1026.19(e)(3)(iv). The effect of these time lines is to impose a seven-day waiting period between loan application and closing, essentially a mandatory delay in mortgage lending. While there is an exception for emergencies, does it generally make sense to build in such a waiting period for obtaining a mortgage loan? How might a waiting period benefit consumers?

The Loan Estimate sets forth a standardized form for disclosure of the key loan terms that are to be estimated in good faith. 12 C.F.R. §§ 1026.19(e)(3), 1026.37. The estimated terms are presumed to be in good faith if the ultimate loan term does not exceed the amount estimated, other than with certain allowed variances. 12 C.F.R. § 1026.19(e)(3). Among the variances allowed is a 10% increase for third-party fees if the third parties are not affiliated with the lender and the fees are not kicked back to the lender, and the consumer can shop for the third-party service. *Id.* This means that the good faith estimate requirement applies to fees paid to the creditor, to a mortgage broker, to an affiliate of the creditor or mortgage broker, and fees paid to unaffiliated third parties if the consumer is not permitted to shop for a third-party service provider.

The apparent purpose of the Loan Estimate is to enable a consumer both to have confidence in the loan terms she will get if she proceeds with a transaction and to readily compare loan terms in order to find the best product for her needs. By getting a binding good faith estimate from the lender, a borrower is able to rely with a reasonable degree of certainty on the loan terms when engaged in comparison shopping. The good faith estimate also ensures that the borrower will not be vulnerable to bait-and-switch tactics in which she is offered one set of appealing loan terms only to learn at closing—when it is too late to be shopping for terms—that the terms are something different and less favorable.

The first page of the Loan Estimate provides a summary of the essential terms—the type of loan (fixed-rate, adjustable-rate, step-rate, plus any features such as interest-only or negative amortization or balloon payments), the principal amount, interest rate, prepayment penalties, or balloon payments, as well as projected monthly payments and estimates of closing costs and the amount of cash that will be necessary to close the transaction.

The Loan Estimate's second page provides a more detailed breakdown of these elements, including explaining which closing services the borrower can shop for (*e.g.*, a survey fee or a pest inspection fee) and which ones the borrower is required to obtain through the lender (*e.g.*, appraisals, title insurance policy).

The Loan Estimate's third page includes a set of four measures for comparison among loans: (1) the total payments to be made in five years, (2) the total principal amount that will be paid off in five years, (3) the APR, and (4) the total amount of interest that will be paid over the loan term as a percentage of the loan amount.

This particular set of comparison metrics reflects that while many mortgage loans are for thirty years, consumers frequently refinance or sell the property within five to seven years. Therefore, a life-of-loan metric is often not useful for consumers. Accordingly, the first two metrics are for five-year payments, while the APR and total amount of interest metrics are life-of-loan.

Two things are worth noting here. First, the APR, which has traditionally been the core of TILA disclosure, is now relegated to the third page of a disclosure and is not even the first comparison metric required. Second, none of the metrics is particularly good at capturing balloon mortgages or for dealing with loans of less than five years' maturity.

The third page of the Loan Estimate also includes disclosure of late fees, any home insurance requirement, a warning that refinancing may not always be possible for the borrower, and a statement of whether the lender intends to transfer servicing of the loan. 12 C.F.R. § 1026.18(t), 1026.37(m). When applicable, the lender is also supposed to include a warning that the borrower might have post-foreclosure liability on the loan. 15 U.S.C. § 129C(g); 12 C.F.R. § 1026.37(m)(7). Finally, the lender is required to disclose that the borrower is not obligated to proceed with the loan because of having received or signed the Loan Estimate. 12 C.F.R. § 1026.37(n).

While the Loan Estimate is meant to facilitate comparison shopping as well as certainty of the terms of the lender's offer, the Closing Disclosure is designed to ensure that consumers are aware of precisely what they will be charged *before* they are contractually bound and to lock the lender into the terms of its offer so there is no possibility of the lender taking advantage of consumer reliance. (As we have seen repeatedly, the problems in consumer finance regulation often arise once a consumer is already committed to a transaction or relationship and no longer has the protection from market competition.)

Consumers have often found themselves surprised by unanticipated costs at closing. The consumer could always complain and refuse to close, but the result might well be that the seller will deem the bid revoked and will sell the house to someone else. Given that homebuyers are also often home sellers and need to coordinate between their purchase and sales transactions to ensure sufficient liquidity, many buyers will grudgingly lump unanticipated closing costs.

Reputational sanctions are of limited strength in mortgage lending because lenders do not generally expect repeat business from a consumer. Therefore they are not especially concerned about losing a consumer's future business by maltreating a consumer. Likewise, reputational consequences may be limited both because consumers may be ashamed at having been overcharged and thus will not share their experience with others, because they may associate a bad experience with a particular loan officer rather than an institution, and because consumers usually shop for mortgages based on rates, rather than the ultimate all-in costs including closing expenses. The Closing Disclosure is meant to prevent lenders from being able to abuse buyers who are effectively unable to refuse small (or not so small) overcharges at settlement.

The Closing Disclosure must be provided to the consumer at least three business days prior to consummation of the transaction, that is, when the consumer becomes legally bound on the loan (which is not the same as closing or settlement). The Closing Disclosure is a five-page-long document. 12 C.F.R. § 1026.38. The first page is almost identical to the first page of the Loan Estimate. The second and third pages include a breakdown of closing costs and other costs, showing which are to be paid by the borrower, which by the seller, and which by others, and when, as well as a summary of both the borrower's and seller's transactions. The fourth and fifth pages contain various disclosures regarding things like late payment fees, whether the lender will accept partial payments, negative amortization, and escrow account requirements.

In addition to the TRID disclosures, the borrower must be informed of its **TILA right of rescission** (discussed below). 15 U.S.C. § 1635; 12 C.F.R. § 1026.23(b). The right of rescission disclosure need not be made prior to consummation of the transaction, but a delayed disclosure will delay the running of the potential rescission period.

TILA and RESPA both require certain post-closing disclosures. TILA requires that a creditor provide periodic statements for residential mortgage loans. These periodic statements must indicate the principal owed, the current interest rate in effect for the loan, the date of any interest rate reset, and the amount of any prepayment or late fees. 15 U.S.C. § 1638(f); 12 C.F.R. § 1026.41. The periodic statement must also contain contact information for the borrower to obtain information about the mortgage and to contact HUD-certified or state-approved housing counselors.

RESPA also requires an annual escrow account statement. 12 C.F.R. § 1024.17(i). Lenders frequently require the funding and maintenance of an escrow fund to cover the borrower's taxes and insurance payments in the event that the borrower fails to make timely payment. The escrowed funds help the lender avoid the creation of a tax lien (for unpaid taxes) and ensure that the collateral property remains covered by insurance. RESPA restricts the initial escrow charges at settlement to the initial charges to be covered by the escrow account plus one-sixth of the total estimated annual payments from the account. 12 C.F.R. § 1024.17(c)(1)(i). (Note that this is not the same as three-twelfths because an insurance premium or tax payment

Figure 29.1 TILA-RESPA Disclosure Timeline

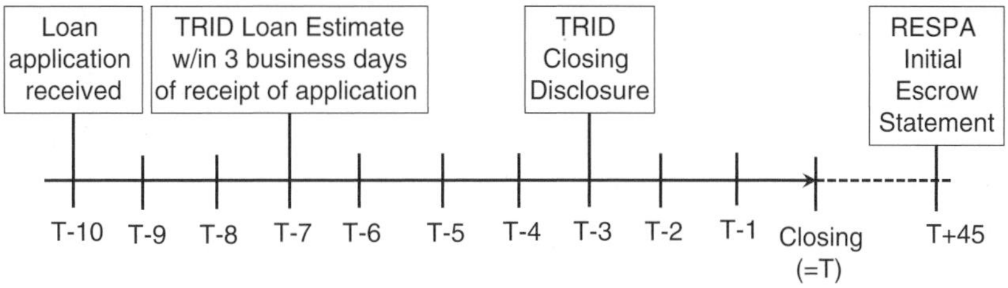

Loan application received
TRID Loan Estimate w/in 3 business days of receipt of application
TRID Closing Disclosure
RESPA Initial Escrow Statement
T-10 T-9 T-8 T-7 T-6 T-5 T-4 T-3 T-2 T-1 Closing (=T) T+45

might be quarterly or annual.) RESPA also limits the amount that may be escrowed in any month to one-twelfth of the total annual estimated charges to be paid from the escrow plus an amount sufficient to maintain a cushion of one-sixth of the estimated total annual payments. 12 C.F.R. § 1024.17(c)(1)(ii).

As most mortgages have monthly payment schedules, TILA periodic disclosures are monthly, whereas the RESPA escrow statement is only made annually. Figure 29.1, below, summarizes the TRID disclosure timeline.

B. TILA & RESPA Remedies

Failure to make the required TILA disclosures triggers civil liability under TILA. 15 U.S.C. § 1640(a). Recall from Chapter 23 that there is a private right of action under TILA, but that liability is limited. TILA general liability for individual plaintiffs is the sum of the actual damages caused by the violation, statutory damages of twice the finance charge (but with a floor of $400 and ceiling of $4,000), and costs and attorney's fees. 15 U.S.C. § 1640(a). For class actions, TILA again gives actual damages, statutory damages, and costs and attorney's fees, but imposes a cap on statutory damages of the lesser of $1 million or 1% of the net worth of the creditor. 15 U.S.C. § 1640(a)(2)(i)(B). TILA disclosure violations are unlikely, however, to trigger a class action because of commonality issues.

In contrast to TILA, RESPA has no private right of action for failure to make disclosures or for improper disclosures. A private right of action exists for other RESPA provisions, but not for its disclosure requirements. Instead, there is only regulatory enforcement. (This might suggest why the TRID was codified in Regulation Z, rather than Regulation X. . . .)

C. TILA Right of Rescission

TILA also includes a powerful, mortgage-specific remedy: the right to rescind the entire transaction. 15 U.S.C. §1635. TILA provides that the borrower may rescind the transaction at any point prior to midnight on the third business day following the later of (1) the closing or (2) the delivery of the TILA right of rescission disclosure and the other required TILA disclosures. 15 U.S.C. § 1635(a). The TILA right of rescission disclosure is a separate and distinct disclosure, and two copies must generally be given to each obligor on the loan. Improper disclosures that are not within the regulatory tolerances for accuracy are equivalent to failure to provide the required disclosures and thus extend the time period for the exercise of the TILA rescission right.

The TILA rescission right generally lapses three years after closing. 15 U.S.C. § 1635(f). Thus, if the TILA right of rescission disclosure isn't made or any other TILA disclosure isn't made or isn't made properly, the borrower can rescind the transaction at any point up to the end of three years from closing. If the borrower signed a statement acknowledging receipt of the disclosures, there is a rebuttable presumption that they were made. 15 U.S.C. § 1635(c). Still, TILA rescission is a strict liability provision. No harm to the borrower need be shown.

The borrower need not have any particular reason for rescinding the transaction; there are automatically three days in which a borrower can change his or her mind about a mortgage. Note that this is not a rescission of the home sale, just a rescission of the mortgage.

There are some important limitations on the TILA right of rescission. The TILA right of rescission does not apply to purchase money mortgages, initial construction mortgages, refinancings by the same creditor that do not include new funding, home equity lines of credit, or mortgages made by state agencies. 15 U.S.C. § 1635(e). In other words, the TILA right of rescission applies primarily to (1) new lender refinancings, (2) same lender refinancings with new advances, and (3) non-purchase money junior mortgages, such as home improvement loans. Why do you think this right applies only to certain types of mortgage lending?

If the consumer rescinds the mortgage, the consumer is not liable for any of the finance charges that have accrued from closing (that is, up to three years of finance charges). 15 U.S.C. § 1635(b). The lender's security interest also becomes void. *Id.* The consumer must return the funds received from the lender, but not until the lender returns any down payment, earnest money, or other fees, which must be done within 20 days of notice of rescission. *Id.* This arrangement enables the consumer to refinance the property: because the property is no longer encumbered by a lien, the consumer can obtain funding prior to having to repay the old lender. In other words, the consumer can take out a new loan to use to pay off the old lender. Were the lien not voided first, the new lender would not loan lest it be making a junior mortgage loan.

If the lender fails to act within the TILA time frame, or if the lender fails to take possession of the property or returned funds, then the property or funds become property of the consumer. *Id.* In other words, the lender may forfeit the entire loan over the failure to provide a single disclosure—about the consumer's right to rescind—and subsequent failure to act in response to the rescission. The TILA right of rescission is potentially one of the harshest remedies in all of commercial law, although this sort of forfeiture is rare.

If the rescission claim is proper and the lender refuses to consent and release the lien, then the borrower may bring suit against the lender for actual damages, statutory damages of $400-$4,000, and attorney's fees. 15 U.S.C. § 1640(a). A lender may be all too happy to consent to rescission, however. If the borrower is able to return the principal, then rescission will at least result in a recovery of principal in full. For a non-performing, underwater loan, this is actually a very good result for the lender because the lender avoids foreclosure expenses and would get only a market value recovery (if that) in foreclosure.

Beyond the general TILA right of rescission, TILA also provides for a right of rescission in foreclosure. 15 U.S.C. § 1635(i). This right is triggered by foreclosure but must be exercised within the regular three-year rescission period. *Id.* The borrower may rescind if a mortgage broker's fee was not properly disclosed in the finance charge (with a $35 variance tolerance) or if the form of the notice of rescission was not proper. *Id.*

What is the point of the TILA right of rescission? Allowing a post-closing cooling off period for a transaction as major as a mortgage may generally make sense to allow a consumer to be sure that s/he wants to commit to the transaction and have a chance to reconsider when not being subjected to high-pressure sales pitches. Prior to the closing, a consumer can feel railroaded into agreeing to the transaction—hence the TILA requirement of a disclosure that the consumer does not have to go through with the transaction. 15 U.S.C. § 1638(b)(2)(B). In particular, Congress seems to have been concerned about unscrupulous home improvement contractors who would obtain liens on customers' homes, frequently without customer knowledge, by having the homeowners sign a contract that would turn out to mortgage the home at exorbitant rates.

But why allow rescission for up to three years simply because the disclosure of the right of rescission hasn't been made? One possibility is that it is a "brown M&M" device. The band Van Halen famously included a provision in their tour contracts requiring that their dressing rooms be stocked with various snacks, including M&Ms. The contract explicitly stated that if there are any brown M&Ms provided, Van Halen will have the unilateral right to terminate the contract without any liability. The provision wasn't meant to simply provide Van Halen with a convenient "out." Instead, it was designed to create a warning bell for more serious contract non-compliance. A tour promoter that fails to have the brown M&Ms removed might also be sloppy with safety, no small issue when performing on a stage with pyrotechnics. Thus, if a brown M&M was spotted, Van Halen would know that it was necessary to do a thorough safety check. Perhaps the TILA right of rescission is expressing the same concern—if the lender wasn't careful enough to include the disclosure, what else might it have been sloppy about?

D. HOEPA Loan Disclosures

The Home Ownership and Equity Protection Act (HOEPA) creates special disclosure and substantive term regulations for high-cost mortgage loans (so-called HOEPA loans).[1] 15 U.S.C. §§ 1602(bb)(1). 1639. While HOEPA's provisions are triggered by various cost measures, certain types of loans are excluded from HOEPA altogether. HOEPA only applies to loans secured by principal residences, so it does not

1. There are also special disclosure requirements for reverse mortgages and home equity loans.

apply to vacation homes or investment properties. 15 U.S.C. §§ 1602(bb)(1)(A); 12 C.F.R. § 1026.32(a)(1). HOEPA also does not apply to reverse mortgages, construction loans, FHA-insured loans, or Rural Development Service loans. 12 C.F.R. § 1026.32(a)(2). This means that HOEPA applies to all other high-cost residential mortgage loans, be they purchase money mortgages, refinancings, or home equity loans or lines of credit. 12 C.F.R. § 1026.32(a)(1).

HOEPA has three separate tests to determine if a loan is a "**high-cost mortgage**": an APR test, a points/fees test, and a prepayment penalty test. If any of the three tests are met, the loan is subject to HOEPA requirements.

The **APR test** looks at whether the APR on the loan is more than 650 basis points above the Average Prime Offer Rate on the date of the loan if the loan is a first-lien loan. 12 C.F.R. § 1026.32(a)(1)(i)(A). Thus, if the Average Prime Offer Rate were 6.00% on the date the loan was made, a first-lien loan could have an APR of up to 12.50% without triggering HOEPA coverage.

For junior liens or small (<$50,000) loans secured by personal property, the APR threshold is 850 basis points above the Average Prime Offer Rate. 12 C.F.R. § 1026.32(a)(1)(i)(B)-(C). When does a mortgage loan ever involve personal property? Some states treat manufactured homes (that's the formal term for what you might know as a mobile home, trailer, or caravan) as personalty, not realty.

The **points-and-fees test** looks to see if the total points and fees on the loan are more than 5% of the total loan amount for loans of at least $20,000. 12 C.F.R. § 1026.32(a)(1)(ii)(A). For loans of less than $20,000, the threshold is the lesser of 8% and $1,000. 12 C.F.R. § 1026.32(a)(1)(ii)(B).

The **prepayment penalty test** looks to see if there is either a prepayment penalty after 36 months from origination or if the prepayment penalty is greater than 2% of the amount prepaid. 12 C.F.R. § 1026.32(a)(1)(iii). Thus, if a loan had a prepayment penalty for the first four years or if the prepayment penalty was equivalent to 3% of the amount prepaid, it would be a HOEPA loan, irrespective of its interest rate or fees. Similarly, if a $200,000 loan had a prepayment penalty of $500 for 36 months, and the homeowner prepaid $20,000, the penalty would be equal to 2.5% of the amount prepaid, and thus the loan would be a HOEPA loan, even though the prepayment penalty is only 0.25% of the total loan amount.[2]

If a loan meets the definition of a "high-cost mortgage," then it is subject to specific disclosure requirements, restrictions on transaction terms, restrictions on fees and practices, ability-to-repay requirements, and a pre-loan counseling requirement. In addition to regular TILA disclosure requirements, HOEPA requires that the creditor include the following disclosure: "You are not required to complete this agreement merely because you have received these disclosures or signed a loan application." and "If you obtain this loan, the lender will have a mortgage on your home. You could lose your home, and any money you have put into it, if you do not meet your obligations under the loan." 15 U.S.C. § 1639(a)(1)(B). The creditor on a

2. A loan could in theory be a HOEPA loan under the prepayment penalty test while still not being a "higher-priced mortgage loan" under 12 C.F.R. § 1026.35(a)(1), and therefore not subject to the prohibition on prepayment penalties for higher-priced mortgage loans. 12 C.F.R. § 1026.43(g)(1)(ii)(C).

HOEPA loan must also disclose the APR and amount of regular monthly payment for fixed-rate loans and for variable rate loans, the APR, the amount of the regular monthly payment, a statement that the rate and monthly payment may increase, and the amount of the maximum monthly payment. 12 C.F.R. §§ 1026.31, 1026.32(c).

HOEPA loans are also subject to pre-closing home ownership counseling requirements. Within three business days of receiving a loan application for a high-cost mortgage loan a creditor must give an applicant a list of HUD-approved housing counselors unaffiliated with the lender. The counseling cannot take place until after consumer gets applicable TILA and RESPA disclosures. 12 C.F.R. § 1026.34(a)(5)(ii). As the TRID is binding on the lender for ten business days, there is basically a two-week window for the counseling to occur.

The housing counselor does not approve or disapprove the loan; the counselor only explains the loan to the consumer and expresses an opinion on the advisability of the mortgage, while the decision to borrow remains the consumer's. The lender can pay for the counseling but cannot condition it on the consumer taking the loan. 12 C.F.R. § 1026.34(a)(5)(v). The lender may not make a HOEPA loan until it has received written certification of the home ownership counseling. 12 C.F.R. § 1026.34(a)(5)(ii).

HOEPA's counseling requirements are nearly unique within the world of consumer finance; consumers are not usually required to consult with a third-party expert before entering into any other sort of transaction, but for high-cost mortgages, an independent, outside check is mandated.[3] The pre-closing homeownership counseling can be seen as a type of particularly intensive and personalized disclosure regime. The homeownership counseling requirement underscores a deep skepticism about whether consumers should ever be taking out such a high-cost mortgage loan: if a loan is priced at more than 650 basis points above prime, HOEPA's requirements are an attempt to signal to the consumer that the loan might not be such a good idea. But HOEPA does not forbid high-cost loans—it just adds frictions to obtaining them. A consumer might well be counseled not to take out a HOEPA loan and still proceed to do so. But at that point, the consumer has been warned.

Why would HOEPA have these particular disclosure and counseling requirements? HOEPA was enacted in part out of concern for less sophisticated consumers getting snookered into high-cost loans through high-pressure sales tactics. Emphasizing to consumers that they do not have to close a loan and the consequences of a default are an attempt to make consumers aware of their rights and the risks they are incurring. Likewise, the counseling requirements are an implicit acknowledgement that regulation through generic disclosures has not been effective in the high-cost mortgage loan market and needs to be supplemented with a personalized social work approach.

3. Counseling is also required for first-time borrowers before taking out loans with negative amortization features. 12 C.F.R. § 1026.36(k).

III. TERM REGULATIONS

A. Federal Preemption of State Law

Federal law includes extensive regulation of mortgage terms. Some of this is in the form of direct regulation, while other is in the form of preemption of state mortgage regulation.

First, the Depositary Institutions Deregulation and Monetary Control Act of 1980 (DIDMCA), the first major bank deregulation act of the 1980s (notably prior to the Reagan "revolution"), exempts all FHA-insured mortgages from state usury laws. 12 U.S.C. § 1735f-7. This meant that state-chartered lending institutions making FHA-insured mortgages were not subject to state usury laws.

Second, the Alternative Mortgage Transactions Parity Act of 1982 (AMTPA), part of the Garn-St. Germain Depository Institutions Act of 1982, provides for preemption of state regulations of "alternative mortgage transactions," meaning any adjustable rate mortgage, mortgage with a maturity shorter than its amortization term (resulting in a balloon payment), or shared equity mortgage. 12 U.S.C. §§ 3802-3803.

Third, another section of the Garn-St. Germain Act preempted state "due-on-sale" prohibitions. 12 U.S.C. § 1710j-3. A due-on-sale clause is a clause in a mortgage that makes the entire debt come due and owing if the collateral property is sold or mortgaged. The Garn-St. Germain Act was reacting to state laws that were prohibiting these due-on-sale clauses in order to facilitate assumable mortgages—in the rising interest rate environment of the 1970s, the original mortgagor would sell the home along with the below-market fixed-rate mortgage to the buyer.

B. Federal Term Regulation

1. Garn-St. Germain Due-on-Sale Restrictions

Garn-St. Germain, however, went further than prohibiting state restrictions on due-on-sale clauses. It also imposes some of its own restrictions on the use of due-on-sale clauses. Garn-St. Germain prohibited due-on-sale clauses from being exercised upon the incurrence of a junior lien on the property, the transfer of the property due to the death of the borrower, the granting of a lease of no more than three years, the transfer of the property to a spouse or children of the borrower, the transfer of ownership due to a divorce or legal separation, or placement of the property into an *inter vivos* trust (often used for asset protection from creditors). 12 U.S.C. § 1710j-3(d). These are some of the most remarkable provisions in the entire galaxy of federal regulation of consumer finance. Garn-St. Germain prevents lenders from being able to control the cumulative loan-to-value ratio on a property. It also prevents a lender from terminating its loan when a major financial event such as death or divorce occurs for a borrower. Garn-St. Germain thus forces mortgage lenders to face much greater risks than those to which they would otherwise consent.

2. Ability to Repay & Qualified Mortgage Safe Harbors

Perhaps the most important mortgage provision in TILA is its ability-to-repay requirement. Since 2010, TILA has provided that:

> no creditor may make a residential mortgage loan unless the creditor makes a reasonable and good faith determination based on verified and documented information that, at the time the loan is consummated, the consumer has a reasonable ability to repay the loan, according to its terms, and all applicable taxes, insurance (including mortgage guarantee insurance), and assessments.

15 U.S.C. § 1639c(a)(1). Ability to repay (ATR) must be calculated based on a payment schedule that fully amortizes the loan over its term and for an adjustable rate mortgage uses the fully indexed rate, rather than a teaser rate. 15 U.S.C. §§ 1639(a)(3), 1639(a)(6), 1639(a)(7).

The ATR requirement applies only to closed-end loans and excludes reverse mortgages, FHA-insured loans, and HELOCs. 12 C.F.R. § 1026.43(a). A separate ability-to-repay requirement applies to open-end HOEPA loans. 15 U.S.C. § 1639(h); 12 C.F.R. § 1026.34(a)(4).

The mortgage ATR requirement is tempered by a presumption of repayment ability for "**qualified mortgages.**" 15 U.S.C. § 1639c(b). This presumption functions to create a safe harbor from ATR liability.

Qualified mortgages or QM are defined by regulation by the CFPB. The CFPB has defined the QM as a mortgage meeting six criteria:

1. The loan is repaid in regular payments that are substantially equal (with an exception for ARMs) and always positively amortizing.
2. The term is no more than 30 years.
3. Fees and points are limited (with a cap varying based on mortgage size).
4. The loan must be underwritten using the maximum interest rate in the first five years.
5. The borrower's income and assets must be verified.
6. The borrower's total monthly payment obligations on of all current debt obligations, not just other mortgages, but also including credit card debt, student loans, auto loans, child support, and alimony, can be no more than 43% of total monthly income. This requirement is called a "back-end debt-to-income ratio" or "back-end DTI."[4]

12 C.F.R. § 1026.43(e)(2). Requirements 4-6 are considered satisfied if the loan is eligible for purchase or guarantee by Fannie Mae or Freddie Mac or for guarantee by the VA, the USDA, or the Rural Housing Service (the "agency loan exception"). 12 C.F.R. § 1026.43(e)(4)(ii). The agency loan exception for Fannie/Freddie purchase/guarantee will cease to meet requirements 4-6 as of 2021. The agency loan exception for VA/USDA/RHS insurance/guarantee will cease to meet requirements 4-6

4. In contrast, a "front-end DTI" would be a ratio of the monthly loan payment for the mortgage to monthly income.

upon the latter of 2021 or when those agencies exercise their power to define QM for the mortgages they insure/guarantee. 12 C.F.R. § 1026.43(e)(4)(iii). The FHA has adopted its own more limited QM definition (incorporating only the CFPB's points/fees limitation), so FHA-insured loans are not covered by the CFPB QM rule. *See* 24 C.F.R. § 203.19(b)(1).

The CFPB's QM rule creates different presumptions of ability to repay depending on the terms of the loan. Non-QMs lack any presumption of ability to repay. Among QMs, the strength of the repayment ability presumption depends on the pricing of the loan. The CFPB QM rule distinguishes between regular QMs and "**higher-priced**" QMs (priced at 150 bps over Prime for first-lien mortgages and 350 bps over Prime for junior liens). 12 C.F.R. § 1026.43(b)(4). Note that this is a different (and lower) threshold than for "**high-cost mortgages**" under HOEPA. Notice that a HOEPA loan could theoretically qualify as a QM but is likely to flunk the back-end DTI test and possibly other tests as well.

Higher-priced QMs have a rebuttable safe harbor for ability to repay. 12 C.F.R. § 1026.43(e)(1)(ii). Regular QMs receive an irrebuttable safe harbor for ability to repay. 12 C.F.R. § 1026.43(e)(1)(i). The result of all of this is to increase the risk of making non-QMs or high-cost QMs. It is widely expected that non-QM lending will be quite limited for the foreseeable future. The FHA QM rule has a similar distinction, but with a different threshold for the irrebutable safe harbor. 24 C.F.R. § 203.19(b)(2)-(3).

What are the consequences for failing to verify ability to repay before making a loan? There is both public and private liability. The CFPB and state attorneys general can bring enforcement action seeking a civil monetary penalty and/or an injunction for an ATR violation, with a three-year statute of limitations. Private liability for an ATR violation works somewhat differently than a typical TILA violation. As with any TILA violation, there is a private right of action for damages, but there is also a special ATR setoff defense that can be raised more broadly that the affirmative suit for damages.

As with all other TILA violations, damages in a private individual action consist of the sum of actual damages, statutory damages ($400-$4,000 for mortgages), and attorney's fees. 15 U.S.C. § 1640(a)(1)-(3). For ATR violations, damages also include all finance charges and fees paid by the consumer unless the creditor demonstrates that its violation was not material (presumably to the actual damages suffered by the consumer). 15 U.S.C. § 1640(a)(4). For a private suit for damages for an ATR violation, there is a three-year statute of limitations running from the occurrence of the violation (the date of the loan). 15 U.S.C. § 1640(e).

Additionally, TILA provides that if anyone attempts to foreclose or otherwise collect on a loan that does not comply with the ATR requirement, a consumer may assert an ATR violation "as a matter of defense by recoupment or set off without regard for the [statute of limitations] for damages. . . ." 15 U.S.C. § 1640(k).[5] This means that the consumer can bring a defense or counterclaim to reduce any judg-

5. The statute does not differentiate between setoff and recoupment, but setoff is a broader concept than recoupment. Setoff involves offsetting any mutual debts, whereas recoupment involves offsetting debts from the same transaction.

ment by the amount of damages that would be awarded for a direct suit for damages for an ATR violation (with the refund of finance charges and fees limited to those in the first three years of the loan). 15 U.S.C. § 1640(k)(2).

The setoff remedy is freed not only from the TILA statute of limitations, but also from the TILA limitation on assignee liability (addressed in more detail in Chapter 32). Assignees are normally liable for TILA violations only if the violation is apparent on "the face of the disclosure statement." 15 U.S.C. § 1640(a). Because an ATR violation is not a disclosure violation, there is no assignee liability for damages for an ATR violation, but this limitation does not apply when the ATR violation is raised as a counterclaim or defense.

It seems unlikely that there will be many direct suits for damages over ATR violations. The statute of limitations is quite short, the defendants are limited, and it would be difficult for a plaintiff to obtain enough facts to adequately plead lack of verification of ability to repay. Moreover, absent a foreclosure on the loan, the consumer is unlikely to have suffered any actual damages and the violation is unlikely to be material. Therefore the damages would be just the statutory damages and an attorney's fee. With such limited damages, it would be difficult for a consumer to obtain counsel on a contingency fee basis, although an ATR violation could be a predicate for a state UDAP cause of action, which might have a more generous damages provision.

Liability for an ATR violation would seem to be greater in cases where it is raised as a defense to reduce the consumer's liability in a collection action. The setoff remedy, however, has important limitations and implications, and is unlikely to be frequently invoked. The setoff remedy does not prevent foreclosure (unless, presumably, the TILA setoff is greater than the unpaid balance on the loan). Instead, it only reduces the collection on the loan. In order to exercise setoff, however, there must be mutually owing debts. Thus, if the money has already been collected from the debtor, there are no longer mutually owing debts, and the funds the debtor has paid cannot be clawed back. Therefore, if a foreclosure sale's proceeds have been distributed, it is too late to raise the defense, other than against the collection of a deficiency judgment. The ATR setoff defense has to be raised before there is a successful collection. (How this works with a non-judicial foreclosure is unclear, as a defense or counterclaim has no application to a non-judicial sale. One possibility is that raising an ATR claim converts a non-judicial foreclosure into a judicial one—and perhaps creates federal question jurisdiction.)

The ATR foreclosure defense is unlikely to be used frequently. In order for there to be ATR liability, several things need to happen. First, there has to be a default on the loan. Second, that default needs to result in a foreclosure. Third, that foreclosure has to be contested. Fourth, the borrower needs to show that the lender did not consider his/her ability to repay when making the loan.

It seems unlikely that many loans will run this gauntlet. If a loan is in fact well-underwritten, but simply doesn't qualify for QM, the default rate should be fairly low. Even then, not all defaults result in foreclosures, and most foreclosures are not contested. So even if ATR was not verified, the likelihood of ATR liability is low.

Despite the limitations noted above, it is worth observing that TILA's mortgage ATR provision is much stronger than TILA's provision regarding ability to pay (ATP) for credit cards. As discussed in Chapter 27, the ATP provision merely requires that the card issuer "consider" the consumer's ability to make *minimum monthly payments*, not repay the balance in full any particular time frame. Likewise, the ATP provision has particular remedy for its violation beyond general TILA liability (actual damages plus twice the finance charge and attorney's fees or the lesser of $1 million or 1% of the creditor's net worth). Taken together, however, ATP and ATR point to a new trend in consumer credit regulation, one that the CFPB has extended to certain small-dollar loan products, as discussed in Chapter 30). This new trend reflects changes in the consumer credit market. Traditionally lenders were assumed to lend only to borrowers who could repay based on their own self-interest. Developments in consumer credit markets such as originate-to-distribute lending, sweat box lending, and a willingness to accept loss leaders on upselling mean that this assumption does not always hold. Hence the regulatory response of mandating consideration of a factor that self-interested lenders traditionally considered as a matter of course.

3. Prepayment Limitations

The CPFB's ability-to-repay rule also restricts prepayment penalties. Prepayment penalties are generally forbidden unless a loan is a fixed-rate, qualified mortgage that is not a higher-priced mortgage loan. 12 C.F.R. § 1026.43(g)(1). When prepayment penalties are allowed, they may not apply after the first three years of the loan. 12 C.F.R. § 1026.43(g)(2)(i). They must also not be more than 2% of the loan balance in the first two years or 1% in the third year. 12 C.F.R. § 1026.43(g)(2)(ii). Moreover, creditors are prohibited from offering loans with prepayment penalties unless the creditor also offers the consumer an alternative fixed-rate loan for the same maturity without a prepayment penalty. 15 U.S.C. § 1639c(4); 12 C.F.R. § 1026.43(g)(3).[6] The restrictions on prepayment penalties are a reaction to mortgages made in the lead up to the 2008 financial crisis; many of these mortgages had low teaser rates, but prepayment penalties that trapped borrowers into the loans once the interest rates reset.

4. HOEPA Loan Rules

High-cost mortgages (HOEPA loans, not to be confused with "higher priced" loans that do not have an irrebuttable presumption of meeting the ability-to-repay requirement under the QM rule) are subject to a battery of substantive term restrictions. HOEPA loans generally may not have balloon payment structures, negative amortization, prepayment penalties, default interest rates, or acceleration clauses triggered by factors other than borrower fraud, payment default, and consumer actions resulting in creditor insecurity. 15 U.S.C. § 1639(c)-(g); 12 C.F.R. § 1026.32(d). The prohibition on prepayment penalties is somewhat confusing. All prepayment penalties are prohibited for HOEPA loans, 12 C.F.R. § 1026.32(d)(6), but a loan might qualify as a high-cost mortgage by virtue of the prepayment penalty test. If so, the prepayment penalty must be stripped out of the loan or else there is a HOEPA violation.

6. This is known as a "plain vanilla" requirement: lenders that sell "Rocky Road" products must also sell plain vanilla products.

Additionally, a creditor may not charge fees for modification, deferral, renewal, amendment or extension of a HOEPA loan or for a payoff statement, and late fees are limited to 4% of the past due amount and may not be pyramided (no late fees on late fees). 12 C.F.R. § 1026.34(a)(7)-(9). Fees and points may not be financed (rolled into the loan amount) on a HOEPA loan, nor may creditors structure transactions to avoid HOEPA requirements by splitting HOEPA loans into two smaller loans. 12 C.F.R. § 1026.34(a)(10), (b). Creditors may not refinance a high-cost mortgage into another one within one year of closing unless the refinancing is in the consumer's interests (meaning lower costs). 12 C.F.R. § 1026.34(a)(3). Creditors are also prohibited from recommending that a defaulted HOEPA loan be refinanced with another high-cost mortgage loan. 12 C.F.R. § 1026.34(a)(6).

A violation of these HOEPA provisions regarding prohibited loan terms or practices is treated as a failure to make a material disclosure and thus as grounds for a TILA rescission for up to three years. 15 U.S.C. §§ 1639(n), 1635; 12 C.F.R. § 1026.23(a)(3)(ii). Thus, even if a lender gave the proper TILA rescission notices on time, there is still a three-year rescission period for loans that violate HOEPA requirements. HOEPA violations also have a three-year statute of limitations, in contrast with the usual one-year limit for TILA violations. 15 U.S.C. § 1640(e).

5. Adjustable Rate Mortgages

Adjustable rate mortgages are required to have rate caps for the maximum rate that may apply during the life of the loan. 12 U.S.C. § 3806. There is no regulation, however, of how high the cap may be, only that a cap be specified.

IV. PROCESS REGULATION

Federal law regulates various aspects of the mortgage origination and servicing process.

A. Mortgage Applications

Regulation B under the Equal Credit Opportunity Act requires that all mortgage loan applications, including refinancings, be in writing. 12 C.F.R. § 1002.4(c). When a mortgage loan application is taken, the creditor must request information on the borrower's ethnicity and race, sex, marital status, and age. 12 C.F.R. § 1002.13(a).

B. Appraisals

TILA requires that real estate appraisals for mortgage loans must be independent. 15 U.S.C. § 1639e. Real estate lending depends heavily on appraisals. The size of a loan and its pricing vary with loan-to-value ratios, and loan-to-value ratios require a property valuation. If the appraisal is too generous, the borrower might get approved for a larger loan or might get approved for a loan where he might not otherwise be approved. This is not always in the borrower's interest, nor is it in the lender's, as the lender may be assuming more risk than intended. But it might be in the interest of the loan officer or mortgage broker, if compensation depends on either (1) making the loan and (2) the size of the loan. Independent appraisals help limit artificial inflation of valuations. In addition to mandating independent appraisals, TILA also requires that appraisers' fees be limited to those that are customary and reasonable in the local market. 15 U.S.C. § 1639e(i).

ECOA requires that borrowers be given copies of all appraisal reports at least three days prior to closing, 15 U.S.C. § 1691(e)(1). The requirement applies even if the loan application is rejected. Applicants may be charged a "reasonable fee" for an appraisal, but if one is undertaken, the the applicant is entitled to receive a copy of the written appraisal for free. 15 U.S.C. § 1691(e)(3)-(4). ECOA also requires that applicants receive a notice of their right to a free copy of any written appraisal 15 U.S.C. § 1691(e)(5). The notice must be provided within three business days of receipt of the loan application. 12 C.F.R. § 1002.14(a)(2). Failure to provide such a notice is a free-standing ECOA violation.

C. Loan Officer Registration and Licensing

The federal Secure and Fair Enforcement for Mortgage Licensing Act of 2008 (the SAFE Act) requires the registration and licensing of "mortgage originators." 12 U.S.C. § 5103. A mortgage originator is anyone who "takes a residential mortgage loan application," "assists a consumer in obtaining or applying to obtain a residential mortgage loan," or "offers or negotiates terms of a residential mortgage loan," excluding clerical employees. 15 U.S.C. § 1602(cc)(2). The registration and licensing is supposed to be done on the state level through a Nationwide Mortgage Licensing System and Registry administered by the Conference of State Bank Supervisors and the American Association of Residential Mortgage Regulators. 12 U.S.C. § 5102(6). Congress, however, can merely authorize the states to act; it cannot mandate their action. The CFPB, however, has authority to take over the system if states fail to act.

D. RESPA Kickback Prohibitions

RESPA prohibits fees, kickbacks, and other exchange of "value pursuant to any agreement or understanding, oral or otherwise, that business incident to or a part of a real estate settlement service involving a federally related mortgage loan shall be referred to any person." 12 U.S.C. § 2607(a). RESPA also prohibits the splitting of real estate settlement fees other than for services actually performed. 12 U.S.C. § 2607(b). A RESPA kickback requires demonstration that a charge was divided between two or more persons. *Freeman v. Quicken Loans, Inc.*, 566 U.S. 624 (2012). Merely charging a fee for which no services are provided is not a RESPA violation. (It may still be a state-law violation.) RESPA also only applies to transactions done in connection with the closing of the mortgage. RESPA does not cover subsequent transactions, such as lender force-placement of insurance, even if they involve kickbacks. *See, e.g., McNeary-Calloway v. JP Morgan Chase Bank, N.A.*, 863 F. Supp. 2d 928 (N.D. Cal. 2012) (overcharges for force-placed insurance years after settlement was not covered by RESPA because it was not related to settlement); *Bloom v. Martin*, 77 F.3d 318 (9th Cir. 1996) (undisclosed demand and reconveyance fees for calculating payoff balance and reconveying a deed of trust were not a RESPA violation because they were not related to settlement).

Excluded from RESPA's kickback and fee-splitting prohibitions are: payment of attorney's fees for actual services, payments to realtors, payments by title companies to their agents, payments by lenders to their agents for actual work done in making the loan (*e.g.*, loan officer or mortgage broker compensation), payments of bona fide salaries or compensation or for goods and services actually provided, and payments to affiliates, as long as the affiliation is disclosed and the affiliate's services are not required. 12 U.S.C. § 2607(c).

There is a private right of action for violation of RESPA kickback provisions, as well as the possibility of CFPB, HUD, and state enforcement. Damages are three times the amount of any settlement charge. 12 U.S.C. § 2607(d)(2). A similar RESPA provision prohibits requiring borrowers to purchase title insurance from any particular insurer. 12 U.S.C. § 2608. Damages are treble the title insurance fees.

The concern that animates the RESPA anti-kickback and fee-splitting provisions appears to be that kickbacks will unnecessarily inflate the price of real estate settlement services for borrowers. 12 U.S.C. § 2601(b)(2). In April 2012, the CFPB announced settlements with several private mortgage insurers for violating the RESPA anti-kickback provisions. CFPB, Press Release, *The CFPB Takes Action Against Mortgage Insurers to End Kickbacks to Lenders*, April 4, 2013. These private mortgage insurers were allegedly ceding reinsurance to captive reinsurance affiliates of the lenders in exchange for the lenders steering business to them. While borrowers often pay for private mortgage insurance, it is priced the same for all insurers and the lender is the loss payee, so the borrower is indifferent as between firms. Kickbacks in the form of reinsurance cessations would benefit the lenders because they would be compensated for holding more of the credit risk on the mortgage but would be able to do so while holding capital only at the much lower level required for their captive reinsurance affiliates, compared to the level that would be required for a depository. The result of this arrangement might have been that borrowers were paying for "insurance" when there really was no risk shift—it was merely being churned back to the lender's affiliate. The CFPB's enforcement action against one of the private mortgage insurers, PHH, resulted in the D.C. Circuit opinion upholding the CFPB's Constitutionality. *PHH Corp. v. CFPB*, 881 F.3d 75 (D.C. Cir. 2018) (en banc).

E. Yield Spread Premiums and Steering Incentives

TILA imposes restrictions on mortgage originators, such as brokers and loan officers, from receiving compensation based on the terms of the loan. 15 U.S.C. § 1639b. Prior to 2010, mortgage brokers would be compensated by lenders for making higher-interest-rate loans. This compensation was called a "Yield Spread Premium" or YSP. The problem with YSPs is that borrowers frequently did not understand that mortgage brokers were acting as agents for the lender, rather than as their agents—many borrowers believed that brokers were under a duty to get them the best possible loan terms. The brokers were incentivized to do just the opposite. Liability for improper steering incentives tracks liability for ATR violations, including the ability to raise a setoff defense without regard to the statute of limitations or to assignee liability limitations. 15 U.S.C. §§ 1640(a)(4), 1640(k).

F. Mortgage Servicing Regulations

1. Servicing Transfers

RESPA includes a number of provisions regulating mortgage servicing—the day-to-day management of mortgage loans, often on behalf of a third party. First, RESPA requires notice to the borrower of any transfer of the servicing of the loan. 12 U.S.C. § 2605(b)-(c). The notice requirement applies to both the transferee and the transferor. *Id.* If payments are received by the transferor for 60 days after the transfer, no late fees may be imposed. 12 U.S.C. § 2605(d). This provision is important because the servicing of loans is frequently transferred, and without proper notice borrowers would be likely to misdirect payments and find themselves delinquent and owing late fees. The servicing transfer notice ensures that borrowers know who is servicing their loans.

2. Qualified Written Requests

RESPA further imposes a duty on loan servicers to respond to borrower inquiries if the inquiry is a "**qualified written request**" (QWR) for information relating to the servicing. 12 U.S.C. § 2605(e). A QWR is written correspondence that allows the servicer to identify the name and account of the borrower and provides a statement for the reasons the borrower believes the account is in error or other sufficient detail regarding the information sought by the borrower. 12 U.S.C. § 2605(e)(1)(B). The servicer must acknowledge a QWR within 20 days and take action regarding the inquiry within 30 business days by correcting the error if any and providing a written explanation of its actions to the borrower and contact information for further assistance. 12 U.S.C. §§ 2605(e)(1)(A), 2605(e)(2); 12 C.F.R. § 1024.35(d)(3)(C). Special shorter timelines apply if the error alleged relates to a foreclosure or loan payoff. 12 C.F.R. § 1024.35(d)(3)(A)-(B). While a QWR is pending, the servicer may not engage in negative credit reporting on the borrower related to the issue raised in the QWR.

The RESPA QWR procedure creates an analog to EFTA and TILA error resolution regimes, which provide a mechanism for informal resolution of disputes. Like those regimes, the RESPA QWR provision is actually a type of disclosure regime in that it enables the borrower to obtain information necessary for evaluating options at a relatively low cost.

There is a private right of action for failure to comply with the RESPA servicing transfer and QWR provisions. Damages are set at actual damages plus statutory damages of up to $2,000 if there is a pattern of non-compliance, plus attorney's fees. Class damages are capped at the lesser of $1 million or 1% of the net worth of the servicer, plus attorney's fees. 12 U.S.C. § 2605(f).

3. Default Servicing and Foreclosures

Regulation X imposes a complex set of rules regarding servicing of delinquent loans and foreclosures. Servicers are not required to engage in any particular substantive loss mitigation, 12 C.F.R. § 1024.41(a), but they are required to undertake particular procedures in regard to delinquent borrowers. First, servicers must engage in early intervention. They must make a good faith effort to contact borrowers by the 36th day of delinquency and provide written information to a delinquent borrower by the 45th day of delinquency. 12 C.F.R. § 1024.39(a)-(b). Second, servicers are required to adopt policies and procedures to maintain continuity of contact with the borrower and ensure that their personnel can access borrower-provided information and provide that information to decision makers. 12 C.F.R. § 1024.40. Third, servicers must screen loss mitigation applications for any loss mitigation options they offer that are received 45 days prior to a foreclosure sale. 12 C.F.R. § 1024.41(b)(2)(i). Servicers must send acknowledgement of having received a loss mitigation application within five business days. 12 C.F.R. § 1024.41(b)(2)(i)(B). They must also exercise reasonable diligence to identify and obtain missing information about the borrower. *Id.*; 12 C.F.R. § 1024.41(c)(2)(ii).

Fourth, if a complete loss mitigation application is received more than 37 days to prior to the foreclosure sale, then the servicer must evaluate the borrower for all loss mitigation options within 30 days and provide written explanation of its decision. 12 C.F.R. § 1024.41(c). Again, however, no loss mitigation is actually required. 12 C.F.R. § 1024.41(a). Fifth, servicers must offer a right of appeal of a loss mitigation decision if the complete application was received 90 or more days before the scheduled foreclosure sale. 12 C.F.R. § 1024.41(h)(1). The appeal must be determined within 30 days by independent servicer personnel. 12 C.F.R. § 1024.41(h)(3)-(4). Again, it bears emphasis that for all of these procedural requirements, if the servicer does not offer loss mitigation options, none of it matters. *See* 12 C.F.R. § 1024.41(a).

Finally, Reg X prohibits referral of loans to foreclosure until they are at least 120 days delinquent. 12 C.F.R. § 1024.41(f). Traditionally, loans were referred to foreclosure at 90 days delinquent. Moreover, no foreclosure is permitted while loss mitigation issues are pending. 12 C.F.R. § 1024.41(g). The result of Reg X should be to substantially slow foreclosure timetables, especially as borrowers can enforce these provisions of Reg X pursuant to 12 U.S.C. § 2605(f). 12 C.F.R. § 1024.41(a).

4. Force-Placed Insurance

Reg X also places restrictions on force-placed insurance fees. Borrowers are generally responsible for taxes and insurance on their properties, and lenders are keen to ensure that there is continuous casualty insurance coverage for their collateral properties. When a borrower defaults on her loan payments, she will also generally fail to make the insurance payments (indeed, what borrower would pay the insurance for a property that is heading toward foreclosure?). Lenders are authorized under the standard Fannie/Freddie uniform security instrument to "force-place" insurance on the property, that is, to take out an insurance policy on the property with the charges added to the borrower's liability. Force-placed insurance tends to be more expensive than regular insurance, not least because borrowers with force-placed insurance tend to be riskier, but also because there is little competition; the lender has no incentive to shop for the lowest price for insurance someone else will be paying.

Reg X provides that that servicers may not charge a borrower for force-placed insurance coverage unless there is notice, unless there is a reasonable basis to believe that the borrower has failed to maintain the required hazard insurance coverage, and the force-placed insurance charges are bona fide and reasonable, meaning that they must bear a reasonable relationship to the servicer's cost of providing the service. 12 C.F.R. §§ 1024.37(b)-(c), 1024.37(h). If an escrow account exists, the servicer may not force-place insurance if it can maintain the borrower's existing coverage by advancing funds from the escrow. 12 C.F.R. § 1024.17(k)(5).

What we see, then, is that federal regulation covers mortgages from loan application all the way up until foreclosure or payoff. It is an incredibly detailed regulatory system combining disclosure regulation, substantive term regulation, and process regulation, with sub-schemes for particular product types. This chapter provides only a high-level overview of this regulatory thicket. Additionally, you should be aware that states have their own sets of mortgage regulations. While many of these regulations are preempted, they include things such as the particular form of the security instrument required (whether a mortgage or deed of trust), closing requirements (*e.g.*, number of witnesses, use of an attorney), occasionally LTV and prepayment regulation, title insurance regulation, and the foreclosure process.

Problem Set 29

1. Your close friends Elisa and Marty D'Souza are a newly married couple excited to be purchasing their first home together. They each currently own their own apartment, and it's taken some work to coordinate the sales of their apartments with the purchase of their new house. The closing of the purchase is scheduled for Monday, while the closings for their sales are scheduled for Wednesday, with the movers scheduled to pack up their apartments on the intervening Tuesday. When Elisa and Marty get to the closing of their purchase, their mortgage lender, Laverna National Bank and Trust, tells them that there's going to be an extra fee of $500 that will have to be paid in cash to cover an unexpected problem with the title search. Elisa calls you from the closing, very upset about this fee. What do you advise her to do? *See* 12 C.F.R. §§ 1026.37, 1026.38.

2. Metropolitan Bancorp is a mid-sized regional mortgage lender. Most of Metropolitan's loans are 30-year, fixed-rate, fully amortized mortgages that Metropolitan keeps in portfolio rather than securitizing. Metropolitan is concerned about its interest rate risk. What could Metropolitan do to minimize its rate risk? *See* 12 C.F.R. §§ 1026.32(b)(6), 1026.43(g).

3. The Banco Merica made a $250,000 non-recourse mortgage loan to Esala Chandrasiri. The loan had a front-end DTI of 40%. Two years later, Chandrasiri defaulted, having paid $1,000 in closing costs, and $50,000 in interest. When Banco Merica forecloses on the loan, it is owed $230,000. Chandrasiri's property sells at foreclosure for $200,000. Chandrasiri, represented by Wachter & Wharton LLP, has vigorously exercised all of his legal rights (for which Wachter & Wharton LLP has charged $25,000). What will the Banco Merica's recovery from the foreclosure sale be? *See* 15 U.S.C. §§ 1639c, 1640(a), 1640(k); 12 C.F.R. §§ 1026.43(c), 1026.43(e)(2)(vi).

4. Jackariah Jenks has a mortgage loan from the Mastodon National Bank. In which of these situations will Jackariah be able to rescind the loan, and what will be the effect of the rescission if allowed?

a. Yesterday Jackariah took out a $50,000 home equity line of credit to finance a remodel of his kitchen. The loan was fully and properly documented. Jackariah paid $500 in closing costs and a $1,000 annual "line availability fee." He also drew down $3,000 on the line for a down payment to his contractor. Today he learned he was fired from his job. *See* 12 C.F.R. §§ 1026.2(a)(24), 1026.4(b)(3), 1026.4(c)(7), 1026.15(a), 1026.15(d).

b. The loan was a purchase money mortgage made two years ago, and Jackariah was never given his TILA rescission right notice. *See* 12 C.F.R. §§ 1026.2(a)(24), 1026.23(a)-(b), 1026.23(f)(1).

c. The loan was made a year ago and was a refinancing of a purchase money loan from the Old Northwest Loans. Jackariah received his TILA rescission right notice, but the APR on the Disclosure Statement was incorrectly listed as 1% lower than what Jackariah was actually charged. *See* 12 C.F.R. §§ 1026.2(a)(24), 1026.23(a)-(b), 1026.23 (d), 1026.23(g)(1).

d. The loan was made a year ago and was a refinancing of a purchase money loan made by the Mastodon National Bank. The closing costs on the refinancing were rolled into the new loan. Jackariah's wife Lorna is a co-signor on this loan. Mastodon National Bank gave Jackariah two copies of the TILA rescission right notice but did not give any to Lorna. *See* 12 C.F.R. §§ 1026.2(a)(24), 1026.23(a)-(b), 1026.23(d), 1026.23(f)(2).

5. Aram Pashigian wants to get a second-lien home equity loan to finance the remediation of a basement drainage problem, but he has terrible credit. The First Bank of Springfield is offering him a loan at 20% APR, when a prime borrower, like his neighbor Fuji Oka, could get a loan at 5%. The loan has a default interest rate of 30%. The loan payments would constitute 50% of Aram's monthly income.

First Bank of Springfield has also insisted that Aram go through housing counseling before proceeding with the loan. The HUD-certified Housing Counselor told Aram that the loan is a very bad idea given his household's finances, but Aram's insistent on going through with the transaction.

Can First Bank of Springfield make the loan? And if so, what risks does First Bank of Springfield face? *See* 15 U.S.C. §§ 1639(d), 1639(n), 1639(u); 12 C.F.R. §§ 1026.23(a)(3)(ii), 1026.32(a)(1)(i)(B)-(C), 1026.32(d)(2), 1026.34(a)(5), 1026.43(e)(2).

6. First Bank of Springfield made a $200,000 purchase money mortgage loan to Sara Coelho. Sara's credit isn't great, and the loan is priced at 8% when the Average Prime

Offer would be for 5%. The loan is a 30-year fixed-rate mortgage with no points or fees, and it complies with Freddie Mac's underwriting guidelines in terms of credit score and debt-to-income ratios. First Bank of Springfield investigated Sara's ability to repay by verifying her employment and salary with her employer, Springfield Public Schools, and pulling her credit report, which lists certain monthly debt payment obligations.

Sara was laid off from her job as a third-grade teacher and has missed her last two mortgage payments. You are counsel to the First Bank of Springfield, and Sara's loan file has been sent to you for review. What do you recommend doing? Based on your recommendations, what should First Bank of Springfield consider in the future when lending to less-than-great credit risks like Sara? *See* 15 U.S.C. §§ 1640(a), 1640(k); 12 C.F.R. §§ 1024.39(a)-(b), 1024.40, 1024.41(a), 1024.41(f)(1), 1026.43(b)(4), 1026.43(c), 1026.43(e).

7. Alan Alright bought a $300,000 home in suburban New Jersey. His lender, Bank of the East, N.A., required him to purchase private mortgage insurance, so that if Alan defaulted, the insurer would cover some of the lender's losses. When Alan asked the lender "where do I get private mortgage insurance?" the loan officer Barry Braun truthfully responded, "There are a bunch of companies that sell this product, but they all charge exactly the same rate. We've always had a good experience working with PRIMICO." With that, Barry handed Alan a PRIMICO brochure and the card for a PRIMICO agent, Claire Chu. "We can even call up Claire now if you'd like," said Barry, as he began dialing Claire's number. Alan ended up purchasing the insurance from PRIMICO through Claire.

Unbeknownst to Alan and other Bank of the East mortgage loan borrowers, however, PRIMICO and Bank of the East have an understanding by which PRIMICO will cede reinsurance to Atlantic Reinsurance, an affiliate of Bank of the East, in relation to the amount of referrals it gets from Bank of the East. Also unbeknownst to Alan, Claire was paying Barry Braun $100—10% of his commission—for every private mortgage insurance referral.

You are a CFPB enforcement attorney, and this fact pattern has been referred to you by CFPB examination staff. What, if any, enforcement actions might you bring and against whom? *See* 12 U.S.C. §§ 2607(a), 5531, 5536.

CHAPTER 30

SMALL-DOLLAR CREDIT

I. SMALL-DOLLAR CREDIT: LIQUIDITY NEEDS

Consumers often have needs for short-term liquidity. Most consumers receive income on a weekly, bi-weekly, or monthly basis. What happens when the consumer has to make a payment in the interim? When consumers face regular payment obligations, they can budget around those obligations to try to match income and expenses. But what happens when a consumer faces an unanticipated liquidity need, such as funeral expenses or a broken-down car or furnace or freezer full of food?

One possibility is that the consumer dips into his or her savings. Savings can be used to smooth over liquidity demands. But not all consumers have savings. When faced with a liquidity need, such a consumer can either sell assets (such as to a pawn shop) or borrow funds. Not all consumers have assets that they can readily turn into cash or want to sell their belongings. Thus, borrowing may be an attractive option.

For many consumers, credit cards fill short-term liquidity needs. The consumer charges expenses to the card throughout the month and then repays later, after having herself been paid. Even if the consumer does not revolve a balance, the credit card lets the consumer smooth over short-term mismatches in income and expenses, and the ability to revolve a balance allows consumers to smooth over income and expense mismatches over a longer term (albeit at a price).

Not all consumers have credit cards, and credit cards have credit limits. Some consumers use bank overdraft for short-term liquidity, but overdraft is not reliable because it typically is not contractual credit. The consumer cannot be sure that the bank will allow the overdraft, and banks do not generally allow consumers to keep large, extended overdrafts outstanding.

Another option for consumers is short-term, small-dollar credit products: signature loans, payday loans, auto title loans, tax-refund anticipation loans, and pawn loans. There are important differences among these products, but also some important similarities. First, excluding signature loans, all of these products necessarily feature enhanced collection mechanisms that make it easier for the lender to get repaid. Second, all of these products are extremely expensive relative to standard credit cards. As a result, the user population for these short-term, small-dollar credit products tends to be less creditworthy and less wealthy. Third, it is important to keep in mind that while some borrowers use short-term, small-dollar credit to deal with unanticipated expenses, many use this credit to cover recurring expenses, such as rent or mortgage payments, credit card bills, utility bills, or groceries.

II. TYPES OF SMALL-DOLLAR CREDIT

A. Signature Loans

The simplest type of small-dollar credit is a "signature loan." It is called that because there is no security or enhanced ability to get payment for the loan. The borrower simply signs a note promising to repay the lender. In this regard, a signature loan is similar to a credit card, but it is not linked with a payment instrument and it is a term loan, rather than a revolving line of credit. Signature loans are offered by a range of institutions from banks and credit unions to online finance company lenders, including peer-to-peer lenders.

Signature loans are not a particularly standardized product, and are more defined by what they lack—enhanced collection mechanisms—than their features. They are usually offered with terms ranging from several months to several years, and in amounts of $500 to as much as $100,000, but typically on the lower end of the range, and rarely for over $40,000.

Most signature loans are amortizing installment loans, meaning that borrowers make regular, periodic payments of both principal and interest so that the principal balance on the loan is reduced with each payment. Some, however, are interest-only (non-amortizing) loans, meaning that the periodic payments are of interest only, with the principal due in a balloon payment at maturity. Signature loans can also be single-payment "bullet" loans, with both principal and interest all due in a single lump sum payment at maturity. Signature loans are generally freely prepayable.

Costs on signature loans vary greatly. Banks and credit unions typically loan at under 36% APR (exclusive of origination fees), while finance companies may charge triple digit APRs. For example, CashCall, a finance company (which you may recall from Chapter 11, where it was the subject of a CFPB enforcement for allegedly abusive collection of debts that exceeded state usury caps), offers a variety of signature loan products both directly and through various affiliates. The loans range from $850 to $10,000, with APRs between 90% and 343%. A typical CashCall loan in California is a $2,600 loan as California's usury law only covers loans smaller than $2,500. Cal. Fin. Code § 22303. The CashCall California loan has a prepayable 42-month term, minimal amortization, simple interest, and a $75 origination fee. The interest rate is either 96% or 135% depending on the borrower's credit profile.

Signature loans are not restricted to any particular use; consumers use them for everything from financing their small businesses to wedding and funeral expenses to education expenses to making home furnishing or remodeling purchases to funding vacations to refinancing other debts.

Other than some general Truth-in-Lending disclosures, regulation of signature loans is primarily on the state level. Finance companies are not usually exempt from usury laws, but often state usury laws have loopholes that allow signature lenders to structure their loans so that the usury laws do not apply, such as with the $2,600 CashCall product in California. State licensing regimes for finance companies may also impose substantive term restrictions on the amount and term length of loans, as well as on amortization requirements and prepayment limitations. The details vary substantially among states.

Signature lenders frequently obtain the borrower's preauthorization to make ACH debits on the borrower's bank account, although this is not a defining feature of a signature loan. The right to make ACH debits on the borrower's bank account gives the lender an enhanced repayment mechanism. If the borrower neglects or chooses not to pay, the creditor can still get repaid without undertaking legal action or any sort of persuasive debt collection activity. The borrower can, of course, withdraw the ACH authorization, but this sort of "**leveraged payment mechanism**"—a special enhanced collection right, is quite valuable and is an essential feature of other types of short-term lending. Because these loans tend to be relatively small, the fixed costs of lending, as well as the cost of underwriting a loan based on the borrower's ability to repay, would be a substantially greater percentage of the loan amount than for larger mortgage loans, auto loans, and credit card lines of credit.

B. Payday Loans

While signature loans have been around forever—they are the most basic type of personal loan—other forms of small-dollar liquidity lending have evolved considerably over the past century. In the early twentieth century, finance companies would "purchase" consumers' paychecks in advance of being paid in exchange for a discount that was effectively an interest rate as high as 400%. In response to concerns about these loans, many states adopted a form of the Uniform Small Loan Law, a model law created by the Russell Sage Foundation. The Uniform Small Loan Law involved a licensing regime and permitted interest of between 24% and 48% annually, much higher than states' existing usury laws.

The small-dollar lending industry remained fairly discrete until the 1990s, when some check cashers would purchase a consumer's personal check, rather than a check from a third party, and agree to hold it for a period of time before cashing it, a process known as "deferred presentment" or "check holding." Typically, check cashers would agree to hold the check until the borrower's next payday. The fees for such deferred presentment were often high and raised questions about whether they were loans and thus subject to state usury laws. Many states clarified this by exempting deferred presentment transactions from their general usury laws, permitting them at APRs of 300%-400%. This was the origin of payday lending.

A **payday loan** is a short-term, small-dollar loan that is backed by a right for the lender in the event of a default to draw on the borrower's bank account for repayment without having to first get a court judgment. In other words, a payday loan gives the lender accelerated repayment ability through a self-help right against the borrower's bank account.

Usually lenders secure the right to draw on the borrower's bank account either by taking a post-dated check from the borrower (dated for the borrower's payday) or by getting an ACH authorization from the borrower (the post-dated check can also be converted to an ACH item). ACH authorization is now the preferred method for payday lenders because an ACH item can be presented up to three times in 180 days, whereas a check can be presented only once. Therefore, even if the borrower does not have funds in the account when the lender makes the first ACH draw, the lender has two more opportunities to engage in the self-help collection. Thus, while a payday loan does not involve a security interest, it functions much like a secured loan.

Payday loans typically have a maturity of between one week and one month, designed to coincide with the borrower's payday (or government benefit distribution date). The idea is that on payday the borrower will have an influx of funds that can be used to repay the lender. If the borrower fails to do so voluntarily, the lender can then exercise its right to draw on the borrower's bank account, which will hopefully be flush with funds on payday.

Because payday lenders rely on an enhanced repayment mechanism, payday loans are only loosely underwritten. Some payday lenders will run credit scores from specialized payday lending credit reporting bureaus, but this is the exception, not the rule. Instead, an applicant typically needs only present identification and evidence of regular income from a third party—either a paycheck or government benefits. The borrower's periodic income may sometimes serve to limit the amount of the borrowing, but frequently it is not a constraint. Instead, the lender will simply have a maximum loan size, irrespective of borrower income, set by regulation.

Payday loans come in both single-payment and installment loan structures, with substantial variation among states due to state law. Payday loans tend to be for amounts between $100 and $500. The typical payday loan from a storefront lender is around $350. The pricing for payday loans is generally in terms of a fixed fee rather than an interest rate. A CFPB study found the median fee to be $15 per $100 borrowed. Fees are generally capped by state law, however, and lenders almost always lend at the maximum permitted rate.

1. Rollovers

The stated maturity date of a payday loan is quite short. Two weeks is the most common term, with the average loan being 18.3 days. Maximum loan length is also frequently governed by state law. While the stated term of payday loans is quite short, loans are frequently rolled over, meaning that the lender extends the loan for another pay period, in exchange for an additional fee (which might be financed into a larger loan). The borrower has not gotten any additional cash disbursed, but instead has the original disbursement for longer.

Not all states permit rollovers, however. Nineteen states allow rollovers, although most limit the number of rollovers. Borrowers will sometimes effectuate something similar to a rollover either by getting back-to-back loans from one lender (paying off one loan and then immediately taking out another) or by refinancing loans between lenders (who might even be located next door to or across the street from each other). Some states limit the number of loans allowed at any one time (and have databases that lenders must check before lending) or have cooling-off periods between loans, but ultimately rollovers are an essential feature of payday lending and are critical to the payday lending business model. The CFPB has found that two-thirds of payday loans were in sequences of at least seven consecutive or near-consecutive loans, and over half of loans were in sequences of ten or more loans. As a result, 90% of payday loan fees were from consumers who borrowed seven or more times and 75% of fees were from consumers who borrowed ten or more times. In other words, the payday loan industry's economics are built on the assumption of rollovers. Thus, a Pew Charitable Trusts study found that they typical borrower takes out eight loans of $375 a year and pays $520 in fees. Pew Charitable Trusts, *Payday Lending in America: Who Borrows, Where They Borrow, and Why* 4 (2012).

Rollovers or reborrowing do not happen automatically with storefront payday lending. If the borrower does nothing, the lender attempts to collect by depositing the check or doing an ACH debit. Neither results in a rollover. Therefore, storefront payday lenders generally encourage or even require borrowers to return to the store on the loan's due date to pay in person. This gives the lender the possibility of selling the borrower on a rollover or a reborrowing after repayment.

The frequency of rollovers makes default rates on payday loans tricky to understand. Default rates are often reported on a per-loan basis, which can be misleading. Thus, if a borrower borrowed $100 and rolled over the loan nine times before defaulting, the borrower would have repaid no principal, meaning a 100% loss rate for the principal, but the reported default rate would be only 10% because only one of the ten loans defaulted. The CFPB has found that 24% of all single-payment payday loans default, and 38% of all loan sequences result in a default. CFPB, *Supplemental Findings on Payday, Payday Installment, and Vehicle Title Loans, and Deposit Advance Products* 22 (June 2016). Note, however, that in the example above that even though the borrower never repaid the $100 principal, the borrower did pay rollover fees of perhaps $180 (at $20 per rollover). Thus, at the end of the day, the lender has made positive revenue of $80 on the loan despite the default. This is the key to the payday lending industry's economics, particularly given the relatively high fixed or semi-variable costs per customer, as discussed below.

The economics of payday lending are best understood in reference to the sweat box model that you learned about in Chapter 27 regarding credit cards. As you'll recall, the sweat box theory hypothesized that credit card issuers lobbied for a reform of bankruptcy laws that delayed consumers' bankruptcy filings because the longer consumers remained in financial distress prior to ultimately filing bankruptcy and defaulting, the more interest and fees would be paid to the card issuer. *See* Ronald J. Mann, *Bankruptcy Reform and the "Sweat Box" of Credit Card Debt*, 2007 Ill. L. Rev. 375. The card issuer could forfeit the principal balance owed without taking a loss if it had made enough in interest and fees prior to the default.

The same model applies to payday lending, in that the lender can profit irrespective of whether the consumer repays the loan. In a sweat box lending model, in contrast, the lender does not need the borrower to repay in full in order to make a profit, as the lender can collect enough in fees and interest prior to a default to offset any lost principal. In a sweat box lending model, the lender's interest is not in lending only to borrowers who can repay in full, but in lending only to borrowers who can make enough payments of fees and interest prior to defaulting. The sweat box lending model, therefore, enables lower lending standards, as payment in full is not required for profitability. Indeed, payday lending is not based on an underwriting of the borrower that assesses the borrower's ability to repay, but on the lender's enhanced collection rights for a relatively small loan amount, making it likely that the payday lender will be the first creditor to grab the debtor's limited assets.

Also key to a sweat box lending model is limiting amortization. If a loan amortizes, it will eventually get paid off, thereby releasing the borrower from the sweat box. Single-payment payday loans do not amortize when they are rolled over. The principal is never reduced until it is paid off or there is a default. Thus, rollovers and lack of amortization raise the concern of consumers getting caught on a "perpetual debt treadmill." S. Rept. 111-176, at 17.

2. Borrower Profile

Approximately 5.5% of the U.S. population reports having used a payday loan in recent years. The typical payday borrower earns less than $40,000 annually (72% of borrowers), and lacks a four-year college degree (85%). Blacks are overrepresented within the payday borrower population, as are divorced or separated individuals and the disabled. Renters are also more likely to be payday borrowers. Pew Charitable Trusts, *Payday Lending in America: Who Borrows, Where They Borrow, and Why* (2012). A key point to see is that while payday borrowers are generally not well-to-do, they must have two things: a bank account and a steady and documentable source of income, that is, either a job or government benefits. In other words, payday loans are not a product used by the unbanked. They are also not a product used by the self-employed.

Most payday borrowers report that they use the loans to pay for recurring expenses—utilities, credit card bills, rent or mortgage, or food. Only 16% say that they borrowed to cover an unexpected expense such as a car repair or emergency medical bill. Pew Charitable Trusts, *Payday Lending in America: Who Borrows, Where They Borrow, and Why* (2012). This indicates that while there are some borrowers who are relying on payday loans as an emergency source of liquidity, many others are using them to bridge a chronic gap between income and expenses that might be better served by a longer-term (and cheaper) source of funding. To use an analogy deployed by the CFPB, a payday loan is like a cab ride. It's sensible for going across town, but not for a cross-country trip.

3. Industry Structure

There are few barriers to entry into the payday lending industry. While every state that permits small-dollar lending requires some sort of registration with the state, the requirements are generally not onerous and are primarily ministerial in nature, rather than merits-based. Payday lenders operate both from physical storefronts and online. There are nearly 16,000 storefront locations, more than McDonald's (over 14,000) or Starbucks (over 13,000) (but contrast the 90,000 bank and 20,000 credit union branches nationwide). Unlike McDonalds or Starbucks, however, these locations are not spread out over all 50 states. Instead, they are clustered within 36 states that lack usury rates or have carve-outs from their usury laws for payday loans. The other 14 states and the District of Columbia either ban payday loans or have usury rates that effectively preclude payday lending. Ten large firms, including some publicly traded ones, account for half of payday storefront locations, but there are also many small lenders with a single storefront or a handful of storefronts.

While there are a large number of payday lending locations, there are a limited number of payday borrowers. Only around 2.4 million households got a payday loan in 2013 (4.2% of the population). That translates into 150 borrowers per lender location. Other studies have found around 500 unique borrowers per storefront. Pew Charitable Trusts, *Auto Title Loans: Market Practices and Borrowers' Experiences* 5 (2015). Whatever the precise number, the general point is that there are a limited number of buyers served by any particular lending location, and the total amount they borrow is relatively limited given loan sizes. There is approximately $2 billion in payday loans outstanding at any point in time, with total annual loans being in the range of $20-$30 billion (counting each rollover as a separate loan).

The small number of borrowers means that there is a relatively small borrower base for lenders to amortize their own fixed costs (overhead and labor), semi-variable costs (costs of funds), and variable costs (lead generation and credit losses). Given the small size of a single loan, a lender is unlikely to recoup its fixed and semi-variable costs, much less make a profit, unless the borrower rolls over the loan.

For example, online payday loans involve a borrower going to a website that is not actually that of the lender, but of a "**lead generator.**" The lead generator auctions off the borrower. The cost of a lead can be as high as $200. In such circumstances, if the lender is charging a $45 fee per loan, the lender needs the original loan plus four rollovers simply to recoup the cost of purchasing the lead, much less its other expenses of overhead, labor, and funds. The same goes for storefront lenders. Although they do not pay for lead generation, they have substantially greater overhead and labor costs from operating a physical establishment.

The implication is that payday lenders need a minimum number of rollovers on a loan to simply break even: a single extension of credit is a money loser for a payday lender. The lender, however, cannot know how many rollovers a borrower will do at the time of the original extension of credit. To the extent that a borrower does less than the minimum number of rollovers for the lender to "break even," that borrower will have to be offset by another borrower who exceeds the break-even point. Thus, the limited subset of borrowers who engage in a large number of rollovers is essential to the economic viability of the payday lending industry. Absent such repeated rollovers, the industry simply cannot recover its fixed and semi-variable expenses. Thus, the low traffic per store means that the operational costs of small-dollar lending have to be amortized over a small customer base in order for the lender to lend profitably, which pushes up borrowing costs.

While there are many competitors within the payday lending industry, competition is not on price; most lenders charge the maximum permitted rate and borrowers do not evince price elasticity beneath the usury cap. Likewise, in the seven states that do not have usury caps for payday loans, competition does not seem to be on price, as prices do not cluster, but instead vary considerably. Competition among payday lenders is on location, convenience, ease of application, certainty of loan approval, and speed of funding. As discuss below in section III.B, this has some unusual effects on the industry.

4. Online Payday Lending

In addition to storefront lending, there is also Internet-based small-dollar lending, mainly payday lending, but also signature lending. For payday loans, approximately one-third of loans originate online. Internet-based small-dollar lending is conducted primarily through **lead generators**. Lead generators are websites that advertise small-dollar loans, often through linked banner advertisements or paid search results on search engines. When the consumer clicks on the banner or the search result, it takes him to a web page that will prompt him to fill out a brief questionnaire that determines the loans for which he may qualify. The lead generator then puts the consumer "lead" up for auction. The lender that wins the bid is then connected with the consumer to consummate the loan.

This lead generation structure has important implications for consumers. First, it means that consumers are not able to comparison shop effectively for online loans. The lead generator does not advertise rates. The only time the consumer is offered a rate is after the loan has been sold to a lender. At that point, the consumer is dealing with a single lender and cannot compare rates. If the consumer goes back to the lead generator to apply again, the consumer's application might be rejected because of the recent application, but even if not, the consumer might just find herself dealing with the very same lender. Not surprisingly, given the lack of consumer choice, online lenders feature higher prices and more abusive collection behavior and loan structures. Pew Charitable Trusts, *Fraud and Online Abuse: Harmful Practices in Internet Payday Lending* 9-12 (Oct. 2014).

Online lending also affects lenders' business models. First, online lending lets lenders avoid the fixed costs of maintaining a storefront presence. Overhead is much lower for online lenders. But they face adverse selection in terms of borrowers, and hence higher loss rates, even while being more selective about borrowers. Not surprisingly, then, online loans are costlier, with a typical APR of 652% in 2014 as compared to 391% for storefront lenders. The use of lead generators enables online lenders to avoid direct advertising costs, but it comes at a price. Leads are not cheap. In 2016 they sold for something in the range of $150-$200 per first-look lead.

Most online loans are single-payment, rather than installment loans, but repayment works differently than with storefront single-payment loans. Whereas storefront lenders want the borrower to come back to the store to pay because it presents a chance to sell the borrower on a new loan or a rollover, online lenders rely on electronic repayment. Instead of in-person sales, online lenders will often do an ACH debit for only the fee, not the principal, so there will be an automatic rollover. Online lenders will also often do multiple ACH debits for the same fee, splitting the debt into multiple debits in order to reduce the chance of a return for insufficient funds; if the second debit is returned for NSF, at least the lender has recovered on the first debit. The reliance on ACH repayment makes online lenders particularly dependent on banks and the ACH system.

Online lending raises important jurisdictional questions. Some jurisdictions forbid various forms of small-dollar lending, while others regulate it, including through usury laws. What usury law applies to a loan made by a Delaware corporation online to a New York consumer? If the Delaware corporation were a national bank, the answer would be easy—the Delaware usury law could be exported. *Marquette Nat'l Bank of Minneapolis v. First of Omaha Service Corp.*, 439 U.S. 299 (1978). But that special rule for national banks is an exception. Normally, the usury law of the borrower's location would apply. Still, jurisdictional issues continue to be contested in online small-dollar lending, including loans made by entities that claim a Native American tribal affiliation or incorporation.

Online lending can also produce a toxic by-product. When consumers apply for a loan through a lead generator, they usually give their bank account and routing information, which a payday lender would use to facilitate an ACH authorization. Many leads, however, are not purchased. What happens with all of that consumer data from unpurchased leads? Unfortunately, in some instances, it is sold to fraudsters who use the bank account and routing information to initiate unauthorized ACH draws. The draws are usually for small amounts ($20 or $40) using an anodyne payday lender-type name, such that the consumer is unlikely to notice. Even if the consumer does notice, the small amounts reduce consumers' incentive to address the fraud, and by their very nature, consumers who have been applying for online payday loans are unlikely to have the time and sophistication to address such frauds.

5. State Level Regulation of Payday Loans

Prior to 2018, payday lending was regulated primarily at the state and local levels. There is now also federal regulation, discussed below, but state-level regulation continues to be significant. As mentioned above, a number of states simply do not allow payday lending. Those that do generally license lenders (often as check cashers under "Deferred Deposit" transaction statutes) and impose disclosure requirements, as well as restrictions on fees, term length, and rollovers or number of loans outstanding at any time. The Louisiana and Mississippi statutes at the end of the chapter are fairly typical of less onerous state regimes. Some states also mandate cooling-off periods between loans. Some states have mandated installment structures and prorated refunds of fees for prepayment in order to reduce incentives to front-load charges on installment loans and have them refinanced repeatedly. Some municipalities have additional payday lending regulations, including anti-agglomeration zoning that attempts to limit the clustering of payday lenders in particular areas.

Lenders have adopted several strategies to circumvent state payday lending regulations. First, they have partnered with banks through "rent-a-bank" operations in order to take advantage of preemption and parity laws. The bank will formally make the loan, but the loan will be marketed, purchased, and administered by the payday lender. Rent-a-bank payday loan operations were once quite common but have become rarer following 2013 OCC and FDIC guidance that emphasized that banks are responsible for third-party relationships and that banks must rigorously underwrite payday-type loans from banks.

Second, some lenders have simply obtained licenses in states with favorable regulatory regimes and then relied on contractual choice of law principles when lending in other states. Third, some lenders have partnered with Native American tribes to make loans. The loan will formally be made by the tribe or a tribal corporation, which is purportedly exempt from state regulations, but most or all of the lending program and its administration, as well as the ultimate source of funds, will be from a non-tribal finance company.

Finally, some Internet lenders have moved to offshore operations on the theory that it makes them somehow not subject to U.S. jurisdiction when lending into the United States. Most recently, payday lenders have been interested in a federal "fintech" charter or a federal payday lending charter as a way of avoiding state regulation. It is important to emphasize that these various regulatory avoidance strategies are far from proven techniques; many are subject to ongoing litigation.

The fact that payday lending relies on the checking and ACH system makes it uniquely susceptible to indirect, "hydraulic" regulation through regulation of the checking and ACH system. Clearinghouse rules and bank risk management both present potential limitations on payday lenders' ability to do business, as discussed in Chapter 17 regarding the Department of Justice's controversial Operation Choke Point.

C. Auto Title Loans

Another way a consumer can borrow is against the value of a vehicle through an auto title loan. An auto title loan is not purchase money financing for a vehicle. Instead, it is a loan secured by a pledge of a vehicle already owned by the borrower as collateral. In an auto title loan, the consumer brings the car in to a prospective lender. The lender physically examines and values the car and makes sure that the consumer has clean title to the car, meaning that the consumer owns the car *and* that there are no prior liens on the car. It is critical that the consumer own the car—or else the consumer cannot pledge it as collateral—and that there be free and clear title because otherwise another creditor would potentially have rights to some or all of the value of the car.

If the lender is satisfied with the vehicle's title, the lender will then extend a loan for a portion of the vehicle's collateral, and will take a pledge of the certificate of title plus a set of keys as collateral while the consumer continues to use the car.

If the consumer fails to repay the loan's principal plus a loan fee (typically at an APR of around 300%), the lender may repossess the car, sell it at a foreclosure sale, and apply the sale proceeds (minus sale costs) to the loan balance (which likely includes various repossession-related fees). UCC §§ 9-609, 9-610. State law gives lenders great leeway in the sale process, requiring only that it be "commercially reasonable." UCC § 9-610(a). Depending on state law, the borrower may be liable for any post-foreclosure balance still owed. Some states require the lender to turn any surplus from the sale over to the borrower, but others treat the vehicle title loan as a pawn transaction and allow the lender to retain the surplus.

The typical auto title loan is structured as a single payment loan, although some title lenders do offer installment loans. In a single-payment structure, the entire principal balance plus all fees must be paid at the loan's maturity. The typical maturity is one month, although terms vary from as short as two weeks to as long as one year.

The stated term and the functional term are often quite different, however, because like a payday loan, if the borrower cannot repay the loan, the borrower has the option of rolling it over for a fee. Because title loans are made based on the collateral value of the vehicle, and not the borrower's independent ability to repay, the payments often exceed borrowers' ability to repay. Indeed, a typical auto title loan has payments that are half of the average borrower's gross monthly income, far more than the typical payday loan, where payments are 36% of gross monthly income. Pew Charitable Trusts, *Auto Title Loans: Market Practices and Borrowers' Experiences* 1 (2015).

Because of the unaffordability of title loans, most title loans are actually rollovers of old loans, instead of new extensions of credit. Borrowers have to roll over the loans because they lack the cash to pay off the loan. Instead, they are only able to produce the rollover fees. Thus, in 2013 some 84% of title loans in Tennessee were rollovers, while in Texas it was 63%.[1] Pew Charitable Trusts, *Auto Title Loans: Market Practices and Borrowers' Experiences* 11 (2015). A CFPB study found that 80% of loans were rolled over or reborrowed on the same day, and only around 12% of loans were single-loan sequences. CFPB, *Single-Payment Vehicle Title Lending* 3 (May 2016). Most loan sequences are for more than three loans, with perhaps a quarter being for ten loans. *Id.* This means that most loans made by title lenders are part of very long sequences. Less than 15% of all loans are part of sequences of three loans or fewer. *Id.* In other words, the title lending business model is based on an expectation that most borrowers will engage in extended rollovers. This implication is that fees may easily exceed the principal loaned out. Thus, for an average title loan of $1,000, total fees average $1,200. Pew Charitable Trusts, *Auto Title Loans: Market Practices and Borrowers' Experiences* 1 (2015). This suggests an average of four to five loans in a sequence, assuming APRs around 300%. Even if many sequences result in a default, the default will not necessarily result in a loss of principal, and even if it does, the fees paid up to that point will exceed the principal lost.

Auto title loans are thus similar to single-payment payday loans in that they are formally closed-end extensions of credit, but function like non-amortizing open-end lines of credit in most situations. The borrower is only able to get out of the sweat box either by defaulting or by finding an irregular source of repayment, such as a tax rebate, an inheritance, or help from family and friends. Note, however, that unlike payday loans, it is generally possible for the borrower to have only one title loan outstanding at a time. This is because the lender will typically take physical possession of the certificate of title, so that the borrower will not be able to produce title certificate to another lender absent fraud.

The size of title loans varies substantially, from roughly $100 to $10,000, depending on the vehicle's value, loan-to-value ratio at which the lender will lend, and state

1. These figures understate the matter because they do not include situations in which the lender treats the first loan as having been paid off and then a second separate loan as having been made, even though there was no actual repayment of principal or new credit extended.

law (some states cap loan amounts), but title loans are usually for around $1,000, substantially larger than the typical payday loan of $375. Pew Charitable Trusts, *Auto Title Loans: Market Practices and Borrowers' Experiences* 1, 3, 5 (2015). Loan-to-value ratios vary by lender, but a 25% LTV ratio is typical. *Id.* at 13. This suggests that the typical title loan borrower has a car worth only around $4,000.

1. The Title Lending Industry

Title lending is a storefront industry because of the need to inspect the vehicle in person. CFPB, *Single-Payment Vehicle Title Lending* 3 (May 2016). There are approximately 8,000 storefront title lending locations nationwide, half of which also offer payday loans. CFPB, *Proposed Rulemaking, Payday, Vehicle Title, and Certain High-Cost Installment Loans*, 81 Fed. Reg. 47863, 47881 (July 22, 2016). While there are lead-generation sites, they still require the borrower to go to a physical location prior to getting the loan. Like storefront payday lenders, title lenders have relatively little traffic per store. The average title lending store serves only around 300 unique customers per year, fewer than payday lenders (500 per year). Pew Charitable Trusts, *Auto Title Loans: Market Practices and Borrowers' Experiences* 5 (2015). This means that overhead is a substantial part of title lenders' expenses.

The title lending industry is somewhat more concentrated than the payday industry. While many title lenders are small operations that also offer payday or pawn loans, the largest title lender, TMX Finance, has about a fifth of the stores nationwide. Pew Charitable Trusts, *Auto Title Loans: Market Practices and Borrowers' Experiences* 5 (2015). TMX and two other firms, Community Loans of America and Select Management Resources, combine for 40% of all title lending locations. CFPB, *Proposed Rulemaking, Payday, Vehicle Title, and Certain High-Cost Installment Loans*, 81 Fed. Reg. 47863, 47881, n.176 (July 22, 2016).

Title lenders' primary risk is non-payment. While the title lender has the vehicle as collateral, it does not always guarantee repayment. The lender has to be able to find the vehicle to repossess it, if the borrower does not voluntarily surrender the vehicle. Vehicles are by nature moveable, and borrowers may attempt to hide their vehicles from repo men. (Electronic vehicle tracking systems can help address this issue, but may not be cost efficient for the lender in many cases.) Even if the lender can find the vehicle to repossess, it might not be worth enough to cover the loan balance. This could be because the lender overvalued the vehicle originally or because the vehicle has been subsequently damaged. (An assignment of insurance rights will not necessarily address this problem because the damage might not be covered by insurance.) When a deficiency judgment is legally allowed, its collectability will be low given that it is just a general unsecured debt of a borrower who, by definition, has few assets.

2. Title Borrower Profile

The auto title loan borrower population is generally similar to the payday borrower population. They tend to be poorer: over half have annual income of under $30,000, and two-thirds have annual income of less than $40,000. *See* Pew Charitable

Trusts, *Auto Title Loans: Market Practices and Borrowers' Experiences* 28 (2015). They also tend to be less well-educated: 83% lack a college degree, and over half have only a high school education or less. *Id.* They also tend to be more heavily male than payday borrowers. *Id.*

While the auto title borrower population tends to be similar to payday borrowers, there is an important potential difference in their credit profiles, namely their potential sources of repayment. To get a payday loan, one needs regular, documentable income (either a job with a steady paycheck or government benefits) and a bank account to facilitate collections; the unbanked cannot get payday loans. Title loans do not require employment or income or a bank account, only clean title to a vehicle. Thus, nearly a quarter of title loan borrowers lack a bank account. Thus, title lending is a form of short-term, small-dollar credit that is available to the unbanked, provided they have clean title to a vehicle.

Title lending is less common than payday lending. There are approximately 2 million title loans made per year, but many fewer individual borrowers. Only around 1% of the population has ever used a title lender versus 5% for payday lenders. Pew Charitable Trusts, *Auto Title Loans: Market Practices and Borrowers' Experiences* 5 (2015). Part of the reason for this is that title lenders only operate in half of the states (as discussed below), and part is likely because there is a limited population of consumers who have clean title to a vehicle and are in the market for short-term, small-dollar credit and would opt for a title loan over other forms of short-term small-dollar credit.

As with payday loans—and small-dollar, short-term credit in general—title borrowers do not shop primarily on price. Title borrowers tend to have immediate liquidity needs that trump any consideration of price beneath some reserve price at which point they would not borrow at all. Because borrowers are not shopping based on price, lenders do not feel pressure to compete on price. Instead, lenders compete mainly on location, convenience, and customer service. The lack of price-based competition suggests that competition is unlikely to provide meaningful consumer protection in the title lending market place.

3. Policy Concerns Regarding Title Loans

Auto title loans raise several policy concerns. First is the lack of ability-to-repay underwriting. Title loans are based on the collateral value of the car, not the borrower's own ability to pay off the loan. Given that the borrower often needs the car for transportation to work, childcare, etc., the idea of simply surrendering the car is often not appealing to borrowers. By pledging the car, the borrower jeopardizes his employment, among other things, if the borrower cannot repay the loan.

As a result, borrowers may well opt to roll over the loan instead of paying it off by surrendering the car, even if over time this may substantially increase the expense of the loan. Indeed, the fact that the loan is collateralized by the borrower's car and not underwritten to an ability to repay (and often requiring a payment that is over half of the borrower's monthly gross income) virtually guarantees that many borrowers will either end up in extended loan sequences or default. Title loans are arguably products that are designed to fail in the sense that they are not really intended to be paid off on their stated maturity date. Instead, given the product's design, it is essentially expected that most borrowers will keep rolling over the loan until they either default or receive unexpected or irregular income and can pay off the loan.

Second is their cost. Title loans are an expensive form of short-term credit, and given that title loans tend to be larger than payday loans, the cost in absolute dollar terms is higher.

Third is their duration. While title loans are nominally short-term credit, they often turn into medium-term loans. Instead of being a one-month extension of credit, they frequently turn into loan sequences of half a year or more. This is problematic because if the consumer ends up in a longer-than-anticipated sequence of loans, the consumer will end up paying much more in absolute dollar terms than anticipated for the loan. A consumer who expects to pay $250 for $1,000 for a month might end up paying $1,500 for having that same $1,000 for six months. It is unclear whether the consumer would make that deal if the consumer knew that it would result in a six-month loan sequence. Thus, while disclosure of nominal terms is generally clear and simple because of the single-payment structure, the total likely cost is never disclosed to borrowers. (Given that cost is not the driving factor for title borrowers, it is unclear whether such disclosure would matter, however.)

Fourth is title loans' lack of amortization. Because title loans tend to be single-payment products, there is no amortization of principal, and when a loan is rolled over, there is no payment of principal, just of the rollover fee (which might itself be financed). The lack of amortization combined with the lack of ability to repay, the cost, and the duration create a sweat box problem, in which the borrower is stuck in a non-amortizing loan for an extended duration, making rollover payments, but not paying down principal because the borrower lacks the financial ability to pay off the loan from regular income and has strong incentives not to pay off the loan by surrendering the vehicle. The result is to substantially increase the cost of the borrowing.

Fifth, the consequences of a default on an auto title loan may be more severe for the borrower than with other types of short-term, small-dollar credit. With an auto title loan, the borrower can potentially lose his car. Estimates regarding default, repossession, and foreclosure rates vary and often use different measures. The CFPB found that there is a 33% sequence-level default rate on auto title loans, meaning that the borrower defaults in one-third of every series of consecutive or near-consecutive loans. CFPB, *Single-Payment Vehicle Title Lending* 4 (May 2016). This compares with a 20% sequence-level default rate for payday loans. CFPB, *Proposed Rulemaking, Payday, Vehicle Title, and Certain High-Cost Installment Loans*, 81 Fed. Reg. 47863, 47883. A sequence-level default rate implies a lower borrower default rate, as a borrower might have multiple loan sequences in a year. Not all defaults result in repossession. A CFPB study found that 20% of sequences resulted in a repossession. CFPB, *Single-Payment Vehicle Title Lending* 4 (May 2016). Another study found that around one in nine auto title borrowers ends up getting his car repossessed. Pew Charitable Trusts, *Auto Title Loans: Market Practices and Borrowers' Experiences*

13 (2015). Some of the repossessed vehicles (perhaps 15%-25%) are redeemed by the borrowers prior to foreclosure, but the rest are sold in foreclosure sales. This means that around 5% to 9% of auto title borrowers lose their cars in a given year.

The loss of a car is not just the loss of an asset. It is often the loss of an asset that is critical for income generation, either because the vehicle is used for business itself or because it is the borrower's form of transportation to and from work. Given that a third of auto title borrowers lack access to another working vehicle, the consequences of a default on an auto title loan can be catastrophic for many borrowers. *See* Pew Charitable Trusts, *Auto Title Loans: Market Practices and Borrowers' Experiences* 1 (2015).

4. State Level Title Loan Regulation

Title lenders only operate in 25 states. The other 25 states and the District of Columbia either prohibit lending against vehicle titles or have usury caps that make title lending unfeasible. Of the states in which title lenders can operate a few require the loans to be installment loans, but generally state regulation consists of fee limits, limitations on the number of rollovers, loan amounts, and number of loans outstanding, and requirements for cooling-off periods between loans. A few states have ability-to-repay requirements, but these tend to be weak, as they can be often satisfied through borrower attestation.

A major problem with title lending regulation is the possibility of regulatory arbitrage between different lending regulation schemes within a state. States often have different regulatory regimes for different types of loans: payday loans, consumer installment loans, title loans, pawn loans, etc. But the definitions of these types of loans sometimes overlap or allow lenders to creatively cast one product as another and thus qualify for a different (and more favorable) regulatory regime.

For example, Missouri regulates title loans, but does not define what a title loan is. Instead, it defines a "title lender" and a "title loan agreement" as a lender or loan agreement that meet certain statutory requirements. Mo. Rev. Stat. 367.500(7), (9). For title loan agreements, however, Missouri law provides that after three rollovers, a title lender may not renew a loan unless the principal is paid down by 10%. Mo. Rev. Stat. 367.512.1(4). Yet Missouri also allows lenders to make "consumer credit loans," which are defined as "loans for personal, family or household purposes in amounts of five hundred dollars or more." Mo. Rev. Stat. § 367.100(1)(b). There are no rollover limitations on "consumer credit loans." As a result, in Missouri, lenders that hold themselves out in their advertising as title lenders make loans that state "This loan is being made pursuant to Missouri Revised Statute 367.100." The Missouri Department of Insurance, Financial Institutions, and Professional Registration believes that such a loan is a consumer credit loan. *See* Matthew Hathaway, *Missouri Lenders Find Ways to Avoid Title-Loan Regulations*, St. Louis Post-Dispatch, Aug. 1, 2010.

D. Tax Refund Anticipation Loans

Consumers can also borrow against an irregular form of income—tax refunds and credits. If a consumer is owed a tax refund from the government—either for overpayment or because of a tax credit such as the Earned Income Tax Credit—the consumer has a money-good one-time income source. The consumer can pledge that future tax refund income as a repayment source for a loan, just as the consumer could pledge her next paycheck for repayment of a payday loan. When a consumer files a tax return, the consumer knows whether he or she anticipates receiving a tax refund. Assuming that the consumer has filed the return correctly, the consumer should receive the refund, but the refund is not paid immediately. A loan against this refund income essentially advances the consumer the tax refund (or a part thereof) earlier. The mechanism for a lender to ensure it gets repaid from the refund before the consumer gets to access the funds is for the tax refund to be deposited in an account controlled by the lender, which then deducts its fees before making the remaining funds available to the consumer. Given that the remaining funds might be made available on a prepaid debit card, the tax refund loan can turn into a second revenue source for the lender through card fees.

The basic idea of tax-refund-based lending is that the lender does not need to worry about the borrower's particular credit profile, only about the whether the borrower has a right to a tax refund. If so, then there is a dedicated repayment source that is backed by full faith and credit of the United States. As long as the lender has first dibs on that refund, the lender need not worry about the borrower's credit quality. Thus, the borrower could be unemployed and it would be irrelevant to the lender.

1. Traditional Refund Anticipation Loans

The nature of tax-refund lending has changed substantially over time. When tax-refund lending began in the 1980s, tax filers often had to wait weeks or months for their refund checks. This meant that a refund anticipation loan was a loan with a potential duration of multiple months. As the tax system became computerized, however, tax returns began to be processed much faster. A taxpayer who files electronically and gets the refund disbursed by direct deposit can often get the refund within five to ten days. As a result, the term of tax refund loans has decreased considerably. Prior to 2010, the typical tax-refund loan was a refund anticipation loan (RAL). The RAL would be for an extremely short term—perhaps 11-12 days—and would have an APR in the triple digits. The relatively high cost of a very short-term advance of the consumer's tax refund raised concerns that there was little consumer benefit relative to the cost of RALs and, given that many RALs were being made against tax credits, that the effectiveness of social welfare programs executed through tax credits was being diminished because of part of the credits were being used by consumers to pay for the RALs.

The tax-refund lending business is mainly run through large tax-preparation services: H&R Block, Jackson Hewitt, Liberty Tax Service, and Santa Barbara Tax Preparation Group. These tax preparers partner with a handful of banks for the RAC and RAL services. Some banks also offer RALs, as do some payday lenders and similar fringe financial service providers. Given that most tax-refund lending is done by banks in a partnership with tax-preparation services, the regulation of tax-refund lending is a hodgepodge. The IRS has authority over tax preparers, but they are also subject to state regulation. In contrast, banks are subject to regulation by their prudential regulators and the CFPB. These different regulatory founts may pursue different policy goals regarding tax-refund lending.

The CFPB has not undertaken any general regulation of tax-refund lending, although the OCC has guidance outstanding as discussed above. A number of states have laws regulating refund anticipation loans. These laws are primarily disclosure statutes (with the disclosure obligation on the tax preparer); a few have restrictions on advertising and usury restrictions (which are generally preempted for national banks).

The IRS requires reporting of RALs and also has regulations governing advertising and the use of consumer tax information absent consumer permission. While the CFPB and prudential regulators have consumer protection concerns regarding tax-refund lending, the IRS has a different set of policy concerns. On the one hand, the IRS faces the concern that tax-refund lending encourages tax preparers to over-claim refunds on tax returns. *See, e.g.*, Leslie Bock, *Refund Anticipation Loans and the Tax Gap*, 20 Stan. L. & Pol'y Rev. 85 (2009). On the other hand, the IRS recognizes that tax-refund lending encourages the filing of tax returns in the first place. RALs create an industry of lenders who are incentivized to encourage consumers to file tax returns. The filing of tax returns is important because tax credits are a major method for distributing social benefits, in particular, the Earned Income Tax Credit, which is the largest anti-poverty program in the United States, assisting over 27 million families.

From 2000 to 2010, tax-refund-based lending was greatly facilitated by the IRS. From 2000 to 2010, the IRS made available to lenders an indicator of whether there were prior claims on tax refunds, such as back taxes, child support obligations, or student loan debt. (The IRS had made this indicator available in the 1990s for a brief time as well.) The IRS debt indicator substantially facilitated refund anticipation lending because it enabled lenders to determine the priority of their claim on the tax refund. If the consumer had prior claims on the refund, the lender would not lend because it was impossible to gauge the repayment risk.

The IRS's provision of a debt indicator facilitated tax-refund lending, while lowering its price, but as the price of tax-refund loans decreased, the combined cost of tax preparation and loans increased. Maggie R. Jones, *A Loan by Any Other Name: How State Policies Changed Advanced Tax Refund Payments*, CARRA Working Paper No. 2016-04, at 4. In 2010, however, the IRS, under pressure from consumer groups, ceased making the debt indicator available. The loss of the IRS debt indicator increased the risk RAL lenders faced because they could not be sure that the consumer would in fact receive a tax refund once prior claims were deducted from any amount owed. At the same time, the OCC and FDIC began a concerted campaign to pressure banks to exit the RAL business. The OCC issued RAL guidance in 2010, OCC Bulletin 2010-7 (Feb. 18, 2010), subsequently updated in 2015, OCC Bulletin 2015-36 (Aug. 4, 2015). This guidance required banks to make certain disclosures to RAL borrowers, to review and approve RAL advertising by tax preparers, to perform due diligence and oversight on tax preparers (including potentially using mystery shoppers), and providing training and certification for tax preparers. The OCC guidance also included an ability-to-repay requirement:

> Safe and sound underwriting criteria should include an evaluation of each applicant's creditworthiness and ability to repay the tax refund-related credit product according to its terms. . . . The bank should evaluate the applicant's independent ability to repay the entire amount of the tax refund-related credit product for which the applicant is approved. Prior evaluation of ability to repay is particularly important if the bank does not receive the tax refund from the applicable tax authority or the amount of the tax refund is less than the amount of the credit extended to the customer.

OCC Bulletin 2015-36 (Aug. 4, 2015). In addition, the OCC made one of the largest RAL lenders sell off its RAL business when that lender became insufficiently well capitalized.

The results from the combination of the IRS and bank regulator actions were staggering. In 2014 there were only 34,000 RAL applications, down from a peak of 12.7 million in 2002. NCLC 2016 RAL Study. Two new tax-refund lending products emerged, however, in the wake of the RAL crackdown: refund anticipation checks (RACs) and a new breed of RALs.[2]

2. Refund Anticipation Checks

RACs are a loan of the tax-preparation fees. When a consumer goes to a tax preparer, the consumer will be charged a tax-preparation fee that might be in the low hundreds of dollars. The consumer can pay the fee upfront or can choose to have the fee deducted from his tax refund (if the preparer believes he is owed one). If the consumer wants to have the fee deducted from his tax refund, he will open a temporary bank account with a bank that has associated with the tax preparer. The IRS will deposit the refund into that bank account. The bank will then issue the consumer a check or direct deposit to the consumer's regular bank account or a pre-paid card for the refund amount minus the tax-preparation fee and a RAC fee (plus any other fees that have been charged). The bank will then close out the temporary account. Obviously, with a prepaid card there may be ongoing fees charged by the issuing bank. The consumer is thus able to pay for the tax-preparation service out of the tax refund, but at a cost. For example, a consumer might pay $35 to defer a $350 tax-preparation fee for three weeks (roughly 173% APR).

Critically, unlike a RAL, the consumer does not get faster access to funds through an RAC, but avoids having to use current funds to pay for the tax-preparation service. In other words, RACs are loans of tax-preparation fees, and the fees for them are therefore finance charges under TILA. *See United States v. ITS Fin., LLC*, 2013 WL 5947222 (S.D. Ohio Nov. 6, 2013); *People v. JTH Tax, Inc.*, 212 Cal. App. 4th 1219 (2013).

---

2. A third type of tax-refund lending product also exists, but is much less common. These are pre-season "paystub" or "holiday" loans, which are loans based on past paystubs but not on a W-2, even though they are "collateralized" by any tax refund owed to the borrower.

RACs are popular products. Some 21 million consumers got RACs in 2014. NCLC 2016 RAL Study. Most were low-income households, and over half qualified for the Earned Income Tax Credit. *Id.*

3. New-Style Refund Anticipation Loans

The new breed of RAL is substantially different from the traditional RAL and is offered by only a handful of lenders. Whereas the traditional RAL had a triple-digit APR, the new-style RAL is interest-free. Whereas the fees on the old RAL were paid by the consumer, the fees on the new-style RAL are paid by the tax preparers (roughly $35/loan). Whereas the traditional RAL was for as much as $1,500 (the maximum EITC), the new RAL is generally capped at $750. Whereas the consumer was liable for any deficiency in the tax refund under the old RAL, the consumer has no liability for deficiencies under the new RALs. The new-style RAL is a way for tax preparers to get business—by advertising the interest-free loan, they are able to generate more tax-preparation customers. RAL lenders claim that tax preparers are forbidden from charging for the RALs, but given the opaque pricing of tax-preparation services, it is hard to tell. Few tax preparers give consumers firm cost estimates in advance, so it is hard for consumers to comparison shop among preparers. Moreover, it is hard to tell if the cost of the RAL is ultimately passed through to borrowers (or all tax-preparation clients) in the form of higher tax-preparation costs or "junk fees" (*e.g.*, a "service bureau fee") or the preparer's share of the fees on the prepaid cards on which the RAL funds are sometimes disbursed.

E. Pawn Loans

A common way that consumers in a pinch for cash get money is by pawning their goods. Pawn shops engage in two related types of transactions. First, pawn shops will simply buy goods outright. In many states a pawn license is actually required to operate a business that purchases used consumer goods (such as used bicycles).

Second, pawn shops make loans secured by a possessory security interest. In a pawn loan transaction, a consumer gets a loan from a pawn shop in exchange for giving the pawn shop certain goods, say an engagement ring or an electric guitar, as a pledge of collateral. As part of the loan agreement, the consumer expressly warrants that he or she has clear title to the items pledged. The loan will only be made for a fraction of the value of the pledged items, with a 40%-60% LTV ratio being typical.

Pursuant to the agreement, the consumer has a fixed amount of time to repay the loan plus any authorized fees. If the consumer repays the loan in a timely fashion, the consumer gets the pledged goods back. (This is known as "**redeeming**" the goods.) If the consumer fails to timely redeem the goods, they become property of the pawn shop, which may then sell them, but the pawn shop may not otherwise attempt to collect from the consumer. Critically, the consumer is not obligated to redeem the goods. In other words, the consumer has a choice of whether to keep the loan proceeds or redeem the goods, and the amount of the pawn loan will reflect the pawn shop's estimate of what it can make selling the goods.

Pawn shops are generally permitted by state law to extend or renew pawn loans indefinitely, and there is usually no maximum term for a loan. *See, e.g.*, 205 ILCS 510/10 ("The parties may agree to extend or renew a loan upon terms agreed upon by the parties, provided the terms comply with the requirements of this Act."). Minimum terms tend to be in the 30- to 90-day range, depending on the state. Rollovers are not a major regulatory concern with pawn loans because anecdotally they are not the mainstay of industry economics the way they are for payday and title loans.

Although there is the rollover risk, pawn loans differ from payday loans in a number of important ways. Pawn loans tend to be much smaller than payday loans. The typical pawn loan is only for around $80, with a 30-day maturity and a fee of perhaps $20. Also, unlike a payday loan, a pawn transaction does not require the borrower to have a bank account or regular source of income, only an asset with some value. This means, however, that there is a forfeiture risk with a pawn loan that does not exist for a payday loan. Although pawn loans are never for anything close to a 100% LTV ratio, the lender gets to keep the full value of the collateral if it is sold rather than redeemed by the borrower. Still, it seems that most borrowers redeem their pledges. The National Pawnbrokers Association reports an 80% redemption rate.

From the lender's perspective, pawn lending is also substantially different from payday lending. There are two main risks in a pawn loan transaction. First is whether the borrower has good title to the goods. If not, the lender could lose its collateral to the rightful owner of the goods. The second is whether the collateral goods (assuming good title) are of sufficient value that their sale will cover the loan if the borrower does not redeem the goods. Neither of these risks relates to the credit quality of the borrower per se. Instead, they relate to the quality of the collateral. Pawn lending is a purely asset-based transaction.

The pawn industry consists primarily of lots of small businesses with one or two storefronts. There are around 13,500 pawns hops in the U.S. and only around 1,000 are part of larger chains. Pawnbrokers are sometimes in a stand-alone line of business, but some also make payday loans or cash checks.

Pawn shops are regulated by states (and sometimes by local government). States generally require a license to engage in pawn transactions. They also specify minimum redemption periods and interest rate or fee limitations, and terms of resale of forfeited goods (generally the pawn shop gets to keep any sale proceeds), and law enforcement reporting requirements (because of the concern over trafficking in stolen goods). Some states also limit the type of collateral that can be pawned. No pledges of false teeth or artificial limbs or wheelchairs in Delaware! 24 Del. Code § 2307(b). Federal law applies to pawn shops only in terms of TILA disclosures and UDAAP liability. The FTC Credit Practices Rule does not apply to pawn transactions because they are possessory security interests, even when they involve household goods.

Rates vary considerably based on state regulation. Some states, like Michigan, have a rate of 3% per month (36% annually), MCL § 446.209; other states permit loans with rates as high as 300% annually. In some states the formal rate that can be charged is capped at a relatively low percentage, (3% per month in Indiana, IC 28-7-5-28; IC 24-4.5-3-508(2), but the lender is also allowed to charge a "service charge" (20% per month in Indiana, IC 28-7-5-28.5, for a total monthly rate of 23% or 276% annually).

Note that in some states, auto title lenders operate under pawn shop laws. For example, in Georgia, a "pawnbroker" is defined as "any person engaged in whole or in part in the business of lending money on the security of pledged goods," but "pledged goods," are defined to mean:

> tangible personal property, including without limitation, all types of motor vehicles or any motor vehicle certificate of title, which property is purchased by, deposited with, or otherwise actually delivered into the possession of a pawnbroker in connection with a pawn transaction. However, for purposes of this Code section, possession of any motor vehicle certificate of title which has come into the possession of a pawnbroker through a pawn transaction made in accordance with law shall be conclusively deemed to be possession of the motor vehicle, and the pawnbroker shall retain physical possession of the motor vehicle certificate of title for the entire length of the pawn transaction but shall not be required in any way to retain physical possession of the motor vehicle at any time.

OCGA §§ 44-12-130(2), 44-12-130(5). Thus, in some states pawn shop regulation is also title lender regulation.

III. POLICY ISSUES WITH SMALL-DOLLAR LOANS

There are three common policy issues that arise with almost all of the different types of small-dollar liquidity lending products: problems with consumer understanding of the likely length and cost of borrowing; the lack of price competition in the market; and concerns that regulation of one product will lead to consumers substituting another, perhaps less salubrious, form of credit.

A. Consumer Optimism

While small-dollar loans are often formally structured as short-term, closed-end loans, they frequently function as non-amortizing, longer-term, open-end loans. This is because of the likelihood of repeat rollovers. Indeed, repeat rollovers are essential to the economics of small-dollar lending.

Do consumers know what they are likely in for with a small-dollar loan? Does the payday borrower know that it is not likely to be a two-week loan, but a sequence of several rolled-over two-week loans? If so, it is easier to conclude that a consumer is making a rational decision to use a small-dollar loan product. If not, however, perhaps because of consumers' overly optimistic assessments of their ability to repay, then one has to question whether consumers are in fact revealing their preferences when they borrow. This issue seems relatively easy to address from a regulatory perspective: longer-term, prepayable loans (with fees prorated) would reduce the chance that consumers do not anticipate a longer borrowing term, while preserving payment timing flexibility.

B. Competition in Small-Dollar Lending Markets

Normally competition among lenders is thought to be an important form of consumer protection. And there's certainly no shortage of small-dollar lenders. So why are small-dollar loan prices so high?

Part of the answer is that the competition that seems so apparent doesn't always exist. In the case of online payday lending there is literally no competition for consumers. Online payday lending is done primarily through lead-generator websites that auction the consumer "lead" to the highest bidder. The consumer cannot compare multiple offers in such a situation. Instead, the highest bidder has an effective monopoly on the consumer. If the consumer resubmits her information to the lead generator's website, she might well end up dealing with the very same lender. To win the lead, however, the lender has to make the high bid, which means that the lender needs to charge higher prices to the consumer be able to recoup its expense in winning the lead.

Another part of the answer is that consumers do not seem particularly price-sensitive. Liquidity borrowers are often desperate for credit and will borrow on almost any terms below some reserve price (a firstborn child, a kidney, etc.). To the extent that borrowers shop, it seems to be mainly on location, convenience, and service, not price. This might actually be completely rational for borrowers. For lower-income borrowers, search costs can be significant. A consumer working two jobs may not have a lot of time to hunt down the best-priced loan. There may be transportation, childcare, and time costs in getting to the lowest-priced lender. A nearby convenient lender may actually be quite valuable to a borrower.

A third part of the answer is the structure of the lending industry—high fixed costs, small customer bases per lender, small loan sizes, and low barriers to entry. Lenders have high fixed costs and relatively small customer bases (with small loans) over which to amortize those costs. The result is that there is a minimum pricing level that lenders cannot price below . . . unless they have other lines of business over which they can amortize their fixed costs. Thus, banks and credit unions, and potentially the Postal Service, have a different cost structure than a stand-alone payday lender. When small-dollar loans are an add-on service, rather than the main offering, the economics of lending is quite different.

Low barriers to entry exacerbate the problem by reducing the borrower base per lender. The low barriers to entry also combine with lenders' ability to differentiate products based on location and convenience to create a situation known "monopolistic competition."[3] In monopolistic competition, producers are able to differentiate

3. Edward Hastings Chamberlin, *Theory of Monopolistic Competition* (1933).

their products in ways other than price that render them imperfect substitutes for each other. Such differentiation might be in terms of product quality, branding, or location. This means that each competitor's product is essentially a market unto itself, enabling the competitor to earn economic profits in the short run. In monopolistic competition, product differentiation leads to higher prices.[4]

In the long run, however, monopolistically competitive firms only break even—their average total costs will increase and demand will decrease resulting eventually in zero economic profit. This happens because there are low or no barriers to entry in the market. (If there were high barriers to entry, then the situation would more closely resemble a monopoly.) Future entrants will eye the economic profits and create substitutes for the differentiated product that will eat into demand.

Thus, if a firm differentiates its product by a unique form factor (*e.g.*, a tablet computer), it will have a monopoly on that differentiated profit and it will earn monopoly profits. But if other firms, eyeing the monopoly profits, copy that unique form factor for its product (*e.g.*, they create their own tablet computers), such that their products are substitutes for the originally differentiated product, then the effect will be to reduce demand for the original firm's product—the aggregate demand will be shared among all three firms, so the demand curve for the original firm will shift leftward. This will result in a new marginal revenue curve for the original firm as well that will result in the original firm producing a lesser quantity for the same price.

In essence the new entrants cannibalize the old firm's monopoly market. The result will eventually be to eliminate all economic profits for all market participants, but without any change in pricing or aggregate production. Thus, long-term equilibrium in monopolistic competition results in higher prices and lower output per firm.[5]

The monopolistic competition model may well describe small-dollar lending markets. Payday lenders, for example, have products that are differentiated in terms of convenience, geographic location, and service, such that the competition is first and foremost locational.

Consider, then, the situation of a payday lender that happens to be the only payday lender in a low-income neighborhood. That lender differentiates its product by its location. It has a local monopoly and will earn monopoly profits. But given low barriers to entry, there is nothing to stop other lenders, eagerly eyeing the monopoly profits, from moving in next door and across the street. Their products are close substitutes for the original lender's previously locationally differentiated payday loan product.

The effect will be that the new entrants will grab some of the market away from the original lender. The aggregate demand for payday loans in the vicinity will remain the same, only it will be shared will be shared among all three firms, so the demand curve for the original payday lender will shift leftward. This will result

4. *See* Steven C. Salop, *Monopolistic Competition with Outside Goods*, 10 Bell J. Econ. 141 (1979); Harold Hotelling, *Stability in Competition*, 39 Econ. J. 41 (1929).

5. *Id.*

in a new marginal revenue curve for the original firm as well that will result in the original firm producing a lesser quantity for the same price. An increase in the number of competitors in this market will not in fact reduce prices.

If monopolistic competition is the problem in small-dollar lending markets, it suggests barriers to entry—reducing competition—as actually being in consumers' interest. Reducing the number of competitors in a market would enable the remaining lenders to amortize their costs over a larger consumer base per lender. The result should be lower costs to consumers even while profit margins for the surviving lenders remain stable. Thus, irrespective of the general consumer welfare effects of small-dollar lending, it may be possible to improve the consumer welfare overall by *decreasing* competition in the industry.[6] This could be done in a number of ways: local anti-agglomeration zoning ordinances limiting how many lenders could be in one small geographic area; more demanding licensing requirements; and substantive term restrictions on products, such as rate caps and rollover limits, that would drive the least efficient players from the market.

C. Substitution Hypothesis

A frequent concern about regulating the terms of small-dollar credit products is that regulation does nothing to address demand for credit, so that if access to one product is constrained because of substantive term regulation, consumers will simply substitute their consumption to another product. This is known as the **substitution hypothesis**. In the most extreme form of the substitution hypothesis, consumers substitute seamlessly between different short-term products: credit cards, overdraft, signature loans, payday loans, title loans, refund anticipation loans, pawn shops, and ultimately to illegal sources of funds—loan sharks, prostitution, drug dealing. Realistically, however, not all consumers are able to substitute. As we have seen, some small-dollar lending products are available only to consumers with bank accounts, with regular income, with clean title to cars, with tax refunds, or with valuable assets. Not all consumers have all of these. Moreover, depending on the substitute options available, a consumer might well decide to reduce his consumption or try to borrow from family or friends. A survey of payday borrowers conducted by the Pew Charitable Trusts found that 81% of payday borrowers said that if they could not get a payday loan they would cut back on expenses, while 62% said they would delay paying bills, 57% said they would borrow from family or friends, and 57% said they would pawn or sell possessions. Pew Charitable Trusts, *Payday Lending in America: Who Borrows, Where They Borrow, and Why* (2012). Thus, even if there is substitution, it hardly follows that it would be a dollar-for-dollar substitution.

While the substitution hypothesis is often taken as a matter of faith, there's surprisingly little evidence on it one way or another. The Pew Charitable Trusts found

6. Yet if what consumers value isn't price, but convenience, then a reduction in competition might not be in consumers' interest. Of course, convenience is likely prized only because it translates into savings more clearly than a lower APR.

that restrictions on storefront payday lending do not result in a shift to online payday loans. Pew Charitable Trusts, *Fraud and Online Abuse: Harmful Practices in Internet Payday Lending* 20 (Oct. 2014). The CFPB, however, examined consumer behavior after banks ceased their "deposit advance programs" in response to regulatory guidance. The CFPB found little evidence of substitution from DAPs to overdraft, to payday, or even to bouncing checks. CFPB, *Supplemental Findings on Payday, Payday Installment, and Vehicle Title Loans, and Deposit Advance Products*, June 2016. It did, however, find substitution to pawn shop lending. *Id.* This comports with another study that found evidence of substitution to pawn shop lending, but not other types of lending when states have banned payday loans. Neil Bhutta et al., *Consumer Borrowing After Payday Loan Bans*, July 13, 2016.

Thus, it appears that there might be some types of substitution occurring, but not the seamless substitution between all forms of short-term credit. Moreover, to the extent that one believes that pawn lending poses fewer consumer protection problems than payday or DAP lending, substitution might in fact be a positive outcome from regulation.

IV. FEDERAL REGULATION OF SMALL-DOLLAR LOANS

Prior to 2018, regulation of small-dollar lending was primarily done on the state level, with regulatory regimes varying substantially among states. A number of federal laws also applied to small-dollar loans, but those laws covered only particular parts of the market—loans made by federal credit unions or loans made to military members and their dependents. In 2018, the CFPB promulgated a regulation covering "Payday, Vehicle Title, and Certain High-Cost Installment Loans" (the "Payday Rule"). The Payday Rule is the first generally applicable federal regulation of small-dollar lending, although it does not cover all types of small-dollar lending.

A. The CFPB Payday Rule

1. The Ability to Repay Requirement

The CFPB's Payday Rule covers three types of loans: (1) short-term loans (loans with a term of 45 days or less); (2) longer-term balloon loans (where one payment is at least twice as large as others); and (3) longer-term loans that have both an APR of greater than 36% and a "leveraged payment mechanism." 12 C.F.R. § 1041.3(b). A "leveraged payment mechanism" is "a right to initiate a transfer of money, through any means, from the consumer's account" to pay the loan. 12 C.F.R. § 1041.3(c). It would, therefore, include a post-dated check or an ACH authorization. Non-recourse pawn loans, overdraft loans, credit cards, and purchase money loans are expressly excluded from the Payday Rule's coverage. 12 C.F.R. § 1041.3(d). Implicitly excluded from coverage are high-cost installment loans and longer-term vehicle title loans. RALs are implicitly covered by the Payday Rule because of their short term.

The Payday Rule deems it to be an abusive and unfair practice for a lender to make such loans without a reasonable determination of the borrower's ability to repay the loan. 12 C.F.R. § 1041.4. Ability to repay is defined for the Payday Rule as the consumer having the ability to: (1) make all payments under the loan; (2) pay all major financial obligations when due; (3) meet "basic living expenses" during the shorter of the term of the loan or 45 days; and (4) being able to meet basic living expenses for 30 days after the largest payment on the loan (such as a balloon payment. 12 C.F.R. § 1041.5(b)(ii). While lenders are required to verify income and certain expenses, lenders are permitted to come up with their own measures of ability to repay. 12 C.F.R. § 1041.5(c).

2. Safe Harbors

The Payday Rule has two safe harbors to the ability to repay requirement, one for shorter-term loans not secured by vehicles and one for longer-term loans. The shorter-term loan safe harbor allows a lender to make a 45-day or shorter amortizing loan of up to $500 (not secured by a vehicle) to a borrower at whatever cost is permitted by applicable state law without an ability-to-repay determination. 12 C.F.R. § 1041.6. The safe harbor allows such a loan to be made only if it would not result in the borrower having had more than six loans outstanding during the previous year or 90 days of continuous short-term indebtedness. 12 C.F.R. § 1041.6(c)(3). For loans made in a sequence, there is a mandated step-down in amount by one-third for each loan. 12 C.F.R. § 1041.6(b)(1).

For longer-term loans, the first safe harbor is for loans that meet the NCUA's Payday Loan Alternative requirements: prepayable, amortizing loans of $200-$1,000, with terms of under six months, at least two level payment installments, no rollovers, an APR of no more than 28%, and no more than three such loans in the previous 180 days. 12 C.F.R. § 1041.3(e)(1).

3. Prohibited Payment Transfer Attempted

The Payday Rule also prohibits as an abusive and unfair practice any attempt to withdraw payment from a consumer's account on such loans after two failed consecutive payment attempts, absent new authorization from the consumer. 12 C.F.R. § 1041.8(b)-(c). In other words, instead of the current three bites at the apple as allowed under NACHA rules, there would only be two bites allowed. Lenders would also be required to provide consumers with advance notice prior to draws on the consumers' accounts. 12 C.F.R. § 1041.9(b).

B. Other Federal Regulation of Small-Dollar Loans

Several other federal laws apply to small-dollar loans in addition to the Payday Rule. First, the Truth in Lending Act's disclosure provisions apply to all types of small-dollar loans, if they are in fact "credit." Payday loans are considered credit under TILA no matter how state law characterizes the fees. Official Interpretation to 12 C.F.R. § 1026.2(a)(14).

Second, the Electronic Fund Transfer Act prohibits conditioning extension of credit on obtaining an authorization for a pre-authorized electronic fund transfer, such as a recurring ACH debit. 15 U.S.C. § 1693k. While this provision does not apply to paper checks or one-time transfers, it would still seem to be an obstacle to installment lenders (including installment payday or title lenders), but consent to ACH draws is almost always obtained, such as by telling the borrower that without the authorization, there will be delayed disbursement of funds.

Third, the Military Lending Act covers all loans (other than mortgages and purchase money financing) to servicemembers and their dependents. 10 U.S.C. § 987. The Military Lending Act imposes a 36% rate cap (covering all costs of credit) on extensions of credit to covered borrowers; prohibits rollovers, taking of checks or ACH draws or vehicle titles as security, mandatory arbitration, or prepayment penalties; and requires certain disclosures. 10 U.S.C. §§ 987(b), 987(c), 987(e). The Military Lending Act is administered by the Department of Defense, not the CFPB. 32 C.F.R. Pt. 232. The rationale behind the Military Lending Act was that indebtedness was creating a force readiness problem for the military and a security clearance problem. Military members who were mired in unaffordable debt were distracted from their jobs, while military members with significant debt often could not get necessary security clearances for fear that they were vulnerable to extortion or bribery.

Fourth, the National Credit Union Administration has an exception to the general 15% usury rate applicable to federal credit unions for "Payday Alternative Loans." 75 Fed. Reg. 58285 (Sept. 24, 2010). The NCUA has authority to waive the 15% usury rate and has generally done so, allowing credit unions to lend at 18% APR. 12 U.S.C. § 1757(5)(A)(vi)(I). The NCUA's Payday Alternative Loan program authorizes amortized installment loans at up to 28% APR plus a $20 application fee with terms of between one and six months, and for amounts between $200 and $1,000. The loans must be made to individuals who have been credit union members for at least one month (no walk-ins!). Rollovers and prepayment limitations are not allowed on the Payday Alternative Loan. Over 700 federal credit unions (around 20% of all federal credit unions) made Payday Alternative Loans in 2015. Total lending volume was quite limited, however, at only $123.3 million, with average loan sizes being close to $700. 81 Fed. Reg. 47864, 48031 (July 22, 2016).

Finally, the Consumer Financial Protection Act's UDAAP provision applies to all small-dollar loans. 12 U.S.C. §§ 5531, 5536. While the CFPB's Payday Rule was promulgated under the UDAAP power, the UDAAP power reaches farther than the Payday Rule. It is possible for a lender to comply with the Payday Rule and still engage in a UDAAP violation in regard to a small-dollar loan. The Payday Rule merely creates an ability-to-repay requirement and safe harbors thereto.

Problem Set 30

1. Themistocles Papanicolauo was raised by his only sister, Lysandra. Lysandra passed away unexpectedly two days ago, on April 10. Her insurance did not cover burial expenses and she died intestate and with few assets. The medical examiner told

Themistocles that they could only keep the body for two weeks, after which it would receive a pauper's burial, unless he claimed the body. Themistocles is determined to give his sister a decent burial, but it will cost at least $1,000. He has savings of $600, but receives a monthly salary, which won't be paid for another few weeks. He owns a late-model Chevy Impala that is probably worth $6,500, and has few valuable possessions other than his Fender Stratocaster guitar that he calls "The Beast" and an amplifier he calls "Big Boy." The guitar and amp might be worth $750 together. How can Themistocles come up with the money for Lysandra's funeral? What are the relative benefits? Risks?

2. Anna Gelpern took out a month-long payday loan that cost $100 and was secured by a $500 check. She defaulted and was charged a $50 late fee. What is the APR on her loan?

3. What is the largest payday loan that can be made at the maximum rate in Mississippi? *See* Miss. Stat. § 75-67-501(4)(b)-(c).

4. What is the maximum APR on a payday loan in Louisiana? *See* La. Rev. Stat. §§ 9:3516(13)-(14), 9:3530(C), 9:3578.3(2)(c), 9:3578.4(A), 9:3578.4(C); 12 C.F.R. § 1026.4(a) ("The finance charge is the cost of consumer credit as a dollar amount. It includes any charge payable directly or indirectly by the consumer and imposed directly or indirectly by the creditor as an incident to or a condition of the extension of credit.").

5. Freedom Financial, a small check casher and payday lender, based on Tupelo, Mississippi, serves a clientele that are primarily elderly Social Security recipients or Social Security Disability recipients, meaning that their sole regular income is a monthly benefit check from the government. Many of the customers have annual incomes of $16,000 or less. Freedom Financial will make deferred deposit transactions on these government checks on what Freedom Financial terms the "1st and 3rd plan." Under this plan, if the consumer qualifies for a $400 loan, the consumer would be given a two-week-long $200 loan (on the first week of the month), and then upon repayment, a second two-week-long loan (on the third week of the month), this time for $400. Freedom Financial's very proud of the 1st and 3rd product. "The 1st and 3rd plan helps us get more cash into our customer's hands," Freedom's owner and CEO, Pierre Pochartrain boasts. Freedom Financial also requires in-person repayment of the loans. "We like to see our customers," Pierre explains. "It's also a chance to inform them of some of our other product offerings, like check cashing, money orders, and tax refund loans."

- **a.** You're an attorney with the Mississippi Department of Financial Regulation reviewing Freedom Financial's license renewal application. Do you have any concerns about the 1st and 3rd product? *See* Miss. Stat. §§ 75-67-501(1), 75-67-501(3), 75-67-501(5).
- **b.** Would the answer to the previous question be different if Freedom Financial operated in Louisiana? *See* La. Rev. Stat. §§ 9:3516(14), 9:3578.6(A)(4), 9:3578.6(A)(6)-(7), 9:3578.6(B).
- **c.** What if Freedom Financial didn't take Social Security checks as collateral, but instead required an ACH authorization for loans when a third-party paycheck was not presented as collateral? *See* 15 U.S.C. §§ 1693(a)(10), 1693k(1).

6. Flavio Carrasco owns The Fast and the Usurious, a Delaware auto title lender. He also owns Fast Flavs, a used car dealership, which sells and leases vehicles. Flavio is frustrated by Delaware's 180-day term limit on auto title loans, including any rollovers. 5 Del. Code §§ 2250(4), 2254. "Many of my customers want to keep extending their loans past 180 days, and I have to tell them that they can't," he says. "It's a real problem because they don't always have the cash to pay off the loan at 180 days, so I have to repossess the cars." Can you come up with a potential workaround for Flavio so that his customers can keep using the cars, while Flavio will keep getting paid and have the security of the vehicle to ensure repayment?

7. You're an enforcement attorney at the CFPB, still working on the QuikiCash case from Chapter 25. QuikiCash is, of course, a lender that offers its customers a product called a "Revolving Credit Plan," which is a revolving line of credit of $500 with a bi-weekly billing cycle date. The Revolving Credit Plan is advertised as a "payday loan alternative." Loans under the Revolving Credit Plan are made in $50 increments. The Revolving Credit Plan has two main price points:

- an interest rate disclosed as 26% APR, assessed on average daily balances during a billing cycle;
- a "Required Account Protection Fee," a mandatory fee of $10 for every $50 in principal balance outstanding. Payment of the RAPF entitles the borrower to payment forbearance in certain situations.

The RAPF is charged once every billing cycle if there is a balance at the end of the day preceding the billing cycle date. The RCP loan documentation also includes a schedule of billing cycle dates for the next year, which states, "Your first payment is due on [second billing cycle date]." The RCP has a minimum payment equal to interest charges and the RAPF "from the current billing cycle," and borrowers are required to authorize ACH debits for minimum payment amounts. Putting aside the TILA issues that you examined in Chapter 25, what potential issues do you see with the QuikiCash Revolving Credit Plan? *See* 12 U.S.C. §§ 5531, 5536.

8. Sir-Lend-a-Lot, a national finance company, wants to make short-term, small-dollar loans but does not think that verifying borrower ability to repay is economically practical for these loans. Sir-Lend-a-Lot wants to know your thoughts on the following products:

a. A $400 46-day, single-payment loan with a $180 fee and no post-dated check or ACH authorization.

b. A 46-day, multiple-payment product with an installment payment of $116 due on days 14, 28, and 42, and a balloon payment of $230 due on day 46; again, no post-dated check or ACH authorization.

c. The same product as in part (b), but a late fee of $15/$100 borrowed; thus, a borrower could miss an installment payment, but be charged a late fee. The installment payment would still be owed, but the first would be waived if the borrower provided an "irrevocable" ACH authorization in exchange for the waiver (not at the time of funding).

See 12 C.F.R. §§ 1041.3(b), (e); 1041.6.

CHAPTER 31

STUDENT LOANS

Student loans are a sensitive topic for law students. Law school is an expensive endeavor and the majority of students borrow to pay for their tuition, books, and living expenses while in law school. This law school debt often comes on top of debt from undergraduate education and possibly from intermediate graduate education. A typical law student graduated in 2012 owing $140,616 in undergraduate and graduate school debt.

Our focus in this chapter is on the financing of education. Before we get into the details, it's important to understand what we are and aren't covering here. First, it's necessary to distinguish between the costs of education and the way those costs are financed. Our concern in this chapter is not why education costs what it does or why the cost of education has been increasing over the past decades, but on how consumers pay for that education. That said, there might be connections between the financing channel and the cost of education, which we will consider.

Second, the boundaries of "education financing" are fuzzy. It's clear to everyone that when a student takes out a loan specifically to cover a tuition payment that it is a "student loan." But what if the student charges the tuition payment to her credit card (or more likely to her parent's credit card)? Yes, it's a loan for financing education, but we're not going to focus on that type of loan here, as it's not materially different from any other purchase on a credit card.

Likewise, there are many forms of borrowing that are not, strictly speaking, student loans, but are related to education finance. For example, if a college student charges $500 of required textbooks on a credit card, that is education finance, but it will appear statistically as credit card debt, not as a "student loan." Our focus in this chapter is solely on loans that are at least in part for tuition, not loans for room and board, for bar exam fees, etc.

With those caveats, let's turn to the student loan market.

I. THE STUDENT LOAN MARKET

There are several ways by which a student can finance an education: contributions from the student's own income and assets, from family members' income and assets, private scholarships, government grants, federal work-study programs that subsidize student employment, and various types of loans. Anyone seeking federal student aid of any sort—grants, work-study, or loans—must first submit a Free Application for Federal Student Aid (FAFSA). The Department of Education processes the FAFSA to determine the student's "Expected Family Contribution" (EFC), which is the amount the student and her family are expected to contribute directly from their income, assets, and other non-government sources, including private loans.

The Department of Education transmits the EFC to schools as requested by the student. The school then calculates the student's "Cost of Attendance"—the sum of tuition, fees, books, room and board, etc.—and deducts the EFC from the Cost of Attendance. This is essentially a calculation of student needs. The school will then offer the student a package of scholarships, federal loans, grants, and federally subsidized work-study income to try to make up the difference. CFPB & Dept. of Education, *Private Student Loans: Report to the Senate Committee on Banking, Housing, and Urban Affairs, the Senate Committee on Health, Education, Labor, and Pensions, the House of Representatives Committee on Financial Services, and the House of Representatives Committee on Education and the Workforce* 10 (Aug. 29, 2012) (hereinafter "CFPB/DoE, *PSL Report*"). There is no guarantee, however, that the school will be able to supply a package that covers all student need. To the extent it does not, the student will have to find other sources of financing or not attend the school.

Student loans thus appear in the education financing mix in two ways. First, they may be part of a package of federal loans, grants, and work-study designed to make up the difference between the Cost of Attendance and the Expected Family Contribution. And second, they may be part of the student's EFC itself. The Department of Education merely calculates a total EFC; it leaves it up to the student how to actually come up with the funds in the EFC. Thus, the EFC can include additional student loans.

Student loans divide into three distinct markets: one for loans made directly by the federal government (**"public student loans"**), a second for loans made by private lenders (**"private student loans"**), and a third, legacy market, for loans made by private lenders, but guaranteed by the federal government (**"guaranteed student loans"**). (Smaller markets exist for state-funded loan programs; those are beyond the scope of this book.) Of the three markets, the public student loan is by far the largest, with over $1 trillion in loans outstanding as of 2017. The private student loan market is relatively small, with $108 billion outstanding. The guaranteed student loan market is still a relatively large market with $320 billion of outstanding loans, but it is a market in wind-down, as the federal government ceased guaranteeing private loans as of 2010. Altogether, the student loan market is, as of the end of 2017, a $1.4 trillion market with over 44 million borrowers.

The regulatory issues are quite different between the markets; private student loans raise many more consumer protection concerns, although public student loans are not free of issues. Regulatory jurisdiction also differs between the markets. The CFPB has jurisdiction over the private student loan market, as well as over the servicers of public student loans, including when they engage in debt collection and credit reporting.

It remains unresolved whether the CFPB has jurisdiction over the origination of public student loans, at least when issued by the federal government. On the one hand, that would raise the strange situation of the CFPB exercising regulatory authority over the Department of Education (or at least over its origination agent, Accenture). On the other hand, there is nothing in the Consumer Financial Protection Act that excludes government units from being "covered persons." There is no question that the CFPB does have regulatory authority over loans issued by state government units. As it happens, the major consumer protection issues with public student loans are not about origination, but about servicing, so the question remains theoretical.

A. Federal Student Loans (Guaranteed and Public)

There are currently two main types of federal student loans: Stafford Loans and PLUS Loans.[1] Stafford Loans are made to student borrowers, while PLUS loans are made to parents or guardians of dependent students or to graduate students. Stafford Loans may be either subsidized or unsubsidized. Subsidized Stafford Loans are need-based. The subsidy comes in the form of the federal government making the interest payments on the loans for those periods when the borrower is enrolled as a student, for a post-graduation grace period, and for any deferment period. Unsubsidized Stafford Loans and PLUS Loans are not need-based. With unsubsidized Stafford and PLUS Loans, interest payments may still be deferred, but the deferred interest is **capitalized**, meaning that it is added to the principal balance of the loan, such that interest will subsequently accrue on the balance as increased by the deferred interest payments. 34 C.F.R. § 685.202(b).

Prior to 1992, all Stafford and PLUS Loans were made through the **Federal Family Education Loan Program** or FFELP. In FFELP, the loans were originated by private lenders that were then guaranteed for repayment by state or non-profit guaranty agencies, which were in turn reinsured by the federal government. 20 U.S.C. §§ 1078(c), 1085(j). FFLEP was discontinued in 2010, but many legacy FFLEP loans remain outstanding.

In 1992, Congress also authorized a federal direct lending program, the William D. Ford Direct Loan Program, today known as the **Direct Loan Program** or **Direct**. 20 U.S.C. § 1087a *et seq*. Direct is the only current federal student loan program. Direct offers both subsidized and unsubsidized Stafford Loans (known in this context as Direct Subsidized and Direct Unsubsidized Loans), as well as Direct PLUS Loans and Direct Consolidation Loans. The Direct Loan programs are summarized in the text box below.

Critically, the various Direct Loan programs fit into the financing mix in different ways. Direct Subsidized Loans are meant to cover part of the difference between the Cost of Attendance and the Expected Family Contribution. Direct Unsubsidized Loans and Direct PLUS loans, in contrast, are designed to be part of the EFC. (Direct Consolidation Loans are subsequent consolidation of other loans, so they are not part of the original financing mix.)

1. A third major federal student loan program, the need-based Perkins Loan program, in which schools made loans using revolving loan funds established with seed money partially contributed by the Department of Education, has gone into wind-down, with the last loans made in 2017.

Federal Direct Loan Programs

Direct Subsidized Loans are currently only for undergraduates with financial need (graduate students were eligible prior to 2012). They include interest deferment during enrollment, grace periods, and forbearance periods (up to three years in case of financial hardship or unemployment). The interest rate on Direct Subsidized Loans is fixed for the life of the loan at 4.45%. There is also a loan fee of 1.066% that is deducted proportionately from each loan disbursement, so that the money the borrower receives is less than the amount actually borrowed. 34 C.F.R. § 685.202(c). This means that the effective interest rate on the loans is actually 5.575%, as the borrower is paying $104.45 to receive $98.93. The maximum annual loan is $5,500.

Direct Unsubsidized Loans are for undergraduate, graduate, and professional degree students. No financial need is required. There is no interest deferment on these loans. The interest rate on Direct Unsubsidized Loans is fixed at 4.45% for undergraduate loans and 6% for graduate loans. Again, there is a 1.066% loan fee, so the real rate on undergraduate loans is 5.575% and on graduate loans it is 7.142%. Maximum annual borrowing is capped at $20,500.

Direct PLUS Loans (originally an acronym for Parent Loan for Undergraduate Students) are for the parents of dependent undergraduates or, as Grad PLUS loans, for graduate or professional degree students. No financial need is required, but the borrower may not have an adverse credit history. The interest rate on all PLUS loans is fixed at 7%. PLUS Loans come with a hefty fee of 4.264%, meaning the real interest rate is 11.766%. This is a substantially higher rate than most borrowers would pay for a loan secured by home equity. The maximum amount for a PLUS Loan is the cost of attendance minus any other financial aid received.

Direct Consolidation Loans are loans that refinance multiple federal education loans into a single loan. Consolidation reduces the number of loan payments for the borrower, as well as the number of servicers with whom the borrower must interact. Consolidation can also result in an extension of loan term, resulting in a smaller monthly payment, although more total payments. Additionally, consolidation can allow a borrower to switch variable-rate loans to a fixed-rate loan and may increase eligibility for various income-based repayment and forgiveness programs. The interest rate on Direct Consolidation Loans is the weighted average rate of the consolidated loans, rounded up to the nearest eighth of a percent. 20 U.S.C. § 1087e(b)(8)(D). There is no fee for a Direct Consolidation Loan; private loan consolidation facilitators will charge fees, however.

The decision to offer direct federal lending was based on an analysis that direct loans would be cheaper and easier to administer than loan guarantees. Not surprisingly, however, FFELP lenders pushed back against this program. After much political wrangling, direct federal lending was preserved, and schools could choose which program they wanted to participate in, with the Department of Education forbidden from encouraging the use of direct lending. Many schools remained in the guaranty program, in part because of strong incentives offered by

FFELP lenders. These incentives were benefits that accrued to the schools, rather than the students, encouraging schools to offer FFELP loans even if they were more expensive than direct loans.

By 2008 only around a quarter of higher education institutions participated in the direct lending program. The 2008 financial crisis, however, resulted in many schools shifting to direct lending because of disruptions in credit markets affecting the non-government lenders. In 2010, in the wake of the crisis, Congress completely eliminated the FFELP.

Today all new government involvement in student loans are Direct Loans; some legacy FFELP and Perkins Loans remain outstanding, however. As of the fourth quarter of 2017, there were over $1 trillion in Direct Loans outstanding to 33 million borrowers, $306 billion in FFELP loans to 14.9 million borrowers, and $7.6 billion in Perkins Loans to 2.5 million borrowers.

1. Loan Underwriting

Perhaps the most remarkable feature of federal education loans compared with most other consumer credit products is that they do not feature risk-based pricing. The loans are not underwritten based on the borrower's repayment capacity. No credit score or collateral is required. Instead, they are awarded based simply on whether the borrower meets the statutory eligibility requirements. It could hardly be any other way; few students have income or assets of their own that are sufficient to support large-scale borrowing. At best, they have prospects of future earnings, assuming they complete their education, but federal loans do not account for the student's choice of school, major, or course selection. Federal student loan funding is indifferent to students' post-graduation employment prospects.

On PLUS Loans, however, the borrower is the student's parent(s), who do(es) have a credit history. PLUS Loans merely require a binary check of whether the borrower has an "adverse credit history," meaning that the borrower cannot have debts of more than $2,085 that are 90 days or more delinquent or were placed in collection or charged off during the two prior years or had a loan default, bankruptcy discharge, foreclosure, repossession, tax lien, or wage garnishment in the prior five years, unless the borrower obtains an indorser (co-signor) who has a good credit history. 34 C.F.R. §§ 682.201(c)(vii), 685.200(c)(2)(viii). Once this basic level of creditworthiness is satisfied, however, pricing on all PLUS Loans is identical regardless of borrower credit quality.

2. Loan Terms

Interest rates on Direct Loans are set by statute. They do not vary by borrower, only by origination year. Thus, all Direct Loans of a particular type made in the same year will have the same interest rate. An engineering major at Caltech will get the same rate as a poetry major at a community college, despite very different post-graduation employment prospects.

The interest rates are based on the ten-year Treasury note rate plus a margin and have a cap. 20 U.S.C. § 1087e(b)(8); 34 C.F.R. §§ 685.202(a)(7)-(8), 685.202(9)(iv). These rates do not include fees, however, which are set separately by statute. (Confusingly for anyone looking up the authorized fee levels in the United States Code, the Budget Control Act of 2011 (the sequester law) has increased the fees beyond their stated statutory rates of 1% and 4%. 2 U.S.C. § 906(b).) Both Direct Loans and FFELP Loans are freely prepayable, 34 C.F.R. § 685.211(a)(2), but may not be refinanced by the existing lender (although consolidation is an option).

Significantly, interest on Direct Loans is calculated using a simply daily interest formula, in which the loan balance is multiplied by the number of days since the last payment date and again by the interest rate factor (the interest rate divided by the number of days in the year—365 or 366). This means that interest does not generally compound on student loans, which is a very pro-borrower feature of Direct Loans. Yet, as we will see below, the capitalization of deferred interest payments can have the same effect as compounding.

3. Repayment Options

Both Direct Loans and FFELP loans have multiple repayment options. 34 C.F.R. § 685.208. The default repayment option has fixed payments for up to ten years (or up to 30 years for Consolidation Loans). 34 C.F.R. § 685.210(a). This option has the highest monthly payments, but the borrower will pay off the loan fastest and will pay the least in total interest.

Borrowers can generally freely choose to change to other repayment options, 34 C.F.R. § 685.210(b)(1), which include a ten-year graduated repayment plan in which payments increase over time, reflecting the hope that the borrower's income will increase over time, and an extended repayment plan that allows fixed or graduated payments over 25 years, resulting in smaller monthly payments, but more total payments.

Additionally, there are several repayment plans that have payments based on the borrower's income (Income-Driven Repayment or IDR) and, in some cases, offer loan forgiveness for any balances remaining at the end of the plan. Most federal student loan borrowers qualify for these IDR plans, yet as of the end of 2017, only 46% were in an IDR plan. (Not all IDR plans are available to FFELP borrowers, and there is no IDR for co-signed loans.)

As Figure 31.1 shows, there are substantial differences in delinquency rates among repayment plans, with IDR plans such as PAYE and IBR having a significantly lower delinquency rate than other types of non-IDR repayment plans for Direct Loan borrowers. This raises the question of why more borrowers are not in IDR plans. The answer appears to be that borrowers are often not informed about IDR options and may not be encouraged by their loan servicers to enroll in IDR plans.

The Department of Education contracts with private companies to service student loans. Servicers are paid on a flat rate per borrower per loan, roughly $2.85/month when a loan is performing and less when it is delinquent. This flat-fee structure means that servicers are disincentivized to spend any additional time on customer contacts, and informing a consumer about IDR options and shifting the consumer to an IDR plan takes time. Likewise, if a borrower invokes the Public Service Loan Forgiveness program, a servicing transfer is automatically triggered (there is a special servicer for these loans), so servicers have no incentive to inform borrowers about the program.

Student loans are not considered to be in default until they are 270 days delinquent, 20 U.S.C. § 1085(l); 34 C.F.R. § 685.102(b), and once a loan has become 360 days delinquent the loan is transferred to a third-party debt collector, so the servicer ceases to be compensated on the loan. This structure means that a servicer has little incentive to attempt to work with a borrower who has defaulted; the servicer's compensation on the loan if it becomes current again is limited and if the servicer is unsuccessful (and redefault rates are very high), it is not compensated for its efforts. Instead, the cost-effective move from a servicer's perspective is to forbear on a student loan borrower who has defaulted (or who is even delinquent), but forbearance does not stop interest from accruing on the loan balance.

4. Postponing Payment

An unusual feature of both Direct and FFELP Loans is that they have provisions that allow for postponement of payments on the loans. First, payment is not due

Figure 31.1 Delinquency Rates by Repayment Plan for Direct Loans[2]

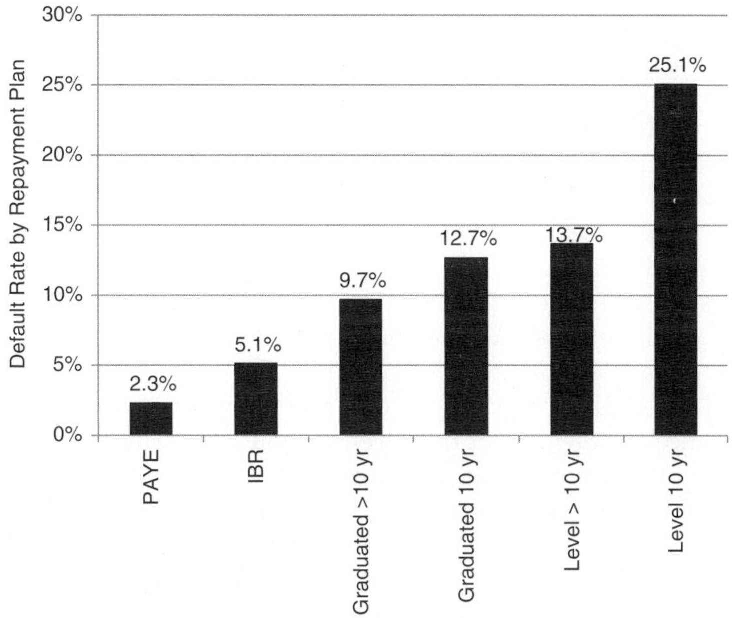

2. CFPB, *Student Loan Servicing: Analysis of Public Input and Recommendations for Reform*, Sept. 2015, at 23 (based on 2014 data).

while the borrower is enrolled in school. For unsubsidized loans, interest will still accrue and be capitalized, but payments are not due.

Second, for Direct Loans (excluding PLUS Loans) there is a six-month **grace period** following the student ceasing to be enrolled at least half-time before repayment commences. There is no grace period for PLUS Loans. Again, interest accrues during the grace period for unsubsidized loans.

Third, loans may go into **deferment**, which means that no interest accrues for subsidized loans, and that no payment is due on any types of loans. Deferment is allowed for specified grounds, including when the borrower (or student for PLUS loans) is enrolled at least half-time at an eligible school, is on active duty military service, unemployed, or unable to find full-time employment (but only for up to three years), or experiencing economic hardship (again only for up to three years). Deferment is not automatic. It requires that the loan not be in default and that the borrower make a formal request and submit supporting documentation to show the grounds for the deferment.

Finally, borrowers can seek **forbearance** on the loan. Forbearance means that no payment is due on the loan. Unlike with deferment, however, interest accrues on the balance of a loan in forbearance. Some forbearance is mandatory, while other forbearance is discretionary for the loan servicer. Mandatory forbearance exists for medical and dental internships and residencies, AmeriCorps service, teaching positions that qualify for loan forgiveness, certain National Guard call-ups, and when the total amount owed each month on all student loans is 20% or more of total monthly gross income (but limited to three years of forbearance). Discretionary forbearance may be granted for medical expenses, changes in employment, or financial difficulties. Forbearances may be granted for no more than a year at a time, although they can be stacked back to back.

As of the end of the fourth quarter of 2017, 39% of Direct Loans by dollar amount (and 43% by number) were not in either repayment or default because the borrowers were in school, in grace period, in deferment, or in forbearance. For FFELP loans the number was only 16% by dollar amount (and 14% by number), with the difference being primarily because few FFELP recipients are still in school or in the six-month post-school grade period.

While it is possible to defer payment in a number of situations, deferred payment does not mean that interest does not accrue; only subsidized loans do not accrue interest when a payment can be deferred. For all other loans, interest is capitalized. Capitalized interest is another way of describing negative amortization, meaning that loan balances get *higher* over time even without new principal being borrowed. And because interest accrues on capitalized interest, capitalization has the same effect as compounding, even though interest does not compound on Direct Loans. Fortunately for student borrowers, capitalization does not occur on a monthly basis, but instead occurs in a lump sum only upon the end of a grace period, deferment, or forbearance. This means there is no compounding of the deferred interest during the deferral period, a very borrower-friendly feature of Direct Loans.

Student loans are the only major class of debt for which negative amortization is common, if not predominant. Negative amortization is part of student loan debt because of the gap in timing between loan disbursement (at the start of education) and subsequent employment (which is when the borrower is presumed to have the cash flow necessary to commence repayment), but it has the effect of making a borrower's debt burden post-graduation substantially larger than the total amount the student borrowed simply because of accrual of interest during the student's education and any grace period thereafter.

5. Loan Forgiveness

Another unusual feature of federal student loans is that they may be "discharged," meaning forgiven or canceled under certain conditions. 34 C.F.R. § 685.212. The Higher Education Act allows for loans to be discharged for both borrower-related factors and school-related factors. Loans may be forgiven if the borrower (or student for a PLUS loan) dies, if the borrower becomes permanently and totally disabled, meaning that the borrower is for the long-term unable to engage in "any substantial gainful activities," 34 C.F.R. § 685.102(b), or if the borrower has a profession that qualifies for loan forgiveness: teaching, military service, or public service. Additionally, the Higher Education Act permits loan cancelation if a school closes before a student completes a program of study, if a school falsifies certification of the borrower's eligibility, or a school fails to pay a refund owed to the student (with only the wrongly withheld refund being canceled).

Together the repayment options, deferment and forbearance options, and loan forgiveness options on Direct Loans represent an important set of consumer protections against unexpected risks. No other type of consumer loans feature these sorts of protections, which are a major benefit from having a government loan program, but also necessitated in part because of the lack of underwriting of Direct Loans.

6. Collections

Direct Loans of all types have a late fee of 6% of a payment that is applied once a payment is 30 days late. 34 C.F.R. §§ 30.61, 685.202(d). The Department of Education is also authorized to recover from borrowers any pre-default collection charges and post-default collection charges, including attorney's fees. 34 C.F.R. §§ 30.60, 685.202(e). Default is defined as occurring when payment is 270 days delinquent. 20 U.S.C. § 1085(l); 34 C.F.R. § 685.102(b). The consequence of default is acceleration of the full loan balance and all accrued interest. 34 C.F.R. § 685.211(d)(1).

The Department of Education has enhanced collection rights relative to private lenders. In addition to bringing suit to collect on a loan, it may simply seek to have the IRS offset any tax refund owed to the borrower or use an administrative wage garnishment procedure that allows the Department of Education to avoid going to court. 34 C.F.R. Part 34, § 685.211(d)(3)(i).

7. Borrower Defenses and Procedural Safeguards

Direct Loans come with a unique set of borrower protections: a borrower may raise as a defense to any attempt to collect the loan "any act or omission of the school that would give rise to a cause of action against the school under applicable State law." 34 C.F.R. § 685.206(c)(1). If other words, if the school were to defraud a student, the student may raise that as a defense to repayment of the loan, even if the school's act or omission was unrelated to the loan. The application of the "Borrower Defense" rule is far from clear under the current regulation, but to the extent that a borrower is relieved of liability on a loan, the Department of Education may pursue the school instead. 34 C.F.R. § 685.206(c)(3).

In November 2016, the Department of Education finalized a revised Borrower Defense rule that made clear that it covered breaches of contract (irrespective of materiality) and substantial misrepresentations with detrimental reliance, as well as any favorable non-default judgment against the school by the borrower. 81 Fed. Reg. 75926-76089. In June 2017, the effective date of the revised rule was postponed indefinitely, as were other provisions that restricted schools' ability to require binding pre-dispute arbitration agreements or rely on arbitration agreements to avoid class actions related to borrower defenses. 82 Fed. Reg. 27621-22. (*See* Chapter 3 for more details.)

B. Private Student Loans

In addition to the federal student loans, there is a market for private student loans (PSLs). As of 2017 there were approximately $108 billion in private student loans outstanding, and 10% of loan originations in 2015-2016 were for PSLs. The vast majority of these loans are made by for-profit financial institution lenders, although some are made by state-affiliated non-profits or directly by schools. CFPB/DoE, *PSL Report* at 9. PSLs are used much more heavily by students at for-profit schools.

Because PSLs are a method for financing students' Expected Family Contribution, they compete with Direct Unsubsidized Loans (which are not based on credit worthiness) and Direct PLUS loans (which require minimum creditworthiness). They also compete with Direct Subsidized Loans, which can always be replaced by a PSL. This means the demand for PSLs is in part a function of federal financial aid program dollar limits and eligibility requirements; to the extent that more federal aid is available, there is less demand for PSLs.

PSLs differ from Direct Loans in several key aspects:

- PSLs are underwritten with risk-based pricing, in contrast to the one-size-fits-all pricing of Direct Loans. Riskier borrowers pay higher rates for PSLs. The underwriting of PSLs generally requires a minimum credit score and often a minimum debt-to-income ratio.
- Because few students will qualify for a PSL themselves, relatedly, PSLs typically require a co-signor. As of 2011, over 90% of PSLs were co-signed, typically by parents or grandparents. Co-signing links the credit of the student and the co-signor, which can have some surprising effects on the student if the co-signor has unrelated financial difficulties.
- PSLs are generally variable-rate loans, whereas Direct Loans are all fixed-rate loans. This means that PSL borrowers bear interest rate risk.

- PSLs have fewer repayment options than Direct Loans. Direct Loans feature a number of income-based and income-contingent repayment options, as well as forbearance options and rehabilitation options if the borrower becomes delinquent. Such features are not standard and are frequently not offered or not offered on equally favorable terms.
- PSLs do not have interest-free deferment options like Direct Subsidized Loans, and they may not allow deferment at all, even with interest capitalization.
- PSLs do not have the discharge options of Direct Loans. As a result, a student who dies or is disabled or whose school closes may still be liable for the loan.
- The definition of "default" is different for PSLs than for Direct Loans. Direct Loans define "default" as a loan being 270 days delinquent. 34 C.F.R. § 685.102(b). For PSLs, delinquency is generally at 120 days. CFPB/DoE *PSL Report* at 11-12. This means that PSLs go into collection much sooner than Direct Loans.

C. PSLs and Secondary Markets

A secondary market in student loans exists through private securitization markets. There is no securitization of Direct Loans, but FFELP loans were securitized, and PSLs are still securitized. Starting in 1972, the federal government engaged in the securitization of FFELP loans through a federally chartered entity called the Student Loan Marketing Association ("Sallie Mae"). Sallie Mae would purchase loans from lenders and pay for those loans by issuing bonds backed by the repayment stream on the loans. The bonds were backed by the full faith and credit of the U.S. government (as were the underlying loans), but with the difference being that the government guarantee of the bonds included a guarantee of *timely* payment of interest and principal, whereas the guaranty on the loans themselves does not guarantee timely payment. The goal of Sallie Mae's operations was to create liquidity for student loans, thus increasing the value of the loans to lenders and thereby reducing their costs to borrowers. Sallie Mae did quite well at this endeavor and by 1991 held 27% of FFELP loans in its securitization vehicles.

Sallie Mae was privatized between 1997 and 2004, however, at which point it became the largest FFELP lender by a substantial margin. After the end of the FFELP, Sallie Mae split into two independent companies in 2014. One, still named Sallie Mae, is a commercial bank that makes and services private student loans. The other, named Navient, is a servicer for federal student loans. Today all securitization of student loans is through private markets; there are no government-sponsored entities engaged in student loan securitization.

The PSL market grew very rapidly from 2001 to 2008, but then quickly contracted after the financial crisis. The market's growth was fueled by securitization, which provided the funding for lenders; when the securitization market collapsed in 2008, so too did the private student lending market. Figure 31.2 illustrates the change in public and private student loan issuance. While issuance has declined in recent years, as shown in Figure 31.3, total debt levels have continued to rise.

Figure 31.2 Public vs. Private Student Loan Issuance[3]

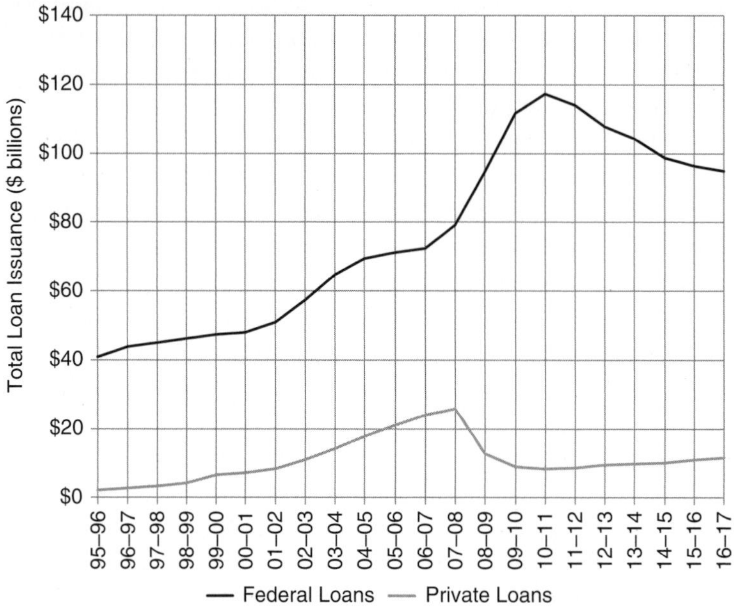

Figure 31.3 U.S. Student Loan Securitization Issuance[4]

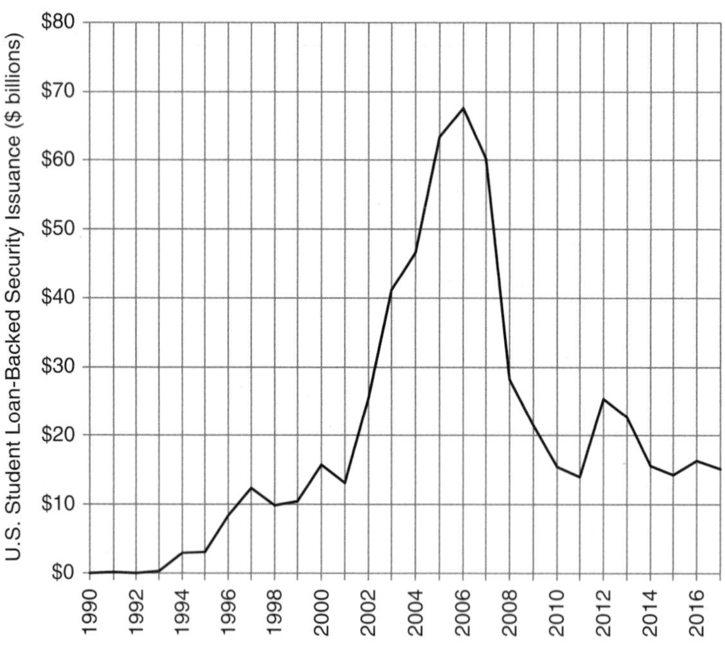

3. College Board, Trends in Student Aid (inflation adjusted to 2016 dollars).
4. SIFMA.

As with securitized mortgage notes, the numerous loan transfers involved in securitization have created problems with missing loan documentation for student loans. Stacy Cowley & Jessica Silver-Greenberg, *As Paperwork Goes Missing, Private Student Loan Debts May Be Wiped Away*, N.Y. Times, July 17, 2017. The CFPB sued one of the largest securitizers of PSLs, the National Collegiate Student Loan Trusts, and their debt collector, Transworld Systems, Inc., for attempting to collect debts for which it lacked proof of ownership. *See* Complaint, *CFPB v. National Collegiate Master Student Loan Trust, et al.*, No. 1:17-cv-01323 (D. Del. Sept. 18, 2017). The complaint and a summary of the settlement are included in Chapter 34.

II. REGULATORY CONCERNS

A. Total Student Indebtedness

The single most pressing regulatory concern about student loans is the marked growth of student loan indebtedness in recent years. At the start of 2003, total balances were $241 billion. By the start of 2017 there was $1.34 trillion in student loan debt outstanding. (*See* Figure 31.4.) On an inflation-adjusted basis this is more than a 417% increase. Not surprisingly, the burden of this increase in student loan debt has fallen disproportionately on younger borrowers. (*See* Figure 31.5.) Part of the increase of student loan debt is simply because of a growth in the number of borrowers. The number of student loan borrowers has doubled during between 2003 and 2017. (*See* Figure 31.6.) But even accounting for the growth in the number of

Figure 31.4 Growth of Student Loan Debt[5]

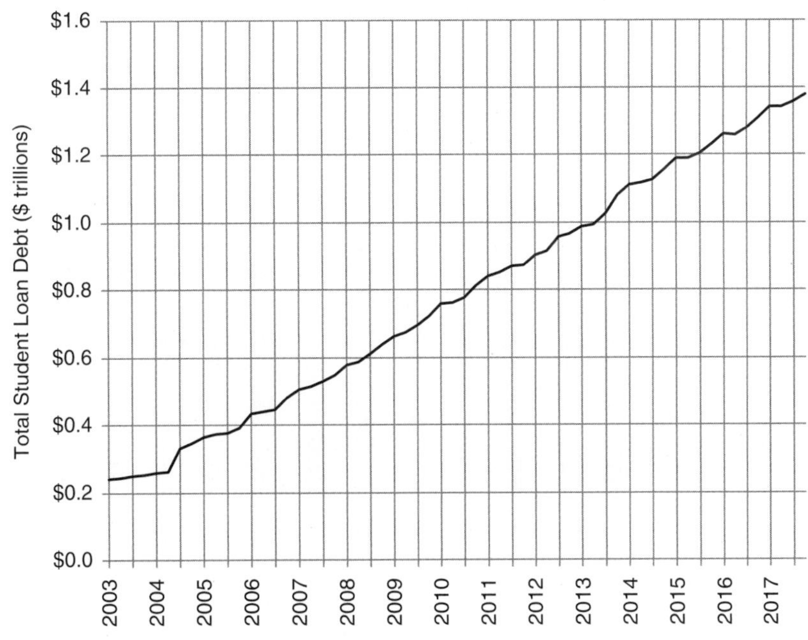

5. New York Fed Consumer Credit Panel/Equifax.

Figure 31.5 Student Loan Debt by Age Group[6]

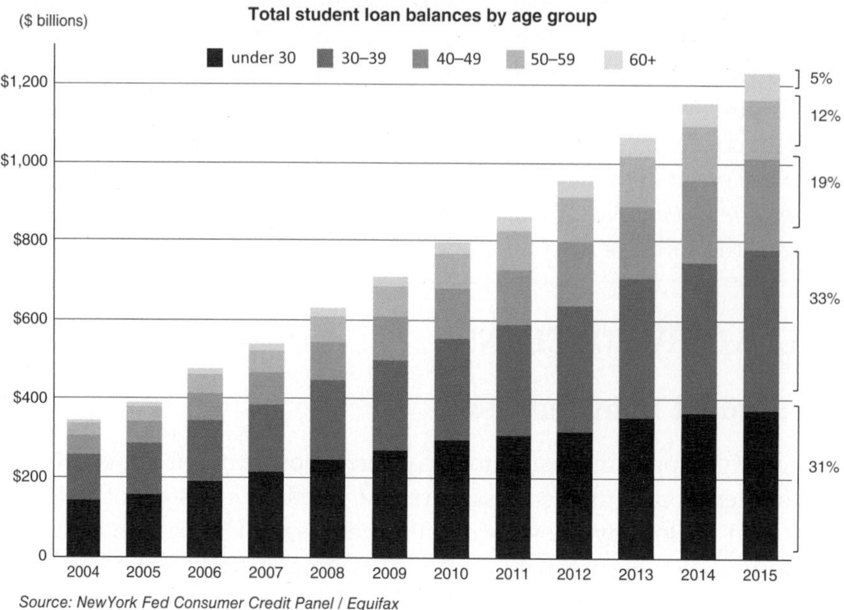

Figure 31.6 Number of Student Loan Borrowers[7]

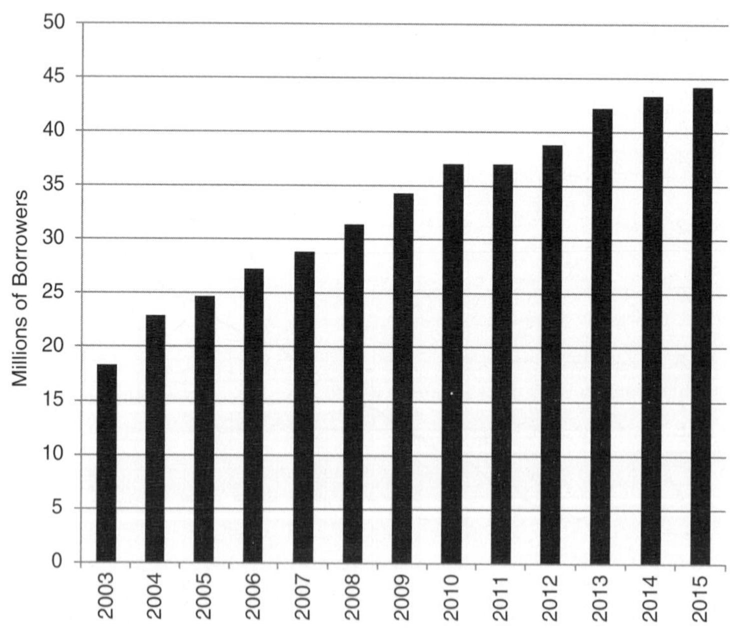

6. New York Fed Consumer Credit Panel/Equifax (2016).
7. New York Fed Consumer Credit Panel/Equifax, author's calculations (2016).

Figure 31.7 Average Student Loan Debt per Borrower in 2015[8]

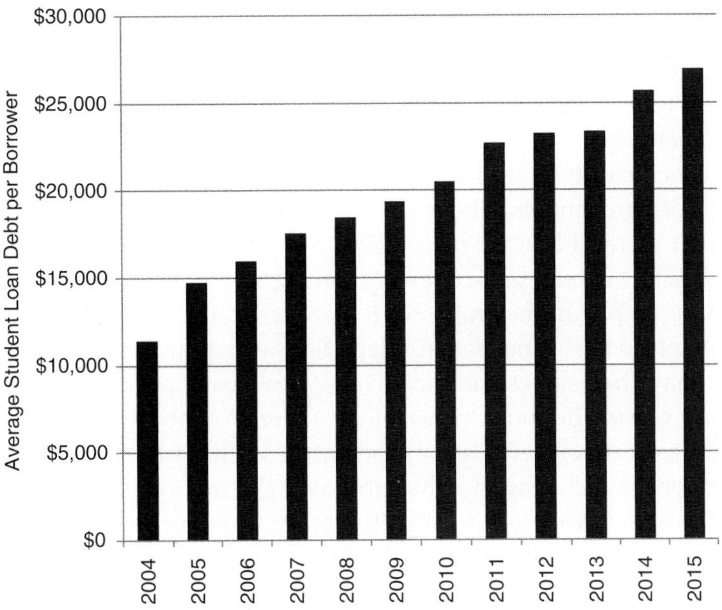

borrowers, per capita student loan debt balances also doubled, rising from $11,387 in 2004 to $26,924 in 2015. (*See* Figure 31.7.) The distribution of balances is quite uneven, however. As of 2015, nearly 40% of consumers with student loan debt had less than $10,000 of debt. Another 47% had balances between $10,000 and $50,000, with only a few percent having balances over $100,000. (*See* Figure 31.8.)

Figure 31.8 Distribution of Student Loan Debt by Balance in 2015[9]

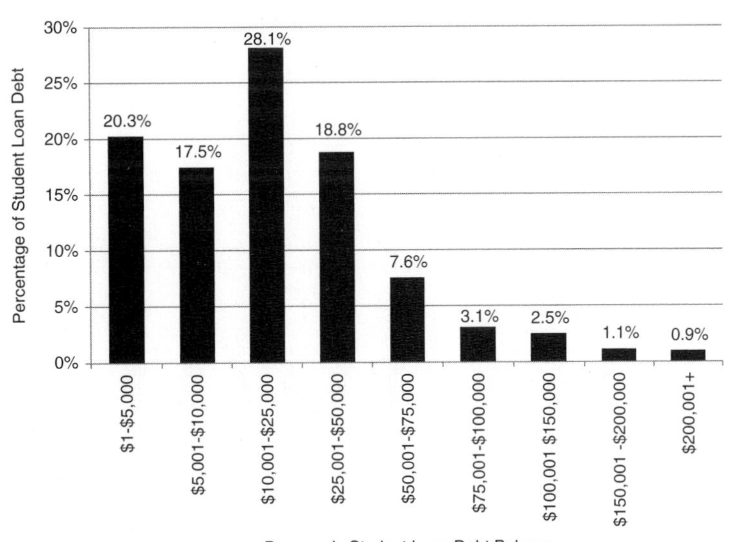

8. New York Fed Consumer Credit Panel/Equifax, author's calculations (2016).
9. New York Fed Consumer Credit Panel/Equifax (2016).

The causes of the rise in student loan debt are a matter of some debate. The expansion of the student population is clearly a factor, but it does not explain the increase in per capita debt. Part of the answer may lie in the increased cost of a degree (including room and board). (*See* Figure 31.9.) On an inflation-adjusted basis, the increase in tuition, fees, and room and board accounts for around 85%-90% of the *per capita* increase in student loan debt from 2004 to 2015.[10]

Other factors include increased costs of graduate school tuition (which accounts for about 10% of enrollments); the relative ease of obtaining a student loan, which requires neither a credit history nor ability to repay; increased time to graduation, which increases living expenses; over-borrowing relative to what students actually need; borrowing to pay higher-rate credit card debt; and, since 2008, increased reliance on financial aid to compensate for depleted savings and home equity. Critically, these factors may themselves interact. The relative ease of obtaining student loan financing may reduce demand constraints, thereby enabling higher tuition rates (this is known as the **Bennett Hypothesis**, after William Bennett, the Secretary of Education under Ronald Reagan, who promoted the theory).

While tuition increases tell most of the story in terms of *per capita* debt loans, *per capita* figures do not tell the whole story of student loan debt. The substantial increase in the number of borrowers is itself an important phenomenon that may reflect the rising cost of tuition and the weakening of middle-class families' financial positions, although there was not a noticeable change in the rate of borrower growth after the 2008 financial crisis.

Figure 31.9. Growth of College Tuition[11]

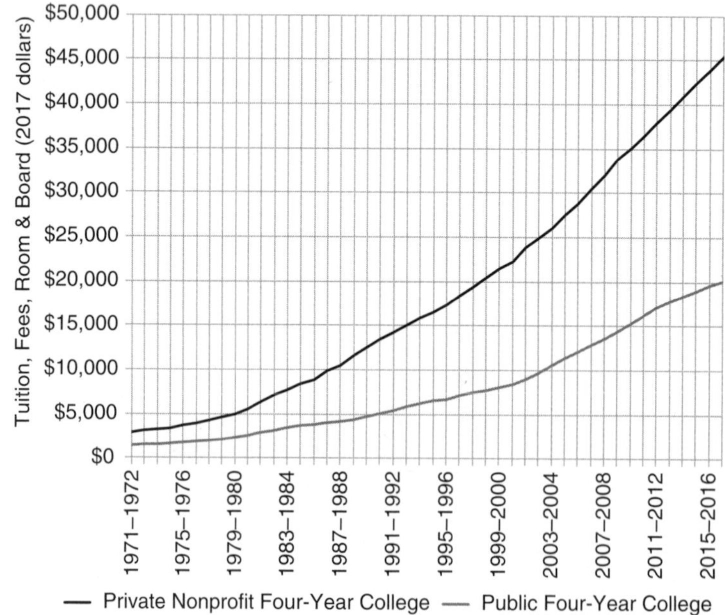

10. Author's calculations.
11. College Board.

Whatever the causes, student loan debt is growing rapidly, particularly for younger consumers. This is a matter of public policy concern for two reasons. The first is simply the hardship that high debt burdens put on individual consumers. The most heavily indebted student borrowers have little prospect of ever paying off their debt, so their consumption ability is limited. Rather than spending funds on new goods and services, part of their income is diverted every month to paying off their student loans.

A subset of students has a particularly unfortunate situation: they have borrowed money for education that has little or no market value, in that it does not translate into job prospects. Sometimes this is because those students knowingly pursued educational paths that always have poor job prospects (*e.g.*, a degree from Upper Vermont Experimental Poets College), but sometimes it is because students were misled by schools or lenders into believing that there were better job prospects than actually exist, and sometimes it is because a school promised job placement support, but the school subsequently closed, leaving the student without support.

Critically, however, increasing student debt burdens are not likely to result in an acute moment of financial crisis, such as when housing prices collapsed in 2007. While defaults on student loans have been rising, they are unlikely to be correlated with each other the way housing prices (and thus mortgage defaults) are. The long repayment periods for student loans plus the availability of deferment and forbearance and forgiveness options mean that student loans are more likely to be a slow-burning policy problem, rather than one that comes to a head with a moment of crisis. Moreover, student loans are not "financialized." Because most student loan debt is held by the government, a rise in defaults does not affect financial markets by threatening the solvency of financial institutions.

Yet rising default rates on both Direct Loans and FFELP loans indicate a mounting problem as shown by Figures 31.10 and 31.11. As of the end of the third quarter of 2017 some 4.4 million borrowers were in default on Direct Loans and another 4.1 million in default on FFELP loans (there may be some overlap between the populations). Recall that "default" for student loans is 270 days delinquent, a much longer delinquency period than for other types of loans, meaning that the percentage of loans that are delinquent (including those in default) is substantially higher. Moreover, it's important to recognize that the growth of borrowing masks the default rates as new loans are included in the denominator of the default rate.

Student loan default rates are not correlated with other types of consumer credit default rates. Figure 31.12 shows that the delinquency rates on mortgages, auto loans, and credit cards all increased in the aftermath of the 2008 financial crisis but began to subside by 2011. Student loan delinquencies (here being shown as 90+ days delinquent) jumped up in 2012. The reason seems to be a coalescence of several factors. First, default rates during the 2008-2011 period were deceptively low because many consumers returned to school after losing their jobs, so a large number of new loans increased the denominator in the default rate, masking an increased number of defaults. Second, by 2012, students who were returning to the labor force would be facing a very soft labor market, particularly for those who did not complete their degrees. And third, deferment and forbearance may mean that defaults generally

Figure 31.10 Percentage of FFELP and Direct Borrowers in Default[12]

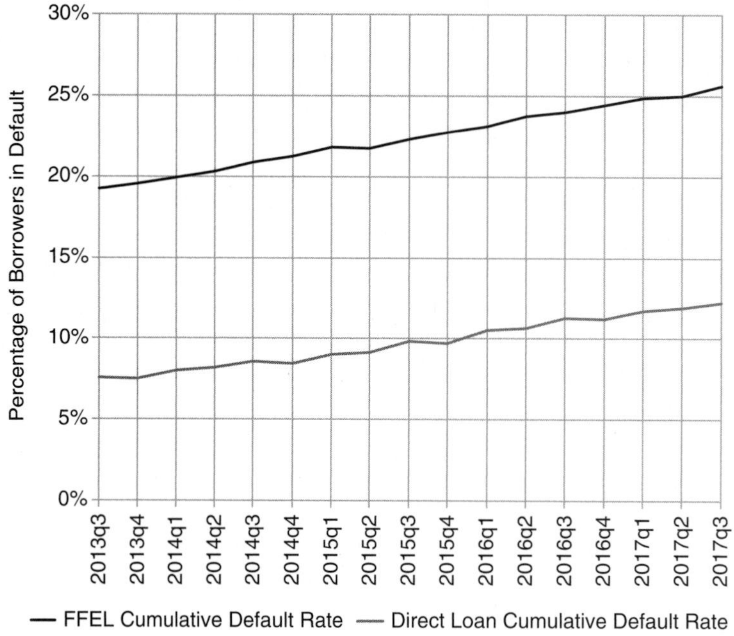

Figure 31.11 Percentage of FFELP and Direct Loans in Default[13]

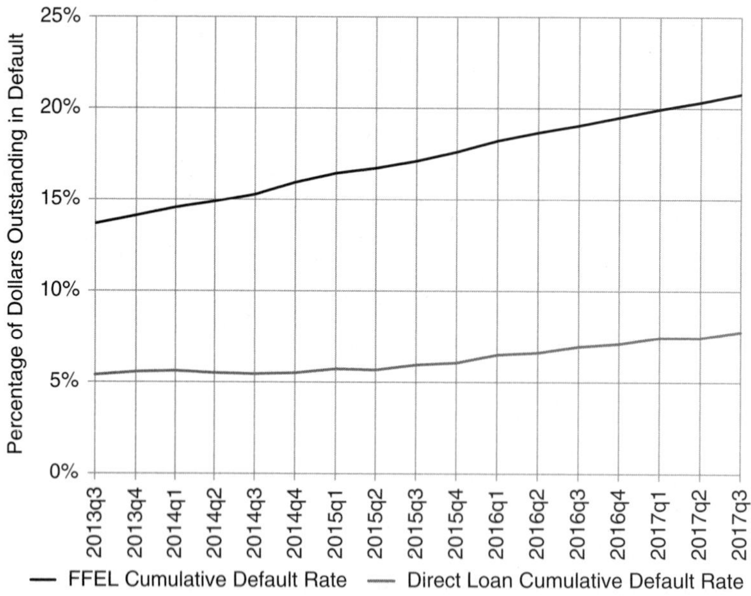

12. Dept. of Education.
13. Dept. of Education.

Figure 31.12 Delinquency Rates (90+ Days) on Various Consumer Financial Products

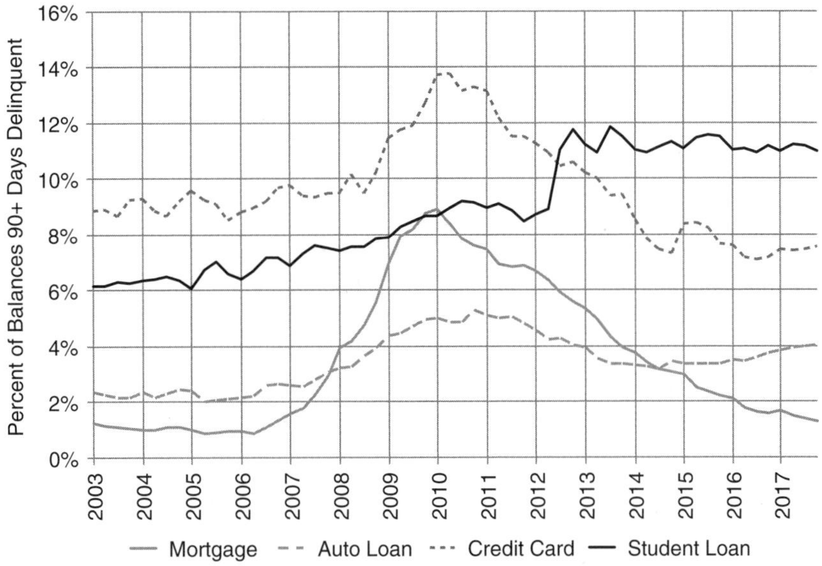

lag in the student loan market. What is notable, however, is that default rates have not fallen post-2012, even as they have for mortgages and credit cards.

The second reason is less of a tearjerker, but perhaps the most important from a public policy perspective: large student debt burdens may have adverse macroeconomic effects. Consumers with high levels of student loan debt are less likely to form households of their own (as that would potentially result in two consumers' worth of student loan debt), much less purchase homes. A lessening of demand from younger consumers for home purchases will reduce home prices, thereby destroying home equity value—a major source of retirement savings—for existing homeowners. Likewise, large student debt burdens may affect the labor market, because the need to pay off loans may lock some consumers into remaining in higher-paying jobs and result in others seeking employment in fields that qualify for federal loan forgiveness. In other words, student loans pose not a financial crisis, but a set of crises for individuals' finances; en masse, that is tied to consumer consumption, which ultimately does connect with the broader economy, just not through the channel of financial institutions.

Over-indebtedness is a concern for all types of consumer debt, but education financing is different in an important way. If a consumer gets in over her head with credit card debt or with an unaffordable mortgage or auto loan, the consumer generally has the option of filing for bankruptcy. Bankruptcy isn't a fun experience for consumers, but at the end of the day, it holds forth the prospect of reducing the consumer's debts, and the mere possibility of a bankruptcy filing gives consumers some negotiating leverage when dealing with creditors. All types of student loans, however, are non-dischargeable in bankruptcy, except in extreme circumstances, when the debtor can show "undue hardship," an exacting standard as applied by the courts. 11 U.S.C. § 523(a)(8). Understanding the harshness of the standard requires some context. Originally, student loans were fully dischargeable after five years, but dischargeable within five years with undue hardship. In that context courts construed undue hardship very strictly. The five-year standard was lengthened and ultimately eliminated, but the body of law interpreting "undue hardship" was left in place, even though it had originally been developed with an assumption that the borrower could discharge the loan, just after five years.

"Undue hardship" is undefined by statute, but courts have generally used one of two tests for undue hardship. Most circuits have adopted the *Brunner* test, which requires that the debtor cannot maintain a "minimal" living standard for himself and his dependents based on current income if forced to repay the loans, that there are additional circumstances (*e.g.*, age, disability) that indicate that this state will persist for most of the repayment period of the loans, that the debtor has made a good faith effort to repay the loans. *Brunner v. N.Y. State Higher Educ. Servs. Corp.*, 831 F.2d 395 (2d Cir. 1987). A minority of courts have adopted a totality of circumstances test that looks at "(1) the debtor's past, present, and reasonably reliable future financial resources; (2) a calculation of the debtor's and her dependent's reasonable necessary living expenses; and (3) any other relevant facts and circumstances surrounding each particular bankruptcy case." *Long v. Educ. Credit Mgmt. Corp. (In re* Long), 322 F.3d 549, 554 (8th Cir. 2003). Additionally, some courts have further required (irrespective of the basic standard) a "certainty of hopelessness" of ever repaying the education loan. *See, e.g., Barrett v. Educ. Credit Mgmt. Corp. (In re* Barrett), 487 F.3d 353, 359 (6th Cir. 2007).

Whatever the test, the threshold for an undue hardship discharge in bankruptcy is extremely high. There is no emergency escape hatch for student loans built into the legal system. For federally made and guaranteed loans, this policy decision is understandable, as taxpayers are on the hook when those loans are not repaid. But the limitation on bankruptcy discharge has, since 2005, also applied to PSLs without any clear policy justification.

B. Private Student Loan-Specific Issues

PSLs raise a number of distinct policy concerns. One is **over-borrowing.** Over-borrowing is distinct from over-indebtedness. Over-borrowing refers to a student taking out more loans than she needs, rather than simply having more debt than she can handle. Suppose a student needs $30,000 to cover her Expected Family Contribution, which is meant, along with an aid package, to cover tuition, fees, living expenses, etc. If the student borrows $35,000 in addition to the aid package, then the student has borrowed $5,000 more than she needs, and will be paying interest on this amount. PSL lenders have an incentive to encourage over-borrowing, as it increases their business volume, but since 2008 they have increasingly required school certification of borrower need. There is no requirement that they do so, however.

Another policy concern with PSLs is the risk of co-signor default. Most PSLs are co-signed and are based on the creditworthiness of the co-signor, even though the borrower is the beneficiary. As a result, most PSL contracts contain an **auto-default clause** that provides that the loan is automatically in default if the co-signor dies or files for bankruptcy, even if the loan is otherwise in good standing. CFPB, *Mid-Year Update on Student Loan Companies*, 12-13 (June 2015). Some PSLs have even further-reaching **universal default clauses**, such as appeared in credit cards before the CARD Act. These clauses provide that a default by the co-signor on any obligation is also a default on the PSL. It is unclear how often PSL lenders take action on such provisions. Note, by way of comparison, though, that similar due-on-sale provisions for mortgages triggered by the borrower's death are prohibited under the Garn-St. Germain Act. 12 U.S.C. § 1701j-3.

An additional policy concern with PSLs is borrower confusion. This can arise in three ways. First, a borrower might not be aware of the possibility of Direct Loans and will instead rely on PSLs that have less favorable terms. Second, a borrower may not understand the differences between a Direct Loan and a private loan, and depending on the marketing of a PSL, the likelihood of confusion might be increased. And third, a borrower might not understand the distinction between a PSL lender and the borrower's school, particularly if the school helps the borrower identify the PSL lender. In such a situation, a borrower might feel compelled to use that particular PSL lender.

PSLs also raise an Equal Credit Opportunity Act issue. One factor in a school's eligibility for funding under the Higher Education Act is its "Cohort Default Rate," a measure of loan defaults by its students and graduates. PSL lenders may use Cohort Default Rates as a proxy for a student's credit risk. That can result in a disparate impact problem because African-American and Hispanic borrowers are disproportionately concentrated at schools with higher Cohort Default Rates, such as historically black colleges.

C. Legacy Issues with FFELP Loans

Although the FFELP has been discontinued, there is still a large volume of FFELP debt outstanding, and this debt continues to have loan servicing issues. When a FFELP loan goes into default, the state or non-profit guaranty agency pays the guarantor on the debt and the loan is transferred to the guaranty agency. If the loan starts to re-perform, the guaranty agency may sell the loan to another lender. When it does so, the guaranty agency is allowed by statute to charge a fee of up to 16% of the loan balance. 20 U.S.C. § 1078-6(a)(1)(D). As a result, a default, even if cured, can be extremely costly to a borrower.

III. REGULATION OF STUDENT LOANS

There are substantially different regulatory regimes for federally made or guaranteed loans and PSLs.

A. Regulation of Direct Loans

Federal education loans are governed by the Higher Education Act and regulations thereunder. Loans that are made or guaranteed by the federal government are made pursuant to Department of Education regulations. Department of Education regulations set forth school eligibility, borrower loan eligibility criteria, loan terms, counseling and disclosure requirements, and various payment deferral or forgiveness options. Loan terms, deferment, and forgiveness are discussed above. Loan eligibility, disclosure, and counseling are discussed below.

Whether state laws of general applicability, such as contract law, debt collection laws, and UDAP statutes, also apply to federal education loans is a matter of contention. Some courts have held that the Higher Education Act preempts these state laws, *see, e.g., Brannan v. United Student Aid Funds*, 94 F.3d 1260 (9th Cir. 1996) (Higher Education Act preempts state debt collection law); *Chae v. SLM Corp.*, 593 F.3d 936 (9th Cir. 2010) (Higher Education Act preempts state UDAP claim), while others have held that there is no preemption, *see, e.g., Bible v. United Student Aid Funds, Inc.*, 799 F.3d 633 (7th Cir. 2015) (state-law contract claim based on promissory note and federal RICO claim not preempted by Higher Education Act); *Weber v. Great Lakes Education Loan Services*, 2013 U.S. Dist. LEXIS 106266 (D. Wisc. July 30, 2013) (state debt collection statute not preempted by Higher Education Act). The Higher Education Act does expressly preempt state usury laws for federal student loans. 20 U.S.C. § 1078(d).

1. Direct Loan Eligibility

An important consumer protection with Direct Loans is limitations on school eligibility. Not all schools are eligible to participate in the Direct Loan program. Participation is limited to "Eligible Institutions," under the Higher Education Act of 1965, 34 C.F.R. § 600.1, which must be either "institutions of higher education," "proprietary institutions of higher education" (that is, for-profit schools), or "post-secondary vocational institutions." 34 C.F.R. § 600.2.

"Institutions of higher education" must operate educational programs that either (1) award "an associate, baccalaureate, graduate, or professional degree," (2) offer at least two-year programs acceptable for full credit toward a baccalaureate degree (thereby covering many community colleges), or (3) offer certificate or non-degree recognized credentials and "prepare[] students for gainful employment in a recognized occupation." 34 C.F.R. §§ 600.4(a)(4), 685.102(a)(2). Similar gainful employment requirements exist for for-profit schools and vocational schools. 34 C.F.R. §§ 600.5(a)(5), 600.6(a)(4).

"Gainful employment" is then separately defined under the Gainful Employment Rule. 34 C.F.R. Part 668, Subpart Q. The Gainful Employment Rule requires that a school meet certain certification requirements, including that its programs meet any educational requirements for the applicable state licensure or certification requirements, 34 C.F.R. §§ 668.403(a)(1), 668.414(d)(3), and that it is not an ineligible program under a debt-to-earnings (D/E) rate metric, 34 C.F.R. § 668.403(a)(2).

The D/E rate is actually two separate measures, a discretionary income rate measure, and an annual earnings rate measure. The discretionary income rate is the quotient of a two-year cohort of graduates' median annual loan payment over a figure that is the higher of the mean or median annual earnings minus 1.5x the poverty rate. 34 C.F.R. § 668.404(a)(1). Annual earning rate is the quotient of the cohort's median annual loan payment over the greater of the mean or median annual earnings. 34 C.F.R. § 668.404(a)(2). (For smaller programs, a four-year cohort is used, 34 C.F.R. § 668.402.)

A passing D/E rate measure requires that the discretionary income rate be ≤ 20% and the annual earnings rate be ≤ 8%. 34 C.F.R. § 668.403(c). Rates of greater than 30% and 12% respectively are failing rates, while rates in between passing and failing are "in the zone." *Id.* In order to remain eligible for participation in Direct Loan programs, a school must not have a failing D/E rate measure in two of three consecutive years or a failing or "in the zone" measure in three of four consecutive years. *Id.*

The point of the Gainful Employment Rule is that federal education funds should not be used to finance education that will leave students indebted, but without job prospects. Notably, however, the Gainful Employment Rule only applies to certificate programs, for-profit schools, and vocational schools. It does not apply to colleges granting associates, baccalaureate, graduate, or professional degrees. Thus, the rule does not prevent Upper Vermont Experimental Poetry College, an accredited baccalaureate granting institution, from arranging Direct Loans for its students, despite their questionable job prospects.

2. Disclosure and Counseling for Direct Loans

Federal student loans are generally exempt from TILA/Reg Z, but are instead covered by the Higher Education Act, 20 U.S.C. § 1001 *et seq.* The Higher Education Act requires disclosures to be made in "simple and understandable terms, in a statement provided to the borrower at or prior to the beginning of the repayment period," as well as requiring additional disclosures between 30 and 150 days before the first payment is due. 34 C.F.R. § 682.205. Additional disclosures explaining options available to avoid default are required if the student runs 60 days delinquent on payments. 34 C.F.R. § 682.205(c). Department of Education regulations also require schools to engage in borrower counseling, 34 C.F.R. § 685.304, both before taking out loans and before graduation. This counseling requirement includes emphasis on the particular terms of the loans.

B. Regulation of Private Student Loans

PSLs are regulated by both state and federal law. The full panoply of state law, including usury statutes, applies to PSLs. On the federal level PSLs are subject to both certain provisions of the Higher Education Act and the Truth in Lending Act. While many of the provisions of these statutes are substantively the same, their application and interpretation by the Department of Education and the CFPB may not always be consistent.

1. Disclosure Requirements

PSLs are subject to the most extensive Truth in Lending Act/Regulation Z disclosures of any product. Since 2010, TILA/Reg Z has required disclosures when a lender solicits a loan or a borrower makes a loan application, when the lender first approves the loan, and at loan disbursement. 15 U.S.C. § 1638(e); 12 C.F.R. § 1026.46-47.

The solicitation or application disclosures must include information on interest rates, fees, repayment terms, including any deferral options and whether interest accrues when the loan is in deferral, cost estimates, and eligibility requirements. Additionally, the lender must disclose that the consumer may qualify for federal student assistance, including Direct Loans, the interest rates available for each Direct Loan program, and whether those rates are fixed or variable. 15 U.S.C. § 1638(e)(1); 12 C.F.R. § 1026.47(a)(6). This sort of mandatory comparison shopping bears some similarities to the "plain vanilla" proposal for standard mortgage offerings to be required when a lender offers a non-standard mortgage.

The loan approval disclosures are substantially similar, except without cost estimates. 15 U.S.C. § 1638(e)(2); 12 C.F.R. § 1026.47(b). TILA and Reg Z require that all PSL approvals be 30-day firm offers of credit from the lender. 15 U.S.C. § 1638(e)(1)(O); 12 C.F.R. § 1026.48(c)(1). This enables consumers to shop for better prices without undue time pressure.

After the borrower has accepted the loan, the lender must make a third set of disclosures. 15 U.S.C. § 1638(e)(4); 12 C.F.R. § 1026.47(c). These are the regular TILA/Reg Z closed-end credit disclosures, but also the student-loan-specific information about interest rates, fees, and repayment terms required in the solicitation disclosures. In addition, the lender must notify the borrower of her right to cancel the loan prior to the expiry of a TILA/Reg Z three-day right of rescission for PSLs. 15 U.S.C. § 1638(e)(7); 12 C.F.R. § 1026.48(d). Finally, prior to closing the loan, each PSL borrower on a loan must receive, sign, and return a "self-certification" form that notes the availability of federal aid and includes a template for computing borrowing need. 15 U.S.C. § 1638(e)(3); 12 C.F.R. § 1026.48(e). The purpose of this requirement is to discourage over-borrowing.

While the TILA disclosure requirements are on lenders, the Higher Education Act requires schools that provide information about PSLs to comply with the TILA loan solicitation disclosures. 20 U.S.C. § 1019a(a)(1)(B)(i); 34 C.F.R. § 601.11. The Higher Education Act also requires schools that provide information about PSLs to inform prospective borrowers that they may qualify for Direct Loans, which may have more favorable terms. The school must also make sure that the information about the PSLs is presented so as to be distinct from that of Direct Loans, in order to avoid borrower confusion.

It's important to recognize, however, the limitation on TILA/Reg Z disclosures for PSLs, namely that they are made after the student has already committed to enroll and may have paid a deposit. Students generally make enrollment decisions in the spring to start the following fall but may not search for a PSL until the summer. By that point the student already has sunk costs and may feel that she has little choice other than to proceed with a PSL.

2. Anti-Inducement/Conflict of Interest Rules

The Higher Education Act requires all higher education institutions to have a "code of conduct." 20 U.S.C. § 1094(a)(25). The code of conduct is required to prohibit all conflicts of interest as a general matter. 20 U.S.C. § 1094(a)(25)(A)(i). It is also required to contain a specific prohibition on revenue-sharing arrangements with lenders that includes any sort of quid pro quo for recommending the lender or its products. 20 U.S.C. § 1094(e)(1). It must also prohibit the school's employees who have any responsibilities with regard to financial aid from soliciting or accepting any gift from a lender or from providing any compensated consulting or contracting services to student lenders. 20 U.S.C. § 1094(e)(2)-(3). These prohibitions also exist as a matter of statute under the Truth in Lending Act. 15 U.S.C. § 1650(b)(1)-(2).

Additionally, higher education institutions are forbidden from requesting or accepting any funds from institution in exchange for being a "preferred lender" for the institution. 20 U.S.C. § 1094(e)(5). Institutions are allowed to have "preferred lender lists" of lenders whose products the school recommends and make them available to students. *See* 20 U.S.C. § 1019(8). Any preferred lender list must have at least two unaffiliated PSL lenders, 20 U.S.C. § 1094(h)(1)(B)(i).

Critically, the conflict of interest rules relate only to student loans; they do not cover other financial products. The Department of Education's Cash Management Rule, 34 C.F.R. Part 668, however, places some additional restrictions on affiliations that involve deposit accounts and debit cards. The Cash Management Rule generally deals with disbursement of student loan funds to students. These disbursements might be handled by the school or by a bank under contract with the school. In the first case, the school might still partner with a bank to market accounts to students into which funds can be disbursed, while in the latter case, the bank handling the disbursements might offer accounts to students. An account is considered to be marketed to students if the school communicates information directly to the students about the account and how it may be opened, if the account or access device for the account is cobranded with the school's name, logo, or mascot and is marketed principally to students, or if the access device also serves as a student ID card. 34 C.F.R. § 668.164 (f)(3).

In either case, if funds are disbursed to the student through electronic fund transfers, then students must be given a choice about how to receive the payments, with no option being preselected and with options presented in "a clear, fact-based, and neutral manner." 34 C.F.R. § 668.164(d)(4)(A). The school must give as the first option for disbursement any bank account the student already has and must list the major features and common fees for each type of account. 34 C.F.R. § 668.164(d)(4)(B).

If any accounts are offered to students from a financial institution that has partnered with the school for marketing the accounts (whether or not the bank handles the disbursements), then the school must ensure that "the terms of the account . . . are not inconsistent with the best financial interests of the students opening them." 34 C.F.R. §§ 668.164(e)(ix), 668.164(f)(viii). That requires that the fees imposed on the account be at or below market. *Id.* Moreover, the school must disclose to the student the terms of the account, 34 C.F.R. §§ 668.164(e)(iii) 668.164(f)(ii), and must also conspicuously disclose on the school's website the contract with the financial institution and the total consideration received by the parties. 34 C.F.R. §§ 668.164(e)(vi)-(vii), 668.164(f)(iii)-(iv). Moreover, in all situations, the school must ensure that the accounts have no opening fees, enable free balance inquiries and ATM withdrawals, and are not converted into credit cards. 34 C.F.R. §§ 668.164(e)(iv)-(v), 668.164(f)(vi)-(vii), 668.164(x).

If a bank is actually involved in disbursing the Direct Loan funds for the school, then, there are a number of substantive restrictions on the account terms, including that there be no cost for point-of-sale transactions or overdrafts. 34 C.F.R. § 668.164(e)(iv).

3. Marketing Restrictions

The Higher Education Act requires that selection of preferred lenders be based on "the best interests of the borrowers," including origination fees, "highly competitive" rates and terms, high-quality servicing, and additional benefits. 20 U.S.C. § 1094(h)(1)(C). Moreover, institutions have a "duty of care and a duty of loyalty to compile the preferred lender list . . . without prejudice and for the sole benefit of the students attending the institution, or the families of such students." 20 U.S.C. § 1094(h)(1)(D).

The educational institution must make clear when presenting its preferred lender list to students that there is no requirement that the student use a preferred lender. 20 U.S.C. § 1094(h)(1). The school must also disclose why it entered into the arrangement with each lender, "particularly with respect to terms and conditions or provisions favorable to the borrower." *Id.*

The Higher Education Act and TILA both prohibit preferred lenders from using the school's name, emblem, mascot, or logo in any way that implies that the school is making the loan. 20 U.S.C. § 1019a(a)(2); 15 U.S.C. § 1650(c); 34 C.F.R. § 601.12. *But see* 12 C.F.R. § 1026.48(a)-(b) (permitting use of school's marks if allowed by other applicable law).

Marketing restriction rules relate only to student loans; they do not cover other financial products. TILA specifically allows schools to enter into marketing contracts with credit card issuers; the schools are merely required to disclose those contracts. 15 U.S.C. § 1650(f).

4. Prepayment Penalties

The sole substantive term restriction on PSLs is a prohibition on prepayment penalties. 15 U.S.C. § 1650(e). Note that an assumption of this particular provision is that a PSL is otherwise freely prepayable; it is not clear, however, whether a loan could simply prohibit prepayment, although it would seem to be inconsistent with the prohibition on prepayment penalties on the theory that the greater includes the lesser.

C. Servicing Regulations

Notably absent from student loan regulation is regulation on loan servicers. Servicers play a critical role in the student loan system. While the Department of Education provides the funds for loans, the loans themselves are made through an origination agent (Accenture) and then serviced by a network of nine non-bank service providers, but this number is deceptively large, as the large servicers subservice for small ones. These servicers are compensated with a fixed monthly fee per loan per borrower. Servicers are not paid for effort or results.

Unlike mortgage servicers and PSL servicers, Direct Loan servicers have no responsibility for advancing delinquent payments. Indeed, Direct Loan servicers do not even collect funds from borrowers, as all payments go to a central lockbox managed by Bank of America for the Department of Education; the servicer merely gets an electronic record of the payment, which means that there is no "float" income for Direct Loan servicers for the period between when payments are received from borrowers and remitted to the lender. PSL servicers can get float income.

All student loan servicers are subject to CFPB rulemaking, supervision, and enforcement; they are "covered persons" by virtue of servicing loans. The Department of Education could, in theory, exercise oversight over Direct Loan servicers, but only contracting officers, rather than a consumer protection unit, exercise oversight over Direct Loan servicers at the Department of Education.

Whereas mortgage loan servicers are subject to significant regulation, including record retention and loss mitigation requirements, there are no equivalent requirements for student loan servicers. There is no equivalent to a RESPA "Qualified Written Request" or to TILA/EFTA error resolution rights in student loan servicing. Student loan servicers are still subject to federal and state debt collection statutes, credit reporting regulations, and contract and tort law, however, as well as to CFPB supervision (if larger participants) and enforcement.

The lack of regulation of servicers is surprising given that most of the complaints in the student loan market (or at least in the public student loan market) relate to servicing, rather than to loan origination or loan terms. Indeed, the servicing gap appears to be among the most serious of consumer protection issues with student loans. Direct Loans have given consumers many rights and protections, but those rights and protections are not effectuated because (1) borrowers are not informed about them by servicers and (2) because of payment processing problems whereby payments are misapplied by servicers.

Problem Set 31

1. Vladlena Gutiérrez, a Nicaraguan immigrant to the United States, is hoping to become the first person in her family to go to college. She was admitted to the prestigious Massachusetts Technical University, her first-choice school, but she's worried how she will be able to afford it, as tuition, fees, room and board are $60,000/year. Vladlena submitted a FAFSA to the Department of Education, which calculated her Expected Family Contribution to be $5,000. Mass Tech has offered Vladlena an aid package of a $10,000 merit scholarship, federal grants of $6,000, a Direct Subsidized Loan of $5,500, and $7,000 in work-study funding.

   a. How can Vladlena finance the Expected Family Contribution and the $31,500 difference between the cost of attendance and the aid package plus the Expected Family Contribution? Will it matter if Vladlena has no credit history? What if her parents have bad credit?

b. Vladlena wants to know if her choice of major will affect the cost of her education. She's interested in studying musicology but knows that Mass Tech has a great engineering program. Will her choice of major affect the terms of her loans?

c. If Vladlena goes to law school after graduation, what will happen to her loans?

d. Vladlena's lined up her financing based on your answer to part (a). How easy will it be for Vladlena to figure out the cost of financing her education in advance?

2. Kevin Carruthers financed part of his education with a Direct PLUS loan on which his mom was the borrower and which was indorsed by Aunt Betsy. Kevin also took out a private student loan that his mother co-signed. Kevin has been successfully repaying the loan post-graduation.

a. What happens if before the loans are paid off Kevin is partially paralyzed (from the waist down) in a car accident? *See* 34 C.F.R. §§ 685.102(b), 685.212.

b. Suppose that following the car accident in part (a) Kevin is unable to continue in his job as a yoga instructor and is temporarily unemployed, during which time bills mount up. Unable to pay down his debt, Kevin files for bankruptcy. What will happen to his loans then? *See* 11 U.S.C. § 523(a)(8).

c. What happens if either Kevin or his mother dies before the loans are paid off? *See* 34 C.F.R. § 685.212.

d. Would the answers to these questions be different if Kevin had used a credit card to pay for his tuition?

3. Eric Tipler graduated six months ago from the College of William & Kate. Eric had borrowed $5,500 in Direct Subsidized Loans and $20,500 in Direct Unsubsidized Loans each of his four years in college. He just got his first student loan bill from the Department of Education.

a. How much money was actually disbursed to Eric?

b. How much does Eric owe today? Do you think Eric will be surprised?

c. How much interest will accrue on the loan next month (December), assuming that Eric does not make a payment?

4. The Anna Nicole Beauty Academy, which awards certificates in cosmetology following a one-year course of study. Anna Nicole students also borrow heavily to pay for their education. A typical Anna Nicole graduate has $20,000 in debt. Fifty students have graduated from Anna Nicole for each of the past two years. Their median annual loan payment is $2,400, while their median (and mean) annual earnings are $25,090. The 2017 federal poverty guideline for a single person is $12,060, and all Anna Nicole graduates are unattached.

a. Will Anna Nicole students be able to get Direct Loans in the future? *See* 34 C.F.R. §§ 600.1, 600.2, 600.4(a)(4), 668.403, 668.404(a), 685.102(a)(2).

b. Would your answer change if Anna Nicole Smith Beauty Academy were instead Andrew Jackson Law School, an accredited for-profit law school that awards J.D. and L.L.M. degrees, but with only a 20% bar passage rate for Ol' Hickory graduates? *See* 34 C.F.R. §§ 600.1, 600.2, 600.4(a)(4).

5. Banco Merica has approached Alaska State University with a proposal that all student ID cards issued at Alaska State also operate as Banco Merica debit cards that can be activated with the opening of a Banco Merica deposit account. The ID card would bear both the Alaska State Roarin' Walrus® logo and the Banco Merica Treasure Galleon® logo. Banco Merica has further proposed that Alaska State offer to open a Banco Merica Student Preferred Checking Account whenever a student enrolls, using the electronic enrollment forms to populate the data fields in an electronic account application, and having Alaska State University employees deputized to verify student identification for the bank. In exchange, Banco Merica has offered to pay Alaska State 5% of all revenue from the debit card plus $1 million annually. Banco Merica has some of the highest overdraft fees of any financial institution in the country. As outside counsel to Alaska State, what are your thoughts on this proposal from a legal perspective? *See* 15 U.S.C. § 1650(b)(1)-(2); 20 U.S.C. §§ 1094(a), 1094(e); 34 C.F.R. §§ 668.164(d), 668.164(f).

6. Devin Mauney was happily enrolled as a junior majoring in bookkeeping at Ionic College, a for-profit educational institution, when the school abruptly shut down mid-year after losing its eligibility for funding under the Higher Education Act. Devin had taken out $80,000 in Direct Subsidized and Unsubsidized Loans, as well as a $10,000 private student loan. No other school will give Devin transfer credit for his work at Ionic College, whose lax academic standards were the source of a national scandal. Will Devin have to repay his loans? *See* 34 C.F.R. §§ 685.212, 685.214.

7. Representative Jake Brooks, a former college economics professor, has a long-standing interest in education policy, and having just assumed the chairmanship of the House Committee on Education and Workforce, he finally has a chance to put some of his ideas into action. Concerned about student debt burdens, Rep. Brooks has proposed a bill that would mandate that federal education funding have risk-based pricing based on students' choice of educational institution and course of study.

In the Senate, however, the Chairwoman of the Senate Committee on Health, Education, Pensions, and Labor, Senator Dalié Jimenez has proposed an "equity financing" bill that would allow students to finance their education by pledging a percentage of their future income for an agreed-upon number of years (including for life) in exchange for an education. The idea is that students with greater earnings would pay more than those with fewer earnings. What would be the effects of adopting either of these proposals?

CHAPTER 32

SECONDARY MARKETS

Consumer debt obligations frequently trade in a secondary market. In this secondary market the holders of the debt obligations are the assignees (directly or indirectly) of the original lender. The situations that result in such assignments vary. Some consumer debt assignments are the result of loans that are originated by a nominal lender, such as an auto dealer, but always intended to be transferred to the ultimate, indirect lender. Some of the obligations in the secondary market consist of financial institutions that for one reason or another are selling off performing loan portfolios. Some secondary market obligations consist of debt buyers that purchase defaulted loans. And some secondary market obligations involve securitization transactions.

Secondary markets in consumer debts play two distinct roles. Some secondary markets are the financing channels for consumer loans. This is the case for auto lending and a great deal of securitization. It is also true for rent-a-bank operations in which a non-bank finance company has a standing agreement to purchase loans made by a bank. In these cases, the originating lenders finance loans by selling them and using the proceeds to make more loans. In these situations, the original lenders would not make the loans unless they had a ready market for them; the loans are made on an "originate-to-distribute" model.

Other secondary markets, however, are more incidental. Debt buyers are not providing the financing for loans in the first instance, although they do contribute capital into the market. Instead, they are buying loans that were made without any intention of resale.

When a loan is transferred in the secondary market, the transfer may well affect the consumer. The incentives of the buyer may be different than those of the originator. Moreover, the sale of the loan may affect the management of the loan. This is particularly true for securitization as securitization transactions bifurcate the ownership of the loan from its management or "servicing."

Securitizations are complicated transactions; this chapter does not aim to teach you all of the ins and outs of securitization, but it is necessary to have at least a high-level understanding of it because it is a major source of funding for many of the key consumer finance markets—mortgages, credit cards, auto loans, and student loans. Securitization is a type of financing transaction in which a pool of loans will be transferred by a financial institution to a specially created entity. That entity will pay for the loans by issuing debt securities that are to be repaid out of the collections on the loan. The specially created entity will have no other assets or liabilities of note, so investors in the debt securities will be assuming the risk on the pool of loans, but not on the general assets and liabilities and operating risks of the financial institution that arranged the deal. Securitizations of consumer debt frequently use a trust for the specially created entity, so there will be a trustee with legal title to the securitized assets. The trust will contract with a third party (often the financial institution that arranged the transaction or one of its affiliates) to "service" the loans, meaning to collect payments from the borrowers and otherwise manage the borrower relationships. Thus the borrower may never know that his loan is securitized as the servicing might remain with the original lender, even though most of the economic interest in the loan is transferred to securitization investors. The interests of the servicer, which depend on the servicer's compensation structure, may be substantially different from those of securitization investors and also from those of homeowners, and this divergence of interests can create problems when dealing with defaults on securitized loans. *See* Adam J. Levitin & Tara Twomey, *Mortgage Servicing*, 28 Yale J. Reg. 1 (2011).

Beyond the incentive problems that can arise from secondary market transactions, there is also a key pair of legal questions. To what extent can the borrower raise the defenses it has against enforcement of the loan by the originator against the assignee? And to what extent is the assignee answerable for claims that the borrower has against the originator?

The starting point for thinking about this is the common law. At common law, an assignee is subject to defenses that the obligor has against the assignor. The assignee is also subject to claims in recoupment against the assignor. But the assignee is not subject to other obligor claims against the assignor. The assignee is, of course, always liable for its own behavior.

Several state and federal laws alter this common law picture for different types of consumer financial products. There is a trade-off involved in these laws. To the extent that assignees are subject to defenses and claims, the substantive rights given to borrowers are more meaningful. For example, if the borrower cannot raise claims against an assignee, then the borrower must pay the assignee on the loan and separately look to the assignor to pay on its claim. That means that the borrower will have to pay out money before having any prospect of recovering the funds. Likewise, if the assignee were not subject to defenses that could be raised against the assignor, bad actor assignors could readily "launder" obligations by selling them into the secondary market, with the result that the defenses could not be raised against anyone.

Yet, to the extent that legal doctrines make assignees liable for the misdeeds of loan originators, secondary market players will take greater care when purchasing loans, demand warranties from assignors, and/or demand greater discounts on purchase prices. This, in turn, will presumably affect the prices originators charge borrowers, particularly in markets where the secondary market is providing the financing, and not just incidental liquidity. In other words, legal rights have a cost.

I. HOLDERS IN DUE COURSE AND STATE-LAW ASSIGNEE LIABILITY

Generally speaking, the transfer of loans in the secondary market is governed by UCC Article 3 (negotiation of promissory notes) and/or UCC Articles 1 and 9 (for sales of or security interests in promissory notes, mortgages, and chattel paper).

The technical details of these transfers need not generally concern us here, with one exception: the effect that a transfer via negotiation (but not via sale) has for assignee liability.

The baseline rule of all commercial law is *nemo dat quod non habet*—no one can transfer rights that they do not have. This means that an assignee takes an assignment subject to all defenses that could be raised against the assignor (as well as claims in recoupment).

There is an important exception to the *nemo dat* rule: the holder in due course rule. A **"holder in due course"** is a party that took physical possession of a negotiable instrument that is indorsed to it or to bearer and did so in good faith, without notice of defenses to or flaws in the instrument, and for value. UCC § 3-302.

A holder in due course takes free from so-called personal defenses to enforcement of the instrument that could be raised against the originator of the instrument: breach of contract or breach of warranty, lack of or failure of consideration, fraud in the inducement (that is, when the borrower was induced to contract through deceit, but understood the terms of the instrument), illegality (if voidable), unadjudicated mental incapacity. UCC § 3-305(b). Thus, holder in due course doctrine means that an assignee that is a holder in due course may actually acquire better rights than its assignor.[1]

The holder in due course is still subject to so-called real defenses that could be raised against the originator: forgery, fraud in the execution (also known as fraud in the factum, namely when the signor was not aware of the essential terms of the instrument), some material alterations, bankruptcy discharge, minority, illegality (if void), adjudicated mental incapacity, and extreme duress. UCC § 3-305(b). Holder in due course status does not provide any immunization against the holder's own wrongdoing.

Holder in due course status is only possible if the debt being assigned is evidenced by a negotiable instrument. For a promissory note to be negotiable, it must be an unconditional promise to pay a fixed amount of money (with or without interest or other charges described in the promise) that is (1) payable to either bear or order, (2) payable on demand or at a definite time, and (3) does not contain any other undertaking or instruction beyond payment of money and grants of collateral or waivers of debtor rights. UCC § 3-104.

Certain types of consumer debt instruments, such as home equity lines of credit and payment-option ARMs, where the date of payment or the amount payable is not fixed, are clearly not negotiable instruments, but it is generally doubtful whether any consumer debt instruments currently meet the requirements of negotiability if applied strictly. *See* Ronald J. Mann, *Searching for Negotiability in Credit and Payment Systems*, 44 UCLA L. Rev. 951 (1997).

Nonetheless, industry practice and assumption is that many types of consumer debt—mortgages and auto loans and student loans in particular, but not credit card debt—are negotiable. What this would mean, if correct, is that the buyers of non-defaulted consumer debt—most notably securitization trusts—might qualify as

1. Likewise, under the "shelter rule," a transferee from a holder in due course acquires all of the holder in due course's rights, even if it is not itself a holder in due course. UCC 3-203 cmts. 2, 4.

holders in due course and thus take free from certain defenses to enforcement of the debt.

Although the UCC undoes assignee liability through holder in due course doctrine, other state laws sometimes expressly provide for assignee liability. For example, California's Automobile Sales Finance Act provides that "An assignee of the seller's right is subject to all equities and defenses of the buyer against the seller, notwithstanding an agreement to the contrary, but the assignee's liability may not exceed the amount of the debt owing to the assignee at the time of the assignment." Cal. Civ. Code § 2983.5(a). If the assignee is liable for the assignor's acts, the assignee may implead the assignor. California law likewise prohibits any waiver of claims or defenses against auto loan assignees. Cal Civ. Code § 2983.7.

II. FTC HOLDER IN DUE COURSE RULE

The FTC's Holder in Due Course Rule (formally, the Rule on Preservation of Consumers' Claims and Defenses, but often simply referred to as the Holder Rule), 16 C.F.R. Pt. 433, provides an important curtailment of holder in due course status and also changes the common law rule regarding an assignee's liability for the obligor's claims against the assignor.

The Holder Rule has an unusual form. It does not directly provide that the holder of the debt is in fact subject to the borrower's claims and defenses. Instead, the Holder Rule requires that any seller of goods or services on installment credit to a consumer include in the contract particular language that says that the holder of the promissory note is "subject to" the consumer's claims and defenses, up to the amount paid by the debtor:

> NOTICE
>
> ANY HOLDER OF THIS CONSUMER CREDIT CONTRACT IS SUBJECT TO ALL CLAIMS AND DEFENSES WHICH THE DEBTOR COULD ASSERT AGAINST THE SELLER OF GOODS OR SERVICES OBTAINED PURSUANT HERETO OR WITH THE PROCEEDS HEREOF. RECOVERY HEREUNDER BY THE DEBTOR SHALL NOT EXCEED AMOUNTS PAID BY THE DEBTOR HEREUNDER.

16 C.F.R. § 433.2(a). The inclusion of this mandatory language (effective in 1977) arguably destroyed the negotiability of promissory notes by making the undertaking in the note conditional because it is "subject to" potential defenses.[2] In 1990, the UCC was amended to provide that the Holder Rule statement does not render the promise conditional, but merely prevents there from being a holder in due course of the instrument. UCC § 3-106(d).

---

2. White & Summers Uniform Commercial Code, § 18:25. For an alternative explanation of the effect of the Holder Rule on negotiable instruments, see Michael F. Sturley, *The Legal Impact of the Federal Trade Commission's Holder in Due Course Notice on a Negotiable Instrument: How Clever Are the Rascals at the FTC*, 68 N.C. L. Rev. 953 (1990).

Note that the Holder Rule only applies to installment credit extended *by the seller* in connection with the purchase of goods or services. Third-party financing is not covered by the rule, so third-party auto loans are not covered. Similarly, the Holder Rule excludes credit cards (third-party financing), and also mortgages (not goods or services). Query whether the rule would apply to student loans made by an educational institution itself.

The effect of the Holder Rule is not merely to defeat holder in due course status for assignees. Merely defeating holder in due course status would mean that the assignee was liable for all defenses that could be raised against the seller, but for claims against the seller. The Holder Rule, however, also makes assignees liable for all that could be raised against the seller, although the assignee's liability in both cases is limited to the amount paid on the contract plus forfeiture of the remaining balance.

While the Holder Rule does not apply to many types of debt, when it does apply it helps borrowers in a few ways. First, because it lets borrowers raise defenses based on the seller's behavior against the holder, it gives borrowers more grounds on which to defend collection actions. Second, by allowing the borrower to bring claims against the seller against the holder, it also enables borrowers to bring counterclaims to collection actions. And third, if the seller is judgment proof, the borrower may still have a remedy from the holder.

III. TILA ASSIGNEE LIABILITY LIMITATIONS

The FTC's Holder Rule applies to all installment credit from sellers of goods and services. The Truth in Lending Act, however, contains a pair of additional assignee liability rules.

First, TILA contains a provision we saw in Chapter 20 regarding the liability of card issuers for claims and defenses that could be raised against merchants. Recall that in a credit card transaction, the consumer's payment obligation to the merchant is sold from the merchant to its acquirer and then to the card issuer. Credit cards are not negotiable instruments and they are excluded from the FTC's Holder in Due Course Rule because they are not seller financing, but card issuers are subject as a matter of common law to all defenses and claims in recoupment that could be raised by the consumer against a merchant. Moreover, under TILA, card issuers are also subject to all non-tort claims as well as all defenses that a consumer could raise against a merchant (that would include statutory claims, such as UDAP claims), 15 U.S.C. § 1666i, although this statutory provision is subject to certain limitations discussed in Chapter 20.

Second, TILA has a more general provision that restricts assignee liability for TILA claims. The general TILA assignability rule is that any TILA violation may be brought against an assignee of the original creditor "only if the violation for which such action or proceeding is brought is apparent on the face of the disclosure statement, except where the assignment was involuntary." 15 U.S.C. § 1641. TILA provides that:

> a violation apparent on the face of the disclosure statement includes, but is not limited to . . . a disclosure which can be determined to be incomplete or inaccurate from the face of the disclosure statement or other documents assigned, or . . . a disclosure which does not use the terms required to be used by [TILA].

15 U.S.C. § 1641(a). An assignee may generally rely on written acknowledgement by a borrower that a disclosure was made. 15 U.S.C. § 1641(b).

There is a quintet of important exceptions to the TILA assignee liability rule. First, the TILA right of rescission for mortgages is unaffected by the assignee liability limitation. 15 U.S.C. § 1641(b)-(c). In other words, a mortgage may be rescinded no matter who holds the note. Second, assignees of HOEPA mortgages are generally excluded from the TILA limitation on assignee liability. 15 U.S.C. § 1641(d). A HOEPA loan's assignee must prove by a preponderance of the evidence that a reasonable person exercising ordinary due diligence could not determine on the basis of the loan documentation that it was in fact a HOEPA loan. Third, assignees remain liable for the ability-to-repay foreclosure defense by way of setoff or recoupment (but not for an affirmative ability-to-repay violation). 15 U.S.C. § 1640(k)(1). Assignees may still shelter in the qualified mortgage safeharbor, however. 15 U.S.C. § 1639c(b)(1). Fourth, mortgage servicers are not treated as assignees unless the servicer is or was the owner of the obligation. 15 U.S.C. § 1641(f). An assignment to the servicer for administrative convenience in a foreclosure does not count as an assignment for TILA liability purposes. This means that mortgage servicers are not answerable for wrongdoings of loan originators. If a loan is securitized, however, the securitization entity, which owns the loan and employs the servicer, would be subject to the TILA assignee liability rule. Finally, TILA requires that upon assignment of any mortgage loan, the new owner must notify the borrower in writing of the transfer within 30 days and include various contact information. 15 U.S.C. § 1641(g). Failure to do so is a free-standing TILA violation for the assignee.

It's easy to miss the forest for the trees here in two ways. First, the TILA assignee liability limitation applies only to TILA claims. It does not govern claims brought under other statutes, including state statutory claims, state UDAP claims, and federal UDAAP claims. Whether a party has liability under those statutes by virtue of merely having purchased a consumer obligation is another matter, but if an assignee has assisted in the design of a consumer financial product, such as setting the underwriting parameters, it would seem to fit within the definition of "service provider" under 12 U.S.C. § 5481(26)(a)(i) as a party that "participates in designing. . .the consumer financial product or service" and thus to have potential UDAAP liability under 12 U.S.C. § 5536.

Second, assignee liability extends only to assignees. It does not extend to shareholders (who are protected by limited liability) or to creditors of the consumer's creditor, even if they are providing the ultimate financing for the loan. Thus, if Firm *X* were to borrow funds from investors *A*, *B*, and *C*, investors *A*, *B*, and *C* would not be assignees, but creditors of Firm *X*, and therefore they would not have potential assignee liability. But the devil here may be in the details. Suppose that Firm *X* had no liabilities except to *A*, *B*, and *C*, and that its liabilities were equal to (or greater than) the expected value of Firm *X*'s assets (which are all consumer loans).

In other words, Firm *X* has no real equity value. In such a situation, it is difficult to distinguish from an economic perspective the creditor-debtor relationship with an assignment, particularly if *A*, *B*, and *C* have voice in the management of Firm *X*'s assets.

In the securitization context this is particularly important. Securitizations involve a series of assignments of loans from the originating creditor to a securitization entity that issues securities backed by the collections on the loans. Assignee liability, to the extent it exists, would normally apply throughout the entire securitization chain. But it does not extend beyond the securitization entity in normal circumstances. The investors in the securitization are shielded by virtue of being either creditors or equity investors in the securitization entity. To the extent that the securitization entity is liable, the investors in the securitization may have smaller returns, but they do not generally face direct liability themselves.

How does the TILA assignee liability limitation interact with the FTC Holder in Due Course rule? The following case takes up the issue.

Walker v. Wallace Auto Sales

155 F.3d 927 (7th Cir. 1998)

Ripple, Circuit Judge.

Carl and Margaret Walker ("the Walkers") brought this lawsuit against Wallace Auto Sales ("Wallace") and Guardian National Acceptance Corporation ("Guardian") on behalf of themselves and all others similarly situated. In their nine-count amended complaint, the Walkers alleged that the defendants systematically imposed hidden finance charges on automobile purchases in violation of the Truth in Lending Act ("TILA"), 15 U.S.C. §§ 1601-1693r, the Racketeer Influenced and Corrupt Organizations Act ("RICO"), 18 U.S.C. §§ 1961-1968, the Illinois Consumer Fraud Act, 815 ILCS 505/2, and the Illinois Sales Finance Agency Act, 205 ILCS 660/8.5. The district court dismissed the Walkers' TILA claim because the conduct alleged by the Walkers did not constitute a violation of that Act. In addition, the court dismissed the Walkers' remaining claims because, in its view, those claims could not survive in the absence of the TILA violation. For the reasons set forth in the following opinion, we reverse the district court's dismissal of the Walkers' TILA claim against Wallace, affirm its dismissal of the TILA claim against Guardian and remand the Walkers' remaining claims to the district court for further consideration.

I. BACKGROUND

A. Facts

On August 31, 1995, the Walkers agreed to purchase a used 1989 Lincoln Continental from Wallace. In order to finance this purchase, the Walkers entered into a retail

2. According to the August 1995 "Blue Book" used car guide, the car purchased by the Walkers had a retail value of $8,300.

installment contract ("the contract") with Wallace. The contract listed the cash price of the automobile as $14,040.[2]

In addition to that amount, the Walkers agreed to pay $699 for an extended warranty and $61 for license, title and taxes. The Walkers made a down payment of $1,500, leaving $13,300 as the amount to be financed on the sales contract. The Walkers agreed to finance this balance at an annual percentage rate of 25% over a period of four years (48 monthly installments of $441 each). Under these terms, the Walkers were to pay $7,868 in interest over the course of those four years, giving the sales contract a total value of $21,168. All of this information was clearly delineated on the face of the contract.

After the sale was complete, Wallace promptly assigned the contract to Guardian, "a specialized indirect consumer finance company engaged primarily in financing the purchase of automobiles through the acquisition of retail installment contracts from automobile dealers." Guardian purchased the contract at a discount of $7,182 from the total value.

. . .

II. DISCUSSION

. . .

A. The Walkers' TILA Claim

. . .

In this case, the Walkers allege that the defendants violated TILA by artificially inflating the "cash price" of the vehicle purchased by the Walkers to cover the cost of the discount at which Guardian purchased the Walkers' sales contract. The Walkers contend that, by passing on the cost of Guardian's discount to the Walkers, the defendants imposed a "hidden finance charge" on them in violation of TILA, 15 U.S.C. § 1638 (a)(3). The defendants, however, contend that the Walkers' TILA claim must be dismissed because the "hidden finance charge" alleged by the Walkers was in fact a "cost of doing business" and was therefore exempt from TILA's disclosure requirements. See 12 C.F.R. Pt. 226, Supp. I at 308-09.

As an initial matter, we note that, under TILA, Guardian may only be charged as an assignee, not a creditor. *See* 15 U.S.C. § 1602(f); 12 C.F.R. Pt. 226, Supp. I at 300. Accordingly, the Walkers must properly allege a cause of action against Wallace (the creditor) before it can assert a claim against Guardian (the assignee). We therefore turn first to the issue of whether the Walkers' amended complaint states a valid TILA claim against Wallace.

1. Wallace's Liability

. . .TILA requires creditors to disclose clearly and accurately any finance charge that the consumer will bear in a particular credit transaction. As the definitions set forth above indicate, this means that a creditor-merchant must disclose to a consumer buying on credit exactly how much he will pay for that credit. *See* 12 C.F.R. § 226.4(a) (defining finance charge as "the cost of consumer credit as a dollar amount"). In this case, the Walkers allege that Wallace is charging higher prices to customers who are buying cars on credit than to customer who are paying cash. In other words, credit customers, such as the Walkers, are paying higher "cash" prices only because they are buying on credit. The higher cash price paid by these customers is therefore part of the cost of buying on credit. Under TILA, such a cost is a finance charge and must be disclosed to the consumer as such. Accordingly, we conclude that the Walkers have alleged sufficient facts to state a cause of action against Wallace under TILA.

. . .

Moreover, our conclusion is further strengthened by this court's recent decision in *Gibson v. Bob Watson Chevrolet-Geo, Inc.*, 112 F.3d 283 (7th Cir. 1997). In that case, we consolidated three appeals from district court decisions dismissing claims that car dealers violated TILA by charging higher prices for warranties in credit transactions than in cash transactions. Specifically, the plaintiffs alleged that the difference between the price of the warranty in credit transactions and the price of the warranty in cash transactions constituted a finance charge that must be disclosed under TILA. In assessing the plaintiffs' allegations, we concluded that the dealers' alleged concealment of credit costs in the warranty price circumvented the objectives of TILA by preventing consumers from accurately gauging the cost of credit.

Indeed, in reversing the district courts' dismissals of plaintiffs' lawsuits, we stressed that the dealers' alleged conduct constituted the "type of fraud that goes to the heart of the concerns that actuate the Truth in Lending Act." *Id.* The same can be said of Wallace's alleged practices in this case. Instead of hiding the additional finance charges in the price of warranties, Wallace allegedly hid a portion of the finance charge in the "cash" price of the cars sold to credit customers. This fraud is no different from that alleged in *Gibson*—in both cases, the dealers allegedly misled the consumers about the true cost of buying on credit.

. . .

In their amended complaint, the Walkers allege that Wallace passed on the cost of the discount imposed by Guardian, that this cost was passed on in credit transactions only and that Wallace failed to disclose it as a finance charge. At this early stage in the proceedings, these allegations are sufficient to prevent the dismissal of the Walkers' TILA claim against Wallace. In order to prevail in the end, however, the Walkers will have to prove their allegation that Wallace separately imposed the cost of Guardian's discount on them. . . .[T]he commentary to Regulation Z makes it clear that it is permissible for a car dealer to assign retail installment contracts to a finance company at a discount, without disclosing the discount to customers. *See* 12 C.F.R. Pt. 226, Supp. I at 308-09. Moreover, the commentary specifically provides that a "charge directly or indirectly imposed by a creditor" is not considered to be a finance charge if the charge "is imposed uniformly in both cash and credit transactions." 12 C.F.R. § 226.4(a) & Pt. 226, Supp. I at 308. Accordingly, Wallace need not disclose the cost of the discount as a finance charge if it attempts to recoup that cost by charging all customers higher prices. Under that scenario, the discounts would not be "separately imposed" on credit consumers like the Walkers, but, like any other overhead item, would be taken into account in the price of all vehicles sold.

Finally, in arriving at the holding we reach today, we stress that nothing in the law prevents a merchant-creditor from passing on the full cost of a discount imposed by an assignee to a credit purchaser. However, if the merchant-creditor chooses this route, TILA requires that it disclose that amount to the purchaser as a finance charge.

2. *Guardian's Liability*

Because we have concluded that the Walkers have stated a claim against Wallace under TILA, we must consider whether they have stated a claim against Guardian.

As we noted earlier, under TILA, Guardian may only be charged as an assignee, not a creditor. Section 131 of TILA, 15 U.S.C. § 1641, limits the liability of subsequent assignees to those situations in which the violation of TILA is "apparent on the face of the disclosure statement." That section provides in pertinent part:

> *Liability of assignees*
> *(a) Prerequisites*
> Except as otherwise specifically provided in this subchapter, any civil action for a violation of this subchapter or proceeding under section 1607 of this title which may be brought against a creditor may be maintained against any assignee of such creditor only if the violation for which such action or proceeding is brought is apparent on the face of the disclosure statement, except where the assignment was involuntary. For the purpose of this section, a violation apparent on the face of the disclosure statement includes, but is not limited to (1) a disclosure which can be determined to be incomplete or inaccurate from the face of the disclosure statement or other documents assigned, or (2) a disclosure which does not use the terms required to be used by this subchapter.

Id.

The Walkers advance two arguments as to why their amended complaint sufficiently states a TILA claim for assignee liability against Guardian. First, the Walkers contend that the limitations on assignee liability in § 131(a) are inapplicable in this case because Guardian is bound by the terms of the retail installment contract it purchased from Wallace. That contract repeats the language of the FTC's Holder Notice (as 16 C.F.R. § 433.2 requires) which provides:

> ANY HOLDER OF THIS CONSUMER CREDIT CONTRACT IS SUBJECT TO ALL CLAIMS AND DEFENSES WHICH THE DEBTOR COULD ASSERT AGAINST THE SELLER OF GOODS OR SERVICES OBTAINED PURSUANT HERETO OR WITH THE PROCEEDS HEREOF. RECOVERY HEREUNDER BY THE DEBTOR SHALL NOT EXCEED AMOUNTS PAID BY THE DEBTOR HEREUNDER.

Id. In the Walkers' view, this provision subjects the holder (Guardian) to "all claims" which the consumer (the Walkers) has against the seller (Wallace), including violations of TILA. In the alternative, the Walkers assert that Guardian is liable under § 131 because Wallace's violation of TILA is apparent on the face of the sales contract. Specifically, in their amended complaint, the Walkers allege that "Guardian is conscious of the fact that the dealer has a strong incentive to pass the discount onto the customer." The Walkers contend that this allegation, combined with their allegation that the purported "cash price" of the vehicle was substantially in excess of its true value, is sufficient to state a TILA claim for assignee liability against Guardian. In short, they maintain that, given Guardian's knowledge of Wallace's incentive to pass the cost of the discount on to its credit customers, Guardian could discern from the exorbitant "cash price" appearing on the face of the sales contract that Wallace had concealed a portion of the finance charge in the cash price.

We turn first to the Walkers' contention that they may maintain a TILA action against Guardian due to the inclusion of the FTC's Holder Notice in their contract with Wallace. In essence, the Walkers assert that, when Guardian accepted the assignment, it voluntarily waived any right to rely on the statutory defense provided by § 131(a). This court recently addressed this very issue in *Taylor v. Quality Hyundai, Inc.*, 150 F.3d 689, 693 (7th Cir. 1998). In that case, the court held that the inclusion of the FTC's Holder Notice in a retail installment contract did not trump the clear command of § 131 that subsequent assignees can be held liable under TILA only when the violation is apparent on the face of the disclosure statement. *See id.* (citing *Robbins v. Bentsen*, 41 F.3d 1195, 1198 (7th Cir. 1994) ("Regulations cannot trump the plain language of statutes . . . .")).

Given our conclusion that the inclusion of the FTC's Holder Notice in the Walkers' sale contract does not override the limitations on assignee liability in § 131, we turn to the Walkers' contention that Guardian may nonetheless be held liable under § 131 because, given Guardian's "knowledge" of Wallace's practices, Wallace's failure to disclose a portion of the finance charge was apparent on the face of the Walkers' retail installment contract. Again, this contention is answered by *Taylor*. In that case, the plaintiffs argued "that the apparentness (or lack thereof) of a violation should be ascertained in light of the knowledge that a reasonable assignee similarly situated to the defendants should have." 150 F.3d at 694. In the *Taylor* plaintiffs' view, the assignees, "as active participants in the financing market," know that creditors often hide finance charges in other items (in that case, the price of an extended warranty, in this case, the "cash price" of the automobile) and therefore must have known that the contracts issued to the plaintiffs contained hidden finance charges. The court rejected the plaintiffs' argument and held that, under the plain wording of the statute, an assignee can be held liable only if the violation is apparent on the face of the documents assigned. *See id.*

In addition to the argument based on Guardian's knowledge of industry practices, the Walkers assert that the TILA violation was apparent on the face of the disclosure statement due to the fact that the "cash price" of the vehicle purchased by the Walkers was substantially in excess of the vehicle's actual value. This argument is also without merit. One cannot assume that Guardian could tell from the face of the sales contract that the auto was overpriced; more importantly, even if Guardian did know that the vehicle was overpriced, such knowledge cannot be equated with knowledge that Wallace was burying a portion of the finance charge in the price of the vehicle.

Finally, even if the Walkers' amended complaint could be construed to allege that Guardian had actual knowledge of Wallace's practice of disguising finance charges, such allegations are not sufficient, under the plain wording of the statute, to state a TILA claim for assignee liability against Guardian. Instead, the Walkers must allege that the violation was "apparent on the face" of the assigned documents. The Walkers do not, and cannot, make such an allegation. Accordingly, we hold that the Walkers have failed to state a TILA claim against Guardian.

B. The Walkers' RICO and State Law Based Claims

In addition to their TILA claim against Wallace and Guardian, the Walkers' amended complaint contains eight other counts alleging that Wallace, Guardian and certain unnamed officers of those companies ("John Does 1-10") violated RICO and two Illinois consumer protection statutes. As we noted earlier, these remaining counts are based on the same factual predicate as the Walkers' TILA claim. Once the district court determined that the Walkers had failed to state a claim under TILA, it dismissed the remaining claims because, in its view, those claims could not survive in the absence of a TILA violation. The court did not independently assess the sufficiency of the Walkers' allegations in the remaining counts.

Because the district court did not reach the issue of whether the plaintiffs' remaining claims are viable and the parties have not briefed that issue on appeal, we remand that issue to the district court for its consideration in the first instance.

In returning these counts to the district court, we also leave for that court's consideration in the first instance the issue of whether, despite the fact that Guardian cannot be held liable as an assignee under TILA, the Walkers may still be able to allege that Guardian had a level of knowledge compatible with liability under RICO (Count II), the Illinois Consumer Fraud Act (Counts VII & VIII) and the Illinois Sales Finance Agency Act (Count IX).

CONCLUSION

We reverse the district court's judgment dismissing the Walkers' TILA claim (Count I) against Wallace, but affirm the dismissal of the TILA claim against Guardian. We also remand the remaining counts (Counts II through IX) to the district court for further consideration consistent with this opinion.

Problem Set 32

Douglas Rand bought a Honda Civic from Rockwell Honda. Douglas paid for the car with a loan from Rockwell Honda. A week after the loan was made, Rockwell Honda assigned the loan to American Honda Finance Corporation (AHFC) (a wholly owned subsidiary of American Honda Motor Corp.). Before making the loan to Douglas, Rockwell Honda had submitted Douglas's loan application to AHFC for approval. American Honda Finance indicated that given Douglas's creditworthiness, it would purchase the loan only if it had a certain minimum interest rate (the "buy rate") and terms. Rockwell Honda made the loan to Douglas at 200 basis points over the minimum "buy rate" indicated by AHFC, and was therefore paid more by AHFC for the loan.

AHFC subsequently assigned Douglas's loan to its wholly owned subsidiary, American Honda Receivables LLC, which in turn then assigned the loan to Citibank, N.A., as Owner Trustee for the Honda Auto Receivables 2016-2 Owner Trust, in exchange for four classes of notes and owner certificates (representing the residual interest in the trust). AHFC ultimately retained the certificates but sold the notes in a registered securities offering pursuant to a trust indenture, with U.S. Bank National Association as indenture trustee for the noteholders. Some of the notes were purchased by the California Public Employees Retirement System. AHFC was also contracted to serve as servicer for the loan by the Honda Auto Receivables 2016-2 Owner Trust. The transaction is depicted graphically below.

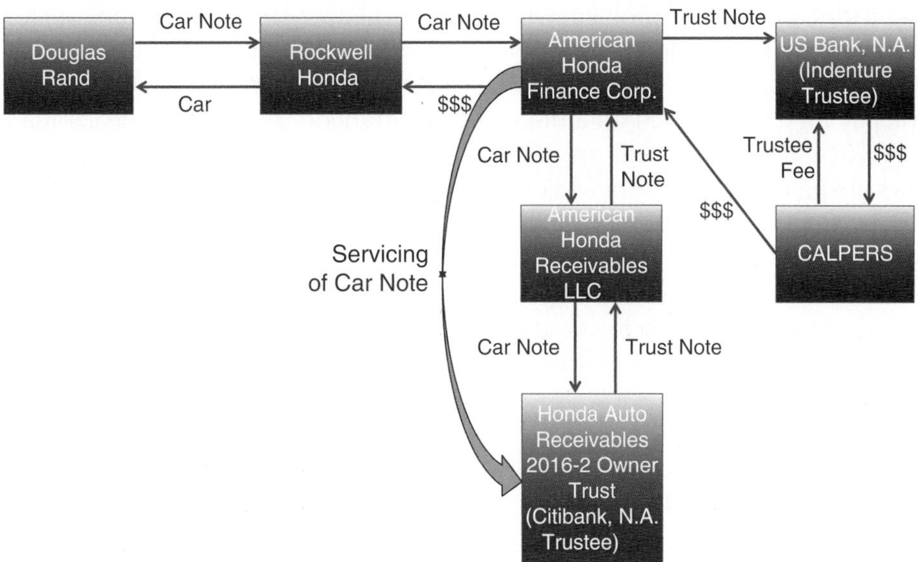

1. The vehicle Douglas purchased broke down after a month, and Rockwell Honda refused to honor the vehicle's warranty, claiming that the problem was due to Douglas's bad driving. Douglas therefore stopped paying on the loan and was promptly sued by AHFC as servicer for the Honda Auto Receivables 2016-2 Owner Trust. Can Douglas raise the breach of warranty as a defense against AHFC? *See* UCC §§ 1-201(b)(21), 3-302, 2-305.

2. Now suppose that Douglas was tricked into buying the car based on misleading promises from the salesperson at Rockwell Honda regarding the gas mileage. Douglas therefore stopped paying on the loan and was promptly sued by AHFC as servicer for the Honda Auto Receivables 2016-2 Owner Trust. Can Douglas raise fraud as a defense against AHFC? *See* UCC §§ 1-201(b)(21), 3-302, 2-305.

3. Douglas is lucky. His cousin, Courtney Weiner, a sharp-eyed consumer attorney, is representing him. Courtney noticed that there was a Truth in Lending Act violation on the loan—the APR was miscalculated on the disclosures and was outside the acceptable error tolerance range. When Douglas brings a counterclaim and impleader for both a TILA violation and fraud, which of the following entities are potentially liable? *See* 15 U.S.C. § 1641.

a. Rockwell Honda
b. AHFC
c. American Honda Motor Corporation
d. American Honda Receivables LLC
e. Citibank, N.A., as Owner Trustee for the Honda Auto Receivables 2016-02 Owner Trust
f. California Public Employees Retirement System
g. U.S. Bank National Association, as Indenture Trustee for the Honda Auto Receivables 2016-02 Notes

4. It turns out that the problem with Douglas's paperwork wasn't the only issue with loans made by Honda dealerships. The CFPB has alleged that AHFC has violated the Equal Credit Opportunity Act by allowing dealers to charge a dealer markup over what it will pay for a loan, based on a disparate impact theory because the dealer markups charged to minority borrowers are higher than those charged to other borrowers. Which parties are potentially liable for an ECOA violation in this context? *See* 15 U.S.C. § 1641.

- **a.** Rockwell Honda
- **b.** AHFC
- **c.** American Honda Motor Corporation
- **d.** American Honda Receivables LLC
- **e.** Citibank, N.A., as Owner Trustee for the Honda Auto Receivables 2016-02 Owner Trust
- **f.** California Public Employees Retirement System
- **g.** U.S. Bank National Association, as Indenture Trustee for the Honda Auto Receivables 2016-02 Notes

---

CHAPTER 33

DEBT COLLECTION I: FAIR DEBT COLLECTION PRACTICES ACT

The consumer finance industry is a complex ecosystem of firms that provide American consumers with historically unparalleled convenience and ease of access to credit. This ecosystem contains both firms that make loans directly to consumers—lenders—and firms that collect those debts—collectors. Lenders and collectors exist in a symbiotic relationship that is necessary for the efficiency and accessibility of consumer credit markets.

The consumer credit system can function only if consumer debts are collectible with reasonable ease. If collection of consumer debts were to become too onerous, the result would be a reduction in credit availability, particularly for higher-risk—and often economically more vulnerable—consumers. At the same time, consumer debtors are often particularly exposed to sharp and aggressive collection practices. Laws regulating debt collection attempt to find a medium balancing business and consumer interests.

In the typical cycle of consumer credit, money is lent, collected (with interest and fees), and then re-lent. The interest and fees pay for the operational costs of the lender and the time value of the funds, offset losses that the lender may incur, and provide a sufficient profit margin to induce the investment. If the losses rise, then the balance in the credit ecosystem is upset. To return to an equilibrium, the lender must reduce operational costs, reduce its profit margins, or raise interest and fees on future borrowers. If the lender is operating reasonably efficiently, it may not be able to meaningfully reduce operational costs, while if profit margins are reduced, the lender may not find the lending to be a sufficiently attractive use of its capital.

Thus, there is a reasonable likelihood that the lender will pass on the cost of losses to future borrowers, to the extent the market will bear. Accordingly, the collectability of consumer debts is essential for making the consumer credit system work as it does for the benefit of hundreds of millions of Americans.

I. DEBT COLLECTION IN AND OUT OF THE COURTS

Debt collection works differently for unsecured creditors (those who do not have a lien on specific collateral property of the debtor) and secured creditors. In the world of consumer finance secured creditors are largely limited to auto and vehicle title lenders, mortgage lenders, pawn lenders, and retail installment lenders. Student loans, most credit cards, payday loans, and signature loans are all unsecured, as well as most other consumer debt. (Recall that the FTC Credit Practices Rule prohibits most non-possessory non-purchase money security interests in personal property.)

Unsecured creditors have two ways of collecting: moral suasion—that is, convincing debtors to repay voluntarily—and compelling repayment through the courts. Within the realm of moral suasion there are different techniques used. Some collectors try to guilt, wheedle, or coax the consumer into making a payment on the debt. Others try to use implied threats to encourage repayment, despite legal limitations on this sort of behavior. It is important to keep in mind that there are no self-help rights for unsecured creditors. An unsecured creditor cannot seize a debtor's assets absent a court judgment, and even then there are procedures that must be followed.

Judicial debt collection involves going to court and getting a judgment against the debtor. In some cases the next step is to use court officers to collect on the judgment, but in other cases the judgment is used as leverage to induce a voluntary payment, combining judicial collection and moral suasion.

Both moral suasion and judicial debt collection start with the same problem: locating the debtor. Moral suasion requires contacting the debtor, whether by phone, mail, or other means of communication, and that necessitates having a phone number or address of some sort. Likewise, any sort of judicial debt collection requires service of process. That too requires being able to locate the debtor. Sometimes locating the debtor is quite easy, but other times, especially with older debts, it has challenges, and not all debtors want to be found. Thus, a foundational part of debt collection work is simply finding the debtor. This process is known as **skip tracing**, with the debtor referred to as the "skip." In an increasingly digital age, there are numerous databases that skip tracers can use to locate debtors, but the possibility of misidentification remains, especially when debtors are identified with partial Social Security numbers or with name and date of birth.

The precise procedures for debt collection through the courts vary by court system. Few consumer debts other than mortgages trigger federal jurisdiction because they do not involve federal questions and the amount in controversy is less than the $75,000 federal diversity jurisdiction threshold, so state court is where most consumer debt collection actions occur. State law provides not only the basis for consumer obligations—contract law—but also the procedural requirements for judicial debt collection, including issues like service of process and for certain non-judicial collections.

A. Unsecured Debts

While state procedure varies, it generally adheres to the following outline. First a creditor must file a lawsuit and obtain a judgment. Obtaining a judgment is a slow and expensive process, especially if the judgment is contested. In federal court it takes a minimum of 21 days to get an uncontested judgment under the Federal Rules of Civil Procedure. A party has 21 days to answer a complaint. Fed. R. Civ. Proc. 12(a)(1). If there is no answer, then the plaintiff may move for a default judgment. Fed. R. Civ. Proc. 55. A contested judgment can easily take a year or longer to achieve with motion practice, discovery, and court calendars; some litigation can drag on for over a decade.

Once the unsecured creditor has gotten a judgment, the unsecured creditor becomes a **judgment creditor**. This is the first step toward collection, but a judgment creditor cannot collect immediately on the judgment. Instead, it must wait for the debtor to have a chance to appeal. In federal court this means a minimum of ten days' wait after a final judgment before proceeding to collection while the debtor can determine whether to appeal, and a longer time if judgment is stayed pending resolution of the appeal, as it often is.

After exhaustion of all appeals, a judgment creditor can try to collect on the court judgment either by **garnishing** the debtor's funds or by **levying** or **executing** on the debtor's property under a writ of execution. Garnishment involves obtaining a court order directing a third party that owes money to a debtor, such as a bank or an employer, to pay the money to the garnishing judgment creditor instead of to the debtor. To levy or execute on the debtor's property means having a law enforcement officer (typically a sheriff or U.S. Marshal) seize and sell the debtor's property pursuant to a writ of execution, with the sale proceeds going to the levying creditor. (The specific procedures and their names vary locally, but do not concern us here.) Once the sheriff or marshal has seized a debtor's property, but before the property is sold, the unsecured creditor becomes a **judgment lien creditor**, which gives the creditor enhanced rights in that particular property—the creditor has a lien on the seized (but not yet sold) property to secure its judgment.

Collection for unsecured creditors is a costly and time-consuming procedure, and it can often be frustrated by the debtor. For natural person debtors, some property is **exempt** by statute from levy. Every state has an **exemption statute** that protects some property from creditors' collection. Exemptions can range from meager amounts of clothing and personal items to unlimited protection of homes from non-mortgage creditors. Federal law, and sometimes state law, imposes limitations on wage garnishment (discussed below). Moreover, the debtor can conceal or move or encumber non-exempt property, making it difficult to find enough property to satisfy the judgment. Even if a debtor is not recalcitrant in paying on a judgment, that is no guarantee of repayment, as the unsecured creditor may be competing with other creditors for repayment from the debtor's limited assets.

B. Secured Debts

Secured creditors may collect through moral suasion or the courts, but they also often have a right to self-help repossession and sale of their collateral. Secured creditors have a lien on certain property of the debtor, known as collateral. A lien is a contingent property right: it is the right to have an obligation satisfied from the proceeds of a forced sale of the collateral property *if* the debtor does not repay the obligation secured by the lien. The lien secures the debt, but the lien is a property right separate and distinct from the debt. The lien gives the secured creditor special rights *only as to the specified collateral*, not as to the rest of the debtor's assets.

As a general matter, a secured creditor may exercise its rights through a self-help repossession of the collateral. Upon default and without a court order, the secured creditor may seize its collateral as long as it does not breach the peace; the state maintains the monopoly on violence. (The repossession process is different for real estate collateral; there is no right to self-help repossession for real estate, as discussed in Chapter 28.) The secured creditor must then either sell the collateral in any commercially reasonable manner or, if the debtor does not object, the secured creditor may keep the property in satisfaction of the debt. This sale is called a **foreclosure sale**. (As discussed in Chapter 28, foreclosure sales in roughly half of states are typically conducted judicially, while the rest have private sales.) The sale forecloses (eliminates) the debtor's equitable right to redeem the collateral by paying off the loan balance. (Some states have a post-sale statutory right of redemption for real property. This is distinct from the pre-sale equitable right of redemption.)

A secured creditor's collection rights may give it an accelerated collection procedure, but only for its collateral; there is no guarantee that the collateral will be enough to pay off the balance of the debt. If a deficiency is owed it must be collected judicially or through moral suasion, and deficiencies are sometimes prohibited by state law.

II. THE DEBT COLLECTION INDUSTRY

Frequently, lenders will collect debts themselves. Lenders will also often place debts for collection on a contingency fee basis—collectors keep a percentage of the any debts collected, but the debts remain on the books on the lender. However, for a variety of reasons—liquidity, regulatory accounting, and customer relations among them—lenders will sell consumer debts to third-party collectors. Sometimes the sale of consumer debts to third-party collectors takes the form of securitization, with consumer debts being sold to trusts that collect them for the benefit of the investors that fund the trusts. Sometimes the sale of consumer debts takes the form of sales to specialty debt collection firms. Indeed, the majority of consumer debt today is sold by lenders to third parties—primarily securitization trusts, but also specialty debt collection firms.

These third-party debt collection firms are often more efficient at collections than the original lenders. FTC, *The Structure and Practices of the Debt Buying Industry*, Jan. 2013, at 11. They frequently have greater expertise in collections, such as familiarity with consumer payment patterns and knowledge of local legal requirements for collection. *Id.* They also often have specialized collections technology for skip tracing and for gauging borrower ability to repay. *Id.*

These efficiencies in collections help reduce total credit losses within the consumer credit ecosystem, which resounds to the benefit of consumers as a whole. As the Federal Trade Commission has observed, "by reducing the losses that creditors incur in providing credit, debt collection also allows creditors to provide more credit at lower prices—that is at lower interest rates." *Id.*

Debt collectors have been around since time immemorial. Traditionally, most debt collection was done on a contingency fee basis, with debts "assigned for collection," meaning that the debt might be legally assigned, but the assignment would be for a share of the collection proceeds, so that the collectors would keep the remaining share of the collection proceeds. (Contingency fees tend to be around 25%-33% of the debt amount.)

Debt collection remained a fairly small-scale and local business through the 1960s, just as consumer credit markets remained highly local, operating through banks that were restricted in interstate lending and retail credit. Technological advances in the 1970s—particularly the invention of the automatic telephone dialer (the "autodialer") started to enable more aggressive collection techniques, and the main federal debt collection law, dating from 1977, was a response to the development of larger-scale collection enterprises, often operating interstate.

The development of large-scale debt collection businesses is a fairly recent phenomenon that arose out of the Savings and Loan crisis. A federal entity called the Resolution Trust Corporation (RTC) took over the assets of many failing savings and loans. The RTC thus found itself with billions of dollars of non-performing loans on its hands. The RTC's solution was to auction off the loans to allow others to try to collect on them. The RTC eventually sold over $500 billion in non-performing loans. The RTC's success showed that there was a market for non-performing loans, and lenders started selling their own non-performing loans directly. At the same time, the credit card market expanded, as the use of risk-based pricing made it possible to offer credit to riskier borrowers. The result was an ongoing expansion in the number of non-performing loans, with lenders that were eager to get the loans off their books because of changes in bank regulatory accounting standards. This same dynamic continues to sustain the debt collection industry, as debt buyers now complement traditional contingency fee debt collectors.

There are numerous participants in both sides of the debt collection business—debt buyers and contingency fee collectors (including collection law firms). While there are many small firms involved, the industry is fairly concentrated, especially among debt buyers, with some of the largest firms being publicly traded. In 2008, 76% of all debt sold was to nine large buyers. FTC, *The Structure and Practices of the Debt Buying Industry*, Jan. 2013, at 14.

The debt buyer business is primarily in credit card debt. In 2008 75% or more of debt sales were of credit card debt. *Id.* at 13. The contingency fee collection business is more diverse in the debts it deals with, including medical debts, health club membership debts, etc. Debt buyers buy primarily "charged-off" debt from banks. Some collectors even have standing arrangements akin to outputs contracts to purchase all charged-off debt meeting particular parameters from particular banks.

"Charged-off" debt refers to obligations that federally regulated depository institutions are not permitted to count as assets for bank regulatory capital purposes. Federally regulated depository institutions (colloquially, banks) are subject to minimum capital requirements. Virtually every depository institution in the

United States is subject to these capital requirements by virtue of having federal deposit insurance, Federal Reserve system membership, or a federal bank charter. These banks must maintain a minimum amount of equity capital relative to their risk-weighted assets. Assets and equity are calculated, in the first instance, according to the banks' balance sheets as computed using generally accepted accounting principles (GAAP).

A "charge-off" is a *regulatory* accounting treatment. It is not part of GAAP accounting, and it applies solely to federally regulated depository institutions. A charged-off debt is not forgiven. The charged-off debt is still owed, but it may not be carried as an asset on a bank's balance sheets for purposes of calculating the bank's capital requirements.

Banks are subject to the Uniform Retail Credit Classification and Account Management Policy (URCCAMP) promulgated by the Federal Financial Institutions Examination Council, the coordinating body for federal bank regulators. Federal Financial Institutions Examination Council, Uniform Retail Credit Classification and Account Management Policy, 65 Fed. Reg. 36903 (June 12, 2000). Virtually every depository institution in the United States is subject to the URCCAMP by virtue of having either federal deposit insurance, Federal Reserve system membership, or a federal bank charter.

The URCCAMP details the classification of non-performing loans on banks' books for regulatory capital purposes. For revolving lines of credit like a credit card, an account must be charged off it is 180 days delinquent, meaning 180 days without receipt of a minimum payment. *Id.* at 36904 (regarding open-end retail loans). (Can you see why banks are incentivized to try to get consumers to make at least a small payment, which resets the charge-off clock?[1]) Closed-end loans are charged off at 120 days delinquency.

Contingency fee collectors have a relationship with the originator of the debt, and thus, in theory, some ability to access the documentation about the debt. Debt buyers operate in a different environment. Debts are often sold and resold, with some firms operating as brokers, but not collectors themselves. When debts are sold, they are typically sold with very limited documentation and sold "as is" with limited warranties. The debt buyers cannot typically access additional documentation about the loans. Instead, usually they only have a "loan tape"—an Excel spreadsheet—to go on. The spreadsheet will contain information about the debtor—name, Social Security number, address, telephone number—and about the debt—the amount owed, the date incurred (or date of account opening or closing), but often little else.

1. On re-aging of delinquent accounts, *see Credit Card Lending: Account Management and Loss Allowance Guidance* (January 2003), joint guidance issued under the auspices of the Federal Financial Institutions Examination Council by the Office of the Comptroller of the Currency (OCC Bulletin 2003-1), Federal Reserve (Supervisory Letter SR-03-1), Federal Deposit Insurance Corporation (Financial Institution Letter, FIL-2-2003), and Office of Thrift Supervision (OTS Release 03-01). The National Credit Union Administration did not issue equivalent guidance for federal credit unions. Lisa Freeman, *NCUA: CUs Aren't Part of the Problem*, Credit Union J., Jan. 16, 2006. The 2003 guidance formalized draft guidance released for comment in July 2002. Press Release, Federal Financial Institutions Examination Council, July 22, 2002, *at* http://www.ffiec.gov/press/pr072202.htm.

Debt buyers rarely receive any dispute history so any dispute process may have to start back at the beginning. While only a small percentage of debts end up being disputed (an estimated 3.2% per year), on the scale of the U.S. economy, that is over 1 million annual disputes. Federal law requires that debt collectors provide consumers within five days of an initial contact with a "validation notice" that sets forth basic information about the debts and the consumer's rights in the collection process. If the consumer disputes the debt within 30 days, then the collector must suspend collection efforts until it has verified the debt. Only around half the debts that trade in the secondary market are verified; once disputed, however, few debts are resold.

Given the limited information plus the fact that the debts are non-performing, consumer debts sell at a significant discount. Older debt sells at a lower price, and after 15 years, it is basically worthless. The average sale price in 2012 was 4¢ on the dollar. FTC, *The Structure and Practices of the Debt Buying Industry*, Jan. 2013, at ii.

Different debt collectors operate with different methods. Some collectors will limit themselves to forms of moral suasion, while others will use the courts, either to bolster their leverage for moral suasion or to take advantage of state collection procedures. The methods employed depend in part on the size and age of the debts. Rationally, no debt collector will spend more than the amount of a debt on that debt's collection, and no collector will want to spend a lot of moral suasion time on a debt that is approaching its statute of limitations. For example, it does not make sense to spend $1,000 to collect a $500 debt, absent compensating general deterrence effects on non-payment by other debtors.

Prior to this point we have seen how the small size of consumer debts inhibits consumer litigation because the costs of litigation are often greater than the harm to the consumer. With debt collection the shoe is on the other foot. The small size of some debts makes collection economically infeasible. Not surprisingly, as we have seen, formal small-dollar lending is almost always secured or otherwise involves the ability of the creditor to be repaid without using the slow and expensive judicial collection system: payday loans, auto title loans, refund anticipation loans, rent-to-own, and pawn are all structured to avoid judicial debt collection. Small-dollar debts exist primarily with credit card balances, where the greatest incentive for repayment is future credit. The economics of collection likely reduce the availability of small-dollar credit in the economy. They also point to a delicate balance in the regulation of debt collection. The empirical literature on consumer finance finds less credit availability and higher costs of credit when credit contracts are harder to enforce.[2] Similar findings exist in the general empirical literature on enforcement of credit contracts in non-consumer settings.[3] To the extent that debt collection

2. *See, e.g.*, Joshua Goodman & Adam J. Levitin, *Bankruptcy Law and the Cost of Mortgage Credit: The Impact of Cramdown on Mortgage Interest Rates*, 57 J. L. & ECON. (2014); Karen Pence, *Foreclosing on Opportunity: State Laws and Mortgage Credit*, 88 Rev. Econ. & Stat. 177 (2006); Daniela Fabbri & Mario Padula, *Does Poor Legal Enforcement Make Households Credit-Constrained?*, 28 J. Bank & Fin. 2369 (2004); Jeremy Berkowitz & Michelle White, *Bankruptcy and Small Firms' Access to Credit*. 35 RAND J. Econ. 69 (2004); Rein Gropp et al., *Personal Bankruptcy and Credit Supply and Demand*, 112 Q.J. Econ. 217 (2004); Emily Y. Lin & Michelle White, *Bankruptcy and the Market for Mortgage and Home Improvement Loans*, 50 J. Urban Econ. 138 (2001).

3. *See, e.g.*, Tullio Jappelli *et al.*, *Courts and Banks: Effects of Judicial Enforcement on Credit Markets*, 37 J. Money, Credit & Banking 223, 223 n.2 (2005); Luc Laeven & Giovanni Majnoni, *Does Judicial Efficiency*

law increases the cost of collection, it is likely to result in an increase in the cost of consumer credit and a reduction in its availability, particularly for more economically vulnerable consumers. Thus, there is a balance between trying to ensure credit availability and ensuring a fair and orderly debt collection process.

There's no getting around the fact that debt collection is on some level ugly. It involves depriving an individual of property against his or her will, whether by the sheriff *vi et armis* or by moral pressure. It is easy in these situations for collectors to overreach and use unduly coercive tactics. The following article gives a taste of the problems that can ensue.

True Debt Collection Horror Tales
3 People Terrorized by Debt Collectors Recount Their Stories

Allie Johnson
CreditCard.com, June 27, 2012

Even a polite call from a debt collector could ruin your day—but imagine if a collector called you names, swore at you, stalked you on Facebook or even threatened to kill your dog.

Bad behavior by debt collectors is on the rise: in 2011, the Federal Trade Commission (FTC) received more than 180,000 consumer complaints regarding abusive debt collection practices, almost 40,000 more than the previous year. "It was an unprecedented number," says Thomas Pahl, assistant director of the division of financial practices for the FTC. And in 2012 so far, Pahl says: "Consumer complaint numbers continue to be very high."

The increase probably results from the bad economy combined with the Federal Trade Commission's stepped-up enforcement of debt collection practices, Pahl says. For example, in 2011, the agency filed a lawsuit against a California debt collector, hired by a funeral home, who threatened to dig up the body of the debtor's daughter—and also to shoot her dog. "The FTC has been more active in bringing cases, so there's more awareness that people can complain to us," Pahl says.

However, a growing number of consumer complaints does not mean that bad behavior is rampant in the industry, says Mark Schiffman, vice president of public affairs for ACA International, a debt collector trade association that trains its members to comply with debt collection laws. "It's really only a tally of complaints to the FTC," Schiffman says. "Someone might say 'Joe's Collection Agency called me at noon on a Tuesday and I didn't like it.' That's a complaint, but [the debt collector] didn't do anything wrong."

While it's true many complaints are fairly routine—for example, allegations of a collector calling too much or being rude—some collectors do resort to extreme tactics. "Most of the industry understands that abusive behavior works," says Ira Rheingold,

---

Lower the Cost of Credit?, 29 J. Banking & Fin. 1791 (2005); Kee-Hong Bae & Vidhan K. Goyal, *Creditor Rights, Enforcement, and Bank Loans*, 64 J. Banking & Fin. 2369 (2004) Marcela Cristini et al., *Inter-American Dev. Bank Research Network Working Papers, The Importance of an Effective Legal System for Credit Markets: The Case of Argentina*, n.R-428 (2001).

executive director of the National Association of Consumer Advocates (NACA). "There's a real pressure on and incentive for people working in those debt-collecting outfits to collect. That's how their compensation works."

These true stories show just how disturbing an encounter with a rogue debt collector can be—and what a consumer can do to fight back.

TALE NO. 1: TERRORIZED BY TEXT

The debt: Jessica Burke had bought a used Pontiac Grand Am and fell a few months behind on payments when she had trouble finding work after a move to California. She called the financing company, and they agreed to give her extra time to pay.

The first call: The very next day, she got a call from a man who called himself "John Anderson," which Burke later found out was a fake name. "He started out by telling me he was a lawyer and would have me sued," says Burke, who found out that was a lie.

The harassment: The bill collector got her address and other private information by calling her cell phone company, impersonating her father and asking to be added to her account. Then, he began a barrage of angry calls and texts. The messages upset Burke so much she called the police, who ordered the collector to stop contacting her. But the texts continued for weeks, coming from a disguised number and implying that he was watching her. In one, he called her "Porky Pig" and a "200-pound slob" and added, "I got picture messages of you today." Late one night, she says, he texted her, claiming he was outside her house. She says: "It was 11 o'clock at night, I lived in a very rural area and I was home by myself. I was terrified."

Fighting back: Burke turned her car over to her creditor, got an attorney and sued the debt collector for multiple violations of the federal Fair Debt Collection Practices Act, including his lies, name-calling, obscenity and repeated calls. "You can't go to jail for owing a debt, but he made that threat a couple of times," says Jeremy Golden, the attorney who represented Burke. "It was really outrageous." But Golden says one of the worst things the debt collector did was pretend to be her dad. "When you couple that with the insults—that's a really scary pattern," Golden says.

The outcome: A federal judge awarded Burke a judgment of $33,312 against the debt collector. But he told her lawyer he did not plan to pay. Burke did some investigating of her own and learned he was broke, so she gave up on trying to collect. She later found online discussions about his tactics. She says: "A lot of people had been getting the same types of phone calls—he was telling them he'd take their dog or have their grandmother arrested."

TALE NO. 2: GET YOUR GUN

The debt: A debt collector called West Virginia homemaker Diana Mey about an old debt, possibly a credit card debt, allegedly owed by her son, who had moved out eight years earlier.

The first call: The debt collector left a message on Mey's home answering machine. "It was a very ominous message that implied legal action," Mey says.

The harassment: The collectors continued to call, threatening to put a lien on Mey's house and to sue her son. She sent a letter telling the company to stop contacting her. Then she started getting hang-up calls that showed up on her caller ID as coming from the local sheriff's department.

"I called the sheriff's department and said, 'Is somebody trying to get ahold of me?' They said 'No.'" One evening, the phone rang again, from the same number. The deep male voice on the other end asked for Diana, using a vulgar slur. He then went on to make graphic threats of sexual assault. Horrified, Mey told him she was recording the call. He responded: "Yay." After she hung up, Mey called 911 to report the incident. Home alone, she got her husband's gun and hung it on her bedpost that night. She says: "I was literally shaking I was so scared."

Fighting back: Later, Mey did some online research and found other complaints about bill collectors from the same company making obscene calls and disguising their phone number as that of the local sheriff's department. Mey found an attorney and sued the company, Global AG, also known by several other names, including Reliant Financial Associates. Her attorney, Martin Sheehan, says Mey's case was bolstered by the recording of the call. "When she came in with that tape recording, that was a game changer," he says. "There was no question how vile it was."

The outcome: The collection company's attorney didn't show up in court, so a judge listened to Mey's testimony and the tape with a local TV station filming. The judge awarded Mey a judgment of more than $10.8 million. "I was stunned," she says. "I never expected that much." Now comes the hard part: trying to collect.

TALE NO. 3: FOLLOWED ON FACEBOOK

The debt: In Florida, Kathryn Haralson bought a used Jeep Grand Cherokee and made monthly payments for more than five years until she fell behind in February 2011. She thought she had only a few more payments left. However, the creditor, MarkOne Financial, claimed she still owed $7,400.

The first call: A bill collector who called himself "Mr. Rice" started making calls to Haralson at home and at the radiology center where she worked, Haralson says.

The harassment: The bill collector called her work number and asked a coworker where Haralson usually parks her car, Haralson says. He also called her father, her brother, her husband and her daughter, who was away at college, according to her lawsuit. The collector dialed her husband's cell phone so much that he had to stop answering it and missed several business calls, she says. The collector called her brother at work enough to jeopardize his job and refused to stop, she says. Then he tracked Haralson down on Facebook and wrote: "Good day. Please contact Mr. Rice at MarkOne regarding a personal business matter," followed by his phone number. Haralson says: "When I started getting Facebook messages, that was very alarming."

Fighting back: Finally, Haralson says she went online and found out that she wasn't the only one having problems with the company. "Everything was the same, the Facebook messages and all the harassment," she says. "I thought they must be doing this to a lot of people." Attorney Billy Howard of Morgan & Morgan law firm, agreed to represent her and filed a lawsuit in state court for violation of Florida law that governs collections practices by creditors. "It got to the point where I couldn't deal with the harassment. It was too much. I was just getting sick of it," Haralson says.

The outcome: Attorney Howard says he and Haralson plan to take the case to trial. "She tried to do the right thing. She was not ducking and trying not to pay her bills—she was in constant contact with them," Howard says. "There was no reason for them to call and bother her daughter and rest of her family but to terrorize her." Haralson says: "I would love nothing more, if I walked away without a penny, than to see them out of business."

III. FAIR DEBT COLLECTION PRACTICES ACT

The debt collection industry is regulated on both federal and state levels, and in some instances, even by local ordinance. These regulations are layered and provide both procedural and substantive limitations on collection. They are mainly aimed at out-of-court collection, although a few do address aspects of judicial collections. This chapter addresses the main federal regulation of debt collection, the Fair Debt Collection Practices Act. The following chapter addresses a range of other federal and state regulations on debt collection.

In 1977, Congress enacted the major federal civil regulation of debt collection, the Fair Debt Collection Practices Act (FDCPA). The FDCPA contains an extensive list of prohibitions on debt collector behavior, as well as some affirmative requirements. The FDCPA applies only to "debt collectors." This means that all of the provisions of the FDCPA hinge on the definition of "debt collector."

A. Definition of Debt Collector

The FDCPA's definition of debt collector has three main parts. First it includes "any person who uses any instrumentality of interstate commerce or the mails in any business the principal purpose of which is the collection of any debts." 15 U.S.C. § 1692a(6). Thus, if a firm does debt collection and little or nothing else, it is a "debt collector" for FDCPA purposes. For purposes of this part of the definition, it does not matter to whom the debts are owed.

Second, it includes "any person who uses any instrumentality of interstate commerce or the mails . . . who regularly collects or attempts to collect, directly or indirectly, debts owed or due or asserted to be owed or due another." 15 U.S.C. § 1692a(6). The critical part of this provision is that it limits "debt collector" to parties collecting debts owed to *someone else*. In other words, when a creditor collects its own accounts, it is not a debt collector for FDCPA purposes, unless it falls into another part of the "debt collector" definition. Excluded, therefore, from this part of the FDCPA's definition of "debt collector" is a party that collects on debts it purchased from a third party when those debts were in default. *Henson v. Santander Consumer United States*, 528 U.S. ___, 2017 U.S. LEXIS 3722 (June 12, 2017).

The third part of the definition is "any creditor who, in the process of collecting his own debts, uses any name other than his own which would indicate that a third person is collecting or attempting to collect such debts."[4] *Id.* A creditor might want to use a different name when engaged in collections in order to avoid any reputational consequences from harsh collection methods. The FDCPA gives creditors a choice between using their own name and incurring reputational consequences or using a third party's name and risking FDCPA liability.

The FDCPA also expressly carves out several groups from the definition of debt collector: government employees, legal process servers, non-profit credit counseling organizations. It also excludes "any officer or employee of a creditor while, in the name of the creditor, collecting debts for such creditor;" and "any person while acting as a debt collector for another person, both of whom are related by common ownership or affiliated by corporate control, if the person acting as a debt collector does so only for persons to whom it is so related or affiliated and if the principal business of such person is not the collection of debts." 15 U.S.C. § 1692a(6)(A)-(B). Thus, a creditor's employees and any affiliate that does not do collection work for unaffiliated third parties and that is not principally a collection affiliate are not debt collectors. A corporate affiliate that handles all collections within a corporate group, however, would not fall into this exemption.

The FDCPA also excludes from the definition of debt collector "any person collecting or attempting to collect any debt owed or due or asserted to be owed or due another to the extent such activity (i) is incidental to a bona fide fiduciary obligation or a bona fide escrow arrangement; (ii) concerns a debt which was originated by such person; (iii) concerns a debt which was not in default at the time it was obtained by such person; or (iv) concerns a debt obtained by such person as a secured party in a commercial credit transaction involving the creditor." 15 U.S.C. § 1692a(6)(F). This provision shields several groups from FDCPA liability.

First, it shields trustees and receivers, including securitization trustees. 15 U.S.C. § 1692a(6)(F)(i). Second, it shields loan servicers if they were also the originator of the debt. 15 U.S.C. § 1692a(6)(F)(ii). This means that a mortgage originator that sells a loan to Fannie Mae but retains the servicing of the loan is not a debt collector for FDCPA purposes. (A third-party servicer, however, would not benefit from this provision.)

Third, it protects debt buyers, as they are not collecting debts owed to another, but collecting debts owed to themselves. 15 U.S.C. § 1692a(6)(F)(iii). In other words, a debt buyer (which would include most securitization conduit parties and vehicles, but not servicers) that purchased a debt and then attempts to collect in its own name is not a debt collector for FDCPA purposes. *Henson v. Santander Consumer USA, Inc.,*

---

4. The definition also includes a category—deed of trust trustees—solely for a prohibition relating to real estate foreclosures. 15 U.S.C. § 1692a(6).

582 U.S. __ (2017). (It is still possible for a debt buyer to qualify as a debt collector if it also regularly acts as a third-party collection agent for debts owed to others or if it engaged in a business the principal purpose of which is debt collection.)

Lastly, this provision protects parties that lend against the security of accounts receivable if they foreclose on the accounts receivable and assume collection of the accounts receivable themselves. 15 U.S.C. § 1692a(6)(F)(iv). A common situation would be a commercial mortgage lender that made a loan to a landlord secured by the rents on the property, including an assignment of rents clause. Upon the landlord's default, the lender could commence collecting the rents itself without being a "debt collector" for FDCPA purposes.

Confusingly, a separate FDCPA provision (not in the FDCPA's definitions section) excludes from the definition of debt collector those private entities that provide administrative support services for state or district attorney pretrial diversion programs for alleged bad check offenders in lieu of criminal prosecution. 15 U.S.C. § 1692p(a). In some states it is a criminal offense to write a bad check, and some states further authorize state or district attorneys to set up bad check units that function as public collection units for creditors under threat of criminal penalty. *See, e.g.*, Ala. Code § 12-17-224. In such programs, the utterers of bad checks are threatened with criminal prosecution unless they pay on the check (cast as restitution), plus a service charge to the state. If this sounds a bit like a kickback racket, well, just note that the power of criminal law enforcement is not otherwise used to enforce private contractual obligations or purely donative gifts.

The FDCPA definition of debt collector includes some parties who might not have realized that they were debt collectors. In particular, attorneys can find themselves liable for FDCPA violations if they are regularly engaged in collection activities. *Heintz v. Jenkins*, 514 U.S. 291 (1995). (Aren't all litigators that represent plaintiffs acting as debt collectors in some sense, then?)

B. FDCPA Prohibitions and Requirements

The FDCPA has some six operative sections regulating what debt collectors may and may not do. These sections address communications with the debtor and with third parties about debt collection, as well as certain unfair collection practices. Most of the provisions in the FDCPA are prohibitions, but there are also some affirmative requirements on debt collectors.

1. Communications with Third Parties

First, the FDCPA prohibits communications with third parties about the debt other than for obtaining location information about the debtor or to effectuate a post-judgment remedy. 15 U.S.C. § 1692c(b). When communicating with third parties when attempting to acquire location information about the consumer, the collector may not indicate that its inquiries relate to a collection matter or state that the consumer owes any debt. 15 U.S.C. § 1692b(1)-(5). In so doing, the FDCPA attempts to the limit debt collectors' ability to leverage social embarrassment into repayment.

2. Validation of Debts

Second, the FDCPA requires the debt collector to attempt to validate any debt that it is trying to collect. 15 U.S.C. § 1692g. The collector must send the consumer a validation notice within five days of initial communication. 15 U.S.C. § 1692g(a). The notice must explain the amount of the debt and the creditor and inform the consumer of some of his or her legal rights, namely that if the validity of the debt is not disputed with 30 days, the collector may assume the debt's validity, while if the debt is disputed, the collector must verify the debt.

Failure to dispute the validity of the debt to the collector is not an admission of the debt's validity, 15 U.S.C. § 1692g(c), and the collector may continue collection activities during the 30-day period. 15 U.S.C. § 1692g(b). A consumer's failure to dispute merely entitles the collector to assume the debt's validity for FDCPA purposes, which creates a safe harbor for some permitted collection activities. Significantly, during the 30 days running from the validation notice until the debt is either verified or not contested, the collector may not undertake any collection action, including communications that overshadow or are inconsistent with the validation notice. 15 U.S.C. § 1692g(b).

The FDCPA is thus structured to enable a consumer to stop a collection action until and unless the creditor takes steps to verify that the debt is actually owed as represented. The FDCPA, however, does not set forth standards for verification of debts, and neither do regulations. This has raised significant issues in mortgage foreclosures and more recently in credit card debt collections, as some collectors have claimed to have verified debts simply by examining their computer systems or computer records created by others but have no actual knowledge of whether there was a debt created. Indeed, in the modern consumer finance world, virtually no one has personal knowledge of a debt obligation being created other than the consumer. Courts have struggled with the question of what verification requires from a collector, with a range of standards applied in different circuits. *See, e.g., Graziano v. Harrison*, 950 F.2d 107 (3d Cir. 1991) (verification requires an itemized accounting of the debt); *Chaudhry v. Gallerizzo*, 174 F.3d 394 (4th Cir. 1999) (verification requires collector confirming in writing that the amount being demanded is what the creditor is claiming is owed, but does not require the collector to keep detailed files of the alleged debt); *Clark v. Capital Credit & Collection Servs.*, 460 F.3d 1162, 1173 (9th Cir. 2006) (adopting Fourth Circuit *Chaudhry* standard); *Dunham v. Portfolio Recovery Assocs., LLC*, 663 F.3d 997, 1004 (8th Cir. 2011) (verification requires that the debtor can sufficiently dispute the payment obligation); *Haddad v. Alexander, Zelmanski, Danner & Fioritto, PLLC*, 758 F.3d 777 (6th Cir. 2014) (verification requires providing "consumer with notice of how and when the debt was originally incurred or other sufficient notice from which the consumer could sufficiently dispute the payment obligation [and] should provide the date and nature of the transaction that led to the debt, such as a purchase on a particular date, a missed rental payment for a specific month, a fee for a particular service provided at a specified time, or a fine for a particular offense assessed on a certain date.").

While the FDCPA does not require that validation notices be clear and readily understandable, courts have read this requirement into the statute; to the extent that the notice contains other information it may constitute a collection activity or communication that "overshadows" or is inconsistent with the disclosure required in the validation notice. *See* 15 U.S.C. § 1692g(b). In this context it is necessary to consider both the language in the actual validation notice and any other communications sent together with the validation notice.

At what point does a communication become inconsistent or overshadow the disclosure? The answer may depend on the consumer. Different circuits use different standards to evaluate communications with consumers. Some circuits use a "least sophisticated" consumer or debtor standard, while others, like the Seventh Circuit in the case below, have a more forgiving "unsophisticated" consumer standard.

In the following case, after determining whether a collector's communication with a consumer would be confusing, Judge Posner tries his hand at drafting a dunning letter, creating a form letter that functions as a safe harbor in the Seventh Circuit.

Bartlett v. Heibl

128 F.3d 497 (7th Cir. 1997)

POSNER, Chief Judge.

The Fair Debt Collection Practices Act, 15 U.S.C. §§ 1692-1692o, provides that within five days after a debt collector first duns a consumer debtor, the collector must send the debtor a written notice containing specified information. The required information includes the amount of the debt, the name of the creditor, and, of particular relevance here, a statement that unless the debtor "disputes the validity of the debt" within thirty days the debt collector will assume that the debt is valid but that if the debtor notifies the collector in writing within thirty days that he is disputing the debt, "the debt collector will obtain verification of the debt [from the creditor] . . . and a copy of [the] verification . . . will be mailed to the consumer." 15 U.S.C. §§ 1692g(a)(1)-(4). A similar provision requires that the debtor be informed that upon his request the debt collector will give him the name and address of his original creditor, if the original creditor is different from the current one. § 1692g(a)(5). If the debtor accepts the invitation tendered in the required notice, and requests from the debt collector either verification of the debt or the name and address of the original debtor, the debt collector must "cease collection of the debt . . . until the [requested information] is mailed to the consumer." § 1692g(b). These provisions are intended for the case in which the debt collector, being a hireling of the creditor rather than the creditor itself, may lack first-hand knowledge of the debt.

If the statute is violated, the debtor is entitled to obtain from the debt collector, in addition to any actual damages that the debtor can prove, statutory damages not to exceed $1,000 per violation, plus a reasonable attorney's fee. § 1692k(a).

A credit-card company hired lawyer John Heibl, the defendant in this case, to collect a consumer credit-card debt of some $1,700 from Curtis Bartlett, the plaintiff. Heibl sent Bartlett a letter, which Bartlett received but did not read, in which Heibl told him that "if you wish to resolve this matter before legal action is commenced, you must do one of two things within one week of the date of this letter": pay $316 toward the satisfaction of the debt, or get in touch with Micard (the creditor) "and make suitable arrangements for payment. If you do neither, it will be assumed that legal action will be necessary." Under Heibl's signature appears an accurate, virtually a literal, paraphrase of section 1692g(a), advising Bartlett that he has thirty days within which to dispute the debt, in which event Heibl will mail him a verification of it. At the end of the paraphrase Heibl adds: "suit may be commenced at any time before the expiration of this thirty (30) days." A copy of Heibl's letter is appended to this opinion.

The letter is said to violate the statute by stating the required information about the debtor's rights in a confusing fashion. Finding nothing confusing about the letter, the district court rendered judgment for the defendant after a bench trial. The plaintiff contends that this finding is clearly erroneous. . . .

The main issue presented by the appeal is whether the district judge committed a clear error in finding that the letter was not confusing. The statute does not say in so many words that the disclosures required by it must be made in a nonconfusing manner. But the courts, our own included, have held, plausibly enough, that it is implicit that the debt collector may not defeat the statute's purpose by making the required disclosures in a form or within a context in which they are unlikely to be understood by the unsophisticated debtors who are the particular objects of the statute's solicitude.

Most of the cases put it this way: the implied duty to avoid confusing the unsophisticated consumer can be violated by contradicting or "overshadowing" the required notice. This sounds like two separate tests, one for a statement that is logically inconsistent with the required notice and the other for a statement that while it doesn't actually contradict the required notice obscures it, in much the same way that static or cross-talk can make a telephone communication hard to understand even though the message is not being contradicted in any way. The required notice might be "overshadowed" just because it was in smaller or fainter print than the demand for payment.

As with many legal formulas that get repeated from case to case without an effort at elaboration, "contradicting or overshadowing" is rather unilluminating—even, though we hesitate to use the word in this context, confusing. The cases that find the statute violated generally involve neither logical inconsistencies (that is, denials of the consumer rights that the dunning letter is required to disclose) nor the kind of literal "overshadowing" involved in a fine-print, or faint-print, or confusing-typeface case. In the typical case, the letter both demands payment within thirty days and explains the consumer's right to demand verification within thirty days. These rights are not inconsistent, but by failing to explain how they fit together the letter confuses.

It would be better if the courts just said that the unsophisticated consumer is to be protected against confusion, whatever form it takes. A contradiction is just one means of inducing confusion; "overshadowing" is just another; and the most common is a third, the failure to explain an apparent though not actual contradiction. . . . On the one hand, Heibl's letter tells the debtor that if he doesn't pay within a week he's going to be sued. On the other hand, it tells him that he can contest the debt within thirty days. This leaves up in the air what happens if he is sued on the eighth day, say, and disputes the debt on the tenth day. He might well wonder what good it would do him to dispute the debt if he can't stave off a lawsuit. The net effect of the juxtaposition of the one-week and thirty-day crucial periods is to turn the required disclosure into legal gibberish. That's as bad as an outright contradiction.

Although the question whether a dunning letter violates the Fair Debt Collection Practices Act does not require evidence that the recipient was confused—or even, as we noted earlier, whether he read the letter—the issue of confusion is for the district judge to decide, subject to light review for "clear error." The cases, however, leave no room to doubt that the letter to Bartlett was confusing; nor as an original matter could we doubt that it was confusing—we found it so, and do not like to think of ourselves as your average unsophisticated consumer. So the judgment must be reversed. But we should not stop here. Judges too often tell defendants what the defendants cannot do without indicating what they can do, thus engendering legal uncertainty that foments further litigation. The plaintiff's lawyer takes the extreme, indeed the absurd, position—one that he acknowledged to us at argument, with a certain lawyerly relish, creates an anomaly in the statutory design—that the debt collector cannot in any way, shape, or form allude to his right to bring a lawsuit within thirty days. That enforced silence would be fine if the statute forbade suing so soon. But it does not. The debt collector is perfectly free to sue within thirty days; he just must cease his efforts at collection during the interval between being asked for verification of the debt and mailing the verification to the debtor. 15 U.S.C. § 1692g(b). In effect the plaintiff is arguing that if the debt collector wants to sue within the first thirty days he must do so without advance warning. How this compelled surprise could be thought either required by the statute, however imaginatively elaborated with the aid of the concept of "overshadowing," or helpful to the statute's intended beneficiaries, eludes us.

The plaintiff's argument is in one sense overimaginative, and in another unimaginative—unimaginative in failing to see that it is possible to devise a form of words that will inform the debtor of the risk of his being sued without detracting from the statement of his statutory rights. We here set forth a redaction of Heibl's letter that complies with the statute without forcing the debt collector to conceal his intention of exploiting his right to resort to legal action before the thirty days are up. We are not rewriting the statute; that is not our business. We are simply trying to provide some guidance to how to comply with it. We commend this redaction as a safe harbor for debt collectors who want to avoid liability for the kind of suit that Bartlett has brought and now won. The qualification "for the kind of suit that Bartlett has brought and now won" is important. We are not certifying our letter as proof against challenges based on other provisions of the statute; those provisions are not before us. With that caveat, here is our letter:

> Dear Mr. Bartlett:
>
> I have been retained by Micard Services to collect from you the entire balance, which as of September 25, 1995, was $1,656.90, that you owe Micard Services on your MasterCard Account No. 5414701617068749.
>
> If you want to resolve this matter without a lawsuit, you must, within one week of the date of this letter, either pay Micard $316 against the balance that you owe (unless you've paid it since your last statement) or call Micard at 1-800-221-5920 ext. 6130 and work out arrangements for payment with it. If you do neither of these things, I will

be entitled to file a lawsuit against you, for the collection of this debt, when the week is over.

Federal law gives you thirty days after you receive this letter to dispute the validity of the debt or any part of it. If you don't dispute it within that period, I'll assume that it's valid. If you do dispute it—by notifying me in writing to that effect—I will, as required by the law, obtain and mail to you proof of the debt. And if, within the same period, you request in writing the name and address of your original creditor, if the original creditor is different from the current creditor (Micard Services), I will furnish you with that information too.

The law does not require me to wait until the end of the thirty-day period before suing you to collect this debt. If, however, you request proof of the debt or the name and address of the original creditor within the thirty-day period that begins with your receipt of this letter, the law requires me to suspend my efforts (through litigation or otherwise) to collect the debt until I mail the requested information to you.

Sincerely,

John A. Heibl

We cannot require debt collectors to use "our" form. But of course if they depart from it, they do so at their risk. Debt collectors who want to avoid suits by disgruntled debtors standing on their statutory rights would be well advised to stick close to the form that we have drafted. It will be a safe haven for them, at least in the Seventh Circuit.

The judgment is reversed and the case is remanded with instructions to enter judgment for the plaintiff and compute the statutory damages, costs, and attorneys' fees to which he is entitled.

Reversed and Remanded.

APPENDIX: HEIBL'S LETTER TO BARTLETT

John A. Heibl
Attorney At Law
900 John Nolen Drive
Suite 210
Madison, Wisconsin 53713

October 4, 1995

Curtis C. Bartlett
11440 Hill Avenue
Edgerton, WI 53534-8700

RE: MasterCard Account No. 5414701617068749

Dear Mr. Bartlett:

I represent MICARD SERVICES. I have been asked to commence such action against you as may be necessary in an attempt to recover the entire balance owed by you because of your failure to make payment when due.

If you wish to resolve this matter before legal action is commenced, you must do one of two things within one week of the date of this letter: (1) Pay $316.00 (unless you have paid that sum since your last statement); or, (2) Contact MICARD SERVICES at 1-800-221-5920 ext. 6130, and make suitable arrangements for payment. If you do neither, it will be assumed that legal action will be necessary. If such action is successful, costs will be added to your balance.

At this time the choice is yours, and I sincerely hope you choose to resolve this matter before legal action is commenced.

Sincerely,
John A. Heibl
JAH/dkf

THIS IS AN ATTEMPT TO COLLECT A DEBT AND ANY INFORMATION OBTAINED WILL BE USED FOR THAT PURPOSE.

THIS INFORMATION THAT I HAVE INDICATES THAT, AS OF September 25, 1995, YOU OWE MICARD SERVICES THE SUM OF $1,656.90. UNLESS YOU, WITHIN THIRTY (30) DAYS AFTER RECEIPT OF THIS NOTICE, DISPUTE THE VALIDITY OF THE DEBT OR ANY PORTION THEREOF, I WILL ASSUME THAT THE DEBT IS VALID. IF YOU DO, I WILL OBTAIN VERIFICATION OF THE DEBT, OR A COPY OF ANY JUDGMENT AGAINST YOU AND A COPY OF SUCH VERIFICATION OR JUDGMENT WILL BE MAILED TO YOU BY ME. UPON YOUR WRITTEN REQUEST WITHIN THE SAME THIRTY (30) DAY PERIOD, I WILL PROVIDE YOU WITH THE NAME AND ADDRESS OF THE ORIGINAL CREDITOR, IF DIFFERENT FROM THE CURRENT CREDITOR. SUIT MAY BE COMMENCED AT ANY TIME BEFORE THE EXPIRATION OF THIS THIRTY (30) DAYS.

---

3. Communications with the Consumer

The FDCPA restricts debt collector communications with the consumer. Collectors are prohibited from communicating with the consumer at inconvenient or unusual times (assumed to be between 9 P.M. and 8 A.M. local time for the consumer), from communicating with the consumer if the consumer is known to be represented by counsel, and from communicating from the consumer at work if the employer prohibits the communication. 15 U.S.C. §§ 1692b(6); 1692c(a). Finally, collectors must cease communication with the consumer if notified in writing that the consumer does not intend to repay the obligation or wants communication to cease. At that point, the collector can only tell the consumer that collection efforts are ceasing or that the creditor may invoke a legal remedy. 15 U.S.C. § 1692c(c).

The FDCPA also contains a trio of sections prohibiting harassment or abuse, false or misleading representations, and unfair practices. 15 U.S.C. §§ 1692d-1692f. Here we see the trio of unfair, deceptive, and abusive, albeit in a rather different context than the Consumer Financial Protection Act's prohibition. 12 U.S.C. § 5136.

Many of these prohibitions are intuitive: threatening violence, using obscene or profane language, making repeated calls for the purpose of harassment, pretending to be affiliated with law enforcement, pretending that a communication is from an attorney, publishing lists of debtors or putting debt up for sale in order coerce payment. 15 U.S.C. § 1692d. Some provisions, however, bear special emphasis, particularly the false representation of amounts owed, 15 U.S.C. § 1692e(2), threatening legal actions that the debt collector does not actually intend to take or cannot legally take, 15 U.S.C. §§ 1692e(4)-(5), 1692f(6), and various provisions about post-dated checks. 15 U.S.C. § 1692f(2)-(4). Query whether Judge Posner's letter in *Bartlett v. Heibel* actually complies with the FDCPA as it implies that there will be litigation if there is non-payment. That seems unlikely for a debt of $1,656.90.

Perhaps the most notable of the FDCPA's prohibitions is attempting to collect any debt that is not actually owed, meaning that the amount must be authorized by contract or by law. 15 U.S.C. § 1692f(1). Some cases have extended the FDCPA to apply to judicial collection actions. Does this mean that any collection suit that does not recover the amount alleged to be owed is a FDCPA violation?

4. FDCPA Damages

The FDCPA imposes liability of actual damages, plus statutory damages of up to $1,000, and reasonable attorneys' fees. 15 U.S.C. § 1692k(a). Actual damages under the FDCPA can include things such as emotional distress. This means an attempt to collect a very small debt can readily result in much greater liability. *See, e.g., Myers v. HR, Inc.*, 543 F. Supp. 2d 1215 (S.D. Cal. 2008) (award of $90,000 in compensatory damages for emotional distress, sleeplessness, upset, and embarrassment for debt collection attempts after statute of limitations for a debt of less than $3,000 had lapsed).

The FDCPA's statutory damages are per action, not per violation. Nothing, however, prevents a consumer from bringing multiple separate actions for each violation, although such atomization might affect what is a "reasonable attorney's fee" under the statute. Class action recoveries are capped at the lesser of $1 million or 1% of the debt collector's net worth, but again, they can be atomized into multiple classes to maximize recoveries. 15 U.S.C. § 1692k(a).

Problem Set 33

1. Your boss, the general counsel of Continental Express Bank, N.A., just read a newspaper story about the CFPB ramping up enforcement actions aimed at debt collection activities and has ordered a top-to-bottom review of Con-Ex's treatment of defaulted accounts. The general counsel wants to know what Con-Ex's options are for collecting on defaulted credit card and auto loan debt and the risk-reward trade-offs with the different options. What's your report to the general counsel?

2. Which of the following parties have potential FDCPA liability if, in a non-judicial foreclosure, they claim a loan balance of $250,000, when the debtor only in fact owes $231,000:

a. Susan Wachter, an attorney with Wachter & Wharton, LLP, a law firm that handles all foreclosures for Home Run Mortgage Servicing Corp. About two-thirds of Susan's work is on foreclosures. *See* 15 U.S.C. § 1692a(6).

b. Wachter & Wharton, LLP, a law firm that handles all foreclosures for Home Run Mortgage Servicing Corp. Non-judicial foreclosures account for 10% of the revenue of Wachter & Wharton, LLP; the rest of its work focuses on consumer finance compliance and tax matters. *See* 15 U.S.C. § 1692a(6).

c. Home Run Mortgage Corp. as servicer for the Fannie Mae AJL-2017 securitization trust. Home Run originated some of the other loans in the Fannie Mae AJL-2019 securitization trust, but not this one. *See* 15 U.S.C. § 1692a(6)(F).

d. Fannie Mae as trustee for the Fannie Mae AJL-2019 securitization trust. Fannie Mae as trustee holds the securitized mortgages in trust for the benefit of various mortgage-backed securities investors. *See* 15 U.S.C. § 1692a(6)(F).

3. A decade ago, when Lisa Mortissier was in graduate school, she ran up a $300 charge on a private label credit card from the retailer Apeture and never paid the bill. The statute of limitations on the debt has long passed. One month ago Lisa got a call from RoundUp LLC seeking repayment of the debt. Lisa said, "That Macy's card? That's ancient. I have no idea what I owe on it." The RoundUp representative told Lisa, "You owe $6,494 plus our $100 collection service fee. That's what happens when you don't pay a debt that has interest accruing on it for ten years." When Lisa said, "That's nuts!" the representative said, "If you don't pay, we'll see you in court." Lisa has since received 20 additional calls from RoundUp at home and at work. Sometimes she's been woken up by calls by RoundUp at 6 in the morning, to hear the words, "Rise and shine you lousy deadbeat! When is your sorry ass going to pay your bills?"

Yesterday, the RoundUp representative called again and told Lisa that "If you don't pay up this week, we're going to file larceny charges against you. Borrowing money and failing to pay it back is theft." Lisa contacted your office today after her friend told her that he saw a tweet from RoundUp saying "Alert: Lisa's Mortissier stiffs her creditors. Don't lend to her."

a. What advice do you have for Lisa? *See* 15 U.S.C. §§ 1692c, 1692d(2), 1692d(5), 1692e(2), 1692e(4)-(5), 1692e(7), 1692(f)(1), 1692g(1), 1692k.

b. Would the result be different if the communications came from Apeture instead of RoundUp? *See* 15 U.S.C. § 1692a(6); Cal. Civ. Code § 1788.2(c).

4. You've been retained as outside counsel for Squeeze Play LLP, a debt buying firm. Squeeze Play purchases portfolios of charged-off credit card debt and medical debt for pennies on the dollar and then proceeds to work the accounts. Squeeze Play has a new general counsel, David Frey, and he wants to know what Squeeze Play has to do to be FDCPA compliant in regarding to debt validation. Squeeze Play has been using a form letter that reads:

Dear [title] [lastname]:

THIS IS A LEGAL DEBT COLLECTION NOTICE.

I AM AN ATTORNEY RETAINED BY SQUEEZE PLAY LLP, A DEBT COLLECTION FIRM. YOU INCURRED A DEBT OF $[debt amount] on account [account number] with [name of original creditor]. Squeeze Play LLP has legally purchased this debt. YOU NOW OWE SQUEEZE PLAY LLP THE DEBT IN THE AMOUNT OF $[debt amount].

If you believe you did not owe this debt to [original creditor], you have thirty days from receipt of this letter to dispute it by sending notice in writing to the address above. Otherwise, Squeeze Play LLP will proceed to take all appropriate actions for collection.

Squeeze Play LLP reserves its right to have me bring legal action against you to collect the debt. Failure to pay the debt you owe could result in a judgment and subsequent wage garnishment and/or execution on your non-exempt property by the [name of county] Sheriff pursuant to a court order. If you wish to avoid legal action and embarrassing public collection activities, you must either send payment of $[debt amount] to Squeeze Play LLP using the enclosed envelope. If you are unable to pay the amount in full, you may arrange a payment plan with Squeeze Play LLP by calling 1-8888-778-3393. FAILURE TO PAY ANY DEBT OWED WILL RESULT IN COLLECTION ACTIONS BY SQUEEZE PLAY LLP.

Sincerely,

David Frey, Attorney-at-law

What are your thoughts on this validation letter? What do you need to do if a consumer disputes the debt? *See* 15 U.S.C. § 1692g; *Bartlett v. Heibl*, 128 F.3d 497 (7th Cir. 1997).

CHAPTER 34

DEBT COLLECTION II: OTHER REGULATIONS

The debt collection industry is regulated on both federal and state levels, and in some instances, even by local ordinance. These regulations are layered and provide both procedural and substantive limitations on collection. They are mainly aimed at out-of-court collection, although a few do address aspects of judicial collections. While the federal Fair Debt Collection Practices Act, covered in the previous chapter, is the most comprehensive regulation of debt collection, it is hardly the only one. Other federal statutes address particular types of debt collection or debtors, and state statutes also regulate the debt collection industry.

I. FEDERAL REGULATION: THE FTC ACT § 5

Like almost all businesses, since 1938 debt collection has been subject to section 5 of the Federal Trade Commission Act, which prohibits unfair and deceptive acts in interstate commerce. 15 U.S.C. § 45. The FTC's Credit Practices Rule (along with similar rules adopted by federal bank regulators) prohibits certain unfair credit practices, some of which relate to collections, including making loans that include a confession of judgment,[1] waiver of property exemption rights, or certain wage future assignments. 16 C.F.R. §§ 444.2(a)(1)-(3). Note that these regulations are applicable to original lenders, not to third-party collectors, but these are regulations of the collection process: a confession of judgment functions as a default judgment in advance in a collection suit, a waiver of property exemption rights waives the consumer's right to keep certain property out of the reach of creditors, and limitations on wage assignments function as a limitation on an agreement to garnish wages. Also note that the limitation on wage assignment applies to assignment of the wages, not of funds that have been commingled in the consumer's bank account with other funds.

1. A confession of judgment is essentially a default judgment obtained in advance. It allows a creditor to submit the confession of judgment to the clerk of the court and requests that a judgment be entered, without ever filing a complaint. *E.g.*, Va. Code § 8.01-432. There is typically a limited time window in which a debtor can contest the confession of judgment.

Complaint
CFPB v. The National Collegiate Master Student Loan Trust *et al.*

No. 1:17-cv-01323 (D. Del. Sept. 18, 2017)

INTRODUCTION

1. Plaintiff, the Consumer Financial Protection Bureau ("Bureau"), brings this action against the fifteen (15) National Collegiate Student Loan Trusts ("Defendants," or "NCSLTs", or "the Trusts") under sections 1031(a), 1036(a), and 1054(a) of the Consumer Financial Protection Act of 2010 ("CFPA"), 12 U.S.C. §§ 5531, 5536(a), 5564(a), to obtain permanent injunctive relief, restitution, refunds, disgorgement, damages, civil money penalties, and other appropriate relief for Defendants' violations of Federal consumer financial law in connection with Defendants' servicing and collection of private student loan debt.

2. The Bureau has reviewed the debt collection and litigation practices of the fifteen (15) Delaware statutory trusts referred to as the National Collegiate Student Loan Trusts, which are the National Collegiate Master Student Loan Trust, NCSLT 2003-1, NCSLT 2004-1, NCSLT 2004-2, NCSLT 2005-1, NCSLT 2005-2, NCSLT 2005-3, NCSLT 2006-1, NCSLT 2006-2, NCSLT 2006-3, NCSLT 2006-4, NCSLT 2007-1, NCSLT 2007-2, NCSLT 2007-3, and NCSLT 2007-4), as performed by Defendants' Servicers and Subservicers (as defined below) pursuant to the various servicing agreements between Defendants and each such Servicer or agreements between a Servicer and a Subservicer.

3. To collect on defaulted private student loans, Defendants' Servicers filed collections lawsuits on behalf of Defendants in state courts across the country. In support of these lawsuits, Subservicers on behalf of Defendants executed and filed affidavits that falsely claimed personal knowledge of the account records and the consumer's debt and, in many cases, personal knowledge of the chain of assignments establishing ownership of the loans. In addition, Defendants' Servicers on behalf of Defendants filed at least 2,000 collections lawsuits without the documentation necessary to prove Trust ownership of the loans or on debt that was time-barred. Finally, notaries for Defendants' Servicers notarized more than 25,000 affidavits even though they did not witness the affiants' signatures.

. . .

DEFENDANTS

. . .

8. Defendants are "covered person[s]" under 12 U.S.C. § 5481(6) because they engaged in "servicing loans, including acquiring, purchasing selling [or] brokering" and in the collection of debt. 12 U.S.C. § 5481(15)(A)(i), (x).

DEFENDANTS' UNLAWFUL ACTS OR PRACTICES

9. The NCSLTs comprise fifteen (15) Delaware statutory trusts created between 2001 and 2007.

10. The basic purpose of each Trust is to acquire a pool of private student loans, execute the indentures and issue notes secured by the pools of student loans, enter into

the so-called trust-related agreements, and provide for the administration of the Trusts and the servicing and collection of student loans.

11. Each Trust is an Owner-directed Delaware statutory trust formed under the laws of Delaware.

12. Defendants do not have employees, and all actions relating to the administration of the Trusts, servicing of the student loans, and collecting debt are carried out by Defendants' Servicers.

13. Defendants' Servicers are any Servicer, Primary Servicer, Subservicer, Special Servicer, Administrator, and any other individual or entity acting on behalf of the Trusts with respect to the servicing and collection of the student loans owned by the Trusts, whether retained directly by Defendants or retained by an individual or entity acting on behalf of Defendants.

14. Each Servicer is a "covered person" under 12 U.S.C. § 5481(6) because it engaged in "servicing loans, including acquiring, purchasing, selling, [or] brokering" and in "collecting debt." 12 U.S.C. § 5481(15)(A)(i), (x).

15. Each Servicer acted as an agent of the Trusts.

16. Since November 1, 2014, Defendants' Subservicer has been Transworld Systems, Inc.

17. The Trusts hold more than 800,000 private student loans sold by originating lenders to the Trusts.

18. Debt-collection activities on behalf of Defendants are carried out by Defendants' Servicers, including the Special Servicer and the Subservicers.

19. Defendants' Servicers and other entities executed, notarized, and filed deceptive affidavits on behalf of Defendants.

20. Defendants' Servicers and other entities, on behalf of Defendants, filed collections lawsuits lacking documentation needed to prove ownership of the loans.

21. In 2009, Defendants entered into a special servicing agreement with the Special Servicer in order to provide for the servicing, collection, and litigation of delinquent and defaulted loans. This agreement required the Special Servicer to hire Subservicers and enter into and adhere to the Default Prevention and Collection Services Agreement of March 1, 2009, as amended.

22. In 2012, upon the resignation of the Special Servicer and pursuant to the terms of the special servicing agreement, the Back-Up Special Servicer assumed the role of Special Servicer.

23. In 2012, the Special Servicer amended the Default Prevention and Collection Services Agreement of March 1, 2009 in order to expand the role of the Subservicer to Defendants with respect to the collection and enforcement of the student loans owned by Defendants.

FALSE AND MISLEADING AFFIDAVITS AND TESTIMONY

24. In connection with collecting or attempting to collect debt from consumers, between November 1, 2012 and April 25, 2016, Subservicers, acting through Defendants' Special Servicer and acting on behalf of Defendants, initiated 94,046 collections lawsuits in courts across the country.

25. In support of the collections lawsuits, Subservicers acting on behalf of Defendants submitted affidavits and documents in support of Defendants' claims that consumers owed debts to Defendants.

26. Affiants on behalf of Defendants executed, notarized, and caused to be filed affidavits—often attaching exhibits—in Defendants' collections lawsuits.

27. In these affidavits, the affiants swore that they had personal knowledge of the education loan records evidencing the debt.

28. In fact, in numerous instances, affiants lacked personal knowledge of the education loan records evidencing the debt when they executed the affidavits.

29. The affiants also swore in the affidavits that they were authorized and competent to testify about the consumers' debts through review of and "personal knowledge" of the business records, including electronic data, in their possession.

30. In fact, in numerous instances, affiants lacked personal knowledge of the business records, including the electronic data, showing that consumers owed debts to the Defendants.

31. Affiants were instructed to review data on a computer screen to verify information in the affidavits about the debts. Affiants, however, did not know the source of the data on that screen, how the data was obtained or maintained, whether it was accurate, or whether those data meant that the debt was in fact owed to Defendants.

32. Each affiant also swore that he or she had "personal knowledge of the record management practices and procedures of Plaintiff [the Trust] and the practices and procedures Plaintiff requires of its loan servicers and other agents."

33. In fact, affiants lacked personal knowledge of the record management practices and procedures of Defendants and the practices and procedures of Defendants' agents.

34. In many affidavits, the affiants also swore, "I have reviewed the chain of title records as business records" regarding the relevant account.

35. In fact, in numerous instances, affiants did not review the chain of assignment records prior to executing the affidavits. In some cases, affiants reviewed only "chain of title" records that had been found online. In fact, at least one of Defendants' Servicers instructed affiants that they did not need to review the chain of assignment records before executing affidavits that represented that the affiant had reviewed those records.

36. In fact, affiants did not have access to deposit and sale agreements—the last link in the chain of assignment transferring loans into the Trust—until May 30, 2014.

37. In many affidavits, the affiants asserted that they had personal knowledge that the loans were transferred, sold, and assigned to the Trusts on dates certain.

38. In fact, affiants lacked personal knowledge of the chain of assignment records necessary to prove that the relevant Trust owned the subject loan.

39. In some instances, when affiants complained to management that they did not have personal knowledge of certain representations made in the affidavits, Defendants' Servicers instructed the affiants to continue signing the affidavits. In some instances, affiants felt "bullied" by management and followed the instructions for fear of losing their jobs.

40. On numerous occasions, to address a backlog of affidavits, employees of Defendants' Servicers such as interns and mailroom clerks were instructed to execute affidavits.

41. On numerous occasions, between November 1, 2012 and September 1, 2013, the Servicers filed stale affidavits that had earlier been executed by a previous Servicer. Contrary to the statements in the affidavits, the affiants in question were no longer "authorized to testify" in the matter and no longer had access or knowledge of the consumer's account records or debt.

42. Affiants also later provided live testimony in court, purportedly based on personal knowledge, similar to the statements made in the affidavits as described in Paragraphs 27–38.

IMPROPERLY NOTARIZED AFFIDAVITS

43. Between November 1, 2012 and August 3, 2014, in connection with collecting or attempting to collect debt from consumers, Defendants' Servicers acting on behalf of Defendants filed at least 11,412 affidavits in collections lawsuits.

44. Between November 1, 2012 and August 3, 2014, Defendants' Servicers acting on behalf of Defendants improperly notarized virtually every affidavit executed and filed.

45. Affiants executed the affidavits on their own outside the presence of the notary.

46. Affiants placed executed affidavits in a specified location.

47. Defendants' Servicers' notaries later notarized stacks of previously signed affidavits all at once at their desks.

48. Contrary to the representations in the affidavits, affiants did not personally appear before notaries.

49. Contrary to the representations in the affidavits, notaries did not place the affiants under oath or witness their signatures.

50. On numerous occasions, notaries notarized affidavits executed by affiants on a prior date. At least one of Defendants' Servicers instructed notaries to ensure that the notarization date matched the date of execution, even if that meant backdating the notarization date.

51. In many cases, the notaries did in fact back date their notarization of the affidavits.

FILING LAWSUITS WITHOUT THE INTENT OR ABILITY TO PROVE THE CLAIMS, IF CONTESTED

52. Defendants filed at least 1,214 collections lawsuits against consumers even though the documentation needed to prove they owned the loans was missing. Through these lawsuits, the Defendants obtained approximately $21,768,807 in judgments against consumers.

53. In these lawsuits, documentation of a complete chain of assignment evidencing that the subject loan was transferred to the Defendants was missing.

54. In addition, the Defendants filed at least 812 collections lawsuits where the documentation did not support Trusts' ownership of the loans. The chain of assignment documentation shows that these loans were allegedly transferred to Defendants before they were in fact disbursed to consumers.

55. In at least 208 other collections lawsuits, the promissory note to prove that a debt was owed did not exist or cannot be located.

56. For each collections lawsuit described in Paragraphs 52–55, Defendants could not prove that a debt was owed to Defendants, if contested.

57. Defendants knew, or their processes should have uncovered, that these chain of assignment documents were missing or flawed, yet Defendants continued to file collections lawsuits.

COLLECTION OF TIME-BARRED DEBT

58. In at least 486 collections lawsuits, in connection with collecting or attempting to collect debt from consumers, Defendants filed a collections lawsuit outside the applicable statute of limitations.

THE CONSUMER FINANCIAL PROTECTION ACT

59. The CFPA provides that it is unlawful for any covered person "to offer or provide to a consumer any financial product or service not in conformity with Federal consumer financial law, or otherwise commit any act or omission in violation of a Federal consumer financial law." 12 U.S.C. § 5536(a)(1)(A). The CFPA grants the Bureau authority to commence a civil action against any person who violates a Federal consumer financial law, such as the CFPA. 12 U.S.C. § 5564(a).

VIOLATIONS OF THE CFPA

60. The CFPA prohibits a covered person from committing or engaging in any "unfair, deceptive, or abusive act or practice" in connection with any transaction with a consumer for a consumer financial product or service, or the offering of a consumer financial product or service. 12 U.S.C. §§ 5531, 5536(a)(1)(B).

61. Servicing loans and collecting debt are "consumer financial products or services" under the CFPA. 12 U.S.C. § 5481(15)(A)(i), (x).

DECEPTIVE ACTS OR PRACTICES

COUNT I

False and Misleading Affidavits and Testimony

62. The Bureau incorporates the allegations in Paragraphs 1–61 by reference.

63. In numerous instances, in connection with collecting or attempting to collect debt, Defendants represented to consumers, directly or indirectly, expressly or by implication, that affiants or witnesses in court had personal knowledge of the education loan records evidencing the debt.

64. In fact, in numerous instances, affiants and witnesses lacked personal knowledge of the education loan records evidencing the debt when they executed the affidavits.

65. In numerous instances, Defendants represented to consumers, directly or indirectly, expressly or by implication, that affiants and witnesses had personal knowledge of the record management practices and procedures of the Trust and the practices and procedures the Trust requires of its loan servicers and other agents.

66. In fact, affiants and witnesses lacked personal knowledge of the record management practices and procedures of the Trusts and the practices and procedures of Trusts' agents.

67. In numerous instances, Defendants represented to consumers, directly or indirectly, expressly or by implication, that affiants and witnesses had reviewed the chain of title records and asserted that they had personal knowledge that the loans were transferred, sold, and assigned to the Trust on dates certain.

68. In fact, on numerous occasions, affiants and witnesses had not reviewed the chain of title records and lacked personal knowledge that the loans were transferred, sold and assigned to the Trust.

69. Defendants' representations set forth in Paragraphs 63–68 are material and likely to mislead consumers acting reasonably under the circumstances.

70. Defendants' representations set forth in Paragraph 63–68 constitute deceptive acts or practices in violation of the CFPA. 12 U.S.C. §§ 5531, 5536(a)(1)(B).

COUNT II

Improperly Notarized Affidavits

71. The Bureau incorporates the allegations in Paragraphs 1–61 by reference.

72. In numerous instances, in connection with collecting or attempting to collect debt, Defendants represented to consumers, directly or indirectly, expressly or by implication, that the affidavits submitted in support of its collections lawsuits were properly sworn and executed before a notary.

73. In fact, in numerous instances, the affidavits were unsworn and executed outside the presence of a notary.

74. Defendants' representations set forth in Paragraphs 72–73 are material and likely to mislead consumers acting reasonably under the circumstances.

75. Defendants' representations set forth in Paragraph 72–73 constitute deceptive acts or practices in violation of the CFPA. 12 U.S.C. §§ 5531, 5536(a)(1)(B).

COUNT III

Filing Lawsuits without the Intent or Ability to Prove the Claims, if Contested

76. The Bureau incorporates the allegations in Paragraphs 1–61 by reference.

77. In numerous instances, in connection with collecting or attempting to collect debt, Defendants represented to consumers, directly or indirectly, expressly or by implication, that collections lawsuits were supported by valid and reliable legal documentation needed to obtain judgment.

78. In fact, in numerous lawsuits, documentation of a complete chain of assignment evidencing that the subject loan was transferred to Defendants was missing.

79. In fact, in numerous lawsuits, a promissory note proving the existence of the debt was missing.

80. In fact, in numerous lawsuits, the Trusts could not prove their claims, if contested.

81. Defendants' representations set forth in Paragraphs 77–80 are material and likely to mislead consumers acting reasonably under the circumstances.

82. Defendants' representations set forth in Paragraph 77–80 constitute deceptive acts or practices in violation of the CFPA. 12 U.S.C. §§ 5531, 5536(a)(1)(B).

COUNT IV.

Collection of Time-Barred Debt

83. The Bureau incorporates the allegations in Paragraphs 1–61 by reference.

84. In numerous instances, in connection with collecting or attempting to collect debt, Defendants represented to consumers, directly or indirectly, expressly or by implication, that the Trusts had a legal right to obtain judgment through its collections lawsuits.

85. In fact, in numerous instances, the statute of limitations on these loans had expired.

86. Defendants' representations set forth in Paragraphs 84–85 are material and likely to mislead consumers acting reasonably under the circumstances.

87. Defendants' representations set forth in Paragraph 84–85 constitute deceptive acts or practices in violation of the CFPA. 12 U.S.C. §§ 5531, 5536(a)(1)(B).

UNFAIR PRACTICES.

COUNT V.

Filing Lawsuits without the Intent or Ability to Prove the Claims, if Contested

88. The Bureau incorporates the allegations in Paragraphs 1–61 by reference.

89. Under section 1031 of the CFPA, an act or practice is unfair if it causes or is likely to cause substantial injury to consumers which is not reasonably avoidable by consumers, and such substantial injury is not outweighed by countervailing benefits to consumers or to competition. 12 U.S.C. §§ 5531(c), 5536(a)(1)(B).

90. In numerous instances, in connection with collecting or attempting to collect debt through collections lawsuits, Defendants filed collections lawsuits without the intent or ability to prove the claims, if contested.

91. Defendants' acts or practices have caused or were likely to cause substantial injury to consumers, estimated to be at least $3.5 million in payments made in connection with these lawsuits.

92. Consumers could not reasonably avoid the harm, and the harm was not outweighed by countervailing benefits to consumers or competition.

93. Defendants' acts or practices set forth in Paragraph 90–92 constitute unfair acts or practices in violation of the CFPA. 12 U.S.C. §§ 5531(c), 5536(a)(1)(B).

CONSUMER INJURY

94. Consumers have suffered or were likely to suffer substantial injury as a result of Defendants' violations of the CFPA. In addition, Defendants have been unjustly enriched as a result of their unlawful acts or practices.

. . . .

Note on National Collegiate Master Student Loan Trust

The CFPB settled with the National Collegiate Master Student Loan Trust and its co-defendants for a monetary penalty of $21.6 million and agreement that there would be an independent audit for ownership and loan validity of all the loans held by the National Collegiate Student Loan Trusts with no collection or credit reporting action on any loan that has not received a positive audit.

II. FEDERAL REGULATION: CRIMINAL LAW

Title II of the federal Consumer Credit Protection Act of 1968 criminalizes the "collection of credit by extortionate means," namely "the use, or an express or implicit threat of use, of violence or other criminal means to cause harm to the person, reputation, or property of any person" as part of the collections process. 18 U.S.C. §§ 891, 894. Title II is an anti-loan sharking provision that also prohibits the making or financing of extortionate extensions of credit. 18 U.S.C. §§ 892-893. Title II is the original federal intervention in the debt collection market and went hand-in-glove with the first federal consumer credit protection regulation: Title I of the Consumer Credit Protection Act is the Truth in Lending Act.

III. FEDERAL REGULATION: SERVICEMEMBERS' CIVIL RELIEF ACT

Federal law provides special protection from collection actions for active duty military servicemembers and their dependents. The Servicemembers Civil Relief Act ("SCRA"), codified at 50 U.S.C. App. §§ 501-597b, is a federal statute dating back to World War II, and is one of the earliest federal interventions in the consumer finance market. While the SCRA affects consumer debt collection, its goal, somewhat like the Military Lending Act of 2006 is not so much consumer protection as ensuring an undistracted military force. Soldiers who are worried about losing their home in foreclosure are likely to be distracted and demoralized; imagine fighting in Afghanistan while back in the U.S. your family was losing its home. While the SCRA is really about trying to remove distractions from the military mission, it nonetheless provides extensive, and yet politically non-controversial, interventions into the consumer credit market.

The SCRA has three main sets of provisions relating to debt collection dealing, respectively, with default judgments, interest rates, and collection actions. The SCRA requires that in any civil action in which the defendant does not make an appearance—which would normally entitle the plaintiff to a default judgment—the plaintiff must file an affidavit with the court regarding the defendant's military service status. 50 U.S.C. App. § 521(a)-(b). Plaintiffs normally use an online system provided free of charge by the Department of Defense's Defense Manpower Data

Center SCRA database, which requires the debtor's last name and either Social Security number or birth date to determine if a defendant is on active duty military service. *See* https://www.dmdc.osd.mil/appj/scra/welcome.xhtml.

If the defendant is on active duty in the military (or a dependent of the active duty servicemember) or military service status cannot be determined, an attorney must be appointed to represent the absent defendant. 50 U.S.C. App. § 521(b)(2). The civil action must be stayed for a minimum of 90 days if there might be a defense to the action that could not be presented without the presence of the defendant or if the appointed counsel cannot determine whether a meritorious defense exists (including because of inability to contact the defendant). 50 U.S.C. App. § 521(d).

If a default judgment is entered during the servicemember's active duty or within 60 days thereafter, it may be vacated if "the servicemember was materially affected by reason of that military service in making a defense to the action" and "the servicemember has a meritorious or legal defense to the action or some part of it." 50 U.S.C. App. § 521(g)(1). An application for vacation must be made within 90 days of release from active duty service. 50 U.S.C. App. § 521(g)(2).

All of this means that in practice it is difficult to obtain a default judgment against an active duty military member. It also means that before proceeding with any sort of judicial debt collection, a collector must ascertain active duty military status and file the SCRA affidavit with the court.

Perhaps the most striking provision of the SCRA is that the SCRA caps interest rates (including service charges, fees, etc.) on debts incurred by the servicemember or dependent before military service at 6% per year for as long as the servicemember is on active duty. 50 U.S.C. App. § 527(a). Any other interest above that is forgiven, rather than forborne and later capitalized or tacked on as a balloon. 50 U.S.C. App. § 527(a)(2). The 6% cap may be raised if servicemember can pay and is not materially affected by reason of the military service. 50 U.S.C. App. § 527(c). The SCRA also prohibits acceleration of debts while the servicemember is on active duty. 50 U.S.C. App. § 527(a)(3). To be effective, however, the servicemember must notify the creditor in writing within 180 days of the servicemember's release from active duty. 50 U.S.C. App. § 527(b).

The SCRA also stays execution of judgments, attachments, and garnishments as long as the court is of the opinion that the servicemenber is materially affected by reason of military service. 50 U.S.C. App. § 524. This stay extends for 90 days past the end of active duty military service. The SCRA additionally prohibits foreclosures during a servicemember's active duty time and for nine months thereafter. 50 U.S.C. App. § 533(c). The SCRA similarly limits eviction actions, 50 U.S.C. App. § 531, and rescission or termination of installment contracts or repossession thereunder for breaches occurring during or before military servicing, 50 U.S.C. App. § 532. For leases of both residential property and motor vehicles and phone contracts, the servicemember lessee may terminate the lease or contract upon entry into military service. 50 U.S.C. App. §§ 535-535a. The SCRA also tolls statutes of limitations on actions brought by servicemembers and on rights of redemption of real property for as long as the servicemember is on active duty. 50 U.S.C. App. § 526. Furthermore, use of SCRA rights cannot affect credit histories. 50 U.S.C. App. § 518.

The effect of the SCRA is that a creditor may not obtain a default judgment easily, will have its interest rate capped at 6% until it obtains that judgment (and presumably also on any post-judgment interest, as federal law should trump any state law on post-judgment interest rates), and will not be able to collect on any judgment as long as the servicemember is on active duty.

Significantly, however, SCRA rights are waivable. 50 U.S.C. App. § 517. Waivers must be in writing and in a separate instrument from the obligation or liability to which they apply. 50 U.S.C. App. § 517(a). Moreover, waivers are only effective to allow modification, termination, or cancellations of loan or lease agreements or to allow repossession or foreclosure if they are made during or after the period of active duty military service. 50 U.S.C. App. § 517(a)-(b).

The SCRA has a private right of action and allows equitable remedies, monetary damages, and recovery of attorney's fees in successful actions. 50 U.S.C. App. § 597a.

IV. FEDERAL REGULATION: GARNISHMENT LIMITATIONS

A. The Garnishment Process

Garnishment is a process in which a debtor of the judgment debtor is directed to turn over funds that are owed to the judgment debtor to the judgment creditor. In other words, the debtor's debtor pays the creditor directly instead of paying the debtor, who will then (possibly) pay the creditor.

Garnishment is typically a remedy that is available only by court order after a money judgment has been entered. Prejudgment garnishment is likely unconstitutional under the Supreme Court's decision in *Sniadach v. Family Finance Corp*, 395 U.S. 337 (1969), which held that Wisconsin's wage garnishment statute was unconstitutional violation of due process because it authorized garnishment without adequate notice or opportunity to be heard. *See also Fuentes v. Shevin*, 407 U.S. 67 (1972) (holding that a pre-judgment seizure of goods under a writ of replevin violated due process).

There are two types of garnishment: wage and non-wage. Wage garnishment involves a court order served on the debtor's employer instructing the employer to withhold a certain amount of the employee's wages and remit them to the creditor.

Technically the employer is the defendant in a wage garnishment action and can either contest the order or comply with it. Failure to comply without contesting can result in the employer being held in contempt of court. It can also result in the creditor being held liable for amounts paid to the employee that should have been garnished, as well as costs, attorney's fees, and possibly even punitive damages. *See, e.g.*, 31 U.S.C. § 3720D(f). Indeed, some states back up garnishment orders with statutory liens on all of the employer's assets to ensure compliance or recovery for the garnishment beneficiary. *See, e.g.*, Cal. Code Civ. Pro. § 706.029. As a result, an employer should not take a garnishment order lightly.

Non-wage garnishment is usually of a bank account. Recall that when you make a bank deposit, you are the bank's creditor; the bank owes you the money you have on deposit. Garnishment is distinct from a levy on a bank account in that a levy is a one-time collection action in which the bank is ordered (usually by the sheriff) to hand over all non-exempt funds in the account, whereas a garnishment order on a bank is usually an evergreen process until the debt is paid off. Under a garnishment order, the bank must divert the non-exempt funds to the creditor as long as the debt is outstanding.

B. Federal Wage Garnishment Limitations

Title III of the Consumer Credit Protection Act of 1968 is the Federal Wage Garnishment Law. The law places restrictions on the garnishment of debtors' wages because of the concern that unrestricted garnishment would encourage predatory lending and could be disruptive to employment. 15 U.S.C. § 1671.

Specifically, the Federal Wage Garnishment Law provides a ceiling for wage garnishment. Garnishments generally may not exceed the lesser of 25% of the employee's disposable income (defined as income after required federal and state tax withholdings, 15 U.S.C. § 1672(b)) or the amount by which the employee's disposable earnings exceed 30 times the hourly minimum wage (currently $7.25/hr). 15 U.S.C. § 1673(a). Thus, if the employee's weekly income is over $290, it is subject to the 25% limit, while if it is under $217.50, it may not be garnished. In other words, the statute assumes that in a 40-hour work week, the most that can be garnished is 10 hours of earnings or 25% of the disposable income.

Not all types of garnishment orders are subject to these limitations, however. Domestic support orders are subject to a cap of 50% of disposable weekly earnings for individuals supporting spouses or dependent children who are not the garnishment beneficiaries and 60% otherwise. 15 U.S.C. § 1673(b)(2). These figures rise for grossly delinquent domestic support obligations. *Id.* Federal law also requires that all child support orders include automatic wage withholding orders, 42 U.S.C. §§ 659, 666.

Payments made in Chapter 13 bankruptcies, and most notably federal and state tax liabilities, are all exempt from any federal garnishment cap. 15 U.S.C. § 1673(b)(1)(B)-(C). Put bluntly, the IRS or state tax authorities can levy on a consumer's entire paycheck. Moreover, the IRS does not need to get a court judgment to pursue a tax levy (the tax term for garnishment). 26 U.S.C. § 6331.

Federal law also facilitates certain non-tax garnishments undertaken by the federal government. Under the Debt Collection Improvement Act, the federal government may garnish up to 15% of disposable income without a court order (but subject to certain administrative procedures) for non-tax debt. 31 U.S.C. § 3720D. A separate provision in the Higher Education Act allows for administrative garnishment of up to 15% for federally made or guaranteed student loans. 20 U.S.C. § 1095a(a)(1). The Department of Education has not been shy in using this provision. Some $665 million of wages were garnished for student loans in 2015-2016.

Conversely, however, federal law prohibits certain types of government benefit payments from garnishment. These prohibitions only apply to the extent that these funds are distinct from the debtor's other funds, however. Treasury regulations require that electronic deposits of exempt government funds be "tagged" so that financial institutions can know which funds are exempt from garnishment without the onus of proof being on the consumer. 31 C.F.R. § 212.

Federal law is just a ceiling for garnishment orders. Individual states frequently further restrict wage garnishment beneath the federal ceiling, although the federal government is not bound by state restrictions. No such restrictions apply to bank account garnishment.

C. Federal Wage Garnishee Employment Protections

Wage garnishment presents real risks for employers. Consider the situation of an employer served with a garnishment order—the employer has to determine how much of the employee's earnings are exempt. If the employer undercalculates or simply fails to respond to the garnishment order, the *employer* is potentially liable to the creditor for the deficiency, whereas if the employer overpays, it may be liable to the employee. Garnishment thus adds both administrative hassle and liability for employers. This means that the employer might have to ask if the employee is really worth keeping around. It might well be easier to fire an employee than to deal with garnishment orders.

Federal law offers some protection for dismissal based on garnishment. The Federal Wage Garnishment Law provides that "No employer may discharge any employee by reason of the fact that his earnings have been subjected to garnishment for any one indebtedness." 15 U.S.C. § 1674. This provision only gives employment protection for discharge based on *one* garnishment order. Debtors, however, often owe more than one debt. Such debtors' employment is not protected by federal law, and multiple garnishment orders increase administrative burdens more than the sum of the individual orders' administrative burdens because of the need to determine the priority of the orders. Generally speaking, domestic support orders have priority over everything else, 42 U.S.C. § 666(b)(7), with other orders being honored in the order received. *See* 34 C.F.R. § 34.20. The federal garnishment caps apply to the aggregate of garnishment orders, not individual ones. *See* 34. C.F.R. § 34.20(b).

Although a debtor can be fired for multiple garnishment orders (certainly simultaneously, perhaps consecutively), such an outcome hardly helps the creditor; how is the debtor to repay the debt without a job? Notice, however, that firing an employee for multiple garnishment orders does not absolve the employer of the need to garnish whatever wages have been accrued and unpaid at the time the order is received; thus there might not be much relief from administrative costs. Dismissal will alleviate future costs, but not existing ones.

The Federal Wage Garnishment Law is enforced by the Department of Labor. There is no private right of action under the Wage Garnishment Law, although private rights of action do exist under the Debt Collection Improvement Act, 31 U.S.C. § 3720D(e), and an employee could always bring a state-law wrongful dismissal suit.

V. DEBT RELIEF SERVICES AND THE TELEMARKETING SALES RULE

When consumers face debt problems they sometimes turn to debt relief companies for assistance. **Debt relief**, which is also known as **debt settlement** or **debt adjustment**, involves the renegotiation of the terms of debts with creditors. Debt relief companies attempt to renegotiate consumers' debts with creditors in exchange for a fee. Usually renegotiations aim for the forgiveness of some amount of the consumer's debt.

There is, of course, no guarantee that creditors will be willing to renegotiate the terms of existing debts; creditors always have the ability to just say "no." Creditors are sometimes concerned about making concessions to debtors who don't actually need relief. Accordingly, some debt relief companies counsel consumers to stop paying on bills, which is a way of getting creditors' attention. The risk from this, however, is that the consumer may incur late fees, penalty interest, and other charges.

Debt relief companies will also often administer repayment plans on which the consumer and lender(s) have agreed. In such situations, the debt relief company will direct the consumer to fund a bank account that the debt relief company manages, for a fee.

Another method of managing debt is **debt consolidation**. Consolidation means that numerous debts will be refinanced with a new single (larger) debt. The consolidated debt will be owed to one creditor that may be either a new or existing creditor. Typically the new, consolidated debt has a longer term than the original debts, but with that longer term it will bear a lower interest rate. Thus, the periodic payments on the consolidated debt will be lower, even if the total payments to pay off the debt will be greater. Debt consolidation's attraction to consumers is from the simplification of multiple payment obligations into a single, smaller one. Debt consolidation is not itself a renegotiation of the debt, but some debt settlement services may effectuate a consolidation.

A third method of managing debt is **credit counseling** from (typically) nonprofit consumer credit counseling services. Credit counselors work with the debtor and creditors to create a debt management plan that is affordable to the debtor. Debt management plans typically require the debtor to make a single periodic payment to the credit counselor, who then makes the periodic payments to the creditors. (This arrangement is similar to that of a trustee in a Chapter 13 bankruptcy.) Whereas debt relief services generally attempt to negotiate a reduction in principal balances, credit counselors' debt management plans typically attempt to lower overall periodic payments through extensions of terms, lower interest rates, and waiver of fees.

The Telemarketing Sales Rules (TSR), 16 C.F.R. Part 310, enacted under the Telemarketing and Consumer Fraud and Abuse Prevention Act (TCFAPA), 15 U.S.C. §§ 6101-08, regulate debt relief services offered via telemarketing. "Telemarketing" is defined as "a plan, program or campaign . . . conducted to induce the purchase of . . . services . . . by use of one or more telephones and which involves more than one instate telephone call." 16 C.F.R. § 310.2. Thus, even if most of the transaction is conducted in person or through the Internet, a transaction could still be considered telemarketing.

The TSR prohibits "deceptive" and "abusive" practices in telemarketing and has an ambit that goes far beyond consumer finance, extending to virtually all telemarketed products and services. In regard to debt relief services, however, the TSR requires that telemarketers make several disclosures to consumers before the consumers consent to pay for debt relief services, which are defined as "any program or service represented, directly or by implication, to renegotiate, settle, or in any way alter the terms of payment or other terms of the debt between a person and one or more unsecured creditors or debt collectors, including, but not limited to, a reduction in the balance, interest rate, or fees owed by a person to an unsecured creditor or debt collector." 16 C.F.R. §§ 310.2(o), 310.3(a)(1)(viii), 310.3(a)(2)(x). Thus, mortgage modification programs are not considered "debt relief" because they deal with secured debt. The same is true for programs dealing with auto loans. Instead, regulated debt relief programs tend to focus on credit card debt. More important than the disclosures required by the TSR is its prohibition on telemarketers "requesting or receiving payment of any fee or consideration for any debt relief service until and unless" the debt has actually been renegotiated, the consumer has made at least one payment on the debt settlement plan, and the fee meets certain requirements about its relationship to the total debt renegotiated. 16 C.F.R. § 310.4(a)(5). The concern the TSR is addressing is that a consumer will sign up with a debt relief service and pay the service's fees, but never actually get any relief, whether because the service undertook no action or because creditors weren't willing to renegotiate the terms of the debt.

TCFAPA has a limited private right of action that extends to the TSR rules thereunder. 15 U.S.C. § 6104(a). Consumers can bring suits under the TSR in federal court if there are $50,000 in actual damages for each person. This high dollar threshold effectively precludes most private actions. Consumers can recover actual damages, costs, attorney's fees, and expert witness fees in successful suits and obtain injunctive relief. 15 U.S.C. §§ 6104(a), 6104(d). While rulemaking for the TSR is the responsibility of the FTC because the TCFAPA is not an "enumerated consumer law," public enforcement of the TSR in regard to debt relief services is administered by the CFPB because TSR violations are treated as UDAAP violations. 15 U.S.C. § 6102(c)(2). Additionally, state attorneys general may enforce the TSR. 15 U.S.C. § 6103.

VI. FEDERAL BANKRUPTCY LAW

Another option consumers have when they cannot manage their debts is to file for bankruptcy. Federal bankruptcy law also affects debt collection. It does so in two ways. First, the filing of a bankruptcy petition immediately triggers a federal injunction against most types of collection activity. This injunction is known as the "automatic stay." 11 U.S.C. § 362(a). The stay covers any attempt to collect from the debtor or the debtor's property, including starting or continuing litigation, creating, perfecting, or enforcing liens, or setting off debts. Violations of the automatic stay are sanctionable by the bankruptcy court.

The filing of a bankruptcy petition creates a new legal entity, known as the bankruptcy estate, consisting of all of the debtor's non-exempt property. State law provides that certain property of a debtor is exempt from creditors' levies. Debtors generally have a choice between using their home state's property exemptions or federal bankruptcy property exemptions, but federal law curtails the unlimited homestead exemption that some states offer. 11 U.S.C. § 522.

The bankruptcy estate is held in trust for the benefit of the debtor's creditors by a trustee in bankruptcy. The combination of the automatic stay and the creation of the bankruptcy estate channels all collection activity against the debtor into a single forum, the bankruptcy court, and thereby enables a fair and orderly distribution to creditors. Creditors file claims with the bankruptcy court detailing what they allege the debtor owes. The claims are presumed valid unless challenged, but they may be disallowed based on state-law defenses, as well as on certain additional bankruptcy-specific defenses. 11 U.S.C. § 502.

The mere fact that a claim is allowed, however, does not mean that it will be paid. Payment of claims depends on the chapter of the Bankruptcy Code under which the consumer filed. In Chapter 7 payment is made out of the debtor's current non-exempt assets, while in Chapter 13 payment is made (primarily) out of the debtor's future income. The choice of what chapter to file under is the consumer's, subject to "means testing." Higher-income consumers (those with more "means") are required to file under Chapter 13 under a complex calculation. As a practical matter, the choice of filing chapter is often determined by the consumer's attorney, with local legal culture playing a large role; there is considerable variation nationally by judicial district in terms of favored filing chapters.

If the consumer files under Chapter 7, the distribution process is fairly automatic. The trustee in bankruptcy will liquidate all of the debtor's non-exempt assets and pay out the proceeds to creditors with allowed claims according to a statutorily defined priority system, with claims being paid pro rata within each priority tier. Secured claims—those secured by collateral, such as a home mortgage or car loan—get paid their collateral or the value thereof. 11 U.S.C. § 725. Next come certain creditors with statutory priorities, most notably domestic support obligations and certain tax obligations, and then, if any funds remain, general unsecured creditors. 11 U.S.C. § 726. In most Chapter 7 cases, there is no recovery for general unsecured creditors. Dalié Jiménez, *The Distribution of Assets in Consumer Chapter 7 Bankruptcy Cases*, 83 Am. Bankr. L.J. 795 (2009).

Note that under Chapter 7, the consumer gives up current assets, but keeps future income. In contrast, if the consumer files for bankruptcy under Chapter 13 (or Chapter 11), the consumer generally keeps his current assets, but instead must devote his future income above a bare minimum for personal upkeep to paying creditors.

The terms under which creditors will be paid in Chapter 13 (or 11) are determined by a "plan" that must be confirmed by the bankruptcy court. Chapter 13 plans last between three and five years and must devote all of the debtor's disposable income to paying creditors. In other words, the debtor is on a court-supervised budget for three to five years. The plan must pay all creditors at least as much as they would receive in a Chapter 7 bankruptcy. Given that most creditors would recover nothing in Chapter 7, this means that a Chapter 13 plan does not need to pay all creditors in full, although some courts will refuse to confirm a plan that does not provide a minimum percentage payment for unsecured creditors.

Significantly, a Chapter 13 plan may provide for the curing and de-acceleration of defaulted debts, including mortgages. 11 U.S.C. § 1322. Chapter 13 generally allows a debtor to retain collateral by paying off the lesser of the value of the property or the face amount of the debt, but this rule does not apply to home mortgages or vehicles purchased in the two-and-a-half years prior to the bankruptcy filing. To retain a home or newish car in Chapter 13, the debtor must pay off the face amount of the debt, even if the market value is substantially lower.

The second way bankruptcy affects debt collection is that a debtor may receive a "discharge" of debts following the bankruptcy. A discharge is a permanent federal injunction against collection of the debts. A discharged debt is still technically owed and can be voluntarily repaid, but post-bankruptcy collection efforts would likely violate the discharge injunction. The discharge injunction does not prevent a creditor from repossessing collateral if the debtor is in default and did not cure the default during the bankruptcy; instead the discharge injunction only shields the debtor from personal liability.

Not all debts are dischargeable in bankruptcy. First, some bankrupts are not eligible for a discharge because they previously received a discharge of debts and not enough time has elapsed. 11 U.S.C. §§ 727, 1328. Second, certain categories of debts are not generally dischargeable, including all student loans, domestic support obligations (child support and alimony), certain tax obligations, debt arising from wrongful or malicious torts, death or personal injury liability from intoxicated driving, and debts incurred based on false representations or fraud, with certain luxury good purchases made prior to bankruptcy presumed to be fraudulent. 11 U.S.C. § 523. To the extent that these debts are not repaid during the bankruptcy they remain owing and are not subject to the discharge injunction. Third, the debtor may choose to "reaffirm" certain debts. Reaffirmed debts are not subject to the discharge injunction, but reaffirmation requires a specific court procedure and sign-off by the debtor's attorney. 11 U.S.C. § 523(c). Debtors will often reaffirm debts in order to retain collateral (especially vehicles) post-bankruptcy because they would not be able to readily purchase an equivalent replacement because they lack the funds for a down payment.

VII. STATE AND LOCAL DEBT COLLECTION REGULATION

While the FDCPA provides federal regulation of "debt collectors," it does not preempt state or local debt collection law to the extent they offer greater consumer protections. 15 U.S.C. § 1692n. Many states have their own FDCPA-type statutes, but their scope does not always track that of the FDCPA. Most notably, California's Rosenthal Fair Debt Collection Practices Act defines debt collector as:

> any person who, in the ordinary course of business, regularly, on behalf of himself or herself or others, engages in debt collection. The term includes any person who composes and sells, or offers to compose and sell, forms, letters, and other collection media used or intended to be used for debt collection, but does not include an attorney or counselor at law.

Cal. Civ. Code § 1788.2(c). While attorneys are exempted from this definition, law firms (as separate legal entities) are not, and California law provides that "An attorney and his or her employees who are employed primarily to assist in the collection of a consumer debt owed to another . . . shall comply with . . . the obligations imposed on debt collectors pursuant to [the Rosenthal Fair Debt Collection Practices Act]." Cal. Bus. & Prof. Code § 6077.5. The substantive provisions of the Rosenthal Fair Debt Collection Practices Act are materially similar to those of the federal FDCPA. A consumer can, of course, bring both federal and state FDCPA actions based on the same behavior, and remedies are likely to be cumulative. Be aware that some states have additional substantive requirements in their debt collection laws. For example, Florida requires that consumers be given notice of any assignment of a debt by a creditor at least 30 days before collection activity begins. Fla. Stat. § 559.715.

Additionally, state UDAP statutes may apply to debt collection. And states often have significant limitations on garnishment beyond the federal ceiling and provide for other consumer property to be exempt from creditors.

Problem Set 34

1. Erin Brown is in-house counsel at Puget Salvage Corp., a Washington-based maritime salvage company. Puget Salvage has just been served with a garnishment order for $11,500 against Jarett Wessel, one of Puget's crane operators, in favor of Continental Express Bank, N.A. This is the fifth garnishment order against Wessel that Puget Salvage has received this month. The others are, in the order received, for $2,500 (Fast Times Automotive Acceptance Corp.), $5,000 (Tom Vasco, a tort victim), $8,000 (Helga Wessel for back child support), and $4,000 (Internal Revenue Service for back taxes). Brown is concerned about complying with all of the garnishment orders. Wessel's take-home pay after taxes and other required withholding is $1,000/week. Jarett has a reputation as a reasonably good employee and just celebrated his third marriage. What are Brown's options? 15 U.S.C. §§ 1673, 1674. (Federal minimum wage is currently $7.25/hr. Assume that Washington state does not impose its own restrictions on garnishment.)

2. Six months ago Army Reserve 1st Lieutenant Andrew Gaughan was deployed to Afghanistan for the third time. The deployments have been tough on Andrew's family and marriage and disruptive to his job as a manager at a recycling plant. In particular, money has been tight for Andrew's family since he's been deployed. Yesterday Andrew came back from a hair-raising patrol to find an email from his wife telling him that she just received a foreclosure notice from their mortgage lender. His wife noted that they hadn't made a mortgage payment since his deployment because money's been so tight that they can't afford the payments at the 8% annual interest rate, and late fees have been racking up on the balance as well. Andrew is due to return stateside in a month

and expects to end his active duty a month thereafter, but he's worried that it will be too late to save his house at that point, and he fears that will also mean the end of his marriage. He's come to see you, a JAG officer assigned as the legal assistance contact for Andrew's base, to see if he has any recourse. What do you tell him? *See* 50 U.S.C. App. §§ 511(2)(A)(i), 523(b), 527(a), 533(b)-(c).

PART II

MARKETS

SECTION C

Data

CHAPTER 35

CREDIT REPORTING

I. CREDIT REPORTING AND CONSUMER CREDIT

The consumer credit system relies on information about consumers. Financial institutions cannot determine whether to lend or on what terms without information about the consumer's ability and likelihood of repayments. Historically, most consumer lending was local, which meant that lenders had the ability to use their own local knowledge to gauge a consumer's credit risk. The loan officer might know something about the consumer's standing and reputation in the community. The loan officer might be familiar with the consumer's employer and know something about the prospective borrower's job security ("John's got a good union job down at the steel mill"), or know if the consumer had a drinking problem or if the consumer took good care of his home or car. As consumer finance markets have become national, this type of local underwriting information has ceased to be readily available to lenders operating nationally. National lenders often lack this type of direct observation of borrowers, and to the extent they have it, its use raises concerns about discriminatory lending and loan officer favoritism.

Today, in a national market, lenders obtain information about consumers from a variety of sources—self-reporting by the consumer, information from consumers' employers or the IRS, valuations from third-party appraisers—their underwriting often relies heavily on data from companies that specialize in collecting data on consumers. These companies are called **consumer reporting agencies**—also known as credit reporting agencies or CRAs. CRAs are businesses that collect a range of data about individual consumers. The CRAs make the data available for purchase, and that data that is sold is known as a **consumer report**.

Consumer reports are often colloquially referred to as credit reports, but this is misleading. The information contained in a consumer report is not always used for credit-granting purposes, and consumer reports do not have to contain any credit information. Consumer reports may include any information that is accurate, complete, and not outdated. Indeed, not all consumer reports are particularly focused on consumers' use of credit, as consumer reports are used for a variety of purposes besides credit transactions. Accordingly, the regulation of consumer reporting affects more than the consumer credit system.

While there are numerous CRAs, the industry is dominated by three national general reporting companies, Equifax, Experian, and Transunion. Other CRAs may be local or may have a national scope, but with a specialized focus such as employment screening, tenant screening, check and bank account screening, personal property insurance, medical, low-income and subprime credit specialists, utilities, retail credit, or gaming credit.

The data gathered by CRAs depends on the particular focus of a CRA. All CRAs collect basic information used to identify the file with a particular consumer, which is essential both to ensure that information obtained by the CRA is matched to the correct file and to ensure that the correct consumer report is furnished to the ultimate user. This basic identification information includes name(s), date of birth, current and past addresses, and Social Security number.

The three national CRAs also collect information about consumers' use of credit, which includes the name of the creditor, the date the account (the "tradeline") was opened (and, if applicable, closed), the type of account, the credit limit or loan amount, the current balance and payment status of the account, and the payment history on the account. They also collect data from public records, such as any history of bankruptcy filings, adverse judgments, and liens. Specialized CRAs collect more focused types of information, for example, history of bank account closures, bad checks, retail fraud, or insurance claims.

While our focus in this chapter will primarily be on the use of consumer reports in the credit context, it is important to recognize that lenders are not the only entities that use consumer reports. Consumer reports are used by banks and credit unions when evaluating prospective depositors because of the overdraft risk of deposit accounts. Financial institutions as well as retailers that accept personal checks will use consumer reports to evaluate check fraud risk. Landlords will use consumer reports to screen potential tenants, and employers (including government agencies) will use consumer reports for employment and background screenings. Insurance companies use consumer reports about accident, prescription drug, and health histories, as well as credit history to evaluate consumer risk. Utility companies and telecoms use consumer reports when screening potential customers for bill repayment risk. And casinos use consumer reports when deciding whether to extend credit to consumers.

While lenders and other users of consumer reports rely on information from CRAs, the CRAs are, in turn, dependent on lenders and other businesses that interface with consumers for the information that they aggregate. Lenders and other businesses are not required to engage in consumer reporting, but virtually all institutional lenders as well as some non-financial institutions, such as hospitals, doctors and dentists offices, utilities, and landlords, do as well.

There are a few reasons why a business would want to engage in consumer reporting. First, credit reporting creates a consequence for non-payment for consumers. That might not only encourage repayment, but might also prioritize the repayment of an obligation owed to a reporting creditor over an obligation owed to a non-reporting creditor.

Second, reporting might help a lender by discouraging other lenders from extending too much credit to the borrower, thus reducing competition for repayment. For example, say a borrower has sufficient income to handle $5,000 in monthly payment obligations. If a lender believes that the borrower has no payment obligations currently, the lender will extend more credit than if the lender believes that there are already $4,700 in monthly payment obligations for the borrower. Thus, consumer reporting is a way for a lender to mark its territory, much like the filing of a financing statement can be used to scare off other potential secured creditors.

Third, lenders might submit consumer reports because consumer reporting affects credit scores produced by CRAs based on consumer report data. Lenders rely on those scores, so they might credit report because they want to improve the quality of the information that they themselves use.

Given that reporting has definite and measurable transaction costs for businesses and even potential liability, it might seem surprising that anyone credit reports: the benefits are more diffuse and reporting creates a set of positive externalities for other businesses that reporting businesses cannot capture. And yet reporting is quite common.

Creditors either report directly to each CRA separately under the terms of a Data Furnisher or Service Agreement or through a processor or "stacking" service that reports to multiple credit reporting agencies. The three national CRAs will only deal with reporting businesses that have a minimum number of active accounts, even if they report through a processor service. Thus, small businesses and consumers cannot engage in credit reporting. As a result, businesses that deal with a smaller number of consumers—such as payday lenders—have developed their own specialty CRAs. The national CRAs also require that reporting businesses report on a monthly basis and that they report data in a particular standardized format (the Metro 2 format, developed by the Consumer Data Industry Association, the trade association for CRAs).

While the consumer reporting system is vital for the operation of the modern consumer finance system, it is important to recognize that CRAs are different from many other types of institutional players in consumer finance in that they do not have a business-to-consumer business model. The CRA business model is to collect information about consumers from businesses and to then sell that information to businesses. The consumer need not have any involvement—or affirmative consent—in the process. This is because consumers do not "own" the data generated by their transactions or any descriptive data generated about them. Consumers are just "product" in the reporting system. This chapter discusses some of the limitations on the use and transfer of consumer data, but the issue is considered more broadly in Chapter 37, which covers consumer financial privacy. As we will see, the fact that consumers are neither sellers nor buyers of consumer reports has resulted in a market that has few incentives to protect consumer interests, as there is no market pressure to do so. Instead, the regulatory regime for consumer reports has adopted a number of moves designed to deal with the lack of consumer market discipline, namely price regulations on the provision of consumer reports to consumers and certain minimum service standards for CRAs.

The following remarks by the CFPB's first Director regarding credit reporting provide an overview of the credit reporting system and its role in the consumer credit economy.

Prepared Remarks by Richard Cordray
Director of the Consumer Financial Protection Bureau

Credit Reporting Field Hearing, Detroit, Michigan
July 16, 2012

Credit reporting plays a critical role in consumers' financial lives, a role that most people do not recognize because it is usually not very visible to them. Credit reports on a consumer's financial behavior can determine a consumer's eligibility for credit cards, car loans, and home mortgage loans – and they often affect how much a consumer is going to pay for that loan. If you have a credit record that appears to show a greater risk that you will fail to repay a loan, then you may be denied credit and you likely will be charged higher interest rates on any loan offered to you.

Our credit reporting system involves several key participants. First are the creditors and others that supply the information about your financial behavior, which can include your credit card issuers, your mortgage company, or companies that are collecting debts they claim you owe, among others. Second are those that collect and sell the information, which are the credit reporting companies. Third are those that use the information, which largely consist of financial institutions, but can also include insurance companies, auto dealers, retail stores, and even prospective employers. Fourth are consumers themselves, who are the object of all this scrutiny and who are immediately affected by it. All of these participants play important roles in ensuring that the credit reporting system operates effectively to help consumer credit markets work better for us all.

The credit reporting market is huge. Almost every adult in America has a credit file. Estimates are that each of the three biggest credit reporting companies maintains files on about 200 million Americans gleaned from over 10,000 providers of information. The amount of information collected and exchanged is astounding. Each year, approximately 3 billion credit reports are issued and more than 36 billion updates are made to consumer credit files.

A credit report contains information about the consumer's transactions – including loans that a consumer has paid on time, has paid late, has not paid, or has paid off, along with current amounts and sources of debt. The credit reporting companies also collect and report on information about consumers' finances available from public records, including civil judgments, liens, and bankruptcies from thousands of federal, state, and local courts and public offices.

The information contained in consumers' credit reports is used to derive their credit scores, such as various versions of the three-digit FICO score. Credit scores translate this great mass of information into a single number that indicates, in shorthand, a consumer's expected likelihood of repaying a loan. Generally, the lower the score, the lower a consumer's likelihood of repaying the loan compared to other consumers.

But credit reports are also used in a wide range of other types of decision-making – including determinations about eligibility for rental housing, what deposits are required for utility or telephone service, and premiums for auto and homeowners' insurance. Credit reports are even sometimes used to determine eligibility for a job. Banks, landlords, cell phone providers, and all kinds of other companies rely on the accuracy of this information to make good decisions and manage their risk of suffering losses.

Credit reporting is an important element in promoting access to credit that a consumer can afford to repay. Without credit reporting, consumers would not be able to get credit except from those who have already had direct experience with them, for example from local merchants who know whether or not they regularly pay their bills. This was the case fifty or a hundred years ago with "store credit," or when consumers really only had the option of going to their local bank. But now, consumers can instantly access credit because lenders everywhere can look to credit scores to provide a uniform benchmark for assessing risk. Conversely, credit reporting may also help reinforce consumer incentives to avoid falling behind on payments, or not paying back loans at all. After all, many consumers are aware that they should make efforts to build solid credit.

So this critical market is at the heart of our lending systems. It has enabled many of us to get credit and to afford a home or a college education.

But it is also clearly a market that can cause considerable problems for consumers. For example, sometimes credit reports contain errors that inaccurately reflect people's financial histories and can unfairly block them from getting approved for credit or can make it cost more than it should. Consumers also can encounter great difficulties at times in getting errors corrected. When the Consumer Bureau first opened its doors almost a year ago, we asked people to share their consumer experiences with us. We have heard reports since from many consumers that their credit reports are not accurate, and it is difficult to get them corrected. Because of the critical role that credit reports play in consumers' lives, it is our job to make sure we understand the full extent of these problems and address them effectively.

Given its enormity, given its influence, and given its wide impact on our overall economy, you can see that there is much at stake in ensuring that the credit reporting market is working properly for consumers.

II. CREDIT SCORES

CRAs do not warrant the accuracy of the information they furnish in consumer reports, and accuracy of reports is a major policy concern, as inaccurate data can result in consumers paying higher prices or not being able to obtain credit, insurance, or other services or in lenders underpricing risk. We will address accuracy issues later in this chapter.

Yet, even if consumer reports contained solely accurate information, they would still provide only a partial picture of the consumer: consumer reporting provides information about the consumer's *past* repayment history and the existence of certain current obligations. It does not indicate what the consumer's current income or assets are. It does not guaranty a potential creditor a total picture of the consumer's financial obligations. Moreover, given the huge range of data contained in standard credit reports, it would be hard for potential creditors to easily digest it and turn it into actionable information. Nonetheless, consumer reports have become the bedrock of the increasingly automated U.S. consumer credit system. They key to this automation are credit scores, which condense the varied information in consumer reports into a single numerical representation of the consumer's creditworthiness.

A. What's in a Credit Score?

A consumer does not have a single credit score. Instead, there are numerous different credit scoring models in use, which mean there are multiple scores in existence for any consumer. These models all use different inputs (with the precise formulas being proprietary trade secrets) and often have different scales. Some may place greater emphasis on certain types of repayment history information than others, such as certain types of obligation or on more recent repayment history. What differences in scores mean may also vary among models. Some models may be scoring the likelihood of timely repayment (*i.e.*, default rate), others ultimate repayment (*i.e.*, default rate and loss severity given default).

One of the most commonly used credit scores is produced by a firm called FICO (originally Fair, Isaac and Company) and is accordingly called a FICO score. Even the term FICO score is imprecise, however, as the Fair Isaac Corporation has several scoring models. Thus, a consumer might well have more than one FICO score. For example, the most recent FICO model is FICO 9, but FICO 8 is the most widely used model for non-mortgage lenders, while mortgage lenders use FICO 4 with Equifax and Transunion data and FICO 98 with Experian data. The other widely used type of credit score is known as a Vantage score, which is a product of a joint venture between Equifax, Experian, and Transunion. (Other brands of credit scores are sometimes derogatively known as "FAKO" scores.)

Perhaps the most important thing to understand about credit scores is that they are largely a black box of proprietary information. Thus, FICO explains in general terms the makeup of its scores: payment history: 35%, amounts owed: 30%; length of credit history: 15%; new credit: 10%; and types of credit in use: 10%. But how much a single late payment or an extra $1,000 of debt will affect the score remains unclear.

The lack of clarity makes it more difficult for consumers to game credit scores, but also to determine the consequences of their behavior on their credit score, much less on their future costs of credit. How much will a later credit card payment affect a consumer's credit score, and how much will that affect the terms on which the consumer gets an auto loan in two years? It's anyone's guess, and the answer may differ by credit score, even as it is clear that there is a connection of some sort.

The black box nature of credit scores also enables credit score providers to engage in product differentiation, thereby limiting competition—lenders have no better understanding than consumers of exactly what is driving any given credit scoring model. How much more likely is repayment from a consumer with a VantageScore Model 4.0 score of 650 than one with a score of 651? Again, it's anyone's guess. This should leave you wondering why lenders would rely on credit scores when they do not fully understand what drives the scores. Nonetheless, the difference in the cost of credit between a 651 and 650 might be quite different than between a 650 and

649, depending on the lender's underwriting model. Indeed, if the lender has a FICO score cutoff of 650, the consumer with a 649 simply won't get a loan.

B. Off-Label Indications of Credit Scores

While credit scores are designed to be a measure of credit risk, they are sometimes used for "off-label" indications, such as insurance and employment. The use of credit scores in these contexts is controversial, because the scores are often alleged to be a proxy for income and to reflect consumers' past financial problems due to medical or economic catastrophes, thin credit files (often a problem for low-income borrowers), and shopping for credit (because more inquiries on a credit report will hurt the score) rather than reflecting a propensity for risky behavior or irresponsibility. California, Massachusetts, and Hawaii have prohibited the use of credit scores for auto insurance, and Maryland and Hawaii have also done so for homeowners' insurance. Scholarly research, however, has not found a connection between credit scores and income. *See* Darcy Steeg Morris, Daniel Schwarcz & Joshua C. Teitelbaum, *Do Credit-Based Insurance Scores Proxy for Income in Predicting Auto Claim Risk?*, 14 J. Empirical Legal Stud. 397, 397-423 (2017) (finding that credit scores are not serving as an income proxy for auto insurance).

Beyond "off-label" uses of credit scores, credit scores have also become a measure of one's standing in society, a way some consumers use to rank and validate themselves. The psychology of this phenomenon is beyond the scope of this chapter other than to note that a quantification of social standing can fill an important need for some individuals, which may make it an important motivator in debt repayment.

C. Invisible and Unscorable Consumers

Not all consumers have credit sores or even files with CRAs. As of 2010, around 26 million consumers—11% of the U.S. adult population—lacked a file with one of the three national general CRAs. These consumers are "credit invisible." CFPB, *Data Point: Credit Invisibles*, May 2015. Additionally, another 19 million consumers—over 8% of the U.S. adult population—were "unscorable," meaning that their files with the CRAs contained insufficient information to generate a score, because the accounts reported were too few or too new or stale. *Id.*

There is a strong correlation between income and having a credit score. In low-income neighborhoods, nearly a third of consumers lack credit files, and another 15% are unscorable, compared to 4% who are credit invisible and 5% who are unscorable in upper-income neighborhoods. *Id.* Other factors, such as race and education, also correlate with lack of a credit score, but the magnitude of the effect is much larger for income. Kenneth Brevoort *et al.*, *Credit Invisibles and the Unscored*, 18 Cityscape 9, 22, 29-31 (2016). Younger consumers are much more likely to be unscorable as they have not yet established a sufficient number of accounts for a score to be generated from their credit file. Thus, nearly two-thirds of 18-19-year olds lack a credit file, but the percentage drops to under 9% for 25-29-year olds. CFPB, *Data Point: Credit Invisibles*, May 2015.

D. The Catch-22 of Establishing Credit

The lack of a credit score is a major obstacle to obtaining formal credit, as most lenders use a credit score in their underwriting. While there are some lenders that specialize in lending to consumers with no or "thin" credit files, they generally charge substantially higher rates than mainstream lenders. There is a Catch-22 with credit scores, in that many of the types of creditors that report to CRAs require a credit score before they will lend. This can make it difficult for consumers to establish credit files.

A simple way to establish credit is being a co-signor on a loan or being made an authorized user of an existing credit card (such as a parent's card). But this requires having someone with existing credit who is willing to work with the consumer and creates a substantial disadvantage for consumers whose parents or close relatives are not themselves in the consumer reporting system.

Another way to establish credit is to use a product, such as a student loan, that does not require a credit score and will result in credit reporting. (Payday and vehicle title loans do not require credit scores, but often do not result in credit reporting to nationwide general CRAs.) Again, however, the ability to obtain a student loan is likely to correlate with one's parents' economic status.

Yet another option is to use a product specifically marketed toward consumers attempting to establish credit: so-called credit builder loans or secured credit cards. Credit builder loans are small loans, secured by a certificate of deposit that cannot be accessed by the borrower until the loan is repaid. Credit builder loans tend to be offered by credit unions and community banks. For example, in order to get a $400 credit builder loan, the consumer must deposit $500, which cannot be recovered until the $500 loan is repaid. The consumer in this situation ends up with no additional liquidity (and in this example gets less liquidity), but establishes a repayment record that gets reported. A secured credit card operates like a credit builder loan, just without the payment feature of the card. Secured credit cards tend to be offered by specialty finance companies with bank partners. Additionally, some landlords will credit report, and there are third-party services that will report on rental payments even if the landlord does not, but these reports are not always accepted by CRAs.

E. Importance of Credit Scores for Modern Life

The key to see here is how credit scores and consumer reporting fit with the entire consumer finance ecosystem. Consumers tend to purchase large-ticket items—homes and cars and major appliances—on credit. To obtain such credit, a consumer needs to have a credit score, which necessitates having a sufficiently robust file with a CRA. For many Americans credit reporting is the initial gateway to home ownership and access to transportation.

Even if a consumer isn't looking to make large credit purchases, a credit score is still essential just for gaining access to the modern payment system. Electronic payments—credit and debit cards and ACH—are the coin of the realm for modern commerce; cash and checks just aren't usable for Internet transactions. To get a debit card or do an ACH transaction one needs a bank account, and banks are unlikely to open an account without first checking the consumer's credit. Likewise, to get a credit card one will need a credit score (and also a bank account to make payments on the card account). Thus, the consumer will need a credit score to access the payments necessary to engage in the modern economy, and in order to get a credit score, the consumer will need to have a sufficiently robust file with a CRA. Consumer reporting doesn't just affect credit. And this is just putting aside insurance and employment uses of consumer reports.

For some consumers, credit scores also function as a metric for self-evaluation, used for comparison with peers. One researcher documented this in interviews with low-income consumers who she finds are often fixated on credit scores. Interviewees described credit scores as:

> "the most important thing in my life, right now, well besides my babies," as "that darned thing that is destroying my life," and as "my ticket to good neighborhoods and good schools for my kids." Many respondents believed that a "good" credit score was the key to financial stability.
>
> One respondent, Maria, told a story about a friend who was able to improve his score. She said, "He figured out some way to get it up. Way up. I wish I knew what he did there, because I would do it. Because after that, everything was easy as pie for him. Got himself a better job, a better place to live, everything better." Maria went to great lengths to try to improve her score so that she, too, could live a life where everything was "easy as pie."

Sara Sternberg Greene, *The Bootstrap Trap*, 67 Duke L.J. 233, 273 (2017). For some consumers, credit scores have become a metric of self-worth and the perceived key to success.

III. REGULATION OF CONSUMER REPORTS

Because of consumer reporting is so foundational to modern life, its regulation is a topic of major concern, even though the harms from problems with consumer reporting may be indirect, collateral consequences.

The consumer reporting system raises three broad categories of policy concern: privacy, usage, and accuracy.

- Privacy concerns deal with what sort of information may be collected, what sort of information may be disseminated, and under what circumstances and to whom the information can be released.
- Accuracy concerns are about the integrity of the data being collected about consumers and what consumers' redress is regarding disputed information.[1]
- Usage concerns relate to how consumer report information may be used.

1. Accuracy concerns also include issues relating to identity theft, in which a consumer's credit identity is misappropriated by another, resulting in inaccurate information being reported about the consumer—what is being reported is really about the thief. Identity theft regulations are addressed in Chapter 37, regarding data security.

These concerns are reflected in the terms of the main regulatory framework for consumer reporting, the Fair Credit Reporting Act ("FCRA"), 15 U.S.C. §§ 1681 *et seq.*, and the regulations thereunder. The CFPB has rulemaking authority under FCRA. 15 U.S.C. § 1681s(e). The CFPB's FCRA regulations are organized as Regulation V, 12 C.F.R. Part 1022.

Many states also have consumer reporting laws, but they often mirror federal law, and may often be preempted by federal law. Our discussion will focus solely on federal regulation.

Federal enforcement of FCRA is divided between the CFPB and the Federal Trade Commission. As FCRA is an "enumerated consumer law" under 12 U.S.C. § 5481(12), it is also a "federal consumer financial law" under 12 U.S.C. § 5481(14), so the CFPB has jurisdiction over the use of consumer reports in connection with consumer financial products or services under 12 U.S.C. § 5512(a). The FTC retains enforcement jurisdiction over the uses of consumer reports in connection with other transactions, such as by insurers, employers, or landlords. 12 U.S.C. § 5581(b)(5)(C)(ii).

The CFPB not only has rulemaking and enforcement authority under FCRA, but also supervision authority over certain CRAs. The CFPB has undertaken a "larger participant" rulemaking defining the scope of market participants under its supervision authority. 12 U.S.C. § 5514(a)(1)(B). CRAs with more than $7 million in annual receipts are subject to CFPB supervision. This covers roughly 30 firms, which together account for nearly 95% of the total consumer reporting market by annual receipts.

FCRA contains a set of restrictions and requirements regarding when consumer reports may be furnished to users by CRAs, what information may be included in such reports, handling of disputed information, duties of the users of consumer reports, and damages for non-compliance. The FRCA also contains a set of provisions relating to identity theft, which we will address in the next chapter. The starting point, however, for understanding the regulation of consumer reports is understanding the scope of FCRA.

A. The Scope of the Fair Credit Reporting Act

As noted above, while the terms "credit report" and "credit reporting agency," are often used colloquially, these are not formal legal categories. Instead, the relevant legal terms under FCRA are "consumer report" and "consumer reporting agency." These terms are critical because they define the scope of FCRA, which regulates the creation, contents, and use of consumer reports.

A "**consumer report**" is defined by FCRA as any:

> written, oral, or other communication of any information by a consumer reporting agency bearing on a consumer's credit worthiness, credit standing, credit capacity, character, general reputation, personal characteristics, or mode of living which is used or expected to be used or collected in whole or in part for the purpose of serving as a factor in establishing the consumer's eligibility for (A) credit or insurance to be used primarily for personal, family, or household purposes; (B) employment purposes; or (c) any other purpose authorized under section 1681b of this title.

15 U.S.C. § 1681a(d)(1). The FCRA definition of "consumer report" is very broad in terms of content, but it has three important limitations. First, it only covers communications that are used or expected to be used in connection with credit, insurance, or employment decisions or other allowed uses of consumer reports. And second, it only applies to communications generated by a "**consumer reporting agency.**" That term is in turn defined as:

> any person which, for monetary fees, dues, or on a cooperative nonprofit basis, regularly engages in whole or in part in the practice of assembling or evaluating consumer credit information or other information on consumers for the purpose of furnishing consumer reports to third parties, and which uses any means or facility of interstate commerce for the purpose of preparing or furnishing consumer reports.

15 U.S.C. § 1681a(f). While a CRA need not be a for-profit venture, it must be collecting information for the purpose of furnishing the reports to third parties. In other words, incidental sharing of information or an email containing salacious gossip does not trigger CRA status. Likewise, FCRA expressly excludes from its coverage internal company reports and information sharing (at least of non-medical information) among corporate affiliates. 15 U.S.C. § 1681a(d)(2)-(3). The following case explores the extent of FCRA's definitions of consumer reporting agency and consumer report.

Holmes v. TeleCheck Int'l, Inc.

556 F. Supp. 2d 819 (M.D. Tenn. 2008)

Todd J. Campbell, U.S.D.J.

. . .

I. INTRODUCTION

This case centers around six checks written by Plaintiff Patricia Holmes and presented by her as payment to four merchants during the period of August 2003 to June 2005. Five of the checks were declined by the merchants at the point of sale upon the recommendation of TeleCheck. With regard to the other check, TeleCheck initially issued a code requiring the merchant to whom Holmes had presented the check to contact TeleCheck to provide additional information regarding the transaction. The merchant ultimately accepted the check.

As a result of TeleCheck's issuance of those recommendations and as a result of TeleCheck's subsequent conduct as Holmes sought additional information from TeleCheck, Holmes brings this action against Defendants TeleCheck International, Inc. and TeleCheck Services, Inc. (collectively referred to as "TeleCheck" unless otherwise indicated), alleging various violations under the Fair Credit Reporting Act ("FCRA"), 15 U.S.C. § 1681, *et seq.* Plaintiff alleges that TeleCheck violated the FCRA when it (1) failed to follow reasonable procedures to assure maximum possible accuracy of the information contained in Holmes' file; (2) failed to respond to Holmes' requests for a file disclosure and for a copy of the report forming the basis for denying Holmes' checks; (3) failed to investigate/

reinvestigate based on a dispute; (4) failed to provide adequate staffing and training to comply with the FCRA; (5) improperly requested, required, or otherwise obtained information from Holmes, namely her social security number; (6) wrongfully disseminated reports, file material and/or other information about Holmes to unauthorized or improper persons, parties, or entities; and (7) failed to include a "Summary of Rights" notice.

Plaintiff has filed a motion for summary judgment on the issue of liability only regarding the first, second, and third alleged violations identified above. Plaintiff asks the Court to find that TeleCheck willfully or negligently violated the FCRA as to those specific claims. . ..

II. OVERVIEW OF FACTS

A. Defendants' Business

TeleCheck represents on its website that it is the "world's leading check acceptance company, providing electronic check conversion, check guarantee, check verification, and collection services to retail, financial institutions, and other industry clients." According to Plaintiff, TeleCheck International, Inc. and TeleCheck Services, Inc. are "consumer reporting agencies" under the FCRA that provide "consumer reports" to merchants. On its website, TeleCheck represents that its check verification service "helps merchants separate good check writers from bad ones," that its databases and risk management systems "identify not only bad check writing risks, but also good ones," and that it can predict "with unmatched accuracy the probability of a check being good." TeleCheck processes approximately 1.2 million check requests each day.

TeleCheck merchants run customers' checks through either a terminal or the cash register to send data to TeleCheck regarding the transaction. TeleCheck's computer system then processes the transaction by running that data through risk models, which draw from hundreds of variables to assess the riskiness of that transaction. According to TeleCheck, the risk models for each merchant are particular to that merchant and are based on the particular merchant's loss experience. TeleCheck typically does not have access to information concerning bank account balances.

Based on the results of the risk model for that particular merchant, TeleCheck then issues one of four numeric codes to the merchant via the terminal or cash register. TeleCheck characterizes these codes as "recommendations" to the merchant as to how to handle the transaction. After receiving one of TeleCheck's numeric codes, the merchant may choose to accept the check, reject the check, or provide additional information to TeleCheck. According to TeleCheck, the decision of check acceptance resides with the merchant, and merchants sometimes choose not to follow TeleCheck's recommendation.[3]

---

3. However, TeleCheck training materials indicate that TeleCheck, not the merchant, issues check declines. TeleCheck training materials, TC00795 (Frequently Asked Question verbiage given to customer care representatives "Customer: Is my check being declined by the merchant or by TeleCheck? Response: The decline is the result of TeleCheck's acceptance guidelines."); *see also* TeleCheck training materials TC000612 ("All declines are based on guidelines set by TeleCheck and only TeleCheck. DO NOT BLAME THE MERCHANT.")(emphasis in original).

"Code 0" indicates that the merchant should call TeleCheck to provide additional information. TeleCheck claims that a "Code 0" is not a recommendation to accept or decline a check; however, in TeleCheck internal documents, a "Code 0" is referred to as a decline.

"Code 1" is an approval code; according to TeleCheck, it is a recommendation to the merchant to accept the check.

"Code 3" is a decline code; according to TeleCheck, it is a recommendation to the merchant to decline the check based on an assessment of the risk of the transaction. When TeleCheck issues a "Code 3," TeleCheck instructs the merchant to provide the checkwriter with a "courtesy card." The "courtesy card" provides TeleCheck's contact information, including a toll-free number, and lists the specific identifying information TeleCheck requires to answer the checkwriter's questions.

"Code 4" is a decline code; according to TeleCheck, it is a recommendation to decline the check based on what the TeleCheck system suggests is an outstanding unpaid check or information that the specific bank account is closed. This case does not involve any "Code 4s."

TeleCheck collects information based on three unique identifiers: bank account number, driver's license number, and/or Social Security number. TeleCheck does not identify checkwriters by name, address, or telephone number because those identifiers may not be unique to that checkwriter. Plaintiff disputes that TeleCheck utilizes Social Security numbers in connection with its check verification and guarantee services and insists that TeleCheck collects consumers' Social Security numbers for improper purposes in violation of the FCRA.

B. TeleCheck's Recommendations Regarding Holmes' Checks

Holmes' claims are based on six check transactions. Five of the transactions involved "Code 3" recommendations. The other transaction involved a "Code 0." With regard to the "Code 0," TeleCheck ultimately recommended that Holmes' check be accepted, and the merchant accepted the check . . .

Plaintiff Holmes alleges that TeleCheck violated the FCRA in a number of ways. The Court will address each claim below. The issues of causation and damages with respect to Plaintiff's FCRA claims will be addressed collectively at the conclusion of this section.

1. *"Inaccuracy of Information/Reasonable Procedures" Claims*

Subparts 3-8 of Holmes' FCRA claim are based on allegations of inaccuracy of information provided to merchants. Holmes brings these claims under 15 U.S.C. § 1681e(b), which requires consumer reporting agencies to "follow reasonable procedures to assure maximum possible accuracy" when preparing a "consumer report".

To establish a prima facie case of inaccuracy under 15 U.S.C. § 1681e(b), a plaintiff must prove: "(1) the defendant reported inaccurate information about the plaintiff; (2) the defendant either negligently or willfully failed to follow reasonable procedures to assure maximum possible accuracy of the information about the plaintiff; (3) the plaintiff was injured; and (4) the defendant's conduct was the proximate cause of the plaintiff's injury." *Nelski v. Trans Union, LLC,* 86 Fed. Appx. 840, 844 (6th Cir. 2004).

TeleCheck contends this claim fails as a matter of law because (1) the recommendations about which Holmes complains were not "consumer reports," and thus are not actionable under the FCRA. . . .

a. TeleCheck is a "consumer reporting agency" under the FCRA.

The FCRA defines a "consumer reporting agency" as "any person which, for monetary fees, regularly engages in the practice of assembling or evaluating consumer credit information or other information on consumers for the purposes of furnishing "consumer reports" to third parties, and which uses any means or facility of interstate commerce for the purpose of preparing or furnishing consumer reports." 15 U.S.C. § 1681a(f). TeleCheck represents itself as a "consumer reporting agency" on its public website ("TeleCheck is also a consumer reporting agency as defined in the Fair Credit Reporting Act"), in its training materials ("Under the FCRA guidelines, TeleCheck is a 'consumer reporting agency' because we render 'consumer reports.'"), in its merchant contracts, and in the "courtesy cards" provided by TeleCheck to merchants to give to consumers following a decline, which advise that consumers have a right to a "free copy of the information held in TeleCheck's files for a period of 60 days following an adverse action" and that "[c]onsumers also may dispute the accuracy or completeness of any information in *TeleCheck's consumer report.*" (Plf.'s App.)(emphasis added). TeleCheck's parent corporation, First Data, also indicates in its SEC filings that TeleCheck is subject to the FCRA "based on TeleCheck's maintenance of a database containing the check-writing histories of consumers and the use of that information in connection with its check verification and guarantee services." (Plf.'s App). The Court finds that, under these facts, TeleCheck is a "consumer reporting agency" under the FCRA.

b. The numeric codes issued to merchants by TeleCheck constitute "consumer reports" under the FCRA.

A "consumer report" is defined under the FCRA as "any written, oral, or other communication of any information by a consumer reporting agency bearing on a consumer's credit worthiness, credit standing, credit capacity, character, general reputation, personal characteristics, or mode of living. . .." 15 U.S.C. § 1681a(d)(1). Further, the information must be "used or collected in whole or in part for the purpose of serving as a factor in establishing the consumer's eligibility for credit or insurance, employment purposes or any other purpose authorized under 15 U.S.C. § 1681b." *Id.* Under § 1681b(a)(3)(F)(i), a "consumer report" may be furnished to a person having "a legitimate business need for the information in connection with a business transaction that is initiated by the consumer."

Defendants argue that the "Code 0" and "Code 3s" disclosed no information about Holmes to merchants bearing on any of the seven characteristics set forth in the FCRA definition of "consumer report," and thus, the FCRA does not apply. Defendants' argument rests on the fact that when TeleCheck issues a "Code 3" to a merchant, it provides the merchant with the following description of the code: "TeleCheck has no negative information on the checkwriter or company, but the check falls outside the guidelines that TeleCheck will guarantee at this time."

The Court is not persuaded by Defendants' argument. A "Code 3" transmittal must be considered alongside all of TeleCheck's representations about its services to merchants. TeleCheck represents that it can predict bad or risky check writers from good ones and that it "contracts with merchants to provide those services (check verification or check guarantee) to assist them in decreasing their risk of bad or fraudulent checks". TeleCheck also states that it "uses the information in its database to determine whether or not a consumer is 'worthy' of writing a check or opening a checking account. TeleCheck's communication of the response codes to the subscriber bears on the consumer's ability to write a check or open a checking account." Thus, when TeleCheck issues a "Code 3" related to a check presented to a merchant, TeleCheck's code communicates a message about an identifiable person's "character, general reputation, personal characteristics, or mode of living," *i.e.,* it is advising the merchant that the checkwriter standing before it poses some kind of risk. TeleCheck is providing this information to a merchant who has a legitimate business need in connection with a business transaction initiated by the consumer, *i.e.,* sales transactions initiated by Holmes at the merchants' stores.

In addition, TeleCheck admits it issues "consumer reports." In documents describing "Code 1," "Code 3," and "Code 4," TeleCheck states that "TeleCheck electronically or verbally communicates these *consumer reports* to its subscribers through the issuance of authorization response codes relating to the consumer's transaction with the subscriber." (Plf.'s App.)(emphasis added). The "courtesy cards" provided by TeleCheck to merchants to give to consumers following a decline advise that consumers have a right to a "free copy of the information held in TeleCheck's files for a period of 60 days following an adverse action" and that "[c]onsumers also may dispute the accuracy or completeness of any information *in TeleCheck's consumer report.*" (Plf.'s App.)(emphasis added).

Courts have held that check verification and guarantee companies are consumer reporting agencies and provide "consumer reports." *See Estiverne v. Sak's Fifth Ave.,* 9 F.3d 1171, 1173-74 (5th Cir. 1993)(holding that a check approval company's report was "consumer report" for FCRA purposes and store's obtaining of report for purpose of deciding whether to accept check was legitimate business need); *Greenway v. Info. Dynamics, Ltd.,* 524 F.2d 1145, 1146 (9th Cir. 1975)(holding that a report of the previous issuance of an unpayable check is a "consumer report," subjecting issuer to requirements of the FCRA as a "consumer reporting agency," inasmuch as report bears on a consumer's credit worthiness, credit standing, credit capacity, character, general reputation, and personal characteristics, and check itself is, essentially, an instrument of credit); *Lofton-Taylor v. Verizon Wireless,* 2006 U.S. Dist. LEXIS 83684 at *3 (S.D. Ala. Nov. 14, 2006)(holding that a "report from a check approval company is a consumer report under § 1681a(d)."); *Alexander v. Moore & Assocs., Inc.,* 553 F. Supp. 948, 950-51 (D.C. Hawaii 1983)(holding that a check guarantee service which gave to tenants a "Code 4" which caused them to later have their checks refused by various merchants issued "consumer reports" and thus was a "credit reporting agency" within the FCRA); *Peasley v. TeleCheck of Kansas,* 6 Kan. App. 2d 990 (Kan. App. 1981)(holding that "the check guarantee and reporting service on bank checks of consumers, which defendant engages in for the benefit of merchant subscribers, falls within the definition of a 'consumer report'" and "defendant in furnishing such service is a 'consumer reporting agency'"). Likewise, the Court finds that the numeric codes issued by TeleCheck to the merchants at issue constituted "consumer reports" under the FCRA.

. . .

While CRAs are at the heart of the consumer reporting process, they are not the only parties involved. Consumer reporting relies on other parties ("**furnishers**") to provide information to CRAs and on parties that use consumer reports in making credit, insurance, and employment decisions ("**users**"). FCRA regulates all furnishers and users, as well as CRAs. The regulatory schemes are substantially different for each group, however.

It is easy to think of FCRA as solely a statute relating to the provision of credit reports, but it has potentially broader reach in consumer financial litigation. When a consumer has a dispute with a lender there may also be a related FCRA issue because the lender has been credit reporting based on the status of the debt it claims. If that debt proves to be inaccurate, then the credit reporting will also be inaccurate. While that will not necessarily result in a FCRA cause of action, it sets the stage for a FCRA claim depending on what actions the creditor and the CRA have taken in regard to the incorrectly reported debt.

IV. PRIVACY REGULATION UNDER FCRA

FCRA contains numerous provisions designed to provide some measure of privacy for consumers while still ensuring that consumer reporting is feasible. FCRA regulates the furnishing of consumer data to CRAs and the provision of the data by CRAs to users.

A. Regulation of Furnishing of Consumer Data to CRAs

FCRA does not regulate when or what type of data may be furnished to CRAs beyond a general accuracy requirement prohibiting the furnishing of data known to be inaccurate. 15 U.S.C. § 1681s-2(a)(1). CRAs are free to gather all types of data.

Once a party furnishes data to a CRA, a number of other obligations apply. First, if party is a "furnisher," a term defined in 12 C.F.R. § 1022.41(c), then Regulation V under FCRA requires that it "must establish and implement reasonable written policies and procedures regarding the accuracy and integrity of the information relating to consumers that it furnishes to a consumer reporting agency. The policies and procedures must be appropriate to the nature, size, complexity, and scope of each furnisher's activities." 12 C.F.R. § 1022.42(a). Second, FCRA creates an obligation for a furnisher to correct and update the information, to report if information has been disputed by the consumer, and to report voluntary account closures by the consumer, 15 U.S.C. § 1681s-2(a)(2)-(4). And third, if a furnisher provides data to a CRA about an account being placed for collection or charged off, it is required to provide information about the date of the delinquency. 15 U.S.C. § 1681s-2(a)(5).

A special duty exists for financial institution furnishers regarding reporting of negative information. While FCRA contains a general definition of "financial institution," 15 U.S.C. § 1681a(5), the term "financial institution" is defined for this particular purpose in reference to 15 U.S.C. § 6809(3), which in turn refers to 12 U.S.C. § 1843(k), which covers institutions engaged in activities that are "financial in nature or incidental to such financial activity." This includes any sort of lending, payments, and deposit taking. Thus, it covers not only banks, but also non-bank lenders, but it would not extend to a dentist's office that provides services for which it bills later. If a financial institution reports negative information on a consumer, the financial institution is required to provide notice to the consumer that it is doing so within 30 days of the reporting. 15 U.S.C. § 1681s-2(a)(7)(A)-(B). The notice must be "clear and conspicuous," but can be included on a notice of default or billing statement. 15 U.S.C. § 1681s-2(a)(7)(C). Only one notice needs to be provided in connection with any single account, transaction, or customer. 15 U.S.C. § 1681s-2(a)(7)(A)(ii). A safe harbor for non-compliance exists if the financial institution has reasonable policies and procedures in place to generally assure compliance. 15 U.S.C. § 1681s-2(b)(7)(F).

B. Regulation of the Provision of Consumer Reports

FCRA allows CRAs to provide consumer reports to users only in specified circumstances. 15 U.S.C. § 1681b(a). Among these specified circumstances are that they be:

(1) to a person whom the consumer reporting agency has reason to believe intends to use the information for a consumer credit transaction involving the consumer;
(2) to servicers, investors, or credit insurers to assess credit or prepayment risks of existing obligations;
(3) to persons with "a legitimate business need for the information" either in connection with a transaction initiated by the consumer or to review an account to determine whether the consumer still meets the terms of the account.
(4) in accordance with written instructions from the consumer to whom the report relates; and
(5) in compliance with certain law enforcement, national security, and court orders.

15 U.S.C. § 1681b(a)(3). Thus, CRAs can provide reports to parties looking to provide credit and to parties who have already provided credit or credit-related services, including for collection purposes (as credit reports will provide a debtor's address).

CRAs are also required to disclose all information in a consumer's file, other than credit scores, to the consumer about whom the report applies. 15 U.S.C. § 1681g(a)(1)(A)-(B). CRAs are generally allowed to charge a fee of up to $8.00 in inflation-adjusted 1997 dollars for the report.[2] 15 U.S.C. § 1681j(f)(1). CRAs must provide free consumer reports, however, in certain circumstances: (1) CRAs operating

2. Inflation adjustment is according to the Consumer Price Index and rounded to the nearest 50¢. For 2018, the maximum charge is $12.00. CFPB, Notice regarding charges for certain disclosures under the Fair Credit Reporting Act, 82 Fed. Reg. 53481 (Nov. 16, 2016).

nationwide must provide one free credit report annually upon request by the consumer; (2) consumers are entitled to a free credit report in the 60 days following receipt of a notice of adverse action based on a credit report; (3) free credit reports must be made available if the consumer is unemployed, on welfare, or has reason to believe that there is inaccurate information in the report due to fraud; and (4) free credit reports must be made available in connection with identity theft. 15 U.S.C. § 1681j(a)-(d).

A special privacy restriction applies to medical information. Federal law is generally quite protective of consumers' medical information, and FCRA is no exception. FCRA prohibits the furnishing of consumer reports with medical information unless (1) the consumer consents, (2) the information is relevant to an employment or credit transaction, or (3) the information is solely about medical debts and is sufficiently redacted so that it does not identify or enable the identification of the nature of the medical services. 15 U.S.C. § 1681b(g)(1). FCRA also separately prohibits disclosure of the name and contact information of any furnisher of medical information, including healthcare-related debt, unless the information does not reveal the service provided. 15 U.S.C. § 1681c(a)(6). Thus, Adelson Cosmetic Dentistry LLP or Phillips Rhinoplasty Associates LLP cannot show up on a consumer report in that form. Instead, the contact information would have to be redacted, such as "Adelson XXXXXX LLP" or "Phillips XXXX Associates LLP." Query whether a dentist office doing business as Big Smile would appear as Big XXX.

Additional regulations relate to provision of credit scores. First, if a consumer report contains a credit score or other risk score or predictor, the CRA must disclose if the number of inquiries was a key factor adversely affecting the score. 15 U.S.C. § 1681c(d)(2). This requirement does not apply to reporting for check verification. *Id.*

Second, if a CRA provides credit scores, the CRA must disclose the score to the consumer, as well as the name of the entity producing the scoring model, the range of scores possible, the key factors in the score (but not exceeding four, excluding the number of inquiries made if that is a key factor), and the date of the score. 15 U.S.C. § 1681g(f). CRAs may charge a "fair and reasonable fee" for credit scores. 15 U.S.C. § 1681g(f)(8).

Beyond these restrictions on CRAs release of information, CRAs are required to maintain reasonable procedures designed to avoid violations of 1681c and 1681b. 15 U.S.C. § 1681e(a). Among other things, CRAs must "require that prospective users identify themselves, certify the purposes for which the information is sought and that it will not be used for other purposes." *Id.* A reasonable effort to verify identity and uses certified is required. *Id.*

V. ACCURACY REGULATION UNDER FCRA

FCRA is also concerned with promoting the accuracy of consumer reports. The accuracy of consumer reports is important both to consumers—as it affects the terms on which they can get credit, insurance, and employment—and to users of consumer reports, who might misprice if using inaccurate information.

FCRA has separate accuracy provisions for CRAs and for **furnishers**, the businesses that supply information to the CRAs.

A. Accuracy Regulation of CRAs

1. General Accuracy Regulation for CRAs

FCRA requires CRAs to "follow reasonable procedures to assure maximum possible accuracy of the information concerning the individual about whom the report relates." 15 U.S.C. § 1681e(b). This standard has been interpreted by some courts to require only what a "reasonably prudent person" would do under the circumstances, which includes "weighing the potential harm from inaccuracy against the burden of safeguarding against such inaccuracy." *Steward v. Credit Bureau, Inc.*, 734 F.2d 47, 51 (D.C. Cir. 1984). Thus, if a CRA has reasonable procedures in place and they are followed, the mere fact of an inaccuracy on a report will not be a FCRA violation. Yet the standard seems to have a tension within it, as it is not simply a reasonableness requirement, but a standard about what is reasonable to achieve "*maximum* possible accuracy," which may not itself be a reasonable goal. Indeed, the idea of "maximum possible accuracy" does not seem to brook the cost-benefit analysis suggested by *Steward*. In any event, what constitutes evidence of unreasonable procedures is a matter of some confusion in the courts, with some courts admitting inaccurate reports as themselves probative of unreasonable procedures.

FCRA does not, however, mandate the inclusion of any particular content in consumer reports, although it does limit what sort of information may be included and also requires that certain information be included if other information is included. CRAs are also required to maintain "reasonable procedures" to avoid violations of these content limitations and requirements. 15 U.S.C. §1681e(a).

2. Limitations on Stale Adverse Information

FCRA places limits on how long certain types of adverse information may stay on a consumer report. If the consumer filed for bankruptcy, that may remain on the report for up to ten years. 15 U.S.C. § 1681c(a)(1). Other types of adverse information—such as foreclosures, paid tax liens, accounts placed for collection or charged off, and civil judgments—may remain on the report for up to seven years. 15 U.S.C. § 1681c(a)(3)-(5). Arrests and civil suits may remain on the report for the longer of seven years or the relevant statute of limitations. 15 U.S.C. § 1681c(a)(2). Criminal convictions may remain on the report indefinitely. 15 U.S.C. § 1681c(a)(5).

3. Indication of Closed or Disputed Accounts and Bankruptcy Chapters

Additionally, FCRA requires consumer reports to indicate if an account was closed by a consumer, if the consumer has disputed an account, and, if a bankruptcy is indicated, what chapter of the Bankruptcy Code the case was filed under. 15 U.S.C. § 1681c(d)-(f).

4. Dispute Procedures for CRAs

When a consumer believes that there is incomplete or inaccurate information on a credit report, the consumer may proceed to dispute the information in one of two ways. The consumer may either attempt to resolve the inaccuracy or incompleteness with the CRA, 15 U.S.C. § 1681i, or it may do so with the furnisher, 15 U.S.C. § 1681s-2(b). This section addresses attempts to resolve such disputes with the CRA; the following section deals with consumers' rights vis-à-vis the furnisher.

If a consumer notifies a CRA of inaccurate or incomplete information, the CRA is required to commence "reasonable reinvestigation," free of charge, or delete the disputed information. 15 U.S.C. § 1681i(a). FCRA does not specify what constitutes a "reasonable reinvestigation." It clearly involves some sort of investigation into the facts, but also clearly has limits. Most critically, it is not subject to the "maximum possible accuracy" standard of 15 U.S.C. § 1681e(b), although that standard would still apply to any ultimate report.

At the very least, the CRA is required to consider any information submitted by the consumer, 15 U.S.C. § 1681i(a)(4), and also double check to make sure that it had correctly recorded the information furnished to it or that it had otherwise collected. That might require contacting a furnisher to verify the information. Thus, FCRA requires CRAs to notify the furnisher of the disputed information about the dispute within five business days. 15 U.S.C. § 1681i(a)(2).

While CRAs must make a "reasonable" investigation, they are not generically required to inquire into the accuracy of the initial source of information. If circumstances indicate that the reliability of the source may be an issue, however, then the CRA might be required to undertake such an inquiry. *See, e.g., Henson v. CSC Credit Serv.*, 29 F.3d 280 (7th Cir. 1994); *Cushman v. Trans Union Corp.*, 115 F.3d 220 (3d Cir. 1997). Some courts have also held that costs relative to possible consumer harm from inaccuracy are a factor that may be considered in terms of what constitutes a reasonable reinvestigation. *See, e.g., Henson v. CSC Credit Serv.*, 29 F.3d 280 (7th Cir. 1994). CRAs are not required to make legal determinations such as interpreting a contract to determine if a vehicle was properly reposed, *Krajewski v. Am. Honda Fin. Corp.*, 557 F. Supp. 2d 596 (2008), or deciding if a mortgage was in fact valid, *De Andrade v. Trans Union LLC*, 523 F.3d 61 (1st Cir. 2008). Ultimately, a CRA receives deference in its determinations, to the extent they are reasonable.

If a CRA cannot verify the disputed information or determines that the information is inaccurate or incomplete, it must delete or modify the information as appropriate within 30 days (extended to 45 days upon receipt of further information from the consumer) as well as notify the furnisher. 15 U.S.C. §§ 1681i(a)(1), 1681i(a)(5)(A). CRAs are also required to maintain reasonable procedures to prevent the reappearance of deleted information. 15 U.S.C. § 1681i(a)(5)(C). CRAs that operate nationwide are also required to maintain systems that share the results of reinvestigations finding incomplete or inaccurate information with other CRAs. 15 U.S.C. § 1681i(a)(5)(D).

A CRA may, however, terminate an investigation at any time if it determines that the dispute is "frivolous or irrelevant," including if the consumer has failed to provide sufficient information for a reinvestigation. 15 U.S.C. § 1681i(a)(3). In such a case, the consumer must be notified within five business days of the decision to terminate the reinvestigation for frivolity or irrelevance, explaining why the investigation was terminated and the type of information needed (in generic terms) in order to investigate. *Id.*

Upon completing a reinvestigation, a CRA must notify the consumer about the results within five business days. 15 U.S.C. § 1681i(a)(6). The notice must explain that the consumer has the right to receive a description of the reinvestigation procedure if requested and that if the consumer is not satisfied with the resolution, the consumer may file a brief statement (which may be limited to 100 words) setting forth the nature of the dispute. 15 U.S.C. § 1681i(a)(6)-(7), 1681i(b). The CRA must include that consumer statement, if submitted, in the consumer report unless it is frivolous or irrelevant, as well as an indication on the report about what information is disputed. 15 U.S.C. § 1681i(d). If a report is modified based on a reinvestigation (including the inclusion of a dispute statement by the consumer), the CRA is required, if the consumer so requests, to send copies of the updated report to certain parties who have previously requested it. 15 U.S.C. § 1681i(d).

B. Accuracy Regulation of Furnishers

While most of FCRA's provisions deal with consumer reporting agencies, some deal with the furnishers of information to consumer reporting agencies. In particular, FCRA creates a duty for furnishers of information to provide accurate information to consumer reporting agencies. This duty has four parts.

1. Duty Not to Provide Information Known to Be Inaccurate

FCRA provides that information shall not be furnished if the furnisher knows or has reasonable cause to believe the information is inaccurate other than from allegations by the consumer, 15 U.S.C. § 1681s-2(a)(1)(A), 1681s-2(a)(1)(D), or that it is in fact inaccurate if the consumer has notified the furnisher of the inaccuracy. 15 U.S.C. § 1681s-2(a)(1)(B). If the furnisher provides an address for the consumer to send notices about inaccurate information, however, the furnisher is liable only for providing inaccurate information if notified by the consumer. 15 U.S.C. § 1681s-2(a)(1)(C).

2. Duty to Promptly Correct and Update Information

FCRA's accuracy obligation is an ongoing responsibility. FCRA requires furnishers to promptly correct and update information about consumers to ensure that the information provided is "complete and accurate." 15 U.S.C. § 1681s-2(a)(2). The duty to provide complete and accurate information includes a duty to provide notices to consumer reporting agencies of information whose completeness or accuracy is disputed by the consumer, as well as of accounts closed by the consumer, and account delinquencies. 15 U.S.C. § 1681s-2(b)(3)-(5). The duty to provide complete and accurate information also requires furnishers to notify consumer reporting agencies of account delinquencies within 90 days of the delinquency. Significantly, there is no private right of action under FCRA for either of these first two data accuracy requirements, only public enforcement. 15 U.S.C. § 1681s-2(c)-(d).

3. Duty to Have Identity Theft Procedures

A particular accuracy concern exists in the context of identity theft. Identity theft is covered in more depth in Chapter 37, but it is worth noting here that FCRA also requires furnishers to have in place "reasonable procedures" to respond to identify theft notifications from consumer reporting agencies to prevent the refurnishing of blocked information. 15 U.S.C. § 1681s-2(b)(6)(A). In the event a consumer submits an identify theft report to the furnisher, the furnisher is then prohibited from furnishing further information about the consumer unless the furnisher affirmatively knows the information is correct or is told by the consumer that the information is correct. 15 U.S.C. § 1681s-2(b)(6)(B).

4. Direct Dispute Procedures for Furnishers

FCRA mandates that furnishers follow certain procedures in regard to information disputed as inaccurate or incomplete, whether the dispute is raised directly with the furnisher or indirectly through the consumer reporting agency. FCRA allows consumers to dispute information directly with furnishers. 15 U.S.C. § 1681s-2(b). To do so, the consumer must provide a dispute notice to the furnisher that identifies the specific information being disputed, explains the basis for the dispute, and includes all the supporting documentation necessary. 15 U.S.C. § 1681s-2(b)(8)(D). After receiving a proper notice about a non-frivolous dispute, the furnisher must conduct a "reasonable investigation" about the dispute information, review all the relevant information provided by the consumer, report the results of the investigation before the expiry of a 30-day period from receipt of the notice (which may be extended to 45 days if further information is received from the consumer during the period), and correct any inaccurate reporting. 15 U.S.C. § 1681s-2(b)(8)(E); 12 C.F.R. § 1022.43(a). If the furnisher determines the dispute is frivolous or irrelevant (such as a re-dispute of the same information), the furnisher must notify the consumer within five business days of the determination explaining why. 12 C.F.R. § 1022.43(f).

FCRA mandates a similar procedure if the furnisher is notified by a consumer reporting agency of a dispute regarding the completeness or accuracy of information it provided. In such a situation, the furnisher must conduct an investigation, report the results to the consumer reporting agency, and correct any inaccurate or incomplete information with all consumer reporting agencies with which it furnished the information, again within 30 days of notification (extendable to 45 days if further information is received during the 30-day period). 15 U.S.C. § 1681s-2(b). Any information the furnisher determines is inaccurate, is incomplete, or cannot be verified must be appropriately modified or deleted or permanently blocked from reporting. 15 U.S.C. § 1681s-2(b)(E). The furnisher is not required to explain its investigation process, however, unlike CRAs.

Notice that while FCRA mandates an investigation process, both for furnishers and CRAs, it does not create any sort of right of appeal. At best, the consumer can have the fact of a dispute noted in a consumer report. Thus, while the consumer can complain and thereby trigger an investigation (if the complaint isn't obviously frivolous), the consumer has no control over or visibility into the scope of the investigation or the standards applied in reaching determinations. A FCRA reinvestigation is not a judicial process. In this regard it is similar to the Electronic Fund Transfer Act and Fair Credit Billing Act (TILA) dispute procedures, and to state UDAP laws that require consumers to first attempt to resolve the issue consensually before proceeding to litigation. *See, e.g.*, Mass. Gen. L. 93A § 9(3). These procedures may generate information for the consumer, which may be useful as a type of pre-discovery if the consumer wishes to pursue the matter through litigation, and may result in a resolution of the dispute, but they do not guarantee any resolution and they preserve the consumers' litigation rights.

The following case illustrates the duty of a furnisher upon a dispute of the reported information.

Jett v. American Home Mortgage Servicing, Inc.

2015 U.S. App. Lexis 8347 (5th Cir. 2015) (unpublished opinion)

Jerry E. Smith, Circuit Judge:

Juliana Jett sued American Home Mortgage Servicing, Incorporated ("American Home"), for allegedly negligently and willfully failing to update her credit information in violation of 15 U.S.C. § 1681s-2(b). The district court entered summary judgment for American Home on both claims. Because there is a genuine dispute of material fact as to negligence, we vacate as to that claim but affirm on the willfulness claim.

I.

Jett fell behind on her mortgage payments and filed for bankruptcy. After she completed her Chapter 13 plan, her Experian Information Solutions, Incorporated ("Experian"), credit report erroneously showed the mortgage as discharged in bankruptcy with a $0 balance. She disputed the listing, and Experian sent an automatic credit dispute verification ("ACDV") form to American Home.[1] Although American Home attempted to report the loan as current with $0 past due and a principal balance of approximately $35,000, Jett's credit report was not updated despite that four ACDV forms were exchanged over two-and-one-half years.

Jett alleges that she was denied refinancing because American Home had negligently and willfully misreported the status of the mortgage. Specifically, she maintains that it failed to update the Metro 2® Consumer Information Indicator ("CII") field properly in

1. When a credit reporting agency ("CRA") receives a dispute from a consumer, it sends an ACDV form to the furnisher of the credit information. The form contains the information that is being reported, what the consumer disputes, and blank fields for the furnisher to edit and return.

the ACDV forms. Instead of changing the CII code to "Q" as instructed by the Consumer Data Industry Association's 2012 Credit Reporting Guide, American Home left the field blank. A blank CII field signals that the CRA should keep reporting the original information, so none of the corrected information was processed by Experian.

The district court entered summary judgment on the negligence claim because "Jett ha[d] failed to adduce any evidence concerning [American Home's] policies and procedures in responding to [the ACDV] requests" and her "evidence that [American Home] knew about [Experian's] policies and procedures [was] insufficient to show that [American Home] had a duty to conform to them." The court entered summary judgment on the willfulness claim because Jett did not respond to that portion of the motion for summary judgment.

II.

If a CRA notifies a furnisher of credit information (a "furnisher") that a consumer disputes the reported information, the furnisher must "review all relevant information provided by the [CRA]," "conduct an investigation," "report the results of the investigation," and "modify . . . delete . . . or . . . permanently block the reporting of [inaccurate or incomplete] information." § 1681s-2(b)(1)(A)–(E). The Fair Credit Reporting Act creates a private cause of action to enforce § 1681s-2(b): "Any person who is negligent in failing to comply with any requirement imposed under this subchapter with respect to any consumer is liable" for actual damages and attorney's fees. Moreover, "[a]ny person who willfully fails to comply with any requirement imposed under this subchapter with respect to any consumer is liable to that consumer" for actual, statutory, and punitive damages and attorney's fees. § 1681n(a).

Relying on *Chiang v. Verizon New England Inc.*, 595 F.3d 26, 38-41 (1st Cir. 2010), American Home urges that summary judgment was proper because Jett failed to show that its policies and procedures were unreasonable. In *Chiang*, summary judgment was affirmed because, *inter alia*, the plaintiff "ha[d] presented no evidence that the procedures employed by [the furnisher] to investigate the reported disputes were unreasonable." *Id.* at 38.

But unlike the furnisher in *Chiang*, American Home knew that Jett's information was being reported inaccurately and attempted to correct it. Regardless of the policies and procedures used to investigate the dispute, the plain language of § 1681s-2(b)(1)(C) and § 1681o makes clear that a furnisher is liable if it negligently reports the results of its investigation to the CRA.[4]

There is a genuine issue of material fact as to whether American Home negligently failed to comply with the reporting requirements. The first ACDV form told it to "[p]rovide complete ID and verify account information" and stated that Jett claimed the

4. Nothing in 12 C.F.R. § 1022.42 alters our understanding of § 1681s-2(b)(1)(C)–(E). Although "[e]ach furnisher must establish and implement reasonable written policies and procedures regarding the accuracy and integrity of the information . . . that it furnishes to a [CRA]," § 1022.42, it is also required to "provide to the [CRA] any correction . . . that is necessary to make the information provided by the furnisher accurate," § 1022.43(e)(4).

mortgage was current and should not be shown as foreclosed. The second form showed that the mortgage was still being reported inaccurately and instructed American Home to "[p]rovide complete ID and verify account information." The third form directed American Home to "[v]erify all amounts" and contained the annotation "Remove" in the CII field in the "Consumer Claims" column. In each instance, American Home tried to correct the information but returned a blank CII field so Experian did not process the updates.

Because there is a genuine dispute of material fact as to American Home's negligence, summary judgment is not appropriate.[6]

III.

For American Home willfully to have violated § 1681s-2(b), it must have "knowingly and intentionally committed an act in conscious disregard for the rights of others."[7]

Jett does not point to any such evidence; rather, she claims that American Home's motion for summary judgment "did not make any mention of an absence of evidence regarding the issue of willfulness." But American Home stated that "there are no genuine issues of material fact, and the summary judgment evidence establishes that [American Home] . . . did not *willfully* or negligently violate any provision of 15 U.S.C [§] 1681s-2(b)." (emphasis added).

The judgment is VACATED as to the negligence claim, AFFIRMED as to the willfulness claim, and REMANDED for further proceedings as needed.

VI. USAGE REGULATION UNDER FCRA

FCRA includes limitations on the use of credit reports. It is illegal to use or obtain a consumer report for any purpose not specifically authorized. 15 U.S.C. § 1681b(f). For private parties this means other than for credit, insurance, employment, or per the consumer's written instructions.

Creditors are also expressly prohibited from using medical information (other than de-identified medical debts) in connection with underwriting decisions. 15 U.S.C. § 1681b(g)(2). This particular prohibition is not limited to medical information obtained from credit reports.

---

6. American Home avers that it was not negligent because the ACDV instructions did not provide notice that it needed to enter a new code and another CRA was able to report the status of the mortgage correctly. Those are issues to be resolved at trial. *See Cousin v. Trans Union Corp.*, 246 F.3d 359, 368 (5th Cir. 2001) ("The adequacy of [a CRA's] procedures is judged according to what a reasonably prudent person would do under the circumstances. In the majority of cases, reasonableness is a question for the jury."

7. *Id.* at 372 (quoting *Pinner v. Schmidt*, 805 F.2d 1258, 1263 (5th Cir. 1986)) (internal quotation marks omitted)).

A. Adverse Actions

Certain FCRA usage regulations apply only to negative actions undertaken based on consumer reports. FCRA also places duties on users of consumer reports that are triggered by an "adverse action" based in whole or part on information contained in a consumer report. 15 U.S.C. § 1681m(a). An "**adverse action**" is defined for credit purposes by reference to the Equal Credit Opportunity Act, which defines the term as:

> a denial or revocation of credit, a change in the terms of an existing credit arrangement, or a refusal to grant credit in substantially the amount or on substantially the terms requested. Such term does not include a refusal to extend additional credit under an existing credit arrangement where the applicant is delinquent or otherwise in default, or where such additional credit would exceed a previously established credit limit.

15 U.S.C. §§ 1681a(k)(1)(A), 1691(d)(6). The term, however, is not limited to credit and also includes unfavorable actions regarding insurance, licenses, employment, and any negative action taken or determination made regarding a consumer-initiated transaction or application. 15 U.S.C. § 1681a(k)(1)(B).

Upon an adverse action, the user of the consumer report must send the consumer a notice that includes, among other information, any numerical credit score used in the credit decision, the name and contact information for the consumer reporting agency that furnished the report, and notice of the right to obtain a free consumer report from the agency and to dispute the accuracy or completeness of any information contained in a consumer report. Further disclosures are required if the creditor relies on information other than from consumer reporting agencies, such as from an affiliate. 15 U.S.C. § 1681m(b). These additional disclosures notify the consumer of the right to inquire about the reasons for the adverse action within 60 days of transmittal of the notice. A safe harbor exists for users that can show that at the time of the alleged failure to comply it maintained reasonable procedures to assure compliance. 15 U.S.C. § 1681m(c). The purpose of the whole adverse action notification requirement is to alert consumers that their consumer reports may contain negative information and enable them to check their reports for accuracy at no cost. The FCRA adverse action notice requirement is separate from the ECOA adverse action notice requirement, 15 U.S.C. § 1691(d), but a combined notice may be provided.

B. Risk-Based Pricing

An adverse action covers an outright denial of credit or the refusal to grant credit on terms requested, but many consumer credit applications do not request a particular rate. Instead, the consumer applies for credit and the lender determines a rate based, in part, on the consumer's risk profile. Thus, the consumer might not be denied credit and may not be getting credit on worse terms than requested, but may still be getting credit on unfavorable terms. A separate FCRA provision covers such "risk-based pricing," and requires certain disclosures be made when a consumer report is used for a consumer credit transaction and the consumer is granted "credit on material terms that are materially less favorable than the most favorable terms available to a substantial proportion of consumers." 15 U.S.C. § 1681m(h). Regulation V provides several methods for determining which consumers must receive a risk-based pricing notice. 12 C.F.R. § 1022.72(b).

When a consumer is granted credit on such less-than-favorable terms, the creditor must provide a notice to the consumer with information similar to an adverse action notice, but also explaining that the terms offered are set based on consumer reporting information, and disclosing the consumer's credit score used in the underwriting and its date, the range of possible credit scores in the model, and the key factors that adversely affected the credit score. 15 U.S.C. §§ 1681m(h), 1681g(f)(1); 12 C.F.R. § 1022.73. Again, the goal is to facilitate the consumer's review of credit reports that may contain negative information for accuracy. The FCRA "risk-based pricing" provision is subject only to public enforcement by the CFPB. 15 U.S.C. § 1681m(h)(8).

Irrespective of the ultimate pricing or loan approval status, FCRA requires that mortgage lenders or brokers disclose to loan applicants any credit score used in the underwriting decision, as well as the date and origin of the score and the range of possible scores. 15 U.S.C. § 1681g(g).

VII. FCRA LIABILITY AND PREEMPTION

FCRA generally permits both public and private enforcement. All FCRA actions must be brought within the earlier of two years after the date of the discovery by the plaintiff of the violation or five years after the date of the violation. 15 U.S.C. § 1681p.

Public enforcement of FCRA is undertaken by the CFPB and the FTC, with state attorneys general also having enforcement authority. 15 U.S.C. § 1681s(a)-(c). Public enforcement agencies can seek monetary penalties or injunctive relief.

For private actors, FCRA imposes two tiers of liability, depending on whether a violation was merely negligent or was willful. 15 U.S.C. § 1681n-1681o. A negligent violation results in liability for actual damages and reasonable attorney's fees. 15 U.S.C. § 1681o(a).

For willful violations, liability is for the sum of actual damages, punitive damages, and reasonable attorney's fees. 15 U.S.C. § 1681n(a). For willful violations only, actual damages are restricted to no less than $100 or more than $1,000, other than for a *natural* person who obtains a consumer report under false pretenses or knowingly without a permissible purpose, in which case actual damages are subject to a $1,000 floor. 15 U.S.C. § 1681n(a)(1)(A)-(B). FCRA damages are *per violation*, so statutory damages for willful non-compliance can add up.

FCRA requires both policies and procedures *and* actual compliance, but policies and procedures can be a safe harbor from compliance. Likewise, lack of a policy or procedure alone is unlikely to be actionable without an allegation of a willful violation because of the need to show damages.

While FCRA provides for statutory damages for willful violations, a consumer must also allege some sort of actual damages, not just a mere procedural violation, in order to have standing to litigate, as the Supreme Court has made clear in the FCRA context. *Spokeo, Inc. v. Robins* 578 U.S. ___, 136 S. Ct. 1540 (2016). Such actual damages alleged must be both particularized and concrete, but intangible injuries may be concrete. In the FCRA context, such intangible injuries could include injury to creditworthiness, harm to reputation, humiliation, and mental distress. Moreover, any attorney's fees incurred prior to litigation of FCRA claims—such as in trying to correct a credit report—would suffice as actual damages for FCRA.

FCRA additionally provides for liability to consumer reporting agencies for *all* persons who obtain consumer reports under false pretenses or without a permissible purpose. Such liability is for the greater of $1,000 or the actual damages sustained by the consumer reporting agency. 15 U.S.C. § 1681n(b). On top of this, FCRA has a built-in sanctions provision that provides for attorney's fees to be awarded for any unsuccessful pleading or motion filed in bad faith. 15 U.S.C. §§ 1681o(b); 1681n(c).

Not all FCRA provisions carry a private right of action. There is no private liability for furnishing inaccurate or incomplete information or failing to send out notices of negative information having been reported. 15 U.S.C. § 1681s-2(c). In 2003 Congress enacted 15 U.S.C. § 1681m(f)-(h). Section 1681m(h) contains a provision stating that there is no private right of action and only federal agency enforcement under this "section." Courts have split on whether this "section" refers solely to subsection 1681m(h) or to the entirety of section 1681m. At the very least, there is no private right of action for users that fail to provide credit scoring model notices when credit is granted on materially less favorable terms than to other borrowers. 15 U.S.C. § 1681m(h)(8)(A). Whether the limitation extends to failure to provide adverse action notices remains unresolved.

FCRA also preempts common law actions for defamation, invasion of privacy, and negligence other than in the context of the provision of false information with malicious intent. 15 U.S.C. § 1681h(e). FCRA preemption protects both CRAs and furnishers.

Problem Set 35

1. Chris Drummer, a young journalist, ordered his credit score from Equifax, a national consumer reporting agency. He was so proud of his 720 FICO that he got it tattooed on his forearm. Chris was understandably confused, then, when he applied for a Continental Express Platinum Card, and the card was issued with a notice stating the rate on the card is set based on Chris's credit score, which it listed as 410 out of a possible range from 0 to 500. Can you explain to Chris what's going on? Why is Chris getting the notice from Continental Express, and how can Chris determine why the scores are so different? *See* 15 U.S.C. §§ 1681g(f), 1681m(h).

2. After learning of the credit score on the Continental Express Platinum Card notice, Chris Drummer (from problem 1) was teased mercilessly about his 720 FICO tattoo by his 23-year-old cousin, Marcus. "Oh yeah, wise guy, what's your score?" asked Chris. "I dunno," said Marcus. "OK, we're going online and ordering your free annual credit report. We'll see who's laughing then," said Chris.

Chris and Marcus went online to order Marcus's free annual credit reports and get Marcus's credit score. To their surprise, they were unable to obtain any reports for Marcus from the three major credit bureaus, much less credit scores. They even double-checked that they had Marcus's Social Security and driver's license numbers correct. "I don't get it," said Chris, "How don't you have a credit report or a score? You've got an apartment and pay rent and utilities and have a bank account and a job." Can you explain to Chris what might be going on and what this means for Marcus?

3. You've been hired to undertake a compliance review of Slick Jimmy Feinerman's Slaab dealership. Jimmy gladly provides financing for his customers. The dealership retains the loans and services them itself. When customers come in to Jimmy's, they are told by the greeter that they need to allow Jimmy's staff to copy their driver's license if they want to test drive a car. Unbeknownst to the consumer, Jimmy's uses the information from the license to pull a consumer report, which Jimmy's salesmen then uses to size up the consumer. What risks is Slick Jimmy running? 15 U.S.C. §§ 1681b(f); 1681n.

4. Kitty Chen ordered her free annual credit report. When she reviewed it she was surprised to see that she was listed as having made a late payment six months ago at Aperture, a clothing store from which she had a private-label credit card. Kitty was sure she had made the payment, which she had sent via check, on time. The bill was due on a Friday, and the check had been cashed on a Monday. Kitty was also puzzled that Aperture hadn't notified her about the late payment previously.

- **a.** Kitty wrote to Aperture to dispute the information, noting that she had mailed the check a week before the bill was due. Aperture responded to Kitty's dispute by with a letter that said it was not undertaking the investigation because it was deeming it frivolous as Kitty admitted the check had been cashed after the due date. What can Kitty do? *See* 12 U.S.C. § 1843(k); 15 U.S.C. §§ 1681s-2(a)(7), 1681s-2(c), 6809(3); 12 C.F.R. §§ 1022.42, 1022.43; UCC § 3-310(b)(1).
- **b.** Now suppose that instead of contacting Aperture, Kitty disputed the information with the CRA, which relayed the dispute to Aperture. Aperture responded that it undertook an investigation and that its files indicate that the check was cashed on the Monday, so that the payment was in fact late. What can Kitty do? *See* 15 U.S.C. §§ 1681i(b)-(c), 1681s-2(b); 12 C.F.R. §§ 1022.42, 1022.43; UCC § 3-310(b)(1).

5. Noah Phillips decided to Google his name after a blind date told him that she had checked him out through a Google search. Among the results Noah found were information about his bankruptcy filing from over a decade ago, a link to a newspaper page advertising his home in a 2008 foreclosure sale, and scurrilous allegations about non-payment from a contractor with whom Noah had had a dispute when renovating his home. A number of the other links returned by the Google search relate to other Noah Phillipses, including one with a criminal conviction for public indecency. Does Noah have any recourse under the Fair Credit Reporting Act? *See* 15 U.S.C. §§ 1681a(d), 1681a(f), 1681b(a), 1681c(a), 1681e(a)-(b), 1681i(a)(1), 1681o.

6. Veracity, a nationwide consumer reporting agency, has been hacked, and millions of consumer files have been stolen. Veracity has not yet revealed the data breach, but it expects an avalanche of litigation after it does. You've been engaged by Veracity to evaluate its legal liability. The general counsel of Veracity understands that there might be a range of theories of liability, but is looking solely for an analysis of its liability under the Fair Credit Reporting Act. What's your analysis? *See* 15 U.S.C. §§ 1681b, 1681e(a), 1681n, 1681o.

7. Last year Tamara West got a new driver's license. The number on her new license was different from that on her old license; her state had adopted a new numbering system. Shortly afterward, Tamara went to pay for groceries with a check as she always did. The cashier took the check and driver's license and ran them through a machine, as she always did. Usually a green light flashed on the machine and the check would be deposited in the register. This time, however, a red light flashed on the machine, and the cashier told Tamara the grocery store could not accept her check. When Tamara asked why, the cashier explained that she had run the driver's license through Check^{2}R, a service that analyzed the payment risk on checks and would either give a green light or red light depending on whether the risk exceeded a certain threshold. As other shoppers looked on in annoyance, Tamara said, "Nothing in my risk profile has changed for the worse. The only difference between today and last week is that I have a new driver's license. How can my check be rejected?" "Take it up with Check^{2}R," said the cashier. "You got another way to pay for those groceries?" Tamara started to dig around in her purse for cash, feeling absolutely humiliated by the experience. What, if anything, can Tamara do? *See* 15 U.S.C. §§ 1681a(d)-(f), 1681b(3)(F), 1681g(a), 1681m(a); UCC § 3-310(b)(1).

8. Tamara West (from problem 6) is back. After spending a lot of time on the phone with folks at Check^{2}R, she's figured out what happened. Check^{2}R tracks consumer files based on driver's license number. Her new driver's license made her appear to be a first-time check writer within the Check^{2}R system, which is why her check was rejected. Does this discovery change Tamara's legal position? *See* 15 U.S.C. §§ 1681e(b), 1681i(a).

CHAPTER 36

FINANCIAL PRIVACY

"Show me where a man spends his money and time and I will show you his God." This aphorism is often attributed to Martin Luther, but whatever its provenance, there is no denying the force of the observation. Spending habits disclose a great deal about a consumer—the consumer's priorities, interests, and to some degree, the consumer's wealth.

Imagine if you could view your neighbor's credit card bills and bank statements for the last year. You might find out that your neighbor subscribes to some objectionable publications, has made purchases of various adult products, given to various political candidates, charities, civic, and religious organizations, has bought drug paraphernalia, firearms, or has obtained pharmaceuticals or medical care. Some of these might be things about which your neighbor is quite open and proud, but perhaps not. Perhaps you learn that your outwardly very pious neighbor has been making donations to various atheist groups or that your militantly straight neighbor has subscribed to gay porn sites or simply that your neighbor is head over heels in debt. At the very least, you'd know quite a bit about your neighbor, which might be useful for all sorts of things: marketing other products to your neighbor, inviting your neighbor to join in some sort of group or activity with you, or targeting your neighbor for opprobrium or avoidance. Now suppose your neighbor . . . or anyone . . . could learn all of this about you. It would be like the ability to read your mail.

All of this speaks to the various reasons why consumers might want to be able to maintain some modicum of privacy or at least control over information about their financial lives. While many consumers might want privacy over their finances for its own sake, consumer financial information is revealing about far more than just finances per se.

At the same time, consumers might sometimes want to share that information because of the benefits it can bring them. Sharing of financial information with a prospective lender is a virtual prerequisite to obtaining credit. But some consumers might also be interested in doing so if it will result in subsequent advertisements and solicitations that are targeted to their interests. In other words, by sharing financial information, consumers can obtain useful information themselves.

Notably, however, obtaining the benefits of either a loan or advertisements and promotions does not require a complete and unlimited sharing of financial information. Financial privacy is not binary. Instead, it is a three-dimensional spectrum, varying in terms of what information is revealed, to whom, and for what purposes. A consumer might be fine with some information being more widely revealed than other information or for it to be revealed but only for a limited purpose, namely obtaining a particular benefit.

A complex web of laws deal with consumer financial privacy and a related topic, financial data security. Privacy deals with the ability to restrict access to information about oneself. Security (covered in the following chapter) is one aspect of ensuring privacy, namely that access to information is limited to authorized parties.

Privacy and security deal with different parts of a financial data life cycle that begins with the collection of data, goes to the storage of the data, and then extends to the sharing of the data. Privacy covers collection and sharing, while security covers storage and sharing.

A range of federal and state laws and regulations affect both of these topics. Some of these statutes are specific to consumer finance, whereas others are more generally applicable.

Privacy concerns arise primarily in regard to four groups: the government, nosy individuals (including family and friends), businesses, and thieves. It's worthwhile understanding the motivations for these different groups. Government is interested in consumer financial data that can be associated with an identifiable consumer primarily for law enforcement purposes. Regulatory interest in data is about data writ large, not individual consumers. Concerns about Big Brother loom, of course, more vividly in the minds of some than others.

A wife concerned about her husband's fidelity might want to be able to review his financial transactions, perhaps without involving him in the process. Likewise, a consumer might simply not want her neighbor to know what sort of intimate purchases she has made, what sort of medical treatment she is receiving, how much she spent on shoes, or to what charities she donates.

The interest of businesses (and thieves, as we will see in the next chapter) in consumer financial data is that it is monetizable. For thieves the data is monetizable, because it can be used to further fraudulent transactions using the consumer's payment data.

For legitimate businesses, however, data is monetizable precisely because of what it reveals about a consumer. Consumers who are interested in one thing are often interested in other related things, and being able to identify a consumer's likely interests is extremely valuable to anyone looking to sell things to consumers. It helps merchants (and that includes financial institutions selling financial products) target likely buyer populations and to tailor their advertisements and even product terms to be more attractive to the buyer population. Thus, if a business can identify consumers who have, for example, made purchases at a baby furniture store recently, it has likely identified a population that will be interested in other baby-related products, and which, in a few years, will be interested in toddler-related products. Similarly, consumers who have recently taken out a purchase money mortgage are likely to be interested in home furnishings, etc. And if the new homebuyer's ZIP code is in a high-income area, it will indicate different likely furnishing purchases than if it's in a moderate-income area. Moreover, different types and sources of consumer data can be combined to produce even richer analytical insights about consumers' likely spending interests.

To the extent that a financial institution can analyze consumer data, it can itself engage in more effective, targeted **cross-selling** (the selling of new products to one's existing consumers). And to the extent that the financial institution can sell consumer data—whether things as basic as a list of customers and their mailing addresses or as complicated as the merchant category code data from credit card transactions—they can extract considerable additional value from a customer relationship.

Put another way, consumers pay for their "free" checking accounts and other "free" financial services. They just pay in data, not dollars, but because data is readily monetizable, it is simply another form of currency.

I. OBTAINING CONSUMER FINANCIAL INFORMATION

Consumer financial information is generated in a number of ways. Most immediately it is generated from consumer transactions with either a merchant or a financial institution. When a consumer makes a purchase or opens an account (or returns an item or closes an account), financial information is generated. Subsequent transactions on an account (and the lack of transactions) also generate consumer financial information. We might call this data original consumer data, in that it originates with the consumer's actions, and we might differentiate between data generated by consumer actions and data generated by consumer inaction (be it non-payment or simply account inactivity). This first level of consumer data is not solely a product of the consumer—data exists only in particular formats, and there is some work that must be done to translate a consumer's activities into formatted data, but this is largely rote, ministerial work performed by a financial institution.

There is also a second level of consumer data that is created by combining and/or analyzing the original raw consumer data. This is derivative consumer data that is created because of substantial action by a financial institution or other non-consumer entity.

The difference between this original level data and the derivative data is important because consumers have no role in the creation of the derivative data once the original data has been generated and may not be aware of its existence. Whereas consumers can, in theory, prevent the creation of original level data by simply not transacting (just say "no"), they lack the ability to prevent the creation of derivative data except by contract or public law.

A. Song-Beverly Credit Card Act

State statutes in 15 states restrict the type of information that *merchants* may obtain from consumers in the course of transactions. Most notable is California's Song-Beverly Credit Card Act, which prohibits any business from requesting a credit cardholder's "personal identification information" (PII) or requiring the cardholder to provide PII "as a condition to accepting" the credit card payment if the PII must be written down or is written down or otherwise recorded by the business.

Cal. Civ. Code § 1747.08(a). "Personal identification information" ("PII") is defined in Song-Beverly as "information concerning the cardholder, other than information set forth on the credit card, and including, but not limited to, the cardholder's address and telephone number." Cal. Civ. Code § 1747.08(b). (Be aware that a number of other statutes use similar terms such as "personally identifiable information," but they are not always defined the same way.)

There are exceptions to the Song-Beverly prohibition for transactions at fuel dispensers, cash advances, obtaining shipping information, when the merchant is contractually obligated to collect the information, or required by other law. Cal. Civ. Code § 1747.08(c). The Song-Beverly prohibition does not prevent the merchant from asking to see identification, only from recording it. Cal. Civ. Code § 1747.08(d). Thus, a merchant can always request a cardholder's driver's license to verify the cardholder's identity.

Song-Beverly has substantial gaps in its coverage. It does not cover debit card or ACH transactions, only credit cards. Cal. Civ. Code §§ 1747.02(a), 1747.03. Song-Beverly has also been interpreted not to apply to online transactions for downloadable products, *Apple, Inc. v. Superior Court*, 56 Cal. 4th 128 (Cal. 2013), or to products ordered online but picked up in person, *Ambers v. Beverages & More, Inc.*, 236 Cal. App. 4th 508 (Cal. Ct. of App. 2d App. Dist. 2015). Consider whether it is possible to make all in-person transactions online by simply having the consumer fill in the payment information at a tablet or computer at point of sale.

Song-Beverly also applies only to requests for PII in connection with a credit card payment. Therefore, it does not apply after payment has been made or to voluntary requests for PII, such as when a consumer chooses to sign up for a loyalty program. This last point is particularly important. Song-Beverly does not prevent merchants from offering rewards or loyalty programs that use separate cards or ID numbers to track consumers and that are correlated with credit card transactions by merchants. The key here is that Song-Beverly prevents consumers from being required to provide PII but does not prohibit collection of PII given voluntarily by the consumer or even if the consumer is incentivized to give it through a rewards program. What Song-Beverly does, however, is impose a bifurcation on the payment and loyalty program sign-up.

The following case both illustrates the operation of Song-Beverly and the type of merchant behavior that Song-Beverly is meant to prevent.

Pineda v. Williams-Sonoma Stores, Inc.

51 Cal. 4th 524 (Cal. 2011)

Moreno, J.—The Song-Beverly Credit Card Act of 1971 (Credit Card Act) (Civ. Code, § 1747 *et seq.*) is "designed to promote consumer protection." (*Florez v. Linens 'N Things, Inc.* (2003) 108 Cal.App.4th 447, 450.) One of its provisions, section 1747.08, prohibits businesses from requesting that cardholders provide "personal identification information" during credit card transactions, and then recording that information. (Civ. Code, § 1747.08, subd. (a)(2).)

Plaintiff sued defendant retailer, asserting a violation of the Credit Card Act. Plaintiff alleges that while she was paying for a purchase with her credit card in one of defendant's stores, the cashier asked plaintiff for her Zip Code. Believing it necessary to complete the transaction, plaintiff provided the requested information and the cashier recorded it. Plaintiff further alleges that defendant subsequently used her name and Zip Code to locate her home address.

(1) We are now asked to resolve whether section 1747.08 is violated when a business requests and records a customer's Zip Code during a credit card transaction. In light of the statute's plain language, protective purpose, and legislative history, we conclude a Zip Code constitutes "personal identification information" as that phrase is used in section 1747.08. Thus, requesting and recording a cardholder's Zip Code, without more, violates the Credit Card Act. We therefore reverse the contrary judgment of the Court of Appeal and remand for further proceedings consistent with our decision.

FACTS AND PROCEDURAL HISTORY

Because we are reviewing the sustaining of a demurrer, we assume as true all facts alleged in the complaint. (*Sheehan v. San Francisco 49ers, Ltd.* (2009) 45 Cal.4th 992, 996 [89 Cal. Rptr. 3d 594, 201 P.3d 472].)

In June 2008, plaintiff Jessica Pineda filed a complaint against defendant Williams-Sonoma Stores, Inc.[3] The complaint alleged the following:

Plaintiff visited one of defendant's California stores and selected an item for purchase. She then went to the cashier to pay for the item with her credit card. The cashier asked plaintiff for her Zip Code and, believing she was required to provide the requested information to complete the transaction, plaintiff provided it. The cashier entered plaintiff's Zip Code into the electronic cash register and then completed the transaction. At the end of the transaction, defendant had plaintiff's credit card number, name, and Zip Code recorded in its database.

Defendant subsequently used customized computer software to perform reverse searches from databases that contain millions of names, e-mail addresses, telephone numbers, and street addresses, and that are indexed in a manner resembling a reverse telephone book. The software matched plaintiff's name and Zip Code with plaintiff's previously undisclosed address, giving defendant the information, which it now maintains in its own database. Defendant uses its database to market products to customers and may also sell the information it has compiled to other businesses.

Plaintiff filed the matter as a putative class action, alleging defendant had violated section 1747.08 and the unfair competition law (UCL) (Bus. & Prof. Code, §§ 17200 *et seq.*). She also asserted an invasion of privacy claim. Defendant demurred, arguing a Zip Code is not "personal identification information" as that phrase is used in section

3. According to its Web site, Williams-Sonoma is "the premier specialty retailer of home furnishings and gourmet cookware in the United States." (Williams-Sonoma, About Us <http://www.williams-sonoma.com/customer-service/about-us.html> [as of Feb. 10, 2011].) The company operates "more than 250 stores nationwide, a direct-mail business that distributes millions of catalogs a year, and a highly successful e-commerce site." (*Ibid.*)

1747.08, that plaintiff lacked standing to bring her UCL claim, and that the invasion of privacy claim failed for, among other reasons, failure to allege all necessary elements. Plaintiff conceded the demurrer as to the UCL claim, and the trial court subsequently sustained the demurrer as to the remaining causes of action without leave to amend. As for the Credit Card Act claim, the trial court agreed with defendant and concluded a Zip Code does not constitute "personal identification information" as that term is defined in section 1747.08.

The Court of Appeal affirmed in all respects. With respect to the Credit Card Act claim, the Court of Appeal relied upon *Party City Corp. v. Superior Court* (2008) 169 Cal.App.4th 497 [86 Cal. Rptr. 3d 721] (*Party City*), which similarly concluded a Zip Code, without more, does not constitute personal identification information.

Plaintiff sought our review regarding both her Credit Card Act claim and her invasion of privacy cause of action. We granted review, but only of plaintiff's Credit Card Act claim.

DISCUSSION

. . .

(3) Section 1747.08, subdivision (a) provides, in pertinent part, "[N]o person, firm, partnership, association, or corporation that accepts credit cards for the transaction of business shall . . . (2) Request, or require as a condition to accepting the credit card as payment in full or in part for goods or services, the cardholder to provide *personal identification information*, which the person, firm, partnership, association, or corporation accepting the credit card writes, causes to be written, or otherwise records upon the credit card transaction form or otherwise." (§ 1747.08, subd. (a)(2), italics added.) Subdivision (b) defines personal identification information as "information concerning the cardholder, other than information set forth on the credit card, and including, but not limited to, the cardholder's address and telephone number." (§ 1747.08, subd. (b).) Because we must accept as true plaintiff's allegation that defendant requested and then recorded her Zip Code, the outcome of this case hinges on whether a cardholder's Zip Code, without more, constitutes personal identification information within the meaning of section 1747.08. We hold that it does.

Subdivision (b) defines personal identification information as "information *concerning* the cardholder . . . including, but not limited to, the cardholder's address and telephone number." (§ 1747.08, subd. (b), italics added.) "Concerning" is a broad term meaning "pertaining to; regarding; having relation to; [or] respecting. . . ." (Webster's New Internat. Dict. (2d ed. 1941) p. 552.) A cardholder's Zip Code, which refers to the area where a cardholder works or lives, is certainly information that pertains to or regards the cardholder.

In nonetheless concluding the Legislature did not intend for a Zip Code, without more, to constitute personal identification information, the Court of Appeal pointed to the enumerated examples of such information in subdivision (b), *i.e.*, "the cardholder's address and telephone number." (§ 1747.08, subd. (b).) Invoking the doctrine *ejusdem generis*, whereby a "general term ordinarily is understood as being '"restricted to those things that are similar to those which are enumerated specifically"'" (*Costco Wholesale*

Corp. v. Superior Court (2009) 47 Cal.4th 725, 743 (conc. opn. of George, C. J.)), the Court of Appeal reasoned that an address and telephone number are "specific in nature regarding an individual." By contrast, the court continued, a Zip Code pertains to the *group* of individuals who live within the Zip Code. Thus, the Court of Appeal concluded, a Zip Code, without more, is unlike the other terms specifically identified in subdivision (b).

(4) There are several problems with this reasoning. First, a Zip Code is readily understood to be part of an address; when one addresses a letter to another person, a Zip Code is always included. The question then is whether the Legislature, by providing that "personal identification information" includes "the cardholder's address" (§ 1747.08, subd. (b)), intended to include components of the address. The answer must be yes. Otherwise, a business could ask not just for a cardholder's Zip Code, but also for the cardholder's street and city in addition to the Zip Code, so long as it did not also ask for the house number. Such a construction would render the statute's protections hollow. Thus, the word "address" in the statute should be construed as encompassing not only a complete address, but also its components.

Second, the court's conclusion rests upon the assumption that a complete address and telephone number, unlike a Zip Code, are specific to an individual. That this assumption holds true in all, or even most, instances is doubtful. In the case of a cardholder's home address, for example, the information may pertain to a group of individuals living in the same household. Similarly, a home telephone number might well refer to more than one individual. The problem is even more evident in the case of a cardholder's *work* address or telephone number—such information could easily pertain to tens, hundreds, or even thousands of individuals. Of course, section 1747.08 explicitly provides that a cardholder's address and telephone number constitute personal identification information (*id.*, subd. (b)); that such information *might also* pertain to individuals other than the cardholder is immaterial. Similarly, that a cardholder's Zip Code pertains to individuals in addition to the cardholder does not render it dissimilar to an address or telephone number.

More significantly, the Court of Appeal ignores another reasonable interpretation of what the enumerated terms in section 1747.08, subdivision (b) have in common, that is, they both constitute information unnecessary to the sales transaction that, alone or together with other data such as a cardholder's name or credit card number, can be used for the retailer's business purposes. Under this reading, a cardholder's Zip Code is similar to his or her address or telephone number, in that a Zip Code is both unnecessary to the transaction and can be used, together with the cardholder's name, to locate his or her full address. (Levitt & Rosch, *Putting Internet Search Engines to New Uses* (May 2006) 29 L.A. LAW. 55, 55; see Solove, *Privacy and Power: Computer Databases and Metaphors for Information Privacy* (2001) 53 STAN. L. REV. 1393, 1406–1408.) The retailer can then, as plaintiff alleges defendant has done here, use the accumulated information for its own purposes or sell the information to other businesses.

There are several reasons to prefer this latter, broader interpretation over the one adopted by the Court of Appeal. First, the interpretation is more consistent with the rule that courts should liberally construe remedial statutes in favor of their protective purpose, which, in the case of section 1747.08, includes addressing "the misuse of personal identification information for, inter alia, marketing purposes." (*Absher v. AutoZone, Inc.* (2008) 164 Cal.App.4th 332, 345.) The Court of Appeal's interpretation, by contrast, would permit retailers to obtain indirectly what they are clearly prohibited from obtaining directly, "end-running" the statute's clear purpose. This is so because information that can be permissibly obtained under the Court of Appeal's construction could easily be used to locate the cardholder's complete address or telephone number. Such an interpretation would vitiate the statute's effectiveness. Moreover, that the Legislature intended a broad reading of section 1747.08 can be inferred from the expansive language it employed, *e.g.,* "concerning" in subdivision (b) and "*any* personal identification information" in subdivision (a)(1). (Italics added.) The use of the broad word "any" suggests the Legislature did not want the category of information protected under the statute to be narrowly construed.

(5) Second, only the broader interpretation is consistent with section 1747.08, subdivision (d). Subdivision (d) permits businesses to "requir[e] the cardholder, as a condition to accepting the credit card . . . , to provide reasonable forms of positive identification, which may include a driver's license or a California state identification card, . . . *provided that none of the information contained thereon is written or recorded.* . . ." (§ 1747.08, subd. (d), italics added.) Of course, driver's licenses and state identification cards contain individuals' addresses, including Zip Codes. Thus, under Civil Code section 1747.08, subdivision (d), a business may require a cardholder to provide a driver's license, but it may not record any of the information on the license, *including the cardholder's Zip Code*. Under the Court of Appeal's interpretation, the Legislature inexplicably permitted in section 1747.08, subdivision (a)(2), what it explicitly forbade in subdivision (d)—the requesting and recording of a Zip Code. We decline to conclude such an inconsonant result was intended.

(6) In light of the foregoing, and particularly given the internal inconsistency that would arise under the Court of Appeal's alternate construction, we conclude that the only reasonable interpretation of section 1747.08 is that personal identification information includes a cardholder's Zip Code. We disapprove *Party City Corp. v. Superior Court, supra,* 169 Cal.App.4th 497, to the extent it is inconsistent with our opinion.

Even were we to conclude that the alternative interpretation urged by defendant and adopted by the Court of Appeal was reasonable, the legislative history of section 1747.08 offers additional evidence that plaintiff's construction is the correct one. . . .

In 1990, the Legislature enacted former section 1747.8, seeking "to address the misuse of personal identification information for, inter alia, marketing purposes, and [finding] that there would be no legitimate need to obtain such information from credit card customers if it was not necessary to the completion of the credit card transaction." (*Absher, supra,* 164 Cal.App.4th at p. 345.) The statute's overriding purpose was to "protect the personal privacy of consumers who pay for transactions with credit cards." (Assem. Com. on Finance and Ins., Analysis of Assem. Bill No. 2920 (1989–1990 Reg. Sess.) as amended Mar. 19, 1990, p. 2.)

The Senate Committee on Judiciary's analysis highlighted the motivating concerns: "The Problem . . . Retailers acquire this additional personal information for their own business purposes—for example, to build mailing and telephone lists which they can subsequently use for their own in-house marketing efforts, or sell to direct-mail or tele-marketing specialists, or to others." (Sen. Com. on Judiciary, Analysis of Assem. Bill No. 2920 (1989–1990 Reg. Sess.) as amended June 27, 1990, pp. 3–4.) To protect consumers, the Legislature sought to prohibit businesses from "requiring information that merchants, banks or credit card companies do not require or need." (Assem. Com. on Finance and Ins., Analysis of Assem. Bill No. 2920 (1989–1990 Reg. Sess.) as amended Mar. 19, 1990, p. 2.)

. . .[T]he [older,] 1990 version of former section 1747.8 forbade businesses from "requir[ing] the cardholder, as a condition to accepting the credit card, to provide personal identification information. . . ." (Stats. 1990, ch. 999, § 1, p. 4191.) In 1991, the provision was broadened, forbidding businesses from "*[r]equest[ing], or* requir[ing] as a condition to accepting the credit card . . . , the cardholder to provide personal identification information. . . ." (Stats. 1991, ch. 1089, § 2, p. 5042, italics added.) "The obvious purpose of the 1991 amendment was to prevent retailers from 'requesting' personal identification information and then matching it with the consumer's credit card number." (*Florez, supra*, 108 Cal.App.4th at p. 453.) "[T]he 1991 amendment prevents a retailer from making an end-run around the law by claiming the customer furnished personal identification data 'voluntarily.' " (*Ibid.*) That the Legislature so expanded the scope of former section 1747.8 is further evidence it intended a broad consumer protection statute.

To be sure, the legislative history does not specifically address the scope of section 1747.08, subdivision (b) or whether the Legislature intended a Zip Code, without more, to constitute personal identification information. However, the legislative history of the Credit Card Act in general, and section 1747.08 in particular, demonstrates the Legislature intended to provide robust consumer protections by prohibiting retailers from soliciting and recording information about the cardholder that is unnecessary to the credit card transaction. Plaintiff's interpretation of section 1747.08 is the one that is most consistent with that legislative purpose.

Thus, in light of the statutory language, as well as the legislative history and evident purpose of the statute, we hold that personal identification information, as that term is used in section 1747.08, includes a cardholder's Zip Code. . . .

DISPOSITION

The judgment of the Court of Appeals is reversed and the case is remanded for further proceedings consistent with this decision.

Other courts have grappled with the same question of whether a ZIP code is personal identification information and come to different answers. The Massachusetts Supreme Judicial Court said that it was, *Tyler v. Michaels Stores*, 464 Mass. 492 (Mass. 2012), but the District Court for the District of Columbia held that by itself it was not. *Hancock v. Urban Outfitters, Inc.*, 32 F. Supp. 3d 26 (D.D.C. 2014), *vacated and remanded with instructions to dismiss for lack of jurisdiction on appeal, Hancock v. Urban Outfitters, Inc.*, 830 F.3d 511 (D.C. Cir. 2016) (plaintiffs failed to allege Article III injury—mere collection of data was not an injury sufficient to create standing).

B. California Online Privacy Protection Act

State laws also require businesses with websites and online services to post privacy policies. Of particular note is the California Online Privacy Protection Act (CalOPPA), Cal. Bus. & Prof. Code §§ 22577-22579. As you're seeing, California is often a leader in this area, as well as being the largest single state consumer market in the United States. For businesses that operate nationally, compliance with California law is essential, and shapes business practices across the board.

CalOPPA applies to any person or company whose website collects personally identifiable information from California consumers. Cal. Bus. & Prof. Code § 22575(a). Such persons must post online a conspicuous privacy policy stating precisely what information is collected and with whom it is shared. *Id.* CalOPPA also requires the person to comply with the privacy policy. Cal. Bus. & Prof. Code § 22576. Violations of CalOPPA are violations of the California Unfair Competition Law, Cal. Civ. Code § 17200.

CalOPPA, like many privacy statutes, is triggered by the collection of "personally identifiable information" (PII), a phrase that is not consistently defined among statutes. For CalOPPA purposes PII means information collected on the Internet about an individual consumer, including first and last name, street address, email address, telephone number, Social Security number, any other information that would enable a specific individual to be contacted either in person or online, or any information collected from the consumer that remains in a personally identifiable form (*e.g.*, a birthdate). Cal. Bus. & Prof. Code § 22577(a). CalOPPA also requires websites to explain in their privacy policy how they respond to "do not track" mechanisms exercised by consumers and whether third parties may collect PII from their websites when a consumer uses the site.

Notice that CalOPPA does not require any real substantive privacy terms. Instead the statute requires disclosure of a privacy policy, the substance of which is left entirely up to the business, and then adherence to whatever that privacy policy is. If consumers do not bother to read the privacy policy or if the policy is written in sufficiently general terms that a consumer cannot determine what is actually happening with his PII, there is no recourse under the statute. Do you think consumers are likely to read privacy policies or change their consumption behavior based on them? If not, what is the point of CalOPPA? And, if they don't read privacy policies, does it indicate that consumers don't really care about privacy, at least in the abstract? If so, why are consumers often so upset when they learn that their PII has been stolen by a hacker?

II. SHARING CONSUMER FINANCIAL INFORMATION

A. Ownership of Financial Data

When a consumer maintains an account or transacts data is created. Who owns such financial data? Consumer financial data is a jointly produced item—it requires the input of the consumer, but the formatting and preservation of that data is done by the financial institution.

Ownership, or at least control rights, over financial data is a big-money issue. Consumer financial data can be mined, giving businesses valuable insights about consumers that can be monetized through targeted advertising and promotions. At the same time, that information can be quite valuable to consumers, who might want to analyze it themselves, often with the assistance of third parties, in order to optimize their consumption habits or simply for accounting purposes.

As a strictly legal matter, it's clear that financial records are property of the financial institution, not the consumer. In *United States v. Miller*, 425 U.S. 435 (1976), the Supreme Court held that consumer financial records are property of the financial institution that holds them. Yet clearly consumers have *some* rights in their financial records, including the ability to force a financial institution to provide them with copies of their records, which they can then share with third parties. But those records are not necessarily the complete set of data generated by the consumer's transactions, nor are they in a format that is easily shareable other than in print. Does a consumer have a right to share account data with third parties in other formats? For example, can a consumer consent to letting a third party "screen scrape" data from its bank account or obtain her complete transaction history in a readily transferrable digital format?

For example, there is a range of non-bank financial services companies that operate without a brick and mortar presence ("**fintechs**"), and some of them provide and/or rely on account data aggregation services. These companies access consumer account data with the consumers' authorization and then provide services to consumers using the data aggregated from the consumers' various financial accounts. The services offered include financial advice and management tools, account and transaction verification, and underwriting and fraud-screening.

Depositaries, however, are sometimes reluctant to facilitate the sharing of this information. First, depositaries may be worried about possibly adverse advice or even competition from the aggregation companies. What if a financial advice tool indicated to a consumer that the consumer could get a much better deal from another bank? Or what if the data aggregator was doing loan underwriting for a competitor of the bank? Fintechs access to consumer data might make financial services more competitive, which is not in the interest of existing market participants because it could result in thinner profit margins.

Second, even when a bank has no competitive concerns, it might still have security concerns. If the consumer shares account login information with a third-party financial services company and that company is then hacked, the consumer's account could be cleaned out, leaving the bank on the hook for the unauthorized transaction(s).

These two factors have created frictions between depositaries and fintechs regarding data sharing, even with consumer authorization. The CFPB has attempted to informally broker a solution through its announcement of "principles" of consumer-authorized financial data sharing and aggregation. The principles are non-binding, of course, but they also set forth the CFPB's policy view, which is that consumers should be able to readily provide third parties with access to their account data (albeit without sharing "account credentials"), but also be able to readily revoke such access.

Consumer Financial Protection Bureau, Consumer Protection Principles: Consumer-Authorized Financial Data Sharing and Aggregation

Oct. 18, 2017

Consumer Protection Principles: Consumer-Authorized Financial Data Sharing and Aggregation

Consumer-authorized access and use of consumer financial account data may enable the development of innovative and improved financial products and services, increase competition in financial markets, and empower consumers to take greater control of their financial lives. To accomplish these objectives, however, such access and use must be designed and implemented to serve and protect consumers. The Bureau intends for the following Consumer Protection Principles to help safeguard consumer interests as the consumer-authorized aggregation services market develops. The Principles are intended to be read together. They are not intended to alter, interpret, or otherwise provide guidance on—although they may accord with—existing statutes and regulations that apply in this market.

1. Access. Consumers are able, upon request, to obtain information about their ownership or use of a financial product or service from their product or service provider. Such information is made available in a timely manner. Consumers are generally able to authorize trusted third parties to obtain such information from account providers to use on behalf of consumers, for consumer benefit, and in a safe manner.

Financial account agreements and terms support safe, consumer-authorized access, promote consumer interests, and do not seek to deter consumers from accessing or granting access to their account information. Access does not require consumers to share their account credentials with third parties.

2. Data Scope and Usability. Financial data subject to consumer and consumer-authorized access may include any transaction, series of transactions, or other aspect of consumer usage; the terms of any account, such as a fee schedule; realized consumer costs, such as fees or interest paid; and realized consumer benefits, such as interest earned or rewards. Information is made available in forms that are readily usable by consumers and consumer-authorized third parties. Third parties with authorized access only access the data necessary to provide the product(s) or service(s) selected by the consumer and only maintain such data as long as necessary.

3. Control and Informed Consent. Consumers can enhance their financial lives when they control information regarding their accounts or use of financial services. Authorized terms of access, storage, use, and disposal are fully and effectively disclosed to the consumer, understood by the consumer, not overly broad, and consistent with the consumer's reasonable expectations in light of the product(s) or service(s) selected by the consumer. Terms of data access include access frequency, data scope, and retention period. Consumers are not coerced into granting third-party access. Consumers understand data sharing revocation terms and can readily and simply revoke authorizations to access, use, or store data. Revocations are implemented by providers in a timely and effective manner, and at the discretion of the consumer, provide for third parties to delete personally identifiable information.

4. Authorizing Payments. Authorized data access, in and of itself, is not payment authorization. Product or service providers that access information and initiate payments obtain separate and distinct consumer authorizations for these separate activities. Providers that access information and initiate payments may reasonably require consumers to supply both forms of authorization to obtain services.

5. Security. Consumer data are accessed, stored, used, and distributed securely. Consumer data are maintained in a manner and in formats that deter and protect against security breaches and prevent harm to consumers. Access credentials are similarly secured. All parties that access, store, transmit, or dispose of data use strong protections and effective processes to mitigate the risks of, detect, promptly respond to, and resolve and remedy data breaches, transmission errors, unauthorized access, and fraud, and transmit data only to third parties that also have such protections and processes. Security practices adapt effectively to new threats.

6. Access Transparency. Consumers are informed of, or can readily ascertain, which third parties that they have authorized are accessing or using information regarding the consumers' accounts or other consumer use of financial services. The identity and security of each such party, the data they access, their use of such data, and the frequency at which they access the data is reasonably ascertainable to the consumer throughout the period that the data are accessed, used, or stored.

7. Accuracy. Consumers can expect the data they access or authorize others to access or use to be accurate and current. Consumers have reasonable means to dispute and resolve data inaccuracies, regardless of how or where inaccuracies arise.

8. Ability to Dispute and Resolve Unauthorized Access. Consumers have reasonable and practical means to dispute and resolve instances of unauthorized access and data sharing, unauthorized payments conducted in connection with or as a result of either authorized or unauthorized data sharing access, and failures to comply with other obligations, including the terms of consumer authorizations. Consumers are not required to identify the party or parties who gained or enabled unauthorized access to receive appropriate remediation. Parties responsible for unauthorized access are held accountable for the consequences of such access.

9. Efficient and Effective Accountability Mechanisms. The goals and incentives of parties that grant access to, access, use, store, redistribute, and dispose of consumer data align to enable safe consumer access and deter misuse. Commercial participants are accountable for the risks, harms, and costs they introduce to consumers. Commercial participants are likewise incentivized and empowered effectively to prevent, detect, and resolve unauthorized access and data sharing, unauthorized payments conducted in connection with or as a result of either authorized or unauthorized data sharing access, data inaccuracies, insecurity of data, and failures to comply with other obligations, including the terms of consumer authorizations.

While consumers can of course agree to the sharing of their own data, what data can be shared by a financial institution without the consumer's specific consent? Financial institutions' ability to share data is limited by several federal statutes.

B. Fair Debt Collection Practices Act

You've already seen the Fair Debt Collection Practices Act, the major statute governing debt collection. While the FDCPA is not usually thought of as a privacy statute, it has some privacy aspects to it, particularly its restrictions on debt collectors contacting third parties about the debt. 15 U.S.C. §§ 1692b, 1692c(b).

The FDCPA's prohibitions privatize the fact of the debt—the debt is left as a matter between the consumer and the debt collector, and no one else. Given the social stigma that can attach to a debt, the financial privacy right created by the FDCPA is an important protection for consumers.

C. Fair Credit Reporting Act

The Fair Credit Reporting Act is also a privacy statute in certain regards. FCRA limits *who* may pull a consumer's credit report, 15 U.S.C. § 1681b. Again, this has the effect of privatizing the facts represented in the credit report—they are not available to the general public.

Additionally, FCRA places a limitation on data sharing between corporate affiliates. If affiliates share information that would constitute a "consumer report" (which, remember, is any communication bearing on a consumer's creditworthiness or personal characteristics that is used or expected to be used for credit, insurance, or employment purposes, 15 U.S.C. § 1681a(d)), then the affiliate that receives the information may not use it for marketing unless there is either a preexisting business relationship between the affiliate and the consumer or the consumer has received a disclosure that information may be shared among affiliates for the purpose of making solicitations of the consumer and been given chance to opt out of the solicitations. 15 U.S.C. § 1681s-3(a)(1). If the consumer opts out, the opt-out is valid for five years, but absent another notice and opt-out opportunity, information sharing would not be possible. 15 U.S.C. § 1681s-3(a)(3). There are a number of exceptions to the FCRA solicitation prohibition, including if there is a preexisting business relationship (defined as either an existing contractual relationship, a recent contract, or a recent inquiry from the consumer about a product or service). 15 U.S.C. § 1681s-3(a)(4).

It is important to recognize that FCRA does not in any way prohibit information sharing among corporate affiliates. Instead, it merely limits the use of certain types of shared information by adding some transactional frictions, namely the need to notify the consumer of an opt-out opportunity.

D. Right to Financial Privacy Act

A particular privacy concerns involves the government's ability to obtain consumer financial records. If the government could do so, it would raise the specter of embarrassing leaks of information or of government programs being tailored to benefit or harm particular consumers.

The Right to Financial Privacy Act, 12 U.S.C. § 3401 *et seq.*, places restrictions on the federal government's ability to obtain financial institution records, generally requiring a warrant or subpoena. 12 U.S.C. § 3402. The regular prudential supervisory process is exempt from RFPA, however, 12 U.S.C. § 3413(b), as are national security activities. 12 U.S.C. § 3414. RFPA does not appear to prohibit the federal government from acquiring financial data in arm's-length marketplace transactions. RFPA does not apply to state governments, but many states have their own equivalent statutes.

E. Gramm-Leach-Bliley Act

The most important federal financial privacy statute is the Gramm-Leach-Bliley Act. GLBA creates an "affirmative and continuing obligation" on every financial institution "to respect the privacy of its customers and to protect the security and confidentiality of those customers' non-public personal information." 15 U.S.C. § 6801(a). GLBA applies to financial institutions engaged in consumer finance, as well as in securities and commodities markets. The CFPB has rulemaking authority under the GLBA for privacy policies in the consumer finance context. The CFPB's rules under GLBA are known as Reg P.

GLBA's privacy protections relate to "nonpublic personal information." That term is defined as "personally identifiable financial information" that the consumer has provided to the financial institution, that results from a transaction the consumer undertakes, or that the financial institution has otherwise obtained (such as from a credit report). 15 U.S.C. § 6809(4). That would include information such as a consumer's name, address, income, and Social Security number, but also account numbers, transactional history, browsing history obtained through "cookies," and even the fact that a person was or is a customer of the financial institution. Publicly available information is not protected.

GLBA's privacy provisions extend to all "financial institutions," a term that is broadly defined as any person that is engaged in financial activities, or activities incidental or complementary to such financial activities. 15 U.S.C. § 6809(3); 12 U.S.C. § 1843(k). Basically any firm that would be a "covered person" under the Consumer Financial Protection Act would readily be a "financial institution" for GLBA purposes.

The basic idea of GLBA is that financial institutions should have to disclose to consumers what they do in terms of sharing consumers' non-public personal information with nonaffiliated third parties and that they should have to obtain consumer consent for such sharing. Consent, however, is *assumed* by GLBA, such that the consumer must affirmatively opt out of information sharing if he does not desire it. Thus, once a financial institution has disclosed its privacy practices to consumers and provided an opt-out opportunity, the financial institution is free to share the information absent consumer objection. For example, a financial institution need only disclose that it sells consumers' contact information to direct marketing companies and, if the consumer does not opt out, the GLBA privacy requirements have been satisfied. Additionally, GLBA contains a number of broad exceptions to the consent requirement.

In other words, GLBA does not present a meaningful activity barrier, especially because information-sharing practices can be described in general terms and because the consumer is unlikely to give the disclosure much attention in the first place because it is one of many account opening disclosures that deluge the consumer with largely non-negotiable terms of the account. In practice, then GLBA functions as a disclosure statute that gives the consumer a very limited right to object to information sharing, and financial institutions can, with transactional planning, largely eliminate the application of that right.

1. Sharing Information with Affiliates

The GLBA privacy provisions all deal with sharing of non-public personal information with nonaffiliated third parties. The negative implication from this is that financial institutions are free under GLBA to share consumers' non-public personal information with affiliated parties without any consumer consent whatsoever. The only restriction on information shared between affiliates is the FCRA limitation on solicitations based on shared information that would constitute a consumer report. 15 U.S.C. § 1681s-3(a)(1).

2. Sharing Information with Nonaffiliated Third Parties

The particular type of privacy practice disclosure and opt-out rights required by GLBA depend on whether an individual is a "consumer" or a "customer" of a financial institution. All individuals transacting for personal, household, or family purposes are "**consumers**," and "**customers**" are that subgroup of consumers with whom a financial institution has an ongoing relationship. For example, a when a consumer cashes a check with a check casher, the consumer is still a "consumer," not a "customer," because there is no ongoing relationship, even if the consumer regularly cashes checks with that check casher. Similarly, a consumer who sends a remittance overseas or who merely applies for a loan is still just a "consumer." But if the consumer has a continuing contractual relationship with the financial institution—such as a loan or lease or line of credit—then the consumer becomes a "customer." The consumer continues to be a customer as long as the relationship is ongoing, but once it ends, the former customer is once again a "consumer." This distinction can get tricky when parts of a relationship are split, such as in a mortgage securitization transaction. One party might own the loan and another might own the servicing rights. In such a case, the borrower is a "consumer" for the purposes of the loan owner and a "customer" for purposes of the servicer. 16 C.F.R. § 1016.3(e)(iv).

For *customers*, GLBA requires that a financial institution provide a **privacy notice** irrespective of whether the financial institution shares customer non-public personal information. 15 U.S.C. § 6803(a). That notice must be provided when the customer relationship is established (or, with consumer consent, shortly thereafter if it would delay a transaction).

The privacy notice must describe when the financial institution shares non-public personal information with third parties and the type of information shared. Specifically, the privacy notice must explain the categories of information collected (*e.g.*, information from an app or from a consumer reporting agency), the categories of information disclosed (*e.g.*, names, contact information, account balances), the categories of affiliates and nonaffiliated third parties to whom information is disclosed or may be disclosed in the future (*e.g.*, insurance companies, direct marketers, non-profit organizations), categories of information disclosed and to whom under joint marketing or service provider agreements, and a statement that the disclosures are made "as permitted by law." 15 U.S.C. § 6803(c); 16 C.F.R. § 1016.6(a). The privacy notice will typically also contain an explanation of opt-out rights (discussed below), although that can be done separately, as well as any Fair Credit Reporting Act affiliate information sharing disclosures, and a statement about the firm's policies and practices for protecting the confidentiality and security of non-public personal information.

The disclosures required in the privacy notice may be quite general. For example, Reg P provides that:

> You satisfy the requirement to categorize the nonpublic personal information that you collect if you list the following categories, as applicable: (i) Information from the consumer; (ii) Information about the consumer's transactions with you or your affiliates; (iii) Information about the consumer's transactions with nonaffiliated third parties; and (iv) Information from a consumer reporting agency.

16 C.F.R. § 1016.6(c)(1). Likewise, for the categories of non-public personal information disclosed or categories of affiliates and nonaffiliated third parties, a statement of general categories and "a few examples to illustrate" suffices. 16 C.F.R. § 1016.6(c)(2)-(3). Thus, it would suffice for a financial institution to disclose that: "We share your non-public personal information with non-financial companies, such as retailers, magazine publishers, airlines, and direct marketers." *See* 16 C.F.R. § 1016.6(c)(3)(ii). Given the level of generality in the GLBA privacy notices, how meaningful are these disclosures? It would seem that the information that they are meant to convey is merely that a consumer's information may be shared, not specifically how it is shared.

In addition, the financial institution must provide an **annual privacy notice** as long as the customer relationship lasts even if there is no information sharing occurring or if it is all occurring through exceptions. 15 U.S.C. § 6803(a); 12 C.F.R. § 1016.5(a). The annual notice need not be provided if the financial institution's privacy practices have not changed and the financial institution does not use the information other than for the normal support of the account and marketing its own products. 15 U.S.C. § 6803(f).

While all customers must receive a privacy notice, 15 U.S.C. § 6803(a), a financial institution still may not share a customer's non-public personal information with nonaffiliated third parties, unless the customer has:

(1) received the GLBA privacy notice, 15 U.S.C. § 6802(a);
(2) been provided with an **opt-out notice** that informs the consumer of his right to opt out of the data sharing and how that right may be exercised;

(3) been given a reasonable way to opt out; and
(4) been given a reasonable amount of time to opt out before his or her non-public personal information is disclosed.

15 U.S.C. § 6802(b)(1). If an institution's privacy practices change, it must provide consumers with a new privacy notice and opt-out opportunity before any subsequent sharing of their non-public personal information other than under a GLBA exception. 12 C.F.R. § 1016.8(a).

For *consumers who are not customers*, GLBA requires that before a financial institution shares non-public personal information with nonaffiliated third parties (other than subject to an exception), that the financial institution first provide the non-customer consumer with a privacy notice and an opt-out notice. 15 U.S.C. §§ 6802(a), 6803. For non-customer consumers, the privacy notice may be provided in a short form that merely states that the full privacy notice is available upon request and explains a reasonable means by which a consumer may obtain it. 12 C.F.R. § 1016.6(d). If a financial institution does not share non-public personal information with non-affiliated third parties or only does so within the permitted exceptions, then neither privacy notice nor opt-out notice need be furnished to non-customer consumers.

3. GLBA Exceptions to Privacy Notice and Opt-Out Opportunity Requirements

The GLBA notice and opt-out requirements do not exist for all types of information disclosure. Neither the notice nor the opt-out requirements apply to information disclosures necessary for effecting, administering, or enforcing a transaction requested or authorized by a consumer. 15 U.S.C. § 6802(e)(1)(A). Thus, when a consumer authorizes a payment on a credit card, non-public personal information, such as name, ZIP code, account number, and the fact that the consumer is a customer, would all normally be transmitted to various payment processors. Consumers do not need to receive a privacy notice for this, nor do they have an opt-out right. If, on the other hand, non-public personal information beyond what is needed for effecting the transaction were to be transmitted—for example a Social Security number or date of birth—then a privacy notice would be required and the consumer would have an opt-out right, at least as to that information.

Likewise, GLBA does not require the privacy notice or opt-out right for information disclosure undertaken with the consent or request of the consumer. 15 U.S.C. § 6802(e)(2). Thus, if the consumer provides access to her bank account to a fintech information aggregator, such as Mint.com, no privacy notice or opt-out right would be required.

Similarly, there is no privacy notice or opt-out right required for disclosure of information for credit reporting, 15 U.S.C. § 6802(e)(6), maintaining or servicing a consumer's account, 15 U.S.C. § 6802(e)(2), or as part of a private label credit card program, which would require sharing information with a merchant. *Id.* There are also exceptions for the purposes, among others, of fraud prevention, protecting confidentiality of data (*e.g.*, sharing with a security software vendor), as part of a securitization or secondary market transaction, including the transfer of servicing rights, ensuring institutional risk control, facilitating a merger or similar transaction, or responding to judicial process or investigation, or complying with federal, state, or local laws. 15 U.S.C. § 6802(e).

GLBA also contains an exception for the opt-out requirement alone. The privacy notice (and any annual notices) must still be provided if this exception is relied on. The exception permits sharing of non-public personal information with a nonaffiliated third party that "performs services for or functions on behalf of the financial institution, including marketing of the financial institution's own products or services," as long as the financial institution fully discloses that it may provide such information and has a contractual confidentiality agreement with the third party. 15 U.S.C. § 6801(b)(2). This provision would cover the marketing of financial products or services through a "joint agreement" between one or more financial institutions. This exception thus covers both **service providers** and **joint marketing**. For example, if a bank contracted with a firm to analyze its accounts to advise it how to optimize its fee structure, that would fall into the "servicer provider" exception, while if a bank partnered with a university alumni association to market the bank's cards to the university's alumni, that would be "joint marketing" and covered by the exception.

The effect of all of these exceptions is that a financial institution may share non-public personal information about a consumer *even if the consumer objects*. The data is effectively not the consumer's to control.

Nonaffiliated third parties that receive non-public personal information from a financial institution under any exception may not themselves reshare the information to nonaffiliated third parties unless the disclosure would itself be lawful if it had been made by the financial institution to the (second) third party. 15 U.S.C. § 6802(c). In no case, however, may account numbers or card numbers be disclosed for marketing purposes to any nonaffiliated third party other than consumer reporting agencies. 15 U.S.C. § 6802(d). Thus, if financial institution *A* was authorized to share the information with financial institution *B*, financial institution *B* could share the information with its affiliates, and, if it solicited consumer consent or could itself rely on an exception, could in turn share the information with nonaffiliated entity *C*.

4. Enforcement of GLBA Privacy Rights

There is no private right of action under GLBA's privacy provisions. Instead, it is enforced by federal regulators according to the regular division of enforcement authority under the Consumer Financial Protection Act. (Note that enforcement authority for the GLBA data security provisions is different, as discussed in the following chapter.) Contrast this with the FCRA provision limiting the use of information sharing between affiliates, which is subject to FCRA's general private right of action.

GLBA does not preempt state laws with more onerous requirements as long as they are not inconsistent with GLBA, 15 U.S.C. § 6807, and some states have more stringent financial privacy laws, most notably requiring consumer opt-ins either for nonaffiliate sharing (California, Connecticut, Florida, Illinois) or for both affiliate and nonaffiliated sharing (Alaska and Vermont). As a result, financial firms will sometimes treat all consumers from particular states as having opted out of information sharing unless a GLBA exception applies.

All in all, then, GLBA does not outright prohibit any information sharing. Instead, it creates a regime in which the default setting is unlimited information sharing provided that the sharing is properly disclosed and the consumer has not opted out of the sharing. As a practical matter, GLBA provides little consumer privacy protection. Indeed, overall, U.S. consumers have very weak financial privacy rights except in regard to the federal government, debt collection, and credit reporting. By and large a consumer's financial information is available for sale without the consumer's affirmative consent.

Problem Set 36

1. Your old law school friend Prehensilia Sharp has become a bit of a privacy nut. Prehensilia is always griping about having to give out her personal information. "Can't I just transact anonymously?" she asks. Can she? If so, how does it affect her? If not, why not?

2. You met up for lunch with Prehensilia (from the previous problem) at a Los Angeles sandwich shop. You pay with your credit card and she pays with a debit card. The merchant swiped the cards using a small device plugged into an iPad and asked for you to sign on the screen. After you signed, a message appeared on the screen asking you for your email address or phone number in order to receive an electronic receipt. "See," Prehensilia says, "They're always asking for your data. It's just so wrong." Is it? *See* Cal. Civ. Code §§ 1747.08(a), 1747.08(c); 15 U.S.C. § 1693d; Visa Rule 5.10.1.1.

3. As a compliance attorney for Mastodon National Bank, you've been asked to review the disclosures on Mastodon's ATMs. The ATMs are used both by Mastodon deposit account holders and consumers with accounts at other financial institutions. Before allowing any ATM withdrawals, Mastodon runs the names and account numbers of all ATM users through a fraud database operated by a third-nonaffiliated-party vendor. Consumers are able to deposit checks at Mastodon ATMs, and when they do so, Mastodon transmits the checks to the payor bank or an intermediate correspondent bank or clearinghouse for payment. What sort of privacy disclosures need to be provided to Mastodon ATM users? *See* 15 U.S.C. §§ 6802(a)-(b), 6802(e), 6803(a); 12 C.F.R. § 1016.6(d).

4. Leviathan Financial is a financial conglomerate that includes both a mortgage lender, Megalodon Mortgage, and a property insurer, Behemoth Beneficial Assurance. Leviathan Financial would like to advertise Behemoth Beneficial Assurance's home insurance products to consumers who obtained mortgages from Megalodon Mortgage. May it do so? *See* 15 U.S.C. §§ 1681a(d), 1681s-3(a); 12 C.F.R. § 1022.23(b).

5. Megalodon Mortgage (from the previous question) would also like to sell information about its mortgage borrowers to home furnishing merchants. These merchants are particularly eager to be able to identify new home purchasers.

   a. Is there a way Megalodon can sell this information without having to provide Gramm-Leach-Bliley Act privacy notices? *See* 15 U.S.C. §§ 6802(a), 6803(a).
   b. Is there a way Megalodon can sell this information without having to solicit consumers for opt-outs? *See* 15 U.S.C. §§ 6802(b)(1)-(2), 6802(c).

6. Your firm has been hired to advise FasterCard, a payment card network, regarding a new data product that Fastercard would like to sell to marketers. FasterCard receives substantial consumer data in the course of processing transactions for banks that issue cards on its network. From these transactions it is able to see the stores and locations where consumers are making purchases, as well as purchase amounts. FasterCard would like to combine this data with anonymized data it purchases from consumer reporting agencies and anonymized data collected from cookies on various online merchants' websites. FasterCard believes that it can link these data sources and possibly other data sources and associate them with particular individuals, creating a much more valuable overview of consumers' purchasing habits. Can FasterCard sell these new combined data profiles without consumer consent? *See* 15 U.S.C. §§ 1681a(d), 1681a(f), 1681b(a), 1681e(a), 6802(b)-(c).

7. Senator Prudence Dogood is a fierce advocate of consumer rights. She's considering introducing legislation that would mandate that depositories and credit card issuers make consumer transaction and account term data (including automatic bill payment information) available to the consumer in a standardized electronic format that the consumer can readily download. The Senator's hope is that this data can be plugged into third-party applications that will analyze the consumer's transactions and see if the consumer is getting the best deal possible from his or her current financial services provider and also facilitate switching of accounts if the consumer so desires. The Senator would like to know your thoughts about the idea, including how it is likely to affect the market if implemented and how it is likely to play politically.

CHAPTER 37

DATA SECURITY AND IDENTITY THEFT

Financial privacy laws generally aim to restrict intentional sharing of consumer data; not all sharing is deliberate. Some is accidental and some is without the consent of the firm holding the data. Data security issues are really a subset of privacy issues.

Federal and state laws impose a number of requirements for protecting financial data. Some of these are general data security requirements that are not specific to financial data, while others are geared to specifically to financial data. Additionally, state law in nearly all states has an ex post security regime that requires notification of certain breaches of data security. On top of all of this, private litigation over data security breaches functions as a type of data security regulation. Finally, federal law has some provisions designed to mitigate the effects of identity theft.

I. DATA SECURITY

A. Gramm-Leach-Bliley Act's "Safeguards" Mandate

The Gramm-Leach-Bliley Act (GLBA) requires financial regulatory agencies to establish standards for the institutions they regulate to ensure sufficient safeguards for the security, confidentiality, and integrity of consumer records. 12 U.S.C. §§ 6801(b), 6805(b). This provision has been implemented for banks through the **Interagency Guidelines Establishing Information Security Standards**, 12 C.F.R. Part 30, app. B (OCC), 12 C.F.R. Part 208, app. D-2 and Part 225, app. F (Fed. Res. Board); and 12 C.F.R. Part 364, app. B (FDIC), and for non-banks through the **FTC's Safeguards Rule**, 16 C.F.R. Part 314.

The basic idea with both the Interagency Guidelines and the FTC Safeguards Rule is that financial institutions must implement "a comprehensive information security program" that has been committed to writing. The program must be "reasonably designed to":

(1) Insure the security and confidentiality of customer information;
(2) Protect against any anticipated threats or hazards to the security or integrity of such information; and
(3) Protect against unauthorized access to or use of such information that could result in substantial harm or inconvenience to any customer.

16 C.F.R. § 314.3(b).

Among other things, an information security program must designate an employee or employees to coordinate the program (for banks, the responsibility is specifically given to the bank's board of directors, which may then delegate it), assess risks, and design safeguards to address those risks. It must also provide for testing of the system and oversight of service providers. The point here is that the implementations of the GLBA Safeguards mandate does not require any particular technology or security measures, but instead requires institutions to address security by having, in the first instance, a written policy about security, and, second, by imposing a standard of care on institutions. If either the information security program or its implementation is inadequate, the institution will be in violation of the GLBA safeguards.

There is no private right of action for failure to comply with the FTC Safeguards Rule or Interagency Guidelines Establishing Information Security Standards. Failure to comply with the GLBA Safeguards requirement might suffice, however, as a predicate for a state-law UDAP or negligence per se claim.

Regulators can themselves enforce compliance, of course. For banks, the sufficiency of information security standards is a major part of the examination process. For non-banks, the FTC has authority to bring unfairness actions under section 5 of the FTC Act for inadequate data security. *See FTC v. Wyndham Worldwide Corp.*, 799 F.3d 236 (3d Cir. 2015).

Whether the CFPB has similar authority under its UDAAP power is untested. The CFPB invoked UDAAP in its consent order with Dwolla over deceptive cybersecurity claims. *In the Matter of Dwolla, Inc.*, Administrative Proceeding, No. 2016-CFPB-0007. *Dwolla*, however, did not involve an actual data security breach, but deceptive statements to consumers about the Dwolla's cybersecurity practices. Whether failure to maintain adequate data security practices is unfair or abusive under the Dodd-Frank Act UDAAP provision remains unresolved. Similarly unresolved is whether the CFPB can investigate data security within the scope of its examination process given that the safeguards section of the GLBA—requiring regulators to establish standards for data security safeguards—is expressly excluded from the enumerated consumer laws. 12 U.S.C. § 5481(12)(J).

The GLBA safeguards apply solely to financial institutions. There are no general federal data security requirements for other businesses, even if they collect and retain consumer financial data, such as credit card account numbers. Yet these institutions might still face liability under the FTC Act's UDAP provision, 15 U.S.C. § 45. The following FTC press release gives some flavor of the type of lax security practices that, when combined with a data breach, may lead to action by a regulator.

Federal Trade Commission Press Release

June 26, 2012

FTC Files Complaint Against Wyndham Hotels for Failure to Protect Consumers' Personal Information

Credit Card Data of Hundreds of Thousands of Consumers Compromised, Millions of Dollars Lost to Fraud

The Federal Trade Commission filed suit against global hospitality company Wyndham Worldwide Corporation and three of its subsidiaries for alleged data security failures that led to three data breaches at Wyndham hotels in less than two years. The FTC alleges that these failures led to fraudulent charges on consumers' accounts, millions of dollars in fraud loss, and the export of hundreds of thousands of consumers' payment card account information to an Internet domain address registered in Russia.

The case against Wyndham is part of the FTC's ongoing efforts to make sure that companies live up to the promises they make about privacy and data security.

In its complaint, the FTC alleges that Wyndham's privacy policy misrepresented the security measures that the company and its subsidiaries took to protect consumers' personal information, and that its failure to safeguard personal information caused substantial consumer injury. The agency charged that the security practices were unfair and deceptive and violated the FTC Act.

Wyndham and its subsidiaries license the Wyndham name to approximately 90 independently-owned hotels, under franchise and management agreements.

Since 2008 Wyndham has claimed, on its Wyndham Hotels and Resorts subsidiary's website that, "We recognize the importance of protecting the privacy of individual-specific (personally identifiable) information collected about guests, callers to our central reservation centers, visitors to our Web sites, and members participating in our Loyalty Program . . ."

According to the FTC's complaint, the repeated security failures exposed consumers' personal data to unauthorized access. Wyndham and its subsidiaries failed to take security measures such as complex user IDs and passwords, firewalls and network segmentation between the hotels and the corporate network, the agency alleged. In addition, the defendants allowed improper software configurations, which resulted in the storage of sensitive payment card information in clear readable text.

Each Wyndham-branded hotel has its own property management computer system that handles payment card transactions and stores information on such things as payment card account numbers, expiration dates, and security codes. According to the FTC, in the first breach in April 2008, intruders gained access to a Phoenix, Arizona Wyndham-branded hotel's local computer network that was connected to the Internet and the corporate network of Wyndham Hotels and Resorts.

Because of Wyndham's inadequate security procedures, the breach gave the intruders access to the corporate network of Wyndham's Hotels and Resorts subsidiary, and the property management system servers of 41 Wyndham-branded hotels. This access enabled the intruders to:

- install "memory-scraping" malware on numerous Wyndham-branded hotels' property management system servers.
- access files on Wyndham-branded hotels' property management system servers that contained payment card account information for large numbers of consumers, which was improperly stored in clear readable text.

Ultimately, the breach led to the compromise of more than 500,000 payment card accounts, and the export hundreds of thousands of consumers' payment card account numbers to a domain registered in Russia.

Even after faulty security led to one breach, the FTC charged, Wyndham still failed to remedy known security vulnerabilities; failed to employ reasonable measures to detect unauthorized access; and failed to follow proper incident response procedures. As a result, Wyndham's security was breached two more times in less than two years.

- In March 2009, intruders again gained unauthorized access to Wyndham Hotels and Resorts' network, using similar techniques as in the first breach. In addition to using memory-scraping malware, they reconfigured software at the Wyndham-branded hotels to obtain clear text files containing the payment card account numbers of guests. In this second incident, the intruders were able to access information at 39 Wyndham-branded hotels for more than 50,000 consumer payment card accounts and use that information to make fraudulent charges using consumers' accounts.
- Later in 2009, intruders again installed memory-scraping malware and thereby compromised Wyndham Hotels and Resorts' network and the property management system servers of 28 Wyndham-branded hotels. As a result of this third incident, the intruders were able to access information for approximately 69,000 consumer payment card accounts and again make fraudulent purchases on those accounts.

The defendants in the case are: Wyndham Worldwide Corporation; its subsidiary, Wyndham Hotel Group, LLC, which franchises and manages approximately 7,000 hotels; and two subsidiaries of Wyndham Hotel Group – Wyndham Hotels and Resorts, LLC and Wyndham Hotel Management, Inc. . . .

B. Fair and Accurate Credit Transactions Act

The Fair and Accurate Credit Transactions Act (FACTA) of 2003, part of the Fair Credit Reporting Act, sets forth a very particular federal data security requirement, namely the truncation of credit and debit card numbers whenever they are printed electronically. Only the last five digits of the number may be printed. 15 U.S.C. § 1681c(g). Liability exists for both negligent non-compliance (for any actual damages caused plus attorney's fees and costs) and for willful non-compliance (for actual damages of at least $100 and no more than $1,000, plus punitive damages, attorney's fees, and costs). 15 U.S.C. §§ 1681n, 1681o. Given that a failure to truncate card numbers is unlikely to be a one-off problem, and that each violation can cost at least $100 if willful, FACTA liability can add up. States have similar card truncation statutes. *See, e.g.*, Cal. Civ. Code § 1747.09.

C. State Data Security Laws

States have their own data security laws. The farthest-reaching state data security law is a regulation from Massachusetts, 201 C.M.R. § 17.00 *et seq.*, implementing

M.G.L. ch. 93H(2). The Massachusetts regulation applies to anyone who owns, licenses, stores, maintains, or processes data about a Massachusetts resident. 201 C.M.R. §§ 17.02, 17.03(1). Because the Massachusetts regulation basically applies to any entity that deals with the data of even a single Massachusetts resident, it essentially sets the bar for compliance nationwide.

The Massachusetts regulation requires that all covered persons adhere to minimum standards for safeguarding "personal information," which is defined as a consumer's first name or initial and last name plus a Social Security number, state-issued ID or driver's license number, financial account number, or credit or debit card number. 201 C.M.R. § 17.02. Persons who deal with Massachusetts residents' personal information must develop, implement, and maintain a comprehensive information security program that is committed to writing. 201 C.M.R. § 17.03. In this regard, the requirement is substantially similar to the FTC's Safeguards Rule, but the Massachusetts data protection regulation applies to more than "financial institutions."

The Massachusetts regulation goes further than the FTC Safeguards Rule and specifically mandates particular data security measures. These measures are arguably required under the FTC Safeguards Rule, but only as part of the "reasonable" measures it mandates, rather than being expressly required. The Massachusetts regulation requires encryption of all personal information stored on laptops or portable devices, 201 C.M.R. § 17.04(5), as well as for all records or files that are transmitted wirelessly or across public networks, 201 C.M.R. § 17.04(3). It also requires covered persons to maintain up-to-date firewall protection and operating security patches if they have personal information on an Internet-connected system, and to have up-to-date security software to protect against malware. 201 C.M.R. § 17.04(6)-(7). Employees must have unique user IDs and passwords (so as to make clear who has accessed information), and their access must be limited to those files needed for their jobs. 201 C.M.R. § 17.04(2). The regulation goes so far as to mandate that access to data must be limited after multiple unsuccessful login attempts. 201 C.M.R. § 17.04(1)(e). Thus, failure to keep anti-virus software up to date would seem to be a violation of Massachusetts law.

There is no private right of action under the regulation or the statutory provision authorizing it. Instead, enforcement is solely by the state attorney general. M.G.L ch. 93H(6). That said, a violation of the Massachusetts data privacy regulation could well be a violation of the Massachusetts UDAP statute, M.G.L. ch. 93A, if the plaintiff could demonstrate harm and the other elements of unfairness. *See Amerifirst Bank v. TJX Cos. (In re TJX Cos. Retail Sec. Breach Litig.),* 564 F.3d 489 (1st Cir. 2009).

Other state data security laws are quite specific. For example, Minnesota prohibits any person or entity conducting business in Minnesota who accepts a credit or debit card from retaining the card security code data, PIN number, or full track contents of the magnetic stripe subsequent to authorization of the transaction (or 48 hours after authorization for PIN debit). Minn. Stat. Ann. § 325E.64. Notably, liability under this statute is owed to the financial institution that issued the card, rather than to the cardholder. Minn. Stat. Ann. § 325E.64.3

D. Private Security Standards

Certain industries have developed their own internal security standards, most notably the payment card industry. The Payment Card Industry Data Security Standard PCI-DSS, discussed in Chapter 21, is a security standard that applies to all merchants that accept payment cards as well as the financial institutions that process the cards. The standard is promulgated by the Payment Card Industry Security Standards Council, an entity created and controlled by American Express, Discover, JCB International, MasterCard, and Visa. The Card Networks require acquirer banks to ensure that merchants comply with PCI-DSS (and hold the acquirers liable for assessments upon non-compliance), so acquirers require merchants to attest compliance with PCI-DSS.

As explained in Chapter 21, PCI-DSS prohibits merchants from retaining payment card data. The only cardholder data that it allows the merchant to retain is the card number, expiration data, cardholder name, and service code. PCI Security Standards Council, PCI-DSS 36 (Version 3.1 2015). The card number, however, must be rendered unreadable anywhere it is stored through encryption, hashing, or truncation methods. *Id.* at 40. PCI-DSS prohibits merchants from storing "sensitive authentication data," such as card verification codes (the unembossed numbers on the back of cards), PIN numbers, and the card's Full Track data (which contains all of the preceding data fields), after authorization of a transaction, even if encrypted. *Id.* at 37.

PCI-DSS also requires that sensitive information be encrypted for transmission over open, public networks, like the Internet. *Id.* at 46-47. The effect is something similar to an end-to-end encryption requirement for card data for merchants.

Beyond PCI-DSS requirements, payments data is also protected through tokenization in some instances. Whereas encryption works by altering text through algorithms, tokenization replaces original data with randomly generated substitute data, making it more akin to a cipher. The key for deciphering the tokenized data is recorded in a secure codebook called a vault. Tokenization can be used with encryption; they are not exclusive technologies. Currently tokenization is not generally required for payments data, although it is increasingly used by digital wallets.

PCI-DSS has even been incorporated into law in a few states. Nevada requires all "data collectors"—that is, parties handling non-public personal information—to comply with PCI-DSS. Nev. Rev. Stat. Ch. 603A.215. Minnesota and Washington both have laws that make merchants that have suffered data breaches of payment card data liable to financial institutions for card reissuance costs and other costs associated with the breach. Minn. Stat. Ann. § 325E.64; Wash. Rev. Code Ann. § 19.255.020(3). Yet Washington exempts companies from data breach liability if they were certified as PCI-DSS compliant within a year of the breach. Wash. Rev. Code Ann. § 19.255.020(2), while Minnesota effectively does so (without expressly invoking PCI-DSS) by making liability contingent on retention of data in violation of PCI-DSS, as discussed in the previous section.

II. DATA BREACHES

Sometimes consumers' financial information is shared involuntarily by a business because of a "data breach," meaning that a hacker has somehow stolen the consumers' data. This data theft might happen if data is intercepted in transmission or it might involve an electronic infiltration of a business's computers to grab data that is in storage. Alternatively, a business might lose a physical computer that contains consumer financial information. However the breach happens, it is a serious event for a business.

A. Costs of Data Breaches

The costs of a data breach are wide-ranging and hard to quantify. Critically, they do not all fall on the breached company; instead breaches create major negative externalities for consumers and other businesses. First, there are costs to the breached firm. At the very least, these include the costs of identifying and then containing a breach—the breached firm has to figure out not just that there is a breach, but the extent of the data that has been compromised and during what period. This involves a certain amount of forensic work from specialist computer security firms. Likewise, once identified, a breach must be fixed, which entails additional expenses.

There will also be legal costs from dealing with a breach, as well as the costs of complying with data breach notification laws (discussed below), and possible post-breach litigation. There are also possible costs from a loss of customer confidence—customers might take their business elsewhere if they are worried that their data is not secure. Some firms will attempt to mitigate such losses of customer goodwill by purchasing various identity theft or fraud monitoring services for affected customers—yet another expense. Finally, the breached data may be used to enter into fraudulent transactions with the breached firm, which will bear the costs of the goods it has shipped to the fraudster.

Data breaches also create costs for consumers. Importantly, as we have seen, consumers are not generally liable for unauthorized payment transactions, so consumers should not bear the direct pecuniary losses from fraudulent transactions made using either their real payment data or payment data from accounts created in their names. As a practical matter, however, consumers may end up bearing direct pecuniary costs if they do not object, and at the very least they will face indirect pecuniary costs of dealing with the possibility of fraudulent use of their accounts or the creation of fake accounts in their name. This includes the costs and time of getting freezes on their files at consumer reporting agencies, getting payment cards reissued, and filing notices with financial institutions that transactions were unauthorized. When other types of data are stolen, additional hassles can ensue, such as changing passwords and security questions for websites, getting other forms of identification reissued, etc.

Finally, data breaches create costs for businesses that have themselves not been breached. When payment credentials are stolen from one merchant, they can be used to make fraudulent purchases from other merchants. The costs of that fraud will either lie on the defrauded merchant or on the card issuer, depending on the details of how the purchase was made. A similar story exists when non-payment credentials are stolen, and then used to open up a new account controlled by a fraudster, but in someone else's name. In such a situation, the named account holder may not even know of the account, and so will not take steps to close it down. In either situation, the losses from fraud resulting from a data breach may well be significantly greater at merchants other than the breached merchant. Indeed, small businesses are likely to be some of the most vulnerable for data breaches because they are unlikely to invest in state-of-the-art security measures. Those small businesses themselves are not particularly appealing targets for the resulting payments fraud with the stolen credentials. Instead, it is larger retailers that are likely to be targeted.

There is a market for cybersecurity insurance, but even when firms have coverage, it is often far too little to cover all of the losses that stem from a major data breach. The policies are never designed to cover the third-party externalities beyond some small amount of litigation liability, and data breach litigation (discussed below) faces many hurdles. Thus, firms with poor security measures are externalizing their costs on third parties. Yet, at the same time, even firms with generally good security measures may still be vulnerable for a security breach. All that is necessary, of course, is for one employee to fall for a phishing attack or the like. In other words, while lack of adequate care may increase the likelihood of a data breach, even substantial care may not be sufficient to prevent one.

B. Data Breach Notification Laws

As of 2018, 48 states plus the District of Columbia, Guam, Puerto Rico, and the U.S. Virgin Islands had data breach notification laws. (Alabama and South Dakota are the exceptions.)

State data breach notification laws all follow the same basic pattern: if the confidentiality, security, or integrity of certain personal consumer information is compromised, then the business must provide notice to the consumers whose information was involved expediently unless law enforcement determines that doing so would impede an investigation.

Within this general framework, there is considerable variation:

- *What types of information are covered by the statute?* States vary in terms of the protected information. Most require a breach to involve an individual's first name or initial and last name plus one or more of (i) Social Security number, (ii) driver's license or state-issued ID card number, or (iii) account number, credit card, or debit card number, as well as any security code needed to access the account, but excludes information that is generally available to the public, such as in public records. Some states, however, also include things such as email addresses and passwords, passport numbers, Social Security numbers, taxpayer ID numbers, biometric data, health insurance policy numbers, and mother's maiden name. A few states make exposure of a financial account number (such as a credit card number) without a password or the like sufficient. For example, would a consumer's email address or user name or security question answer be covered?

- *What forms of information are covered by the statute?* Only electronic information, or also tangible records? For most states only electronic information is covered.
- *What constitutes a breach?* There is substantial variation in the way breach is defined among states. A common formulation is "The unlawful and unauthorized acquisition of personal information that compromises the security, confidentiality, or integrity of personal information." If an employee gains unauthorized access, but in good faith, and doesn't disclose information further, is that a breach?
- *Is the notification triggered by a determination of harm?* Most states do not require notification if the breached entity determines that the breach does not present a reasonable likelihood of harm to the consumer. Yet the 11 states and 3 territories that require notification irrespective of harm include California, Georgia, Illinois, New York, and Texas.
- *Is there an encryption safe harbor?* Many states do not require notification if the breached data is encrypted, provided that the encryption key is not also compromised.
- *Who must be notified?* All states require that the affected consumers be notified, but some require notice to go to consumer reporting agencies, while others require notice to go to governmental officials, primarily state attorneys general, but sometimes also law enforcement. Additionally, some state data breach notification statutes require notice to be given to third parties if the breached party was storing data on the third party's behalf.
- *What is the procedure and timing of notice?* Must it be given to government officials too?
- *What are the penalties for failure to comply, and is there a private right of action?* Some states have private rights of action for data breach notification failures, some do not. Penalties vary considerably.

Additional statutes may apply if the compromised information includes medical information.

Given the variation among state data breach notification laws, how does a business know which law applies? Most states' laws are keyed to a breach affecting the information of their residents. For example, Illinois law provides that "Any data collector that owns or licenses personal information concerning an Illinois resident shall notify the resident at no charge that there has been a breach of the security of the system data following discovery or notification of the breach." 815 ILCS 530/10.

Some further require the breached business to operate within the state. New York's statute requires "[a]ny person or business which conducts business in New York state, and which owns or licenses computerized data which includes private information shall disclose any breach of the security of the system following discovery or notification of the breach in the security of the system to any resident of New York state whose private information was, or is reasonably believed to have been, acquired by a person without valid authorization." N.Y. Gen. Bus. L. § 899-aa. Thus, a data breach can readily result in 51 different statutes applying to the breached firm. This is a compliance nightmare for a firm that is already dealing with the immediate problem of the breach itself.

C. What's the Point of Data Breach Notification Laws?

While data breach notification statutes are the primary legal response to the problem of hacking, it is unclear how much good they do. One possibility is that notification statutes help limit fraud losses by alerting consumers (and sometimes consumer reporting agencies) that data has been compromised, so that the consumer can then put a freeze on his or her credit report or monitor his or her accounts, etc. The benefits here, however, depend on (1) the notification being timely relative to the breach, (2) consumers responding diligently, and (3) the stolen information being used to either create counterfeit payment credentials or open new accounts. There is reason to doubt all of these conditions.

Many breaches are not discovered until weeks or months after they occur. In such cases, notification may simply be too late to do any good, no matter what the consumer does. Statutes require timely notification after discovery, not after the actual breach itself.

Even if notification is timely, many consumers are not going to respond diligently. The fraud losses do not fall on the consumer, however, as we have seen, even if fraudulent charges and fake accounts can cause consumers lots of problems. If consumers do not respond diligently, notification is of little use.

Even if consumers respond diligently, a credit freeze does not prevent the use of stolen payment credentials, only the opening of new accounts in the consumer's name. A consumer might seek to get payment cards reissued, but many do not.

Finally, not all stolen information is being used to create new accounts or conduct payments fraud. Some is used to create other types of credentials (which may in turn be used to create fake accounts). In such cases, breach notifications are likely of little use.

Another possibility is that notification statutes are not at all about loss mitigation on the consumer side but help incentivize better data security practices by businesses. Notification statutes *increase* the cost of breaches for firms. In so doing, they arguably increase the incentive for firms to invest in data security. But a breach might not be the result of inadequate care and investment in data security. The nature of computer technology is that it is changing, and it may have latent flaws that a firm cannot identify with reasonable diligence. In such cases, the increased costs of a breach from notification do not incentivize better behavior by businesses.

Given that the benefits of breach notification laws are questionable, at best, why are they so pervasive? The answer seems to be political: data breaches are a huge problem, and consumers are poorly equipped to evaluate the risks they pose. State legislatures want to do something helpful, and at first blush a breach notification law seems like a good idea—let me know if my data has been compromised so I can take steps to protect myself. So why not give it a try? Yet even accepting this logic, the current non-uniform state-based regime makes little sense. Why have 51 different data breach notifications rather than a single federal one or a uniform state one?

D. Private Data Breach Litigation

When a data breach occurs, litigation is likely to ensue, usually in the form of class action suits, typically by consumers, but sometimes by banks. The particular theories behind these suits vary substantially. Negligence, negligent misrepresentation, and negligence per se are often alleged (the latter often incorporating the standards in the FTC Safeguards Rule as the standard of care), but other common causes of action are various state UDAP and other consumer protection statutes, breach of contract claims, bailment claims, breach of fiduciary duty claims, state data breach notification law violation claims, fraud claims, and the Federal Stored Communications Act. While negligence is the most common theory in data breach litigation, it faces a major hurdle in many states: the economic loss doctrine. This doctrine limits recovery in negligence actions to losses from physical harm; purely economic losses are not recoverable. The following case illustrates how successful various theories of liability are in a suit brought by a number of financial institutions against retailer TJX, the parent company of TJ Maxx, relating to a data breach.

In re TJX Cos. Retail Security Breach Litigation

524 F. Supp. 2d 83 (D. Mass. 2007)

William G. YOUNG, D.J.

I. INTRODUCTION

In what has been described as the largest retail security breach ever, criminals hacked into the computer systems of TJX Companies, Inc. ("TJX") and compromised the security of at least 45,700,000 customer credit and debit accounts. *See* Joseph Pereira, *Breaking the Code: How Credit-Card Data Went Out Wireless Door,* WALL ST. J., May 4, 2007, at Al. Financial institutions have brought suit seeking to recover their costs arising out of the resulting fraudulent transactions and the need to replace the compromised cards.

II. PROCEDURAL BACKGROUND

As described in *McMorris* v. *TJX Companies, Inc.,* 493 F. Supp. 2d 158, 160-61 (D. Mass. 2007), numerous cases were filed after TJX disclosed that its data security had been compromised. Almost immediately, this Court began consolidating the cases filed in the District of Massachusetts. *See id.* The Multi-District Litigation Panel subsequently entered an order transferring to this session of the Court all the cases filed in federal courts wherever located. *In re TJX Cos. Customer Data Sec. Breach Litig.,* 493 F. Supp. 2d 1382, 1383 (J.P.M.L. 2007).

Once consolidated, this case proceeded on two separate tracks: a Consumer Track for a putative class action brought by consumers, and a Financial Institutions Track for a putative class action brought by issuing banks. The issuing banks asserted claims against TJX as well as Fifth Third Bank and Fifth Third Bancorp ("Fifth Third") for (1) breach of contract; (2) negligence; (3) negligent misrepresentation; and (4) [state UDAP violations]. The issuing banks further assert claims against Fifth Third based on negligence per se.

TJX and Fifth Third moved to dismiss both tracks. The Consumer Track has since settled in principle, thus apparently mooting the motions to dismiss that track. The motions to dismiss the Financial Track are the subject of this memorandum.

III. FACTUAL ALLEGATIONS IN THE AMENDED COMPLAINT

In July 2005, computer hackers began hacking into TJX's systems to access the personal and financial information of shoppers. The stolen information was used to make fraudulent purchases. TJX did not discover the security breaches until fourteen months later, in December 2006.

At the heart of this case is a complex web of relationships between TJX and financial institutions. The plaintiffs are issuing banks that issued credit cards and debit cards to consumers, who used these cards to make purchases at TJX's stores. When customers presented a credit or debit card during a sale, TJX sent the account information to its bank, Fifth Third, for verification. Fifth Third then transmitted the account information to the issuing banks, who would authorize the transaction, through credit card networks operated by Visa and MasterCard.

Card Operating Regulations issued by Visa ("Visa Operating Regulations") and MasterCard ("MasterCard Operating Regulations") mandate that retailers safeguard cardholder information. Fifth Third has contracts with Visa and MasterCard that require Fifth Third to comply with these regulations. TJX and Fifth Third have a contract that similarly requires TJX to comply with the Visa and MasterCard Operating Regulations. TJX and Fifth Third allegedly failed to take necessary steps to safeguard consumer information, leading to the security breach and thereby violating the Operating Regulations.

Fifth Third submitted the MasterCard Operating Regulations (which are allegedly confidential) to the Court for in camera review with the consent of the issuing banks; this Court also received portions of the Visa Operating Regulations. In analyzing the contract claims, it is appropriate to consider these materials. *See, e.g., Beddall* v. *State St. Bank & Trust. Co.,* 137 F.3d 12, 17 (1st Cir. 1998). The parties must understand, however, that while the Court can well appreciate why MasterCard and Visa keep these regulations confidential in order to protect all parties (and consumers as well), this Court cannot base its public conclusions on data it keeps secret. *See Richardson v. United States,* 477 F. Supp. 2d 392, 405 n.18 (D. Mass. 2007). Submission of such documentation, therefore, constitutes a waiver of confidentiality to the extent the Court relies on these materials.

IV. DISCUSSION

To survive the motion to dismiss, the issuing banks must set forth factual allegations which, if taken as true, provide "plausible grounds" from which to draw the reasonable inference of each fact essential to each element of a claim. *Bell Atl. Corp.* v. *Twombly,* 550 U.S. 544, 556 (2007). The Supreme Court explained that "more than labels and conclusions" are required and that "a formulaic recitation of the elements of a cause of action will not do." *Id.*

. . .

A. Contract Claims

The issuing banks allege that they are third-party beneficiaries of contracts between TJX and Fifth Third and between Fifth Third and credit card associations such as Visa and MasterCard. These contracts required TJX and Fifth Third to safeguard consumer data. TJX and Fifth Third have both moved to dismiss this claim.

The parties agree on the law but disagree on its application to this case. Massachusetts employs the standard set forth in the Restatement (Second) of Contracts § 302 to identify intended beneficiaries who have enforceable rights under contracts.[2] *Rae* v. *Air-Speed, Inc.,* 386 Mass. 187, 195 (Mass. 1982). Section 302 states:

> (1) Unless otherwise agreed between promisor and promisee, a beneficiary of a promise is an intended beneficiary if recognition of a right to performance in the beneficiary is appropriate to effectuate the intent of the parties and . . .
> (b) the circumstances indicate that the promisee intends to give the beneficiary the benefit of the promised performance.

The case law makes clear that, pursuant to the "unless otherwise agreed" language in section 302, a promisor and promisee may expressly disclaim the existence of intended third-party beneficiaries. When this is the case, no third parties have enforceable rights under the contract. *See, e.g., Pennsylvania State Employees Credit Union* v. *Fifth Third Bank,* 398 F. Supp. 2d 317, 324 (M.D. Pa. 2005). The rationale is "contracting parties should be able to control who may sue on the contract." *Id.* at 325.

Here, the parties dispute whether there are effective express disclaimers that would prevent the issuing banks from being considered intended beneficiaries. TJX and Fifth Third point to a provision in the Merchant Agreements, which reads:

> This Agreement is for the benefit of, and may be enforced only by, Bank and Merchant and their respective successors and permitted transferees and assignees, and is not for the benefit of, and may not be enforced by any third party.

Bryan R. Blais Decl. ("Blais Decl."); *see also* G. Shaun Richardson Decl. ("Richardson Decl.") (containing identical wording).

The issuing banks respond that the Merchant Agreements incorporate the MasterCard and Visa Operating Regulations and provide that, in the event of conflict, the Operating Regulations prevail over the Merchant Agreements:

> Merchant agrees to participate in Networks in compliance with, and subject to, the by-laws, operating regulations and/or other rules, policies and procedures of such

---

2. Ohio, which is specified as the governing law in the contracts between Fifth Third and TJX, has also adopted section 302. *Hill* v. *Sonitrol of Sw. Ohio, Inc.,* 36 Ohio St. 3d 36, 521 N.E.2d 780, 784 (Ohio 1988).

> organizations and subject to any rules which may be published by Bank and distributed to Merchant . . . . In the event of a conflict between the Operating Regulations and this Agreement, the Operating Regulations shall prevail.

Richardson Decl.; *see also* Blais Decl. ("Merchant agrees to participate in VISA, MasterCard, and Other Associations in compliance with, and subject to, the by-laws, operating regulations and/or all other rules, policies and procedures of such organizations as in effect from time to time . . . .").

The MasterCard Operating Regulations include the following passage:

> The basic purpose of the Corporation [MasterCard] is to provide to its members the advantages of widespread interchange while modifying each member's local operations as little as possible. In keeping with this philosophy, the specifications as to forms and procedures contained in these rules are considered to be the minimum standards necessary to make credit and debit interchange workable.
>
> These rules are intended to be solely for the benefit of the corporation and its members.

MasterCard Operating Regulations, at 1. The issuing banks allege that they are members and, as such, are intended beneficiaries of the MasterCard Operating Regulations. The issuing banks further note that the MasterCard Operating Regulations include an indemnity provision. MasterCard Operating Regulations § 1.1.

The MasterCard Operating Regulations state, however, that MasterCard "shall have the sole right to interpret and enforce" the MasterCard Operating Regulations. MasterCard Operating Regulations § 1.2. Although the MasterCard Operating Regulations include a forum selection clause, the MasterCard Operating Regulations state that this "provision shall in no way limit or otherwise impact" MasterCard's sole right to interpret and enforce the MasterCard Operating Regulations. *Id.* § 1.4.

Consequently, while the issuing banks may be intended beneficiaries of the MasterCard Operating Regulations, the MasterCard Operating Regulations make clear that only MasterCard can enforce their terms and thus that the issuing banks have no right to file suit to achieve that end. As a result, the MasterCard Operating Regulations do not conflict with the provisions in the TJX and Fifth Third contracts denying third parties, such as the issuing banks, the ability to enforce the terms of the contracts.

The Visa Operating Regulations are similarly consistent with the Merchant Agreements. The Visa Operating Regulations may be designed to ensure the vitality of the Visa network and consequently benefit those who are members of that network. Like the MasterCard Operating Regulations, however, the Visa Operating Regulations fail to require that the issuing banks be allowed to assert third-party beneficiary claims. Indeed, the Visa Operating Regulations appear expressly to negate such a theory insofar as they "do not constitute a third-party beneficiary contract as to *any* entity or person . . . or confer any rights, privileges, or claims of any kind as to any third parties." Visa Operating Regulations, § 1.2C (emphasis added). Furthermore, the Middle District of Pennsylvania, which apparently is privy to a greater portion of the Visa Operating Regulations than this Court, indicated that, like MasterCard, Visa reserves the right to interpret the Operating Regulations and to determine when they have been violated. *See Sovereign Bank* v. *BJ's Wholesale Club, Inc.*, 2006 U.S. Dist. LEXIS 40063, 2006

WL 1722398, at *4, *5 (M.D. Pa. 2006); *see also id.* 2006 U.S. Dist. LEXIS 40063, [WL] at *7 (quoting Visa representative's statement that the Operating Regulations were not intended to create "'direct rights of enforcement between' [members]").

In sum, the issuing banks' argument that the contracts between Fifth Third and Visa and MasterCard empower them to bring suit is undermined fatally by the fact that the Operating Regulations, which were incorporated into these contracts, themselves appear to deny third parties the ability to bring suit. The issuing banks' assertion that the Operating Regulations conflict with the portions of the Merchant Agreements disclaiming the existence of intended beneficiaries is, for similar reasons, unavailing. Accordingly, this Court dismisses the contract claims.

B. Negligence

Under Massachusetts law, which the parties assume applies here, "purely economic losses are unrecoverable in tort and strict liability actions in the absence of personal injury or property damage." *Aldrich* v. *ADD Inc.,* 437 Mass. 213, 222 (Mass. 2002) (quotation marks and citations omitted). The rationale is partly that "a commercial user can protect himself by seeking express contractual assurances concerning the product (and thereby perhaps paying more for the product) or by obtaining insurance against losses." *Bay State-Spray & Provincetown S.S., Inc.* v. *Caterpillar Tractor Co.,* 404 Mass. 103, 109-110 (Mass. 1989).

In *CUMIS Insurance Society, Inc.* v. *BJ's Wholesale Club, Inc.,* No. 05-1158, slip op. at 8-9, 2005 Mass. Super. LEXIS 696 (Mass. Super. Ct. Dec. 1, 2005) (Quinlan, J.), the Massachusetts Superior Court held that the Massachusetts formulation of the doctrine barred the negligence claims in that case. Furthermore, in cases from the Middle District of Pennsylvania, the judge held that the doctrine barred the negligence claims arising out of security breaches such as those present in the instant case. *See, e.g., Pennsylvania State,* 398 F. Supp. 2d at 326-330 (applying Pennsylvania law that is identical to Massachusetts law).

The issuing banks cite *Banknorth, N.A.* v. *BJ's Wholesale Club, Inc.,* 394 F. Supp. 2d 283 (D. Me. 2005), a retail security breach action that applied Maine law, which is more permissive of negligence claims than the Massachusetts standard. That case, however, expressed no opinion on whether negligence claims in a situation such as that in the instant case were in fact barred by the economic loss doctrine under Maine law. *Id.* at 287. A later case out of the Middle District of Pennsylvania, however, applied Maine law to facts much like those here and held that, even under Maine law, the economic loss doctrine barred the negligence claims. *Banknorth, N.A.* v. *BJ's Wholesale Club, Inc.,* 442 F. Supp. 2d 206, 211-14 (M.D. Pa. 2006). Whatever the proper application of Maine law, case law is unanimous in holding that the Massachusetts formulation of the economic loss doctrine applies to negligence actions such as the instant one.

The issuing banks fall back on the argument that the economic loss doctrine does not, in any event, bar their negligence claim because they have incurred damage to property in that the compromised cards could no longer be used and that loss card verification codes were lost. The Middle District of Pennsylvania, however, has rejected this argument:

> Plaintiff's . . . argument is that the economic loss doctrine does not apply here because BJ's did nonetheless cause property damage to the cards that had to be replaced. [The credit union] bases this argument on the fact that the cards are tangible property and that the loss of the use of these cards, "physical tangible items[,] constitutes property damage that obviates the economic loss doctrine." We disagree. A plaintiff must show physical damage to property, not its tangible nature, to avoid the application of the economic loss doctrine. The damages sought here, the costs of replacing the cards, are economic losses.

Pennsylvania State, 398 F. Supp. 2d at 330 (citation omitted). This Court adopts this reasoning and holds that the alleged "physical" destruction of the credit cards, debit cards, and security codes should instead be considered economic losses.

For these reasons, this Court grants the motions by TJX and Fifth Third to dismiss the negligence claims.[4]

C. Negligent Misrepresentation

Under Massachusetts law, which the parties again assume applies here, the economic loss doctrine does not apply to negligent misrepresentation claims. *Nota Constr. Corp.* v. *Keyes Assocs.,* 45 Mass. App. Ct. 15 (Mass. Ct. App. 1998); *CUMIS Ins. Soc'y, Inc.* v. *BJ's Wholesale Club, Inc.,* No. 05-1158, slip op. at 7-8 n.4, 2005 Mass. Super. LEXIS 696 (Mass. Super. Ct. Dec. 1, 2005) (Quinlan, J.).

Massachusetts courts follow the Restatement of Torts (Second) section 552. As described in *Nota Construction,* the elements of negligent misrepresentation are:

> In order to recover for negligent misrepresentation a plaintiff must prove that the defendant (1) in the course of his business, (2) supplies false information for the guidance of others (3) in their business transactions, (4) causing and resulting in pecuniary loss to those others (5) by their justifiable reliance upon the information, and (6) with failure to exercise reasonable care or competence in obtaining or communicating the information.

45 Mass. App. Ct. at 19-20. "A claim of negligent misrepresentation is ordinarily one for the jury, unless the undisputed facts are so clear as to permit only one conclusion." *Id.* at 20.

TJX contends that there can be no negligent misrepresentation because there is no fiduciary relationship. For this proposition, TJX points to this Court's holding in *Berenson* v. *Nat'l Fin. Servs,, LLC,* 403 F. Supp. 2d 133 (D. Mass. 2005), that on the facts there presented, no negligent misrepresentation arose from a failure to disclose where no fiduciary relationship existed. *Id.* at 147. This Court did not, however, hold that a fiduciary relationship was a *necessary* condition for a successful negligent misrepresentation claim based on nondisclosure. On the contrary, the nondisclosure rule has not been restricted to the fiduciary context; as the First Circuit explained, nondisclosure can form the basis of a negligent misrepresentation claim whenever there is a duty to

---

4. The issuing banks further allege a claim against Fifth Third for negligence per se. Massachusetts does not, however, recognize such a claim. *See Berish* v. *Bornstein,* 437 Mass. 252, 273, 770 N.E.2d 961 (2002). Consequently, this Court must dismiss that claim.

disclose. *First Marblehead Corp.* v. *House,* 473 F.3d 1, 9-10 (1st Cir. 2006); *see also Berenson,* 403 F. Supp. 2d at 147 (providing a fiduciary relationship only as example of when required duty to disclose exists). Consequently, the issuing banks need not establish a fiduciary relationship with TJX or Fifth Third in order to prevail on a claim for negligent misrepresentation.[5]

In this case, the negligent misrepresentation claim is based on implied representations that TJX and Fifth Third made to the issuing banks that they took the security measures required by industry practice to safeguard personal and financial information. Even if neither TJX nor Fifth Third had direct contact with the issuing banks, TJX and Fifth Third knew that the issuing banks were part of a financial network that relies on members taking appropriate security measures. *See Nycal Corp.* v. *KPMG Peat Marwick LLP,* 426 Mass. 491, 497-98 (Mass. 1998); Restatement (Second) of Torts § 552, cmts. g, h (1977). Whether the issuing banks' reliance on the implied security assurances was justifiable is a factual issue inappropriate for resolution on a motion to dismiss. *See First Marblehead,* 473 F.3d at 11 ("Massachusetts courts have expressed a strong preference that reliance, in the context of negligent misrepresentation claims, be determined by a jury . . . ."). Finally, this case is indistinguishable from *CUMIS,* in which the Superior Court denied a motion to dismiss a claim for negligent misrepresentation. Slip op. at 7-8, 2005 Mass. Super. LEXIS 696. For these reasons, this Court denies the motions by TJX and Fifth Third to dismiss the negligent misrepresentation claims.

. . .[Discussion of UDAP claims omitted]. . .

V. CONCLUSION

For the reasons described in this memorandum, this Court grants the motions to dismiss the contract claims as well as the negligence and negligence per se claims. This Court denies the motions to dismiss the negligent misrepresentation claims. . . .

The largest question looming over data breach class actions is standing. Courts have taken different views on the subject, and the issue has been complicated by the Supreme Court's decision in *Spokeo v. Robins,* 136 S. Ct. 1540 (2016), which held that Congress could not confer Article III standing on a plaintiff for a mere statutory violation. Instead, the plaintiff must always prove an injury in fact, which must be pleaded with both concreteness and particularity. The following case illustrates the difficulties that standing doctrine can create for a class of consumers alleging harm from a data breach.

5. The issuing banks must nevertheless still establish that TJX and Fifth Third had a duty to disclose that it was taking deficient security measures. Since no party addressed this issue in the motions to dismiss, this Court will not address that issue at this time.

Alleruzzo v. SuperValu, Inc. (In re SuperValu, Inc., Customer Data Security Breach Litigation)

870 F.3d 763 (8th Cir. 2017)

KELLY, Circuit Judge.

In 2014, retail grocery stores owned and operated by defendants SuperValu, Inc., AB Acquisition, LLC, and New Albertsons, Inc. suffered two cyber attacks in which their customers' financial information was allegedly accessed and stolen. Following the data breaches, customers who shopped at the affected stores brought several putative class actions, which were subsequently centralized in the United States District Court for the District of Minnesota by the Judicial Panel on Multidistrict Litigation. The district court dismissed the plaintiffs' consolidated complaint . . . concluding that plaintiffs failed to allege facts establishing Article III standing. Plaintiffs appealed, and we affirm. . . .

I. BACKGROUND

. . .Plaintiffs are sixteen customers who purchased goods from defendants' grocery stores in Missouri, Illinois, Maryland, Pennsylvania, Delaware, Idaho, and New Jersey using credit or debit cards during the period between June and September 2014. From June 22, 2014, to July 17, 2014, cyber criminals accessed the computer network that processes payment card transactions for 1,045 of defendants' stores. The hackers installed malicious software on defendants' network that allowed them to gain access to the payment card information of defendants' customers (hereinafter, Card Information), including their names, credit or debit card account numbers, expiration dates, card verification value (CVV) codes, and personal identification numbers (PINs). By harvesting the data on the network, the hackers stole customers' Card Information.

On August 14, 2014, defendants issued a press release notifying customers of the computer intrusion at their stores. The press release acknowledged that the attack "may have resulted in the theft" of Card Information, but it had not yet been determined that "any such cardholder data was in fact stolen," and, at that point, there was "no evidence of any misuse of any such data." Defendants also announced that they were conducting an on-going investigation into the incident, which might uncover additional "time frames, locations and/or at-risk data" exposed in the intrusion.

On September 29, 2014, defendants announced a second data breach that took place in late August or early September 2014. The press release stated that an intruder installed different malicious software onto the same network. Defendants acknowledged that the software may have captured Card Information from debit and credit cards used to purchase goods at their stores but, at the time of the press release, there had been no determination that such information "was in fact stolen." Once again, defendants affirmed that their investigation was ongoing, and that further information on the scope of the intrusion could be identified in the future. Although defendants' release states that the second intrusion was separate from the one announced on August 14, 2014, plaintiffs dispute this contention in their complaint, alleging that the two breaches were related and stemmed from the same security failures.

According to the complaint, hackers gained access to defendants' network because defendants failed to take adequate measures to protect customers' Card Information. Defendants used default or easily guessed passwords, failed to lock out users after several failed login attempts, and did not segregate access to different parts of the network or use firewalls to protect Card Information. By not implementing these measures, defendants ran afoul of best practices and industry standards for merchants who accept customer payments via credit or debit card. Moreover, defendants were on notice of the risk of consumer data theft because similar security flaws had been exploited in recent data breaches targeting other national retailers.

As a result of the breaches, plaintiffs' Card Information was allegedly stolen, subjecting plaintiffs "to an imminent and real possibility of identity theft." Specifically, plaintiffs contend that the hackers can use their Card Information to siphon money from their current accounts, make unauthorized credit or debit card charges, open new accounts, or sell the information to others who intend to commit fraud. Identity thieves can use the stolen Card Information to commit fraud for an "extended period of time after" the breach, and the information is often traded on the cyber black market "for a number of years after the initial theft." In support of these allegations, plaintiffs cite a June 2007 United States Government Accountability Office (GAO) report on data breaches. *See* U.S. Gov't Accountability Off., GAO-07-737, Personal Information: Data Breaches are Frequent, but Evidence of Resulting Identity Theft is Limited; However, the Full Extent is Unknown (2007), http://www.gao.gov/assets/270/262899.pdf.

Customers allegedly affected by the breaches filed putative class actions in several district courts. The Judicial Panel on Multidistrict Litigation transferred the related actions to the United States District Court for the District of Minnesota for coordinated or consolidated pretrial proceedings. Pursuant to the district court's order, plaintiffs filed a consolidated amended complaint on June 26, 2015, with sixteen named plaintiffs bringing claims on behalf of a putative class of persons affected by defendants' data breaches.

Each of the sixteen plaintiffs shopped at defendants' affected stores using a credit or debit card, and their Card Information was allegedly compromised in the data breaches. After the data breaches were announced, each plaintiff "spent time determining if [his or her] card was compromised" by reviewing information released about the breaches and the impacted locations and monitoring account information to guard against potential fraud. . . .

The complaint states six claims for relief for: (1) violations of state consumer protection statutes, (2) violations of state data breach notification statutes, (3) negligence, (4) breach of implied contract, (5) negligence per se, and (6) unjust enrichment. Defendants moved to dismiss the complaint under Federal Rules of Civil Procedure 12(b)(1) and 12(b)(6). The district court granted the . . . motion and dismissed the complaint. . . finding that none of the plaintiffs had alleged an injury-in-fact and thus they did not have standing. . .

II. DISCUSSION

Article III of the Constitution limits the jurisdiction of the federal courts to cases or controversies. *Spokeo, Inc. v. Robins*, 136 S. Ct. 1540, 1547 (2016). A plaintiff invoking the jurisdiction of the court must demonstrate standing to sue by showing that she has suffered an injury in fact that is fairly traceable to the defendant's conduct and that is likely to be redressed by the relief she seeks. *Id.* This case primarily concerns the injury in fact and fairly traceable elements. To establish an injury in fact, a plaintiff must show that her injury is "'concrete and particularized' and 'actual or imminent, not conjectural or hypothetical.'" *Id.* at 1548 (quoting *Lujan v. Defs. of Wildlife,* 504 U.S. 555, 560 (1992)). An injury is fairly traceable if the plaintiff shows "a causal connection between the injury and the conduct complained of" that is "not . . . th[e] result [of] the independent action of some third party not before the court." *Lujan,* 504 U.S. at 560.

Because this case is at the pleading stage, plaintiffs "must 'clearly allege facts' demonstrating" the elements of standing. *Spokeo,* 136 S. Ct. at 1547. . . .

The district court evaluated the standing of all the named plaintiffs collectively. As relevant here, the court concluded that . . . there was insufficient evidence of misuse of plaintiffs' Card Information connected to defendants' data breaches to "plausibly suggest[] that the hackers had succeeded in stealing the data and were willing and able to use it for future theft or fraud." On appeal, plaintiffs argue that they have sufficiently alleged an injury in fact because the theft of their Card Information in the data breaches at defendants' stores created a substantial risk that they will suffer identity theft in the future. In addition, plaintiff Holmes specifically argues that his allegations of actual misuse of his Card Information are sufficient to allege a present injury in fact causally connected to defendants' careless security practices. Although we conclude that the complaint does not sufficiently allege a substantial risk of future identity theft, we nonetheless find that the court has subject matter jurisdiction over this action because plaintiff Holmes has alleged facts giving rise to standing.

A. Future Injury

Plaintiffs argue that they have sufficiently alleged an injury in fact because the theft of their Card Information due to the data breaches at defendants' stores creates the risk that they will suffer identity theft in the future. The Supreme Court has recognized that future injury can be sufficient to establish Article III standing. *See Clapper v. Amnesty Int'l USA,* 568 U.S. 398, 409 (2013). In future injury cases, the plaintiff must demonstrate that "the threatened injury is 'certainly impending,' or there is a '"substantial risk" that the harm will occur.'" *Susan B. Anthony List v. Driehaus,* 134 S. Ct. 2334, 2341 (2014). The question here is whether the complaint adequately alleges that plaintiffs face a "certainly impending" or "substantial risk" of identity theft as a result of the data breaches purportedly caused by defendants' deficient security practices.

Although we have not had occasion to address this question, several circuits have applied *Clapper* to determine whether an increased risk of future identity theft constitutes an injury in fact. *See Attias,* 2017 U.S. App. Lexis 13913, 2017 WL 3254941, at *3-7; *Whalen v. Michaels Stores, Inc.,* No. 16-260 (L), 689 Fed. Appx. 89 (2d Cir. May 2, 2017) (Summ. Order); *Beck v. McDonald,* 848 F.3d 262, 273-76 (4th Cir. 2017); *Galaria v. Nationwide Mut. Ins.,* 663 F. App'x 384, 387-90 (6th Cir. 2016); *Lewert v. P.F. Chang's China Bistro, Inc.,* 819 F.3d 963, 966-69 (7th Cir. 2016); *Remijas v. Neiman Marcus Grp., LLC,* 794 F.3d 688, 692-93 (7th Cir. 2015). These cases came to differing conclusions on the question of standing. We need not reconcile this out-of-circuit precedent because the cases ultimately turned on the substance of the allegations before each court. Thus, we begin with the facts pleaded by plaintiffs here.

Defendants argue that plaintiffs have at most alleged only that the intruders accessed the card data, not that they stole it. We disagree. At several points, the complaint alleges that the malware the hackers installed on defendants' network allowed them to "harvest" plaintiffs' Card Information, that defendants' security practices "allow[ed] and ma[de] possible the theft" of plaintiffs' Card Information, and that plaintiffs have actually "suffered theft" of their Card Information. Moreover, defendants' own press releases, which are appended to the complaint, acknowledge that the data breaches "may have resulted in the theft of" Card Information. Defendants argue that the allegations are conclusory, but "on a motion to dismiss we presum[e] that general allegations embrace those specific facts that are necessary to support the claim." *Lujan*, 504 U.S. at 561. Drawing all inferences in the plaintiffs' favor, we are satisfied that the complaint sufficiently alleges that the hackers stole plaintiffs' Card Information.

Plaintiffs, however, ask us to go further and conclude that the complaint has adequately alleged that their Card Information has been misused. . . .[T]he named plaintiffs have not alleged that they have suffered fraudulent charges on their credit or debit cards or that fraudulent accounts have been opened in their names. Plaintiffs point to the allegations that, on information and belief, illicit websites are selling their Card Information to counterfeiters and fraudsters, and that plaintiffs' financial institutions are attempting to mitigate their risk. Not only are these allegations speculative, they also fail to allege any injury "to the plaintiff[s]." *Friends of the Earth, Inc. v. Laidlaw Envtl. Servs. (TOC), Inc.*, 528 U.S. 167, 181 (2000); *see Spokeo*, 136 S. Ct. at 1548 (injury "must affect the plaintiff in a personal and individual way"). Therefore, setting aside Holmes, plaintiffs sufficiently allege that their Card Information was stolen by hackers as a result of defendants' security practices, but not that it was misused.

Plaintiffs argue that the theft of their Card Information creates a substantial risk that they will suffer identity theft. According to the GAO report cited in the complaint, "identity theft" "encompasses many types of criminal activities, including fraud on existing accounts—such as unauthorized use of a stolen credit card number—or fraudulent creation of new accounts—such as using stolen data to open a credit card account in someone else's name." U.S. Gov't Accountability Off., *supra*, at 2. Defendants appear to concede that identity theft constitutes an actual, concrete, and particularized injury. *See Attias*, 2017 U.S. App. LEXIS 7717, 2017 WL 3254941, at *5 ("Nobody doubts that identity theft, should it befall one of these plaintiffs, would constitute a concrete and particularized injury."). Our task is to determine whether plaintiffs' allegations plausibly demonstrate that the risk that plaintiffs will suffer future identity theft is substantial.

Although others have ruled that a complaint could plausibly plead that the theft of a plaintiff's personal or financial information creates a substantial risk that they will suffer identity theft sufficient to constitute a threatened injury in fact, *see, e.g., Remijas*, 794 F.3d at 692-93, we conclude that plaintiffs have not done so here. As factual support for the otherwise bare assertion that "[d]ata breaches facilitate identity theft," the complaint relies solely on the 2007 GAO report. *See generally* U.S. Gov't Accountability Off., *supra*. This report fails to support plaintiffs' contention.

Initially, we note that the allegedly stolen Card Information does not include any personally identifying information, such as social security numbers, birth dates, or driver's license numbers. As the GAO report points out, compromised credit or debit card information, like the Card Information here, "generally cannot be used alone to open unauthorized new accounts." *Id.* at 30 ("The type of data compromised in a breach can effectively determine the potential harm that can result."). As such, pursuant to the factual evidence relied on in the complaint, there is little to no risk that anyone will use the Card Information stolen in these data breaches to open unauthorized accounts in the plaintiffs' names, which is "the type of identity theft generally considered to have a more harmful direct effect on consumers." *Id.* We are left with the risk that plaintiffs' Card Information could be used to commit credit or debit card fraud, in which criminals make unauthorized charges to or siphon money from those existing accounts.

Ultimately, the findings of the GAO report do not plausibly support the contention that consumers affected by a data breach face a substantial risk of credit or debit card fraud. Although the report acknowledges that there are some cases in which a data breach appears to have resulted in identity theft, it concludes based on the "available data and information" that "most breaches have not resulted in detected incidents of identity theft." *Id.* at 21. Among other evidence, the report reviews the 24 largest data breaches reported between January 2000 and June 2005, and finds only four were known to have resulted in some form of identity theft, and only three of those were believed to be incidents of account fraud. *Id.* at 24-25. Because the report finds that data breaches are unlikely to result in account fraud, it does not support the allegation that defendants' data breaches create a substantial risk that plaintiffs will suffer credit or debit card fraud. *See Beck*, 848 F.3d at 276.

The 2007 report found that "[c]omprehensive information on the outcomes of data breaches is not available," U.S. Gov't Accountability Off., *supra* at 21, and the "extent to which data breaches result in identity theft is not well known," *id.* at 5. It is possible that some years later there may be more detailed factual support for plaintiffs' allegations of future injury. But such support is absent from the complaint here, and a mere possibility is not enough for standing. *See Clapper*, 568 U.S. at 409 ("'[A]llegations of possible future injury' are not sufficient.")

Plaintiffs also argue that the costs they incurred to mitigate their risk of identity theft, including time they spent reviewing information about the breach and monitoring their account information, constitute an injury in fact for purposes of standing. Because plaintiffs have not alleged a substantial risk of future identity theft, the time they spent protecting themselves against this speculative threat cannot create an injury. *See Clapper*, 133 S. Ct. at 1151 (plaintiffs "cannot manufacture standing merely by inflicting harm on themselves based on their fears of hypothetical future harm that is not certainly impending"); *Beck*, 848 F.3d at 276-77 ("[S]elf-imposed harms cannot confer standing.").

Accordingly, we conclude that the complaint has not sufficiently alleged a substantial risk of identity theft, and plaintiffs' allegations of future injury do not support standing in this case. . . .

III. CONCLUSION

For the foregoing reasons, we . . . affirm the dismissal as to the . . . plaintiffs [other than Holmes]. . . .

III. IDENTITY THEFT PREVENTION

Identity theft is an issue closely related to, but distinct from, data security and management of data breaches. Identity theft falls into two categories—existing account fraud and new account fraud. Existing account from involves nothing more than a fraudster using someone else's existing, legitimate account information, such as if your credit card were stolen and the thief were to use it. The thief is claiming to be you (at least implicitly). New account fraud is more complex. It involves the fraudster opening up a new account that is in somebody else's name. The person named on the account may not even know that there is an account opened. To open up a new account, however, typically requires obtaining a few different real identifiers of a consumer.

While identity theft can involve many types of accounts—Social Security, healthcare, government identification, for example—the most common type of identity theft is simply payments fraud. Indeed, most of the time when people speak of identity theft, they mean payments fraud. This should not be surprising as the goal of most identity thieves is monetary return. Putting aside those with nefarious espionage purposes or the like, a typical identity thief is looking for data that can be readily monetized. In this regard, payment information—credit card account numbers with expiry dates and security codes, or bank account numbers with consumers' names, or bank account login information—is exactly what fraudsters want. It is much easier to use a stolen credit card account number to make a purchase than to take the steps to assemble the data to apply for a new card in someone else's name. That said, if successful, the new card in someone else's name may ultimately be more rewarding because the named account holder doesn't know about the account and won't act to shut it down in response to suspicious activity.

Identity theft of all sorts obviously falls under various criminal laws. But there are also a couple of federal law provisions designed to detect and mitigate the effects of identity theft. Note that this is different from data breach notification laws—a data breach need never ripen into identity theft. Instead, it only raises the possibility of future identity theft. But there are also situations where it is clear that identity theft has occurred, or at least where there are clear warning signs that it may be occurring.

A. FTC's Red Flags Rule

The FTC's **Red Flags Rule**, 16 C.F.R. Part 681, requires "financial institutions" (defined as depositories and credit unions) and "creditors" (defined parties who regularly obtain or use creditor reports for credit transactions, furnish information to consumer reporting agencies, or who regular extend credit) that offer or maintain accounts that permit multiple payments or transactions (credit cards, but also checking accounts, installment loans, and cell phone and utility accounts) to "develop and implement a written Identity Theft Prevention Program (Program) that is designed to detect, prevent, and mitigate identity theft in connection with the opening of a covered account or any existing covered account."16 C.F.R. § 681(d)(1). The program must include "reasonable policies and procedures" to identify, detect, and respond to "Red Flags," meaning "patterns, practices, or specific activities that indicate the possible existence of identity theft." 16 C.F.R. §§ 681(b)(9), 681(d)(2). The program must be approved by the board of directors or an appropriate committee of the board, senior management or the board must be involved with running the program, and staff must be trained to implement the program. 16 C.F.R. § 681(e).

The **Interagency Guidelines on Identity Theft Detection, Prevention, and Mitigation** provide further details about factors a Red Flags program should consider in identifying relevant Red Flags, detecting Red Flags, and preventing and mitigating identity theft. 16 C.F.R. Part 681, app. A. A supplement to the Guidelines provides a long list of suspicious activities, such as warnings from consumer reporting agencies, the use of documents that appear altered, forged, or inconsistent with other information, mismatched personal information, invalid phone numbers being provided, unissued Social Security Numbers, material changes in purchasing patterns by the consumer, or a material increase in the use of available credit. Some of these activities might be completely benign—a form might have a typo or a consumer's spending needs might have changed. But they are also consistent with identity theft and warrant greater care from the financial institution.

B. Fair Credit Reporting Act Identity Theft Provisions

The Fair Credit Reporting Act has a pair of provisions dealing with identity theft. These provisions give consumers a right to put an "initial fraud alert" on their file with a consumer reporting agency (CRA), 15 U.S.C. § 1681c-1(a)(1), which must be included in any consumer report provided for at least the next 90 days. Such an alert merely requires that the consumer or his representative provide appropriate proof of the identity of the requester and assert in good faith a suspicion that the consumer has been or is about to become the victim of fraud or related crime, including identity theft.

If the consumer provides an "identity theft report," then there is an "extended fraud alert" that continues for seven years (unless otherwise requested by the consumer). 15 U.S.C. § 1681c-1(b). An identity theft report is a report filed, under penalty of perjury, that alleges an identity theft and that is a copy of a report filed with an appropriate law enforcement agency. 15 U.S.C. § 1681a(q)(4). CRAs must share alerts with other CRAs. 15 U.S.C. § 1681c-1(b)(1)(C).

CRAs are also required to block reporting of any information that a consumer claims is from an alleged identity theft, 15 U.S.C. § 1681c-2(a), and must notify the furnisher of the block, 15 U.S.C. § 1681c-2(b). The CRA is allowed to decline to approve or lift the block if it determines that the information was blocked in error, that the consumer made a misrepresentation of a material fact relevant to the block, or that the consumer obtained possession of goods, services, or money because of the blocked transaction, but the consumer must be notified of any decline or lifting. 15 U.S.C. § 1681c-2(c).

Users and prospective users of credit reports may not open new accounts, issue new cards, or increase credit limits if there is an initial fraud alert unless they have utilized "reasonable policies and procedures to form a reasonable belief that the user knows the identity of the person making the request." 15 U.S.C. § 1681c-1(h)(1)(B)(i). If there is an extended alert, no new account may be opened unless the creditor contacts the consumer using contact information provided with the creation of the extended fraud alert to verify the request. 15 U.S.C. § 1681c-1(h)(2)(B).

C. State Security Freeze Laws

State law in all 50 states and the District of Columbia permit consumers to place a "security freeze" on their credit report. Such a freeze prohibits the consumer reporting agency from releasing a consumer report without the consumer's consent. *See, e.g.,* Md. Comm. Code § 14-1212.1(b)-(c).

The effect of a freeze is more drastic than a FCRA identity theft report, as it is a blanket prohibition on releasing a consumer report, rather than requiring some sort of verification prior to releasing the information. A freeze does not, however, prevent reporting of information to the CRA.

Generally the state security freeze statutes prescribe an official way to request a freeze, and do not require consumers to present any actual evidence supporting identity theft concerns. Security freezes under state law are generally for an indefinite time. Some states limit the fees that may be charged by CRAs for such a freeze (or for lifting a freeze), while others require a free freeze and yet others do not regulate freeze fees.

Problem Set 37

1. Joshua Goodman loves the food from the Golden Gate restaurant in San Francisco, California.

   a. The first time Joshua ordered over the phone for delivery, he gave Golden Gate his credit card number. Joshua was surprised the next time that he ordered that Golden Gate seemed to already know his credit card number based on his phone number. Should Joshua be concerned? What, if anything, can he do about it?

   b. When Joshua got the Golden Gate order, he gave the delivery person his credit card, which was swiped through a knucklebuster containing carbon copy paper. Joshua signed the paper and kept one copy himself. Separately stapled to the bag containing the delicious food was a receipt that listed out the items in the order. It also contained Joshua's complete credit card number and expiry date. Should Joshua be concerned? What, if anything, can he do about it? *See* 15 U.S.C. §§ 1681c(g), 1681(n), 1681(o); Cal. Civ. Code § 1747.09.

2. You are the chief compliance officer for a marketplace lender that makes installment loans to customers acquired over the Internet. Following a high-profile data breach incident at a competitor, the company's board has asked you for a report on what the company's obligations are regarding data security and how the company is complying with those obligations. Explain to the board what the company's obligations are and what you think is required in terms of compliance. *See* 16 C.F.R. Parts 314, 681; 201 C.M.R. § 17.00 *et seq.*

3. First Bank of Springfield (total assets $12 billion) emailed all of its account holders about its refreshed online and mobile banking experience. It told all of its account holders that the first time that they signed in after the upgrade, they would need to use a temporary password. The temporary password was the first four letters of the account holder's last name plus the last four digits of the account holder's Social Security number: XXXX####. Heidi Schooner, an account holder at First Bank of Springfield, tried logging on to her account after the upgrade but found that she wasn't able to do so. After much back and forth with customer support, she learned that her temporary password had been changed by someone else and her account had been cleaned out with a foreign wire transfer of $3,700. Heidi's situation turns out to be typical of many First Bank of Springfield account holders. You are general counsel for the First Bank of Springfield. What concerns do you have?

4. Equifax, one of the three major consumer reporting agencies, announced that it had suffered a massive data breach, with information on over a hundred million consumers being compromised.

a. Dennis Hoofnagle is worried that his data might have been affected and that he'll become the victim of identity theft. What steps can Chris take to mitigate his risk, and what costs or burdens will these steps pose for him? *See* 15 U.S.C. §§ 1681c-1, 1681c-2.

b. Dennis would like to sue Equifax over the data breach. What theories might he sue on and what obstacles do you foresee for his suit? *See* 15 U.S.C. §§ 1681b(a), 1681e(a); 16 C.F.R. § 314.3(b).

5. Senator Prudence Dogood has reached out to you for advice about identity theft policy. The Senator is very concerned about what seems to be a rise in data breaches and identity thefts, and she wants to do something about it. She's wondering what you think of the following policy proposals:

a. Creating a federal data breach notification law.

b. Creating a federal private right of action for consumers whose data has been stolen in a data breach, with statutory damages.

c. Prohibiting firms from storing consumer financial account data.

d. Requiring that all consumer financial data be stored in encrypted form.

e. Prohibiting the issuance of consumer reports except with specific consent by the consumer, whose identity must be verified in a reasonable fashion.

INDEX